The **Rough G**

Thailand

written and researched by

Paul Gray and Lucy Ridout

with additional contributions by

John Clewley, Ron Emmons, Felix Hude and Neil Pettigrew

NEW YORK • LONDON • DELHI

www.roughguides.com

Contents

Loy Krathong insert following p.264

The wat insert following p.496

Thai cuisine insert following p.680

◀◀ Boat on Krabi River ◀ Rice paddies in northern Thailand

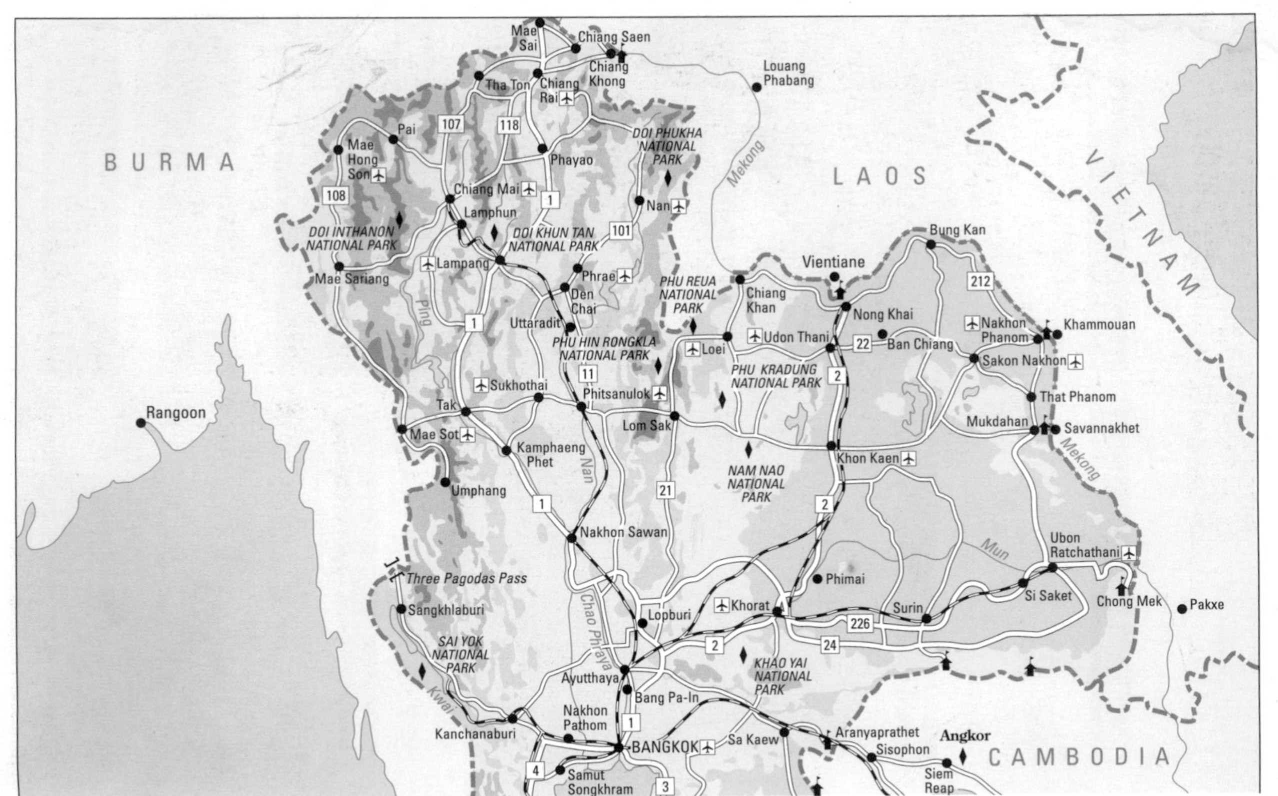
BURMA
LAOS
VIETNAM
CAMBODIA
Mae Sai
Chiang Saen
Chiang Khong
Louang Phabang
Tha Ton
Chiang Rai
Pai
107
118
DOI PHUKHA NATIONAL PARK
Mekong
Mae Hong Son
Phayao
Chiang Mai
1
Nan
108
Lamphun
DOI INTHANON NATIONAL PARK
DOI KHUN TAN NATIONAL PARK
101
Bung Kan
Lampang
Vientiane
Mae Sariang
Phrae
PHU REUA NATIONAL PARK
212
Den Chai
Chiang Khan
Ping
Nong Khai
Uttaradit
Nakhon Phanom
Khammouan
PHU HIN RONGKLA NATIONAL PARK
Udon Thani
Ban Chiang
22
Loei
Sakon Nakhon
PHU KRADUNG NATIONAL PARK
11
2
Sukhothai
That Phanom
Rangoon
Phitsanulok
Tak
Lom Sak
Mukdahan
Savannakhet
Mae Sot
Kamphaeng Phet
Khon Kaen
Nan
NAM NAO NATIONAL PARK
Umphang
21
Nakhon Sawan
Mun
Ubon Ratchathani
Three Pagodas Pass
Phimai
Chao Phraya
Sangkhlaburi
Khorat
Si Saket
Chong Mek
Pakxe
Lopburi
Surin
226
SAI YOK NATIONAL PARK
KHAO YAI NATIONAL PARK
24
Kwai
Ayutthaya
Bang Pa-In
Nakhon Pathom
Kanchanaburi
Aranyaprathet
Angkor
BANGKOK
Sa Kaew
Sisophon
4
Samut Songkhram
3
Siem Reap

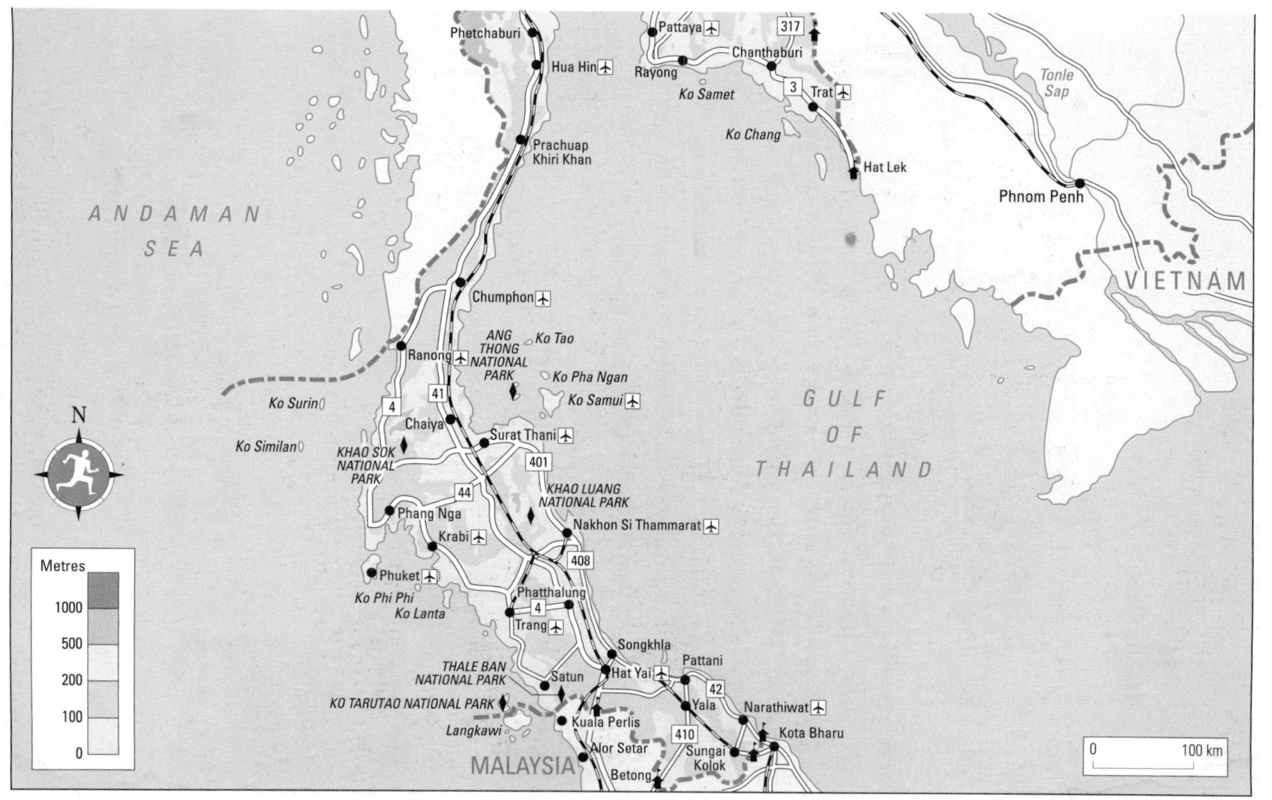
ANDAMAN SEA
GULF OF THAILAND
VIETNAM
MALAYSIA
Phetchaburi
Hua Hin
Pattaya
Rayong
Chanthaburi
Ko Samet
Trat
Ko Chang
Hat Lek
Tonle Sap
Phnom Penh
Prachuap Khiri Khan
Chumphon
ANG THONG NATIONAL PARK
Ko Tao
Ko Pha Ngan
Ko Samui
Ranong
Ko Surin
Ko Similan
Chaiya
Surat Thani
KHAO SOK NATIONAL PARK
KHAO LUANG NATIONAL PARK
Nakhon Si Thammarat
Phang Nga
Krabi
Phuket
Ko Phi Phi
Ko Lanta
Phatthalung
Trang
Songkhla
Hat Yai
Pattani
THALE BAN NATIONAL PARK
Satun
KO TARUTAO NATIONAL PARK
Langkawi
Kuala Perlis
Alor Setar
Betong
Yala
Narathiwat
Kota Bharu
Sungai Kolok
317
3
4
41
401
44
408
42
410
N
Metres
1000
500
200
100
0
0
100 km

Introduction to

Thailand

With over eleven million foreigners flying into the country each year, Thailand has become Asia's primary holiday destination. Yet despite this vast influx of tourists and their cash, Thailand's cultural integrity remains largely undamaged – a country that adroitly avoided colonization has been able to absorb Western influences without wholly succumbing to them. Though the high-rises and neon lights occupy the foreground of the tourist picture, the typical Thai community is still the traditional farming village. Almost fifty percent of Thais earn their living from the land, based around the staple, rice, which forms the foundation of the country's unique and famously sophisticated cuisine.

Tourism has been just one factor in the country's development which, once the deep-seated regional uncertainties surrounding the Vietnam War had faded, was free to proceed at an almost death-defying pace. Indeed, Thailand enjoyed the fastest-expanding economy in the world, at an average of nine percent growth a year, until it overstretched itself in 1997, sparking a regional financial crisis – but already, with remarkable resilience, the economy is growing rapidly again. Politics in Thailand, however, has not been able to keep pace. Coups d'état, which used to be the commonest method of changing government, seem to be a thing of the past, but despite a recently revised constitution and robust criticism from students, grass-roots activists and parts of the press, the malnourished democratic system is characterized by corruption and cronyism.

Through all the changes of the last sixty years, the much-revered constitutional monarch, King Bhumibol, who sits at the pinnacle of an elaborate hierarchical system of deference covering the whole of Thai society, has lent a large measure of stability. Furthermore, some ninety percent of the population are still practising Theravada Buddhists, a unifying faith that colours all aspects of daily life – from the tiered temple rooftops that dominate every skyline, to the omnipresent saffron-robed monks and the packed calendar of festivals; it is still the norm for a Thai man to spend time as a monk at some period during his life.

Where to go

The clash of tradition and modernity is most intense in **Bangkok**, the first stop on almost any itinerary. Within its historic core you'll find resplendent temples, canalside markets and the opulent indulgence of the eighteenth-century **Grand Palace**, while downtown Bangkok's forest of skyscrapers shelters cutting-edge fashion and decor boutiques and some achingly hip bars and clubs. After touchdown in Bangkok, much of the package-holiday traffic flows

▲ Thai silk

Fact file

• Known as **Siam** until 1939, Thailand lies wholly within the tropics, covering an **area** of 511,770 square kilometres and divided into 76 provinces or changwat. The **population** of 63 million is made up of ethnic Thais (75 percent) and Chinese (14 percent), with the rest comprising mainly immigrants from neighbouring countries as well as hill-tribespeople; the national language is *phasaa Thai*. Buddhism is the national **religion**, with some 90 percent followers, and Islam the largest of the minority religions at around 5 percent. Average **life expectancy** is 71 years.

• Since 1932 the country has been a **constitutional monarchy**; King Bhumibol, also known as Rama IX (being the ninth ruler of the Chakri dynasty), has been on the throne since 1946. The elected **National Assembly** (Rathasapha) has five hundred MPs in the House of Representatives (Sapha Phuthaen Ratsadon), led by a prime minister, and two hundred members of the Senate (Wuthisapha).

• Tourism is the country's main **industry**, and its biggest **exports** are computers and components, vehicles and vehicle parts, textiles and rubber.

The gecko

Whether you're staying on a beach or in a town, chances are you'll be sharing your room with a few **geckos**. These pale green tropical lizards, which are completely harmless to humans and usually measure a cute four to ten centimetres in length, mostly appear at night, high up on walls and ceilings, where they feed on insects. Because the undersides of their flat toes are covered with hundreds of microscopic hairs that catch at even the tiniest of irregularities, geckos are able to scale almost any surface, including glass, which is why you usually see them in strange, gravity-defying positions. The largest and most vociferous gecko is known as the **tokay** in Thai, named after the disconcertingly loud sound it makes. Tokays can grow to an alarming 35cm, but are welcomed by most householders, as they devour insects and mice; Thais also consider it auspicious if a baby is born within earshot of a crowing tokay. There's more about Thailand's fauna and flora on p.891.

▲ Fishing boats, Hua Hin

east to **Pattaya**, the country's first and most congested seaside resort, but for prettier beaches you're far better off venturing slightly further afield, to the islands of **Ko Samet** and the **Ko Chang archipelago**, with their squeaky white sand and shorefront bungalows.

The southern reaches of Isaan hold some of Thailand's best-kept secrets.

Fewer tourists strike north from the east coast into **Isaan**, the poorest and in some ways the most traditionally Thai region. Here, a trip through the gently modulating landscapes of the **Mekong River** valley, which defines Thailand's northeastern extremities, takes in archetypal agricultural villages and a fascinating array of religious sites, while the southern reaches of Isaan hold some of Thailand's best-kept secrets – the magnificent stone temple complexes of **Phimai**, **Phanom Rung** and **Khao Phra Viharn**, all built by the Khmers of Cambodia almost ten centuries ago. Closer to the capital, in the southwestern corner of Isaan, **Khao Yai National Park** encapsulates the phenomenal diversity of Thailand's flora and fauna, which here range from wild orchids to strangling figs, elephants to hornbills, tigers to macaques.

At the heart of the northern uplands, **Chiang Mai** is both an attractive historic city and a vibrant cultural centre, with a strong tradition of arts, crafts and festivals. It does a burgeoning line in self-improvement courses – from ascetic meditation to the more earthly pleasures of Thai cookery classes – while the overriding enticement of the surrounding region is the prospect of **trekking** through villages inhabited by a richly mixed population of tribal peoples. Plenty of outdoor activities and courses, as well as spas and

▲ Wat Yai Suwannaram, Phetchaburi

Thai boxing

Such is the national obsession with *muay thai*, or Thai boxing, that when Wijan Ponlid returned home from the Sydney 2000 Olympics with the country's only gold medal (for international flyweight boxing), he was paraded through town at the head of a procession of 49 elephants, given a new house and over 20 million baht, and offered a promotion in the police force. Belatedly perhaps, *muay thai* has recently entered the canon of martial-arts cinema: *Ong Bak* (2003) and *Tom Yum Goong* (2005) were global box-office hits, and their all-punching, all-kicking star, Tony Jaa, who performed all his own stunts, has been appointed Cultural Ambassador for Thailand.

Though there are boxing venues all around the country, the very best fights are staged at Bangkok's two biggest stadiums, Rajdamnoen and Lumphini, which are well worth attending as a cultural experience even if you have no interest in the sport itself; see p.202 for times and ticket prices and p.62 for more on the rules and rituals of *muay thai*.

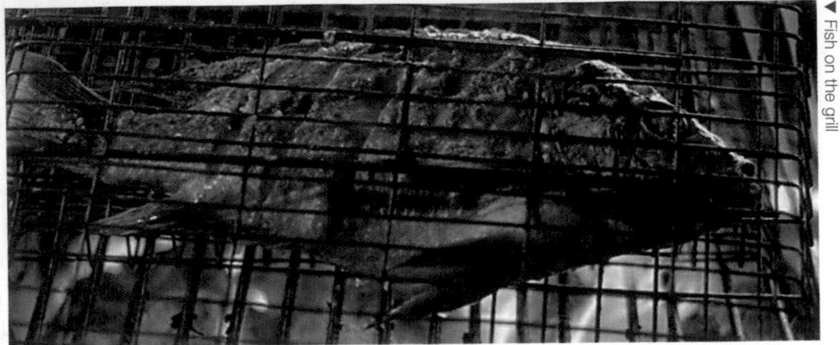

▼ Fish on the grill

massages, can be enjoyed at **Pai**, a surprisingly cosmopolitan hill station for travellers, four hours northwest of Chiang Mai.

With Chiang Mai and the north so firmly planted on the independent tourist trail, the intervening **central plains** tend to get short shrift. Yet there is rewarding trekking around **Umphang**, near the Burmese border, and the elegant ruins of former capitals **Ayutthaya** and **Sukhothai** embody a glorious artistic heritage, displaying Thailand's distinctive ability to absorb influences from quite different cultures. **Kanchanaburi**, stunningly located on the **River Kwai** in the western reaches of the central plains, tells of a much darker episode in Thailand's past, for it was along the course of this river that the Japanese army built the Thailand–Burma Railway during World War II, at the cost of thousands of POW lives.

Hill-tribe trekking

Trekking in northern Thailand isn't just about walking through beautiful, rainforested mountain scenery, it also brings you into contact with the hill tribes or *chao khao*, fascinating ethnic minorities who are just clinging on to their traditional ways of life. Sometimes termed Fourth World people, in that they are migrants who continue to migrate without regard for national boundaries, the hill tribes have developed sophisticated customs, laws and beliefs to harmonize relationships between individuals and their environment. Despite the disturbance caused by trekking, most *chao khao* are genuinely hospitable to foreigners, but it's important that you go with a knowledgeable guide who has the interests of the local people at heart – and that you act as a sensitive guest in the face of their hospitality. For more on the hill tribes, see p.912; for trekking practicalities, see p.331.

Bangkok's forest of skyscrapers shelters cutting-edge fashion and decor boutiques and some achingly hip bars and clubs.

Sand and sea are what most Thai holidays are about, though, and the pick of the coasts are in southern Thailand, where the Samui archipelago off the **Gulf coast** is one of the highlights. **Ko Samui** itself has the most sweeping white-sand beaches, and the greatest variety of accommodation and facilities to go with them. **Ko Pha Ngan** next door is still pure backpacker territory, where you have a stark choice between desolate coves and **Hat Rin**, Thailand's party capital. The remotest island, rocky **Ko Tao**, is acquiring increasing sophistication as Southeast Asia's largest dive-training centre.

Across on the other side of the peninsula, the **Andaman coast** boasts even more exhilarating scenery and the finest coral reefs in the country, in particular around the spectacular **Ko Similan** island chain, which ranks as one of the best dive sites in the world. The largest Andaman coast island, **Phuket**, is one of Thailand's top tourist destinations and is graced with a dozen fine beaches, though several of these have been over-developed with a glut of high-rises and tacky nightlife. Phuket was one of many places along the Andaman coast to suffer extensive damage in the December 2004 tsunami, but regeneration along the entire coastline has been relatively swift, and few first-time visitors will notice the effects. **Ko Phi Phi** was particularly badly hit, but tourists have returned in droves to rekindle the island's party atmosphere, and to enjoy the coral-rich sea and breathtakingly beautiful limestone cliffs that characterize the coastline of all the islands in

▲ Samlor in for a service, Nonthaburi

▲ Thonburi longthai

Krabi province. The island of **Ko Lanta** has a more understated charm and is a popular destination for both families and backpackers. Inland attractions generally pale in comparison to the coastal splendours, but the rainforests of **Khao Sok National Park** are a notable exception.

Further down the Thai peninsula, in the provinces of the **deep south**, the teeming sea life and unfrequented sands of the **Trang islands** and the **Ko Tarutao National Marine Park** are the main draws.

Spirit houses

Although the vast majority of Thais are Buddhist, nearly everyone also believes that the physical world is inhabited by **spirits**. These spirits can cause trouble if not given enough care and attention, and are apt to wreak havoc when made homeless. Therefore, whenever a new building is constructed – be it a traditional village house or a multi-storey office block – the owners will also construct a home for the spirits who previously occupied that land. Crucially, these spirit houses must be given the best spot on the site – which in Bangkok often means on the roof – and must also reflect the status of the building in question, so their architecture can range from the simplest wooden structure to an elaborate scale model of a particularly ornate temple or even a sleek little icon of modernism. Daily **offerings** of flowers, incense and candles are set inside the spirit house, sometimes with morsels of food. For an introduction to animist and Buddhist practices in Thailand, see p.884.

When to go

The **climate** of most of Thailand is governed by three seasons: rainy (roughly May–Oct), caused by the southwest monsoon dumping moisture gathered from the Andaman Sea and the Gulf of Thailand; cool (Nov–Feb); and hot (March–May). The **rainy season** is the least predictable of the three, varying in length and intensity from year to year, but usually it gathers force between June and August, coming to a peak in September and October, when unpaved roads are reduced to mud troughs and whole districts of Bangkok are flooded. The **cool season** is the pleasantest time to visit, although temperatures can still reach a broiling 30°C in the middle of the day. In the **hot season**, when temperatures often rise to 35°C in Bangkok, the best thing to do is to hit the beach.

Rat or raja?

There's no standard system of transliterating Thai script into Roman, so you're sure to find that the Thai words in this book don't always match the versions you'll see elsewhere. Maps and street signs are the biggest sources of confusion, so we've generally gone for the transliteration that's most common on the spot. However, sometimes you'll need to do a bit of lateral thinking, bearing in mind that a classic variant for the town of Ayutthaya is Ayudhia, while among street names, Thanon Rajavithi could come out as Thanon Ratwithi – and it's not unheard of to find one spelling posted at one end of a road, with another at the opposite end. See p.933 for an introduction to the Thai language.

Within this scheme, slight variations are found from region to region. The less humid **north** experiences the greatest range of temperatures: at night in the cool season the thermometer occasionally approaches zero on the

▲ Bed Supperclub, Bangkok

higher slopes, and this region is often hotter than the central plains between March and May. It's the **northeast** that gets the very worst of the hot season, with clouds of dust gathering above the parched fields, and humid air too. In **southern Thailand**, temperatures are more consistent throughout the year, with less variation the closer you get to the equator. The rainy season hits the **Andaman coast** of the southern peninsula harder than anywhere else in the country – heavy rainfall usually starts in May and persists until November.

One area of the country, the **Gulf coast** of the southern peninsula, lies outside this general pattern. With the sea immediately to the east, this coast and its offshore islands feel the effects of the northeast monsoon, which brings rain between October and January, especially in November, but suffers less than the Andaman coast from the southwest monsoon.

Overall, the **cool season** is generally the **best time** to come to Thailand: as well as having more manageable temperatures and less rain, it offers waterfalls in full spate and the best of the upland flowers in bloom. Bear in mind, however, that it's also the busiest season, so forward planning is essential.

Thailand's Climate

Average daily temperatures (°C) and monthly rainfall (mm)

	Jan	Feb	Mar	Apr	May	Jun	Jul	Aug	Sep	Oct	Nov	Dec
Bangkok												
Max temp (°C)	26	28	29	30	30	29	29	28	28	28	27	26
Rainfall (mm)	11	28	31	72	190	152	158	187	320	231	57	9
Chiang Mai												
Max temp (°C)	21	23	26	29	29	28	27	27	27	26	24	22
Rainfall (mm)	8	6	15	45	153	136	167	227	251	132	44	15
Pattaya												
Max temp (°C)	26	28	29	30	30	29	29	28	28	28	27	26
Rainfall (mm)	12	23	41	79	165	120	166	166	302	229	66	10
Ko Samui												
Max temp (°C)	26	26	28	29	29	28	28	28	28	27	26	25
Rainfall (mm)	38	8	12	63	186	113	143	123	209	260	302	98
Phuket												
Max temp (°C)	27	28	28	29	28	28	28	28	27	27	27	27
Rainfall (mm)	35	31	39	163	348	213	263	263	419	305	207	52

38 things not to miss

It's not possible to see everything that Thailand has to offer in one trip – and we don't suggest you try. What follows is a selective taste of the country's highlights: beautiful beaches, outstanding national parks, magnificent temples, and even good things to eat and drink – arranged in five colour-coded categories to help you find the very best things to see, do and experience. All entries have a page reference to take you straight into the Guide, where you can find out more.

01 Khao Sok National Park Page **714** • Mist-clad outcrops, steamy jungle populated by whooping gibbons, and the vast Cheow Lan lake all make Khao Sok a rewarding place to explore.

02 Tom yam kung See *Thai cuisine* **colour section** • Delicious hot and sour soup with prawns and lemon grass, that typifies the strong, fresh flavours of Thai food.

04 Diving and snorkelling off Ko Similan Page **727** • The underwater scenery at this remote chain of national park islands is among the finest in the world.

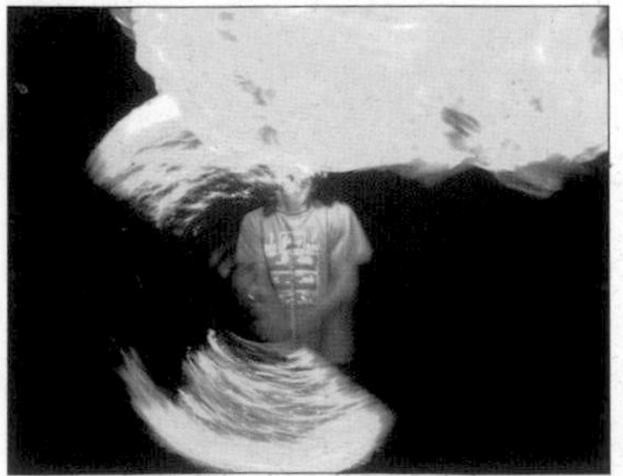

05 Full moon party at Hat Rin, Ko Pha Ngan Page **663** • *Apocalypse Now* without the war . . .

03 Umphang treks Page **320** • The best way to reach mighty Tee Lor Su Falls from Umphang is by rafting and hiking your way through the jungle.

06 Phetchaburi Page **607** • Many of the temples in this charming, historic town date back three hundred years and are still in use today.

07 Night markets Page **53** • Evening gatherings of pushcart kitchens, which are usually the best-value and most entertaining places to eat in any Thai town.

08 The National Museum, Bangkok Page **143** • A colossal hoard of Thailand's artistic treasures.

09 Ko Samet Page **471** • Petite and pretty, Ko Samet is justifiably popular for its gorgeous white-sand beaches and its proximity to Bangkok.

10 Ko Chang archipelago Page **491** • Enjoy the beaches and forests of Thailand's second-largest island, or escape to a more peaceful corner of the archipelago.

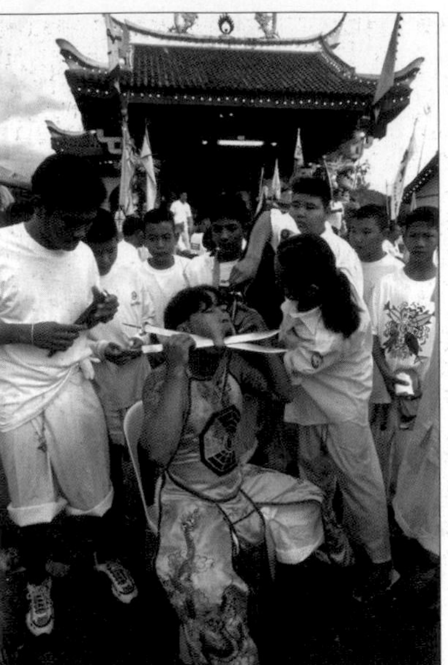

11 Vegetarian festival, Phuket Page **738** • During Taoist Lent, fasting Chinese devotees test their spiritual resolve with acts of gruesome self-mortification.

12 Amulet market, Bangkok Page **149** • Nearly everyone wears a sacred talisman – often a miniature Buddha image – to ward off misfortune, and the huge amulet market at Wat Rajnadda is a great place for browsing.

13 Ko Tarutao National Marine Park Page **844** • Spectacular and relatively peaceful islands, sheltering a surprising variety of landscapes and fauna.

14 Jim Thompson's House, Bangkok Page **169** • The house of the legendary American adventurer, entrepreneur and art collector is a small, personal museum of Thai crafts and architecture.

15 Rock-climbing on Laem Phra Nang Page **781** • Even novice climbers can scale the cliffs here for unbeatable views of the stunning Andaman coastline.

16 Folklore Museum, Phitsanulok Page **288** • One of Thailand's best ethnology museums, complete with a reconstructed village home and a fascinating array of traditional kitchen implements.

17 Ayutthaya Page **267** • An hour to the north, this former capital provides a sharp contrast to Bangkok, an atmospheric graveyard for temples flanked by good museums and some appealing guest houses.

18 Wat Pho, Bangkok Page **139** • A lively and lavish temple, encompassing the awesome Reclining Buddha and a great massage school.

19 Thai cookery classes in Chiang Mai Page **348** • Of the many courses now on offer in the town, cookery classes are the most instantly gratifying, including first-class meals and colourful market visits.

20 Sukhothai Page **291** • Stay in one of the many welcoming guest houses in New Sukhothai and hire a bicycle to explore the elegant ruins of the nearby old city, Thailand's thirteenth-century capital.

21 Axe pillows Page **564** • Much more comfortable than they look, traditional axe pillows are used eveywhere in Thailand, and sold very cheaply in the village of Ban Sri Than.

22 Nan Page **388** • Few travellers make the trip out to Nan, but it's a likeable town set in rich mountain scenery, with a strong handicraft tradition and some intriguing Lao-influenced temples, including the beautiful murals at Wat Phumin.

23 Khao Yai National Park Page **522** • Explore Thailand's most popular national park by bicycle, on foot, or by going on night safari.

24 Ko Lanta Page **806** • Dubbed "the island of long beaches", Ko Lanta makes an appealingly low-key destination for backpackers and families alike.

25 Khmer ruins Page **535** • When the ancient Khmers controlled northeast Thailand in the ninth century, they built a chain of magnificent Angkor Wat-style temple complexes, including this one at Phimai.

26 Ko Tao Page **673** • Take a dive course, or just explore this remote island's contours by boat or on foot.

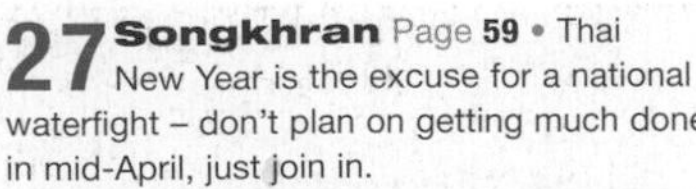

27 Songkhran Page **59** • Thai New Year is the excuse for a national waterfight – don't plan on getting much done in mid-April, just join in.

28 Chatuchak Weekend Market, Bangkok Page **179** • Thailand's top shopping experience features over eight thousand stalls selling everything from wood-carvings to designer lamps and hill-tribe jewellery to jeans.

29 The Mekong River Page **582** • Forming 750km of the border between Thailand and Laos, the mighty Mekong provides an endlessly fascinating scenic backdrop to travels in the northeast.

30 Riding the Death Railway, River Kwai Page **251** • Thailand's most scenic train journey is also its most historic, using the track constructed by World War II POWs, whose story is movingly told in the nearby Hellfire Pass Museum.

31 The Mae Hong Son loop Page **395** • A spectacular 600km trip, winding over steep forested mountains and through tightly hemmed farming valleys.

32 Sea-canoeing in Ao Phang Nga Page **766** • Low-impact paddling is the best way to explore the secret island-lagoons and mangrove swamps of this extraordinary bay.

33 Loy Krathong **See** *Loy Krathong* **colour section** • At this nationwide festival held in honour of the water spirits, Thais everywhere float miniature baskets filled with flowers and lighted candles on canals, rivers, ponds and seashores.

34 Traditional massage Page **64** • Combining elements of acupressure and yoga, a pleasantly brutal way to help shed jet lag, or simply to end the day.

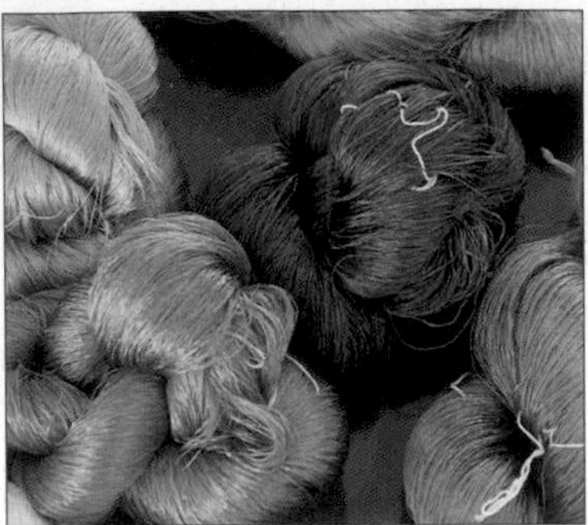

35 **Silk** Page **547** • Sericulture is an important village industry in the northeast, whose weavers produce the country's most exquisite designs, though high-quality silk is sold all over Thailand.

36 **Wat Phu Tok** Page **595** • A uniquely atmospheric meditation temple on a steep, wooded outcrop – clamber around for the spectacular views, if nothing else.

37 **Wat Phra That Doi Suthep, Chiang Mai** Page **368** • One of the most harmonious ensembles of temple architecture in the country, with mountaintop views over half of northern Thailand thrown in.

38 **The Grand Palace, Bangkok** Page **131** • No visitor should miss this huge complex, which encompasses the country's holiest and most beautiful temple, Wat Phra Kaeo, and its most important image, the Emerald Buddha.

Basics

Basics

Getting there

Thailand currently has six **international airports**, in Bangkok, Chiang Mai, Hat Yai, Krabi, Phuket and Ko Samui. The vast majority of travellers fly into Bangkok. At the time of writing, all international flights into Bangkok use Don Muang, but when the capital's new Suvarnabhumi Airport is completed, possibly in late 2006, all international flights will land there instead. See p.98 for more information about both airports.

Air fares to Thailand always depend on the **season**, with the highest being around mid-November to mid-February, when the weather is best (with premium rates charged for flights between mid-Dec and New Year), and in July and August to coincide with school holidays. You will need to book several months in advance to get reasonably priced tickets during these peak periods.

The cheapest way of getting straight to most **regional Thai airports** is usually to buy a flight to Bangkok and then a domestic add-on;

Fly less – stay longer! Travel and climate change

Climate change is a serious threat to the ecosystems that humans rely upon, and air travel is the fastest-growing contributor to the problem. Rough Guides regard travel, overall, as a global benefit, and feel strongly that the advantages to developing economies are important, as is the opportunity of greater contact and awareness among peoples. But we all have a responsibility to limit our personal impact on global warming, and that means giving thought to how often we fly, and what we can do to redress the harm that our trips create.

Flying and climate change

Pretty much every form of motorized travel generates CO_2 (the main cause of human-induced climate change) but planes are far and away the worst offenders, not just because of the sheer distances they allow us to travel, but because they release a selection of greenhouse gases high into the atmosphere. Two people taking a return flight between Europe and the US will contribute as much to climate change as an average household's gas and electricity over a whole year.

Fuel-cell and other less harmful types of plane may emerge eventually. But until then, there are really just two options for concerned travellers: to reduce the amount we travel by air (take fewer trips – stay for longer!), and to make the trips we do take "climate neutral" via a carbon offset scheme.

Carbon offset schemes

Offset schemes run by climatecare.org, carbonneutral.com and others allow you to make up for some or all of the greenhouse gases that you are responsible for releasing. To do this, they provide "carbon calculators" for working out the global-warming contribution of a specific flight (or even your entire existence), and then let you contribute an appropriate amount of money to fund offsetting measures. These include rainforest and other indigenous reforestation, and initiatives to reduce future energy demand – often run in conjunction with sustainable development schemes.

Rough Guides, together with Lonely Planet and other concerned partners in the travel industry, are supporting a carbon offset scheme run by climatecare.org. Please take the time to view our website and see how you can help to make your trip climate neutral.

Ⓦ www.roughguides.com/climatechange

see p.42 for details of domestic airlines. An alternative option for **Phuket** would be to fly there with Malaysia Airlines via Kuala Lumpur, or Singapore Airlines via Singapore, avoiding Bangkok altogether. You can also go via Singapore for direct connections to **Chiang Mai** (with Silk Air or Tiger Airways), **Ko Samui** (Bangkok Airways) and **Krabi** (Tiger Airways). Air Asia's direct Kuala Lumpur–Chiang Mai flights, Berjaya Airlines' KL–Samui flights and Bangkok Airways' Hong Kong–Samui route might also be useful options if you want to miss out Bangkok.

Flights from the UK and Ireland

The fastest and most comfortable way of reaching Thailand **from the UK** is to fly nonstop from London to Bangkok with Qantas/British Airways, Thai Airways or Eva Airways – a journey time of about eleven and a half hours. These airlines usually keep their prices competitive, at around £510/730 plus tax in low season/high season. Fares on indirect scheduled flights to Bangkok – with a change of plane en route – are always cheaper than nonstop flights and start at £330/590, though these journeys can take anything from two to twelve hours longer.

There are no nonstop flights from any regional airports in Britain or from any **Irish airports**, and rather than routing via London, you may find it convenient to fly to another hub such as Amsterdam (with KLM), Frankfurt (with Lufthansa), Paris (with Air France), Zurich (with Swiss) or even Dubai (with Emirates), and take a connecting flight from there. Note, however, that changing planes at Charles de Gaulle airport in Paris is a perennial nightmare, partly due to the huge queues at security checks in the transit area, and that KLM can be less than reliable. Flights from Glasgow via Dubai with Emirates, for example, start at around £490, from Dublin via Zurich with Swiss, at around €690.

Flights from the US and Canada

Thai Airways operate **nonstop flights** to Bangkok from New York (4 weekly; around US$1100/1250 low season/high season) and Los Angeles (4–6 weekly; US$1150/1350). Otherwise, plenty of airlines run daily flights to Bangkok from major East and West Coast cities with only **one stop** en route; it's generally easier to find a reasonable fare on flights via Asia than via Europe, even if you're departing from the East Coast. From New York expect to pay around US$1100/1250 in low season/high season, from LA US$825/950.

Air Canada has the most convenient service to Bangkok from the largest number of Canadian cities; from Vancouver, expect to pay around C$1400/1600 in low season/high season; from Toronto, C$1600/1850. Cheaper rates are often available if you're prepared to make two or three stops and take more time.

Although layover times can vary, the actual **flying time** is approximately 17 hours from either New York or LA. From Canada, you can expect to spend something like 16 hours in the air flying from Vancouver (via Tokyo) or at least twenty hours from Montréal (via Europe).

Flights from Australia and New Zealand

There's no shortage of **scheduled flights** to Bangkok **from Australia**, with direct services from major cities operated by Thai Airways, Qantas/British Airways and Emirates (around nine hours from Sydney and Perth), and plenty of indirect flights via Asian hubs, which take at least eleven and a half hours. There's often not much difference between the fares on nonstop and indirect flights, with fares starting from around A$800/1200 (excluding taxes) in low/high season from Sydney and most major eastern Australian cities; special promotions are quite common, however, so you could be looking at low-season flights for as little as A$730. Fares from Perth and Darwin are up to A$100/200 cheaper.

From **New Zealand**, Thai Airways runs nonstop twelve-hour flights between Auckland and Bangkok, charging from NZ$1250/1700 (excluding taxes) in low/high season. BA/Qantas and Emirates flights from Auckland make brief stops in Sydney, adding at least a couple of hours to the trip, and other major Asian airlines offer indirect flights via their hubs (from 17 hours): fares for indirect flights also start at about NZ$1250/1700. From Christchurch and Wellington you'll pay NZ$150–300 more than from Auckland.

Flights from South Africa

There are no nonstop flights **from South Africa** to Thailand, but Singapore Airlines can get you from Johannesburg to Bangkok, via a brief stop in Singapore, in 14 hours. From Cape Town it's a minimum of 18 hours, going via Kuala Lumpur. Other airlines, including South African Airways, make a stop either in the Middle East or in Hong Kong or Southeast Asia. Fares start at about R10,000/7600 for high/low season, including taxes.

Online booking

Ⓦ**www.expedia.co.uk** (in UK), Ⓦ**www.expedia.com** (in US), Ⓦ**www.expedia.ca** (in Canada)
Ⓦ**www.lastminute.com** (in UK)
Ⓦ**www.opodo.co.uk** (in UK)
Ⓦ**www.orbitz.com** (in US)
Ⓦ**www.travelocity.co.uk** (in UK), Ⓦ**www.travelocity.com** (in US), Ⓦ**www.travelocity.ca** (in Canada), Ⓦ**www.zuji.com.au** (in Australia), Ⓦ**www.zuji.co.nz** (in New Zealand)

Airlines

Air France US Ⓣ1-800/237-2747, Canada Ⓣ1-800/667-2747, UK Ⓣ0870/142-4343, Australia Ⓣ1300/390-190, Ⓦwww.airfrance.com.
Air New Zealand US Ⓣ1-800/262-1234, Canada Ⓣ1-800/663-5494, UK Ⓣ0800/028-4149, Republic of Ireland Ⓣ1800/551-447, New Zealand Ⓣ0800/737 000, Ⓦwww.airnewzealand.com.
Bangkok Airways Ⓦwww.bangkokair.com.
British Airways US and Canada Ⓣ1-800/AIRWAYS, UK Ⓣ0870/850 9850, Republic of Ireland Ⓣ1890/626 747, Australia Ⓣ1300/767 177, New Zealand Ⓣ09/966 9777, Ⓦwww.ba.com.
Cathay Pacific US Ⓣ1-800/233-2742, UK Ⓣ020/8834 8888, Australia Ⓣ13 1747, New Zealand Ⓣ09/379 0861, Ⓦwww.cathaypacific.com.
China Airlines US Ⓣ917/368-2003, UK Ⓣ020/7436 9001, Australia Ⓣ02/9232 3336, New Zealand Ⓣ09/308 3364, Ⓦwww.china-airlines.com.
Delta US and Canada Ⓣ1-800/221-1212, Ⓦwww.delta.com.
Emirates US Ⓣ1-800/777-3999, UK Ⓣ0870/243 2222, Australia Ⓣ02/9290 9700, New Zealand Ⓣ09/968 2200, South Africa Ⓣ0861-364728, Ⓦwww.emirates.com.
Etihad Airways Canada Ⓣ905 858 8998, UK Ⓣ020/8735 6700, South Africa Ⓣ0861-ETIHAD, Ⓦwww.etihadairways.com.
EVA Air US and Canada Ⓣ1-800/695-1188, UK Ⓣ020/7380 8300, Australia Ⓣ02/8338 0419, New Zealand Ⓣ09/358 8300, Ⓦwww.evaair.com.
Finnair US Ⓣ1-800/950-5000, UK Ⓣ0870/241 4411, Republic of Ireland Ⓣ01/844 6565, Australia Ⓣ02/9244 2299, Ⓦwww.finnair.com.
Garuda Indonesia US Ⓣ212/279-0756, UK Ⓣ020/7467 8600, Australia Ⓣ1300/365 330 or 02/9334 9944, New Zealand Ⓣ09/366 1862, Ⓦwww.garuda-indonesia.com.
KLM US Ⓣ1-800/225-2525, UK Ⓣ0870/507 4074, Australia Ⓣ1300 303 747, New Zealand Ⓣ09/309 1782, Ⓦwww.klm.com.
Korean Air US and Canada Ⓣ1-800/438-5000, UK Ⓣ0800/0656-2001, Republic of Ireland Ⓣ01/799 7990, Australia Ⓣ02/9262 6000, New Zealand Ⓣ09/914 2000, Ⓦwww.koreanair.com.
Lufthansa US Ⓣ1-800/645-3880, Canada Ⓣ1-800/563-5954, UK Ⓣ0870/837 7747, Republic of Ireland Ⓣ01/844 5544, Australia Ⓣ1300 655 727, New Zealand Ⓣ09/303 1529, Ⓦwww.lufthansa.com.
Malaysia Airlines US Ⓣ1-800/552-9264, UK Ⓣ0870/607 9090, Republic of Ireland Ⓣ01/676 2131, Australia Ⓣ293/13 26 27, New Zealand Ⓣ0800/777 747, South Africa Ⓣ011/880-9614, Ⓦwww.malaysia-airlines.com.
Northwest/KLM US Ⓣ1-800/225-2525, Ⓦwww.nwa.com.
Qantas Airways US and Canada Ⓣ1-800/227-4500, UK Ⓣ0845/774 7767, Republic of Ireland Ⓣ01/407 3278, Australia Ⓣ13 13 13, New Zealand Ⓣ0800/808 767 or 09/357 8900, Ⓦwww.qantas.com.
Qatar Airways US Ⓣ1-877/777-2827, Canada Ⓣ1-888/366-5666, UK Ⓣ020/7896 3636, Ⓦwww.qatarairways.com.
Royal Brunei UK Ⓣ020/7584 6660, Australia Ⓣ1300-721271, New Zealand Ⓣ09/977 2209, Ⓦwww.bruneiair.com.
Royal Jordanian US Ⓣ1-800/223-0470, Canada Ⓣ1-800/363-0711 or 514/288-1647, UK Ⓣ020/7878 6300, Australia Ⓣ02/9244 2701, New Zealand Ⓣ03/365 3910, Ⓦwww.rj.com.
Silk Air Ⓦwww.silkair.com.
Singapore Airlines US Ⓣ1-800/742-3333, Canada Ⓣ1-800/663-3046, UK Ⓣ0844/800-2380, Republic of Ireland Ⓣ01/671 0722, Australia Ⓣ13 1011, New Zealand Ⓣ0800/808-909, South Africa Ⓣ021/674-0601, Ⓦwww.singaporeair.com.
South African Airways US and Canada Ⓣ1-800/722-9675, UK Ⓣ0870/747 1111, Australia Ⓣ1800/221 699, New Zealand Ⓣ09/977 2237, South Africa Ⓣ011/978-1111, Ⓦwww.flysaa.com.
Swiss US and Canada Ⓣ1-877/359-7947, UK Ⓣ0845/601 0956, Republic of Ireland Ⓣ1890/200

515, Australia ⓣ 1300 724 666, New Zealand ⓣ 09/977 2238, South Africa ⓣ 0860 040506, ⓦ www.swiss.com.

Thai Airways US ⓣ 212/949-8424, Canada ⓣ 416/971-5181, UK ⓣ 0870/606 0911, Australia ⓣ 1300 651 960, New Zealand ⓣ 09/377 3886, ⓦ www.thaiair.com.

Tiger Airways ⓦ www.tigerairways.com.

Turkish Airlines ⓣ 1-800/874-8875, UK ⓣ 020/7766 9300, Australia ⓣ 02/9299 8400, ⓦ www.thy.com.

Travel agents and tour operators worldwide

Adventure Center US ⓣ 1-800/228-8747 or 510/654-1879, ⓦ www.adventurecenter.com. Hiking and "soft adventure" specialist agent, offering dozens of packages to Thailand with well-regarded tour operators from all over the world.

Asian Pacific Adventures US ⓣ 1-800/825-1680 or 818/881 2745, ⓦ www.asianpacificadventures.com. Individualized, small-group tours and tailor-mades, including activities such as canoeing, rafting, cruises, trekking and Thai cooking.

Asian Trails Thailand ⓣ 02 626 2000, ⓦ www.asiantrails.net. Well-regarded company that does self-drive tours, cycling and motorcycling adventures, home-stay programmes, river- and sea cruises, plus more typical package tours.

Bike and Travel Thailand ⓣ 02 990 0274, ⓦ www.cyclingthailand.com. Organizes joint and private cycling holidays across Thailand, including around the River Kwai, in Khao Yai national park, and to north and south Thailand. Mountain bikes and support vehicle provided.

Creative Events Asia Thailand ⓦ www.creativeeventsasia.com. Wedding specialists for everything from paperwork to the ceremony and guest accommodation.

Crooked Trails US ⓣ 206/372-4405, ⓦ www.crookedtrails.com. Not-for profit community-based tourism organization offering home-stays in hill-tribe villages and along the Andaman coast, usually featuring volunteer work as well as cultural tours.

ebookers UK ⓣ 0800/082 3000, ⓦ www.ebookers.com, Republic of Ireland ⓣ 01/488-3507 ⓦ www.ebookers.ie. Low fares on an extensive selection of scheduled flights and package deals.

Educational Travel Center US ⓣ 1-800/747-5551 or 608/256-5551, ⓦ www.edtrav.com. Low-cost fares, student/youth discount offers, car rental and tours.

ETC (Educational Travel Centre) Thailand ⓣ 02 224 0043, ⓦ www.etc.co.th. Tour operator whose highlights include overnight rice barge cruises from Bangkok to Ayutthaya, Khao Sok safaris and treks in the Chiang Mai region.

Flight Centre US ⓣ1-866 967 5351, Canada ⓣ1-877 967 5302, UK ⓣ0870/499 0040, Australia ⓣ13 31 33, New Zealand ⓣ0800/243 544, South Africa ⓣ0860 400 727, ⓦwww.flightcentre.com. Guarantee to offer the lowest air fares; also sell a wide range of package holidays and adventure tours.
Gecko Travel UK ⓣ023/9225 8859, Thailand ⓣ081 885 9490, ⓦwww.geckotravel.com. Southeast Asia specialist operating small-group adventure holidays with off-the-beaten-track itineraries; their 21-day tour of Thailand's northern mountains and southern beaches includes treks, rafting and a cookery course. Also offers motorbike tours, family-oriented tours and shorter trips out of Bangkok.
gohop Republic of Ireland ⓣ01/241 2389, ⓦwww.gohop.ie. Irish-owned agent, offering flights, packages, hotels and car rental.
Intrepid Travel US ⓣ1-866/847 8192, Canada ⓣ1-866/732 5885, UK and Ireland ⓣ0800/917 6456, Australia ⓣ1300/360 887 New Zealand ⓣ0800/174 043, ⓦwww.intrepidtravel.com. Well-regarded small-group adventure tour operator that uses local transport and travellers'-style accommodation. Plenty of options, ranging from eight days' trekking and rafting in the north to a 29-day tour of northern hills, western rivers and southern beaches.
Journeys International US ⓣ1-800/255-8735 or 734/665-4407, ⓦwww.journeys-intl.com. Long-standing, award-winning operator focusing on eco-tourism and small-group or customized trips. Their eight-day "Secrets of Siam" tour, for example, puts the emphasis on appreciating local culture in northern Thailand, with optional extras such as bird-watching and classes in cooking and massage.
Lost Horizons Thailand ⓣ081 910 4525, ⓦlosthorizonsasia.com. Eco-minded activity packages, including yoga holidays and turtle-conservation projects, plus cycling, kayaking, trekking etc. Destinations include Khao Sok, the River Kwai, Mae Hong Son and southern beaches.
Nature Trails Thailand ⓣ02 735 0644, ⓦwww.naturetrailsthailand.com. Specialist bird-watching tours in Thailand's national parks.
North South Travel UK ⓣ01245/608 291, ⓦwww.northsouthtravel.co.uk. Competitive travel agency, offering discounted fares worldwide. Profits are used to support projects in the developing world, especially the promotion of sustainable tourism.
Open World Thailand ⓣ02 974 3866, ⓦwww.openworldthailand.com. Award-winning operator offering a diverse programme of trips, notably bird-watching expeditions, cultural tours and Buddhism and meditation trips.
Origin Asia Thailand ⓣ02 259 4896, ⓦwww.alex-kerr.com. Cultural programmes that teach and explain living Thai arts such as dance, music, martial arts, textiles, flower offerings and cooking. Courses last from one day to a week and are held in Bangkok and Chiang Mai.
Real Traveller Canada ⓣ1-888/800-4100, ⓦwww.realtraveller.com. Vancouver-based agent for a multitude of adventure companies all over the world, specializing in small-group and customized trips.
Responsible Ecological Social Tours (REST) Thailand ⓦwww.rest.or.th. Long-running promoter of community-based tourism that operates home-stay programmes in Chiang Mai, Mae Hong Son, Samut Songkhram, Nakhon Si Thammarat and Ko Yao Noi.
Spice Roads Thailand ⓣ02 712 5305, ⓦwww.spiceroads.com. Escorted bike tours to north and south Thailand. Tailor-made itineraries also available.
STA Travel US ⓣ1-800/781-4040, Canada ⓣ1-888/427-5639, UK ⓣ0870/1630-026, Australia ⓣ1300/733 035, New Zealand ⓣ0508/782 872, South Africa ⓣ0861 781 781, ⓦwww.statravel.com. Worldwide specialists in independent travel; also student IDs, travel insurance, car rental, rail passes, and more. Good discounts for students and under-26s.
Telltale Travel UK ⓣ0800/011 2571, ⓦwww.telltaletravel.co.uk. Tailor-made tours that aim to offer as authentic an experience as possible, with accommodation mainly in home-stays (many of them quite upmarket) in Bangkok and around the country.
Thompsons Tours South Africa ⓣ011/770-7700, ⓦwww.thompsons.co.za. Flights and package holidays.
Trailfinders UK ⓣ0845/058 5858, Republic of Ireland ⓣ01/677 7888, Australia ⓣ1300/780 212, ⓦwww.trailfinders.com. One of the best-informed and most efficient agents for independent travellers.
Travel Cuts US ⓣ1-800/592-CUTS, Canada ⓣ1-866/246-9762, ⓦwww.travelcuts.com. Popular, long-established specialists in budget travel, including student and youth discount offers.
USIT Republic of Ireland ⓣ01/602 1904, Northern Ireland ⓣ028/9032 7111, with branches in Athlone, Belfast, Cork, Dublin, Galway, Limerick and Waterford, ⓦwww.usit.ie. Ireland's main outlet for discounted, youth and student fares.

Travel via neighbouring countries

Sharing land borders with Burma, Laos, Cambodia and Malaysia, Thailand works well as part of many overland itineraries, both across Asia and between Europe and Australia. In addition, Bangkok is one of the major regional flight hubs for Southeast Asia.

The main restrictions on overland routes in and out of Thailand are determined by **visas**, and by where the permitted land crossings lie. At any of the land borders described below, most passport holders should be able to get an on-the-spot thirty-day entry stamp into Thailand, which can be extended for ten days at Thai provincial immigration offices for a swingeing B1900. It's easy enough, however, to hop across one of the land borders and return on the same day with another, free thirty-day stamp, or you might want to apply for a sixty-day tourist visa instead, obtainable in advance from Thai embassies.

Full details of **visa requirements** are given on p.88.

You may need to buy visas for your next port of call when in Thailand; details of visa requirements for travel to Thailand's immediate neighbours are outlined below, but these can change so it's worth checking in advance before you travel. All **Asian embassies** are located in Bangkok (see p.216 for contact details), but several countries also have visa-issuing consulates outside the capital, where waiting times can be shorter: China and India run consulates in Chiang Mai (see p.367), and Laos and Vietnam have consulates in Khon Kaen (see p.571). Many Khao San tour agents offer to get your visa for you, but beware: some are reportedly **faking the stamps**, which could get you in pretty serious trouble, so it's safer to go to the embassy yourself.

The right paperwork is also crucial if you're planning to **drive your own car or motorbike** into Thailand. For advice on this, consult the Golden Triangle Rider website (ⓦ www.gt-rider.com/crossingborders.html), which has up-to-date, first-hand accounts of border crossings with a vehicle between many Southeast Asian countries, with lots of detail on Thailand.

Burma

At the time of writing, there is no overland access from **Burma** into Thailand and access in the opposite direction is restricted: Western tourists are only allowed to make limited-distance day-trips into Burma at Three Pagodas Pass near Kanchanaburi (see p.265), at Myawaddy near Mae Sot (see p.316), at Mae Sai (where longer trips to Kentung and back are also possible, see p.435), and at Kaw Thaung (Victoria Point) near Ranong. In some of these places you may be required officially to exit Thailand, enter Burma on a temporary **visa** (for a fee of US$5–10), and then re-enter Thailand for a new thirty-day stay; see relevant accounts in the guide chapters for details. Tourists who intend to enter Burma by air can buy four-week tourist visas at the Burmese embassy in Bangkok (see p.216) for about B800; apply to the embassy and you may be able to collect the same day, or definitely the following day.

Cambodia

At the time of writing, six overland crossings on the **Thai-Cambodia border** are open to non-Thais, but check with the Cambodian Embassy in Bangkok as well as with other travellers first, as regulations are changeable. See the relevant town accounts for specific details on all the border crossings – and for travellers' up-to-the-minute experiences, check out ⓦ www.talesofasia.com/cambodia-overland.htm.

Most travellers use either the crossing at Poipet, which has transport connections to Sisophon, Siem Reap and Phnom Penh and lies just across the border from the Thai town of Aranyaprathet (see p.484), with its transport to Chanthaburi and Bangkok; or they follow the route from Sihanoukville in Cambodia via Koh Kong and Hat Lek to Trat (see p.488), which is near Ko Chang on Thailand's east coast. The Trat route is the fastest option if you're travelling nonstop from Bangkok to Cambodia.

The crossings in northeast Thailand include the Chong Chom–O'Smach border pass, near Kap Choeng in Thailand's Surin province (see p.544), and the Sa Ngam–Choam border in Si Saket province (see p.553) – from both these borders there's transport to Anlong Veng and Siem Reap. There are also two crossings in Chanthaburi province (see p.484), with transport to and from Pailin in Cambodia.

Visas for Cambodia are issued to travellers on arrival at Phnom Penh and Siem Reap airports, and at the Aranyaprathet–Poipet, Hat Lek–Koh Kong, Chong Chom–O'Smach and Ban Pakkard–Phsa Prom (Chanthaburi) land borders; you need US$20 and two photos for this. You may also want to bring a (real or self-made) International Quarantine Booklet showing dates of your vaccinations, as border guards at overland crossings have been known to (illegally) charge foreigners without vaccination cards a US$5 penalty fee. If you do need to buy an advance thirty-day visa, you can do so from the Cambodian Embassy in Bangkok (see p.216). This costs about B1000; apply before noon and you can collect your visa the following day after 5pm.

Laos and Vietnam

There are currently five points along the **Lao border** where it's permissible for tourists to cross into Thailand: Houayxai (for Chiang Khong; see p.443); Vientiane (for Nong Khai; see p.589); Khammouan (aka Tha Khaek, for Nakhon Phanom; see p.596); Savannakhet (for Mukdahan; see p.599); and Pakxe (for Chong Mek; see p.563). Provided you have the right visa, all these borders can be used as exits into Laos; see relevant town account for transport details.

Visas are required for all non-Thai visitors to Laos. A fifteen-day **visa on arrival** can be bought for US$30 (plus two photos) at Vientiane Airport, Louang Phabang Airport, and all the above-listed land borders. However, these visas cost roughly the same but are valid for half the period of **visas bought in advance** from either the Lao Embassy in Bangkok (see p.216) or the Lao Consulate in Khon Kaen (see p.571), both of whom issue thirty-day visas for around B1400, depending on nationality. For this, you need two passport photos; processing takes up to three days – or less than an hour if you pay an extra B200.

If you have the right Lao visa and Vietnamese exit stamp, you can travel **from Vietnam** to Thailand via Savannakhet in a matter of hours; you'll need to use Vietnam's Lao Bao border crossing, west of Dong Ha, where you can catch a bus to Savannakhet and then a ferry across the Mekong to Mukdahan (a bridge across the river near Mukdahan is due to be completed by the end of 2007, which should make the journey even quicker). All travellers into Vietnam need to buy a visa in advance. Thirty-day visas can take up to four working days to process at the embassy in Bangkok (see p.216) and cost about B1800, depending on your nationality; the same visas are issued in 24 hours at the Vietnamese consulate in Khon Kaen (see p.571).

Malaysia and Singapore

Travelling between Thailand and **Malaysia and Singapore** has in the past been a straightforward and very commonly used overland route, with plentiful connections by bus, minibus, share-taxi and train, most of them routed through the southern Thai city and transport hub of Hat Yai. However, because of the ongoing **violence in Thailand's deep south** (see p.825), all major Western governments are currently advising people not to travel to or through Songkhla, Pattani, Yala and Narathiwat provinces, unless essential. This encompasses Hat Yai and the following border crossings to and from Malaysia: at Padang Besar, on the main rail line connecting Butterworth in Malaysia (and, ultimately, Kuala Lumpur and Singapore) with Hat Yai and Bangkok; at Sungai Kolok, terminus of a railway line from Hat Yai and Bangkok, and at adjacent Ban Taba, both of which are connected by road to nearby Kota Bharu in Malaysia; and at the road crossings at Sadao, south of Hat Yai, and at Betong, south of Yala. (The routes towards Kota Bharu and Betong pass through particularly volatile territory, with martial law declared in Pattani, Yala and Narathiwat provinces; however, martial law is not in effect in Hat Yai itself nor the districts of Songkhla province through which the Bangkok–Butterworth rail line and the Hat Yai–Sadao road pass.)

Nevertheless, the provinces of Trang and Satun on the west coast are not affected, and it's still perfectly possible to travel **overland via Satun**: by share-taxi between Satun town and Alor Setar via Thale Ban National Park, or by ferry between Satun's Thammalang pier and Kuala Perlis or the island of Langkawi (see p.841); or by irregular boats between Ko Lipe and Langkawi (see p.845). For up-to-the-minute advice, consult your government travel advisory (see p.81).

Most Western tourists can spend thirty days in Malaysia and fourteen days in Singapore without having bought a visa beforehand, and there are useful Thai embassies or consulates in Kuala Lumpur, Kota Bahru, Penang and Singapore (see p.90).

Health

Although Thailand's climate, wildlife and cuisine present Western travellers with fewer health worries than in many Asian destinations, it's as well to know in advance what the risks might be, and what preventive or curative measures you should take.

For a start, there's no need to bring huge supplies of non-prescription medicines with you, as Thai **pharmacies** (*raan khai yaa*; typically open daily 8.30am–8pm) are well stocked with local and international branded medicaments, and of course they are generally much less expensive than at home. Nearly all pharmacies are run by trained English-speaking pharmacists, who are usually the best people to talk to if your symptoms aren't acute enough to warrant seeing a doctor.

Hospital (*rong phayaabahn*) cleanliness and efficiency vary, but generally hygiene and healthcare standards are good and the ratio of medical staff to patients is considerably

A traveller's first-aid kit

Among items you might want to carry with you – especially if you're planning to go trekking – are:

- Antiseptic.
- Antihistamine cream.
- Plasters/band-aids.
- Lints and sealed bandages.
- Insect repellent, sunscreen and calamine lotion or similar, to soothe sunburn or insect bites.
- Imodium, Lomotil or Arret for emergency diarrhoea relief.
- Paracetamol/aspirin.
- Rehydration sachets.
- Hypodermic needles and sterilized skin wipes.

higher than in most parts of the West. As with head pharmacists, doctors speak English. Several Bangkok hospitals are highly regarded (see p.217), and all provincial capitals have at least one hospital: if you need to get to one, ask at your accommodation for advice on, and possibly transport to, the nearest or most suitable. In the event of a major health crisis, get someone to contact your embassy (see p.216) and insurance company – it may be best to get yourself transported to Bangkok or even home.

There have been outbreaks of **Avian Influenza (bird flu)** in domestic poultry and wild birds in Thailand which have led to a small number of human fatalities, believed to have arisen through close contact with infected poultry. There has been no evidence of human-to-human transmission in Thailand, and the risk to humans is believed to be very low. However, as a precaution, you should avoid visiting live animal markets and other places where you may come into close contact with birds, and ensure that poultry and egg dishes are thoroughly cooked.

Inoculations

There are no compulsory **inoculation** requirements for people travelling to Thailand from the West, but you should consult a doctor or other health professional, preferably at least four weeks in advance of your trip, for the latest information on recommended immunizations. Most doctors strongly advise vaccinations or boosters against polio, tetanus, typhoid, diphtheria and hepatitis A, and in some cases they might also recommend protecting yourself against Japanese B encephalitis, rabies, hepatitis B and tuberculosis. There is currently no vaccine against malaria; for information on prophylaxis, see below. If you forget to have all your inoculations before leaving home, or don't leave yourself sufficient time, you can get them in Bangkok at, for example, the Thai Red Cross Society's Queen Saovabha Institute or the Travmin Medical Centre; see p.217 for details.

Mosquito-borne diseases

Mosquitoes in Thailand spread not only malaria, but also diseases such as dengue fever, especially during the rainy season. The main message, therefore, is to **avoid being bitten** by mosquitoes. You should smother yourself and your clothes in **mosquito repellent** containing the chemical compound DEET, reapplying regularly (shops, guest houses and department stores all over Thailand stock it, but if you want the highest-strength repellent, or convenient roll-ons or sprays, do your shopping before you leave home). DEET is strong stuff, and if you have sensitive skin, a natural alternative is citronella (available in the UK as Mosi-guard), made from a blend of eucalyptus oils.

At night you should sleep either under a **mosquito net** sprayed with DEET or in a bedroom with **mosquito screens** across the windows (or in an enclosed air-con room). Accommodation in tourist spots nearly always provides screens or a net (check both for holes), but if you're planning to go way off the beaten track or want the security of having your own mosquito net just in case, wait until you get to Bangkok to buy one, where department stores sell them for much less than you'd pay in the West. Plug-in insecticide vaporizers, knock-down insect sprays and mosquito coils – also widely available in Thailand – help keep the insects at bay; electronic "buzzers" are useless.

Malaria

Thailand is **malarial**, with the disease being carried by mosquitoes that bite from dusk to dawn, but the risks involved vary across the country.

There is a significant risk of malaria, mainly in rural and forested areas, in a narrow strip along the **borders with Burma, Laos and Cambodia** (including Ko Chang). The only anti-malarial drugs that are currently likely to be effective in these areas are **Doxycycline** and **Malarone**, whose use should be discussed with your travel health adviser, especially as prophylaxis advice can change from year to year.

Elsewhere in Thailand the risk of malaria is considered to be so low that anti-malarial tablets are not advised.

The **signs of malaria** are often similar to flu, but are very variable. The incubation period for malignant malaria, which can be fatal, is usually 7–28 days, but it can take up to a year for symptoms of the benign form to occur. The most important symptom is a raised temperature of at least 38°C beginning a week or more after the first potential exposure to malaria: if you suspect anything, go to a hospital or clinic immediately.

Dengue fever

Dengue fever, a debilitating and occasionally fatal viral disease that is particularly prevalent during and just after the rainy season, is on the increase throughout tropical Asia, and is endemic to many areas of Thailand, especially in the south. Unlike malaria, dengue fever is spread by mosquitoes that can bite during daylight hours, so you should also use mosquito repellent during the day. Ko Pha Ngan seems to suffer a higher than usual incidence of dengue fever. Symptoms include fever, headaches, fierce joint and muscle pain ("breakbone fever" is another name for dengue), and possibly a rash, and usually develop between five and eight days after being bitten.

There is no vaccine against dengue fever; the only treatment is lots of rest, liquids and paracetamol (or any other acetaminophen painkiller, not aspirin), though more serious cases may require hospitalization.

Other health problems

Wearing protective clothing is a good idea when **swimming** or **snorkelling**: a T-shirt will stop you from getting sunburnt in the water, while long trousers can guard against coral grazes. Should you scrape your skin on coral, wash the wound thoroughly with boiled water, apply antiseptic and keep protected until healed.

Thailand's seas are home to a few dangerous creatures that you should look out for, notably **jellyfish**, which tend to be washed towards the beach by rough seas during the monsoon season. All manner of stinging and non-stinging jellyfish can be found in Thailand – as a general rule, those with the longest tentacles tend to have the worst stings – but reports of serious incidents are rare; before swimming at this time of the year, ask around at your resort or at a local dive shop to see if there have been any sightings of poisonous varieties. You also need to be wary of poisonous **sea snakes**, **sea urchins** and a couple of less conspicuous species – **stingrays**, which often lie buried in the sand, and **stonefish**, whose potentially lethal venomous spikes are easily stepped on because the fish look like stones and lie motionless on the sea bed.

If **stung or bitten** you should always seek medical advice as soon as possible, but there are a few ways of alleviating the pain or administering your own first aid in the meantime. If you're stung by a jellyfish, wash the affected area with salt water (not fresh water) and, if possible, with vinegar (failing that, ammonia, citrus fruit juice or even urine may do the trick), and try to remove the fragments of tentacles from the skin with a gloved hand, forceps, thick cloth or credit card. The best way to minimize the risk of

Carrying essential medications

Make sure that you take sufficient supplies of any **essential medications** and carry the complete supply with you whenever you travel – including on public transport – in case of loss or theft (or possibly carry more than you need and split it between your baggage). You should also carry a prescription that includes the **generic name** in case of emergency. It might also be a good idea to carry a **doctor's letter** about your drugs prescriptions with you at all times, partly as this will ensure you don't get hauled up for narcotics transgressions when passing through customs.

If your medication has to be kept cool, buy a thermal insulation bag and a couple of freezer blocks before you leave home. That way you can refreeze one of the two blocks every day, while the other is in use; staff in most hotels, guest houses, restaurants and even some bars should be happy to let you use their freezer compartment for a few hours. If you use needles and syringes, you should also take a small sharps bin with you, as garbage disposal in Thailand is haphazard and your used syringes might harm someone.

stepping on the toxic spines of sea urchins, stingrays and stonefish is to wear thick-soled shoes, though these cannot provide total protection; sea urchin spikes should be removed after softening the skin with ointment, though some people recommend applying urine to help dissolve the spines; for stingray and stonefish stings, alleviate the pain by immersing the wound in hot water while awaiting help.

In the case of a **poisonous snake bite**, don't try sucking out the poison or applying a tourniquet: wrap up and immobilize the bitten limb and try to stay still and calm until medical help arrives; all provincial hospitals in Thailand carry supplies of antivenins. For more on Thai snakes, see p.897.

Rabies

Rabies is widespread in Thailand, mainly carried by dogs (between four and seven percent of stray dogs in Bangkok are reported to be rabid), but also cats and monkeys. It is transmitted by bites, scratches or even licks. Dogs are everywhere in Thailand and even if kept as pets they're never very well cared for; hopefully their mangy appearance will discourage the urge to pat them, as you should steer well clear of them. Rabies is invariably fatal if the patient waits until symptoms begin, though modern vaccines and treatments are very effective and deaths are rare. The important thing is, if you are bitten, licked or scratched by an animal, to vigorously clean the wound with soap and disinfect it, preferably with something containing iodine, and to seek medical advice regarding treatment right away.

Worms and flukes

Worms can be picked up through the soles of your feet, so avoid going barefoot. They can also be ingested by eating undercooked meat, and liver **flukes** by eating raw or undercooked freshwater fish. Worms which cause schistosomiasis (bilharziasis) by attaching themselves to your bladder or intestines can be found in freshwater rivers and lakes. The risk of contracting this disease is low, but you should avoid swimming in the southern reaches of the Mekong River and in most freshwater lakes.

Digestive problems

By far the most common travellers' complaint in Thailand, **digestive troubles** are often caused by contaminated food and water, or sometimes just by an overdose of unfamiliar foodstuffs. Break your system in gently by avoiding excessively spicy curries and too much raw fruit in the first few days, and then use your common sense about choosing where and what to eat: if you stick to the most crowded restaurants and noodle stalls you should be perfectly safe (for more on food hygiene, see p.52). You need to be more rigorous about **drinking water**, though: stick to bottled water (even when brushing your teeth), which is sold everywhere, or else opt for boiled water or tea.

Stomach trouble usually manifests itself as simple **diarrhoea**, which should clear up without medical treatment within three to seven days and is best combated by drinking lots of fluids. If this doesn't work, you're in danger of getting **dehydrated** and should take some kind of rehydration solution, either a commercial sachet of ORS (oral rehydration solution), sold in all Thai pharmacies, or a do-it-yourself version, which can be made by adding a handful of sugar and a pinch of salt to every litre of boiled or bottled water (soft drinks are not a viable alternative). If you can eat, avoid fatty foods.

Anti-diarrhoeal agents such as **Imodium** are useful for blocking you up on long bus journeys, but only attack the symptoms and may prolong infections; an antibiotic such as ciprofloxacin, however, can often reduce a typical attack of self-limiting traveller's diarrhoea to one day. If the diarrhoea persists for a week or more, or if you have blood or mucus in your stools, or an accompanying fever, go to a doctor or hospital.

HIV and AIDS

AIDS is widespread in Thailand, primarily because of the sex trade (see p.176). **Condoms** (*meechai*) are sold in pharmacies, department stores, hairdressers and even street markets.

Should you need to have treatment involving an **injection** at a hospital, try to check that the needle has been sterilized first; this is not always practicable, however, so you might consider carrying your own syringes. Due to rigorous screening methods, Thailand's medical blood supply is now considered safe from HIV/AIDS infection.

Medical resources for travellers

UK and Ireland

British Airways Travel Clinics London ⓣ0845/600 2236, ⓦwww.ba.com/travel/healthclinintro.
Hospital for Tropical Diseases Travel Clinic London ⓣ020/7387-5000 or ⓣ0845/155-5000, ⓦwww.thehtd.org.
MASTA (Medical Advisory Service for Travellers Abroad) UK ⓦwww.masta.org or ⓣ0113/238-7575 for the nearest clinic.
NHS Travel Health Website ⓦwww.fitfortravel.scot.nhs.uk.
Royal College of Surgeons Travel Health Centre Dublin ⓣ01/402 2337.
Travel Medicine Services Belfast ⓣ028/9031 5220.
Tropical Medical Bureau Dublin ⓣ1850/487 674, ⓦwww.tmb.ie.

US and Canada

Canadian Society for International Health ⓦwww.csih.org. Extensive list of travel health centres.
CDC ⓦwww.cdc.gov/travel. Official US government travel health site.
International Society for Travel Medicine ⓦwww.istm.org. Lists travel health clinics.

Australia, New Zealand and South Africa

Travellers' Medical and Vaccination Centre ⓦwww.tmvc.com.au, in Australia ⓣ1300/658 844. Lists travel clinics in Australia, New Zealand and South Africa.

Getting around

Travel in Thailand is both inexpensive and efficient, if not always speedy. Unless you travel by plane, long-distance journeys in Thailand can be arduous, especially if a shoestring budget restricts you to hard seats and no air-conditioning.

Nonetheless, the wide range of transport options makes travelling around Thailand easier than elsewhere in Southeast Asia. **Buses** are fast and frequent, and can be quite luxurious; **trains** are slower but safer and offer more chance of sleeping during overnight trips; moreover, if travelling by day you're likely to follow a more scenic route by rail than by road. Inter-town **songthaews**, **share-taxis** and air-con **minibuses** are handy, and **ferries** provide easy access to all major islands. Local transport comes in all sorts of permutations, both public and chartered.

For an idea of the frequency and duration of bus, train, air and ferry services, check the **travel details** section at the end of each chapter.

Inter-town buses

Buses, overall the most convenient way of getting around the country, come in two main categories: **ordinary** (*rot thammadaa*; orange-coloured) and **air-con** (*rot air* or *rot thua*; usually blue). Ordinary and many air-con buses are run by Baw Khaw Saw, the government transport company, while privately owned air-con buses also ply the most popular long-distance routes. Be warned that long-distance overnight buses, particularly the private air-con buses, seem to be involved in more than their fair share of accidents; because of this, some travellers prefer to do the overnight journeys by train and then make a shorter bus connection to their destination.

Ordinary buses

Ordinary buses are incredibly inexpensive and cover most short-range routes between main towns (up to 150km), running very frequently during daylight hours. Each bus is staffed by a team of two or three – the driver, the fare collector and the optional "stop" and "go" yeller – who often personalize the vehicle with stereo systems, stickers, jasmine garlands and the requisite Buddha image or amulet. With an entertaining team and eye-catching scenery, journeys can be fun, but there are drawbacks. For a start, the teams work on a commission basis, so they pack as many people in as possible and might hang around for thirty minutes after they're due to leave in the hope of cramming in a few extra. They also stop so often that their average speed of 60kph can only be achieved by hurtling along at breakneck speeds between pick-ups, often propelled by amphetamine-induced craziness. To flag down an ordinary bus from the roadside you should wait at the nearest **bus shelter**, or **sala**, usually located at intervals along the main long-distance bus route through town or on the fringes of any decent-sized settlement, for example on the main highway that skirts the edge of town. Where there is only a bus shelter on the "wrong" side of the road, you can be sure that buses travelling in both directions will stop there for any waiting passengers. If you're in the middle of nowhere with no *sala* in sight, any ordinary bus should stop for you if you flag it down.

Air-con buses

Most Thais making journeys of 100km or more choose to travel by **air-con bus**, and on some routes non-air-con options have anyway been phased out. On the busiest routes air-con services depart every 20–30 minutes, while on less popular journeys there may be only three or four a day. Whatever the frequency, most air-con services stop just a few times en route and are usually quite comfortable: passengers are generally allotted specific seats, and on the longest journeys get blankets, snacks and nonstop videos.

On some routes you have a choice of three or even four classes of air-con bus, with the **second-class** service (distinguished by an orange flash on their blue livery and the number "2" appended to the vehicle and route number) being the slowest, cheapest and least comfortable, and the **VIP** (or even "super VIP") services having the fewest seats (generally 24–32 instead of 44) and more leg room for reclining.

Air-con services can cost up to twice as much as the ordinary buses (two or three times as much for VIP buses). Not all air-con buses have toilets, so it's always worth using bus station facilities before you board; and make sure you have some warm clothes, as temperatures can get chilly, even with the blanket.

On a lot of long-distance routes **private air-con buses** are indistinguishable from government ones and operate out of the same Baw Khaw Saw bus terminals. The major private companies, such as Nakhonchai (Ⓣ02 936 3355, Ⓦwww.nca.co.th), have roughly similar fares, though naturally with more scope for price variation, and offer comparable facilities and standards of service. The opposite is unfortunately true of a number of the smaller private companies, several of which have a poor reputation for service and comfort, but attract farang customers with bargain fares and convenient timetables. The long-distance tour buses that run **from Thanon Khao San** in Banglamphu to Chiang Mai and Surat Thani are a case in point; travellers on these routes frequently complain about shabby furnishings, ineffective air-conditioning, unhelpful (even aggressive) drivers and a frightening lack of safety awareness – and there are frequent reports of theft from luggage on these routes, too. If you're planning to travel either of these routes, you are strongly recommended to travel with the government or private bus companies from the main bus terminals (who have a reputation with their regular Thai customers to maintain) or to go by train instead – the extra comfort and peace of mind are well worth the extra baht.

Tickets and timetables

Tickets for all buses can be bought from the departure terminals, but for ordinary buses it's normal to buy them on board. Air-con buses may operate from a separate station or office, and tickets for the more popular routes should be booked a day in advance. As a rough indication of **fares**, a trip from Bangkok to Surat Thani, a distance of 640km, costs B530–700 for VIP, B450 for first-class air-con and B350 for second-class air-con.

Long-distance buses often depart in clusters around the same time (early morning or late at night for example), leaving a gap of five or more hours during the day with no services at all. Local TAT offices often keep up-to-date bus **timetables** in English, or you can consult ⓦwww.transport.co.th/Eng/HomeEnglish.htm for services in and out of Bangkok. Or go to the bus terminal the day before you want to leave and check with staff there. That said, if you turn up at a bus terminal in the morning for a medium-length journey (150–300km), you're almost always guaranteed to be on your way within two hours.

Songthaews, share-taxis and air-conditioned minibuses

In rural areas, the bus network is supplemented – or even substantially replaced – by **songthaews** (literally "two rows"), which are open-ended vans (or occasionally cattle-trucks) onto which the drivers squash as many passengers as possible on two facing benches, leaving latecomers to swing off the running board at the back. As well as their essential role within towns (see "Local transport" on p.42), songthaews ply set routes from larger towns out to their surrounding suburbs and villages, and, where there's no call for a regular bus service, between small towns: some have destinations written on in Thai, but few are numbered. In most towns you'll find the songthaew "terminal" near the market; to pick one up between destinations just flag it down. To indicate to the driver that you want to get out, the normal practice is to rap hard with a coin on the metal railings as you approach the spot (or press the bell if there is one).

In the deep south (see p.827) they do things with a little more style – **share-taxis**, often clapped-out old limos, connect all the major towns, though they are inexorably being replaced by more comfortable **air-conditioned minibuses**. Similar private air-con minibuses are now cropping up on popular routes elsewhere in the country (eg Ayutthaya–Bangkok, Pattaya–Ban Phe, Ranong–Chumphon and Chiang Mai–Pai), while government-run versions are the norm on certain routes in the Central Plains, most usefully on the Kanchanaburi–Sangkhlaburi and Tak–Mae Sot runs. Air-con minibuses generally depart frequently and cover the distance faster than the ordinary bus service, but can be uncomfortably cramped when full and are not ideal for travellers with huge rucksacks.

In many cases, long-distance songthaews and air-con minibuses will drop you at an exact address (for example a particular guest house) if you warn them far enough in advance – it's generally an expected part of the service. As a rule, the **cost** of inter-town songthaews is comparable to that of air-con buses, that of air-con minibuses perhaps a shade more.

Trains

Managed by the State Railway of Thailand (SRT), the **rail** network consists of four main lines and a few branch lines. The **Northern Line** connects Bangkok with Chiang Mai via Ayutthaya, Lopburi, Phitsanulok and Lampang. The **Northeastern Line** splits into two just beyond Ayutthaya, the lower branch running eastwards to Ubon Ratchathani via Khorat and Surin, the more northerly branch linking the capital with Nong Khai via Khon Kaen and Udon Thani. The **Eastern Line** also has two branches, one of which runs from Bangkok to Aranyaprathet on the Cambodian border, the other of which connects Bangkok with Si Racha and Pattaya. The **Southern Line** extends via Hua Hin, Chumphon and Surat Thani, with spurs off to Trang and Nakhon Si Thammarat, to Hat Yai (see the travel warning on p.825), where it branches: one line continues down the west coast of Malaysia, via Butterworth, where you change trains for Kuala Lumpur and Singapore; the other heads down the eastern side of the peninsula to Sungai Kolok on the Thailand–Malaysia border (20km from Pasir Mas on Malaysia's interior railway). At Nakhon Pathom a branch of this line veers

Train information

For 24hr **train information**, phone the State Railway of Thailand (SRT) in Bangkok on ⓣ02 220 4334, or on its free Hotline ⓣ1690. The SRT website (ⓦwww.railway.co.th or ⓦwww.thailandrailway.com) carries English-language timetables and gives a breakdown of ticket prices from Bangkok.

off to Nam Tok via Kanchanaburi – this is all that's left of the Death Railway, of *Bridge on the River Kwai* notoriety (see p.242).

Fares depend on the class of seat, whether or not you want air-conditioning, and on the speed of the train; those quoted here exclude the "speed" supplements, which are discussed below. Hard, wooden or thinly padded third-class seats cost about the same as an ordinary bus (Bangkok–Surat Thani B227, or B297 with air-conditioning), and are fine for about three hours, after which numbness sets in. For longer journeys you'd be wise to opt for the padded and often reclining seats in second class (Bangkok–Surat B368, or B478 with air-conditioning). On long-distance trains, you also usually have the option of second-class berths (Bangkok–Surat B498–568, or B658–748 with air-conditioning), with day seats that convert into comfortable curtained-off bunks in the evening; lower bunks, which are more expensive than upper, have a few cubic centimetres more of space, a little more shade from the lights in the carriage, and a window. Female passengers can sometimes request a berth in an all-female section of a carriage. Travelling first class (Bangkok–Surat B1179) means a two-person air-con sleeping compartment, complete with washbasin.

There are several different **types of train**: slowest of all is the third-class-only Ordinary service, which is generally (but not always) available only on short and medium-length journeys and has no speed supplement. Next comes the misleadingly named Rapid train (B60 supplement), a trip on which from Bangkok to Surat Thani, for example, takes twelve or thirteen hours; the Express (B80 supplement) which does the same route in around twelve hours; the Special Express (B100 supplement) covers the ground in around eleven hours; and fastest of all is the Special Express Diesel Railcar (B120 supplement), which does the journey in nine or ten hours. Note that nearly all long-distance trains have **dining cars**, and rail staff will also bring meals to your seat.

Booking at least one day in advance is strongly recommended for second- and first-class seats on all lengthy journeys, and sleepers should be booked as far in advance as possible (all reservations open thirty days before departure). It's possible to make bookings for any journey in Thailand at the train station in any major town, or by **email** (ⓔpassenger-ser@railway.co.th) or **fax** (ⓕ02 226 6068) to the SRT, at least fifteen days before the start of your journey; you should receive an email confirmation of your booking and then pay for your tickets at the departure station at least an hour before leaving. Otherwise, you can arrange advance bookings over the Internet with reputable Thai travel agencies such as Traveller 2000 (ⓦwww.traveller2000.com) or Thai Focus (ⓦwww.thaifocus.com). For details on how to book trains out of Bangkok **in person**, see p.212.

The SRT publishes clear and fairly accurate free **timetables** in English, detailing types of trains and classes available on each route, as well as fares; the best place to get hold of them is over the counter at Bangkok's Hualamphong Station or, if you're lucky, the TAT office in Bangkok. These English-only timetables cover the services that the SRT think will appeal to tourists; a wider range of trains are shown on part-Thai, part-English national timetables, and there are more detailed local timetables covering, for example, the Bangkok–Ayutthaya route via Don Muang Airport.

The SRT also sells twenty-day **rail passes** (available only in Thailand), covering unlimited train journeys in second- (or third-) class seats for B1500, or B3000 with all supplements thrown in. However, unless you're on a whistle-stop tour of all four corners of the country, the rail network is not really extensive enough to make them pay.

Ferries

Regular **ferries** connect all major islands with the mainland, and for the vast majority of crossings you simply buy your ticket on board. Safety standards are generally just about adequate but there have been a small number of sinkings in recent years – avoid travelling on boats that are clearly overloaded or in poor condition. In tourist areas competition ensures that prices are kept low, and fares tend to vary with the speed of the crossing, if anything: thus Chumphon–Ko Tao costs between B300 (6hr) and B550 (2hr).

On the east coast and the Andaman coast boats generally operate a reduced service during the monsoon season (May–Oct), when the more remote spots become inaccessible. Ferries in the Samui archipelago are fairly constant year-round. Details on island connections are given in the relevant chapters.

Flights

The domestic arm of **Thai Airways** (in Bangkok ⓣ1566, elsewhere in Thailand ⓣ02 1566, ⓦwww.thaiair.com) still has the lion's share of the internal flight network, which extends to all extremities of the country – around two dozen airports. However, with deregulation, several smaller airlines have now broken into the volatile market, including one or two cheap, no-frills companies. **Bangkok Airways** (ⓣ1771 or 02 265 5555, ⓦwww.bangkokair.com) is still Thai Airways' main competitor at home, covering useful routes such as Bangkok–Ko Samui, Bangkok–Trat and Bangkok–Phuket, Chiang Mai–Ko Samui, a Pattaya–Ko Samui–Phuket triangle and a Bangkok–Sukhothai–Chiang Mai triangle.

Among the newcomers on the scene, **Air Asia** (ⓣ02 515 9999, ⓦwww.airasia.com) currently flies from Bangkok to Chiang Mai, Chiang Rai, Krabi, Phuket, Surat Thani, Ubon Ratchathani and Udon Thani; **Nok Air** (ⓣ1318 or 02 900 9955, ⓦwww.nokair.com) covers Bangkok to Chiang Mai, Nakhon Si Thammarat, Phuket and Trang, Chiang Mai to Mae Hong Son and a Bangkok–Loei–Udon Thani triangle; **One-Two-Go** (in Bangkok ⓣ1126, elsewhere in Thailand ⓣ1141, ext 1126, ⓦwww.fly12go.com), operated by Orient Thai Airlines, has flights from Bangkok to Chiang Mai, Chiang Rai, Khon Kaen, Krabi, Phuket and Surat Thani; and **PB Air** (ⓣ02 261 0220–8, ⓦwww.pbair.com) flies from Bangkok to Buriram, Krabi, Lampang, Mae Hong Son, Nakhon Phanom, Nakhon Si Thammarat, Nan, Roi-Et and Sakon Nakhon. Note that these routings change surprisingly frequently and that at the very minor airports, schedules are erratic and flights are sometimes cancelled, so always check ahead.

In some instances a flight can save you days of travelling: a flight from Chiang Mai to Phuket with Thai Airways, for example, takes two hours, as against a couple of days by meandering train and/or bus. To give an idea of **fares**, on the Bangkok–Chiang Mai route Thai and Bangkok Airways both charge around B2600 one-way, while on certain One-Two-Go flights to Chiang Mai you can get seats for B1399.

If you're planning to use the internal network a lot, you can save money by buying an **airpass**, which must be bought outside Thailand from one of the airlines' offices or a travel agent. Of the two available, Bangkok Airways' Discovery Airpass is the easier to use: you buy between three and six flight coupons, generally for US$50 each, confirming the first flight before departure, though the others can be left open; a coupon for Bangkok–Ko Samui costs US$60, while the coupons are not valid on the Chiang Mai–Ko Samui route. Thai Airways' Discover Thailand Airpass covers three one-way flights for US$169; you fix the routes when you buy the pass, but dates of travel can be changed in Thailand. Up to five additional flights can be added for US$59 each.

Local transport

Most sizeable towns have some kind of **local transport system**, comprising a network of buses, songthaews or even longtail boats, with set fares and routes but not rigid timetabling – in many cases vehicles wait until they're full before they leave.

Buses and songthaews

Larger cities like Bangkok, Chiang Mai, Khorat, Ubon Ratchathani and Phitsanulok have a **local bus** network which usually extends to the suburbs and operates from dawn till dusk (through the night in Bangkok). Most vehicles display route numbers in Western numerals, and you pay the conductor B6–10 depending on your destination (on some routes you can choose to take air-con buses, for which you pay a few baht extra).

Within medium-sized and large towns, the main transport role is often played by **songthaews**. The size and shape of vehicle used varies from town to town – and in some places they're known as "tuk-tuks" from the noise they make, not to be confused with the smaller tuk-tuks, described below, that operate as private taxis – but all have the telltale two facing benches in the back. In some towns, especially in the northeast, songthaews follow fixed routes; in others they act as communal taxis, picking up a number of people who are going in roughly the same direction and taking each of them right to their destination. To hail a songthaew just flag it down, and to indicate that you want to get out, either rap hard with a coin on the metal railings, or ring the bell if there is one. Fares within towns range between B10 and B20, depending on distance.

Longtail boats

Wherever there's a decent public waterway, there'll be a **longtail boat** ready to ferry you along it. Another great Thai trademark, these elegant, streamlined boats are powered by deafening diesel engines – sometimes custom-built, more often adapted from cars or trucks – which drive a propeller mounted on a long shaft that is swivelled for steering. Longtails carry between ten and twenty passengers: in Bangkok and Krabi the majority follow fixed routes, but elsewhere they're for hire at about B200 an hour per boat.

Taxi services

Taxis also comes in many guises, and in bigger towns you can often choose between taking a tuk-tuk, a samlor and a motorbike taxi. The one thing common to all modes of chartered transport, bar Bangkok and Chiang Mai's metered taxis, is that you must establish the **fare** beforehand: although drivers nearly always pitch their first offers too high, they do calculate with traffic and time of day in mind, as well as according to distance – if successive drivers scoff at your price, you know you've got it wrong.

Tuk-tuks

Named after the noise of its excruciatingly unsilenced engine, the three-wheeled, open-sided **tuk-tuk** is the classic Thai vehicle. Painted in primary colours, tuk-tuks blast their way round towns and cities on two-stroke engines, zipping around faster than any car and taking corners on two wheels. They aren't as dangerous as they look though, and can be an exhilarating way to get around, as long as you're not too fussy about exhaust fumes. Fares come in at around B50 for a medium-length journey (more like B100 in Bangkok) regardless of the number of passengers – three is the safe maximum, though six is not uncommon. See p.113 for advice on how to avoid being ripped off by Bangkok tuk-tuk drivers.

Samlors

Tuk-tuks are also sometimes known as samlors (literally "three wheels"), but the original **samlors** are tricycle rickshaws propelled by pedal power alone. Slower and a great deal more stately than tuk-tuks, samlors still operate in one or two towns around the country. Forget any qualms you may have about being pedalled around by another human being: samlor drivers' livelihoods depend on having a constant supply of passengers, so your most ethical option is to hop on and not scrimp on the fare.

A further permutation are the motorized samlors (often called "skylabs" in north-eastern Thailand), where the driver relies on a motorbike rather than a bicycle to propel passengers to their destination. They look much the same as cycle samlors, but often sound as noisy as tuk-tuks.

Motorbike taxis

Even faster and more precarious than tuk-tuks, **motorbike taxis** feature both in towns and in out-of-the-way places. In towns – where the drivers are identified by coloured, numbered vests – they have the advantage of being able to dodge traffic jams, but are obviously only really suitable for the single traveller, and motorbike taxis aren't the easiest mode of transport if you're carrying luggage. In remote spots, on the other hand, they're often the only alternative to hitching or walking, and are especially useful for getting between bus stops on main roads and to national parks or ancient ruins.

Within towns motorbike-taxi fares can start at B10 for short journeys, but for trips to the outskirts the cost rises steeply – about B150–200 for a twenty-kilometre round trip.

Vehicle rental

Despite first impressions, a high accident rate and the obvious mayhem that characterizes Bangkok's roads, **driving** yourself around Thailand can be fairly straightforward. Many roads, particularly in the northeast and the south, are remarkably uncongested. Major routes are clearly signed in English, though this only applies to some minor roads; unfortunately there is no perfect English-language map to compensate (see p.84).

Outside the capital, its immediate environs and the eastern seaboard, local drivers are generally considerate and unaggressive; they very rarely use their horns for example, and will often indicate and even swerve away when it's safe for you to overtake. The most inconsiderate and dangerous road-users in Thailand are bus drivers and lorry drivers, many of whom drive ludicrously fast, hog the road, race round bends on the wrong side of the road and use their horns remorselessly; worse still, many of them are tanked up on amphetamines, which makes them quite literally fearless.

Bus and lorry drivers are at their worst after dark (many of them only drive then), so you are strongly advised **never to drive at night** – a further hazard being the inevitable stream of unlit bicycles and mopeds in and around built-up areas, as well as poorly signed roadworks, which are often not made safe or blocked off from unsuspecting traffic.

As for local **rules of the road**, Thais drive on the left, and the speed limit is 60km/h within built-up areas and 90km/h outside them. Beyond that, there are few rules that are generally followed – you'll need to keep your concentration up and expect the unexpected from fellow road-users. Watch out especially for vehicles pulling straight out of minor roads, when you might expect them to give way. An oncoming vehicle flashing its lights means it's coming through no matter what; a right indicator signal from the car in front usually means it's not safe for you to overtake, while a left indicator signal usually means that it is safe to do so.

Theoretically, foreigners need an international **driver's licence** to rent any kind of vehicle, but most companies accept national licences, and the smaller operations (especially bicycle rentals) have been known not to ask for any kind of proof whatsoever. A popular current rip-off, notably on Ko Pha Ngan and Ko Tao, is for small agents to charge renters exorbitant amounts for any minor damage to a jeep or motorbike, even paint chips, that they find on return – they'll claim that it's very expensive to get a new part shipped over from the mainland, but for something as small as a paint chip it's unlikely that they're actually going to replace a panel or whatever. Check out any vehicle carefully before renting; on the two islands mentioned, we've tried to recommend agents who don't indulge in this practice.

Petrol (*nam man*, which can also mean oil) costs around B26 a litre. The big fuel stations are the least costly places to fill up (*hai taem*), and many of these also have toilets and simple restaurants, though some of the more decrepit-looking fuel stations on the main highways only sell diesel. Most small villages have easy-to-spot roadside huts where the fuel is pumped out of a large barrel.

Renting a car

If you decide to **rent a car**, go to a reputable dealer, such as Avis, Budget, Hertz or SMT (see below), or a rental company recommended by TAT, and make sure you get insurance from them. There are international car-rental places at many airports, including Bangkok's Don Muang, which is not a bad place to kick off, as you're on the edge of the city and within fairly easy, signposted reach of the major regional highways; returning a car to Don Muang, however, is less straightforward, because of the jumble of roads and flyovers on the way into Bangkok – try to get detailed instructions, or a map, when you start your rental.

Car-rental places in provincial capitals and resorts are listed in the relevant accounts in this book. The price of a small car at a reputable company is generally about B1500 per day. In some parts of the country, where there are no dedicated car-rental agencies, you'll still be able to rent a car or air-con minibus with driver, for around B1800 per day.

Jeeps are a lot more popular with farangs, especially on beach resorts and islands like Pattaya, Phuket and Ko Samui, but they're notoriously **dangerous**; a huge number of tourists manage to roll their jeeps on steep hillsides and sharp bends. Jeep rental usually works out somewhere between B800 and B1200 per day.

International companies will accept your credit-card details as surety, but smaller agents will often ask for a deposit of at least B2000 and/or will want to hold on to your passport.

Car rental agencies

Avis US ⓣ1-800/230-4898, Canada ⓣ1-800/272-5871, UK ⓣ0870/606 0100, Republic of Ireland ⓣ021/428 1111, Australia ⓣ13 63 33 or 02/9353 9000, New Zealand ⓣ09/526 2847 or 0800/655 111, South Africa ⓣ0861/113748, ⓦwww.avis.com.
Budget US ⓣ1-800/527-0700, Canada ⓣ1-800/268-8900, UK ⓣ08701/565656, Republic of Ireland ⓣ09/0662 7711, Australia ⓣ1300/362 848, New Zealand ⓣ0800/283-438, South Africa ⓣ011/398 0123 or 0861/016622, ⓦwww.budget .com.
Hertz US ⓣ1-800/654-3131, Canada ⓣ1-800/263-0600, UK ⓣ020/7026-0077, Republic of Ireland ⓣ01/870-5777, Australia ⓣ08/9921-4052, New Zealand ⓣ0800/654 321, South Africa ⓣ021/935 4800, ⓦwww.hertz.com.
National US ⓣ1-800/CAR-RENT, UK ⓣ0870/400-4581, Ireland ⓣ021/432 0755, Australia ⓣ02/13 10 45, New Zealand ⓣ03/366-5574, South Africa ⓣ011/570 1900 or 0800/011323, ⓦwww.nationalcar.com.

Renting a motorbike

One of the best ways of exploring the countryside is to **rent a motorbike**, an especially popular option in the north of the country. Two-seater 80cc bikes with automatic gears are best if you've never ridden a motorbike before, but aren't really suited for long slogs. If you're going to hit the dirt roads you'll certainly need something more powerful, like a 125cc trail bike. These have the edge in gear choice and are the best bikes for steep slopes, though an inexperienced rider may find these machines a handful; the less widely available 125cc road bikes are easier to control and much cheaper on fuel.

Rental **prices** for the day usually work out at somewhere between B100 (for a fairly beat-up 80cc) and B350 (for a good trail bike), though you can bargain for a discount on a long rental. As with cars, the renters will often ask for a deposit and your passport or credit-card details, though you're unlikely to have to prove that you've ridden a bike before. Insurance is not often available, so it's a good idea to make sure your travel insurance covers you for possible mishaps.

Before signing anything, **check the bike** thoroughly – test the brakes, look for oil leaks, check the treads and the odometer, and make sure the chain isn't stretched too tight (a tight chain is more likely to break) – and preferably take it for a test run. As you will have to pay an inflated price for any damage when you get back, make a note on the contract of any defects such as broken mirrors, indicators and so on. Make sure you know what kind of fuel the bike takes as well.

As far as **equipment** goes, a helmet is essential – most rental places provide poorly made ones, but they're better than nothing. Helmets are obligatory on all motorbike journeys, and the law is often rigidly enforced with on-the-spot fines in major tourist resorts. You'll need sunglasses if your helmet doesn't have a visor. As well as being more culturally appropriate, long trousers, a long-sleeved top and decent shoes will provide a second skin if you go over, which most people do at some stage. Pillions should wear long trousers to avoid getting nasty burns from the exhaust. For the sake of stability, leave most of your luggage in baggage storage and pack as small a bag as possible, strapping it tightly to the bike with bungy cords – these are usually provided. Once on the road, oil the chain at least every other day, keep the radiator topped up and fill up with oil every 300km or so.

For expert **advice** on motorbike travel in Thailand, check out David Unkovich's website (Ⓦwww.gt-rider.com), which covers everything from how to ship a bike to Thailand to which are the best off-road touring routes in the country.

Cycling

Though long-distance **cycling** is not a popular Thai pastime, an increasing number of travellers are choosing to explore the country by bicycle. The options are numerous, whether you choose to ride the length of the country from Surat Thani to Chiang Mai, or opt for a dirt-road adventure in the mountains north of Fang. And if you don't want to import your own bike, you can buy or rent one locally or join an organized tour. Most Thai roads are in good condition and clearly signposted; although the western and northern borders are mountainous, the rest of the country is surprisingly flat. Traffic is reasonably well behaved and personal safety is not a major concern as long as you "ride to survive". There are bike shops in nearly every town and basic equipment and repairs are cheap. Unless you head into the remotest regions around the Burmese border you are rarely more than 25km from food, water and accommodation. Overall, the best time to cycle is during the cool, dry season from November to February and the least good from April to July (see p.13 for climate information).

Local one-day cycle tours and **bike-rental outlets** (B30–50/day) are listed throughout this book.

Cycling routes

When designing your itinerary, plan on an average of 50km per day, based on 100-kilometre cycling days with rest days every other day; see p.84 for advice on maps. The main arteries carry a high volume of traffic and are to be avoided, if possible. The secondary **roads** (distinguished by their three-digit numbers) are paved but carry far less traffic and are the preferred cycling option. The tertiary roads are unpaved and turn to mud during the rainy season. Note that crossing into Burma from Thailand by land is not possible, but into and out of Laos and Cambodia is hassle-free; see the travel warning on p.825 concerning crossing into Malaysia.

The traffic into and out of **Bangkok** is dense so it's worth hopping on a bus or train for the first 50–100km to your starting point. The Bangkok Skytrain and city trains, intercity air-con buses, taxis and Thai domestic airplanes (no bike box required) will **carry your bike** free of charge. The Bangkok subway does not allow bikes. Intercity trains will only transport your bike (for a fare – about the price of a person) if there is a luggage carriage attached, unless you dismantle it and carry it as luggage in the compartment with you. Intercity non-air-con buses and songthaews will carry your bike on the roof for a fare (about the price of a person).

Due **north** out of Bangkok it's a mostly flat 700-kilometre-plus run (depending on your route) **to Chiang Mai** through historic Ayutthaya and Sukhothai in the central plains. Avoid Highway 1 where possible. To the northwest, **Mae Sot to Mae Hong Son** (360km minimum) along the mountainous Thai-Burmese border is a more adventurous ride through hill-tribe country. Between **Mae Hong Son and Chiang Rai** and around **Nan** on the Lao border are forested and mountainous areas that are especially good for dirt-road and off-road cycling (Thailand has few restrictions on off-road cycling).

From Bangkok to the **northeastern** cities of Nong Khai (minimum 620km) and Ubon Ratchathani (minimum 630km) are flat, easy and laid-back runs, while the route **along the Mekong** from Chiang Khan to Mukdahan (around 600km) is a little hillier, but more interesting. Further south (200km) to Chong Mek and the Lao border is very scenic, if pretty flat.

Heading **south** out of Bangkok, the picturesque and mainly flat route to **Surat Thani** (minimum 650km) runs along the Gulf coast. It's best to begin riding in **Phetchaburi** or **Hua Hin** and avoid Highway 4/41 where possible. The Andaman coast of the peninsula is more spectacular and sometimes mountainous, leading down through **Ranong** (570km minimum from Bangkok) and **Krabi** (940km plus) and on to **Malaysia** via Trang and Satun.

For more detailed itineraries and links to other accounts of cycling in Thailand see Biking Southeast Asia with Mr Pumpy at Ⓦwww.mrpumpy.net.

Cycling practicalities

Strong, light, quality **mountain bikes** are the most versatile choice. 26-inch wheels are standard throughout Thailand and are strongly recommended; dual-use (combined road and off-road) tyres are best for touring. As regards panniers and **equipment**, the most important thing is to travel light. Carry a few spare spokes, but don't overdo it with too many tools and spares; parts are cheap in Thailand and most problems can be fixed quickly at any bike shop.

Bringing your bike from home is the best option as you are riding a known quantity. **Importing** it by plane should be straightforward, but check with the airlines for details. Asian airlines do not charge extra.

Buying in Thailand is also a possibility; the range is reasonable and prices tend to be cheaper than in the West or Australia. In Bangkok, the best outlet is Probike, next to Lumphini Park at 237/2 Thanon Rajdamri (ⓣ02 253 3384, ⓦwww.probike.co.th). There are also a couple of good outlets in Chiang Mai (see also ⓦwww.chiangmaicycling.org): Chaitawat, on Thanon Phra Pokklao, south off Thanon Ratchamankha, on the right (ⓣ053 279890); and Canadian-owned Top Gear, 173 Thanon Chang Moi (ⓣ053 233450).

You can also **rent** Trek 4500 mountain bikes through the Bangkok cycle-tour operator Spice Roads (ⓣ02 712 5305, ⓦwww.spiceroads.com), from US$7/day.

Organized tours by bike

Bangkok-based Spice Roads (ⓣ02 712 5305, ⓦwww.spiceroads.com) and Bike & Travel (ⓣ02 990 0274, ⓦwww.cyclingthailand.com) both run varied programmes of **escorted bike tours** in Thailand, including ten-day trips in the north or south (US$950). In Chiang Mai, Click and Travel (ⓣ053 281553, ⓦwww.clickandtravelonline.com), who offer tours of the north, can also provide kids' mountain bikes and bike seats.

Hitching

Public transport being so inexpensive, you should only have to resort to **hitching** in the most remote areas, in which case you'll probably get a lift to the nearest bus or songthaew stop quite quickly. On routes served by buses and trains, hitching is not standard practice, but in other places locals do rely on regular passers-by (such as national park officials), and as a farang you can make use of this "service" too. As with hitching anywhere in the world, think twice about hitching solo or at night, especially if you're female. Like bus drivers, truck drivers are notorious users of amphetamines, so you may want to wait for a safer offer.

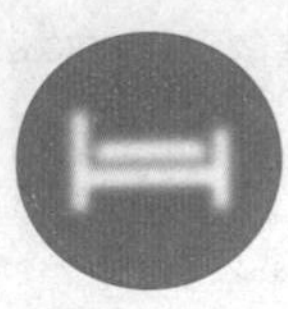

Accommodation

Cheap accommodation can be found all over Thailand. For the simplest double room prices generally start at around B150 in the outlying regions, B200 in Bangkok, and B350 in some of the pricier resorts. Tourist centres invariably offer a huge range of more upmarket choices, and you'll have little problem finding luxury hotels in these places. In most resort areas rates fluctuate according to demand, plummeting during the off-season and, in some places, rising at weekends throughout the year.

Guest houses, bungalows and hostels

Guest houses and **bungalows** are small budget hotels aimed specifically at Western travellers and designed to offer cheap accommodation plus a range of other traveller-oriented facilities, usually including an inexpensive restaurant, a safety deposit system for valuables and luggage storage, and perhaps extending to Internet access, a tour operator desk, and a poste restante service. The difference between guest houses and bungalows is often academic, though "bungalows", which are generally found on the beach and in rural resorts, do often comprise rooms in huts, villas, chalets or indeed bungalows, while the term "guest house" is more common in urban areas and villages where rooms are likely to be in a purpose-built hotel-style building or a converted home. En-suite showers and flush toilets are common, but at the cheaper places you might be showering with a bowl dipped into a large water jar, and using squat toilets.

Both guest houses and bungalows are increasingly offering a spread of options to cater for all budgets: their **cheapest rooms** will often be furnished with nothing more than a double bed, a blanket and a fan (window optional, private bathroom extra) and might cost anything from B100–300 for two people, depending on the location and the competition; Bangkok and the big beach resorts are the least good value. A similar room with **en-suite** bathroom, and possibly more stylish furnishings generally comes in at B180–500, while for a room with **air-con**, and perhaps a TV and fridge as well, you're looking at B200–800.

Accommodation prices

Throughout this guide, guest houses, hotels and bungalows have been categorized according to the **price codes** given below. These categories represent the **minimum** you can expect to pay in the **high season** (roughly July, Aug and Nov–Feb) for a **double room**; note, though, that there may be an extra "peak" supplement for the Christmas–New Year period. If travelling on your own, expect to pay anything between sixty and one hundred percent of the rates quoted for a double room. Wherever a price range is indicated, this means that the establishment offers rooms with varying facilities – as explained in the write-up. Where an establishment also offers **dormitory beds**, the price per bed is given in the text, instead of being indicated by a price code. Top-whack hotels will add **seven percent tax** and **ten percent service charge** to your bill – the price codes below are based on net rates after taxes have been added.

1 Under B200
2 B200–350
3 B350–500
4 B500–700
5 B700–1000
6 B1000–1500
7 B1500–2500
8 B2500–4000
9 Over B4000

In the most popular tourist centres at the busiest times of year, the best-known guest houses are often full night after night. An increasing number will take **bookings** and advance payment via their websites, but for those that don't it's usually a question of turning up and waiting for a vacancy. At most guest houses **checkout time** is either 11am or noon.

Generally you should avoid taking advice from a **tout** or tuk-tuk driver, as they demand commission from guest-house owners, which, if not passed directly on to you via a higher room price, can have a crippling effect on the smaller guest houses. If a tout claims your intended accommodation is "full" or "no good" or has "burnt down", it's always worth phoning to check yourself. However, during the busiest periods at popular resorts, you may find yourself turning to the touts, since at least they'll know a place that has vacant rooms.

With just 27 officially registered **youth hostels** in the whole country, it's not worth becoming a YHA member just for your trip to Thailand, especially as card-holders get only a small discount anyway. In general, youth-hostel prices work out the same as guest-house rates and rooms are open to all ages, whether or not you're a member. They are mostly aimed towards Thai students and so may not be staffed by English-speakers. Online reservations can be made via the Thai Youth Hostels Association website (Ⓦwww.tyha.org).

Budget hotels

Thai sales reps and other people travelling for business rather than pleasure rarely use guest houses, opting instead for **budget hotels**, which offer rooms from B150–700. Beds in these places are large enough for a couple, and it's quite acceptable for two people to ask and pay for a "single" room (*hawng thiang diaw*, literally a "one-bedded room"). Usually run by Chinese-Thais, these three- or four-storey places are found in every sizeable town, often near the bus station. Though the rooms are generally clean and en suite, and come with either fan or air-con, the atmosphere in these places is generally less convivial than at guest houses and there's rarely an on-site restaurant. A number of budget hotels also double as brothels, though as a farang you're unlikely to be offered this sideline, and you might not even notice the goings-on.

Advance reservations are accepted over the phone, but this is rarely necessary, as such hotels rarely fill up. The only time you may have difficulty finding a budget hotel room is during Chinese New Year (a moveable three-day period in late January or February), when many Chinese-run hotels close and others get booked up fast.

Moderate hotels

Moderate hotels – priced between B700 and B1500 – can sometimes work out to be good value, offering many of the trimmings of a top-end hotel (air-con, TV, fridge, pool, restaurant, nightclub), but none of the prestige. They're often the kind of places that once stood at the top of the range, but were downgraded when the multinational luxury hotels muscled in and hogged the poshest clientele. Bed size varies more than in the budget hotels, with some making the strict Western distinction between singles and doubles. You're unlikely to have trouble finding a room on spec, though advance reservations are accepted by phone and booking online through one of the accommodation finders listed below can sometimes save you quite a lot of money.

Upmarket and boutique hotels

Many of Thailand's **upmarket hotels** belong to international chains like Holiday Inn, Marriott and Sheraton, and home-grown chains such as Amari and Dusit, maintaining top-quality standards in Bangkok and major resorts at prices of B2500 (£40/US$60) and upward for a double – far less than you'd pay for equivalent accommodation in the West.

Thailand also boasts an increasing number of exceptionally stylish **super-deluxe hotels**, many of them designed as intimate, small-scale **boutique** hotels, with chic minimalist decor and excellent facilities that often include a **spa** (see p.64 for more on spas). A night in one of these places will rarely cost you less than B4000 (£100/US$150) – and may set you back more than twice as much; see accommodation listings for Bangkok, Chiang Mai, Hua Hin, Ko Samui and Phuket for some suggestions. A note of caution about the term "boutique", however: as in the West, accommodation owners have latched onto it for marketing purposes – sometimes, in practice, a "boutique" guest house or hotel is little more than "small".

Many luxury hotels quote rates in US dollars, though you can always pay in baht. It's a good idea to **reserve ahead** in Bangkok, Chiang Mai, Phuket, Ko Samui, Ko Phi Phi or Pattaya during peak season. And consider checking online accommodation-booking services (listed below) as many of these offer big discounts on top hotels.

Online booking agents

Asia Hotels ⓦ www.asia-hotels.com
Hotel Thailand ⓦ hotelthailand.com
Passion Asia ⓦ www.passionasia.com
Sawadee ⓦ www.sawadee.com
Thai Focus ⓦ www.thaifocus.com

Home-stays

As guest houses have become increasingly hotel-like and commercial in their facilities and approach, many tourists looking for old-style local hospitality are choosing **home-stay accommodation** instead. Home-stay facilities are nearly always simple, and cheap at around B100–150 per person per night, with guests staying in a spare room and eating with the family. Home-stays give an unparalleled insight into typical Thai (usually rural) life and can often be incorporated into a programme that includes experiencing village activities such as rice-farming, squid-fishing, rubber-tapping or silk-weaving. They are also a positive way of supporting small communities, as all your money will feed right back into the village. As well as listed home-stays in Amphawa (see p.233), Ban Prasat (see p.535), Pha To (see p.633), Khuraburi (see p.712), Ko Yao Noi (see p.765) and Krabi (see p.777), there are many others bookable either through REST (Responsible Ecological Social Tours; Ⓦwww.rest.or.th) or as part of a holiday organized via Telltale Travel (Ⓦwww.telltaletravel.co.uk).

National parks and camping

Nearly all the **national parks** have accommodation facilities, usually comprising a series of simple concrete bungalows that cost an average B800 for two or more beds plus a basic bathroom. Because most of their custom comes from Thai families and student groups, park officials are sometimes loath to discount them for lone travellers, though a few parks do offer dorm-style accommodation at around B100 a bed. In many parks, advance booking is unnecessary except at weekends and national holidays.

If you do want to pre-book, the easiest option is to do it online at Ⓦwww.dnp.go.th/National_park.asp – though, as credit-card payment is not yet possible, you need to pay in cash or via bank draft within three days of booking, most conveniently at any branch of Krung Thai bank, or at designated international banks, or at the National Park headquarters in question; see the "Reservation" section of individual national park webpages at the site given above for comprehensive details. The alternatives are to pay on the spot in Bangkok at the offices of the National Park, Wildlife and Plant Conservation Department (Mon–Fri 8.30am–4.30pm; Ⓣ02 562 0760), located in the Ministry of Natural Resources and Environment (MONRE), near Kasetsart University at 61 Thanon Phaholyothin, about 4km north of the Mo Chit Skytrain terminus and Chatuchak Park subway stop; or to book on the phone (not much English spoken), then pay as above. A few national parks accept phone bookings themselves; these are highlighted in the guide chapters. If you turn up without booking, check in at the park headquarters, which is usually adjacent to the visitor centre.

In a few parks, private operators have set up low-cost guest houses on the outskirts, and these generally make more attractive and economical places to stay.

Camping

You can usually **camp** in a national park for a nominal fee of B30, and some national parks also rent out fully equipped tents at anything from B100 to B400. Unless you're planning an extensive tour of national parks, though, there's little point in lugging a tent around Thailand: accommodation everywhere else is too inexpensive to make camping a necessity, and anyway there are no campsites inside town perimeters.

Camping is allowed on nearly all **islands and beaches**, many of which are national parks in their own right. Few travellers bother to bring tents for beaches, though, opting instead for inexpensive bungalow accommodation or simply sleeping out under the stars.

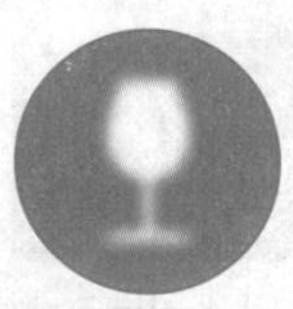

Food and drink

Bangkok and Chiang Mai are the country's big culinary centres, boasting the cream of gourmet Thai restaurants and the best international cuisines. The rest of the country is by no means a gastronomic wasteland, however, and you can eat well and cheaply in even the smallest provincial towns, many of which offer the additional attraction of regional specialities. In fact you could eat more than adequately without ever entering a restaurant, as itinerant food vendors hawking hot and cold snacks materialize in even the most remote spots, as well as on trains and buses – and night markets often serve customers from dusk until dawn.

Hygiene is a consideration when eating anywhere in Thailand, but being too cautious means you'll end up spending a lot of money and missing out on some real local treats.

Wean your stomach gently by avoiding excessive amounts of chillies and too much fresh fruit in the first few days, and always drink either bottled or boiled water.

You can be pretty sure that any noodle stall or curry shop that's permanently packed with customers is a safe bet. Furthermore, because most Thai dishes can be cooked in under five minutes, you'll rarely have to contend with stuff that's been left to smoulder and stew. Foods that are generally considered high risk include salads, raw or undercooked meat, fish or eggs, ice and ice cream. If you're really concerned about health standards you could stick to restaurants and food stalls displaying a "**Clean Food Good Taste**" sign, part of a food sanitation project set up by the Ministry of Public Health, TAT and the Ministry of Interior. The criteria for awarding the logo seem to have some rigour: less than half of applicants pass muster, and thirty percent of awardees are randomly chosen and reassessed each year.

The glorious range and flavours of **Thai cuisine** are discussed in the colour insert later on in this book. For those interested in **learning Thai cookery**, short courses designed for visitors are held in Bangkok, Chiang Mai, Kanchanaburi, Ko Samui, Krabi, Pai, Phuket and Sukhothai; see the relevant accounts for details.

Where to eat

A lot of tourists eschew the huge range of Thai **places to eat**, despite their obvious attractions, and opt instead for the much "safer" restaurants in guest houses and hotels. Almost all tourist accommodation has a kitchen, and while some are excellent, the vast majority serve up bland imitations of Western fare alongside equally pale versions of common Thai dishes. Having said that, it can be a relief to get your teeth into a processed-cheese sandwich after five days' trekking in the jungle, and guest houses do serve comfortingly familiar Western breakfasts.

Throughout the country most **inexpensive Thai restaurants** and cafés specialize in one general food type or preparation method, charging around B30 a dish – a "noodle shop", for example, will do fried noodles and/or noodle soups, plus maybe a basic fried rice, but they won't have curries or meat or fish dishes. Similarly, a restaurant displaying whole roast chickens and ducks in its window will offer these sliced, usually with chillies and sauces and served over rice, but their menu probably won't extend to noodles or fish, while in "curry shops" your options are limited to the vats of curries stewing away in the hot cabinet.

To get a wider array of low-cost food, it's sometimes best to head for the local **night market** (*talat yen*), a term for the gatherings of open-air night-time kitchens found in every town. Often operating from 6pm to 6am, they are typically to be found on permanent patches close to the fruit and vegetable market or the bus station, and as often as not they're the best and most entertaining places to eat, not to mention the least expensive – after a lip-smacking feast of savoury dishes, a fruit drink and a dessert you'll come away no more than B100 poorer.

A typical night market has some thirty-odd "specialist" pushcart kitchens (*rot khen*) jumbled together, each fronted by several sets of tables and stools. Noodle and fried-rice vendors always feature prominently, as do sweets stalls, heaped high with sticky rice cakes wrapped in banana leaves or thick with bags of tiny sweetcorn pancakes hot from the griddle – and no night market is complete without its fruit-drink stall, offering banana shakes and freshly squeezed orange, lemon and tomato juices. In the best setups you'll find a lot more besides: curries, barbecued sweetcorn, satay sticks of pork and chicken, deep-fried insects, fresh pineapple, watermelon and mango and – if the town's by a river or near the sea – heaps of fresh fish. Having decided what you want, you order from the cook (or the cook's dogsbody) and sit down at the nearest table; there is no territorialism about night markets, so it's normal to eat several dishes from separate stalls and rely on the nearest cook to sort out the bill.

For a detailed **food and drink glossary**, turn to p.938.

Fruits of Thailand

One of the most refreshing snacks in Thailand is **fruit** (*phonlamai*), and you'll find it offered everywhere – neatly sliced in glass boxes on hawker carts, blended into delicious shakes at night market stalls and served as a dessert in restaurants. The fruits described below can be found in all parts of Thailand, though some are seasonal. The country's more familiar fruits are not listed here, but include forty varieties of **banana** (*kluay*), dozens of different **mangoes** (*mamuang*), three types of **pineapple** (*sapparot*), **coconuts** (*maprao*), **oranges** (*som*), **lemons** (*manao*) and **watermelons** (*taeng moh*).

To avoid stomach trouble, **peel all fruit** before eating it, and use common sense if you're tempted to buy it pre-peeled on the street, avoiding anything that looks fly-blown or seems to have been sitting in the sun for hours.

Custard apple (soursop; *noina*; July–Sept). Inside the knobbly, muddy green skin you'll find creamy, almond-coloured blancmange-like flesh, having a strong flavour of strawberries and pears, with a hint of cinnamon, and many seeds.

Durian (*thurian*; April–June). Thailand's most prized, and expensive, fruit (see p.181) has a greeny-yellow, spiky exterior and grows to the size of a football. Inside, it divides into segments of thick, yellow-white flesh which gives off a disgustingly strong stink that's been compared to a mixture of mature cheese and caramel. Not surprisingly, many airlines and hotels ban the eating of this smelly delicacy on their premises. Most Thais consider it the king of fruits, while most foreigners find it utterly foul in both taste and smell.

Guava (*farang*; year-round). The apple of the tropics has green textured skin and sweet, crisp flesh that can be pink or white and is studded with tiny edible seeds. Has five times the vitamin C content of an orange and is sometimes eaten cut into strips and sprinkled with sugar and chilli.

Jackfruit (*khanun*; year-round). This large, pear-shaped fruit can weigh up to twenty kilograms and has a thick, bobbly, greeny-yellow shell protecting sweet yellow flesh. Green, unripe jackfruit is sometimes cooked as a vegetable in curries.

Longan (*lamyai*; July–Oct). A close relative of the lychee, with succulent white flesh covered in thin, brittle skin.

Lychee (*linjii*; April–May). Under rough, reddish-brown skin, the lychee has sweet, richly flavoured white flesh, rose-scented and with plenty of vitamin C, round a brown, egg-shaped pit.

Mangosteen (*mangkut*; April–Sept). The size of a small apple, with smooth, purple skin and a fleshy inside that divides into succulent white segments that are sweet though slightly acidic.

Papaya (paw-paw; *malakaw*; year-round). Looks like an elongated watermelon, with smooth green skin and yellowy-orange flesh that's a rich source of vitamins A and C. It's a favourite in fruit salads and shakes, and sometimes appears in its green, unripe form in salads, notably *som tam*.

Pomelo (*som oh*; Oct–Dec). The largest of all the citrus fruits, it looks rather like a grapefruit, though it is slightly drier and has less flavour.

Rambutan (*ngaw*; May–Sept). The bright red rambutan's soft, spiny exterior has given it its name – *rambut* means "hair" in Malay. Usually about the size of a golf ball, it has a white, opaque flesh of delicate flavour, similar to a lychee.

Rose apple (*chomphuu*; year-round). Linked in myth with the golden fruit of immortality; small and egg-shaped, with white, rose-scented flesh.

Sapodilla (sapota; *lamut*; Sept–Dec). These small, brown, rough-skinned ovals look a bit like kiwi fruit and conceal a grainy, yellowish pulp that tastes almost honey-sweet.

Tamarind (*makhaam*; Dec–Jan). A Thai favourite and a pricey delicacy – carrying the seeds is said to make you safe from wounding by knives or bullets. Comes in rough, brown pods containing up to ten seeds, each surrounded by a sticky, dry pulp which has a sour, lemony taste.

Some large markets, particularly in Chiang Mai and Bangkok, have separate **food court** areas where you buy coupons first and select food and drink to their value at the stalls of your choice. This is also the modus operandi in the food courts found on the top floor of department stores and shopping centres across the country.

For a more relaxing ambience, Bangkok and the larger towns have a range of **upmarket restaurants**, some specializing in **"royal" Thai cuisine**, which differs from standard fare mainly in the quality of the ingredients and the way the food is presented. Great care is taken over how individual dishes look: they are served in small portions and decorated with carved fruit and vegetables in a way that used to be the prerogative of royal cooks, but has now filtered down to the common folk. The cost of such delights is not prohibitive, either – a meal in one of these places is unlikely to cost more than B500 per person.

Vegetarians and vegans

Although very few Thais are **vegetarian** (*mangsawirat*), it's usually possible to persuade cooks to rustle up a vegetable-only fried rice or noodle dish, though in more out-of-the-way places that's often your only option unless you eat fish – so you'll need to supplement your diet with the nuts, barbecued sweetcorn, fruit and other non-meaty goodies sold by food stalls. In tourist spots, vegetarians can happily splurge on specially concocted Thai and Western veggie dishes, and some restaurants will come up with a completely separate menu if requested.

If you're **vegan** (*jeh*) you'll need to stress when you order that you don't want egg, as they get used a lot; cheese and other dairy produce, however, don't feature at all in Thai cuisine. Many towns will have one or more **vegan restaurants** (*raan ahaan jeh*), which are usually run by members of a temple or Buddhist sect and operate from unadorned premises off the main streets; because strict Buddhists prefer not to eat late in the day, most of the restaurants open early, at around 6 or 7am and close by 2pm. Very few of these places have an English-language sign, but they all display the Thai character for vegan, a "jeh" (a little like the letter "q" with an elongated arching tail that curves over its head to the left), in yellow on a red background. Nor is there ever a menu: customers simply choose from the trays of veggie stir-fries and curries, nearly all of them made with soya products, that are laid out canteen-style. Most places charge around B30 for a couple of helpings served over a plate of brown rice.

How to eat

Thai food is eaten with a **fork** (left hand) and a **spoon** (right hand); there is no need for a knife as food is served in bite-sized chunks, which are forked onto the spoon and fed into the mouth. Steamed **rice** (*khao*) is served with most meals, and indeed the most commonly heard phrase for "to eat" is *kin khao* (literally, "eat rice"). **Chopsticks** are provided only for noodle dishes, and north-eastern sticky-rice dishes are always eaten with the **fingers of your right hand**. Never eat with the fingers of your left hand, which is used for washing after going to the toilet.

So that complementary taste combinations can be enjoyed, the dishes in a Thai meal are served all at once, even the soup, and shared communally. The more people, the more taste and texture sensations; if there are only two of you, it's normal to order three dishes, plus your own individual plates of steamed rice, while three diners would order four dishes, and so on. Only put a serving of one dish on your rice plate each time, and then only one or two spoonfuls.

Bland food is anathema to Thais, and restaurant tables everywhere come decked out with a **condiment set** featuring the four basic flavours (salty, sour, sweet and spicy): fish sauce with chopped chillies; vinegar with chopped chillies; sugar; and dried chillies – and often extra bowls of ground peanuts and a bottle of chilli ketchup as well. If you do bite into a **chilli**, the way to combat the searing heat is to take a mouthful of plain rice: swigging water just exacerbates the sensation.

Drinks

Thais don't drink water straight from the tap, and nor should you; plastic bottles of drinking **water** (*nam plao*) are sold countrywide, in even the smallest villages, for around

B5–10. Cheap restaurants and hotels generally serve free jugs of boiled water, which should be fine to drink, though they are not as foolproof as the bottles.

Night markets, guest houses and restaurants do a good line in freshly squeezed **fruit juices** such as lemon (*nam manao*) and orange (*nam som*), which often come with salt and sugar already added, particularly upcountry. The same places will usually do **fruit shakes** as well, blending bananas (*nam kluay*), papayas (*nam malakaw*), pineapples (*nam sapparot*) and others with liquid sugar or condensed milk (or yoghurt, to make lassi). Fresh **coconut water** (*nam maprao*) is another great thirst-quencher – you buy the whole fruit dehusked, decapitated and chilled; Thais are also very partial to freshly squeezed **sugar-cane juice** (*nam awy*), which is sickeningly sweet.

Bottled and canned brand-name **soft drinks** are sold all over the place, with a particularly wide range in the ubiquitous 7–11 chain stores. Soft-drink bottles are returnable, so some shops and drink stalls have an amazing system of pouring the contents into a small plastic bag (fastened with an elastic band and with a straw inserted) rather than charging you the extra for taking away the bottle. The larger restaurants keep their soft drinks refrigerated, but smaller cafés and shops add **ice** (*nam khaeng*) to glasses and bags. Most ice is produced commercially under hygienic conditions, but it might become less pure in transit so be wary – and don't take ice if you have diarrhoea. For those travelling with children, or just partial themselves to **dairy products**, UHT-preserved milk and chilled yoghurt drinks are widely available (especially 7–11 stores), as are a variety of soya drinks.

Weak Chinese **tea** (*nam chaa*) makes a refreshing alternative to water and often gets served in Chinese restaurants and roadside cafés. Posher restaurants keep stronger Chinese and Western-style teas and **coffee** (*kaafae*), which is nowadays mostly the ubiquitous instant Nescafé. This is usually the coffee offered to farangs, even if freshly ground Thai-grown coffee – notably several kinds of hill-tribe coffee from the mountains of the north – is available. If you would like to try traditional Thai coffee, most commonly found at Chinese-style cafés in the south of the country or at outdoor markets, and prepared through filtering the grounds through a cloth, ask for *kaafae thung* (literally, "bag coffee"), normally served very bitter with sugar as well as sweetened condensed milk alongside a glass of black tea to wash it down with. Fresh Western-style coffee (*kaafae sot*), whether filtered, espresso or percolated, is mostly limited to farang-oriented places, international-style coffee bars and big hotels, in Bangkok, Chiang Mai and beach areas. Tea and coffee are normally served black, perhaps with a sachet of coffee whitener on the side.

Alcoholic drinks

Beer (*bia*) is one of the few consumer items in Thailand that's not a bargain due to the heavy taxes levied on the beverage – at around B50 for a 330ml bottle in the shops, it works out roughly the same as what you'd pay in the West (larger, 660ml bottles, when available, are always slightly better value). The two most famous local beers are Singha, which now has six percent alcohol content and an improved taste (ask for "*bia sing*"), and the cheaper Chang, which weighs in at a head-banging seven percent alcohol. All manner of foreign beers are now brewed in Thailand, including Heineken and Asahi, and in the most touristy areas you'll find imported bottles from all over the world.

Wine attracts even higher taxation than beer. It's now found on plenty of upmarket and tourist-oriented restaurant menus, but expect to be disappointed both by the quality and by the price. Thai wine is now produced at several vineyards, notably at Château de Loei near Phu Reua National Park in the northeast, which produces quite tasty reds, whites, a rosé, a dessert wine and brandy (see p.581).

At about B75 for a hip-flask-sized 375ml bottle, the local **whisky** is a lot better value, and Thais think nothing of consuming a bottle a night, heavily diluted with ice and soda or Coke. The most palatable and widely available of these is Mekong, which is very pleasant once you've stopped expecting it to taste like Scotch; distilled from rice, Mekong is 35 percent proof, deep gold in colour and tastes slightly sweet. If that's not to your taste, a pricier Thai **rum** is also available, Sang Thip, made from sugar cane, and even stronger than the whisky at forty percent proof. Check the menu carefully when ordering a bottle of Mekong from a bar in a tourist area, as they often ask up to five times more than you'd pay in a guest house or shop.

You can **buy** beer and whisky in food stores, guest houses and most restaurants at any time of the day; **bars** aren't really an indigenous feature as Thais rarely drink out without eating, but you'll find a fair number of Western-style drinking holes in Bangkok and larger centres elsewhere in the country, ranging from ultra-hip haunts in the capital to basic, open-to-the-elements "**bar-beers**".

The media

To keep you abreast of world affairs, there are several English-language newspapers in Thailand, though a mild form of censorship affects the predominantly state-controlled media, even muting the English-language branches on occasion.

Newspapers and magazines

Of the hundreds of **Thai-language newspapers and magazines** published every week, the sensationalist tabloid *Thai Rath* attracts the widest readership, and the independent *Siam Rath*, founded by M.R. Kukrit Pramoj (see p.178), and the broadly similar *Matichon*, are the most intellectual.

Alongside these, two daily **English-language papers** – the *Bangkok Post* (Ⓦwww.bangkokpost.com) and the *Nation* (Ⓦwww.nationmultimedia.com) – are capable of adopting a fairly critical attitude to governmental goings-on and cover major domestic and international stories as well as tourist-related issues. Of the two, the *Bangkok Post* tends to focus more on international stories, while the *Nation* has the most in-depth coverage of Thai and Southeast Asian issues. Both are sold at most newsstands in the capital as well as in major provincial towns and tourist resorts; the more isolated places receive their few copies at least one day late. *Bangkok Metro*, the capital's monthly English-language listings **magazine**, as well as reviews and previews of events in the city, carries lively articles on cultural and contemporary life in Thailand.

The more traveller-oriented monthly magazine *Untamed Travel* (formerly *Farang*) reviews bars, clubs, restaurants and guest houses in Thailand's most popular dozen tourist destinations and also prints some interesting features on contemporary Southeast Asian culture; it is sold most widely in Bangkok but is also available in some major tourist centres.

You can also pick up **foreign publications** such as *Newsweek*, *Time* and the *International Herald Tribune* in Bangkok, Chiang Mai, and the major resorts; from Monday to Friday, the *IHT* now carries an English-language supplement devoted to Thailand, *Thai Day*. English-language bookstores such as Bookazine and some expensive hotels carry air-freighted copies of foreign national newspapers for at least B50 a copy. The weekly current affairs magazine *Far Eastern Economic Review* is also worth looking out for; available in major bookshops and at newsstands in tourist centres, it generally offers a very readable selection of articles on Thailand and the rest of Asia.

Television

There are five government-controlled **TV channels** in Thailand: channels 3, 5, 7 and

9 transmit a blend of news, documentaries, soaps, talk and quiz shows, while the more serious-minded 11 is a public-service channel, owned and operated by the government's public relations department. ITV is the only supposedly independent channel, owned and operated by Shin Corp, a communications conglomerate that was founded by Thaksin Shinawatra, but was recently sold, under controversial circumstances, to Temasek Holdings of Singapore; what effect, if any, this will have on editorial policy is unclear. **Cable** networks – available in many mid-range and most upmarket hotel rooms – carry channels from all around the world, including CNN from the US, BBC World from the UK, ABC from Australia, English-language movie channels, MTV and various sports and documentary channels. Both the *Bangkok Post* and the *Nation* print the daily TV and cable **schedule**.

Radio

Thailand boasts over five hundred **radio stations**, mostly music-oriented, ranging from Virgin Radio's Eazy (105.5 FM), which serves up Western pop, to Fat Radio, which plays Thai Indie sounds (104.5 FM). At the opposite end of the taste spectrum, Chulalongkorn University Radio (101.5 FM) plays classical music from 9.30pm to midnight every night. Meanwhile, the government-controlled Radio Thailand broadcasts news in English on 95.5 FM and 105 FM every day at 7am, noon and 7pm.

With a shortwave **radio** – or by going **online** – you can pick up the BBC World Service (ⓦwww.bbcworldservice.com), Radio Australia (ⓦwww.abc.net.au/ra), Voice of America (ⓦwww.voa.gov), Radio Canada (ⓦwww.rcinet.ca) and other international stations right across Thailand. Times and wavelengths change regularly, so get hold of a recent schedule just before you travel or consult the websites for frequency and programme guides.

Festivals

Nearly all Thai festivals have some kind of religious aspect. The most theatrical are generally Brahmanic (Hindu) in origin, honouring elemental spirits with ancient rites and ceremonial costumed parades. Buddhist celebrations usually revolve round the local temple, and while merit-making is a significant feature, a light-hearted atmosphere prevails, as the wat grounds are swamped with food and trinket vendors and makeshift stages are set up to show *likay* folk theatre, singing stars and beauty contests; there may even be funfair rides as well.

Many of the **secular festivals** (like the elephant roundups and the Bridge over the River Kwai spectacle) are outdoor local culture shows, geared specifically towards Thai and farang tourists. Others are thinly veiled trade fairs held in provincial capitals to show off the local speciality, which nevertheless assume all the trappings of a temple fair and so are usually worth a look.

Few of the **dates** for religious festivals are fixed, so check with TAT for specifics or consult ⓦwww.thailandgrandfestival.com. The names of the most touristy celebrations are given here in English; the more low-key festivals are more usually known by their Thai name (*ngan* means "festival").

A festival calendar

January–March

Bangkok International Film Festival (usually takes place over ten days in Feb; ⓦwww.bangkokfilm.org). An annual chance to preview new and unusual Thai films alongside features and documentaries from around the world.

Nakhon Sawan *Chinese New Year* (three days anytime between mid-Jan and late Feb). The new Chinese year is welcomed in with exuberant parades of dragons and lion dancers, Chinese opera performances, an international lion dance competition and a fireworks display. Also celebrated in Chinatowns across the country, especially in Bangkok and Phuket.

Chiang Mai *Flower Festival* (usually first weekend in Feb). Enormous floral sculptures are paraded through the streets. See p.352.

Nationwide *Maha Puja* (particularly Wat Benjamabophit in Bangkok and Wat Phra That Doi Suthep in Chiang Mai; Feb full-moon day). A day of merit-making marks the occasion when 1250 disciples gathered spontaneously to hear the Buddha preach, and culminates with a candlelit procession round the local temple's bot.

Nakhon Si Thammarat *Hae Pha Khun That* (for Maha Puja at Feb full moon). Southerners gather to pay homage to the Buddha relics at Wat Mahathat, including a procession of long saffron cloth around the chedi. See p.682.

Phra Phutthabat, near Lopburi *Ngan Phrabat* (early Feb and early March). Pilgrimages to the Holy Footprint attract food and handicraft vendors and travelling players. See p.283.

Phitsanulok *Ngan Phra Buddha Chinnarat* (mid-Feb). Thailand's second most important Buddha image is honoured with music, dance and *likay* performances.

Phetchaburi *Phra Nakhon Khiri fair* (mid-Feb). *Son-et-lumière* at Khao Wang palace.

Lopburi *King Narai Reign Fair* (Feb). Costumed processions and a *son-et-lumière* show at Narai's palace.

That Phanom *Ngan Phra That Phanom* (Feb). Thousands come to pay homage at the holiest shrine in Isaan, which houses relics of the Buddha.

Nationwide *Kite fights and flying contests* (particularly Sanam Luang, Bangkok; late Feb to mid-April). There's also an International Kite Festival, held in Cha-am in March. See p.142.

April and May

Mae Hong Son and Chiang Mai *Poy Sang Long* (early April). Young Thai Yai boys precede their ordination into monkhood by parading the streets in floral headdresses and festive garb. See pp.408 and 352.

Nationwide *Songkhran* (particularly Chiang Mai, and Bangkok's Thanon Khao San; usually April 13–15). The most exuberant of the national festivals welcomes the Thai New Year with massive waterfights, sandcastle building in temple compounds and the inevitable parades and "Miss Songkhran" beauty contests. See p.352.

Prasat Hin Khao Phanom Rung *Ngan Phanom Rung* (usually April). Daytime processions up to the eleventh-century Khmer ruins, followed by a *son-et-lumière*. See p.540.

Samphran Elephant Ground, near Nakhon Pathom *Jumbo Queen* (May 1; ⓦwww.jumboqueen.com). Elephants show off their skills and engage in a costumed re-enactment of a sixteenth-century battle before being rewarded by a huge buffet. The Jumbo Queen contest is a beauty pageant for graceful larger ladies, the winner of which becomes an ambassador for elephant conservation.

Nationwide *Visakha Puja* (particularly Bangkok's Wat Benjamabophit and Nakhon Si Thammarat; May full-moon day). The holiest day of the Buddhist year, commemorating the birth, enlightenment and death of the Buddha all in one go; the most public and photogenic part is the candlelit evening procession around the wat.

Sanam Luang, Bangkok *Raek Na* (early May). The royal ploughing ceremony to mark the beginning of the rice-planting season; ceremonially clad Brahmin leaders parade sacred oxen and the royal plough, and interpret omens to forecast the year's rice yield. See p.142.

Yasothon *Rocket Festival* (*Bun Bang Fai*; weekend in mid-May). Beautifully crafted painted wooden rockets are paraded and fired to ensure plentiful rains; celebrated all over Isaan, but especially lively in Yasothon. See p.564.

June–September

Hua Hin *Jazz Festival* (a weekend in late June). Well-known musicians from Thailand and abroad play for free at various special outdoor venues throughout the beach resort.

Dan Sai, near Loei *Phi Ta Khon* (end June or beginning July). Masked re-enactment of the Buddha's penultimate incarnation. See p.576.

Ubon Ratchathani *Candle Festival* (*Asanha Puja*) (July, three days around the full moon). Ubon citizens celebrate the nationwide festival to mark the Buddha's first sermon and the subsequent beginning of the annual Buddhist retreat period (Khao Pansa) with parades of enormous wax sculptures. See p.554.

Hua Hin *Elephant Polo Tournament* (five days in late September). Teams from around the world compete on elephant-back in this variation on the traditional game. Also features an elephant parade and various other elephant-related events.

Nakhon Si Thammarat *Tamboon Deuan Sip* (Sept or Oct). Merit-making ceremonies to honour dead relatives accompanied by a ten-day fair on the town field. See p.682.

Ko Si Chang *King Chulalongkorn's Birthday* (Sept 20). Islanders honour the memory of their patron-king Rama V with a *son et lumière* and a beauty contest staged entirely in nineteenth-century dress. See p.455.

October–December

Phuket and Trang *Vegetarian Festival* (*Ngan Kin Jeh*; Oct or Nov). Chinese devotees become vegetarian for a nine-day period and then parade through town performing acts of self-mortification such as pushing skewers through their cheeks. Celebrated in Bangkok's Chinatown by most food vendors and restaurants turning vegetarian for about a fortnight. See p.738.

Nong Khai and around *Bang Fai Phaya Nak* (usually Oct). The strange appearance of pink balls of fire above the Mekong River draws sightseers from all over Thailand. See p.588.

Nationwide *Tak Bat Devo* and *Awk Pansa* (especially Ubon Ratchathani and Nakhon Phanom; Oct full-moon day). Offerings to monks and general merrymaking to celebrate the Buddha's descent to earth from Tavatimsa heaven and the end of the Khao Pansa retreat. Celebrated in Ubon with a procession of illuminated boats along the river and lots of firecrackers, and in Nakhon Phanom with another illuminated boat procession and Thailand–Laos dragon-boat races along the Mekong. See p.596.

Surat Thani *Chak Phra* (mid-Oct). The town's chief Buddha images are paraded on floats down the streets and on barges along the river. See p.636.

Nan and Phimai *Boat Races* (mid-Oct to mid-Nov). Longboat races and barge parades along town rivers. See p.389.

Nationwide *Thawt Kathin* (the month between Awk Pansa and Loy Krathong, generally Oct to Nov). During the month following the end of the monks' rainy-season retreat, it's traditional for the laity to donate new robes to the monkhood and this is celebrated in most towns with parades and a festival.

Nationwide *Loy Krathong* (particularly Sukhothai and Chiang Mai; full moon in Nov). Baskets (*krathong*) of flowers and lighted candles are floated on any available body of water (such as ponds, rivers, lakes, canals and seashores) to honour water spirits and celebrate the end of the rainy season. Nearly every town puts on a big show, with bazaars, public entertainments, fireworks, and in Chiang Mai, the release of paper hot-air balloons; in Sukhothai it is the climax of a nine-day *son-et-lumière* festival. See p.352 and *Loy Krathong* colour insert.

Wat Saket, Bangkok *Ngan Wat Saket* (first week of Nov). Probably Thailand's biggest temple fair, held around the Golden Mount, with all the usual festival trappings.

Surin *Elephant Roundup* (third weekend of Nov). Two hundred elephants play team games, perform complex tasks and parade in battle dress. See p.547.

Kanchanaburi *River Kwai Bridge Festival* (ten nights from the last week of Nov into the first week of Dec). Spectacular *son et lumière* at the infamous bridge.

Khon Kaen *Silk and Phuk Siao Festival* (Nov 29–Dec 10). Weavers from around the province come to town to sell their lengths of silk. See p.567.

Ayutthaya *World Heritage Site Festival* (mid-Dec). Week-long celebration, including a nightly historical *son-et-lumière* romp, to commemorate the town's UNESCO designation. See p.268.

Nationwide *New Year's Eve Countdown* (Dec 31). Most cities and tourist destinations welcome in the new year with fireworks, often backed up by food festivals, beauty contests and outdoor performances.

Entertainment and sport

Most travellers confine their experience of Thai traditional culture to a one-off attendance at a Bangkok tourist show, not least because it can be hard to locate, let alone understand, more authentic folk theatre and music (see p.903) performances. Traditional sport is more accessible, however, and just as much of a performance, especially in the case of Thai boxing.

Bangkok has a few authentic fixed venues for dance and a couple for Thai boxing; otherwise it's a question of keeping your eyes open in upcountry areas for signs that a travelling troupe may soon turn up. This is most likely at festivals and fairs, which sometimes also feature some of the more traditional pastimes such as (illegal) gambling on the outcome of cock fights and fighting fish contests.

Drama and dance

Drama pretty much equals **dance** in classical Thai theatre, and many of the traditional dance-dramas are based on the Hindu epic the *Ramayana* (in Thai, *Ramakien*), an adventure tale of good versus evil which is taught in all the schools. Not understanding the plots can be a major disadvantage, so try reading an abridged version beforehand (see "Books" p.927, or p.61 for an outline) and check out the wonderfully imaginative murals at Wat Phra Kaeo in Bangkok, after which you'll certainly be able to sort the goodies from the baddies, if little else. There are three broad categories of traditional Thai dance-drama – *khon*, *lakhon* and *likay* – described below in descending order of refinement.

Khon

The most spectacular form of traditional Thai theatre is **khon**, a stylized drama performed in masks and elaborate costumes by a troupe of highly trained classical dancers. There's little room for individual interpretation in these dances, as all the movements follow a strict choreography that's been passed down through generations: each graceful, angular gesture depicts a precise event, action or emotion which will be familiar to educated *khon* audiences. The dancers don't speak, and the story is chanted and sung by a chorus who stand at the side of the stage, accompanied by a classical *phipat* orchestra.

A typical *khon* performance features several of the best-known **Ramayana** episodes, in which the main characters are recognized by their masks, headdresses and heavily brocaded costumes. Gods and humans don't wear masks, but it's generally easy enough to distinguish the hero Rama and heroine Sita from the action; they always wear tall gilded headdresses and often appear in a threesome with Rama's brother Lakshaman. Monkey **masks** are always open-mouthed, almost laughing, and come in several colours: monkey army chief Hanuman always wears white, and his two right-hand men – Nilanol, the god of fire, and Nilapat, the god of death – wear red and black respectively. In contrast, the demons have grim mouths, clamped shut or snarling out of usually green faces; Totsagan, king of the demons, wears a green face in battle and a gold one during peace, but always sports a two-tier headdress carved with two rows of faces.

Khon is performed at Bangkok's National Theatre and is also featured within the various cultural **shows** staged by tourist restaurants in Bangkok, Phuket and Pattaya. Even if you don't see a show, you're bound to come across copies of the masks worn by the main *khon* characters, which are sold as souvenirs all over the country and constitute an art form in their own right.

Lakhon

Serious and refined, **lakhon** is derived from *khon* but is used to dramatize a greater range of stories, including Buddhist *Jataka* tales, local folk dramas and of course the *Ramayana*. The form you're most likely to come across is *lakhon chatri*, which is performed at shrines like Bangkok's Erawan and *lak muang* as entertainment for the spirits and a token of gratitude from worshippers. Usually female, the *lakhon chatri* dancers perform as a group rather than as individual characters, executing sequences which, like *khon* movements, all have minute and particular symbolism. They wear similarly decorative costumes but no masks, and dance to the music of a *phipat* orchestra.

Unfortunately, as resident shrine troupes tend to repeat the same dances a dozen times a day, it's rarely the sublime display it's cracked up to be. Bangkok's National Theatre stages fairly regular performances of the more elegantly executed *lakhon nai*, a dance form that used to be performed at the Thai court and often retells the *Ramayana*.

Likay

Likay is a much more popular derivative of *khon* – more light-hearted, with lots of comic interludes, bawdy jokes and over-the-top acting and singing. Some *likay* troupes perform *Ramayana* excerpts, but a lot of them adapt pot-boiler romances or write their own. Depending on the show, costumes are either traditional as in *khon* and *lakhon*, modern and Western as in films, or a mixture of both. *Likay* troupes travel around the country doing shows on make-shift outdoor stages wherever they think they'll get an audience; temples sometimes hire them out for fairs and there's usually a *likay* stage of some kind at a festival.

Performances are often free and generally last for about five hours, with the audience strolling in and out of the show, cheering and joking with the cast throughout. Televised *likay* dramas get huge audiences and always follow romantic plot-lines. Short *likay* dramas are also performed regularly at Bangkok's National Theatre.

Nang

Nang, or shadow plays, are said to have been the earliest dramas performed in Thailand, but now are rarely seen except in the far south, where the Malaysian influence ensures an appreciative audience for *nang thalung*. Crafted from buffalo hide, the two-dimensional *nang thalung* puppets play out scenes from popular dramas against a back-lit screen, while the storyline is told through songs, chants and musical interludes. An even rarer *nang* form is the *nang yai*, which uses enormous cut-outs of whole scenes rather than just individual characters, so the play becomes something like an animated film. For more on shadow puppets and puppetry, see p.686.

Film and video

All sizeable towns have a **cinema** or two (Bangkok has over forty; see p.201) and tickets generally start at B80. In some rural areas, villagers still have to make do with the travelling cinema, or *nang klarng plaeng*, which sets up a mobile screen in wat compounds or other public spaces, and often entertains the whole village in one sitting (see p.918 for more on these). However makeshift the cinema, the **king's anthem** is always played before every screening, during which the audience is expected to stand up.

Fast-paced Chinese blockbusters have long dominated the programmes at Thai cinemas, serving up a low-grade cocktail of sex, spooks, violence and comedy. Not understanding the dialogue is rarely a draw-back, as the storylines tend to be simple and the visuals more entertaining than the words. In the cities, **Western films** are also pretty big, and new releases often get **subtitled** rather than dubbed.

In recent years Thailand's own film industry has been enjoying a bit of a boom, and in the larger cities and resorts you may be lucky enough to come across one of the bigger Thai hits showing with English subtitles.

The website Ⓦwww.movieseer.com lists the weekly schedule for many cinemas around the country. See "Contexts" on p.918 for an introduction to Thai cinema.

Thai boxing

Thai boxing (*muay Thai*) enjoys a following similar to soccer or baseball in the West: every province has a stadium and whenever the sport is shown on TV you can be sure that large noisy crowds will gather round the sets in streetside restaurants and noodle shops. The best place to see Thai boxing is at one of Bangkok's two main stadia, which between them hold bouts every night of the week and on some afternoons as well (see p.202).

There's a strong spiritual and **ritualistic** dimension to *muay Thai*, adding grace to an otherwise brutal sport. Each boxer enters the ring to the wailing music of a three-piece *phipat* orchestra, often flamboyantly attired in a lurid silk robe over the statutory red or blue boxer shorts. The fighter then bows, first in the direction of his birthplace and then to the north, south, east and west, honouring both his teachers and the spirit of the ring. Next he performs a slow dance, claiming the audience's attention and demonstrating his prowess as a performer.

Any part of the body except the head may be used as an **offensive weapon** in *muay Thai*, and all parts except the groin are fair targets. Kicks to the head are the blows which cause most knockouts. As the action hots up, so the orchestra speeds up its tempo and the betting in the audience becomes more frenetic. It can be a gruesome business, but it was far bloodier before modern boxing gloves were made compulsory in the 1930s – combatants used to wrap their fists with hemp impregnated with a face-lacerating dosage of ground glass.

A number of *muay Thai* gyms and camps offer training **courses** for foreigners, including the Muay Thai Institute in Bangkok (Ⓣ02 992 0096, Ⓦwww.muaythai-institute.net); Fairtex Muay Thai (Ⓦwww.fairtexbkk.com), which has centres in Samut Prakan, near Bangkok (Ⓣ02 755 3329) and in Pattaya (Ⓣ038 488675); Lanna Muay Thai in Chiang Mai (Ⓣ053 892102, Ⓦwww.lannamuaythai.com); the Muay Thai Martial Arts Academy (MTMAA) in Surat Thani (Ⓣ077 282816, Ⓦwww.muaythaitraining.com); and Suwit Gym on Phuket (Ⓣ076 381167, Ⓦwww.bestmuaythai.com). You can also do one-off training sessions at a couple of gyms in central Bangkok; see p.202 for details.

Takraw

Whether in Bangkok or upcountry, you're quite likely to come across some form of **takraw** game being played in a public park, a wat compound or just in a backstreet alley. Played with a very light rattan ball (or one made of plastic to look like rattan), the basic aim of the game is to keep the ball off the ground. To do this you can use any part of your body except your hands, so a well-played *takraw* game looks extremely balletic, with players leaping and arching to get a good strike.

There are at least five versions of **competitive takraw**, based on the same principles. The version featured in the Southeast Asian Games and most frequently in school tournaments is played over a volleyball net and involves two teams of three; the other most popular competitive version has a team ranged round a basketball net trying to score as many goals as possible within a limited time period before the next team replaces them and tries to outscore them.

Other *takraw* games introduce more complex rules (like kicking the ball backwards with your heels through a ring made with your arms behind your back) and many assign points according to the skill displayed by individual players rather than per goal or dropped ball. Outside of school playing fields, proper *takraw* tournaments are rare, though they do sometimes feature as entertainment at Buddhist funerals.

Spas and traditional massage

The last few years have seen an explosion in the number of spas being opened around Thailand – mainly in the grounds of the poshest hotels, but also as small, affordable walk-in centres in towns. With their focus on indulgent self-pampering, spas are usually associated with high-spending tourists, but the treatments on offer at Thailand's five-star hotels are often little different from those used by traditional medical practitioners, who have long held that massage and herbs are the best way to restore physical and mental well being.

Thai massage (*nuad paen boran*) is based on the principle that many physical and emotional problems are caused by the blocking of vital energy channels within the body. The masseur uses his or her feet, heels, knees and elbows, as well as hands, to exert a gentle pressure on these channels, supplementing this acupressure-style technique by pulling and pushing the limbs into yogic stretches. This distinguishes Thai massage from most other massage styles, which are more concerned with tissue manipulation. One is supposed to emerge from a Thai massage feeling both relaxed and energized, and it is said that regular massages produce long-term benefits in muscles as well as stimulating the circulation and aiding natural detoxification. Thais will visit a masseur for many conditions, including fevers, colds and muscle strain, but bodies that are not sick are also considered to benefit from the restorative powers of a massage, and nearly every hotel and guest house will be able to put you in touch with a masseur. On the more popular beaches, it can be hard to walk a few hundred metres without being offered a massage – something Thai tourists are just as enthusiastic about as foreigners. Thai masseurs do not use oils or lotions and the client is treated on a mat or mattress; you'll often be given a pair of loose-fitting trousers and perhaps a loose top to change into. English-speaking masseurs will often ask if you have any problem areas on your body that you want them to avoid; if your masseur doesn't speak English, the simplest way to signal this is to point at the offending area while saying *mai sabai* ("not well"); if you're in pain during a massage, wincing usually does the trick, perhaps adding *jep* ("it hurts"). A session should ideally last two hours and will cost from around B200–300.

The **science** behind Thai massage has its roots in Indian Ayurvedic medicine, which classifies each component of the body according to one of the four elements (earth, water, fire and air), and holds that balancing these elements within the body is crucial to good health. Many of the stretches and manipulations fundamental to Thai massage are thought to have derived from yogic practices introduced to Thailand from India by Buddhist missionaries in about the second century BC; Chinese acupuncture and reflexology have also had a strong influence. In the nineteenth century, King Rama III ordered a series of murals illustrating the principles of Thai massage to be painted around the courtyard of Bangkok's Wat Pho, and they are still in place today, along with statues of ascetics depicted in typical massage poses. **Wat Pho** has been the leading school of Thai massage for hundreds of years, and it is possible to take courses there as well as to receive a massage; see p.141 for details. Masseurs who trained at Wat Pho are considered to be the best in the country and masseurs all across Thailand advertise this as a credential, whether or not it is true. Many Thais consider blind masseurs to be especially sensitive practitioners. While Wat Pho is the most famous place to take a **course** in Thai massage, many foreigners interested in learning this ancient science head for Chiang Mai, which offers the biggest concentration of massage schools (including a new satellite branch of the Wat Pho school), though you will find others all over Thailand, including in Bangkok and at southern beach resorts.

All **spas** in Thailand feature traditional Thai massage and herbal therapies in their programmes, but most also offer dozens of other international treatments, including facials, aromatherapy, Swedish massage and various body wraps. Spa centres in upmarket hotels and resorts are usually open to non-guests but generally need to be booked in advance; day spas that are not attached to hotels are found in some of the bigger cities and resorts, including Bangkok, Chiang Mai, Ko Samui and Phuket, and some of these may not require reservations.

Thailand's most famous deluxe spas include the very exclusive Chiva Som holistic therapy centre in Hua Hin (see p.617); the Oriental Spa, run by the renowned five-star *Oriental Hotel* in Bangkok (see p.218); the Banyan Tree spas at the hotels of the same name in Bangkok (see p.218) and Phuket (see p.743); the spas at the *Dhara Devi* (see p.346) and *Four Seasons* (see p.375) hotels in Chiang Mai; the Six Senses spas at the *Evason* in Pak Nam Pran (see p.623) and the *Sila Evason* on Ko Samui (see p.650); and the Prana Spa at the *Tongsai Bay* on Samui (see p.650).

Meditation centres and retreats

Of the hundreds of meditation temples in Thailand, a few cater specifically for foreigners by holding meditation sessions and retreats in English; novices and practised meditators alike are generally welcome. The meditation taught is mostly Vipassana, or "insight", which emphasizes the minute observation of internal sensations; the other main technique you'll come across is Samatha, which aims to calm the mind and develop concentration (these two techniques are not entirely separate, since you cannot have insight without some degree of concentration).

Longer **retreats** are for the serious-minded only. All the temples listed below welcome both male and female English-speakers, but strict segregation of the sexes is enforced and many places observe a vow of silence. Reading and writing are also discouraged, and you'll generally not be allowed to leave the retreat complex unless absolutely necessary, so try to bring whatever you'll need in with you. Some retreats require you to wear modest, white clothing – check ahead whether there is a shop at the retreat complex or whether you are expected to bring this with you.

An average day at any one of these monasteries starts with a **wake-up call** at 4am and includes several hours of **group meditation** and chanting, as well as time put aside for chores and personal reflection. However long their stay, visitors are usually expected to keep the eight Buddhist precepts, the most restrictive of these being the abstention from food after midday and from alcohol, tobacco, drugs and sex at all times. Most wats ask for a minimal daily **donation** (around B150) to cover the costs of the simple accommodation and food.

Further details about many of the temples listed below – including how to get there – are given in the relevant sections in the guide chapters. Though a little out of date, *A Guide to Buddhist Monasteries and Meditation Centres in Thailand* contains plenty of useful general information; originally published by the World Fellowship of Buddhists, it's now accessible online at ⓦwww.dharmanet.org/thai_94.html. An even more useful Internet resource is ⓦ**www.dhammathai.org**, which provides lots of general background, practical advice and details of meditation temples and centres around Thailand.

Meditation centres and retreat temples

For information on **Wat Khao Tham** on Ko Pha Ngan, see p.663; **Wat Mahathat** in Bangkok, p.143; **Wat Phra That Doi Suthep** near Chiang Mai, p.349; **Wat Phra That Si Chom Thong** near Chiang Mai, p.397; **Wat Ram Poeng** in Chiang Mai, see p.349; and **Wat Suan Mokkh** in Chaiya, p.635.

House of Dhamma Insight Meditation Centre 26/9 Soi Lardprao 15, Chatuchak, Bangkok ⓣ02 511 0439, ⓦwww.houseofdhamma.com. Vipassana meditation classes in English on the second and third Sunday of the month, plus regular introductory two-day courses, and day, weekend and week-long retreats. Courses in reiki and other subjects available.

International Meditation Club 138 Soi 53, Thanon Sukhumvit, Bangkok ⓣ081 622 4507, ⓦwww.intlmedclub.org. Regular, two-day, meditation workshops in Bangkok and three-day retreats in Pattaya and Cha-am.

Thailand Vipassana Centre ⓦwww.dhamma.org. Dhamma Kamala, 200 Ban Nernpasuk, Prachinburi, near Bangkok; and at Dhamma Abha, 138 Ban Huayplu, Phitsanulok. Frequent ten-day residential courses in a Burmese Vipassana tradition. Foreign students must pre-register by email (application form available on the website) with Khun Thaveephol or Khun Warattada on ⓔbehappy@loxinfo.co.th.

Wat Pah Nanachat Ban Bung Wai, Amphoe Warinchamrab, Ubon Ratchathani 34310, ⓦwww.watpahnanachat.org. A group of foreign monks have established this forest monastery, 17km west of Ubon Ratchathani, specifically for farangs who want to immerse themselves in Anapanasati meditation (mindfulness with breathing, a form of Samatha). Short- and long-term visitors are welcome, but the atmosphere is serious and intense and not for beginners or curious sightseers, and accommodation for students is limited, so you should write to the monastery before visiting, allowing several weeks to receive a written response.

World Fellowship of Buddhists (WFB) 616 Benjasiri Park, Soi Medhinivet off Soi 24, Thanon Sukhumvit, Bangkok ⓣ02 661 1284–7, ⓦwww.wfb-hq.org. The main information centre for advice on English-speaking retreats in Thailand. Holds a Buddhist discussion group and meditation session in English on the first Sunday of every month, with dharma lectures and discussions on the second Sunday.

Culture, etiquette and the law

Tourist literature has marketed Thailand as the "Land of Smiles" so successfully that a lot of farangs arrive in the country expecting to be forgiven any outrageous behaviour. This is just not the case: there are some things so universally sacred in Thailand that even a hint of disrespect will cause deep offence. TAT publishes a special leaflet on the subject, entitled *Dos and Don'ts in Thailand*, reproduced at ⓦwww.tourismthailand.org.

The monarchy

It is both socially unacceptable and a criminal offence to make critical or defamatory remarks about the **royal family**. Thailand's monarchy might be a constitutional one, but almost every household displays a picture of King Bhumibol and Queen Sirikit in a prominent position, and respectful crowds mass whenever either of them makes a public appearance. The second of their four children, Crown Prince Vajiralongkorn, is the heir to the throne; his younger sister, Princess Royal Maha Chakri Sirindhorn, is often on TV and in the English newspapers as she is involved in many charitable projects. When addressing or speaking about royalty, Thais use a special language full of deference, called *rajasap* (literally "royal language").

Aside from keeping any anti-monarchy sentiments to yourself, you should be prepared to stand when the **king's anthem** is played at the beginning of every cinema programme, and to stop in your tracks if the town you're in plays the **national anthem** over its public address system – many small towns do this twice a day at 8am and again at 6pm, as do some train stations and airports. A less obvious point: as the king's head features on all Thai currency, you should never step on a coin or banknote, which is tantamount to kicking the king in the face.

Religion

Almost equally insensitive would be to disregard certain **religious** precepts. **Buddhism** plays an essential part in the lives of most Thais, and Buddhist monuments should be treated with respect – which basically means wearing long trousers or knee-length skirts, covering your arms and removing your shoes whenever you visit one.

All **Buddha images** are sacred, however small, tacky or ruined, and should never be used as a backdrop for a portrait photo, clambered over, placed in a position of inferiority or treated in any manner that could be construed as disrespectful. In an attempt to prevent foreigners from committing any kind of transgression the government requires a special licence for all Buddha statues exported from the country (see p.82).

Monks come only just beneath the monarchy in the social hierarchy, and they too are addressed and discussed in a special language. If there's a monk around, he'll always get a seat on the bus, usually right at the back. Theoretically, monks are forbidden to have any close contact with women, which means, as a female, you mustn't sit or stand next to a monk, or even brush against his robes; if it's essential to pass him something, put the object down so that he can then pick it up – never hand it over directly. Nuns, however, get treated like ordinary women.

See Contexts p.884 for more on religious practices in Thailand.

The body

The Western liberalism embraced by the Thai sex industry is very unrepresentative of the majority Thai attitude to the body. **Clothing** – or the lack of it – is what bothers Thais most about tourist behaviour. As mentioned above, you need to dress modestly when entering temples, but the same also applies to other important buildings and all public places. Stuffy and sweaty as it sounds, you should keep short shorts and vests for the real tourist resorts, and be especially diligent about covering up and, for women, wearing bras in rural areas. Baring your flesh on beaches is very much a Western practice: when Thais go swimming they often do so fully clothed, and they find topless and nude bathing extremely unpalatable.

According to ancient Hindu belief, the **head** is the most sacred part of the body and the **feet** are the most unclean. This belief, imported into Thailand, means that it's very rude to touch another person's head or to point your feet either at a human being or at a sacred image – when sitting on a temple floor, for example, you should **tuck your legs beneath you** rather than stretch them out towards the Buddha. These hierarchies also forbid people from wearing **shoes** (which are even more unclean than feet) inside temples and most private homes, and – by extension – Thais take offence when they see someone sitting on the "head", or prow, of a boat. **Putting your feet up** on a table, a chair or a pillow is also considered very uncouth, and Thais will always take their shoes off if they need to stand on a train or bus seat to get to the luggage rack, for example. On a more practical note, the **left hand** is used for washing after defecating, so Thais never use it to put food in their mouth, pass things or shake hands – as a farang though, you'll be assumed to have different customs, so left-handers shouldn't worry unduly.

Social conventions

Thais very rarely shake hands, instead using the **wai** to greet and say goodbye and to acknowledge respect, gratitude or apology. A prayer-like gesture made with raised hands, the *wai* changes according to the relative status of the two people involved: Thais can instantaneously assess which *wai* to use, but as a farang your safest bet is to go for the "stranger's" *wai*, which requires that your hands be raised close to your chest and your fingertips placed just below your chin. If someone makes a *wai* at you, you should generally *wai* back, but it's safer not to initiate.

Public displays of **physical affection** in Thailand are more common between friends of the same sex than between lovers, whether hetero- or homosexual. Holding hands and hugging is as common among male friends as with females, so if you're caressed by a Thai acquaintance of the same sex, don't assume you're being propositioned.

Finally, there are three specifically Thai **concepts** you're bound to come across, which may help you comprehend a sometimes laissez-faire attitude to delayed buses and other inconveniences. The first, **jai yen**, translates literally as "cool heart" and is something everyone tries to maintain – most Thais hate raised voices, visible irritation and confrontations of any kind, so losing one's cool can have a much more inflammatory effect than in more combative cultures. Related to this is the oft-quoted response to a difficulty, **mai pen rai** – "never mind", "no problem" or "it can't be helped" – the verbal equivalent of an open-handed shoulder shrug, which has its basis in the Buddhist notion of karma (see "Religion", p.889). And then there's **sanuk**, the wide-reaching philosophy of "fun", which, crass as it sounds, Thais do their best to inject into any situation, even work. Hence the crowds of inebriated Thais who congregate at waterfalls and other beauty spots on public holidays (travelling solo is definitely not *sanuk*), the inability to do almost anything without high-volume musical accompaniment, and the national waterfight which takes place every April on streets right across Thailand.

Thai names

Although all Thais have a first **name** and a family name, everyone is addressed by their first name – even when meeting strangers – prefixed by the title "**Khun**" (Mr/Ms); no one is ever addressed as Khun Surname, and even the phone book lists people by their given name. In Thailand you will often be addressed in an Anglicized version of this convention, as "Mr Paul" or "Miss Lucy" for example. Bear in mind though, that when a man is introduced to you as Khun Pirom, his wife will definitely not be Khun Pirom as well (that would be like calling them, for instance, "Mr and Mrs Paul"). Among friends and relatives, **Phii** ("older brother/sister") is often used instead of Khun when addressing older familiars (though as a tourist you're on surer ground with Khun), and **Nong** ("younger brother/sister") is used for younger ones.

Many Thai **first names** come from ancient Sanskrit and have an auspicious meaning; for example, Boon means good deeds, Porn means blessings, Siri means glory and Thawee means to increase. However, Thais of all ages are commonly known by the **nickname** given them soon after birth rather than by their official first name. This tradition arises out of a deep-rooted superstition that once a child has been officially named the spirits will begin to take an unhealthy interest in them, so a nickname is used instead to confuse the spirits. Common nicknames – which often bear no resemblance to the adult's personality or physique – include Yai (Big), Oun (Fat) and Muu (Pig); Lek or Noi (Little), Nok (Bird), Noo (Mouse) and Kung (Shrimp); Neung (Number One/Eldest), Sawng (Number Two), Saam (Number Three); and English nicknames like Apple, Joy or even Pepsi.

Family names were only introduced in 1913 (by Rama VI, who invented many of the aristocracy's surnames himself), and are used only in very formal situations, always in conjunction with the first name. It's quite usual for good friends never to know each other's surname. Ethnic Thais generally have short surnames like Somboon or Srisai, while the long, convoluted family names – such as Sonthanasumpun – usually indicate Chinese origin, not because they are phonetically Chinese but because many Chinese immigrants have chosen to adopt new Thai surnames and Thai law states that every newly created surname must be unique. Thus anyone who wants to change their surname must submit a shortlist of five unique Thai names – each to a maximum length of ten Thai characters – to be checked against a database of existing names. As more and more names are taken, Chinese family names get increasingly unwieldy, and more easily distinguishable from the pithy old Thai names.

Age restrictions and other laws

Thai law requires that tourists **carry their original passports** at all times, though sometimes it's more practical to carry a photocopy and keep the original locked in a safety deposit. It is illegal for **under-18s** to buy cigarettes or alcohol, to drive, or to have sex, and you must be 21 or over to be allowed into a **bar or club** (ID checks are often enforced in Bangkok). It is illegal for anyone to **gamble** in Thailand (though many do). **Smoking** is prohibited in all air-conditioned public buildings (including restaurants but usually excluding bars and clubs) and on air-conditioned trains, buses and planes; violators are subject to a B2000 fine. Dropping cigarette butts, **littering** and spitting in public places can also earn you a B2000 fine. There are fines for **overstaying your visa** (see p.89), **working without a permit**, and **not wearing a motorcycle helmet** and violating other **traffic laws** (see p.44).

Drugs

Drug-smuggling carries a maximum penalty in Thailand of death. **Dealing drugs** will get you anything from four years to life in a Thai prison; penalties depend on the drug and the amount involved. Travellers caught with even the smallest amount of drugs at airports and international borders are prosecuted for trafficking, and no one charged with trafficking offences gets bail. Heroin, amphetamines, LSD and ecstasy are classed as Category 1 drugs and carry the most severe penalties: even **possession** of Category 1 drugs for personal use can result in a **life sentence**. Away from international borders, most foreigners arrested in possession of small amounts of cannabis are released on bail, then fined and deported, but the law is complex and prison sentences are possible.

Despite occasional royal pardons, don't expect special treatment as a farang: you only need to read one of the first-hand accounts by foreign former prisoners (reviewed in "Books" on p.924) to get the picture, but if that doesn't put you off you could always visit an inmate in a Bangkok jail – details on how to do this are given on p.218. The **police** actively look for tourists doing drugs, reportedly searching people regularly and randomly on Thanon Khao San, for example. They have the power to order a urine test if they have reasonable grounds for suspicion, and even a positive result for marijuana consumption could lead to a year's imprisonment. Be wary also of **being shopped** by a farang or local dealer keen to earn a financial reward for a successful bust (there are setups at the Ko Pha Ngan full moon parties, for example), or having substances slipped into your luggage (simple enough to perpetrate unless all fastenings are secured with padlocks).

If you are arrested, ask for your embassy to be contacted immediately, which is your right under Thai law (see p.216 for phone numbers), and embassy staff will talk you through procedures. The British charity Prisoners Abroad (Ⓦwww.prisonersabroad.org.uk) carries a detailed Survival Guide on its website, which outlines what to expect if arrested in Thailand, from the point of apprehension through trial and conviction to life in a Thai jail; if contacted, the charity may also be able to offer direct support to a British citizen facing imprisonment in a Thai jail.

Outdoor activities

The vast majority of travellers' itineraries take in a few days' trekking in the north and a stint snorkelling or diving off the beaches of the south. The big beach resorts of Pattaya, Phuket and Ko Samui also offer dozens of other watersports, and for the wildlife enthusiast there are plenty of national parks to explore. There is also a developing interest in more unusual outdoor activities, such as rock-climbing and kayaking.

Trekking is concentrated in the north, so we've covered the practicalities of trekking in that chapter (see p.331), but there are smaller, less touristy trekking operations in Kanchanaburi (see p.248), Sangkhlaburi (see p.259) and Umphang (see p.320), all of which are worth considering. **Golf** has also taken off in Thailand, and there are dozens of courses across the country, the best of them concentrated near the resort towns of Hua Hin (see p.619) and Pattaya (see p.465). Details of watersports at the major resorts are given in the relevant accounts.

Diving and snorkelling

Clear, warm waters (averaging 28°C), prolific marine life and affordable prices make Thailand a very rewarding place for **diving** and **snorkelling**. Almost every island or beach resort has at least one dive shop that organizes diving and snorkelling trips to outlying islands, trains novice divers and rents out equipment, and in the bigger resorts there are dozens of dive centres to choose from.

Thailand's three coasts are subject to different monsoon **seasons**, so you can dive all year round; the diving seasons run from November to April along the Andaman coast (though there is sometimes good diving here up until late August), and all year round on the Gulf and east coasts. Though every diver has their favourite reef, Thailand's premier diving destinations are generally considered to be Ko Similan, Ko Surin, Burma Banks and Hin Muang and Hin Daeng – all of them off the Andaman coast. To many people's surprise, the 2004 tsunami caused relatively little damage to the Andaman Coast's top reefs; dive companies simply bypass those sites that were affected. As an accessible base for diving, Ko Tao off the Gulf coast is hard to beat, with deep, clear inshore water and a wide variety of dive sites in very close proximity.

Whether you're snorkelling or diving, you should be aware of your effect on the fragile reef structures. Try to minimize your impact by **not touching the reefs** and asking your boatman not to anchor in the middle of one, and **don't buy coral souvenirs**, as tourist demand only encourages local entrepreneurs to dynamite reefs.

Thailand's best dives and dive resorts

The east coast
Pattaya (p.465)

The Andaman coast
Ao Nang (p.789)
Burma Banks (p.751)
Hin Muang and Hin Daeng (p.808)
Ko Lanta (p.808)
Ko Phi Phi (p.794)
Ko Racha (p.751)
Ko Similan (p.727)
Ko Surin (p.712)
Phuket (p.750)

The Gulf coast
Ko Pha Ngan (p.661)
Ko Samui (p.640)
Ko Tao (p.674)

The deep south
Ko Lipe (p.849)

Diving

It's always worth having a look at several **dive centres** before committing yourself to a trip or a course. Always verify the dive instructors' PADI (Professional Association of Diving Instructors) or equivalent accreditation and check to see if the dive shop is a member of PADI's International Resorts and Retailers Association (IRRA) as this guarantees a certain level of professionalism. You can view a list of IRRAs in Thailand at Ⓦwww.padi.com.

We've highlighted IRRA dive shops that are accredited Five-Star centres, as these are considered by PADI to offer very high standards, but you should always check with other divers first if possible, no matter how many stars your chosen dive centre has garnered. Some dive operators do fake their PADI credentials, which is why it's good to get a second opinion. Avoid booking ahead over the Internet without knowing anything else about the dive centre, and be wary of any operation offering extremely cheap courses: maintaining diving equipment is an expensive business in Thailand so any place offering unusually good rates will probably be cutting corners and compromising your safety. Ask to **meet your instructor** or dive leader, find out how many people there'll be in your group, check out the kind of instruction given (some courses are over-reliant on videos) and look over the equipment, checking the quality of the air in the tanks yourself and also ensuring there's an oxygen cylinder on board. Most novice and experienced divers prefer to travel to the dive site in a decent-sized **boat** equipped with a radio and emergency medical equipment rather than in a longtail. If this concerns you, ask the dive company about their boat before you sign up – any company with a good boat will have photos of it to impress potential customers – though you'll find firms that use longtails will probably charge less.

Insurance should be included in the price of courses and introductory dives; for qualified divers, you're better off checking that your general travel insurance covers diving, though some of the more reputable diving operators in Thailand can organize cover for you. There are several **recompression chambers** in Thailand, including two in Sattahip on the east coast near Pattaya and one in Pattaya itself (see p.470), one on Ko Samui (see p.640), one on Ko Tao (see p.674) and three on Phuket (see p.750). It's a good idea to check whether your dive centre is a member of one of these outfits, as recompression services are extremely expensive for anyone who's not.

For books on diving in Thailand see p.926.

Trips and courses

All dive centres run programmes of one-day **dive trips** (featuring two dives), **wreck dives** and **night dives** for B1300–4500 plus equipment, and many of the Andaman coast dive centres (Khao Lak, Phuket, Ko Phi Phi, Ao Nang) also do three- to seven-day **live-aboards** to the exceptional reefs off the remote Similan and Surin islands (from B11,000) and even further afield to the impressive Burma Banks.

Renting a full set of diving **gear**, including wetsuit, from a dive centre costs B300–1000 per day; most dive centres also rent

underwater cameras for B1000–1500 per day.

Phuket, Khao Lak, Ao Nang, Ko Phi Phi, Ko Lanta, Ko Tao and Pattaya are the best places to **learn**, and dive centres at all these places offer a range of **courses** from beginner to advanced level, with equipment rental usually included in the cost; Ko Tao is now the largest dive-training centre in Southeast Asia, with around fifty dive companies including plenty of PADI Five-Star centres. The most popular courses are the one-day **introductory** or resort dive (a pep talk and escorted shallow dive), which costs anything from B2000 for a very local dive to B5000 for an all-inclusive day-trip to the fabulous Similan Islands; and the four-day **open-water course** which entitles you to dive without an instructor (B8000–13,500 including at least two dives a day). Kids' Bubblemaker courses, for children aged 8–10, cost around B1500.

Snorkelling

Most beaches offer organized **snorkelling** trips to nearby reefs and many dive operators welcome snorkellers to tag along with the divers for discounts of thirty percent or more; not all diving destinations are rewarding for snorkellers though, so check the relevant account in this book first. As far as snorkelling **equipment** goes, the most important thing is that you buy or rent a mask that fits. To check the fit, hold the mask against your face, then breathe in and remove your hands – if it falls off, it'll leak water. If you're buying equipment, you should be able to kit yourself out with a mask, snorkel and fins for about B1000, available from most dive centres. Few places rent fins, but a mask and snorkel set usually costs about B100 a day to rent, and if you're going on a snorkelling day-trip they are often included in the price.

National parks

Over the last half-century more than a hundred areas across Thailand have been singled out for conservation as **national parks**, with the dual aim of protecting the country's natural resources and creating educational and recreational facilities for the public.

These parks generally make the best places to **observe wildlife**. One of the best for seeing larger animals is **Khao Yai** (see p.522), the most popular national park, about three hours northeast of Bangkok. If you join a night safari here, you could be rewarded with sightings of elephants, deer, civets, even tigers, whilst during the day you'll come across gibbons and hornbills at the very least. Bird-watchers consider the national park mountains of **Doi Suthep** (see p.368) and **Doi Inthanon** (see p.396) – both close to Chiang Mai – primary observation areas, and the coastal flats at **Khao Sam Roi Yot** (see p.624) and the sanctuary of **Thale Noi** (see p.829) in the south are also good spots.

Many of southern Thailand's protected reserves are **marine parks**, including the archipelagoes of **Ko Similan** (see p.727), **Ko Surin** (see p.712), **Ang Thong** (see p.655) and **Ko Tarutao** (see p.847).

All the national parks are administered by the National Park, Wildlife and Plant Conservation Department, part of the Ministry of Natural Resources and Environment (MONRE), which is located near Kasetsart University at 61 Thanon Phaholyothin, Chatuchak District, Bangkok 10900 (Mon–Fri 8.30am–4.30pm; ⓣ02 562 0760, ⓦwww.dnp.go.th/National_park.asp); easiest access is by Skytrain to Mo Chit or subway to Chatuchak Park, then take a bus or taxi about 4km up Phaholyothin to the office, which is north of the Thanon Ngam Wong Wan junction. To book national park bungalows in advance (advisable for weekends and public holidays) you usually need to pay up front; see "Accommodation" on p.51 for details.

For all their environmental benefits, national parks are a source of **controversy** in Thailand, with vested interests such as fishermen, farmers, loggers, poachers and the tourist industry pitted against environmentalists and certain sections of the government. The parks administration has itself come in for voluble criticism over the last few years, particularly over the filming of *The Beach* on the national park island of Ko Phi Phi Leh, and in 2000 when – without warning – it raised the **foreigners' entrance fee** levied at most national parks from B20 to B200 (B100 for children). See "Flora, Fauna and Environmental Issues" on p.891 for a fuller account of these issues and for a more detailed introduction to Thailand's wildlife.

Most parks have limited public facilities, very few signposted walking trails and a paucity of usable maps. Nor are many of the parks well served by public transport – some can take a day to reach from the nearest large town, via a route that entails several bus and songthaew changes and a final lengthy walk. This, combined with the expense and poor quality of most national park accommodation, means that if you're planning to do a serious tour of the parks you should consider **bringing a tent** (all parks allow this; see p.51 for details) and be prepared to rent your own transport.

Rock-climbing

The limestone karsts that pepper southern Thailand's Andaman coast make ideal playgrounds for **rock-climbers**, and the sport has really taken off here in the last decade. Most climbing is centred round **East Railay** and **Ton Sai** beaches on Laem Phra Nang in Krabi province (see p.781), where there are dozens of routes within easy walking distance of tourist bungalows, restaurants and beaches. Several **climbing schools** have already established centres here, providing instruction, guides and all the necessary equipment. Half-day introductory courses at East Railay and Ton Sai cost B800, a full day's guided climbing is B1500 and a three-day course B5000. **Equipment rental** is charged at about B1000 per day for two people. Ko Phi Phi (see p.795) also offers a few interesting routes and a couple of climbing schools, as does Ko Yao Noi (see p.761). There are also less developed climbing areas near Chiang Mai (see p.339) and Ko Tao (see p.673), as well as in Lopburi (see p.279) and Phetchaburi. For an introduction to climbing in Thailand, plus advice on where to climb and what equipment to bring, as well as reviews of climb shops and a climbers' forum, see Ⓦwww.simonfoley.com/climbing.

Sea-kayaking and whitewater rafting

Sea-kayaking is also centred around Thailand's Andaman coast, where the limestone outcrops, sea caves, *hongs* (hidden lagoons), mangrove swamps and picturesque shorelines of Ao Phang Nga in particular (see p.766) make for rewarding paddling. Kayaking day-trips around Ao Phang Nga can be arranged from any resort in Phuket, at Khao Lak, at all Krabi beaches and islands, and on Ko Yao Noi; three-to-six-day kayaking expeditions are also possible. The longest-established sea-kayaking operator in this area is the famous and highly reputable John Gray's Sea Canoe (Ⓦwww.johngray-seacanoe.com), whose trips cost from B3000. Paddle Asia (Ⓦwww.paddleasia.com) offer 4–6-day sea-kayaking trips around the Trang islands and the Tarutao National Marine Park islands (from US$675 per person) and over on Ko Samui, Blue Stars (see p.645) organize kayaking trips around the picturesque islands of the Ang Thong National Marine Park. Many other beach resorts rent kayaks for low-key, independent coastal exploration; prices average B100–200 per hour for a one- or two-person kayak.

You can go **river-kayaking** and **whitewater rafting** on several rivers in north, west and south Thailand. Some stretches of these rivers can run quite fast, particularly during the rainy season from July to November, but there are plenty of options for novices, too. The best time is from October through February; during the hot season (March–June), many rivers run too low. The most popular whitewater-rafting rivers include the Umphang and Mae Khlong rivers near Umphang (see p.320) and the Pai River near Pai (see p.418). Gentler rafting excursions take place on the River Kwai and its tributaries near Kanchanaburi (see p.235), on the Kok River from Tha Ton (see p.423) and on the Sok River in Khao Sok National Park (see p.718). Southwest of Chiang Mai, rafts can be rented from the adjacent national park headquarters for trips in Ob Luang Gorge (see p.400).

Gay and lesbian Thailand

Buddhist tolerance and a national abhorrence of confrontation and victimization combine to make Thai society relatively tolerant of homosexuality, if not exactly positive about same-sex relationships. Most Thais are extremely private and discreet about being gay, generally pursuing a "don't ask, don't tell" understanding with their family. The majority of people are horrified by the idea of gay-bashing and generally regard it as unthinkable to spurn a child or relative for being gay.

Hardly any Thai celebrities are out, yet the predilections of several respected social, political and entertainment figures are widely known and accepted. **Transvestites** (known as *katoey* or "ladyboys") and **transsexuals** are also a lot more visible in Thailand than in the West. You'll find cross-dressers doing ordinary jobs, even in small upcountry towns, and there are a number of transvestites and transsexuals in the public eye too – including national volleyball stars and champion *muay Thai* boxers. The government tourist office vigorously promotes the transvestite cabarets in Pattaya, Phuket and Bangkok, all of which are advertised as family entertainment. *Katoey* also regularly appear as characters in soap operas, TV comedies and films, where they are depicted as harmless figures of fun. Richard Totman's *The Third Sex* offers an interesting insight into Thai *katoey*, their experiences in society and public attitudes towards them; see "Books" on p.925 for a review.

There is no mention of homosexuality at all in Thai law, which means that the age of consent for gay sex is sixteen, the same as for heterosexuals. However, this also means that gay rights are not protected under Thai law.

The scene

Thailand's gay scene is mainly focused on **mainstream venues** like karaoke bars, restaurants, massage parlours, gyms, saunas and escort agencies. For the sake of discretion, gay venues are usually intermingled with equivalent straight venues. As in the straight scene, venues reflect class and status differences. Expensive international-style places are very popular in Bangkok, attracting upper- and middle-class gays, many of whom have travelled or been educated abroad and developed Western tastes. These places also attract a contingent of Thais seeking foreign sugar daddies. The biggest concentrations of farang-friendly gay bars and clubs are found in Bangkok, Chiang Mai, Phuket and Pattaya, and are listed in the relevant accounts in the guide chapters (note that you must be 20 years old to enter a nightclub in Thailand, and ID checks are often enforced). The gay communities of Bangkok, Phuket and Pattaya all host flamboyant annual **Gay Pride festivals** (check upcoming dates on the websites listed below). For a detailed guide to the gay and lesbian scene throughout the country, see the *Utopia Guide to Thailand* by John Goss, which can be downloaded via Ⓦwww.utopia-asia.com.

Thailand's gay scene is heavily male, and there are hardly any **lesbian**-only venues, though Bangkok has a few mixed gay bars. Thai lesbians generally eschew the word lesbian, which in Thailand is associated with male fantasies, instead referring to themselves as either *tom* (for tomboy) or *dee* (for lady). Where possible, we've listed lesbian meeting-places, but unless otherwise specified, gay means male throughout this guide.

Although excessively physical displays of affection are frowned upon for both heterosexuals and homosexuals, Western gay couples should get no hassle about being seen together in public – it's much more acceptable, and common, in fact, for friends of the same sex (gay or not) to walk hand-in-hand, than for heterosexual couples to do so.

The farang-oriented gay **sex industry** is a tiny but highly visible part of Thailand's gay scene. With its tawdry floor shows and host services, it bears a dispiriting resemblance to the straight sex trade, and is similarly most active in Bangkok, Pattaya, Patong (on Phuket) and Chiang Mai. Like their female counterparts in the heterosexual fleshpots, many of the boys working in the gay sex bars that dominate these districts are underage; note that anyone caught having sex with a prostitute below the age of 18 faces imprisonment. A significant number of gay prostitutes are gay by economic necessity rather than by inclination. As with the straight sex scene, we do not list commercial gay sex bars in the guide.

Information and contacts for gay travellers

Anjaree PO Box 322, Rajdamnoen PO, Bangkok 10200 Ⓔ anjaree@loxinfo.com. General information on the lesbian community in Thailand.

Dreaded Ned's Ⓦ www.dreadedned.com. Events listings and information on almost every gay venue in the country.

Lesla Ⓦ www.lesla.com. Thailand's largest lesbian organization hosts regular events and runs a webboard.

Long Yang Club Ⓦ www.longyangclub.org/thailand. This international organization was founded to promote friendship between men of Western and Eastern origin and runs regular socials.

Utopia Ⓦ www.utopia-asia.com and Ⓦ www.utopia-asia.com/womthai.htm. Asia's best gay and lesbian website lists clubs, events, accommodation and organizations for gays and lesbians and has useful links to other sites in Asia and the rest of the world. Its offshoot, Utopia Tours, is a gay-oriented travel agency offering trips and guides within Thailand and the rest of Asia; tours can be booked through Door East, *Tarntawan Palace Hotel*, 119/5–10 Thanon Suriwong (Ⓣ 02 238 3227, Ⓦ www.utopia-tours.com).

Travelling with kids

There's plenty in Thailand to appeal to children – especially the beach, the swimming pools and the water-based activities in the more developed resorts.

Many **dive centres** will teach the PADI children's scuba courses on request: their Bubblemaker programme is open to 8-year-olds and the Junior Open Water is designed for anyone over ten. An increasing number of **upmarket hotels** in the big resorts arrange special activities for kids: the *Laguna Resort* hotels complex on Ao Bang Tao, Phuket (see p.742) is particularly recommended for its family-friendly accommodation and kids' activities camp, as are the *Novotel Phuket Resort*, and the *Holiday Inn*, both on Patong Beach, Phuket (p.747), and the *JW Marriott Phuket Resort and Spa* on Phuket's Hat Mai Khao (p.739). The activity-centred Club Med chain of hotels (Ⓦ www.clubmed.com) also has a resort on Phuket (see p.754). Other hotels that offer plenty of diversions for active teenagers include *Le Royal Meridien Baan Taling Ngam* on Ko Samui (see p.660) and the *Amari Trang* in Trang (see p.833). Most of these hotels will also provide a **babysitting** service.

Older children will relish the cheap supply of electronic games and brand-name clothing on sale in the main tourist centres, and might enjoy taking up the countless offers from beach masseuses to "plait your hair" and "have manicure".

Despite its lack of obvious child-centred activities, many parents find that the moderately developed island of Ko Lanta makes a good destination for kids of all ages, with reasonably priced accommodation, fairly uncrowded sandy beaches and safe seas. However, as with almost any non-mainstream destination in Thailand, the nearest top-class health centre is several hours' away from Ko Lanta, in Phuket. On Ko Lanta and many other beaches, open-air shorefront restaurants are the norm, so adults can eat in relative peace while kids play within view.

Active children also enjoy the **national parks** and their waterfalls, plus the opportunities to go **rafting** – available in both sedate and whitewater versions – and **elephant-riding**. Kanchanaburi is a rewarding centre for all these outdoor pursuits, with the added attraction that many of the town's guest houses are set round decent-sized lawns. Chiang Mai can also offer these activities, as well as elephant-logging shows, an attractive, modern zoo, watching umbrella-makers and other craftspeople at work, and a trip to the Mae Sa valley, which is lined with many family-oriented attractions, such as the botanical gardens and **butterfly farms**. Bangkok has several child-friendly **theme parks** and activity centres, listed on p.200, as does the beach resort of Pattaya (see p.466).

Practicalities

Many of the expensive **hotels** listed in this guide offer special deals for families, usually allowing one or two under-twelves to share their parents' room for free, as long as no extra bedding is required. It's often possible to cram two adults and two children into the double rooms in inexpensive and mid-range hotels (as opposed to guest houses), as beds in these places are usually big enough for two. An increasing number of guest houses now offer three-person rooms, and some even provide special family accommodation: see accommodation listings throughout the book for details. Decent cots are provided free in the bigger hotels, and in some smaller ones (though cots in these places can be a bit grotty).

Few museums or transport companies offer student reductions, but in some cases children get **discounts**; these vary a lot, one of the more bizarre provisos being the State Railway's regulation that a child aged three to twelve qualifies for half-fare only if under 150cm tall; in some stations you'll see a measuring scale painted onto the ticket-hall wall. On most domestic flights, under-twos pay ten percent of the full fare, and under-twelves pay fifty percent.

Although most Thai babies don't wear them, **disposable nappies** (diapers) are sold in Thailand at convenience stores, pharmacies and supermarkets in big resorts and sizeable towns; for longer, more out-of-the-way journeys and stays on lonely islands and beaches, consider bringing some washable ones as back-up. A **changing mat** is another necessity as there are few public toilets in Thailand, let alone ones with baby facilities (though posh hotels are always a useful option). If your baby is on powdered milk, it might be an idea to bring some of that; you can certainly get it in Thailand but it may not taste the same as at home. Thai women do not **breastfeed** in public. Dried **baby food**, too, could be worth taking, though you can get international-brand baby food in big towns and resorts, and some parents find restaurant-cooked rice and bananas go down just as well.

For touring, child-carrier backpacks are ideal. Opinions are divided on whether or not it's worth bringing a **buggy** or three-wheeled **stroller**. Where they exist, Thailand's pavements are bumpy at best, and there's an almost total absence of ramps; sand is especially difficult for buggies, though less so for three-wheelers. Buggies and strollers do, however, come in handy for feeding and even bedding small children, as highchairs and cots are only provided in the more upmarket hotels. You can buy buggies fairly cheaply in most moderate-sized Thai towns, but if you bring your own and then wish you hadn't, most hotels and guest houses will keep it for you until you leave. Taxis and car-rental companies never provide baby **car seats**, and even if you bring your own you'll often find there are no seatbelts to strap them in with.

Children's **clothes** are also very cheap in Thailand, and have the advantage of being designed for the climate. Even if you've forgotten a crucial piece of children's equipment, you'll probably find it in the nearest big-city department store, nearly all of which have dedicated kids' sections selling everything from bottles and dummies. There's even a branch of Mothercare in Bangkok.

Even more than their parents, children need protecting from the sun, unsafe drinking water, heat and unfamiliar **food**. All that chilli in particular may be a problem, even with older kids; consider packing a jar of Marmite or equivalent child's favourite, so that you can always rely on toast if the local food doesn't go down so well. As with adults, you should be careful about unwashed fruit and salads and about dishes that have been left uncovered for a long time. As diarrhoea could be dangerous for a child, rehydration solutions (see under "Health", p.37) are vital if your child goes down with it. Other significant **hazards** include thundering traffic; huge waves, strong currents and jellyfish; and the **sun** – not least because many beaches offer only limited shade, if at all. Sunhats, sunblock and waterproof suntan lotions are essential, and can be bought in the major resorts. You should also make sure, if possible, that your child is aware of the dangers of **rabies**; keep children away from **animals**, especially dogs and monkeys, and ask your medical advisor about rabies jabs.

Information and advice

Bambi ⓦwww.bambi-bangkok.org. The website of the Bangkok-based expat parents' group has tips on parents' common concerns, in particular health issues, as well as ideas for child-friendly activities in Thailand.

Kids To Go ⓦthorntree.lonelyplanet.com. The Kids To Go branch of this travel forum gets quite a lot of postings from parents who've already taken their kids to Thailand.

Thailand 4 Kids ⓦwww.thailand4kids.com. Sells an e-book guide covering the practicalities of family holidays in Thailand.

Travel essentials

Addresses

Thai **addresses** can be immensely confusing, mainly because property is often numbered twice, first to show which real estate lot it stands in, and then to distinguish where it is on that lot. Thus 154/7–10 Thanon Rajdamnoen means the building is on lot 154 and occupies numbers 7–10. There's an additional idiosyncrasy in the way Thai roads are sometimes named: in large cities a minor road running off a major road is often numbered as a soi ("lane" or "alley", though it may be a sizeable thoroughfare), rather than given its own street name. Thanon Sukhumvit for example – Bangkok's longest – has minor roads numbered Soi 1 to Soi 103, with odd numbers on one side of the road and even on the other; so a Thanon Sukhumvit address could read something like 27/9–11 Soi 15, Thanon Sukhumvit, which would mean the property occupies numbers 9–11 on lot 27 on minor road number 15 running off Thanon Sukhumvit.

Charities and volunteer projects

Reassured by the plethora of well-stocked shopping plazas, efficient services and apparent abundance in the ricefields, it is easy to forget that life is extremely hard for many people in Thailand. Countless **charities** work with Thailand's many poor and disadvantaged communities: listed below are a few that would welcome help in some way from visitors. The website of the *Bangkok Post* also carries an extensive list of charitable foundations and projects in Thailand at ⓦwww.bangkokpost.com/outlookwecare.

Baan Unrak, Home of Joy Sangkhlaburi ⓣ034 595428, ⓦwww.geocities.com/baanunrak. Based north of Kanchanaburi, this project houses and educates destitute orphans, most of whom are ethnic minority refugees from Burma. It was founded by a woman working with the international Neo Humanist Foundation of Ananda Marga and now has two homes in the Sangkhlaburi area, where it cares for over 60 children, as well as a weaving centre and community outreach and education programmes. The easiest way to support Baan Unrak is to drop by their Bakery café and handicrafts shop in Sangkhlaburi, where you can also find out how to visit the school. Donations of books, clothes and money may also be welcome.

Chiang Mai Disabled Centre 133/1 Thanon Ratchaphakinai, Chiang Mai ⓣ053 852172, ⓦdisabled.infothai.com. Centrally placed, disabled-managed outlet for a foundation that provides, among other things, a training, resource and social centre for disabled people. Skilled long-term volunteers, donations and wheelchair sponsorships are sought, or just take your custom there for such services as Internet access, laundry and massage.

Human Development Foundation 100/11 Kae Ha Klong Toey 4, Thanon Damrongrathhaphipat, Klong Toey, Bangkok ⓣ02 671 5313, ⓦwww.mercycentre.org. Since 1972, this organization – founded by locally famous Catholic priest Father Joe Maier – has been providing education and support for Bangkok's street kids and slum-dwellers as well as caring for those with HIV-AIDS. It now runs more than thirty kindergartens in Bangkok's slums and is staffed almost entirely by people who grew up in the slums themselves. Contact the centre for information about donations, sponsorship and volunteering, or visit it to purchase cards and gifts. Father Joe's book, *The Slaughterhouse: Stories from Bangkok's Klong Toey Slum*, is an eye-opening insight into this side of Thai life that tourists rarely encounter; it's available from most Bangkok bookshops and profits go to the Foundation (see p.924 for a review).

Mae Tao Clinic Mae Sot ⓦwww.burmachildren.org. Every year, thousands of refugees from Burma's pernicious military regime flee across Thailand's western borders in search of sanctuary. Many are housed in refugee camps, where they at least have access to food and medical care, but thousands more fall outside the remit of the refugee camps and end up at the Mae Tao Clinic. The clinic, which provides free medical care for around 30,000 Burmese refugees a year, was founded in 1989 by a Karen refugee, Dr Cynthia, now internationally renowned for her work. Several guest houses and restaurants in Mae Sot accept donations of clothes, medical supplies and money for the Mae Tao clinic, and can also advise on where to go to give blood. The town is also home to a number of other organizations concerned with the welfare of the refugee communities. See p.316 for details.

The Mirror Art Group 106 Moo 1, Ban Huay Khom, Tambon Mae Yao, Chiang Rai ⓣ053 737412, ⓦwww.mirrorartgroup.org. NGO working with the hill tribes in the Mae Yao sub-district of Chiang Rai province to help combat such issues as drug abuse, erosion of culture and trafficking of women and children. Volunteers with IT, English and teaching skills are sought, as well as donations such as second-hand books, clothes, toys and videos.

North Andaman Tsunami Relief (NATR) Khuraburi ⓣ087 917 7165, ⓦwww.northandamantsunamirelief.com. This farang-Thai NGO has initiated a lot of post-tsunami reconstruction projects for the many devastated villages in the Khuraburi area and welcomes donations to help maintain the good work. It has also established a home-stay programme at local fishing villages, Andaman Discoveries (ⓦwww.andamandiscoveries.com), to help revitalize the local economy; for more details about this see p.711.

The Students' Education Trust (SET) ⓦwww.thaistudentcharity.org. High-school and further education in Thailand is a luxury that the poorest kids cannot afford – not only is there a lack of funds for fees, books, uniforms and even bus fares, but they often need to work to help support the family. Many are sent to live in temples to ease the burden on their relatives. The SET was founded by British-born Phra Peter Pannapadipo to help these kids pursue their education and escape from the poverty trap. He lived as a Thai monk for ten years and tells the heart-breaking stories of some of the boys at his temple in his book, *Little Angels: The Real-Life Stories of Twelve Thai Novice Monks* (see p.924 for a review). SET welcomes donations and sponsorship; see their website for details.

Thai Child Development Foundation Pha To ⓦwww.thaichilddevelopment.org. This small Thai-Dutch-run village project in south Thailand helps house and educate needy local children. The foundation welcomes donations of games, toys, clothes and money, and takes on volunteers for 1–3 months, but you can also support it by joining one of the eco-tours or home-stay programmes organized by its sister outfit Runs 'N Roses (ⓣ086 172 1090, ⓦwww.runsnroses.com), described on p.633.

Tsunami Volunteer Center Khao Lak ⓣ089 882 8840, ⓦwww.tsunamivolunteer.net. Within days of the 2004 tsunami, a Thai NGO established this project in Khao Lak, site of the worst devastation along Thailand's Andaman coast. In its first year of operation the centre coordinated reconstruction and regeneration tasks for hundreds of volunteers but there are still many projects on the go and the centre continues to welcome donations as well as volunteers. The main projects involve construction work, IT and English teaching; minimum commitment is two weeks. Several other tsunami relief organizations also work in the Khao Lak area; see p.720 for more details.

We-Train International House Bangkok ⓣ02 967 8550–4, ⓦwww.we-train.co.th. Run by the Association for the Promotion of the Status of Women

(APSW), this is a hotel close to Bangkok airport whose profits go towards helping APSW support, house and train disadvantaged women and children. See p.102 for details.

Contact lens solutions

Opticians in all reasonable-sized towns sell international brand-name **contact lens** cleaning and disinfection solutions.

Contraceptives

Condoms (*meechai*) are sold in all pharmacies and in many hairdressers and village shops as well. Birth-control **pills** can be bought in Bangkok (see p.217) and at some pharmacies in major towns and resorts; supplies of any other contraceptives should be brought from home.

Costs

Thailand can be a very cheap place to travel. At the bottom of the scale, you can manage on a **daily budget** of about B600 (£9/US$15) if you're willing to opt for basic accommodation, stay away from the more expensive resorts like Phuket, Ko Samui and Ko Phi Phi, and eat, drink and travel as the locals do. On this budget, you'll be spending under B200 for a dorm bed or single room (less if you share the cost of a double room), around B200 on three meals (eating mainly at night markets and simple noodle shops, and eschewing beer), and the rest on travel (sticking mainly to non-air-con buses and third-class trains) and incidentals. With extras like air-conditioning in rooms and on long-distance buses and trains, taking the various forms of taxi rather than buses or shared songthaews for cross-town journeys, and a meal and a couple of beers in a more touristy restaurant, a day's outlay would look more like B1000 (£15/US$25). Staying in comfortable, upmarket hotels and eating in the more exclusive restaurants, you should be able to live in great comfort for around B2000 a day (£30/US$50).

Travellers soon get so used to the low cost of living in Thailand that they start **bargaining** at every available opportunity, much as Thai people do. Although it's expected practice for a lot of commercial transactions, particularly at markets and when hiring tuk-tuks and taxis (though not in supermarkets or department stores), bargaining is a delicate art that requires humour, tact and patience. If your price is way out of line, the vendor's vehement refusal should be enough to make you increase your offer: never forget that the few pennies or cents you're making such a fuss over will go a lot further in a Thai person's hands than in your own.

It's rare that foreigners can bargain a price down as low as a Thai could, anyway, while **two-tier pricing** has been made official at government-run sights, as a kind of informal tourist tax: at national museums and historical parks, for example, foreigners often pay a B30–40 admission charge while Thais get in for B10; and at national parks, foreigners have to pay B200 entry while Thais pay just B20. A number of privately owned tourist attractions follow a similar two-tier system, posting an inflated price in English for foreigners and a lower price in Thai for locals.

Crime and personal safety

As long as you keep your wits about you, you shouldn't encounter much trouble in Thailand. **Theft** and **pickpocketing** are two of the main problems – not surprising considering that a huge percentage of the local population scrape by on under US$5 per day – but the most common cause for concern is the number of **con-artists** who dupe gullible tourists into parting with their cash.

To **prevent theft**, most travellers prefer to carry their valuables with them at all times, but it's sometimes possible to leave your valuables in a hotel or guest-house locker – the safest lockers are those that require your own padlock, as there are occasional reports of valuables being stolen by hotel staff. **Padlock your luggage** when leaving it in hotel or guest-house rooms, as well as when consigning it to storage or taking it on public transport. Padlocks also come in handy as extra security on your room, particularly on the doors of beachfront bamboo huts.

Theft from some long-distance **overnight buses** is also a problem, with the majority of reported incidents taking place on the temptingly cheap buses run by private companies direct from Bangkok's Thanon Khao San (as opposed to those that depart from the government bus stations) to destinations such as Chiang Mai and southern beach resorts. The best solution is to go direct from the bus stations.

Personal safety

On any bus, private or government, and on any train journey, never keep anything of value in luggage that is stored out of your sight and be wary of accepting food and drink from fellow passengers as it may be drugged. This might sound paranoid, but there have been enough **drug-muggings** for TAT to publish a specific warning about the problem. Drinks can also be spiked in bars and clubs, especially by sex-workers who later steal from their victim's room.

Violent crime against tourists is not common, but it does occur, and there have been several serious attacks on women travellers in the last few years. However, bearing in mind that over five million foreign tourists visit Thailand every year, the statistical likelihood of becoming a victim is extremely small. **Obvious precautions** for travellers of either sex include locking accessible windows and doors at night – preferably with your own padlock (doors in many of the simpler guest houses and beach bungalows are designed for this) – and not travelling alone at night in a taxi or tuk-tuk. Nor should you risk jumping into an unlicensed taxi at the airport in Bangkok at any time of day: there have been some very violent robberies in these, so take the well-marked licensed, metered taxis instead, or one of the airport buses.

Unfortunately, it is also necessary for female tourists to think twice about spending time alone with a **monk**, as not all men of the cloth uphold the Buddhist precepts and there have been rapes and murders committed by men wearing the saffron robes of the monkhood. See p.888 for more about the changing Thai attitudes towards the monkhood.

Though unpalatable and distressing, Thailand's high-profile **sex industry** is relatively unthreatening for Western women, with its energy focused exclusively on farang men; it's also quite easily avoided, being contained within certain pockets of the capital and a couple of beach resorts.

As for **harassment** from men, it's hard to generalize, but most Western women find it less of a problem in Thailand than they do back home. Outside the main tourist spots, you're more likely to be of interest as a foreigner rather than a woman and, if travelling alone, as an object of concern rather than of sexual aggression.

Among hazards to watch out for in the natural world, **riptides** claim a number of tourist lives every year, particularly off Phuket, Ko Chang (Trat), Hua Hin, Cha-am and Ko Samui during stormy periods of the monsoon season, so always pay attention to warning signs and red flags, and always ask locally if unsure. **Jellyfish** can be a problem on any coast, especially just after a storm (see p.36 for further advice). For advice on **road safety** see p.44.

Regional issues

It's advisable to travel with a guide if you're going off the main roads in certain **border areas** or, if you're on a motorbike, to take advice before setting off. As these regions are generally covered in dense unmapped jungle, you shouldn't find yourself alone in the area anyway, but the main stretches to watch are the immediate vicinity of the Burmese border north of Three Pagodas Pass, between Mae Sot and Mae Sariang, around Mae Sai, and between Umphang and Sangkhlaburi – where villages, hideaways and refugee camps occasionally get shelled either by the Burmese military or by rebel Karen or Mon forces – and the border between Cambodia and southern Isaan, which is littered with unexploded mines.

Because of the **violence in the deep south**, all Western governments are currently advising against travel to or through the border provinces of Songkhla, Yala, Pattani and Narathiwat, unless essential – see p.825 for further details. For up-to-the-minute advice on current political troublespots, consult your government's travel advisory.

Scams

Despite the best efforts of guidebook writers, TAT and the Thai tourist police, countless travellers to Thailand get scammed every

Governmental travel advisories

Australian Department of Foreign Affairs Ⓦwww.dfat.gov.au, Ⓦwww.smartraveller.gov.au.
British Foreign & Commonwealth Office Ⓦwww.fco.gov.uk.
Canadian Department of Foreign Affairs Ⓦwww.dfait-maeci.gc.ca.
Irish Department of Foreign Affairs Ⓦwww.foreignaffairs.gov.ie.
New Zealand Ministry of Foreign Affairs Ⓦwww.mft.govt.nz.
South African Department of Foreign Affairs Ⓦwww.dfa.gov.za.
US State Department Ⓦtravel.state.gov.

year. Nearly all **scams** are easily avoided if you're on your guard against anyone who makes an unnatural effort to befriend you. We have outlined the main scams in the relevant sections of this guide, but con-artists are nothing if not creative, so if in doubt walk away at the earliest opportunity. The worst areas for scammers are the busy tourist centres, including many parts of Bangkok and the main beach resorts.

Many **tuk-tuk drivers** earn most of their living through securing **commissions** from tourist-oriented shops; this is especially true in Bangkok, where they will do their damnedest to get you to go to a gem shop (see below). The most common tactic is for drivers to pretend that the Grand Palace or other major sight you intended to visit is closed for the day (they usually invent a plausible reason, such as a festival or royal occasion; see p.113 for more), and to then offer to take you on a round-city tour instead, perhaps even for free. The tour will invariably include a visit to a gem shop. The easiest way to avoid all this is to take a **metered taxi**; if you're fixed on taking a tuk-tuk, ignore any tuk-tuk that is parked up or loitering and be firm about where you want to go.

Self-styled **tourist guides**, **touts** and anyone else who might introduce themselves as **students** or **businesspeople** and offer to take you somewhere of interest, or invite you to meet their family, are often the first piece of bait in a well-honed chain of con-artists. If you bite, chances are you'll end up either at a gem shop or in a gambling den, or, at best, at a tour operator or hotel that you had not planned to patronize. This is not to say that you should never accept an invitation from a local person, but be extremely wary of doing so following a street encounter in Bangkok or the resorts. Tourist guides' ID cards are easily faked.

For many of these characters the goal is to get you inside a dodgy **gem shop**, nearly all of which are located in Bangkok. There is a full run-down of advice on how to avoid falling for the notorious low-grade gems scam on p.210, but the bottom line is that if you are not experienced at buying and trading in valuable gems you will definitely be ripped off, possibly even to the tune of several thousand pounds or dollars. Check the 2Bangkok website's account of a typical gem scam (Ⓦwww.2bangkok.com/2bangkok/Scams/Sapphire.shtml) before you shell out any cash at all.

A less common but potentially more frightening scam involves a similar cast of warm-up artists leading tourists into a **gambling** game. The scammers invite their victim home on an innocent-sounding pretext, get out a pack of cards, and then set about fleecing the incomer in any number of subtle ways. Often this can be especially scary as the venue is likely to be far from hotels or recognizable landmarks. You're unlikely to get any sympathy from police, as gambling is **illegal** in Thailand.

Reporting a crime or emergency

In emergencies, contact the English-speaking **tourist police**, who maintain a 24-hour toll-free nationwide line (Ⓣ1155) and have offices in the main tourist centres – getting in touch with the tourist police first is invariably more efficient than directly contacting the local police, ambulance or fire service. The tourist police's job is to offer advice and tell you what to do next, but they do not file crime reports, which must be done at the nearest police station. TAT has a special department for mediating between tourists, police and accused persons (particularly shopkeepers and tour agents) – the Tourist Assistance Center, or **TAC**; it's based in the TAT office on Thanon Rajdamnoen Nok, Bangkok (daily 8.30am–4.30pm; ⓣ02 281 5051).

Customs regulations

The **duty-free** allowance on entry to Thailand is 200 cigarettes (or 250g of tobacco) and a litre of spirits or wine.

To **export antiques or religious artefacts** – especially Buddha images – from Thailand, you need to have a licence granted by the Fine Arts Department, which can be obtained through the Office of Archeology and National Museums, 81/1 Thanon Si Ayutthaya (near the National Library), Bangkok (ⓣ02 628 5032), or through the national museums in Chiang Mai (see p.352) or Phuket (see p.760). Applications take at least two working days in Bangkok, generally more in the provinces, and need to be accompanied by the object itself, two postcard-sized colour photos of it, taken face-on and against a white background, and photocopies of the applicant's passport; furthermore, if the object is a Buddha image, the passport photocopies need to be certified by your embassy in Bangkok. Some antiques shops can organize all this for you.

Departure taxes

The international **departure tax** on all foreigners leaving Thailand by air is B500, due to rise to B700 on February 1, 2007. Domestic departure taxes are included in the price of the ticket, except at Bangkok Airways' Samui Airport, where a departure tax of B400 is payable.

Electricity

Mains **electricity** is supplied at 220 volts AC and is available at all but the most remote villages and basic beach huts. Where electricity is supplied by generators and/or solar power, for example on the smaller, less populated islands, it is often rationed to evenings only. If you're packing phone and camera chargers, a hair-dryer, laptop or other appliance, you'll need to take a set of travel-plug adapters with you as several plug types are commonly in use, most usually with two round pins, but also with two flat-blade pins, and sometimes with both options. Check out ⓦwww.kropla.com for a very helpful list, complete with pictures, of the different sockets, voltage and phone plugs used in Thailand.

Insurance

Most visitors to Thailand will need to take out **specialist travel insurance**, though you should check exactly what's covered. Policies generally exclude so-called **dangerous sports** unless an extra premium is paid: in Thailand this can mean such things as scuba-diving, whitewater rafting and trekking.

Rough Guides has teamed up with Columbus Direct to offer you travel insurance that can be tailored to suit your needs. Products include a low-cost **backpacker** option for long stays; a **short break** option for city getaways; a typical **holiday package** option; and others. There are also annual **multi-trip** policies for those who travel regularly. Different sports and activities, such as trekking, can be usually be covered if required. See our website (ⓦwww.roughguidesinsurance.com) for eligibility and purchasing options. Alternatively, call in the UK ⓣ0870/033 9988, in the US ⓣ1-800/749-4922, in Australia ⓣ1-300/669 999 or elsewhere ⓣ+44 870/890 2843.

Internet

Internet access is very widespread and very cheap in Thailand. You'll find traveller-oriented **Internet cafés** in every touristed town and resort in the country – there are at least twenty in the Banglamphu district of Bangkok, for example – and even remote islands like Ko Mak and Ko Phayam provide Internet access via satellite phones. Competition keeps prices low: upcountry you could expect to pay as little as B20 per hour, while rates in tourist centres average B1 per minute. Nearly every mid-sized town in Thailand also offers a public Internet service, called **Catnet**, at the government telephone office (usually located inside or adjacent to the main post office). To use the service, you need to buy a B100 card with a Catnet PIN (available at all phone offices), which gives you around three hours of Internet time at any of these public terminals.

If you plan to email from your **laptop** in Thailand, be advised that very few budget guest houses and cheap hotels have telephone sockets in the room. At the other end of the scale, luxury hotels charge astronomical rates for international calls, though many now offer broadband, or even wireless access. One potentially useful way round the cost issue is to become a temporary subscriber to the Thai ISP CS Loxinfo (ⓣ02 263 8222, ⓦwww.csloxinfo.com). Their Webnet deal, for example, with local dial-up numbers in every province in Thailand, is aimed at international businesspeople and tourists and can be bought online; it allows you 12 hours of Internet access for B160, 30 hours for B380 or 63 hours for B750. The usual phone plug in Thailand is the American standard RJ11 phone jack. See ⓦwww.kropla.com for detailed advice on how to set up your modem before you go, and how to hardwire phone plugs where necessary.

Laundry

Guest houses and hotels all over the country run low-cost, same-day **laundry** services. In some places you pay per item, in others you're charged by the kilo (generally from B30–50/kg); ironing is often included in the price.

Left luggage

Most major train stations have **left luggage** facilities, where bags can be stored for up to twenty days (from B10–40 per item per day); at bus stations you can usually persuade someone official to look after your stuff for a few hours. Many guest houses and hotels also offer an inexpensive and reliable service.

Living in Thailand

The most common source of **employment** in Thailand is **teaching English**, and Bangkok and Chiang Mai are the most fruitful places to look for jobs. You can search for openings at schools all over Thailand on ⓦwww.ajarn.com; the website also features extensive advice on all sorts of issues to do with teaching and living in Thailand. In addition, keep an eye on guest-house noticeboards in the two cities as teachers often advertise for replacements here. The *Bangkok Post* and *Bangkok Metro* listings magazine also sometimes carry teachers-wanted ads.

If you're a qualified **dive instructor**, you might be able to get seasonal work at one of the major resorts – in Phuket, Khao Lak and Ao Nang and on Ko Phi Phi, Ko Lanta, Ko Samui and Ko Tao, for example. Guest-house noticeboards occasionally carry adverts for more unusual jobs, such as playing extras in Thai movies. A tourist visa does not entitle you to work in Thailand, so, legally, you'll need to apply for a **work permit**.

Study and work programmes

For volunteer placements at smaller grassroots projects, see p.77.

AFS Intercultural Programs US ⓣ1-800/AFS-INFO, Canada ⓣ1-800/361-7248 or 514/288-3282, UK ⓣ0113/242 6136, Australia ⓣ1300/131 736 or ⓣ02/9215-0077, New Zealand ⓣ0800/600 300 or 04/494 6020, South Africa ⓣ011/339-2741, international enquiries ⓣ+1-212/807-8686, ⓦwww.afs.org. Global UN-recognized organization running summer programmes to foster international understanding.

Council on International Educational Exchange (CIEE) US ⓣ1-800/40-STUDY or ⓣ207/533-7600, UK ⓣ020/8939 9057, ⓦwww.ciee.org. Leading NGO that organizes paid year-long placements as English teachers in schools in central and northern Thailand.

Earthwatch Institute US ⓣ1-800/776-0188 or 978/461-0081, UK ⓣ01865/318 838, ⓦwww.earthwatch.org. Long-established charity whose international environmental research projects include coral-reef monitoring in Thailand; participants pay to join.

Go MAD: Go Make A Difference ⓦwww.go-mad.org. Designed by and for travellers who want to volunteer at small, local organizations in Thailand and elsewhere. No fees or forms.

i to i International Projects US ⓣ1-800/985 4864, UK ⓣ0800/011 1156, Australia ⓣ03/9775 2086, ⓦwww.i-to-i.com. Short-term voluntary placements teaching English or doing community or conservation work in Thailand; participants pay to join and may get some training.

Volunthai Thailand ⓦwww.volunthai.com. Invites young volunteers to teach English in rural schools in northeast Thailand; minimum one-month commitment.

Thai language classes

The most popular places to **study Thai** are Chiang Mai and Bangkok, where there's plenty of choice, including private and group lessons for both tourists and expats. AUA (American University Alumni; Ⓦwww.auathai.com) has outlets in both Bangkok and Chiang Mai (described on p.349). In Bangkok, there's also Jentana and Associates (Ⓦwww.thai-lessons.com), and Nisa Thai Language School (Ⓔnisathai@cscoms.com). For more information and directories of language schools, see Ⓦwww.learningthai.com.

Mail

Overseas mail usually takes around seven days from Bangkok, a little longer from the more isolated areas. **Post office hours** are generally Mon–Fri 8.30am–4.30pm, Sat 9am–noon; some close Mon–Fri noon–1pm and may stay open until 6pm. Almost all main post offices across the country operate a **poste restante** service and will hold letters for one to three months. Mail should be addressed: *Name* (family name underlined or capitalized), Poste Restante, GPO, *Town or City*, Thailand. It will be filed by surname, though it's always wise to check under your first initial as well. The smaller post offices pay scant attention to who takes what, but in the busier GPOs you need to show your passport, pay B1 per letter or B2 per parcel received, and sign for them.

Post offices are the best places to buy **stamps**, though hotels and guest houses often sell them too, charging an extra B1 per stamp. An airmail letter of under 10g costs B17 to send to Europe or Australia and B19 to North America; standard-sized postcards cost B12, larger ones and aerogrammes B15, regardless of where they're going. All **parcels** must be officially boxed and sealed (for a small fee) at special counters within main post offices, or in a private outlet just outside. In tourist centres (especially at Bangkok's GPO) be prepared to queue, first for the packaging, then for the weighing and then again for the buying of stamps. The **surface** rate for parcels to the UK is B950 for the first kg, then B175/kg; to the US B550 for the first kg, then B140/kg; and to Australia B650 for the first kg, then B110/kg; the package should reach its destination in three months. The **airmail** rate for parcels to the UK is B900 for the first kg, then B380/kg; to the US B950 for the first kg, then B500/kg; and to Australia B750 for the first kg, then B350/kg; the package should reach its destination in one or two weeks.

Maps

For most major destinations, the **maps** in this book should be all you need, though you may want to supplement them with larger-scale maps of Bangkok and the whole country. Bangkok bookshops are the best source of these; where appropriate, detailed local maps and their stockists are recommended in the relevant chapters of this guide. If you want to buy a map before you get there, Rough Guides' 1:1,200,000 map of Thailand is a good option – and, since it's printed on special rip-proof paper, it won't tear. Reasonable alternatives include the 1:1,500,000 maps produced by Nelles and Bartholomew.

For **drivers**, PN Map Centre's large-format atlas *Thailand Highway Map* is good, and is updated regularly; it's available at most bookstores in Thailand where English-language material is sold. If you can't get hold of that, you could go for the relevant 1:300,000 maps of each province published by PN Map Centre and sold at better bookshops in Bangkok and all over the country; some of the detail on these maps is only in Thai, but they should have enough English to be useful. Better than both the above are the excellent World Class Drives map-booklets, which are handed out free to customers of Budget car rental: detailed and almost unfailingly accurate, these are designed for tourists, but only cover certain parts of the country.

Trekking maps are hard to come by, except in the most popular national parks where you can usually pick up a free hand-out showing the main trails.

Money

Thailand's unit of currency is the **baht** (abbreviated to "B"), divided into 100 satang – which are rarely seen these days. Notes come in B20, B50, B100, B500 and B1000 denominations, inscribed with Western as well as Thai numerals, and increasing in size according to value. The coinage is more confusing, because new shapes and sizes circulate alongside older ones, which sometimes have only Thai numerals. There are three different silver one-baht coins, all legal tender; the smallest of these is the newest version, and the one accepted by public call-boxes. Silver two-baht pieces are slightly bigger; silver five-baht pieces are bigger again and have a copper rim; ten-baht coins have a small brass centre encircled by a silver ring.

At the time of writing, **exchange rates** were averaging B40 to US$1, B50 to €1 and B70 to £1. A good site for current exchange rates is Ⓦwww.xe.com. Note that Thailand has no black market in foreign currency. Because of severe currency fluctuations in the late 1990s, some tourist-oriented businesses now quote their prices in **US dollars**, particularly luxury hotels and dive centres.

Banking hours are Monday to Friday from 8.30am to 3.30 or 4.30pm, but exchange kiosks in the main tourist centres are always open till at least 5pm, sometimes 10pm, and upmarket hotels change money 24 hours a day. The Don Muang Airport exchange counters also operate 24 hours, while exchange kiosks at overseas airports with flights to Thailand usually keep Thai currency.

Sterling and US dollar **traveller's cheques** are accepted by banks, exchange booths and upmarket hotels in every sizeable Thai town, and most places also deal in a variety of other currencies; everyone offers better rates for cheques than for straight cash. Generally, a total of B33 in commission and duty is charged per cheque – though kiosks and hotels in isolated places may charge extra – so you'll save money if you deal in larger cheque denominations.

American Express, Visa and MasterCard **credit and debit cards** are accepted at top hotels as well as in some posh restaurants, department stores, tourist shops and travel agents, but surcharging of up to seven percent is rife, and theft and forgery are major industries – always demand the carbon copies, and never leave cards in baggage storage. If you have a personal identification number (PIN) for your debit or credit card, you can also withdraw cash from hundreds of 24-hour **ATMs** around the country. Almost every town now has at least one bank with an ATM that accepts Visa/Plus cards and MasterCard/Cirrus cards, and there are a growing number of stand-alone ATMs in supermarkets. For an up-to-the-minute list of ATM locations in Thailand, check Ⓦwww.mastercard.com and Ⓦwww.visa.com.

Opening hours and public holidays

Most **shops** open at least Monday to Saturday from about 8am to 8pm, while department stores operate daily from around 10am to 9pm. Private office hours are generally Monday to Friday 8am to 5pm and Saturday 8am to noon, though in tourist areas these hours are longer, with weekends worked like any other day. Government offices work Monday to Friday 8.30am to noon and 1 to 4.30pm, and national museums tend to stick to these hours too, but some close on Mondays and Tuesdays rather than at weekends.

Many tourists only register **national holidays** because trains and buses suddenly get extraordinarily crowded: although banks and government offices shut on these days, most shops and tourist-oriented businesses carry on regardless, and TAT branches continue to dispense information. The only time an inconvenient number of shops, restaurants and hotels do close is during **Chinese New Year**, which, though not marked as an official national holiday, brings many businesses to a standstill for several days in late January or February. You'll notice it particularly in the south, where most service industries are Chinese-managed.

Thais use both the Western Gregorian **calendar** and a Buddhist calendar – the Buddha is said to have died (or entered Nirvana) in the year 543 BC, so Thai dates start from that point: thus 2007 AD becomes 2550 BE (Buddhist Era).

National holidays

Jan 1 Western New Year's Day
Feb (day of full moon) Maha Puja: commemorates the Buddha preaching to a spontaneously assembled crowd of 1250.

April 6 Chakri Day: the founding of the Chakri dynasty.
April (usually 13–15) Songkhran: Thai New Year.
May 1 National Labour Day
May 5 Coronation Day
May (early in the month) Royal Ploughing Ceremony: marks start of rice-planting season.
May (day of full moon) Visakha Puja: the holiest of all Buddhist holidays, which celebrates the birth, enlightenment and death of the Buddha.
July (day of full moon) Khao Pansa: the start of the annual three-month Buddhist rains retreat, when new monks are ordained.
Aug 12 Queen's birthday
Oct 23 Chulalongkorn Day: the anniversary of Rama V's death.
Dec 5 King's birthday: also celebrated as national Fathers' Day.
Dec 10 Constitution Day
Dec 31 Western New Year's Eve

Phones

Local **calls within Thailand** are very cheap (as little as B1 for 3min from a coin payphone), but inter-provincial rates can be as high as B12/minute. To save fiddling around with coins, which will soon be gobbled up on a long-distance call, you may well be better off buying a domestic TOT **phone card** for B100; this comes with a PIN number, is available from hotels and a wide variety of shops, and can be used in designated orange or green cardphones or in stainless steel payphones. In some provincial towns, enterprising mobile-phone owners hang out on the main streets, often with a simple fold-out table and makeshift cardboard sign, offering cheap long-distance, and sometimes international, calls.

When **dialling** any number in Thailand, you must now always preface it with what used to be the area code, even when dialling from the same area; in this book we've separated off this code, for easy recognition (you'll still come across plenty of business cards and brochures which give only the old local number, to which you'll need to add the area code). Where we've given several line numbers – eg ⓣ02 431 1802–9 – you can substitute the last digit, 2, with any digit between 3 and 9. For **directory enquiries** within Thailand, call ⓣ1133.

All mobile phone numbers in Thailand have recently been changed from nine to ten digits, by adding the lucky number "8" after the initial zero (again you're likely to come across cards and brochures giving the old number). Note also, however, that Thais tend to change mobile-phone providers – and therefore numbers – comparatively frequently, in search of a better deal.

One final local idiosyncrasy: Thai phone books list people by their first name, not their family name.

Mobile phones

An increasing number of tourists are taking their **mobile phones** to Thailand. Visitors from the US may well need to have a dual- or tri-band phone, but GSM 900Hz and 1800Hz, the systems most commonly found in other parts of the world, are both available in Thailand. Most foreign networks have links with Thai networks, but it's worth checking with your phone provider before you travel; it's also worth checking how much coverage there is for your network within Thailand. For a full list of network types and providers in Thailand, along with coverage maps and roaming partners, go to ⓦwww.gsmworld.com/roaming.

If you want to use your mobile a lot in Thailand, it may well be worth getting hold of a rechargeable **Thai SIM card** with a local phone number. An AIS 1-2-Call card (ⓦwww.ais.co.th) will give you the widest coverage in Thailand, and top-up cards are available at 7-11 stores across the country. Their call rates aren't the cheapest, however, at B5 for the first minute, then B2 per minute within Thailand; international calls can cost as much as around B30 per minute, but you can get far cheaper rates (B7/min to the UK, for example) by using voice-over-internet protocol (VOIP; see below), prefixing the relevant country code with ⓣ009; texts cost B2 domestic, around B9 international.

Your own network operator may be able to give you useful advice about **exchanging SIM cards** before you leave home, but the best place in Thailand to buy a card and have any necessary technical adjustments made is the Mah Boon Krong Centre in Bangkok (see p.204); an AIS 1-2-Call SIM card, for example, will cost you around B220, including your first B50 worth of calls. Because of heightened security fears, you'll need to take your passport along and fill in a simple registration form when you buy a rechargeable Thai SIM card.

International calls

There are two basic ways of making **international calls** from Thailand: by international direct-dialling (IDD), prefixing the relevant country code with ⓣ**001**; and far more cheaply, by voice-over-internet protocol (VOIP), prefixing the relevant country code with ⓣ**009**.

001 calls to North America cost B9/minute, to Australia or the UK B18/minute and to New Zealand B22/minute. For most other countries, there are three time periods with different **rates**: the most expensive, or standard, time to call is from 7am to 9pm (economy rate applies on Sundays); the economy period runs from 9pm to midnight and 5am to 7am; the reduced rate applies between midnight and 5am. The per-minute rate for a direct-dial call to Ireland is B30 standard, B24 economy and B24 reduced, to South Africa B45/B36/B32.

You can use these government rates by buying a **Thaicard**, the international phone card issued by CAT (Communications Authority of Thailand). Available in B100–3000 denominations at post offices and many shops, Thaicards can be used in designated purple cardphones – if you can't happen to find one, head for the nearest government telephone centre, which is usually located within or adjacent to a town's main post office.

There's also a private international cardphone system called **Lenso**, which operates in Bangkok and the biggest resorts. To use Lenso's yellow phones, you either need a special Lenso phone card (available from shops near the phones in B200, B300 and B500 denominations), or you can use a credit card. Rates, however, are ten percent higher than government IDD rates.

You can take advantage of the cheaper rates of **009 calls** by buying one of CAT's **Phone Net** cards, which come in denominations of B300 and B500. They're available from the same outlets as Thaicards (see above) and can be used in the same cardphones. Whatever time of day it is, tariffs are B5/minute to North America, B6/minute to Australia, South Africa and the UK, B14/minute to New Zealand and B24/minute to Ireland. Many private international call offices (where your call is timed and you pay at the end) in tourist areas such as Bangkok's Thanon Khao San now use VOIP to access these rates – plus a service charge to the customer, of course.

International dialling codes

Calling from abroad, the international **country code** for Thailand is ⓣ**66**, after which you leave off the initial zero of the Thai number.

Calling from Thailand, for Burma, Cambodia, Laos or Malaysia dial ⓣ007 then the subscriber number, or for cheap-rate calls to Malaysia ⓣ002 then the subscriber number. For anywhere else, dial ⓣ001 or ⓣ009 (see above) and then the relevant country code:

Australia ⓣ61
Canada ⓣ1
Ireland ⓣ353
New Zealand ⓣ64
South Africa ⓣ27
UK ⓣ44
US ⓣ1

For **international directory enquiries** and operator services, call ⓣ100.

Photography

Most towns and all resorts have at least one **camera shop** where you will be able to download digital pictures on to a CD for B100–150 per CD. They all have card readers so there's no need to bring cables. In tourist centres many Internet cafés also offer CD-burning services, though if you want to email your pictures bringing your own cable will make life easier. For expert advice on digital image storage while travelling see ⓦadrianwarren.com.

Tampons

Few Thai women use **tampons**, which are not widely available, except from branches of Boots in Bangkok and the resorts, and from a few tourist-oriented minimarkets in the biggest resorts.

Time

Bangkok is seven hours ahead of GMT, twelve hours ahead of US Eastern Standard Time and three hours behind Australian Eastern Standard Time.

Tipping

It is usual to **tip** hotel bellboys and porters B20, and to round up taxi fares to the nearest B10. Most guides, drivers, masseurs, waiters and maids also depend on tips, and although some upmarket hotels and restaurants will add an automatic ten percent service charge to your bill, this is not always shared out.

Tourist information

The **Tourism Authority of Thailand**, or **TAT** (Ⓦwww.tourismthailand.org) maintains offices in several cities abroad and has 24 branches within Thailand (all open daily 8.30am–4.30pm, though a few close noon–1pm for lunch). Regional offices should have up-to-date information on local festival dates and transport schedules, but none of them offers accommodation booking, and service can be variable. You can contact the TAT tourist assistance phoneline from anywhere in the country for free on Ⓣ1672 (daily 8am–8pm). In Bangkok, TAT plays second fiddle to the Bangkok Tourist Bureau, details of which can be found on p.104. In some smaller towns that don't qualify for a local TAT office, the information gap is filled by a **municipal tourist assistance office**, though at some of these you may find it hard to locate a fluent English speaker.

TAT offices abroad

Australia and New Zealand Level 2, 75 Pitt St, Sydney, NSW 2000 Ⓣ02/9247 7549, Ⓦwww.thailand.net.au.
South Africa Contact the UK office.
UK and Ireland 3rd Floor, Brook House, 98–99 Jermyn St, London SW1Y 6EE Ⓣ020/7925 2511, recorded information on Ⓣ0870/900 2007, Ⓦwww.thaismile.co.uk.
US and Canada 61 Broadway, Suite 2810, New York, NY 10006 Ⓣ212/432-0433, Ⓔinfo@tatny.com; 611 North Larchmont Blvd, 1st Floor, Los Angeles, CA 90004 Ⓣ323/461-9814, Ⓔtatla@ix.netcom.com.

Travellers with disabilities

Thailand makes few provisions for its disabled citizens and this obviously affects **travellers with disabilities**, but taxis, comfortable hotels and personal tour guides are all more affordable than in the West and most travellers with disabilities find Thais only too happy to offer assistance where they can. Hiring a local tour guide to accompany you on a day's sightseeing is particularly recommended: government tour guides can be arranged through any TAT office.

Most **wheelchair-users** end up driving on the roads because it's too hard to negotiate the uneven pavements, which are high to allow for flooding and invariably lack dropped kerbs. Crossing the road can be a trial, particularly in Bangkok and other big cities, where it's usually a question of climbing steps up to a bridge rather than taking a ramped underpass. Few buses and trains have ramps but in Bangkok some Skytrain stations and all subway stations have lifts.

Several **tour companies** in Thailand specialize in organizing trips featuring adapted facilities, accessible transport and escorts. The Pattaya-based Adventure Holidays Thailand (Ⓣ038 233502, Ⓦwww.adventure-holidays-thailand.com) has a reputation for its can-do attitude to travel for disabled and physically challenged people and its tailor-made tours of Thailand can be designed to include elephant-riding and rafting as well as more traditional sightseeing. The Bangkok-based Help and Care Travel Company (Ⓣ02 720 5395, Ⓦwww.wheelchairtours.com), which designs accessible holidays in Thailand for slow walkers and wheelchair users, can provide transport and escort services; its website carries a (short) list of wheelchair-accessible hotels in the main tourist centres. In Chiang Mai, *Baan Khun Daeng* (Ⓣ053 242874, Ⓦmembers.chello.nl/danblokker/e_home.html) is a wheelchair-accessible guest house run by a wheelchair-user who can also arrange accessible tours around north Thailand. Mermaid's Dive Centre in Pattaya (Ⓣ038 232219, Ⓦwww.learn-in-asia.com/handicapped_diving.htm; see p.465) runs International Association of Handicapped Divers programmes for **disabled divers** and instructors.

Visas

There are three main entry categories for visitors to Thailand; for all of them your

passport must be valid for at least six months from the date of entry. As **visa** requirements are often subject to change, you should always check before departure with a Thai embassy or consulate, a reliable travel agent, or on the Thai Ministry of Foreign Affairs' website at Ⓦwww.mfa.go.th/web/12.php. For further, unofficial details on related matters, such as the perils of overstaying your visa, go to Ⓦwww.thaivisa.com.

Most Western passport holders (that includes citizens of the UK, Ireland, the US, Canada, Australia, New Zealand and South Africa) are allowed to enter the country for **stays of up to thirty days** without having to apply for a visa (officially termed the "tourist visa exemption"); the period of stay will be stamped into your passport by immigration officials upon entry. You're supposed to be able to somehow show proof of means of living while in the country (B10,000/person, B20,000/family), and in theory you may be put back on the next plane without it or sent back to get a sixty-day tourist visa from the nearest Thai embassy, but this is unheard of. It's easy to get a new thirty-day stay by hopping across the border into a neighbouring country and back, including taking a day-trip into Burma at Kaw Thaung (see p.700), Myawaddy (see p.316) or Thachileik (see p.435).

If you're fairly certain you may want to stay longer than thirty days, then from the outset you should apply for a **sixty-day tourist visa** from a Thai embassy or consulate, accompanying your application – which generally takes several days to process – with your passport and two photos. The sixty-day visa currently costs B1000 or equivalent (though it's a rip-off £25 in the UK); multiple-entry versions are available, costing B1000 per entry, which may be handy if you're going to be leaving and re-entering Thailand. Tourist visas are valid for three months, ie you must enter Thailand within three months of the visa being issued by the Thai embassy or consulate. Visa application forms can be downloaded from, for example, Ⓦwww.thaiembassyuk.org.uk/visaapplicationform_internet.pdf.

Thai embassies also consider applications for **ninety-day non-immigrant visas** (B2000 or equivalent single entry, B5000 multiple-entry) as long as you can offer a good reason for your visit, such as study or business (there are different categories of non-immigrant visa for which different levels of proof are needed). As it's quite a hassle to organize a ninety-day visa from outside the country (and generally not feasible for most tourists), it's generally easier, though more expensive, to apply for a thirty-day extension to your sixty-day visa once inside Thai borders.

It's not a good idea to **overstay** your visa limits. Once you're at the airport or the border, you'll have to pay a fine of B500/day before you can leave Thailand. More importantly, however, if you're in the country with an expired visa and you get involved with police or immigration officials for any reason, however trivial, they are obliged to take you to court, possibly imprison you, and deport you.

Extensions and re-entry permits

Thirty-day stays can be **extended** in Thailand for a further ten days, sixty-day tourist visas for a further thirty days, at the discretion of officials; extensions cost B1900 and are issued over the counter at immigration offices (*kaan khao muang*; Ⓦwww.immigration.go.th) in nearly every provincial capital – most offices ask for one or two photos as well, plus two photocopies of the main pages of your passport including your Thai arrival card, arrival stamp and visa. Many Khao San tour agents offer to get your visa extension for you, but beware: some are reportedly faking the stamps, which could get you into serious trouble. Immigration offices also issue **re-entry permits** (B1000 single re-entry, B3800 multiple) if you want to leave the country and come back again while maintaining the validity of your existing visa.

Thai embassies and consulates abroad

For a full listing of Thai diplomatic missions abroad, consult the Thai Ministry of Foreign Affairs' website at Ⓦwww.mfa.go.th/web/10.php.

Australia 111 Empire Circuit, Yarralumla, Canberra ACT 2600 Ⓣ02/6273 1149, Ⓦwww.thaiembassy.org.au; plus consulate at 131 Macquarrie St, Sydney, NSW 2000 Ⓣ02/9241 2542–3, Ⓦthaisydney.idx.com.au.

Burma 73 Manawhari Street, Dagon Township, Rangoon ⓣ01/224647.
Cambodia 196 Preah Norodom Blvd, Sangkat Tonle Bassac, Khan Chamcar Mon, Phnom Penh ⓣ023/726306–10, ⓦwww.thaiembassy.org/phnompenh.
Canada 180 Island Park Drive, Ottawa, ON, K1Y 0A2 ⓣ613/722-4444, ⓦwww.magma.ca/~thaiott; plus consulate at 1040 Burrard St, Vancouver, BC, V6Z 2R9 ⓣ604/687-1143, ⓦwww.thaicongenvancouver.org.
Laos Route Phonekheng, Vientiane, PO Box 128 ⓣ021/214581–3; plus consulate at Khanthabouly District, Savannakhet Province, PO Box 513 ⓣ041/212373.
Malaysia 206 Jalan Ampang, 50450 Kuala Lumpur ⓣ03/2148 8222; plus consulates at 4426 Jalan Pengkalan Chepa, 15400 Kota Bharu ⓣ09/748 2545; and 1 Jalan Tunku Abdul Rahman, 10350 Penang ⓣ04/226 9484.
New Zealand 2 Cook St, PO Box 17226, Karori, Wellington 6005 ⓣ04/476 8618–9, ⓦwww.thaiembassynz.org.nz.
Singapore 370 Orchard Road, Singapore 238870 ⓣ6737 2158 or 6835 4991, ⓦwww.thaiembsingapore.org.
South Africa 428 Pretorius/Hill St, Arcadia, Pretoria 0083 ⓣ012/342 1600.
UK and Ireland 29–30 Queens Gate, London SW7 5JB ⓣ020/7589 2944, ⓦwww.thaiembassyuk.org.uk. Visa applications by post are not accepted here, but can be sent to various honorary consulates around the UK and Ireland – see ⓦwww.thaiembassyuk.org.uk/instruction.htm.
US 1024 Wisconsin Ave NW, Suite 401, Washington, DC 20007 ⓣ202/944-3600, ⓦwww.thaiembdc.org; plus consulates at 700 North Rush St, Chicago, IL 60611 ⓣ312/664-3129, ⓦwww.thaichicago.net; 351 E 52nd St, New York, NY 10022 ⓣ212/754-1770, ⓦwww.thaiconsulnewyork.com; and 611 North Larchmont Blvd, 2nd Floor, Los Angeles, CA 90004 ⓣ323/962-9574–7, ⓦwww.thai-la.net.
Vietnam 63–65 Hoang Dieu St, Hanoi ⓣ04/823-5092–3; plus consulate at 77 Tran Quoc Thao St, District 3, Ho Chi Minh City ⓣ08/932-7637–8, ⓦwww.thaiembassy.org/hochiminhcity.

Guide

Guide

Bangkok

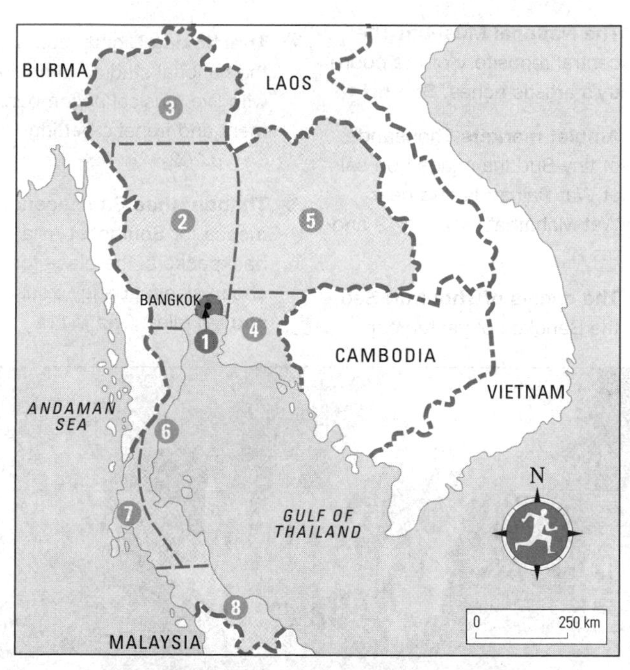
BURMA
LAOS
BANGKOK
CAMBODIA
VIETNAM
ANDAMAN SEA
GULF OF THAILAND
MALAYSIA
N
0 250 km

CHAPTER 1 Highlights

* **The Grand Palace** The country's least missable sight, incorporating its holiest and most dazzling temple, Wat Phra Kaeo. See p.131
* **Wat Pho** Admire the Reclining Buddha and the lavish architecture, and leave time for a relaxing massage. See p.139
* **The National Museum** The central repository of the country's artistic riches. See p.143
* **Amulet markets** Thousands of tiny Buddha images on sale at Wat Rajnadda and near Wat Mahathat. See p.149 and p.142
* **The canals of Thonburi** See the Bangkok of yesteryear on a touristy but memorable longtail boat ride. See p.160
* **Jim Thompson's House** An elegant Thai design classic. See p.169
* **Chatuchak Weekend Market** Eight thousand stalls selling everything from triangular pillows to second-hand Levis. See p.179
* **Thai boxing** Nightly bouts at the national stadia, complete with live musical accompaniment and frenetic betting. See p.202
* **Thanon Khao San** Legendary mecca for Southeast Asia backpackers; the place for cheap sleeps, baggy trousers and tall tales. See p.114

△ Restoring the murals at Wat Phra Kaeo

1

Bangkok

The headlong pace and flawed modernity of Bangkok match few people's visions of the capital of exotic Siam. Spiked with scores of high-rise buildings of concrete and glass, it's a vast flatness that holds a population of at least nine million, and feels even bigger. But under the shadow of the skyscrapers you'll find a heady mix of chaos and refinement, of frenetic markets and hushed golden temples, of dispiriting, zombie-like sex shows and early-morning alms-giving ceremonies. One way or another, the place will probably get under your skin – and if you don't enjoy the challenge of slogging through jams of buses and tuk-tuks, which fill the air with a chainsaw drone and clouds of pollution, you can spend a couple of days on the most impressive temples and museums, have a quick shopping spree and then strike out for the provinces.

Most budget travellers head for the **Banglamphu** district, where if you're not careful you could end up watching DVDs all day long and selling your shoes when you run out of money. The district is far from having a monopoly on Bangkok accommodation, but it does have the advantage of being just a short walk from the major sights in the **Ratanakosin** area: the dazzling ostentation of the **Grand Palace** and **Wat Phra Kaeo**, lively and grandiose **Wat Pho** and the **National Museum**'s hoard of exquisite works of art. Once those cultural essentials have been seen, you can choose from a whole bevy of lesser sights, including **Wat Benjamabophit** (the "Marble Temple"), especially at festival time, and **Jim Thompson's House**, a small, personal museum of Thai design.

For livelier scenes, explore the dark alleys of **Chinatown's** bazaars or head for the water: the great **Chao Phraya River**, which breaks up and adds zest to the city's landscape, is the backbone of a network of **canals** that remains fundamentally intact in the west-bank Thonburi district. Inevitably the waterways have earned Bangkok the title of "Venice of the East", a tag that seems all too apt when you're wading through flooded streets in the rainy season; indeed, the city is year by year subsiding into the marshy ground, literally sinking under the weight of its burgeoning concrete towers.

Shopping on dry land varies from touristic outlets pushing silks, handicrafts and counterfeit watches, through home-grown boutiques selling street-wise fashions and stunning contemporary decor, to thronging local markets where half the fun is watching the crowds. Similarly, the city offers the country's most varied **entertainment**, ranging from traditional dancing and the orchestrated bedlam of Thai boxing, through hip bars and clubs playing the latest imported sounds, to the farang-only sex bars of the notorious Patpong district, a tinsel-town Babylon that's the tip of a dangerous iceberg. Even if the above doesn't appeal, you'll almost certainly pass through Bangkok once, if not several times

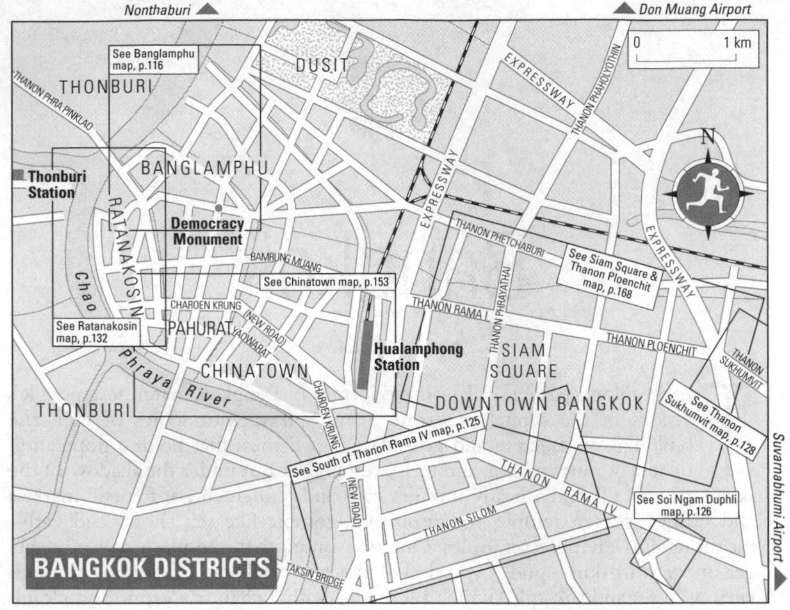

– not only is it Thailand's main port of entry, it's also the obvious place to sort out **onward travel**, with good deals on international air tickets, as well as a convenient menu of embassies for visas to neighbouring countries.

A little history

Bangkok is a relatively young capital, established in 1782 after the Burmese sacked Ayutthaya, the former capital. A temporary base was set up on the western bank of the Chao Phraya River, in what is now **Thonburi**, before work started on the more defensible east bank, where the French had built a grand, but short-lived fort in the 1660s. The first king of the new dynasty, Rama I, built his palace at **Ratanakosin**, within a defensive ring of two (later expanded to three) canals, and this remains the city's spiritual heart.

Initially, the city was largely **amphibious**: only the temples and royal palaces were built on dry land, while ordinary residences floated on thick bamboo rafts on the river and canals; even shops and warehouses were moored to the river bank. A major shift in emphasis came in the second half of the nineteenth century, first under Rama IV (1851–68), who as part of his effort to restyle the capital along European lines built Bangkok's first roads, and then under Rama V (1868–1910), who constructed a new residential palace in Dusit, north of Ratanakosin, and laid out that area's grand boulevards.

Since World War II, and especially from the mid-1960s onwards, Bangkok has seen an explosion of **modernization**, which has blown away earlier attempts at orderly planning and left the city without an obvious centre. Most of the canals have been filled in, to be replaced by endless rows of cheap, functional concrete shophouses, high-rises and housing estates, sprawling over a built-up area of 330 square kilometres. The benefits of Thailand's **economic boom** since the 1980s have been concentrated in Bangkok, attracting migration from all over the country and making the capital ever more dominant: the population, over half of which is under 30 years of age, is now forty times that of the second city, Chiang Mai. Every aspect of national life is centralized in the city, but the governor of Bangkok is not granted enough power to deal with the ensuing problems, notably that of **traffic** – which in Bangkok now comprises four-fifths of the nation's automobiles. The Skytrain and the subway have undoubtedly helped, but the governor was unable to get the competing systems to intersect properly or ticket jointly, and it's left to ingenious, local solutions such as the Khlong Saen Saeb canal boats and side-street motorbike taxis to keep the city moving. And there's precious little chance to escape from the pollution in green space: the city has only 0.4 square metres of public parkland per inhabitant, the lowest figure in the world, compared, for example, to London's 30.4 square metres per person.

Arrival, information, transport and accommodation

Finding a place to stay in Bangkok is usually no problem: the city has a huge range of **accommodation**, from the murkiest backstreet bunk to the plushest five-star riverside suite, and you don't have to spend a lot to get a comfortable place. Getting to your guest house or hotel, however, is unlikely to put you in a good mood, for there can be few cities in the world where **transport** is such a headache. Bumper-to-bumper vehicles create fumes so bad that some days the city's carbon monoxide emissions come close to the international danger level, and it's not unusual for residents to spend three hours getting to work – and these are people who know where they're going. However, the recent openings of the subway system and the elevated train network called the Bangkok Transit System, or BTS Skytrain, have radically improved public transport in downtown areas of the city. Unfortunately for tourists, these systems do not stretch as far as Ratanakosin or Banglamphu, where boats still provide the fastest means of hopping from one sight to another.

City of angels

When Rama I was crowned in 1782, he gave his new capital a grand 43-syllable name to match his ambitious plans for the building of the city. Since then, 21 more syllables have been added. Krungthepmahanakhornbowornrattanakosinmahintarayutthaya - maha-dilokpopnopparatratchathaniburiromudomratchaniwetmahasathanamornpiman-avatarnsathitsakkathattiyavisnukarprasit is certified by the Guinness Book of Records as the longest place name in the world, roughly translating as "Great city of angels, the supreme repository of divine jewels, the great land unconquerable, the grand and prominent realm, the royal and delightful capital city full of nine noble gems, the highest royal dwelling and grand palace, the divine shelter and living place of the reincarnated spirits". Fortunately, all Thais refer to the city simply as **Krung Thep**, "City of Angels", though plenty can recite the full name at the drop of a hat. **Bangkok** – "Village of the Plum Olive" – was the name of the original village on the Thonburi side; with remarkable persistence, it has remained in use by foreigners since the time of the French garrison.

Arriving in Bangkok

Unless you arrive in Bangkok by train, be prepared for a long slog into the city. Both the old Don Muang Airport and the new Suvarnabhumi Airport are a slow 25km from the city centre. Even if you arrive by coach, you'll still have a lot of work to do to get into the centre.

At the time of writing, the new **Suvarnabhumi Airport** (Ⓦwww.suvarnabhumiairport.com, or go to Ⓦwww.2bangkok.com for the latest news) is under construction, 25km east of central Bangkok off the main highway towards Chonburi, at inauspiciously named Nong Ngu Hao (meaning "cobra swamp"). All scheduled international and domestic flights are slated to arrive here, while Don Muang will handle only charter airlines. Full details of the new airport's facilities, transport into town and so on are not yet available, however.

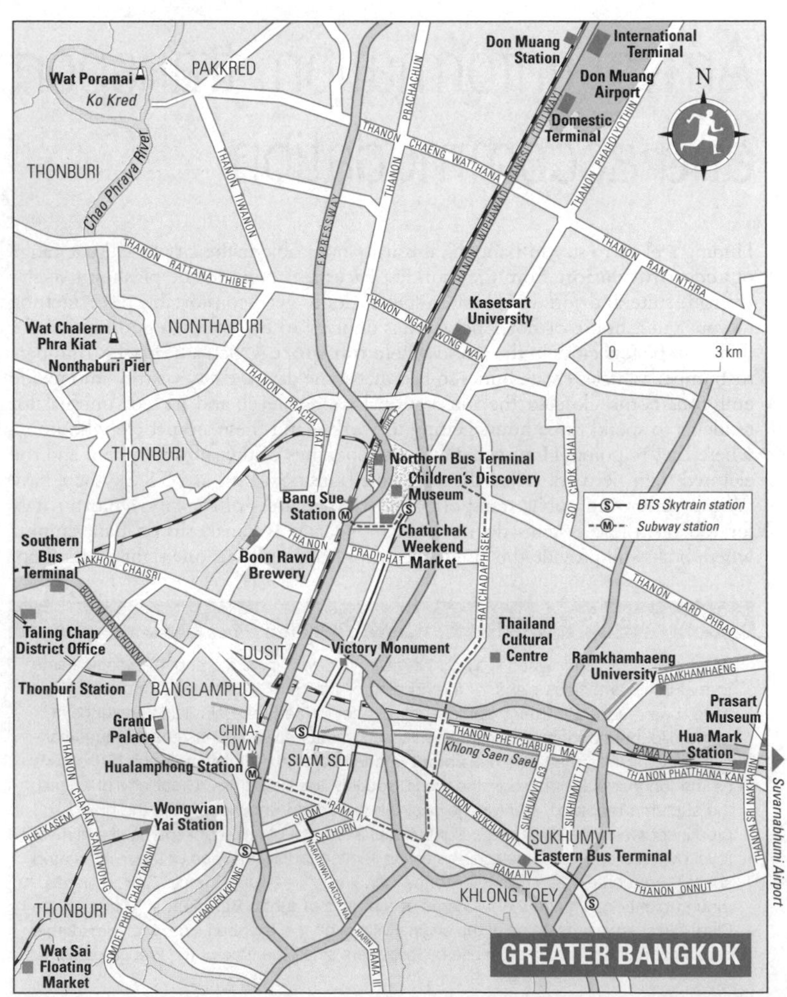

There'll certainly be plenty of cafés and restaurants and an airport hotel, the *Novotel Suvarnabhumi* (ⓣ02 131 1111,ⓦwww.accorhotels.com; ⑨), offering Thai, Japanese and international restaurants, a swimming pool, health spa and fitness centre. Inter-provincial air-con buses (ⓣ02 936 2841–8, ⓦwww.transport.co.th/eng/homeenglish.htm) will run direct from the airport to Pattaya, Rayong and Trat on the east coast, as well as to Hua Hin, and further routes may appear. A high-speed rail link is also planned, running downtown to Phaya Thai Skytrain station (via a city check-in at Makkasan, connected to Phetchaburi subway station), but this will not be ready until at least 2008. Otherwise, you can expect similar facilities to Don Muang (see below), with a B50 airport pick-up fee for taxis mooted, as well as four airport bus routes (ⓦwww.bmta.co.th), serving Banglamphu, Hualamphong train station, Thanon Witthayu (via Thanon Sukhumvit) and Thanon Silom. At the moment, Suvarnabhumi is set to open before the end of 2006, but there have been a fair few slippages since the land for the airport was bought – in 1973.

By air

At **Don Muang Airport** you'll find 24-hour exchange booths and ATMs; tourist police booths and a couple of helpful TAT information desks (daily 8am–midnight; ⓣ02 504 2701–3); round-the-clock Thai Hotels Association accommodation desks, with prices generally cheaper than rack rates; post offices with international telephone and Internet access facilities; Avis car-rental desks (see p.216); an emergency clinic (near Arrivals in Terminal 1); cafés, restaurants, bookshops and pharmacies; and several pricey left-luggage depots, charging B90 per item per day.

Getting into town

The most economical way of getting into the city is by **public bus**, but this can be excruciatingly slow and the invariably crowded vehicles are totally unsuitable for heavily laden travellers. The bus stop is outside the northern end of Arrivals on the main highway, which runs north–south in front of the airport buildings; see the box on p.108 for a rough sketch of the most useful routes.

Unless you're already counting your baht, you're better off getting into the city by air-conditioned **airport bus** (daily 5am–midnight; at least every 30min; B100); the buses depart from outside Terminal 1, Terminal 2 and the domestic terminal (clearly signposted outside each building). Four routes are covered: route A1 runs along to the west end of Thanon Silom, via Pratunam and Thanon Rajdamri; route A2 goes to Thanon Phra Athit in Banglamphu, via Victory Monument, Thanon Phetchaburi, Democracy Monument, Thanon Phra Athit and Thanon Tanao (for Thanon Khao San); route A3 heads down the Dindaeng Expressway and runs the length of Thanon Sukhumvit to Soi Thonglor via the Eastern Bus Terminal; and route A4 (no service between 3pm and 6pm) runs to Hualamphong Railway Station, via Thanon Rajaprarop, Siam Square, Thanon Phrayathai and Thanon Rama IV. The TAT offices at the airport have further details of both public and airport buses.

The **train** to Hualamphong Station (see p.102) is the quickest way into town during morning and evening rush hours, and ideal if you want to stay in Chinatown or change onto the subway system (either at Hualamphong or at Bang Sue Station), but services are irregular. To reach the station at Don Muang Airport, which stands beside the big *Amari Airport Hotel*, follow the signs from arrivals in Terminal 1. More than thirty trains a day make the fifty-minute trip to Hualamphong (B5–30), with services most frequent between 6 and 8am and

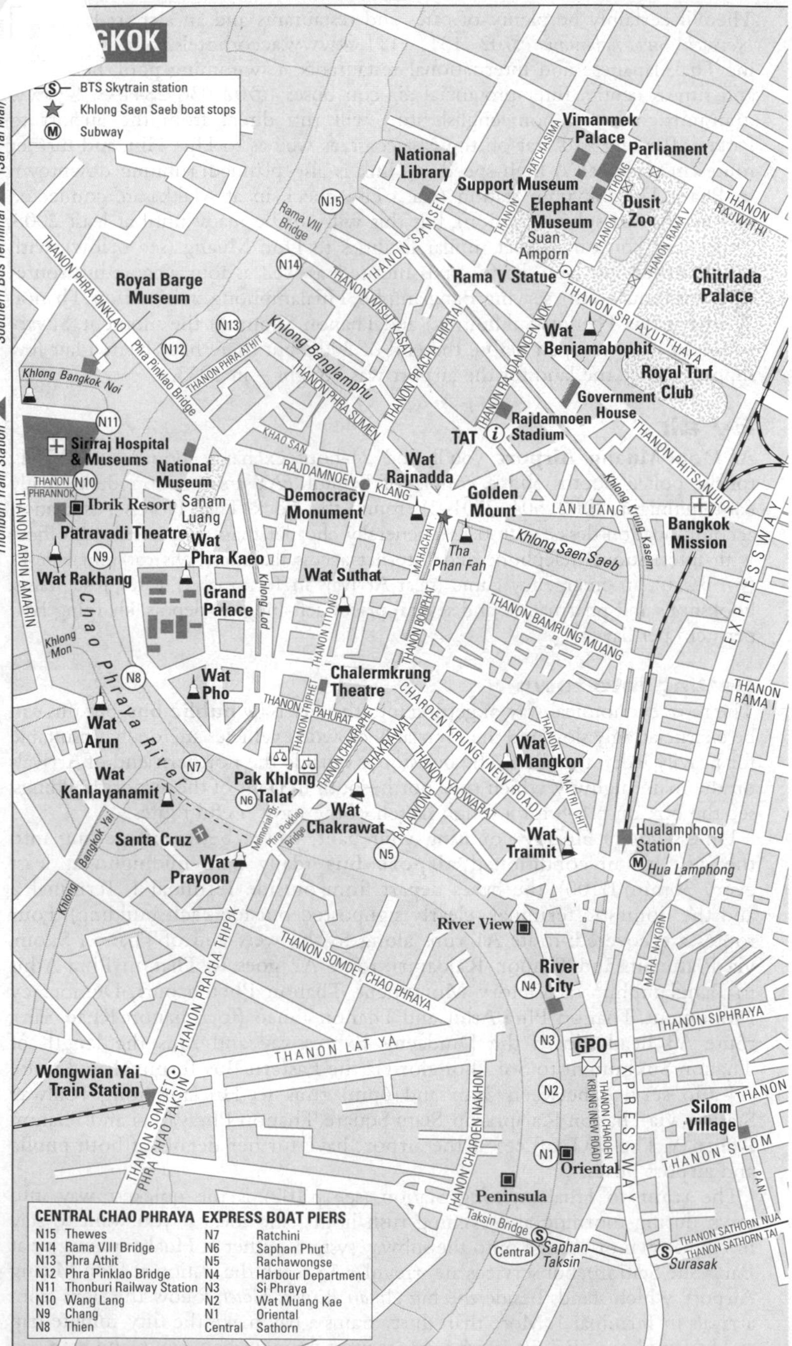
Nonthaburi
BANGKOK
BTS Skytrain station
Khlong Saen Saeb boat stops
Subway
Southern Bus Terminal (Sai Tai Mai)
Thonburi Train Station
Vimanmek Palace
Parliament
National Library
Support Museum
Elephant Museum
Suan Amporn
Dusit Zoo
Rama V Statue
Chitrlada Palace
Royal Barge Museum
Wat Benjamabophit
Royal Turf Club
Government House
Rajdamnoen Stadium
TAT
Siriraj Hospital & Museums
National Museum
Wat Rajnadda
Democracy Monument
Golden Mount
Tha Phan Fah
Bangkok Mission
Ibrik Resort
Sanam Luang
Patravadi Theatre
Wat Phra Kaeo
Wat Rakhang
Grand Palace
Wat Suthat
Wat Pho
Chalermkrung Theatre
Wat Arun
Chao Phraya River
Wat Mangkon
Wat Kanlayanamit
Pak Khlong Talat
Wat Chakrawat
Santa Cruz
Wat Prayoon
Wat Traimit
Hualamphong Station
Hua Lamphong
River View
River City
GPO
Wongwian Yai Train Station
Silom Village
Oriental
Peninsula
Saphan Taksin
Central
Surasak
Thanon Rajwithi
Thanon Samsen
Thanon Ratchasima
Thanon U-Thong
Thanon Rama V
Thanon Sri Ayutthaya
Thanon Phitsanulok
Thanon Phra Pinklao
Phra Pinklao Bridge
Rama VIII Bridge
Khlong Bangkok Noi
Thanon Phra Athit
Khlong Banglamphu
Thanon Phra Sumen
Thanon Wisut Kasat
Thanon Pracha Thipatai
Thanon Rajdamnoen Nok
Khao San
Rajdamnoen Klang
Lan Luang
Khlong Krung Kasem
Khlong Saen Saeb
Thanon Phrannok
Thanon Arun Amarin
Mahachai
Khlong Lod
Thanon Titong
Thanon Boriphat
Thanon Bamrung Muang
Expressway
Thanon Rama I
Khlong Mon
Thanon Pahurat
Thanon Triphet
Thanon Chakraphet
Chakrawat
Charoen Krung (New Road)
Thanon Yaowarat
Thanon Maitri Chit
Rajawong
Memorial Br.
Phra Pokklao Bridge
Khlong Bangkok Yai
Thanon Somdet Chao Phraya
Thanon Pracha Thipok
Maha Nakorn
Thanon Siphraya
Thanon Lat Ya
Thanon Charoen Nakhon
Thanon Charoen Krung (New Road)
Thanon Somdet Phra Chao Taksin
Thanon Silom
Pan
Taksin Bridge
Thanon Sathorn Nua
Thanon Sathorn Tai
Bangkok Marriott Resort & Krungthep Bridge
CENTRAL CHAO PHRAYA EXPRESS BOAT PIERS
N15 Thewes
N14 Rama VIII Bridge
N13 Phra Athit
N12 Phra Pinklao Bridge
N11 Thonburi Railway Station
N10 Wang Lang
N9 Chang
N8 Thien
N7 Ratchini
N6 Saphan Phut
N5 Rachawongse
N4 Harbour Department
N3 Si Phraya
N2 Wat Muang Kae
N1 Oriental
Central Sathorn

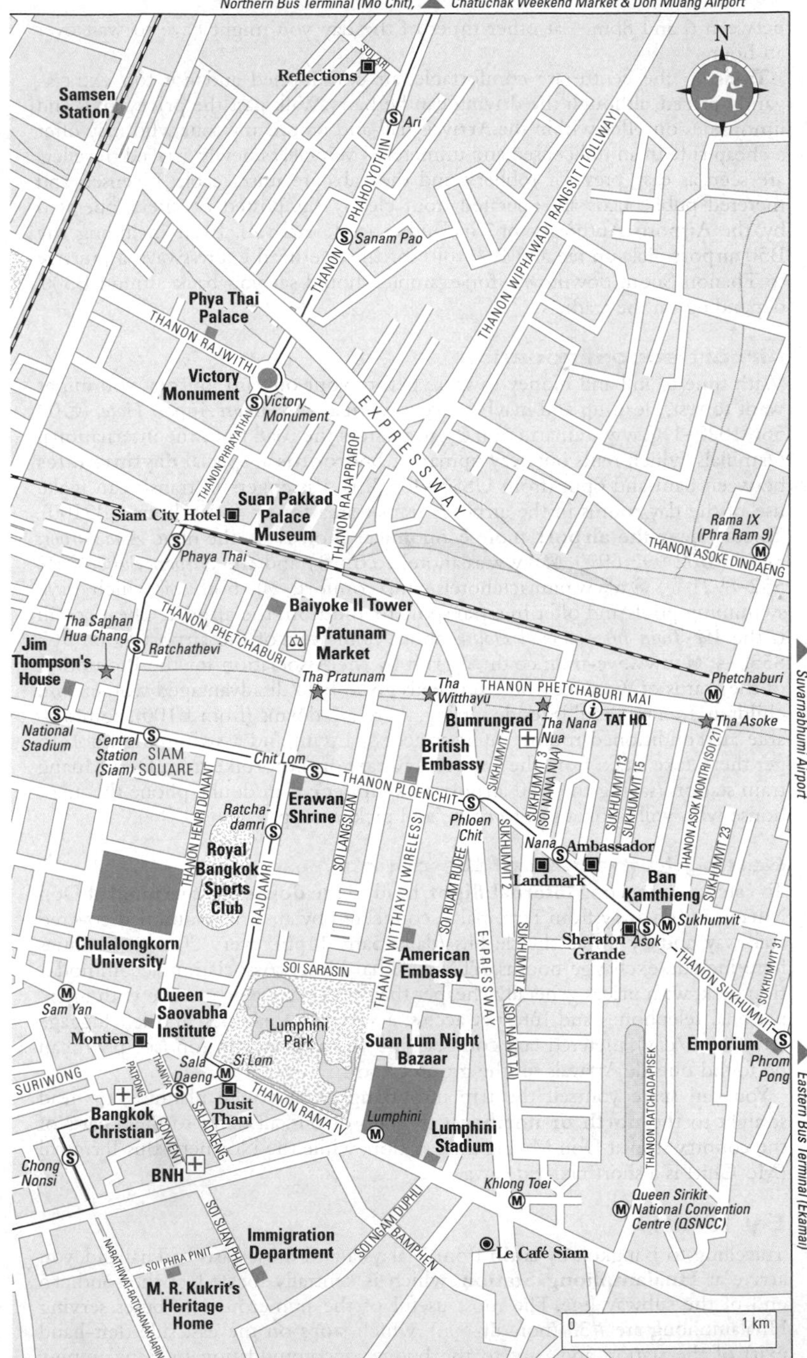
Northern Bus Terminal (Mo Chit), Chatuchak Weekend Market & Don Muang Airport
N
Reflections
Samsen Station
Ari
Sanam Pao
THANON PHAHOLYOTHIN
THANON WIPHAWADI RANGSIT (TOLLWAY)
Phya Thai Palace
THANON RAJWITHI
Victory Monument
Victory Monument
THANON PHRAYATHAI
EXPRESSWAY
THANON RAJAPRAROP
Siam City Hotel
Suan Pakkad Palace Museum
Phaya Thai
Rama IX (Phra Ram 9)
THANON ASOKE DINDAENG
Baiyoke II Tower
THANON PHETCHABURI
Tha Saphan Hua Chang
Ratchathevi
Pratunam Market
Jim Thompson's House
Tha Pratunam
Tha Witthayu
THANON PHETCHABURI MAI
Phetchaburi
Suvarnabhumi Airport
National Stadium
Central Station (Siam)
SIAM SQUARE
Bumrungrad
Tha Nana Nua
TAT HQ
Tha Asoke
British Embassy
Chit Lom
THANON PLOENCHIT
Erawan Shrine
SOI LANGSUAN
THANON WITTHAYU (WIRELESS)
Phloen Chit
SUKHUMVIT 3 (SOI NANA NUA)
SUKHUMVIT 13
SUKHUMVIT 15
THANON ASOK MONTRI (SOI 21)
SUKHUMVIT 23
THANON HENRI DUNANT
Ratchadamri
Royal Bangkok Sports Club
RAJDAMRI
SOI RUAM RUDEE
SUKHUMVIT 2
Nana
Ambassador
Landmark
Ban Kamthieng
SUKHUMVIT
Sukhumvit
Sheraton Grande
Asok
Chulalongkorn University
American Embassy
EXPRESSWAY
SUKHUMVIT 4 (SOI NANA TAI)
SOI SARASIN
THANON SUKHUMVIT
SUKHUMVIT 31
Sam Yan
Queen Saovabha Institute
Lumphini Park
Montien
Suan Lum Night Bazaar
Emporium
Phrom Pong
SURIWONG
PATPONG
THANIYA
Sala Daeng
Si Lom
THANON RAMA IV
Eastern Bus Terminal (Ekamai)
Bangkok Christian
Dusit Thani
SALADAENG
CONVENT
Lumphini
Lumphini Stadium
THANON RATCHADAPISEK
Chong Nonsi
BNH
Khlong Toei
Queen Sirikit National Convention Centre (QSNCC)
SOI SUAN PHLU
Immigration Department
SOI NGAM DUPHLI
BAMPHEN
Le Café Siam
NARATHIWAT-RATCHANAKHARIN
SOI PHRA PINIT
M. R. Kukrit's Heritage Home
0
1 km

between 6 and 8pm – at other times of the day you might have to wait over an hour.

Taxis to the centre are comfortable, air-conditioned and not too extravagantly priced, although the driving can be hairy. Walk past the pricey taxis and limousines on offer within the Arrivals hall and ignore any tout who may offer a cheap ride in an unlicensed and unmetered vehicle, as newly arrived travellers are seen as easy prey for robbery, and the cabs are untraceable. Licensed and metered public taxis are operated from clearly signposted counters, operated by the Airports Authority of Thailand, outside Arrivals. Even including the B50 airport pick-up fee and B60 tolls for the overhead expressways, a journey to Thanon Silom downtown, for example, should set you back around B300, depending on the traffic.

Airport accommodation

With time to kill and money to spare before your onward journey, you might want to rest, clean up and maybe have a swim at the *Amari Airport Hotel* (ⓣ02 566 1020–1, ⓦwww.amari.com; ❾), just across the road from the international terminals, which rents out very upmarket **bedrooms** at special **daytime rates** between 8am and 6pm (from US$39 for 3hr). Passengers in transit can make use of the day rooms in the airport's transit area for up to six hours (B2100). To **stay near the airport**, more economical choices are the huge *Asia Airport Hotel* (ⓣ02 992 6999, ⓦwww.asiahotel.co.th; ❽) and the *Airport Suite* (ⓣ02 552 8921–9, ⓦwww.pinnaclehotels.com/comfort; ❼), both of which have swimming pools and offer free transport to and from the airport. Cheaper still is the *We-Train International House*, about 3km west of the airport (ⓣ02 967 8550–4, ⓦwww.we-train.co.th; ❸), run by the Association for the Promotion of the Status of Women, where proceeds go to help disadvantaged women and children. In a peaceful lakeside setting, there are dorms (from B100), comfortable air-conditioned rooms, Internet access, a gym and a swimming pool. To get there, take a taxi from the airport, or a taxi or motorbike from Don Muang train station (saving the B50 airport pick-up fee); if in doubt, phone the guest house who will book a taxi to come and pick you up.

Getting to the rest of the country

To catch a connecting **internal flight**, head to the **domestic terminal** at Don Muang, 500m away from Terminal 2, connected by an air-conditioned covered walkway and by a free shuttle bus (daily 5am–11pm; every 20min). Facilities here include exchange booths, ATMs, a Thai Hotels Association accommodation desk, with prices generally cheaper than rack rates, a post office with international telephones and Internet access, a variety of eateries, and left luggage (B70/item/day); metered taxi counters and the airport bus stop (see p.99) can be found outside Arrivals on the ground floor.

You can spare yourself the trip into Bangkok if you're planning to head straight to the **north or northeast** by train or bus: all trains to these parts of the country stop at Don Muang train station, while the Northern Bus Terminal (Mo Chit) is a short taxi-ride away.

By train

Travelling to Bangkok by **train** from Malaysia and most parts of Thailand, you arrive at **Hualamphong Station**, which is centrally located, at the southern end of the subway line. The most useful of the numerous city buses serving Hualamphong are #53 (non-air-con), which stops on the east side (left-hand exit) of the station and runs to the budget accommodation in Banglamphu;

and the #25 (ordinary and air-con), which runs east to Siam Square and along Thanon Sukhumvit to the Eastern Bus Terminal, or west through Chinatown to Tha Chang (for the Grand Palace). See box on p.108 for bus-route details. Station **facilities** include a post office, an exchange booth, several ATMs, an Internet centre and a **left-luggage** office (daily 4am–11pm), which charges B20–30 per day, depending on the size of the bag (almost any rucksack counts as large). A more economical place to store baggage is at the *TT2 Guest House* (see p.122), about fifteen minutes' walk from the station, which provides the same service for only B10 per item per day, whatever the size.

One service the station does not provide is itinerant tourist assistance staff – anyone who comes up to you in or around the station concourse and offers help/information/transport or ticket-booking services is almost certainly a **con-artist**, however many official-looking ID tags are hanging round their neck. This is a well-established scam to fleece new arrivals and should be avoided at all costs (see p.81 for more details). For train-related questions, contact the 24-hour "Information" counter close by the departures board (there's more information on buying onward rail tickets on p.212). The station area is also fertile ground for **dishonest tuk-tuk drivers**, so you'll need to be extra suspicious to avoid them – take a metered taxi or public transport instead.

Note that, to ease congestion, the State Railways of Thailand have a phased, long-term plan to move long-distance services out to a new terminal at **Bang Sue Station**, on the Northern, Northeastern and Southern lines, 7km north of Hualamphong and close to Mo Chit Northern Bus Terminal. The timetable for this plan is uncertain, but you can check when booking your ticket. Suburban and short-distance trains would continue to operate from Hualamphong, providing frequent links with Bang Sue, which is also at one end of the city's subway system.

Trains from Kanchanaburi pull in at the small and not very busy **Thonburi Station**, from where it's a short ride in a red public songthaew or an 850-metre walk east to the N11 (Bangkok Noi) express-boat stop, just across the Chao Phraya River from Banglamphu and Ratanakosin.

By bus

Buses come to a halt at a number of far-flung spots. All services from the north and northeast terminate at the **Northern Bus Terminal** (**Mo Chit**) on Thanon Kamphaeng Phet 2; some east-coast buses also use Mo Chit (rather than the Eastern Terminal), including several daily services from Pattaya, Rayong (for Ko Samet), Chanthaburi and Trat (for Ko Chang and the Cambodian border). The quickest way to get into the city centre from Mo Chit is to hop onto the Skytrain (see p.111) at the Mo Chit Station, or the subway at the adjacent Chatuchak Park Station (see p.111), fifteen minutes' walk from the bus terminal on Thanon Phaholyothin, and then change onto a city bus if necessary. Otherwise, it's a long bus or taxi ride into town: city buses from the Northern Bus Terminal include ordinary #159 to Siam Square, Hualamphong Station, Banglamphu and the Southern Bus Terminal; and ordinary and air-conditioned #3, and air-conditioned #509 and #512 to Banglamphu; for details of these routes see the box on pp.108–9.

Most buses from the east coast use the **Eastern Bus Terminal** (**Ekamai**) between sois 40 and 42 on Thanon Sukhumvit. This bus station is right beside the Ekamai Skytrain stop (see p.111), and is also served by lots of city buses, including air-conditioned #511 to Banglamphu and the Southern Bus Terminal (see box on pp.108–9 for details), or you can take a taxi down Soi 63 to Tha Ekamai, a pier on Khlong Saen Saeb, to pick up the canal boat service to the Golden Mount near Banglamphu (see p.110). There's a left-luggage booth at the bus terminal (daily 8am–6pm; B30/day).

Bus services from Malaysia and the south, as well as from Kanchanaburi, use the **Southern Bus Terminal** (**Sai Tai Mai**) at the junction of Thanon Borom Ratchonni and the Nakhon Chaisri Highway, west of the Chao Phraya River in Thonburi. Drivers on these services always make a stop to drop passengers on the east side of Thanon Borom Ratchonni, in front of a Toyota dealer, before doing a time-consuming U-turn for the terminus on the west side of the road; if you're heading across the river to Banglamphu or downtown Bangkok you should get off here, along with the majority of the other passengers. Numerous **city buses** cross the river from this bus stop, including air-con #507 to Banglamphu, Hualamphong Station and Thanon Rama IV, air-con #511 to Banglamphu and Thanon Sukhumvit, and non-air-con #159 to the Northern Bus Terminal (see box on pp.108–9 for routes). This is also a better place to grab a **taxi** into town, as rides are faster and cheaper when started from here.

Orientation and information

Bangkok can be a tricky place to get your bearings as it's huge and ridiculously congested, with largely featureless modern buildings and no obvious centre. The boldest line on the map is the **Chao Phraya River**, which divides the city into Bangkok proper on the east bank, and **Thonburi**, part of Greater Bangkok, on the west.

The historical core of Bangkok proper, site of the original royal palace, is **Ratanakosin**, which nestles into a bend in the river. Three concentric canals radiate eastwards around Ratanakosin: the southern part of the area between the canals is the old-style trading enclave of **Chinatown** and Indian **Pahurat**, linked to the old palace by Thanon Charoen Krung (aka New Road); the northern part is characterized by old temples and the **Democracy Monument**, west of which is the backpackers' ghetto of **Banglamphu**. Beyond the canals to the north, **Dusit** is the site of many government buildings and the nineteenth-century Vimanmek Palace, and is linked to Ratanakosin by the three stately avenues, Thanon Rajdamnoen Nok, Thanon Rajdamnoen Klang and Thanon Rajdamnoen Nai.

"New" Bangkok begins to the east of the canals and beyond the main rail line and Hualamphong Station, and stretches as far as the eye can see to the east and north. The main business district and most of the embassies are south of **Thanon Rama IV**, with the port of Khlong Toey at the southern edge. The diverse area north of Thanon Rama IV includes the sprawling campus of Chulalongkorn University, huge shopping centres around **Siam Square** and a variety of other businesses. A couple of blocks northeast of Siam Square stands the tallest building in Bangkok, the 84-storeyed **Baiyoke II Tower** whose golden spire makes a good point of reference. To the east lies the swish residential quarter off **Thanon Sukhumvit**.

Information and maps

The official source of information on the capital is the Bangkok Tourist Bureau (BTB). Its main office is at the **Bangkok Information Centre**, next to Phra Pinklao Bridge at 17/1 Thanon Phra Athit in Banglamphu (daily 9am–7pm; Ⓣ02 225 7612–4, Ⓦwww.bangkoktourist.com), and this is supported by 27 strategically placed satellite booths around the capital (daily 9am–5pm), including in front of the Grand Palace, at the Erawan Shrine, at River City and Mah

Boon Krong shopping centres, in front of Robinson Department Store on Thanon Silom, and in front of Banglamphu's Wat Chana Songkhram.

For advice on destinations further afield you need to visit the **Tourism Authority of Thailand (TAT)** which maintains a Tourist Service Centre within walking distance of Banglamphu, at 4 Rajdamnoen Nok (daily 8.30am–4.30pm; ⓣ02 283 1500, freephone tourist assistance 8am–8pm ⓣ1672, ⓦwww.tourismthailand.org), a twenty-minute stroll from Thanon Khao San, or a short ride in air-conditioned bus #503. TAT also has a couple of booths in the airport arrivals concourse (daily 8am–midnight), but its headquarters (daily 8.30am–4.30pm; ⓣ02 250 5500) is rather inconveniently located out at 1600 Thanon Phetchaburi Mai, 350m west of the junction with Sukhumvit Soi 21 and the Phetchaburi subway stop, or 150m east of the junction with Sukhumvit Soi 3 and Tha Nana Nua on the Khlong Saen Saeb canal boat service (see the Thanon Sukhumvit map on p.128). Note, however, that the many other shops and offices across the capital displaying signs announcing "TAT Tourist Information" or similar are **not official Tourism Authority of Thailand centres** and will not be dispensing impartial advice: the Tourism Authority of Thailand never uses the acronym TAT on its office-fronts or in its logo. Other useful sources of information, especially about what to avoid, are the travellers' **noticeboards** in some Banglamphu guest houses.

The monthly expats-oriented **listings magazine** *Metro* (B100) details upcoming art exhibitions and gigs and includes useful sections on restaurants, cinemas, nightlife and gay life. The backpackers' monthly, *Untamed Travel* (B120), is more hip and straight-talking and though it doesn't carry events listings it does review some guest houses, bars, clubs, restaurants and sights in Bangkok as well as in the rest of the country and other Southeast Asian destinations. Both magazines are sold at bookstores, hotel shops and 7–11 stores.

To get around Bangkok on the cheap, you'll need to buy a **bus map**. Of the several available at bookshops, hotels and some guest houses, the most useful is Bangkok Guide's *Bus Routes & Map*, which not only maps all major air-conditioned and non-air-conditioned bus routes but also carries detailed written itineraries of some two hundred bus routes. The long-running bright blue and yellow bus map published by Tour 'n' Guide also maps bus routes and dozens of smaller sois, but its street locations are not always reliable, and it can be hard to decipher exact bus routings. The bus routes on *Litehart's Groovy Map and Guide* are clearly colour-coded but only selected ones are given. Serious shoppers will want to buy a copy of the idiosyncratic *Nancy Chandler's Map of Bangkok*, which has lots of annotated recommendations on shops, markets and interesting neighbourhoods across the city and is reliably accurate; it's available in most tourist areas and from ⓦwww.nancychandler.net.

City transport

The main form of transport in the city is **buses**, and once you've mastered the labyrinthine complexity of the route maps you'll be able to get to any part of the city, albeit slowly. Catching the various kinds of **taxi** is more expensive, and you'll still get held up by the daytime traffic jams. **Boats** are obviously more limited in their range, but they're regular and as cheap as buses, and you'll save a lot of time by using them whenever possible – a journey between Banglamphu and the GPO, for instance, will take around thirty minutes by water, half what it would take on land. The **Skytrain** and **subway** each have a similarly limited range but are also worth using whenever suitable for all or part of your journey;

△ The Chao Phraya River

Tours of the city

If you can't face negotiating the public transport network, any taxi or tuk-tuk driver can be hired for the day to take you around the major or minor sights (B700–800), and every travel agent in the city can arrange this for you as well; read the advice on avoiding tuk-tuk tout scams on p.81 first. Alternatively, the Bangkok Tourist Bureau (BTB; see p.104) runs occasional **tours of the capital**, including a night-time bicycle tour of Ratanakosin (Sat 6.30–9.30pm; minimum five people; B390 including bicycle), weekend walking tours according to demand (B100), and a tourist "tram" (more like an open-topped single-decker bus) which covers a forty-minute circuit from the Grand Palace down to Wat Pho, up to Banglamphu, and back to the palace, roughly every half an hour (daily 9.30am–5pm; B30). Real Asia (Ⓣ02 665 6364, Ⓦwww.realasia.net) does canal and walking tours through Thonburi and leads outings to the historic fishing port of Samut Sakhon (from B1800), and Tamarind Tours runs imaginative and well-regarded tours of the city and nearby provinces, including specialized options such as Bangkok X-Files and Bangkok After Dark (Ⓣ02 238 3227, Ⓦwww.tamarindtours.com; from US$59).

Unlikely as it sounds, there are several companies offering **cycle tours** of the city's outer neighbourhoods and beyond; these are an excellent way to gain a different perspective on Thai life and offer a unique chance to see traditional communities close up. The most popular, longest running bicycle tour is the ABC Amazing Bangkok Cyclist Tour, which starts in the Thanon Sukhumvit area and takes you across the river to surprisingly rural khlong- and riverside communities; tours operate every day year-round, cover up to 30km depending on the itinerary, and need to be reserved in advance through Real Asia (Ⓣ02 665 6364, Ⓦwww.realasia.net; B1000–2000 including bicycle). Bangkok Bike Rides (Ⓣ02 712 5305 Ⓦwww.bangkokbikerides.com; $25–50 per person, minimum two people) also operates from the Sukhumvit area and runs a programme of different daily tours within Greater Bangkok as well as to the floating markets and canalside neighbourhoods of Damnoen Saduak and Samut Songkhram in the Central Plains. **Grasshopper Adventures** runs half-day cycle tours from Banglamphu around the sights of Ratanakosin (departs every Sun at 8am from the *Viengtai Hotel* on Thanon Ram Bhuttri; Ⓣ087 929 5208, Ⓦwww.grasshopperadventures.com; B800).

For details of Thonburi canal tours, see p.160; for Chao Phraya Express tourist boats, see p.109; and for dinner cruises along the Chao Phraya River, see p.186.

their networks roughly coincide with each other at the east end of Thanon Silom, at the corner of Soi Asoke and Thanon Sukhumvit, and on Thanon Phaholyothin by Chatuchak Park (Mo Chit), while the Skytrain joins up with the Chao Phraya River express boats at the vital hub of Sathorn/Saphan Taksin (Taksin Bridge) and the subway intersects the mainline railway at Hualamphong and Bang Sue stations. **Walking** might often be quicker than travelling by road, but the heat can be unbearable, distances are always further than they look on the map, and the engine fumes are stifling.

Buses

Bangkok is served by over four hundred bus routes, reputedly the world's largest bus network, on which operate three main types of bus service. On **ordinary** (non-air-con) buses, which are either red and white, blue and white, or small and green, fares range from B6 to B9; most routes operate from about 4am to 10pm, but some maintain a 24-hour service, as noted in the box on p.108. **Air-conditioned** buses are either blue, orange or white (some are articulated) and charge between B12 and B24 according to distance travelled; most stop in the late evening, but a few of the more popular routes run 24-hour services. As buses can only go as fast as the car in front, which at the moment is averaging 4 kilometres per hour, you'll probably be spending a long time on each journey, so you'd be well advised to pay the extra for cool air – and the air-conditioned buses are usually less crowded, too. It's also possible to travel certain routes (until 9pm) on pink, air-conditioned private **microbuses**, which were designed with the commuter in mind and offer the certainty of a seat (no standing allowed). The fare is generally a flat B25 (exact money only), which is dropped into a box beside the driver's seat.

Some of the most useful city-bus routes are described in the box on p.108; for a comprehensive roundup of bus routes in the capital, buy a copy of Bangkok Guide's *Bus Routes & Map* (see p.105), or log onto the Bangkok Mass Transit Authority website (Ⓦ www.bmta.co.th), which gives details of all city-bus routes, bar microbuses and airport buses.

Boats

Bangkok was built as an amphibious city around a network of canals – or **khlongs** – and the first streets were constructed only in the second half of the nineteenth century. Many canals remain on the Thonburi side of the river, but most of those on the Bangkok side have been turned into roads. The Chao Phraya River itself is still a major transport route for residents and non-residents alike, forming more of a link than a barrier between the two halves of the city.

Express boats

The Chao Phraya Express Boat Company operates the vital **express-boat** (*reua duan*; Ⓦ www.chaophrayaboat.co.th) service, using large water buses to plough up and down the river, between clearly signed piers (*tha*), which appear on all Bangkok maps. Tha Sathorn, which gives access to the Skytrain network at Saphan Taksin Station, has been designated "Central Pier", with piers to the south of here numbered S1, S2, etc, those to the north N1, N2 and so on – the important stops in the centre of the city are outlined in the box on p.110 and marked on our city map (see p.100). Its basic route, one hour thirty minutes in total, runs between Wat Rajsingkorn, just upriver of Krung Thep Bridge, in the south, and Nonthaburi in the north. These "**standard**" boats set off every fifteen to twenty minutes between around 6am and 7.30pm (6.40pm on Sat & Sun). Boats do not necessarily stop at every landing – they only pull in if

Useful bus routes

For more details on Banglamphu bus stops and routes, see p.118.

#3 (ordinary and air-con, 24hr): Northern Bus Terminal–Chatuchak Weekend Market–Thanon Phaholyothin–Thanon Samsen–Thanon Phra Athit (for Banglamphu guest houses)–Thanon Sanam Chai–Thanon Triphet–Memorial Bridge (for Pak Khlong Talat)–Taksin Monument–Wat Suwan.

#15 (ordinary): Krung Thep Bridge–Thanon Charoen Krung–Thanon Silom–Thanon Rajdamri–Siam Square–Thanon Lan Luang–Sanam Luang–Thanon Phra Athit.

#16 (ordinary and air-con): Thanon Srinarong–Thanon Samsen–Thewes (for guest houses)–Thanon Phitsanulok–Thanon Phrayathai–Siam Square–Thanon Suriwong.

#25 (ordinary and air-con, 24hr): Eastern Bus Terminal–Thanon Sukhumvit–Siam Square–Hualamphong Station–Thanon Yaowarat (for Chinatown)–Pahurat–Wat Pho–Tha Chang (for the Grand Palace). Note, however, that some #25 buses (ordinary only) only go as far as Hualamphong Station, while during rush hours some #25 buses take the expressway, missing out Siam Square.

#29 (ordinary and air-con): Don Muang Airport–Chatuchak Weekend Market–Siam Square–Thanon Phrayathai–Thanon Rama IV–Hualamphong Station.

#38 (ordinary): Chatuchak Weekend Market–Victory Monument–Thanon Phrayathai–Thanon Phetchaburi–Thanon Asok Montri–Thanon Sukhumvit–Eastern Bus Terminal.

#39 (ordinary, 24hr): Chatuchak Weekend Market–Victory Monument–Thanon Phetchaburi–Thanon Lan Luang–Democracy Monument–Rajdamnoen Klang (for Thanon Khao San guest houses)–Sanam Luang. Note, however, that some #39 buses only run as far south as Victory Monument.

#53 circular (also anti-clockwise; ordinary): Thewes–Thanon Krung Kasem–Hualamphong Station–Thanon Yaowarat–Pahurat–Pak Khlong Talat–Thanon Maharat (for Wat Pho, the Grand Palace and Wat Mahathat)–Sanam Luang (for National Museum)–Thanon Phra Athit and Thanon Samsen (for Banglamphu guest houses)–Thewes.

#56 circular (also clockwise; ordinary): Thanon Phra Sumen–Wat Bowoniwes–Thanon Pracha Thipatai–Thanon Ratchasima (for Vimanmek Palace)–Thanon Rajwithi–Krung Thon Bridge–Thonburi–Phrapokklao Bridge–Thanon Chakraphet (for Chinatown)–Thanon Mahachai–Democracy Monument–Thanon Tanao (for Khao San guest houses)–Thanon Phra Sumen.

#59 (ordinary and air-con, 24hr): Don Muang Airport–Chatuchak Weekend Market–Victory Monument–Thanon Phrayathai–Thanon Phetchaburi–Phan Fah (for Khlong Saen Saeb and Golden Mount)–Democracy Monument (for Banglamphu guest houses)–Sanam Luang.

people want to get on or off, and when they do stop, it's not for long – so when you want to get off, be ready at the back of the boat in good time for your pier. During busy periods, certain "**special express**" boats operate limited-stop services on set routes, flying either a **blue flag** (Nonthaburi to Tha Sathorn in 35min, stopping only at Wang Lang; Mon–Fri roughly 6–9am & 5–7pm), a **yellow flag** (Nonthaburi to Rajburana, far downriver beyond Krung Thep Bridge, in about 50min; Mon–Fri roughly 6–9am & 4–7.30pm) or an **orange flag** (Nonthaburi to Wat Rajsingkorn in 1hr; Mon–Fri roughly 6–9am & 2.30–7pm).

Tickets can be bought on board, and cost B9–13 on standard boats according to distance travelled, B13 flat rate on orange-flag boats, B18–27 on yellow-flag boats and B22–32 on blue-flag boats. Don't discard your ticket until you're off

#124 (ordinary): Southern Bus Terminal–Phra Pinklao Bridge–Sanam Luang (for Banglamphu guest houses).

#159 (ordinary): Southern Bus Terminal–Phra Pinklao Bridge–Democracy Monument–Hualamphong Station–MBK Shopping Centre–Thanon Ratchaprarop–Victory Monument–Chatuchak Weekend Market–Northern Bus Terminal.

#503 (air-con): Sanam Luang (for Banglamphu guest houses)–Democracy Monument–Rajdamnoen Nok (for TAT and boxing stadium)–Wat Benjamabophit–Thanon Sri Ayutthaya (for Thewes guest houses)–Victory Monument–Chatuchak Weekend Market–Rangsit. Note, however, that during rush hours, some #503 buses take the expressway, missing out Chatuchak Weekend Market.

#504 (air-con): Don Muang Airport–Thanon Rajaprarop–Thanon Rajdamri–Thanon Silom–Thanon Charoen Krung–Krungthep Bridge.

#507 (air-con): Southern Bus Terminal–Phra Pinklao Bridge (for Banglamphu guest houses)–Sanam Luang–Thanon Charoen Krung (New Road)–Thanon Chakraphet–Thanon Yaowarat (for Chinatown and Wat Traimit)–Hualamphong Station–Thanon Rama IV (for Soi Ngam Duphli guest houses)–Bang Na Intersection–Pak Nam (for Ancient City buses).

#508 (air-con): Thanon Maharat–Grand Palace–Thanon Charoen Krung–Siam Square–Thanon Sukhumvit–Eastern Bus Terminal–Pak Nam (for Ancient City buses). Note, however, that during rush hours, some #508 buses take the expressway, missing out the Eastern Bus Terminal.

#509 (air-con): Northern Bus Terminal–Chatuchak Weekend Market–Victory Monument–Thanon Rajwithi–Thanon Sawankhalok–Thanon Phitsanulok–Thanon Rajdamnoen Nok–Democracy Monument–Rajdamnoen Klang (for Banglamphu guest houses)–Phra Pinklao Bridge–Thonburi.

#511 (air-con, 24hr): Southern Bus Terminal–Phra Pinklao Bridge–Wat Bowoniwes (for Banglamphu guest houses)–Democracy Monument–Thanon Lan Luang–Thanon Phetchaburi–Thanon Sukhumvit–Eastern Bus Terminal–Pak Nam (for Ancient City buses). Note, however, that during the day, some #511 buses take the expressway, missing out the Eastern Bus Terminal.

#512 (air-con): Northern Bus Terminal–Chatuchak Weekend Market–Thanon Phetchaburi–Thanon Lan Luang–Democracy Monument (for Banglamphu guest houses)–Sanam Luang–Tha Chang (for Grand Palace)–Pak Khlong Talat.

#513 (air-con): Don Muang Airport–Victory Monument–Thanon Phraya Thai–Thanon Sri Ayutthaya–Thanon Rajaprarop–Eastern Bus Terminal–Thanon Sukhumvit. Note, however, that some #513 buses take the expressway, missing out the section from Victory Monument to the Eastern Bus Terminal.

the boat, as the staff at some piers impose a B1 fine on anyone disembarking without one.

The Chao Phraya Express Boat Company also runs **tourist boats**, distinguished by their light-blue flags, between Sathorn (departs every 30min 9.30am–3pm on the hour and half-hour) and Banglamphu piers (departs every 30min 10am–3.30pm on the hour and half-hour). In between (in both directions), these boats call in at Oriental, Si Phraya, Rachawongse, Saphan Phut, the Princess Mother Memorial Park in Thonburi, Thien, Maharaj (near Wat Mahathat and the Grand Palace) and Wang Lang; there are also free connecting boats from Tha Banglamphu across to the Royal Barge Museum. On-board guides provide running commentaries, and a one-day ticket for unlimited trips, which also allows you to use other express boats within the same route between 9am

Central stops for the Chao Phraya express boats

N15 Thewes (all boats except blue flag) – for Thewes guest houses.

N14 Rama VIII Bridge (standard) – for Samsen Soi 5.

N13 Phra Athit (standard and orange flag) – for Thanon Phra Athit, Thanon Khao San and Banglamphu guest houses.

N12 Phra Pinklao Bridge (all boats except blue flag) – for Royal Barge Museum and Thonburi shops.

N11 Thonburi Railway Station (or Bangkok Noi; standard) – for trains to Kanchanaburi.

N10 Wang Lang (or Siriraj; all standard and special express boats) – for Siriraj Hospital and hospital museums.

N9 Chang (standard and orange flag) – for the Grand Palace.

N8 Thien (standard) – for Wat Pho, and the cross-river ferry to Wat Arun.

N7 Ratchini (aka Rajinee; standard).

N6 Saphan Phut (Memorial Bridge; standard and orange flag) – for Pahurat, Pak Khlong Talat and Wat Prayoon.

N5 Rachawongse (aka Rajawong; all standard and special express boats) – for Chinatown.

N4 Harbour Department (standard and orange flag).

N3 Si Phraya (all boats except blue flag) – walk north past the *Sheraton Royal Orchid Hotel* for River City shopping complex.

N2 Wat Muang Kae (standard) – for GPO.

N1 Oriental (standard and orange flag) – for Thanon Silom.

Central Sathorn (all standard and special express boats) – for the Skytrain (Saphan Taksin Station) and Thanon Sathorn.

Piers are marked on the map on p.100.

and 7.30pm, costs B100; one-way tickets are also available, costing, for example, B20 from Tha Sathorn to Maharaj.

Cross-river ferries

Smaller than express boats are the slow **cross-river ferries** (*reua kham fak*), which shuttle back and forth between the same two points. Found at or beside every express stop and plenty of other piers in between, they are especially useful for exploring Thonburi and for connections to Chao Phraya special express-boat stops during rush hours. Fares are B2–3, which you usually pay at the entrance to the pier.

Longtail boats

Longtail boats (*reua hang yao*) ply the khlongs of Thonburi like commuter buses, stopping at designated shelters (fares are in line with those of express boats), and are available for individual rental here and on the river (see box on p.160). On the Bangkok side, **Khlong Saen Saeb** is well served by longtails, which run at least every fifteen minutes during daylight hours from the Phan Fah pier at the Golden Mount (handy for Banglamphu, Ratanakosin and Chinatown), and head way out east to Wat Sribunruang, with useful stops at Thanon Phrayathai, aka Saphan Hua Chang (for Jim Thompson's House and Ratchathevi Skytrain stop); Pratunam (for the Erawan Shrine); Soi Chitlom; Thanon Witthayu (Wireless Road); and Soi Nana Nua (Soi 3), Thanon Asok

Montri (Soi 21, for TAT headquarters and Phetchaburi subway stop), Soi Thonglo (Soi 55) and Soi Ekamai (Soi 63), all off Thanon Sukhumvit. This is your quickest and most interesting way of getting between the west and east parts of town, if you can stand the stench of the canal. You may have trouble actually locating the piers as few are signed in English and they all look very unassuming and rickety; see the map on p.100 for locations and keep your eyes peeled for a plain wooden jetty – most jetties serve boats running in both directions. Once on the boat, state your destination to the conductor when he collects your fare, which will be between B8 and B18. Due to the construction of some low bridges, all passengers change onto a different boat at Tha Pratunam and then again at the stop way out east on Sukhumvit Soi 71 – just follow the crowd.

The Skytrain

Although its network is limited, the **BTS Skytrain**, or *rot fai faa* (Ⓦwww.bts.co.th; see p.112), provides a much faster alternative to the bus, and is clean, efficient and vigorously air-conditioned. There are only two Skytrain lines, both running every few minutes from around 6am to midnight, with **fares** of B10–40 per trip depending on distance travelled. You'd really have to be motoring to justify buying a day **pass** at B100, while the ten-trip, fifteen-trip and thirty-trip cards, for B250, B300 and B540 respectively (valid for thirty days), are designed for long-distance commuters.

The **Sukhumvit Line** runs from Mo Chit (stop #N8) in the northern part of the city (near Chatuchak Market and the Northern Bus Terminal) south via Victory Monument (N3) to the interchange, **Central Station**, at Siam Square, and then east along Thanon Ploenchit and Thanon Sukhumvit, via the Eastern Bus Terminal (Ekamai; E7), to On Nut (Soi 77, Thanon Sukhumvit; E9); the whole journey to the eastern end of town from Mo Chit takes around thirty minutes.

The **Silom Line** runs from the National Stadium (W1), just west of Siam Square, through Central Station, and then south along Thanon Rajdamri, Thanon Silom and Thanon Sathorn, via Sala Daeng near Patpong (S2), to Saphan Taksin (Sathorn Bridge; S6), to link up with the full gamut of express boats on the Chao Phraya River. Free feeder buses for Skytrain passholders, currently covering six circular routes, mostly along Thanon Sukhumvit, are geared more for commuters than visitors, but pick up a copy of the ubiquitous free BTS **map** if you want more information.

The subway

Bangkok's underground rail system, the **subway** (or metro; in Thai, *rot fai tai din*; Ⓦwww.bangkokmetro.co.th; see p.112), has similar advantages to the Skytrain, though its current single line connects few places of interest for visitors. With fares of between B14 and B36, the subway runs a frequent service (every 2–7min) between around 6.30am and 11.30pm from Hualamphong train station, first heading east along Thanon Rama IV, with useful stops at Sam Yan (for Si Phraya and Phrayathai roads), Silom (near the Sala Daeng Skytrain station) and Lumphini (Thanon Sathorn/southeast corner of Lumphini Park). The line then turns north up Thanon Asok Montri/Thanon Ratchadapisek via the Queen Sirikit National Convention Centre, Sukhumvit Station (near Asoke Skytrain station), Phetchaburi (handy for Khlong Sen Seb boats) and the Thailand Cultural Centre, before looping around via Chatuchak Park (near Mo Chit Skytrain station) and Kampaeng Phet (best stop for the weekend market) to terminate at Bang Sue railway station in the north of the city.

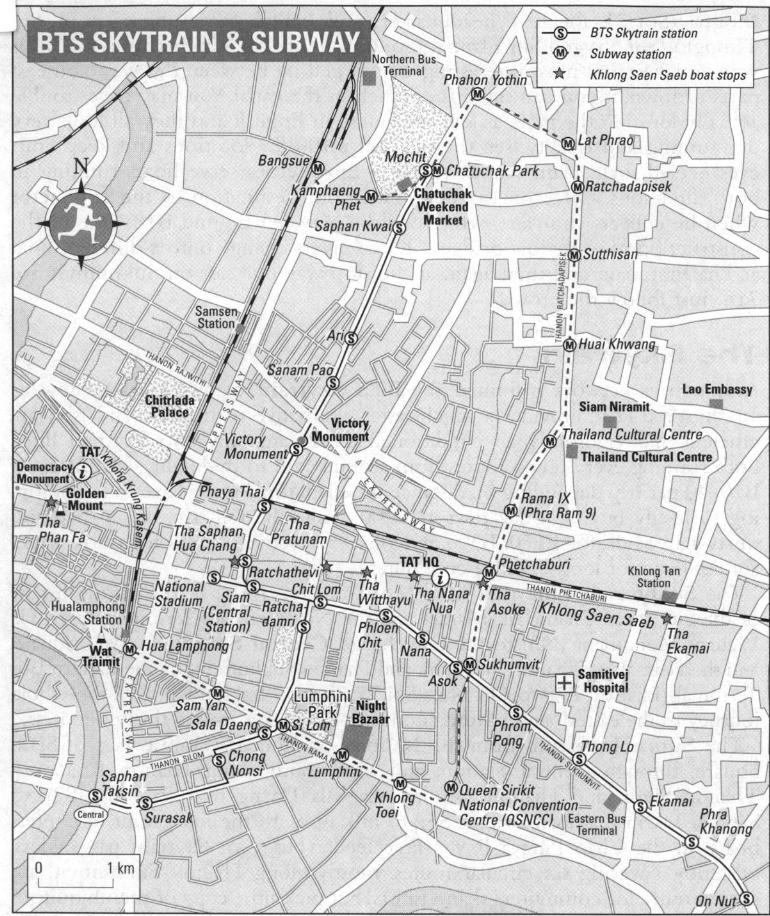

Taxis

Bangkok **taxis** come in three forms, and are so plentiful that you rarely have to wait more than a couple of minutes before spotting an empty one of any description. Neither tuk-tuks nor motorbike taxis have meters, so you should agree on a price before setting off, and expect to do a fair amount of haggling.

For nearly all journeys, the best and most comfortable option is to flag down one of Bangkok's metered, air-conditioned **taxi cabs**; look out for the "TAXI METER" sign on the roof, and a red light in the windscreen in front of the passenger seat, which means the cab is available for hire. Fares start at B35, and are displayed on a clearly visible meter that the driver should reset at the start of each trip, and increase in stages on a combined distance/time formula; as an example, a medium-range journey from Thanon Ploenchit to Thanon Sathorn will cost around B50 at a quiet time of day. Try to have change with you as cabs tend not to carry a lot of money; tipping of up to ten percent is common, though occasionally a cabbie will round down the fare on the meter. If a driver tries to quote a flat fare rather than using the meter, let him go, and avoid the now-rare unmetered cabs (denoted by a "TAXI" sign on the roof). If you want to book a metered taxi (B20 surcharge), call Siam Taxi Co-operative on ⓣ1661 or Taxi Radio on ⓣ1681.

Somewhat less stable though typically Thai, **tuk-tuks** have little to recommend them. These noisy, three-wheeled, open-sided buggies, which can carry three medium-sized passengers comfortably, fully expose you to the worst of Bangkok's pollution and weather. Locals might use tuk-tuks for short journeys – though you'll have to bargain hard to get a fare lower than the taxi-cab flag-fall of B35 – while a longer trip from Thanon Ploenchit to Thanon Sathorn, for example, will set you back up to B100. Be aware, also, that tuk-tuk drivers tend to speak less English than taxi drivers – and there have been cases of robberies and attacks on women passengers late at night. During the day it's quite common for tuk-tuk drivers to try and **con** their passengers into visiting a jewellery or expensive souvenir shop with them, for which they get a hefty commission; the usual tactic involves falsely informing tourists that the Grand Palace, or whatever their destination might be, is closed (see p.131), and offering instead a ridiculously cheap, even free, city tour.

Motorbike taxis generally congregate at the entrances to long sois – pick the riders out by their numbered, coloured vests – and charge around B10 for short trips down into the side streets. If you're short on time and have nerves of steel, it's also possible to charter them for hairy journeys out on the main roads (a trip from Thanon Ploenchit to Thanon Sathorn should cost around B50). Crash helmets are compulsory on all main roads in the capital (traffic police fine non-wearers on the spot), though they're rarely worn on trips down the sois and the local press has reported complaints from people who've caught head-lice this way (they suggest wearing a headscarf under the helmet).

Accommodation

If your time in Bangkok is limited, you should think especially carefully about what you want to do in the city before deciding which part of town to stay in. Traffic jams are so appalling here that easy access to relevant train networks and river transport can be crucial.

For double rooms under B400, your widest choice lies with the **guest houses** of Banglamphu and the smaller, dingier travellers' ghetto that has grown up around Soi Ngam Duphli, off the south side of Thanon Rama IV. The most inexpensive rooms here are no-frills crash-pads – small and often windowless, with thin walls and shared bathrooms. Unless you pay cash in advance, bookings are rarely accepted by guest houses, but it's often worth phoning to establish whether a place is full already. During peak season (Nov–Feb) you may have difficulty getting a room after noon.

Banglamphu is also starting to cater for the slightly better-off tourist and you'll find some good mid-priced options along and around Thanon Khao San. But the majority of the city's **moderate and expensive** rooms are concentrated downtown around Siam Square and Thanon Ploenchit and in the area between Thanon Rama IV and Thanon Charoen Krung (New Road), along Thanon Sukhumvit, and to a lesser extent in Chinatown. Air-conditioned rooms with hot-water bathrooms can be had for around B500 in these areas, but for that you're looking at a rather basic cubicle; you'll probably have to ˀre like B800 for smart furnishings and a swimming pool. The cream ...ngkok's **deluxe** tourist accommodation, with rates starting from B4000, ... scenically sited along the banks of the Chao Phraya River, though there are a few top-notch hotels in the downtown area too, which is also where you'll find the best business hotels. Details of accommodation **near the airport** are given on p.102.

For **long-stay accommodation**, the most economical option is usually a room with a bathroom in an apartment building, which is likely to set you back at least B5000 a month. Many foreigners end up living in apartments off Thanon Sukhumvit, around Victory Monument and Pratunam, or on Soi Boonprarop, off Thanon Rajaprarop just north of Pratunam. Visit the Teaching in Thailand website, Ⓦwww.ajarn.com, for links to a roomfinder website and tips on living in Bangkok, or try Ⓦwww.sabaai.com for serviced apartments. The *Bangkok Post* (Ⓦwww.bangkokpost.com) carries rental ads in its Thursday property section, as well as online, as does the monthly listings magazine *Metro*; vacancies are also sometimes advertised on the noticeboards in the AUA Language Centre on Thanon Rajdamri.

Banglamphu

Nearly all backpackers head straight for **Banglamphu**, Bangkok's long-established travellers' ghetto, location of the cheapest accommodation and some of the best nightlife in the city, and arguably the most enjoyable area to base yourself in the city. It's within easy reach of the Grand Palace and other major sights in **Ratanakosin** (which has only one, very plush, accommodation option of its own), and has enough bars, restaurants and shops to keep any visitor happy for a week or more, though some people find this insularity tiresome after just a few hours.

At the heart of Banglamphu is the legendary **Thanon Khao San** (Ⓦwww.khaosanroad.com), almost a caricature of a travellers' centre, crammed with Internet cafés, dodgy travel agents and restaurants serving yoghurt shakes and muesli, the sidewalks lined with stalls and shops flogging cheap backpackers' fashions, racks of bootleg music and video CDs, tattooists and hair-braiders. It's a lively, high-energy base: great for shopping and making travel arrangements (though beware the innumerable Khao San scams, as outlined on p.80) and a good place to meet other travellers. It's especially fun at night when young Thais from all over the city gather here to browse the temporary clothes stalls, mingle with the crowds of foreigners and squash into the bars and clubs that have made Khao San *the* place to party.

The increasingly sophisticated nightlife scene has enticed more moneyed travellers into Banglamphu and a growing number of Khao San **guest houses** are reinventing themselves as good-value mini-hotels boasting chic decor, swimming pools, and even views from the windows – a remarkable facelift from the cardboard cells of old. The cheap sleeps are still there though – in the darker corners of Khao San itself, as well as on the smaller, quieter roads off and around it. Rooms overlooking Thanon Khao San are noisy late into the night, and the same is increasingly true of accommodation on parallel **Thanon Ram Bhuttri**, where a plethora of bars keeps the street busy at all hours. Things are a little quieter on the roads that encircle the nearby temple, Wat Chana Songkhran, namely **Soi Ram Bhuttri** and its feeder alley, **Soi Chana Songkhram**; along **Phra Athit**, which runs parallel to the Chao Phraya River and is packed with trendy Thai café-bars and restaurants (and also has a useful express-boat stop); and in the residential alleyways that parallel Thanon Khao San to the south:

Trok Mayom and **Damnoen Klang Neua**. About ten minutes' walk north from Thanon Khao San, the handful of guest houses scattered amongst the neighbourhood shophouses of the **Thanon Samsen sois** offer a more authentically Thai atmosphere. A further fifteen minutes' walk in the same direction will take you to **Thanon Sri Ayutthaya**, behind the National Library in **Thewes** (a seven-minute walk from the express-boat stop), the calmest area in Banglamphu, where rooms are larger and guest houses smaller.

We've listed only the cream of what's on offer in each small enclave of Banglamphu: if your first choice is full there'll almost certainly be a vacancy somewhere just along the soi, if not right next door. **Theft** is a problem in Banglamphu, particularly at the cheaper guest houses, so don't leave anything valuable in your room and heed the guest houses' notices about padlocks and safety lockers.

Banglamphu is served by plenty of **public transport**. All the guest houses listed lie only a few minutes' walk from Chao Phraya **express boat** stops N13 (Phra Athit, sometimes known as Banglamphu), N14 (Rama VIII Bridge) and N15 (Thewes), as detailed in the box on p.110. Note that if you're using the boat service in the evening to head downtown via the Central BTS train station at Saphan Taksin, the last boat leaves N13 at about 7.15pm. Banglamphu is also served by **public longtail boats** along Khlong Saen Saeb (see p.110), which leave from Phan Fah and have a particularly useful stop at Saphan Huachang, which is a few minutes' walk from both **BTS** Ratchathewi and BTS Siam (about every 10mins during daylight hours; B8; 10mins). The other fast way to get on to the BTS system is to take a taxi from Banglamphu to BTS National Stadium. For details of the most useful **buses** in and out of Banglamphu and where to catch them, see the box on p.118. **Airport bus** A2 from Don Muang runs to Banglamphu, as will AE2 from Suvamabhumi Airport (see p.98). For the cheapest route from Don Muang Airport to Banglamphu, take ordinary bus #29 from the road 100m right of International Terminal 1 as far as Mo Chit Skytrain station and change onto ordinary bus #3, which will take you to Thanon Phra Athit in Banglamphu: the trip will probably take about 90

△ Thanon Khao San

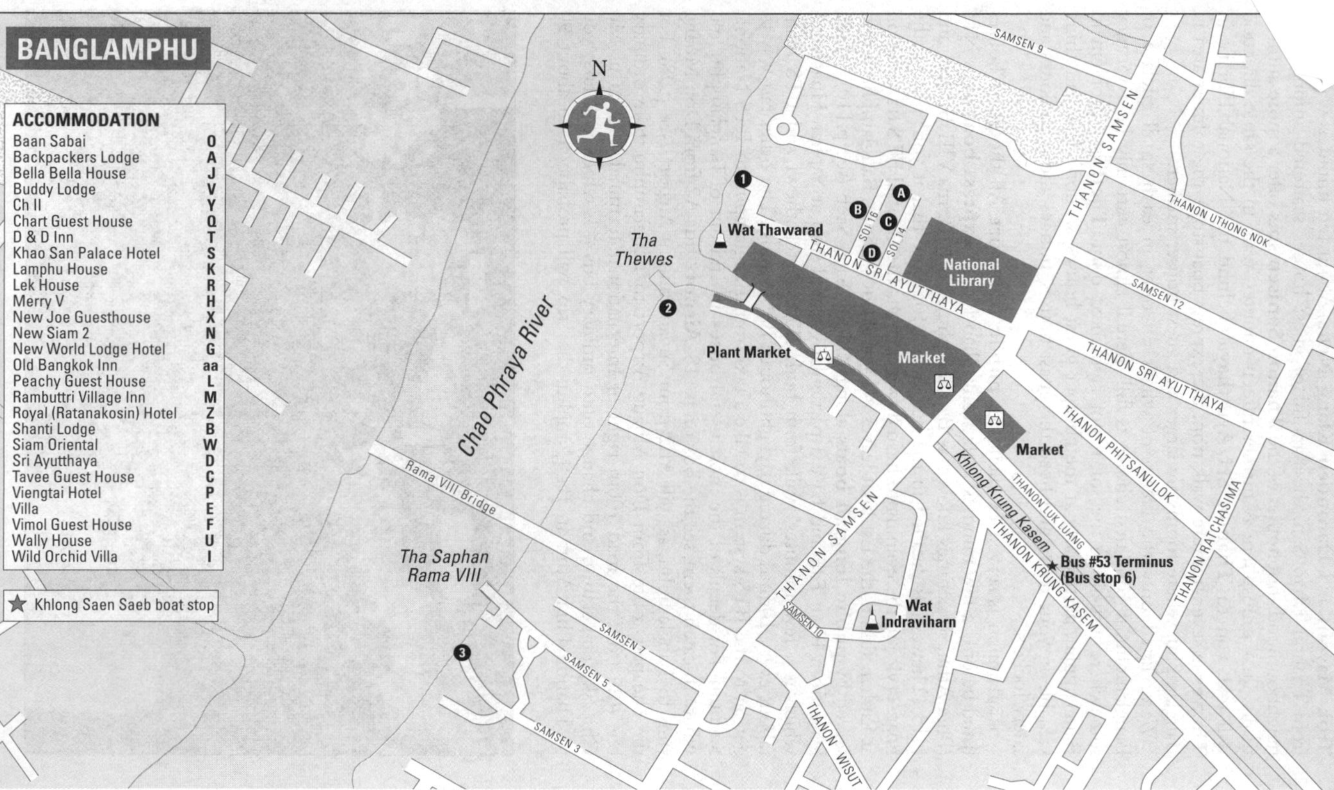
BANGLAMPHU
ACCOMMODATION
Baan Sabai O
Backpackers Lodge A
Bella Bella House J
Buddy Lodge V
Ch II Y
Chart Guest House Q
D & D Inn T
Khao San Palace Hotel S
Lamphu House K
Lek House R
Merry V H
New Joe Guesthouse X
New Siam 2 N
New World Lodge Hotel G
Old Bangkok Inn aa
Peachy Guest House L
Rambuttri Village Inn M
Royal (Ratanakosin) Hotel Z
Shanti Lodge B
Siam Oriental W
Sri Ayutthaya D
Tavee Guest House C
Viengtai Hotel P
Villa E
Vimol Guest House F
Wally House U
Wild Orchid Villa I
Khlong Saen Saeb boat stop
N
Chao Phraya River
Tha Thewes
Wat Thawarad
National Library
Market
Plant Market
Market
THANON SRI AYUTTHAYA
SOI 16
SOI 14
THANON SAMSEN
SAMSEN 9
THANON UTHONG NOK
SAMSEN 12
THANON PHITSANULOK
THANON RATCHASIMA
THANON LUK LUANG
Khlong Krung Kasem
THANON KRUNG KASEM
Bus #53 Terminus (Bus stop 6)
Wat Indraviharn
SAMSEN 10
THANON WISUT
SAMSEN 7
SAMSEN 5
SAMSEN 3
Rama VIII Bridge
Tha Saphan Rama VIII

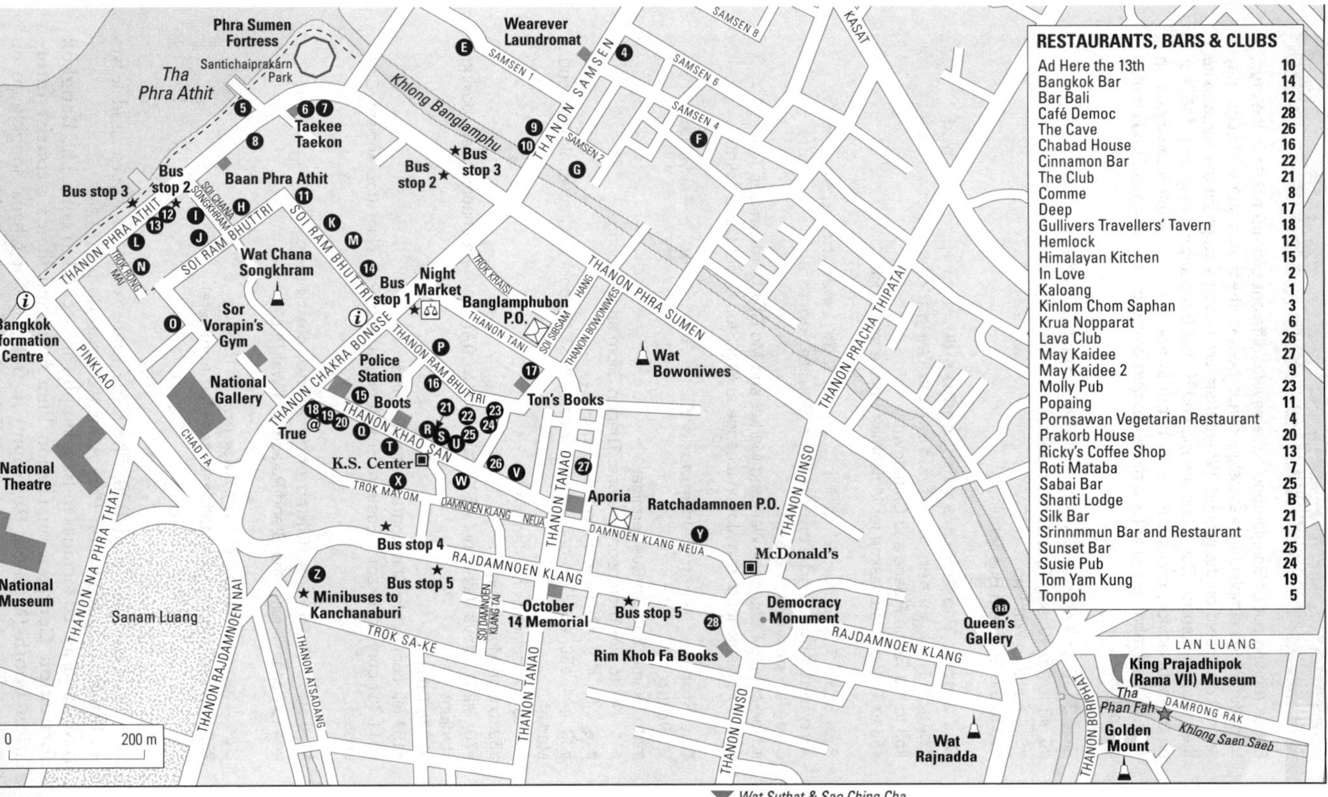
RESTAURANTS, BARS & CLUBS
Ad Here the 13th 10
Bangkok Bar 14
Bar Bali 12
Café Democ 28
The Cave 26
Chabad House 16
Cinnamon Bar 22
The Club 21
Comme 8
Deep 17
Gullivers Travellers' Tavern 18
Hemlock 12
Himalayan Kitchen 15
In Love 2
Kaloang 1
Kinlom Chom Saphan 3
Krua Nopparat 6
Lava Club 26
May Kaidee 27
May Kaidee 2 9
Molly Pub 23
Popaing 11
Pornsawan Vegetarian Restaurant 4
Prakorb House 20
Ricky's Coffee Shop 13
Roti Mataba 7
Sabai Bar 25
Shanti Lodge B
Silk Bar 21
Srinnmmun Bar and Restaurant 17
Sunset Bar 25
Susie Pub 24
Tom Yam Kung 19
Tonpoh 5
Phra Sumen Fortress
Santichaiprakarn Park
Tha Phra Athit
Wearever Laundromat
Khlong Banglamphu
Taekee Taekon
Baan Phra Athit
Bus stop 3
Bus stop 2
Bus stop 1
Bus stop 4
Bus stop 5
Wat Chana Songkhram
Sor Vorapin's Gym
Bangkok Information Centre
National Gallery
National Theatre
National Museum
Sanam Luang
Night Market
Banglamphubon P.O.
Police Station
Boots
True
K.S. Center
Ton's Books
Wat Bowoniwes
Aporia
Ratchadamnoen P.O.
McDonald's
Democracy Monument
October 14 Memorial
Rim Khob Fa Books
Minibuses to Kanchanaburi
Queen's Gallery
King Prajadhipok (Rama VII) Museum
Tha Phan Fah
Golden Mount
Wat Rajnadda
Khlong Saen Saeb
THANON PHRA ATHIT
SOI CHANA SONGKHRAM
SOI RAM BHUTTRI
TROK RONG MAI
PINKLAO
CHAD FA
THANON NA PHRA THAT
THANON RAJDAMNOEN NAI
THANON ATSADANG
TROK SA-KE
THANON CHAKRA BONGSE
THANON RAM BHUTTRI
THANON KHAO SAN
TROK MAYOM
DAMNOEN KLANG NEUA
RAJDAMNOEN KLANG
SOI DAMNOEN KLANG TAI
THANON TANAO
THANON TANI
TROK KRAISI
HANG
SOI SIBSAM
THANON BOWONIWES
THANON PHRA SUMEN
THANON SAMSEN
SAMSEN 1
SAMSEN 2
SAMSEN 4
SAMSEN 6
SAMSEN 8
KASAT
THANON PRACHA THIPATAI
THANON DINSO
LAN LUANG
DAMRONG RAK
THANON BORIPHAT
0 200 m
Wat Suthat & Sao Ching Cha

…lamphu's bus stops and routes

…uses running out of Banglamphu have several different pick-up points in the area: to make things simpler, we've assigned numbers to these bus stops, though they are not numbered on the ground. Where there are two bus stops on the same route they share a number. Bus stops are marked on the Banglamphu map on p.116. For on-the-spot advice, contact the BTB booth in front of Wat Chana Songkhram on Thanon Chakrabongse, and for a more detailed breakdown of Bangkok's bus routes see p.108.

Bus Stop 1: Thanon Chakrabongse, near the 7–11
#6, #9 to Pak Khlong Talat flower market
#6, #9, #32 to Wat Pho
#30 to the Southern Bus Terminal

Bus Stop 2: Thanon Phra Athit, south side, near *Hemlock*; and Thanon Phra Sumen, south side, near *Banglumpoo Place* hotel
#53 to the Grand Palace and Chinatown
#56 to Thanon Ratchasima for Vimanmek Palace and Dusit

Bus Stop 3: Thanon Phra Athit, north side, near the cross-river ferry entrance; and Thanon Phra Sumen, north side, opposite *Banglumpoo Place* hotel
#3 (air-con) to Chatuchak Weekend Market and Mo Chit Northern Bus Terminal
#53 to Hualamphong train station (change at Bus Stop 6, but same ticket)

Bus Stop 4: Thanon Rajdamnoen Klang, north side, outside Lottery Building
#2 to Ekamai Eastern Bus Terminal
#15, #47 to Jim Thompson's House, Thanon Silom and Patpong
#15, #47, #79, #79 (air-con) to Siam Square
#39, #44, #59, #503 (air-con), #509 (air-con), #157 (air-con) to Chatuchak Weekend Market
#47 to Lumphini boxing stadium
#59 to Don Muang Airport
#70, #201, #503 (air-con), #509 (air-con) to TAT and Ratchadamnoen boxing stadium
#70 to Dusit
#157 (air-con) to Mo Chit Northern Bus Terminal
#511 (air-con) to Ekamai Eastern Bus Terminal and Pak Nam (for Ancient City buses)

Bus Stop 5: Thanon Rajdamnoen Klang, south side
#44 to Sanam Luang, the Grand Palace and Wat Pho

Bus Stop 6: Thanon Krung Kasem, north side
#53 to Hualamphong train station (buses start from here)

minutes but costs less than B20. The same route works in reverse, and leaves from Bus Stop 3 on Thanon Phra Athit (see map on p.116).

Traveller-oriented facilities in Banglamphu are second to none. The **Bangkok Information Centre** is on Thanon Phra Athit, and there's a **tourist information booth** (Mon–Sat 9am–5pm) in front of Wat Chana Songkhram on Thanon Chakrabongse, near the Soi Ram Bhuttri junction. The closest **poste**

restante service to Khao San is at Ratchadamnoen Post Office on the eastern stretch of Soi Damnoen Klang Neua, but the one at Banglamphubon Post Office near Wat Bowoniwes is also handy (for full details see p.218). Almost every alternate building on Thanon Khao San, Thanon Ram Bhuttri and Soi Ram Bhuttri offers **Internet access**, as do many of the guest houses; intense competition keeps the rates very low (B40/hour or less) and there's an especially enticing cyber lounge, *True*, on Khao San (details on p.217). There are also Catnet Internet terminals (see Basics, p.82) at the Ratchadamnoen Post Office. As well as numerous money **exchange** places on Thanon Khao San, you'll find two branches of national banks, several ATMs, an outlet for Boots the Chemist and a couple of self-service **laundries**; at the Wearever laundromat on Thanon Samsen, between sois 1 and 3, you can also lounge on sofas, drink coffee, and enjoy free wi-fi acess. Several places will download your digital pictures on to a CD (see Listings p.218).

Thanon Khao San, Thanon Ram Bhuttri and Soi Damnoen Klang Neua

Buddy Lodge 265 Thanon Khao San ⓣ02 629 4477, ⓦwww.buddylodge.com. The most stylish and expensive hotel on Khao San and right in the thick of the action. The charming, colonial-style rooms are done out in cream, with louvred shutters, balconies, air-con and polished dark-wood floors, though they are not as pristine as you might expect for the price. There's a beautiful rooftop pool, a spa (see p.218), and several bars and restaurants downstairs in the Buddy Village complex. Specify an upper-floor location away from Khao San to ensure a quieter night's sleep. ❼

Chart Guest House 62 Thanon Khao San ⓣ02 282 0171, ⓔchartguesthouse@hotmail.com. Clean, comfortable enough hotel in the heart of the road; the cheapest rooms have no view and share a bathroom; the priciest have air-con and windows. Rooms in all categories are no frills and a little cramped. ❷ Fan and bathroom ❸–❹

Ch II 85 Soi Damnoen Klang Neua ⓣ02 282 1596. Shabby but cheap rooms, some with windows and some en suite, in a fairly quiet location, though you may be woken by the 5am prayer calls at the local mosque. There are only a couple of other guest houses on this road, so it has a local feel to it, even though Khao San is less than 200m away. Fan ❶, fan and bathrom ❷

D & D Inn 68–70 Thanon Khao San ⓣ02 629 0526, ⓦwww.khaosanby.com. The delightful rooftop pool, with expansive views, is the clincher at this good-value, mid-sized hotel located in the midst of the throng. Rooms all have air-con and satellite TV and are comfortably furnished and perfectly fine, if not immaculate. The cheapest single rooms have no window. ❺

Khao San Palace Hotel 139 Thanon Khao San ⓣ02 282 0578. Clean and well-appointed hotel with a rooftop pool. All rooms have bathrooms and windows and some also have air-con and TV. The best rooms are in the new wing – they're nicely tiled and some have panoramic views. Fan ❸, air-con ❸–❹

Lek House 125 Thanon Khao San ⓣ02 281 8441. Classic old-style Khao San guest house, with 20 small, basic rooms and shared facilities, but less shabby than many others in the same price bracket and a lot friendlier than most. Could get noisy at night as it's right next to the popular *Silk Bar*. ❷

New Joe Guesthouse 81 Trok Mayom ⓣ02 281 2948, ⓦwww.newjoe.com. Very basic rooms in a block just behind Khao San, but they all have fans and private bathrooms. ❷

Royal (Ratanakosin) Hotel 2 Thanon Rajdamnoen Klang ⓣ02 222 9111. Determinedly old-fashioned hotel that's used mainly by older Thai tourists and for conferences. Air-con rooms in the new wing are decent enough if unexciting and there's a pool and a restaurant, but the chief attraction is the location, just a 5-min stroll from Sanam Luang (or a further 10min to the Grand Palace) – though getting to Thanon Khao San entails a life-endangering leap across 12 lanes of traffic. Old wing ❻, new wing ❼

Siam Oriental 190 Thanon Khao San ⓣ02 629 0312, ⓔsiam_oriental@hotmail.com. Small hotel right in the middle of Thanon Khao San, offering spartan but clean rooms, all with attached bathrooms and most with window s. Some rooms have air-con and a few also have balconies. Fan ❸, air-con ❸–❺

Viengtai Hotel 42 Thanon Ram Bhuttri ⓣ02 280 5392, ⓦwww.viengtai.co.th. The second best of the options in Banglamphu's upper price bracket, with a good location just a few metres from the shops and restaurants of Thanon Khao San, though street-facing rooms get noise from the burgeoning number of Ram Bhuttri bars. Rooms are a decent size if not especially stylish, they all have air-con and TV, and there's a big pool. ❼

Wally House 189/1–2 Thanon Khao San ⓣ02 282 7067. Small guest house behind the restaurant and Internet café of the same name, with a range of very cheap, simple rooms, some of them en suite, the nicest of which are in a big, old, wooden-floored teak house set back from Khao San above a small courtyard. Fan ❶, fan and bathroom ❷

Ram Bhuttri, Chana Songkhram and Phra Athit

Baan Sabai 12 Soi Rong Mai, between Soi Ram Bhuttri and Thanon Chao Fa ⓣ02 629 1599, ⓔbaansabai@hotmail.com. Built round a courtyard, this large, upbeat, hotel-style guest house has a range of bright, fresh and decent-sized en-suite rooms, some of them air-con, though the cheapest have no windows. Fan ❷, air-con ❹

Bella Bella House Soi Ram Bhuttri ⓣ02 629 3090. The pale-pink rooms in this guest house are decently priced and some boast lovely views over Wat Chana Songkhram. The cheapest share bathrooms, and the most expensive have air-con. Fan ❷, air-con ❸

Lamphu House 75 Soi Ram Bhuttri ⓣ02 629 5861, ⓦwww.lamphuhouse.com. With smart bamboo beds, coconut-wood clothes rails and elegant rattan lamps in even its cheapest rooms, this travellers' hotel has a cheery, modern feel. Cheapest rooms share facilities and have no outside view; the pricier ones have air-con and balconies overlooking the courtyard. Fan ❷, fan and bathroom ❸, air-con ❹

Merry V Soi Ram Bhuttri ⓣ02 282 9267. Large, efficiently run guest house offering some of the cheapest accommodation in Banglamphu. Rooms are basic and small, many share bathrooms and it's pot luck whether you get a window or not. Useful noticeboard in the downstairs restaurant. Fan ❶, fan and bathroom ❸.

New Siam 2 50 Trok Rong Mai ⓣ02 282 2795, ⓦwww.newsiamguesthouse.com. Very pleasant and well run small hotel whose en-suite fan and air-con rooms stand out for their thoughtfully designed extras such as in-room safes, cable TV and drying rails on the balconies. Occupies a quiet but convenient location and has a small streetside pool. Popular with families and triple rooms are also available. Fan ❹, air-con ❹

Peachy Guest House 10 Thanon Phra Athit ⓣ02 281 6471. Popular, good value, very cheap place set round a small courtyard, with lots of clean, simple rooms, most with shared bathrooms but some with air-con. Fan and shared bathroom ❶, air-con and shared bathroom ❷, air-con and bathroom ❸

Rambuttri Village Inn 95 Soi Ram Bhuttri ⓣ02 282 9162, ⓦwww.khaosan-hotels.com. The draw at this otherwise rather characterless six-storey hotel is the good-sized rooftop swimming pool. Rooms are plain and unadorned, either with or without bathroom and air-con, and the plaza out front is full of tailors' shops – and their touts. Book online only, and at least five days ahead. Fan and shared bathroom ❸, air-con and bathroom ❺

Wild Orchid Villa 8 Soi Chana Songkhram ⓣ02 629 4378, ⓔwild_orchid_villa@hotmail.com. Painted in an appropriately wild colour scheme of lemon, aqua and blackberry, this hotel features some cosily furnished air-con rooms at the top of its price range (though their bathrooms are inconveniently accessed via the balcony), and some much less interesting windowless options, with shared bathrooms, at the bottom end. Has a very pleasant seating area out front. Fan and shared bathroom ❷, air-con and bathroom ❹

Samsen sois, Thewes and the fringes

Backpackers Lodge 85 Soi 14, Thanon Sri Ayutthaya ⓣ02 282 3231. Quiet, family-run place in the peaceful Thewes quarter of north Banglamphu. Just 12 simple partition-walled rooms, all with shared bathroom, and a communal area downstairs. ❷

New World Lodge Hotel Samsen Soi 2 ⓣ02 281 5596, ⓦwww.newworldlodge.com. Friendly, well-run Muslim hotel in an interesting traditional neighbourhood. Rooms are large, smartly outfitted and have air-con, TV and tiny balconies; some have khlong views. There's also a pleasant canalside seating area and café. The cheapest rooms in the much less appealing guest-house wing are shabby and share bathrooms. Guest house ❷, hotel ❻

Old Bangkok Inn 609 Thanon Phra Sumen ⓣ02 629 1785, ⓦwww.oldbangkokinn.com. This chic little boutique guest house has just ten air-con rooms, each of them styled in dark wood, with antique north-Thai partitions and antique Burmese doors, beds and ironwork lamps, plus elegant contemporary-accented bathrooms. All rooms have a PC with free broadband access and DVD player. Some also have a tiny private garden. Very convenient for the Khlong Saen Saeb canal-boat service and 15 minutes' walk from Tha Phra Athit express-boat pier or 10 minutes' walk from Khao San. ❽

Shanti Lodge 37 Soi 16,Thanon Sri Ayutthaya ⓣ02 281 2497, ⓦwww.shantilodge.com. Quiet place with an appealingly laid-back, whole-earth vibe and a variety of small but characterful rooms – some have rattan walls, others are decorated with Indian motifs. The cheapest share bathrooms, the most expensive have air-con. Has a very good, predominantly vegetarian restaurant downstairs (see p.188). Fan ❷, fan and bathroom ❸, air-con ❹

Sri Ayutthaya 23/11 Soi 14, Thanon Sri Ayutthaya ⓣ02 282 5942. The most attractive guest house in Thewes, where the good-sized rooms (choose between fan rooms with or without private bathroom and en suites with air-con) are elegantly done out with beautiful wood-panelled walls and polished wood floors. Fan ❸, air-con ❹

Tavee Guest House 83 Soi 14, Thanon Sri Ayutthaya ⓣ02 282 5983. Decent-sized rooms; quiet and friendly and one of the cheaper places in the Thewes quarter. Offers rooms with shared bathroom plus some en-suite ones with air-con. Fan ❷, air-con ❹

Villa 230 Samsen Soi 1 ⓣ02 281 7009. One of Banglamphu's more therapeutic guest houses, in a lovely old Thai home and garden with just ten large rooms, each idiosyncratically furnished in simple, semi-traditional style; bathrooms are shared and rooms are priced according to their size. Just five minutes' walk from Khao San. ❸–❹

Vimol Guest House 358 Samsen Soi 4 ⓣ02 281 4615. Old-style, family-run guest house in a quiet but interesting neighbourhood that has just a smattering of other tourist places. The simple, cramped, hardboard-walled rooms are ultra basic and have shared bathrooms but are possibly the cheapest in Banglamphu. ❶

Ratanakosin

Chakrabongse Villas 396 Thanon Maharat ⓣ02 224 6686, ⓦwww.thaivillas.com; see Ratanakosin map on p.132. Riverside luxury accommodation with a difference: in the luxuriant gardens of hundred-year-old Chakrabongse House, overlooking Wat Arun and within walking distance of Wat Pho, three tranquil villas beautifully furnished in dark wood and silk, with polished teak floors. All have air-con and cable TV, and there's a small, attractive swimming pool and an open-sided riverfront pavilion for relaxing or dining (if ordered in advance). ❾

Chinatown and Hualamphong Station area

Not far from the Ratanakosin sights, and within fifteen minutes' walk of Siam Square, **Chinatown (Sampeng)** is one of the most frenetic and quintessentially Asian parts of Bangkok. Staying here, or in one of the sois around the conveniently close **Hualamphong Station**, can be noisy, but there's always plenty to look at, and some people choose to base themselves in this area in order to get away from the travellers' scene in Banglamphu. All listed accommodation is marked on the map on p.153.

Hualamphong is on the **subway** system, and Chinatown is served by a number of useful **bus** routes, including west-bound air-conditioned #507 and ordinary buses #25, #40 and #53, which all go to Ratanakosin (for Wat Pho and the Grand Palace); the east-bound #16, #25 and #40 buses all go to Siam Square, where you change onto the Skytrain. For more details, see box on p.108.

Baan Hualamphong 336/20 Soi Chalong Krung ⓣ02 639 8054, ⓦwww.baanhualampong.com. Custom-built wooden guest house that's attractively designed, has a stylish modern decor and is fitted with contemporary bathrooms and furnishings. There are big, bright, double rooms plus five-person dorms at B200 per bed, but all rooms share bathrooms. Has kitchen facilities, inviting lounging areas and a roof terrace, and provides a left-luggage service. ❹

Bangkok Center 328 Thanon Rama IV ⓣ02 238 4848, ⓦwww.bangkokcentrehotel.com. Handily placed upper-mid-range option with efficient service right by the subway station and just across the road from the train station. Rooms are smartly furnished if a little old-fashioned, and all have air-con and TV; there's a pool, restaurant and Internet access on the premises. ❻

FF Guest House 338/10 Trok La-O, off Thanon Rama IV ⓣ02 233 4168.Tiny, family-run guest house offering ten cheap, basic rooms with shared bathrooms. Located at the end of an alley just a 5-min walk from the train and subway stations. ❷

Grand China Princess 215 Thanon Yaowarat ⓣ02 224 9977, ⓦwww.grandchina.com. The poshest hotel in Chinatown boasts fairly luxurious accommodation in its 27-storey-high tower close to the heart of the bustle, with stunning views over all the city landmarks, a small rooftop swimming pool, revolving panoramic restaurant and several other food outlets. ❼

New Empire Hotel 572 Thanon Yaowarat ⓣ 02 234 6990, ⓦ www.newempirehotel.com. Medium-sized hotel right in the thick of the Chinatown bustle, offering pretty decent superior (renovated) rooms with air-con and TV and some slightly cheaper, rather faded versions. In either category, it's worth requesting a room on the seventh floor to get panoramic views towards the river. ④–⑤

River View Guest House 768 Soi Panurangsri, Thanon Songvad ⓣ 02 235 8501, ⓔ riverview_bkk@hotmail.com. Large, plain, old-style rooms, with fans at the lower end of the range, air-con, and TVs at the top. Great views over the bend in the river from upper-floor rooms. Located in a lively if hard-to-find spot right next to the Chinese temple San Jao Sien Khong: head north for 400m from River City shopping centre (on the express-boat line) along Soi Wanit 2, before following signs to the guest house to the left. Fan ③, air-con ④

TT2 Guest House 516 Soi Kaeo Fa (formerly Soi Sawang and known to taxi drivers as such), off Thanon Maha Nakorn ⓣ 02 236 2946, ⓔ ttguesthouse@hotmail.com. A long-running, traveller-friendly budget place, this guest house is clean, friendly and well run, has Internet access and stores left luggage at B10 a day. All rooms share bathrooms. During high season, there are B100 beds in a three-person dorm. Roughly a 15min walk from either Hualamphong or the N3 Si Phraya express-boat stop; from Hualamphong, cross Thanon Rama IV, then walk left for 250m, cross Thanon Maha Nakorn and walk down it (following signs for *TT2*) for 275m as far as Soi Kaeo Fa, where you turn left and then first right. The guest house is opposite Wat Kaeo Jam Fa. ②

Thonburi

Few tourists stay on the **Thonburi** side of the river, though many visit its canals and temples (see p.158). It's suprisingly convenient, with express boats and cross-river shuttles serving Banglamphu and Ratanakosin across on the other bank.

Ibrik Resort by the River 256 Soi Wat Rakang ⓣ 02 848 9220, ⓦ www.ibrikresort.com. With just three rooms, this is the most bijou of boutique resorts. Each room is beautifully appointed in boho-chic style, with traditional wood floors, modernist white walls and sparkling silk accessories – and two of them have balconies right over the Chao Phraya River. It's just like staying at a trendy friend's in a neighbourhood that sees hardly any other tourists. It's right next door to *Supatra River House* restaurant and five minutes' walk from express-boat stop Tha Wang Lang/Phrannok. ⑧

Siam Square, Thanon Ploenchit and northern downtown

Siam Square – not really a square, but a grid of shops and restaurants between Thanon Phrayathai and Thanon Henri Dunant – and nearby **Thanon Ploenchit** are as central as Bangkok gets, at the heart of the Skytrain system and with all kinds of shopping on hand. There's no ultra-cheap accommodation here, but a few scaled-up guest houses complement the expensive hotels. Concentrated in their own small "ghetto" on **Soi Kasemsan 1**, which runs north off Thanon Rama I just west of Thanon Phrayathai and is the next soi along from Jim Thompson's House (see p.169), these offer an informal guest-house atmosphere, with hotel comforts – air-conditioning and en-suite hot-water bathrooms – at moderate prices. Several luxury hotels have set up on **Thanon Witthayu**, aka **Wireless Road**, home of the American and British embassies (among others). Accommodation here is marked on the **maps** on p.100 and p.168.

Inexpensive and moderate

A-One Inn 25/13 Soi Kasemsan 1, Thanon Rama I ⓣ 02 215 3029, ⓦ www.aoneinn.com. The original upscale guest house, and still justifiably popular, with Internet access and a reliable left-luggage room. Bedrooms all have satellite TV and come in a variety of sizes, including family rooms (but no singles). ④

The Bed & Breakfast 36/42 Soi Kasemsan 1, Thanon Rama I ⓣ 02 215 3004, ⓕ 02 215 2493.

Bright, clean and family-run, though the rooms – carpeted and with en-suite and telephones – are a bit cramped. As the name suggests, a simple breakfast – coffee, toast and fruit – is included. ❹

Far East Inn 20/8–11 Soi Bangkok Bazaar, Soi Chitlom ⓣ02 255 4041–5, ⓦwww.geocities.com/fareastinn or ⓦwww.tyha.org. The large rooms here are unexceptional but well-equipped – air-con, cable TV, mini-bars and baths with hot water – and the place is friendly, very central and reasonably quiet. Discounts for YHA members. ❻

Patumwan House 22 Soi Kasemsan 1, Thanon Rama I ⓣ02 612 3580–99, ⓦwww.patumwanhouse.com. Around the corner at the far end of the soi, with very large, though rather bare rooms with satellite TV, fridges and wardrobes; facilities include a café and Internet access. At the lower end of this price code. Discounted weekly and monthly rates. ❻

Reno Hotel 40 Soi Kasemsan 1, Thanon Rama I ⓣ02 215 0026, ⓔrenohotel@bblife.com. Friendly hotel, boasting large, comfortable, en-suite rooms with air-con, hot water and TV, a small swimming pool and a stylishly refurbished bar-restaurant where breakfast is served (included in the price). Internet access; small discounts for stays of a fortnight or a month. ❺

VIP Guest House 1025/5–9 Thanon Ploenchit ⓣ02 252 9535–8, ⓔghouse_g@hotmail.com. Very clean, self-styled "boutique" hotel in a peerless location. In the attractive, parquet-floored rooms (all with air-con and hot water), large beds leave just enough space for a couple of armchairs and a dressing table, as well as cable TV, mini-bar and tea- and coffee-making facilities. Breakfast included. ❻

Wendy House 36/2 Soi Kasemsan 1, Thanon Rama I ⓣ02 214 1149–50, ⓦwww.wendyguesthouse.com. Friendly and well-run guest house, with smart, clean and comfortable rooms, some with fridge and cable TV. Internet and wireless access in the ground-floor café, where breakfast (included in the price) is served. Discounted weekly rates. ❺

White Lodge 36/8 Soi Kasemsan 1, Thanon Rama I ⓣ02 216 8867 or 215 3041, ⓕ02 216 8228. Cheapest guest house on the soi, with well-maintained, shining white cubicles, a welcoming atmosphere, and good breakfasts at *Sorn's* next door. ❸

Expensive

Conrad All Seasons Place, 87 Thanon Witthayu ⓣ02 690 9999, ⓦwww.conradhotels.com. A recent addition to the city's luxury hotel scene, which places a high premium on design, aiming to add a cutting edge to traditional Thai style. Bathroom fittings include free-standing baths, glass walls and huge shower heads, and there's an enticing pool, spa, gym and two floodlit tennis courts. Eating options include the modern Chinese *Liu*, a branch of Beijing's hottest restaurant. ❾

Holiday Mansion Hotel 53 Thanon Witthayu ⓣ02 255 0099, ⓔhmtel@ksc.th.com. Handily placed opposite the British Embassy, this hotel's main selling point is its large, attractive swimming pool. The bright and spacious bedrooms are nothing to write home about, but come with cable TV, air-con and hot water. Rates include breakfast. ❼

Jim's Lodge 125/7 Soi Ruam Rudee, Thanon Ploenchit ⓣ02 255 3100, ⓦwww.jimslodge.com. In a relatively peaceful residential area, convenient for the British and American embassies, with friendly and helpful staff; offers international standards, including satellite TV and mini-bars, on a smaller scale and at bargain prices (towards the lower end of this price code); no swimming pool, but there is a roof garden with outdoor Jacuzzi. ❼

Pathumwan Princess Hotel 444 Thanon Phrayathai ⓣ02 216 3700, ⓦwww.pprincess. com. At the southern end of the Mah Boon Krong (MBK) Shopping Centre, affordable luxury that's recently been refurbished in a crisp, modern style and is popular with families and businessmen. Facilities run to Korean and Japanese restaurants, a large, salt-water swimming pool with hot and cold Jacuzzis, a health spa and a huge fitness club (including jogging track and squash and tennis courts). ❽

Reflections 81 Soi Ari (aka Thanon Phaholyothin Soi 7), between sois 2 and 3 ⓣ02 270 3344, ⓦwww.reflections-thai.com. An oasis of kitsch in a neighbourhood busy with food stalls and office workers, the *Reflections* compound is centred around an intriguingly camp-pop hotel plus a similarly styled gift shop and restaurant. The 28 rooms in the hotel come in two sizes and all have air-con, but otherwise each is entirely individual as every room was designed by a different artist. You might choose, for example, to stay in the all-pink "princess" room, in the one that evokes beachfront life, or in the one influenced by Parisian boho style (browse the website to see the full range). Though it's outside main shopping and entertainment districts, the hotel is just 5 minutes' walk from BTS Ari, five stops north of Siam Square and three stops south of Chatuchak Weekend Market; see map on p.100. Has a spa and pool. ❽

Siam City Hotel 477 Thanon Sri Ayutthaya ⓣ02 247 0123, ⓦwww.siamhotels.com. Elegant, welcoming luxury hotel on the northern side of downtown (next to Phaya Thai Skytrain station and opposite Suan Pakkad). Rooms are tastefully done out in dark wood and subdued colours, and there's a spa, health club, swimming pool and a comprehensive array of restaurants: Thai, Chinese, Japanese, Italian, international and a bakery. ❽

Swissôtel Nai Lert Park 2 Thanon Witthayu Ⓣ02 253 0123, Ⓦwww.nailertpark.swissotel.com. The main distinguishing feature of this welcoming, low-rise hotel is its lushly beautiful gardens, overlooked by many of the chic and spacious, balconied bedrooms; set into the grounds are a landscaped swimming pool, tennis courts, squash court and popular spa and health club. Good deli-café, cool bar (see p.197) and Japanese (see p.190), French and Chinese restaurants. ❾

Downtown: south of Thanon Rama IV

South of Thanon Rama IV, the left bank of the river contains a full cross-section of places to stay. Tucked away at the eastern edge of this area is **Soi Ngam Duphli**, a small ghetto of cheap guest houses that is often choked with traffic escaping the jams on Thanon Rama IV. The neighbourhood is generally on the slide, but is close to Lumphini subway station and a lot handier for the downtown areas and the new airport than Banglamphu.

Some medium-range places are scattered between Thanon Rama IV and the river, ranging from the notorious (the *Malaysia*) to the sedate (the *Bangkok Christian Guest House*). The area also lays claim to the capital's biggest selection of top hotels, which are among the most opulent in the world. Traversed by the Skytrain, this area is especially good for eating and nightlife. Staying by the river itself off **Thanon Charoen Krung**, aka **New Road**, has the added advantage of easy access to express boats, which will ferry you upstream to view the treasures of Ratanakosin.

Inexpensive

ETC Guest House 5/3 Soi Ngam Duphli Ⓣ02 287 1477–8, Ⓔetc@etc.co.th. Above a branch of the recommended travel agent of the same name, and very handy for Thanon Rama IV, though consequently a little noisy. Friendly, helpful and very clean, catering mainly to Japanese travellers. Rooms come with fans and are further cooled by air-conditioning in the corridors; hot-water bathrooms are either shared or en suite. Breakfast is included and Internet access is available. ❷

Freddy's 2 27/40 Soi Sri Bamphen Ⓣ02 286 7826, Ⓕ02 213 2097. Popular, clean, well-organized guest house with a variety of rooms with shared bathrooms and plenty of comfortable common areas, including a small café and beer garden at the rear. Rather noisy. ❶

Lee 3 Guest House 13 Soi Saphan Khu Ⓣ02 679 7045. In an old wooden house, the best of the Lee family of guest houses spread around this and adjoining sois. Decent, quiet and very cheap, with shared cold-water bathrooms. ❶

Madam Guest House 11 Soi Saphan Khu Ⓣ02 286 9289, Ⓕ02 213 2087. Cleanish, often cramped, but characterful bedrooms, some with their own cold-water bathrooms, in a warren-like, balconied wooden house. ❶

Sala Thai Daily Mansion 15 Soi Saphan Khu Ⓣ02 287 1436, Ⓕ02 677 6880. The pick of the area. A clean and efficiently run place at the end of this quiet, shaded alley, with bright, modern rooms with wall fans, sharing hot-water bathrooms. Especially good for lone travellers, as singles are half the price of doubles. ❸

Moderate

Charlie House 1034/36–37 Soi Saphan Khu Ⓣ02 679 8330–1, Ⓦwww.charliehousethailand.com. Good mid-range alternative to the crash-pads of Soi Ngam Duphli: bright, clean lobby restaurant, serving good, reasonably priced food, and small, non-smoking carpeted bedrooms with hot-water bathrooms, air-con and TV, close to Thanon Rama IV. Internet access. ❹

Intown Residence 1086/6 Thanon Charoen Krung Ⓣ02 639 0960–2, Ⓔintownbkk@hotmail.com. Clean, welcoming, rather old-fashioned and very good-value hotel sandwiched between shops on the noisy main road (ask for a room away from the street). Slightly chintzy but comfortable rooms, at the lower end of their price code, come with air-con, hot-water bathrooms, mini-bars, satellite TVs and phones. Weekly and monthly discounts available. ❹

Malaysia Hotel 54 Soi Ngam Duphli Ⓣ02 679 7127–36, Ⓦwww.malaysiahotelbkk.com. Once a travellers' legend famous for its compendious noticeboard, now better known for its seedy 24hr

DOWNTOWN: SOUTH OF THANON RAMA IV

RESTAURANTS & BARS	
Angelini's	19
Anna's Café	21
Aoi	12
Baan Khanitha	27
Ban Chiang	23
The Barbican	7
Celadon	P
Chai Karr	13
Charuvan	11
Cy'an	N
Deen	16
Dick's Café	3
Eat Me	22
Harmonique	2
Himali Cha-Cha	4 & 15
Hu'u	26
Indian Hut	8
Irish Xchange	14
Ishq	25
Jim Thompson's Saladaeng Café	24
Khrua Aroy Aroy	18
La Boulange	20
Le Bouchon	5
Lucifer	10
Mei Jiang	G
River View	1
The Sky Bar & Distil	17
Somboon Seafood	6
Tawandaeng German Brewery	28
Thien Duong	I
Tongue Thai	9
Zen	14

ACCOMMODATION	
Bangkok Christian Guest House	K
Dusit Thani Hotel	I
Intown Residence	A
La Residence	F
Luxx	H
Metropolitan	N
Montien Hotel	C
Niagara	M
Oriental Hotel	E
Peninsula Bangkok	G
Rose Hotel	D
Sofitel Silom	J
Sukhothai	P
Swiss Lodge	L
Woodlands Inn	B
YWCA	O

BTS Skytrain station
Subway station

Hualamphong Station
28 & M. R. Kukrit's Heritage Home
Immigration Office

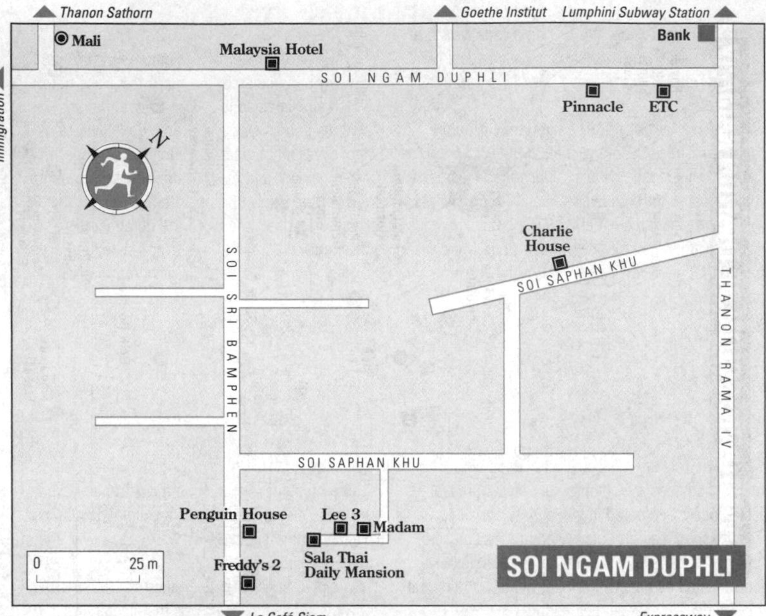

coffeeshop and massage parlour. The accommodation itself is reasonable value though: the rooms are large and have air-con, mini-bars and hot-water bathrooms; some have cable TV. There's a swimming pool (B50/day for non-guests) and Internet access. ④

Niagara 26 Soi Suksa Witthaya, off the south side of Thanon Silom ⓣ 02 233 5783, ⓕ 02 233 6563. No facilities other than a coffeeshop, but the clean bedrooms, with air-con, hot-water bathrooms, TV, telephones and rates at the lower end of this price code, are a snip. ⑤

Penguin House 27/23 Soi Sri Bamphen ⓣ 02 679 9991–2, ⓦ www.geocities.com/penguinhouse. New, modern block with a ground-floor café and large, reasonably attractive rooms above, featuring air-con, hot water, cable TV and fridges; ask for one away from the busy road. Discounted monthly rates available. ⑤

Pinnacle 17 Soi Ngam Duphli ⓣ 02 287 0111–31, ⓦ www.pinnaclehotels.com. Bland but reliable international-standard place, with rooftop Jacuzzi and fitness centre; rates include breakfast. ⑥

Woodlands Inn 1158/5–7 Soi 32, Thanon Charoen Krung ⓣ 02 235 3894, ⓦ www.woodlandsinn.org. Simple but well-run hotel next to the GPO, under South Indian management and popular with travellers from the subcontinent. All rooms have air-con, cable TV and hot-water bathrooms, and there's a good-value South Indian restaurant on the ground floor. ④

YWCA 13 Thanon Sathorn Tai ⓣ 02 287 3136, ⓦ www.ywcabangkok.com. Reliable, low-rise accommodation for women in neat standard or spacious deluxe rooms, all with air-con and hot water. Breakfast included. Deeply discounted monthly rates. ⑥

Expensive

Bangkok Christian Guest House 123 Soi 2, Saladaeng, off the eastern end of Thanon Silom ⓣ 02 233 2206, ⓦ www.bcgh.org. Well-run, orderly missionary house in a shiny, modern building, where plain but immaculately kept rooms come with air-con and hot-water bathrooms. At the lower end of this price code, with breakfast included. ⑦

Bangkok Marriott Resort & Spa 257 Thanon Charoennakorn ⓣ 02 476 0022, ⓦ www.marriott.com. A luxury retreat from the frenetic city centre, well to the south on the Thonburi bank, but connected to Taksin Bridge (for the Skytrain and Chao Phraya express boats), 10min away, by hotel ferries every 15min. Arrayed around a highly appealing swimming pool, the tranquil, riverside gardens are filled with vegetation and birdsong, while the stylish and spacious bedrooms come with polished hardwood floors and balconies. There's a fitness centre, a branch of the classy Mandara Spas, and among a wide choice of eateries, a good Japanese teppanyaki house and a bakery-café. Good value, at the lower end of this price code. ❾

Dusit Thani Hotel 946 Thanon Rama IV, on the corner of Thanon Silom ⓣ02 236 9999, ⓦwww.dusit.com. Elegant, centrally placed top-class hotel, geared for both business and leisure, with very high standards of service. The hotel is famous for its restaurants, including *Thien Duong* (see p.192) and the French *D'Sens*, which has some spectacular top-floor views. ❾

La Residence 173/8–9 Thanon Suriwong ⓣ02 266 5400–1, ⓦwww.laresidencebangkok.com. A small, intimate boutique hotel where the tasteful, individually decorated rooms stretch to mini-bars, safes and cable TV. Continental breakfast included. ❼

Luxx 6/11 Thanon Decho ⓣ02 635 8800, ⓦwww.staywithluxx.com. Welcoming boutique hotel offering a good dose of contemporary style at reasonable prices. Decorated in white, grey and plain, unvarnished teak, the rooms feature DVD players, safes, dressing gowns and cute wooden baths surmounted by outsized shower heads. Continental or American breakfast included. ❽

Metropolitan 27 Thanon Sathorn Tai ⓣ02 625 3333, ⓦwww.metropolitan.como.bz. The height of chic, minimalist urban living, where the largest standard hotel rooms in the city (the "Metropolitan" rooms) are stylishly decorated in dark wood, creamy Portuguese limestone and lotus-themed contemporary artworks, while Yohji Yamamoto outfits adorn all the staff. There's a very seductive pool, a fine spa, a well-equipped fitness centre with a daily schedule of complimentary classes, ranging from t'ai chi to Pilates, an excellent restaurant, *Cyan* (see p.191), and a fiercely hip private bar. ❾

Montien Hotel 54 Thanon Surawongse, on the corner of Rama IV ⓣ02 233 7060, ⓦwww.montien.com. Grand, airy and solicitous luxury hotel, with a strongly Thai character, very handily placed for business and nightlife. ❾

Oriental Hotel 48 Oriental Avenue, off Thanon Charoen Krung ⓣ02 659 9000, ⓦwww.mandarinoriental.com. One of the world's best, this effortlessly stylish riverside hotel boasts immaculate standards of service. ❾

Peninsula Bangkok 333 Thanon Charoennakorn, Klongsan ⓣ02 861 2888, ⓦwww.peninsula.com. Superb top-class hotel which self-consciously aims to rival the *Oriental* across the river. Service is flawless, the decor stylishly blends traditional and modern Asian design, and every room has a panoramic view of the Chao Phraya. Although it's on the Thonburi side of the river, the hotel operates a shuttle boat across to a pier and reception area by the *Shangri-La Hotel* off Thanon Charoen Krung. ❾

Rose Hotel 118 Thanon Suriwong ⓣ02 266 8268–72, ⓦwww.rosehotelbkk.com. Set back from the main road but very handy for the city's nightlife, this thirty-year-old hotel has just been cleverly refurbished: the simple, compact rooms now boast a stylish, retro look, in keeping with the age of the place. The ground-floor public rooms, where breakfast (included in the price) is served, are more elegant again, and a swimming pool is planned. Internet access. Towards the lower end of this price code. ❼

Sofitel Silom 188 Thanon Silom ⓣ02 238 1991, ⓦwww.sofitel.com. Towards the quieter end of Thanon Silom, a clever renovation combines contemporary Asian artworks and furnishings with understated French elegance. A wine bar and Mediterranean, Japanese and rooftop Chinese restaurants, as well as a fitness club and small pool, complete the picture. ❾

Sukhothai 13/3 Thanon Sathorn Tai ⓣ02 287 0222, ⓦwww.sukhothai.com. The most elegant of Bangkok's top hotels, its decor inspired by the walled city of Sukhothai: low-rise accommodation coolly furnished in silks, teak and granite, around six acres of gardens and lotus ponds. Excellent restaurants including the Thai *Celadon* (see p.191). ❾

Swiss Lodge 3 Thanon Convent ⓣ02 233 5345, ⓦwww.swisslodge.com. Swish, friendly, good-value, boutique hotel, with high standards of service, just off Thanon Silom and ideally placed for business and nightlife. *Café Swiss* serves fondue, raclette and all your other Swiss favourites, while the tiny terrace swimming pool confirms the national stereotypes of neatness and clever design. ❽

Thanon Sukhumvit

Thanon Sukhumvit is Bangkok's longest road – it keeps going east all the way to Cambodia – but for such an important artery it's way too narrow for the volume of traffic that needs to use it, and is further hemmed in by the overhead Skytrain line that runs above its entire course. Packed with high-rise hotels and office blocks, an amazing array of specialist restaurants (from Lebanese

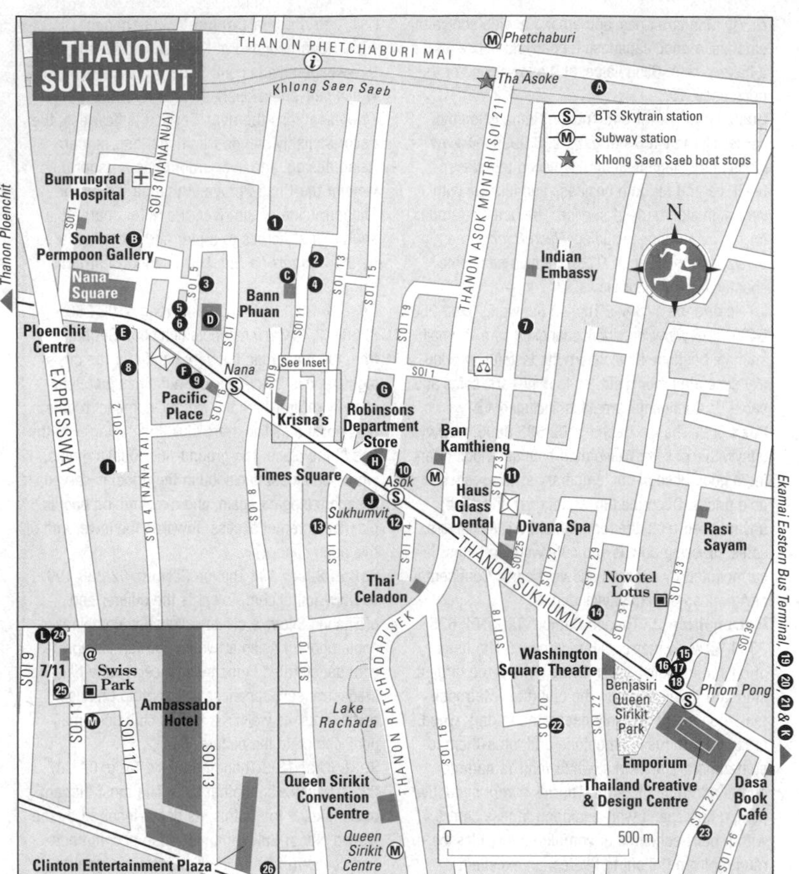

ACCOMMODATION		RESTAURANTS, BARS & CLUBS		Himali Cha-Cha	17
Amari Atrium	A	Al Ferdoss	6	Le Dalat Indochine	11
Amari Boulevard Hotel	D	Baan Khanitha	7	Lemongrass	23
The Atlanta	I	The Ball in Hand	8	Londoner Brew Pub	16
Federal Hotel	C	Ban Rie Coffee	20	MahaNaga	14
Grand Business Inn	M	Bed Supperclub	2	Nipa	9
J.W. Marriott Hotel	E	The Bull's Head	15	Pizza Venezia	4
The Landmark Bangkok	F	Cabbages and Condoms	13	Q Bar	1
Rex Hotel	K	Cheap Charlie's	25	Robin Hood	18
Sheraton Grande Sukhumvit	J	Dosa King	10	Suda Restaurant	12
Suk 11	L	Face Bangkok (La Na Thai & Hazara)	21	Tamarind Café	22
SV Guest House	G	Gaeng Pa Lerd Rod	17	Took Lae Dee	5
Westin Grande Sukhumvit	H	Gallery 11	24	Vientiane Kitchen (Khrua Vientiane)	19
Zenith Hotel	B	Gullivers Traveler's Tavern	3	Yong Lee	26

to Laotian), tailors, bookstores and stall after stall selling cheap souvenirs and T-shirts, it's a lively place that attracts a high proportion of single male tourists to its enclaves of girlie bars on Soi Nana Tai, Soi Cowboy and the Clinton Entertainment Plaza. But for the most part it's not a seedy area, and is home to many expats and middle-class Thais.

Although this is not the place to come if you're on a tight budget, Sukhumvit has one exceptional mid-priced guest house; its four- and five-star hotels tend to be oriented towards business travellers, but facilities are good and the downtown views from the high-rise rooms a real plus. The best accommodation here is between and along sois 1 to 21; many of the sois are surprisingly quiet, even leafy, and offer a welcome breather from the congested frenzy of Thanon Sukhumvit itself – transport down the longer sois is provided by motorbike-taxi (*mohtoesai*) drivers who wait at the soi's mouth, clad in numbered waistcoats. Advance reservations are recommended during high season.

Staying here, you're well served by the **Skytrain**, which has stops all the way along Thanon Sukhumvit, while the Sukhumvit **subway** stop at the mouth of Soi 21 (Thanon Asok Montri) makes it easy to get to Hualamphong Station and Chinatown. On the downside, you're a long way from the main Ratanakosin sights, and the volume of traffic on Sukhumvit means that travelling by **bus** across town can take an age – if possible, try to travel to and from Thanon Sukhumvit outside rush hour (7–9am & 3–7pm); it's almost as bad in a taxi, which will often take at least an hour to get to Ratanakosin. Useful buses for getting to Ratanakosin include #508 (air-con) and #25 (ordinary); full details of bus routes are given on p.108. Airport bus A3 from Don Muang stops all the way along Thanon Sukhumvit, as will AE3 from Suvamabhumi (see p.99).

A much faster way of getting across town is to hop on one of the **longtail boats** that ply the canals: Khlong Saen Saeb, which begins near Democracy Monument at Phan Fah in the west of the city, runs parallel with part of Thanon Sukhumvit and has stops at the northern ends of Soi Nana Nua (Soi 3) and Thanon Asok Montri (Soi 21), from where you can either walk down to Thanon Sukhumvit, or take a motorbike taxi. This reduces the journey between Thanon Sukhumvit and the Banglamphu/Ratanakosin area to about thirty minutes; for more details on boat routes, see p.110.

Inexpensive and moderate

The Atlanta At the far southern end of Soi 2 ⓣ 02 252 1650, ⓦ www.theatlantahotel.bizland.com. Classic, old-style, five-storey hotel with lots of colonial-era character and some of the cheapest accommodation on Sukhumvit. However, rooms are simple and some are pretty scruffy, though they are all en suite and some have air-con while others have small balconies. There are two swimming pools, Internet access and a left-luggage facility. The hotel restaurant serves an extensive Thai menu, including lots of vegetarian dishes, and shows classic movies set in Asia. Fan ❹, air-con ❹–❺

Federal Hotel 27 Soi 11 ⓣ 02 253 0175, ⓦ www.federalbangkok.com. Efficiently run, mid-sized, old-style hotel at the far end of Soi 11 so there's a feeling of space and a relatively uncluttered skyline; many rooms look out on the poolside seating area, though the cheapest have no window. All rooms have air-con and cable TV; the upstairs ones are smart and good value and worth paying a little extra for. ❺–❻

Rex Hotel Between sois 32 and 34 (opposite Soi 49), about 300m west from Thong Lo Skytrain station Exit 2 ⓣ 02 259 0106, ⓕ 02 258 6635. The best value accommodation close to the Eastern Bus Terminal (one stop on the BTS), this old-fashioned hotel is comfortable and well maintained and has a pool and a restaurant to complement its sizeable air-con rooms, but is too isolated from the best of Sukhumvit for a longer stay. ❺–❻

Suk 11 Behind the 7–11 store at 1/3 Soi 11 ⓣ 02 253 5927, ⓦ www.suk11.com. One of the most unusual and characterful little hotels in Bangkok, this is also the most backpacker-orientated guest house in the area. The interior of the apparently ordinary apartment-style building has been transformed to resemble a village of traditional wooden houses, accessed by a dimly lit plankway that winds past a variety of guest rooms, terraces and lounging areas. The rooms themselves are simple but comfortable and very clean, they're all air-conditioned and some are en suite. In high season, B250 beds in five-person air-con dorms are also available. It's friendly, well run and thoughtfully appointed, keeps informative noticeboards, provides free breakfast, has wi-fi Internet capability and washing machines, stores left luggage (B20/day), and accepts advance reservations via the website. Shared bathroom ❹, en suite ❺

SV Guest House Soi 19 ⓣ 02 253 1747, ⓕ 02 255 7174. Some of the least expensive beds in the area in this long-running, clean and well maintained guest house. All double rooms have air-con, the cheapest share bathrooms and have no outside window, the best are very good value and have private bathrooms, air-con and cable TV. Shared bathroom ❸, en suite ❹

Expensive

Amari Atrium 1880 Thanon Phetchaburi Mai ⓣ02 718 2000–1, ⓦwww.amari.com. Welcoming, efficiently run and environmentally friendly luxury hotel, earning the government's highest seal of eco-approval. There's a lively range of restaurants and bars, a small but attractive outdoor pool, a well-equipped gym, steam room, sauna and Jacuzzi. Many rooms have been adapted for the disabled and elderly. The hotel's a little out on a limb, but is handy for the subway, boats on Khlong Saen Saeb and TAT's main office, and there's a free shuttle bus to the major shopping centres. ❾

Amari Boulevard Hotel Soi 5 ⓣ02 255 2930, ⓦwww.amari.com. Medium-sized, unpretentious and friendly upmarket tourist hotel. Rooms are comfortably furnished and all enjoy fine views of the Bangkok skyline from their balcony or terrace. There's an attractive rooftop swimming pool and garden terrace which becomes the Thai-food restaurant *Season* in the evenings. ❽

Grand Business Inn 2/4-2/11 Soi 11 ⓣ02 254 7981, ⓦwww.awgroup.com. Good-value mid-range hotel offering 66 large, comfortable, standard-issue air-con rooms, all with bathtubs and cable TV. In a very central location just a few metres from BTS Nana. ❼

J.W. Marriott Hotel Soi 2 ⓣ02 656 7700, ⓦwww.marriotthotels.com. Deluxe hotel, offering comfortable rooms geared towards business travellers, six restaurants (including the *Marriott Cafe*, known for its exceptionally good all-day buffets), a swimming pool, spa and fitness centre. ❾

The Landmark Bangkok Between sois 4 and 6 ⓣ02 254 0404 ⓦwww.landmarkbangkok.com Although many of its customers are business people, *The Landmark*'s welcoming atmosphere also makes it a favourite with tourists and families. Rooms are of a very high standard without being offputtingly plush, facilities include a rooftop pool, squash court and health club, and there's broadband access in every room. ❾

Sheraton Grande Sukhumvit Between sois 12 and 14 ⓣ02 649 8888, ⓦwww.sheratongrandesukhumvit.com. Deluxe accommodation in stylishly understated rooms, all of which offer fine views of the cityscape (the honeymoon suites have their own rooftop plunge pools). Facilities include a gorgeous free-form swimming pool and tropical garden on the ninth floor, a spa with a range of treatment plans, the trendy *Basil* Thai restaurant and the *Living Room* bar, which is famous for its jazz singers. Those aged 17 and under stay for free if sharing adults' room. ❾

Westin Grande Sukhumvit Above Robinson's Department Store, between sois 17 and 19 ⓣ02 651 1000, ⓦwww.westin.com/bangkok. Conveniently located four-star hotel that's aimed at the fashion-conscious business traveller but would suit holidaymakers too. The decor is modish but cheerful, with groovy pale-wood desks, flat-screen TVs and Westin's trademark super-deluxe "heavenly" mattresses. Facilities include several restaurants, a swimming pool, gym and spa, a kids' club and a business centre. Good value for its class. ❾

Zenith Hotel 29 Soi 3 ⓣ02 655 4999, ⓦwww.zenith-hotel.com. Central and reasonably smart if fairly bland upper-mid-range option, where the high-rise rooms are large and sleek (all have air-con and TV) and there's a rooftop swimming pool. ❽

The City

Bangkok is sprawling, chaotic and exhausting: to do it justice and keep your sanity, don't try to do too much in too short a time. The place to start is **Ratanakosin**, the royal island on the east bank of the Chao Phraya, where the city's most important and extravagant sights are to be found. On the edges of this enclave, the area around the landmark **Democracy Monument** includes some interesting and quirky religious architecture, a contrast with the attractions of neighbouring **Chinatown**, whose markets pulsate with the much more aggressive business of making money. Quieter and more European in ambience are the stately buildings of the new royal district of **Dusit**, 2km northeast of Democracy Monument. Very little of old Bangkok remains, but the back canals of **Thonburi**, across the river from Ratanakosin and Chinatown, retain a traditional feel quite at odds with the modern high-rise jungle of **downtown Bangkok**, which has evolved across on the eastern perimeter of the city and can take an hour to reach by bus from Ratanakosin. It's here that you'll find the best shops, bars, restaurants and nightlife, as well as several worthwhile sights. Greater Bangkok now covers an area some 30km in diameter; though unsightly urban development predominates, an expedition to **the outskirts** is made worthwhile by several museums and the city's largest market, **Chatuchak**.

Ratanakosin

When Rama I developed **Ratanakosin** as his new capital in 1782, after the sacking of Ayutthaya and a temporary stay across the river in Thonburi, he paid tribute to its precursor by imitating Ayutthaya's layout and architecture – he even shipped the building materials downstream from the ruins of the old city. Like Ayutthaya, the new capital was sited for protection beside a river and turned into an artificial island by the construction of defensive canals, with a central **Grand Palace** and adjoining royal temple, **Wat Phra Kaeo**, fronted by an open cremation field, **Sanam Luang**; the Wang Na (Palace of the Second King), now doing service as the **National Museum**, was also built at this time. **Wat Pho**, which predates the capital's founding, was further embellished by Rama I's successors, who have consolidated Ratanakosin's pre-eminence by building several grand European-style palaces (now housing government institutions); Wat Mahathat, the most important centre of Buddhist learning in southeast Asia; the National Theatre; the National Gallery; and Thammasat and Silpakorn universities.

Bangkok has expanded eastwards away from the river, leaving the Grand Palace a good 5km from the city's commercial heart, and the royal family have long since moved their residence to Dusit, but Ratanakosin remains the ceremonial centre of the whole kingdom – so much so that it feels as if it might sink into the boggy ground under the weight of its own mighty edifices. The heavy, stately feel is lightened by traditional shophouses and noisy markets along the riverside strip and by **Sanam Luang**, still used for cremations and royal ceremonies, but also functioning as a popular open park and the hub of the modern city's bus system. Despite containing several of the country's main sights, the area is busy enough in its own right not to have become a swarming tourist zone, and strikes a neat balance between liveliness and grandeur.

Ratanakosin is within easy walking distance of Banglamphu, but is best approached from the river, via the **express-boat piers** of Tha Chang (the former bathing place of the royal elephants, which gives access to the Grand Palace) or Tha Thien (for Wat Pho). A **word of warning**: when you're heading for the Grand Palace or Wat Pho, you may well be approached by someone pretending to be a student or an official, who will tell you that the sight is closed when it's not, because they want to lead you on a shopping trip. Although the opening hours of the Grand Palace are sometimes erratic because of state occasions, it's far better to put in a bit of extra legwork and check it out for yourself.

Wat Phra Kaeo and the Grand Palace

Hanging together in a precarious harmony of strangely beautiful colours and shapes, **Wat Phra Kaeo** (Ⓦwww.palaces.thai.net) is the apogee of Thai

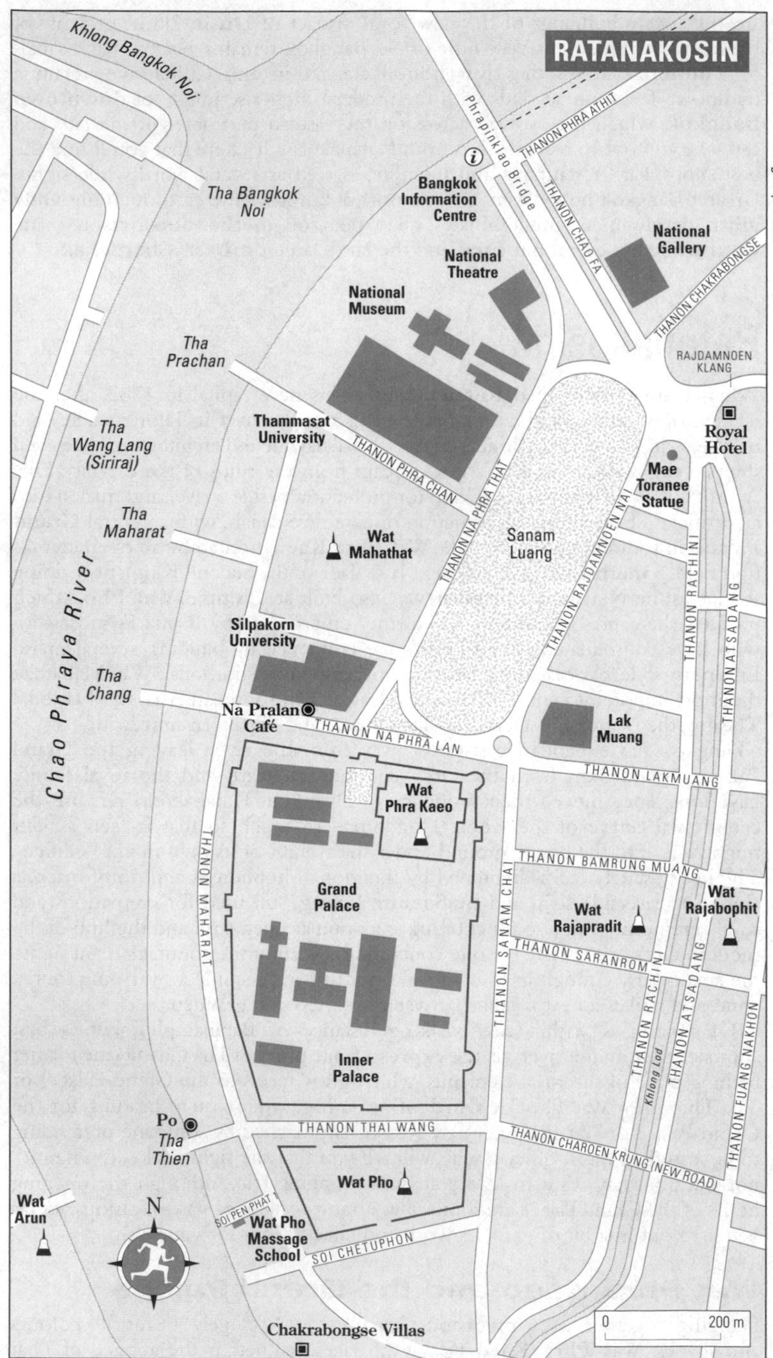
RATANAKOSIN
Khlong Bangkok Noi
Phrapinklao Bridge
THANON PHRA ATHIT
THANON CHAO FA
Banglamphu
Bangkok Information Centre
Tha Bangkok Noi
National Gallery
National Theatre
National Museum
THANON CHAKRABONGSE
RAJDAMNOEN KLANG
Tha Prachan
Royal Hotel
Thammasat University
Tha Wang Lang (Siriraj)
THANON PHRA CHAN
Mae Toranee Statue
THANON NA PHRA THAT
THANON RAJDAMNOEN NAI
Tha Maharat
Wat Mahathat
Sanam Luang
THANON RACHINI
Chao Phraya River
Silpakorn University
THANON ATSADANG
Tha Chang
Na Pralan Café
THANON NA PHRA LAN
Lak Muang
THANON LAKMUANG
Wat Phra Kaeo
THANON MAHARAT
THANON BAMRUNG MUANG
Grand Palace
Wat Rajapradit
Wat Rajabophit
THANON SANAM CHAI
THANON SARANROM
Khlong Lod
THANON FUANG NAKHON
Inner Palace
Po Tha Thien
THANON THAI WANG
THANON CHAROEN KRUNG (NEW ROAD)
Wat Pho
Wat Arun
N
SOI PEN PHAT 1
Wat Pho Massage School
SOI CHETUPHON
0
200 m
Chakrabongse Villas

religious art and the holiest Buddhist site in the country, housing the most important image, the **Emerald Buddha**. Built as the private royal temple, Wat Phra Kaeo occupies the northeast corner of the huge **Grand Palace**, whose official opening in 1785 marked the founding of the new capital and the rebirth of the Thai nation after the Burmese invasion. Successive kings have all left their mark here, and the palace complex now covers 61 acres, though very little apart from the wat is open to tourists.

The only **entrance** to the complex in 2km of crenellated walls is the Gate of Glorious Victory in the middle of the north side, on Thanon Na Phra Lan. This brings you onto a driveway with a tantalizing view of the temple's glittering spires on the left and the dowdy buildings of the Offices of the Royal Household on the right: this is the powerhouse of the kingdom's ceremonial life, providing everything down to chairs and catering, even lending an urn when someone of rank dies (a textile museum under the auspices of the queen is scheduled to open among these buildings, perhaps in 2007). Turn left at the end of the driveway for the ticket office and entrance turnstiles: **admission** to Wat Phra Kaeo and the palace is B250 (daily 8.30am–3.30pm, palace halls and weapons museum closed Sat & Sun; 2hr personal audioguide B200, with passport or credit card as surety), which includes a free brochure and map, as well as admission (within seven days) to the Vimanmek Palace in the Dusit area (see p.165). As it's Thailand's most sacred site, you have to show respect by **dressing in smart clothes** – no vests, shorts, see-through clothes, sarongs, mini-skirts or fisherman's trousers – but if your rucksack won't stretch that far, head for the office to the right just inside the Gate of Glorious Victory, where suitable garments can be provided (free) as long as you leave some identification (passport or driver's licence) as surety or pay a deposit of B100 per item.

Wat Phra Kaeo

Entering the temple is like stepping onto a lavishly detailed stage set, from the immaculate flagstones right up to the gaudy roofs. Although it receives hundreds of foreign sightseers and at least as many Thai pilgrims every day, the temple, which has no monks in residence, maintains an unnervingly sanitized look, as if it were built only yesterday. Its jigsaw of structures can seem complicated at first, but the basic layout is straightforward: the turnstiles in the west wall open onto the back of the bot, which contains the Emerald Buddha; to the left, the upper terrace runs parallel to the north side of the bot, while the whole temple compound is surrounded by arcaded walls, decorated with extraordinary murals of scenes from the *Ramayana* (see box on p.137).

The approach to the bot

Immediately inside the turnstiles, you're confronted by six-metre tall *yaksha*, gaudy demons from the *Ramayana*, who watch over the Emerald Buddha from every gate of the temple and ward off evil spirits. Less threatening is the toothless old codger, cast in bronze and sitting on a plinth by the back wall of the bot, who represents a Hindu hermit credited with inventing yoga and herbal medicine. In front of him is a large grinding stone where previously herbal practitioners could come to grind their ingredients – with enhanced powers, of course. Skirting around the bot, you'll reach its **main entrance** on the eastern side, in front of which stands a cluster of grey **statues**, which have a strong Chinese feel: next to Kuan Im, the Chinese goddess of mercy, are a sturdy pillar topped by a lotus flower, which Bangkok's Chinese community presented to Rama IV during his 27 years as a monk, and two handsome cows which commemorate Rama I's birth in the Year of the Cow. Worshippers make their

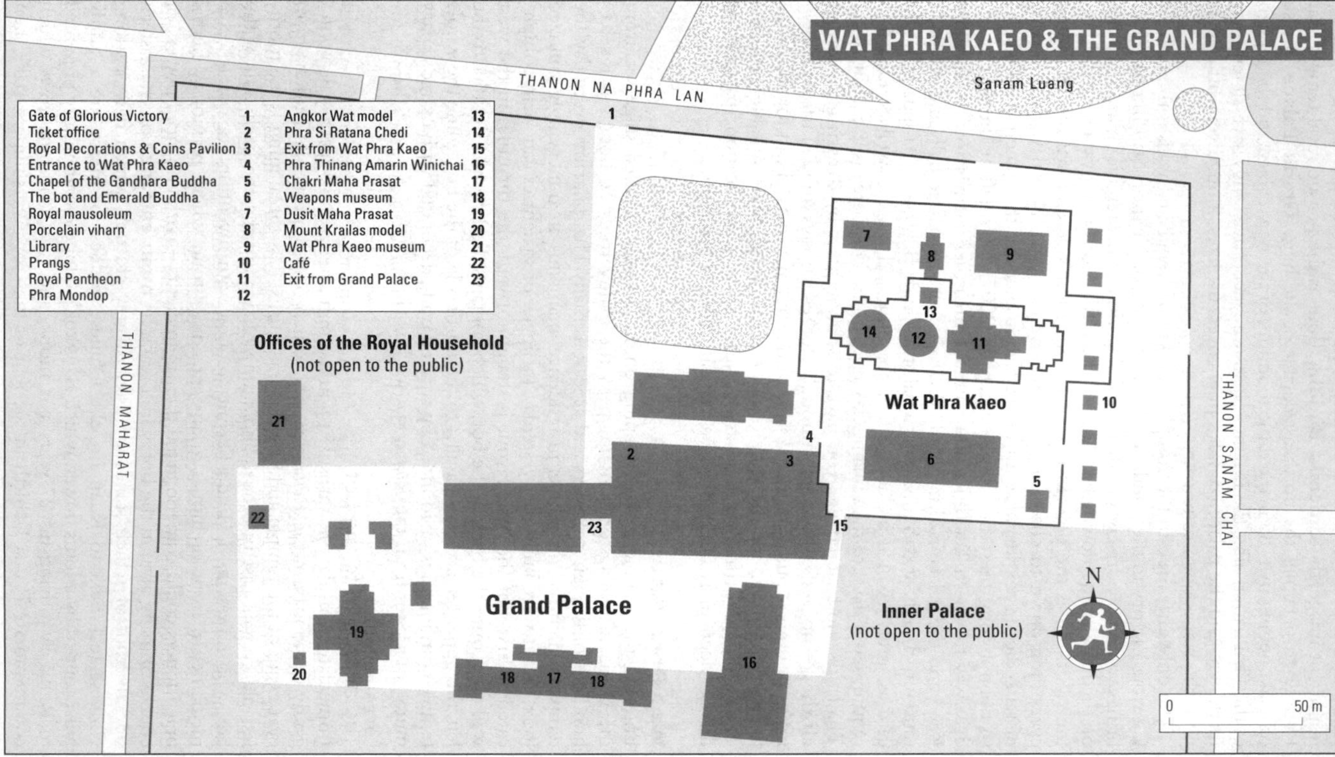
WAT PHRA KAEO & THE GRAND PALACE
Gate of Glorious Victory 1
Ticket office 2
Royal Decorations & Coins Pavilion 3
Entrance to Wat Phra Kaeo 4
Chapel of the Gandhara Buddha 5
The bot and Emerald Buddha 6
Royal mausoleum 7
Porcelain viharn 8
Library 9
Prangs 10
Royal Pantheon 11
Phra Mondop 12
Angkor Wat model 13
Phra Si Ratana Chedi 14
Exit from Wat Phra Kaeo 15
Phra Thinang Amarin Winichai 16
Chakri Maha Prasat 17
Weapons museum 18
Dusit Maha Prasat 19
Mount Krailas model 20
Wat Phra Kaeo museum 21
Café 22
Exit from Grand Palace 23
Tha Chang
THANON NA PHRA LAN
Sanam Luang
THANON MAHARAT
THANON SANAM CHAI
Offices of the Royal Household
(not open to the public)
Wat Phra Kaeo
Grand Palace
Inner Palace
(not open to the public)
N
0
50 m

offerings to the Emerald Buddha in among the statues, where they can look at the image through the open doors of the bot without messing up its pristine interior with candle wax and joss-stick ash.

Nearby, in the southeastern corner of the temple precinct, look out for the beautiful country scenes painted in gold and blue on the doors of the **Chapel of the Gandhara Buddha**, a building which was crucial to the old royal rain-making ritual and which is still used during the Royal Ploughing Ceremony (see p.142). Adorning the roof are thousands of nagas (serpents), symbolizing water; inside the locked chapel, among the paraphernalia used in the ritual, is kept the Gandhara Buddha, a bronze image in the gesture of calling down the rain with its right hand, while cupping the left to catch it. In times of drought the king would order a week-long rainmaking ceremony to be conducted, during which he was bathed regularly and kept away from the opposite sex while Buddhist monks and Hindu Brahmins chanted continuously.

The bot and the Emerald Buddha

The **bot**, the largest building of the temple, is one of the few original structures left at Wat Phra Kaeo, though it has been augmented so often it looks like the work of a wildly inspired child. Eight *sema* stones mark the boundary of the consecrated area around the bot, each sheltering in a psychedelic fairy castle, joined by a low wall decorated with Chinese porcelain tiles, which depict delicate landscapes. The walls of the bot itself, sparkling with gilt and coloured glass, are supported by 112 golden garudas (birdmen) holding nagas, representing the god Indra saving the world by slaying the serpent-cloud that had swallowed up all the water. The symbolism reflects the king's traditional role as a rain maker.

Inside the bot, a nine-metre-high pedestal supports the tiny **Emerald Buddha**, a figure whose mystique draws pilgrims from all over Thailand – as well as politicians accused of corruption, who traditionally come here to publicly swear their innocence. Here especially you must act with respect, sitting with your feet pointing away from the Buddha. The spiritual power of the sixty-centimetre jadeite image derives from its legendary past. Reputed to have been created in Sri Lanka, it was discovered when lightning cracked open an ancient chedi in Chiang Rai in the early fifteenth century. The image was then moved around the north, dispensing miracles wherever it went, before being taken to Laos for two hundred years. As it was believed to bring great fortune to its possessor, the future Rama I snatched it back when he captured Vientiane in 1779, installing it at the heart of his new capital as a talisman for king and country.

The Emerald Buddha has three costumes, one for each season: the crown and ornaments of an Ayutthayan king for the hot season; a gilt monastic robe dotted with blue enamel for the rainy season, when the monks retreat into the temples; and a full-length gold shawl to wrap up in for the cool season. To this day it's the job of the king himself to ceremonially change the Buddha's costumes – though in recent years, due to the present king's age, the Crown Prince has conducted proceedings. (The Buddha was granted a new set of these three costumes in 1997: the old set is now in the Wat Phra Kaeo Museum – see p.138 – while the two costumes of the new set that are not in use are put on display among the blinding glitter of crowns and jewels in the Royal Decorations and Coins Pavilion, which lies between the ticket office and the entrance to Wat Phra Kaeo.) Among the paraphernalia in front of the pedestal is the tiny, black Victory Buddha, which Rama I always carried with him into war for luck. Did it work? Eh?

The upper terrace

The eastern end of the **upper terrace** is taken up with the **Prasat Phra Thep Bidorn**, known as the **Royal Pantheon**, a splendid hash of styles. The pantheon has its roots in the Khmer concept of *devaraja*, or the divinity of kings: inside are bronze and gold statues, precisely life-size, of all the kings since Bangkok became the Thai capital. The building is open only on special occasions, such as Chakri Day (April 6), when the dynasty is commemorated.

From here you get the best view of the **royal mausoleum**, the **porcelain viharn** and the **library** to the north (all of which are closed to the public), and, running along the east side of the temple, a row of eight bullet-like **prangs**, each of which has a different nasty ceramic colour. Described as "monstrous vegetables" by Somerset Maugham, they represent, from north to south, the Buddha, Buddhist scripture, the monkhood, the nunhood, the Buddhas who attained enlightenment but did not preach, previous emperors, the Bodhisattva and the future Buddha.

In the middle of the terrace, dressed in deep-green glass mosaics, the **Phra Mondop** was built by Rama I to house the *Tripitaka*, or Buddhist scripture. It's famous for the mother-of-pearl cabinet and solid-silver mats inside, but is never open. Four tiny **memorials** at each corner of the mondop show the symbols of each of the nine Chakri kings, from the ancient crown representing Rama I to the present king's sun symbol, while the bronze statues surrounding the memorials portray each king's lucky white elephants, labelled by name and pedigree. A contribution of Rama IV, on the north side of the mondop, is a **scale model of Angkor Wat**, the prodigious Cambodian temple, which during his reign (1851–68) was under Thai rule. At the western end of the terrace, you can't miss the golden dazzle of the **Phra Si Ratana Chedi**, which Rama IV erected to enshrine a piece of the Buddha's breastbone.

The murals

Extending for over a kilometre in the arcades that run inside the wat walls, the **murals of the Ramayana** depict every blow of this ancient story of the triumph of good over evil, using the vibrant buildings of the temple itself as backdrops, and setting them off against the subdued colours of richly detailed landscapes. Because of the damaging humidity, none of the original work of Rama I's time survives: maintenance is a never-ending process, so you'll always find an artist working on one of the scenes. The story is told in 178 panels, labelled and numbered in Thai only, starting in the middle of the northern side: in the first episode, a hermit, while out ploughing, finds the baby Sita, the heroine, floating in a gold urn on a lotus leaf and brings her to the city. Panel 109 shows the climax of the story, when Rama, the hero, kills the ten-headed demon Totsagan (Ravana), and the ladies of the enemy city weep at the demon's death. Panel 110 depicts his elaborate funeral procession, and in 113 you can see the funeral fair, with acrobats, sword-jugglers and tightrope-walkers. In between, Sita – Rama's wife – has to walk on fire to prove that she has been faithful during her fourteen years of imprisonment by Totsagan. If you haven't the stamina for the long walk round, you could sneak a look at the end of the story, to the left of the first panel, where Rama holds a victory parade and distributes thankyou gifts.

The palace buildings

The exit in the southwest corner of Wat Phra Kaeo brings you to the palace proper, a vast area of buildings and gardens, of which only the northern edge is on show to the public. Though the king now lives in the Chitrlada Palace in Dusit, the Grand Palace is still used for state receptions and official ceremonies, during which there is no public access to any part of the palace; in addition the

The Ramayana

The **Ramayana** is generally thought to have originated as an oral epic in India, where it appears in numerous dialects. The most famous version is that of the poet Valmiki, who as a tribute to his king drew together the collection of stories over two thousand years ago. From India, the *Ramayana* spread to all the Hindu-influenced countries of South Asia and was passed down through the Khmers to Thailand, where as the **Ramakien** it has become the national epic, acting as an affirmation of the Thai monarchy and its divine Hindu links. As a source of inspiration for literature, painting, sculpture and dance-drama, it has acquired the authority of holy writ, providing Thais with moral and practical lessons, while its appearance in the form of films and comic strips shows its huge popular appeal. The version current in Thailand was composed by a committee of poets sponsored by Rama I, and runs to three thousand pages (available in an abridged English translation by M.L. Manich Jumsai – see p.927).

The central story of the *Ramayana* concerns **Rama** (in Thai, Phra Ram), son of the king of Ayodhya, and his beautiful wife **Sita**, whose hand he wins by lifting and stringing a magic bow. The couple's adventures begin when they are exiled to the forest, along with Rama's good brother, **Lakshaman** (Phra Lak), by the hero's father under the influence of his evil stepmother. Meanwhile, in the city of Lanka (Longka), the demon king **Ravana** (Totsagan) has conceived a passionate desire for Sita and, disguised as a hermit, sets out to kidnap her. By transforming one of his subjects into a beautiful deer, which Rama and Lakshaman go off to hunt, Ravana catches Sita alone and takes her back to Lanka. Rama then wages a long war against the demons of Lanka, into which are woven many battles, spy scenes and diversionary episodes, and eventually kills Ravana and rescues Sita.

The Thai version shows some characteristic differences from the Indian. Hanuman, the loyal monkey king, is given a much more playful role in the *Ramakien*, with the addition of many episodes which display his cunning and talent for mischief, but the major alteration comes at the end of the story, when Phra Ram doubts Sita's faithfulness after rescuing her from Totsagan. In the Indian story, this ends with Sita being swallowed up by the earth so that she doesn't have to suffer Rama's doubts any more; in the *Ramakien* the ending is a happy one, with Phra Ram and Sita living together happily ever after.

weapons museum and the interiors of the Phra Thinang Amarin Winichai and the Dusit Maha Prasat are closed at weekends.

Phra Maha Monthien

Coming out of the temple compound, you'll first of all see to your right a beautiful Chinese gate covered in innumerable tiny porcelain tiles. Extending in a straight line behind the gate is the **Phra Maha Monthien**, which was the grand residential complex of earlier kings.

Only the **Phra Thinang Amarin Winichai**, the main audience hall at the front of the complex, is open to the public. The supreme court in the era of the absolute monarchy, it nowadays serves as the venue for the king's birthday speech; dominating the hall is the *busbok*, an open-sided throne with a spired roof, floating on a boat-shaped base. The rear buildings are still used for the most important part of the elaborate coronation ceremony, and each new king is supposed to spend a night there to show solidarity with his forefathers.

Chakri Maha Prasat and the Inner Palace

Next door you can admire the facade of the "farang with a Thai hat", as the **Chakri Maha Prasat** is nicknamed. Rama V, whose portrait you can see over its entrance, employed an English architect to design a purely Neoclassical residence, but other members of the royal family prevailed on the king to add the three Thai spires. This used to be the site of the elephant stables: the large red tethering posts are still there and the bronze elephants were installed as a reminder. The building displays the emblem of the Chakri dynasty on its gable, which has a trident (*ri*) coming out of a *chak*, a discus with a sharpened rim. The only part of the Chakri Maha Prasat open to the public is the **weapons museum**, which occupies two rooms on the ground floor on either side of the grand main entrance, and houses a forgettable display of hooks, pikes, tridents, guns and cannon.

The **Inner Palace**, which used to be the king's harem (closed to the public), lies behind the gate on the left-hand side of the Chakri Maha Prasat. The harem was a town in itself, with shops, law courts and a police force for the huge all-female population: as well as the current queens, the minor wives and their servants, this was home to the daughters and consorts of former kings, and the daughters of the aristocracy who attended the harem's finishing school. Today, the Inner Palace houses a school of cooking, fruit-carving and other domestic sciences for well-bred young Thais.

Dusit Maha Prasat

On the western side of the courtyard, the delicately proportioned **Dusit Maha Prasat**, an audience hall built by Rama I, epitomizes traditional Thai architecture. Outside, the soaring tiers of its red, gold and green roof culminate in a gilded *mongkut*, a spire shaped like the king's crown, which symbolizes the 33 Buddhist levels of perfection. Each tier of the roof bears a typical *chofa*, a slender, stylized bird's-head finial, and several *hang hong* (swans' tails), which represent three-headed nagas. Inside, you can still see the original throne, the **Phra Ratcha Banlang Pradap Muk**, a masterpiece of mother-of-pearl inlaid work. When a senior member of the royal family dies, the hall is used for the lying-in-state: the body, embalmed and seated in a huge sealed urn, is placed in the west transept, waiting up to two years for an auspicious day to be cremated.

To the right and behind the Dusit Maha Prasat rises a strange model mountain, decorated with fabulous animals and topped by a castle and prang. It represents **Mount Krailas**, a version of Mount Meru, the centre of the Hindu universe, and was built as the site of the royal tonsure ceremony. In former times, Thai children had shaved heads, except for a tuft on the crown, which, between the age of five and eight, was cut in a Hindu initiation rite to welcome adolescence. For the royal children, the rite was an elaborate ceremony that sometimes lasted five days, culminating with the king's cutting of the hair knot. The child was then bathed at the model Krailas, in water representing the original river of the universe flowing down the central mountain.

The Wat Phra Kaeo Museum

In the nineteenth-century Royal Mint in front of the Dusit Maha Prasat – next to a small, basic **café** and an incongruous hair salon – the **Wat Phra Kaeo Museum** houses a mildly interesting collection of artefacts associated with the Emerald Buddha along with architectural elements rescued from the Grand Palace grounds during restoration in the 1980s. Highlights include the bones of various kings' white elephants, and upstairs, the Emerald Buddha's original costumes and two useful scale models of the Grand Palace, one as it is now, the other as it was when first built. Also on the first floor stands the grey stone slab of the Manangasila Seat, where Ramkhamhaeng, the great thirteenth-century king of Sukhothai, is said to have sat and taught his subjects. It was discovered in 1833 by Rama IV during his monkhood and brought to Bangkok, where Rama VI used it as the throne for his coronation.

Wat Pho

Where Wat Phra Kaeo may seem too perfect and shrink-wrapped for some, **Wat Pho** (daily 8.30am–6pm; B20; personal guides available, charging B200/300/400 for 1, 2 or 3 visitors; Ⓦwww.watpho.com), covering twenty acres to the south of the Grand Palace, is lively and shambolic, a complex

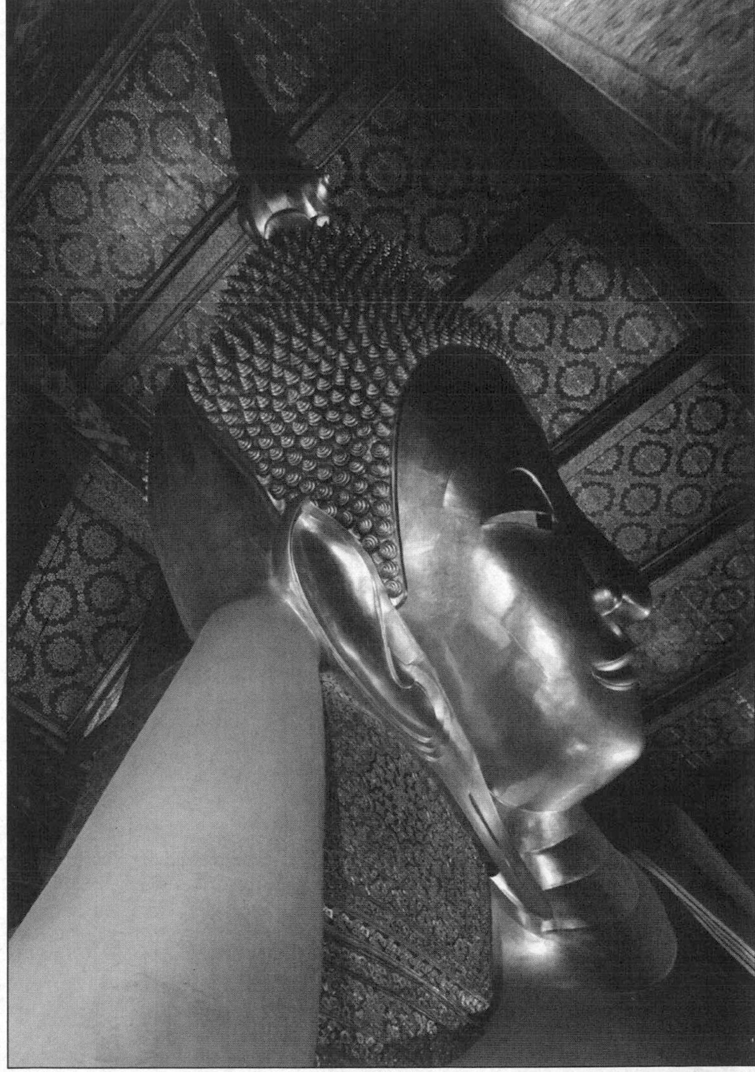

△ The Reclining Buddha, Wat Pho

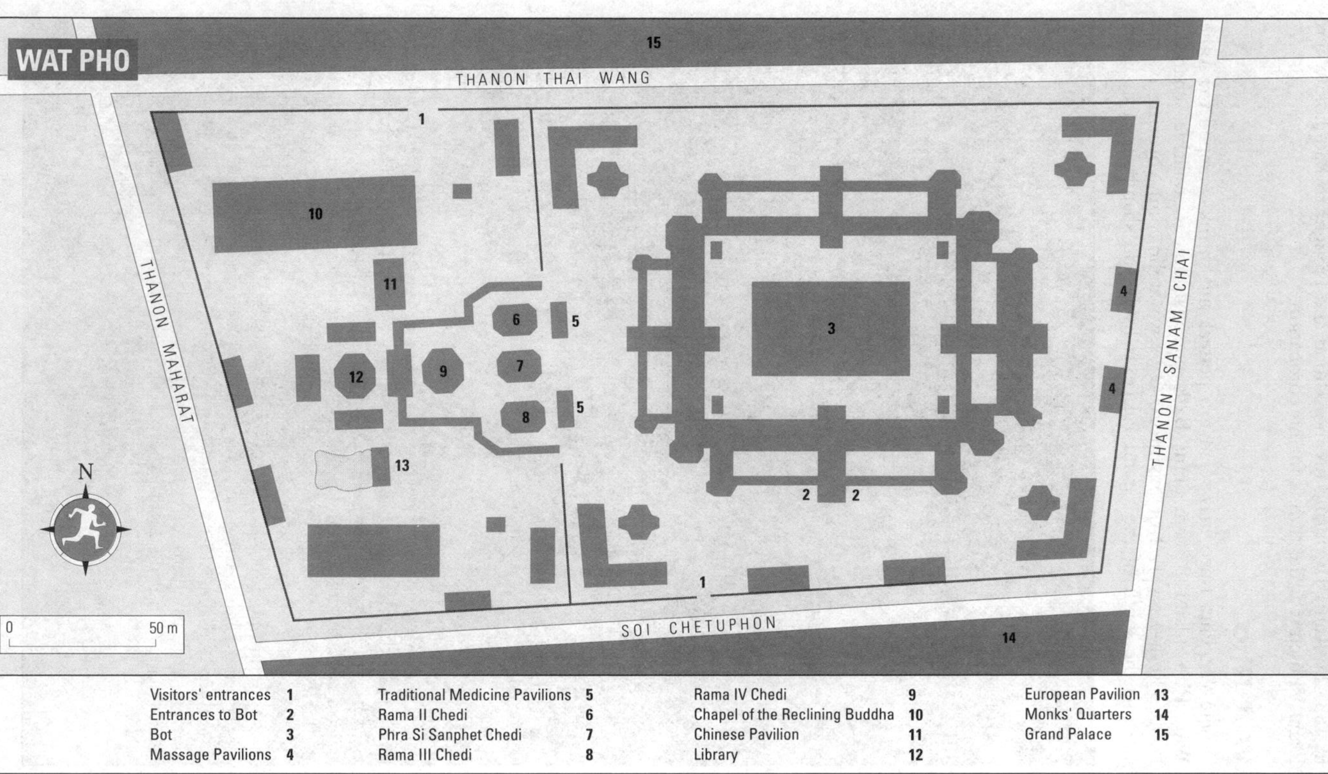
WAT PHO
THANON THAI WANG
THANON MAHARAT
THANON SANAM CHAI
SOI CHETUPHON
Tha Thien
N
0
50 m
1
2
3
4
5
6
7
8
9
10
11
12
13
14
15
Visitors' entrances 1
Entrances to Bot 2
Bot 3
Massage Pavilions 4
Traditional Medicine Pavilions 5
Rama II Chedi 6
Phra Si Sanphet Chedi 7
Rama III Chedi 8
Rama IV Chedi 9
Chapel of the Reclining Buddha 10
Chinese Pavilion 11
Library 12
European Pavilion 13
Monks' Quarters 14
Grand Palace 15

arrangement of lavish structures which jostle with classrooms, basketball courts and a turtle pond. Busloads of tourists shuffle in and out of the **north entrance**, stopping only to gawp at the colossal Reclining Buddha, but you can avoid the worst of the crowds by using the **main entrance** on Soi Chetuphon to explore the huge compound, where you're likely to be approached by friendly young monks wanting to practise their English.

Wat Pho is the oldest temple in Bangkok and older than the city itself, having been founded in the seventeenth century under the name Wat Photaram. Foreigners have stuck to the contraction of this old name, even though Rama I, after enlarging the temple, changed the name in 1801 to Wat Phra Chetuphon, which is how it is generally known to Thais. The temple had another major overhaul in 1832, when Rama III built the chapel of the Reclining Buddha, and turned the temple into a public centre of learning by decorating the walls and pillars with inscriptions and diagrams on subjects such as history, literature, animal husbandry and astrology. Dubbed Thailand's first university, the wat is still an important centre for traditional medicine, notably **Thai massage**, which is used against all kinds of illnesses, from backaches to viruses. Excellent massages are available in the ramshackle buildings on the east side of the main compound; allow two hours for the full works (B300/hr; foot reflexology massage B300/45min). Wat Pho's massage school also conducts thirty-hour training courses in English, over a five- to ten-day period, costing B7000, as well as foot-massage courses for B5500; courses, as well as air-conditioned massages, are held in new premises just outside the temple, at 392/25–28 Soi Pen Phat 1, Thanon Maharat (Ⓣ02 221 3686 or Ⓦwww.watpomassage.com for more information).

The eastern courtyard

The main entrance on Soi Chetuphon is one of a series of sixteen monumental gates around the main compound, each guarded by stone **giants**, many of them comic Westerners in wide-brimmed hats – ships which exported rice to China would bring these statues back as ballast.

The entrance brings you into the eastern half of the main complex, where a courtyard of structures radiates from the bot in a disorientating symmetry. To get to the bot, the principal congregation and ordination hall, turn right and cut through the two surrounding cloisters, which are lined with hundreds of Buddha images. The elegant **bot** has beautiful teak doors decorated with mother-of-pearl, showing stories from the *Ramayana* in minute detail. Look out also for the stone bas-reliefs around the base of the bot, which narrate a longer version of the *Ramayana* in 152 action-packed panels. The plush interior has a well-proportioned altar on which ten statues of disciples frame a graceful, Ayutthayan Buddha image containing the remains of Rama I, the founder of Bangkok (Rama IV placed them there so that the public could worship him at the same time as the Buddha).

Back outside the entrance to the double cloister, keep your eyes open for a miniature mountain covered in statues of naked men in tall hats who appear to be gesturing rudely: they are *rishis* (hermits), demonstrating various positions of healing massage. Skirting the southwestern corner of the cloisters, you'll come to two pavilions between the eastern and western courtyards, which display plaques inscribed with the precepts of traditional medicine, as well as anatomical pictures showing the different pressure points and the illnesses that can be cured by massaging them.

The western courtyard

Among the 99 chedis strewn about the grounds, the four **great chedis** in the western courtyard stand out as much for their covering of garish tiles as for their size. The central chedi is the oldest, erected by Rama I to hold the remains of the most sacred Buddha image of Ayutthaya, the Phra Si Sanphet. Later, Rama III built the chedi to the north for the ashes of Rama II and the chedi to the south to hold his own remains; Rama IV built the fourth, with bright blue tiles, though its purpose is uncertain.

In the northwest corner of the courtyard stands the chapel of the **Reclining Buddha**, a 45-metre-long gilded statue of plaster-covered brick which depicts the Buddha entering Nirvana, a common motif in Buddhist iconography. The chapel is only slightly bigger than the statue – you can't get far enough away to take in anything but a surreal close-up view of the beaming five-metre smile. As for the feet, the vast black soles are beautifully inlaid with delicate mother-of-pearl showing the 108 *lakshanas*, or auspicious signs, which distinguish the true Buddha. Along one side of the statue are 108 bowls which will bring you good luck and a long life if you put a coin in each.

Sanam Luang

Sprawling across thirty acres north of the Grand Palace, **Sanam Luang** is one of the last open spaces left in Bangkok, a bare field where residents of the capital gather in the early evening to meet, eat and play. The nearby pavements are the marketplace for some exotic spiritual salesmen: on the eastern side sit astrologers and palm-readers, and sellers of bizarre virility potions and contraptions; on the western side and spreading around Thammasat University and Wat Mahathat, scores of small-time hawkers sell amulets, taking advantage of the spiritually auspicious location. In the early part of the year, especially in March during the Thai Sports and Kite Festival, the sky is filled with kite-fighting contests (see box below).

As it's in front of the Grand Palace, the field is also the venue for national ceremonies, such as royal funerals and the **Ploughing Ceremony**, held in May at a time selected by astrologers to bring good fortune to the rice harvest. The elaborate Brahmin ceremony is led by an official from the Ministry of

Kite-flying

Flying intricate and colourful **kites** is now done mostly for fun in Thailand, but it has its roots in more serious activities. Filled with gunpowder and fitted with long fuses, kites were deployed in the first Thai kingdom at Sukhothai (1240–1438) as machines of war. In the same era, special *ngao* kites, with heads in the shape of bamboo bows, were used in Brahmin rituals: the string of the bow would vibrate in the wind and make a noise to frighten away evil spirits (nowadays noisy kites are still used, though only by farmers, to scare the birds). By the height of the Ayutthayan period (1351–1767) kites had become largely decorative: royal ceremonies were enhanced by fantastically shaped kites, adorned with jingling bells and ornamental lamps.

In the nineteenth century, Rama V, by his enthusiastic lead, popularized kite-flying as a wholesome and fashionable recreation. **Contests** are now held all over the country between February and April, when winds are strong and farmers traditionally have free time after harvesting the rice. These contests fall into two broad categories: those involving manoeuvrable flat kites, often in the shapes of animals; and those in which the beauty of static display kites is judged. The most popular contest of all, which comes under the first category, matches two teams, one flying star-shaped *chula*s, two-metre-high "male" kites, the other flying the smaller, more agile *pakpao*s, diamond-shaped "females". Each team uses its skill and teamwork to ensnare the other's kites and drag them back across a dividing line.

Agriculture, who stands in for the king in case the royal power were to be reduced by any failure in the ritual. At the designated time, the official cuts a series of circular furrows with a plough drawn by two oxen, and scatters rice that has been sprinkled with lustral water by the Brahmin priests of the court. When the ritual is over, spectators rush in to grab handfuls of the rice, which they then plant in their own paddies for good luck.

The lak muang

At 6.54am on April 21, 1782 – the astrologically determined time for the auspicious founding of Bangkok – a pillar containing the city's horoscope was ceremonially driven into the ground opposite the northeast corner of the Grand Palace. This phallic pillar, the **lak muang** – all Thai cities have one, to provide a home for their guardian spirits – was made from a four-metre tree trunk carved with a lotus-shaped crown, and is now sheltered in an elegant shrine surrounded by immaculate gardens. It shares the shrine with the taller *lak muang* of Thonburi, which was recently incorporated into Greater Bangkok.

Hundreds of worshippers come every day to pray and offer flowers, particularly childless couples seeking the gift of fertility. In one corner of the gardens you can often see short performances of **classical dancing**, paid for by well-off families when they have a piece of good fortune to celebrate.

Wat Mahathat

On Sanam Luang's western side, with its main entrance on Thanon Maharat, **Wat Mahathat** (daily 9am–5pm; free), founded in the eighteenth century, provides a welcome respite from the surrounding tourist hype, and a chance to engage with the eager monks studying at **Mahachulalongkorn Buddhist University** here. As the nation's centre for the Mahanikai monastic sect (where Rama IV spent 24 years as a monk before becoming king in 1851), and housing one of the two Buddhist universities in Bangkok, the wat buzzes with purpose. It's this activity, and the chance of interaction and participation, rather than any special architectural features, which make a visit so rewarding. The many university-attending monks at the wat are friendly and keen to practise their English, and are more than likely to approach you: diverting topics might range from the poetry of Dylan Thomas to English football results gleaned from the BBC World Service.

Situated in Section Five of the wat is its **Vipassana Meditation Centre**, where sitting and walking meditation practice is available in English (daily 7–10am, 1–4pm & 6–8pm; Ⓣ02 222 6011 or 623 5613 or go to Ⓦwww.section-5.org for further information). Participants generally stay in the simple surroundings of the meditation building itself (donation requested), and must wear white clothes (available to rent at the centre) and observe the eight main Buddhist precepts (see p.65). Talks in English on meditation and Buddhism are held here every evening (8–9pm), as well as at the International Buddhist Meditation Centre (Room 106 or 209; Ⓣ02 623 5881, Ⓦwww.mcu.ac.th/ibmc) in the Mahachulalongkorn University building on the second and fourth Saturdays of every month (3–5pm).

The National Museum

Near the northwest corner of Sanam Luang, the **National Museum** (Wed–Sun 9am–4pm; B40 including free leaflet with map; Ⓦwww.thailandmuseum.com) houses a colossal hoard of Thailand's chief artistic riches, ranging from sculptural treasures in the north and south wings, through bizarre decorative objects in the older buildings, to outlandish funeral chariots and the exquisite Buddhaisawan Chapel, as well as occasionally staging worthwhile temporary exhibitions (details on ☎02 224 1333). It's worth making time for the free **guided tours in English** (Wed & Thurs 9.30am): they're generally entertaining and their explication of the choicest exhibits provides a good introduction to Thai religion and culture. By the ticket office are a bookshop and a pleasant, air-conditioned **café**, serving drinks, sandwiches and cakes, while the **restaurant** inside the museum grounds, by the funeral chariots building, dishes up decent, inexpensive Thai food.

The first building you'll come to near the ticket office houses an informative overview of the history of Thailand, including a small archeological gem: a black stone **inscription**, credited to King Ramkhamhaeng of Sukhothai, which became the first capital of the Thai nation (c.1278–99) under his rule. Discovered in 1833 by the future Rama IV, it's the oldest extant inscription using the Thai alphabet. This, combined with the description it records of prosperity and piety in Sukhothai's Golden Age, has made the stone a symbol of Thai nationhood.

The main collection: southern building

At the back of the compound, two large modern buildings, flanking an old converted palace, house the museum's **main collection**, kicking off on the ground floor of the **southern building**. Look out here for some historic sculptures from the rest of Asia, including one of the earliest representations of the Buddha, from Gandhara in northwest India. Alexander the Great left a garrison at Gandhara, which explains why the image is in the style of Classical Greek sculpture: for example, the *ushnisha*, the supernatural bump on the top of the head, which symbolizes the Buddha's intellectual and spiritual power, is rationalized into a bun of thick, wavy hair.

Upstairs, the **prehistory** room displays axe heads and spear points from Ban Chiang in the northeast of Thailand (see p.574), one of the earliest Bronze Age cultures ever discovered. Alongside are many roughly contemporaneous metal artefacts from Kanchanaburi province, as well as some excellent examples of the developments of Ban Chiang's famous pottery. In the adjacent **Dvaravati** room (S7; sixth to eleventh centuries), the pick of the stone and terracotta Buddhas is a small head in smooth, pink clay, whose downcast eyes and faintly smiling full lips typify the serene look of this era. At the far end of the first floor, you can't miss a voluptuous Javanese statue of elephant-headed Ganesh, Hindu god of wisdom and the arts, which, being the symbol of the Fine Arts Department, is always freshly garlanded. As Ganesh is known as the clearer of obstacles, Hindus always worship him before other gods, so by tradition he has grown fat through getting first choice of the offerings – witness his trunk jammed into a bowl of food in this sculpture.

Room S9 next door contains the most famous piece of **Srivijaya** art (seventh to thirteenth centuries), a bronze Bodhisattva Avalokitesvara found at Chaiya (according to Mahayana Buddhism, a *bodhisattva* is a saint who has postponed his passage into Nirvana to help ordinary believers gain enlightenment). With its pouting face and sinuous torso, this image has become the ubiquitous emblem of southern Thailand. The rough chronological order of the collection continues back downstairs with an exhibition of **Khmer** and **Lopburi** sculpture (seventh to fourteenth centuries), most notably some dynamic bronze statuettes and stone lintels. Look out for an elaborate lintel that depicts Vishnu reclining on a dragon in the sea of eternity, dreaming up a new universe after the old one has been annihilated in the Hindu cycle of creation and destruction. Out of his navel comes a lotus, and out of this emerges four-headed Brahma, who will put the dream into practice.

The main collection: northern building

The second half of the survey, in the northern building, begins upstairs with the **Sukhothai** collection (thirteenth to fifteenth centuries), which features some typically elegant and sinuous Buddha images, as well as chunky bronzes of Hindu gods and a wide range of ceramics. The **Lanna** rooms (roughly thirteenth to sixteenth centuries) include a miniature set of golden regalia, among them tiny umbrellas and a cute pair of filigree flip-flops, which would have been enshrined in a chedi. An ungainly but serene Buddha head, carved from grainy, pink sandstone, represents the **Ayutthaya** style of sculpture (fourteenth to eighteenth centuries): the faintest incision of a moustache above the lips betrays the Khmer influences that came to Ayutthaya after its conquest of Angkor. A sumptuous scripture cabinet, showing a cityscape of old Ayutthaya, is a more unusual piece, one of a surviving handful of such carved and painted items of furniture.

Downstairs in the section on **Bangkok** or **Ratanakosin** art (eighteenth century onwards), a stiffly realistic standing bronze brings you full circle. In his zeal for Western naturalism, Rama V had the statue made in the Gandhara style of the earliest Buddha image displayed in the first room of the museum.

The funeral chariots

To the east of the northern building, beyond the café on the left, stands a large garage where the fantastically elaborate **funeral chariots** of the royal family are stored. Pre-eminent among these is the Vejayant Rajarot, built by Rama I in 1785 for carrying the urn at his own funeral. The thirteen-metre-high structure symbolizes heaven on Mount Meru, while the dragons and divinities around the sides – piled in five golden tiers to suggest the flames of the cremation – represent the mythological inhabitants of the mountain's forests. Each weighing around forty tonnes and requiring the pulling power of three hundred men, the teak chariots last had an outing in 1996, for the funeral of the present king's much-revered mother (see p.434).

Wang Na (Palace of the Second King)

The sprawling central building of the compound was originally part of the **Wang Na**, a huge palace stretching across Sanam Luang to Khlong Lod, which housed the "second king", appointed by the reigning monarch as his heir and deputy. When Rama V did away with the office in 1887, he turned the "Palace of the Second King" into a museum, which now contains a fascinating array of Thai *objets d'art*. As you enter (room 5), the display of sumptuous rare gold pieces behind heavy iron bars includes a well-preserved armlet taken from the ruined prang of fifteenth-century Wat Ratburana in Ayutthaya. In adjacent room 6, an intricately carved ivory seat turns out, with gruesome irony, to be a *howdah*, for use on an elephant's back. Among the masks worn by *khon* actors next door (room 7), look out especially for a fierce Hanuman, the white monkey-warrior in the *Ramayana* epic, gleaming with mother-of-pearl.

The huge and varied ceramic collection in room 8 includes some sophisticated pieces from Sukhothai, while the room behind (9) holds a riot of mother-of-pearl items, whose flaming rainbow of colours comes from the shell of the turbo snail from the Gulf of Thailand. It's also worth seeking out the display of richly decorated musical instruments in room 15.

The Buddhaisawan chapel

The second holiest image in Thailand, after the Emerald Buddha, is housed in the **Buddhaisawan chapel**, the vast hall in front of the eastern entrance to the Wang Na. Inside, the fine proportions of the hall, with its ornate coffered ceiling and lacquered window shutters, are enhanced by painted rows of divinities and converted demons, all turned to face the chubby, glowing **Phra Sihing Buddha**, which according to legend was magically created in Sri Lanka and sent to Sukhothai in the thirteenth century. Like the Emerald Buddha, the image was believed to bring good luck to its owner and was frequently snatched from one northern town to another, until Rama I brought it down from Chiang Mai in 1795 and installed it here in the second king's private chapel. Two other images (in Nakhon Si Thammarat and Chiang Mai) now claim to be the authentic Phra Sihing Buddha, but all three are in fact derived from a lost original – this one is in a fifteenth-century Sukhothai style. It's still much loved by ordinary people and at Thai New Year is carried out onto Sanam Luang, where worshippers sprinkle it with water as a merit-making gesture.

The careful detail and rich, soothing colours of the surrounding 200-year-old **murals** are surprisingly well preserved; the bottom row between the windows narrates the life of the Buddha, beginning in the far right-hand corner with his parents' wedding.

Tamnak Daeng

On the south side of the Buddhaisawan chapel, the sumptuous **Tamnak Daeng** (Red House) stands out, a large, airy Ayutthaya-style house made of rare golden teak, surmounted by a multi-tiered roof decorated with carved foliage and swan's-tail finials. Originally part of the private quarters of Princess Sri Sudarak, elder sister of Rama I, it was moved from the Grand Palace to the old palace in Thonburi for Queen Sri Suriyen, wife of Rama II; when her son became second king to Rama IV, he dismantled the edifice again and shipped it here to the Wang Na compound. Inside, it's furnished in the style of the early Bangkok period, with some of the beautiful objects that once belonged to Sri Suriyen, a huge, ornately carved box bed, and the uncommon luxury of an indoor toilet and bathroom.

The National Gallery and Silpakorn University Gallery

If the National Museum hasn't finished you off, two other lesser galleries nearby might. The **National Gallery**, across from the National Theatre on the north side of Sanam Luang at 4 Thanon Chao Fa (Wed–Sun 9am–4pm; B30; ⓣ02 282 2639–40, ⓦwww.thailandmuseum.com), displays in its upstairs gallery some rather beautiful early-twentieth-century temple banners depicting Buddhist subjects, but houses a permanent collection of largely uninspiring and derivative twentieth-century Thai art downstairs. Its temporary exhibitions can be pretty good however. The fine old wooden building that houses the gallery is also worth more than a cursory glance – it used to be the Royal Mint, and is constructed in typical early-twentieth-century style, around a central courtyard.

The **Silpakorn University Gallery** (Mon–Fri 9am–7pm, Sat 10am–4pm; free; ⓣ02 623 6120, ext 1418) on Thanon Na Phra Lan, across the road from the entrance to the Grand Palace, also stages regular exhibitions, by students, teachers and artists-in-residence. The country's first art school, the university was founded in 1943 by Professor Silpa Bhirasri, the much-revered, naturalized Italian sculptor (see p.881).

Banglamphu and the Democracy Monument area

Best known as the site of the travellers' mecca, Thanon Khao San (for more on which, see p.114), the **Banglamphu** district (see map on p.116) also has a couple of noteworthy temples. But the most interesting sights in this part of the city are found to the south and east of **Democracy Monument**, within walking distance of Khao San guest houses and equally accessible from the Grand Palace. If coming from downtown Bangkok, the fastest way to get to this area is by longtail canal boat along Khlong Saen Saeb (see p.110): the Phan Fah terminus for this boat service is right next to the Golden Mount compound. For details on bus and express-boat services to Banglamphu, see p.118.

Wat Chana Songkhram

Sandwiched between Thanon Khao San and the Chao Phraya River at the heart of the Banglamphu backpackers' ghetto stands the lusciously renovated eighteenth-century **Wat Chana Songkhram**. As with temple compounds throughout the country, Wat Chana Songkhram is used for all sorts of neighbourhood activities (including car-parking and football games) and is not at all an ivory tower; in this instance, part of the temple yard has been appropriated by stallholders selling second-hand books and travellers' clothes, making the most of the constant stream of tourists who use the wat as a shortcut between the river and Khao San. It's worth slowing down for a closer look though, as the gables of the bot roof are beautifully ornate, embossed with a golden relief of Vishnu astride Garuda enmeshed in an intricate design of red and blue glass mosaics, and the golden finials are shaped like nagas. Peeking over the compound walls onto the guest houses and bars of Soi Ram Bhuttri are a row of *kuti*, or monks' quarters: elegantly simple wooden cabins on stilts with steeply pitched roofs.

Phra Athit

Thanon **Phra Athit**, the Banglamphu road that runs alongside the (mostly obscured) Chao Phraya River, is known for its arty atmosphere and numerous little bar-restaurants that draw crowds of students from nearby Thammasat University. Many of these places open only in the evenings, but some serve passing tourists during daylight hours. The northern stretch of Thanon Phra Athit is dominated by the crenellated whitewashed tower of **Phra Sumen Fortress** (Phra Sumeru), a renovated corner of the original eighteenth-century city walls that stands beside the river and its juncture with Khlong Banglamphu. The fortress was the northernmost of fourteen octagonal towers built by Rama I in 1783 to protect the royal island of Ratanakosin and originally contained 38 rooms for storing ammunition. (The only other surviving tower, also renovated, is Phra Mahakan Fortress, next to the Golden Mount. Nowadays there's nothing to see inside the Phra Sumen tower, but the area around it has been made into a pleasant grassy riverside recreation area, **Santichaiprakarn Park**, with English-language signs describing the history of the fortifications. A park sign also highlights one of the last remaining lamphu trees (*duabanga grandiflora*) in the area, which continues to grow in a muddy pool on the edge of the river to the left of the royal *sala*; lamphu trees were once so common in this neighbourhood that they gave the area its name: Banglamphu means "the place with lamphu trees", though they've all but disappeared now.

The fort marks the northernmost limit of a **riverside walkway** that runs down to the Bangkok Information Centre at Phra Pinklao Bridge, passing en route the front entrances of two very grand old buildings from the late nineteenth and early twentieth centuries, both of them beautifully restored and currently occupied by international organizations. They show their most elegant faces to the river, as in those days most visitors would have arrived by boat. On the eastern side of Thanon Phra Athit, there's another fine early-twentieth-century mansion, **Baan Phra Athit**, at #201/1; most of this building is now occupied by a private company, but one wing has been turned into the café-bar *Coffee and More*, with views onto the courtyard.

Wat Indraviharn

Located in the northern reaches of the Banglamphu district on Thanon Wisut Kasat, **Wat Indraviharn** (also spelt Wat Intharawihan or Wat In) is famous for the enormous standing Buddha that dominates its precincts. Commissioned by Rama IV in the mid-nineteenth century, the 32-metre-high image is the tallest such representation – depicting the Buddha holding an alms bowl from beneath the folds of his robe – in the world, and is covered all over in gold mirror-mosaic; the topknot enshrines a Buddha relic from Sri Lanka. Though it's hardly the most elegant of statues, the beautifully pedicured foot-long toenails peep out gracefully from beneath devotees' garlands of fragrant jasmine, and you can get reasonable views of the neighbourhood by climbing the stairways of the tower supporting the statue from behind; when unlocked, the doorways in the upper part of the tower give access to the interior of the hollow image, affording vistas from shoulder level. Elsewhere in the wat's compact grounds you'll find the usual amalgam of architectural and spiritual styles, including a Chinese shrine and statues of Ramas IV and V.

Wat Indraviharn is one of an increasing number of favourite hangouts for **con-artists**, and the popular scam here is to offer tourists a tuk-tuk tour of Bangkok for a bargain B20, which invariably features a hard-sell visit to a jewellery shop – see p.210 for more on the famous Bangkok jewellery scam and p.80 for more on con-artists. Avoid all these hassles by hailing a passing metered taxi instead, or move on by **public transport**: Chao Phraya express boat stops N14 and N15 are within reach, and bus #3 runs from Thanon Samsen to Thanon Phra Athit.

Democracy Monument and October 14 Memorial

About 300m southeast of Thanon Khao San and midway along Rajdamnoen Klang, the avenue that connects the Grand Palace and the new royal district of Dusit, looms the imposing **Democracy Monument** (*Anu Sawari Pracha Tippatai*). Designed in 1939 by Italian sculptor Corrado Feroci (who founded Thailand's first Institute of Fine Arts and is often known by his Thai name, Silpa Bhirasri), it was conceived as a testimony to the ideals that fuelled the 1932 revolution and the changeover to a constitutional monarchy, hence its symbolic positioning between the royal residences. It contains a copy of the constitution and its dimensions are also significant: the four wings tower to a height of 24m, the same as the radius of the monument – allusions to June 24, the date the system was changed – and the 75 cannons around the perimeter refer to the year, 2475 BE (1932 AD).

Rajdamnoen Klang and Democracy Monument have long been the rallying point for political demonstrations, including the fateful student-led protests of October 14, 1973, when half a million people gathered here to demand a new constitution and an end to the autocratic regime of the so-called "Three

Tyrants". The October 14 demonstration was savagely repressed: it turned into a bloody riot and culminated in the death of several hundred protesters at the hands of the police and the military. After years of procrastination, the events of this catastrophic day were finally commemorated in 2002 with the erection of the **October 14 Memorial**, a small granite amphitheatre encircling an elegant modern chedi bearing the names of some of the dead; photographs of the demonstration fill the back wall. The memorial stands in front of the former headquarters of Colonel Narong Kittikachorn, one of the Three Tyrants, 200m west of Democracy Monument, at the corner of Rajdamnoen Klang and Thanon Tanao.

The Queen's Gallery

It's an easy stroll from the long-running, rather staid, National Gallery to the newest high-profile art museum in the area, **The Queen's Gallery** (Thurs–Tues 10am–7pm; B20; Ⓦwww.queengallery.org), a privately funded five-storey space on the corner of Rajdamnoen Klang and Thanon Phra Sumen that stages temporary exhibitions of contemporary Thai art, plus the occasional show by foreign artists. Reading rooms on each floor contain a vast selection of artists' monographs, many of them with English-language texts, and the bookshop beside the gallery entrance sells hard-to-find Thai art books.

King Prajadhipok (Rama VII) Museum

Appropriately located just 400m east of Democracy Monument, within the rather elegant European-style walls of an early-twentieth-century shop, the **King Prajadhipok Museum** (Tues–Sun 9am–4pm; B40; Ⓦwww.kpi.ac.th/museum) on Thanon Lan Luang charts the life and achievements of **Rama VII**, the king whose ten-year reign embraced Thailand's 1932 transition from rule by absolute monarchy to rule by democratic constitutional monarchy. Though the museum is hardly an unmissable attraction, the section explaining the background to the 1932 revolution is important, and there's also a miniature replica of one of Thailand's earliest cinemas here, the extant Chalermkrung Theatre in Chinatown, which was commissioned by Rama VII in 1933; the king was a keen amateur film-maker and old films from his era are screened at the museum's cinema twice daily, at 10am and 2pm.

Wat Rajnadda, Loh Prasat and the amulet market

Five minutes' walk southeast of Democracy Monument, at the point where Rajdamnoen Klang meets Thanon Mahachai, stands the assortment of religious buildings known collectively as **Wat Rajnadda**. It's immediately recognizable by the multi-tiered, castle-like structure called **Loh Prasat**, or "Iron Monastery" – a reference to its 37 forbiddingly dark metal spires, which represent the 37 virtues necessary for attaining enlightenment. The only structure of its kind in Bangkok, Loh Prasat is the dominant and most bizarre of Wat Rajnadda's components. Each tier is pierced by passageways running north–south and east–west (fifteen in each direction at ground level), with small meditation cells at each point of intersection. The Sri Lankan monastery on which it is modelled contained a thousand cells; this one probably has half that number.

In the southeast (Thanon Mahachai) corner of the temple compound, Bangkok's biggest amulet market, the **Wat Rajnadda Buddha Center**, comprises at least a hundred stalls selling tiny Buddha images of all designs, materials and prices. Alongside these miniature charms are statues of Hindu deities, dolls and carved wooden phalluses, also bought to placate or ward off disgruntled spirits, as well as love potions and tapes of sacred music. While the amulet market at Wat

Amulets

To gain protection from malevolent spirits and physical misfortune, Thais wear or carry at least one **amulet** at all times. The most popular **images** are copies of sacred statues from famous wats, while others show revered holy men, kings (Rama V is a favourite), healers or a many-armed monk depicted closing his eyes, ears and mouth so as to concentrate better on reaching Nirvana – a human version of the hear-no-evil, see-no-evil, speak-no-evil monkeys. On the reverse side a *yantra* is often inscribed, a combination of letters and figures also designed to ward off evil, sometimes of a very specific nature: protecting your durian orchards from gales, for example, or your tuk-tuk from oncoming traffic. Individually hand-crafted or mass-produced, amulets can be made from bronze, clay, plaster or gold, and some even have sacred ingredients added, such as the ashes of burnt holy texts. But what really determines an amulet's efficacy is its history: where and by whom it was made, who or what it represents and who consecrated it. Monks are often involved in the making of the images and are always called upon to consecrate them – the more charismatic the monk, the more powerful the amulet. Some of the most sought-after amulets are those that have been blessed by the famously influential octogenarian abbot of Wat Ban Rai in Nakhon Ratchasima province, Luang Paw Khoon. The proceeds from the sale of amulets contribute to wat funds and good causes.

The **belief in amulets** is thought to have originated in India, where tiny images were sold to pilgrims who visited the four holy sites associated with the Buddha's birth, enlightenment, first sermon and death. But not all amulets are Buddhist-related – there's a whole range of other enchanted objects to wear for protection, including tigers' teeth, rose quartz, tamarind seeds, coloured threads and miniature phalluses. Worn around the waist rather than the neck, the phallus amulets provide protection for the genitals as well as being associated with fertility, and are of Hindu origin.

For some people, amulets are not only a vital form of spiritual protection, but valuable **collectors' items** as well. Amulet-collecting mania is something akin to stamp collecting – there are at least half a dozen Thai magazines for collectors, which give histories of certain types, tips on distinguishing between genuine items and fakes, and personal accounts of particularly powerful amulet experiences. The most rewarding places to watch the collectors and browse the wares yourself are at Wat Rajnadda Buddha Center (see p.149); along "Amulet Alley" on Trok Mahathat, between Wat Mahathat (see p.142) and the river; and at Chatuchak Weekend Market (see p.179).

Rajnadda is probably the best in Bangkok, you'll find less pricey examples from the streetside vendors who congregate daily along the pavement in front of Wat Mahathat. Prices start as low as B20 and rise into the thousands.

Wat Saket and the Golden Mount

Beautifully illuminated at night, when it seems to float unsupported above the neighbourhood, the gleaming gold chedi across the road from Wat Rajnadda actually sits atop a structure known as the Golden Mount, within the compound of the late-eighteenth-century **Wat Saket**. The main temple was built by Rama I just outside his new city walls to serve as the capital's crematorium and over the next century became the dumping ground for some sixty thousand plague victims, most of whom were too poor to afford funeral pyres and so were left to the vultures.

The **Golden Mount**, or Phu Khao Tong, is a later addition and dates back to the early nineteenth century, when Rama III commissioned a huge chedi to be constructed here on ground that proved too soft to support it. The whole thing collapsed into a hill of rubble, but as Buddhist law states that a religious building can never be destroyed, however tumbledown, so fifty years later Rama V bricked in the debris and crowned it with the more sensibly sized chedi we see today, in which he placed some relics, believed by some to be the Buddha's teeth.

To reach the base of the mount, follow the renovated crenellations of the eighteenth-century Phra Mahakan Fortress and the old city wall, past the small bird and antiques market that operates from one of the recesses. Climbing to the top, you'll pass remnants of the collapsed chedi and plaques commemorating donors to the temple. The **terrace** surrounding the base of the new chedi offers an impressive panorama of landmark roofs: the gleaming gables of Wat Rajnadda and the spikes of neighbouring Loh Prasat immediately to the west, the golden spires of the Grand Palace behind them, and further beyond, the finely proportioned prangs of Wat Arun on the other side of the river.

Wat Saket hosts an enormous annual **temple fair** in the first week of November, when the mount is illuminated with coloured lanterns and the whole compound seethes with funfair rides, food-sellers and travelling performers.

Wat Suthat, Sao Ching Cha and Thanon Bamrung Muang

Located about 700m southwest of the Golden Mount, or a similar distance directly south of Democracy Monument along Thanon Dinso, **Wat Suthat** (daily 9am–9pm; B20) is one of Thailand's six most important temples and contains Bangkok's tallest **viharn**, built in the early nineteenth century to house the meditating figure of **Phra Sri Sakyamuni Buddha**. This eight-metre-high statue was brought all the way down from Sukhothai by river, and now sits on a glittering mosaic dais surrounded with surreal **murals** that depict the last twenty-four lives of the Buddha rather than the more usual ten. The galleries that encircle the viharn contain 156 serenely posed Buddha images, making a nice contrast to the **Chinese statues** dotted around the viharn's courtyard and that of the bot in the adjacent compound, most of which were brought over from China during Rama I's reign, as ballast in rice boats: check out the depictions of gormless Western sailors and the pompous Chinese scholars.

The area just in front of Wat Suthat is dominated by the towering, red-painted teak posts of **Sao Ching Cha**, otherwise known as the **Giant Swing**, once the focal point of a Brahmin ceremony to honour Shiva's annual visit to earth. Teams of two or four young men would stand on the outsized seat (now missing) and swing up to a height of 25m, to grab between their teeth a bag of gold suspended on the end of a bamboo pole. The act of swinging probably symbolized the rising and setting of the sun, though legend also has it that Shiva and his consort Uma were banned from swinging in their heavenly abode because doing so caused cataclysmic floods on earth – prompting Shiva to demand that the practice be continued on earth as a rite to ensure moderate rains and bountiful harvests. Accidents were so common with the terrestrial version that it was outlawed in the 1930s.

The streets leading up to Wat Suthat and Sao Ching Cha are renowned as the best place in the city to buy **religious paraphernalia**, and are well worth a browse even for tourists. **Thanon Bamrung Muang** in particular is lined with shops selling everything a good Buddhist could need, from household offertory tables to temple umbrellas and two-metre Buddha images. They also sell special alms packs for devotees to donate to monks; a typical pack is contained within a (holy saffron-coloured) plastic bucket (which can be used by the monk for washing his robes, or himself), and comprises such daily necessities as soap, toothpaste, soap powder, toilet roll, candles and incense.

Wat Rajabophit

From Wat Suthat, walk south down Thanon Titong for a few hundred metres before turning right (west) onto Thanon Rajabophit, on which stands **Wat Rajabophit** (see map on p.132), one of the city's prettiest temples and another example of Chinese influence. It was built by Rama V and is characteristic of this progressive king in its unusual design, with the rectangular bot and viharn connected by a circular cloister that encloses a chedi. Every external wall in the compound is covered in the pastel shades of Chinese *bencharong* ceramic tiles, creating a stunning overall effect, while the bot interior looks like a tiny banqueting hall, with gilded Gothic vaults and intricate mother-of-pearl doors.

If you now head west towards the Grand Palace from Wat Rajabophit, you'll pass a gold **statue of a pig** as you cross the canal. The cute porcine monument was erected in tribute to one of Rama V's wives, born in the Chinese Year of the Pig. Alternatively, walking in a southerly direction down Thanon Fuang Nakhon to its continuation, Thanon Banmo, will lead you all the way down to the Chao Phraya River and Memorial Bridge, taking in some fine old Chinese shophouses and the exuberant flower and vegetable market, Pak Khlong Talat, along the way (see p.158 for a description of this route).

Chinatown and Pahurat

When the newly crowned Rama I decided to move his capital across to the east bank of the river in 1782, the Chinese community living on the proposed site of his palace was given no choice but to relocate downriver, to the **Sampeng** area. Two hundred years on, **Chinatown** has grown into the country's largest Chinese district, a sprawl of narrow alleyways, temples and shophouses packed between Charoen Krung (New Road) and the river, separated from Ratanakosin by the Indian area of **Pahurat** – famous for its cloth and dressmakers' trimmings – and bordered to the east by Hualamphong train station. Real estate in this part of the city is said to be amongst the most valuable in the country, and there are over a hundred gold and jewellery shops along Thanon Yaowarat alone. For the tourist, Chinatown is chiefly interesting for its markets, shophouses, open-fronted warehouses and remnants of colonial-style architecture, though it also harbours a few noteworthy temples. The following account covers Chinatown's main attractions and most interesting neighbourhoods, sketching a meandering and quite lengthy route which could easily take a whole day to complete on foot. For the most authentic Chinatown experience it's best to come during the week, as some shops and stalls shut at weekends; on weekdays they begin closing around 5pm.

Easiest access is either by **subway** to Hualamphong Station, or by Chao Phraya **express boat** to Tha Rachawongse (Rajawong; N5) at the southern end of Thanon Rajawong, which runs through the centre of Chinatown. This part of the city is also well served by **buses** from downtown Bangkok, as well as from Banglamphu and Ratanakosin (see box on p.108); from Banglamphu either take any Hualamphong-bound bus and then walk from the train station, or catch the non-air-conditioned bus #56, which runs along Thanon Tanao at the end of Thanon Khao San and then goes all the ...wn Mahachai and Chakraphet roads in Chinatown – get off just after ...rry King department store for Sampeng Lane. Coming from down... Bangkok and/or the Skytrain network, either switch to the subway,

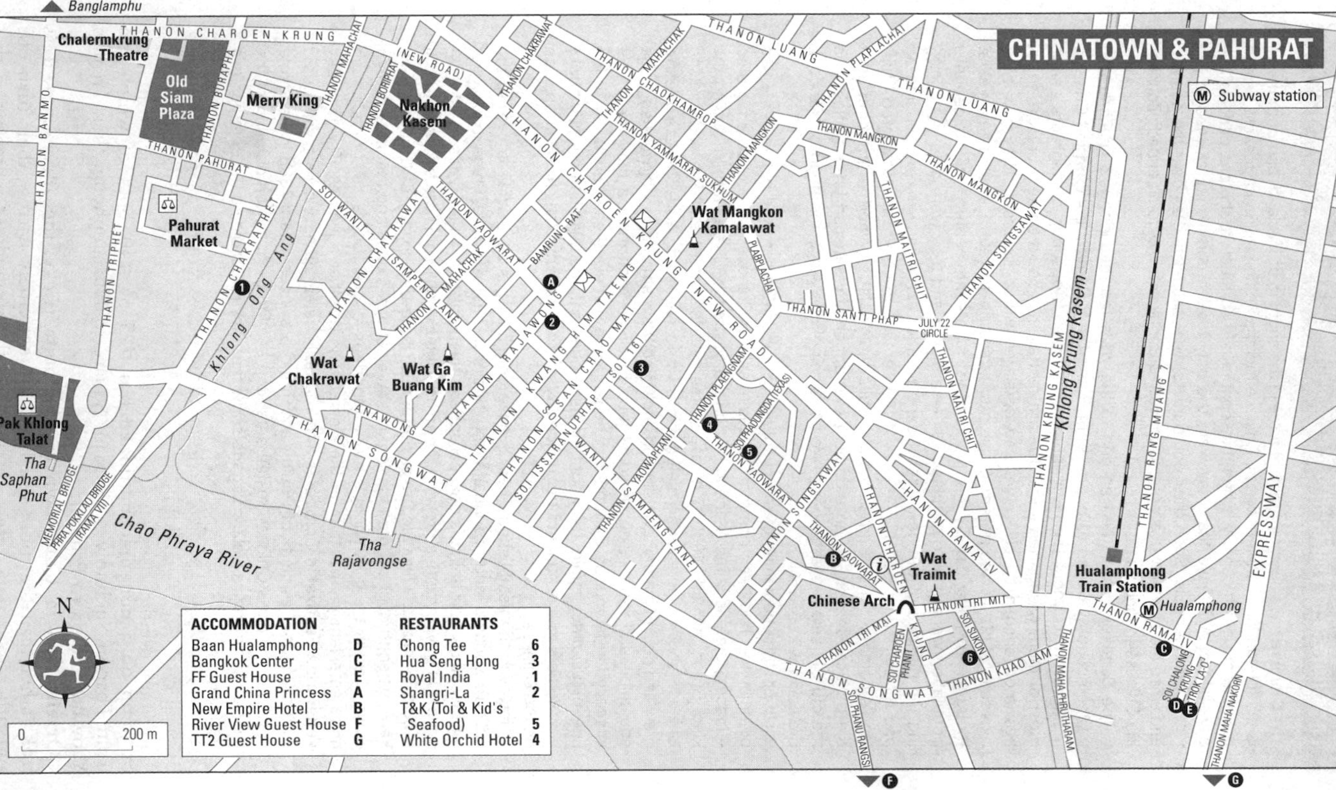
CHINATOWN & PAHURAT
M Subway station
Banglamphu
Chalermkrung Theatre
Old Siam Plaza
Merry King
Nakhon Kasem
Pahurat Market
Pak Khlong Talat
Tha Saphan Phut
Wat Chakrawat
Wat Ga Buang Kim
Wat Mangkon Kamalawat
Wat Traimit
Chinese Arch
Hualamphong Train Station
Hualamphong
Tha Rajavongse
Chao Phraya River
Khlong Ong Ang
Khlong Krung Kasem
EXPRESSWAY
THANON CHAROEN KRUNG
(NEW ROAD)
THANON BANMO
THANON TRIPHET
THANON BURAPHA
THANON PAHURAT
THANON CHAKRAPHET
THANON MAHACHAI
THANON BORIPHAT
THANON CHAKRAWAT
THANON MAHACHAK
THANON CHAOKHAMROP
THANON YAMMARAT SUKHUM
THANON MANGKON
THANON LUANG
THANON PLAPLACHAI
THANON YAOWARAT
THANON CHAKRAWAT
SOI WANIT 1 (SAMPENG LANE)
THANON RAJAWONG
THANON KWANG HIM TAENG
SOI SAN CHAO MAI (SO 16)
SOI ISSARANUPHAP
THANON YAOWAPHANIT
THANON PLAENGNAM
SOI PHADUNGDAO (TEXAS)
THANON SONGSAWAT
THANON SONGWAT
ANAWONG
BAMRUNG RAT
PLABPLACHAI
THANON SANTI PHAP
JULY 22 CIRCLE
THANON MAITRI CHIT
THANON KRUNG KASEM
THANON RONG MUANG 7
THANON RAMA IV
THANON TRI MIT
THANON TRI MAI
SOI CHAROEN PHANIT
SOI SUKON 1
THANON KHAO LAM
THANON MAHA PHRUTHARAM
SOI PHANU RANGSI
SOI CHALONG KRUNG
TROK LA-O
THANON MAHA NAKORN
MEMORIAL BRIDGE
PHRA POKKLAO BRIDGE (RAMA VIII)
N
0 200 m
F
G
ACCOMMODATION
Baan Hualamphong D
Bangkok Center C
FF Guest House E
Grand China Princess A
New Empire Hotel B
River View Guest House F
TT2 Guest House G
RESTAURANTS
Chong Tee 6
Hua Seng Hong 3
Royal India 1
Shangri-La 2
T&K (Toi & Kid's Seafood) 5
White Orchid Hotel 4

The Chinese in Thailand

The **Chinese** have been a dominant force in the shaping of Thailand, and **commerce** is the foundation of their success. Chinese merchants first gained a toehold here in the mid-fourteenth century, when they contributed so much to the prosperity of the city-state of Ayutthaya that they were the only foreign community allowed to live within the city walls. Soon their compatriots were established all over the country, and when the capital was eventually moved to Bangkok it was to an already flourishing Chinese trading post.

The Bangkok era marked an end to the wars that had dogged Thailand and as the economy began to boom, both Rama I and Rama II encouraged Chinese immigration to boost the indigenous workforce. Thousands of migrants came, most of them young men eager to earn money that could be sent back to families impoverished by civil wars and persistently bad harvests. They saw their overseas stints as temporary measures, intending to return after a few years, though many never did. By the middle of the nineteenth century half the capital's population were of pure or mixed Chinese blood, and they were quickly becoming the masters of the new import-export trade, particularly the burgeoning tin and rubber industries. By the end of the century, the Chinese dominated Thailand's commercial and urban sector, while the Thais remained in firm control of the political domain, an arrangement that apparently satisfied both parties – as the old Chinese proverb goes, "We don't mind who holds the head of the cow, providing we can milk it".

Up until the beginning of the twentieth century, **intermarriage** between the two communities had been common, because so few Chinese women had emigrated – indeed, there is some Chinese blood in almost every Thai citizen, including the king. But in the early 1900s Chinese women started to arrive in Thailand, making Chinese society increasingly self-sufficient and enclosed. **Anti-Chinese feeling** grew and discriminatory laws ensued, including the restricting of Chinese-language education and the closing of some jobs to Chinese citizens, a movement that increased in fervour as Communism began to be perceived as a threat. Since the late 1970s, strict immigration controls have been enforced, limiting the number of new settlers to one hundred per nationality per year, a particularly harsh imposition on the Chinese.

However, the established Thai-Chinese community is as crucial as ever to the nation's success and, as wealth and business interests take precedence over military influence within the political sphere, the number of Thai-Chinese business-people in government is growing. The Thai-Chinese still dominate the commercial sector, as can be witnessed over the annual three-day holiday at **Chinese New Year**, when throughout the kingdom nearly all shops, hotels and restaurants shut down. This is the community's most important festival, but is celebrated much more as a family affair than in the Chinatowns of other countries. The nine-day **Vegetarian Festival** in October is a more public celebration, observed with gusto by the Chinese residents of Phuket and Trang provinces (see p.738); in Bangkok, nearly all the city's Chinese restaurants stop serving meat for the duration of the festival, flying special yellow flags to show that they're upholding the community's tradition.

or jump on a non-air-conditioned bus #25 or #40, both of which run from Thanon Sukhumvit, via Siam Square to Hualamphong, then Thanon Yaowarat and on to Pahurat.

Orientation in Chinatown can be quite tricky: the alleys (known as trok rather than the more usual soi) are extremely narrow, their turn-offs and other road signs often obscured by the mounds of merchandise that

△ Chinatown

clutter the sidewalks and the surrounding hordes of buyers and sellers. For a detailed tour of the alleys and markets, use *Nancy Chandler's Map of Bangkok*; alternatively, ask for help at the BTB **tourist information** booth (Mon–Sat 9am–5pm) just northwest of the Chinese Arch on Thanon Yaowarat.

Wat Traimit and the Golden Buddha

Given the confusing layout of the district, it's worth starting your explorations at the eastern edge of Chinatown, just west of Hualamphong train and subway stations, with the triangle of land occupied by **Wat Traimit** (daily 9am–5pm; B20). Cross the khlong beside the station and walk 200m down (signed) Thanon Tri Mit to enter the temple compound. Outwardly unprepossessing, the temple boasts a quite stunning interior feature: the world's largest solid-gold Buddha is housed here, fitting for a community so closely linked with the gold trade, even if the image has nothing to do with China's spiritual heritage. Over 3m tall and weighing five and a half tons, the **Golden Buddha** gleams as if coated in liquid metal, seated amidst candles and surrounded with offerings of lotus buds and incense. A fine example of the curvaceous grace of Sukhothai art, the beautifully proportioned figure is best appreciated by comparing it with the cruder Sukhothai Buddha in the next-door bot, to the east.

Cast in the thirteenth century, the image was brought to Bangkok by Rama III, completely encased in stucco – a common ruse to conceal valuable statues from would-be thieves. The disguise was so good that no one guessed what was underneath until 1955 when the image was accidentally knocked in the process of being moved to Wat Traimit, and the stucco cracked to reveal a patch of gold. The discovery launched a country-wide craze for tapping away at plaster Buddhas in search of hidden precious metals, but Wat Traimit's is still the most valuable – it's valued, by weight alone, at over US$10 million. Sections of the stucco casing are now on display alongside the Golden Buddha.

Sampeng Lane, Soi Issaranuphap and Wat Mangkon Kamalawat

Leaving Wat Traimit by the Charoen Krung/Yaowarat exit (at the back of the temple compound), walk northwest along Thanon Yaowarat, and make a left turn onto Thanon Songsawat, to reach **Sampeng Lane** (also signposted as Soi Wanit 1), an area that used to thrive on opium dens, gambling houses and brothels, but now sticks to a more reputable (if tacky) commercial trade. Stretching southeast–northwest for about 1km, Sampeng Lane is a fun place to browse and shop, unfurling itself like a ramshackle department store selling everything from Chinese silk pyjama pants to computer games at bargain-basement rates. Like goods are more or less gathered in sections, so at the eastern end you'll find mostly cheap jewellery and hair accessories, for example, before passing through stalls specializing in ceramics, Chinese lanterns and shoes, followed by clothes (west of Thanon Rajawong), sarongs and haberdashery.

For a rather more sensual experience, take a right about halfway down Sampeng Lane, into **Soi Issaranuphap** (also signed in places as Soi 16). Packed with people from dawn till dusk, this long, dark alleyway, which also traverses Charoen Krung (New Road), is where you come in search of ginseng roots (essential for good health), quivering fish heads, cubes of cockroach-killer chalk and pungent piles of cinnamon sticks. You'll see Chinese grandfathers discussing business in darkened shops, ancient pharmacists concocting bizarre potions to order, alleys branching off in all directions to gaudy Chinese temples and market squares. Soi Issaranuphap finally ends at the Thanon Plaplachai intersection amid a flurry of shops specializing in paper **funeral art**. Believing that the deceased should be well provided for in their afterlife, Chinese people buy miniature paper replicas of necessities to be burned with the body: especially popular are houses, cars, suits of clothing and, of course, money.

If Soi Issaranuphap epitomizes traditional Chinatown commerce, then **Wat Mangkon Kamalawat** (also known as **Wat Leng Nee Yee** or, in English, "Dragon Flower Temple") stands as a superb example of the community's spiritual practices. Best approached via its dramatic multi-tiered gateway 10m up Thanon Charoen Krung (New Road) from the Soi Issaranuphap junction, Wat Mangkon receives a constant stream of devotees, who come to leave offerings at one or more of the small altars inside this important Mahayana Buddhist temple. As with the Theravada Buddhism espoused by the Thais, Mahayana Buddhism (see "Religion: Thai Buddhism" in Contexts) fuses with other ancient religious beliefs, notably Confucianism and Taoism, and the statues and shrines within Wat Mangkon cover the whole spectrum. Passing through the secondary gateway, under the glazed ceramic gables topped with undulating Chinese dragons, you're greeted by a set of four outsize statues of bearded and rather forbidding sages, each clasping a symbolic object: a parasol, a pagoda, a snake's head and a mandolin. Beyond them, a series of Buddha images swathed in saffron netting occupies the next chamber, a lovely open-sided room of gold paintwork, red-lacquered wood, lattice lanterns and pictorial wall panels inlaid with mother-of-pearl. Elsewhere in the compound are little booths selling devotional paraphernalia, a Chinese medicine stall and a fortune-teller.

Wat Ga Buang Kim and Wat Chakrawat

Less than 100m up Thanon Charoen Krung (New Road) from Wat Mangkon, a left turn into Thanon Rajawong, followed by a right turn into Thanon Anawong and a further right turn into the narrow, two-pronged Soi Krai brings you to the typical neighbourhood temple of **Wat Ga Buang Kim**. Here, as at Thai temples upcountry, local residents socialize in the shade of the tiny, enclosed courtyard and the occasional worshipper drops by to pay homage at the altar. This particular wat is remarkable for its exquisitely ornamented "vegetarian hall", a one-room shrine with altar centre piece framed by intricately carved wooden tableaux – gold-painted miniatures arranged as if in sequence, with recognizable characters reappearing in new positions and in different moods. The hall's outer wall is adorned with small tableaux, too, the area around the doorway at the top of the stairs peopled with finely crafted ceramic figurines drawn from Chinese opera stories. The other building in the wat compound is a stage used for Chinese opera performances.

Back on Anawong, a right turn down Thanon Chakrawat leads to the quite dissimilar **Wat Chakrawat**, home to several long-suffering crocodiles, not to mention monkeys, dogs and chess-playing local residents. **Crocodiles** have lived in the tiny pond behind the bot for about fifty years, ever since one was brought here after being hauled out of the Chao Phraya, where it had been endangering the limbs of bathers. The original crocodile, stuffed, sits in a glass case overlooking the current generation in the pond. Across the other side of the wat compound is a grotto housing two unusual Buddhist relics. The first is a black silhouette on the wall, decorated with squares of gold leaf and believed to be the Buddha's shadow. Nearby, the statue of a fat monk looks on. The story goes that this monk was so good-looking that he was forever being tempted by the attentions of women; the only way he could deter them was to make himself ugly – which he did by gorging himself into obesity.

Pahurat

The ethnic emphasis changes west of Khlong Ong Ang, where **Pahurat** begins, for here, in the small square south of the intersection of Chakraphet and Pahurat roads, is where the capital's sizeable Indian community congregates. Unless you're looking for *bindi* cigarettes or Bollywood VCDs, curiosity-shopping is not as rewarding here as in Chinatown, but if you're interested in buying **fabrics** this is definitely the place; Thanon Pahurat is chock-a-block with cloth merchants specializing in everything from curtain materials, through saree lengths to *lakhon* dance costumes complete with accessories.

Also here, at the Charoen Krung (New Road)/Thanon Triphet intersection, is the **Old Siam Plaza**: its mint-green and cream exterior, resplendent with shutters and balustraded balconies, is redolent of a colonial summer palace, and its airy, three-storey interior is filled with a strange combination of shops selling either upmarket gifts or hi-tech consumer goods. Most rewarding are the half-dozen shops on the ground floor that carry an excellent range of silk from north and northeast Thailand; many of them offer dressmaking services as well. But most of the ground floor is taken up by a permanent food festival and is packed with stalls selling snacks, sweets and sticky desserts. Pahurat is also renowned for its Indian restaurants, and a short stroll along Thanon Chakraphet takes you past a choice selection of curry houses and street vendors.

Pak Khlong Talat

A browse through the 24-hour flower and vegetable market, **Pak Khlong Talat**, is a fine and fitting way to round off a day in Chinatown, though if you're an early riser it's also a great place to come before dawn, when market gardeners from Thonburi boat and truck their freshly picked produce across the Chao Phraya ready for sale to the shopkeepers, restaurateurs and hoteliers. Occupying an ideal position close to the river, the market has been operating from covered halls between the southern ends of Khlong Lod, Thanon Banmo, Thanon Chakraphet and the river bank since the nineteenth century and is the biggest wholesale market in the capital. The flower stalls, selling twenty different varieties of cut orchids and myriad other tropical blooms, spill onto the streets along the riverfront as well and, though prices are lowest in the early morning, you can still get some good bargains here in the afternoon. The riverside end of nearby Thanon Triphet and the area around the base of Memorial Bridge (Saphan Phut) hosts a huge **night bazaar** (nightly 8pm–midnight) that's dominated by cheap and idiosyncratic fashions – and by throngs of teenage fashion victims.

For the most interesting **approach** to the flower market from the Old Siam Plaza, turn west across Thanon Triphet to reach Thanon Banmo, and then follow this road south down towards the Chao Phraya River. As you near the river, notice the facing rows of traditional Chinese shophouses, still in use today, which retain their characteristic (peeling) pastel-painted facades, shutters and stucco curlicues. There's an entrance into the market on your right and just after sundown this southernmost stretch of Thanon Banmo fills with handcarts and vans unloading the most amazing hordes of fresh blooms. The Chao Phraya **express boat** service stops just a few metres from the market at Tha Saphan Phut (N6). Numerous city **buses** stop in front of the market and pier, including the northbound non-air-conditioned #3 and air-conditioned #512, which both run to Banglamphu (see box on p.108).

Thonburi

Bangkok really began across the river from Ratanakosin in the town of **Thonburi**. Devoid of grand ruins and isolated from central Bangkok, it's hard to imagine Thonburi as a former capital of Thailand, but so it was for fifteen years, between the fall of Ayutthaya in 1767 and the establishment of Bangkok in 1782. General Phraya Taksin chose to set up his capital here, strategically near the sea and far from the marauding Burmese, but the story of his brief reign is a chronicle of battles that left little time and few resources to devote to the building of a city worthy of its predecessor. When General Chao Phraya displaced the by now demented Taksin to become Rama I, his first decision as founder of the Chakri dynasty was to move the capital to the more defensible site across the river. It wasn't until 1932 that Thonburi was linked to its replacement by the **Memorial Bridge**, or **Saphan Phut**, built to commemorate the 150th anniversary of the foundation of the Chakri dynasty and of Bangkok, and dedicated to Rama I (or Phra Buddha Yodfa, to give him his official title), whose bronze statue sits at the Bangkok approach. It proved to be such a crucial river-crossing that the bridge has since been supplemented by the adjacent twin-track Saphan Phra Pokklao. Thonburi retained its separate identity for another forty years until, in 1971, it officially became part of Bangkok.

While Thonburi may lack the fine monuments of Thailand's other ancient capitals, it nevertheless contains some of the most traditional parts of Bangkok and makes a pleasant and evocative place to explore, either on foot, by boat or even by bicycle (see box on p.106). As well as the imposing riverside structure of **Wat Arun**, Thonburi is home to the **Royal Barge Museum**, the bizarre anatomical exhibits of the **Siriraj Hospital museums**, and the moderately interesting temples of **Wat Rakhang** and **Wat Prayoon.** In addition, life on this side of the river still revolves around the khlongs: vendors of food and household goods paddle their boats along the canals that crisscross the residential areas, and canalside factories use them to transport their wares to the

△ A Thonburi khlong

Chao Phraya River artery. Venture onto the Thonburi backroads just three or four kilometres west of the river and you find yourself surrounded by market gardens and rural homes, with no hint of the throbbing metropolis across on the other bank. Modern Thonburi, on the other hand, sprawling to each side of Thanon Phra Pinklao, consists of the prosaic line-up of department stores, cinemas, restaurants and markets found all over urbanized Thailand.

Getting to Thonburi is simply a matter of crossing the river – use one of the numerous bridges (Memorial/Phra Pokklao and Phra Pinklao are the most central), take a cross-river ferry, or hop on the express ferry, which makes several stops on the Thonburi bank. Thonburi Station, 850m west of the Tha Bangkok Noi (Railway Station; N11) ferry stop, is the departure point for trains to

Exploring Thonburi by boat

The most popular way to explore the sights of Thonburi is by **boat**, taking in Wat Arun and the Royal Barge Museum, then continuing along Thonburi's network of small canals. The easiest option is to take a fixed-price trip from one of the piers on the Bangkok side of the Chao Phraya, and most of these companies also feature visits to Thonburi's two main **floating markets**, both of which are heavily touristed and rather contrived. **Wat Sai** floating market happens daily from Monday to Friday but is very commercialized, and half of it is land-based anyway, while **Taling Chan** floating market is also fairly manufactured but more fun, though it only operates on Saturdays and Sundays. Taling Chan market is held on Khlong Chak Phra and is easily woven in to a private boat tour as described below; it's held in front of Taling Chan District Office, a couple of kilometres west of Thonburi train station, and can also be reached by taking bus #79 from Democracy Monument/Ratchadamnoen Klang to Khet Taling Chan. Arguably more photogenic, and certainly a lot more genuine, are the individual **floating vendors** who continue to paddle from house-to-house touting anything from hot food to plastic buckets: you've a good chance of seeing some of them in action on almost any private boat tour on any day of the week, particularly in the morning. For an authentic floating-market experience, consider heading out of Bangkok to Amphawa, in Samut Songkhram province, described on p.234.

Fixed-priced trips with The Boat Tour Centre (Ⓣ02 235 3108) at Tha Si Phraya cost B800 per boat for one whistle-stop hour, B1500 for two hours and go either to Wat Sai (for which you need to be at the pier by about 8am; Mon–Fri only), or around the Thonburi canals, taking in Wat Arun and the Royal Barge Museum (can depart any time). The Mitchaopaya Travel Service (Ⓣ02 623 6169), operating out of Tha Chang, offers trips of varying durations that all take in the Royal Barge Museum and Wat Arun: in one hour (B800), you'll go out along Khlong Bangkok Noi and back via Khlong Mon, in ninety minutes (B1000) you'll come back along Khlong Bangkok Yai, while in two hours (B1200) you'll have time to go right down the back canals on the Thonburi side and visit an orchid farm. From Monday to Friday, all of these Mitchaopaya trips stop off at the tiny so-called "Thonburi Floating Market", which even their own staff can't recommend, but on Saturdays and Sundays they take in the much livelier Taling Chan floating market. Real Asia (Ⓣ02 665 6364, Ⓦwww.realasia.net) runs guided full-day walking and boat tours of the Thonburi canals for B1800 per person. For details of dinner cruises down the Chao Phraya River, see p.186.

It's also possible to **organize your own longtail boat trip** around Thonburi from other piers, including Tha Oriental (at the *Oriental Hotel*), the pier at the River City Shopping Centre, Tha Wang Nah, next to the Bangkok Information Centre on Thanon Phra Athit in Banglamphu, and the Tha Phra Athit pier that's across from *Ricky's Coffee Shop* on Thanon Phra Athit (200m south of the N13 Tha Phra Athit express boat pier), but bear the above prices in mind and be prepared for some heavy bargaining. An enjoyable 90-minute loop from Tha Phra Athit, via Khlong Bangkok Noi, Khlong Chak Phra and Khlong Bangkok Yai, should cost B700 for a private two-person trip and will take in a variety of different khlongside residences, temples and itinerant floating vendors, but won't include any stops.

Kanchanaburi, but should not be confused with Thonburi's other even smaller train station, Wongwian Yai (for trains to Samut Sakhon), which is further south. The Southern Bus Terminal is also in Thonburi, at the junction of Thanon Borom Ratchonni and the Nakhon Chaisri Highway, and all public and air-conditioned buses to southern destinations leave from here.

Getting around Thonburi is a bit more complicated: the lack of footbridges over canals means that walking between sights often involves using the heavily trafficked Thanon Arun Amarin, so for these stretches it's more comfortable to hop onto a motorbike taxi, though there is a peaceful riverside walkway between Wat Kanlayanamit and Memorial Bridge. The slower, more convoluted alternative would be to leapfrog your way up or down the river by boat, using the numerous cross-river ferries that sail from small piers all the way down the Thonburi bank to link up with the Chao Phraya express-boat stops on the other side.

Royal Barge Museum

Since the Ayutthaya era, kings of Thailand have been conveyed along their country's waterways in royal barges. For centuries these slender, exquisitely elegant, black-and-gold wooden vessels were used on all important royal outings, and even up until 1967 the current king used to process down the Chao Phraya River to Wat Arun in a flotilla of royal barges at least once a year, on the occasion of Kathin, the annual donation of robes by the laity to the temple at the end of the rainy season. But the 100-year-old boats are becoming quite frail, so such an event is now rare: the last full-scale royal processions were floated in 1999, to mark the king's 72nd birthday, and in 2006 to celebrate his sixtieth year on the throne. A **royal barge procession** along the Chao Phraya is a magnificent event, all the more spectacular because it happens so infrequently. Fifty or more barges fill the width of the river and stretch for almost 1km, drifting slowly to the measured beat of a drum and the hypnotic strains of ancient boating hymns, chanted by over two thousand oarsmen dressed in luscious brocades.

The eight beautifully crafted vessels at the heart of the ceremony are housed in the **Royal Barge Museum** on the north bank of Khlong Bangkok Noi (daily 9am–5pm; B30; Ⓦwww.thailandmuseum.com). Up to 50m long and intricately lacquered and gilded all over, they taper at the prow into imposing mythical figures after a design first used by the kings of Ayutthaya. Rama I had the boats copied and, when those fell into disrepair, Rama VI commissioned the exact reconstructions still in use today. The most important is *Sri Suphanahongse*, which bears the king and queen and is graced by a glittering five-metre-high prow representing the golden swan Hamsa, mount of the Hindu god Brahma. In front of it floats *Anantanagaraj*, fronted by a magnificent seven-headed naga and bearing a Buddha image. The newest addition to the fleet is *Narai Song Suban*, which was commissioned by the current king for his golden jubilee in 1996; it is a copy of the mid-nineteenth-century original and is crowned with a black Vishnu (Narai) astride a garuda figurehead. A display of miniaturized royal barges at the back of the museum recreates the exact formation of a traditional procession.

The museum is a feature of most canal tours but is easily visited on your own. Just take the Chao Phraya **express boat** to Tha Phra Pinklao (N12) or, if coming from Banglamphu, take the cheaper, more frequent cross-river ferry (B3) from under Pinklao bridge, beside the Bangkok Information Centre, to Tha Phra Pinklao across the river, then walk up the road a hundred metres and take the first left down Soi Wat Dusitaram. If coming by **bus** from the Bangkok side (air-con buses #503, #507, #509, #511 and #32 all cross the river here), get off at the first stop on the Thonburi side, which is right beside the mouth of Soi Wat Dusitaram. Signs from Soi Wat Dusitaram lead you through a jumble of walkways and stilt-houses to the museum, about ten minutes' walk away.

Siriraj Hospital Museums

For some bizarre reason, a surprising number of tourists make a point of visiting the **Anatomical Museum** (Mon–Fri 9am–noon & 1–4pm; free; Ⓦwww.si.mahidol.ac.th/eng), one of six small collections of medical curiosities housed in Thonburi's enormous Siriraj teaching hospital. The Anatomical Museum was set up to teach students how to dissect the human body, but its most notorious exhibits are the specimens of conjoined twins kept in jars in a couple of old wooden display cabinets. There is also a picture of the most famous conjoined twins in history, the genuinely Siamese twins, Chang and Eng, who were born just outside Bangkok in Samut Songkhram (see p.231). The collection was established in 1927 and looks very dated in comparison to modern museums; there is almost no information in English. Exit right from the back door of the Anatomical Building and take the first left to find the **Museum of History of Thai Medicine** (Mon–Fri 9am–noon & 1–4pm; free), a potentially more stimulating exhibition whose wax tableaux recreate the traditional medical practices of midwives, masseuses, pharmacists and yogis, though these also have no English-language captions.

Easiest **access** to the hospital is by Chao Phraya express boat to Tha Wang Lang/Siriraj (downstream service; N10) or nearby Tha Phrannok (upstream service; N10). From the piers walk a few metres up Thanon Phrannok and enter the hospital via its side entrance. Follow the road through the hospital compound for about 350m, turn left just before the (signed) Museum of History of Thai Medicine, and the Anatomical Museum is the first building on your left.

Wat Rakhang

The charming riverside temple of **Wat Rakhang** (Temple of the Bells) gets its name from the five large bells donated by King Rama I and is notable for the hundreds of smaller chimes that tinkle away under the eaves of the main bot and, more accessibly, in the temple courtyard, where devotees come to strike them and hope for a run of good luck. To be extra certain of having wishes granted, visitors sometimes also buy turtles from the temple stalls outside and release them into the Chao Phraya River below. Behind the bot stands an attractive eighteenth-century wooden *ho trai* (scripture library) that still boasts some original murals on the wooden panels inside, as well as exquisitely renovated gold-leaf paintwork on the window shutters and pillars. A cross-river **ferry** shuttles between Wat Rakhang's pier and the Tha Chang (Grand Palace) express-boat pier, or you can **walk** to Wat Rakhang in five minutes from the Tha Wang Lang/Siriraj and Phrannok express-boat piers: turn south (left) through the Phrannok pierside market and continue until you reach the temple, passing the posh *Supatra River House* restaurant (see p.201), the tiny *Ibrik Resort by the River* boutique hotel (see p.122), and Patravadi Theatre on the way.

Wat Arun

Almost directly across the river from Wat Pho rises the enormous, five-spired prang of **Wat Arun** (daily 7am–5pm; B20; Ⓦwww.watarun.org), the Temple of Dawn, probably Bangkok's most memorable landmark and familiar as the silhouette used in the TAT logo. It looks particularly impressive from the river as you head downstream from the Grand Palace towards the *Oriental Hotel*, but is ornate enough to be well worth stopping off for a closer look. All boat tours include half an hour here, but Wat Arun is also easily visited by yourself, although tour operators will try to persuade you otherwise: just take a B3 cross-river ferry from the pier adjacent to the Chao Phraya express-boat pier at Tha Thien.

A wat has occupied this site since the Ayutthaya period, but only in 1768 did it become known as the Temple of Dawn – when General Phraya Taksin reputedly reached his new capital at the break of day. The temple served as his royal chapel and housed the recaptured Emerald Buddha for several years until the image was moved to Wat Phra Kaeo in 1785. Despite losing its special status after the relocation, Wat Arun continued to be revered and its corncob prang was reconstructed and enlarged to its present height of 81m by Rama II and Rama III.

The prang that you see today is classic Ayutthayan style, built as a representation of Mount Meru, the home of the gods in Khmer cosmology. Climbing the two tiers of the square base that supports the **central prang**, you not only enjoy a good view of the river and beyond, but also get a chance to examine the tower's distinctive decorations. Both this main prang and the four minor ones that encircle it are studded all over with bits of broken porcelain, ceramic shards and tiny bowls that have been fashioned into an amazing array of polychromatic flowers. The statues of mythical *yaksha* demons and half-bird, half-human *kinnari* that support the different levels are similarly decorated. The crockery probably came from China, possibly from commercial shipments that were damaged at sea, but whatever its provenance, the overall effect is highly decorative and far more subtle than the dazzling glass mosaics that clad most wat buildings. On the first terrace, the mondops at each cardinal point contain statues of the Buddha at the most important stages of his life: at birth (north), in meditation (east), preaching his first sermon (south) and entering Nirvana (west). The second platform surrounds the base of the prang proper, whose closed entranceways are guarded by four statues of the Hindu god Indra on his three-headed elephant Erawan. In the niches of the smaller prangs stand statues of Phra Pai, the god of the wind, on horseback.

Santa Cruz and Wat Prayoon

About 700m downstream of Wat Arun, the bot at **Wat Kanlayanamit** stands very tall in order to accommodate its 15-metre-high nineteenth-century seated Buddha image, the largest in Bangkok, but is chiefly of interest because it marks the start of the riverside walkway to Memorial Bridge. En route, you'll pass the distinctive pastel facade and pretty stained-glass windows of **Santa Cruz** (also known as **Wat Kudi Jeen**), a Catholic church that sits at the heart of what used to be Thonburi's Portuguese quarter. The Portuguese came to Thailand both to trade and to proselytize, and by 1856 had established the largest of the European communities in Bangkok: four thousand Portuguese Christians lived in and around Thonburi at this time, about one percent of the total population. The Portuguese ghetto is a thing of the distant past, but plenty of local residents still have Portuguese blood in them and the church and its adjacent school continue to be well attended.

The walkway stops at the base of Memorial Bridge, where cross-river ferries shuttle back and forth to Tha Saphan Phut (N6) across the water. Before leaving Thonburi, however, it's worth stopping off at nearby **Wat Prayoon** (officially Wat Prayurawongsawat) for a wander around the temple's **Khao Mor cemetery**, which is located in a separate compound to the southeast side of the wat, just off Thanon Pracha Thipok, three minutes' walk from the bridge. The cemetery's unusual collection of miniature chedis and shrines are set on an artificial hill, which was constructed on a whim of Rama III's, after he'd noticed the pleasing shapes made by dripping candle wax. Wedged in among the grottoes, caverns and ledges of this uneven mass are numerous shrines to departed devotees, forming a phenomenal gallery of different styles, from traditional Thai chedis, bots or prangs to such obviously foreign designs as the tiny Wild West house complete with cactuses at the front door. Turtles fill the pond surrounding the mound – you can feed them with the bags of banana and papaya sold nearby. At the edge of the pond stands a memorial to the unfortunate few who lost their lives when one of the saluting cannons exploded at the temple's dedication ceremony in 1836.

Dusit

Connected to Ratanakosin via the boulevards of Rajdamnoen Klang and Rajdamnoen Nok, the spacious, leafy area known as **Dusit** has been a royal district since the reign of Rama V, King Chulalongkorn (1860–1910). The first Thai monarch to visit Europe, Rama V returned with radical plans for the modernization of his capital, the fruits of which are most visible in Dusit: notably at **Vimanmek Palace** and **Wat Benjamabophit**, the so-called "Marble Temple". Even now, Rama V still commands a loyal following and his statue, which stands at the Thanon U-Thong-Thanon Sri Ayutthaya crossroads, is presented with offerings every week and is also the focus of celebrations on Chulalongkorn Day (Oct 23). Today, the peaceful Dusit area retains its European feel, and much of the country's decision-making goes on behind the high fences and impressive facades along its tree-lined avenues: the building that houses the National Parliament is here, as is Government House (used mainly for official functions), and the King's official residence, Chitrlada Palace, occupies the eastern edge of the area. On December 2 Dusit is also the venue for the spectacular annual **Trooping the Colour**, when hundreds of magnificently uniformed Royal Guards demonstrate their allegiance to the king by parading around Suan Amporn, across the road from the Rama V statue. Across from Chitrlada Palace, **Dusit Zoo** makes a pleasant enough place to take the kids.

From Banglamphu, you can get to Dusit by taking the #70 **bus** from Rajdamnoen Klang and getting off outside the zoo and Elephant Museum on Thanon U-Thong, or the #56 from Thanon Phra Athit or Thanon Phra Sumen and alighting at the Thanon Ratchasima entrance to Vimanmek Palace (see box on p.1118); alternatively, take the **express boat** to Tha Thewes and then walk. From downtown Bangkok, easiest access is by bus from the Skytrain and subway stops at Victory Monument; there are many services from here, including air-con #510 and #16, both of which run all the way along Thanon Rajwithi.

△ Receiving alms at Wat Benjamabophit

Vimanmek Palace and the Royal Elephant National Museum

Breezy, elegant **Vimanmek Palace** (daily 9.30am–4pm; compulsory free guided tours every 30min, last tour 3.15pm; B100, or free with a Grand Palace ticket, which remains valid for one week; Ⓦwww.palaces.thai.net) was built by Rama V as a summer retreat on Ko Si Chang, from where it was transported bit by bit in 1901. The ticket price also covers entry to a dozen other specialist collections in the palace grounds, including the Support Museum and Elephant Museum. All visitors are treated to free performances of traditional Thai dance daily at 10.30am and 2pm. Note that the same **dress rules** apply here as to the Grand Palace (see p.133). The main **entrance** to the extensive Vimanmek Palace compound is on Thanon Rajwithi, but there are also ticket gates on Thanon Ratchasima, and opposite Dusit Zoo on Thanon U-Thong.

Vimanmek Palace

Built almost entirely of golden teak without a single nail, the coffee-coloured, L-shaped Vimanmek Palace is encircled by delicate latticework verandas that look out onto well-kept lawns, flower gardens and lotus ponds. Not surprisingly, this "Celestial Residence" soon became Rama V's favourite palace, and he and his enormous retinue of officials, concubines and children stayed here for lengthy periods between 1902 and 1906. All of Vimanmek's 81 rooms were out of bounds to male visitors, except for the king's own apartments in the octagonal tower, which were entered by a separate staircase.

On display inside is Rama V's collection of artefacts from all over the world, including *bencharong* ceramics, European furniture and bejewelled Thai betel-nut sets. Considered progressive in his day, Rama V introduced many new-fangled ideas to Thailand: the country's first indoor bathroom is here, as is the earliest typewriter with Thai characters, and some of the first portrait paintings – portraiture had until then been seen as a way of stealing part of the sitter's soul.

The Support Museum

Elsewhere in the Vimanmek grounds a dozen handsome, pastel-painted royal residences have been converted into tiny, specialist interest museums, including collections of antique textiles, photographs taken by the King, royal ceremonial paraphernalia and antique clocks. The most interesting of these is the **Support Museum Abhisek Dusit Throne Hall**, which is housed in another very pretty building, formerly used for meetings and banquets, immediately behind (to the east of) Vimanmek. The Support Museum showcases the exquisite handicrafts produced under Queen Sirikit's charity project, Support, which works to revitalize traditional Thai arts and crafts. Outstanding exhibits include a collection of handbags, baskets and pots woven from the *lipao* fern that grows wild in southern Thailand; jewellery and figurines inlaid with the iridescent wings of beetles; gold and silver nielloware; and lengths of intricately woven silk from the northeast.

Chang Ton Royal Elephant National Museum

Just behind (to the east of) the Support Museum, inside the Thanon U-Thong entrance to the Vimanmek compound, stand two whitewashed buildings that once served as the stables for the king's white elephants. Now that the sacred pachyderms have been relocated, the stables have been turned into the **Royal Elephant National Museum** (Ⓦwww.thailandmuseum.com). Inside you'll find some interesting pieces of elephant paraphernalia, including sacred ropes,

The royal white elephants

In Thailand the most revered of all elephants are the so-called **white elephants** – actually tawny brown albinos – which are considered so sacred that they all, whether wild or captive, belong to the king by law. Their special status originates from Buddhist mythology, which tells how the previously barren Queen Maya became pregnant with the future Buddha after dreaming one night that a white elephant had entered her womb. The thirteenth-century King Ramkhamhaeng of Sukhothai adopted the beast as a symbol of the great and the divine, and ever since, a Thai king's greatness is said to be measured by the number of white elephants he owns. The present king, Rama IX, has twelve, the largest royal collection to date.

Before an elephant can be granted official "white elephant" status, it has to pass a stringent assessment of its physical and behavioural **characteristics**. Key qualities include a paleness of seven crucial areas – eyes, nails, palate, hair, outer edges of the ears, tail and testicles – and an all-round genteel demeanour, manifested, for instance, in the way in which it cleans its food before eating, or in a tendency to sleep in a kneeling position. The most recent addition to King Bhumibol's stables was first spotted in Lampang in 1992, but experts from the Royal Household had to spend a year watching its every move before it was finally given the all-clear. Tradition holds that an elaborate ceremony should take place every time a new white elephant is presented to the king: the animal is paraded with great pomp from its place of capture to Dusit, where it's anointed with holy water in front of an audience of the kingdom's most important priests and dignitaries, before being housed in the royal stables. Recently though, the king has decreed that as a cost-cutting measure there should be no more ceremonies for new acquisitions, and only one of the royal white elephants is now kept inside the royal palace; the others live in less luxurious rural accommodation.

The expression "white elephant" probably derives from the legend that the kings used to present certain enemies with one of these exotic creatures. The animal required expensive attention but, being royal, could not be put to work in order to pay for its upkeep. The recipient thus went bust trying to keep it.

mahouts' amulets and magic formulae, as well as photos of the all-important ceremony in which a white elephant is granted royal status (see above).

Dusit Zoo (Khao Din)

Across Thanon U-Thong from the Elephant Museum is the side entrance into **Dusit Zoo**, also known as **Khao Din** (daily 8am–6pm; B30, children B5), which was once part of the Chitrlada Palace gardens, but is now a public park; the main entrance is on Thanon Rajwithi, and there's a third gate on Thanon Rama V, within walking distance of Wat Benjamabophit. All the usual suspects are here in the zoo, including big cats, elephants, orang-utans, chimpanzees and a reptile house, but the enclosures are pretty basic. However, it's a reasonable place for kids to let off steam, with plenty of shade, a full complement of English-language signs, a lake with pedalos and lots of foodstalls.

Wat Benjamabophit

Wat Benjamabophit (aka Wat Bencha; daily 7am–5pm; B20) is the last major temple to have been built in Bangkok. It's an interesting fusion of classical Thai and nineteenth-century European design, with its Carrara marble walls – hence the touristic tag "The Marble Temple" – complemented by the bot's unusual stained-glass windows, Victorian in style but depicting figures from

Thai mythology. Inside, a fine replica of the highly revered Phra Buddha Chinnarat image of Phitsanulok presides over the small room containing Rama V's ashes. The courtyard behind the bot houses a gallery of Buddha images from all over Asia, set up by Rama V as an overview of different representations of the Buddha.

Wat Benjamabophit is one of the best temples in Bangkok to see religious **festivals** and rituals. Whereas monks elsewhere tend to go out on the streets every morning in search of alms, at the Marble Temple the ritual is reversed, and merit-makers come to them. Between about 6 and 7.30am, the monks line up on Thanon Nakhon Pathom, their bowls ready to receive donations of curry and rice, lotus buds, incense, even toilet paper and Coca-Cola; the demure row of saffron-robed monks is a sight that's well worth getting up early for. The evening candlelight processions around the bot during the Buddhist festivals of Maha Puja (in Feb) and Visakha Puja (in May) are among the most entrancing in the country.

Wat Benjamabophit is just a two-hundred-metre walk south of the zoo's Thanon Rama V entrance, or about 600m from Vimanmek's U-Thong gate. Coming by bus #70 from Banglamphu, get off at the crossroads in front of the Rama V statue and walk east along Thanon Sri Ayutthaya.

Downtown Bangkok

Extending east from the rail line and south to Thanon Sathorn, **downtown Bangkok** is central to the colossal expanse of Bangkok as a whole, but rather peripheral in a sightseer's perception of the city. This is where you'll find the main financial district, around Thanon Silom, and the chief shopping centres, around Siam Square and Thanon Ploenchit, in addition to the smart hotels and restaurants, the embassies and airline offices. Scattered widely across the downtown area are four attractive museums housed in traditional teak buildings: **Jim Thompson's House**, the **Ban Kamthieng**, the **Suan Pakkad Palace Museum** and **M.R. Kukrit's Heritage Home**. Downtown's other tourist attractions are far more diverse: **Siam Ocean World**, a hi-tech aquarium that both kids and adults can enjoy; the noisy and glittering **Erawan Shrine**; and the Art Nouveau **Phya Thai Palace**, a quirky, half-restored royal dwelling. The infamous **Patpong** district hardly shines as a tourist sight, yet, lamentably, its sex bars still provide a huge draw for foreign men.

If you're heading downtown from Banglamphu, allow at least an hour to get to any of the places mentioned here by **bus**. Depending on the time of day, it may be quicker to take an **express boat** downriver, and then change onto the **Skytrain**. It might also be worth considering the regular **longtails** on Khlong Saen Saeb, which runs parallel to Thanon Phetchaburi. They start at the Golden Mount, near Democracy Monument, and have useful stops at Saphan Hua Chang on Thanon Phrayathai (for Jim Thompson's House) and Pratunam (for the Erawan Shrine).

Siam Square to Thanon Sukhumvit

Though **Siam Square** has just about everything to satisfy the Thai consumer boom – big shopping centres, Western fast-food restaurants, cinemas – don't come looking for an elegant commercial piazza: the "square" is in fact a grid of small streets on the south side of Thanon Rama I, between Thanon Phrayathai and Thanon Henri Dunant, and the name is applied freely to the surrounding area.

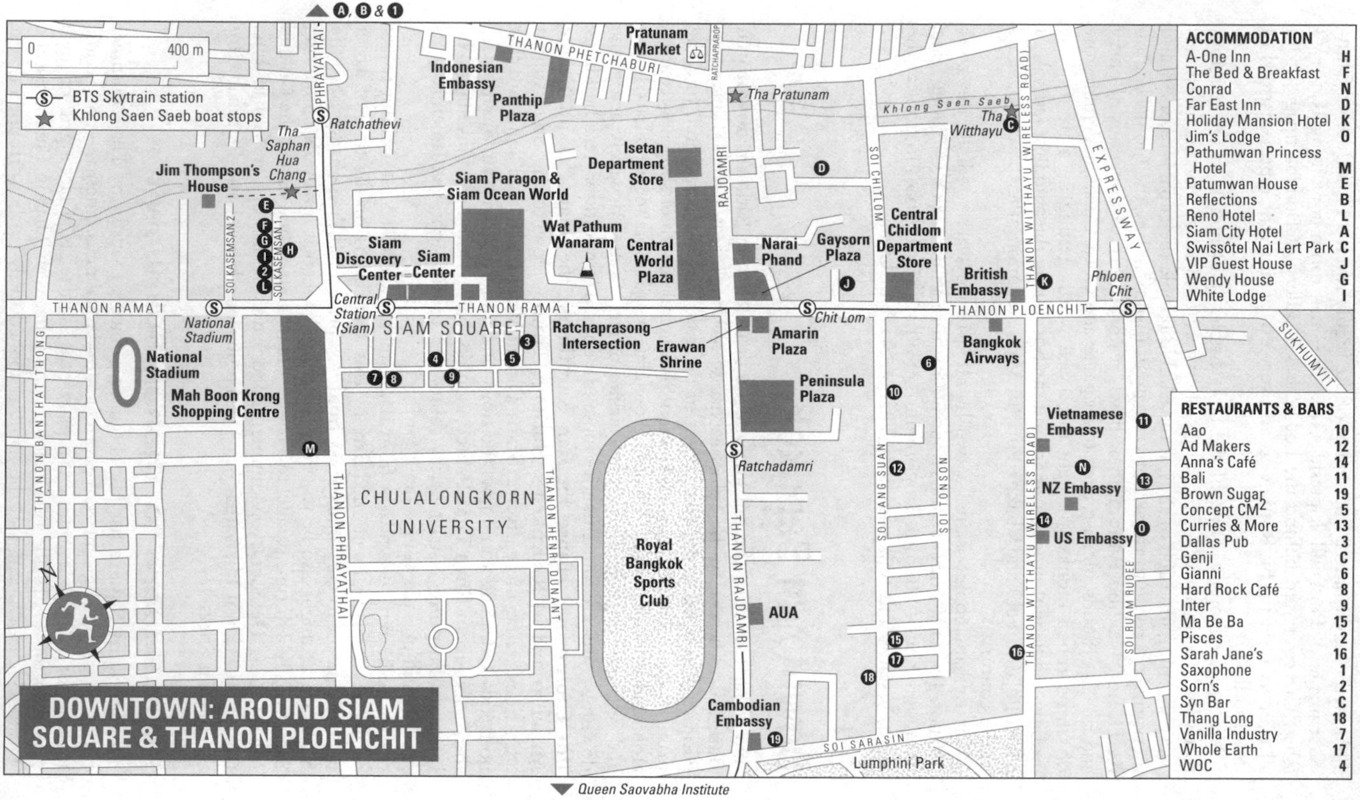

DOWNTOWN: AROUND SIAM SQUARE & THANON PLOENCHIT

0 400 m

- (S) BTS Skytrain station
- ★ Khlong Saen Saeb boat stops

ACCOMMODATION

A-One Inn	H
The Bed & Breakfast	F
Conrad	N
Far East Inn	D
Holiday Mansion Hotel	K
Jim's Lodge	O
Pathumwan Princess Hotel	M
Patumwan House	E
Reflections	B
Reno Hotel	L
Siam City Hotel	A
Swissôtel Nai Lert Park	C
VIP Guest House	J
Wendy House	G
White Lodge	I

RESTAURANTS & BARS

Aao	10
Ad Makers	12
Anna's Café	14
Bali	11
Brown Sugar	19
Concept CM2	5
Curries & More	13
Dallas Pub	3
Genji	C
Gianni	6
Hard Rock Café	8
Inter	9
Ma Be Ba	15
Pisces	2
Sarah Jane's	16
Saxophone	1
Sorn's	2
Syn Bar	C
Thang Long	18
Vanilla Industry	7
Whole Earth	17
WOC	4

▲ A, B & 1

Thanon Phetchaburi
Pratunam Market
Indonesian Embassy
Panthip Plaza
Ratchaprarop
Tha Pratunam
Khlong Saen Saeb
Tha Witthayu
Phrayathai
Ratchathevi
Tha Saphan Hua Chang
Jim Thompson's House
Soi Kasemsan 2
Soi Kasemsan 1
Siam Paragon & Siam Ocean World
Isetan Department Store
Wat Pathum Wanaram
Central World Plaza
Rajdamri
Narai Phand
Gaysorn Plaza
Soi Chitlom
Central Chidlom Department Store
British Embassy
Thanon Witthayu (Wireless Road)
Expressway
Phloen Chit
Siam Discovery Center
Siam Center
Thanon Rama I
National Stadium
Central Station (Siam)
Siam Square
Ratchaprasong Intersection
Erawan Shrine
Chit Lom
Amarin Plaza
Thanon Ploenchit
Bangkok Airways
Sukhumvit
Peninsula Plaza
Vietnamese Embassy
National Stadium
Mah Boon Krong Shopping Centre
Thanon Banthat Thong
Chulalongkorn University
Thanon Phrayathai
Thanon Henri Dunant
Ratchadamri
Royal Bangkok Sports Club
Thanon Rajdamri
AUA
Soi Lang Suan
Soi Tonson
NZ Embassy
US Embassy
Soi Ruam Rudee
Cambodian Embassy
Soi Sarasin
Lumphini Park

▼ Queen Saovabha Institute

△ The Erawan Shrine

Just to the northwest of Siam Square, at the corner of Phrayathai and Rama I roads, a spanking new contemporary art museum is under construction, though agreement has yet to be reached about what to display inside. Further east, you'll find yet more shopping malls around the Erawan Shrine, where Rama I becomes Thanon Ploenchit, an intersection sometimes known as **Ratchaprasong**. Life becomes marginally less frenetic around **Ploenchit**, which is flanked by several grand old embassies, but picks up again once you pass under the expressway flyover and enter the shopping and entertainment quarter of **Thanon Sukhumvit**.

Jim Thompson's House

Just off Siam Square at the north end of Soi Kasemsan 2, Thanon Rama I, and served by the National Stadium Skytrain station, **Jim Thompson's House** (daily from 9am, viewing on frequent 30–40min guided tours in several languages, last tour 5pm; B100, students & under-25s B50; Ⓦwww.jimthompsonhouse.org) is a kind of Ideal Home in elegant Thai style, and a peaceful refuge from downtown chaos. The house was the residence of the legendary American adventurer, entrepreneur, art collector and all-round character whose mysterious disappearance in the jungles of Malaysia in 1967 has made him even more of a legend among Thailand's farang community.

Apart from putting together this beautiful home, Thompson's most concrete contribution was to turn traditional silk-weaving from a dying art into the highly successful international industry it is today. The complex now includes a **shop** (closes 6pm), part of the Jim Thompson Thai Silk Company chain (see p.206), above which a new **gallery** hosts temporary exhibitions on textiles and the arts, such as royal maps of Siam in the nineteenth century. There's also an excellent **bar-restaurant** (last food orders 4.30pm), which serves a similar menu to *Jim Thompson's Saladaeng Café* (see p.191). Ignore any con men at the entrance to the soi looking for mugs to escort on rip-off shopping trips, who'll tell you that the house is closed when it isn't.

The legend of Jim Thompson

Thai silk-weavers, art-dealers and conspiracy theorists all owe a debt to **Jim Thompson**, who even now, forty years after his disappearance, remains Thailand's most famous farang. An architect by trade, Thompson left his New York practice in 1940 to join the Office of Strategic Services (later to become the CIA), a tour of duty that was to see him involved in clandestine operations in North Africa, Europe and, in 1945, the Far East, where he was detailed to a unit preparing for the invasion of Thailand. When the mission was pre-empted by the Japanese surrender, he served for a year as OSS station chief in Bangkok, forming links that were later to provide grist for endless speculation.

After an unhappy and short-lived stint as part-owner of the *Oriental Hotel*, Thompson found his calling in the struggling **silk-weavers** of the area near the present Jim Thompson House, whose traditional product was unknown in the West and had been all but abandoned by Thais in favour of less costly imported textiles. Encouragement from society friends and an enthusiastic write-up in *Vogue* convinced him there was a foreign market for Thai silk, and by 1948 he had founded the Thai Silk Company Ltd. Success was assured when, two years later, the company was commissioned to make the costumes for the Broadway run of *The King and I*. Thompson's celebrated eye for colour combinations and his tireless promotion – in the early days, he could often be seen in the lobby of the *Oriental* with bolts of silk slung over his shoulder, waiting to pounce on any remotely curious tourist – quickly made his name synonymous with Thai silk.

Like a character in a Somerset Maugham novel, Thompson played the role of Western exile to the hilt. Though he spoke no Thai, he made it his personal mission to preserve traditional arts and architecture (at a time when most Thais were more keen to emulate the West), assembling his famous Thai house and stuffing it with all manner of Oriental *objets d'art*. At the same time he held firmly to his farang roots and society connections: no foreign gathering in Bangkok was complete without Jim Thompson, and virtually every Western luminary passing through Bangkok – from Truman Capote to Ethel Merman – dined at his table.

If Thompson's life was the stuff of legend, his disappearance and presumed death only added to the mystique. On Easter Sunday, 1967, Thompson, while staying with friends in a cottage in Malaysia's Cameron Highlands, went out for a stroll and never came back. A massive search of the area, employing local guides, tracker dogs and even shamans, turned up no clues, provoking a rash of fascinating but entirely unsubstantiated theories. The grandfather of them all, advanced by a Dutch psychic, held that Thompson had been lured into an ambush by the disgraced former prime minister of Thailand, Pridi Panyonyong, and spirited off to Cambodia for indeterminate purposes; later versions, supposing that Thompson had remained a covert CIA operative all his life, proposed that he was abducted by Vietnamese Communists and brainwashed to be displayed as a high-profile defector to Communism. More recently, an amateur sleuth claims to have found evidence that Thompson met a more mundane fate, having been killed by a careless truck driver and hastily buried.

The grand, rambling **house** is in fact a combination of six teak houses, some from as far afield as Ayutthaya and most more than two hundred years old. Like all traditional houses, they were built in wall sections hung together without nails on a frame of wooden pillars, which made it easy to dismantle them, pile them onto a barge and float them to their new location. Although he had trained as an architect, Thompson had more difficulty in putting them back together again; in the end, he had to go back to Ayutthaya to hunt down a group of carpenters who still practised the old house-building methods. Thompson added a few unconventional touches of his own, incorporating the elaborately carved front wall of a Chinese pawnshop between the drawing room and the bedroom, and reversing the other walls in the drawing room so that their carvings faced into the room.

The impeccably tasteful **interior** has been left as it was during Thompson's life, even down to the cutlery on the dining table. Complementing the fine artefacts from throughout Southeast Asia is a stunning array of Thai arts and crafts, including one of the best collections of traditional Thai paintings in the world. Thompson picked up plenty of bargains from the Thieves' Quarter (Nakhon Kasem) in Chinatown, before collecting Thai art became fashionable and expensive. Other pieces were liberated from decay and destruction in upcountry temples, while many of the Buddha images were turned over by ploughs, especially around Ayutthaya. Some of the exhibits are very rare, such as a headless but elegant seventh-century Dvaravati Buddha and a seventeenth-century Ayutthayan teak Buddha, but Thompson also bought pieces of little value and fakes simply for their looks – a shopping strategy that's all the more sensible in the jungle of today's Thai antiques trade.

After the guided tour, you're free to wander round the former rice barn and gardener's and maid's houses in the small **garden**, which display some gorgeous traditional Thai paintings and drawings, as well as small-scale statues and Chinese ceramics.

Siam Ocean World

Spreading over two spacious basement floors of the Siam Paragon shopping centre on Thanon Rama I, **Siam Ocean World** is a highly impressive, Australian-built aquarium (daily 9am–10pm, last admission 9pm; B450, children between 80 and 120cm tall B280; audioguide B100; Ⓦ www.siamoceanworld.com). Despite the relatively high admission price, it gets packed at weekends and during holidays, and there are often long queues for the twenty-minute glass-bottomed boat rides (B150), which give a behind-the-scenes look at the aquarium's workings. Among other outstanding features of this US$30-million development are an eight-metre-deep glass-walled tank, which displays the multi-coloured variety of a coral reef drop-off to great effect, touch tanks for handling starfish, and a long, under-ocean tunnel where you can watch sharks and rays swimming over your head. In this global piscatorial display of around 400 species, locals such as the Mekong giant catfish and the Siamese tigerfish are not forgotten, while regularly spaced touch-screen terminals allow you to glean further information in English about the creatures on view. Popular daily highlights include shark feeds, currently at 1.30pm and 5.30pm, and it's even possible to dive with the sharks here, costing from B5300 for an experienced diver to B6600 for a first-timer (Ⓦ www.sharkdive.org).

The Erawan Shrine

For a glimpse of the variety and ubiquity of Thai religion, drop in on the **Erawan Shrine** (*Saan Phra Prom* in Thai), at the corner of Thanon Ploenchit and Thanon Rajdamri underneath Chit Lom Skytrain station. Remarkable as much for its setting as anything else, this shrine to Brahma, the ancient Hindu creation god, and Erawan, his elephant, squeezes in on one of the busiest and noisiest corners of modern Bangkok, in the shadow of the *Grand Hyatt Erawan Hotel* – whose existence is the reason for the shrine. When a string of calamities held up the building of the original hotel in the 1950s, spirit doctors were called in, who instructed the owners to build a new home for the offended local spirits: the hotel was then finished without further mishap. Ill fortune struck the shrine itself, however, in early 2006, when a young, mentally disturbed, Muslim man smashed the Brahma statue to pieces with a hammer – and was then brutally beaten to death by an angry mob. It's expected that an exact replica of the statue will quickly be installed, incorporating the remains of the old statue to preserve the spirit of the deity.

Be prepared for sensory overload here: the main structure shines with lurid glass of all colours and the overcrowded precinct around it is almost buried under scented garlands and incense candles. You might also catch a lacklustre group of traditional dancers performing here to the strains of a small classical orchestra – worshippers hire them to give thanks for a stroke of good fortune. To increase their future chances of such good fortune, visitors buy a bird or two from the flocks incarcerated in cages here; the bird-seller transfers the requested number of captives to a tiny hand-held cage, from which the customer duly liberates the animals, thereby accruing merit. People set on less abstract rewards will invest in a lottery ticket from one of the physically handicapped sellers: they're thought to be the luckiest you can buy.

Ban Kamthieng (Kamthieng House)

Another reconstructed traditional Thai residence, **Ban Kamthieng** (Tues–Sat 9am–5pm; B100; Ⓦwww.siam-society.org) was moved in the 1960s from Chiang Mai to 131 Thanon Asok Montri (Soi 21), off Thanon Sukhumvit, and set up as an ethnological museum by the Siam Society. The delightful complex of polished teak buildings makes a pleasing oasis beneath the towering glass skyscrapers that dominate the rest of Sukhumvit, and is easily reached from the Asok Skytrain and Sukhumvit subway stops. It differs from Suan Pakkad, Jim Thompson's House and M.R. Kukrit's Heritage Home in being the home of a rural family, and the objects on display give a fair insight into country life for the well-heeled in northern Thailand, though unless you've already visited the north you may find the twenty-first-century metropolitan context unhelpfully anomalous.

The house was built on the banks of the Ping River in the mid-nineteenth century, and the ground-level display of farming tools and fish traps evokes the upcountry practice of fishing in flooded rice paddies to supplement the supply from the rivers. Upstairs, the main display focuses on the ritual life of a typical Lanna household, explaining the role of the spirits, the practice of making offerings, and the belief in talismans, magic shirts and male tattoos. The rectangular lintel above the door is a *hum yon*, carved in floral patterns that represent testicles and designed to ward off evil spirits. Walk along the open veranda to the authentically equipped kitchen to see a video lesson in making spicy frog soup, and to the granary to find an interesting exhibition on the ritual practices associated with rice-farming. Elsewhere in the Siam Society compound you'll find an esoteric bookshop (see p.209) and an antiques outlet.

Thailand Creative and Design Centre (TCDC)

Appropriately located on the sixth floor of the Emporium, one of Bangkok's most fashion-conscious shopping plazas, the **Thailand Creative and Design Centre** (Tues–Sun 10.30am–10pm; Ⓦwww.tcdc.or.th) seeks to celebrate, promote and inspire the nation's design innovations through its permanent display on international design and society, and through its programme of national and international exhibitions and talks. As well as its sleekly functional exhibition spaces, there's a resource centre, café and shop. The Emporium Shopping Centre is on Thanon Sukhumvit between sois 22 and 24, right alongside BTS Phrom Pong station.

Northern downtown

The area above Thanon Phetchaburi, which becomes increasingly residential as you move north, is cut through by two major roads lined with monolithic company headquarters: Thanon Phaholyothin, which runs past the Northern Bus Terminal and the weekend market, and Thanon Wiphawadi Rangsit, leading eventually to Don Muang Airport. The start of Thanon Phaholyothin is marked by the stone obelisk of **Victory Monument** (*Anu Sawari Chaisamoraphum*, or just *Anu Sawari*), which can be seen most spectacularly from Skytrains as they snake their way round it. It was erected after the Indo-Chinese War of 1940–41, when Thailand pinched back some territory in Laos and Cambodia while the French government was otherwise occupied in World War II, but nowadays it commemorates all of Thailand's past military glories.

Suan Pakkad Palace Museum

The **Suan Pakkad Palace Museum** (daily 9am–4pm; B100; ⓦwww.suanpakkad.com), five minutes' walk from Phaya Thai Skytrain station, at 352–4 Thanon Sri Ayutthaya, stands on what was once a cabbage patch but is now one of the finest gardens in Bangkok. Most of this private collection of beautiful Thai objects from all periods is displayed in four groups of traditional wooden houses, which were transported to Bangkok from various parts of the country. You can either take a guided tour in English (free) or explore the loosely arranged collection yourself (a leaflet and bamboo fan are handed out at the ticket office, and some of the exhibits are labelled). The attached **Marsi Gallery**, in the modern Chumbhot-Pantip Center of Arts on the east side of the garden, displays some interesting temporary exhibitions of contemporary art (ⓣ02 246 1775–6 for details).

The highlight of Suan Pakkad is the renovated **Lacquer Pavilion**, across the reedy pond at the back of the grounds. Set on stilts, the pavilion is actually an amalgam of two eighteenth- or late-seventeenth-century temple buildings, a *ho trai* (library) and a *ho khien* (writing room), one inside the other, which were found between Ayutthaya and Bang Pa-In. The interior walls are beautifully decorated with gilt on black lacquer: the upper panels depict the life of the Buddha while the lower ones show scenes from the *Ramayana*. Look out especially for the grisly details in the tableau on the back wall, showing the earth goddess drowning the evil forces of Mara. Underneath are depicted some European dandies on horseback, probably merchants, whose presence suggests that the work was executed before the fall of Ayutthaya in 1767.

The carefully observed details of daily life and nature are skilful and lively, especially considering the restraints which the **lacquering technique** places on the artist, who has no opportunity for corrections or touching up. The design has to be punched into a piece of paper, which is then laid on the panel of black lacquer (a kind of plant resin); a small bag of chalk dust is pressed on top so that the dust penetrates the minute holes in the paper, leaving a line of dots on the lacquer to mark the pattern; a gummy substance is then applied to any background areas that are to remain black, before the whole surface is covered in microscopically thin squares of gold leaf; thin sheets of blotting paper, sprinkled with water, are then laid over the panel, which when pulled off bring away the gummy substance and the unwanted pieces of gold leaf. This leaves the rest of the gold decoration in high relief against the black background.

Divided between House no. 8 and the Ban Chiang Gallery in the Chumbhot-Pantip Center of Arts is a very good collection of elegant, whorled pottery and bronze jewellery, which the former owner of Suan Pakkad Palace,

Princess Chumbhot, excavated from tombs at Ban Chiang, the major Bronze Age settlement in the northeast. Scattered around the rest of the museum are some attractive Thai and Khmer religious sculptures among an eclectic jumble of artefacts, including fine ceramics and some intriguing kiln-wasters, failed pots which have melted together in the kiln to form weird, almost rubbery pieces of sculpture; an extensive collection of colourful papier-mâché *khon* masks; beautiful betel-nut sets (see box on p.361); monks' elegant ceremonial fans; and some rich teak carvings, including a 200-year-old temple door showing episodes from *Sang Thong*, a folk tale about a childless king and queen who discover a handsome son in a conch shell.

Phya Thai Palace

An intriguing way to spend a Saturday in Bangkok is to explore **Phya Thai Palace**, a grandiose and eccentric relic of the early twentieth century on Thanon Rajwithi, about ten minutes' walk west of Victory Monument and its Skytrain station. Built mostly by **Vajiravudh**, Rama VI, who lived here from 1919 for the last six years of his reign, it initially became the most luxurious hotel in Southeast Asia after his death, incorporating Thailand's first radio station, then after the 1932 coup, a military hospital. Parts of the airy, rambling complex have been splendidly restored by the Palace Fan Club, while others show nearly a century's worth of wear and tear, and one building is still used as offices by Phra Mongkutklao Army Hospital; you're quite likely to come across a musical performance or rehearsal as you're being guided round the otherwise empty rooms. Engaging **tours** in English (90min–2hr; free), led by volunteer guides, usually kick off at 9.30am and 1.30pm on Saturdays. It is also possible to visit on weekdays, as long as you make an appointment and pay B500. For further information, contact Miss Pisadaporn Rupramarn on Ⓣ02 354 7660 (Mon–Fri ext. 93646 or 93694, Sat ext. 93698). It's well worth buying the excellent guidebook, not only to help the palace restoration fund, but also to read the extraordinary story of **Dusit Thani**: this miniature utopian city was set up by King Vajiravudh on an acre of the palace grounds (now dismantled), as a political experiment complete with two daily newspapers, elections and a constitution – only a decade or so before a real constitution was forcibly imposed on the monarchy after the coup of 1932.

Most of the central building, the **Phiman Chakri Hall**, is in a sumptuous, English, Art Nouveau style, featuring silk wallpaper, ornate murals, Italian marble – and an extravagant but unusable fireplace that reminded Vajiravudh of his schooling in England. The king's first bedroom, decorated in royal red and appointed with a huge, step-down, marble bath, later went for B120 a night as a hotel suite. Outside in the grounds, between a pond used for bathing and the canal which gave access to Khlong Samsen, Vajiravudh first constructed for himself a simple wooden house so that he could keep an eye on the builders, the **Mekhala Ruchi Pavilion**, which later became the king's barber's. In front of the Phiman Chakri Hall, the **Thewarat Sapharom Hall**, a neo-Byzantine teak audience hall, is still used for occasional **classical concerts**. Don't leave without sampling the lovely, Art Nouveau **coffee shop**, a former waiting room covered in ornate teak carving.

Southern downtown

South of Thanon Rama I, commercial development gives way to a dispersed assortment of large institutions, dominated by Thailand's most prestigious centre of higher learning, Chulalongkorn University, and the green expanse of **Lumphini Park**. Thanon Rama IV marks another change of character: downtown proper, centring around the high-rise, American-style boulevard of Thanon Silom, heart of the financial district, extends from here to the river. Alongside the smoked-glass banks and offices, the plush hotels and tourist shops, and opposite Bangkok's Carmelite convent, lies the dark heart of Bangkok nightlife, **Patpong**. Further west along Silom, at the corner of Thanon Pan, lies the colourful landmark of the Maha Uma Devi Temple (aka Sri Mahamariamman or Wat Khaek), a gaudy South Indian, Hindu shrine built in 1895 in honour of Uma Devi. Carrying on to the river, the strip west of Charoen Krung (New Road) reveals some of the history of Bangkok's early dealings with foreigners in the fading grandeur of the old trading quarter. Here you'll find the only place in Bangkok where you might be able to eke out an architectural walk, though it's hardly compelling. Incongruous churches and "colonial" buildings (the best of these is the Authors' Wing of the *Oriental Hotel*, where nostalgic afternoon teas are served) are hemmed in by the spice shops and *halal* canteens of the growing Muslim area around Thanon Charoen Krung.

The Queen Saovabha Memorial Institute (Snake Farm)

The **Queen Saovabha Memorial Institute** (*Sathan Saovabha*), often simply known as the **Snake Farm**, at the corner of Thanon Rama IV and Thanon Henri Dunant (a 10min walk from Sala Daeng Skytrain station or Sam Yan or Si Lom subway stations), is a bit of a circus act, but an entertaining, informative and worthy one at that. Run by the Thai Red Cross, it has a double function: to produce snake-bite serums, and to educate the public on the dangers of Thai snakes. The latter mission involves putting on displays (Mon–Fri 10.30am & 2pm, Sat, Sun & hols 10.30am; B70; ⓣ02 252 0161–4, ⓦwww.redcross.or.th) that begin with a slick half-hour slide-show illustrating, among other things, how to apply a tourniquet and immobilize a bitten limb. Things warm up with a live, half-hour demonstration of snake-handling and -feeding and venom extraction, which is well presented and safe, and gains a perverse fascination from the knowledge that the strongest venoms of the snakes on show can kill in only three minutes. If you're still not herpetologically sated, a wide range of Thai snakes can be seen live in cages around the grounds, as well as preserved and bottled in a small snake museum.

Lumphini Park

If you're sick of cars and concrete, head for **Lumphini Park** (*Suan Lum*; daily 5am–7pm), at the east end of Thanon Silom, where the air is almost fresh and the traffic noise dies down to a low murmur. Named after the town in Nepal where the Buddha was born, it was the country's first public park, donated by Rama VI, whose statue by Silpa Bhirasri (see p.881) stands at the main, southwest entrance. The park is arrayed around two lakes, where you can join the locals in feeding the turtles and fish with bread or take out a pedalo or rowing boat, and is landscaped with a wide variety of local trees and numerous pagodas and pavilions, usually occupied by chess-players. In the early morning and at dusk, exercise freaks hit the outdoor gym on the southwest side of the park, or en masse do some jogging along the yellow-marked circuit or some balletic t'ai chi, stopping for the twice-daily broadcast of the national anthem. On Sunday afternoons in the cool season, free classical concerts draw in scores of urban picnickers. The park is a popular area for gay cruising, and you might be offered dope, though the police patrol regularly – for all that, it's not at all

Thailand's sex industry

Bangkok owes its reputation as the carnal capital of the world to a highly efficient sex industry adept at peddling fantasies of cheap sex on tap. More than a thousand sex-related businesses operate in the city, but the gaudy neon fleshpots of Patpong give a misleading impression of an activity that is deeply rooted in Thai culture – the overwhelming majority of Thailand's prostitutes of both sexes (estimated at anywhere between 200,000 and 700,000) work with Thai men, not farangs.

Prostitution and polygamy have long been intrinsic to the Thai way of life. Until Rama VI broke with the custom in 1910, Thai kings had always kept a retinue of concubines around them, a select few of whom would be elevated to the status of wife and royal mother, the rest forming a harem of ladies-in-waiting and sexual playthings. The practice was aped by the status-hungry nobility and, from the early nineteenth century, by newly rich merchants keen to have lots of sons and heirs. Though the monarch is now monogamous, many men of all classes still keep mistresses, known as *mia noi* (minor wives), a tradition bolstered by the popular philosophy that an official wife (*mia luang*) should be treated like the temple's main Buddha image – respected and elevated upon the altar – whereas the minor wife is an amulet, to be taken along wherever you go. For those not wealthy enough to take on *mia noi*, prostitution is a far less costly and equally accepted option. Statistics indicate that at least two-fifths of sexually active Thai men are thought to use the services of prostitutes twice a month on average, and it's common practice for a night out with the boys to wind up in a brothel or massage parlour.

The **farang sex industry** is a relatively new development, having had its start during the Vietnam War, when the American military set up seven bases around Thailand. The GIs' appetite for "entertainment" fuelled the creation of instant red-light districts near the bases, attracting women from surrounding rural areas to cash in on the boom; Bangkok joined the fray in 1967, when the US secured the right to ferry soldiers in from Vietnam for R&R breaks. By the mid-1970s, the bases had been evacuated, but the sex infrastructure remained and tourists moved in to fill the vacuum, lured by advertising that diverted most of the traffic to Bangkok and Pattaya. Sex tourism has since grown to become an established part of the Thai economy and has spread to Phuket and Ko Samui.

The majority of the women who work in the Patpong bars come from the poorest rural areas of north and northeast Thailand. **Economic refugees** in search of a better life, they're easily drawn into an industry in which they can make in a single night what it takes a month to earn in the rice fields. In some Isaan villages, money sent home by prostitutes in Bangkok far exceeds financial aid given by the government. Women from rural communities have always been expected to contribute an equal share to the family income, and many opt for a couple of lucrative years in the sex bars and brothels as the most effective way of helping to pay off family debts and improve the living conditions of parents stuck in the poverty trap. Reinforcing this

an intimidating place. To recharge your batteries, make for the inexpensive garden restaurant in the northwest corner, or the pavement foodstalls at the northern edge of the park.

Patpong

Concentrated into a small area between the eastern ends of Thanon Silom and Thanon Suriwong, the neon-lit go-go bars of the **Patpong** district loom like rides in a tawdry sexual Disneyland. In front of each bar, girls cajole passers-by with a lifeless sensuality while insistent touts proffer printed menus and photographs detailing the degradations on show. Inside, bikini-clad women gyrate social obligation is the pervasive Buddhist notion of karma, which holds that your lot, however unhappy, is the product of past-life misdeeds and can only be improved by making sufficient merit to ensure a better life next time round.

While most women enter the racket presumably knowing at least something of what lies ahead, younger girls definitely do not. **Child prostitution** is rife: an estimated ten percent of prostitutes are under 14, some are as young as 9. They are valuable property: a prepubescent virgin can be rented to her first customer for US$1000, as sex with someone so young is believed by some to have rejuvenating properties. Most child prostitutes have been sold by desperate parents as **bonded slaves** to pimps or agents, and are kept locked up until they have fully repaid the money given to their parents, which may take two or more years.

Despite its ubiquity, prostitution has been **illegal** in Thailand since 1960, but sex-industry bosses easily circumvent the law by registering their establishments as bars, restaurants, barbers, nightclubs or massage parlours, and making payoffs to the police. Sex workers, on the other hand, often endure exploitation and violence from employers, pimps and customers rather than face fines and long rehabilitation sentences in prison-like reform centres. Life is made even more difficult by the fact that abortion is illegal in Thailand. A 1996 amendment to the **anti-prostitution law** attempts to treat sex workers as victims rather than criminals, penalizing parents who sell their children to the flesh trade and punishing owners, managers and customers of any place of prostitution with a jail sentence or a heavy fine, but this has reportedly been haphazardly enforced, owing to the number of influential police and politicians allegedly involved in the sex industry. Under this amendment anyone caught having sex with an under-15 is charged with rape, though this has apparently resulted in an increase in trafficking of young children from neighbouring countries as they are less likely to seek help.

In recent years, the spectre of **AIDS** has put the problems of the sex industry into sharp focus: UN AIDS statistics from 2003 reported that about one in five sex workers in Thailand was infected with HIV/AIDS and about one in seventy-five of the general adult Thai population; in the same year there were 58,000 AIDS-related deaths in the country. However, the rate of new HIV infections is in decline – down from 143,000 in 1991 to 21,000 in 2003 – thanks to an aggressive, World Health Organization-approved AIDS awareness campaign conducted by the government and the Population and Community Development Association (PDA), a Bangkok-based NGO, a vital component of which was to send health officials into brothels to administer blood tests and give out condoms. Though the government no longer funds many AIDS-awareness initiatives, the high-profile PDA (Ⓦ www.pda.or.th/eng), which also runs the famous *Cabbages and Condoms* restaurant on Thanon Sukhumvit, continues to campaign and educate the public, spurred on by fears that young Thais are too complacent about the virus, and by recent reports of a worrying rise in new infections.

to Western music and play hostess to the (almost exclusively male) spectators; upstairs, live shows feature women who, to use Spalding Gray's phrase in *Swimming to Cambodia*, "do everything with their vaginas except have babies".

Patpong was no more than a sea of mud when the capital was founded on the marshy river bank to the west, but by the 1960s it had grown into a flash district of nightclubs and dance halls for rich Thais, owned by a Chinese millionaire godfather who gave his name to the area. In 1969, an American entrepreneur turned an existing teahouse into a luxurious nightclub to satisfy the tastes of soldiers on R&R trips from Vietnam, and so Patpong's transformation into a Western sex reservation began. At first, the area was rough and violent, but over the years it has wised up to the desires of the affluent farang, and now markets itself as a packaged concept of Oriental decadence. The centre of the skin trade lies along the interconnected sois of **Patpong 1 and 2**, where lines of go-go bars share their patch with respectable restaurants, a 24-hour supermarket and an overabundance of pharmacies. By night, it's a thumping theme park, whose blazing neon promises tend towards self-parody, with names like *Thigh Bar* and *Chicken Divine*. Budget travellers, purposeful besuited businessmen and noisy lager louts throng the streets, and even the most demure tourists – of both sexes – turn out to do some shopping at the night market down the middle of Patpong 1, where hawkers sell fake watches, bags and designer T-shirts. By day, a relaxed hangover descends on the place. Bar-girls hang out at foodstalls and cafés in respectable dress, often recognizable by faces that are pinched and strained from the continuous use of antibiotics and heroin in an attempt to ward off venereal disease and boredom. Farang men slump at the bars on Patpong 2, drinking and watching videos, unable to find anything else to do in the whole of Bangkok.

The small dead-end alley to the east of Patpong 2, **Silom 4** (ie Soi 4, Thanon Silom), hosts some of Bangkok's hippest nightlife, its bars, clubs and pavements heaving at weekends with the capital's bright young things. Several gay venues can be found on Silom 4, but the focus of the scene has shifted to **Silom 2**, while in between, **Thanon Thaniya**'s hostess bars and restaurants cater to Japanese tourists.

M.R. Kukrit's Heritage Home

Ten minutes' walk south of Thanon Sathorn and twenty minutes from Chong Nonsi Skytrain station, at 19 Soi Phra Pinit (Soi 7, Thanon Narathiwat Ratchanakharin), lies **M.R. Kukrit's Heritage Home**, the beautiful traditional house and gardens of one of Thailand's leading figures of the twentieth century (*Baan Mom Kukrit*; Sat, Sun & public hols 10am–5pm; B50). M.R. (*Mom Rajawongse*, a princely title) **Kukrit Pramoj** (1911–95) was a remarkable all-rounder, descended from Rama II on his father's side and, on his mother's side, from the influential ministerial family, the Bunnags. Kukrit graduated in Philosophy, Politics and Economics from Oxford University and went on to become a university lecturer back in Thailand, but his greatest claim to fame is probably as a writer: he founded, owned and penned a daily column for *Siam Rath*, the most influential Thai-language newspaper, and wrote short stories, novels, plays and poetry. He was also a respected performer in classical dance-drama (*khon*), and he starred as an Asian prime minister, opposite Marlon Brando, in the Hollywood film, *The Ugly American*. In 1974, during an especially turbulent period for Thailand, life imitated art, when Kukrit was called on to become Thailand's PM at the head of a coalition of seventeen parties. However, just four hundred days into his premiership, the Thai military leadership dismissed him for being too anti-American.

The **residence**, which has been left just as it was when Kukrit was alive, reflects his complex character. In the large, open-sided *sala* (pavilion) for public functions near the entrance is an attractive display of *khon* masks, including a gold one which Kukrit wore when he played the demon king, Totsagan (Ravana). In and around the adjoining Khmer-styled garden, keep your eyes peeled for the the *mai dut*, sculpted miniature trees similar to bonsai, some of which Kukrit worked on for decades. The living quarters beyond are made up of five teak houses on stilts, assembled from various parts of central Thailand and joined by an open veranda. The bedroom, study and various sitting rooms are decked out with beautiful *objets d'art*; look out especially for the carved bed that belonged to Rama II and the very delicate, 200-year-old nielloware (gold inlay) from Nakhon Si Thammarat in the formal reception room. In the small family prayer room, Kukrit Pramoj's ashes are enshrined in the base of a reproduction of the Emerald Buddha.

Chatuchak and the outskirts

The amorphous clutter of Greater Bangkok doesn't harbour many attractions, but there are a handful of places – principally **Chatuchak Weekend Market**, the cultural theme park of **Muang Boran**, the rather more esoteric **Prasart Museum**, the upstream town of **Nonthaburi** and the tranquil artificial island of **Ko Kred** – which make pleasant half-day escapes.

Chatuchak Weekend Market (JJ)

With over eight thousand open-air stalls to peruse, and wares as diverse as Lao silk, Siamese kittens and designer lamps to choose from, the enormous **Chatuchak Weekend Market**, or **JJ** as it's usually abbreviated, from "Jatu Jak" (Sat & Sun 7am–6pm), is Bangkok's most enjoyable – and exhausting – shopping experience. It occupies a huge patch of ground between the Northern Bus Terminal and Mo Chit Skytrain (N8)/Chatuchak Park subway stations, and is best reached by Skytrain or subway if you're coming from downtown areas; Kamphaeng Phet subway station is the most convenient as it exits right into the most interesting, southwestern, corner of the market. Coming from Banglamphu, you can either get a bus to the nearest Skytrain stop (probably National Stadium or Ratchathewi) and then take the train, or take the #503 or #509 bus all the way from Rajdamnoen Klang (about 1hr); see p.118 for details.

Though its primary customers are Bangkok residents in search of idiosyncratic fashions and homewares, Chatuchak also has plenty of collector- and tourist-oriented **stalls**. Aside from trendy one-off clothes and accessories, best buys include antique lacquerware, unusual sarongs, traditional cotton clothing and crafts from the north, jeans, silver jewellery, and ceramics, particularly the five-coloured *bencharong*. The market is divided into 26 numbered **sections**, plus a dozen unnumbered ones, each of them more or less dedicated to a particular genre, for example household items, young fashions, plants, second-hand books, or crafts. If you have several hours to spare, it's fun just to browse at whim, but if you're looking for souvenirs, handicrafts or traditional textiles you should start with sections 22, 24, 25 and 26, which are all in a cluster at the southwest (Kamphaeng Phet subway) end of the market; sections A, B and C, behind the market's head office and information centre is also full of interesting artefacts. *Nancy Chandler's Map of Bangkok* has a fabulously detailed and informatively annotated **map** of all the sections in the market, it's best bought before you arrive but is available at Teak House Art in Section 2, near Kamphaeng Phet subway's exit 2. Maps are also posted at various points around the market and for specific help you can also ask at the market office near Gate 1 off Thanon Kamphaeng Phet 2.

The market also contains a controversial, **wildlife** section that has long doubled as a clearing-house for protected and endangered species such as gibbons, palm cockatoos and Indian pied hornbills, many of them smuggled in from Laos and Cambodia and sold to private animal collectors and foreign zoos. The illegal trade goes on beneath the counter, and may be in decline following a spate of crackdowns, but you're bound to come across fighting cocks around the back (demonstrations are almost continuous), miniature flying squirrels being fed milk through pipettes, and iridescent red and blue Siamese fighting fish, kept in individual jars and shielded from each other's aggressive stares by sheets of cardboard.

There's no shortage of **foodstalls** inside the market compound, particularly at the southern end, where you'll find plenty of places serving inexpensive *phat thai* and Isaan snacks. Close by these stalls is a classy little juice bar called *Viva* where you can rest your feet while listening to the manager's jazz tapes. The biggest restaurant here is *Toh Plue*, whose main branch is on the edge of the block containing the market office and makes a good rendezvous point (there's a second branch beside Kamphaeng Phet subway station's exit 1). For veggie food, head for *Chamlong's* (also known as *Asoke*), an ultra-cheap food-court-style restaurant just outside the market on Thanon Kamphaeng Phet (across Thanon Kamphaeng Phet 2; 5 mins' walk from Kamphaeng Phet subway's exit 1; Sat & Sun 8am–noon). You can **change money** (Sat & Sun 8am–6pm) in the market building at the south end of the market, and there are several ATMs here too. A few very small electric **trams** circulate around the market's main inner ringroad, transporting weary shoppers for free, though they always seem to be full.

The Prasart Museum

Located right out on the eastern edge of the city (and still surrounded by fields), the **Prasart Museum** at 9 Soi 4A, Soi Krungthep Kreetha, Thanon Krungthep Kreetha (Tues–Sun 10am–3pm; B1000 for one or two people; call ⓣ02 379 3601 to book the compulsory tour) is an unusual open-air exhibition of traditional Asian buildings, collected and reassembled by wealthy entrepreneur and art-lover Khun Prasart. The museum is rarely visited by independent tourists – partly because of the intentionally limited opening hours and inflated admission price, and partly because it takes a long time to get there by public transport – but it makes a pleasant day out and is worth the effort.

Set in a gorgeously lush tropical garden, the museum comprises about a dozen replicas of **traditional buildings**, including a golden teak palace inspired by the royal residence now housed at the National Museum, a Chinese temple and water garden, a Khmer shrine, a Sukhothai-era teak library set over a lotus pond, and a European-style mansion, fashionable with Bangkok royalty in the late nineteenth century. Some of these structures have been assembled from the ruins of buildings found all over Asia, but there's no attempt at purist authenticity – the aim is to give a flavour of architectural styles, not an exact reproduction. Many of the other buildings, including the Thai wat and the Chinese temple, were constructed from scratch, using designs dreamt up by Khun Prasart and his team. Whatever their ancestry, all the buildings are beautifully crafted, with great attention paid to carvings and decorations, and many are filled with antique **artefacts**, including Burmese woodcarvings, prehistoric pottery from Ban Chiang and Lopburi-era statuettes. There are also some unusual pieces of royal memorabilia and an exquisite collection of *bencharong* ceramics. Khun Prasart also owns a ceramics workshop, which produces reproductions of famous designs; they can be bought either at the museum, or at his showroom, the Prasart Collection, on the second floor of the Peninsula Plaza shopping centre on Thanon Rajdamri.

Regular **bus** #93 runs almost to the door: pick it up near its starting point on Thanon Si Phraya near River City and the GPO, or anywhere along its route on Phetchaburi and Phetchaburi Mai roads (both the Khlong Saen Saeb canal boats and the subway have potentially useful stops at the Thanon Asok Montri/ Sukhumvit Soi 21 junction with Thanon Phetchaburi Mai). The #93 terminates on Thanon Krungthep Kreetha, but you should get off a couple of stops before the terminus, at the first stop on Thanon Krungthep Kreetha, as soon as you see the sign for the Prasart Museum (about 1hr 15min by bus from Si Phraya). Follow the sign down Soi Krungthep Kreetha, go past the golf course and, after about a fifteen-minute walk, turn off down Soi 4A.

Nonthaburi

A trip to **NONTHABURI**, the first town beyond the northern boundary of Bangkok, is the easiest excursion you can make from the centre of the city and affords a perfect opportunity to recharge your batteries. Nonthaburi is the last stop upriver for express boats, around one hour fifteen minutes from Central Pier (Sathorn) on a "standard" boat, under an hour if you catch a "special express". The ride itself is most of the fun, weaving round huge, crawling sand barges and tiny canoes, and the slow pace of the boat gives you plenty of time to take in the sights on the way. On the north side of Banglamphu, beyond Thewes flower market, the Art Nouveau Bangkhunprom Palace and the elegant, new Rama VIII Bridge, you'll pass the royal boat house in front of the National Library on the east bank, where you can glimpse the minor ceremonial boats that escort the grand royal barges. Further out are dazzling Buddhist temples and drably painted mosques, catering for Bangkok's growing Muslim population, as well as a few remaining communities who still live in houses on stilts or houseboats – around Krungthon Bridge, for example, you'll see people living on the huge teak vessels used to carry rice, sand and charcoal.

Durians

The naturalist Alfred Russel Wallace, eulogizing the taste of the **durian**, compared it to "rich butter-like custard highly flavoured with almonds, but intermingled with wafts of flavour that call to mind cream cheese, onion sauce, brown sherry and other incongruities". He neglected to discuss the smell of the fruit's skin, which is so bad – somewhere between detergent and dogshit – that durians are barred from Thai hotels and aeroplanes. The different **varieties** bear strange names which do nothing to make them more appetizing: "frog", "golden pillow", "gibbon" and so on. However, the durian has fervent admirers, perhaps because it's such an acquired taste, and because it's considered a strong aphrodisiac. Aficionadoes discuss the varieties with as much subtlety as if they were vintage champagnes, and they treat the durian as a social fruit, to be shared around, despite a price tag of up to B3000 each.

Durian season is roughly April to June and the most famous durian orchards are around Nonthaburi, where the fruits are said to have an incomparably rich and nutty flavour due to the fine clay soil. If you don't smell them first, you can recognize durians by their sci-fi appearance: the shape and size of a rugby ball, but slightly deflated, they're covered in a thick, pale-green shell which is heavily armoured with short, sharp spikes (*duri* means "thorn" in Malay). By cutting along one of the faint seams with a good knife, you'll reveal a white pith in which are set a handful of yellow blobs with the texture of a wrinkled soufflé: this is what you eat. The taste is best when the smell is at its highest, about three days after the fruit has dropped. Be careful when out walking near the trees: because of its great weight and sharp spikes, a falling durian can lead to serious injury, or even an ignominious death.

Disembarking at suburban Nonthaburi, on the east bank of the river, you won't find a great deal to do, in truth. There's a market that's famous for the quality of its fruit, while the attractive, old Provincial Office across the road is covered in rickety wooden latticework. To break up your trip with a slow, scenic drink or lunch, you'll find a floating seafood restaurant, *Rim Fang*, to the right at the end of the prom which, though a bit overpriced, is quiet and breezy.

Set in relaxing grounds about 1km north of Nonthaburi pier on the west bank of the river, elegant **Wat Chalerm Phra Kiat** injects a splash of urban refinement among a grove of breadfruit trees. You can get there from the express-boat pier by taking the ferry straight across the Chao Phraya and then catching a motorbike taxi. The beautifully proportioned temple, which has been lavishly restored, was built by Rama III in memory of his mother, whose family lived and presided over vast orchards in the area. Entering the walls of the temple compound, you feel as if you're coming upon a stately folly in a secret garden, and a strong Chinese influence shows itself in the unusual ribbed roofs and elegantly curved gables, decorated with pastel ceramics. The restorers have done their best work inside: look out especially for the simple, delicate landscapes on the shutters.

Ko Kred

About 7km north of Nonthaburi, the tiny island of **KO KRED** lies in a particularly sharp bend in the Chao Phraya, cut off from the east bank by a waterway created to make the cargo route from Ayutthaya to the Gulf of Thailand just that little bit faster. Although it's slowly being discovered by day-trippers from Bangkok, this artificial island remains something of a time capsule, a little oasis of village life completely at odds with the metropolitan chaos downriver. Roughly ten square kilometres in all, Ko Kred has no roads, just a concrete path that follows its circumference, with a few arterial walkways branching off towards the interior. Villagers, the majority of whom are Mon (see box on p.261), use a small fleet of motorbike taxis to cross their island, but as a sightseer you're much better off on foot: a round-island walk takes less than an hour and a half.

There are few sights as such on Ko Kred, but its lushness and comparative emptiness make it a perfect place in which to wander. You'll no doubt come across one of the island's potteries and kilns, which churn out the regionally famous earthenware flower-pots and small water-storage jars and employ a large percentage of the village workforce; several shops dotted around the island sell Ko Kred terracotta, including what's styled as the Ancient Mon Pottery Centre near the island's northeast corner, which also displays delicate and venerable museum pieces and Mon-style Buddha shrines. The island's clay is very rich in nutrients and therefore excellent for fruit-growing, and banana trees, coconut palms, pomelo, papaya, mango and durian trees all grow in abundance on Ko Kred, fed by an intricate network of irrigation channels that crisscrosses the interior. In among the orchards, the Mons have built their wooden houses, mostly in traditional style and raised high above the marshy ground on stilts. A handful of attractive riverside wats complete the picture, most notably **Wat Paramaiyikawat** (aka Wat Poramai), at the main pier at the northeast tip of the island. This engagingly ramshackle eighteenth-century temple was restored by Rama V in honour of his grandmother, with a Buddha relic placed in its white, riverside chedi, which is a replica of the Mutao Pagoda in Hanthawadi, capital of the Mon kingdom in Burma. Among an open-air scattering of Burmese-style alabaster Buddha images, the tall bot shelters some fascinating nineteenth-century murals, depicting scenes from temple life at ground level and the life of the Buddha above, all set in delicate imaginary landscapes.

Practicalities

The best time to go to Ko Kred is the weekend, when the Chao Phraya Express Boat Company (Sun only; B300; ⓣ02 623 6001–3, ⓦwww.chaophrayaboat.co.th) and Mitchaopaya Travel Service (Sat & Sun; B250; ⓣ02 623 6169) run **tours** there from central Bangkok. They both head upriver at 9am (Chao Phraya Express Boat Company from Tha Sathorn via Tha Maharat, Mitchaopaya from Tha Chang), taking in Wat Poramai and the Ancient Mon Pottery Centre, before circling the island via Ban Khanom Thai, where you can buy traditional sweets and watch them being made. Chao Phraya Express Boat Company arrives back, via Wat Sangsiritham floating market, at Tha Maharat at about 3pm (Tha Sathorn at 3.30pm), while Mitchaopaya also takes in the Royal Barge Museum (see p.161) and Wat Chalerm Phra Kiat in Nonthaburi (see opposite), returning to Tha Chang at around 4.30pm.

At other times, the main drawback of a day-trip to Ko Kred is the difficulty of **getting there**. Your best option is to take a Chao Phraya express boat to Nonthaburi, then bus #32 to Pakkred pier – or, if you're feeling flush, a chartered longtail boat direct to Ko Kred (about B200–300). From Pakkred, the easiest way of getting across to the island is to hire a longtail boat, although shuttle boats cross at the river's narrowest point to Wat Poramai from Wat Sanam Nua, about a kilometre's walk or a short samlor or motorbike-taxi ride south of the Pakkred pier.

Muang Boran Ancient City

A day-trip out to the **Muang Boran Ancient City** open-air museum (daily 8am–5pm; B300, children B200 including bicycle rental or tram ticket; ⓦwww.ancientcity.com), 33km southeast of Bangkok, is a great way to enjoy the best of Thailand's architectural heritage in relative peace and without much effort. Occupying a huge park shaped like Thailand itself, the museum comprises more than 116 traditional Thai buildings scattered around pleasantly landscaped grounds and is best toured by rented **bicycle** (B50; B150/tandem; B200/three-seater), though you can also make use of the circulating **tram** (B150 round trip, kids B75), and doing it on foot is just about possible. Many of the buildings are copies of the country's most famous monuments, and are located in the appropriate "region" of the park, with everything from Bangkok's Grand Palace (central region) to the spectacularly sited hilltop Khmer Khao Phra Viharn sanctuary (northeast) represented here. There are also some original structures, including a rare scripture repository (library) rescued from Samut Songkhram (south), as well as some painstaking reconstructions from contemporary documents of long-vanished gems, of which the Ayutthaya-period Sanphet Prasat palace (central) is a particularly fine example. A sizeable team of restorers and skilled craftspeople maintains the buildings and helps keep some of the traditional techniques alive; if you come here during the week you can watch them at work.

To get to Muang Boran from Bangkok, take air-conditioned **bus** #511 to **Samut Prakan** on the edge of built-up Greater Bangkok, then change onto songthaew #36, which passes the entrance to Muang Boran. Although bus #511 runs from Banglamphu via Thanon Rama I and Thanon Sukhumvit (see p.108 for the route), wherever you're starting from, the journey is likely to be much faster if you cover downtown Bangkok by Skytrain (and boat and/or subway if necessary) and pick up the #511 at the Ekamai Skytrain stop.

A couple of kilometres east of Samut Prakan, the **Crocodile Farm** (daily 7am–6pm; B300, kids B200) figures on tour-group itineraries, but is a depressing place. The thirty thousand reptiles kept here are made to "perform" for their trainers in hourly shows (daily 9, 10 & 11am & 1, 2, 3 & 4pm) and are subsequently turned into handbags, shoes, briefcases and wallets, a selection of which are sold on site. Songthaews run from Samut Prakan. There's also a dinosaur museum at the farm, which features 13 life-sized models and replica skeletons (B60).

Food, entertainment, shopping and moving on

As you'd expect, nowhere in Thailand can compete with Bangkok's diversity when it comes to eating and entertainment, and, although prices are generally higher here than in the provinces, it's still easy to have a good time while on a budget. Bangkok boasts an astonishing fifty thousand **places to eat** – that's almost one for every hundred citizens – ranging from grubby streetside noodle shops to the most elegant of restaurants. Here we run through the best of the city's indigenous eateries, with a few representatives of the capital's numerous ethnic minorities.

Bangkok nightlife has at last outgrown its reputation for catering only to single men and now centres around dozens of fashionable **bars** and sophisticated **clubs**, where hip design and trend-setting DJs draw in capacity crowds of stylish young Thais and partying travellers. Getting back to your lodgings is no problem in the small hours: many bus routes run a (reduced) service throughout the night, and tuk-tuks and taxis are always at hand – though it's probably best for unaccompanied women to avoid using tuk-tuks late at night.

Introductions to more traditional elements of Thai culture are offered by the raucous ambience of the city's **boxing arenas**, its **music and dancing** troupes and its profusion of **shops**, stalls and markets – all of them covered here. This section concludes with an overview of the options for **moving on** from the city – not only to elsewhere in Thailand, but to other countries too, as Bangkok is one of Asia's bargain counters when it comes to buying flights.

Eating

Thai eateries of all types are found all over Bangkok. The best **gourmet Thai** restaurants in the country operate from the downtown districts around Thanon Sukhumvit and Thanon Silom, proffering wonderful royal, traditional and regional cuisines that definitely merit a visit. Over in Banglamphu, Thanon Phra Athit has become famous for its dozen or so trendy little restaurant-bars,

△ Bangkok curry shop

each with distinctive decor and a contemporary Thai menu that's angled at young Thai diners. At the other end of the scale there are the **night markets** and **street stalls**, so numerous in Bangkok that we can only flag the most promising areas – but wherever you're staying, you'll hardly have to walk a block in any direction before encountering something appealing.

For the non-Thai cuisines, Chinatown naturally rates as the most authentic district for pure **Chinese** food; likewise neighbouring Pahurat, the capital's Indian enclave, is best for unadulterated **Indian** dishes; and good, comparatively cheap **Japanese** restaurants are concentrated on Soi Thaniya, at the east end of

Dinner, lunch and cocktail cruises

The **Chao Phraya River** looks fabulous at night, when most of the noisy longtails have stopped terrorizing the ferries, and the riverside temples and other grand monuments – including the Grand Palace and Wat Arun – are elegantly illuminated. Joining one of the nightly **dinner cruises** along the river is a great way to appreciate it all. Call ahead to reserve a table and check departure details – some places offer free transport from hotels, and some cruises may not run during the rainy season (May to October). If you have other plans for dinner, it's now possible to take a cruise at other times of the day: the *Manohra* (see below) runs **cocktail cruises** between 6 and 7pm (B750), while the *Shangri-La Horizon* (see below) sails off on a **lunch cruise** at noon (international buffet; B1850), returning to the hotel pier around 2.30pm, with optional drop-offs at the Grand Palace or Wat Arun.

Loy Nava ⓣ02 235 3108. Departs Si Phraya pier at 8pm (returning 10pm). Thai set meal. B1200.

Maeyanang Run by the *Oriental Hotel* ⓣ02 236 0400. Departs *Oriental* at 7.30pm (not Mon), returning at 9.30pm. Thai buffet. B1600.

Manohra Beautiful converted rice barge operated by the *Marriott Bangkok Resort*, south of Taksin Bridge in Thonburi ⓣ02 477 0770, ⓦwww.manohracruises.com. Departs hotel at 7.30pm, returning 10pm, with pick-ups at Tha Sathorn and Tha Oriental possible. Thai set dinner, accompanied by live traditional music, B1500.

Pearl of Siam ⓣ02 225 6179. Departs River City at 7.30pm, returning at 9.30pm. Thai and international buffet. B1200.

Shangri-La Horizon ⓣ02 236 7777. Departs *Shangri-La Hotel* pier, north of Taksin Bridge, at 7.30pm, returning at 9.30pm. International buffet. B2200.

Wan Fah ⓣ02 222 8679, ⓦwww.wanfah.com. Departs River City at 7pm, returning at 9pm. Thai or seafood set menu. B1200.

Thanon Silom. The place to head for Western, **travellers' food** – from herbal teas and hamburgers to muesli – as well as a hearty range of veggie options, is Thanon Khao San, packed with small, inexpensive tourist restaurants; standards vary, but there are some definite gems among the blander establishments.

Besides the night markets and street stalls, **fast food** comes in two main forms: the Thai version is the upper-floor **food courts** of shopping centres and department stores all over the city, dishing up mostly one-dish meals from around the country, while the old Western favourites like *McDonald's* and *Kentucky Fried Chicken* mainly congregate around Thanon Sukhumvit and Siam Square. In addition, downtown Bangkok has a good quota of **coffee shops**, including several branches of local company *Black Canyon* and *Starbucks*, the latter expensive but usually graced with armchairs and free newspapers.

In the more expensive restaurants listed below you may have to pay a ten percent service charge and seven percent government tax. Telephone numbers are given for the more popular or out-of-the-way establishments, where booking may be advisable. Most restaurants in Bangkok are open every day for lunch and dinner; we've noted exceptions in the listings below.

Banglamphu and the Democracy Monument area

Banglamphu is a great area for eating. **Khao San** is stacked full of guest-house restaurants serving the whole range of cheap and familiar travellers' fare; there are also some good Thai places here, as well as veggie, Indian,

Israeli and Italian joints. For a complete contrast you need only walk a few hundred metres down to riverside **Thanon Phra Athit**, where the pavement heaves with arty little café-restaurants; these are patronized mainly by students from Thammasat University up the road, but most offer English-language menus to any interested tourists. The food in these places is generally modern Thai, nearly always very good and reasonably priced. There are also some recommended trendy Thai places on the Banglamphu **fringes**, plus a few traditional options too. Hot-food stalls serving very cheap **night-market** fare pop up nightly all over the Khao San area, so there's always something available to soak up the beer. For restaurant locations see the map on p.116.

Around Khao San

Chabad House 96 Thanon Ram Bhuttri, ⓦwww.jewishthailand.com. A little piece of Israel, run by the Bangkok branch of the Jewish Chabad-Lubavitch movement. Serves a well-priced kosher menu (B75–130) of falafels, baba ganoush, schnitzels, hummus, salads and Jewish breads in air-conditioned calm, on the ground floor of a long-established community centre and guest house. Sun–Thurs 10am–10pm, Fri 10am–3pm.

Himalayan Kitchen 1 Thanon Khao San. One of only a handful of places serving South Asian food in the area, this first-floor restaurant – which gives good bird's-eye views of Khao San action – is decorated with Nepalese *thanka* paintings and dishes out decent Nepalese veg and non-veg thalis (from B160).

May Kaidee 117/1Thanon Tanao, though actually on the parallel soi to the west; easiest access is to take first left on Soi Damnoen Klang Neua; ⓦwww.maykaidee.com. Simple, neighbourhood restaurant serving the best vegetarian food in Banglamphu. Try the tasty green curry with coconut, the Vietnamese-style veggie spring rolls or the sticky black-rice pudding. May Kaidee herself also runs veggie cookery classes, detailed on p.216. Most dishes B50–60.

Popaing Soi Ram Bhuttri. Popular place for cheap seafood: mussels and cockles cost just B50 per plate, squid B70, or you can get a large helping of seafood noodles for B100. Eat in the low-rent restaurant area or on the street beneath the temple wall.

Prakorb House Thanon Khao San. Archetypal travellers' haven, with only a few tables, and an emphasis on wholesome ingredients. Herbal teas, mango shakes, delicious pumpkin curry, and lots more besides (B40–60). Inexpensive.

Srinnmmun Bar and Restaurant 335 Thanon Ram Bhuttri. This funky little cabin of a place with just a handful of tables and a penchant for soft country music serves delicious Thai food (cooked on the street), especially shrimps drizzled with coconut sauce, spicy *yam* salads and stir-fried veg with pineapple, cashews and tofu. Most dishes B40–60. Cheap.

Sunset Bar Sunset Street, 197–201 Thanon Khao San. Turning off Khao San at the Sunset Street sign, ignore the street-view tables of *Sabai Bar* and follow the narrow passageway as it opens out into a tranquil, shrub-filled courtyard, occupied by the *Sunset Bar* coffee shop and restaurant – the perfect place to escape the Khao San hustle with a mid-priced juice or snack. The courtyard's handsome, mango-coloured, 1907 villa is another enticement: a discreet branch of *Starbucks*, complete with sofas, occupies its ground floor, while the upper floor is given over to the Kraichitti Gallery, a commercial art outlet.

Tom Yam Kung Thanon Khao San. Occasionally mouth-blastingly authentic Thai food served in the courtyard of a beautiful early-twentieth-century villa that's hidden behind Khao San's modern clutter. The menu (B60–150) includes spicy fried catfish, coconut-palm curry with tofu and shrimps in sugar cane. Well-priced cocktails, draught beer and a small wine list. Open 24hr.

Phra Athit area

Hemlock 56 Thanon Phra Athit, next door but one from *Pra Arthit Mansion*; the sign is visible from the road but not from the pavement ⓣ02 282 7507. Small, stylish, highly recommended air-con restaurant that's very popular with students and young Thai couples. Offers a long and interesting menu of unusual Thai dishes (mostly about B60), including banana-flower salad (*yam hua plii*), coconut and mushroom curry, grand lotus rice and various *larb* and fish dishes. The traditional *miang* starters (shiny green wild tea leaves filled with chopped vegetables, fish and meat) are also very tasty, and there's a good vegetarian selection. Mon–Sat 5pm–midnight; worth reserving a table on Friday and Saturday nights.

Krua Nopparat 130–132 Thanon Phra Athit. The decor in this unassuming air-con restaurant is noticeably plain compared to all the arty joints on this road, but the Thai food (B60–100) is good, especially the eggplant wing-bean salad and the battered crab.

Ricky's Coffee Shop 22 Thanon Phra Athit. With its atmospherically dark woodwork, red lanterns and marble-top tables, this contemporary take on a traditional Chinese coffee house is an enjoyable spot to idle over fresh coffee (choose from several blends: B50) and feast on the deli-style offerings – pastrami, imported cheeses – served over baguettes and croissants, not to mention the all-day breakfasts and veggie lunch menu (most dishes B70–120). Daily 7.30am–8pm.

Roti Mataba 136 Thanon Phra Athit. Famous outlet for the ever-popular fried Indian breads, or rotis, served here in lots of sweet and savoury varieties, including with vegetable and meat curries, and with bananas and condensed milk (from B20). Closed Sun.

Tonpoh Thanon Phra Athit, next to Tha Phra Athit express-boat pier. Sizeable, good-value seafood menu (B60–220) and a relatively scenic riverside location; good place for a beer and a snack at the end of a long day's sightseeing.

Thanon Samsen, Thewes and the fringes

In Love Beside the Tha Thewes express-boat pier at 2/1 Thanon Krung Kasem. Popular place for seafood – and riverine breezes – with decent Chao Phraya views, an airy upstairs terrace, and a huge menu including baked cottonfish in mango sauce, steamed sea bass with lime and chilli, and *tom yam kung*. Most dishes B160–190.

Isaan restaurants Behind the Rajdamnoen Boxing Stadium on Thanon Rajdamnoen Nok. A cluster of restaurants serving cheapish north-eastern fare (from B60) to hungry boxing fans: take your pick for hearty plates of *kai yang* and *khao niaw*.

Kaloang Beside the river at the far western end of Thanon Sri Ayutthaya. Flamboyant service and excellent seafood attracts an almost exclusively Thai clientele to this open-air riverside restaurant. Dishes (from B120–250) well worth shelling out for include the fried rolled shrimps served with a sweet dip, the roast squid cooked in a piquant sauce and the steamed butter fish.

Kinlom Chom Saphan Riverside end of Thanon Samsen Soi 3. This sprawling, waterside seafood restaurant boasts close-up views of the lyre-like Rama VIII Bridge and is always busy with a youngish Thai crowd. The predominantly seafood menu (from B120–250) features everything from crab to grouper cooked in multiple ways, including with curry, garlic or sweet basil sauces. As well as the usual complement of tom yam and *tom kha* soups, there are *yam* salads and meat options including stir-fried ostrich with herbs. Daily 11am–2am.

May Kaidee 2 33 Thanon Samsen, between the khlong and Soi 1 ⓦ www.maykaidee.com. This air-con branch of Banglamphu's best loved Thai veggie restaurant may lack the ad hoc character of the original (see p.187), but the menu is the same – pumpkin soup, banana-flower salad, curry-fried tofu with vegetables – and equally cheap (most dishes B50–60). See p.216 for details of owner May Kaidee's veggie cookery classes.

Na Pralan Café Almost opposite the main entrance to the Grand Palace, Thanon Na Phra Lan. Technically in Ratanakosin (it's marked on the map on p.132) but very close to Banglamphu, this small, cheap café, only a couple of doors up the street from the Silpakorn University Art College, is ideally placed for refreshment after your tour of the Grand Palace. Popular with students, it occupies a quaint old air-con shophouse with battered, artsy decor. The menu, well thought out with some unusual twists, offers mostly one-dish meals with rice, and a range of ice creams, coffees, teas and beers. Mon–Sat 10am–midnight, Sun 10am–6pm.

Pornsawan Vegetarian Restaurant 80 Thanon Samsen, between sois 4 and 6. Cheap, no-frills Thai veggie café that uses soya products instead of meat in its curries and stir-fries. Daily 7am–6.30pm.

Shanti Lodge 37 Soi 16,Thanon Sri Ayutthaya. The restaurant attached to the famously chilled-out guest house serves an exceptionally innovative menu of predominantly vegetarian dishes, including tofu stuffed with brown rice, assorted curries and vegetables; and mushroom *larb*. Most dishes around B75.

Chinatown and Pahurat

The places listed below are marked on the map on p.153. In the evenings, night-time hot-food stalls open up all along Thanon Yaowarat and Soi Phadungdao: the Bangkok Tourist Bureau information booth (Mon-Sat 9am-5pm), at the east (Chinese Arch) end of Thanon Yaowarat, has a brochure detailing some of the specialist stalls.

Yellow-flag heaven for veggies

Every autumn, for nine days during the ninth lunar month (October or November), Thailand's Chinese community goes on a **meat-free** diet in order to mark the onset of the Vegetarian Festival (Ngan Kin Jeh), a sort of Taoist version of Lent. Though the Chinese citizens of Bangkok don't go in for skewering themselves like their compatriots in Trang and Phuket (see p.738), they do celebrate the Vegetarian Festival with gusto: some people choose to wear only white for the duration, all the temples throng with activity, and nearly every restaurant and foodstall in Chinatown turns vegetarian for the period, flying small yellow flags to show that they are upholding the tradition. For vegetarian tourists this is a great time to be in town – just look for the yellow flag and you can be sure all dishes will be one hundred percent vegan. Soya substitutes are a popular feature on the vegetarian Chinese menu, so don't be surprised to find pink prawn-shaped objects floating in your noodle soup or unappetizingly realistic slices of fake duck. Many hotel restaurants also get in on the act during the Vegetarian Festival, running special veggie promotions for a week or two.

Chong Tee 84 Soi Sukon 1, Thanon Trimit, between Hualamphong Station and Wat Traimit. Delicious and moreishly cheap pork satay and sweet toast.

Hua Seng Hong 371 Thanon Yaowarat. Thai birds' nest soup is one of the specialities here, but locals tend to go for the tasty wonton noodle soup or the stir-fried crab noodles (dishes from B160).

Royal India Just off Thanon Chakraphet at 392/1. Famously good curries (from B60) served in the heart of Bangkok's most Indian of neighbourhoods to an almost exclusively South Asian clientele. Especially renowned for its choice Indian breads.

Shangri-La 306 Thanon Yaowarat (cnr of Thanon Rajawong). Cavernous place serving Chinese classics (B80–300), including lots of seafood, and lunchtime *dim sum*. Very popular, especially for family outings.

T&K (Toi & Kid's Seafood) 49 Soi Phadungdao, just off Thanon Yaowarat. Famously good barbecued seafood, with everything from prawns (B150 a serving) to oysters (B30 each) on offer. Daily 4.30pm–2am.

White Orchid Hotel 409–421 Thanon Yaowarat. Recommended for its *dim sum*, with bamboo baskets of prawn dumplings, spicy spare ribs, stuffed beancurd and the like, served in three different portion sizes at fairly high prices. *Dim sum* 11am–2pm & 5–10pm. All-you-can-eat lunchtime buffets also worth stopping by for.

Downtown: Around Siam Square and Thanon Ploenchit

The map on p.168 shows the places listed below. In this area, there are also branches of *Anna's Café* (see p.191), in Diethelm Tower B, Thanon Witthayu (ⓣ02 252 0864), and *Aoi* (see p.191), in the Siam Paragon shopping centre on Thanon Rama I (ⓣ02 129 4348).

Aao 45/4–8 Soi Lang Suan, Thanon Ploenchit ⓣ02 254 5699. Bright, almost unnerving retro-Sixties decor is the setting for friendly service and very tasty Thai dishes – notably *kaeng phanaeng kai* (B90) and wing-bean salad – most of which are available spiced to order and/or in vegetarian versions. Closed Sun.

Bali 15/3 Soi Ruam Rudee ⓣ02 250 0711. Top-notch, moderately priced Indonesian food in a cosy nook. Blow out on seven-course *rijstaffel* for B340. Closed Sun.

Curries & More 63/3 Soi Ruam Rudee ⓣ02 253 5408–9. And a whole lot more . . . this offshoot of *Baan Khanitha* (see p.192) offers something for everyone, including European-style fish, steaks and pasta, as well as curries from around the country (from around B300). Try the delicious *chu chi khung nang*, deep-fried freshwater prawns with mild, Indian-style curry, or the prawn and pomelo salad. The modern, white-painted interior is hung with contemporary paintings, but the garden, surrounded by waterfalls and with water flowing over the transparent roof, is the place to be.

Food for Fun Floor 4, Siam Center. Highly enjoyable, inexpensive, new food court, decorated in startling primary colours. Lots of traditional Thai drinks and all manner of tasty one-dish meals – *khao man kai*, *khanom jiin* and *laab* and *som tam* from the Isaan counter – as well as pizza, pastas, Vietnamese and Korean food.

Food Loft Floor 7, Central Chidlom, Thanon Ploenchit. Bangkok's top department store lays on a suitably upscale food court of all hues – Thai, Vietnamese, Malay, Chinese, Japanese, Indian, Italian. Choose your own ingredients and watch them cooked in front of you, eat in the stylish, minimalist seating areas and then ponder whether you have room for a Thai or Western dessert.

Genji *Swissôtel Nai Lert Park*, 2 Thanon Witthayu ⓣ02 253 0123. Excellent, genteel Japanese restaurant overlooking the hotel's beautiful gardens, with a sushi bar, teppanyaki grill tables and private dining rooms. The sushi and tempura set (B900) is especially delicious.

Gianni 34/1 Soi Tonson, Thanon Ploenchit ⓣ02 252 1619. One of Bangkok's best independent Italian restaurants, successfully blending traditional and modern in both its decor and food. Offerings include a belt- (and bank-) busting tasting menu for B1190 and innovative pastas.

Inter 432/1–2 Soi 9, Siam Square. Honest, efficient Thai restaurant that's popular with students and shoppers, serving good one-dish meals for around B50, as well as curries, salads and Isaan food, in a no-frills, fluorescent-lit canteen atmosphere.

Ma Be Ba 93 Soi Lang Suan ⓣ02 254 9595. Lively, spacious and extravagantly decorated Italian restaurant dishing up a good variety of antipasti, excellent pastas (around B300 and upwards) and pizzas (in two sizes), and traditional main courses strong on seafood. Live music nightly, mostly pop covers, country and Latin, plus jazz piano early evenings Wed–Fri.

Mah Boon Krong Food Centre north end of Floor 6, MBK shopping centre, corner of Thanon Rama I and Thanon Phrayathai. Increase your knowledge of Thai food here: ingredients, names and pictures of a wide variety of tasty, cheap one-dish meals from all over the country are displayed at the various stalls, as well as fresh juices and a wide range of desserts. Other cuisines, such as Vietnamese, Chinese, Indian, Japanese and Italian are now also represented, charging slightly higher prices.

Pisces 36/6 Soi Kasemsan 1, Thanon Rama I. Drawing plenty of custom from the local guest houses, a friendly, family-run restaurant, neat and colourful, serving a wide variety of breakfasts and cheap, tasty Thai food, with lots of vegetarian options. Daily 8am–1pm & 5–10.30pm.

Sarah Jane's Ground Floor, Sindhorn Tower 1, 130–132 Thanon Witthayu ⓣ02 650 9992–3. Long-standing restaurant, popular with Bangkok's Isaan population, serving excellent, simple northeastern dishes, as well as Italian food. It's in slick but unfussy modern premises that can be slightly tricky to find at night, towards the rear of a modern office block. Moderate.

Sorn's 36/8 Soi Kasemsan 1, Thanon Rama I. In this quiet lane of superior guest houses, a laid-back, moderately priced hangout decorated with black-and-white prints of Thailand by the photographer owner. Delicious versions of standard Thai dishes – the *tom kha kai* is especially good – as well as Western meals, a huge breakfast menu including reasonably priced set meals, and good teas and coffees. Daily 7am–noon & 5–11pm.

Thang Long 82/5 Soi Lang Suan ⓣ02 251 3504. Excellent Vietnamese food, such as lemon grass fish (B175) in this stylish, minimalist and popular restaurant, all stone floors, plants and whitewashed walls.

Vanilla Industry Soi 11, Siam Square. Small, sophisticated, good-value, first-floor restaurant that's a shrine to Western gourmet delights (backed up by a cookery school on the floor above): smoked salmon finger sandwiches, spot-on desserts such as strawberry panna cotta, pastas, salads and other main courses, and excellent teas and coffees.

Whole Earth 93/3 Soi Lang Suan ⓣ02 252 5574. Long-standing veggie-oriented restaurant, serving interesting and varied Thai and Indian-style dishes (B100 and under) for both vegetarians and omnivores in a relaxing atmosphere.

Zen Floor 6, Central World Plaza, corner of Thanon Ploenchit and Thanon Rajdamri ⓣ02 255 6462; Floor 3, MBK shopping centre, corner of Thanon Rama I and Thanon Phrayathai ⓣ02620 9007–8; and Floor 4, Siam Center, Thanon Rama I ⓣ02 658 1183–4. Good-value Japanese restaurant with wacky modern wooden design and seductive booths. Among a huge range of dishes, the complete meal sets (with pictures to help you choose) are filling and particularly good.

Downtown: south of Thanon Rama IV

The places listed below are marked on the maps on p.100, p.125 and p.126. In this area, there are also branches of *Baan Khanitha* (see p.192) at 67 Thanon Sathorn Tai, at the corner of Soi Suan Phlu (ⓣ02 675 4200), and *Zen* (see above), at 1/1 Thanon Convent (ⓣ02 266 7150–1).

Angelini's *Shangri-La Hotel*, 89 Soi Wat Suan Plu, Thanon Charoen Krung ⓣ02 236 7777. One of the capital's best Italians, pricey but not too extravagant. The setting is lively and relaxed, with open-plan kitchen and big picture windows onto the pool and river. There are some unusual main courses as well as old favourites like *ossobucco*, or you can invent your own wood-oven-baked pizza.

Anna's Café 118 Thanon Saladaeng ⓣ02 632 0619–20. In a large, elegant villa between Silom and Sathorn roads, reliable, varied and very reasonably priced Thai and Western dishes and desserts, including a very good *som tam, kai yang* and sticky rice combo.

Aoi 132/10–11 Soi 6, Thanon Silom ⓣ02 235 2321–2. The best place in town for a Japanese blowout, justifiably popular with the expat community. Excellent authentic food and elegant decor. Good-value lunch sets (from B250) available and a superb sushi bar.

Ban Chiang 14 Soi Srivieng, off Thanon Surasak, between Thanon Silom and Thanon Sathorn ⓣ02 236 7045. Fine, reasonably priced central and northeastern Thai cuisine in an elegant, surprisingly quiet wooden house with garden tables.

Celadon *Sukhothai Hotel*, 13/3 Thanon Sathorn Tai ⓣ02 287 0222. Consistently rated as one of the best hotel restaurants in Bangkok and a favourite with locals, serving outstanding traditional and contemporary Thai food in an elegant setting surrounded by lotus ponds.

Chai Karr 312/3 Thanon Silom, opposite *Holiday Inn* ⓣ02 233 2549. Folksy, traditional-style wooden decor is the welcoming setting for a wide variety of well-prepared, modestly priced Thai and Chinese dishes, followed by home-made coconut ice cream. Closed Sun.

Charuvan 70–2 Thanon Silom, near the entrance to Soi 4. Cheap but lackadaisical place to refuel, with an air-con room, specializing in tasty duck on rice; the beer's a bargain too.

Cy'an *Metropolitan Hotel*, 27 Thanon Sathorn Tai ⓣ02 625 3333. Expensive but highly inventive cooking, fusing Asian and Mediterranean elements to produce strong, clean flavours, with great attention to detail. Charming service to go with it, in a stylish room with the best tables on a terrace overlooking the pool.

Deen 786 Thanon Silom, almost opposite Silom Village. Small, basic, air-con Muslim café (no alcohol), which offers Thai and Chinese standard dishes with a southern Thai twist, as well as spicy Indian-style curries and specialities such as *grupuk* (crispy fish) and *roti kaeng* (Muslim pancakes with curry).

Eat Me 1/6 Soi Phiphat 2, Thanon Convent ⓣ02 238 0931. Highly fashionable art gallery and restaurant in a striking, white, modernist building, with changing exhibitions on the walls and a temptingly relaxing balcony. The pricey, far-reaching menu is more international – tenderloin steak fillet with Dijon sauce, pancetta-wrapped chicken breast with grape salad – than fusion, though the lemon grass crème brûlée is not to be missed. Daily 3pm–1am.

Harmonique 22 Soi 34, Thanon Charoen Krung, on the lane between Wat Muang Kae express-boat pier and the GPO ⓣ02 237 8175. A relaxing, welcoming, moderately priced restaurant that's well worth a trip: tables are scattered throughout several converted shophouses, decorated with antiques, and a quiet, leafy courtyard, and the Thai food is varied and excellent – among the seafood specialities, try the crab or red shrimp curries. Closed Sun.

Himali Cha-Cha 1229/11 Soi 47/1, Thanon Charoen Krung, south of GPO ⓣ02 235 1569 (plus a branch down a short alley off the north end of Thanon Convent, opposite *Irish Xchange*). Fine, moderately priced North Indian restaurant, founded by a character who was chef to numerous Indian ambassadors, and now run by his son. Homely atmosphere, attentive service and a good vegetarian selection.

Indian Hut 311/2–5 Thanon Suriwong, ⓣ02 237 8812. Bright, white-tablecloth, North Indian restaurant – look out for the *Pizza Hut*-style sign – that's reasonably priced and justly popular with local Indians. For carnivores, tandoori's the thing, with an especially good kastoori chicken kebab with saffron and cumin. There's a huge selection of mostly vegetarian pakoras as appetizers, as well as plenty of veggie main courses and breads, and a hard-to-resist house dahl.

Ishq 142 Thanon Sathorn Nua ⓣ02 634 5398–9. A beautiful Portuguese colonial-style mansion, with especially opulent bathrooms, set back from the main road and Surasak BTS station amidst fountains. Pricey but very good food from all over southeast Asia, including tasty Lao mushroom soup and Vietnamese beef balls.

Jim Thompson's Saladaeng Café 120/1 Soi 1, Thanon Saladaeng ⓣ02 266 9167. A civilized, moderately priced haven with tables in the elegantly informal air-con interior or out in the leafy garden. Thai food stretches to some unusual dishes such as deep-fried morning glory with spicy shrimp and minced pork. There's pasta, salads and other Western dishes, plus a few stabs at fusion including delicious spaghetti *sai ua* (with northern Thai sausage and tomato sauce) and linguini *tom yam kung*. The array of desserts is mouthwatering, rounded off by good coffee and a wide choice of teas.

Khrua Aroy Aroy 3/1 Thanon Pan. In a fruitful area for cheap food (including a night market across Silom on Soi 20), this simple shophouse restaurant stands out for its choice of tasty, well-prepared dishes from all around the kingdom, notably *khao soi*, *kaeng matsaman* and *khanom jiin*. Lunchtimes only.

La Boulange 2–2/1 Thanon Convent. A fine choice for breakfast with great croissants and all sorts of tempting patisserie made on the premises. For savoury lunches and dinners, choose from a variety of quiches, sandwiches, salads and typical brasserie fare such as *gigot d'agneau*.

Le Bouchon 37/17 Patpong 2, near Thanon Suriwong ⓣ02 234 9109. Cosy, welcoming bar-bistro that's much frequented by the city's French expats, offering French home-cooking, such as lamb shank in a white bean sauce (B490); booking is strongly recommended. Closed Sun lunchtime.

Le Café Siam 4 Soi Sri Akson, Thanon Chua Ploeng ⓣ02 671 0030, ⓦwww.lecafesiam.com. An early-twentieth-century Sino-Thai mansion in a tranquil garden that's difficult to find off the eastern end of Soi Sri Bamphen, but well worth the effort (the restaurant suggests the number of a taxi company – ⓣ02 611 6499 – or you can download a map from their website). The French and Thai food, with main courses starting at B200, is superb, served in a relaxing ambience that subtly blends Chinese and French styles, with an especially seductive bar area upstairs. Evenings only.

Mali Soi Jusmag, just off Soi Ngam Duphli. Cosy, informal, low-lit restaurant, mostly air-con with a few cramped tables out front. The Thai menu specializes in salads and northeastern food, with plenty of veggie options, while Western options run as far as burgers, potato salad, all-day breakfasts, delicious banana pancakes and a few Mexican dishes. Moderate.

Mei Jiang *Peninsula Hotel*, 333 Thanon Charoennakorn, Klongsan ⓣ02 861 2888. Probably Bangkok's best Chinese restaurant, with beautiful views of the hotel gardens and the river night and day. It's designed like an elegant teak box, and staff are very attentive and graceful. Specialities include duck smoked with tea and excellent lunchtime *dim sum* – a bargain, starting at B80 a dish.

River View Floor 2, River City Shopping Centre, off Thanon Charoen Krung ⓣ02 237 0077–8, ext 233. A bit cheesy – waiters with jazzy waistcoats and truly awful muzzak – but the views of the river are great and the food's very tasty, including lots of fish dishes, salads and a vegetarian selection; the deep-fried chicken with cashewnuts (B150) and deep-fried pompanos fish with mango salad are recommended.

Somboon Seafood Thanon Suriwong, corner of Thanon Narathiwat Ratchanakharin ⓣ02 234 4499. Highly favoured seafood restaurant, known for its crab curry (B250) and soy-steamed sea bass, with simple, smart decor and an array of marine life lined up in tanks outside awaiting its gastronomic fate.

Thien Duong *Dusit Thani Hotel*, cnr Silom and Rama IV roads ⓣ02 236 9999. Probably Bangkok's finest Vietnamese, a classy and expensive restaurant serving beautifully prepared dishes such as succulent *salat cua*, deep-fried soft-shell crab salad with cashew nuts and herb dressing, and zesty *goi ngo sen*, lotus-stem salad with shrimp and pork.

Tongue Thai 18–20 Soi 38, Thanon Charoen Krung ⓣ02 630 9918–9. In front of the Oriental Place shopping mall. Very high standards of food and cleanliness, with charming, unpretentious service, in a 100-year-old shophouse elegantly decorated with Thai and Chinese antiques and contemporary art. Veggies are very well catered for with delicious dishes such as tofu in black bean sauce and deep-fried banana-flower and corn cakes, while carnivores should try the fantastic beef curry (*panaeng neua*; B170).

Thanon Sukhumvit

See the map on p.128 for locations of the places listed below. In this area, there are also branches of *Aoi* (see p.191), Floor 4, Emporium shopping centre (ⓣ02 664 8590–2), and *Himali Cha-Cha* (see p.191), 2 Soi 35, Thanon Sukhumvit (ⓣ02 258 8846). For those restaurants east of sois 39 and 26 that are not shown on the map, we've given directions from the nearest Skytrain station.

Al Ferdoss Soi 3/1. Long-running Lebanese and Turkish restaurant in the heart of Sukhumvit's Middle Eastern soi, where you can smoke hookah pipes on the streetside terrace and choose from a menu (B70–150) that encompasses shish, hummus, tabouleh and the rest.

Baan Khanitha 36/1 Soi 23 ⓣ02 258 4128. The big attraction at this long-running favourite haunt of Sukhumvit expats is the setting in a traditional Thai house. The food is upmarket Thai and fairly pricey, and includes lots of fiery salads (*yam*), and a good range of *tom yam* soups, green curries and seafood curries.

Ban Rie Coffee Opposite Ekamai Eastern Bus Station and beside the Ekamai Skytrain station on the corner of Soi 63. Surely the perfect place to await your next east-coast bus, this chic teakwood pavilion welcomes you via a wooden walkway across a narrow fringe of ricefields and works hard to create a soothing ambience inside. It serves a decent selection of mid-priced hot and iced coffees, as well as Thai desserts, and also offers Internet access and terrace seating.

Bangkok Baking Company Ground Floor, *JW Mariott Hotel*, between sois 2 and 4. Exceptionally delicious cakes, pastries and breads: everything from rosemary focaccia to tiramisu cheesecake (B65–100).

Basil *Sheraton Grande Hotel*, between sois 12 and 14. Mouthwateringly fine traditional Thai food with a modern twist is the order of the day at this trendy, relatively informal though high-priced restaurant in the super-deluxe five-star *Sheraton*. Recommendations include the grilled river prawns with chilli, the *matsaman* curry (both served with red and green rice) and the surprisingly delicious durian cheesecake. Vegetarian menu on request. Also offers cooking classes (see p.216).

Cabbages and Condoms 6–8 Soi 12, ⓦwww.pda.or.th/restaurant. Run by the Population and Community Development Association of Thailand (PDA; see p.177) – "our food is guaranteed not to cause pregnancy" – so diners are treated to authentic Thai food in the Condom Room, and relaxed scoffing of barbecued seafood in the beer garden. Try the spicy catfish salad (B130) or the prawns steamed in a whole coconut (B250). All proceeds go to the PDA, and there's an adjacent shop selling double-entendre T-shirts, cards, key rings and of course, condoms.

Dosa King Mouth of Soi 19. Informal, all-vegetarian Indian cafe serving good, unpretentious food from both north and south, including twenty different dosa (southern pancake) dishes, tandooris, etc. An alcohol-free zone so you'll have to make do with sweet lassi instead. Most dishes B120–180.

Face Bangkok: La Na Thai and Hazara 29 Soi 38; about 150m walk from BTS Thong Lo Exit 4 ⓣ02 713 6048, ⓦwww.facebars.com. Two restaurants, a bar, a bakery and a spa occupy this attractive compound of traditional, steeply gabled wooden Thai houses. Each restaurant is tastefully styled with appropriate artefacts and fabrics, and the adjacent *Face Bar* makes a chic 'n' funky place for a pre- or post-dinner drink. All venues offer an extensive list of imported wines. The very upmarket *Lan Na Thai* restaurant (daily 11.30am–2.30pm & 6.30–11.30pm) serves quality Thai food, such as Chiang Mai-style pork curry (B390) and deep-fried grouper with tamarind sauce (B460), while the *Hazara* (daily 6.30–11.30pm) specializes in Afghani and north-Indian tandoor cuisine, including murgh Peshwar chicken (B390) and the signature cardamon–marinated lamb (B590).

Gaeng Pa Lerd Rod Soi 33/1; no English sign but it's just before the *Bull's Head*. Hugely popular outdoor restaurant whose tables are clustered under trees in a streetside yard and get packed with office workers at lunchtime. Thai curries (from B40) are the speciality here, with dishes ranging from conventional versions, like catfish and beef curries, to more adventurous offerings like fried cobra with chilli, and curried frog. Inexpensive.

Gallery 11 Soi 11. Sharing the traffic free sub-soi with the idiosyncratic *Suk 11* guest house, this restaurant fosters a similarly laid-back rustic atmosphere, with its wooden building, plentiful foliage and moody lighting. The food is good, authentic, mid-price Thai, with plenty of spicy *yam* salads, seafood and curries, mostly B100–200. Also serves lots of cocktails and imported wines by the glass (B150).

Le Dalat Indochine 14 Soi 23 ⓣ02 661 7967. There's Indochinese romance aplenty at this delightfully atmospheric restaurant, which is housed in an early-twentieth-century villa decked out in homely style with plenty of photos, pot plants at every turn and eclectic curiosities in the male and female toilets. The extensive, Vietnamese menu features favourites such as a *goi ca* salad of aromatic herbs and shredded pork, *chao tom* shrimp sticks and *ga sa gung*, chicken curry with caramelized ginger. Set dinners from B1000.

Lemongrass 5/1 Soi 24 ⓣ02 258 8637. Known for its delicious Thai nouvelle cuisine (B120–500), including a particularly good minced chicken with ginger, and for its pleasant setting in a converted traditional house. A vegetarian menu is available on request. Advance reservations recommended. Daily 6–11pm.

MahaNaga 2 Soi 29, ⓦwww.mahanaga.com. The dining experience at this tranquil enclave is best appreciated after dark, when the fountain-courtyard tables are romantically lit and the air-con interior seduces with its burgundy velvet drapes. Cuisine is fusion fine-dining, though some east-west combos work better than others and the vegetarian selection is underwhelming. Grilled salmon in red curry is a winner (B350), or you might brave the rack of lamb served with spicy vegetables, egg noodles and mango sauce (B450).

Nipa 3rd Floor, Landmark Plaza, between sois 4 and 6. Tasteful traditional Thai-style place, run by the adjacent hotel, *The Landmark Bangkok*, whose classy menu features an adventurous range of dishes, including spicy fish curry (B180), several *matsaman* and green curries (B220), excellent *som tam* and mouthwatering braised spare ribs. Also offers a sizeable vegetarian selection. Regular cookery classes are held here – see "Listings" on p.216 for details.

Pizza Venezia Soi 11 ⓦwww.veneziabangkok.com. Fairly formal Italian place that's a favourite with Sukhumvit expats for its pizzas (B180–360). Also offers a diverse roster of daily specials, plus classic pasta, meat and fish dishes, including a good oven-baked sea bass in white-wine sauce (B590).

Suda Restaurant Soi 14. Unpretentious shop-house restaurant whose formica tables and plastic chairs spill out onto the soi and are mainly patronized by budget-conscious expats and their Thai friends. The friendly proprietor serves a good, long menu of Thai favourites (from B40), including deep-fried chicken in banana leaves, battered shrimps, fried tuna with cashews and chilli, and sticky rice with mango.

Tamarind Café 300m down Soi 20 ⓦwww.tamarind-cafe.com. This stylish vegetarian café and photo gallery serves an eclectic menu that fuses flavours from Korea, Malaysia, Thailand, Japan and the Mediterranean in a refreshingly innovative menu. Wild mushroom steak (B280), Malaysian-style quesadilla (B95) and triple-bean salad (B110) all feature, as does all-day brunch. There are changing photo exhibitions, lounge-style seating, free wi-fi Internet access, and a roof terrace. Mon–Fri 11am–11pm, Sat & Sun 9am–11pm.

Took Lae Dee Inside the Foodland supermarket on Soi 5. The place to come for very cheap breakfasts: hearty American breakfasts eaten at the counter cost just B55.

Vientiane Kitchen (Khrua Vientiane) 8 Soi 36, about 50m south off Thanon Sukhumvit. Just a 3min walk west then south from Thong Lo Skytrain station (Exit 2) and you're transported into a little piece of Isaan, where the menu's stocked full of northeastern delicacies, a live band sets the mood with heart-felt folk songs, and there are even occasional performances by a troupe of upcountry dancers. The Lao- and Isaan-accented menu (B120–250) includes vegetable curry with ants' eggs, spicy-fried frog, jackfruit curry, and farm chicken with cashews, plus there's a decent range of veggie options such as meat-free *larb* and sweet and sour dishes. With its airy, barn-like interior and a mixed clientele of Thais and expats, it all adds up to a very enjoyable dining experience.

Yong Lee Corner of Soi 15. One of the few refreshingly basic – and brusque – rice-and-noodle shops on Sukhumvit; dishes cost from just B40. Daily 11.30am–2.30pm & 5.30–9.30pm.

Nightlife and entertainment

For many of Bangkok's male visitors, nightfall is the signal to hit the city's sex bars, most notoriously in the area off Thanon Silom known as Patpong (see p.176). Fortunately, Bangkok's **nightlife** has thoroughly grown up and left these neon sumps behind in the last ten years, offering everything from microbreweries and vertiginous, roof top cocktail bars to fiercely chic clubs and dance bars, hosting top-class DJs: within spitting distance of the beer bellies flopped onto Patpong's bars, for example, lies Soi 4, Thanon Silom, one of the city's most happening after-dark haunts. Along with Silom 4, the high-concept clubs and bars of Sukhumvit and the lively, teeming venues of Banglamphu pull in the style-conscious cream of Thai youth and are tempting an increasing number of travellers to stuff their party gear into their rucksacks. Though Silom 4 started out as a purely **gay** area, it now offers a range of styles in gay, mixed and straight pubs, DJ bars and clubs, while the city's other main gay area is the more exclusive Silom 2 (towards Thanon Rama IV). As with the straight scene, many gay bars feature go-go dancers and live sex shows. Those listed here do not. Most bars and clubs operate nightly until 1am, while clubs on Silom 4 and Silom 2 can stay open until 2am, with closing time strictly enforced under the current government's Social Order Policy. This has also involved occasional clampdowns on illegal drugs, including urine testing of bar customers, and more widespread ID checks to curb under-age drinking (you have to be 21 or over to drink in bars and clubs) – it's worth bringing your passport out with you, as ID is often requested however old you are.

On the cultural front, the most accessible of the capital's performing arts are **Thai dancing**, particularly when served up in bite-size portions in tourist shows, and the graceful and humorous performances at the **Traditional Thai Puppet Theatre** on Thanon Rama IV. **Thai boxing** is also well worth watching: the live experience at either of Bangkok's two main national stadia far outshines the TV coverage.

Bars and clubs

For convenient drinking and dancing, we've split the most recommended of the city's bars and clubs into four central areas. The travellers' enclave of Banglamphu takes on a new personality after dark, when its hub, Thanon Khao San, becomes a "walking street", closed to all traffic but open to almost any kind of makeshift stall, selling everything from fried bananas and cheap beer to bargain fashions and idiosyncratic art works. Young Thais crowd the area to browse and snack before piling in to Banglamphu's countless bars and clubs, most of which host a good mix of local and foreign drinkers and ravers. Venues here tend to be low-key, with free entry (though some places ask you to show ID first), reasonably priced drinks and up-to-date sounds, or there's always plenty of kerbside restaurant tables, which make great places to nurse a few beers and watch the parade. Away from Khao San and nearby Soi Ram Bhuttri, Thanon Phra Athit is famous for its style-conscious little restaurant-bars where tables spill over onto the pavement, and the live music is likely to be a lone piano-player or guitarist.

Downtown bars, which tend to attract both foreign and Thai drinkers, are concentrated on adjoining Soi Lang Suan and Soi Sarasin (between Thanon Ploenchit and Lumphini Park), and in studenty Siam Square, as well as around the east end of Thanon Silom. Lang Suan and Sarasin boast several live-music bars, while the western end of the latter (between the jazz bar, *Brown Sugar*, and Thanon Rajdamri) supports a gaggle of good-time, gay and straight, DJ bars that are very popular with young Thais at weekends. On Silom 4, while most of the gay venues have been around for some years now, other bars and clubs have opened and closed with bewildering speed. All the same – once you've passed through the ID check at the entrance – on a short, slow bar-crawl around this wide, traffic-free alley lined with pavement tables, it would be hard not to find somewhere to enjoy yourself. If, among all the choice of nightlife around Silom, you do end up in one of Patpong's sex shows, watch out for hyper-inflated bar bills and other cons – plenty of customers get ripped off in some way, and stories of menacing bouncers are legion. Thanon Sukhumvit also has its share of girlie bars and bar-beers (open-sided drinking halls with huge circular bars) packed full of hostesses, but it's also garnering quite a reputation for high-concept "destination bars" (where the decor is as important as the drinks menu), as well as being the home of several long-established British-style pubs.

During the cool season (Nov–Feb), an evening out at one of the seasonal **beer gardens** is a pleasant way of soaking up the urban atmosphere (and the traffic fumes). You'll find them in hotel forecourts or sprawled in front of dozens of shopping centres all over the city.

Banglamphu and Ratanakosin

Except where indicated, all bars listed below are marked on the map on p.116.

Ad Here the 13th 13 Thanon Samsen. Friendly, intimate little jazz bar where half a dozen tables of Thai and expat musos congregate to listen to nightly sets from the in-house blues 'n' jazz quartet (about 10pm onwards). Well-priced beer and plenty of cocktails. Nightly 6pm–midnight.

Bangkok Bar Next to *Sawasdee Inn* at 149 Soi Ram Bhuttri. This skinny two-storey dance bar is fronted by a different DJ every night whose pop and house beats draw capacity crowds nightly. Nightly 6pm–1am.

Bar Bali 58 Thanon Phra Athit. Typical Phra Athit bar-restaurant, with just a half-dozen tables, a small menu of salads and drinking foods and a decent selection of well-priced cocktails. Nightly 6pm–1am.

Café Democ 78 Thanon Rajdamnoen Klang. Fashionable, dark and dinky bar that overlooks Democracy Monument and is spread over one and a half cosy floors, with extra seating on the semi-circular mezzanine. Lots of cocktails, nightly sessions from up-and-coming Thai DJs, and regular hip-hop evenings. Tues–Sun 4pm–2am.

The Cave Thanon Khao San. Feel like climbing the walls after your tenth bottle of Singha? This bar comes complete with indoor climbing wall, charging B100 per climb or B200/hour. Also sells climbing shoes and gear. Nightly 5pm–midnight.

Cinnamon Bar 106 Thanon Ram Bhuttri. Drink at little tables on the narrow outside terrace, beneath the waterfall wall and plastic bamboo trees, or join the fashionable, well-behaved student crowd around the pool table inside. Nightly 6pm–1am.

The Club Thanon Khao San. The kitsch, pseudo Italianate interior – designed to evoke a classical courtyard garden, complete with central fountain and statue of a chubby child hugging a fish – is unlikely to appeal to many Western clubbers, but Thais love this place, putting up with the ID checks at the door and making the most of the two bars and resident DJs. Also serves food. Daily 11am–1am.

Comme Thanon Phra Athit. Live music from enthusiastic cover bands, easy chairs and an open frontage mean that this inviting bar-restaurant, one of the largest on Phra Athit, nearly always gets a good crowd. Also serves some food (mostly Thai standards). 6pm–1am.

Deep 329/1-2 Thanon Ram Bhuttri. Get here early if you want a table on a Friday or Saturday night as the bands draw eager crowds that pack out the tiny bar. 6pm–1am.

Gulliver's Traveler's Tavern Thanon Khao San, ⓦ www.gulliverbangkok.com. Infamous, long-established backpacker-oriented air-con pub with pool tables, sports TV and reasonably priced beer (happy hours 3–9pm). Also does international food and has another branch on Thanon Sukhumvit. Daily 11am–1am.

Lava Club Basement, Bayon Building, 209 Thanon Khao San. Self-consciously sophisticated basement lounge bar done out in "volcanic" red and black with laser displays to enhance the look. DJs play mainly house and rave. Nightly 8pm–1am; ID sometimes required.

Molly Pub Thanon Ram Bhuttri. The attractive, colonial-style facade, complete with pastel-coloured shutters, make a pleasant backdrop for the outdoor tables and low-slung wooden chairs that are perfectly located for people-watching over a Beer Chang or two. Also serves food. Daily 11am–1am.

Po 230 Tha Thien, Thanon Maharat (see map on p.132). When the Chao Phraya express boats start to wind down around 6pm, this bar takes over the rustic wooden pier and the balcony above with their great sunset views across the river. Beer and Thai whisky with accompanying Thai food and loud Thai and Western pop music – very popular with local students.

Sabai Bar Mouth of Sunset Street, 197 Thanon Khao San. Open-sided, three-storey, streetside bar that's the perfect spot for watching the Khao San parade. Nightly 6pm–1am.

Silk Bar 129–131 Thanon Khao San. The tiered outdoor decks are a popular spot for sipping cocktails while watching the nightly Khao San hustle; inside there's air-con, a pool table, a DJ and a small menu of standard Thai fare. Daily 6am–1am.

Susie Pub Next to *Marco Polo Guest House* on the soi between Thanon Khao San and Thanon Ram Bhuttri. Big, dark, phenomenally popular pub that's usually standing-room-only after 9pm. Has a pool table, decent music, resident DJs and cheapish beer. Packed with young Thais. Daily 11am–1am; ID sometimes required.

Siam Square, Thanon Ploenchit and northern downtown

The venues listed below are marked on the map on p.168.

Ad Makers 51/51 Soi Langsuan ⓣ 02 652 0168. Friendly, spacious bar with Wild West-style wooden decor and good food, attracting a cross-section of Thais and foreigners and featuring nightly folk and rock bands.

Brown Sugar 231/19–20 Soi Sarasin ⓣ 02 250 1826. Chic, pricey, lively bar, acknowledged as the capital's top jazz venue.
Concept CM² *Novotel*, Soi 6, Siam Square ⓣ 02 209 8888. More theme park than nightclub, with live bands and various, barely distinct entertainment zones, including karaoke, an Italian restaurant and everything from bhangra to hip-hop in the Boom Room. Admission B550 (including two drinks) Fri & Sat, B220 (including one drink) Sun–Thurs.
Dallas Pub Soi 6, Siam Square ⓣ 02 255 3276. Typical dark, noisy "songs for life" hangout – buffalo skulls, Indian heads, American flags – but a lot of fun: singalongs to decent live bands, dancing round the tables, cheap beer and friendly, casual staff.
Hard Rock Café Soi 11, Siam Square. Genuine outlet of the famous chain, better for drink than food. Brash enthusiasm and big sounds, with predictable live bands nightly.
Saxophone 3/8 Victory Monument (southeast corner), Thanon Phrayathai ⓣ 02 246 5472. Lively, spacious venue that hosts nightly jazz, blues, folk and rock bands and attracts a good mix of Thais and farangs; decent food, relaxed drinking atmosphere and, all things considered, reasonable prices.
Syn Bar *Swissôtel Nai Lert Park*, 2 Thanon Witthayu. Hip hotel bar, popular at weekends, decorated retro style with bubble chairs and sparkling fibre-optic carpet. Excellent cocktails and nightly DJs playing house and Latin; happy hour Mon–Fri 5–9pm.
WOC 264/4–6 Soi 3, Siam Square. Smart, modernist but easy-going hangout for students and 20-somethings, with reasonably priced drinks, a good choice of accompanying snacks and some interesting Thai/Italian pastas for main dishes. A little hard to find up some stairs by Siam Square's Centerpoint.

Southern downtown: south of Thanon Rama IV

See the map on p.125 for locations of the venues listed below.

The Barbican 9/4–5 Soi Thaniya, east end of Thanon Silom ⓣ 02 234 3590. Stylishly modern fortress-like decor to match the name: dark woods, metal and undressed stone. With Guinness on tap and the financial pages posted above the urinals, it could almost be a smart City of London pub – until you look out of the windows onto the soi's incongruous Japanese hostess bars. Good food, DJ sessions and happy hours Mon–Fri 5–7pm.
Hu'u Ascott Building, 187 Thanon Sathorn Tai. Moody, elegant and dimly lit bar in Asian minimalist style, playing hot or cool sounds according to the time of night and serving excellent cocktails, alongside snacks and tapas; be prepared for a stylish surprise at the toilet washbasins.
Irish Xchange 1/5 Thanon Convent, off the east end of Thanon Silom ⓣ 02 266 7160. Blarney Bangkok-style: a warm, relaxing Irish pub, tastefully done out in dark wood and familiar knick-knacks and packed with expats, especially on Fri night. Guinness and Kilkenny Bitter on tap, expensive food such as Irish stew and beef and Guinness pie, and a rota of house bands.
Lucifer 76/1–3 Patpong 1. Popular dance club in the dark heart of Patpong, largely untouched by the sleaze around it. Done out with mosaics and stalactites like a satanic grotto, with balconies to look down on the dance-floor action. Free entry, except Fri & Sat, B150 including one drink. *Radio City*, the interconnected bar downstairs, is only slightly less raucous, with jumping live bands, including famous Elvis and Tom Jones impersonators, and tables out on the sweaty pavement.
Noriega's Soi 4, Thanon Silom. Unpretentious, good-time bar at the end of the alley, with nightly live bands playing jazz, blues and rock; salsa lessons followed by big Latin sounds on Sun evenings.
The Sky Bar & Distil Floor 63, State Tower, 1055 Thanon Silom, cnr of Thanon Charoen Krung ⓣ 02 624 9555. Thrill-seekers and view addicts shouldn't miss forking out for an al fresco drink here, 275 metres above the city's pavements – come around 6pm to enjoy the stunning panoramas in both the light and the dark. It's standing only at *The Sky Bar*, a circular restaurant bar on the edge of the building with almost 360° views, but for the sunset itself, you're better off on the outside terrace of *Distil* on the other side of the building (where bookings are accepted), which has a wider choice of drinks, charming service and huge couches to recline on.
Speed Soi 4, Thanon Silom. Dance bar with an industrial feel in black and silver, popular at the weekend, playing hip-hop and R'n'B. Fri & Sat B100, including one drink.
Tapas Bar Soi 4, Thanon Silom ⓦ www.tapasroom.com. Vaguely Spanish-oriented, pricey bar (but no tapas) with Moorish-style decor, whose outside tables are probably the best spot for checking out the comings and goings on the soi; inside, music ranges from house and hip-hop to Latin jazz and funk, often with an accompanying percussionist (Fri & Sat admission B100).
Tawandaeng German Brewery 462/61 Thanon Rama III ⓣ 02 678 1114–5. A

△ The Sky Bar

taxi-ride south of Thanon Sathorn down Thanon Narathiwat Ratchanakharin – and best to book a table in advance – this vast all-rounder is well worth the effort. Under a huge dome, up to 1600 revellers enjoy good food and great micro brewed beer every night, but the main attraction is the mercurial cabaret (not Sun), featuring Fong Naam, led by Bruce Gaston, who blend Thai classical and popular with Western styles of music.

Thanon Sukhumvit

The places listed below are marked on the map on p.128. Note that many clubs in Sukhumvit require you to show ID when you enter, to prove that you are 21.

The Ball in Hand Ist floor of the *Sin* building, behind 7/11 on Soi 4, ⓦ www.theballinhand.com. In notoriously sleazy Soi 4, better known as Soi Nana, this vast pool hall and bar stands out from all the other places with pool tables because of its dozen or so high-quality imported tables, its strict no-hustle policy and its regular competitions. Daily from about 1pm–1am.

Bed Supperclub 26 Soi 11 ⓣ 02 651 3537, ⓦ www.bedsupperclub.com. Worth visiting for the futuristic visuals alone, this seductively curvaceous spacepod bar squats self-consciously in an otherwise quite ordinary soi. Inside, the all-white interior is dimly lit and surprisingly cosy, with deep couches inviting drinkers to recline around the edges of the upstairs gallery, getting a good view of the downstairs bar and DJ. The vibe is always welcoming and a lot less pretentious than you might expect; some nights are themed, including a weekly gay night (check listings mags or website for details), when a B500 cover charge is redeemble against two drinks of the equivalent price. The restaurant section is starker, lit with glacial ultra-violet, and serving a Pacific Rim fusion menu from 7.30–9pm (reservations essential). Bar opens nightly from 8pm–2am; ID required.

The Bull's Head Soi 33/1. A Sukhumvit institution that takes pride in being Bangkok's most authentic British pub, right down to the horse brasses, jukebox and typical pub food. Famous for its Sunday evening "toss the boss" happy hours (5–7pm), when a flip of a coin determines whether or not you have to pay for your round. Daily 11am–1.30am.

Cheap Charlie's Soi 11. Idiosyncratic, long-running pavement bar that's famous for its cheap beer and lack of tables and chairs. A few lucky punters get to occupy the bar-stools but otherwise it's standing room only. Daily 3pm–2am.

Gulliver's Traveler's Tavern 6 Soi 5, ⓦ www.gulliverbangkok.com. An offshoot of the original Khao San sports bar, this cavernous branch has tables inside and out at which it serves draught Guinness and the rest (happy hour lasts from midday–9pm), as well as an international menu. Shows live sporting fixtures on TV and has table football, pool tables and Internet access. Daily 11am–1am.

Londoner Brew Pub Mouth of Soi 33, Ⓦwww.the-londoner.com. Aside from the pool table, darts board, big-screen sports TV and live music (nightly from about 9pm), it's the specially brewed pints of Londoner's Pride Cream Bitter and London Pilsner 33 that draw in the punters. Happy hours 4–7pm & 11pm–1am. Also has free wi-fi Internet access. Daily 11am–1am.

Q Bar 34 Soi 11, Ⓦwww.qbarbangkok.com. Very dark, very trendy, New York-style bar occupying two floors and a terrace. Famous for its wide choice of chilled vodkas, and for its music, *Q Bar* appeals to a mixed crowd of fashionable people, particularly on Friday and Saturday nights when the DJs fill the dance floor. Arrive before 11pm if you want a seat, and don't turn up in shorts, singlets or sandals if you're male. Mon–Thurs B400 incl 2 free drinks, Fri–Sun B600. Daily 8pm–1am; ID required.

Robin Hood Mouth of Soi 33/1. Another popular British pub, with pool table, sports TV and English food, plus an all-day breakfast for B280. Daily 11am–1am.

Gay scene

The bars, clubs and bar-restaurants listed here are the most notable of Bangkok's gay nightlife venues; *Bed Supperclub* (see opposite) also hosts a regular gay night. For more general background on gay life in Thailand, contacts and sources of information, most of them concentrated in Bangkok, see p.74. Don't forget **Bangkok Pride** (Ⓦwww.bangkokpride.org) in mid-November, when the capital's gay community struts its stuff in a week of parades, cabarets, fancy-dress shows and sports contests.

The Balcony Soi 4, Thanon Silom. Unpretentious, fun place with a large, popular terrace, reasonably priced drinks, karaoke and decent Thai and Western food.

Dick's Café Duangthawee Plaza, 894/7–8 Soi Pratuchai, Thanon Suriwong. Stylish day-and-night café-restaurant (daily 10.30am–2am), hung with exhibitions by gay artists, on a traffic-free soi opposite the prominent Wall St Tower, ideal for drinking, eating decent Thai and Western food or just chilling out.

Disgo Disgo Soi 2, Thanon Silom. Small, well-designed bar-disco with a retro feel, playing good dance music to a fun young crowd.

DJ Station Soi 2, Thanon Silom. Highly fashionable but unpretentious disco, packed at weekends, attracting a mix of Thais and farangs; cabaret show nightly at 11.30pm. B100 including one drink (B200 including two drinks Fri & Sat).

Expresso Soi 2, Thanon Silom. Immaculately designed bar-lounge with cool water features and subtle lighting.

Freeman Dance Arena, 60/18–21 Soi 2/1, Thanon Silom (in a small soi between Soi Thaniya and Soi 2). Busy disco, somewhat more Thai-oriented than *DJ Station*, with slick cabaret shows at 11.30pm and 1am. B150 including one drink (B250 including two drinks Fri & Sat). Under the same management is *Richard's*, a smart, pre-club bar-restaurant next door.

JJ Park 8/3 Soi 2, Thanon Silom. Classy, Thai-oriented bar-restaurant, for relaxed socializing rather than raving, with nightly singers, comedy shows and good food.

Sphinx 98–104 Soi 4, Thanon Silom. Chic decor, terrace seating and very good Thai and Western food attract a sophisticated crowd to this ground-floor bar and restaurant; karaoke and live music upstairs at *Pharoah's*.

Telephone Pub 114/11–13 Soi 4, Thanon Silom. Cruisey, dimly lit, long-standing eating and drinking venue with a terrace on the alley and telephones on the tables inside.

Vega Soi 39, Thanon Sukhumvit. Trendy bar-restaurant run by a group of lesbians. The live music, karaoke and dance floor attract a mixed, fashionable crowd. Mon–Sat 11am–1pm.

Culture shows and performing arts

Because of the language barrier, most Thai theatre is inaccessible to tourists and so, with a few exceptions, the best way to experience the traditional **performing arts** is usually at shows designed for tourists. You can, however, witness Thai dancing being performed for its original ritual purpose, usually several times

Bangkok for kids

The following theme parks and amusement centres are all designed for kids, the main drawback being that many are located a long way from the city centre. Other attractions kids should enjoy include the Siam Ocean World aquarium (see p.171), Dusit Zoo (see p.166), the Snake Farm (see p.175), cycling around Muang Boran Ancient City (see p.183), feeding the turtles at Wat Prayoon (see p.163), pedal-boating in Lumphini Park (see p.175), and the Traditional Thai Puppet Theatre at Suan Lum Night Bazaar (see p.200). There are also Saturday afternoon classes in kids' traditional Thai dance at the Patravadi Theatre (see opposite). For general tips on kids' Thailand, see p.75.

Children's Discovery Museum Opposite Chatuchak Weekend Market on Thanon Kamphaeng Phet 4 (Tues–Fri 9am–5pm, Sat & Sun 10am–6pm; B150, kids B120; ⓣ02 615 7333, ⓦwww.bkkchildrenmuseum.com/english). Interactive and hands-on displays covering science, the environment, human and animal life. Mo Chit Skytrain or Chatuchak Park subway or, from Banglamphu, any bus bound for Chatuchak or the Northern Bus Terminal.

Dream World Ten minutes' drive north of Don Muang Airport at kilometre-stone 7 Thanon Rangsit-Ongharak (Mon–Fri 10am–5pm, Sat & Sun 10am–7pm; B120, children B95; ⓣ02 533 1152, ⓦwww.dreamworld-th.com). Theme park with different areas such as Fantasy Land, Dream Garden and Adventure Land. Water rides, a hanging coaster and other amusements. Non-air-con buses #39 and #59 from Rajdamnoen Klang in Banglamphu to Rangsit, then songthaew or tuk-tuk to Dream World; or bus, Skytrain or subway to Mo Chit/Chatuchak Park, then air-con bus #523.

Safari World On the northeastern outskirts at 99 Thanon Ramindra, Minburi (daily 9am–4.30pm; B700, children B450; ⓣ02 518 1000, ⓦwww.safariworld.com). Drive-through safari park, complete with monkeys, lions, rhinos, giraffes and zebras, plus a sea-life area with dolphins and sea lions. If you don't have your own car, you can be driven through the park in a Safari World coach. Take air-con bus #60 from Rajdamnoen Klang in Banglamphu or air-con #26 from Victory Monument, then a songthaew to Safari World.

Siam Park On the far eastern edge of town at 101 Thanon Sukhapiban 2 (daily 10am–6pm; B400, children B300; ⓣ02 919 7200, ⓦwww.siamparkcity.com). Waterslides, whirlpools and artificial surf, plus rollercoasters, a small zoo and a botanical garden. Air-con bus #60 from Rajdamnoen Klang in Banglamphu or air-con #501/#1 from Hualamphong Station.

a day, at the Lak Muang Shrine behind the Grand Palace (see p.143) and the Erawan Shrine on the corner of Thanon Ploenchit (see p.171). For background on Thai classical dance and traditional theatre, see p.61.

The easiest place to get a glimpse of the variety and spectacle intrinsic to traditional Thai theatre is at the unashamedly tourist-oriented **Siam Niramit cultural extravaganza** (nightly from 6pm, show starts at 8pm; B1500; ⓣ02 649 9222, ⓦwww.siamniramit.com; tickets can be bought on the spot or through most travel agents). The eighty-minute show presents a history of regional Thailand's culture and beliefs in a hi-tech spectacular of fantastic costumes and huge chorus numbers, enlivened by acrobatics and flashy special effects. It's staged in the 2000-seat Ratchada theatre at 19 Thanon Tiam Ruammit, a five-minute walk from the Thailand Culture Centre subway, following signs for the South Korean embassy (see map on p.98); the theatre complex also includes crafts outlets and a buffet restaurant (dinner costs B500).

The **Traditional Thai Puppet Theatre** (ⓣ02 252 9683–4, ⓦwww.thaipuppet.com), at Suan Lum Night Bazaar on Thanon Rama IV, stages entertaining tourist-oriented performances, which, though pricey, are well worth it for both adults and children. The puppets in question are jointed stick-puppets (*hun lakhon lek*), an art form that was developed in the early twentieth century and had all but died out before the owner of the theatre, Sakorn Yangkeowsod (aka Joe Louis), came to its rescue in the 1980s. Each sixty-centimetre-tall puppet is manipulated by three puppeteers, who are accomplished Thai classical dancers in their own right, complementing their charges' elegant and precise gestures with graceful movements in a harmonious ensemble. Hour-long shows (B900, kids B300) are put on daily at the theatre at 7.30pm, preceded by a video documentary in English at 7pm. The puppets perform mostly stories from the *Ramakien*, accompanied by surtitles or synopses in English and live traditional music of a high standard.

Many tourist restaurants offer low-tech versions of the Siam Niramit experience, in the form of nightly **culture shows** – usually a hotchpotch of Thai dancing and classical music, with a martial-arts demonstration thrown in; it's always worth calling ahead to reserve, especially if you want a vegetarian version of the set menu. Worth checking out are the upmarket, riverside *Supatra River House* at 266 Soi Wat Rakhang in Thonburi (Ⓣ02 411 0305), where twice a week diners are entertained by performers from the nearby Patravadi Theatre (Fri & Sat at 8.30pm; B650–850 including food); and Silom Village (Ⓣ02 234 4581) on Thanon Silom, which stages a nightly fifty-minute indoor show (8.30pm; B600) to accompany a set menu of Thai food (available from 7pm), as well as a rather desultory free show at 7.45pm at its outdoor restaurant.

More glitzy and occasionally ribald entertainment is the order of the day at the capital's two **ladyboy cabaret shows**, where a bevy of luscious transvestites dons glamorous outfits and performs over-the-top song and dance routines: Mambo Cabaret plays at the theatre in Washington Square, between Sukhumvit sois 22 and 24 (Ⓣ02 259 5715; nightly 8pm; Nov–Feb also at 10pm; B600–800), and New Calypso Cabaret performs inside the *Asia Hotel*, close by Ratchathewi Skytrain station at 296 Thanon Phayathai (Ⓣ02 216 8937, Ⓦwww.calypsocabaret.com; nightly 8.15 & 9.45pm; B1000 or half-price if booked online 5 days ahead).

Other **venues** that stage traditional or contemporary performances accessible to non-Thai speakers (checking listings magazines for details) include:

National Theatre Next to the National Museum on the northwest corner of Sanam Luang Ⓣ02 224 1342 or 02 222 1012. Roughly weekly shows of music, *lakhon* (classical dance-drama) and *likay* (folk drama) – a programme in English is posted up in the theatre foyer, or contact the nearby Bangkok Information Centre (see p.104), who keep a copy of the programme in Thai; plus outdoor shows of classical music and dancing at the National Museum in the dry season (Dec–April Sat & Sun 5pm; B20).

Patravadi Theatre 69/1 Soi Wat Rakhang, Thonburi Ⓣ02 412 7287, Ⓦwww.patravaditheatre.com; free shuttle boat transport from Tha Maharaj in front of Wat Mahathat). Experimental, contemporary theatre. Also runs open-to-all mostly hour-long classes (B150) in *khon* dance (Fri 5pm), drumming (Sat 2pm, Sun 2.30pm), Thai classical dance (kids Sat 2.30pm, adults 4.30–6pm), whose participants stage free shows every Sun 6pm.

Sala Chalermkrung 66 Thanon Charoen Krung (New Road), on the intersection with Thanon Triphet in Pahurat, next to Old Siam Plaza Ⓣ02 225 8757; see p.152 for transport details. Mainstream traditional and contemporary theatre.

Thailand Cultural Centre Thanon Ratchadapisek Ⓣ02 247 0028, ext 4280, Ⓦwww.thaiculturalcenter.com; BTS Thailand Cultural Centre. Mainstream classical concerts, traditional and contemporary theatre, and visiting international dance and theatre shows.

Cinemas

Central Bangkok has more than forty **cinemas**, many of which show recent American and European releases with their original dialogue and Thai subtitles. Most cinemas screen shows around four times a day: rough programme details are given every day in the *Nation* but your best bet is to go to Ⓦwww.movieseer.com, which allows you to search by movie or by area in Bangkok (or indeed around the country), up to a week ahead; cinema locations are printed on *Nancy Chandler's Map of Bangkok*. Seats cost around B100; whatever cinema you're in, you're expected to stand for the king's anthem, which is played before every performance. See p.58 for information about Bangkok's annual film festival.

There are half a dozen cinemas in and around Siam Square, and nearly every major downtown shopping plaza has two or three screens on its top floor. Movies at the French and German cultural centres, the Alliance Française, 29 Thanon Sathorn Tai (Ⓣ02 670 4200, Ⓦwww.alliance-francaise.or.th), and the Goethe Institut, 18/1 Soi Goethe, between Thanon Sathorn Tai and Soi Ngam Duphli (Ⓣ02 287 0942, Ⓦwww.goethe.de), are often subtitled in English. And if it's been a while since you've caught up on the new releases, check out the dozens of video-showing restaurants along Banglamphu's Thanon Khao San, where recent blockbusters are screened back-to-back every day and night of the year, all for the price of a banana smoothie or a cheese sandwich.

Thai boxing

The violence of the average **Thai boxing** match may be offputting to some, but spending a couple of hours at one of Bangkok's two main stadia can be immensely entertaining, not least for the enthusiasm of the spectators and the ritualistic aspects of the fights. Bouts, advertised in the English-language newspapers, are held in the capital every night of the week at the **Rajdamnoen Stadium**, next to the TAT office on Rajdamnoen Nok (Ⓣ02 281 4205; Mon, Wed, Sun 6pm, Thurs 5pm), and at **Lumphini Stadium** on Thanon Rama IV (Ⓣ02 252 8765; Tues & Fri 6.30pm, Sat 2pm & 6.30pm). Tickets cost B1000–2000 (at Rajdamnoen the view from the B1000 seats is partially obscured). Sessions usually feature ten bouts, each consisting of five three-minute rounds (with two-minute rests in between each round), so if you're not a big fan it may be worth turning up an hour late, as the better fights tend to happen later in the billing. It's more fun if you buy one of the less expensive standing tickets, enabling you to witness the frantic gesticulations of the betting aficionadoes at close range. For more on Thai boxing and on training camps outside the city, see p.63.

To engage in a little *muay Thai* yourself, visit Sor Vorapin's Gym at 13 Trok Kasap off Thanon Chakrabongse in Banglamphu, which holds *muay Thai* **classes** twice daily (B400/session, B2500/7 sessions; Ⓣ02 282 3551, Ⓦwww.thaiboxings.com). Jitti's Gym on Soi Amon off Sukhumvit Soi 49 also offers well-regarded training sessions for foreigners (Ⓣ02 2392 5890, Ⓦwww.thailandroad.com/jittigym). For more in-depth training and further information about Thai boxing, contact the Muay Thai Institute on the far northern outskirts of Bangkok (Ⓣ02 992 0096, Ⓦwww.muaythai-institute.net), which runs training courses for foreigners (B6400 for 40hr), including practical instruction, as well as history and theory.

Shopping

Bangkok has a good reputation for shopping, particularly for silk, gems and fashions, where the range and quality are streets ahead of other Thai cities, and antiques and handicrafts are good buys too. As always, watch out for **fakes**: cut glass masquerading as precious stones (see p.210 for advice on this), old,

△ Mah Boon Krong Shopping Centre

damaged goods being passed off as antiques, and counterfeit designer labels. Bangkok also has the best English-language bookshops in the country. Department stores and tourist-oriented shops in the city keep late hours, opening daily at 10 or 11am and closing at about 9pm; many small, upmarket boutiques, for example along Thanon Charoen Krung and Thanon Silom, close on Sundays.

Counterfeit culture

Faking it is big business in Bangkok, a city whose copyright regulations carry about as much weight as its anti-prostitution laws. Forged **designer clothes** and accessories are the biggest sellers; street vendors along Patpong, Silom, Sukhumvit and Khao San roads will flog you a whole range of inexpensive lookalikes, including Burberry shirts, Diesel jeans, Calvin Klein wallets, Prada bags and Hermes scarves.

Along Patpong, after dark, plausible would-be Rolex, Cartier and Tag **watches** from Hong Kong and Taiwan go for under B1000 if you bargain hard – and are fairly reliable considering the price. If your budget won't stretch to a phoney Rolex Oyster, there's plenty of opportunities for lesser expenditure here and at the stalls concentrated on Thanon Khao San, where pirated **DVDs and music and video CDs** and **software and games CD-ROMs** are sold at a fraction of their normal price. Quality is usually fairly high but the choice is often limited. Finally, several stallholders along Thanon Khao San even make up passable international **student and press cards** as well as international driver's licences – though travel agencies and other organizations in Bangkok aren't easily fooled.

Downtown Bangkok is full of smart, multi-storeyed **shopping plazas** like Siam Paragon, Siam Centre, Emporium and Gaysorn Plaza, which is where you'll find the majority of the city's fashion stores, as well as designer lifestyle goods and bookshops. The plazas tend to be pleasantly air-conditioned and thronging with trendy young Thais, but don't hold much interest for tourists unless you happen to be looking for a new outfit. You're more likely to find useful items in one of the city's numerous **department stores**, most of which are also scattered about the downtown areas. Seven-storey Central Chidlom on Thanon Ploenchit, which boasts handy services like watch-, garment- and shoe-repair booths as well as a huge product selection (including large sizes), is probably the city's best (with other Central branches on Thanon Silom and around town), but the Siam Paragon department store (which also offers garment and shoe repairs), in the shopping centre of the same name on Thanon Rama I, and Robinson's (on Sukhumvit Soi 19, at the Silom/Rama IV junction and on Thanon Charoen Krung near Thanon Sathorn) are also good. They all have **children's** departments selling bottles, slings and clothes, or there's the branch of Mothercare inside the Emporium between Sukhumvit sois 22 and 24. The British chain of **pharmacies**, Boots the Chemist, has lots of branches across the city, including on Thanon Khao San, in the Siam Centre opposite Siam Square, on Patpong, in the Times Square complex between Sukhumvit sois 12 and 14, and in Emporium on Sukhumvit; Boots is the easiest place in the city to buy tampons.

The best place to buy anything to do with **mobile phones**, including rechargeable Thai SIM cards with a local phone number (see p.86), is the scores of small booths on Floor 4 of Mah Boon Krong (MBK) Shopping Centre at the Rama I/Phrayathai intersection. For **computer** hardware and software, the undisputed mecca is Panthip Plaza, across from Pratunam Market at 604/3 Thanon Phetchaburi (BTS Ratchathevi or canal stop Tha Pratunam), crammed with new and used, genuine and pirated hardware and software.

Markets

For travellers, spectating, not shopping, is apt to be the main draw of Bangkok's neighbourhood **markets** – notably the bazaars of Chinatown and the blooms and scents of Pak Khlong Talat, the flower and vegetable market just west of

Memorial Bridge. The massive Chatuchak Weekend Market is an exception, being both a tourist attraction and a marvellous shopping experience (see p.179 for details). If you're planning on some serious market exploration, get hold of *Nancy Chandler's Map of Bangkok*, an enthusiastically annotated creation with special sections on the main areas of interest. With the chief exception of Chatuchak, most markets operate daily from dawn till early afternoon; early morning is often the best time to go to beat the heat and crowds. The Patpong **night market**, which also spills out onto Thanon Silom and Thanon Suriwong, is *the* place to stock up on fake designer goods, from pseudo-Rolex watches to Burberry shirts; the stalls open at about 5pm until late into the evening. A recent arrival on the evening shopping scene is the **Suan Lum Night Bazaar**, opposite Lumphini Park at the corner of Thanon Rama IV and Thanon Witthayu (Wireless Road; Ⓦwww.thainightbazaar.com), a huge development of more than three thousand booths, which is at its best between 6 and 10pm. Down the narrow alleys of tiny booths, you'll find colourful street fashions, jewellery and lots of soaps, candles and beauty products, as well as some interesting contemporary decor: lighting, paintings, ceramics and woodcarving. At the centre stands the Traditional Thai Puppet Theatre (see p.200), with a popular Thai terrace-restaurant in front, and the attractive women's clothes and furnishings, notably rugs, of the Doi Tung by Mae Fah Luang shop (see p.206), with a hip Doi Tung coffee house attached. Other options for eating and drinking are uninspiring – your best bet is probably the open-air food court and beer garden, with a stage for nightly live music, by Thanon Witthayu.

Handicrafts, textiles and contemporary interior design

Samples of nearly all regionally produced **handicrafts** end up in Bangkok, so the selection is phenomenal. Many of the shopping plazas have at least one classy handicraft outlet, and competition keeps prices in the city at upcountry levels, with the main exception of household objects – particularly wickerware and tin bowls and basins – which get palmed off relatively expensively in Bangkok. Handicraft sellers in Banglamphu tend to tout a limited range compared to the shops downtown, but several places on and around Thanon Khao San sell reasonably priced triangular "axe" pillows (*mawn khwaan*) in traditional fabrics, which make fantastic souvenirs but are heavy to post home; some places, including one dedicated outlet between *Bella House* and *Baan Sabai* on Banglamphu's Soi Chana Songkhram, sell unstuffed versions which are simple to mail home, but a pain to fill when you return. The cheapest outlet for traditional northern and northeastern textiles – including sarongs, axe pillows and farmers' shirts – is **Chatuchak Weekend Market** (see p.179), where you'll also able to nose out some interesting handicrafts. Bangkok is also rapidly establishing a reputation for its **contemporary interior design**, fusing minimalist Western ideals with traditional Thai and other Asian craft elements. The best places to sample this, as detailed in the reviews below, are on Floor 4 of the Siam Discovery Centre and Floor 4 of the Siam Paragon shopping centre, both on Thanon Rama I, and Floor 3 of the Gaysorn Plaza on Thanon Ploenchit.

Noted for its thickness and sheen, **Thai silk** became internationally recognized only about fifty years ago after the efforts of American Jim Thompson (see box on p.170). Much of it comes from the northeast, but you'll find a good range of outlets in the capital. Prices start at about B500 per metre for two-ply silk (suitable for thin shirts and skirts), or B750 for four-ply (for suits).

Banglamphu

Taekee Taekon 118 Thanon Phra Athit. Tasteful assortment of traditional textiles and scarves, plus a selection of Thai art cards, black-and-white photocards and Nancy Chandler greetings cards.

Downtown: around Siam Square and Thanon Ploenchit

Ayodhya Floor 4, Siam Paragon, Thanon Rama I, Floor 3, Gaysorn Plaza, Thanon Ploenchit and Floor 4, Emporium, Thanon Sukhumvit. With the same owners and designers as Panta (see below), but specializing in smaller items, such as gorgeous cushion covers, pouffes covered in dried water-hyacinth stalks, bowls, trays and stationery.

Come Thai Floor 3, Amarin Plaza, Thanon Ploenchit. Wide range of unusual handwoven silk and cotton fabrics from all over southeast Asia.

Doi Tung by Mae Fah Luang 4th Floor, Siam Discovery Centre, Thanon Rama I, and Suan Lum Night Bazaar, Thanon Rama IV Ⓦwww.doitung.org. Part of the late Princess Mother's development project based at Doi Tung, selling very attractive fabrics (silk, cotton and linen) in warm colours, either in bolts or made up into clothes, cushion covers, rugs and so on.

Earthasia 1045 Thanon Ploenchit (opposite Soi Ruam Rudee). Contemporary basketware, furniture, rugs and beautiful lotus-bud lamps in vivid colours.

Exotique Thai Floor 4, Siam Paragon, Thanon Rama I. A collection of small outlets from around the city and the country – including silk-makers and clothes designers down from Chiang Mai – that makes a good, upmarket one-stop shop, much more interesting than Narai Phand (see below). There's everything from jewellery, through mother-of-pearl furniture, to beauty products, with a focus on home decor and contemporary adaptations of traditional crafts.

Lamont Contemporary Floor 3, Gaysorn Plaza, Thanon Ploenchit. Beautiful lacquerware bowls, vases and boxes in Imaginative contemporary styles, as well as bronze and ceramic objects.

Narai (or Narayana) Phand 127 Thanon Rajdamri (Ⓦwww.naraiphand.com). This souvenir centre was set up to ensure the preservation of traditional crafts and to maintain standards of quality, as a joint venture with the Ministry of Industry in the 1930s, and it looks it: its layout is wholly unappealing, though it makes a reasonable one-stop shop for last-minute presents. It offers a huge assortment of very reasonably priced goods from all over the country, including silk and cotton, *khon* masks and musical instruments, *bencharong*, nielloware and celadon, woodcarving, silver, basketware and beauty products.

Niwat (Aranyik) Floor 3, Gaysorn Plaza, Thanon Ploenchit. A good place to buy that chunky, elegant Thai-style cutlery you may have been eating your dinner with in Bangkok's posher restaurants, with both traditional and contemporary hand made designs.

Panta Floor 4, Siam Discovery Centre, and Floor 4, Siam Paragon. Modern design store which stands out for its experimental furniture, including way-out-there items made of woven rattan and wood and cushions covered in dried water-hyacinth stalks, string and rag clippings.

Thann Native Floor 3, Gaysorn Plaza, Thanon Ploenchit. Contemporary rugs, cushion covers and furniture, and some very striking glass candle-holders.

Triphum Floor 3, Gaysorn Plaza, Thanon Ploenchit, and Floor 4, Siam Paragon. Affordable, hand-painted reproductions of temple mural paintings, Buddhist manuscripts from Burma, repro Buddha statues in many styles, lacquerware, framed amulets and even Buddha's footprints.

Downtown: south of Thanon Rama IV

Jim Thompson's Thai Silk Company Main shop at 9 Thanon Suriwong (including a branch of their very good café – see p.191), plus branches in Isetan in the Central World Plaza, Central Chidlom department store on Thanon Ploenchit, at Emporium on Thanon Sukhumvit, at the Jim Thompson House Museum, and at many hotels around the city, Ⓦwww.jimthompson.com. A good place to start looking for traditional Thai fabric, or at least to get an idea of what's out there. Stocks silk and cotton by the yard and ready-made items from dresses to cushion covers, which are well designed and of good quality, but pricey. They also have a home furnishings section and a good tailoring service. A couple of hundred metres along Thanon Suriwong from the main branch, at no. 149/4–6, a Jim Thompson Factory Sales Outlet sells remnant home-furnishing fabrics and home accessories at knock-down prices (if you're really keen on a bargain, they have a much larger factory outlet way out east of the centre on Soi 93, Thanon Sukhumvit).

The Legend Floor 3, Thaniya Plaza, Thanon Silom. Stocks a small selection of well-made Thai handicrafts, from wood and wickerware to pretty fabrics and celadon and other ceramics, at reasonable prices.

Silom Village 286/1 Thanon Silom. A complex of low-rise buildings that attempts to create a relaxing, upcountry atmosphere as a backdrop for its pricey fabrics and jewellery, and occasionally unusual souvenirs, such as woven rattan goods and grainy *sa* paper made from mulberry bark.

Tamnan Mingmuang 3rd Floor, Thaniya Plaza, Soi Thaniya, east end of Thanon Silom. Subsidiary of The Legend opposite (see above) which concentrates on basketry from all over the country. Among the unusual items on offer are trays and boxes for tobacco and betel nut made from *yan lipao* (intricately woven fern vines), and bambooware sticky rice containers, baskets and lampshades. The Legend's other subsidiary, the adjacent Eros, sells rather tacky erotic craft items such as naked chess sets.

Thai Home Industries Oriental Avenue, in front of the *Oriental Hotel.* Huge, characterful museum-piece of an old shop, which seems to have surprisingly little for sale on its dusty shelves. However, you'll find attractive, traditional cutlery and some nice, plain cotton shirts and dressing gowns in amongst the basketware and bamboo trays.

Thanon Sukhumvit

Rasi Sayam 82 Soi 33. Very classy handicraft shop, specializing in eclectic and fairly pricey decorative and folk arts such as tiny betel-nut sets woven from *lipao* fern, sticky-rice lunch baskets, coconut wood bowls and *mutmee* textiles. Mon–Sat 9am–5.30pm.

Thai Celadon Soi 16 (Thanon Ratchadapisek). Classic celadon stoneware made without commercial dyes or clays and glazed with the archetypal blues and greens that were invented by the Chinese to emulate the colour of precious jade. Mainly dinner sets, vases and lamps, plus some figurines.

Tailored clothes

Inexpensive **tailoring shops** crowd Silom, Sukhumvit and Khao San roads, but the best single area to head for is the short stretch of Thanon Charoen

Having clothes tailor-made

Bangkok can be an excellent place to get tailor-made suits, dresses, shirts and trousers at a fraction of the price you'd pay in the West. Tailors here can copy a sample brought from home and will also work from any photographs you can provide; most also carry a good selection of catalogues. The bad news is that many tourist-oriented tailors aren't terribly good, often attempting to get away with poor work and shoddy materials, so lots of visitors end up wasting their time and money. However, with a little effort and thought, both men and women can get some fantastic clothes made to measure.

Choosing a tailor can be tricky, and unless you're particularly knowledgeable about material, shopping around won't necessarily tell you much. However, don't make a decision wholly on prices quoted – picking a tailor simply because they're the cheapest usually leads to poor work, and cheap suits don't last. Special deals offering two suits, two shirts, two ties and a kimono for US$99 should be left well alone. Above all, ignore recommendations by anyone with a vested interest in bringing your custom to a particular shop.

Prices vary widely depending on material and the tailor's skill. As a very rough guide, for labour alone expect to pay B5000–6000 for a two-piece suit, though some tailors will charge rather more. For middling **material**, expect to pay about the same again, or anything up to four times as much for top-class cloth. With the exception of silk, local materials are frequently of poor quality and for suits in particular you're far better off using English or Italian cloth. Most tailors stock both imported and local fabrics, but bringing your own from home can work out significantly cheaper. Give yourself as much **time** as possible. For suits, insist on two fittings. Most good tailors require around three days for a suit (some require ten days or more), although a few have enough staff to produce good work in a day or two. The more **detail** you can give the tailor the better. As well as deciding on the obvious features such as single- or double-breasted and number of buttons, think about the width of lapels, style of trousers, whether you want the jacket with vents or not, and so forth. Specifying factors like this will make all the difference to whether you're happy with your suit, so it's worth discussing them with the tailor; a good tailor should be able to give good advice. Finally, don't be afraid to be an awkward customer until you're completely happy with the finished product – after all, the whole point of getting clothes tailor-made is to get exactly what you want.

Krung between the GPO and Thanon Silom, close by the Chao Phraya express boat stops at Tha Oriental and Tha Wat Muang Kae, or ten minutes' walk from Saphan Taksin Skytrain station. It's generally best to avoid tailors in tourist areas such as Thanon Khao San, shopping malls and Thanon Sukhumvit's Soi Nana and Soi 11, although if you're lucky it's still possible to come up trumps here: one that stands apart is Banglamphu's well-regarded Chang Torn, located at 95 Thanon Tanao (ⓣ02 282 9390). All the outlets listed below are recommended. See the box on p.207 for advice on having clothes tailor-made.

For cheap and reasonable shirt and dress material other than silk go for a browse around **Pahurat** market (see p.157), though the suit materials are mostly poor, and best avoided.

A Song Tailor 8 Trok Chartered Bank, off Thanon Charoen Krung, near the *Oriental Hotel* ⓣ02 630 9708. Friendly, helpful and a good first port of call if you're on a budget.

Ah Song Tailor 1203 Thanon Charoen Krung (opposite Soi 36) ⓣ02 233 7574. Meticulous tailor who takes pride in his work. Men's and women's suits.

Golden Wool 1340–1342 Thanon Charoen Krung ⓣ02 233 0149; and **World Group** 1302–1304 Thanon Charoen Krung, ⓣ02 234 1527. Part of the same company, they can turn around decent work in a couple of days, though prefer to have a week. One of the tailors here has made suits for the king.

Marco Tailor Soi 7, Siam Square ⓣ02 252 0689 or 02 251 7633. Long-established tailor with a good reputation, though not cheap by Bangkok standards; they require two or three weeks for a suit. Men's only.

Marzotto Tailor 3 Soi Shangri-la Hotel, Thanon Charoen Krung ⓣ02 233 2880. Friendly business which makes everything from trousers to wedding outfits, and can make a suit in two days, with just one fitting, if necessary.

Fashions

Thanon Khao San is lined with stalls selling low-priced **fashions**: the tie-dyed vests, baggy cotton fisherman's trousers and embroidered blouses are all aimed at backpackers, but they're supplemented by cheap contemporary fashions that appeal to urban Thai trendies as well. The stalls of Banglamphu Market, around the edges of the abandoned New World department store, have the biggest range of inexpensive Thai fashions in this area. For the best and latest trends from Thai designers, however, check out the shops in Siam Square and across the road in the more upmarket Siam Centre. Prices vary considerably: street gear in Siam Square is undoubtedly inexpensive, while genuine Western brand names are generally competitive but not breathtakingly cheaper than at home; larger sizes can be hard to find. **Shoes** and **leather goods** are good buys in Bangkok, being generally hand made from high-quality leather and quite a bargain: check out branches of the stylish, Italian-influenced Ragazze in the Silom Complex (Floor 2), Thanon Silom, in the menswear department at Isetan in the Central World Plaza or on Floor 3 of the MBK Shopping Centre (both Thanon Rama I).

Emporium Thanon Sukhumvit, between sois 22 and 24. Enormous and rather glamorous shopping plaza, with a good range of fashion outlets, from exclusive designer wear to trendy high-street gear. Genuine brand name outlets include Versace, Prada, Gucci, Chanel Louis Vuitton – and Mango.

Gaysorn Plaza Thanon Ploenchit. The most chic of the city's shopping plazas: in amongst Burberry, Emporio Armani and Louis Vuitton, a few Thai names have made it, notably Fly Now, which mounts dramatic displays of women's party and formal gear, alongside more casual wear, and Fashion Society, a gathering of cutting-edge local designers in one store.

Mah Boon Krong (MBK) At the Rama I/Phrayathai intersection. Labyrinthine shopping centre which houses hundreds of small, mostly fairly inexpensive outlets, including plenty of high-street fashion shops.

Siam Centre Thanon Rama I, across the road from Siam Square. Particularly good for hip local labels, such as Greyhound, Jaspal and Fly Now, as well as international names like Ecko and Mambo.

Siam Square Worth poking around the alleys here, especially near what's styled as the area's "Centerpoint" between sois 3 and 4. All manner of inexpensive boutiques, some little more than booths, sell colourful street gear to the capital's fashionable students and teenagers.

Books

English-language **bookstores** in Bangkok are always well stocked with everything to do with Thailand, and most carry fiction classics and popular paperbacks as well. The capital's **second-hand** bookstores are not cheap, but you can usually part-exchange your unwanted titles.

Aporia 131 Thanon Tanao, Banglamphu. This is one of Banglamphu's main outlets for new books and keeps a good stock of titles on Thai and Southeast Asian culture, a decent selection of travelogues, plus some English-language fiction. Also sells second-hand books.

Asia Books Branches on Thanon Sukhumvit between sois 15 and 19, in Landmark Plaza between sois 4 and 6, in Times Square between sois 12 and 14, and in Emporium between sois 22 and 24; in Peninsula Plaza and in the Central World Plaza, both on Thanon Rajdamri; in Siam Discovery Centre and in Siam Paragon, both on Thanon Rama I; and in Thaniya Plaza near Patpong off Thanon Silom. English-language bookstore that's especially recommended for its books on Asia – everything from guidebooks to cookery books, novels to art (the Sukhumvit 15–19 branch has the very best Asian selection). Also stocks bestselling novels and coffee-table books.

B2S Floor 7, Central Chidlom, Thanon Ploenchit. Department-store bookshop with a decent selection of English-language books, but most notable for its huge selection of magazines and newspapers.

Bookazine Branches on Thanon Silom in the CP Tower (Patpong) and in the Silom Complex; on Thanon Rama I opposite the Siam Centre; in the Amarin Plaza on Thanon Ploenchit; in All Seasons Place on Thanon Witthayu; in Gaysorn Plaza on Thanon Ploenchit; and at the mouth of Sukhumvit Soi 5. Alongside a decent selection of English-language books about Asia and novels, these shops stock a huge range of foreign newspapers and magazines.

Books Kinokuniya 3rd Floor, Emporium Shopping Centre, between sois 22 and 24 on Thanon Sukhumvit, with branches at Floor 6, Isetan, in the Central World Plaza, Thanon Rajdamri, and Floor 3, Siam Paragon, Thanon Rama I. Huge English-language bookstore with a broad range of books ranging from bestsellers to travel literature and from classics to sci-fi; not so hot on books about Asia though.

Dasa Book Cafe between sois 26 and 28, Thanon Sukhumvit ⓦ www.dasabookcafe.com. Appealingly calm second-hand bookshop that's intelligently, and alphabetically, categorized, with sections on everything from Asia to chick-lit, health to gay and lesbian interest. Browse its stock online, or enjoy coffee and cakes in situ. Daily 10am–9pm.

Rim Khob Fa Bookshop Democracy Monument roundabout, Rajdamnoen Klang, Banglamphu. Useful outlet for the more obscure and esoteric English-language books on Thailand and Southeast Asia, as well as mainstream titles on Thai culture.

Robinson's Department Store at the mouth of Sukhumvit Soi 19. The third-floor book department stocks a decent range of English-language fiction and non-fiction, plus lots of books about Asia as well as local and international magazines.

Shaman Books Thanon Khao San, Banglamphu. Well-stocked second-hand bookshop where all books are logged on the computer. Lots of books on Asia (travel, fiction, politics and history) as well as a decent range of novels and general interest books.

Siam Society Bookshop: Libreria 131 Sukhumvit Soi 21, inside the Ban Kamthieng compound. Extensive collection of esoteric and academic books about Thailand, including many ethnology studies published by White Lotus and by the Siam Society itself. Tues-Sat 9am-6pm, Sun noon-5pm.

Silpakorn Book Centre Corner of Na Phra Lan and Na Phra That roads. Very handily placed opposite the entrance to the Grand Palace, this smart little bookshop keeps a good selection of English-language titles, especially on Thailand and Southeast Asia.

Ton's Bookseller 327/5 Thanon Ram Bhuttri, Banglamphu. Exceptionally well stocked with titles about Thailand and Southeast Asia, particularly political commentary and language studies; also sells some English-language fiction.

Jewellery, gems and other rare stones

Bangkok boasts the country's best **gem and jewellery** shops, and some of the finest lapidaries in the world, making this *the* place to buy cut and uncut stones such as rubies, blue sapphires and diamonds. However, countless gem-buying tourists get badly **ripped off**, so be extremely wary. Never buy anything through a tout or from any shop recommended by a "government official"/"student"/"businessperson"/tuk-tuk driver who just happens to engage you in conversation on the street, and note that there are no government jewellery shops despite any information you may be given to the contrary. Always check that the shop is a member of the **Thai Gem and Jewelry Traders Association** by calling the association or visiting their website (Ⓣ02 630 1390–7, Ⓦwww.thaigemjewelry.or.th). To be doubly sure, you may want to seek out shops that also belong to the TGJTA's **Jewel Fest Club** (Ⓦwww.jewelfest.com), which guarantees quality and will offer refunds; see their website for a directory of members. For independent professional advice or precious stones certification, contact the Asian Institute of Gemological Sciences, located on the sixth floor of the Jewelry Trade Center Building, 919/1 Thanon Silom (Ⓣ02 267 4325–7, Ⓦwww.aigsthailand.com), which also runs reputable **courses**, such as a five-day (15hr) introduction to gemstones (B7500) and one day on rubies and sapphires (B1500). A common **scam** is to charge a lot more than what the gem is worth based on its carat weight. Get it tested on the spot, ask for a written guarantee and receipt. Don't even consider **buying gems in bulk** to sell at a supposedly vast profit elsewhere: many a gullible traveller has invested thousands of dollars on a handful of worthless multi-coloured stones, believing the vendor's reassurance that the goods will fetch a hundred times more when resold at home. Gem scams are so common in Bangkok that TAT has published a brochure about it and there are several websites on the subject, including the very informative Ⓦwww.2bangkok.com/2bangkok/Scams/Sapphire.shtml, which describes the typical scam in detail and advises on what to do if you get caught out; it's also continuously updated with details of the latest scammers. Most victims get no recompense at all, but you have more chance of doing so if you contact the website's recommended authorities while still in Thailand. See p.80 for more on common scams in Thailand.

The most exclusive of the reputable **gem outlets** are scattered along Thanon Silom, but many tourists prefer to buy from hotel shops, like the very upscale Kim's in Oriental Place in front of the *Oriental*, where reliability is assured. Other recommended outlets include Johnny's Gems at 199 Thanon Fuang Nakhon, near Wat Rajabophit in Ratanakosin; and Merlin et Delaunay at 1 Soi Pradit, off Thanon Suriwong. Thongtavee, Floor 2, River City, an outlet of a famous Burmese **jade** factory in Mae Sai in northern Thailand, sells beautiful jade jewellery, as well as carved Buddha statues, chopsticks and the like. The hub of Bangkok's **gold** trade is Chinatown, specifically Thanon Yaowarat, which boasts over a hundred outlets. For cheap **silver** earrings, bracelets and necklaces, you can't beat the traveller-orientated jewellery shops along Trok Mayom in Banglamphu.

Among the more esoteric of Bangkok's outlets is the **Rare Stone Museum** at 1048–1054 Thanon Charoen Krung (Ⓣ02 236 5655, Ⓦwww.rarestonemuseum.com), near Soi 26 and the GPO. Here, for B50–100, you can buy tektites, pieces of glassy rock found in Thai fields and thought to be the 750,000-year-old products of volcanic activity on the moon, as well as fossilized plants and shells, 60- to 200-million-year-old petrified dinosaur droppings (properly known as coprolite) unearthed in Thailand's Isaan region, and some fantastic rock formations. Of these last-mentioned, the best, resembling anything from owls and polar bears to grander scenes such as a dog contemplating the moon, are kept for display in the adjoining museum (daily 10am–5.30pm; B100).

Antiques and paintings

Bangkok is the entrepôt for the finest Thai, Burmese and Cambodian **antiques**, but the market has long been sewn up, so don't expect to happen upon any undiscovered treasure. Even experts admit that they sometimes find it hard to tell real antiques from fakes, so the best policy is just to buy on the grounds of attractiveness. The River City shopping complex, off Thanon Charoen Krung (New Road), devotes its third and fourth floors to a bewildering array of pricey treasures, as well as holding an auction on the first Saturday of every month (viewing during the preceding week). Worth singling out here are Old Maps and Prints on the fourth floor (Ⓦwww.classicmaps.com), which has some lovely old prints of Thailand and Asia (averaging around B3500), as well as rare books and maps; and Ingon on the third floor, which specializes in small Chinese pieces made of jade and other precious stones, such as snuff boxes, jewellery, statuettes and amulets. The other main area for antiques is the section of Charoen Krung that runs between the GPO and the bottom of Thanon Silom, and the stretch of Silom running east from here up to and including the multi-storey Silom Galleria. Here you'll find a good selection of largely reputable individual businesses specializing in woodcarvings, ceramics, bronze statues and stone sculptures culled from all parts of Thailand and neighbouring countries as well. The owners of Old Maps and Prints have a second outlet, the Old Siam Trading Company in the Nailert Building at the mouth of Thanon Sukhumvit Soi 5 (Ⓦwww.oldsiamtrading.com). Remember that most antiques require an export permit (see p.82).

Street-corner stalls all over the city sell poor-quality mass-produced traditional Thai **paintings**, but for a huge selection of Thai art, especially oil paintings, visit Sombat Permpoon Gallery on Sukhumvit Soi 1, which carries thousands of canvases, framed and unframed, spanning the range from classical Ayutthayan-era-style village scenes to twenty-first-century abstracts. The gallery does have works by famous Thai artists like Thawan Duchanee.

Moving on from Bangkok

Bangkok is the terminus of all major highways and rail lines, and **public transport** between the capital and the provinces is inexpensive and plentiful, if not always speedy. Bangkok is also the best place to make arrangements for onward travel from Thailand – the city's travel agents can offer some good flight deals and all the major Asian embassies are here, so getting the appropriate **visas** should be no problem.

Travel within Thailand

All the Bangkok travel agents listed on p.218 offer day and overnight **excursions** to popular destinations; prices start at around B1000 for two-day packages, including transport and budget accommodation. Typical programmes include trekking, river-rafting and elephant-riding in the Kanchanaburi and Sangkhlaburi area (1–2 nights); trekking from Umphang (3–5 nights); trekking, river-rafting and elephant-riding around Chiang Rai, Chiang Mai or Pai (2–3 nights); and trekking, river-rafting and elephant-riding in Khao Sok national park (2–4 nights). For details of **specialist Thai tour operators** offering more distinctive cultural, cycling and trekking packages, see Basics p.30. For info on Thailand's **domestic flight network**, see Basics p.42; the domestic departure tax is included in the price of the ticket.

By train

Nearly all trains depart from **Hualamphong Station** (but see p.103 concerning Bang Sue Station), whose 24-hour "Information" booth keeps English-language **timetables**, or you can try phoning the Train Information Hotline on ⓣ1690; the State Railway of Thailand website (ⓦwww.railway.co.th) also carries timetables and a fare chart. For a guide to destinations and journey times from Bangkok, see "Travel details" on p.219. For details on city transport to and from Hualamphong, left-luggage facilities at the station, and a warning about **con-artists** operating at the station, see the section on "Arriving in Bangkok" on p.102. **Tickets** for overnight trains and other busy routes should be booked at least a day in advance (or at least a week in advance for travel on national holidays), and are best bought from Hualamphong. During normal office hours you can buy rail tickets from the clearly signed State Railway **advance booking office** at the back of the station concourse (daily 8.30am–4pm); at other times you can buy them from ticket counters #2, which is labelled "foreign tourist priority"; counters #1 and #2 deal with ticket refunds and alterations. Train tickets can also be bought through almost any travel agent and through some hotels and guest houses for a booking fee of about B50. In addition to all types of normal rail ticket, the Advance Booking Office sells **joint rail and boat or rail and bus tickets** to Ko Samui, Ko Pha Ngan, Ko Tao, Krabi and Ko Phi Phi. Sample prices include B668 to Surat Thani (second-class air-con sleeper), plus B150 for bus and boat connections to Ko Samui or B200 for bus connections to Krabi.

A few other services leave from sleepy **Thonburi Station** (sometimes still referred to by its former name, **Bangkok Noi Station**), across the river from Banglamphu in Thonburi. Chief among these is the twice-daily run to Nam Tok via Nakhon Pathom and Kanchanaburi; in addition there are a handful of commuter services (not listed on English-language timetables)to Prachuap Khiri Khan, Ractchaburi or Lang Suan. Thonburi Station is about 850 metres walk west of the Railway Station N11 express-boat pier: frequent red songthaews run passengers between the pier and the train station (B5; 5 mins), or you can walk it in about 15 minutes by heading up the only road that runs away from the pier, passing a temple, walking under the flyover, and turning right at the far edge of the market when you see the station sign.

The other non-Hualamphong departure is the service to Samut Sakhon, which leaves from **Wongwian Yai Station**, also in Thonburi, hidden behind market stalls on the west side of Thanon Somdet Phra Chao Taksin, just south of the Wongwian Yai roundabout with its horseback statue of King Taksin. You can get to the roundabout on non-air-con bus #6 from Ratchadamnoen Klang in Banglamphu, or by taking the cross-river ferry from River City to Khlong San and then either walking or hopping on almost any bus.

By bus

Bangkok's three main bus terminals are distributed around the outskirts of town. Leave plenty of time to get to the bus terminals, especially if setting off from Banglamphu, from where you should allow at least an hour and a half (outside rush hour) to get to the Eastern Bus Terminal, and a good hour to get to the Northern or Southern terminals. Seats on the most popular long-distance air-con bus services (such as to Chiang Mai, Krabi, Phuket and Surat Thani) should be **reserved** ahead of time, ideally at the relevant bus station as hotels and guest houses may book you on to one of the dodgy tourist services described opposite.

The **Northern Bus Terminal**, or **Sathaanii Mo Chit** (ⓣ02 936 2852–66), is the departure point for all buses to northern and northeastern towns, including

Chiang Mai, Chiang Rai, Nong Khai and Pak Chong (for Khao Yai), and for most destinations in the central plains, including Ayutthaya, Sukhothai and Mae Sot (but excluding Nakhon Pathom and Kanchanaburi, services to which run from the Southern Bus Terminal). Mo Chit also runs a few buses to the east-coast destinations of Pattaya, Chanthaburi and Trat: though there are more regular services to the east coast from the Eastern Bus Terminal, journey times from Mo Chit are usually slightly shorter. The Northern Bus Terminal is on Thanon Kamphaeng Phet 2, near Chatuchak Weekend Market in the far north of the city; Mo Chit Skytrain station and Kamphaeng Phet subway station are within a short motorbike taxi or tuk-tuk ride, or take a city bus direct to the bus terminal: air-con #503, #512 and #157 run from Banglamphu and non-air-con #159 runs from the Southern Bus Terminal; see box on p.108 for bus route details.

The **Eastern Bus Terminal**, or **Sathaanii Ekamai** (ⓣ02 391 8097), between Sukhumvit sois 40 and 42, serves east-coast destinations such as Pattaya, Ban Phe (for Ko Samet) and Trat (for Ko Chang). The Skytrain stops right by the bus terminal at Ekamai Station, as do city buses #511 (from Banglamphu) and #59 (from the Northern Bus Terminal); see box on p.108 for bus route details. Alternatively you can take the Khlong Saen Saeb boat service from the Golden Mount (see p.110) to Tha Ekamai (Sukhumvit Soi 63) and then hop into a taxi down Soi 63 to the bus terminal. There's a rudimentary **left-luggage** service at Ekamai (daily 8am–6pm; B30/day). If you happen to have time to kill at Ekamai, you could sip coffee and check emails at the plush *Ban Rie Coffee* experience across the road (see p.193), or there's a cineplex a few minutes' walk west, between sois 61 and 63.

The **Southern Bus Terminal**, or **Sathaanii Sai Tai Mai** (ⓣ02 435 1199), is at the junction of Thanon Borom Ratchonni and the Nakhon Chaisri Highway, west of the Chao Phraya River in Thonburi. It handles departures to all points south of the capital, including Hua Hin, Chumphon (for Ko Tao), Surat Thani (for Ko Samui and Ko Pha Ngan), Phuket and Krabi, as well as departures for destinations west of Bangkok, such as Nakhon Pathom and Kanchanaburi. To get here, take city bus #507 (air-con) from Banglamphu or Hualamphong Station, air-con #511 from Banglamphu or Thanon Sukhumvit, or non-air-con #159 from the Northern Bus Terminal (see box on p.108 for bus route details).

Budget transport

Many Bangkok tour operators offer **budget transport** to major tourist destinations such as Chiang Mai, Surat Thani, Krabi, Ko Samet and Ko Chang. This often works out as cheap if not cheaper than the equivalent fare on a public air-con bus and, as most of the budget transport deals leave from the Thanon Khao San area in Banglamphu, they're often more convenient. The main drawbacks, however, are the **lack of comfort** and **poor safety**: some travellers end up wishing they'd taken a public air-con bus instead (see below, and Basics p.39 for more info), and in many cases that's what we'd advise. It is standard practice for **tour operators**, especially those on Thanon Khao San, to assure you that transport will be in a large, luxury VIP bus despite knowing it's actually a clapped out old banger. Also be aware that tour operators open up and go bust all the time, again, particularly in the Thanon Khao San area, so consult other travellers for recommendations; never hand over any money until you see the ticket. If you do use budget transport, keep your valuables on your person with you at all time during your journey: this is especially crucial on overnight services.

For the shorter trips, for example to **Ko Samet** (B200–250 excluding boat), **Laem Ngop**, departure point for Ko Chang (B180–350 excluding boat), and **Kanchanaburi** (B120), transport operators nearly always take passengers in minibuses which, if crowded, can be unbearably cramped, and often have insufficient air-conditioning. Drivers usually go as fast as possible, which some travellers find scary. Another dedicated minibus service to Kanchanaburi, used mainly by Thai travellers, leaves from outside the *Royal Hotel* on Ratchadamnoen Klang in Banglamphu, departing when full throughout the day from 5am–8pm (2hr; B100). For destinations further afield, such as **Chiang Mai** (11hr) and **Surat Thani** (11hr), travellers are usually taken by larger tour bus; again these tend to be worn-out old things (despite invariably being advertised as VIP-style) and drivers on these journeys have an even worse safety record. **Security** on these buses is a serious problem, and because they're run by private companies there is no insurance against loss or theft of baggage: don't keep anything of value in luggage that's stored out of sight, even if it's padlocked as luggage gets slashed and rifled in the roomy luggage compartment. In addition, passengers often find themselves dumped on the outskirts of their destination city, at the mercy of unscrupulous touts. If you are planning a journey to Chiang Mai or Surat Thani, consider taking the train instead – the extra comfort and peace of mind are well worth the extra baht – or at the least, opt for a government bus from the relevant terminal.

If you're heading for an **island** (such as **Ko Samui**, **Ko Tao** or **Ko Chang**), your bus should get you to the ferry port in time to catch the boat, though there have been complaints from travellers that this does not always happen; check whether your bus ticket covers the ferry ride.

Leaving Thailand

Bangkok is one of the best places in the world to buy low-priced **international air tickets**. You'll get the rock-bottom deals from agents who don't belong to the **Association of Thai Travel Agents** (ATTA), but as with their Western counterparts many of these are transient and may not be trustworthy.

Getting to Don Muang Airport

The fastest, most expensive way of getting to Don Muang Airport is by **metered taxi,** which can cost anything from B120 to B350 (plus up to B70 in expressway tolls), depending on where you are and how bad the traffic is. If you leave the downtown areas before 7am you can get to the airport in half an hour, but at other times you should set off an hour and a half before you have to check in. A cheaper and (during rush hour) faster option from downtown areas is to take the **Skytrain** or **subway** to Mo Chit/Chatuchak Park in the north of the city and then either take bus #29 or #510 for the last few kilometres to Don Muang, or flag down a taxi.

Every guest house and travel agent in Banglamphu, and many hotels elsewhere in the city, can book you onto one of the **private minibuses** to Don Maung Airport. Those running from Banglamphu depart approximately every hour, day and night, and cost B60–80; though you'll get picked up from your accommodation, you should book yourself onto a minibus that leaves at least an hour and a half before check-in commences as it can take up to 45 minutes to pick up all passengers, after which there's the traffic to contend with.

The **airport bus services** that are so useful when arriving at Don Muang are less reliable on the outward journey, mainly because the traffic often makes it impossible for them to stick to their half-hourly schedules; at B100 it's not a risk worth taking. As with in-bound **trains**, schedules for trains from Hualamphong to Don Muang are not helpfully spread throughout the day (ask at the station for the timetable), but the service is cheap and fast. A number of **city buses** run from the city to the airport and are detailed in the box on p.108; they are slow and crowded however.

Thanon Khao San is a notorious centre for dodgy operators who flee with travellers' money overnight: if you buy from a non-ATTA outlet, don't hand over any money until you've called the airline to check your reservation personally, and have been given the ticket. To check if an agency is affiliated, ask for proof of membership and check with the ATTA office (ⓣ02 237 6046–8, ⓦwww.atta.or.th). Some tried and tested travel agents are given in "Listings", p.218.

All major **airline offices** are in downtown Bangkok. There's no advantage in buying tickets directly from the airlines – their phone numbers are given in "Listings", below, so you can confirm reservations or change dates.

The **international departure tax** on all foreigners leaving Thailand by air is B500, but will rise to B700 on February 1, 2007; buy your voucher near the check-in desks at the airport. For advice on getting to Don Muang Airport see the box opposite; for information on the new Suvarnabbhumi Airport, see p.98.

Getting to other Asian countries

For details of **flights** from Bangkok and regional airports to neighbouring countries, see Basics pp.32–34. Most travellers who choose to make their way **overland from Thailand** to Laos, Cambodia or Malaysia do so slowly, stopping at various places in Thailand en route, but it is possible to make these overland trips in one swoop from Bangkok, though in most cases you'll need to spend a night somewhere on the way. To get **from Bangkok to Laos**, you have to take a train or bus to the border at Chiang Khong, Nong Khai, Nakhon Phanom, Mukdahan or Chong Mek. For transport **to Cambodia**, you'll need to begin by either taking a bus from Bangkok to Trat; a train or bus from Bangkok to Aranyaprathet (see p.484); or a bus or train to Surin. The easiest way of travelling from Bangkok **to Malaysia** is by train to the west coast of the peninsula. There is currently one train a day from Bangkok's Hualamphong Station to Butterworth (for Penang; 21hr), which costs about B1100 in a second-class sleeper. It's also possible to make onward train connections to Kuala Lumpur (for an extra B450) and Singapore (for an extra B900); see Basics p.33 for more.

All the **foreign embassies and consulates** in Bangkok are located in the downtown area; see "Listings", p.216, for details. Before heading off to the embassy, ring ahead to check on the opening hours (usually very limited) and documentation required. For an overview of visa requirements and travel options for Burma, Cambodia, Laos, Malaysia, Singapore and Vietnam see Basics, pp.32–34. Some travellers prefer to avoid the hassle of trudging out to the relevant embassy by paying one of the Khao San travel agencies to get their visa for them; beware of doing this, however, as some agencies are reportedly **faking the stamps**, which causes serious problems at immigration.

Listings

Airlines, domestic Air Asia ⓣ02 515 9999; Bangkok Airways, 99/14 Thanon Wibhawadi Rangsit ⓣ1771 or 02 265 5555; Nok Air ⓣ1318 or 02 900 9955; One-Two-Go ⓣ1126; PB Air, UBC 2 Bldg, 591 Sukhumvit Soi 33 ⓣ02 261 0220–8; Phuket Airlines, 1168/102 34th Floor Lumphini Tower Bldg, Thanon Rama IV ⓣ02 679 8999; SGA, Domestic Terminal, Don Muang Airport ⓣ02 535 7050; Thai Airways, 485 Thanon Silom and 6 Thanon Lan Luang near Democracy Monument ⓣ02 356 1111.

Airlines, international Aeroflot ⓣ02 254 1180–2; Air Asia ⓣ02 515 9999; Air Canada ⓣ02 670 0400; Air France ⓣ02 635 1186–7; Air India ⓣ02 235 0557–8; Air New Zealand ⓣ02 254 8440; Bangkok Airways ⓣ02 265 5555; Biman

Bangladesh Airlines ⓣ02 233 3896–7; British Airways ⓣ02 627 1701; Cathay Pacific ⓣ02 263 0606; China Airlines ⓣ02 250 9888; Druk Air ⓣ02 535 1960; Emirates ⓣ02 664 1040; Eva Air ⓣ02 240 0890; Finnair ⓣ02 635 1234; Garuda ⓣ02 679 7371–2; Gulf Air ⓣ02 254 7931–4; Japan Airlines ⓣ02 649 9500; KLM ⓣ02 679 1100; Korean Air ⓣ02 635 0465–9; Lao Airlines ⓣ02 236 9822; Lauda Air ⓣ02 267 0873; Lufthansa ⓣ02 264 2400; Malaysia Airlines ⓣ02 263 0565–71; Pakistan International (PIA) ⓣ02 234 2961–5; Philippine Airlines ⓣ02 633 5713; Qantas Airways ⓣ02 627 1701; Royal Brunei ⓣ02 637 5151; Singapore Airlines ⓣ02 353 6000; Sri Lankan Airlines ⓣ02 236 8450; Swiss ⓣ02 636 2150; Thai Airways ⓣ02 356 1111; United Airlines ⓣ02 253 0558; Vietnam Airlines ⓣ02 655 4137–40.

Airport enquiries Don Muang: general enquiries ⓣ02 535 1111; international departures ⓣ02 535 1386; international arrivals ⓣ02 535 1149; domestic departures ⓣ02 535 1277; domestic arrivals ⓣ02 535 1305.

Car rental Avis, ⓦwww.avis.com: 2/12 Thanon Witthayu (Wireless Road) ⓣ02 255 5300–4; Don Muang international airport ⓣ02 535 4052. Budget, ⓦwww.budget.co.th: 19/23 Building A, Royal City Avenue, Thanon Phetchaburi Mai ⓣ02 203 0250; Don Muang Airport train station, Thanon Vibhavadi Rangsit ⓣ02 566 5067. SMT Rent-A-Car (part of National), ⓦwww.smtrentacar.com: 727 Thanon Srinakharin ⓣ02 722 8487; Don Muang Airport train station, Thanon Vibhavadi Rangsit ⓣ02 928 2500.

Cookery classes Nearly all the five-star hotels will arrange Thai cookery classes for guests if requested; the most famous are held at the *Oriental Hotel* (ⓣ02 659 9000; US$120/day), which mainly focus on demonstrating culinary techniques (Mon–Thurs each week), with a chance for hands-on practice on Fri and Sat. There's a more hands-on approach at the *Nipa* restaurant (ⓣ02 254 0404, ⓦwww.landmarkbangkok.com), which runs one- to five-day cookery courses on demand (B1950/person/day, but cheaper in groups and for longer courses), and add-on fruit-carving lessons (daily 2–4pm; B450) at the restaurant on the third floor of the Landmark Plaza, between sois 4 and 6 on Thanon Sukhumvit. *Basil* at the *Sheraton Grande*, between sois 12 and 14 on Thanon Sukhumvit runs afternoon classes (Mon–Sat ⓣ02 649 8366, ⓦwww.sheratongrandesukhumvit.com; B1950). In a grand, century-old building at 233 Thanon Sathorn Tai (ⓣ02 673 9353–8, ⓦwww.blueelephant.com), the *Blue Elephant* offers courses that range from B2800 for a half-day to a five-day private course for professional chefs for B68,000, while Banglamphu's famous veggie cook, May Kaidee, shares her culinary expertise at her restaurant at 117/1Thanon Tanao (ⓣ089 137 3173, ⓦwww.maykaidee.com; see p.187) for B1000 per day. Set in an orchard in a rural part of Nonthaburi, *Thai House* (ⓣ02 903 9611 or 997 5161, ⓦwww.thaihouse.co.th) runs one- (B3500) to three-day (B16,650) cooking courses, the latter including vegetable- and fruit-carving and home-stay accommodation in traditional wooden houses.

Couriers DHL Worldwide has several central Bangkok depots, including on Thanon Silom and Thanon Sukhumvit; call ⓣ02 345 5000 or visit ⓦwww.dhl.co.th for details.

Embassies and consulates See ⓦwww.mfa.go.th for a full list, with links. Australia, 37 Thanon Sathorn Tai ⓣ02 344 6300; Burma (Myanmar), 132 Thanon Sathorn Nua ⓣ02 233 2237; Cambodia, 185 Thanon Rajdamri (enter via Thanon Sarasin) ⓣ02 254 6630; Canada, 15th floor, Abdulrahim Place, 990 Thanon Rama IV ⓣ02 636 0540; China, 57 Thanon Rajadapisek ⓣ02 245 7030–45; Germany, 9 Thanon Sathorn Tai ⓣ02 287 9000; India, 46, Sukhumvit Soi 23 ⓣ02 258 0300–5; Indonesia, 600–602 Thanon Phetchaburi ⓣ02 252 3135–40; Ireland, 12th Floor, Tisco Tower, 48/20 Thanon Sathorn Nua ⓣ02 638 0303; Laos, 502/1–3 Soi Sahakarnpramoon, Thanon Pracha Uthit ⓣ02 539 6667–8, ext 1053; Malaysia, 35 Thanon Sathorn Tai ⓣ02 679 2190–9; Nepal, 189 Sukhumvit Soi 71 ⓣ02 391 7240; Netherlands, 15 Soi Tonson, between Thanon Witthayu (Wireless Road) and Soi Langsuan ⓣ02 309 5200; New Zealand, 14th Floor, M Thai Tower, All Seasons Place, 87 Thanon Witthayu ⓣ02 254 2530; Pakistan, 31 Sukhumvit Soi 3 ⓣ02 253 0288; Philippines, mouth of Sukhumvit Soi 30/1, ⓣ02 259 0139–40; Singapore, 129 Thanon Sathorn Tai ⓣ02 286 2111; South Africa, 6th Floor, The Park Place, 231 Thanon Sarasin ⓣ02 253 8473-6; Sri Lanka, 13th Floor, Ocean Tower II, Sukhumvit Soi 19 ⓣ02 261 1934; UK, 14 Thanon Witthayu ⓣ02 305 8333; US, 120 Thanon Witthayu ⓣ02 205 4000; Vietnam, 83/1 Thanon Witthayu ⓣ02 251 5836–8, ext. 112.

Emergencies For all emergencies, either call the tourist police (free 24hr phoneline ⓣ1155), who also maintain a booth in the Suan Lum Night Bazaar on Thanon Rama IV, visit the Banglamphu Police Station at the west end of Thanon Khao San, or contact the Tourist Police Headquarters, CMIC Tower, 209/1 Soi 21 (Thanon Asok Montri), Thanon Sukhumvit ⓣ02 664 4000.

Exchange The Don Muang Airport exchange desks and those in the upmarket hotels are open 24 hours; many other exchange booths stay open till 8pm, especially along Khao San, Sukhumvit and Silom. If you have a MasterCard/Cirrus or Visa debit or credit card, you can also withdraw cash from hundreds of ATMs around the city and at the airport.

Hospitals, clinics and dentists Most expats rate the private Bumrungrad International Hospital, 33 Sukhumvit Soi 3 ⓣ02 667 1000, emergency ⓣ02 667 2999, ⓦwww.bumrungrad.com, with its famously five-star accommodation, as the best and most comfortable in the city, followed by the BNH (Bangkok Nursing Home) Hospital, 9 Thanon Convent ⓣ02 686 2700, ⓦwww.bnhhospital.com; Bangkok International Hospital, 2 Soi Soonvijai 7, Thanon Phetchaburi Mai, ⓣ02 310 3000, emergency ⓣ02 310 3102, ⓦwww.bangkokhospital.com; and the Samitivej Sukhumvit Hospital, 133 Sukhumvit Soi 49 ⓣ02 711 8000, ⓦwww.samitivej.co.th. Other recommended private hospitals include Bangkok Mission Hospital, 430 Thanon Phitsanulok, cnr Thanon Lan Luang, just east of Banglamphu ⓣ02 282 1100, ⓦwww.tagnet.org/mission-net, and Bangkok Christian Hospital, 124 Thanon Silom ⓣ02 233 6981–9. You can get vaccinations and malaria advice, as well as rabies advice and treatment, at the Thai Red Cross Society's Queen Saovabha Memorial Institute (QSMI) and Snake Farm on the corner of Thanon Rama IV and Thanon Henri Dunant (Mon–Fri 8.30am–noon & 1–4.30pm; ⓣ02 252 0161–4, ⓦwww.redcross.or.th). Among general clinics, the Australian-run Travmin Bangkok Medical Centre, 8th Floor, Alma Link Building, next to the Central Department Store at 25 Soi Chitlom, Thanon Ploenchit (ⓣ02 655 1024–5; B650/consultation), is recommended. For dental problems, try the Bumrungrad Hospital's dental department on ⓣ02 667 2300, or the following dental clinics (not 24hr): Care Dental Clinic 120/26 Soi Prasamnit 3, Sukhumvit Soi 23 ⓣ02 259 1604; Dental Hospital 88/88 Sukhumvit Soi 49 ⓣ02 260 5000–15, ⓦwww.dentalhospitalbangkok.com; Glas Haus Dental Centre, mouth of Sukhumvit Soi 25, ⓣ02 260 6120–2; Siam Family Dental Clinic 292/6 Siam Square Soi 4 ⓣ02/255 6664–5, ⓦwww.siamfamilydental.com.

Immigration office About 600m down Soi Suan Phlu, off Thanon Sathorn Tai (Mon–Fri 8.30am–4.30pm; ⓣ02 287 3101–10; ⓦwww.immigration.go.th); visa extensions take about an hour. They also send a weekly mobile office to Bumrungrad Hospital, 3rd Floor, Sukhumvit Soi 3 (Wed 9am–3pm). It's difficult to get through to the Suan Phlu office by phone, so you may be better off calling the Department of Employment's One-Stop Service Centre for advice on ⓣ02 693 9333–9. Be very wary of any Khao San tour agents who offer to organize a visa extension for you: some are reportedly faking the relevant stamps and this has caused problems at immigration. However, many places organize "visa-run" trips, which take you and your passport, usually in a minivan, to the Cambodian border at Poipet and back within a day, charging around B2000 all in (the 30-day visa itself is free); East Meets West Travel, Sukhumvit Soi 12 (ⓣ02 251 5230, ⓦwww.eastmeetswesttravel.com), specializes in this service.

Internet access Banglamphu is packed with places offering Internet access, in particular along Thanon Khao San, where competition keeps prices very low. To surf in style, head for *True*, housed in a beautiful early-twentieth century villa at the back of *Tom Yam Kung* restaurant at the western end of Thanon Khao San, where you also can sip coffee, recline on retro sofas and browse lifestyle mags. The Ratchadamnoen Post Office on Banglamphu's Soi Damnoen Klang Neua (Mon–Fri 8.30am–4.30pm) also has very cheap public Catnet Internet booths, and there's also a cheap TNet centre next door. Outside Banglamphu, mid-range and upmarket hotels also offer Internet access, but at vastly inflated prices. Thanon Sukhumvit has a number of makeshift phone/Internet offices, as well as several more formal and more clued-up Internet cafés, including one opposite the 7/11 on Soi 11 (daily 9am–midnight), and the Time Internet Centre on the second floor of Times Square, between sois 12 and 14 (daily 9am–midnight). On the north side of Thanon Silom, between Soi 4 and Soi 2/1, *Mr Bean* offers civilized surfing (daily 9am–10pm) and very good coffee. Elsewhere in the downtown area, during the day, there are several, rather noisy, places on Floor 7 of the MBK Shopping Centre, while *Chart Café* on the ground floor of River City shopping centre offers a bit more style and tranquility, as well as food and drink while you're online. There are Catnet centres in the public telephone office adjacent to the GPO on Thanon Charoen Krung (daily 7am–8pm), and at both international terminals of Don Muang Airport, in the check-in areas, as well as at the domestic terminal.

Laundry Nearly all guest houses and hotels offer same-day laundry services, or there are several self-service laundries on Thanon Khao San.

Left luggage At Don Muang Airport (international B90/day, domestic B70/day); Don Muang train station (B30/day); Ekamai Eastern Bus Terminal (B30/day), Hualamphong train station (B20–30/day), and at most hotels and guest houses (B10–20/day).

Mail The GPO is at 1160 Thanon Charoen Krung, a few hundred metres left of the exit for Wat Muang

Kae express-boat stop. Poste restante, which is kept for two months, can be collected here. This and most other services at the GPO are open Mon–Fri 8am–8pm, Sat & Sun 8am–1pm; the parcel-packing service, however, operates Mon–Fri 8.30am–4.30pm, Sat 9am–noon. If you're staying on or near Thanon Khao San in Banglamphu, it's more convenient to use the poste restante service at one of the two post offices in Banglamphu itself. The one closest to Khao San is Ratchadamnoen Post Office on the eastern stretch of Soi Damnoen Klang Neua (Mon–Fri 8am–5pm, Sat 9am–1pm); letters are kept for two months and should be addressed c/o Poste Restante, Ratchadamnoen PO, Bangkok 10200. There's an efficient parcel packing and sending service in the same building. Banglamphu's other post office is on Soi Sibsam Hang, just west of Wat Bowoniwes (Mon–Fri 8am–5pm, Sat 9am–1pm); its poste restante address is Banglamphubon PO, Bangkok 10203. In the Thanon Sukhumvit vicinity, poste restante can be sent to the Thanon Sukhumvit post office between sois 4 and 6, c/o Nana PO, Thanon Sukhumvit, Bangkok 10112 (Mon–Fri 8.30am–5.30pm, Sat 9am–noon).

Massage and spas Traditional Thai massage sessions and courses are held at Wat Pho (see p.141), and at dozens of guest houses in Banglamphu. More luxurious and indulgent spa and massage treatments are available at many posh hotels across the city, including most famously at the *Banyan Tree Hotel* on Thanon Sathorn Tai (Ⓣ 02 679 1054, Ⓦ www.banyantreespa.com) and the *Oriental* on Thanon Charoen Krung (Ⓣ 02 439 7613, Ⓦ www.mandarinoriental.com), and more affordably at *Buddy Lodge* on Thanon Khao San in Banglamphu (Ⓣ 02 629 4477; Thai massage B800/60min; aromatic scrub B1500). One of Banglamphu's most popular massage centres is Pian's on Soi Susie Pub (daily 8am–10pm, Ⓣ 02 629 0924, Ⓦ www.piangroup.com), where a Thai massage costs B180/hr and you can study Thai, Swedish, herbal and foot massage (about B30,000 for a 30-hour course, or B250 for a one-hour introduction). In the Silom area, Ruen Nuad, 42 Thanon Convent (Ⓣ 02 632 2662–3; daily 10am–9pm), offers excellent Thai massages (B550 for 2hr), as well as aromatherapy and herbal massages, in an air-conditioned, characterful wooden house, down an alley opposite the BNH Hopsital and behind *Naj* restaurant. In Sukhumvit, Bann Phuan on Soi 11 is a recommended massage centre (Thai massage B200/hr), or for spa treatments there's Divana Massage and Spa at 7, Soi 25 (Ⓣ 02 661 6784, Ⓦ www.divanaspa.com; 2-hour spa from B2350). For more on spa treatments see Basics p.64.

Pharmacies There are English-speaking staff at most of the capital's pharmacies, including the city-wide branches of Boots the Chemist (most usefully on Thanon Khao San, in the Siam Centre on Thanon Rama I, on Patpong, and inside the Emporium on Thanon Sukhumvit).

Photographic services Most photo shops will download your digital photos onto a CD for about B150; there's no need to bring your own cables as they have card readers. In Banglamphu, try Center Digital Lab at 169 Thanon Khao San, next to *Grand Guest House*; on Sukhumvit, 11 Digital Photo has branches in Nana Square at the mouth of Soi 3 and near the *Federal Hotel* on Soi 11.

Prison visits A number of foreigners are serving long sentences in Bangkok's prisons, most of them in Nonthaburi's Bang Kwang jail, and they appreciate visits from other foreigners. When visiting, you need to know the name of the prisoner, which block number they're in, and the relevant visiting hours. Embassy staff keep this information, and guest-house noticeboards often have more details as well as accounts from recent prison visitors; similar info is available at Ⓦ www.bangkwang.net and Ⓦ www.khaosanroad.com/bangedup.htm. Prisoners are only allowed one visitor at a time, and visitors must look respectable (no shorts or singlets); all visitors must show their passports at the jail. You can only bring certain gifts with you (such as books, newspapers, fruit, sweets and clothes), as other stuff has to be bought at the prison shop. For directions to Nonthaburi, see p.181; at Nonthaburi pier, take the road ahead, and then turn first left for the prison visitor centre.

Telephones International cardphones are dotted all over the city, so there's now little call for the public telephone offices in or adjacent to post offices, though their booths do at least guarantee some peace and quiet. The largest and most convenient public telephone office is in the compound of the GPO on Thanon Charoen Krung (daily 7am–8pm), which also offers a fax and Internet service, a free collect-call service and even video-conferencing (see above for location details). The post offices at Hualamphong Station, on Thanon Sukhumvit (see above), and in Banglamphu (see above) also have international telephone offices attached, but these close at 5pm. Many entrepreneurs, particularly on Thanon Khao San, advertise very cheap international calls through the Internet: see Basics for details.

Travel agents Diethelm Travel has branches all over Thailand and Indochina and is especially good for travel to Burma, Cambodia, Laos and Vietnam: 12th Floor, Kian Gwan Building II, 140/1 Thanon Witthayu Ⓣ 02 255 9205–18, Ⓦ www.diethelm-travel.com; Asian Trails sells flights, does interesting Thailand tours (see p.30) and runs scheduled and private transfers to many coastal destinations from Bangkok hotels and the airport: 9th Floor, SG Tower, 161/1 Soi Mahadlek Luang 3, Thanon Rajdamri %02 626 2000 ⓦwww.asiantrails.net; Educational Travel Centre (ETC) sells air tickets and Thailand tours and has offices inside the *Royal Hotel*, 2 Thanon Rajdamnoen Klang, Banglamphu ⓣ02 224 0043, ⓦwww.etc.co.th, at 180 Thanon Khao San, Banglamphu ⓣ02 282 7021, and at 5/3 Soi Ngam Duphli ⓣ02 286 9424; Olavi Travel sells air tickets and budget transport within Thailand and is opposite *Gulliver's Traveler's Tavern* at 53 Thanon Chakrabongse, Banglamphu ⓣ02 629 4711–4, ⓦwww.olavi.com; the helpful Thai Overlander at 407 Thanon Sukhumvit, between sois 21 and 23, ⓣ02 258 4778-80, ⓦwww.thaioverlander.com does train tickets (B50 fee), day trips and air tickets; Royal Exclusive is good for travel to Burma, Cambodia, Laos and Vietnam, and also sells air and train tickets: 21 Thanon Silom ⓣ02 267 1536, ⓦwww.royalexclusive.com; and the Bangkok branch of the worldwide STA Travel is a reliable outlet for cheap international flights: 14th Floor, Wall Street Tower, 33 Thanon Suriwong ⓣ02 236 0262, ⓦwww.statravel.co.th. For Bangkok tour operators specializing in trips within Thailand see p.30.

Travel details

Trains

Bangkok Hualamphong Station to: Aranyaprathet (2 daily; 5–6hr); Ayutthaya (30 daily; 1hr 30min); Butterworth (Malaysia; 1 daily; 21hr); Chiang Mai (7 daily; 12–14hr); Chumphon (11 daily; 6hr 45min–8hr 20min); Don Muang airport (27 daily; 50min); Hua Hin (12 daily; 3–4hr); Khon Kaen (5 daily; 7hr 30min–10hr 30min); Khorat (11 daily; 4–5hr); Lampang (7 daily; 10–12hr); Lamphun (6 daily; 12–14hr); Lopburi (15 daily; 2hr 30min–3hr); Nakhon Pathom (12 daily; 1hr 20min); Nakhon Si Thammarat (2 daily; 15–16hr); Nong Khai (4 daily; 10hr 30min–12hr 30min); Pak Chong (for Khao Yai National Park; 11 daily; 2hr 45min–3hr 30min); Pattaya (1 daily; 3hr 45min); Phatthalung (5 daily; 12–15hr); Phitsanulok (10 daily; 5hr 15min–9hr 30min); Si Racha (1 daily; 3hr 15min); Surin (10 daily; 7–10hr); Trang (2 daily; 15–16hr); Ubon_ Ratchathani (7 daily; 10hr 20min–13hr 15min); Udon Thani (5 daily; 10–12hr).

Don Muang Airport to: Ayutthaya (23 daily; 40min); Chiang Mai (7 daily; 10hr 20min–13hr 25min); Khon Kaen (5 daily; 6hr 40min–9hr 40min); Khorat (11 daily; 3hr 10min–4hr 10min); Lampang (7 daily; 10hr); Lamphun (6 daily; 12hr); Lopburi (15 daily; 1hr 25min–2hr 10min); Nong Khai (4 daily; 10–12hr); Pak Chong (for Khao Yai National Park; 11 daily; 2hr–2hr 40min); Phitsanulok (11 daily; 4hr 25min–8hr 40min); Surin (10 daily; 6–9hr); Ubon Ratchathani (7 daily; 9hr 30min–12hr 25min); Udon Thani (5 daily; 10hr).

Thonburi (Bangkok Noi) Station to: Hua Hin (5 daily; 4hr–4hr 30min); Kanchanaburi (2 daily; 2hr 40min); Nakhon Pathom (7 daily; 1hr 10min); Nam Tok (2 daily; 4hr 35min).

Wongwian Yai Station to: Samut Sakhon (hourly; 1hr).

Buses

Eastern Bus Terminal to: Ban Phe (for Ko Samet; 12 daily; 3hr–3hr 30min); Chanthaburi (every 30min; 4–5hr); Pattaya (every 30min; 2hr 30min–3hr 30min); Rayong (every 40min; 2hr 30min–3hr); Si Racha (for Ko Si Chang; every 30min; 2–3hr); Trat (for Ko Chang; at least every 90min; 5–6hr).

Northern Bus Terminal to: Aranyaprathet (hourly; 4hr 30min); Ayutthaya (every 20min; 2hr); Chanthaburi (5 daily; 3–4hr); Chiang Khong (10 daily; 13–14hr); Chiang Mai (19 daily; 10–11hr); Chiang Rai (16 daily; 12hr); Chong Mek (daily; 11hr); Kamphaeng Phet (7 daily; 6hr 30min); Kanchanaburi (9 daily; 2hr 30min); Khon Kaen (29 daily; 6–7hr); Khorat (every 30min; 2hr 30min–3hr); Kong Chiam (4 daily; 11hr); Lampang (18 daily; 8hr); Loei (20 daily; 10hr); Lopburi (every 20min; 2hr 30min–3hr); Mae Hong Son (2 daily; 18hr); Mae Sai (8 daily; 13hr); Mae Sot (11 daily; 8hr 30min); Mukdahan (13 daily; 11hr); Nakhon Phanom (17 daily; 12hr); Nan (8 daily; 10hr); Nong Khai (13 daily; 10hr); Pak Chong (for Khao Yai National Park; every 30min; 3hr); Pattaya (every 30min; 2–3hr); Phitsanulok (up to 19 daily; 5–6hr); Rayong (5 daily; 3hr); Si Racha (every 30min; 2hr); Sukhothai (17 daily; 6–7hr); Surin (up to 20 daily; 8–9hr); Tak (13 daily; 7hr); Trat (5 daily; 4–5hr); Ubon Ratchathani (19 daily; 10–12hr); Udon Thani (every 15min; 9hr).

Southern Bus Terminal to: Cha-am (every 40min; 2hr 45min–3hr 15min); Chumphon (12 daily;

7–9hr); Damnoen Saduak (every 20min; 2hr); Hua Hin (every 40min; 3–4hr); Kanchanaburi (every 15min; 2hr); Ko Samui (8 daily; 12–13hr); Krabi (8 daily; 12–14hr); Nakhon Pathom (every 10min; 40min–1hr 20min); Nakhon Si Thammarat (11 daily; 12hr); Phang Nga (3 daily; 11hr–12hr 30min); Phatthalung (4 daily; 13hr); Phetchaburi (every 30min; 2hr); Phuket (15 daily; 14–16hr); Prachuap Khiri Khan (every 30min; 4–5hr); Pranburi (every 40min; 3hr 30min); Ranong (6 daily; 9–10hr); Samut Songkhram (every 20min; 1hr 30min); Satun (2 daily; 16hr); Surat Thani (10 daily; 10–11hr); Takua Pa (10 daily; 12–13hr); Trang (6 daily; 12–14hr).

Flights

Bangkok to: Buriram (3 weekly; 55min); Chiang Mai (25–27 daily; 1hr); Chiang Rai (5 daily; 1hr 15min); Hua Hin (3 daily; 40min); Khon Kaen (3 daily; 55min); Ko Samui (20 daily; 1hr–1hr 30min); Krabi (4 daily; 1hr 20min); Lampang (2 daily; 1hr); Loei (2 weekly; 1hr 25min); Mae Hong Son (2 weekly; 1hr 20min); Nakhon Phanom (1–2 daily; 1hr 5min); Nakhon Si Thammarat (3–5 daily; 1hr 15min); Nan (5 weekly; 1hr 40min); Phitsanulok (2–3 daily; 45min); Phuket (15 daily; 1hr 20min); Roi Et (daily; 1hr); Sukhothai (1–2 daily; 1hr 10min); Surat Thani (4 daily; 1hr 10min); Trang (1–2 daily; 1hr 30min); Trat (3 daily; 50min); Ubon Ratchathani (5 daily; 1hr 5min); Udon Thani (9 daily; 1hr).

2

The central plains

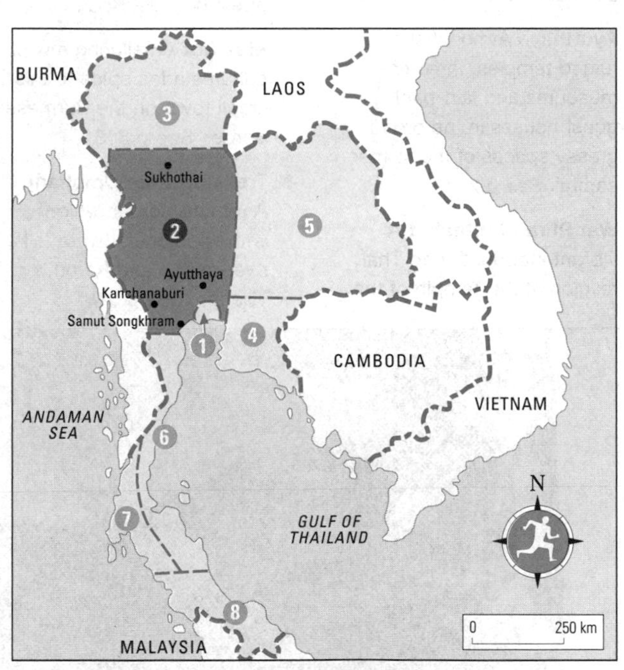

CHAPTER 2

Highlights

* **Kanchanaburi and the River Kwai** Stay in a raft house, take a scenic train ride along the Death Railway and visit some moving World War II memorials. See p.235
* **Sangkhlaburi** Peaceful lakeside town near the Burmese border. See p.259
* **Ayutthaya** Atmospheric ruined temples, three fine museums and laid-back guest houses in the broad, grassy spaces of the former capital. See p.267
* **Wat Phra Phutthabat** A vibrant introduction to Thai religion at the Temple of the Buddha's Footprint. See p.282
* **Phitsanulok Folklore Museum** A fascinating look at traditional rural life. See p.288
* **Sukhothai** The nation's first capital is packed with elegant thirteenth-century ruins and many inviting guest houses. See p.291
* **Mae Sot** An alluring mix of cultures adds spice to this small town on the Burmese border. See p.313
* **Trekking from Umphang** A remote border region with spectacular waterfalls, river-rafting and Karen villages. See p.318

△ The Death Railway, River Kwai

2

The central plains

North and west of the capital, the unwieldy urban mass of Greater Bangkok peters out into the vast, well-watered **central plains**, a region that for centuries has grown the bulk of the nation's food and been a tantalizing temptation for neighbouring power-mongers. The most densely populated region of Thailand, with sizeable towns sprinkled among patchworks of paddy, orchards and sugar-cane fields, the plains are fundamental to Thailand's agricultural economy. Its rivers are the key to this area's fecundity, especially the Nan and the Ping, whose waters irrigate the northern plains before merging to form the Chao Phraya, which meanders slowly south through Bangkok and out into the Gulf of Thailand. Further west, the Mae Khlong River sustains the many market gardens and fills the canals that dominate the hinterlands of the estuary at **Samut Songkhram**.

Sited at the confluence of the Kwai Yai and Kwai Noi rivers, the town of **Kanchanaburi** has long attracted visitors to the notorious Bridge over the River Kwai and is now well established as a travellers' hangout, mainly because of its unique raft-house accommodation. Few tourists venture much further upriver, except as passengers on the remaining stretch of the **Death Railway** – the most tangible wartime reminder of all – but the remote and tiny hilltop town of **Sangkhlaburi** holds enough understated allure to make the extra kilometres worthwhile.

On the plains north of Bangkok, the historic heartland of the country, the major sites are the ruined ancient cities, which cover the spectrum of Thailand's art and architecture. Closest to Bangkok, **Ayutthaya** served as the country's capital for the four hundred years prior to the 1782 foundation of Bangkok, and its ruins evoke an era of courtly sophistication. A short hop north of here, the remnants of **Lopburi** hark back to an earlier time, when the predominantly Hindu Khmers held sway over this region, building a constellation of stone temples across central and northeastern Thailand and introducing a complex grammar of sacred architecture that still dictates aspects of wat design today.

A separate nucleus of sites in the northern neck of the plains centres on **Sukhothai**, birthplace of the Thai kingdom in the thirteenth century. The buildings and sculpture produced during the Sukhothai era are the acme of Thai art, and the restored ruins of the country's first official capital are the best place to appreciate them, though two satellite cities – **Si Satchanalai** and **Kamphaeng Phet** – provide further incentives to linger in the area, and the engaging city of **Phitsanulok** also serves as a good base. West of Sukhothai, on the Burmese border, the town of **Mae Sot** makes a refreshing change from ancient history and is the departure point for the rivers and waterfalls of

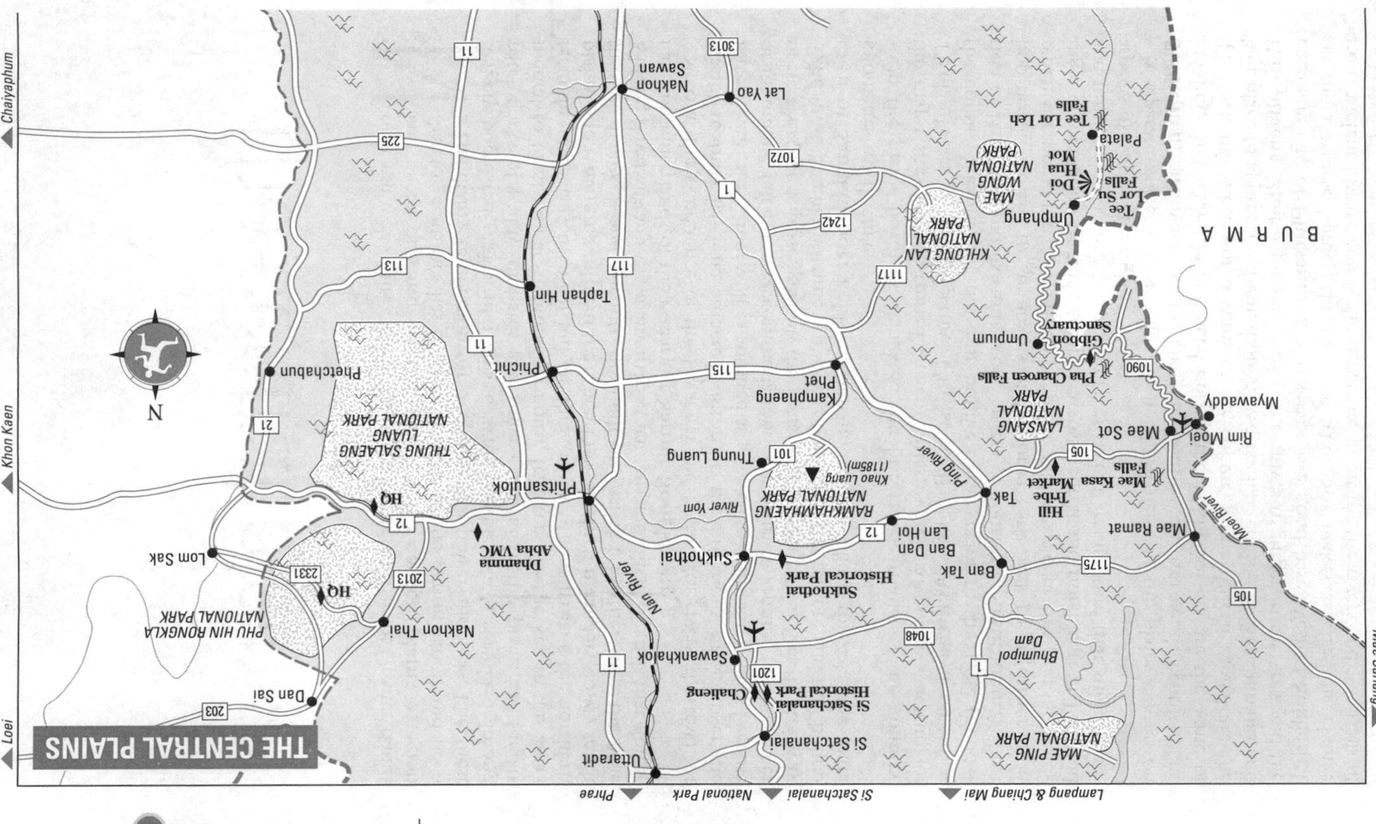
THE CENTRAL PLAINS
Loei
Khon Kaen
Chaiyaphum
Phrae
National Park
Si Satchanalai
Lampang & Chiang Mai
Mae Sariang
N
PHU HIN RONGKLA NATIONAL PARK
THUNG SALAENG LUANG NATIONAL PARK
RAMKHAMHAENG NATIONAL PARK
Khao Luang (1185m)
KHLONG LAN NATIONAL PARK
MAE WONG NATIONAL PARK
LANSANG NATIONAL PARK
MAE PING NATIONAL PARK
Bhumipol Dam
BURMA
Dan Sai
Lom Sak
Nakhon Thai
HQ
Phetchabun
Dhamma Abha VMC
Phitsanulok
Phichit
Taphan Hin
Nakhon Sawan
Lat Yao
Uttaradit
Nan River
Sawankhalok
Si Satchanalai
Si Satchanalai Historical Park
Chalieng
Sukhothai
Sukhothai Historical Park
River Yom
Thung Luang
Kamphaeng Phet
Ban Dan Lan Hoi
Ping River
Ban Tak
Tak
Hill Tribe Market
Mae Kasa Falls
Mae Ramat
Mae Sot
Rim Moei
Myawaddy
Moei River
Pha Charoen Falls
Gibbon Sanctuary
Umpium
Umphang
Doi Hua Mot
Tee Lor Su Falls
Palata
Tee Lor Leh Falls
203
2331
2013
12
21
11
113
225
117
115
101
1201
1048
1
1175
105
1090
1117
1242
1072
3013

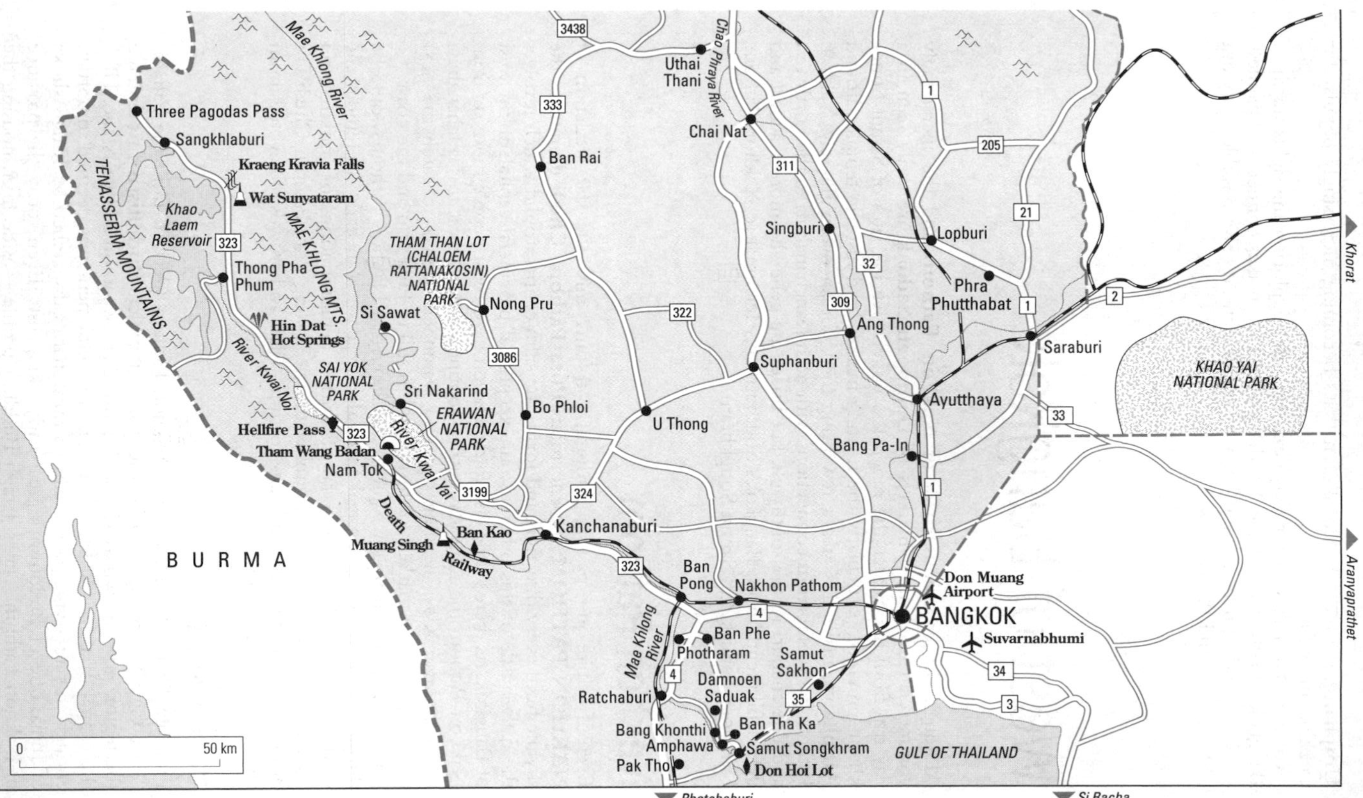
Khorat
Aranyaprathet
Si Racha
Phetchaburi
KHAO YAI NATIONAL PARK
Saraburi
Lopburi
Phra Phutthabat
Ayutthaya
Bang Pa-In
Ang Thong
Singburi
Chai Nat
Chao Phraya River
Uthai Thani
Suphanburi
U Thong
Ban Rai
Nong Pru
Bo Phloi
THAM THAN LOT (CHALOEM RATTANAKOSIN) NATIONAL PARK
ERAWAN NATIONAL PARK
Sri Nakarind
River Kwai Yai
Si Sawat
SAI YOK NATIONAL PARK
Hin Dat Hot Springs
Hellfire Pass
Tham Wang Badan
Nam Tok
Death Railway
Muang Singh
Ban Kao
Kanchanaburi
Ban Pong
Nakhon Pathom
Don Muang Airport
BANGKOK
Suvarnabhumi
Samut Sakhon
Ban Phe
Photharam
Damnoen Saduak
Ratchaburi
Mae Khlong River
Ban Tha Ka
Bang Khonthi
Amphawa
Samut Songkhram
Don Hoi Lot
Pak Tho
GULF OF THAILAND
Mae Khlong River
MAE KHLONG MTS.
River Kwai Noi
Thong Pha Phum
Wat Sunyataram
Kraeng Kravia Falls
Khao Laem Reservoir
Sangkhlaburi
Three Pagodas Pass
TENASSERIM MOUNTAINS
BURMA
0
50 km
1
2
3
4
21
32
33
34
35
205
309
311
322
323
324
333
3086
3199
3438

Umphang, a remote border region that's becoming increasingly popular for trekking and rafting.

Chiang Mai makes an obvious next stop after exploring the sights north of Bangkok, chiefly because the Northern Rail Line makes connections painless. Or you could branch east into Isaan, by train or bus. It's also possible to fly out of Sukhothai and Phitsanulok.

West of Bangkok

Although the enormous chedi of **Nakhon Pathom** and the increasingly commercialized floating markets of **Damnoen Saduak** are easily seen in a day-trip from the capital, the much less visited riverine sites of Samut Songkhram province, particularly the floating markets and historic temples around **Amphawa**, make this area a rewarding focus for an overnight stay. Nakhon Pathom has useful **train** connections with both Kanchanaburi to the northwest and Phetchaburi to the southwest, but **buses** are generally more practical and depart frequently from Bangkok's Southern Bus Terminal to Nakhon Pathom, Damnoen Saduak and Samut Songkhram.

Nakhon Pathom

Even if you're just passing through, you can't miss the star attraction of **NAKHON PATHOM**: the enormous **Phra Pathom Chedi** dominates the skyline from every direction, and forms the calm centre around which revolves the daily bustle of this otherwise unexceptional provincial capital, 56km west of Bangkok. As there's little else to detain you here, most people move on from Nakhon Pathom the same day, either continuing northwest to Kanchanaburi and the River Kwai, heading south to Damnoen Saduak to catch the next morning's floating markets, or further south still to Hua Hin and the coast.

The one time you might want to stay longer in Nakhon Pathom would be during either of its two annual **festivals**: for a week in early September the town hosts a food and fruits fair, featuring demonstrations of cooking and fruit-carving; then in mid-November the week-long Phra Pathom Chedi fair brings together itinerant musicians, fortune-tellers and crowds of devotees from all over central Thailand.

The Town

Probably Thailand's oldest town, Nakhon Pathom (derived from the Pali for "First City") is thought to be the point at which **Buddhism** first entered the region now known as Thailand, more than two thousand years ago. Then the capital of a sizeable Mon kingdom, the settlement was deemed important enough to rate a visit from a pair of missionaries dispatched by King Ashoka of India, one of Buddhism's great early evangelists. Even today, the province of Nakhon Pathom retains a high Buddhist profile – aside from housing the country's holiest chedi, it also contains Phuttamonthon, Thailand's most important Buddhist sanctuary and home of its supreme patriarch.

Arriving at Nakhon Pathom's **train station**, a two-hundred-metre walk south across the khlong and through the market will get you to the chedi compound's north gate. Try to avoid being dumped at the **main bus terminal**, which is about 1km east of the town centre: most buses pass the chedi first, dropping passengers either in front of the police station across from the chedi's southern entrance, or beside the khlong, 100m from the northern gate. Staff at the train station will look after luggage for an hour or two, as will ticket collectors at the booth inside the chedi's south gate, a few metres from the bus drop. Finding your way around town is no problem as the chedi is an omnipresent landmark: nearly everything described below is within ten minutes' walk of it.

Phra Pathom Chedi

Phra Pathom Chedi (daily dawn–dusk; B20) has been twice rebuilt since its initial construction, its earliest fragments remaining entombed within the later layers. The origin of the chedi has become indistinguishable from folklore; although the Buddha never actually came to Thailand, legend has it that he rested here after wandering the country, and the original Indian-style (inverted bowl-shaped) chedi, similar to Ashoka's great stupa at Sanchi in India, may have been erected to represent this. Local chronicles, however, tell how the chedi was built in the sixth century as an act of atonement by the patricidal Phraya Pan. Abandoned at birth because of a prediction that he would one day murder his father, the Mon king, Pan was found by a village woman and raised to be a champion of the downtrodden. Vowing to rid the Mon of oppressive rule, Pan killed the king, and then, learning that he had fulfilled the tragic prophecy, blamed his adoptive mother and murdered her as well. To expiate his sin, the monks advised him to build a chedi "as high as the wild pigeon flies", and thus the original 39-metre-high stupa was born. Statues of both father and son stand inside the viharns of the present chedi.

Whatever its true beginnings, the first chedi fell into disrepair, only to be rebuilt with a **Khmer** prang during the time the Khmers controlled the

△ Courtyard, Phra Pathom Chedi

region, between the eighth and twelfth centuries. Once again it was abandoned to the jungle until the future Rama IV rediscovered it during his 27-year monkhood. Mindful of the Buddhist tradition that all monuments are sacred, in 1853 Rama IV set about encasing the old prang in the enormous new 120-metre-high plunger-shaped **chedi** (making it reputedly the tallest stupa in the world), adding four viharns, a circular cloister and a bot as well as a model of the original prang. Rama IV didn't live to see the chedi's completion, but his successors covered it in golden-brown tiles from China and continued to add statues and murals as well as new buildings.

Around the chedi

Approaching the chedi from the main (northern) staircase, you're greeted by the eight-metre-high Sukhothai-style Buddha image known as **Phra Ruang Rojanarit**, installed in front of the north viharn. Each of the viharns – there's one at each of the cardinal points – has an inner and an outer chamber containing tableaux of the life of the Buddha. The figures in the outer chamber of the **north viharn** depict two princesses paying homage to the newly born Prince Siddhartha (the future Buddha), while the inner one shows a monkey and an elephant offering honey and water to the Buddha at the end of a forty-day fast.

Proceeding clockwise around the chedi, as is the custom at all Buddhist monuments, you can weave between the outer promenade and the inner cloister via ornate doors that punctuate the dividing wall; the promenade is dotted with **trees**, many of which have religious significance, such as the bodhi tree (*ficus religiosa*) under one of which the Buddha was meditating when he achieved enlightenment. Moving on, you come to the **east viharn**, on whose wall is painted a clear cross-section of the chedi that shows the encased original at its core. Flanking the staircase that leads up to the **south viharn** are a three-dimensional replica of the original chedi with its Khmer prang (east side) and a model of the venerated chedi at Nakhon Si Thammarat (west side). The west viharn houses two reclining Buddhas: a sturdy, nine-metre-long figure in the outer chamber and a more delicate portrayal in the inner one.

The museums

There are two, similarly named, museums within the chedi compound. The newer, more formal setup, the **Phra Pathom Chedi National Museum** (Wed–Sun 9am–noon & 1–4pm; B30; Ⓦ www.thailandmuseum.com), is clearly signposted from the bottom of the chedi's south staircase. It displays a good collection of Dvaravati-era (sixth to eleventh centuries) artefacts excavated nearby, including Wheels of Law – an emblem introduced by Theravada Buddhists before naturalistic images were permitted – and Buddha statuary with the U-shaped robe and thick facial features characteristic of Dvaravati sculpture.

For a broader, more contemporary overview, hunt out the other magpie's nest of a collection, the **Phra Pathom Chedi Museum** (Wed–Sun 9am–noon & 1–4pm; free), which is halfway up the steps near the east viharn. More a curiosity shop than a museum, the small room is an Aladdin's cave of Buddhist amulets, seashells, gold and silver needles, Chinese ceramics, Thai musical instruments and ancient statues.

Sanam Chan Palace

A ten-minute walk west of the chedi along Thanon Rajdamnoen takes you through a large park to the moderately interesting **Sanam Chan Palace** (Sanam Chandra) complex (Thurs–Sun 9am–4pm; B50; Ⓦ www.palaces.thai.net), which was built as the country retreat of Rama VI in 1907. Sanam Chan is located across the road from the main campus of Silpakorn University and can also be reached by following signs for the university: from the chedi's southwest corner head west along Thanon Rajvithee, continue past the *Whale Hotel* for about 1km and then turn right down Thanon Rajamanka Nai – a B20 ride on a motorbike taxi.

The **palace** was designed to blend Western and Eastern styles: its principal structure, the Chaeemongkolosana Hall, evokes a miniature Bavarian castle, complete with turrets and red-tiled roof; the Mareeratcharatabulung Hall is a more oriental-style pavilion, built of teak and painted a deep rose colour inside and out; and the Thubkwan Hall is an unadorned traditional Thai-style house of polished, unpainted golden teak. Behind the Thubkwan Hall, in among a complementary series of pretty white wooden villas, stands a sizeable **art gallery**, which stages temporary exhibitions of modern works.

Practicalities

The most traveller-friendly of Nakhon Pathom's **accommodation** options is the conveniently located *Mitpaisal Hotel* (Ⓣ034 242422, Ⓔmitpaisal@hotmail.com; fan ❷, air-con ❸). Less than 200m from the chedi's north gateway, it has one entrance just a few metres to the right of the station exit, and another across from the north bank of the khlong (near the stop for buses to Bangkok), at 120/30 Thanon Phaya Pan. Rooms are a good size and are all en suite, and you can choose between fan or air-con. The other passable budget option is the less central and shabbier *Mitrsampant Hotel* (Ⓣ034 242422; ❷), located above a shop opposite the west gate of the chedi compound at the Lang Phra/Rajdamnoen intersection; all rooms here have fan and shower. There's more upmarket accommodation at the mid-range *Nakorn Inn Hotel* on Soi 3, just off Thanon Rajvithee, which starts at the southwestern corner of the chedi compound (Ⓣ034 251152, Ⓕ034 254998; ❸); rooms here all have air-con and TV.

For inexpensive Thai and Chinese food head for any of the **restaurants** along the eastern arm of Thanon Phraya Gong, which runs along the south (chedi) side of the canal; the place with the "Thai Food" sign is used to serving foreigners. Or try one of the garden restaurants along Thanon Rajdamnoen, which runs west from the chedi's west gate. Night-time foodstalls on Thanon Rajvithee are another good bet, and during the day the market in front of the station serves the usual takeaway goodies, including reputedly the tastiest *khao laam* (bamboo cylinders filled with steamed rice and coconut) in Thailand.

You can **change money** at the exchange booth (open banking hours only) on Thanon Phaya Pan, beside the bridge over the khlong, one block south of the train station; several nearby banks also have ATMs. There's **Internet access** on the road between the khlong and the chedi.

Buses heading for Kanchanaburi, Damnoen Saduak and Phetchaburi collect passengers from stops outside the police station across Thanon Kwaa Phra from the chedi's southern gate, and further west along Thanon Rajvithee, near the *Nakorn Inn Hotel*. Buses bound for Bangkok pick up from Thanon Phaya Pan on the north bank of the khlong, across from the *Mitpaisal Hotel*.

Damnoen Saduak floating markets

To get an idea of what shopping in Bangkok used to be like before all the canals were tarmacked over, many people take an early-morning trip to the **floating markets** (*talat khlong*) of **DAMNOEN SADUAK**, 60km south of

Nakhon Pathom. Vineyards and orchards here back onto a labyrinth of narrow canals, and every morning between 6 and 11am local market gardeners ply these waterways in paddle boats full of fresh fruit, vegetables and tourist-tempting soft drinks and souvenirs. Most dress in the deep-blue jacket and high-topped straw hat traditionally favoured by Thai farmers, so it all looks very picturesque, but the setup feels increasingly manufactured, and some visitors have complained of seeing more tourists than vendors, however early they arrive. For a more authentic version, consider going instead to the floating market near Amphawa, 10km south of Damnoen Saduak (see p.234).

The target for most tourists is the main **Talat Khlong Ton Kem**, 2km west of Damnoen Saduak's tiny town centre at the intersection of Khlong Damnoen Saduak and Khlong Thong Lang. Many of the wooden houses here have been converted into warehouse-style souvenir shops and tourist restaurants, diverting trade away from the khlong vendors and into the hands of large commercial enterprises. But, for the moment at least, a semblance of the traditional water trade continues, and the two bridges between Ton Kem and **Talat Khlong Hia Kui** (a little further south down Khlong Thong Lang) make decent vantage points. Touts invariably congregate at the Ton Kem pier to hassle you into taking a **boat trip** around the khlong network (asking an hourly rate of around B150–200/person), but there are distinct disadvantages in being propelled between markets at top speed in a noisy motorized boat. For a less hectic and more sensitive look at the markets, explore via the walkways beside the canals.

Practicalities

Damnoen Saduak is 109km from Bangkok, so to reach the market in good time you have to catch one of the earliest **buses** from the capital's Southern Bus Terminal (from 6am; 2hr 30min). Or join one of the numerous half- or full-day trips (from B250, or B360 including Nakhon Pathom and the River Kwai). In Nakhon Pathom, buses and songthaews pick up passengers outside the police station and outside *Nakorn Inn Hotel* (from 6am; 1hr). From Kanchanaburi, take bus #461 to Ban Phe (every 15min from 5.25am; 1hr 15min), then change to bus #78. To get to Damnoen Saduak from Phetchaburi or any points further south, catch any Bangkok-bound bus and, depending on which route it takes, change either at Samut Songkhram or at the Photharam intersection.

Damnoen Saduak's **bus terminal** is just north of Thanarat Bridge and Khlong Damnoen Saduak, on the main Bangkok/Nakhon Pathom–Samut Songkhram road, Highway 325. Frequent yellow **songthaews** cover the 2km to Ton Kem, but walk if you've got the time: a walkway follows the canal, which you can get to from Thanarat Bridge, or you can cross the bridge and take the road to the right (west), Thanon Sukhaphiban 1, through the orchards. Drivers on the earliest buses from Bangkok sometimes do not terminate at the bus station but instead cross Thanarat Bridge and then drop tourists at a pier a few hundred metres along Thanon Sukhaphiban 1.

The best way to see the markets is to stay overnight in Damnoen Saduak and get up at dawn, well before the buses and coach tours from Bangkok arrive. There's decent budget **accommodation** at the *Little Bird Hotel*, also known as *Noknoi* (Ⓣ032 254382; fan ❷, air-con ❸), whose sign is clearly visible from the main road and Thanarat Bridge. Rooms here are good value with enormous en suite bathrooms and air-con if you want it. Staff can also arrange floating market boat trips.

Samut Songkhram and around

Rarely visited by foreign tourists and yet within easy reach of Bangkok, the tiny estuarine province of **SAMUT SONGKHRAM** is nourished by the Mae Khlong River as it meanders through on the last leg of its route to the Gulf. Fishing is an important industry round here, and big wooden boats are still built in riverside yards near the estuary, within easy reach of the Gulf waters;

Eng and Chang, the Siamese twins

Eng (In) and Chang (Chan), the "original" **Siamese twins**, were born in Samut Songkhram in 1811, when Thailand was known as Siam. The boys' bodies were joined from breastbone to navel by a short fleshy ligament, but they shared no vital organs and eventually managed to stretch their connecting tissue so that they could stand almost side by side instead of permanently facing each other.

In 1824, the boys were spotted by entrepreneurial Scottish trader Robert Hunter, who returned five years later with an American sea merchant, Captain Abel Coffin, to convince the twins' mother to let them take her sons on a world tour. Hunter and Coffin anticipated a lucrative career as producer-managers of an exotic **freak show**, and were not disappointed. They launched the twins in Boston, advertising them as "the Monster" and charging the public 50 cents to watch the boys demonstrate how they walked and ran. Though shabbily treated and poorly paid, the twins soon developed a more theatrical show, enthralling their audiences with impressive acrobatics and feats of strength, and earning the soubriquet "the eighth wonder of the world". At the age of 21, having split from their exploitative managers, the twins became self-employed, but continued to tour with other companies across the world. Wherever they went, they would always be given a thorough examination by local **medics**, partly to counter accusations of fakery, but also because this was the first time the world and its doctors had been introduced to conjoined twins. Such was the twins' international celebrity that the term "Siamese twins" has been used ever since. Chang and Eng also sought advice from these doctors on surgical separation – an issue they returned to repeatedly right up until their deaths but never acted upon, despite plenty of gruesome suggestions.

By 1840 the twins had become quite wealthy and decided to settle down. They were granted American citizenship, assumed the family name Bunker, and became slave-owning **plantation farmers** in North Carolina. Three years later they married two local sisters, Addie and Sally Yates, and between them went on to father 21 children. The families lived in separate houses and the twins shuttled between the two, keeping to a strict timetable of three days in each household; for an intriguing imagined account of this bizarre state of affairs, read Darin Strauss's novel ***Chang and Eng***, reviewed on p.929. Chang and Eng had quite different personalities, and relations between the two couples soured, leading to the division of their assets, with Chang's family getting most of the land, and Eng's most of the slaves. To support their dependants, the twins were obliged to take their show back on the road several times, on occasion working with the infamous showman P.T. Barnum. Their final tour was born out of financial desperation following the 1861–65 Civil War, which had wiped out most of the twins' riches and led to the liberation of all their slaves.

In 1874, Chang succumbed to bronchitis and died; Eng, who might have survived on his own if an operation had been performed immediately, died a few hours later, possibly of shock. They were 62. The twins are buried in White Plains in North Carolina, but there's a **memorial** to them near their birthplace in Samut Songkhram, where a statue and the small, makeshift In-Chan Museum (Mon–Fri 8.30am–4.30pm; free) have been erected 4km north of the provincial capital's centre on Thanon Ekachai (Route 3092).

further inland, fruit is the main source of income, particularly pomelos, lychees, guavas and coconuts. But for visitors it is the network of three hundred canals woven around the river, and the traditional way of life the waterways still support, that is most intriguing. As well as some of the most genuine floating markets in Thailand, there are chances to witness traditional cottage industries such as palm-sugar production and *bencharong* ceramic painting, plus more than a hundred historic temples to admire, a number of them dating back to the reign of Rama II, who was born in the province. The other famous sons of the region are Eng and Chang, the "original" Siamese twins, who grew up in Samut Songkhram and are commemorated with a small museum in the town.

Despite the region's tangible charm, tourism is very much in its infancy here, so hotel options are limited. If you're dependent on public transport, your first stop will be the provincial capital of Samut Songkhram, also commonly known as Mae Khlong, after the river that cuts through it. It's a pleasant enough market town, but there's little reason to linger as the sights and most of the accommodation are out of town, mainly in the **Amphawa** district a few kilometres upriver.

If you get the chance, it's well worth venturing out onto the canals after dark to **watch the fireflies** twinkling romantically in their favourite *lamphu* trees like delicate strings of fairylights; any boatman will ferry you to the right spot.

Practicalities

The most enjoyable way of travelling to Samut Songkhram is by **train** from Bangkok – a scenic, albeit rather convoluted route that has three stages and involves going via Samut Sakhon. It's a very unusual line, being single track and for much of its route literally squeezed in between homes, palms and mangroves, and, most memorably, between market stalls, so that at both the Samut Sakhon and Samut Songkhram termini the train really does chug to a standstill amidst the trays of seafood. Trains to Samut Sakhon leave approximately hourly from Bangkok's **Wongwian Yai station** in southern Thonburi (not to be confused with Thonburi train station further north; see p.212), but for the fastest onward connections catch the 5.30am, 8.35am, 12.15pm or 3.25pm. The train pulls up right inside the wet market at **Samut Sakhon**, also known as **Mahachai**, where you need to take a ferry across the Maenam Tha Chin to get the connecting train from **Ban Laem** on the other bank. Exiting the train, cross the track and continue in the same direction as the train was going, through a clothes market, until you emerge on to a shopping street. Cross the street to the five-storey blue-painted *Tarua Restaurant*, right on the estuary, adjacent to the busy fishing port, where you'll find two piers. The pier on the right of the restaurant is served by frequent shuttle boats (B2) to the Chinese temple directly across the river, from where you should turn right and walk about 15–20 minutes upriver, via a Thai temple, to reach Ban Laem station. The boat departing the pier on the left of the restaurant goes direct to Ban Laem station, further upstream (5min; B5), and times its journeys to meet the Ban Laem trains. There are only four trains a day in each direction from **Ban Laem** to Samut Songkhram at the end of the line (1hr), a journey through marshes, lagoons, shrimp farms, salt flats and mangrove and palm growth. Once again, at **Samut Songkhram**, the station is literally enveloped by the town-centre market, with traders gathering up their goods and awnings from the trackside for the arrival and departure of the service. From the station it's 50m due west to the river and the pier for cross-river ferries and taxi-boats.

The **bus** ride to Samut Songkhram from Bangkok's Southern Bus terminal (every 20min; 1hr 30min) is faster than the train, but the views are dominated by urban sprawl until the last stretch, when Highway 35 runs through a swathe of **salt farms** whose windmills pump in the sea water via a web of canals, leaving the brine to evaporate into photogenic little pyramids of white crystals. Buses also run direct to **Amphawa** from Bangkok's southern bus terminal (every 20min; 2hr). Samut Songkhram's bus station is south of the market, across from the Siam Commercial Bank off Thanon Ratchayadruksa. When returning to Bangkok, there's also a minibus service to the Northern Mo Chit bus terminal (approximately hourly; B70; about 1hr 30min), which departs from Thanon Si Jumpa, about 100m east of from the *Maeklong Hotel*.

Once in Samut Songkhram, you have various options for local transport, though routes don't encompass all the sights. **Songthaews** to Amphawa and **local buses** to Amphawa and Damnoen Saduak, via Highway 325, leave from the north edge of the central market, and from the bus station. However, a more appealing way of exploring this area is by boat: **taxi-boats** and other chartered river transport operate from the Mae Khlong River pier, 50m west of the train station and market in the town centre, or, most rewardingly, once in Amphawa, you can take a **boat tour** from Amphawa's *Baan Tai Had Resort* (B150–200/person) or one of the nearby home-stays (B300–700/boat). Independent exploration is possible if you have your own vehicle, and *Baan Tai Had* rents out bicycles, kayaks and jet skis. Alternatively, you could join a one-day **cycling tour** of the area from Bangkok for about US$50 with either Spice Roads (ⓣ02 712 5305, ⓦwww.spiceroads.com) or Bike and Travel (ⓣ02 990 0274, ⓦwww.cyclingthailand.com).

All the central branches of the main banks around the edge of Samut Songkhram market offer **currency exchange**.

Accommodation and eating

If you want cheap **accommodation** then you should stay in Samut Songkhram town centre, at the welcoming and well kept *Maeklong Hotel* (ⓣ034 711150; fan ❷, air-con ❸), which has large en-suite rooms about 150m due north of the train station, beyond the edge of the market, at 526/10-13 Thanon Si Jumpa. To get the most out of the area however, it's worth splashing out on the luxurious but good-value *Baan Tai Had Resort* (ⓣ034 767220, ⓦwww.hotelthailand.com/samutsongkram/baantaihad; ❻), located beside the Mae Khlong River in the Amphawa district, about 6km upstream from Samut Songkhram (a 15-minute, B60 ride by taxi-boat from Samut Songkhram's pier; if coming by car, email the hotel for a map). With its stylish, comfortable bungalows set around a Bali-style garden, swimming pool and restaurant, *Baan Tai Had* makes a good base, not least because of its local tour programmes and English-speaking guides. There's also a potentially interesting **home-stay programme** in two nearby villages, Ban Tha Ka (15km north of Samut Songkhram) and Plai Phong Pang (9km west of Samut Songkhram on Route 3093), where many households have joined together to offer accommodation and meals in their traditional homes (B400/person half-board), though their English is likely to be rudimentary at best. Home-stays must be booked through the headman (*kamnan*) of each village: for Plai Phong Pang call ⓣ081 403 7907, and for Ban Tha Ka call ⓣ034 766208. There's also the independent *Baan Rim Khong* home-stay (ⓣ034 752775, ⓔsruangkamol@hotmail.com; B700 for two-days and a night, all inclusive) in Plai Phong Pang.

Seafood is the obvious regional speciality and the most famous local dish is *hoi lot pat cha*, a spicy stir-fry that centres round the tubular molluscs, known as **hoi lot** or "worm shells", that are harvested in their sackloads at low tide from a muddy sandbank known as Don Hoi Lot at the mouth of the Mae Khlong estuary. Don

Hoi Lot is probably the most famous spot in the province to eat seafood, and a dozen restaurants occupy the area around the nearby pier, many offering views out over the Gulf and its bountiful sandbar; the pier is 5km south of Highway 35 and served by songthaews from Samut Songkhram market. If you're staying at *Baan Tai Had*, make use of the free taxi-boat service to the canalside *Chao Lay* restaurant whose mid-priced menu features plenty of fresh fish and seafood, usually including locally caught giant prawns (*kung yai*). In Samut Songkhram itself, the food stalls alongside the pier make a pleasant spot for a lunch of cheap seafood *phat thai*.

Tha Ka Floating Market and the palm-sugar centres

Unlike at the over-touristed markets of nearby Damnoen Saduak, the **floating market at Tha Ka** is still the province of local residents. Market gardeners paddle up here in their small wooden sampans, or motor along in their noisy longtails, the boats piled high either with whatever's in season, be it pomelos or betel nuts, rambutans or okra, or with perennially popular snacks like hot noodle soup and freshly cooked satay. Their main customers are canalside residents and other traders, so the atmosphere is still pleasingly but not artificially traditional and as yet the market is not a major feature on the coach-tour trail. Thai tourist groups do visit, but mainly if market day happens to fall on a weekend. The Tha Ka market operates only six times a month, on a **timetable** that's dependent on the tides (for boat access) and is therefore dictated by the moon; thus market days are restricted to the second, seventh and twelfth mornings of every fifteen-day lunar cycle, from around 7 to 11am (contact any TAT office for exact dates). The market takes place on Khlong Phanla in the village of Ban Tha Ka, a half-hour **boat ride** from *Baan Tai Had Resort*, or ten to forty minutes from the home-stays, and about an hour from Damnoen Saduak; it's usually incorporated into a day-trip (about B200/person). The boat ride to the market is half the fun, but you can also get there by **road**, following Highway 325 out of Samut Songkhram for 10km, then taking a five-kilometre access road to Ban Tha Ka.

Most boat trips to Tha Ka also make a stop at one of the nearby **palm-sugar-making centres**. The sap of the coconut palm is a crucial ingredient in many Thai sweets and the fertile soil of Samut Songkhram province supports many small-scale sugar-palm plantations. Several palm-sugar cottage industries between Amphawa and Ban Tha Ka are open to the public; they're signed off Highway 325 and if you're not on a tour you can reach them by car or by Damnoen Saduak-bound bus.

Amphawa and around

The district town of **AMPHAWA** is smaller and more atmospheric than Samut Songkhram, retaining original charm alongside modern development. Its old neighbourhoods hug the banks of the Mae Khlong River and the Khlong Amphawa tributary, the wooden homes and shops facing the water and accessed either by boat or on foot along one of the waterfront walkways. Frequent **songthaews** and local **buses** (both approximately every 30min; 15min) connect Samut Songkhram market with Amphawa market, which sets up beside the khlong, just back from its confluence with the river.

King Rama II Memorial Park and Wat Amphawan

King Rama II was born in Amphawa (his mother's home town) in 1767 and is honoured with a memorial park and temple erected on the site of his probable birthplace, beside the Mae Khlong River on the western edge of Amphawa town, five minutes' walk west of Amphawa market and khlong. It's accessible both by boat and by road, 6km from Samut Songkhram on the Amphawa–Bang Khonthi road.

Rama II, or Phra Buddhalertla Naphalai as he is known in Thai, was a famously cultured king and a respected poet and playwright, and the **museum** (Wed–Sun 9am–4pm; B10) at the heart of the **King Rama II Memorial Park** (daily 9am–6pm) displays lots of rather esoteric Rama II memorabilia, including a big collection of nineteenth-century musical instruments and a gallery of *khon* masks used in traditional theatre. On the edge of the park, **Wat Amphawan** is graced with a statue of the king and decorated with murals that depict scenes from his life, including a behind-the-altar panorama of nineteenth-century Bangkok, with Ratanakosin Island's Grand Palace, Wat Pho and Sanam Luang still recognizable to modern eyes.

Wat Chulamani and Ban Pinsuwan bencharong workshop

The canalside **Wat Chulamani** was until the late 1980s the domain of the locally famous abbot Luang Pho Nuang, a man believed by many to possess special powers, and followers still come to the temple to pay respects to his body, which is preserved in a glass-sided coffin in the main viharn. The breathtakingly detailed decor inside the viharn is testament to the devotion he inspired: the intricate black-and-gold lacquered artwork that covers every surface has taken years and cost millions of baht to complete. Across the temple compound, the bot's modern, pastel-toned murals tell the story of the Buddha's life, beginning inside the door on the right with a scene showing the young Buddha emerging from a tent (his birth) and being able to walk on lilypads straightaway. The death of the Buddha and his entry into nirvana is depicted on the wall behind the altar. Wat Chulamani is located beside Khlong Amphawa, a twenty-minute walk east of Amphawa market, or a five-minute boat-ride. It is also signed off Highway 325, so any bus going to Damnoen Saduak from Samut Songkhram will drop you within reach.

A few hundred metres down the road from Wat Chulamani, and also accessible on foot, by bus and by canal, the Ban Pinsuwan **bencharong workshop** specializes in reproductions of famous antique *bencharong* ceramics, the exquisite five-coloured pottery that used to be the tableware of choice for the Thai aristocracy and is now a prized collector's item. A *bencharong* museum, exhibiting the chronology of styles, is planned.

Kanchanaburi and the River Kwai valleys

Set in a landscape of limestone hills just 120km from Bangkok, the provincial capital of **Kanchanaburi** occupies a strategic and scenic spot at the point where the **River Kwai Noi** merges with the **River Kwai Yai** to become the Mae Khlong (though Kwai Yai is just the name that's been appropriated for the

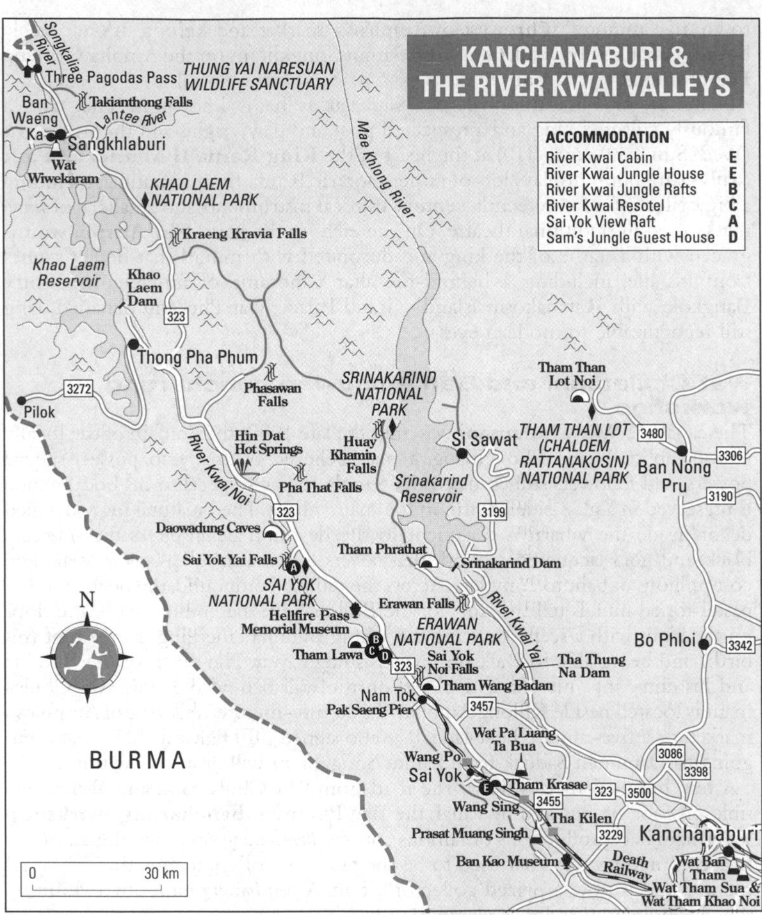

Mae Khlong as it flows through this region). The town is most famous for its World War II role as a POW camp and base for construction work on the Thailand–Burma Railway, chiefly because of the notorious Bridge over the River Kwai, which spans the river here. But there are plenty more important wartime sights in and around Kanchanaburi, and the town is also an appealing destination in its own right, with lots of riverside guest houses that make enjoyable places to unwind for a few days. The surrounding area offers numerous caves, wats and historical sites to explore, some of them easily reached by bicycle, and organized treks and rafting trips are also a major feature.

Beyond Kanchanaburi, the main area of interest is the Kwai Noi Valley as this was the route followed by the **Death Railway**. Riding the train along the remaining section of this line is a popular activity and combines well with a visit to the sobering museum north of the current terminus at the aptly named **Hellfire Pass**. Following the Kwai Noi to its headwaters brings you to the unhyped, ethnically mixed little lakeside town of **Sangkhlaburi**, close by the

Burmese border at **Three Pagodas Pass**. Further east, the Kwai Yai valley offers fewer obvious attractions, but is the site of the much-visited **Erawan Falls**, while nearby **Tham Than Lot National Park** appeals to hikers because of its impressive caves.

Kanchanaburi

With its plentiful supply of traveller-oriented accommodation and countless possibilities for easy forays into the surrounding countryside, **KANCHANABURI** makes the perfect getaway from Bangkok, a two-hour bus ride away. The big appeal here is the river: that it's the famous River Kwai is a bonus, but the more immediate attractions are the guest houses whose rooms overlook the waterway, most of them offering fine views of the serrated limestone hills beyond. The heart of this ever-expanding travellers' scene dominates the southern end of Thanon Maenam Kwai (also spelt Kwae) and is within easy reach of the train station, but the real town centre is some distance away, running north from the bus station up Kanchanaburi's main drag, Thanon Saeng Chuto.

Nearly all Kanchanaburi's official attractions relate to World War II and the building of the Thailand–Burma Railway. Day-trippers and tour groups descend in their hundreds on the infamous **Bridge over the River Kwai**, the symbol of Japanese atrocities in the region, though the town's main **war museums** and **cemeteries** are much more moving. Many veterans returning to visit the graves of their wartime comrades are understandably resentful that others have in some cases insensitively exploited the POW experience – the commercial paraphernalia surrounding the Bridge is a case in point. On the other hand, the Death Railway Museum (aka Thailand–Burma Railway Centre) provides shockingly instructive accounts of a period not publicly documented outside this region. The town's main war sights are located along the east bank of the Kwai Yai and Mae Khlong, but it's easy to cross the river – by road, ferry or longtail – and explore some of the more tranquilly located temples along the Kwai Noi and west bank of the Mae Khlong.

The Bridge forms the dramatic centrepiece of the annual *son et lumière* **River Kwai Bridge Festival**, held over ten nights from the end of November to commemorate the first Allied bombing of the Bridge on November 28, 1944; Kanchanaburi gets packed out during this time, so book accommodation well ahead.

Arrival

Trains are the most scenic way to get to Kanchanaburi, but there are only two daily from Bangkok's Thonburi station, via Nakhon Pathom. The State Railway also runs special day-trips from Bangkok's Hualamphong Station, which include short stops at Nakhon Pathom, the Bridge over the River Kwai and Nam Tok, the terminus of the line (Sat, Sun & holidays only; advance booking essential, see p.212). Coming from Hua Hin, Chumphon and points further south, take the train to Ban Pong and then change to a Kanchanaburi-bound train (or bus). The main **Kanchanaburi train station** (Ⓣ034 511285) is on Thanon Saeng Chuto, about 2km north of the town centre, but within walking distance of some of the riverside accommodation along Soi Rongheabaow and Thanon Maenam Kwai. However, if you're staying at *Bamboo House* or the *Felix River Kwai*, or are doing a day-trip and want to see the Bridge, get off at the **River**

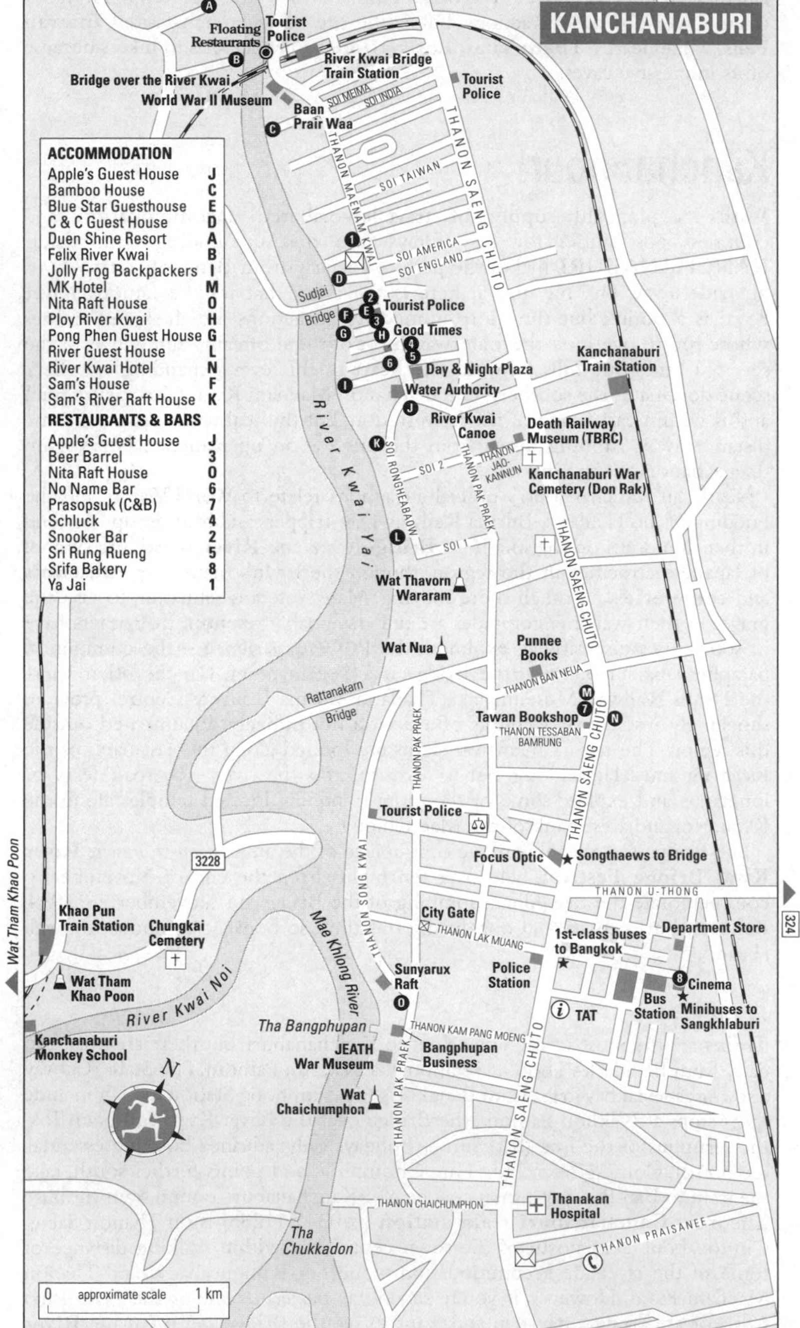
KANCHANABURI
ACCOMMODATION
Apple's Guest House J
Bamboo House C
Blue Star Guesthouse E
C & C Guest House D
Duen Shine Resort A
Felix River Kwai B
Jolly Frog Backpackers I
MK Hotel M
Nita Raft House O
Ploy River Kwai H
Pong Phen Guest House G
River Guest House L
River Kwai Hotel N
Sam's House F
Sam's River Raft House K
RESTAURANTS & BARS
Apple's Guest House J
Beer Barrel 3
Nita Raft House 0
No Name Bar 6
Prasopsuk (C&B) 7
Schluck 4
Snooker Bar 2
Sri Rung Rueng 5
Srifa Bakery 8
Ya Jai 1
Floating Restaurants
Tourist Police
River Kwai Bridge Train Station
Bridge over the River Kwai
World War II Museum
Baan Prair Waa
Soi Meima
Soi India
Thanon Maenam Kwai
Thanon Saeng Chuto
Soi Taiwan
Soi America
Soi England
Sudjai Bridge
Good Times
Day & Night Plaza
Water Authority
Kanchanaburi Train Station
River Kwai Canoe
Death Railway Museum (TBRC)
Thanon Jaokannun
Soi 2
Soi Rongheabaow
Thanon Pak Praek
Kanchanaburi War Cemetery (Don Rak)
River Kwai Yai
Soi 1
Wat Thavorn Wararam
Wat Nua
Punnee Books
Rattanakarn Bridge
Thanon Ban Neua
Tawan Bookshop
Thanon Tessaban Bamrung
Tourist Police
Focus Optic
Songthaews to Bridge
Wat Tham Khao Poon
3228
Thanon U-Thong
324
City Gate
Thanon Song Kwai
Thanon Lak Muang
Department Store
1st-class buses to Bangkok
Khao Pun Train Station
Chungkai Cemetery
Wat Tham Khao Poon
Mae Khlong River
Sunyarux Raft
Police Station
Cinema
Bus Station
Minibuses to Sangkhlaburi
TAT
River Kwai Noi
Tha Bangphupan
Thanon Kam Pang Moeng
Kanchanaburi Monkey School
JEATH War Museum
Bangphupan Business
N
Wat Chaichumphon
Thanon Chaichumphon
Thanakan Hospital
Thanon Praisanee
Tha Chukkadon
0 approximate scale 1 km
Wat Tham Mangkon
Thong & Wat Ban Tham
Wat Tham Sua

Moving on from Kanchanaburi

Hair-raisingly fast **tourist minibuses** run to Bangkok's **Thanon Khao San** two or more times a day (2hr; B120) and can be booked through most Kanchanaburi guest houses and tour operators; a chartered minivan to the **airport** in Bangkok costs around B2000 for up to nine people. There's also a tourist minibus service between Kanchanaburi guest houses and **Ayutthaya** (2hr; B450 per person). Government buses leave from the main **bus station** (see below); the first-class ticket office and departure point is right beside the main road on the edge of the bus station, while the main ticket office for all other services is further back inside the depot. Minibuses to **Sangkhlaburi** depart from the back of the bus station.

If heading north, to **Ayutthaya** and/or **Chiang Mai**, you'll need to first take a bus to Suphanburi, as described in "Arrival". For any long-distance journey to **southern Thailand**, the best option is to take a train or bus to Nakhon Pathom and change to a **night train** headed for **Chumphon, Surat Thani** or beyond; reservations for any rail journey can be made at Kanchanaburi train station, described on p.237.

Kwai Bridge train station instead, five minutes further down the line, on the east bank of the river.

Faster than the train are the **buses** from Bangkok's Southern Bus Terminal (every 15min; 2hr) and Northern Bus Terminal (9 daily; 2hr 30min). From Lopburi, Ayutthaya (for trains from Chiang Mai), or points further north, you'll have to return to Bangkok or change buses at Suphanburi, about 90km north of Kanchanaburi (#411; every 20min; 2hr). From Phetchaburi and Hua Hin you need to change buses at Ratchaburi for connections to Kanchanaburi (#461; every 15min; 1hr 45min). Arriving at Kanchanaburi **bus station** (ⓣ034 511182), at the southern edge of the town centre, it's a ten- to twenty-minute walk, B15 motorbike-taxi ride or B40–50 samlor ride along Thanon Lak Muang to the raft houses off Thanon Song Kwai; to get to the Soi Rongheabaow and Thanon Maenam Kwai guest houses, either take a B40–50 samlor or tuk-tuk ride, or travel part way on the public songthaew service described below.

If you're coming from Bangkok, the fastest transport of all is to take one of the **tourist minibuses** from Thanon Khao San, which travel at breakneck speeds and take just two hours door to door (B120), though they generally only drop passengers at *Jolly Frog*, despite advertising otherwise. Another dedicated Bangkok-Kanchanaburi minibus service leaves from outside Bangkok's *Royal Hotel* on Ratchadamnoen Klang in Banglamphu, departing when full throughout the day from 5am–8pm (generally hourly) and dropping you wherever you want (2hr; B100).

Town transport and information

Orange public **songthaews** run along Thanon Saeng Chuto, originating from outside the Focus Optic optician's, one block north of the bus station, and travelling north via the Kanchanaburi War Cemetery (Don Rak), Death Railway Museum, train station and access road to the Bridge (every 15min; 15min to the Bridge turn-off; B8).

A scenic way of travelling between riverine sights is by chartered **longtail boat** from one of the small piers in the tourist areas. At the Bangphupan pier, secreted amongst the trinket shops 100m north of the JEATH Museum at 21 Thanon Pakpraek, boats operated by Bangphupan Business (ⓣ034 620126) cost a hefty B200 for the trip up to the Bridge, or a more reasonable B600 for a two-hour trip out to Khao Poon and Chungkai and back to the Bridge (maximum six people). Or you can paddle yourself in a **kayak** (see p.248 for details).

By far the best way to see the main town sights, and the surrounding countryside, is by **bicycle**; most guest houses and many tour agencies rent out bikes for B20–30 per day (B50 for mountain bikes), and several also have **motorbikes** (B200–350/day) and **jeeps** (from B1000) for hire. There are dozens of outlets along Thanon Maenam Kwai, as well as one up at the Bridge.

The **TAT** office (daily 8.30am–4.30pm; ⓣ034 511200, ⓔtatkan@tat.or.th) is south of the bus station on Thanon Saeng Chuto and keeps up-to-date bus and train timetables.

Accommodation

Many people choose to make the most of the inspiring scenery by staying on or near the river, in either a **raft house** (often just a rattan hut balanced on a raft of logs) or a **guest house.** The most popular area is around **Thanon Maenam Kwai,** which stretches 2km from Soi Rongheabaow to the Bridge, and is *the* backpackers' hub, crammed with bars, restaurants and tour operators; most guest houses are at the riverside end of the small sois running off this thoroughfare, though the premier views are bagged by the hotels on the west bank of the Kwai Yai, to the **north of the Bridge**. Riverside **Soi Rongheabaow** (or Rong Heeb Oil, as it's sometimes spelt) abuts Thanon Maenam Kwai to the south and is much quieter, little more than a narrow village lane, where bicycles and dogs constitute the main traffic. South again, **Thanon Song Kwai** is the departure point for raft-house tours and with one exception its accommodation is mainly patronized by holidaying groups of Thai students. The **Thanon Saeng Chuto** hotels, away from the river in the centre of town, have the least interesting outlooks but the most convenient locations. Details of raft-house accommodation further **upstream** are given under the relevant accounts: Tham Lawa on p.256, Sai Yok on p.257 and Thong Pha Phum on p.258.

Despite the tranquil views, riverside accommodation can be **noisy**, plagued by roaring longtail engines during the day and karaoke-bar sound systems at night; with this in mind, it can be expedient to book in for just one night until you've experienced the decibel levels for yourself. As Kanchanaburi province levies a one-percent **local government tax** from all tourist accommodation providers, you may find this added on to your bill.

Soi Rongheabaow and Thanon Maenam Kwai area

Apple's Guest House 52 Soi Rongheabaow 3 ⓣ034 512017, ⓦwww.applenoi-kanchanaburi.com. Small, welcoming guest house, away from the river, whose owners run well-regarded tours and have made their restaurant the town's best. The twenty spotless rooms are set round a lawn fringed with shrubs, and are all en suite; price depends on size, furnishings and whether you want fan or air-con. Fan ❷–❸, air-con ❹

Bamboo House Soi Vietnam, off the Bridge end of Thanon Maenam Kwai ⓣ034 624470. One of Kanchanaburi's more secluded options, this place sits on a pretty stretch of the river not far from the Bridge, though it is 2km from the shops and restaurants of southern Thanon Maenam Kwai. Accommodation in all categories is pretty basic, ranging from simple floating huts with a mattress on the floor and shared bathrooms, to en-suite bungalows and a few air-con rooms on dry land, but many are set round the huge lawn and pretty flower garden. If arriving by train, get off at the River Kwai Bridge station, which is closer than Kanchanaburi station. Floating hut ❷, en-suite bungalow ❷, air-con ❹

Blue Star Guesthouse 241 Thanon Maenam Kwai, ⓣ034 512161, ⓔbluestar_guesthouse@yahoo.com. Popular, clued-up guest house with a wide range of good-value accommodation including cheap fan rooms in a row house, attractive, well-priced bungalows set over a lotus swamp, and raised tree-house cabins with downstairs bathrooms. All rooms are en suite and the land runs down to the river area, though there are few views. Fan ❷, air-con ❸–❹

C & C Guest House Soi England, 265/2 Thanon Maenam Kwai ⓣ034 624547. Genially managed riverside compound of basic and very cheap floating huts with shared bathrooms, plus some simple en-suite huts (with the option of air-con and connecting rooms) set in the garden. It's a very quiet spot, at the end of a winding soi. The owners also run tours, heavily promoted on Bangkok's Thanon Khao San, to their "jungle lodge" near Erawan Falls. Call for free transport from the bus or train station. Fan ❶, air-con ❷

Jolly Frog Backpackers 28 Soi China, just off the southern end of Thanon Maenam Kwai ⓣ034 514579. Most backpackers' first choice, this large, efficiently run complex features comfortable en-suite rooms in bamboo huts (some with air-con) plus a few cheap singles with shared bathrooms, all ranged around a riverside garden. You can swim off the jetty (though be careful of the strong current), and the lawn's invitingly large. On the down side, the place can be noisy at night and is quite impersonal. Fan ❶–❷, air-con ❷

Ploy River Kwai Thanon Maenam Kwai ⓣ034 515804, ⓦwww.ploygh.com. Strikingly different in style from everywhere else in Kanchanaburi, this is a smart little enclave set back off the road but with distant river views only from the restaurant. The chic, sleek, contemporary-look rooms each have a platform bed and air-con, with extra charged for those with garden-style bathrooms or TVs. ❹–❺

Pong Phen Guest House 5 Soi Bangladesh (Bangklated), off Thanon Maenam Kwai ⓣ034 512981, ⓦwww.pongphen.com. Small, smartly outfitted modern raft-house rooms with shared bathrooms but great views from the common veranda. On land, choose between well-designed fan and air-con rooms, all en suite, set in a row around the lawn area. Fan ❶, fan and bathroom ❷, air-con ❸–❺

River Guest House 42 Soi Rongheabaow ⓣ034 511637, ⓦwww.riverguesthouse.net. Occupying a tranquil spot, the dozen bright green terraced stilt-houses here all enjoy uninterrupted river views and, being Turkish owned, are each named after a place in Turkey. Rooms are no frills but spruce and all have private bathrooms; some also have air-con. Fan ❷, air-con ❸

Sam's House Thanon Maenam Kwai ⓣ034 515956, ⓦwww.samsguesthouse.com. The poshest and most popular of the *Sam*'s places, this one features a set of attractively positioned timber huts on stilts among a dense tangle of lotuses – all are en suite, furnished to a high standard, and fronted by a small private balcony, and some have air-con. There are some less interesting fan and air-con rooms on the river bank. Fan ❶–❸, air-con ❸–❹

Sam's River Raft House 48/1 Soi Rongheabaow ⓣ034 624231, ⓦwww.samsguesthouse.com. This arm of the *Sam*'s empire offers twenty comfortably equipped floating rooms, built on pontoons, some with direct access to the riverfront walkway, others with river-bank views, but all of them en suite and with optional air-con. There are cheaper, surprisingly cute rooms in the garden across the road. Floating room with fan ❷, with air-con ❸; garden room with fan ❶, with air-con ❷

North of the Bridge

Duen Shine Resort On the west bank of the Kwai Yai ⓣ034 653345, ⓦwww.duenshine.com. Upmarket riverside resort that gets more Thai tourists than international guests and offers pretty good-value rooms, all with air-con and TV, in raft houses, cottages and a small hotel block. There's a swimming pool in the landscaped tropical garden, and a restaurant. ❻–❽

Felix River Kwai On the west bank of the Kwai Yai ⓣ034 515061, ⓦwww.felixriverkwai.co.th. Occupying a lovely riverside spot within walking distance of the Bridge (or a 2km drive from Thanon Maenam Kwai – a little inconvenient if you don't have transport), this is the most upmarket resort in the area and offers over two hundred large deluxe rooms with air-con, TV and mini-bar, plus two swimming pools. Rates depend on whether or not you want a river view, and are sometimes discounted during the week; reservations are essential for weekends. ❼–❽

Thanon Song Kwai area

Nita Raft House 271/1 Thanon Pak Praek ⓣ034 514521, ⓔnita_rafthouse@yahoo.com. Located away from the main Thanon Song Kwai fray, near the JEATH Museum, this is a genuine, old-style guest house with a very laid-back atmosphere that's been run by the same couple for years. The fourteen simple floating rooms are among the cheapest in town and all offer some sort of river view; some are also en suite. There's a nice floating lounge for watching DVDs, and sampling the tasty guest-house food. Shared bathroom ❶, en suite ❷

Thanon Saeng Chuto

MK Hotel 277/41 Thanon Saeng Chuto ⓣ034 621143. Friendly, smartly maintained, city-style little hotel that lacks character but compensates with genuinely comfortable air-con rooms and reasonable prices. ❸

River Kwai Hotel 284/3–16 Thanon Saeng Chuto ⓣ034 510111, ⓦwww.riverkwai.co.th. The town centre's top hotel is nowhere near the river, but it's very good value even if it lacks the atmosphere of its riverside competitors. Rooms are of a very high standard, and all have air-con and cable TV. Hotel facilities include a pool, nightclub and Internet access. ❻

The Town

Strung out along the east bank of the River Kwai and its continuation, south of the Kwai Noi confluence, as the Mae Khlong, Kanchanaburi is a long, narrow ribbon of a town. The **war sights** are sandwiched between the river and the busy main drag, Thanon Saeng Chuto, with the Bridge over the River Kwai

The Death Railway

Shortly after entering World War II in December 1941, Japan, fearing an Allied blockade of the Bay of Bengal, began looking for an alternative supply route to connect its newly acquired territories that stretched from Singapore to the Burma–India border. In spite of the almost impenetrable terrain, the River Kwai basin was chosen as the route for a new **Thailand–Burma Railway**, the aim being to join the existing terminals of Nong Pladuk in Thailand (51km southeast of Kanchanaburi) and Thanbuyazat in Burma – a total distance of 415km.

About 60,000 Allied POWs were shipped up from captured Southeast Asian territories to work on the link, their numbers later augmented by as many as 200,000 conscripted Asian labourers. Work began at both ends in June 1942. Three million cubic metres of rock were shifted and 14km of bridges built with little else but picks and shovels, dynamite and pulleys. By the time the line was completed, fifteen months later, it had more than earned its nickname, the **Death Railway**: an estimated 16,000 POWs and 100,000 Asian labourers died while working on it.

The appalling conditions and Japanese brutality were the consequences of the **samurai code**: Japanese soldiers abhorred the disgrace of imprisonment – to them, ritual suicide was the only honourable option open to a prisoner – and therefore considered that Allied POWs had forfeited any rights as human beings. Food rations were meagre for men forced into backbreaking eighteen-hour shifts, often followed by night-long marches to the next camp. Many suffered from beri-beri, many more died of dysentery-induced starvation, but the biggest killers were cholera and malaria, particularly during the monsoon. It is said that one man died for every sleeper laid on the track.

The two lines finally met at Konkuita, just south of present-day Sangkhlaburi. But as if to underscore its tragic futility, the Thailand–Burma link saw less than two years of active service: after the Japanese surrender on August 15, 1945, the railway came under the jurisdiction of the British who, thinking it would be used to supply Karen separatists in Burma, tore up 4km of track at Three Pagodas Pass, thereby cutting the Thailand to Burma link forever. When the Thais finally gained control of the rest of the railway, they destroyed the track all the way down to Nam Tok, apparently because it was uneconomic. Recently, however, an Australian-Thai group of volunteers and former POWs has salvaged sections of track near the fearsome stretch of line known as Hellfire Pass, clearing a memorial walk at the pass and founding an excellent museum at the site, described on p.256. There have been a number of books written about the Death Railway, including several by former POWs; the Thailand–Burma Railway Centre's bookshop stocks a selection, as do the town's bookshops, listed on p.249.

marking the northern limit, and the JEATH Museum towards the town's southern edge. If you have the time, it makes sense to start with the fairly central Death Railway Museum, across the road from the train station, which offers a good introduction to the World War II sights.

Death Railway Museum (Thailand–Burma Railway Centre)

The **Death Railway Museum** (formerly known as the Thailand–Burma Railway Centre; daily 9am–5pm; B60, kids B30; Ⓦwww.tbrconline.com) is the best place to start any tour of Kanchanaburi's World War II memorials. Located across the road from the train station, next to the Don Rak Kanchanaburi War Cemetery on Thanon Jaokannun, it was founded by the local supervisor of the Commonwealth War Graves Commission, Rod Beattie, specifically to provide an informed context for the thousands of people who visit the POW graves every week. He spent years exploring the entire route of the Thailand–Burma Railway and the result is a comprehensive and sophisticated history of the line itself, with plenty of original artefacts, illustrations and scale models, and particularly strong sections on the planning and construction of the railway, and on the subsequent operation, destruction and decommissioning of the line. There is more of a focus on the line itself here than at the more emotive Hellfire Pass Memorial Museum (see p.256), but the human stories are well documented too, notably via some extraordinary original photographs and video footage shot by Japanese engineers, as well as through unique interviews with surviving Asian labourers on the railway.

The shop inside the entrance stocks some interesting books on the railway and also sells products made by the Women for Weaving project in Sangkhlaburi (see p.260).

The Kanchanaburi War Cemetery (Don Rak)

Thirty-eight Allied POWs died for each kilometre of track laid on the Thailand–Burma Railway, and many of them are buried in Kanchanaburi's two war cemeteries. Of all the region's war sights, the cemeteries are the only places to have remained untouched by commercial enterprise. Opposite the train station on Thanon Saeng Chuto, the **Kanchanaburi War Cemetery** (**Don Rak**; daily 8am–4pm; free), is the bigger of the two (the other cemetery, Chungkai, is described on p.245), with 6982 POW graves laid out in straight lines amid immaculately kept lawns and flowering shrubs. It was established after the war, on a plot adjacent to the town's Chinese cemetery, as the final resting place for the remains that had been hurriedly interred at dozens of makeshift POW-camp gravesites all the way up the course of the railway line. Many of the identical stone memorial slabs in Don Rak state

△ Kanchanaburi War Cemetery

simply, "A man who died for his country"; others, inscribed with names, dates and regiments, indicate that the overwhelming majority of the dead were under 25 years old. A commemorative service is held here every year on April 25, Anzac Day.

The Bridge over the River Kwai

For most people, the plain steel arches of the **Bridge over the River Kwai** come as a disappointment: as a war memorial it lacks both the emotive punch of the museums and the perceptible drama of spots further up the line, and as a bridge it looks nothing out of the ordinary – certainly not as awesomely hard to construct as it appears in David Lean's famous 1957 film, *Bridge on the River Kwai* (which was in fact shot in Sri Lanka). But it is the link with the multi-Oscar-winning film, of course, that draws tour buses by the dozen, and makes the Bridge approach seethe with trinket-sellers and touts. For all the commercialization of the place, however, you can't really come to the Kwai and not see it. To get here, take any songthaew heading north up Thanon Saeng Chuto and then walk the 850m from the junction, hire a samlor, or cycle – it's 5km from the bus station. You can charter longtails from the pier beside the Bridge for trips to JEATH or out to sights along the Kwai Yai (B800 for an hour's outing).

The fording of the Kwai Yai at the point just north of Kanchanaburi known as Tha Makkham was one of the first major obstacles in the construction of the Thailand–Burma Railway. Sections of a steel bridge were brought up from Java and reassembled by POWs using only pulleys and derricks. A temporary **wooden bridge** was built alongside it, taking its first train in February 1943; three months later the steel bridge was finished. Both bridges were severely damaged by Allied bombers (rather than commando-saboteurs as in the film) in 1944 and 1945, but the steel bridge was repaired after the war and is still in use today. In fact the best way to see the Bridge is by taking the train over it: the Kanchanaburi–Nam Tok train crosses it three times a day in each direction, stopping briefly at the River Kwai Bridge station on the east bank of the river; or you can take the yellow **tourist tram** that shuttles the 1km back and forth across the Bridge (daily 8–10am & 12–2pm; 15min return; B20 return), departing from River Kwai Bridge station.

World War II Museum and Art Gallery

While at the Bridge, you can't fail to see the advertisements for the nearby **World War II Museum** (daily 8am–6pm; B30), 30m south along Thanon Maenam Kwai. Despite mendacious signs that call this the "World War II Museum and JEATH War Museum", it should not be confused with the real JEATH War Museum (see below), for this is an entirely different, privately owned collection that cynically uses the war to pull in the coach parties. The war section comprises an odd mixture of memorabilia (a rusted bombshell, the carpet used by the local Japanese commander) and reconstructed tableaux featuring emaciated POWs, while the top-floor gallery in the same building displays selected "Miss Thailand" portraits from 1934 onwards. Across the courtyard, a second building seeks to present an overview of Thailand's most venerated institutions with the help of specially commissioned wall-paintings: Buddhism on the ground floor, prime ministers and kings on the middle storeys, and family portraits of the museum's founders – the Chansiris – at the top.

The JEATH War Museum

Founded by the chief abbot of Wat Chaichumpon and housed within the temple grounds in a reconstructed Allied POW hut of thatched palm, the ramshackle and unashamedly low-tech **JEATH War Museum** (daily 8.30am–6pm; B30) was the town's first public repository for the photographs and memories of the POWs who worked on the Death Railway. The name JEATH is an acronym of six of the countries involved in the railway: Japan, England, Australia, America, Thailand and Holland. The museum has since been surpassed by the slicker and more informative exhibitions at the Death Railway Museum (see p.243) and the Hellfire Pass Memorial Museum (see p.256) and is now of most interest for its small collection of wartime photographs and for its archive of newspaper articles about and letters from former POWs who have revisited the River Kwai. The museum is located beside the Mae Khlong on Thanon Pak Praek, at the southern end of town. It's about 700m from the TAT office, or 5km from the Bridge. From the nearby pier, Tha Banphuphan, you can take a longtail boat ride up to the Bridge and out to sights along the Kwai Noi.

Across the river

Kanchanaburi's other war cemetery, at **Chungkai**, and a handful of moderately interesting temples – including cave temples at **Wat Tham Khao Poon** and **Wat Ban Tham**, the hilltop twins of **Wat Tham Sua** and **Wat Tham Khao Noi**, and a wat featuring a rather bizarre **floating nun** – provide the focus for pleasurable trips west of the town centre, to various locations along the Kwai Noi and the Mae Khlong. All these sights are accessible by bicycle from central Kanchanaburi, and can also be reached by longtail (hired through guest houses or at one of the east-bank piers), or even by kayak (see p.248).

Chungkai Cemetery, the Monkey School and Wat Tham Khao Poon

Scrupulously well-trimmed **Chungkai Cemetery** occupies a fairly tranquil roadside spot on the west bank of the Kwai Noi, at the site of a former POW camp. Some 1750 POWs are buried here; most of the gravestone inscriptions include a name and regimental insignia, but a number remain unnamed – at the upcountry camps, bodies were thrown onto mass funeral pyres, making identification impossible. The cemetery is a pleasant 2km cycle from Kanchanaburi's Rattanakarn Bridge, along Route 3228; much of the land in this area is sugar-cane country, for which Kanchanaburi has earned the title "sugar capital of Thailand".

One kilometre further west along Route 3228 from Chungkai Cemetery, a side track that runs alongside the railway line from Khao Pun train station (on the Kanchanaburi-Nam Tok line) takes you down to the river and the **Kanchanaburi Monkey School** (daily 9am–5pm; B150). Here some 17 stump-tailed, pig-tailed and crab-eating macaques (some of whom are said to have been rescued from abusive homes) have been trained in the varyingly useful arts of picking coconuts (still said to be the most efficient way of doing this job: a macaque can pluck 600 in a day, a human only 200), riding bicycles and performing memory tricks.

A further kilometre west along Route 3228 (4km from Rattanakarn Bridge), at the top of the road's only hill, sits the cave temple **Wat Tham Khao Poon** (daily 8am–6pm; B20). The attraction here is a nine-chambered cave connected by a labyrinth of dank stalactite-filled passages, where almost every ledge and knob of rock is filled with religious icons, the most important being the Reclining Buddha in the main chamber. Once out of the cave system, follow the track through the temple compound for 150m to reach a good vantage point over the Kwai Noi, just above the train tracks, presided over by an outsized, pot-bellied golden Buddha statue; arriving by boat, you enter the wat compound via the cliff-side steps here.

Wat Tham Mangkon Thong (Floating Nun Temple)

The impressive scenery across on the east of the River Kwai Noi makes for an equally worthwhile bike trip, but the cave temple on this side – **Wat Tham Mangkon Thong**, otherwise known as the **Floating Nun Temple** – is fairly tacky. The draw here is a Thai nun who, clad in white robes, will get into the temple pond and float there, meditating – if tourists give her enough money to make it worth her while. It's difficult not to be cynical about such a commercial stunt, though Taiwanese visitors are said to be particularly impressed. The floating takes place on a round pond at the foot of the enormous dragon staircase that leads up to the temple embedded in the hillside behind. The temple comprises an unexceptional network of low, bat-infested limestone caves, punctuated at intervals with Buddha statues.

There's no direct access from the west to the east bank of the Kwai Noi, so to get to Wat Tham Mangkon Thong from Chungkai and Wat Tham Khao Poon you have to return to town and start again. Travelling by bicycle or motorbike, take the ferry across the Mae Khlong River at Tha Chukkadon and then follow the road on the other side for about 4km. By car, turn west off Thanon Saeng Chuto (Highway 323) about 3km south of TAT onto Route 3429, which bridges the river and takes you north then west to the temple. Alternatively, take **bus** #8191 (every 30min; 20min) from Kanchanaburi bus station; the last return bus passes the temple at about 4.15pm.

Wat Ban Tham

Because of the limestone landscape, caves are all too common around Kanchanaburi and many of them have been sanctified as shrines. **Wat Ban Tham** is yet another example, but is intriguing enough to make the twelve-kilometre trip from the town centre worthwhile. Travelling south down the Mae Khlong to get to the temple is especially pleasant by longtail or kayak, but can also be done by road: cross the river at Thanon Mae Khlong, then turn left for the six-kilometre ride along a partially unmade road or, if combining with Wat Tham Mangkon, see directions above and then head south.

Wat Ban Tham was founded around 600 years ago but its fame rests on the seventeenth-century love story that was supposedly played out in a cave on this site. A young woman called Nang Bua Klee was forced to choose between duty to her criminal father and love for the local hero by whom she had fallen pregnant; her father eventually persuaded Bua Klee to poison her sweetheart's food, but the soldier learned of the plot and killed both his wife and their unborn son, whose souls are now said to be trapped in the cave at Wat Ban Tham. The cave is approached via an ostentatious Chinese-style dragon's mouth staircase, whose upper levels relate the legend in a gallery of brightly painted modern murals on the right-hand walls. Inside the cave, a woman-shaped stone has been painted in the image of the dead mother and is a popular object of worship for women trying to conceive: hopeful devotees bring pretty dresses and shoes for the image, which are hung in wardrobes to the side of the shrine when not in use, as well as toys for her son.

Wat Tham Sua and Wat Tham Khao Noi

If you're in the mood for more temples, continue south along the Mae Khlong from Wat Ban Tham for another 5km to reach the modern hilltop wats of Tham Sua and Tham Khao Noi, which both afford expansive views over the river valley and out to the mountains beyond. Coming by car, the quickest route is to head south out of town along Highway 323 and cross the river via the signed Mae Khlong Dam. Otherwise, take any local bus as far as Tha Muang, 12km south along Highway 323, then change to a motorbike taxi to the temples (about B40).

Designed by a Thai architect at the end of the twentieth century, **Wat Tham Sua** was conceived in typical grandiose style around a massive chedi covered with tiles similar to those used at Nakhon Pathom. Inside, a placid seated Buddha takes centre stage, his huge palms raised to show the Wheels of Law inscribed like stigmata across them; a conveyor belt transports devotees' offerings into the enormous alms bowl set into his lap. The neighbouring Chinese-designed **Wat Tham Khao Noi** was built at the same time and is a fabulously gaudy, seven-tiered Chinese pagoda within which a laughing Buddha competes for attention with a host of gesturing and grimacing statues and painted characters.

Eating and drinking

All of Kanchanaburi's guest houses and raft houses have **restaurants**, and there's a cluster of floating restaurants beside the Bridge, serving authentic if rather pricey seafood to accompany the river views. Except where stated, all listed restaurants open daily from breakfast until late. A cheaper place to enjoy genuine local food is at the ever-reliable **night market**, which sets up alongside Thanon Saeng Chuto on the edge of the bus station. There are also a few foodstalls at the thrice-weekly **night bazaar**, which operates in front of the train station every Monday, Thursday and Saturday evening from 6 to 10pm, but the focus here is mainly on cheap fashions, CDs and sarongs.

A recent influx of small, farang-managed **bars** has added a new dimension to a previously very low-key nightlife and there are now some 15 tiny one-room bars competing for attention on Thanon Maenam Kwai, between *Phon Phen Guest House* and *Apple's Guest House*. Most of the new places offer a similar diet of loud music and cheapish beer, usually with bar girls and/or sports TV as an added attraction – many will not make their first birthday, but those listed here have been around long enough to last.

Restaurants

Apple's Guest House 52 Soi Rongheabaow 3. Exceptionally delicious food, prepared to traditional Thai recipes by Kanchanaburi's most famous cooking school. The extensive menu includes coconut- and cashew-laced *matsaman* curries (B65) – both meat and vegetarian varieties – as well as outstanding yellow curries and multi-course set dinners. Because every dish is prepared to order, service can be slow.

Nita Raft House Thanon Pak Praek. Home-style cooking is the thing at the kitchen attached to this raft house (see p.241), especially the famous "no name" deep-fried vegetable and chicken fritters. Seating is home-style too, on floor cushions, and there are usually DVD screenings in the evenings.

Prasopsuk (C&B) Opposite the *River Kwai Hotel* at 277 Thanon Saeng Chuto. The streetside restaurant attached to the *Prasopsuk Hotel* is a good place for *som tam* and sticky rice (B40/set), but it also serves a full menu of stir-fries, curries, seafood, rice and noodle dishes.

Schluck Thanon Maenam Kwai. Cosy air-con restaurant that entices a regular crowd of expats with its menu of pizzas (from B130), salads and steaks (from B130), plus its decent selection of authentically spicy fish and *yam* dishes. Also has a few tables outside. Daily 4pm–2am.

Sri Rung Rueng Thanon Maenam Kwai. Popular, well-priced, bamboo-roofed restaurant with a huge menu of *tom kha, tom yam* and curries (yellow, red, green, Penang, and matsaman), all available in veg and non-veg versions (B60), plus steaks, seafood (B120) and cocktails (B100).

Srifa Bakery At the back of the bus station. The place to come for your Thai bakery items – including chicken doughnuts, tuna puffs and coconut buns (B10–20) – as well as lattes and cappuccinos.

Ya Jai 301/1 Thanon Maenam Kwai. Kanchanaburi's VIPs congregate here to clinch business deals and entertain clients so the atmosphere at this open-walled restaurant is more upmarket than at many others in town. The menu focuses on a short but authentic selection of soups, curries, seafood and spicy salads: B120–220. There's live music too.

Bars

Beer Barrel Thanon Maenam Kwai. Rustic-styled outdoor beer garden where the decking is made from Death Railway sleepers and you sit at rough-hewn wooden tables amid a jungle of low-lit trees

Day-trips, rafting and trekking

All the places listed below advertise **day- and overnight trips** around the Kanchanaburi and Sangkhlaburi areas. Few itineraries feature much trekking: most concentrate on waterfalls, elephant rides and river-rafting. Prices listed are per person in a group of four people minimum; smaller groups usually have to pay proportionally more. Rates fluctuate a little according to season, demand and competition. All the tour operators listed below also do tailor-made guided tours to the war sights (often by boat or raft) and to Damnoen Saduak floating markets, and most will also provide a cheap transport service – car plus driver but no guide – for the more accessible sights.

A.S. Mixed Travel 52 Soi Rongheabaow 3 ⓣ034 512017, ⓦwww.applenoi-kanchanaburi.com. Small and friendly operation that runs out of *Apple's Guest House*, is led by enthusiastic and well-informed guides, and gets lots of positive feedback. Their specialities include cycling expeditions, around Hellfire Pass, Tham Lawa and elsewhere (from B950), and overnight stays in the Thung Yai area near Sangkhlaburi and on the lake at Thong Pha Phum. They also run three- and four-day treks, plus standard one-day combinations of Erawan Falls, elephant-riding, rafting and the Death Railway (B400–950).

C&C Soi England, 265/2 Thanon Maenam Kwai ⓣ034 624547. The most popular of these trips run by *C&C Guest House* (and also sold direct from several Thanon Khao San travel agents in Bangkok), are those that feature canoeing, Erawan Falls, and a night at *C&C*'s waterside outpost, *Erawan Jungle Huts*, which is built near Tha Thung Na dam on the upper Kwai Yai about 20km south of Erawan (from B750).

Good Times Travel 63/1 Thanon Maenam Kwai ⓣ034 624441, ⓦwww.good-times-travel.com. Energetically run, competitively priced day- and half-day trips (B120–890) that generally get good reviews. Especially popular for its late-afternoon programme where tourists get to soap and shower elephants (and themselves) in the river and then have a barbecue dinner, they also offer infinite permutations of rafting, elephant-riding, Erawan Falls, Hellfire Pass and the Death Railway, plus a two-day trip to a Karen area near Hin Dat hot springs, which includes four hours' trekking each day (B2100).

River Kwai Canoe Next door but one to the Death Railway Museum on Thanon Jaokannun ⓣ087 001 9137. Kayaking specialist offering two and three-hour paddling trips (B300/350) down the main stretch of the river, beginning some way north of the *Felix* hotel.

Sunyarux Raft Thanon Song Kwai ⓣ081 856 5848, ⓔsunyaruxtravel@hotmail.com. Being tugged down the river on a floating raft "hotel" is the most popular activity for Thai holidaymakers in Kanchanaburi, but Sunyarux is one of the only outfits to offer it to English-speaking tourists. The two-storey raft hotel, with camp beds both on the roof and under cover, is pulled by a longtail down the Mae Khlong River to the Mae Khlong Dam, making stops at various temples and other sights en route, with plenty of chances to swim and go inner-tubing (B2000 per person including all meals, minimum 6 people; the trip lasts 24hr; book 24 hours ahead).

and vines. The star feature here is the ice-cold draught beer, but there's also a short menu of bar meals including *som tam, kai pat bai kaphrao* (chicken with basil) and *khao pat kung*. Nightly 4pm–1am.

No Name Bar Thanon Maenam Kwai. Popular farang-run travellers' hangout that invites punters to "get shit-faced on a shoestring". Key attractions are the satellite TV screenings of major sporting events, the pool table and the well-priced beer. Also serves British food, including roast beef and Yorkshire pudding. Open evenings till the early hours.

Snooker Bar Thanon Maenam Kwai. Standard travellers' fare plus back-to-back video shows nightly. Open daily until late.

Listings

Airline tickets Domestic and international tickets (issued in 24hr) from Good Times Travel, 63/1 Thanon Maenam Kwai ⓣ034 624441, ⓦwww.good-times-travel.com.

Books For the town's best selection of books about Thailand and English-language novels head for Tawan bookshop and stationery store at 275/1-2 Thanon Saeng Chuto. The shop at the Death Railway Museum on Thanon Jaokannun is the best outlet for books about the Death Railway. *Punnee Bar* on Thanon Ban Neua buys and sells second-hand titles as does *Jolly Frog* guest house on Thanon Maenam Kwai.

Cinema At the back of the bus station; see ⓦwww.movieseer.com for programmes.

Cookery classes Most famously at *Apple's Guest House*, 52 Soi Rongheabaow 3: shop at the morning market and learn how to cook the seven basic Thai dishes (minimum three participants; book the day before (10am–4pm; B950).

Emergencies For all emergencies, call the tourist police on the free, 24hr phone line ⓣ1155, or contact them at one of their booths in town (daily 9am–6pm): right beside the Bridge ⓣ034 512795; on Thanon Song Kwai; and on Thanon Saeng Chuto (ⓣ034 512668).

Exchange There are several banks with money-changing facilities and ATMs on the stretch of Thanon Saeng Chuto immediately to the north of the Thanon U Thong junction and around the bridge.

Hospitals The private Thanakan Hospital is at 20/20 Thanon Saeng Chuto, at the southern end of town, near the junction with Thanon Chukkadon ⓣ034 622366-75; the government-run Phahon Phonphayulasena Hospital is further south at 572/1 Thanon Saeng Chuto, near the junction with Thanon Mae Khlong ⓣ034 622999.

Immigration office At 100/22 Thanon Mae Khlong ⓣ034 564265.

Internet access Available at almost every guest house on Thanon Maenam Kwai, as well as at several dedicated Internet centres on Thanon Maenam Kwai.

Mail The GPO is 1km south of the TAT office on Thanon Saeng Chuto, but there's a more central postal agent just north of Sudjai Bridge on Thanon Maenam Kwai.

Pharmacies Several dispensaries in the fresh-market area south of Wat Thavorn and one near the Day and Night Plaza on Thanon Maenam Kwai.

Telephones The CAT international telephone office (daily 8.30am–8pm) is on a side road near the GPO, about 1.2km south of the TAT office, on Soi Praisanee/ Soi 38, off Thanon Saeng Chuto. There are several private telephone offices at guest houses and on Thanon Maenam Kwai.

Around Kanchanaburi

After the war sights and a ride on the Death Railway, the most popular attraction around Kanchanaburi is the seven-tiered **Erawan Falls**, sometimes combined with a trek to the caves of **Tham Than Lot National Park**.

Erawan and Srinakarind national parks

Chances are that when you see a poster of a waterfall in Thailand, you'll be looking at a picture of the falls in **Erawan National Park** (daily 8am–4pm; ⓣ034 574222; B200), 65km northwest of Kanchanaburi. The seven-tiered waterfall, topped by a triple cascade, is etched into the national imagination not just for its beauty, but also for its alleged resemblance to a three-headed elephant; this elephant (*erawan* in Thai) is the former national symbol and the usual mount of the Hindu god Indra.

Although the park covers an area of 550 square kilometres, the main **trail** follows the course of the rivulet, past all seven tiers. Each of these levels comprises a waterfall feeding a pool of invitingly clear water partly shaded by bamboos, rattans and lianas. It's a fairly easy climb up to the fifth stage, but the route onto the sixth and seventh levels is steep and slippery and features some dilapidated bridges and ladders: wear appropriate shoes, and avoid doing the last bit alone if you can. The best pools for swimming are level two (which gets the most crowded) and level seven (which is a hard slog but rarely busy, and also boasts stunning views over the jungle).

If you follow the main road along its westerly branch from Srinakarind market for another 10km you'll reach Wat Phrathat, from where it's a five-hundred-metre walk to **Tham Phrathat** (last entry at 3pm); a chartered songthaew from the market to the wat costs about B300: buses don't come this far. The stalactite cave has several large chambers, but is of interest to geologists for the fault lines that run under the Kwai Noi and are clearly visible in the disjointed strata.

A few kilometres north of the turn-off to Erawan, the landscape is dominated by the scenic **Srinakarind Reservoir**, which is fed by the dammed waters of the Mae Khlong and the Kha Khaeng and gives rise to the Kwai Yai. It's a popular recreation spot and site of several resorts, all of which lie within the **Srinakarind National Park** (also known as Khuean Srinagarindra National Park; ⓣ034 516667). From the dam you can hire boats (about B1500) to make the two-hour journey northwest across the reservoir to **Huay Khamin Falls**, which are said to be the most powerful in the district, and reputedly get the name "Turmeric Streak" from the ochre-coloured limestone rockface. However, it's quicker and less hassle to join one of the tours from Kanchanaburi.

Practicalities

Buses to Erawan (#8170; 2hr) leave Kanchanaburi every fifty minutes between 8am and 5.20pm and stop at **Srinakarind** market, from where it's a one-kilometre walk to the National Park headquarters and trailhead; if you miss the 4pm bus back, you'll probably be there for the night. Erawan features on many tours, and most Kanchanaburi guest houses will also arrange **songthaew** transport to and from the falls for about B100 per person, giving you around five hours in the park. If you have your own transport, simply follow signs from Kanchanaburi for Route 3199 and the falls.

It's possible to stay in the Erawan National Park **bungalows** (❺), though these are often full and should ideally be reserved ahead via the National Parks office in Bangkok (ⓣ02 562 0760, ⓦwww.dnp.go.th/National_park.asp; see Basics p.51 for details, or try the local office on ⓣ034 574222, ⓔerawan_np@yahoo.com); you can also pitch your own tent for a nominal fee. Several **foodstalls**, restaurants and shops near the trailhead open daily until about 8pm.

Tham Than Lot (Chaloem Rattanakosin) National Park

Ninety-seven kilometres north of Kanchanaburi, off Route 3086, tiny little **Tham Than Lot National Park** (also known as **Chaloem Rattanakosin National Park;** ⓣ034 519606, ⓦwww.dnp.go.th/National_park.asp) covers just 59 square kilometres but boasts two very nice caves, a decent waterfall and an enjoyable hiking trail that links them; wear comfortable shoes and bring a torch.

It's possible but time consuming to get to the park without your own transport and would be rather rushed as a day-trip. Take regular **bus** #325 from Kanchanaburi and get off at **BAN NONG PRU** (every 20min; 2–3hr), then change onto a motorbike taxi (B100) for the 22-kilometre ride to the park entrance and visitors' centre. There are a few **national park bungalows** (B700 for up to four people; ⓣ02 562 0760) near the visitor centre, which should be booked in advance for weekends. Alternatively, rent your own motorbike from Kanchanaburi, or take a tour (see p.248).

From the visitor centre, follow the signed trail for about ten minutes to reach the first cave, **Tham Than Lot Noi**, which is 400m deep and illuminated if there are enough people (for example at weekends). A very picturesque 2.5-kilometre, two-hour trail runs on from the other side of Tham Than Lot Noi, along a stream and through a ravine to the first of three **waterfalls**, about an hour and a half's easy walk away and passing towering dipterocarps, fine jungle views and plenty of butterflies en route. The path gets more difficult after the first waterfall, and dangerously slippery in the wet season, running via another couple of waterfalls before coming to the larger of the park's two caves, the impressively deep sink-hole **Tham Than Lot Yai**, site of a small Buddhist shrine. Another ten minutes along the trail brings you to a small forest temple, from where you'll need to retrace your steps to return to the visitor centre.

The Death Railway: to Nam Tok and Hellfire Pass

The two-hour journey along the notorious Thailand–Burma **Death Railway** from Kanchanaburi to **Nam Tok** is one of Thailand's most scenic, and most popular. Though the views are lovely, it's the history that makes the ride so special, so it's worth visiting the Death Railway Museum in town (see p.243) before making the trip, as this provides a context for the enormous loss of human life and the extraordinary feat of engineering behind the line's construction (see the box on p.242). Alternatively, take the bus straight up to the **Hellfire Pass Memorial Museum**, just north of the line's current Nam Tok terminus, which provides an equally illuminating introduction to the railway's history, then return to Kanchanaburi by train. The peaceful stretch of the River Kwai Noi between Nam Tok and Hellfire Pass is now the site of a few low-key riverside hotels, in particular around **Tham Lawa**.

The obvious way to travel through this area is by train, though the #8203 **bus** service from Kanchanaburi to Nam Tok (every 30min; 1hr 30min) and beyond is faster and more frequent. If you are planning to use the train as transport to sights, be aware that they often run very late. With your own transport, you have the chance to visit some of the less mainstream sights between Kanchanaburi and Nam Tok, notably the region's Stone Age artefacts at the **Ban Kao Museum**, and the nearby ruins of a twelfth-century Khmer temple sanctuary at **Muang Singh**.

Riding the Death Railway

Three **trains** run daily along the Death Railway in both directions, which means it's possible to make day-trips from Kanchanaburi to Muang Singh and Nam Tok if you get the timing right, though most tourists simply enjoy the ride as an attraction itself. At the time of writing, the train is scheduled to leave

Kanchanaburi at 6.07am, 10.30am and 4.30pm and to return from Nam Tok at 5.25am, 1pm and 3.15pm; Kanchanaburi TAT keeps up-to-date **timetables**. If you're up at the Bridge, you can join the train five minutes later. As it's such a popular trip, the State Railway adds a couple of **Special Cars** for tourists on the 10.30am Kanchanaburi–Nam Tok train, for which they charge B150 instead of the usual B17; the seats are exactly the same as those in the cheap carriages, but you get a reserved place and several soft drinks and snacks. Whatever ticket you opt for, sit on the left-hand side of the train for the best views, or the right-hand side for shade.

Leaving Kanchanaburi via the Bridge over the River Kwai, the train chugs through the Kwai Noi valley, stopping frequently at country stations decked with frangipani and jasmine. The first stop of note is Tha Kilen (1hr 15min), where you can alight for Prasat Muang Singh (see opposite), and about twenty minutes later the most hair-raising section of track begins. At **Wang Sing**, also known as Arrow Hill, the train squeezes through thirty-metre-deep solid rock cuttings, dug at the cost of numerous POW lives; 6km further, it slows to a crawl at the approach to the **Wang Po viaduct**, where a 300-metre-long trestle bridge clings to the cliff face as it curves with the Kwai Noi – almost every man who worked on this part of the railway died. The station at the northern end of the trestle bridge is called **Tham Krasae**, after the cave that's hollowed out of the rockface beside the bridge; you can see the cave's resident Buddha image from the train. A couple of raft-house operations have capitalized on the drama of the stretch of river alongside Wang Po. On the viaduct side, *River Kwai Cabin* (ⓣ081 944 0898, ⓦwww.suansaiyok.com; ❺–❻) offers fairly rustic bungalow accommodation; on the other bank, *River Kwai Jungle House* (ⓣ034 561052, ⓦwww.banrimkwae.com; ❼) has well-positioned raft houses. At both places meals are included in the nightly package rates quoted here and accommodation should be booked in advance. North of Tham Krasae, the train pulls in at **Wang Po Station** before continuing alongside a particularly lovely stretch of the Kwai Noi, its banks thick with jungle and not a raft house in sight, the whole vista framed by distant tree-clad peaks. Thirty minutes later, the train reaches Nam Tok, a small town that thrives chiefly on its position at the end of the line.

To Nam Tok by road

For most people, the main reason for heading out of Kanchanaburi towards Nam Tok is to take the train along the infamous Death Railway, but there are several sights along the way that can only be visited by road, either with your own transport or as part of a tour (perhaps combined with a one-way trip on the train). Chief among these are the prehistoric relics at **Ban Kao Museum** and the Khmer ruins of nearby **Prasat Muang Singh**.

Ban Kao Museum

The **Ban Kao Museum** (daily 8.30am–4.30pm; B30) is devoted to relics from an advanced prehistoric civilization (8000 to 1000 BC) that once settled on the banks of the Kwai Noi. Items on display include unique, curiously designed pots dated to around 1770 BC that were found buried at the head and feet of fifty skeletons; polished stone tools from around 8000 BC; and inscribed bronze pots and bangles transferred from a nearby bronze-culture site, which have been placed at around 1000 BC – somewhat later than the bronze artefacts from Ban Chiang in the northeast (see p.574). The hollowed-out tree trunks in front of the museum are also unusual: they may have been used as boats or as coffins – or possibly as a metaphorical combination of the two.

The museum is 35km west of Kanchanaburi and 8km from Prasat Muang Singh. Follow Highway 323 north out of Kanchanaburi until you get to the junction with minor road 3229, then follow this road southwest for about 16km before veering on to minor road 3445 for the last couple of kilometres. There's no public transport.

Prasat Muang Singh

Eight hundred years ago, the Khmer empire extended west as far as Muang Singh (City of Lions), an outpost strategically sited on the banks of the River

△ Avalokitesvara statue, Prasat Muang Singh

Kwai Noi, 43km west of present-day Kanchanaburi. Thought to have been built at the end of the twelfth century, the temple complex of **Prasat Muang Singh** (daily 9am–4.30pm; B40) follows Khmer religious and architectural precepts (see p.537), but its origins are obscure – the City of Lions gets no mention in any of the recognized chronicles until the nineteenth century.

Prasat Muang Singh covers one-third of a square kilometre, bordered by moats and ramparts that probably had cosmological as well as defensive significance, and with an enclosed **shrine complex** at its heart. Restorations now give an idea of the crude grandeur of the original structure, which was constructed entirely from blocks of rough russet laterite.

As with all Khmer prasats, the pivotal feature of Muang Singh is the main prang, as always surrounded by a series of walls and a covered gallery, with gateways marking the cardinal points. The prang faces east, towards Angkor, and is guarded by a fine sandstone statue of **Avalokitesvara**, one of the five great Bodhisattvas of Mahayana Buddhism, would-be Buddhas who have postponed their entrance into nirvana to help others attain enlightenment. He's depicted here in characteristic style, his eight arms and torso covered with tiny Buddha reliefs and his hair tied in a top knot. In Mahayanist mythology, Avalokitesvara represents mercy, while the other statue found in the prasat, the female figure of **Prajnaparamita**, symbolizes wisdom – when wisdom and mercy join forces, enlightenment ensues. Just visible on the inside of the north wall surrounding the prang is the only intact example of the stucco carving that once ornamented every facade. Other fragments and sculptures found at this and nearby sites are displayed beside the north gate; especially tantalizing is the single segment of what must have been a gigantic face hewn from several massive blocks of stone.

Muang Singh is 8km northwest of Ban Kao Museum, on minor road 3445. Easiest **access** from Kanchanaburi is by road: either follow directions as for Ban Kao Museum, above, or continue along Highway 323 as far as kilometre-stone 15 to take Route 3445 southwest to Muang Singh. You can also get to Muang Singh by taking the Death Railway train: get off at Tha Kilen (1hr 15min from Kanchanaburi), walk straight out of the station for 500m, turn right at the crossroads and continue for another 1km to reach the ruins.

Wat Pa Luang Ta Bua Yannasampanno: the Tiger Sanctuary Temple

Kanchanaburi's oddest and most controversial attraction is the chance to stroke a tiger at the so-called "Tiger Sanctuary Temple", **Wat Pa Luang Ta Bua Yannasampanno** (Ⓦwww.tigertemple.com; afternoons only; B300 donation; do not wear red clothes, which antagonize the tigers). Many tourists are seduced by the idea and join one of the numerous tours to the temple, but a lot of people return discouraged by the experience, not least because the animals are housed in small bare cages and only let out to be paraded in front of visitors in the afternoons.

Temples are traditionally regarded as sanctuaries for unwanted and illegally captured animals and Wat Pa Luang Ta Bua has been taking in tigers since 1999, when a distressed young tiger cub was brought to them, probably orphaned by poachers keen to tap into the lucrative trade in tiger body parts. The temple has attracted a lot of media interest and has been accused of exploiting the animals as a money-making tourist attraction; there was more negative publicity after one of the tigers mauled a Thai tourist. The abbot is now soliciting donations for the construction of an ambitious "Tigers' Island" reserve within the temple grounds. The temple is 37km from town and signed off Highway

323 at kilometre-stone 21, a few kilometres beyond the Route 3445 turn-off to Muang Singh.

Nam Tok and around

There's not much to **NAM TOK**, the terminus of the Death Railway line. The **train station** is at the top of the town, 900m north of Highway 323, and a further 2km from the Kwai Noi; buses usually stop near the T-junction of the highway and the station road.

On rainy-season weekends, Thais flock to Nam Tok's roadside **Sai Yok Noi Falls**, but if you're filling time between trains, you'd be better off stretching your legs on the short trek to the nearby Wang Badan cave or taking a boat trip from the town's Pak Saeng pier to Tham Lawa or Sai Yok Yai Falls (see p.257). Impressive stalactites, fathomless chambers and unnerving heat make **Tham Wang Badan** (daily 8.30am–4.30pm) one of the more interesting underground experiences in the region and it's easily reached by a trail that begins from Highway 323 about 1500m northwest of the train station. From the station, walk up the station approach road, cross the tracks, turn left at the roundabout, then first right through the small town, passing a water tower on your left; you'll reach the T-junction with Highway 323 after 900m. The **trail** to the cave is signposted 600m northwest (right) up Highway 323, from the right-hand (east) side of the road. About 1km into the trail, you arrive at the park warden's office where you can rent feeble torches; it's better to bring your own or to pay the warden at least B50 to accompany you and turn on the cave lights, which is well worth the money. From the office it's 2km of easy walking to the cave.

Longtail **boats** can be rented from the restaurant beside **Pak Saeng pier** for the forty-minute boat ride upstream to Tham Lawa and its nearby riverside accommodation, described below. To reach the pier from the Highway 323 T-junction, cross the road, turn left (southeast) towards Kanchanaburi, then take the first road on your right. The return journey to the cave takes roughly two hours, including half an hour there, and costs about B850 for the eight-seater boat. Add on at least four more hours and another B850 if you want to continue on to Sai Yok Yai Falls.

Few tourists stay in Nam Tok unless desperate so **accommodation** here is no great shakes and it's all quite a way from the train station. *Sai Yok Noi Bungalows* (ⓣ034 634397; ❶) has basic fan rooms; from the train station, turn northwest at the T-junction (towards Sangkhlaburi), walk about ten minutes and then turn right at the hotel sign by the fuel station. Or you can sleep in a floating room, comfortably kitted out with attached bathroom and veranda, beside Pak Saeng pier, at *Kitti Raft* (ⓣ034 634168; ❸–❹).

Tham Lawa and around

About 10km north of Nam Tok, a side road turns off Highway 323 at kilometre-stone 54 and runs down to the river, giving access to a beautiful stretch of the Kwai Noi, the *Resotel* pier, and several pleasant places to stay. Any Kanchanaburi-Thong Pha Phum bus will drop you at the turn-off, or join a cycling tour here from A.S. Mixed Travel in Kanchanaburi (see p.248). The most famous attraction around here is **Tham Lawa** (B200 entry), the largest stalactite cave in the area and home to three species of bat; it's a ten-minute longtail ride upriver from the pier. The river is about 50m wide at this point, embraced by sheer limestone cliffs that are artistically pitted, dramatically streaked in red and white, and grown thick with lianas and bamboos tumbling down to the water's edge – be careful when swimming as the current is very strong (hotels should have lifejackets available). There's no development along the banks apart from a few raft houses and shore-bound little hotels, and **boat** rental at the *Resotel* pier (for up to eight people, prices quoted are for return trips) to Tham Lawa cave (10min; B700), Hellfire Pass (B800 to the nearest pier, then a 4km walk), and Sai Yok Yai Falls (1hr 30min; B1400). You might also want to visit the **Mon Village** behind the *River Kwai Jungle Rafts* resort, where you're encouraged to browse the sarongs and other artefacts made and sold by the villagers, take an elephant-ride, and visit the school. The Mon villagers fled here from Burma in the late 1950s but have still not been granted Thai ID papers, which means the children can't study at Thai secondary schools and adults have difficulty finding work. This village has close links with *Jungle Rafts* and many of its residents work at the hotel. For more on the Mon people, see p.261.

Occupying a large swathe of steep and densely grown river bank about 1km off the highway at kilometre-stone 54, *Sam's Jungle Guest House* (Ⓣ081 948 3448; ❶–❹) offers a range of well-priced **accommodation** in a strange and rather unstylish assortment of buildings that nonetheless enjoy an exceptionally tranquil setting. The cheapest rooms share facilities, the better ones have bathrooms, balconies and air-con, and there's a swimming pool. The nearby *Resotel* pier is the departure point for the two other places to stay around here, both of them owned by the River Kwai Floatel company (Ⓣ02 642 6361, Ⓦwww.riverkwaifloatel.com). Located on the west bank of the river, a few metres downstream from Tham Lawa, *River Kwai Resotel* (❼) is the more upmarket of the two, comprising some charming thatched riverside huts and a swimming pool. A short distance upstream, the more rustic but very popular *River Kwai Jungle Rafts* (B1600 per person full board) offers simple but tasteful floating rooms, complete with hammocks, a swimming area, canoe rental and a bar. Rooms have no electricity so there are no fans or air-con and only oil-lamps at night.

Hellfire Pass

Although the rail line north of Nam Tok was ripped up soon after the end of World War II, it casts its dreadful shadow all the way up the Kwai Noi valley into Burma. The remnants of track are most visible at **Hellfire Pass**, and many of the villages in the area are former POW sites – locals frequently stumble across burial sites, now reclaimed by the encroaching jungle. To keep the Death Railway level through the uneven course of the Kwai valley, the POWs had to build a series of embankments and trestle bridges and, at dishearteningly frequent intervals, gouge deep cuttings through solid rock. The most concentrated digging was at **Konyu**, 18km beyond Nam Tok, where seven separate cuttings were made over a 3.5-kilometre stretch. The longest and most brutal of these was Hellfire Pass, which got its name from the hellish-looking lights and shadows of the fires the POWs used when working at night. The job took three months of round-the-clock labour with the most primitive tools.

Hellfire Pass has now been turned into a memorial walk in honour of the POWs who worked and died on it, and their story is documented at the beautifully designed **Hellfire Pass Memorial Museum** (daily 9am–4pm; donation) which stands at the trailhead. This is the best and most informative of all the World War II museums in the Kanchanaburi region, using war time relics, and POW memorabilia, photos and first-hand accounts to tell the sobering history of the construction of this stretch of the Thailand–Burma Railway. Founded by an Australian-Thai volunteer group, the museum now serves as a sort of pilgrimage site for the families and friends of Australian POWs.

The same Australian-Thai group has also cleared a four-kilometre, ninety-minute circular **memorial walk**, which begins at the museum and follows the old rail route through the eighteen-metre-deep cutting and on to Hin Tok creek along a course relaid with some of the original narrow-gauge track. The creek was originally forded by a trestle bridge so unstable that it was nicknamed the Pack of Cards Bridge, but this has long since crumbled away. The trail doubles back on itself, passing through bamboo forest and a viewpoint that gives some idea of the phenomenal depth of rock the POWs had to dig through.

Most Kanchanaburi tour operators (see p.248) offer **day-trips** featuring Hellfire Pass. It's also quite easy to get to Hellfire Pass on your own, and to combine it with your own trip on the Death Railway: from Kanchanaburi or Nam Tok, take any **bus** bound for Thong Pha Phum or Sangkhlaburi and ask to be dropped off at Hellfire Pass, which is signposted on the west side of Highway 323 just after kilometre-stone 64; it's about a 75-minute journey from Kanchanaburi or 20 minutes from Nam Tok. The last return bus to Kanchanaburi passes Hellfire Pass at about 4.45pm; if you're continuing to Sangkhlaburi, the last onward bus comes past at about 1.15pm.

North to Thong Pha Phum

Expanses of impenetrable mountain wilderness characterize the Kwai Noi valley to the north of Hellfire Pass, a landscape typified by the dense monsoon forests of **Sai Yok National Park**, which stretches all the way to the Burmese border. The first significant town beyond Sai Yok is **Thong Pha Phum** (147km from Kanchanaburi), which sits at the southern edge of the massive **Khao Laem Reservoir** and features some pleasant waterside accommodation.

Sai Yok National Park, Pha That Falls and Hin Dat hot springs

Signed off the highway between kilometre-stones 80 and 81, 104km north of Kanchanaburi, **Sai Yok National Park** (Ⓣ034 516163; B200 entry) is best known for its much-photographed though unexceptional **Sai Yok Yai Falls** and for the stalactite-filled Daowadung Caves. It's also home to the smallest-known mammal in the world, the elusive hog-nosed or bumblebee bat, which weighs just 1.75g and has a wingspan of 1.6cm. The park makes a refreshing enough stopover between Nam Tok and Sangkhlaburi, particularly if you have your own transport, and you can stay in the national park **bungalows** (Ⓦwww.dnp.go.th/National_park.asp; B800 for up to four people) or the more inviting *Sai Yok View Raft* (Ⓣ034 514194; ❸–❺), one of several raft houses near the waterfall; get there early to secure a room. The raft house serves food and there are plenty of hot-food stalls (daily 6am–8pm) near the visitor centre. Any of the Kanchanaburi–Thong Pha Phum **buses** will stop at the road entrance to Sai Yok, from where it's a three-kilometre walk to the **visitor centre**, trailheads and river. The last buses in both directions pass the park at about 4.30pm. Motorbike taxis sometimes hang around the road entrance, but a more scenic approach would be by longtail from Nam Tok (see p.255). All the trails start from near the visitor centre, and are clearly signposted from there as well as being marked on the map available from the centre.

North of Sai Yok National Park, signs off Highway 323 direct you to the two long, gently sloping cascades of **Pha That Falls** (12km east of the highway's kilometre-stone 103), accessible only with your own transport or on a tour; and to **Hin Dat** (Hindad) **hot springs** (1km east off the highway's kilometre-stone 105; B20 entry), where you can immerse yourself in a big pool of soothingly warm water, and make use of the nearby showers and foodstalls. Any Thong Pha Phum bus will drop you at the access track, and the restaurant near the springs has a couple of basic rooms for rent (B300), though there's not much to detain you here.

Thong Pha Phum and the lakeside hotels

From Sai Yok National Park, Highway 323 continues northwest, following the course of the Kwai Noi. Forty-seven kilometres on, the road skirts **THONG PHA PHUM**, a mid-sized market town with bus connections to Sangkhlaburi and Kanchanaburi and plenty of small food shops. If you need **accommodation**, the bungalow-hotel *Som Chainuk* (Ⓣ034 599067; ❶–❹) offers basic fan rooms and better air-con versions on the main street, within easy walking distance of the bus drop. Alternatively there's the similar *Boonyong Bungalow* hotel (Ⓣ034 599441; ❶–❹), further along the same street, across from the minivan bus station.

With your own transport, a much more scenic overnight option is to drive 12km west of Thong Pha Phum market to the southeastern fringes of nearby **Khao Laem Reservoir**. Also known as the Kreung Kra Wia Reservoir, this vast body of water stretches all the way to Sangkhlaburi 73km to the north and, when created in the early 1980s, flooded every village in the vicinity. The former villagers have been rehoused along the reservoir's banks, and hotels have sprung up here too, making the most of the refreshing, almost Scandinavian, landscape of forested hills and clear, still water that's perfect for swimming. Here you'll find a string of appealing **raft-house hotels** including *Phae VIP* (*Phae Wang Ing Pha*; Ⓣ034 599001), which has both simple, family-sized raft houses (B3000 for up to ten people) as well as more comfortable air-conditioned doubles (❹). Even if you've no intention of staying, *VIP*'s moderately priced lakeside restaurant makes a soothing place for an hour's break on the way to or from Sangkhlaburi. To get there, follow signs from Thong Pha Phum for the Khao Laem Dam, but instead of turning right for the dam continue along the left-hand branch of the road for another 7km.

Sangkhlaburi and Three Pagodas Pass

Beyond Thong Pha Phum the views get increasingly spectacular as Highway 323 climbs through the remaining swathes of montane rainforest, occasionally hugging Khao Laem's eastern shore, until 73km later it comes to an end at the small town of **Sangkhlaburi**, just across the lake from the Mon village of Ban Waeng Ka and a mere 18km short of the Burmese border at **Three Pagodas Pass**. Note that even if you have a visa you won't be allowed to travel any more than 1km into Burma at the pass.

Sangkhlaburi is easily reached by bus from Kanchanaburi, and runs transport to Three Pagodas Pass. Travelling to Sangkhlaburi under your own steam can be tiring as the **road** is full of twists after Thong Pha Phum; the last 25km are particularly nerve-wracking for bikers because of the gravel spots in the many bends. Nonetheless, the scenery is fabulous, particularly at the **viewpoint** just north of kilometre-stone 35 (about 40km south of Sangkhlaburi), where there's a lakeside lay-by that's just perfect for taking photos. You may also be tempted to stop at the roadside **Kraeng Kravia Falls**, 1km south of the viewpoint at kilometre-stone 34, beside the army checkpoint. Though not very high, the three-tiered cascade does get quite powerful during and just after the rainy season, and makes a pleasant spot for picnicking on barbecued chicken sold at the nearby stall.

Sangkhlaburi and around

In the early 1980s, the old town of **SANGKHLABURI** (often called Sangkhla for short) was lost under the rising waters of the newly created Khao Laem Reservoir. Its residents were relocated to the northeastern tip of the lake, beside the Songkalia River, where modern-day Sangkhla now enjoys an eerily beautiful view of semi-submerged trees and raft houses. It's a tiny town with no unmissable attractions, but the atmosphere is pleasantly low-key and the best of the tourist accommodation occupies scenic spots along the lake-shore. Cultural interest is to be found in the villages, markets and temples of the area's Mon, Karen and Thai population, and there's natural beauty in various waterfalls, whitewater rivers, and the remote Thung Yai Naresuan Wildlife Sanctuary. Though it sees relatively few farang tourists, Sangkhla is getting increasingly popular among weekending Thais, so come during the week for a bit of peace and better deals on accommodation.

The two guest houses in Sangkhlaburi both run **organized trips** in the area for their guests. As well as their accommodation and activities package described on p.260, *Burmese Inn* does one-day rafting excursions on the Songkalia River (B500); two- and three-day treks in the Thung Yai Naresuan Wildlife Sanctuary, around the Karen village of Ban Sane Pong (B1700–1850); and two-day cooking classes (B500). They also keep a book of useful information on motorbike routes in the area, including to Takianthong waterfall and Sawan Badan cave, both accessed via the road to Three Pagodas Pass.

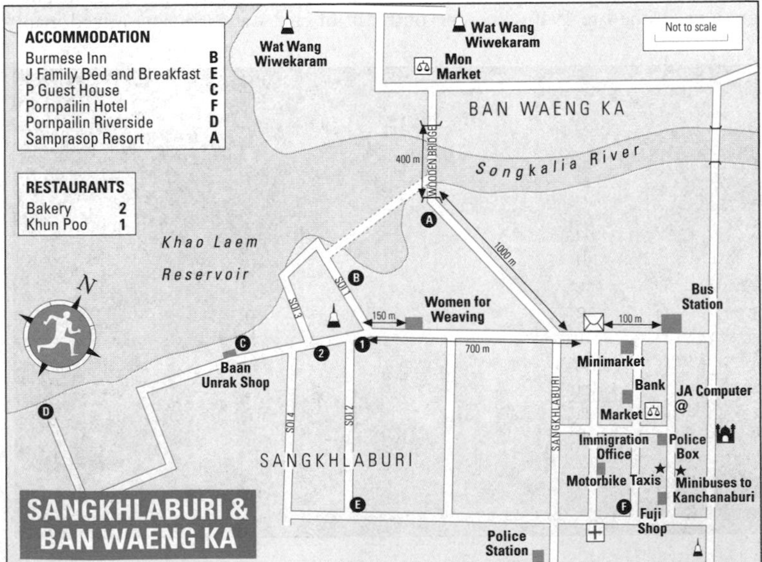

Sangkhlaburi town

Aside from crossing the famous wooden bridge over the lake to the Mon village of Ban Waeng Ka (see below), the other main pastime in Sangkhlaburi is **boating** across the reservoir in search of the **sunken temple** Wat Sam Phrasop, a former village temple that once stood on a hill but was almost completely submerged when the valley was flooded. When water levels are high you can only glimpse the top of its spire, but by the end of the dry season you get to see at least part of the temple's upper storey as well; it's close to the confluence of the three rivers that feed the reservoir. *P Guest House* rents out two-person **canoes** for independent exploring (B100/hour), or you can join a sunset longtail-boat trip from either *P Guest House* or *Burmese Inn* (B350–500/boat depending on number of passengers).

Sangkhla's location so close to the Burmese border, along with the upheavals caused by the creation of the Khao Laem Reservoir, mean that the town is full of displaced people, many of whom are in dire straits. Several organizations work with refugees in the area, including **Baan Unrak**, a farang-managed programme that has run an orphans' home here since 1991 and has also established a school and a weaving project. You can buy handicrafts at the Baan Unrak shop next to *P Guest House*, and find out more about the project, make donations and sample the food at their *Bakery* café (see p.264); for more information on Baan Unrak, see Basics p.77. Another community project that's worth supporting is **Women for Weaving**, set up by a group of Karen refugees in 1989. Their Hilltribe Handicrafts shop is located about 450m down the hill from the post office, or 150m up the hill from the turn-off to *Burmese Inn*, and carries a huge selection of hand-woven items, much of it in *mut mee* design and all of it made from good-quality Chiang Mai cotton, including tablecloths, sarongs, shirts and bags; for more on the Karen, see the box on p.312.

The wooden bridge, Ban Waeng Ka and Wat Wang Wiwekaram

The Mon village of **BAN WAENG KA**, across the reservoir from Sangkhlaburi, grew up in the late 1940s after the outbreak of civil war in Burma forced many

△ The sunken temple of Wat Sam Phrasop

to flee across the Thai border (see box below). The **Mon** people's homeland, Mon State, lies just west of the Tenasserim Mountains, so thousands of Mon ended up in Sangkhlaburi. Illegal immigrants in Thailand, their presence was permitted but not officially recognized, so that thirty years later, when the dam was constructed and

The Mon in Thailand

Dubbed by some "the Palestinians of Asia", the **Mon** people – numbering roughly one million in Burma and an estimated 50,000 in Thailand (chiefly in the western provinces of Kanchanaburi and Ratchaburi, and in Nonthaburi and Pathum Thani just north of Bangkok) – have endured centuries of persecution, displacement and forced assimilation.

Ethnologists speculate that the Mon originated either in India or Mongolia, travelling south to settle on the western banks of the Chao Phraya valley in the first century BC. Here they founded the **Dvaravati kingdom** (sixth to eleventh centuries AD), building centres at U Thong, Lopburi and Nakhon Pathom and later consolidating a northern kingdom in Haripunchai (modern-day Lamphun). They probably introduced Theravada Buddhism to the region, and produced some of the earliest Buddhist monuments, particularly Wheels of Law and Buddha footprints.

Over on the Burmese side of the border, the Mon kingdom had established itself around the southern city of Pegu well before **the Burmese** filtered into the area in the ninth century, but by the mid-eighteenth century they'd been stripped of their homeland and were once again relocating to Thailand. The Thais welcomed them as a useful source of labour, and in 1814 the future Rama IV arrived at the Kanchanaburi border with three royal warboats and a guard of honour to chaperone the exiles. Whole swathes of undeveloped jungle were given over to them, many of which are still Mon-dominated today.

The **persecution** of Burmese Mon continues to this day under Burma's repressive regime, the State Peace and Development Council (SPDC; see box on p.312), and the Mon continue to struggle for the right to administer their own independent Mon State in their historical homelands opposite Kanchanaburi province in lower Burma. Though the New Mon State Party entered into a ceasefire agreement with the Burmese junta in June 1995, international human rights organizations continue to report gross violations against civilian Mon living in Burma. Hundreds of thousands of Mon and Karen men, women and children have been press-ganged into unpaid labour; furthermore, deaths from malnutrition, malaria and cholera have been reported, as have beatings and gang rapes. Other captive workers are used as human land-mine detectors, and as porters to transport arms for the Burmese attacks on their own rebel army. The junta has also banned the teaching of Mon language and literature in schools, to which the Mon have responded by setting up their own literacy groups during school holidays.

Not surprisingly, Mon have been fleeing these atrocities in droves, the majority ending up in the Halockhani **refugee camp** right on the Thai-Burma border, near Sangkhlaburi but in a Mon-controlled area; the 5315 Mon living there as of June 2005 have no right of entry into Thailand. For more information, see the website of the Mon Human Rights Foundation of Monland (HURFOM; ⓦwww.rehmonnya.org).

Like Thais, the Mon are a predominantly Buddhist, rice-growing people, but they also have strong animist beliefs. All Mon families have totemic **house spirits**, such as the turtle, snake, chicken or pig, which carry certain taboos; if you're of the chicken-spirit family, for example, the lungs and head of every chicken that you cook have to be offered to the spirits, and although you're allowed to raise and kill chickens, you must never give one away. Guests belonging to a different spirit group from their host are not allowed to stay overnight. Mon **festivals** also differ slightly from Thai ones – at Songkhran (Thai New Year), the Mon spice up the usual water-throwing and parades with a special courtship ritual in which teams of men and women play each other at bowling, throwing flirtatious banter along with their wooden discs.

the valley villages flooded, the Mon refugees were entitled to neither compensation nor new agricultural land. Despite this, an influential local Mon abbot, Luang Pho Uttama, managed to secure the right to relocate five hundred submerged households to the northern shore of the reservoir, a settlement that has mushroomed into the one-thousand-household village of Ban Waeng Ka. Although most of the original Mon villagers now have official Sangkhlaburi residency, they still have limited rights and must apply for expensive seven-day permits if they wish to travel out of the district, a system that lends itself to corruption.

Getting to the village is simply a matter of crossing the narrow northern neck of the lake, near the influx of the Songkalia River. Pedestrians can use the spider's web of a **wooden bridge** that is Sangkhla's unofficial town symbol: at almost 400m it is said to be the longest hand-built wooden bridge in the world and can be reached either by following signs from near the post office to *Samprasop Resort*, which overlooks the structure, or by using the new connecting footbridge near the *Burmese Inn*. If you're on a motorbike or in a car, you'll have to use the concrete roadbridge several hundred metres further north. Once across the wooden bridge, turn left to get into the village – a sprawling collection of traditional wooden houses lining a network of steep tracks, with a small but lively dry-goods market at its heart.

About 2km west from the bridgehead – you might want to hail a B10 motorbike taxi to get here – **Wat Wang Wiwekaram** (or Wat Luang Pho Uttama) is Ban Waeng Ka's most dramatic sight, its massive, golden **chedi** clearly visible from Sangkhlaburi. Built in a fusion of Thai, Indian and Burmese styles, the imposing square-sided stupa is modelled on the centrepiece of India's Bodh Gaya, the sacred site of the Buddha's enlightenment, and contains a much-prized Buddha relic (said to be a piece of his skeleton) brought to Ban Waeng Ka from Sri Lanka. The wat is hugely popular with Buddhist pilgrims from all over Thailand, and is also a focal point for the Mon community on both sides of the Thai–Burma border; at Mon New Year in April, the wat is packed with Mon people paying their respects. Mon, Karen, Burmese and Thai devotees donate enormous sums of money to the temple coffers in honour of **Luang Pho Uttama**, the wat's abbot, who has been revered as a unifying force and champion of Mon culture ever since he crossed the border into Thailand in 1955. Now in his nineties and in poor health, Luang Pho Uttama is mostly confined to a Bangkok hospital, but his photograph is displayed in the temple compound, and the opulence of the wat buildings is testimony to his status. There's a good **tourist market** in the covered cloisters at the chedi compound, with plenty of reasonably priced Burmese woodcarvings, checked *longyis* and jewellery. The wat is spread over two compounds, with the gleaming new bot, **viharn** and monks' quarters about 1km away from the chedi, at the end of the right-hand fork in the road. The interior of the viharn is decorated with murals showing tableaux from the five hundred lives of the Buddha, designed to be viewed in anticlockwise order.

Practicalities

Sangkhlaburi is connected to Kanchanaburi by three different **bus services**. The fastest option is the air-conditioned **minibus** service (up to 10 daily; 3hr) which departs from the office in the far southeast corner of Kanchanaburi bus station and should be reserved at least a few hours in advance. The minibuses only pick up in Thong Pha Phum, and terminate on the northern edge of Sangkhla, departing from the same spot (up to 10 daily between 6.30am and 3.30pm; 3hr; reserve ahead): find the adjacent ticket office (unsigned in English) next to a small restaurant in a row of shops diagonally across from the Fuji shop and police box. If you have lots of luggage or can't face being cramped in a minivan,

air-con buses are a faster alternative (4 daily 7.30am–3pm; 4hr; last departure from Kanchanaburi at 3.30pm and from Sangkhla at 2.30pm) than the **non-air-con** buses (4 daily; 5–6hr; last departure from Kanchanaburi at midday and from Sangkhlaburi at 1.15pm); both these services terminate at the bus station on the western edge of Sangkhla.

Motorbike taxis usually charge B15 from the bus station to the guest houses and around B50 for a ride from the guest houses to Wat Wang Wiwekaram across the water. Sangkhlaburi itself is small enough to walk round in an hour; alternatively, *P Guest House* rents **motorbikes** (B200/day) and *Khun Poo* restaurant has **mountain bikes** (B30/day), while *Burmese Inn* should be able to arrange a pick-up **truck** and driver.

The reservoir marks the western limit of Sangkhla. The town's westernmost (signless) road is the most useful thoroughfare, with the bus station at its northern end, *P Guest House* 1.3km down the hill towards the southern end, and the post office, *Burmese Inn* and *Bakery* in between. The **market** is the focus of the tiny grid of streets that runs east of the bus station and post office. JA Computer and Internet, about 50m east of the bus station, has several **Internet** terminals and there's also Internet access at Baan Unrak's *Bakery* café. Traveller's cheques and dollars can be changed at the **bank**, on the edge of the market in the town centre, which also has an ATM. Sangkhla's **immigration** office (daily 6am–6pm) is 150m east of the post office, though if you're simply visiting the market on the Burmese side of the border at Three Pagodas Pass, you can get all the necessary documentation, photos and currency exchange done at the border itself. Should you want to get a couple of passport photos in advance, however, the Fuji shop two blocks north of the immigration office can do this; its **photographic services** also include downloading digital photos on to CDs.

Accommodation

Not many independent foreign travellers make it to Sangkhlaburi, but there are some attractive accommodation options on offer for those who do. The two guest houses are used by backpacking tour groups, so it's often worth reserving ahead, and this is essential at all accommodation for weekends and national holidays.

Burmese Inn 700m down the hill from the bus station, then right down Soi 1 ⓣ086 168 1801, ⓦwww.sangkhlaburi.com. This traveller-oriented guest house overlooks the northeastern spur of the lake just behind the new bridge, offering easy access to the Mon village, but slightly truncated lake views. Most of the rooms and bungalows look right over the water and nearly all are en suite; the more expensive are attractively furnished and some have air-con and TV. Shared bathroom ❶, fan and bathroom ❶–❸, air-con ❺

J Family Bed and Breakfast (Kumsai Soonpoy) 17/1 Soi 2 ⓣ034 595511. A genuine home-stay offering four big rooms with fan and shared bathroom in the large family home of the Mon woman, Kumsai Soonpoy, who runs the Baan Unrak shop. ❷

P Guest House About 1.3km down the hill from the bus station, ⓣ034 595061, ⓦwww.pguesthouse.com. Efficiently run, Mon-owned place that sits prettily on the banks of the reservoir and offers comfortable travellers' accommodation in stone huts with shared bathrooms, and en-suite rooms with air-con. However, as priority is given to guests booking *P*'s special packages, which include one night's accommodation plus a day of rafting, elephant-riding and a trip on the lake, you may find it hard to stay here on a room-only basis. Fan and shared bathroom ❷, air-con ❺

Pornpailin Hotel ⓣ034 595039, ⓦwww.ppailin.com. Standard, fairly cheap and not at all scenic hotel that's on the edge of the market and nowhere near the lake but offers large en-suite rooms with fan or air-con. Fan ❷, air-con ❸–❺

Pornpailin Riverside About 2km down the hill from the bus station ⓣ034 595355, ⓦwww.ppailin.com. Very attractive sister outfit to the *Pornpailin Hotel* (ask there for transport) whose wooden fan and air-con bungalows are gorgeously located right on the lake; all have enormous lake-view windows and some even have steps dropping right into the water. Rates rise by 20 percent on Fri & Sat. ❺–❻

Eating

Day and night, the cheapest places to **eat** are at and around the market in the town centre. *P's* large but cosy restaurant offers fine lake views and serves good Thai, Burmese and European food. The welcoming *Bakery* (8am–8pm), midway between the turn-offs for *Burmese Inn* and *P Guest House*, makes a nice chilled-out spot to sample brown-bread sandwiches, veggie pizzas and banana cake and is staffed by volunteers from the nearby Baan Unrak orphans' home; it has Internet access too. At night, travellers tend to congregate at nearby *Khun Poo* (no English sign but you can't miss the big crab sign; 8am–10pm), where members of the gregarious owner's family perform live music (Fri & Sat from 8.30pm), and there are frequent video screenings of *Bridge Over the River Kwai* and *Return to the River Kwai*. The wide-ranging menu (averaging B70 a dish) includes beef steak in white wine sauce, chicken in Vietnamese-style tomato sauce, and plenty of veggie dishes.

Three Pagodas Pass (Ban Chedi Sam Ong) and the Burmese border

Four kilometres before Sangkhlaburi, a road branches off Highway 323 to **Three Pagodas Pass** (signed as **Jadee Sam Ong**), winding its way through cloud-capped, forested hills and passing a few Karen and Mon settlements before reaching the border terminus 18km further on. Songthaews for the pass leave Sangkhlaburi bus station every forty minutes from 6am until about 5pm and take forty minutes; the last songthaew back to Sangkhla leaves at 6pm.

All **border trade** for hundreds of kilometres north and south has to come through Three Pagodas Pass: textiles, sandals, bicycles and medical supplies go to Burma, in return for cattle and highly profitable teak logs – the felling of which has been illegal in Thailand since 1989. Over the last fifty years, the Mon, the Karen and the Burmese government have vied with each other constantly for supremacy at the pass, the rebels relying on the tax on smuggled goods to finance their insurgency campaigns, the government desperate to regain its foothold in rebel territory. However, since 1990, the pass has remained under the control of the Burmese government.

It must be the romantic image of a hilltop smuggling station that attracts the few foreign tourists to the 1400-metre-high pass, because there's nothing substantial to see here. The **pagodas** themselves are diminutive whitewashed structures, said to have been erected in the eighteenth century by the kings of Burma and Thailand as a symbolic peace gesture (during the Ayutthayan period, Burmese troops would regularly thunder through here on elephant-back on their way to attack the capital). Each king supposedly built a chedi on his own side of the border and, at the foot of the central, borderline pagoda, the two kings signed an agreement never to war with each other again. Another interpretation holds that the pagodas represent the three strands of Buddhism – the Buddha, the Dharma (teaching) and the Sangha (monkhood) – and were erected here to boost the morale of Thai soldiers going to and from battle in Burma.

All three pagodas are now on Thai soil, at the edge of **BAN CHEDI SAM ONG**, a tiny village comprising not much more than a few foodstalls, a wat, and a small market selling brightly coloured Karen trousers and jackets, sarongs made of Burmese batik, Burmese face powder – applied as protection against the elements – cheroots, orchids, and teak artefacts and furniture. Though there's not much else to do, you can **stay** here at *Three Pagodas Resort* (Ⓣ081 922 6231, Ⓕ02 412 6578; fan ❷, air-con ❹), whose polished teakwood fan and air-con

Loy Krathong: the Festival of Light

Every year on the evening of the full moon of the twelfth lunar month (usually in November), Thais all over the country celebrate the end of the rainy season with the festival of Loy Krathong. One of Thailand's most beautiful festivals, it's held to honour the spirits of the water at a time when all the fields are flooded and the canals and rivers are overflowing their banks.

▲ *Krathong* on sale

Honouring the water goddess

To thank and appease Phra Mae Khong Kha, the goddess of water, to ask forgiveness for polluting her waters, and to cast adrift any bad luck that may have accrued over the past year, nearly everyone makes or buys a **krathong** and sets it afloat (*loy*) on the nearest body of water. These miniature basket-boats are fashioned from banana leaves and filled with flowers and lighted candles; usually people release them at around the same time and the bobbing lights of thousands of them floating on neighbourhood rivers, beachfronts, ponds, canals and even swimming pools make a fantastic spectacle. It's traditional to make a wish or a prayer as you launch your *krathong* and to watch until it disappears from view: if your candle burns strong, your wishes will be granted and you will live long. And if you launch a *krathong* with your beloved, your union will be blessed.

The krathong

Though it's increasingly popular to take the easy option and buy your **krathong** ready-made from the market, often with an eco-unfriendly polystyrene base, some people still create their own in the traditional manner. Around a base made from a ten-centimetre slice of banana tree trunk, a crown of sepals is fashioned from rectangles of banana leaf that are folded and pinned with slivers of wood into elegant origami-style shapes. The lotus-like crown is filled with flowers – often orange marigolds or purple orchids – and then spiked with three sticks of incense and some candles. Some people slip tiny objects between the flowers, such as hair and fingernail clippings to represent sinful deeds that will then be symbolically released along with the *krathong*, or a coin or two to persuade the spirits to take away any bad luck that has been dogging them (opportunist young boys often take on this role, raiding the floating *krathong* for small change). Large organizations usually commission their own outsized krathong and these sometimes compete for a best-in-show award, judged by local bigwigs.

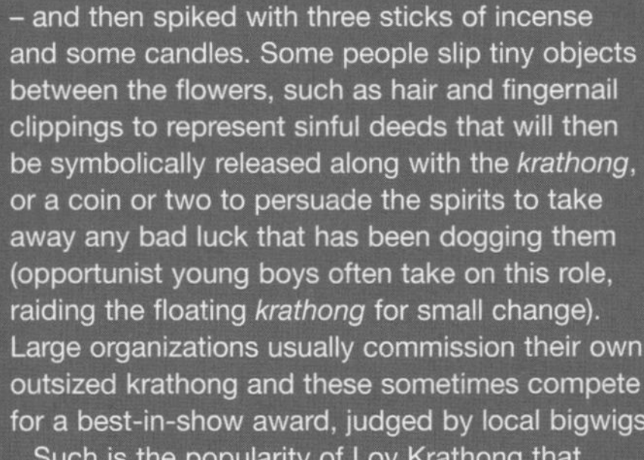

Such is the popularity of Loy Krathong that the morning-after debris on waterways leaves a significant **environmental hazard** quite at odds with the original aims of the thanksgiving festival. Some *krathong*-makers have tried to address this by inventing fish-friendly krathong, using bread for leaves and replacing flowers with sugar confections, but the traditional banana-leaf offering is such an icon that variations seem unlikely to catch on.

▼ Making *krathong*, Warorot market, Chiang Mai

Nationwide celebrations

▲ A Miss Loy Krathong contestant awaits the verdict

The festival is said to have originated seven hundred years ago, when the consort of a Sukhothai king, Nang Noppamas, adapted the ancient Brahmin custom of paying homage to the water goddess and began the tradition of placing *krathong* on the lotus ponds. The thirteenth-century temple ruins of **Sukhothai Historical Park** are now one of the most popular places to watch the Loy Krathong festivities: not only do its ponds shimmer beneath thousands of floating candles, but for the nine nights around the full moon the ruins are wreathed in lights and illuminated during a nightly *son-et-lumière* performance, and there are firework displays, concerts and street-theatre shows, not to mention a parade of graceful Nang Noppamas (Miss Loy Krathong) lookalikes.

Every community designs its own celebration and the Loy Krathong festivities in **Chiang Mai** – where the festival is also known as Yipeng – are famous nationwide. Here, not only does the Ping River shine with thousands of *krathong*, but the skies are also alight, speckled with hundreds of glowing giant paper lanterns, or **khom loy**, drifting in the breeze. In **Tak**, not far from Sukhothai, townspeople and villagers make their krathong from burning coconut husks rather than banana leaves and thread them together in chains (hence the local name for the festival, Loy Krathong Sai, or Loy Krathong "Line") so that as they glide along the many meanders of the town's zigzagging river they make an especially graceful sight.

Outside urban centres there's often a more earthy, irreverent flavour to the celebrations, with the entire community turning up to drink a great deal of Chang beer and local firewater and to heckle at the inevitable Miss Loy Krathong contest. Entrants might be under five, over eighty, male, female or transsexual, but they'll all be dancing to the famous **Loy Krathong song**, which fills the airwaves across the nation.

Lanterns in the sky

As with the *krathong*, a **khom loy** will also carry vices and misfortunes away when it's released in the breeze. Part lantern, part hot air-balloon, *khom loy* are usually made from local mulberry paper, to various shapes and designs, but most often with the dimensions of a large sack, up to two metres high. The power to keep it aloft comes from candles or a small bowl of flaming oil hung at the base of the lantern. Some people tuck coins inside the lantern, or paste their address inside so that the finder can claim a small reward. *Khom loy* are also said to represent the Buddha's topknot, which he cut off when he renounced the life of a prince. In the past they were used as distinctly un-Buddhist weapons, designed to explode when they touched down in enemy territory.

▼ Releasing a *khom loy*

The Loy Krathong song

Wan pen duan sip sawng	The full moon of the twelfth month
Nam koh nawng taem taling	As water fills the banks
Rao tanglai chai ying	We all, men and women
Sanuk ganjing wan Loy Krathong	Have really good fun on Loy Krathong day
Loy loy krathong	Float, float the krathong
Loy loy krathong	Float, float the krathong
Loy krathong gan laew	And after we have floated our krathong
Kaw choen nawng kaew	I invite you my dear
Awk maa ramwong	To come out and dance ramwong
Ramwong wan Loy Krathong	Ramwong on Loy Krathong day
Ramwong wan Loy Krathong	Ramwong on Loy Krathong day
Bun ja song hai rao suk jai	Making merit will bring us happiness
Bun ja song hai rao suk jai	Making merit will bring us happiness

bungalows are set round a pretty garden, under the lip of a limestone cliff on the edge of Ban Sam Phra Chedi Ong; they're just across the fence from Burma (but don't try to cross here) and within 150 metres of its hilltop pagoda.

The Burmese side of the border is occupied by the village of **Payathonzu**. At the time of writing, foreign nationals are allowed to **cross the border** (daily 6am–6pm; border passes cost B500 or $10, you must surrender your passport, and you also need 2 passport photos, available at the adjacent shop), but access is restricted to about 1.5km, with the main attraction being the Mon temple **Wat Sao Roi Ton**, known in Burmese as **Tai Ta Ya temple**, or the Temple of One Hundred Teakwood Posts. Commissioned by Ban Waeng Ka's revered Mon abbot Luang Pho Uttama, this stately two-storey structure was built in Burmese style and designed around the eponymous one hundred polished-wood pillars. From the temple grounds, a long, evocative line of life-sized concrete statues depicting monks on their alms round runs back towards the limestone crags behind; it's a work in progress, with currently some 150 of the total 500 completed. About 750m behind the temple, a golden, Burmese-style hilltop pagoda offers breathtaking views over the hills of Burma and Thailand. Payathonzu **market** is about 1km away, or 1.5km direct from the border checkpoint, and is the place to buy jade jewellery and sample Burmese curries. Wat Sao Roi Ton is about fifteen minutes' walk from the border, or a short **motorbike-taxi** ride. For B150, motorcycle taxi drivers will give you the full one- to two-hour tour of the temple, hilltop pagoda and market.

Ayutthaya and the Chao Phraya basin

Bisected by the country's main artery, the **Chao Phraya River**, and threaded by a network of tributaries and canals, the fertile plain to the north of the capital retains a spectrum of attractions from just about every period of the country's history. The monumental kitsch of the nineteenth-century palace at **Bang Pa-In** provides a sharp contrast with the atmospheric ruins at the former capital of **Ayutthaya**, where ancient temples, some crumbling and overgrown, others alive and kicking, are arrayed in a leafy, riverine setting. **Lopburi**'s disparate remains, testimony to more than a millennium of continuous settlement, are less compelling, but you'll get a frenetic, noisy insight into Thai religion if you visit the nearby **Wat Phra Phutthabat** (Temple of the Buddha's Footprint), still one of Thailand's most popular pilgrimage sites after three and a half centuries.

Each of the attractions of this region can be visited on a day-trip from the capital – or, if you have more time to spare, you can slowly work your way through them before heading north or northeast. **Trains** are the most useful means of getting around, as plenty of local services run to and from Bangkok (note that the State Railway's standard English-language timetables do not list all the local services – phone the railway's hotline on ⓣ1690 for more comprehensive information).

The line from the capital takes in Bang Pa-In and Ayutthaya before forking at Ban Phachi: the northern branch heads for Lopburi and goes on to Phitsanulok and Chiang Mai; the northeastern branch serves Isaan. **Buses** between towns are regular but slow, while Bang Pa-In and Ayutthaya can also be reached on scenic **boat** trips up the Chao Phraya.

Bang Pa-In

Little more than a roadside market, the village of **BANG PA-IN**, 60km north of Bangkok, has been put on the tourist map by its extravagant and rather surreal **Royal Palace** (daily 8.30am–4.30pm, ticket office closes 3.30pm; visitors are asked to dress respectfully, so no vests, shorts or sandals; B100; Ⓦ www.palaces.thai.net), even though most of the buildings can be seen only from the outside. King Prasat Thong of Ayutthaya first built a palace on this site, 20km downstream from his capital, in the middle of the seventeenth century, and it remained a popular country residence for the kings of Ayutthaya. The palace was abandoned a century later when the capital was moved to Bangkok, only to be revived in the middle of the nineteenth century when the advent of steamboats shortened the journey time upriver. Rama IV (1851–68) built a modest residence here, which his son Chulalongkorn (Rama V), in his passion for westernization, knocked down to make room for the eccentric melange of European, Thai and Chinese architectural styles visible today.

The palace

Set in manicured grounds on an island in the Chao Phraya River, and based around an ornamental lake, the palace complex is flat and compact – a free brochure from the ticket office gives a diagram of the layout. On the north side of the lake stand a two-storey, colonial-style residence for the royal relatives and the Italianate **Warophat Phiman** (Excellent and Shining Heavenly Abode), which housed Chulalongkorn's throne hall and still contains private apartments where the present royal family sometimes stays. A covered bridge links this outer part of the palace to the **Pratu Thewarat Khanlai** (The King of the Gods Goes Forth Gate), the main entrance to the inner palace, which was reserved for the king and his immediate family. The high fence that encloses half of the bridge allowed the women of the harem to cross without being seen by male courtiers. You can't miss the photogenic **Aisawan Thiphya-art** (Divine Seat of Personal Freedom) in the middle of the lake: named after King Prasat Thong's original palace, it's the only example of pure Thai architecture at Bang Pa-In. The elegant tiers of the pavilion's roof shelter a bronze statue of Chulalongkorn.

In the inner palace, the **Uthayan Phumisathian** (Garden of the Secured Land), recently rebuilt by Queen Sirikit in grand, neo-colonial style, was Chulalongkorn's favourite house. After passing the **Ho Withun Thasana** (Sage's Lookout Tower), built so that the king could survey the surrounding countryside, you'll come to the main attraction of Bang Pa-In, the **Phra Thinang Wehart Chamrun** (Palace of Heavenly Light). A masterpiece of Chinese design, the mansion and its contents were shipped from China and presented as a gift to Chulalongkorn in 1889 by the Chinese Chamber of Commerce in Bangkok. You're allowed to take off your shoes and feast your eyes on the interior, which drips with fine porcelain and embroidery, ebony furniture inlaid with mother-of-pearl and fantastically intricate woodcarving. This residence was the favourite of Rama VI, whose carved and lacquered writing table can be seen on the ground floor.

The simple marble **obelisk** behind the Uthayan Phumisathian was erected by Chulalongkorn to hold the ashes of Queen Sunandakumariratana, his favourite wife. In 1881, Sunanda, who was then 21 and expecting a child, was taking a trip on the river here when her boat capsized. She could have been rescued quite easily, but the laws concerning the sanctity of the royal family left those around her no option: "If a boat founders, the boatmen must swim away; if they remain near the boat [or] if they lay hold of him [the royal person] to rescue him, they are to be executed." Following the tragedy, King Chulalongkorn became a zealous reformer of Thai customs and strove to make the monarchy more accessible.

Turn right out of the main entrance to the palace grounds and cross the river on the small cable car, and you'll come to the greatest oddity of all: **Wat Nivet Dhamapravat**. A grey Buddhist viharn in the style of a Gothic church, it was built by Chulalongkorn in 1878, complete with wooden pews and stained-glass windows.

Practicalities

Bang Pa-In can easily be visited on a day-trip from Bangkok or Ayutthaya. The best way of getting here **from Bangkok** is by **train** from Hualamphong station; the journey takes just over an hour. All trains continue to Ayutthaya, with half going on to Lopburi. From Bang Pa-In station (note the separate station hall built by Chulalongkorn for the royal family) it's a two-kilometre hike to the palace, or you can take a motorbike taxi for about B30. Slow **buses** leave Bangkok's Northern Terminal roughly every half-hour and stop at Bang Pa-In market, a motorbike-taxi ride from the palace.

Every Sunday, the Chao Phraya Express Boat company (Ⓣ02 623 6001–3, Ⓦwww.chaophrayaboat.co.th) runs **river tours** to Bang Pa-In, taking in Wat Phailom, a breeding ground for open-billed storks escaping the cold in Siberia, from November to June (during the rest of the year they visit Wat Chalerm Phra Kiat in Nonthaburi instead, see p.182), plus a shopping stop at Bang Sai folk arts and handicrafts centre. The boats leave Tha Sathorn at 7.30am, calling at Tha Maharat at 8am, and return to Maharat at 6pm, Sathorn at 6.30pm; tickets, available from the piers, are B430 (B350 one-way), not including lunch and admission to the palace and the handicrafts centre (B200). The Mitchaopaya company, based at Tha Chang (Ⓣ02 623 6169), also runs similar cruises on certain Sundays, and luxury cruises to Ayutthaya (see p.269) also stop at Bang Pa-In.

From Ayutthaya, large songthaews leave Thanon Naresuan roughly every half-hour for the thirty-minute-plus journey to Bang Pa-In market; irregular trains from Ayutthaya's inconveniently located station are quicker (15min) but probably less useful for this short hop; or if you're feeling flush, you could ask about chartering a boat to the palace, through, for example, *Ayutthaya Guest House* (see p.270).

Ayutthaya

In its heyday as the booming capital of the Thai kingdom, **AYUTTHAYA**, 80km north of Bangkok, was so well endowed with temples that sunlight

reflecting off their gilt decoration was said to dazzle from three miles away. Wide, grassy spaces today occupy much of the atmospheric site, which now resembles a graveyard for temples: grand, brooding red-brick ruins rise out of the fields, satisfyingly evoking the city's bygone grandeur while providing a soothing contrast to the brashness of modern temple architecture. A few intact buildings help form an image of what the capital must have looked like, while three fine museums flesh out the picture.

The core of the ancient capital was a four-kilometre-wide **island** at the confluence of the Lopburi, Pasak and Chao Phraya rivers, which was once encircled by a twelve-kilometre wall, crumbling parts of which can be seen at the Phom Phet fortress in the southeast corner. A grid of broad roads now crosses the island, known as Ko Muang, with recent buildings jostling uneasily with the ancient remains; the hub of the small, grim and lifeless modern town rests on the northeast bank of the island around the corner of Thanon U Thong and Thanon Naresuan although the newest development is off the island to the east.

Ayutthaya comes alive each year for a week in mid-December, when a **festival** is organized to commemorate the town's listing as a **World Heritage Site** by UNESCO on December 13, 1991. The highlight of the celebrations is the nightly *son et lumière* show, a grand historical romp featuring fireworks and elephant-back fights and the like, staged at Wat Phra Si Sanphet, Wat Phra Ram or one of the other ancient sites.

Some history

Ayutthaya takes its name from the Indian city of Ayodhya (Sanskrit for "invincible"), the legendary birthplace of Rama, hero of the *Ramayana* epic (see p.137). It was founded in 1351 by U Thong – later **Ramathibodi I** – after Lopburi was ravaged by smallpox, and it rose rapidly through exploiting the expanding trade routes between India and China. Stepping into the political vacuum left by the decline of the Khmer empire at Angkor and the first Thai kingdom at Sukhothai, by the mid-fifteenth century Ayutthaya controlled an empire covering most of the area of modern-day Thailand. Built entirely on canals, few of which survive today, Ayutthaya grew into an enormous amphibious city, which by 1685 had one million people – roughly double the population of London at the same time – living largely on houseboats in a 140-kilometre network of waterways.

Ayutthaya's great wealth attracted a swarm of **foreign traders**, especially in the seventeenth century. At one stage around forty different nationalities, including Chinese, Portuguese, Dutch, English and French, were settled here, many of whom lived in their own ghettos and had their own docks for the export of rice, spices, timber and hides. With deft political skill, the kings of Ayutthaya maintained their independence from outside powers, while embracing the benefits of their cosmopolitan influence: they employed foreign architects and navigators, used Japanese samurai as royal bodyguards, and even took on outsiders as their prime ministers, who could look after their foreign trade without getting embroiled in the usual court intrigues.

In 1767, this 400-year-long **golden age** of stability and prosperity came to an abrupt end. After more than two centuries of recurring tensions, the Burmese captured and ravaged Ayutthaya, taking tens of thousands of prisoners back to Burma with them. With even the wats in ruins, the city had to be abandoned to the jungle, but its memory endured: the architects of the new capital on Ratanakosin island in Bangkok perpetuated Ayutthaya's layout in every possible way.

Arrival

The best way of getting to Ayutthaya **from Bangkok** is by **train** – there are about thirty a day, concentrated in the early morning and evening; trains continue on to Nong Khai and Ubon Ratchathani in the northeast, and to the north and Chiang Mai (if you're moving on to Chiang Mai, there's now also the convenient option of a nightly VIP bus, which picks up from Ayutthaya's "Little Khao San Road" – contact the *Ayutthaya Guest House* for further information). To get to the centre of town from the station on the east bank of the Pasak, take the ferry from the jetty 100m west of the station (last ferry around 8pm; B2) across and upriver to Chao Phrom pier; it's then a five-minute walk to the junction of Thanon U Thong and Thanon Naresuan (if you're going to stay or eat at *Bann Kun Pra*, take the other ferry from the neighbouring jetty, which runs directly across the river and back). The station has a useful left-luggage service (24hr; B10/piece/day). Though frequent, **buses** to Ayutthaya are slower and less convenient, as they depart from Bangkok's distant Northern Terminal. Most buses from Bangkok pull in at the bus stop on Thanon Naresuan, just west of the centre of Ayutthaya, though some, mainly those on long-distance runs, will only stop at Ayutthaya's Northern Bus Terminal, 2km to the east of the centre near the *U-Thong Inn* on Thanon Rojana. Private, air-con minibuses from Bangkok's Victory Monument and Southern Bus Terminal finish their routes opposite the Thanon Naresuan bus stop (both about every 20min during daylight hours; 1–2hr depending on traffic). It's also possible to get here by scenic **boat tour** on the Chao Phraya River from Bangkok via Bang Pa-In Palace: River Sun Cruises (ⓣ02 266 9125–6 or 02 266 9316) based at River City, for example, runs swanky day-trips for B1800 per person, including buffet lunch, with one leg of the journey – either up to Ayutthaya or back to Bangkok – completed in a coach or air-con minibus. A couple of plushly converted teak rice barges do luxury overnight **cruises** to Bang Pa-In and Ayutthaya: the *Manohra 2* (ⓣ02 477 0770, ⓦwww.manohracruises.com) takes three leisurely days and two nights over the trip, while the *Mekhala* (ⓦwww.mekhalacruise.com) does it in one and a half days and one night, with one leg between Bangkok and Ayutthaya by air-con minibus and one leg between Ayutthaya and Bang Pa-In by longtail boat.

From Kanchanaburi, it's possible to bypass the Bangkok gridlock, either by hooking up with an air-con tourist minibus (2hr 30min; arranged through guest houses in Kanchanaburi) or, under your own steam, by taking a public bus to Suphanburi (every 20min; 1hr 30min), then changing to an Ayutthaya bus (every 30min; 1hr), which will drop you off at Chao Phrom market.

Information

Once in Ayutthaya, the helpful **TAT** office (daily 8.30am–4.30pm; ⓣ035 246076–7 or 035 322730–1, ⓔtatyutya@tat.or.th) can be found in the former city hall on the west side of Thanon Si Sanphet, opposite the Chao Sam Phraya National Museum. It's well worth heading upstairs here to the smartly presented multi-media **exhibition** on Ayutthaya (daily except Wed 8.30am–4.30pm; free), which provides an engaging introduction to the city's history, an overview of all the sights, including a scale-model reconstruction of Wat Phra Si Sanphet, and insights into local traditional ways of life. The **tourist police** (ⓣ035 242352 or 1155) have their office just to the north of TAT on Thanon Si Sanphet. You can access the **Internet** at most of the guest houses, or there are plenty of Internet cafés around Chao Phrom market and on Thanon Pamaphrao.

Accommodation

Although Ayutthaya is usually visited on a day-trip, there's a good choice of **accommodation**, including a small ghetto of budget guest houses on an unnamed lane, running north from Chao Phrom market to Thanon Pamaphrao, which has earned the ironic nickname "Little Khao San Road".

Ayutthaya Guest House 12/34 Thanon Naresuan ⓣ035 232658, ⓔayutthaya_guesthouse@yahoo.com. Large, modern, friendly establishment, with all manner of useful services including Internet access, bike and motorbike rental, and minibuses and tours to Kanchanaburi. Accommodation is in

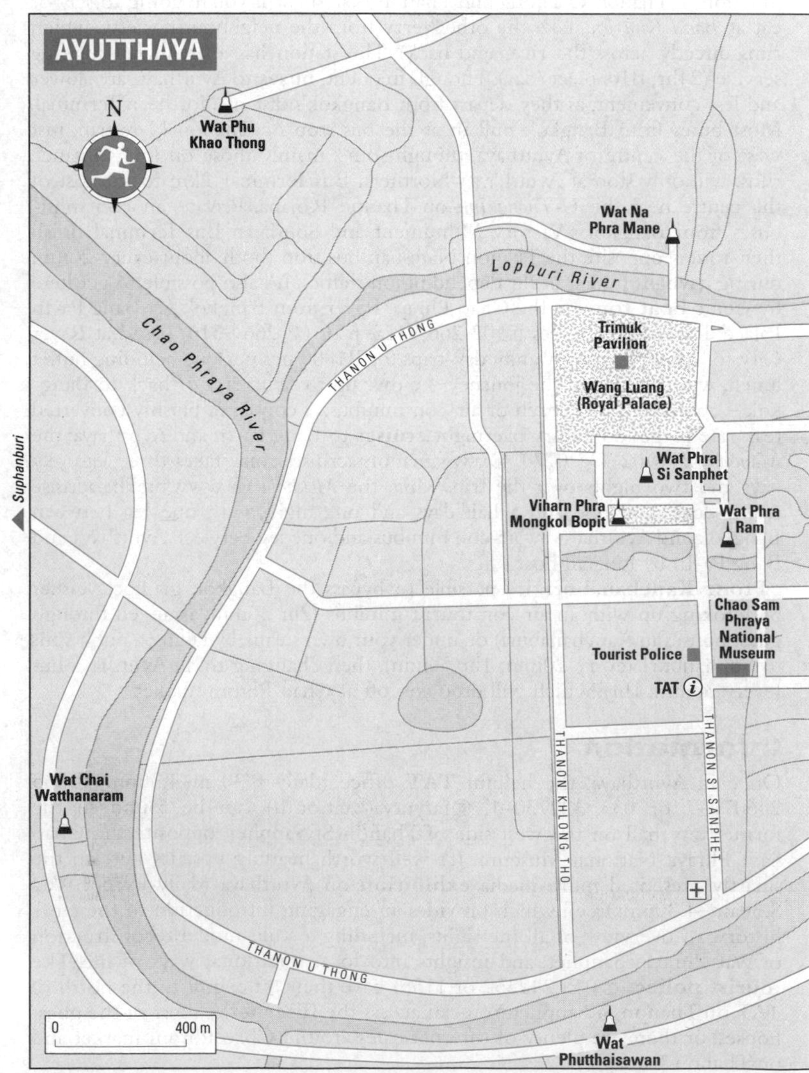

clean, wooden-floored rooms with hot showers available, either shared or en suite, fan-cooled or air-con. ❶–❸

Baan Lotus Guest House Thanon Pamaphrao ⓣ035 251988. Large, tranquil traditional house with polished teak floorboards and balconies, at the end of a long garden with a lotus pond at the back; rooms are clean, simple and en suite. ❷

Baan Suan Guest House 23/1 Thanon Chakrapat ⓣ035 242394, ⓦwww.baansuanguesthouse.com. Quiet, homely, balconied house with bright, clean and simple rooms, some with air-con, sharing cold-water bathrooms. In the pleasant, well-kept garden, sturdy wooden bungalows with hot showers, some with air-con, give a foretaste of beach life. Internet access. Good rates for singles. Fan ❷–❹, air-con ❸–❹

Bann Kun Pra Thanon U Thong, just north of Pridi Damrong Bridge ⓣ035 241978, ⓦwww.bannkunpra.com. Airy, attractive rooms

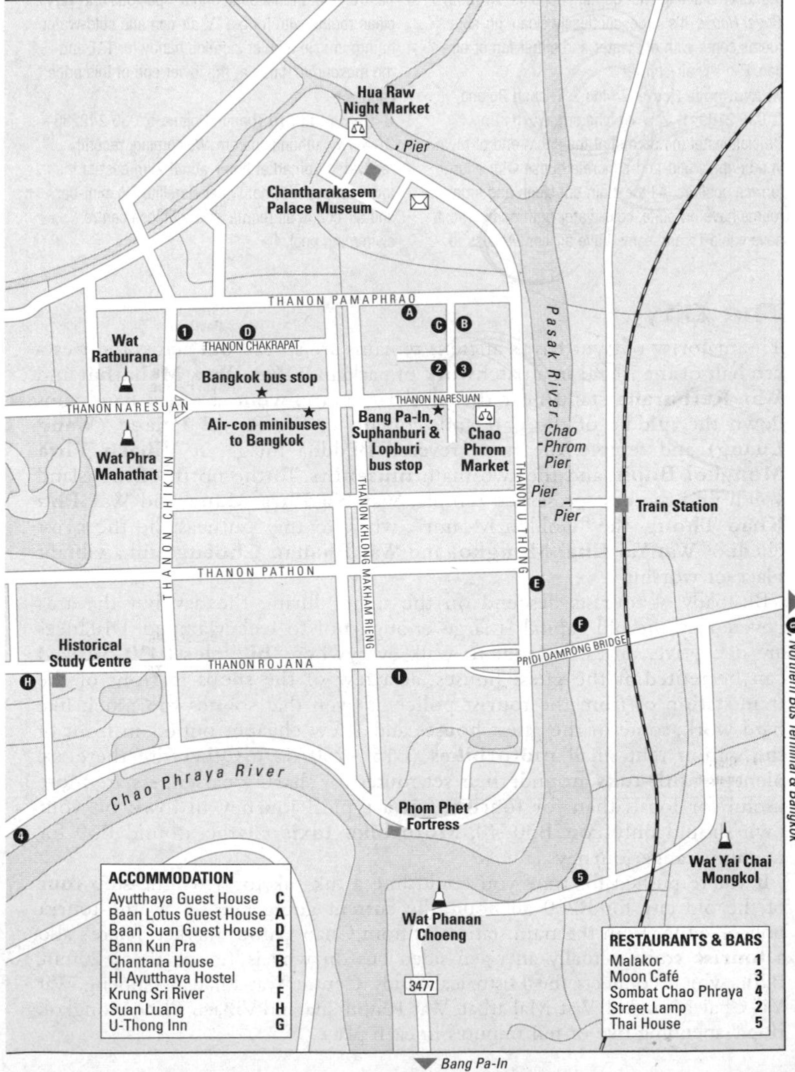

spread across two buildings: a rambling, hundred-year-old riverside teak house with a large, comfy chillout terrace, where some rooms have river-view balconies; and a newer block near the road, where all rooms have en-suite cold-water bathrooms and some have air-con; all have access to smart, shared, hot showers. Internet access, bike rental, healthy breakfasts and a warm welcome. Fan ❸, air-con ❺, dorms B250.

Chantana House 12/22 Thanon Narsuan Ⓣ035 323200 or 089 885 0257, Ⓔchantanahouse@yahoo.com. Smart, welcoming guest house in an attractive building with garden, opposite *Ayutthaya Guest House*. It's large, spotlessly clean, en-suite rooms come with hot water and either fan or air-con. Fan ❸, air-con ❹

HI Ayutthaya Hostel 7 Moo 2, Thanon Rojana Ⓣ035 210941, Ⓦwww.tyha.org/ayuyh.html. Official hostel (no dorms) at the south end of town, in a bright, wood-and-concrete house with a large terrace upstairs. All the plain but clean and smart rooms have en-suite, cold-water bathrooms, most have cable TV and some have air-con. Access to a kitchen (with free hot drinks), laundry and the Internet is available, bikes can be rented, and a simple continental breakfast is included in the price. Fan ❷, air-con ❸

Krung Sri River 27/2 Moo 11, Thanon Rojana Ⓣ035 244333–7, Ⓦwww.krungsririver.com. Luxury hotel with swanky lobby, gym and attractive pool, occupying a prime, but noisy, position at the eastern end of the Pridi Damrong Bridge. ❼

Suan Luang Thanon Rojana Ⓣ & Ⓕ035 245537. This training ground for hotel and catering students at Rajabhat University, next to the Historical Study Centre, offers functional, bright, spacious and very clean rooms with fridge, TV, air-con and cold-water bathrooms, in a quiet location handy for TAT and the museums. Rates at the lower end of this price code. ❹

U-Thong Inn 210 Thanon Rojana Ⓣ035 242236–9, Ⓦwww.uthonginn.com. Welcoming, recently renovated upmarket hotel, about 2km east of the town centre, with hot water, satellite TV, mini-bar and air-con in all rooms, and a fitness centre swimming pool. ❻

The City

The majority of Ayutthaya's ancient remains are spread out across the western half of the island in a patchwork of parkland: **Wat Phra Mahathat** and **Wat Ratburana** stand near the modern centre, while a broad band runs down the middle of the parkland, containing the **Royal Palace (Wang Luang)** and temple, the most revered Buddha image, at **Viharn Phra Mongkol Bopit**, and the two main **museums**. To the north of the island you'll find the best-preserved temple, **Wat Na Phra Mane**, and **Wat Phu Khao Thong**, the "Golden Mount", while to the southeast lie the giant chedi of **Wat Yai Chai Mongkol** and **Wat Phanan Choeng**, still a vibrant place of worship.

Busloads of tourists descend on the sights during the day, but the area covered by the old capital is large enough not to feel swamped. Distances are deceptive, so it's best not to walk everywhere: **bicycles** (B30–50/day) can be rented at the guest houses, at a few of the shops in front of the train station or from the tourist police. If even that sounds too much like hard work, some of the guest houses and a few cheaper outlets in front of the station rent small **motorbikes** (B150–250/day). Otherwise there are plenty of **tuk-tuks** around: their set routes for sharing passengers are more useful for locals than for tourists, but a typical journey in town on your own should only cost B30–40. **Motorbike taxis** charge around B30 for medium-range journeys.

If you're pushed for time you could hire a tuk-tuk for a whistle-stop **tour** of the old city for B200 an hour (the current going rate set by the tourist police), either from the train station or from Chao Phrom market. There's also a **tourist train**, actually an open-sided bus on wheels (every 15 or 20min; B20), which connects the Historical Study Centre, Wat Phanan Choeng, Wat Yai Chai Mongkol, Wat Mahathat, Wat Ratburana and Viharn Phra Mongkok Bopit, spending five or ten minutes in each place.

Tour **boats**, generally accommodating up to eight passengers and charging around B700 for a two-hour trip, can be chartered from the pier outside the Chantharakasem Palace, from Wat Phanan Choeng or through guest houses. A typical tour takes in **Wat Phutthaisawan**, built around a gleaming white prang by Ramathibodi I in 1353, only two years after the city's foundation, and the recently restored **Wat Chai Watthanaram**, which was built by King Prasat Thong in 1630 to commemorate his victory over Cambodia, taking as its model the imposing symmetry of the Baphuon temple at Angkor. It's also possible to take an **elephant-ride** (Ⓣ035 211001; B400/person for 20min, B500 for 30min) around the central ruins from behind the TAT office off Thanon Pathon. (You're quite likely to spot these photogenically caparisoned animals in the early evening as they rumble across to the northeast side of town to their home in the restored sixteenth-century kraal, into which wild elephants were formerly driven for capture and taming.)

Wat Phra Mahathat and Wat Ratburana

Heading west out of the new town centre along Thanon Naresuan, after about 1km you'll come to the first set of ruins, a pair of temples on opposite sides of the road. The overgrown **Wat Phra Mahathat**, on the left (daily 8am–5pm; B30), is the epitome of Ayutthaya's nostalgic atmosphere of faded majesty. The name "Mahathat" (Great Relic Chedi) indicates that the temple was built to house remains of the Buddha himself: according to the royal chronicles – never renowned for historical accuracy – King Ramesuan (1388–95) was looking out of his palace one morning when ashes of the Buddha materialized out of thin air here. A gold casket containing the ashes was duly enshrined in a grand 38-metre-high prang. The prang later collapsed, but the reliquary was unearthed in the 1950s, along with a hoard of other treasures, including a gorgeous marble fish, which opened to reveal gold, amber, crystal and porcelain ornaments – all now on show in the Chao Sam Phraya National Museum (see p.275).

You can climb what remains of the prang to get a good view of the broad, grassy complex, with dozens of brick spires tilting at impossible angles and headless Buddhas scattered around like spare parts in a scrapyard – look out for the serene head of a stone Buddha that has become nestled in the embrace of a bodhi tree's roots. To the west you'll see a lake, now surrounded by a popular park, where Ramathibodi I discovered an auspicious conch shell, symbol of victory and righteousness, which confirmed his choice of site for his new city, and the slender prang of **Wat Phra Ram**, built in the late fourteenth century on the site of Ramathibodi's cremation by his son and successor as king, Ramesuan.

Across the road from Wat Phra Mahathat, the towering **Wat Ratburana** (daily 8am–5pm; B30) was built in 1424 by King Boromraja II to commemorate his elder brothers, Ay and Yi, who managed to kill each other in an elephant-back duel over the succession to the throne, thus leaving it vacant for Boromraja. Here, four elegant Sri Lankan chedis lean outwards as if in deference to the main prang, on which some of the original stucco work can still be seen, including fine statues of garudas swooping down on nagas. It's possible to descend steep steps inside the prang to the crypt, where on two levels you can make out fragmentary murals of the early Ayutthaya period. Several hundred Buddha images were buried down here, most of which were snatched by grave robbers, although some can be seen in the Chao Sam Phraya Museum (see p.275). They're in the earliest style that can be said to be distinctly Ayutthayan – an unsmiling Khmer expression, but on an oval face and elongated body that show the strong influence of Sukhothai.

Wat Phra Si Sanphet and the Wang Luang (Royal Palace)

Nearly a kilometre west of Wat Ratburana is **Wat Phra Si Sanphet** (daily 8am–5pm; B30), built in 1448 by King Boromatrailokanat as his private chapel. Formerly the grandest of Ayutthaya's temples, and still one of the best preserved, it took its name from one of the largest standing metal images of the Buddha ever known, the **Phra Si Sanphet**, erected here in 1503. Towering 16m high and covered in 173kg of gold, it did not survive the ravages of the Burmese, though Rama I rescued the pieces and placed them inside a chedi at Wat Pho in Bangkok. The three remaining grey chedis in the characteristic style of the old capital were built to house the ashes of three kings, and have now become the most hackneyed image of Ayutthaya.

The site of this royal wat was originally occupied by Ramathibodi I's wooden palace, which Boromatrailokanat replaced with the bigger **Wang Luang** (Royal Palace; same hours and ticket as Wat Phra Si Sanphet), stretching to the Lopburi River on the north side. Successive kings turned the Wang Luang into a vast complex of pavilions and halls, with an elaborate system of walls designed to isolate the inner sanctum for the king and his consorts. The palace was destroyed by the Burmese in 1767 and plundered by Rama I for its bricks, which he needed to build the new capital at Bangkok. Now you can only trace the outlines of a few walls in the grass and inspect an unimpressive wooden replica of an open pavilion – better to consult the model of the whole complex in the Historical Study Centre (see opposite).

Viharn Phra Mongkol Bopit and the cremation ground

Viharn Phra Mongkol Bopit (Mon–Fri 8.30am–4.30pm, Sat & Sun 8.30am–5.30pm; free), on the south side of Wat Phra Si Sanphet, attracts tourists and Thai pilgrims in about equal measure. The pristine hall – a replica of a typical Ayutthayan viharn, with its characteristic chunky lotus-capped columns around the outside – was built in 1956, with help from the Burmese to atone for their flattening of the city two centuries earlier, in order to shelter the revered **Phra Mongkol Bopit**, one of the largest bronze Buddhas in Thailand. The powerfully austere image, with its flashing mother-of-pearl eyes, was cast in the fifteenth century, then sat exposed to the elements from the time of the Burmese invasion until its new home was built. During restoration, the hollow image was found to contain hundreds of Buddha statuettes, some of which were later buried around the shrine to protect it.

The car park in front of the viharn used to be the **cremation site** for Ayutthayan kings and high-ranking members of the royal family. Here, on a propitious date decided by astrologers, the embalmed body was placed on a towering *meru* (funeral pyre), representing Mount Meru, the centre of the Hindu-Buddhist universe. These many-gabled and pinnacled wooden structures, which had all the appearance of permanent palaces, were a miracle of architectural technology: the *meru* constructed for King Phetracha in 1704, for example, was 103m tall and took eleven months to raise, requiring thousands of tree trunks and hundreds of thousands of bamboo poles. The task of building at such great heights was given to *yuan-hok*, a particular clan of acrobats who used to perform at the top of long poles during special festivals. Their handiwork was not consigned to the flames: the cremation took place on a pyramid erected underneath the central spire, so as not to damage the main structure, which was later dismantled and its timber used for building temples. The cremation ground is now given over to a picnic area and a clutch of souvenir and refreshment stalls.

The museums

A ten-minute walk south of the viharn brings you to the largest of the town's three museums, the **Chao Sam Phraya National Museum** (Wed–Sun 9am–4pm, last admission 3.30pm; B30; Ⓦwww.thailandmuseum.com), where most of the moveable remains of Ayutthaya's glory – those that weren't plundered by treasure-hunters or taken to the National Museum in Bangkok – are exhibited. The museum itself was funded by a Fine Arts Department sale of the Buddhist votive tablets excavated from Wat Ratburana in the late 1950s, and given the original name (Chao Sam Phraya) of King Boromraja II, who built the wat. Apart from numerous Buddhas and some fine woodcarving, the museum is bursting with **gold treasures** in all shapes and sizes – the original relic casket from Wat Mahathat, betel-nut sets and model chedis, a royal wimple in gold filigree, a royal sword and scabbard and a fifteenth-century crouching elephant, both dripping with gems and both found in the crypt of the main prang of Wat Ratburana.

The **Historical Study Centre** (Mon–Fri 9am–4.30pm, Sat & Sun 9am–5pm; B100), five minutes' walk away along Thanon Rotchana, is a more modern showpiece museum. The visitors' exhibition upstairs puts the ruins in context, dramatically presenting a wealth of background detail through videos, sound effects and reconstructions of temple murals, along with model ships, a peasant's wooden house and a small-scale model of the Royal Palace that all build up a broad social history of Ayutthaya.

In the northeast corner of the island, the **Chantharakasem Palace Museum** (Wed–Sun 8.30am–4.30pm; B30; Ⓦwww.thailandmuseum.com) was traditionally the home of the heir to the Ayutthayan throne. The Black Prince, Naresuan, built the first *wang na* (palace of the front) here in about 1577 so that he could guard the area of the city wall that was most vulnerable to enemy attack. Rama IV (1851–68) had the palace rebuilt and it now displays many of his possessions, including a throne platform overhung by a white *chat*, a ceremonial nine-tiered parasol that is a vital part of a king's insignia. The rest of the museum features beautiful ceramics and Buddha images, and a small arsenal of cannon and musketry from the late Ayutthaya and early Bangkok periods.

Wat Na Phra Mane

Wat Na Phra Mane (Mon–Fri 8am–5pm, Sat & Sun 8am–6pm; B20), on the north bank of the Lopburi River opposite the Wang Luang, is Ayutthaya's most rewarding temple, as it's the only one from the town's golden age that survived the ravages of the Burmese. The story goes that when the Burmese were on the brink of capturing Ayutthaya in 1760, a siege gun positioned here burst, mortally wounding their king and prompting their retreat; out of superstition, they left the temple standing when they came back to devastate the city in 1767.

The main **bot**, built in 1503, shows the distinctive features of Ayutthayan architecture – outside columns topped with lotus cups, and slits in the walls instead of windows to let the wind pass through. Inside, underneath a rich red-and-gold coffered ceiling that represents the stars around the moon, sits a powerful six-metre-high Buddha in the disdainful, over-decorated royal style characteristic of the later Ayutthaya period.

In sharp contrast is the dark-green **Phra Khan Thavaraj** Buddha, which dominates the tiny viharn behind to the right. Seated in the "European position", with its robe delicately pleated and its feet up on a large lotus leaf, the gentle figure conveys a reassuring serenity. It's advertised as being from Sri Lanka, the source of Thai Buddhism, but more likely is a seventh- to ninth-century Mon image from Wat Phra Mane at Nakhon Pathom.

Wat Phu Khao Thong

Head 2km northwest of Wat Na Phra Mane and you're in open country, where the fifty-metre chedi of **Wat Phu Khao Thong** rises steeply out of the fields. In 1569, after a temporary occupation of Ayutthaya, the Burmese erected a Mon-style chedi here to commemorate their victory. Forbidden by Buddhist law from pulling down a sacred monument, the Thais had to put up with this galling reminder of the enemy's success until it collapsed nearly two hundred years later, when King Borommakot promptly built a truly Ayutthayan chedi on the old Burmese base – just in time for the Burmese to return in 1767 and flatten the town. This "Golden Mount" has recently been restored and painted toothpaste-white, with a colossal equestrian statue of King Naresuan, conqueror of the Burmese, to keep it company. You can climb 25m of steps up the side of the chedi to look out over the countryside and the town, with glimpses of Wat Phra Si Sanphet and Viharn Phra Mongkok Bopit in the distance. In 1956, to celebrate 2500 years of Buddhism, the government placed on the tip of the spire a ball of solid gold weighing 2500g, of which there is now no trace.

Wat Yai Chai Mongkol

To the southeast of the island, if you cross the suspension bridge over the Pasak River and the rail line, then turn right at the major roundabout, you pass through Ayutthaya's new business zone and some rustic suburbia before reaching the ancient but still functioning **Wat Yai Chai Mongkol**, about 2km from the bridge (daily 8am–5pm; B20). Surrounded by formal lawns, flowerbeds and much-photographed saffron-draped Buddhas, the wat was established by Ramathibodi I in 1357 as a meditation site for monks returning from study in Sri Lanka. King Naresuan put up the celebrated **chedi** to mark the decisive victory over the Burmese at Suphanburi in 1593, when he himself had sent the enemy packing by slaying the Burmese crown prince in an elephant-back duel. Built on a colossal scale to outshine the Burmese Golden Mount on the opposite side of Ayutthaya, the chedi has come to symbolize the prowess and devotion of Naresuan and, by implication, his descendants right down to the present king. By the entrance, a **reclining Buddha**, now gleamingly restored in white, was also constructed by Naresuan.

△ Wat Yai Chai Mongkol

Wat Phanan Choeng

In Ayutthaya's most prosperous period, the docks and main trading area were located near the confluence of the Chao Phraya and Pasak rivers, to the west of Wat Yai Chai Mongkol. This is where you'll find the oldest and liveliest working temple in town, **Wat Phanan Choeng** (daily 8am–5pm; B20). The main viharn is often filled with the sights, sounds and smells of an incredible variety of merit-making activities, as devotees burn huge pink Chinese incense candles, offer food and rattle fortune sticks. It's even possible to buy tiny golden statues of the Buddha to be placed in one of the hundreds of niches that line the walls, a form of votive offering peculiar to this temple. If you can get here during a festival, especially Chinese New Year, you're in for an overpowering experience.

The nineteen-metre-high Buddha, which almost fills the hall, has survived since 1324, shortly before the founding of the capital, and tears are said to have flowed from its eyes when Ayutthaya was sacked by the Burmese. However, the reason for the temple's popularity with the Chinese is to be found in the early eighteenth-century shrine by the pier, with its image of a beautiful Chinese princess who drowned herself here because of a king's infidelity: his remorse led him to build the shrine at the place where she had walked into the river.

Eating and drinking

The main travellers' hangout in the evening is the small, laid-back *Moon Café*, on the same lane as the *Ayutthaya Guest House*, which has regular live music and serves good Western and Thai **food**; under the same ownership, *Street Lamp* across the road is a congenial restaurant, with good espressos and Internet access. Many riverside restaurants in Ayutthaya are slightly expensive and disappointing: the best bets are the atmospheric terrace at *Bann Kun Pra* (see p.271), which specializes in reasonably priced fish and seafood, notably prawns; and the congenial *Sombat Chao Phraya*, Thanon U Thong on the south side of town, where, on river bank terraces or a moored boat with views of Wat Phutthaisawan's white prang, you can dine on such delicacies as royal tofu with wild mushrooms, crab, cashew nuts and prawns. Around the central ruins, your best bet is *Malakor*, a simple, wooden house with covered balconies on Thanon Chaikun, offering tasty Thai and Western food and views of Wat Ratburana (floodlit at night). On the road between Wat Yai Chai Mongkol and Wat Phanan Choeng, *Thai House* serves a huge variety of excellent Thai food, including delicious deep-fried banana flowers, and a choice of Thai desserts; prices are reasonable and tables are arrayed around several stilted, wooden, traditional-style houses.

Lopburi and around

Mention the name **LOPBURI** to a Thai and the chances are that he or she will start telling you about monkeys – the central junction of this drab provincial capital, 150km due north of Bangkok, swarms with macaques. So beneficial are the beasts to the town's tourist trade that a local hotelier treats six hundred of them to a sit-down meal at Phra Prang Sam Yod temple every November, complete with menus, waiters and napkins, as a thank you for their help. In fact, the monkeys can be a real nuisance, but at least they add some life to the town's central **Khmer buildings**, which, though historically important, are rather unimpressive. More illuminating is the **Narai National Museum**, housed in a partly reconstructed seventeenth-century palace complex, and distant **Wat Phra Phutthabat**, a colourful eye-opener for non-Buddhists. Lopburi's main festival is the five-day **King Narai Reign Fair** in February, to commemorate the seventeenth-century king's birthday, featuring costumed processions, cultural performances, traditional markets and a *son et lumière* show at Phra Narai Ratchanivet.

Originally called Lavo, Lopburi is one of the longest-inhabited towns in Thailand, and was a major centre of the Mon (Dvaravati) civilization from around the sixth century. It maintained a tenuous independence in the face of the advancing Khmers until as late as the early eleventh century, when it was incorporated into the empire as the provincial capital for much of central Thailand. Increasing Thai immigration from the north soon tilted the balance against the Khmers, and Lopburi was again independent from some time early in the thirteenth century until the rise of Ayutthaya in the middle of the fourteenth. Thereafter, Lopburi was twice used as a second capital, first by King Narai of Ayutthaya in the seventeenth century, then by Rama IV of Bangkok in the nineteenth, because its remoteness from the sea made it less vulnerable to European expansionists. Rama V downgraded the town, turning the royal palace into a provincial government office and museum; Lopburi's modern role is as the site of several huge army barracks.

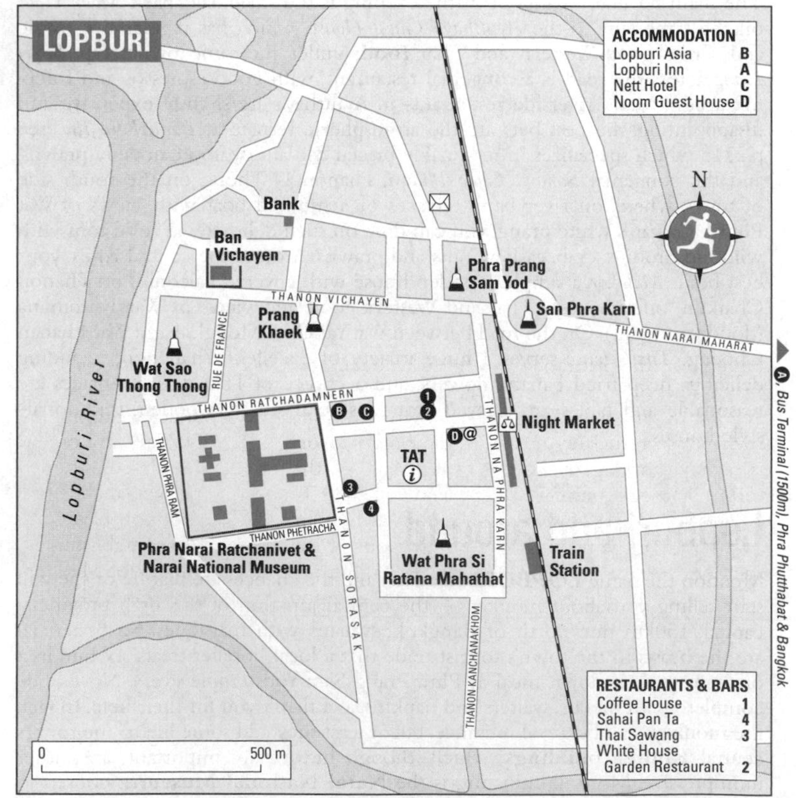

Arrival and information

As it's on the main line north to Chiang Mai, Lopburi is best reached by **train**. Fifteen services a day, concentrated in the early morning and evening, run here from Bangkok's Hualamphong station (3hr) via Ayutthaya (1hr 30min): a popular option is to arrive in Lopburi in the morning, leave your bags at the conveniently central **station** while you look around the town, then catch one of the night trains to the north. **Buses** from Ayutthaya (every 20min) take around two hours to reach Lopburi; from Bangkok's Northern Bus Terminal (every 20min) around three hours. Several companies now also operate **air-con minibuses** between Bangkok's Victory Monument and Lopburi, which leave when full and take around two hours; their offices are on Thanon Na Phra Karn, north of Lopburi's train station. If you happen to be coming here from Kanchanaburi, it's possible to bypass Bangkok by taking a public bus to Suphanburi (every 20min; 1hr 30min), then changing to a Lopburi bus (hourly; 3hr). The long-distance bus **terminal** is on the south side of the huge Sakeo roundabout, 2km east of the town centre: a blue city bus or red songthaew heading west on Thanon Narai Mahathat to Narai's Palace will save you the walk.

TAT has an office in a restored, wooden, colonial-style building on the north side of Wat Phra Si Ratana Mahathat (daily 8.30am–4.30pm; ⓣ036 422768–9, ⓔtatlobri@tat.or.th), and **Internet access** is available just around the corner on Thanon Praya Kumjud, at an unnamed shop next to *Noom Guest House*.

Accommodation

Lopburi's choice of **accommodation** is poor, and not helped by Thanon Na Phra Karn, a minefield of seedy budget hotels in front of the train station. The best option in the heart of town is the clean and friendly *Nett Hotel*, announced by a multi-coloured mosaic of a dragon and a cock at 17/1–2 Soi 2, Thanon Ratchadamnern (ⓣ036 411738 or 036 421460; ❶–❷), offering recently renovated, en-suite fan or air-con rooms, the latter with hot water, TV and fridge. The town's most prominent hotel, the *Lopburi Asia*, opposite the entrance to Narai's palace, has also recently been refurbished, but still comes in a distant second, with a choice of rooms with fan and bathroom, or with air-con and hot water, all with TV (ⓣ036 618894; ❷). The town's cheapest digs – decent enough for the price – are in an old wooden house above a bar at *Noom Guest House*, Thanon Praya Kumjud (ⓣ036 427693, ⓦwww.tourburi.com; ❶), where you'll get a mattress on the floor, a fan and a shared hot-water bathroom; the owners also **rent bicycles** (B80/day) and **motorbikes** (B250/day) and organize rock-climbing trips. About 3km east of the centre, the air-conditioned rooms at the recommended *Lopburi Inn*, 28/9 Thanon Narai Maharat (ⓣ036 412609, ⓕ036 412457; ❹), are as posh as Lopburi town gets; if you have your own transport, you might be tempted out of town to its sister establishment, the *Lopburi Inn Resort*, off the Saraburi road, an overblown complex of Mediterranean-style buildings with a large swimming pool and gym (ⓣ036 614790–2, ⓦwww.lopburiinnresort.com; ❻).

The Town

The old centre of Lopburi sits on an egg-shaped island between canals and the Lopburi River, with the rail line running across it from north to south. **Thanon Vichayen**, the main street, crosses the rail tracks at the town's busiest junction before heading east – now called Thanon Narai Maharat – through the newest areas of development towards Highway 1. All of the sights below are easily walkable from the train station.

Wat Phra Si Ratana Mahathat

As you come out of the station, the first thing you'll see are the sprawled grassy ruins of **Wat Phra Si Ratana Mahathat** (daily 7am–6pm; B30), where the impressive centrepiece is a laterite prang in the Khmer style of the twelfth century, decorated with finely detailed stucco work and surrounded by a ruined cloister. Arrayed in loose formation around this central feature are several more rocket-like Khmer prangs and a number of graceful chedis in the Ayutthayan style, among them one with a bulbous peak and faded bas-reliefs of Buddhist saints. On the eastern side of the main prang, King Narai added to the mish-mash of styles by building a "Gothic" viharn, now roofless, which is home to a lonely, headless stone Buddha, draped in photogenic saffron.

Phra Narai Ratchanivet (King Narai's palace)

The imposing gates and high crenellated walls of the **Phra Narai Ratchanivet**, a short walk northwest of the wat, might promise more than the complex delivers, but the museum in its central courtyard is worth a look, and the grounds are a green and relaxing spot. King Narai, with the help of French architects, built the heavily fortified palace in 1666 as a precaution against any possible confrontation with the Western powers, and for the rest of his reign he was to spend eight months of every year here, entertaining foreign envoys and indulging his love of hunting. After Narai's death, Lopburi was left forgotten until 1856, when Rama IV – worried about British and French colonialism – decided to make this his second capital and lavishly restored the central buildings of Narai's palace.

The outer courtyard

The main **entrance** to the palace complex is through the Phayakkha Gate on Thanon Sorasak (the gate is open daily 7am–5.30pm, giving access to the palace grounds, but during museum opening hours – see below – the admission fee is collected here). You'll see the unusual lancet shape of this arch again and again in the seventeenth-century doors and windows of Lopburi – just one aspect of the Western influences embraced by Narai. Around the **outer courtyard**, which occupies the eastern half of the complex, stand the walls of various gutted buildings – twelve warehouses for Narai's treasures, stables for the royal hunting elephants, and a moated reception hall for foreign envoys. With their lily ponds and manicured lawns, these well-shaded grounds are ideal for a picnic or a siesta.

The central courtyard and the Narai National Museum

Straight ahead from the Phayakkha Gate another arch leads into the **central courtyard**, where the typically Ayutthayan **Chanthara Phisan Pavilion** contains a fascinating exhibition on Narai's reign – check out the pointed white cap typical of those worn by noblemen of the time, which increased their height by no less than 50cm.

To the left is the colonial-style Phiman Mongkut Hall, now the **Narai National Museum** (Wed–Sun 8.30am–4.30pm; B30; Ⓦwww.thailandmuseum.com), whose exhibits concentrate on the period following the Khmer subjugation of Lopburi in the eleventh century. Inevitably there's a surfeit of Buddhas, most of them fine examples of the Khmer style and the distinctive **Lopburi style**, which emerged in the thirteenth and fourteenth centuries, mixing traditional Khmer elements – such as the conical *ushnisha*, or flame on the crown of the Buddha's head – with new features such as a more oval face and slender body. On the top floor is **King Mongkut's bedroom**, filled with his furniture and assorted memorabilia of his reign, including his very short and uncomfortable-looking bed and eerie painted statues of his equally vertically challenged near-contemporaries, Napoleon and Queen Victoria.

On the south side of the museum lies the shell of the **Dusit Sawan Hall**, where foreign dignitaries came to present their credentials to King Narai. Inside you can still see the niche, raised 3.5m above the main floor, where the throne was set; beneath the niche, a modern plaque showing Narai receiving the French envoy, the Chevalier de Chaumont, in 1685, is revered as an icon of the king, with offerings of gold leaf, joss sticks and garlands. The whole building is divided in two around the throne: the front half has "foreign" doors and windows with pointed arches; the rear part, from where the king would have made his grand entrance, has traditional Thai openings. The hall used to be lined with French mirrors in imitation of Versailles, with Persian carpets and a pyramidal roof of golden glazed tiles rounding off the most majestic building in the palace.

The private courtyards

King Narai's private courtyard, through whose sturdy walls only the trusted few were admitted, occupied the southwest corner of the complex. During Narai's time, hundreds of lamps were placed in niches around the walls of this courtyard by night, shedding a fairy-like light on the palace. Now there's not much more than the foundations left of his residence, the **Sutha Sawan Hall**, and its bathing ponds and artificial grotto.

Rama IV's private courtyard was built to house his harem in the northwest corner of the grounds, behind the present site of the museum. In what used to be the kitchen there's now a small folk museum of central Thai life, containing a loom and various pieces of farming and fishing equipment. In front, you can consult a crude model of the palace as it looked in Narai's time.

Wat Sao Thong Thong and Ban Vichayen

The north gate (now closed) to the palace is called the Vichayen Gate after **Constantine Phaulkon**, a Greek adventurer who came to Ayutthaya with the English East India Company in 1678 and ultimately became *ookya vichayen*, or prime minister (his story is told in *Falcon* by John Hoskins – see p.925). It leads directly to the aptly named Rue de France, the approach to the remains of his grand residence. Halfway along this road, set back on the left, you'll pass a building whose plain terracotta roof tiles and whitewashed exterior give it a strangely Mediterranean look. This is in fact the viharn of **Wat Sao Thong Thong**, and is typical of Narai's time in its combination of Thai-style tiered roof with "Gothic" pointed windows. Erected as either a Christian chapel or a mosque for the Persian ambassador's residence, it was later used as a Buddhist viharn and has now been tastefully restored, complete with brass door-knockers and plush red carpet. Inside there's an austere Buddha image of the Ayutthaya period and, in the lamp niches, some fine Lopburi-style Buddhas.

The complex of **Ban Vichayen** (daily 7am–6pm; B30) had been built by Narai as a residence for foreign ambassadors, with a Christian chapel incongruously stuccoed with Buddhist flame and lotus-leaf motifs. Though now just a nest of empty shells, it still conjures up the atmosphere of court intrigue and dark deeds which, towards the end of Narai's reign, centred on the colourful figure of its chief resident, Phaulkon. He entered the royal service as interpreter and accountant, rapidly rising to the position of Narai's *ookya vichayen* (prime minister). It was chiefly due to his influence that Narai established close ties with Louis XIV of France, a move that made commercial sense but also formed part of Phaulkon's secret plan to turn Narai and his people to Christianity, with the aid of the French. Two missions were sent from Versailles, but both failed in their overt aim of signing a political alliance and their covert attempt at religious conversion. (It was around this time that the word for Westerner, *farang*, entered the Thai language, from the same derivation as *français*, which the Thais render *farangset*.) In 1688, a struggle for succession broke out, and leading officials persuaded the dying Narai to appoint as regent his foster brother, Phetracha, a great rival of Phaulkon's. Phetracha promptly executed Phaulkon on charges of treason, and took the throne himself when Narai died. Under Phetracha, Narai's open-door policy towards foreigners was brought to a screeching halt and the Thai kingdom returned to traditional, smaller-scale dealings with the outside world.

Prang Khaek, Phra Prang Sam Yod and San Phra Karn

Near the northeast corner of the palace, the junction of Thanon Vichayen and Thanon Sorasak is marked by an unusual traffic island, on which perch the three stubby red-brick towers of **Prang Khaek**, a well-preserved Hindu shrine, possibly to the god Shiva, and dating from as early as the eighth century. The nearby **Phra Prang Sam Yod** (daily 7am–6pm; B30), at the top of Thanon Na Phra Karn, seems also to have been a Hindu temple, later converted to Buddhism under the Khmers. The three chunky prangs, made of dark laterite with some restored stucco work, and symbolizing the Hindu triumvirate of Brahma, Vishnu and Shiva, are Lopburi's most photographed sight, though they'll only detain you for a minute or two – at least check out some carved figures of seated hermits at the base of the door columns. The shrine's grassy knoll is a good spot for monkey-watching – they run amok all over this area, so keep an eye on your bags and pockets. Across the rail line at the modern red-and-gold shrine of **San Phra Karn**, there's even a monkey's adventure playground for the benefit of tourists, beside the base of what must have been a huge Khmer prang.

Eating

Lopburi's **restaurants** present an even sorrier selection than its hotels. The cheap, air-con *Thai Sawang*, on Thanon Sorasak near the palace, offers simple Western breakfasts, as well as Thai and recommended Vietnamese food, while the friendly, stylish *Coffee House* on Thanon Ratchadamnern serves good espressos, as well as Western breakfasts and one or two hot dishes such as soup noodles with pork or chicken. Otherwise, try the classier, open-air *White House Garden Restaurant* on Thanon Praya Kumjud (parallel to and south of Ratchadamnern), which specializes in rich seafood dishes at reasonable prices. *Sahai Pan Ta*, near the northwest corner of Wat Mahathat, is a dark and rowdy Wild-West-style place, with food and live music.

Wat Phra Phutthabat (Temple of the Buddha's Footprint)

Seventeen kilometres southeast of Lopburi along Highway 1 stands the most important pilgrimage site in central Thailand, **Wat Phra Phutthabat**, which is believed to house a footprint made by the Buddha. Any of the frequent **buses** to Saraburi or Bangkok from Lopburi's Sakeo roundabout will get you there in thirty minutes. The souvenir village around the temple, which is on the southern side of Highway 1, includes plenty of foodstalls for day-trippers.

The **legend** of Phra Phutthabat dates back to the beginning of the seventeenth century, when King Song Tham of Ayutthaya sent some monks to Sri Lanka to worship the famous Buddha's footprint of Sumankut. To the monks' surprise, the Sri Lankans asked them why they had bothered to travel all that way when, according to the ancient Pali scriptures, the Buddha had passed through Thailand and had left his footprint in their own backyard. As soon as Song Tham heard this he instigated a search for the footprint, which was finally discovered in 1623 by a hunter named Pram Bun, when a wounded deer disappeared into a hollow and then emerged miraculously healed. The hunter pushed aside the bushes to discover a foot-shaped trench filled with water, which immediately cured him of his terrible skin disease. A temple was built on the spot, but was destroyed by the Burmese in 1765 – the present buildings date from the Bangkok era.

A staircase flanked by nagas leads up to a marble platform, where an ornate mondop with mighty doors inlaid with mother-of-pearl houses the **footprint**, which in itself is not much to look at. Sheltered by a mirrored canopy, the stone print is nearly 2m long and obscured by layers of gold leaf presented by pilgrims; people also throw money into the footprint, some of which they take out again as a charm or merit object. The hill behind the shrine, which you can climb for a fine view over the gilded roofs of the complex to the mountains beyond, is covered in shrines.

During the dry season in January, February and March, a million pilgrims from all over the country flock to the **Ngan Phrabat** (Phrabat Fair), when other pilgrims are making their way to the other major religious sites at Doi Suthep, Nakhon Si Thammarat and That Phanom. During the fair, which reaches its peak in two week-long lunar periods, one usually at the beginning of February, the other at the beginning of March, stalls selling souvenirs and traditional medicines around the entrance swell to form a small town, and traditional entertainments, magic shows and a Ferris wheel are laid on. The fair is still a major religious event, but before the onset of industrialization it was the highlight of social and cultural life for all ages and classes; it was an important place of courtship, for example, especially for women at a time when their freedom was limited. Another incentive for women to attend the fair was the belief that visiting the footprint three times would ensure a place in heaven – for many women, the Phrabat Fair became the focal point of their lives, as Buddhist doctrine allowed them no other path to salvation. Up to the reign of Rama V (1868–1910) even the king used to come, performing a ritual lance dance on elephant-back to ensure a long reign.

The northern plains

Heading north from Lopburi, road and rail plough through Thailand's "rice bowl", a landscape of lurid green paddies interrupted only by the unwelcoming sprawl of **Nakhon Sawan**, located at the confluence of the Ping, Wang, Yom and Nan rivers, which merge here to create the Chao Phraya. A prosperous city of about 100,000 predominantly Chinese inhabitants, Nakhon Sawan plays a vital role as the region's main market and distribution centre for rice, but is of interest to tourists only as a place to change buses for Kamphaeng Phet or Phitsanulok. The bus station is in the town centre and there are a couple of passable budget hotels close by as a last resort. All Bangkok–Chiang Mai trains stop in Nakhon Sawan, but as the station is 10km out of town, with skeletal local transport and no station hotels, breaking your journey 130km further north at Phitsanulok makes much more sense. The one time the city deserves a special visit is during **Chinese New Year** (between late January and mid-February, see Basics p.59), which is celebrated here with more vigour than anywhere else in the country. The place gets transformed for the three-day festival, decked out with Chinese lanterns and decorative arches, as visitors from all over Thailand gather to watch the Chinese dragons and lion-dancers snaking through the streets. Chinese opera troupes, an international lion-dance competition, fireworks and countless foodstalls complete the scene.

Many tourists bypass the lush northern reaches of the central plains, fast asleep in an overnight train from Bangkok to Chiang Mai, yet it was here, during the thirteenth, fourteenth and fifteenth centuries, that the kingdom of Thailand first began to cohere and assume its present identity. Some of Thailand's finest buildings and sculpture were produced in **Sukhothai**, once the most powerful city in Thailand. Abandoned to the jungle by the sixteenth century, it has now been extensively restored, the resulting historical park making an attractive open-air museum. Less complete renovations have made Sukhothai's satellite cities of **Si Satchanalai** and **Kamphaeng Phet** worth visiting, both for their relative wildness and lack of visitors.

The nearest hills in which to clear the cobwebs are in **Ramkhamhaeng National Park** near Sukhothai; further west, the Burmese border town of **Mae Sot** is the departure point for the **Umphang** region, which offers excellent trekking and whitewater-rafting.

Phitsanulok stands at the hub of an efficient **transport** network that works well as a transit point between Bangkok, the far north and Isaan. Nearly every Bangkok–Chiang Mai train stops here, and assorted buses head east towards the Isaan towns of Loei and Khon Kaen. It's also possible to fly in and out of the northern plains via Phitsanulok and Sukhothai.

Phitsanulok and around

Equipped with decent hotels and pleasantly located on the east bank of the Nan River, **PHITSANULOK** makes a handy base for exploring the historical centres of Sukhothai and Kamphaeng Phet, but boasts only a couple of unmissable sights of its own. Chief of these is the country's second most important Buddha image, enshrined in historic Wat Mahathat and the focus of pilgrimages from all over Thailand; complementing this sacred sight is one of the best ethnology collections in Thailand, at the Folklore Museum. There are also several potentially rewarding national parks within an hour or two's drive along Highway 12, the so-called "Green Route".

Phitsanulok hosts two lively food **festivals** every year, once during the Western New Year period (December 25 to January 1) and again at Songkhran, the Thai New Year (April 9–15); almost every restaurant in town participates, selling their trademark dishes from special stalls set up along the east bank of the river.

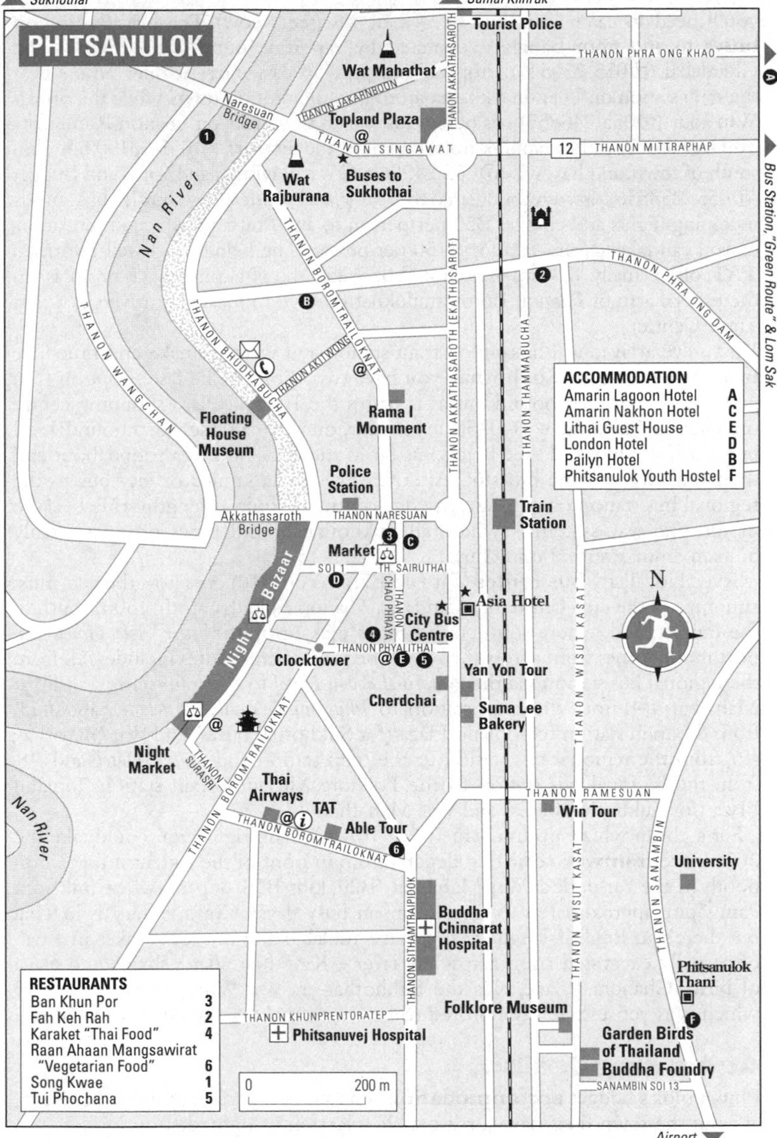

Entertainment includes performances of traditional Thai dance. Later in the year, on the third weekend of September, traditional longboat races are staged on the Nan River, in front of Wat Mahathat.

Arrival, information and transport

Phitsanulok **train station** (ⓣ055 258005) is in the town centre, but to get into town from the regional **bus station** (ⓣ055 242430), 2km east on Highway 12, you'll need to catch local bus #1, #2 or #8 (see below). The private **air-con buses** to and from Bangkok, operated by Yan Yon Tour (ⓣ055 258647) and Cherdchai (ⓣ055 230541), drop off and pick up passengers at their offices near the train station on Thanon Akkathasaroth (Ekathosarot) in town, while the similar Win Tour (ⓣ055 246857) has offices just across the tracks on Thanon Ramesuan. You can also fly to Phitsanulok from Bangkok; the **airport** (ⓣ055 301002) is 7km south of town, and has Avis (ⓣ055 242060, ⓦwww.avisthailand.com) and Budget (ⓣ055 258556, ⓦwww.budget.co.th) car-rental outlets. A shuttle bus meets incoming flights and charges B50 per person to any Phitsanulok accommodation, or you can take a share-taxi for B150 per person. The helpful and well-informed **TAT** office (daily 8.30am–4.30pm; ⓣ055 252742, ⓔtatphlok@tat.or.th) is on the eastern arm of Thanon Boromtrailoknat (known to local taxi drivers as Surasi Trade Centre).

If you've arrived at Phitsanulok train station and want to make an immediate **bus connection to Sukhothai**, you have two choices. The fastest option is to pick up a Sukhothai-bound bus as it passes the Topland Plaza shopping centre on Thanon Singawat – B40–50 by samlor, or you can use northbound local buses #5, #8 and #11 (see below) as far as the Topland Plaza roundabout and then walk west to the bus stop. Alternatively, take a samlor or city bus to the regional bus station on the eastern edge of town – quite a lengthy ride because of the one-way system – where all Sukhothai-bound buses originate (daily 5.30am–6pm; every 30min; 1hr).

Several local city **bus routes** (flat fare B7, air-con B10) crisscross the city, most running via the city-centre bus stands on Thanon Akkathasaroth, 150m south of the train station, where southbound buses pick up outside the *Asia Hotel*, and northbound ones from across the road. The most useful routes include: #1, from the regional bus station via the *Amarin Lagoon Hotel* to the train station and Wat Mahathat; #4, from the train station to *Phitsanulok Youth Hostel*; #5 and #11, from the train station to Topland Plaza (for Sukhothai buses) and Wat Mahathat; #6, from the regional bus station to the train station and *Pailyn Hotel*; and #8, from the regional bus station to the Folklore Museum, train station, Topland Plaza (for Sukhothai buses) and Wat Mahathat.

For a cheap whizz around some of the town's main sights you could take the 30-minute **tramway tour** that departs from in front of the tourist information booth in the car park at Wat Mahathat (B20, kids B10; departs when full from 9am–3pm, approximately every 30min on busy days). Commentary is in Thai but there's an English-language summary available and the route takes in a trio of partially excavated ruins across the river – King Naresuan's shrine and place of birth, Chandra Palace, plus the Sukhothai-era Wat Wihanthong – none of which is as yet sufficiently restored to be worth making the effort to walk to.

Accommodation

Phitsanulok's budget **accommodation** is nowhere near as inviting as Sukhothai's, but the town does have a reasonable selection of upmarket options.

Amarin Lagoon Hotel 52/299 Thanon Phra Ong Khao ⓣ055 220999, ⓕ055 220944. One of the poshest places in Phitsanulok, this low-rise hotel is prettily set in landscaped gardens and has 300 attractively furnished rooms with air-con and TV, plus a swimming pool, sauna, Internet access and three restaurants. It's 3km east of the town centre, but there's a hotel shuttle-bus service, and city buses #1 and #2 run past the entrance. ❺–❾

Amarin Nakhon Hotel 3/1 Thanon Chaophraya ⓣ055 219069, ⓕ055 219500. Very central and good-value tourist-oriented hotel, with dated but comfortable air-con rooms; those on the uppermost of the hotel's eleven floors enjoy panoramic views of the city. ❸

Lithai Guest House 73/1–5 Thanon Phayalithai ⓣ055 219629, ⓕ055 219627. Centrally located, and sharing the Lithai Building with a travel agency and a couple of restaurants, this is a recommended lower- to mid-range option, offering big, clean, bright rooms with fan and shared bathrooms or en-suite air-con options with cable TV. Fan and shared bathroom ❷, air-con ❸

London Hotel 21–22 Soi Buddhabucha (Phuttabucha) 1 ⓣ055 225145. The cheapest place in town, this converted family home has lots of character and just eight tiny, cosy, fan rooms, all painted to a funky mint-green and yellow colour scheme and all sharing bathrooms. ❶

Pailyn Hotel 38 Thanon Boromtrailoknat ⓣ055 252411, ⓦwww.pailynhotel.phitsanulok.com. Popular, long-running tourist hotel, and the best of the central options, where many of the sizeable air-con rooms in the thirteen-storey tower offer long-range river views from their balconies. It's handy for Wat Mahathat, and there's a free ride to transport terminals. Also has two good restaurants and regular live music. Served by city bus #6. ❺–❻

Phitsanulok Youth Hostel 38 Thanon Sanambin ⓣ055 242060, ⓦwww.tyha.org. Set in a large compound full of greenery and antique wooden doors, panels and shutters, this place has lots of atmosphere despite being a bit rough round the edges. The fan rooms are uniquely designed with wood panelling, antique furniture and idiosyncratic bathrooms; air-con versions are slightly less characterful. There's also a B120 dorm as well, and free breakfasts. Youth-hostel membership is not required. The hostel is a 1.5km walk from the centre: take bus #4 from the train station and get off outside the *Phitsanulok Thani Hotel* next door; from the regional bus station take any bus to the train station, then a #4. Fan ❷, air-con ❸

The Town

Typically for a riverside town, "Phi-lok", as it's often nicknamed, is long and narrow, and – while the centre is small enough to cover on foot – its two main sights lie at opposite extremities. Huge swathes of the town were destroyed by fire in 1957, but Phitsanulok's history harks back to a heyday in the late fourteenth and early fifteenth centuries when, with Sukhothai waning in power, it rose to prominence as the favoured home of the crumbling capital's last rulers. After supremacy was finally wrested by the emerging state of Ayutthaya in 1438, Phitsanulok was made a provincial capital, subsequently becoming a strategic army base during Ayutthaya's wars with the Burmese, and adoptive home to Ayutthayan princes. The most famous of these was **Naresuan**, a notoriously courageous warrior who was governor of Phitsanulok before he assumed the Ayutthayan crown in 1590. The ruins of Naresuan's Chandra Palace, where both he and his younger brother Akkathasaroth were born, are currently under excavation in the grounds of a former school northwest of the bridge that bears his name; the tramway tour makes a stop there.

Wat Mahathat (Wat Yai)

Officially called Wat Phra Si Ratana Mahathat (and known locally as **Wat Mahathat** or **Wat Yai**), this fourteenth-century temple was one of the few buildings miraculously to escape Phitsanulok's great 1957 fire. Standing at the northern limit of the town on the east bank of the Nan River (and served by city buses #1, #5, #8 and #11), it receives a constant stream of worshippers eager to pay homage to the highly revered Buddha image inside the viharn. Because the image is so sacred, a **dress code** is strictly enforced here – shorts and skimpy clothing are definitely forbidden – and there's an entrance fee of B40.

Delicately inlaid mother-of-pearl doors mark the entrance to the viharn, opening onto the low-ceilinged interior, painted mostly in dark red and black, with gold leaf motifs, and dimly lit by narrow slits along the upper walls. In the centre of the far wall sits the much-cherished **Phra Buddha Chinnarat**: late Sukhothai in style and probably cast in the fourteenth century, this gleaming, polished-bronze Buddha is one of the finest of the period and, for Thais, second in importance only to the Emerald Buddha in Bangkok. Tales of the statue's miraculous powers have fuelled the devotion of generations of pilgrims – one legend tells how the Buddha wept tears of blood when Ayutthayan princes arrived in Phitsanulok to oust the last Sukhothai regent. The Phra Buddha Chinnarat stands out among Thai Buddha images because of its *mandorla*, the flame-like halo that symbolizes extreme radiance and frames the upper body and head like a chair-back, tapering off into nagas at the arm rests. There's an almost perfect replica of the Phitsanulok original in Bangkok's Marble Temple, commissioned by Rama V in 1901. Every February, Phitsanulok honours the Phra Buddha Chinnarat with a week-long **festival**, which features *likay* folk-theatre performances and dancing.

Behind the viharn, the gilded mosaic **prang** houses the holy relic that gives the wat its name (Mahathat means "Great Relic Stupa") – though which particular remnant lies entombed here is unclear – and the cloister surrounding both structures contains a gallery of Buddha images of different styles (Wed–Sun 9am–5.30pm; free).

The east bank

South of Wat Mahathat and Naresuan Bridge, **the east bank** of the Nan River has been landscaped into a pleasant riverside park that runs all the way down to Akkathasaroth (Ekathosarot) Bridge. There are no exceptional attractions along its course, but you may want to make a stop at **Wat Rajburana**, just south of Naresuan Bridge and across the road from the river, which also survived the 1957 fire. Recognizable by the dilapidated brick-based chedi that stands in the compound, the wat is chiefly of interest for the *Ramayana* murals (see p.137) that cover the interior walls of the bot. Quite well preserved, they were probably painted in the mid-nineteenth century. Traditional Thai massage is available in the open-sided *sala* at the heart of the wat compound.

The most attractive feature of the riverside park is the **Floating House Museum** (open all hours; free), about 500m south of Wat Rajburana and diagonally across from the post office. Understated in style and completely empty, but beautifully fashioned from teak wood, it replicates a (classy) traditional river home, comprising three *sala* connected by a roofed walkway, walls of split reeds, carved window frames and elegant wood-panelled interiors. The house floats in a lily pond beside the road, high above the river. Akkathasaroth Bridge marks the riverside park's southern boundary, beyond which the bank is dominated by the permanent stalls of the **night bazaar**, *the* place for locals and tourists to shop for bargain-priced fashions and a cheap meal.

The Folklore Museum, Buddha Foundry and Garden Bird Park

Across town on Thanon Wisut Kasat, southeast of the train station, the **Sergeant Major Thawee Folklore Museum** (Jatawee Buranaket; Tues–Sun 8.30am–4.30pm; B50) puts a different slant on the region's culture; its fascinating look at traditional rural life makes this one of the best ethnology museums in the country. Local bus #8 will drop you close by. The collection, which is housed in a series of wooden pavilions, belongs to former sergeant major Dr Thawee, who has pursued a lifelong personal campaign to preserve and document a way of life that's gradually disappearing. Highlights include the reconstructed kitchen, veranda and birthing room of a typical village house, known as a "tied house" because its split bamboo walls are literally tied together with rattan cane, and an exceptionally comprehensive gallery of traps – dozens of specialized contraptions designed to ensnare everything from cockroaches to birds perched on water buffaloes' backs. The weaving and natural dyes exhibition is also worth dwelling on, as is the blow-by-blow account – complete with photos – of the routine castration of bullocks and water buffalo.

Cross the road from the museum and walk south about 50m for a rare chance to see Buddha images being forged at the **Buranathai Buddha Bronze-Casting Foundry**, located at 26/43 Thanon Wisut Kasat. The foundry, which also belongs to Dr Thawee, is open during working hours (usually daily 8am-5pm) and anyone can drop in to watch the stages involved in moulding and casting a Buddha image. It's a fairly lengthy procedure and best assimilated from the illustrated explanations inside the foundry. Images of all sizes are made here, from thirty-centimetre-high household icons to mega-models destined for wealthy temples. The Buddha business is quite a profitable one: worshippers can earn a great deal of merit by donating a Buddha statue, particularly a precious one, to their local wat, so demand rarely slackens. There's a gift shop on site.

Adjacent to the Buddha Foundry, and accessible from it, as well as via Soi 17, **Garden Birds of Thailand** (*Suan Nok*; daily 8.30am-5pm; B100; Ⓦwww.geocities.com/Thaibirdgarden) is Dr Thawee's most recent enthusiasm: a zoo containing hundreds of breathtakingly beautiful Thai birds, each one segregated and informatively described. It's an astonishing collection that offers a unique chance to admire at close range such beauties as a silver pheasant, an Asian fairy bluebird, and a rhinoceros hornbill, as well as highly endangered species such as the jambu fruit dove and the helmeted hornbill. As is often the case in such places, however, the cages are very small and few of the birds are in pairs or groups.

The Green Route

East of Phitsanulok, Highway 12 has been tagged **"the Green Route"** by TAT because it gives access to several national parks and waterfalls and provides an excuse for a pleasant day or two's excursion from the city. TAT has produced a sketch map outlining car and motorbike routes. **Phu Hin Rongkla National Park** (Ⓣ055 233527, Ⓦwww.dnp.go.th/National_park.asp; B200), about 100km northeast of Phitsanulok (turn north off Highway 12 at kilometre-stone 68, on to Route 2013, then east on to Route 2331 to reach the visitor centre), was the notorious stronghold of the insurgent Communist Party of Thailand from 1967–1982 and still contains some relics from that period, though its short trails through montane forests and natural rock gardens are now its main point of interest. Or consider organizing a day's mountain-biking in **Thung Salaeng Luang National Park** (Ⓣ055 268019, Ⓦwww.dnp.go.th/National_park.asp; B200), 82km east of Phitsanulok (turn south off Highway 12 at kilometre-stone 79). Thung Salaeng is famous for the flowers that carpet its grasslands after the end of the rainy season (the flower meadows are only open from October 23 into December) and has two designated mountain-bike trails as well as rafting opportunities: see Listings on p.290 for details of the mountain-bike rental and rafting outlet in Phitsanulok.

The Dhamma Abha **Vipassana meditation centre** (Ⓣ055 268049, Ⓦwww.dhamma.org/schthaia.htm), which holds two ten-day meditation courses every month, is also in this area, in Ban Huayplu (turn north off Highway 12 at km-stone 49); see Basics p.66 or details.

Eating

In the evening, **night market** stalls set up within the night bazaar along the east bank of the river, south of Akkathasaroth Bridge. Fish and mussels are a speciality, but the most famous dish is "flying vegetables", in which strong-tasting morning-glory (*phak bung*) is stir-fried before being tossed flamboyantly in the air towards the plate-wielding waiter or customer.

Ban Khun Por Opposite the *Amarin Nakhon* hotel on Thanon Chao Phraya, just south off Thanon Naresuan. This cosy, parlour-style dining room is full of curios (sepia-tinted royal photos, old telephones, collectors' porcelain) and serves an impressively long mid-priced menu (most dishes B60–90). The focus is on Thai food, with lots of spicy *yam* salads – wing-bean, glass-noodle and ear-mushroom to name a few – masses of seafood and stir-fries, chicken in pandanus leaves, plus a selection of royal Thai desserts. Japanese dishes, including sashimi, also feature prominently. Daily 11am–2pm & 6–11pm.

Fah Keh Rah Just east of the railway line on Thanon Phra Ong Dam. A small, family-run Muslim restaurant that specializes in *lassi* yoghurt drinks and thick *roti* breads served with ladlefuls of the daily curry (from B20). Shuts around 7pm.

Karaket "Thai Food" Thanon Phaylithai. Tasty Thai curry shop, where you make your selection from the metal trays set out on the pavement trestle, then eat in air-conditioned comfort inside. Very popular for family takeaways. Most dishes B20. Shuts around 8.30pm.

Raan Ahaan Mangsawirat "Vegetarian Food" Thanon Sithamtraipidok, north around the corner from the TAT Road. There are two tiny vegetarian restaurants here, almost next door to each and both signed "Vegetarian Food". Food in both places is exceptionally cheap (from B5 a serving) and consists of a plate of brown rice plus spoonfuls from the array of veggie stir-fries and curries. The one closest to TAT also does veggie noodle soups to order. Daily 6am–3pm.

Song Kwae (signed "The Song Kheaw") Thanon Wangchan. One of several long-running floating restaurants on the west bank of the river, this place has a nice atmosphere, pleasing river views and a decent menu of fresh fish and seafood (mostly B60–80), plus standard Thai-Chinese dishes accompanied by rice. Daily 11am–11pm.

Tui Phochana Thanon Phyalithai. One of several cheap Thai curry shops on this road, this one is famous for its curries made with jackfruit (B20–40). Shuts about 7pm.

Listings

Airline The Thai Airways office is near TAT on Thanon Boromtrailoknat ☎055 242971-2; tickets also available from the tour operators listed below.

Car rental Budget and Avis both have desks at the airport (see p.286), and Able Tour (see below) is a Budget agent. For hiring a car with a driver, see "Tour operators" below.

Emergencies For all emergencies, call the tourist police on the free 24hr phoneline ☎1155, or contact them at their office north of Wat Mahathat on Thanon Akkathasaroth ☎055 245358.

Exchange There are banks with money-changing facilities and ATMs on Thanon Naresuan and Thanon Boromtrailokanat. The out-of-hours exchange booth on the corner of Naresuan and Chao Phraya roads opens Mon–Fri 5–8pm, Sat & Sun 8.30am–noon, 1–5pm & 6–8pm.

Hospitals Both Rattanavej Hospital on Thanon Phra Ong Dam ☎055 210819-21, and Inter Medical Hospital, Thanon Boromtrailokanat ☎055 284228–32 are private hospitals; and there's also the government-run Buddha Chinnarat Hospital, Thanon Sithamtraipidok ☎055 219844–52.

Internet access Catnet terminals inside the telephone office on Thanon Bhudhabucha (daily 8am–6pm) and at several private Internet centres in town (see map).

Left luggage At the train station (24hr; B10/item).

Mail The GPO is near the river on Thanon Bhudhabucha.

Motorbike rental At PN Motor, inside the bus terminal on Thanon Mittraphap ☎055 242424; around B200 per day.

Telephones The CAT overseas telephone office is next to the GPO on Thanon Bhudhabucha (daily 8am–4.30pm).

Tour operators Able Tour and Travel (Mon–Fri 8am–6pm, Sat 8am–4.30pm; ☎055 242206, Ⓔabletour_phs@yahoo.com), near the TAT office on Thanon Boromtrailokanat, sells air tickets and can arrange minivans to Sukhothai or Kamphaeng Phet (B1200, plus B1000 for optional guide). Lithai Travel at 73/1-5 Thanon Phyalithai (☎055 219626) also sells air tickets. For mountain-bike and rafting trips in Thung Salaeng Luang National Park, contact the Samai Klinruk bike shop and Nature Camp tour office (☎& Ⓕ055 213541) at 193/6 Mu 5 Tambon Hua Ro, which is about 1.5km north of Topland Plaza on the east side of Thanon Akkathasaroth, opposite a big sports complex.

Sukhothai

For a brief but brilliant period (1238–1376), the walled city of **SUKHOTHAI** presided as the capital of Thailand, creating the legacy of a unified nation of Thai peoples and a phenomenal artistic heritage. Now an impressive assembly of elegant ruins, the Old City, 58km northwest of Phitsanulok, has been preserved as **Sukhothai Historical Park** and is one of Thailand's most visited ancient sites.

There are only a few accommodation options near the historical park, and not many other facilities, so most travellers stay in so-called **NEW SUKHOTHAI**, a modern market town 12km to the east, which has good travel links with the Old City and is also better for restaurants and long-distance bus connections. Straddling the Yom River, it's a small, friendly town, used to seeing tourists but by no means overrun with them. The new town also makes a peaceful and convenient base for visiting Ramkhamhaeng National Park, as well as the outlying ruins of Si Satchanalai and Kamphaeng Phet.

Sukhothai Historical Park is the most famous place in Thailand to celebrate **Loy Krathong**, the festival of light, and the ruins are the focus of a spectacular festival held over nine nights around the full moon of the twelfth lunar month (Oct/Nov). Not only are the pond surfaces of the Old City aglow with candles, but the ruins are wreathed in lights and illuminated during a nightly *son et lumière* performance at Wat Mahathat, and there are firework displays at nearby Wat Trapang Ngoen, plus lots of parades, concerts and street-theatre shows; see the colour section for more on Loy Krathong. All accommodation gets packed out during the festival, so book in advance unless you're willing to sleep sardine-style on a guest-house floor.

Arrival and transport

New Sukhothai has direct bus connections with many major provincial capitals and makes a good staging point between Chiang Mai and Bangkok. All buses use the Sukhothai **bus terminal**, located about 3km west of New Sukhothai's town centre, just off the bypass. Despite what obstructive samlor drivers might tell you, it is possible to **walk** from the bus terminal to some accommodation – *Number 4*, *J&J* and *99* guest houses – in New Sukhothai: see relevant guest house accounts for details. For transport to other New Sukhothai guest houses, there are public **songthaews** (B10, or B30–40 if you're the only passenger), motorbike taxis (B30) and tuk-tuks (B30), or B80–100 to the Old City; rates are posted on the wall. If taking the public songthaew, either get off at the songthaew stop for the Old City, just before crossing the river, or in front of Wat Ratchathani, just after crossing the river; none of the New Sukhothai guest houses is more than ten minutes' walk from the river. There's a small place offering backpackers' rooms (B100) in the bus station compound, where you can also leave luggage (B10/day). Note, however, that if you're arriving by bus **from Mae Sot or Tak** you will pass via the Old City before reaching New Sukhothai's bus terminal, so get off there if you're intending to stay in the Old City.

A more comfortable, though not necessarily faster, option is to take the **train** from Bangkok, Chiang Mai or anywhere in between as far as Phitsanulok and then change onto one of the half-hourly buses to New Sukhothai (1hr; for details see p.286). This bus service also makes Sukhothai feasible as a day-trip from Phitsanulok, and vice versa.

You can also **fly** to Sukhothai from Bangkok and Chiang Mai with Bangkok Airways; the airport is about 25km north of town (half-way to Si Satchanalai),

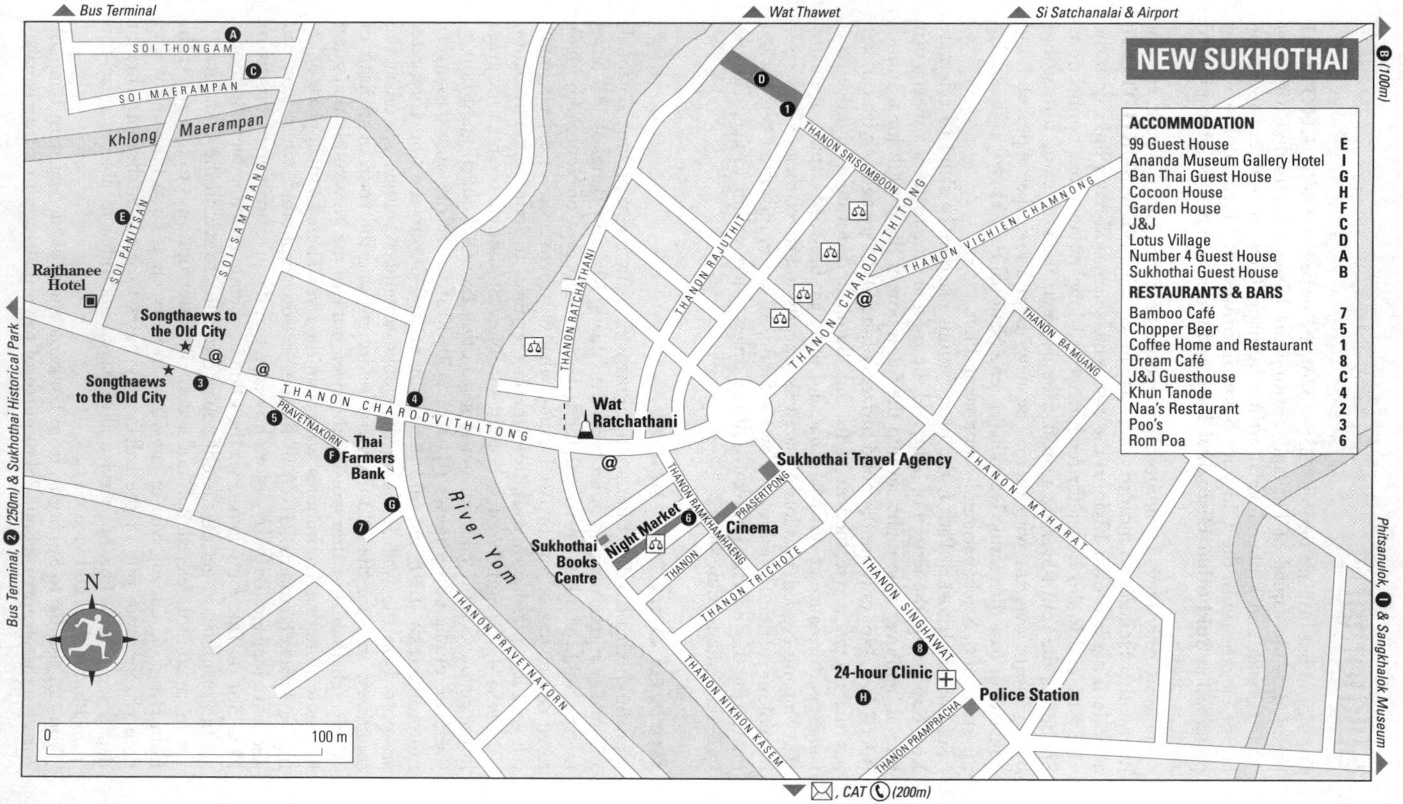

NEW SUKHOTHAI

ACCOMMODATION	
99 Guest House	E
Ananda Museum Gallery Hotel	I
Ban Thai Guest House	G
Cocoon House	H
Garden House	F
J&J	C
Lotus Village	D
Number 4 Guest House	A
Sukhothai Guest House	B
RESTAURANTS & BARS	
Bamboo Café	7
Chopper Beer	5
Coffee Home and Restaurant	1
Dream Café	8
J&J Guesthouse	C
Khun Tanode	4
Naa's Restaurant	2
Poo's	3
Rom Poa	6

Bus Terminal
Wat Thawet
Si Satchanalai & Airport
B (100m)
Phitsanulok, I & Sangkhalok Museum
✉, CAT ✆ (200m)
Bus Terminal, 2 (250m) & Sukhothai Historical Park

SOI THONGAM
SOI MAERAMPAN
Khlong Maerampan
SOI PANITSAN
SOI SAMARANG
Rajthanee Hotel
Songthaews to the Old City
Songthaews to the Old City
THANON CHARODVITHITONG
PRAVETNAKORN
Thai Farmers Bank
River Yom
THANON PRAVETNAKORN
THANON RATCHATHANI
Wat Ratchathani
THANON RAJUTHIT
THANON SRISOMBOON
THANON CHARODVITHITONG
THANON VICHIEN CHAMNONG
THANON BA MUANG
THANON MAHARAT
Sukhothai Travel Agency
PRASERTPONG
Cinema
THANON RAMKHAMHAENG
Night Market
Sukhothai Books Centre
THANON
THANON TRICHOTE
THANON NIKHON KASEM
THANON SINGHAWAT
24-hour Clinic
Police Station
THANON PRAMPRACHA
N
0 100 m

and shuttle buses transfer passengers to hotels and guest houses for B120 per person; the return shuttle to the airport departs from the Sukhothai Travel Agency only (see p.303), though most guest houses offer a transfer service direct to the airport for about B200 per person. *J&J* guest house offers transport to Phitsanulok airport for B1000 per car. Passengers departing from Sukhothai Airport are subject to a B200 tax (as this is a privately run airport). The local Bangkok Airways office (ⓣ055 647224) is located here, though you can also buy air tickets from the more central Sukhothai Travel Agency (see Listings).

For **local transport**, frequent songthaews shuttle between New Sukhothai and the Old City 12km away, departing from a signed depot west of the river on Thanon Charodvithitong (every 15min during daylight hours; 15min; B15). **Cycling** is also a good way of getting around, and bikes are available for rent in both New Sukhothai and the historical park, see Listings for details.

Accommodation

New Sukhothai has a particularly good selection of guest-house **accommodation**. Though most travellers opt to commute to the Old City for sightseeing, staying on the edge of the historical park makes it easy to revisit the ruins at sunrise and sunset, even if it is a songthaew ride away from most restaurants, markets and shops.

New Sukhothai

99 Guest House 234/6 Soi Panitsan (Panichsan) ⓣ055 611315, ⓔninetynine_gh@yahoo.com. Tiny, homely guest house run by clued-up tour guide and restaurateur Naa and her family. There are just five double rooms (with fan and shared bathroom), plus a spacious, typically Thai seating area downstairs, filled with axe pillows. Guests are welcome to join the family meals and Naa also runs cooking classes (see p.303). *99* is a 10-minute walk from the town centre, following signs from the bus stop for the Old City. It's also about 10 minutes' walk from the bus station: an indistinct track runs from just in front of the main bus terminal building (step outside the terminal building as if heading to the highway and with your back to the terminal, it's on the left, between the spirit house and the first shop); within 100m you'll see signs for *Number 4* and 200m beyond that, having passed through a field, turn left when you reach the tarmacked road and follow signs. ❶

Ananda Museum Gallery Hotel Beside the Sangkhalok Museum on the bypass, about 2km east of the town centre ⓣ055 622428, ⓦwww.ananda-hotel.com. Thirty-four-room boutique hotel that's stylishly furnished with *teen jok* textiles from Si Satchanalai and locally made furniture and artefacts, though the location is not ideal and the outlook is dominated by the highway (not all rooms have much of a window). Nonetheless it's the most modern of Sukhothai's poshest options and is right next to the ceramics museum. There's a spa and restaurant on site. ❼–❽

Ban Thai Guest House 38 Thanon Pravetnakorn ⓣ055 610163, ⓔbanthai_guesthouse@yahoo.com. Set in a garden on the west bank of the Yom River, this comfortable budget option comprises several attractive wood-panelled rooms with shared bathroom in a small purpose-built house with a terrace out front, plus some nice, idiosyncratic wooden bungalows with private bathroom and the option of air-con. Home-made yoghurt is a breakfast favourite, and there's a long menu of Thai and Western main courses too. ❶–❷

Cocoon House 86/1 Thanon Singhawat ⓣ055 612081, ⓕ055 622157. Set way back off the street behind its sister outfit *Dream Café*, this collection of rooms and bungalows is full of arty touches, from the individually decorated interiors to the romantically designed garden that's dotted with curios and caged birds and is prettily lit at night. Service can be a little haphazard however. Choose between air-con rooms in a small house and large, stylish bungalows. ❹–❻

Garden House Thanon Pravetnakorn ⓣ055 611395. Characterful, well-priced guest house offering rooms with shared bathrooms in the wood-floored area above the restaurant, plus cute wooden en-suite bungalows (fan or air-con) with nice verandas strung down the long, narrow garden path. Room with shared bathroom ❶, fan bungalows ❷, air-con bungalows ❸

J&J 122/1 Soi Maerampan, off Thanon Charodvithitong ⓣ055 620095, ⓔjjguest@hotmail.com. Very traveller-oriented place offering en-suite fan and air-con rooms in a terraced row, detached air-con bungalows, plus a couple of deluxe versions. The restaurant bakes its own delicious bread, there's a book exchange, and the Belgian-Thai managers run well-reviewed tours to nearby national parks (see p.301). Within walking distance of the bus station (see *99 Guest House*, above), or a 10-minute walk from the town centre, following signs from the bus stop for the Old City. Fan rooms ❷, air-con rooms ❸, bungalows ❹–❺

Lotus Village 170 Thanon Ratchathani, also accessible from Thanon Rajuthit ⓣ055 621484, ⓦwww.lotus-village.com. Stylish, mid-priced accommodation in a traditional Thai compound of beautiful teak houses set around a mature tropical garden with lotus ponds. Most rooms have polished teak floors and all are elegantly furnished; some are in self-contained bungalows, some share bathrooms (four rooms per house, with one bathroom between them) and a few have air-con. Internet rates include breakfast, those quoted here don't. Run by a well-informed Thai-French couple who organize tours around the region. Reception shuts at 9pm. Shared bathroom ❷, fan bungalows ❹, air-con ❺–❻

Number 4 Guest House Soi Thongam ⓣ055 610165. Partly managed by *99 Guest House* (ask there if you get no answer here), this place comprises ten charming, if simple, wood and bamboo bungalows, each with a bathroom and a veranda (some also have daybeds). It's within 5 minutes' walk of the bus station (see *99 Guest House*, above), or a 10-minute walk from the town centre, following signs from the bus stop for the Old City. ❷

Sukhothai Guest House 68 Thanon Vichien Chamnong, about 200m walk northeast from the junction with Thanon Ba Muang ⓣ055 610453, ⓦwww.sukhothaiguesthouse.com. This welcoming if rather compact compound of 12 terraced rooms – cocooned amidst masses of plants and set back off the street – is run by a genial Indian-Thai family. Accommodation consists of several clusters of terraced, en-suite, fan and air-con rooms; there's a restaurant and Internet access, and staff can arrange massages, motorbike rental and cooking classes. They also run tours to the rarely visited temple and bat caves of Ban Dan Lan Hoi, west of the Old City. Phone (until 10pm) for a free pick-up from the bus station. Fan ❸, air-con ❺

The Old City and around

Old City Guest House Opposite the entrance to the museum on Thanon Charodvithitong, just outside the central zone ⓣ055 697515. Thai-oriented guest house offering a big range of accommodation options, from small, rather dark but very cheap rooms with shared bathrooms to large, quite plush, air-con en suites with TV. Fan ❶, air-con ❸–❹

Orchid Hibiscus Guest House About 2km south-west of the main entrance to the historical park, on Route 1272 ⓣ081 962 7698, ⓦwww.asiatravel.com/thailand/orchid_hibiscus/index.html. Delightfully tranquil Italian-Thai-managed garden haven partly surrounded by fields. The eight brick bungalows are furnished with four-poster beds, air-con (and mosquito nets) and ranged around a pretty tropical flower garden and swimming pool. It also has a couple of deluxe teak houses with separate living rooms plus two four-bed family houses for rent. Rates include breakfast. Bungalows ❺, teak/family house ❻

Pailyn Sukhothai Hotel 4km east of the historical park at 10/1 Thanon Charodvithitong ⓣ055 633336, ⓕ055 613317. Fairly upmarket if rather old-fashioned package-oriented hotel with 200-plus comfortable air-con rooms plus a swimming pool, sauna and disco on site. ❺–❻

Vitoon Guest House Opposite the entrance to the museum on Thanon Charodvithitong, just outside the central zone ⓣ055 697045, ⓔkok_2@hotmail.com. Sprucely kept, very clean rooms with fan and bath in a rather characterless purpose-built little block, plus a separate building containing more appealing, wood-panelled, air-con rooms with TV. Rents bicycles and has a restaurant and Internet acess. Fan ❷, air-con ❹

Sukhothai Historical Park (Muang Kao Sukhothai)

In its prime, the Old City boasted around forty separate temple complexes and covered an area of about 70 square kilometres between the Yom River and the low range of hills to the west. At its heart stood the walled royal city, protected by a series of moats and ramparts. **SUKHOTHAI HISTORICAL PARK**, or **MUANG KAO SUKHOTHAI** (daily 6am–6pm), covers all this area and is

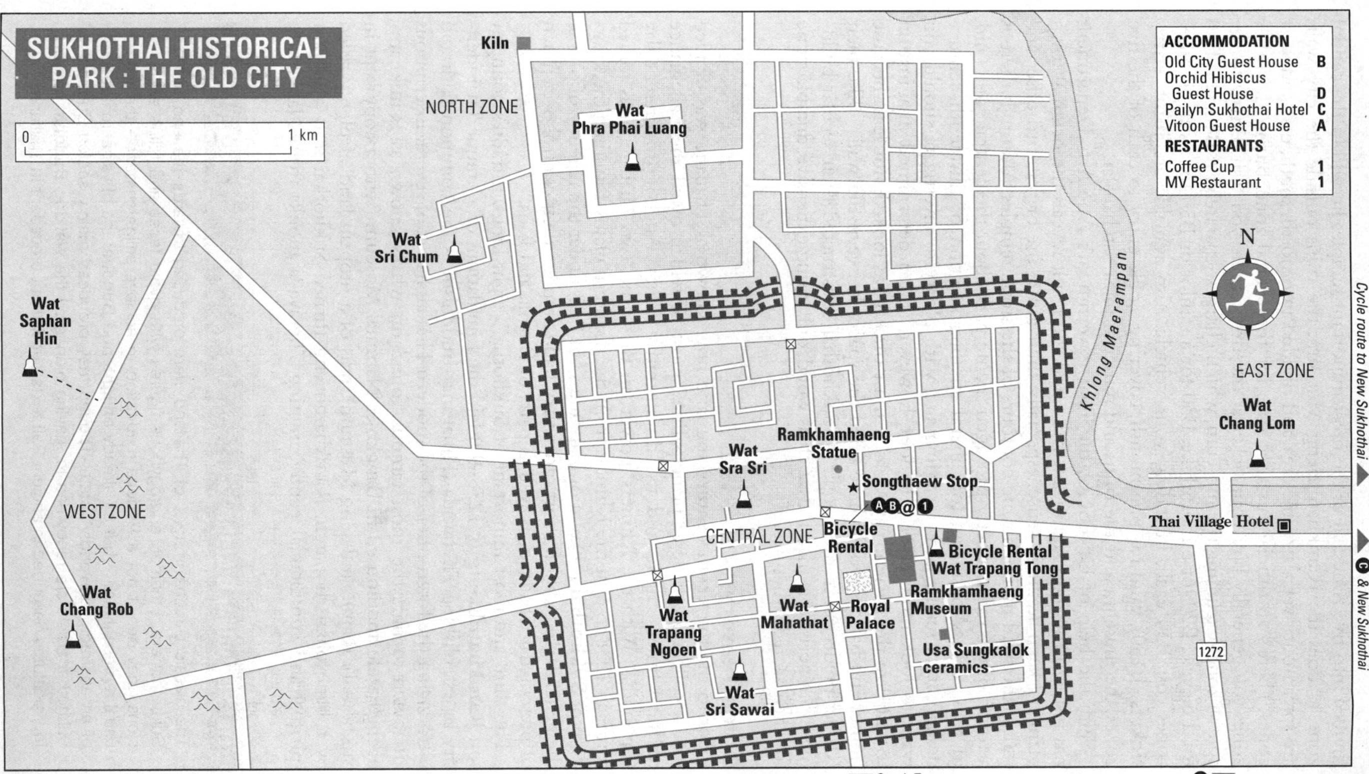
SUKHOTHAI HISTORICAL PARK : THE OLD CITY
0
1 km
Tak
Kiln
NORTH ZONE
Wat Phra Phai Luang
Wat Sri Chum
Wat Saphan Hin
WEST ZONE
Wat Chang Rob
ACCOMMODATION
Old City Guest House B
Orchid Hibiscus Guest House D
Pailyn Sukhothai Hotel C
Vitoon Guest House A
RESTAURANTS
Coffee Cup 1
MV Restaurant 1
N
Khlong Maerampan
EAST ZONE
Wat Chang Lom
Cycle route to New Sukhothai
C & New Sukhothai
Thai Village Hotel
1272
Ramkhamhaeng Statue
Wat Sra Sri
Songthaew Stop
A B @ 1
CENTRAL ZONE
Bicycle Rental
Bicycle Rental
Wat Trapang Tong
Ramkhamhaeng Museum
Wat Trapang Ngoen
Wat Mahathat
Royal Palace
Usa Sungkalok ceramics
Wat Sri Sawai
South Zone
D

divided into five zones: all of the most important temples lie within the central zone, as does the Ramkhamhaeng Museum; the ruins outside the city walls are spread out over a sizeable area and divided into north, south, east and west zones. There's an official entrance gate for the central zone, but in the other zones you generally buy your ticket at the first temple you visit. **Entry** to the central zone (excluding the museum, which charges separately) is B40, plus B10 for a bicycle, B20 for a motorbike, B30 for a samlor or B50 for a car; all other zones cost B30 each, including your vehicle. Also available are **joint entry tickets** (B150), valid for one month, covering single entry to each of the five zones, the museum and the ruins and museum in Si Satchanalai.

With the help of UNESCO, the Thai government's Fine Arts Department has restored the most significant ruins and the result reveals the original town planners' keen aesthetic sense, especially their astute use of water to offset and reflect the solid monochrome contours of the stone temples. Although there is a touch of the too perfectly packaged theme park about the central zone (and, in some critics' opinions, too liberal an interpretation of thirteenth-century design), it's a serene and rewarding site, with plenty to investigate should you want to look more closely. It does, however, take a determined imagination to visualize the ancient capital as it must once have looked, not least because houses and palaces would have filled the spaces between the wats – like their Khmer predecessors, the people of Sukhothai constructed their secular buildings from perishable materials such as wood, only using expensive, durable stone for their sacred structures.

Some history

Prior to the thirteenth century, the land now known as Thailand was divided into a collection of petty principalities, most of which owed their allegiance to the Khmer empire and its administrative centre Angkor (in present-day Cambodia). With the Khmers' power on the wane, two Thai generals joined forces in 1238 to oust the Khmers from the northern plains, founding the kingdom of **Sukhothai** ("Dawn of Happiness" in Pali) under the regency of one of the generals, Intradit. In short order they had extended their control over much of present-day Thailand, as well as parts of Burma and Laos.

The third and most important of Sukhothai's eight kings, Intradit's youngest son **Ramkhamhaeng** (c.1278–99) laid the foundations of a unique Thai identity by establishing Theravada (Hinayana) Buddhism as the common faith and introducing the forerunner of the modern Thai alphabet; of several inscriptions attributed to him, the most famous, found on what's known as Ramkhamhaeng's Stele and housed in Bangkok's National Museum (with a copy kept in Sukhothai's Ramkhamhaeng Museum), tells of a utopian land of plenty ruled by a benevolent monarch. Ramkhamhaeng turned Sukhothai into a vibrant spiritual and commercial centre, inviting Theravada monks from Nakhon Si

The Sukhothai Buddha

The classic Buddha images of Thailand were produced towards the end of the Sukhothai era. Ethereal, androgynous figures with ovoid faces and feline expressions, they depict not a Buddha meditating to achieve enlightenment – the more usual representation – but an already **enlightened Buddha**: the physical realization of an abstract, "unworldly" state. Though they produced mainly seated Buddhas, Sukhothai artists are renowned for having pioneered the **walking Buddha**, one of four postures described in ancient Pali texts but without precedent in Thailand.

Thammarat and Sri Lanka to instruct his people in the religion that was to supplant Khmer Hinduism and Mahayana Buddhism, and encouraging the growth of a ceramics industry with the help of Chinese potters. By all accounts, Ramkhamhaeng's successors lacked his kingly qualities and so, by the second half of the fourteenth century, Sukhothai had become a vassal state of the newly emerged kingdom of Ayutthaya; finally, in 1438, it was forced to relinquish all vestiges of its independent identity.

Practicalities

Songthaews from New Sukhothai (every 15min; 15min; B15) stop just east of the museum and central zone entrance point. Alternatively you can **cycle from New Sukhothai** to the historical park along a peaceful canalside track. To pick up the track, start from the bridge in New Sukhothai, cycle west along the main road to the historical park for about 3km until you reach a temple (with an impressive gold and white decorated gateway) on the right-hand side. A narrow track between this temple and the adjacent Caltex petrol station takes you via a small bridge to a track that runs along the north bank of Khlong Maerampan, nearly all the way to the Old City. It's an easy ride of about 14km, through very pleasant, and frequently shaded, traditional canalside neighbourhoods. Near the end of the ride you cross a major road to pick up the final stretch of track; then, after reaching the elephant statues at the ruins of Wat Chang Lom (see p.300), cross the bridge on your left to regain the main road into the historical park, about 1.5km away. Any New Sukhothai guest house can help you with bicycle rental, and both *Number 4 Guest House* and *Ban Thai* can provide maps of the khlong route.

Even if you don't arrive at the Old City on one, it's a good idea to **rent a bicycle** there for touring the ruins: outlets near the songthaew stop rent them out for B20. Alternatively, you could hop onto the **trolley bus** that, during busy times only, starts from near the museum and takes groups round the central zone for B20 per person. Tuk-tuks at the New Sukhothai bus station and in the town offer a four-hour tour of the ruins plus return transport for B450.

There's a **currency exchange** booth (daily 8.30am–12.30pm) inside the park, next to the museum, and several small **restaurants** serving both Thai and Western food near the songthaew drop on the main road, including *Coffee Cup* and *MV Restaurant*. *Coffee Cup* and *Vitoon Guest House* both have **Internet** access. For details of accommodation close to the historical park, see p.294. Several shops just outside the park entrance sell reproduction antique furniture and ceramics, but for a better range of **traditional style ceramics**, especially copies of historic Sangkhalok and Sukhothai designs and glazes, visit the Usa Sungkalok Sukhothai ceramics factory, which is located outside the central zone on the narrow road that runs between the museum and Wat Trapang Tong.

Ramkhamhaeng National Museum

The well-presented **Ramkhamhaeng National Museum** (daily 9am–4pm; B30; Ⓦwww.thailandmuseum.com), located just outside the main entrance to the central zone, features several illuminating exhibitions and contains some of the finest **sculptures** and reliefs found at the temples of Sukhothai's Old City and nearby Si Satchanalai. Outstanding artefacts in the downstairs gallery of the main building include the 14th-century bronze statue of a walking Buddha, and the large Buddha head that was found at Wat Phra Phai Luang in the north zone of Sukhothai Historical Park. Also here is a useful guide to the many different **stucco motifs** that once decorated every Sukhothai-era temple, along with a copy of one of the finest local examples of stucco relief, depicting the Buddha being sheltered by a naga, whose original is still in situ at Si Satchanalai's Wat Chedi Jet Taew. The wide-ranging section on Ramkhamhaeng's famous **stele** features a complete translation of the inscription, plus a detailed look at the origins and evolution of the original "Tai" script. The upstairs gallery concentrates on **Sangkhalok ceramics** and provides a much more informative introduction than the kiln museum in Si Satchanalai.

The central zone

The **central zone** covers three square kilometres so a bike is recommended, though not essential. Of the eleven ruins here, Wat Mahathat is the one that should definitely not be missed.

A modern **statue** of King Ramkhamhaeng sits to the right just inside the zone entrance: cast in bronze, he holds a palm-leaf book in his right hand – a reference to his role as founder of the modern Thai alphabet. Close by stands a large bronze **bell**, a replica of the one referred to on the famous stele (also reproduced here), which told how the king had the bell erected in front of his palace so that any citizen with a grievance could come by and strike it, whereupon the king himself would emerge to investigate the problem.

Wat Mahathat

Turn left inside the gate for Sukhothai's most important site, the enormous **Wat Mahathat** compound, packed with the remains of scores of monuments and surrounded, like a city within a city, by a moat. This was the spiritual focus of the city, the king's temple and symbol of his power; successive regents, eager to add their own stamp, restored and expanded it so that by the time it was abandoned in the sixteenth century it numbered ten viharns, one bot, eight mondops and nearly two hundred small chedis. Looking at the wat from ground level, it's hard to distinguish the main structures from the minor ruins. Remnants of the viharns and the bot dominate the present scene, their soldierly ranks of pillars, which formerly supported wooden roofs, directing the eye to the Buddha images seated at the far western ends.

The principal chedi complex, which houses the Buddha relic, stands grandly – if a little cramped – at the heart of the compound, built on an east-west axis in an almost continuous line with two viharns. Its elegant centrepiece follows a design termed **lotus-bud chedi** (after the bulbous finial ornamenting the top of a tower), and is classic late Sukhothai in style. This lotus-bud reference is an established religious symbol: though Sukhothai architects were the first to incorporate it into building design – since when it's come to be regarded as a hallmark of the era – the lotus bud had for centuries represented the purity of the Buddha's thoughts battling through the clammy swamp and finally bursting out into flower. The chedi stands surrounded by eight smaller towers – some with their stucco decoration partially reapplied, and some with a Buddha image in one of their four alcoves – on a square platform decorated with a procession of walking Buddha-like monks, another artistic innovation of the Sukhothai school, here depicted in stucco relief. Flanking the chedi platform are two square mondops, built for the colossal standing Buddhas still inside them today.

The grassy patch across the road from Wat Mahathat marks the site of the former palace, of which nothing now remains.

Around Wat Mahathat

A few hundred metres southwest, the triple corn-cob-shaped prangs of **Wat Sri Sawai** make for an interesting architectural comparison with Wat

Mahathat. Just as the lotus-bud chedi epitomizes Sukhothai aspirations, the prang represents Khmer ideals – Wat Sri Sawai was probably conceived as a Hindu shrine several centuries before the Sukhothai kingdom established itself here. The stucco reliefs decorating the prangs feature a few weatherworn figures from both Hindu and Buddhist mythology, which suggests that the shrine was later pressed into Buddhist service; the square base inside the central prang supported the Khmer Shiva lingam (phallus), while the viharn out front is a later, Buddhist addition.

Just west of Wat Mahathat, the particularly fine lotus-bud chedi of **Wat Trapang Ngoen** rises gracefully against the backdrop of distant hills. Aligned with the chedi on the symbolic east–west axis are the dilapidated viharn and, east of that, on an island in the middle of the "silver pond" after which the wat is named, the remains of the bot. Walk the connecting plank to the bot to appreciate the setting from the water. North of the chedi, notice the fluid lines of the walking Buddha mounted onto a brick wall – a classic example of Sukhothai sculpture.

Taking the water feature one step further, **Wat Sra Sri** commands a fine position on two connecting islands north of Wat Trapang Ngoen. The bell-shaped chedi with a tapering spire and square base shows a strong Sri Lankan influence, and the metallic replica of a freestanding walking Buddha is typical Sukhothai.

The outer zones

There's a much less formal feel to the ruins in the four **outer zones**, where you're as likely to find cows trampling through the remains as tourists. You'll need a bicycle or car to get around, but all sites are clearly signposted from the gates encircling the central zone. The north zone is the closest and most rewarding, followed by the east zone just off the road to New Sukhothai. If you're feeling energetic, head for the west zone, which requires a much longer bike ride and some hill climbing. The ruins to the south aren't worth the effort.

The north zone

Exiting the central zone north of Wat Sra Sri, the road bisects the earthen ramparts of the old city walls and enters the **north zone**. About 500m north of the walls, a footbridge (also accessible to bicycles and motorbikes) leads you across to **Wat Phra Phai Luang**, one of the ancient city's oldest structures. The three prangs, only one of which remains intact, were built by the Khmers before the Thais founded their own kingdom here and, as at the similar Wat Sri Sawai, you can still see some of the stucco reliefs showing both Hindu and Buddhist figures. Others are displayed in Ramkhamhaeng National Museum. It's thought that Wat Phra Phai Luang was at the centre of the old Khmer town and that it was as important then as Wat Mahathat later became to the Thais. When the shrine was converted into a Buddhist temple,

△ Seated Buddha, Wat Sri Chum

the viharn and chedi were built to the east of the prangs: the reliefs of the (now headless and armless) seated Buddhas are still visible around the base of the chedi. Also discernible among the ruins are parts of a large reclining Buddha and a mondop containing four huge standing Buddhas in different postures.

About 500m west from the Wat Phra Phai Luang compound, **Wat Sri Chum** boasts Sukhothai's largest surviving Buddha image. The enormous, heavily restored brick-and-stucco seated Buddha, measuring more than 11m from knee to knee and almost 15m high, peers through the slit in its custom-built mondop. Check out the elegantly tapered fingers, complete with gold-leaf nail varnish. A passageway – rarely opened up, unfortunately – runs inside the mondop wall, taking you from ground level on the left-hand side to the Buddha's eye level and then up again to the roof, affording a bird's-eye view of the image. Legend has it that this Buddha would sometimes speak to favoured worshippers, and this staircase would have enabled tricksters to climb up and hold forth, unseen; one of the kings of Sukhothai is said to have brought his troops here to spur them on to victory with encouraging words from the Buddha.

The east zone

About 1.5km east of the main entrance, the only temple of interest in the **east zone** is canalside **Wat Chang Lom**, beside the bicycle track to New Sukhothai and just off the road to the new city, behind *Thai Village Hotel*. Chang Lom means "surrounded by elephants" and the main feature here is a large, Sri Lankan-style, bell-shaped chedi encircled by a frieze of elephants.

The west zone

Be prepared for a long haul out to the **west zone**, in the forested hills off the main road to Tak. Marking the western edge of the Old City, almost 5km west of the main entrance, the hilltop temple of **Wat Saphan Hin** should – with sufficiently powerful telescopic lenses – give a fantastic panorama of the old city's layout, but with the naked eye conjures up only an indistinct vista of trees and stones. If you make it this far, chances are you'll share the view only with the large standing Buddha at the top. The wat is reached via a steep 200-metre-long pathway of stone slabs (hence the name, which means "Stone Bridge") that starts from a track running south from the Tak road. This is the easiest approach if you're on a bike as it's completely flat; the shorter route, which follows a lesser, more southerly, road out of the old city, takes you over several hills and past the elephant temple of **Wat Chang Rob**, 1km short of Saphan Hin, where it joins the other track.

Around New Sukhothai

Though the historical park is the main draw for visitors to New Sukhothai, there are enough other attractions in the area to make it worth staying on for a couple of extra days. Many of these places – such as Si Satchanalai and Kamphaeng Phet – can be fairly easily reached by public transport, but you'll need to **rent your own vehicle** (see p.303) for trips to Wat Thawet and Ramkhamhaeng National Park.

Lotus Village guest house does **day-trips** to Kamphaeng Phet historical park and to Si Satchanalai's ruins, textile museum and gold workshop (B2300 for the group, excluding fuel and guide), and can arrange return transport for anyone wanting to climb Khao Luang in Ramkhamhaeng National Park (B600/car). Ronnie at *Ban Thai Guest House* leads enjoyable two-hour **bicycle tours** around local villages and farmland most afternoons from 4.30pm (B2000 including bike) and can also provide route maps for his guests. *Number 4 Guest House* keeps a resource book detailing interesting motorbike and bicycle routes through the area, including via the canal track to the historical park and to Thung Luang pottery village, and *Bamboo Café*'s information book is also full of unusual local itineraries. *J&J* guest house runs unusual overnight B2000 excursions to the caves, waterfalls and lakeside accommodation of Si Satchanalai National Park (as distinct from Si Satchanalai Historical Park), as well as a one-day version (B1000) and half-day trips to Tham Kham Khao National Park for a swim in the lake and a chance to watch the millions of bats streaming out of a nearby cave at dusk (B500).

Sangkhalok Museum

If you have a serious interest in ceramics you'll probably enjoy the Sukhothai-era exhibits at the privately owned **Sangkhalok Museum** (Mon–Fri 8am–6pm, Sat & Sun 10am–8pm; B100, children B50; ask for one of the informative museum booklets at the ticket desk), a couple of kilometres east of New Sukhothai on Highway 101, close to the junction with Highway 12, the road to Phitsanulok. A samlor ride from central New Sukhothai should cost no more than B40.

The ground floor of the museum displays ceramic artefacts from twelfth- to sixteenth-century Sukhothai, including **water pipes** used in the city's widely admired irrigation system, and the lotus-bud **lamps** whose gracefully shaped perforations both protect the flame and diffuse its light and are still as popular in Thailand today. Some of the finest pieces are the **bowls** with scalloped rims and bluish-green patterns and the characteristically expressive **figurines**; unusually, many of these works are signed by the potter. This style of pottery has become known as Sangkhalok, after the prosperous city of Sawankhalok, near Si Satchanalai, which was part of the kingdom of Sukhothai at that time (see p.306 for a description of the Sangkhalok kilns in Si Satchanalai). Also on show are ceramics from twelfth-century Burma, China and Vietnam, all of which were found in the area and so show who the citizens of Sukhothai were trading with at that time, as well as some of the most exquisite ceramics that were produced in northern Thailand during the Lanna era (thirteenth to sixteenth centuries). Upstairs, the focus is on the cultural significance of certain artefacts and their recurring motifs.

Wat Thawet

Famous for its one hundred different brightly painted concrete statues depicting morality tales and Buddhist fables, **Wat Thawet** is quite a popular sight for Thai tourists, though some farangs find it a bit tacky. The temple **sculpture park** was conceived by a local monk in the 1970s, with the aim of creating a "learning garden", where visitors could learn about the Buddhist ideas of hell and karmic retribution. For example, people who have spent their lives killing animals are depicted here with the head of a buffalo, pig, cock or elephant, while those who have been greedy and materialistic stand naked and undernourished, their ribs and backbones sticking out. Then there's the alcoholic who is forced to drink boiling liquids that literally make his concrete guts explode on to the ground.

Part of the appeal of Wat Thawet is that it makes a good focus for a very pleasant **bicycle** trip from Sukhothai, a sixteen-kilometre round-trip that is almost entirely along peaceful canalside tracks. From New Sukhothai, follow riverside Thanon Ratchathani north beyond *Lotus Village* until you hit the bypass. Cross the bypass and take the concrete path from the west edge of the bridge. Stay on this calm, scenic track for the next 8km, passing typical wooden houses, several banana plantations, a wooden suspension bridge and, about 1km before the temple, going beneath a major flyover; Wat Thawet is beside the second wooden suspension bridge.

Ramkhamhaeng National Park, Khao Luang and Thung Luang Pottery Village

The forested area immediately to the southwest of Sukhothai is protected as **Ramkhamhaeng National Park** (ⓣ055 619200, ⓦwww.dnp.go.th/National_park.asp; B20) and makes a pleasant day-trip on a motorbike, with the possibility of a challenging mountain climb at the end of it. To get to the main park entrance from New Sukhothai, follow Highway 101 towards Kamphaeng Phet for 19km, then take side road 1319, signed to Khao Luang, for the final 16km to park headquarters. Although any Kamphaeng Phet-bound bus will take you as far as the junction, you'll have trouble hitching into the park from here, so hiring private transport from Sukhothai is best. You can rent national park **bungalows** (ⓦwww.dnp.go.th/National_park.asp; B500 for up to six people) at the park's headquarters.

The headquarters stands at the foot of the eastern flank of the highest peak, **Khao Luang** (1185m), which can be climbed in around four hours, but only safely from November through February. Several very steep trails run up to the summit from here, but they are not very clearly marked; the first couple of kilometres are the worst, after which the incline eases up a little. From the top you should get a fine view over the Sukhothai plains. If you want to camp on the summit, simply alert the rangers at park headquarters, and they will arrange for their colleague at the summit to rent you a tent; you need to take your own food and water.

En route to or from Ramkhamhaeng National Park you could make a detour to **Thung Luang Pottery Village**, signed 16km out of New Sukhothai on Highway 101, where nearly every household is involved in the production of earthenware pots, vases and statuary. Once you've turned off the main road, you'll pass a line of roadside stalls, but to enter the heart of the pottery neighbourhoods continue for another kilometre or so, past a school and two temples.

Eating and drinking

One of the best places to **eat** in New Sukhothai is the nightly gathering of hot-food stalls and streetside tables in front of Wat Ratchathani on Thanon Charodvithitong. There's also a permanent covered area for night market-style restaurants on the soi between Thanon Ramkhamhaeng and Thanon Nikhon Kasem and a weekly night bazaar with food stalls, which sets up every Tuesday at New Sukhothai's Old City songthaew depot on Thanon Charodvithitong.

Bamboo Café off Thanon Pravetnakorn. Tiny Japanese café-restaurant serving a menu of various teas (green, wheat, oolong) plus miso soup (B35) and onigiri rice-ball sets (B75). It's worth coming just for the books of local information, which are full of ideas on unusual things to do in and around Sukhothai. Tues–Sun 10am–9pm.

Chopper Beer Thanon Pravetnakorn. Farang-oriented upstairs bar with nightly live music and a menu that runs to steak as well as seafood.

Coffee Home and Restaurant At the entrance to *Lotus Village* on Thanon Rajuthit. Cute garden restaurant serving fresh coffee and ice creams, as well as baked spare-ribs with pineapple, seafood soup, various spicy *yam* salads and Chinese-style baked rice with olives (B65–165). Daily 2–11pm.

Dream Café 88/1 Thanon Singhawat. A cosy, cool, dark, coffee-shop atmosphere, with walls and windowsills full of curios and Thai antiques, twenty different ice-cream sundaes on the menu and a range of stamina-enhancing herbal drinks. Among its fairly pricey substantial fare (two courses for around B300) are authentically fiery Thai curries, fresh Vietnamese-style spring rolls, deep-fried banana-flower fritters, seafood – and gin-and-tonics.

J&J Guesthouse 122/1 Soi Maerampan. Delicious home-made bread that's perfect for breakfast or lunch.
Khun Tanode Beside the bridge on Thanon Charodvithitong. Low-key, laid-back, well-priced little riverside restaurant that's popular with locals and is prettily illuminated at night. Try the local speciality – crispy-fried chicken drumsticks in Sukhothai sauce (B60) – or mussels cooked in a herb sauce (B60). Daily 10am–midnight.
Naa's Restaurant 40/4 Thanon Charodvithitong; about 300m west of the Old City songthaew depot. *99 Guesthouse* owner and cookery teacher Naa runs a restaurant that's famous for its spicy southern fare, especially yellow curries (B30 over rice or B60 for two). She also offers lots of milder dishes, as well as veggie options. Daily 8am–8pm.
Poo's Across from the Old City songthaew depot on Thanon Charodvithitong. Relaxed and welcoming spot that serves Thai food, rents motorbikes and gives Thai massage but comes into its own in the late afternoon when it begins to shake and stir Sukhothai's biggest selection of cocktails, many of which are a bargain B60.
Rom Poa At the edge of the covered night market between Thanon Ramkhamhaeng and Thanon Nikhon Kasem. Popular place with pushy touts but a perfectly decent menu of spicy jelly-thread noodle salads (*yam wun sen*), curries, lots of seafood dishes, fruit shakes and a decent vegetarian selection. Most dishes B40–60, though that's still more expensive than many other stalls in the night market.

Listings

Banks and exchange There are several banks with money-changing facilities and ATMs on Thanon Singhawat.
Bicycle rental Most guest houses offer mountain bikes for B50–80 and town bicycles for B30 per day. There are plenty of bicycles for rent in the historical park too (B20).
Books A few English-language books and touring maps are available at Sukhothai Books Centre on Thanon Nikhon Kasem.
Cookery courses One and two-day courses led by the woman behind *Naa's Restaurant* and *99 Guest House* (B750/day); shorter, cheaper courses at *Ban Thai* and *Sukhothai* guest houses.
Emergencies For all emergencies, call the tourist police on ⓣ1155, or go to the local police station on Thanon Singhawat.
Hospital The government-run Sukhothai Hospital (ⓣ055 610280) is a couple of kilometres west of New Sukhothai on the road to Sukhothai Historical Park; there's a more central 24hr clinic on Thanon Singhawat.
Internet access There are plenty of Internet centres in New Sukhothai (see map for locations) and the CAT phone office on Thanon Nikhon Kasem has public Catnet terminals (Mon–Fri 8.30am–4.30pm). In the Old City, there's access at *Coffee Cup* restaurant and *Vitoon Guest House*.
Mail The GPO is on Thanon Nikhon Kasem, 200m southeast from the junction with Thanon Prampracha.
Motorbike rental Motorbikes can be rented through almost any guest house for B200 per day and at *Poo* bar and restaurant across from the Old City songthaew depot.
Shopping The *Ananda Museum Gallery Hotel* plaza, beside the Sangkhalok Museum on the bypass, sells very classy handicrafts, particularly celadon and ceramics in both traditional and modern styles. Also try Usa Sungkalok near the Old City (see p.297).
Telephones The CAT overseas phone centre (Mon–Fri 8.30am–4.30pm) is next to the post office on Thanon Nikhon Kasem, 200m southeast from the junction with Thanon Prampracha.
Travel agent Domestic and international air tickets from Sukhothai Travel Agency, 10–12 Thanon Singhawat (ⓣ055 613075, ⓔsukhothaitravelservice@yahoo.com; Mon–Fri 7.30am–4.30pm, Sat & Sun 7.30am–3pm).
Visa run *J&J Guest House* does a day-trip visa run to the Burmese border near Mae Sot for anyone needing a new 30-day visa (B1500 per person excluding entry into Burma).

Si Satchanalai and around

In the mid-thirteenth century, Sukhothai cemented its power by establishing several satellite towns, of which the most important was **SI SATCHANALAI**, 57km upriver from Sukhothai on the banks of the Yom. Now a historical park, the restored ruins of **Muang Kao Si Satchanalai** have a quieter ambience than the grander models at Sukhothai Historical Park, and the additional attractions of the riverside wat in nearby **Chalieng**, the **Sangkhalok pottery kilns** in Bang Ko Noi, and the **Sathorn Textile Museum** in New Si Satchanalai combine to make the area worth exploring.

Practicalities

Si Satchanalai works best as a day-trip from Sukhothai, though there are a couple of places to stay near the historical park. The fastest way to get there is on one of the air-con **buses** bound for Chiang Rai; these depart New Sukhothai bus station at 6.40am, 9am, 10.30am and 11.30am and take just over an hour. Though there are local buses to Si Satchanalai, which depart New Sukhothai bus station about every 30min, these take about 1hr 45min and sometimes require a change of bus in Sawankhalok. The last conveniently timed air-con bus back to New Sukhothai passes Old Si Satchanalai at about 4.30pm (just flag it down from the highway); if you miss it, you'll have to wait till about 8pm. Hardly any local buses run in the afternoon. All buses drop passengers on Highway 101 at the signpost for Chalieng's Wat Phra Si Ratana Mahathat, beside a pink archway gate and a shop that does **bicycle rental**. This is the best place to rent a bike (B20) as, though it's less than 500m to Wat Mahathat from here, it's almost another 2km further to reach the next rental place, at the entry to Muang Kao Si Satchanalai proper. Pass through the pink archway and cross the Yom River via a wooden suspension bridge (open to bikes and motorbikes) to reach the first temple, Wat Phra Si Ratana Mahathat in Chalieng. Coming by car you'll need to use the road bridge about 1km further west up Highway 101. Alternatively, you could either rent a motorbike in New Sukhothai or join a tour from there.

There are **food** stalls and small restaurants at every juncture, including at Wat Mahathat, between the road bridge and Muang Kao, and beside the Muang Kao ticket gate. If you want to **stay** right on the doorstep, you have just a couple of less than perfect options: *Ta Bee Guest House* (Ⓣ089 702 7720, Ⓦwww.su-kho-thai.com; B200–300) is a tiny place, still partly under construction, offering just a couple of simple fan rooms on the north bank of the River Yom, right beside the road bridge, about 1500m from Muang Kao. *Wang Yom Resort* (Ⓣ055 631380; fan ❹, air-con ❺) is a more pretentious place, with overpriced, slightly dilapidated fan and air-con bungalows set around quite an attractive garden on the south bank of the River Yom, about 500m southeast of the park entrance, or 1km from the road bridge.

Chalieng and Wat Phra Si Ratana Mahathat

Before Sukhothai asserted control of the region and founded Si Satchanalai, the Khmers governed the area from **Chalieng**, cradled in a bend in the Yom River just over 2km to the east of Muang Kao Si Satchanalai. Just about all that now remains of Chalieng is **Wat Phra Si Ratana Mahathat** (dawn to dusk; B10), whose compound, aligned east–west and encircled by a now sunken wall of laterite blocks, contains structures thought to date back to the Khmer era, but with later additions by Sukhothai and Ayutthayan builders. Approaching from the wooden suspension bridge you'll enter via the semi-submerged eastern gateway, passing beneath a hefty Khmer-style carved lintel that was hewn from a single block of stone. Inside, the compound is dominated by a towering corncob prang, the main shrine, which was likely remodelled during the Ayutthayan era and whose exterior has recently been renovated with all-over stucco decorations. The ruined viharn in front of the prang enshrines a large seated Buddha sculpted in typical Sukhothai style, with hand gestures symbolizing his triumph over temptation. The tall stucco relief of a walking Buddha to the left is also classic Sukhothai and is regarded as one of the finest of its genre. Immediately to the west of the prang, the remains of the octagonal laterite platform and its bell-shaped chedi are believed to date from a different era, possibly considerably earlier. A mondop containing a large standing Buddha guards one side and looks towards the River Yom; a second viharn, containing two Buddha images, occupies the other flank.

Muang Kao Si Satchanalai

From the Wat Mahathat compound it's a two-kilometre ride northwest along the quiet riverside road to the entrance point to **Muang Kao Si Satchanalai** (daily 8am–4pm; B40 plus B10–50 surcharge depending on your vehicle, or free if you have a combined Sukhothai–Si Satchanalai ticket). You can rent bikes here (B20), and there are food stalls and a trolley bus (operates during busy times only). Though it was built to emulate its capital, Si Satchanalai is much less hyped than Sukhothai, sees fewer tourists and is less manicured than the more popular site.

Most circuits begin with the most striking set of ruins, the elephant temple of **Wat Chang Lom**, whose centrepiece is a huge, Sri Lankan-style, bell-shaped chedi set on a square base studded with 39 life-sized elephant buttresses (those in Sukhothai and Kamphaeng Phet are smaller). A mahout and his elephant sometimes hang out here to prove the point. Many of the elephant reliefs are in good repair, with much of their stucco flesh still intact; others now have their bulky laterite-brick innards exposed.

Across the road from Wat Chang Lom, **Wat Chedi Jet Taew** has seven rows of small chedis thought to enshrine the ashes of Si Satchanalai's royal rulers, which makes this the ancient city's most important temple. One of the 34 chedis is an elegant scaled-down replica of the hallmark lotus-bud chedi at Sukhothai's Wat Mahathat; some of the others are copies of other important wats from the vicinity. Several have fine stucco-covered Buddha images in their alcoves, including a famously beautiful one of the Buddha sheltered by a naga (now with restored head), also reproduced in Ramkhamhaeng National Museum.

A few hundred metres along the road from Wat Chedi Jet Taew, **Wat Nang Phya** is remarkable for the original stucco reliefs on its viharn wall, which remain in fine condition; stucco is a hardy material that sets soon after being first applied, and becomes even harder when exposed to rain – hence its ability to survive seven hundred years in the open. The balustraded wall has slit windows and is entirely covered with intricate floral motifs.

North of Wat Chang Lom, the hilltop ruins of Wat Khao Phanom Pleung and Wat Khao Suan Khiri afford splendid aerial views of different quarters of the ancient city. The sole remaining intact chedi of **Wat Khao Phanom Pleung** sits on top of the lower of the hills and used to be flanked by a set of smaller chedis built to entomb the ashes of Si Satchanalai's important personages – the ones who merited some special memorial, but didn't quite make the grade for Wat Chedi Jet Taew. The temple presumably got its name, which means "mountain of sacred fire", from the cremation rituals held on the summit. **Wat Khao Suan Khiri's** huge chedi, which graces the summit 200m northwest, has definitely seen better days, but the views from its platform – south over the main temple ruins and north towards the city walls and entrance gates – are worth the climb.

The Sangkhalok kilns

Endowed with high-quality clay, the area around Si Satchanalai – known as Sawankhalok or Sangkhalok during the Ayutthaya period – commanded an international reputation as a ceramics centre from the mid-fourteenth to the end of the fifteenth century, producing pieces still rated among the finest in the world. More than two hundred **kilns** have been unearthed in and around Si Satchanalai to date, and it's estimated that there could once have been a thousand in all. One of the main groups of kilns is in the village of **Ban Ko Noi**, which is about 7km upstream from the park entry point and can be reached by bicycle by following the very pleasant, almost traffic-free road beside the river (not the one going into the park) through hamlets fringed with flowering shrubs and fruit trees. At Ban Ko Noi, four excavated kilns have been roofed and turned into the **Sangkhalok Kiln Preservation Centre** (daily 9am–4.30pm; B30 or free if you bought the joint Sukhothai–Si Satchanalai ticket), but, unfortunately, they are poorly served by almost non-existent English-language captions (you'll have a much better idea of what you're looking at if you've already been to the Ramkhamhaeng National Museum in Sukhothai Historical Park). Two of the kilns are up-draught kilns and two are cross-draught kilns. Up-draught kilns were fairly crude cylindrical structures whose maximum temperature was 1000 degrees centigrade and so could only be used for earthenware; cross-draught kilns were large and spatula shaped, with the fire set at the opposite end to the chimney, thus generating a greater and more consistent heat, up to 1350 degrees centigrade, which enabled the production of glazed ware. A small display of **Sangkhalok ceramics** gives a hint of the pieces that were fired here. Works fall into three broad categories: domestic items such as pots, decorated plates and lidded boxes; decorative items like figurines, temple sculptures and temple roof tiles; and items for export, particularly to Indonesia and the Philippines, where huge Sangkhalok storage jars were used as burial urns. Most Sangkhalok ceramics were glazed – the grey-green celadon, probably introduced by immigrant Chinese potters, was especially popular – and typically decorated with fish or chrysanthemum motifs. Several of Thailand's major museums feature collections of ceramics from both Si Satchanalai and Sukhothai under the umbrella label of Sangkhalok, and there's a dedicated collection of Sangkhalok wares just outside New Sukhothai, described on p.301. Stalls across the road from the Preservation Centre sell reproduction ceramics and "antiques".

The Sathorn Textile Museum

Eleven kilometres north of the Si Satchanalai ruins, modern Si Satchanalai is worth visiting for the **Sathorn Textile Museum**, located at the northern end of the ribbon-like new town, on the east side of Highway 101. The museum houses the private collection of Khun Sathorn, who also runs the adjacent textile shop, and he or his staff open up the one-room exhibition for anyone who shows an interest. *Lotus Village* guest house in New Sukhothai includes a visit to the museum on its Si Satchanalai day-trip, or you can come here on the bus from New Sukhothai, getting off in modern Si Satchanalai rather than at the ruins.

Most of the **textiles** on show come from the nearby village of Hat Siew, whose weavers have long specialized in the art of *teen jok*, or hem embroidery, whereby the bottom panel of the sarong or *phasin* (woman's sarong) is decorated with a band of supplementary weft, usually done in exquisitely intricate patterns. Some of the textiles here are almost a hundred years old and many of the *teen jok* **motifs** have symbolic meaning showing what the cloths would have been used for – a sarong or *phasin* used for a marriage ceremony, for example, tends to have a double image, such as two birds facing each other. Elephants also feature quite a lot in Hat Siew weaving, probably a reference to the village custom in which young men who are about to become monks parade on elephants to their ordination ceremony. The tradition continues to this day and elephant parades are held at the mass ordination ceremony every year on April 7 and 8. Modern Hat Siew textiles are sold at the adjacent Sathorn shop and at other outlets further south along the main road.

Kamphaeng Phet

KAMPHAENG PHET, 77km south of Sukhothai, was probably founded in the fourteenth century by the kings of Sukhothai as a buffer city between their capital and the increasingly powerful city-state of Ayutthaya. Strategically sited 100m from the east bank of the Ping, the ruined old city has, like Sukhothai and Si Satchanalai before it, been partly restored and opened to the public as a historical park. The least visited of the three, it rivals Si Satchanalai for your attention mainly because of the untamed setting and the gracefully weathered statues of its main temple. A new city has grown up on the southeastern boundaries of the old, the usual commercial blandness offset by a riverside park, plentiful flowers and an unusual number of historic wooden houses dotted along the main thoroughfares. You can even swim off an island in the middle of the river, accessible via a footbridge near Soi 21, a few hundred metres south of the night market. Should you decide to linger for a few days, *Three J Guest House* not only makes a pleasant base but can also arrange rafting and bird-watching trips in nearby national parks.

The town is served by direct **buses** from Bangkok, Chiang Mai and Tak, but most travellers come here on a day-trip from Sukhothai or Phitsanulok.

Practicalities

Arriving by bus from Sukhothai or Phitsanulok, you'll enter Kamphaeng Phet from the east and should get off either inside the old city walls or at the Thanon Tesa roundabout rather than wait to be dumped across the river at the **terminal** 2km west of town on Highway 1. If you are coming from the bus terminal, you'll need to hop on a red town **songthaew**, which will take you to the Thanon Tesa roundabout just east of the river (the most convenient disembarkation point for the ruins), or further into the town centre for most of the hotels and restaurants. From the roundabout, songthaews generally do a clockwise circle around the new town, running south along Thanon Rajdamnoen (get off at the intersection with Rajdamnoen Soi 4 for *Three J Guest House*), then west along Bumrungrat, north up Thanon Tesa 1 and west out to the bus station. There's a **bank** with an exchange counter and ATM close to the roundabout and several more banks on Thanon Charoensuk. The main **post office** is on Thanon Tesa 1, about 200m south of the roundabout; it has a Catnet **Internet** terminal or there are several other Internet places in town (see map on p.308 for locations).

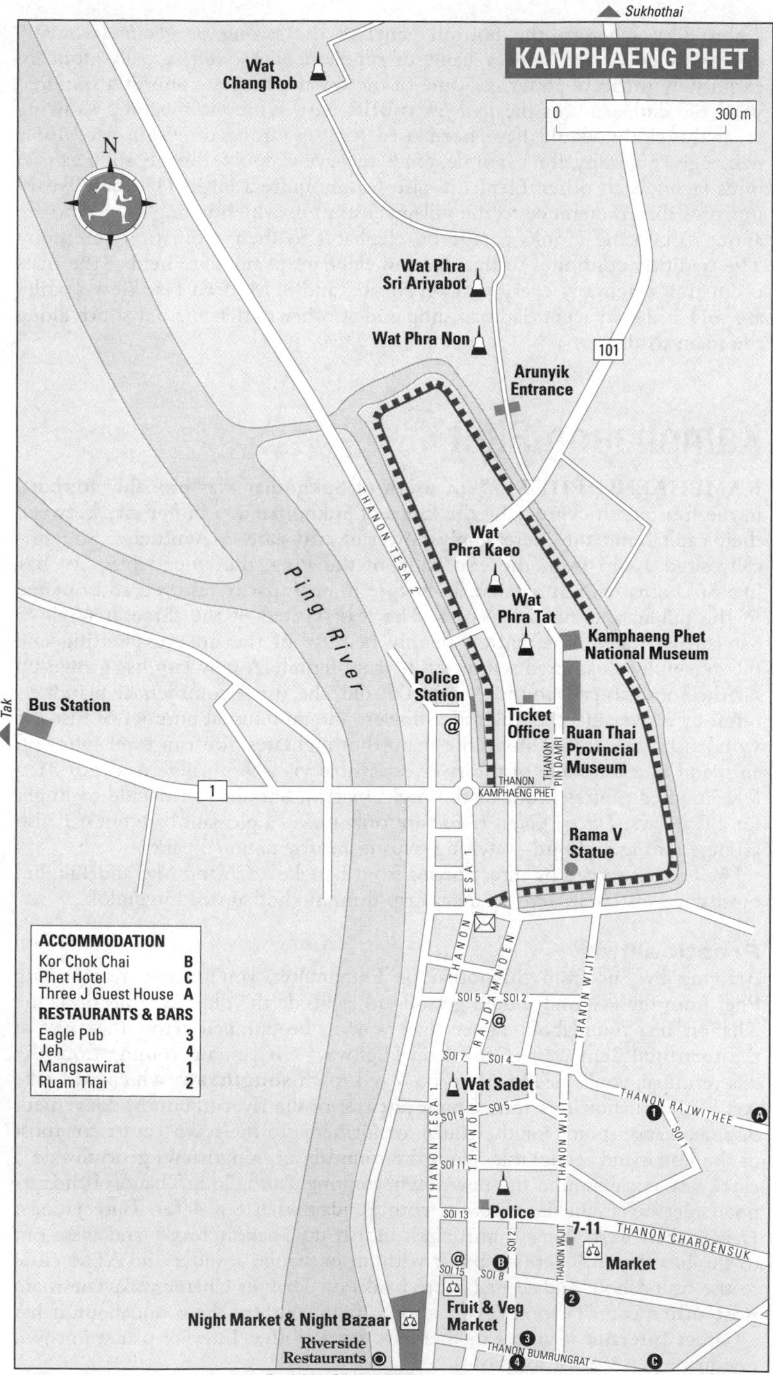

KAMPHAENG PHET
0
300 m
Sukhothai
N
Wat Chang Rob
Wat Phra Sri Ariyabot
Wat Phra Non
101
Arunyik Entrance
THANON TESA 2
Ping River
Wat Phra Kaeo
Wat Phra Tat
Kamphaeng Phet National Museum
Police Station
Bus Station
Tak
Ticket Office
THANON PIN DAMRI
Ruan Thai Provincial Museum
1
THANON KAMPHAENG PHET
Rama V Statue
THANON TESA 1
THANON RAJDAMNOEN
THANON WIJIT
SOI 5
SOI 2
SOI 7
SOI 4
Wat Sadet
SOI 9
SOI 5
THANON RAJWITHEE
SOI 1
SOI 11
Police
SOI 13
7-11
THANON CHAROENSUK
Market
SOI 15
SOI 8
Fruit & Veg Market
Night Market & Night Bazaar
Riverside Restaurants
THANON BUMRUNGRAT
Footbridge & island
ACCOMMODATION
Kor Chok Chai B
Phet Hotel C
Three J Guest House A
RESTAURANTS & BARS
Eagle Pub 3
Jeh 4
Mangsawirat 1
Ruam Thai 2

Accommodation

The most traveller-oriented **place to stay** in Kamphaeng Phet is *Three J Guest House*, located 600m east of the main drag, Thanon Rajdamnoen, at 79 Thanon Rajwithee (Ⓣ055 713129, Ⓦ360.yahoo.com/threejguesthouse; fan ❷, air-con ❷–❸). Run by an enthusiastic bank-worker and his family, it's a pleasant, secluded home-stay with ten comfortable bungalows built from rough-cut logs and set in a Chinese-style rock garden at the back of the family home. All rooms have cosy verandas; the cheapest options share bathrooms and the priciest have air-con. There's bicycle and motorbike rental, Internet access, and tours to national parks at weekends, especially to the owner's home-stay in Khlong Mod Daeng National Park (B1000 per person for a day and a night). The main budget alternative is *Kor Chok Chai* (Ⓣ055 713532; ❷), with its fan and air-con rooms, east of the fruit and veg market on Rajdamnoen Soi 8; the hotel is unsigned but recognizable by its pair of Chinese stone lions guarding the door. Most of *Kor Chok Chai*'s customers are salespeople, so there's some call-girl activity after hours, but it's clean, comfortable and recently renovated. The best of the town's central hotels, and the usual choice of tour groups, is the *Phet Hotel* on the southeastern edge of town at 189 Thanon Bumrungrat (Ⓣ055 712810; ❹). It has good upper-mid-range rooms, all with air-con, (Thai) TV and mini-bar, wide views over KP's skyline, and there's a restaurant, bar and nightclub on the premises; it's also wi-fi compatible and has Internet in the lobby.

Eating and drinking

The huge range of cheap noodles, stir-fries and over-rice dishes served at *Ruam Thai*, south of the Charoensuk intersection on Thanon Wijit, make this very popular, unpretentious **restaurant** a reliable choice at any time of day, but after dark the night market is the most enjoyable place to eat. It sets up in a covered area in the southern part of the new town, between the river and Thanon Tesa 1; try asking here for the special local noodle dish, *kway tiaw cha kang rao*, made with cow peas and pork. There are a couple of vegetarian restaurants in town, both of them typical cheap canteens that open daily from about 7am to 2pm and offer very good deals of rice plus a couple of stews, curries or stir-fries for B15–20: *Mangsawirat* (no English sign but look for the red Chinese character for "vegetarian" against a yellow background) is on Thanon Rajwithee, at the junction with Soi 1, about 300m east of Thanon Rajdamnoen and 300m west of *Three J Guest House*; *Jeh* (flagged only by the Thai letter for "Jeh" in red against yellow) is right next to a formal dress shop just off Thanon Bumrungrat on Soi 2 at 68/3. If you're after beer, whisky and live music (from 9pm), the *Eagle Pub*, one block south and east of *Kor Chok Chai* on Thanon Bumrungrat, is one of the livelier spots in town.

Muang Kao Kamphaeng Phet

Ruins surround modern Kamphaeng Phet on all sides, but **Muang Kao Kamphaeng Phet** (daily 6am–7pm; B40 plus B10/bicycle, B20/motorbike and B50/car) takes in the two most interesting areas: the oblong zone inside the old city walls and the forested area just north of that. A tour of both areas involves a five-kilometre round-trip, so the best option is to rent a **bicycle** or **motorbike** from *Three J Guest House* in the new town, though you could also strike a deal with a samlor driver; there's no rental outlet at the historical park. If you are coming on a day-trip from Sukhothai or Phitsanulok, consider hiring your own transport there. The ruins that dot the landscape across the Ping River, west of the Thanon Tesa roundabout, belong to the even older city of Nakhon Chum, but are now too tumbledown to be worth the effort.

Inside the city walls

Parts of the **city walls** that gave Kamphaeng Phet its name are still in good condition, though Highway 101 to Sukhothai now cuts through the enclosed area and a few shops have sprung up along the roadside, making it hard to visualize the fortifications as a whole. Approaching from the Thanon Tesa roundabout, you can either head up Thanon Pin Damri and start your tour at Wat Phra That and the Provincial Museum, or you enter the compound from the western gate and come in at the back end of **Wat Phra Kaeo**. Built almost entirely of laterite and adorned with laterite Buddhas, this was the city's central and most important structure, and given the name reserved for temples that have housed the kingdom's most sacred image: the Emerald Buddha, now in the wat of the same name in Bangkok, is thought to have been set down here to rest at some point. Seven centuries later, the Buddha images have been worn away into attractive abstract shadows, often aptly compared to the pitted, spidery forms of Giacometti sculptures, and the slightly unkempt feel to the place makes a perfect setting. Few tools have been unearthed at any of the Kamphaeng Phet sites, giving weight to the theory that the sculptors moulded their statues from the clay-like freshly dug laterite before leaving it to harden. Small, overgrown laterite quarry pits are still visible all over the old city. The statues would originally have been faced with stucco, and restorers have already patched up the central tableau of one reclining and two seated Buddhas. The empty niches that encircle the principal chedi were once occupied by statues of bejewelled lions.

Adjoining Wat Phra Kaeo to the east are the three chedis of **Wat Phra That**. The central bell-shaped chedi, now picturesquely wreathed in lichen and stray bits of vegetation, is typical of the Sri Lankan style and was built to house a sacred relic. Just east of Wat Phra That, **Kamphaeng Phet National Museum** (Wed–Sun 9am–4pm; B30; Ⓦwww.thailandmuseum.com) displays the artistic and archeological heritage of Kamphaeng Phet. The exhibition on the ground floor looks at the historical development of the city, while upstairs is given over to a display of sculptures found in the locality. The prize exhibit up here is the very fine bronze standing Shiva: cast in the sixteenth century in Khmer-Ayutthayan style, the statue has had a chequered history – including decapitation by a keen nineteenth-century German admirer. Also on this floor is an unusual seventeenth- or eighteenth-century Ayutthayan-style standing Buddha in wood, whose diadem, necklace and even hems are finely carved.

While you're at the National Museum you can't fail to see the alluring group of recently built traditional-style teak wood *salas* in the adjacent compound which, though unsigned in English, are in fact the **Kamphaeng Phet Ruan Thai Provincial Museum** (daily 9am–4.30pm; B10). Inside, exhibits and scale models labelled in English and Thai introduce the history, traditions and contemporary culture of Kamphaeng Phet province.

The arunyik temples

The dozen or so ruins in the forested area north of the city walls – east 100m along Highway 101 from behind Wat Phra Kaeo, across the moat and up a road to the left – are all that remains of Kamphaeng Phet's **arunyik** (forest) temples, built here by Sukhothai-era monks in a wooded area to encourage meditation. It's an enjoyably tranquil and atmospheric area to explore if you have your own wheels, with the tumbledown structures peeking out of the thinly planted groves that line the access road; the road winds around a fair bit before eventually rejoining the Sukhothai-Kamphaeng Phet highway to the north of the walled city.

Once you're through the entrance, the first temple on the left is **Wat Phra Non**, otherwise known as the Temple of the Reclining Buddha, though you need a good imagination to conjure up the indistinct remains into the once enormous Buddha figure. Gigantic laterite pillars support the viharn that houses the statue; far more ambitious than the usual brick-constructed jobs, these pillars were cut from single slabs of stone from a nearby quarry and would have measured up to 8m in height.

Immediately to the north, the four Buddha images of **Wat Phra Sri Ariyabot** are in better condition. With cores of laterite and skins of stucco, the restored standing and walking images tower over the viharn, while the seated (south-facing) and reclining (north-facing) Buddhas have been eroded into indistinct blobs. The full-grown trees rooted firmly in the raised floor are evidence of just how old the place is.

Follow the road around the bend to reach **Wat Chang Rob**, crouched on top of a laterite hill 1km from the entrance gate. Built to the same Sri Lankan model as its sister temples of the same name in Sukhothai and Si Satchanalai, this "temple surrounded by elephants" retains only the square base of its central bell-shaped chedi. Climb one of its four steep staircases for a view out over the mountains in the west, or just for a different perspective of the 68 elephant buttresses that encircle the base. Sculpted from laterite and stucco, they're dressed in the ceremonial garb fit for such revered animals; floral reliefs can just be made out along the surfaces between neighbouring elephants – the lower level was once decorated with a stucco frieze of flying birds.

West of Sukhothai

Highway 12 heads west from Sukhothai, crossing the westernmost reaches of the northern plains before arriving at the provincial capital of **TAK** (79km), on the east bank of the Ping River. Historically important as the birthplace of King Taksin of Thonburi (who attached the name of his hometown to the one he was born with), Tak is of little interest to tourists except as a place to change **buses** for continuing north to Lampang and Chiang Mai, south to Kamphaeng Phet and Bangkok, or west to Mae Sot and the Burmese border; Tak **bus station** is about 3km east of the town centre. **TAT** has a regional office in the town centre at 193 Thanon Taksin (daily 8.30am–4.30pm; ⓣ055 514341, ⓔtattak@tat.or.th). The one time it's worth making a special effort to visit Tak is for **Loy Krathong**, the nationwide festival of light that's held here over eight nights around the full moon of the twelfth lunar month (Oct/Nov; see colour section for details). The idiosyncratic Tak celebration is known as Loy Krathong Sai and involves the nightly floating of thousands of lighted coconut husks (rather than the usual banana-leaf baskets) on the Ping River. If you need a **hotel** in Tak, there are the very cheap, very basic fan rooms at *Mae Ping*, across the road from the fruit and veg market at 231 Thanon Mahattai Bamroong (ⓣ055 511807; ❶), or the medium-sized, comfortably furnished *Viang Tak 2* (ⓣ055 511910, ⓦwww.visit-mekong.com/the-viang-tak-2-hotel/; ❺), one block southwest of the fruit and veg market at 236 Thanon Chumphon, which has air-con rooms, some of them with nice river views, and a swimming pool.

Most travellers ignore Tak, however, and go straight **on to Mae Sot**, reached by either of two roads through the stunning western mountain range that divides the northern plains from the Burmese border. **Highway 105**, the more direct route, is served by fast and frequent, if cramped, government minibuses between Tak and Mae Sot. If following this route with your own transport,

Refugees from Burma: the Karen

With a population of five to seven million, the **Karen** are Burma's largest ethnic minority, but their numbers have offered no protection against persecution by the Burmese. This mistreatment has been going on for centuries, and entered a new phase after Burma won its independence from Britain in 1948. Unlike many other groups in Burma, the Karen had remained loyal to the British during World War II and were supposed to have been rewarded with autonomy when Britain pulled out; instead they were left to battle for that themselves. Fourteen years after the British withdrawal, the **Burmese army** took control, setting up an isolationist state run under a bizarre ideology compounded of militarist, socialist and Buddhist principles. In 1988, opposition to this junta peaked with a series of pro-democracy demonstrations that were suppressed by the slaughter of thousands.

The army subsequently felt obliged to hold elections, which resulted in an overwhelming majority for the **National League for Democracy** (NLD), led by **Aung San Suu Kyi**, recipient of the 1991 Nobel Peace Prize. In response, the military placed Aung San Suu Kyi under house arrest (where she has remained on and off ever since) and declared all opposition parties illegal. The disenfranchised MPs then joined the thousands of ordinary citizens who, in the face of the savagery of the Burmese militia against the country's minorities, had fled east to jungle camps along the Thai border and beyond, into Thailand itself.

Armed wings of Burma's numerous minority groups have been fighting from their jungle bases ever since and, although many factions have reached temporary ceasefire agreements with the Burmese junta, **persecution** of minority peoples continues. The Karen, whose homeland state of Kawthulay borders northwest Thailand from Mae Sariang down to Three Pagodas Pass, have been particularly vulnerable: their soldiers, the Karen National Union (KNU), are the only major rebel group not to have reached a formal ceasefire agreement with the junta. (The Karen are distinct from the Karenni, or Red Karen, whose homeland is north of Kawthulay and borders Thailand's Mae Hong Song province.) Common tactics employed by the Burmese army against the Karen and other minority groups include the forcible razing and relocation of villages, systematic murder, rape and robbery, and the rounding-up of slave labour: according to the International Confederation of Free Trade Unions, on any given day several hundred thousand men, women, children and elderly people are subjected to forced labour in Burma, mainly for the building of roads, railways and military projects, and as porters for the Burmese army.

As a result of these ongoing atrocities, as many as one thousand Burmese are thought to flee across the Thai border every month, the majority of them Karen. Of the 151,000 registered refugees living at the eleven **refugee camps** along the Thailand–Burma border in June 2005, some 130,000 were Karen. One of the biggest camps near Mae Sot is the village-like Umpium, on the road to Umphang, which is

there are a couple of attractions en route, beginning at kilometre-stone 12, 20km west of Tak, with **Lansang National Park** (dawn to dusk; B200; Ⓣ055 519278, Ⓦwww.dnp.go.th/National_park.asp; bungalows from B400), which has trails and waterfalls and is reached via a three-kilometre side road off Highway 105; some Mae Sot tour operators run trips here too. This region is home to Lisu, Lahu and Maew hill tribes, many of whom live on the cool slopes of 840-metre-high Doi Muser where they grow coffee, fruit and vegetables that they trade, along with hill-tribe crafts, at the **hill-tribe market** alongside the highway between kilometre-stones 28 and 29.

Rickety but roomy ordinary buses take twice as long to ply **Route 1175** between Tak and Mae Sot, which follows a winding and at times hair-raising course across the thickly forested range, affording great views over the valleys home for about 19,000 Karen, but the largest is Mae La, near Tha Song Yang, about 60km north of Mae Sot, which houses over 48,000. However, following a decision in 2005 by the Thai government to finally allow resettlement of Burmese refugees to a third country, some of these camps may not last too much longer. Previously the Thai government had resisted agreeing to the resettlement programme fearing that this would encourage even more refugees to cross its borders.

Registered refugees are by no means the whole story, however, as for many years **Thai government policy** has been to admit only those who are fleeing active fighting, not human rights violations. Thailand is not a signatory to the 1951 Convention Relating to the Status of Refugees and has no legal framework for processing asylum seekers. The hundreds of thousands who have left their homeland because of politically induced economic hardship – forced labour, theft of their land and livestock, impossibly high taxation and corruption, among other factors – are therefore obliged either to try and enter the refugee camps illegally, or to attempt to make a living as **migrant workers**. Without refugee status, Burmese exiles are extremely vulnerable to abuse, both from corrupt officials and from exploitative employers. In Mae Sot, for example, where Burmese migrants are a mainstay of the local economy, many of them are paid as little as B20 a day (less than twenty percent of Thailand's minimum wage) to work in the worst jobs available, in gem and garment factories, and as prostitutes, though recent work-permit amnesties have made it harder for police officers to further exploit the migrants. Demands for better wages and improved conditions, however, nearly always result in deportation.

Reactions in the **Thai press** to the Burmese refugee issue are mixed, with humanitarian concerns tempered by economic hardships in Thailand and by high-profile cases of illegal Burmese workers involved in violent crimes and drug-smuggling (Burma is now one of the world's leading producers and smugglers of methamphetamines, also known as *ya baa*, or Ice, much of which finds its way into Thailand). Relations between the neighbours have been volatile ever since the Burmese razed Ayutthaya in 1767, and there are still occasional high-level political spats today, but Thailand's politicians are conscious above all of Burma's potential as a lucrative trading partner and of its geographical importance in expanding overland trade routes. As well as acting as peace broker between the junta and some ethnic minority groups, the Thai government has also made a show of cracking down on Burmese dissidents and deporting thousands of migrant works back to Burma.

For recent **news** and archive reports on the situation in Burma and on its borders, see Ⓦwww.irrawaddy.org. For information on how to offer **support** to refugees from Burma, see p.78. For a deeper insight into the Karen struggle and the refugee situation in Mae Sot, read *Restless Souls: Rebels, Refugees, Medics and Misfits* by Phil Thornton, a Mae Sot-based journalist, reviewed on p.925.

on either side and passing through makeshift roadside settlements built by hill tribes. The road eventually descends into the valley of the **Moei River** – which forms the Thai–Burmese border here – and joins the northbound section of Highway 105 at the lovely, traditional village of **Mae Ramat** before continuing south to Mae Sot. Highway 105 carries on north, reaching Mae Sariang (see p.400) after a five-hour songthaew ride – a bumpy but scenic journey through rugged border country.

Mae Sot and the border

Located 100km west of Tak and only 6km from Burma, **MAE SOT** is very much a border town, populated by a rich ethnic mix of Burmese, Karen, Hmong

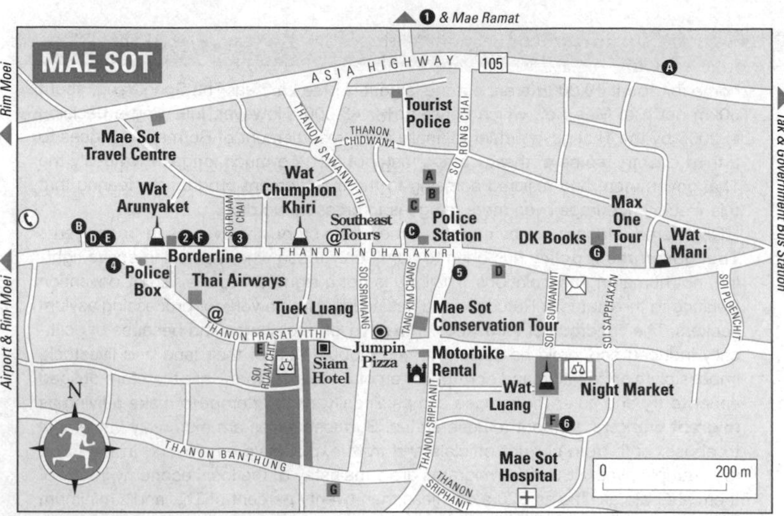

ACCOMMODATION

- Bai Fern F
- Ban Thai B
- Central Mae Sot Hill Hotel A
- Duang Kamol (D.K.) Hotel G
- Fortune D
- Green Guest House C
- Number 4 Guest House E

RESTAURANTS AND BARS

- Aiya 4
- Bai Fern F
- Crocodile Tear 3
- Khao-Mao Khao-Fang 1
- Kung's 2
- Krua Canadian Restaurant 5
- Raan Ahaan Mangsawirat Vegetarian Restaurant 6

TRANSPORT

- Minivans to Tak A
- Night Buses to Bangkok B
- Songthaews to Mae Sariang, Mae Ramat & Mae Salid C
- Buses to Chiang Mai, Chiang Rai, Mae Sai, Lampang & Lamphun D
- Songthaews to Rim Moei E
- Songthaews to Umphang F
- Songthaews & minibuses to Pha Charoen, KM 48, Phitsanulok and Sukhothai G

and Thais (plus a lively injection of committed NGO expats), and dependant both on its thriving trade in Burmese gems and teak as well as, reportedly, on an even more lucrative cross-border black market in drugs, labourers and sex workers. For the casual visitor, however, it's a relaxed place to hang out, with a burgeoning number of good restaurants to enjoy, albeit no real sights. The short ride to the border market provides additional, if low-key, interest, and there are several caves and waterfalls within day-tripping distance.

Mae Sot's main selling point, however, is as a stopover on the way to **Umphang** (see p.318), a remote village 164km further south, which is starting to get a name as a centre for interesting rafting and trekking adventures. The journey to Umphang takes about four hours in a bumpy songthaew, so it's usually worth staying the night in Mae Sot; you can also organize treks to Umphang through Mae Sot tour operators. If you need to change money for the trip, you should do so in Mae Sot (see "Listings", p.318) as there are no exchange facilities anywhere in Umphang.

Arrival and information

Mae Sot's buses and songthaews use a variety of different **transport terminals** around town (see the map for details), as well as the government bus station east of town near the Highway 105/1090 intersection. Although there are a few direct **buses** between Mae Sot and northern and central provincial capitals, as well as to and from Bangkok (mostly overnight), many people travel via Tak instead, which operates more frequent long-distance services and has good government **minivan** connections with Mae Sot (every 30min; 1hr 30min). If you're arriving on a government minibus from Tak, you may be dropped off at your chosen guest house. Local services include **songthaews** to Umphang (for details see p.318) and to the border towns of Mae Ramat (every 30min; 45min) and Mae Sariang (hourly 6am–midday; 5hr). Various airlines have tried to make a success out of running **flights** to Mae Sot's tiny airstrip, 3km west of town on the Asia Highway, but at the time of writing there were none in operation; contact the Thai Airways office in Mae Sot (Ⓣ055 531730) for latest developments.

There is no TAT office here, but both *Bai Fern* and *Khrua Canadian* restaurants are good sources of local **information**, and the best guest houses should also be able to help.

Accommodation

Because of the many volunteers in town, most guest houses offer weekly and monthly discounts.

Bai Fern 660/2 Thanon Indharakiri Ⓣ055 533343, Ⓔrungrapee@hotmail.com. Well-run, traveller-oriented guest house that's attached to one of the town's best restaurants. All rooms are pretty simple and share bathrooms: the better ones are quite large and light and are on the floor above the restaurant and in the house at the back; the ones immediately behind the restaurant are dark and quite noisy. Bicycle, motorbike and car rental available. ❶

Ban Thai 740/1 Thanon Indharakiri Ⓣ055 531590, Ⓔbanthai_mth@hotmail.com. The most appealing guest house in Mae Sot occupies several traditional-style, wooden-floored houses in a peaceful garden compound at the west end of town. All rooms are tastefully and comfortably furnished; those in the main house share bathrooms, while those in the more expensive compound houses are en suite and have cable TV. The compound is wi-fi compatible. As the guest house is popular with long-stay NGO volunteers, it's worth phoning ahead to check for vacancies. Also runs cookery courses. ❸

Central Mae Sot Hill Hotel 100 Asia Highway/Highway 105 Ⓣ055 532601, Ⓦwww.centralhotelsresorts.com. The most upmarket accommodation in the area, but a 10min drive from the town centre. All rooms are air-con, smartly furnished and have TV, and there's a swimming pool and tennis courts. ❼

Duang Kamol (D.K.) Hotel 298 Thanon Indharakiri Ⓣ055 531699, Ⓕ055 542651. The nicest and best value of the town-centre hotels is set above the bookshop of the same name, and has huge clean rooms, many of them with little balconies and some with air-con and TV. Fan ❷, air-con ❸

Fortune 738/1 Thanon Indharakiri Ⓣ055 536392 or 085 054 2683, Ⓔjaruneetana@yahoo.com. Large, clean and bright single, double and triple rooms in a purpose-built guest house run by an eager Burmese family at the west end of town. Some of the en-suite rooms are noisy as they're close to the road, but the singles are good value and air-con is also available. Phone for a pick-up from the bus terminal. Fan ❷, air-con ❸

Green Guest House Across the stream from the Tak/Mae Sariang bus station at 460/8 Thanon Indharakiri Ⓣ055 533207, Ⓔkritsanaya@yahoo.com. Small, friendly, clued-up place with a complex of ten good, clean rooms, all of them en suite. Those upstairs are nicest: large, light and with wooden floors, hot water and TV; downstairs ones are slightly cheaper and have cold water, no TV and concrete floors. Central, and especially handy for transport to Tak and Mae Sariang. Bikes and motorbikes for rent. ❷

Number 4 Guest House 736 Thanon Indharakiri Ⓣ & Ⓕ055 544976, Ⓦwww.geocities.com/no4guesthouse. Located in an old teak house about 15min walk west of the town centre, this place has the cheapest rooms in Mae Sot, though there's nothing more to them than a mattress and a fan. The emphasis is very much on self-service and doing your own thing, which can make it hard to get information, though Khun Om runs well-reviewed treks (see p.321) and has bicycles for rent. ❶

The Town

Over the last two decades the **Burmese population** of Mae Sot and its environs has swelled enormously (see the box on p.312) and the Burmese influence in Mae Sot is palpable in everything from food to fashions; many of the guest houses are run by Burmese staff, who often speak good English, and the only real sights in the town are its handful of glittering Burmese-style temples.

There are currently eleven camps for refugees from Burma along the border, to the north and south of Mae Sot, and Mae Sot itself is the headquarters for several related international **aid projects**; many of these organizations welcome donations of clothes and medicines, which can be left at *Ban Thai* and *Number 4* guest houses, and at *Krua Canadian* and *Bai Fern* restaurants. One of the most famous organizations in Mae Sot is the **Mae Tao clinic** (Ⓦwww.burmachildren.org), which provides free medical care for over 30,000 Burmese refugees a year, focusing on those who fall outside the remit of the refugee camps and cannot use the Thai health system. The clinic was founded in 1989 by a Karen refugee, Dr Cynthia, who has won several prestigious international awards for her work; her clinic also trains and equips "backpack teams" of mobile medics who spend months travelling through the Burmese jungle providing healthcare to internally displaced peoples. To help the clinic by giving blood or financial aid, contact one of the above-mentioned guest-houses or restaurants.

A number of places in town sell **Karen crafts**, including the Borderline shop next to Wat Arunyaket on Thanon Indharakiri, which is an outlet for shoulder-bags, sarongs and other items made by Karen women living in refugee camps along the border. For fashions, Burmese sarongs and daily necessities, you can't beat the well-stocked day market that runs south off Thanon Ruamchit. Mae Sot is most famous, however, as a good place to buy jewellery: the **gem and jade shops** clustered around the *Siam* hotel on Thanon Prasat Vithi offer a larger and less expensive selection than the stalls at the Rim Moei border market, and even if you don't intend to buy, just watching the performance-like haggling is half the fun.

Rim Moei market and the Burmese border

Frequent B10 songthaews ferry Thai traders and a meagre trickle of tourists the 6km from Mae Sot to the border at **RIM MOEI**, where a market for Burmese goods has grown up along the high street and beside the banks of the Moei River. It's a bit tacky, and not as fun to browse as Mae Sot's markets, but it's not a bad place to pick up Burmese **handicrafts**, particularly wooden artefacts like boxes and picture frames, woven Karen shoulder-bags and checked *longyis*. The best buys are chunky teak tables and chairs, most of them polished up to a fine golden brown sheen; vendors will arrange shipping.

At the time of writing, access to the Burmese village of **Myawaddy**, across the Thailand–Burma Friendship Bridge on the opposite bank of the Moei River, is open to any foreign national for a fee of B500, payable at the bridge, though foreign visitors are allowed no further **into Burma** than this, and must return to Thailand on the same day. When coming back through Thai customs (daily 6.30am–6.30pm; last exit from Burma at 5.30pm Thai time, 5pm Burmese time, and last entry into Thailand at 6pm) you will automatically be given a new one-month Thai visa on the spot, which is handy if your existing visa is running out, but not so great if you've still got the best part of a sixty-day visa (see Basics p.89 for how to pre-empt this problem). There's nothing much to see in Myawaddy save for an awful lot of samlor drivers touting for business, a few places to eat and a number of clothes stalls and the odd lacquerware outlet.

Around Mae Sot

There are several minor caves and waterfalls **around Mae Sot**, which are easy enough to explore if you have your own transport (see "Listings" on p.318 for rental outlets), though none can compare with Umphang's far mightier Thi Lor Su Falls.

Heading north out of Mae Sot, along Highway 105 towards Mae Ramat, take a side road at around kilometre-stone 13 for 7km to reach the three-tiered **Mae Kasa Falls** (rainy season only) and hot springs. Much further north, just after kilometre-stone 95 on Highway 105, a sign directs you the 2km off the highway to the enormous 800-metre-deep bat-cave, **Tham Mae Usu** (inaccessible from July to October because of flooding). South out of town, off Route 1090 to Umphang, the 97 tiers of **Pha Charoen Falls** are 41km from Mae Sot. A couple of kilometres on from the falls, **Highland Farm Gibbon Sanctuary** (ⓣ089 958 0821, ⓦwww.highland-farm.org) cares for over forty injured and abandoned gibbons, most of whom have been rescued from abusive owners and are unable to live in the wild. The sanctuary welcomes day-trippers and homestay visitors (minimum stay 3 nights full board at $25 per person per day), and also offers one-month placements ($600 all-inclusive). It's located beside the road at kilometre-stone 42.8. To get to the falls or the sanctuary (known as Baan Farang), take any songthaew bound for kilometre-stone 48 from the depot on the southern edge of Mae Sot.

Eco-conscious Mae Sot Conservation Tour, at 415/17 Thanon Tang Kim Chang (ⓣ055 532818, ⓔmaesotco@cscoms.com), runs **trips** to the upland jungle around Mae Lamao, home to Karen and Hmong hill tribes, about 25km east of Mae Sot off Highway 105. The jungle-craft day-trip includes an interpretative two-hour trek and whitewater-rafting (B2100, minimum four people); the overnight version adds a stay in a Karen village plus a side-trip to the gibbon sanctuary (B3500). Max One Tour, based in the *D.K. Hotel* plaza at 296/1 Thanon Indharakiri (ⓣ055 542942, ⓦwww.maxonetour.com), offers a one-day tour that covers the hot springs, Rim Moei border market, Pha Charoen Falls and the gibbon sanctuary for B1500 (minimum two people), or B2000 if you want to see Tham Mae Usu cave as well.

Eating and drinking

Thanon Prasat Vithi is well stocked with noodle-shops and night-market stalls, there's lots of Muslim and Burmese food for sale in the market, and the NGO presence ensures a good spread of restaurants and bars catering to Western palates.

Aiya Thanon Indharakiri, west of the Prasat Vithi junction. Thai and Burmese food, including especially good spiced Burmese-style curries made with seafood and with tofu and pineapple (from B60). Daily 4–10pm.

Bai Fern 660/2 Thanon Indharakiri. Highly recommended restaurant, attached to the guest house of the same name, which serves some of the best and most imaginative food in the region. The menu includes pepper steaks served with a variety of unusual sauces, salmon salad (B180), authentic Italian carbonara (B90), traditional Thai curries and lots of vegetarian options, as well as brownies, apple pie, chocolate cake and mixed-grain bread. Daily 7.30am–10pm.

Crocodile Tear Thanon Indharakiri. The place to head for cocktails and draught beer, and live performances of blues, Latin and folk music every night from around 9pm.

Khao-Mao Khao-Fang Out of town, 2km north towards Mae Ramat up Highway 105. A garden restaurant extraordinaire, where the artfully landscaped cascades, rivers, lianas, rock features and mature trees make you feel as if you're sitting in a primeval forest film set, especially at night when sea-green lighting adds to the effect. A popular spot for dates and VIP lunches, it serves fairly pricey food that's nothing special, but the cocktails are fun and as one of Mae Sot's most famous attractions, it's worth the hassle to get here. During the day you could use the Mae Ramat/Mae Sariang songthaew service, but after dark you'll need your own transport.

Kung's 668/3 Thanon Indharakiri (no English sign). Characterful bar-restaurant that's a favourite haunt of NGOs thanks to its delicious Thai food (from B60), including recommended snakehead orange curry, rice with Chiang Mai sausage, and morning-glory tempura, plus great-value margaritas. Sit at the low-slung tables and chairs outdoors or play pool and ponder the arty table-displays inside.

Krua Canadian Restaurant Near the police station, just off Thanon Indharakiri. There's a great menu of delicious dishes at this NGO favourite (mostly B40–80), including local specialities such as stir-fried frog and bird curry, mango catfish salad and *matsaman* curries, plus tofu steak and chips. Also serves several blends of local hill-tribe coffee, plus a long menu of veggie options. DVD screenings in the evening.

Raan Ahaan Mangsawirat Vegetarian Restaurant Right next to the Umphang songthaew stop off Thanon Sriphanit. Tiny vegetarian food shop serving ultra-cheap veggie curries with rice (B15–20) daily until about 3pm.

Listings

Airlines The office for Thai and Andaman Airways is in the town centre at 76/1 Thanon Prasat Vithi ⓣ055 531730. You can also buy domestic and international air tickets at Mae Sot Conservation Tour, 415/17 Thanon Tang Kim Chang (ⓣ055 532818), and at Southeast Tours Internet centre and travel agent on Thanon Indharakiri ⓣ089 142 6664, ⓦwww.travelsoutheastasia.com.

Banks and exchange There are several banks with money-changing facilities and ATMs on Thanon Prasat Vithi.

Bicycle, car and motorbike rental Most guest houses have rental bicycles for guests. *Bai Fern* restaurant rents cars (B1200), motorbikes (B150) and bicycles (B50).

Books A few English-language books are on sale at D.K. Books on Thanon Indharakiri.

Cookery lessons Available through *Ban Thai* guest house (B500).

Emergencies For all emergencies, call the tourist police on the free, 24hr phoneline ⓣ1155, or contact them at the police station on Thanon Indharakiri.

Hospitals Mae Sot Hospital is on the southeastern edge of town and Pha Wawa Hospital is on the southwestern edge.

Immigration office At Rim Moei border crossing.

Language lessons Thai lessons through *Krua Canadian Restaurant*, just off Thanon Indharakiri. Burmese lessons available through most guest houses and several restaurants.

Massage Herbal massage at Tuek Luang Yellow House, opposite *Siam* hotel on Thanon Prasat Vithi. Herbal saunas (3–7pm) at Wat Mani, on Thanon Indharakiri.

Telephone International calls from the government telephone office at the far west end of Thanon Indharakiri.

Umphang

Even if you don't fancy doing a trek, consider making the spectacular trip 164km south from Mae Sot to the village of **UMPHANG**, both for the stunning mountain scenery you'll encounter along the way, and for the buzz of being in such an isolated part of Thailand. Umphang-bound songthaews leave Mae Sot from a spot two blocks south of Thanon Prasat Vithi, departing every hour between 7.30am and 3.30pm and costing B120, or B170 if you're lucky enough to get the front seat. The drive generally takes about four hours and for the first hour proceeds in a fairly gentle fashion through the maize, cabbage and banana plantations of the Moei valley. The fun really begins when you start climbing into the mountains and the road – accurately dubbed the "Sky Highway" – careers round the edges of steep-sided valleys, undulating like a fairground rollercoaster (there are said to be 1219 bends in all). The scenery is glorious, but if you're prone to car-sickness, take some preventative tablets before setting out, as this journey can be very unpleasant, not least because the songthaews get so crammed with people and produce that there's often no possibility of distracting yourself by staring out of the window. Karen, Akha, Lisu and Hmong people live in the few hamlets along the route, many growing cabbages along the cleared lower slopes with the help of government incentives (part of a national campaign to steer upland farmers away from the opium trade). The Hmong in particular are easily recognized by their distinctive

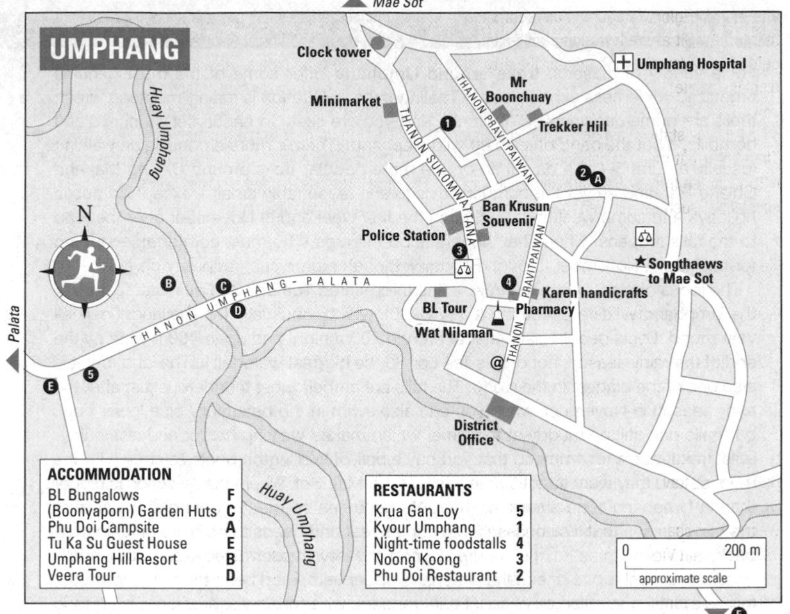

embroidered jackets and skirts edged in bright pink, red and blue bands (see p.914). In 2000, the local Karen population mushroomed when three refugee camps from the Rim Moei area were relocated to the purpose-built village of Umpium alongside the Sky Highway midway between Mae Sot and Umphang, just beyond the checkpoint (see the box on p.312 for more on Karen refugees from Burma). As of June 2005 Umpium was home to 19,000 Karen refugees. In fact the Umphang region was inhabited by Karen hill tribes before the Thais came to settle in the area in the early twentieth century; later when the Thais began trading in earnest with their neighbours across the Burmese border, the Karen traders from Burma used to carry their identification documents into Thailand in a bamboo container which they called an "umpha" – this is believed to be the origin of the name Umphang.

Surrounded by mountains and situated at the confluence of the Mae Khlong and Umphang rivers, Umphang itself is small and very quiet, made up of little more than a thousand or so wooden houses and a wat. It won't take long to explore the minute grid of narrow roads that dissects the village, but independent tourists are still relatively rare here, so you should get a friendly reception. Bring some warm clothes as it can get pretty cool at night and in the early mornings – and the songthaew ride from Mae Sot is often windy.

Practicalities

A few very shaky **mountain bikes** can be rented from *Tu Ka Su Guest House*; there's no official motorbike rental, but some guest-house owners will oblige. When it comes to public transport, Umphang is effectively a dead end, so the only way to travel on from here is to go back to Mae Sot first. **Songthaews** to Mae Sot leave at least hourly until noon from the top of the town, 300m uphill from Thanon Pravitpaiwan, but they always circulate around town

Trekking around Umphang

For a variety of reasons, **treks around Umphang** offer some of the most genuine organized wilderness experiences in Thailand; the vegetation is mainly montane forest, there are numerous varieties of orchid, and you are likely to encounter monkeys and hornbills, if not the band of resident wild elephants. There's more emphasis on walking (usually around 3–4hr a day) than on the more popular treks around Chiang Mai and Chiang Rai, and as yet the number of visitors is reasonably small – except on public holidays and some weekends, including the first weekend in November after the road to the falls reopens, when Thai trippers flood the area. The most comfortable **season** for trekking is November through February, though nights can get pretty chilly.

The focus of most Umphang treks is the three-tiered **Tee Lor Su Falls**, star feature of the Umphang Wildlife Sanctuary (entry B200), which, unusually for Thailand, flows all year round. Local people claim that at around 200m high, and up to 400m wide by the end of the rainy season, not only is Tee Lor Su the biggest waterfall in Thailand, but it is also one of the biggest in the world. The falls are at their most thunderous just after the rainy season in November, when you can also swim in the beautifully blue lower pool, but trails can still be muddy at this time, which makes walking harder and less enjoyable; trek leaders recommend that you buy a pair of Wellington boots to cope with the mud, so you may want to anticipate this when in Mae Sot, where the selection is bigger than in Umphang. One stretch of the route becomes so muddy during and just after the rainy season that it's impassable to human feet and needs to be done on elephant-back, a ride of three to four hours. During the dry season (Dec–April), it's usually possible to climb up to one of the waterfall's upper tiers, mud permitting. Access to the falls is strictly controlled by national park rangers, who forbid visitors from taking food or plastic water bottles beyond the ranger station and campsite, which is 1.5km from the falls. Trekkers reach Tee Lor Su Falls via a fairly challenging combination of rafting and walking, but from November 1 to May 30 the **4WD road** to the ranger station is opened to the public, which means you only have to walk the 1.5km route to the falls. During this period some tour operators offer this car-plus-hike option as a day-trip from Umphang, usually throwing in a rafting session as well, or you could rent a car from one of the Umphang operators, such as Umphang Hill, and drive yourself.

A **typical trek** lasts three days and follows something like the following itinerary. Day one: rafting down the Mae Khlong River via Tee Lor Jor Falls and some impressively honeycombed cliffs; camp overnight at hot springs or beside the river. Day two: a three- to four-hour jungle trek to Tee Lor Su Falls; camp near the falls. Day three: a three-hour trek to a Karen village; a two-hour elephant-ride; return to Umphang. Longer or shorter treks are possible.

Although Tee Lor Su is the most famous destination in the Umphang area, a couple of other programmes that emphasize whitewater-rafting are also becoming popular. From June through October there's whitewater-rafting from the Karen village of **Umphang Khi** via the forty-plus rapids of the Umphang River, which can also include a fairly long trek and a night in the village. Alternatively, there are one- and two-day rafting trips to **Thi Lor Leh Falls**, which involve four to eight hours' rafting (depending on water levels) via a series of cataracts along the Mae Khlong River, and the possibility of a seven-hour trek on the second day.

It's possible to **arrange your trek** in Mae Sot, or even in Bangkok, but the best place to set up a trip is in Umphang itself. Not only are trips from here usually cheaper and better value (you don't waste half a trek day getting to Umphang), but trek leaders are more flexible and happy to take small groups and to customize itineraries. They are experts on the area, and your custom helps boost the economy of the village. The best time to contact trek leaders at the smaller outfits is often after about 4pm, when they've returned from their last trip. Guides should provide tents, bedrolls, mosquito nets and sleeping bags, plus food and drinking water; trekkers may be asked to help carry some of the gear.

Mae Sot trekking operators

In addition to the specialist agencies listed below, you can also try asking at *Fortune* guest house and at *Bai Fern* and *Krua Canadian* restaurants.

Khun Om C/o *Number 4 Guest House*, 736 Thanon Indharakiri ⓣ & ⓕ 055 544976, ⓦwww.geocities.com/no4guesthouse. The treks run by the taciturn Khun Om get rave reviews. He offers a four-day Tee Lor Su programme for B4500 and an extended five-day four night version featuring a hearty climb up Doi Phuwatoo (B5600) as well as – his *pièce de résistance* – a seven-day expedition all the way down to Sangkhlaburi for US$400 per person. Although it can be hard to elicit information from the staff at *Number 4*, full details of the treks are given on their website; book ahead if possible.

Mae Sot Conservation Tour 415/17 Thanon Tang Kim Chang ⓣ055 532818, ⓔmaesotco@cscoms.com. This eco-conscious outfit offers the four-day Tee Lor Su option for B5800.

Max One Tour In the *D.K. Hotel* plaza at 296/1 Thanon Indharakiri ⓣ055 542942, ⓦwww.maxonetour.com and at SP Tour ⓣ055 531409, at the Mae Sot Travel Centre on the northern outskirts of town at 14/21 Asia Highway (Highway 105). Prices start at B5700 per person (minimum two people) for three days and two nights to Tee Lor Su if departing from Mae Sot, or B3700 if you make your own way to Umphang. Their three-day trek with rafting on the Umphang River costs B5750 from Mae Sot or B4000 from Umphang. See Umphang Hill below for full details.

Umphang trekking operators

The main English-speaking trek leaders operating out of Umphang at the time of writing are listed below, but you can also arrange treks through staff at *Umphang House* and *Tu Ka Su Guest House*. Note that there are **no exchange facilities** in Umphang so you must bring enough cash to cover the cost of your trek.

BL Tour 1/438 Thanon Umphang-Palata ⓣ055 561021. As well as the standard three-day trips to Tee Lor Su (from B3800), BL also runs one- and two-day options to Umphang Khi (from B2500).

Mr Boonchuay 360 Thanon Pravitpaiwan ⓣ055 561020, ⓔboonchuay_umpang @hotmail.com. Umphang-born and bred, Mr Boonchuay knows the area well and has a good reputation; though his English is not perfect, he has English-speaking guides. He does three-day treks for B3300 per person and four-day treks for B4000 (minimum two). Trekkers can stay in the basic concrete rooms behind his office (B200/dble) or in nicer bungalows down by the river (B250/dble).

Phu Doi 637 Thanon Pravitpaiwan ⓣ055 561049, ⓦwww.phudoi.com. Two- and three-day treks to Tee Lor Su (from B2500/3200), and one-day dry-season outings by car (B1700); half and one-day-trips around the Umphang area from B750/1500. Good bungalow accommodation at *Phu Doi Campsite* in Umphang (see p.322).

Trekker Hill Off Thanon Pravitpaiwan ⓣ055 561090, ⓕ055 561328. Mr Tee and his "jungle team" of five guides get good reviews. Runs three- and four-day treks to Tee Lor Su (B4000/B5000) and can also arrange dry season drive-trek-and-raft tours to Tee Lor Su, one-day raft trips around Umphang Khi, and day-trips to view Doi Hua Mot mountain range. Offers accommodation for trekkers in simple, en-suite double bungalows at B250.

Umphang Hill At *Umphang Hill Resort* on Thanon Umphang-Palata, but can also be booked through Max One Tour in Mae Sot ⓣ055 561063, ⓦwww.umphanghill.com. Efficiently run, this place often undercuts rival outfits and has English-speaking staff at the office throughout the day. They do more than a dozen itineraries and tailor-made permutations; most are led by local Karen guides and get enthusiastic reviews. Two-day treks cost from B3000; three-day treks cost B4000, or about B3500 for the Umphang Khi whitewater trip; four days B4500 (minimum two people; prices drop with larger groups). From Dec–May, with advance notice, they can also arrange a challenging seven-day trek to Sangkhlaburi (B9000/person, minimum four people).

before heading off so your guest house can arrange for the songthaew to pick you up. After noon you'll probably need to charter the whole vehicle. There's an **Internet** centre (daily 8am–8pm) to the south of the temple on Thanon Pravitpaiwan, a **pharmacy** near the temple on Thanon Pravitpaiwan, and a basic **hospital** on the northeast edge of town.

Accommodation and eating

Most of the **accommodation** in Umphang is geared either towards groups of trekkers accompanied by Thai guides, or towards independent travellers who are overnighting just before or after their trek. Because of this, many places charge per person rather than per room; the categories listed below are for two people sharing a room, so expect to pay half if you're on your own. Most trekking companies have their own accommodation (see p.321).

There are several **places to eat** along Thanon Umphang-Palata, including *Krua Gan Loy* just east of *Tu Ka Su*, which does good cheap Thai standards and stays opens late; the riverside restaurant at *Umphang Hill Resort,* which has no English-language menu but serves good authentic Thai restaurant food and features karaoke in the evenings; and nearby *Boonyaporn Garden Huts,* site of a pleasantly situated riverside bar. Elsewhere, *Phu Doi Restaurant* has an English-language menu of curries and meat-over-rice dishes; *Kyour Umphang*, west down a lane across from Mr Boonchuay, does cheap and tasty crispy-fried catfish, Isaan sausage, fried frog with garlic and simpler rice and noodle dishes (B30–60); *Noong Koong* does cheap noodles during the day; and at dusk night-time foodstalls set up close by the temple and the pharmacy.

BL Bungalows 2km east of Umphang, bookable through the central tour office at 1/438 Thanon Umphang-Palata ⓣ055 561021, ⓕ055 561322. Nice, simple, en-suite bungalows in a stunning spot a couple of kilometres east of town, surrounded by fields and with fine hill views. There's a restaurant here too. ❹

(Boonyaporn) Garden Huts 106 Thanon Umphang-Palata, ⓣ055 561093, ⓦwww.boonyaporn.com. A spread of accommodation options, set around a riverside garden, ranging from fairly simple wooden huts with shared bathrooms to quite attractive wooden en-suite bungalows with decks and partial river-views. The most expensive rooms have air-con and TV. Fan ❷–❹, air-con ❻

Phu Doi Campsite 637 Thanon Pravitpaiwan ⓣ055 561049, ⓦwww.phudoi.com. Decent set of comfortable fan rooms in a couple of wooden houses with verandas overlooking a pond, plus some rooms above the office. All rooms have private bathrooms. ❸

Tu Ka Su Guest House 129 Thanon Umphang-Palata ⓣ055 561295, ⓦwww.tukasu.com. In a pretty garden up the hill from the river, this quite stylish place offers nicely designed en-suite wooden cabins, with TV; some with cute, semi-garden-style bathrooms. ❹

Umphang Hill Resort 99 Thanon Umphang-Palata ⓣ055 561063, ⓦwww.umphanghill.com. Attractively set in a flower garden on a slope leading down to the river, with views of the surrounding mountains. Large, basic chalets with veranda, fan or air-con, TV and hot water, plus some ultra-cheap tiny trekkers' huts fashioned out of converted ox-carts and with just enough room for a double mattresses and nothing else plus a veranda overlooking the river. Ox cart hut ❶, fan ❹, air-con ❺

Veera Tour Thanon Umphang-Palata ⓣ055 561239. Decent enough if rather dark rooms with mattresses and shared bathrooms in a large timber house. ❷

Travel details

Trains

Ayutthaya to: Bangkok Hualamphong Station (30 daily; 1hr 30min); Chiang Mai (6 daily; 12hr); Lopburi (20 daily; 1hr–1hr 30min); Nong Khai (4 daily; 9hr 30min); Phitsanulok (12 daily; 4hr 30min–5hr 30min); Ubon Ratchathani (7 daily; 8hr 30min–10hr).

Kanchanaburi to: Bangkok Thonburi (2 daily; 3hr); Nakhon Pathom (2 daily; 2hr); Nam Tok (3 daily; 2hr–2hr 30min).
Lopburi to: Ayutthaya (20 daily; 1hr–1hr 30min); Bangkok Hualamphong Station (15 daily; 2hr 30min–3hr); Chiang Mai (6 daily; 11hr); Phitsanulok (12 daily; 3hr–5hr 15min).
Nakhon Pathom to: Bangkok Hualamphong (12 daily; 1hr 40min); Bangkok Thonburi (2 daily; 1hr 10min); Butterworth (Malaysia; 1 daily; 19hr 50min); Chumphon (11 daily; 5hr 45 min–8hr 30min); Hat Yai (5 daily; 12hr 15min–16hr); Hua Hin (12 daily; 2hr 15min–3hr 15min); Kanchanaburi (2 daily; 1hr 35min); Nakhon Si Thammarat (2 daily; 15hr); Nam Tok (2 daily; 3hr 30min); Padang Besar (Malaysia; 1 daily; 15hr 30min); Phetchaburi (10 daily; 1hr 20min–2hr 20min); Sungai Kolok (2 daily; 18hr 30min–20hr); Surat Thani (11 daily; 8hr–11hr 30min); Trang (2 daily; 14–15hr).
Nam Tok to: Bangkok Thonburi (2 daily; 5hr).
Phitsanulok to: Ayutthaya (11 daily; 4hr–5hr 30min); Bangkok Hualamphong (10 daily; 5hr 30min–8hr); Chiang Mai (6 daily; 5hr 50min–7hr 40min); Don Muang Airport (11 daily; 4hr 50min–7hr); Lamphun (6 daily; 5hr 40min–7hr 20min); Lopburi (10 daily; 3hr–5hr 15min).
Samut Sakhon (Mahachai) to: Bangkok Wongwian Yai (17 daily; 1hr).
Samut Songkhram (Maeklong) to: Ban Laem (4 daily; 1hr).

Buses

Ayutthaya to: Bangkok (every 20min; 2hr); Chiang Mai (14 daily; 9hr); Lopburi (every 20min; 2hr); Phitsanulok (10 daily; 5hr); Sukhothai (11 daily; 6hr); Suphanburi (every 30min; 1hr); Tak (15 daily; 6hr).
Bang Pa-In to: Bangkok (every 30min; 2hr).
Damnoen Saduak to: Bangkok (every 20min; 2hr).
Kamphaeng Phet to: Bangkok (7 daily; 6hr 30min); Sukhothai (hourly; 1hr–1hr 30min); Tak (hourly; 1hr).
Kanchanaburi to: Bangkok (Northern Bus Terminal; 9 daily; 2hr 30min); Bangkok (Southern Bus Terminal; every 15min; 2hr); Erawan (every 50min; 1hr 30min–2hr); Nam Tok (every 30min; 1hr 30min); Ratchaburi (every 15min; 2hr); Sai Yok (every 30min; 2hr 30min); Sangkhlaburi (11–18 daily; 3–6hr); Suphanburi (every 20min; 2hr); Thong Pha Phum (every 30min; 3hr).
Lopburi to: Bangkok (every 20min; 2hr 30min–3hr), via Wat Phra Phutthabat (30min); Chiang Mai (3 daily; 9hr); Khorat (9 daily; 3hr 30min); Phitsanulok (3 daily; 4hr); Suphanburi (hourly; 3hr).
Mae Sot to: Bangkok (13 daily; 8hr 30min); Chiang Mai (4 daily; 6hr 30min–7hr 30min); Chiang Rai (2 daily; 11hr); Mae Ramat (every 30min; 45min); Mae Sai (2 daily; 12hr); Mae Sariang (7 daily; 5hr); Phitsanulok (7 daily; 3hr 15min–5hr); Sukhothai (6 daily; 2hr 30min–3hr); Tak (every 30min; 1hr 30min–3hr); Umphang (9 daily; 4hr).
Nakhon Pathom to: Bangkok (every 10min; 40min–1hr 20min); Damnoen Saduak (every 20min; 1hr); Kanchanaburi (every 10min; 1hr 45min).
Nam Tok to: Sangkhlaburi (4 daily; 3hr 30min).
Phitsanulok to: Bangkok (up to 19 daily; 5–6hr); Chiang Mai (up to 18 daily; 5–6hr); Chiang Rai (17 daily; 6–7hr); Kamphaeng Phet (hourly; 3hr); Khon Kaen (10 daily; 5–6hr); Khorat/Nakhon Ratchasima (21 daily; 6–7hr); Loei (15 daily; 5hr); Lomsak (hourly; 2hr); Mae Sot (7 daily; 3hr 15min–5hr); Phrae (7 daily; 2–3hr); Sukhothai (every 30min; 1hr); Tak (every 30min; 2–3hr); Ubon Ratchathani (7 daily; 12hr); Udon Thani (5 daily; 7hr).
Samut Songkhram to: Bangkok (every 20min; 1hr 30min).
Sukhothai to: Bangkok (up to 17 daily; 6–7hr); Chiang Mai (up to 16 daily; 5–6hr); Chiang Rai (4 daily; 8–9hr); Kamphaeng Phet (hourly; 1hr–1hr 30min); Khon Kaen (11 daily; 6–7hr); Mae Sot (9 daily; 2hr 30 min–3hr); Nan (2 daily; 6hr); Phitsanulok (every 30min; 1hr); Phrae (4 daily; 4hr); Si Satchanalai (every 30min; 1hr); Tak (every 30min; 1hr).
Tak to: Bangkok (13 daily; 7hr); Chiang Mai (8 daily; 4–6hr); Kamphaeng Phet (hourly; 1hr); Mae Sot (every 30min; 1hr 30min–3hr); Phitsanulok (every 30min; 2hr); Sukhothai (every 30min; 1hr).

Flights

Phitsanulok to: Bangkok (2–3 daily; 45min).
Sukhothai to: Bangkok (1–2 daily; 1hr 10min); Chiang Mai (2 daily; 40min).

3

The north

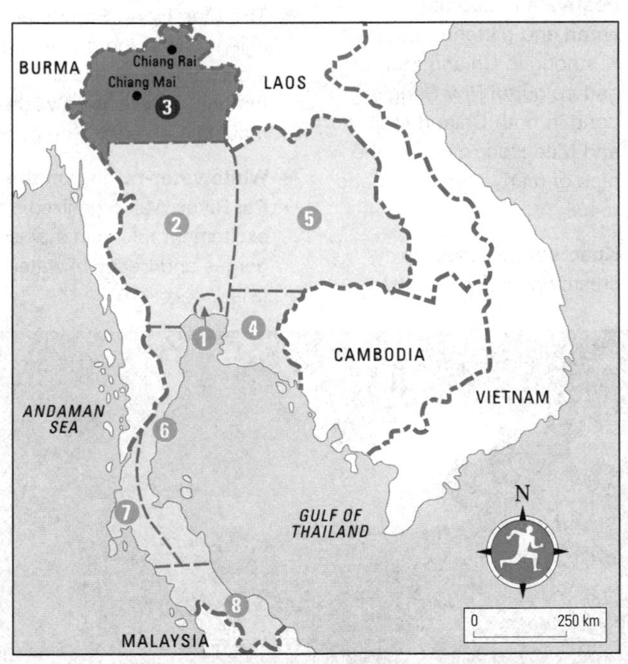
BURMA
Chiang Rai
Chiang Mai
3
LAOS
2
5
1
4
CAMBODIA
VIETNAM
ANDAMAN SEA
6
7
GULF OF THAILAND
N
8
0
250 km
MALAYSIA

CHAPTER 3

Highlights

- **Hill-tribe trekking** A chance to visit these fascinating peoples and explore the dramatic countryside. See p.331
- **Chiang Mai** Old-town temples, cookery courses, the best of Thai crafts, fine restaurants – still a great place to hang out. See p.334
- **Festivals** Exuberant Songkhran and glittering Loy Krathong in Chiang Mai, and colourful Poy Sang Long in both Chiang Mai and Mae Hong Son are the pick of many. See p.352 and p.408
- **Khao soi** Delicious, spicy, creamy noodle soup, the northern Thai signature dish. See p.362
- **Wat Phra That Doi Suthep** Towering views from this stunning example of temple architecture. See p.368
- **Nan** An underrated all-rounder, offering beautiful temple murals, handicrafts and landscapes. See p.388
- **The Mae Hong Son loop** A roller-coaster journey – with a chill-out break in Pai – through the country's wildest mountain scenery. See p.395
- **Whitewater-rafting on the Pai River** Well-organized excitement taking in rapids, gorges and beautiful waterfalls. See p.418

△ The Mae Hong Son loop

3

The north

Travelling up through the central plains, there's no mistaking when you've reached the **north** of Thailand: somewhere between Uttaradit and Den Chai, the train slows almost to a halt, as if approaching a frontier post, to meet the abruptly rising mountains that continue largely unbroken to the borders of Burma and Laos. Beyond this point the climate becomes more temperate, nurturing the fertile land which gave the old kingdom of the north the name of **Lanna**, "the land of a million rice fields". Although only one-tenth of the land can be used for rice cultivation, the valley rice fields here are three times more productive than those in the dusty northeast, and the higher land yields a great variety of fruits, as well as beans, groundnuts and tobacco.

Until the beginning of the last century, Lanna was a largely independent region. On the back of its agricultural prosperity, it developed its own styles of art and architecture, which can still be seen in its flourishing temples and distinctive handicraft traditions. The north is also set apart from the rest of the country by its exuberant festivals, a cuisine which has been heavily influenced by Burma and a dialect quite distinct from central Thai. Northerners proudly call themselves *khon muang*, "people of the principalities", and their gentle sophistication is admired by the people of Bangkok, whose wealthier citizens build their holiday homes in the clean air of the north's forested mountains.

Chiang Mai, the capital and transport centre of the north, is a great place just to hang out or to prepare for a journey into the hills. For many travellers, this means joining a trek to visit one or more of the **hill tribes**, who comprise one-tenth of the north's population and are just about clinging onto the ways of life which distinguish them from one another and the Thais around them. For those with qualms about the exploitative element of this ethnological tourism, there are plenty of other, more independent options. To the west, the trip to **Mae Hong Son** takes you through the most stunning mountain scenery in the region into a land with its roots across the border in Burma, with the option of looping back through **Pai**, a laid-back hill station for travellers. Bidding to rival Chiang Mai as a base for exploring the countryside is **Chiang Rai** to the north; above Chiang Rai, the northernmost tip of Thailand is marked by the fascinating border town of **Mae Sai**, and the junction of Laos and Burma at **Sop Ruak**. Fancifully dubbed the "Golden Triangle", Sop Ruak is a must on every bus party's itinerary – you're more likely to find peace and quiet among the ruins of nearby **Chiang Saen**, set on the leafy banks of the Mekong River. Few visitors backtrack south from Chiang Mai, even though the towns of **Lamphun**, **Lampang** and **Phrae** are packed with artistic and historical goodies. Further out on a limb to the east, **Nan** is even less popular, but combines rich mountain scenery with eclectic temple art.

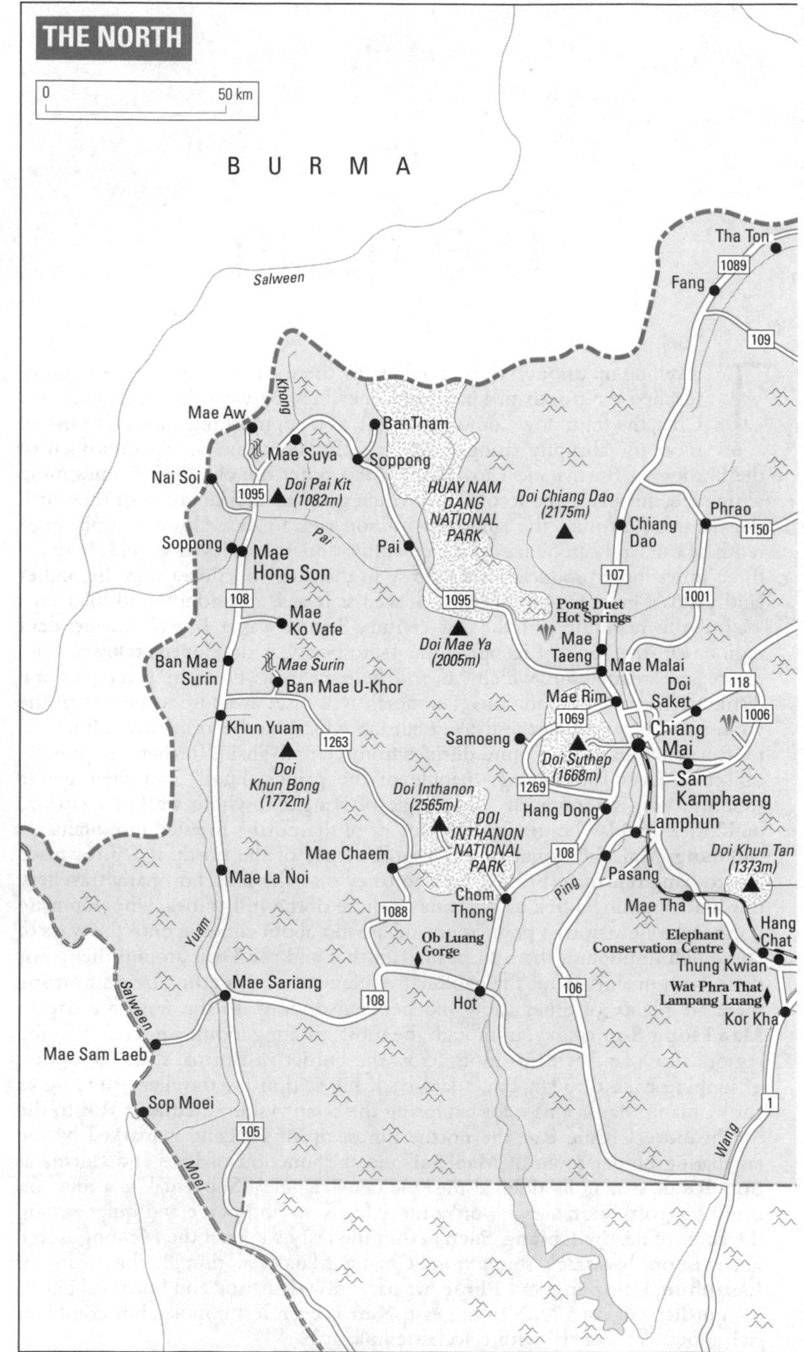
THE NORTH
0
50 km
B U R M A
Salween
Tha Ton
1089
Fang
109
Khong
Mae Aw
BanTham
Mae Suya
Soppong
Nai Soi
1095
Doi Pai Kit (1082m)
HUAY NAM DANG NATIONAL PARK
Doi Chiang Dao (2175m)
Chiang Dao
Phrao
1150
Pai
Soppong
Mae Hong Son
Pai
107
108
1001
1095
Pong Duet Hot Springs
Mae Ko Vafe
Doi Mae Ya (2005m)
Mae Taeng
Ban Mae Surin
Mae Surin
Mae Malai
Ban Mae U-Khor
Doi Saket
118
Mae Rim
1006
Khun Yuam
1069
Chiang Mai
1263
Samoeng
Doi Suthep (1668m)
Doi Khun Bong (1772m)
San Kamphaeng
Doi Inthanon (2565m)
1269
Hang Dong
Lamphun
DOI INTHANON NATIONAL PARK
Mae Chaem
108
Doi Khun Tan (1373m)
Mae La Noi
Pasang
Chom Thong
Ping
Mae Tha
11
1088
Hang Chat
Yuam
Ob Luang Gorge
Elephant Conservation Centre
Thung Kwian
Mae Sariang
Wat Phra That Lampang Luang
108
Hot
106
Kor Kha
Salween
Mae Sam Laeb
Sop Moei
1
105
Wang
Moei
Mae Sot
Tak

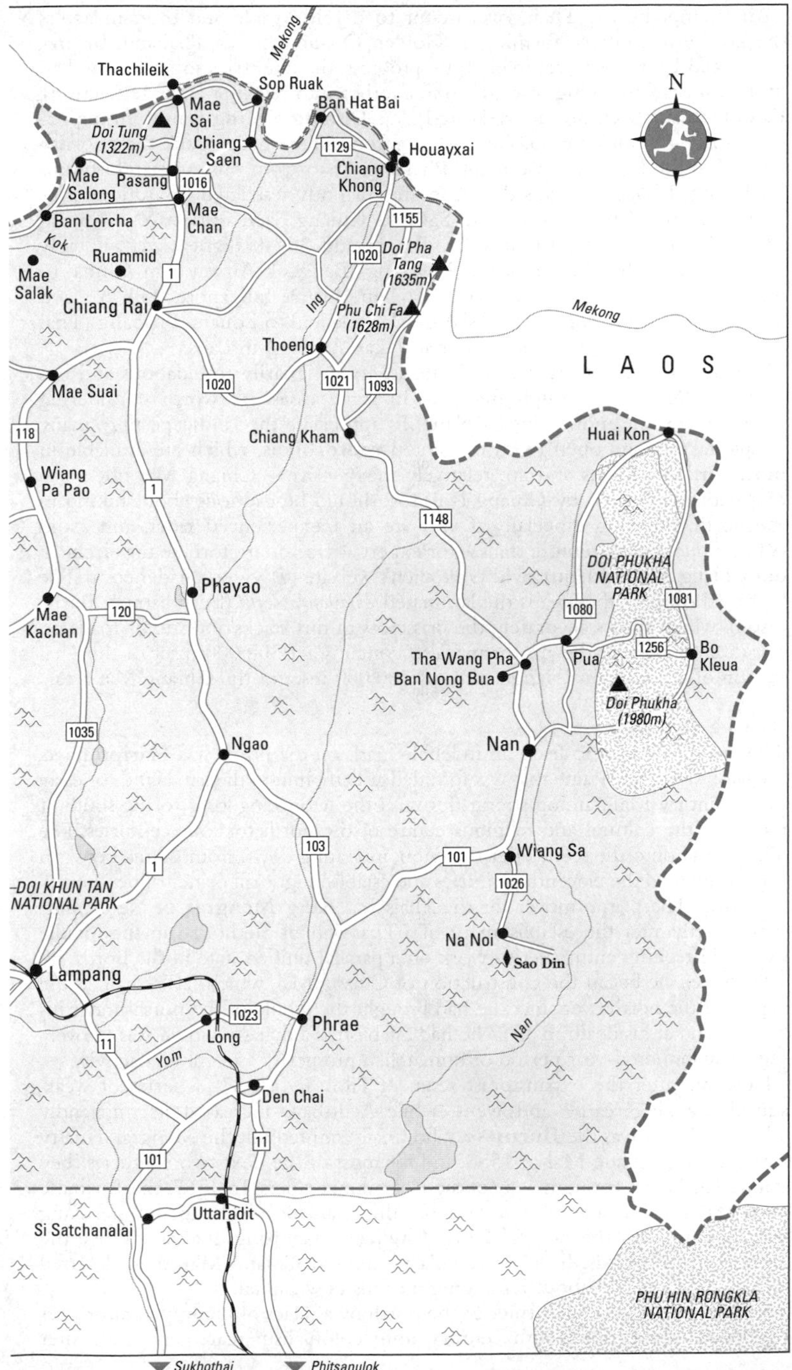

Mekong
Thachileik
Sop Ruak
Ban Hat Bai
Mae Sai
Doi Tung (1322m)
Chiang Saen
1129
Houayxai
Chiang Khong
Mae Salong
Pasang
1016
Mae Chan
Ban Lorcha
1155
Kok
Ruammid
1020
Doi Pha Tang (1635m)
Mae Salak
1
Chiang Rai
Ing
Phu Chi Fa (1628m)
Mekong
Thoeng
L A O S
1020
1021
1093
Mae Suai
118
Chiang Kham
Huai Kon
Wiang Pa Pao
1
1148
DOI PHUKHA NATIONAL PARK
Phayao
1081
1080
Mae Kachan
120
1256
Pua
Bo Kleua
Tha Wang Pha
Ban Nong Bua
Doi Phukha (1980m)
1035
Ngao
Nan
103
101
Wiang Sa
1
DOI KHUN TAN NATIONAL PARK
1026
Na Noi
Sao Din
Lampang
1023
Phrae
Long
Nan
11
Yom
Den Chai
11
101
Uttaradit
Si Satchanalai
PHU HIN RONGKLA NATIONAL PARK
Sukhothai
Phitsanulok
N

An attempt by the Thai government to develop trade and tourism across the northern frontiers, forming a "Golden Quadrangle" of Thailand, Burma, China and Laos, has as yet made little progress, the countries so far having had limited success in trying to cajole one another into relaxing entry restrictions. East of Chiang Saen on the Mekong River, **Chiang Khong** is now an important crossing point to Houayxai in Laos, from where boats make the two-day trip down the Mekong to Louang Phabang. Apart from this, overland options for leaving Thailand in this direction are currently restricted to arduous trips to Burma and China, from Mae Sai and Chiang Saen respectively. Chiang Mai International Airport now handles around 30–40 flights a day, notably to Kunming (Thai Airways) and Jinghong (Bangkok Airways) in China, to Rangoon and Mandalay (Air Mandalay) in Burma, Singapore (Silk Air and Tiger Air), Kuala Lumpur (Air Asia) in Malaysia and to Louang Phabang (Thai Airways and Lao Airlines) and Vientiane (Lao Airlines) in Laos.

Transport routes in northern Thailand are necessarily roundabout and bus services often slow, though frequent: in some cases, it's worth considering hopping over the mountains by plane. To appreciate the landscape fully, many people take to the open roads on rented **motorbikes**, which are available in most northern towns and are relatively inexpensive – Chiang Mai offers the best choice, followed by Chiang Rai. You should be cautious about biking in the north, however, especially if you are an inexperienced rider, and avoid riding alone on any remote trails – for expert advice on motorbike travel, check out Chiang Mai resident David Unkovich's website (Ⓦwww.gt-rider.com). The best road **map** of the area is the laminated *Thailand North* (Berndtson & Berndtson), which shows accurately the crisscross of dirt tracks and minor roads on a 1:750,000 map of the north, and also contains a 1:500,000 inset of the Thai section of the Golden Triangle and a 1:300,000 inset of the Chiang Mai area.

Some history

The first civilization to leave an indelible mark on the north was **Haripunjaya**, the Mon (Dvaravati) state that was founded at Lamphun in the late eighth or early ninth century. Maintaining strong ties with the Mon kingdoms to the south, it remained the cultural and religious centre of the north for four centuries. The Thais came onto the scene after the Mon, migrating down from China between the seventh and the eleventh centuries and establishing small principalities around the north. The prime mover for the Thais was **King Mengrai** of Ngon Yang, who, shortly after the establishment of a Thai state at Sukhothai in the middle of the thirteenth century, set to work on a parallel unified state in the north. By 1296, when he began the construction of Chiang Mai, which has remained the capital of the north ever since, he had brought the whole of the north under his control, and at his death in 1317 he had established a dynasty which was to oversee a two-hundred-year period of unmatched prosperity and cultural activity.

However, after the expansionist reign of Tilok (1441–87), a series of weak, squabbling kings came and went, while Ayutthaya increased its unfriendly advances. But it was the **Burmese** who finally snuffed out the Mengrai dynasty by capturing Chiang Mai in 1558, and for most of the next two centuries they controlled Lanna through a succession of puppet rulers. In 1767, the Burmese sacked the Thai capital at Ayutthaya, but the Thais soon regrouped under King Taksin, who with the help of **King Kawila** of Lampang gradually drove the Burmese northwards. In 1774 Kawila recaptured Chiang Mai, then deserted and in ruins, and set about rebuilding it as his new capital.

Kawila was succeeded as ruler of the north by a series of incompetent princes for much of the nineteenth century, until colonialism reared its head. After

Britain took control of Upper Burma, **Rama V** of Bangkok began to take an interest in the north – where, since the Bowring Treaty of 1855, the British had established lucrative logging businesses – to prevent its annexation. He forcibly moved large numbers of ethnic Thais northwards, in order to counter the British claim of sovereignty over territory occupied by Thai Yai (Shan), who also make up a large part of the population of Upper Burma. In 1877 Rama V appointed a commissioner over Chiang Mai, Lamphun and Lampang to better integrate the region with the centre, and links were further strengthened in 1921 with the arrival of the railway from Bangkok. Since then the north has built on its agricultural richness to become relatively prosperous, though the economic booms of the last two decades have been concentrated, as elsewhere in Thailand, in the towns, due in no small part to the increase in tourism. The eighty percent of Lanna's population who live in rural areas – of which the vast majority are subsistence farmers – are finding it increasingly difficult to earn a living off the soil, due to rapid population growth and land speculation for tourism and agro-industry.

Hill-tribe treks

Trekking in the mountains of north Thailand differs from trekking in most other parts of the world in that the emphasis is not primarily on the scenery but on the region's inhabitants. Northern Thailand's **hill tribes**, now numbering over 800,000 people living in around 3500 villages, have preserved their subsistence-oriented way of life with comparatively little change over thousands of years; see p.913 for more on the tribes themselves. In recent years, the term **mountain people** (a translation of the Thai *chao khao*) is increasingly used as a less condescending way to describe them; since these groups have no chief, they are technically not tribes. While some of the villages are near enough to a main road to be reached on a day-trip from a major town, to get to the other, more traditional villages usually entails joining a guided party for a few days, roughing it in a different place each night. For most visitors, however, these hardships are far outweighed by the experience of encountering peoples of so different a culture, travelling through beautiful tropical countryside and tasting the excitement of elephant-riding and river-rafting.

On any trek you are necessarily confronted by the **ethics** of your role. Over a hundred thousand travellers now go trekking in Thailand each year, the majority heading to certain well-trodden areas such as the Mae Taeng valley, 40km northwest of Chiang Mai, and the

△ Akha women making handicrafts, Mae Salong

hills around the Kok River west of Chiang Rai. Beyond the basic level of disturbance caused by any tourism, this steady flow of trekkers creates pressures for the traditionally insular hill tribes. Foreigners unfamiliar with hill-tribe customs can easily cause grave offence, especially those who go looking for drugs. Though tourism acts as a distraction from their traditional way of life, most tribespeople are genuinely welcoming and hospitable to foreigners, appreciating the contact with Westerners and the minimal material benefits which trekking brings them. Nonetheless, to minimize disruption, it's important to take a responsible attitude when trekking. While it's possible to trek **independently**, the lone trekker will learn very little without a guide as intermediary, and is far more likely to commit an unwitting offence against the local customs, so it's best to go with a sensitive and knowledgeable **guide** who has the welfare of the local people in mind, and follow the basic guidelines on etiquette outlined in the box below. If you don't fancy an organized trek in a group as described below, it's possible to hire a personal guide from an agent, for which rates begin at about B700 per day.

Trekking etiquette

As the guests, it's up to farangs to adapt to the customs of the hill tribes and not to make a nuisance of themselves. Apart from keeping an open mind and not demanding too much of your hosts, a few **simple rules** should be observed.

- Dress modestly, in long trousers or skirt (or at least knee-length shorts if you must) and a T-shirt or shirt.
- Loud voices and boisterous behaviour are out of place. Smiling and nodding establishes good intent. A few hill-tribe phrasebooks and dictionaries are available from bookshops and you'll be a big hit if you learn some words of the relevant language.
- If travelling with a loved one, avoid displays of public affection such as kissing, which are extremely distasteful, and disrespectful, to local people.
- Before entering a hill-tribe village, look out for taboo signs (*ta-laew*), woven bamboo strips on the ground outside the village entrance; these mean a special ceremony is taking place and that you should not enter. Similar signs stuck on the roof above a house entrance or a fresh tree branch mean the same thing. Be careful about what you touch; in Akha villages, keep your hands off cult structures like the entrance gates and the giant swing. Ask first before entering a house, and do not step or sit on the door sill, which is often considered the domain of the house spirits. If the house has a raised floor on stilts, take off your shoes. Most hill-tribe houses contain a religious shrine: do not touch or photograph this shrine, or sit underneath it. If you are permitted to watch a ceremony, this is not an invitation to participate unless asked. Like the villagers themselves, you'll be expected to pay a fine for any violation of local customs.
- Some villagers like to be photographed, most do not. Point at your camera and nod if you want to take a photograph. Never insist if the answer is an obvious "no". Be particularly careful with the sick and the old, and with pregnant women and babies – most tribes believe cameras affect the soul of the foetus or new-born.
- Taking gifts can be dubious practice. If you want to take something, writing materials for children and clothing are welcome, as well as sewing tools (like needles) for women – ask your guide to pass any gifts to the village headman for fair distribution. However, money, sweets and cigarettes may encourage begging and create unhealthy tastes.
- Do not ask for opium, as this will offend your hosts. Getting dressed or changing your clothes in front of villagers is also offensive.

The hill tribes are big business in northern Thailand: in **Chiang Mai** there are over two hundred agencies which between them cover just about all the trekkable areas in the north. **Chiang Rai** is the second-biggest trekking centre, and agencies can also be found in **Mae Hong Son**, **Pai** and **Nan**, which usually arrange treks only to the villages in their immediate area. Guided trekking on a much smaller scale than in the north is available in Umphang (see p.320), Kanchanaburi (see p.248) and Sangkhlaburi (see p.259).

The basics

The right **clothing** is the first essential on any trek. Strong boots with ankle protection are the best footwear, although in the dry season training shoes are adequate. Wear thin, loose clothes – long trousers should be worn to protect against thorns and, in the wet season, leeches – and a hat, and cover your arms if you're prone to sunburn. Antiseptic, antihistamine, anti-diarrhoea **medicine** and insect repellent are essential, and a mosquito net is a good idea. At least two changes of clothing are needed, plus a sarong or towel (women in particular should bring a sarong to wash or change underneath).

If you're going on an organized trek, **water** is usually provided by the guide, as well as a small backpack. **Blankets** or, preferably, a **sleeping bag** are also supplied, but might not be warm enough in the cool season, when night-time temperatures can dip to freezing; you should bring at least a sweater, and buy a cheap, locally made balaclava to be sure of keeping the chill off.

It's wise not to take anything valuable with you; most guest houses in trekking-orientated places like Chiang Mai have safes and left-luggage rooms, but check that the guest house is long-established and has a good reputation before you consider leaving your things, and then make sure you sign an inventory.

Organized treks

Organized treks can be as short as two days or as long as ten, but are typically of three or four days' duration. The standard size of a group is between six and twelve people, with an average size of eight; being part of a small group is preferable, enabling you to strike a more informative relationship with your guides and with the villagers. Everybody in the group usually sleeps on a bamboo floor or platform in the headman's hut, with a guide cooking communal meals, for which some ingredients are brought from outside and others are found locally.

Each trek usually follows a regular **itinerary** established by the agency, although they can sometimes be customized, especially for smaller groups and with agencies in the smaller towns. Some itineraries are geared towards serious hikers while others go at a much gentler pace, but on all treks much of the walking will be up and down steep forested hills, often under a burning sun, so a reasonable level of fitness is required. Many treks now include a ride on an elephant and a trip on a bamboo raft – exciting to the point of being dangerous if the river is running fast. The typical trek of three days' duration costs about B2000–2500 in Chiang Mai (including transport, accommodation, food and guide), sometimes less in other towns, much less without rafting and elephant-riding.

There are several features to look out for when **choosing a trek**. If you want to trek with a small group, get an assurance from your agency that you won't be tagged onto a larger group. Make sure the trek has at least two guides – a leader and a back-marker; some trekkers have been known to get lost for days after becoming separated from the rest of the group. Ask about transport from base at the beginning and end of the trek; most treks begin with a pick-up ride out of town, but on rare occasions the trip can entail a long public bus ride. If at all possible, meet and chat with the other trekkers, as well as the guides, who should speak reasonable English and know about hill-tribe culture, especially the details of etiquette in each village. Finally, ask what food will be eaten, check how much walking is involved per day and get a copy of the route map to gauge the terrain.

While everybody and their grandmother act as **agents**, only a few know their guides personally, so choose a reputable agent. (Note that many guest houses who offer trekking don't employ their own guides and so on, but just take a commission from outside trekking agents.) When picking an agent, you should check whether they and their guides have licences and certificates from the Tourist Authority of Thailand, which they should be able to show you: this ensures at least a minimum level of training, and provides some comeback in case of problems. Word of mouth is often the best recommendation, so if you hear of a good outfit, try it. Each trek should be **registered** with the tourist police, stating the itinerary, the duration and the participants, in case the party encounters any trouble – it's worth checking with the agency that the trek has been registered with the tourist police before departure.

Independent trekking

The options for **independent trekking** are limited, chiefly by logistics, security risks and poor mapping of the area. A series of green Royal Thai Survey Department 1:50,000 maps are available at Suriwong bookshop on Thanon Sri Dornchai in Chiang Mai at B135 each, but each one covers a very limited area. For most independent travellers, the only feasible approach is to use as a base one of the few farang-oriented rural **guest houses** in the north, such as *Wilderness Lodge* near Mae Suya (see p.412), *Cave Lodge* at Tham Lot (see p.413), and *Malee's Nature Lovers Bungalows* and *Chiang Dao Nest* near Chiang Dao (see p.421). They're generally set deep in the countryside, within walking range of several hill-tribe villages, about which the owner can give information in English.

If you're confident about finding your way round, it's possible to find **accommodation** in hill-tribe villages themselves. It helps if you speak some Thai, but most villagers, if you hang around for any time, will ask (with the usual "sleep" gesture) if you want to stay. It is usual to stay in the headman's house on a guest platform; expect to pay at least B100 per night – for this, you will often be offered dinner and breakfast. It's safe to accept plain rice, boiled drinks and food that's boiled or fried in your presence, but you're taking a risk with anything else, as it's not unusual for foreigners to suffer food poisoning. Most villages are safe to stay in; to safeguard yourself against the risk of armed bandits who sporadically rob foreigners, try to check with local guides and the district police in the area where you intend to trek.

Chiang Mai

Although rapid economic progress in recent years – due largely to tourism – has brought its share of problems, not least concern about traffic jams and fumes, **CHIANG MAI** manages to preserve some of the atmosphere of an ancient settlement alongside its modern urban sophistication. It's regarded as the kingdom's second city, with a population of about 250,000, but the contrast with the maelstrom of Bangkok is pronounced: the people here are famously easy-going and even speak more slowly than their cousins in the capital, while the old quarter, set within a 1.5-kilometre-square moat, has retained many of its traditional wooden houses and quiet, leafy gardens. Chiang Mai's elegant temples are the primary tourist sights, but these are no pre-packaged museum pieces – they're living community centres, where you're quite likely to be approached by monks keen to chat and practise their English. Inviting craft shops, good-value accommodation, rich cuisine and riverside bars further enhance the city's allure, making Chiang Mai a place that detains many travellers longer than they expected. Local environmentalists, however, are concerned that planned developments such as a cable car up the mountain and a theme park, of which the new Chiang Mai Night Safari is just the first step, could put an indelible stain on the city's enticing character. Several colourful festivals (see box on p.352) attract throngs of visitors here too: Chiang Mai is considered one of the best places in Thailand to see in the Thai New Year – Songkhran – in mid-April, and to celebrate Loy Krathong at the full moon in November, when thousands of candles are floated down the Ping River in lotus-leaf boats.

Founded as the capital of Lanna in 1296, on a site indicated by the miraculous presence of deer and white mice, Chiang Mai – "New City" – has remained the north's most important settlement ever since. Lanna's golden age under the Mengrai dynasty, when most of the city's notable temples were founded, lasted until the Burmese captured the city in 1558. Two hundred years passed before the Thais pushed the Burmese back beyond Chiang Mai to roughly where they are now, and the **Burmese influence** is still strong – not just in art and architecture, but also in the rich curries and soups served here. After the recapture of the city, the *chao* (princes) of Chiang Mai remained nominal rulers of the north until 1939, but, with communications rapidly improving from the beginning of the last century, Chiang Mai was brought firmly into Thailand's mainstream as the region's administrative and service centre.

The traditional tourist activities in Chiang Mai are visiting the **temples** and **shopping** for handicrafts, pursuits which many find more appealing here than in the rest of Thailand. These days, increasing numbers of travellers are taking advantage of the city's relaxed feel to indulge in a burst of self-improvement, enrolling for **courses** in **cookery**, **massage** and the like (see box on p.348). However, a pilgrimage to **Doi Suthep**, the mountain to the west of town, should not be missed, to see the sacred temple and the towering views over the valley of the Ping River, when weather permits. Beyond the city limits, a number of other day-trips can be made, such as to the ancient temples of Lamphun or to the orchid farms and elephant shows of the Mae Sa valley – and, of course, Chiang Mai is the main centre for hill-tribe **trekking** (see box on p.339).

Arrival

Bounded by a huge ring road, the Superhighway, Chiang Mai divides roughly into two main parts: the **old town**, surrounded by the well-maintained moat and occasional remains of the city wall, where you'll find most of Chiang Mai's traditional wats, and the **new town centre**, between the moat and the Ping River to the east, for hotels, shops, banks and travel agents. The main concentration of guest houses and restaurants hangs between the two, centred on the landmark of **Tha Pae Gate** (*Pratu Tha Pae*) in the middle of the east moat.

Many people arrive at the **train station** (which has a left-luggage office) on Thanon Charoen Muang, just over 2km from Tha Pae Gate on the eastern

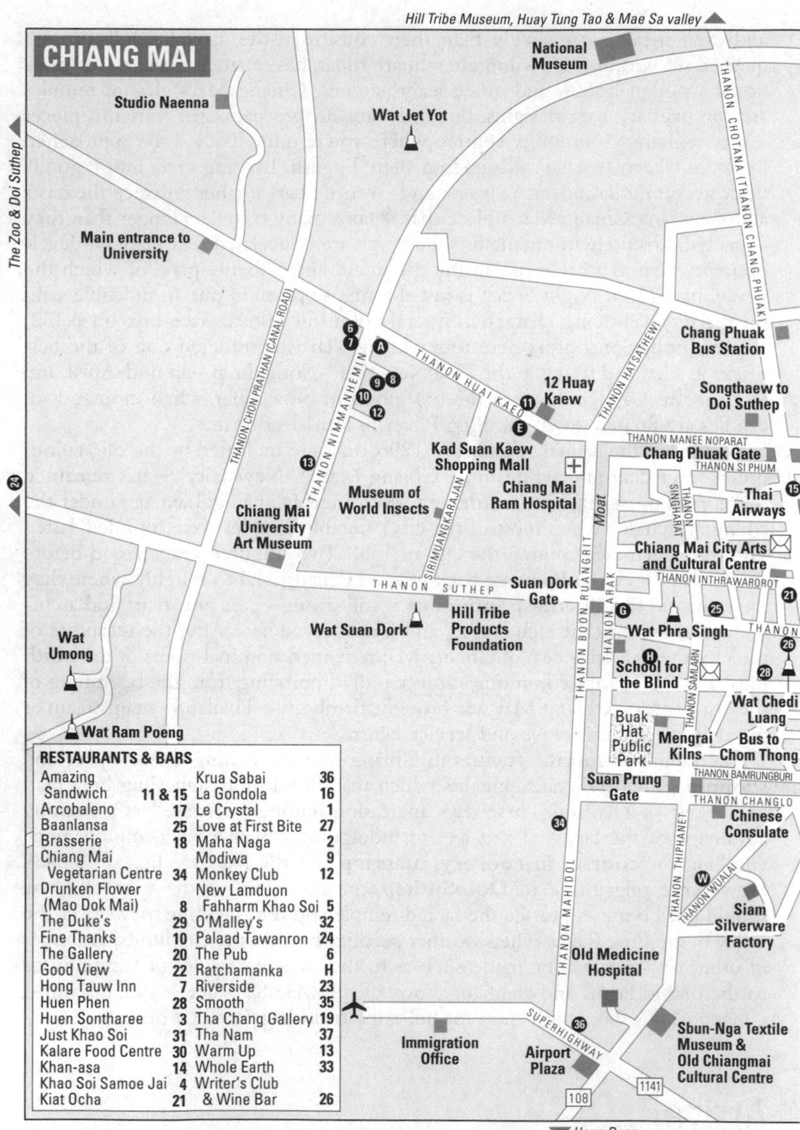

side of town (☎053 244795 or 053 245363–4), or at the **Arcade bus station** on Thanon Kaeo Nawarat (☎053 242664), 3km out to the northeast. Getting from either of these to the centre is easy by bus #4 (to Tha Pae Gate), songthaew or tuk-tuk (see "City transport" p.340). Coming south from Fang or Tha Ton, you'll wind up at the **Chang Phuak bus station** on Thanon Chotana (Thanon Chang Phuak), 500m from the city centre's northern Chang Phuak Gate and 2km northwest of the accommodation concentration around Tha Pae Gate. If you insist on travelling with one of the low-cost private bus

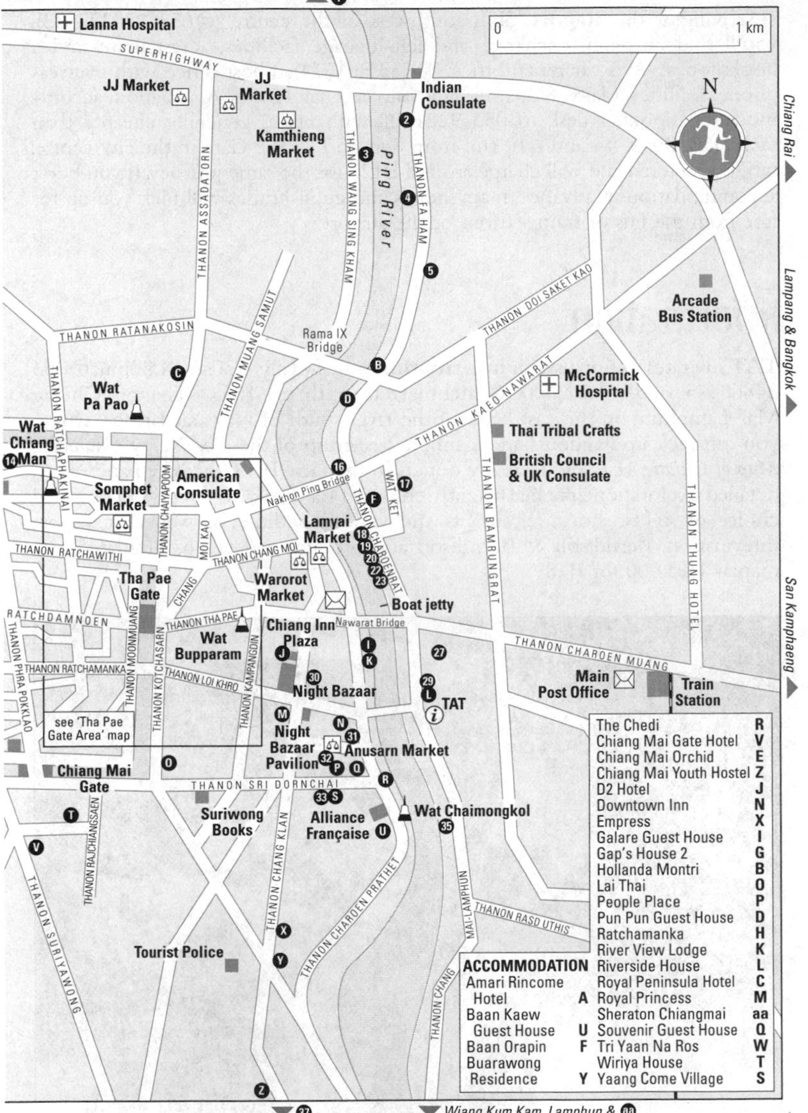

companies (see p.39) on Bangkok's Thanon Khao San, find out exactly where you'll be dropped in Chiang Mai before making a booking: many of these companies' buses stop on a remote part of the Superhighway, where they "sell" their passengers to various guest-house touts. There's no obligation to go with the touts, but if you try to duck out you'll have a hard job getting downtown and you'll certainly come in for a lot of hassle. The better guest houses – certainly including those we've listed – don't involve themselves in such shenanigans.

Arriving at the **airport**, 3km southwest of the centre (ⓣ053 270222–33), you'll find currency exchange and left-luggage facilities, a restaurant and a bookshop, an Avis car rental office (ⓣ053 201574), a post office with overseas phone facilities (daily 8.30am–8pm) and a Thai Hotels Association accommodation booking desk (ⓣ053 922129), with prices generally cheaper than rack rates. Buses #4 and #10 run from here to Tha Pae Gate in the city centre, while a metered taxi will charge around B120 for the same journey. If you book accommodation in advance, many hotels and guest houses will pick you up for free from the bus or train stations or the airport.

Information

TAT operates out of a swish **information** office (daily 8.30am–4.30pm; ⓣ053 248604–5 or 053 302500, ⓔtatchmai@tat.or.th) at 105/1 Thanon Chiang Mai–Lamphun, on the east bank of the river south of Nawarat Bridge, where you can pick up handouts and a simple free **map** of the city. *Nancy Chandler's Map of Chiang Mai*, sold in many outlets in the city (B160), is very handy for a detailed exploration: like her brightly coloured Bangkok map, it gives a personal choice of sights, shops, restaurants and various oddities, as well as transport information. Berndtson & Berndtson also produce a detailed, laminated city map at 1:13,000 for B189.

△ Chiang Mai samlor

Trekking and other outdoor activities around Chiang Mai

The **trekking** industry in Chiang Mai offers an impressive variety of itineraries, with over two hundred agencies covering nearly all trekkable areas of the north (see p.333 for general advice on how to choose an agency). Most treks include a ride on an elephant and a bamboo-raft excursion, though the amount of actual walking included can vary greatly. A few operators offer something a little different. The reliable Eagle House (16 Thanon Chang Moi Kao Soi 3 ⓣ053 235387, ⓦwww.eaglehouse.com) runs the standard type of trek, with elephants and rafting, but to carefully chosen quiet areas, and passes on a proportion of costs towards funding projects in hill-tribe villages. Moving upmarket, the Trekking Collective (25/1 Thanon Ratchawithi ⓣ053 418432, ⓦwww.trekkingcollective.com) can arrange pricey but high-quality customized treks from one to twenty days and can cater for specific interests such as bird-watching; it too is involved in community programmes to help tribal people. Also upscale and also with a strong eco-tourism element, the *Lisu Lodge* (office at 172/1–11 Thanon Loi Khro ⓣ053 281789, ⓦwww.lisulodge.com) lays on trekking, elephant- and oxcart-riding, mountain-biking and river-rafting, from its luxurious soft-adventure base an hour north of Chiang Mai.

As well as treks, which all begin with orientation at the Tribal Museum, Chiangmai Green Alternative Tours, 31 Thanon Chiangmai–Lamphun (ⓣ053 247374, ⓔcmgreent@cmnet.co.th), offers a diversity of other trips lasting anything from a half-day to a week, including nature field trips, bird-watching and **mountain-biking**. The last-mentioned is the speciality of Velocity (see p.340) and of Northern Trails (ⓦwww.northerntrails.com), who organize one-day rides near Chiang Dao, as well as multiple-day tours and customized itineraries in Thailand, Laos or Cambodia, with guide and support vehicle. Northern Trails are represented by adventure tourism agency Contact Travel, 73/7 Thanon Charoen Prathet (ⓣ053 277178, ⓦwww.activethailand.com), who also offer treks, lake- and river-kayaking and Thai Adventure Rafting's excellent two-day **whitewater-rafting** trips on the Pai River (see p.414). Or you can squeeze rafting on the Mae Taeng River, mountain-biking and elephant-riding into one day with Chiangmai Adventure, 23/1 Thanon Si Phum (ⓣ053 418197, ⓦwww.chiangmaiadventure.co.th). There's a fifteen-metre **rock-climbing** wall at The Peak on Thanon Chang Klan (ⓣ053 820777 or 081 716 4032, ⓦwww.thepeakadventure.com), where you can take three-day courses and arrange one-day trips to Crazy Horse Buttress, a limestone outcrop in the San Kamphaeng area, 50km east of town, which offers highly varied climbing with more than seventy routes, or longer climbing trips to Kiew Lom Reservoir near Lampang, including camping and kayaking. Chiang Mai Rock Climbing Adventures, 55/3 Thanon Ratchaphakinai (ⓣ086 911 1470, ⓦwww.thailandclimbing.com), also lead climbing and caving trips and a wide range of courses to Crazy Horse, with experienced US-trained guides, and offer equipment rental, crag info and a partner-finding service. For the thrills of bungy-jumping, paintball, off-road buggies or go-karting, head for the X Centre in the Mae Sa Valley (ⓣ053 297700, ⓦwww.junglebungy.com). Finally, for a panoramic view of the city and the Ping Valley, contact Chiang Mai Sky Adventure (ⓣ053 868460, ⓦwww.skyadventures.info), who organize 15- or 30-minute microlight flights, or Oriental Balloon Flights (ⓣ085 040 2001, ⓦwww.orientalballoonflights.com), who offer short balloon flights over the Ping Valley early in the morning from November to February. Call either of these places for free transport to the site.

Several free, locally published **magazines**, including *Citylife*, *Guidelines* and *Welcome to Chiang Mai and Chiang Rai*, contain information about upcoming events in town, and articles about local culture; they're distributed in spots where tourists tend to congregate, including money-exchange booths and hotel lobbies. The latter magazine's **website** (ⓦwww.chiangmai-chiangrai.com), includes extensive listings of the hotels and other businesses in the city and the north, as well as information about entertainment and community events, while the latest edition of *Citylife* can be perused online each month at Ⓦwww.chiangmainews.com. Another website loaded with information about the local area is 1stopchiangmai.com. The *Chiang Mai Mail* **newspaper**, an affiliate of the *Pattaya Mail*, is good for local news and entertainment listings, coming out every Saturday. If you expect to stay in Chiang Mai for any length of time, *Exploring Chiang Mai – City, Valley and Mountains* (B495), a **guidebook** by local resident Oliver Hargreave, is packed with useful information about lesser-known temples and attractions, and suggestions for trips out of town.

City transport

Although you can comfortably walk between the most central temples, **bicycles** are the best way of getting around the old town and, with a bit of legwork, out to the attractions beyond the moat too. Trusty sit-up-and-beg models and basic mountain bikes are available at many outlets on the roads along the eastern moat for B30–50 a day, while Velocity, 177 Thanon Chang Phuak (Ⓣ053 410665 or 081 595 5975, Ⓔvelocity@thaimail.com), rents (B150/day) and sells better-quality road and mountain bikes and organizes guided cycling tours. If you don't fancy pedalling through the heat and pollution, consider a **motorbike** – there are plenty for rent (from around B150/day; see p.368 for addresses of outlets), though these really come into their own for exploring places around Chiang Mai and in the rest of the north.

Chiang Mai now has a fledgling, air-conditioned **bus** system, covering five routes around town; many free publications include a map of the routes, which are described in the box below. Each service charges a fixed B10 fare and runs about every fifteen minutes, beginning at 6am and ending at 10pm. Red **songthaews** act as shared taxis within the city, picking up a number of people headed in roughly the same direction and taking each to their specific destination. A sample fare from Tha Pae Gate to Wat Phra Singh is currently B15, but it'll naturally cost more to go somewhere off the beaten track or if the driver thinks you want to charter (*mao*) the whole vehicle.

Bus routes in Chiang Mai

#2: Chiang Mai Area Office (Nong Hoi)–Thanon Chiang Mai-Lamphun–Thanon Charoenrat–Superhighway–Thanon Chotana–7th Field Artillery Battalion.

#4: Airport–Thanon Wualai–Thanon Bamrungburi–Thanon Moonmuang–Thanon Chang Moi–Thanon Charoen Muang–Thanon Thung Hotel–Thanon Kaew Nawarat–Carrefour superstore.

#6: Chiang Mai Area Office (Nong Hoi)–Superhighway–Arcade Bus Station–Superhighway–Thanon Chotana–Chang Puak Bus Station–Superhighway–Thanon Huai Kaeo–Thanon Chon Prathan–Thanon Suthep–Thanon Arak–Suan Prung Gate–Thanon Mahidol–Airport–Superhighway–Thanon Chang Klan–Thanon Charoen Prathet–Thanon Tha Pae–Thanon Chang Klan–Chiang Mai Area Office (Nong Hoi).

#8: Airport–Thanon Mahidol–Thanon Boonruang Rit–Thanon Maneenoparat–Thanon Chang Puak–Thanon Chotana–City Hall.

#10: Kwan Vieng Village–Airport–Thanon Mahidol–Thanon Boonruang Rit–Thanon Maneenoparat–Thanon Phrapokklao–Thanon Ratchawithi–Thanon Moonmuang–Thanon Chang Moi–Thanon Tha Pae–Thanon Chang Klan–Thanon Sridornchai–Thanon Wualai–Kwan Vieng Village.

Metered taxis have a B40 flag fare, which includes the first two kilometres, and cost B5/km after that; they charge B40 for a pick-up call (☎053 279291 or 081 952 0900), but can be flagged down on the street if not busy. The meter service is limited to locations within the third ring road around the city; for destinations beyond you'll be quoted a fixed fare. Chiang Mai is also stuffed with **tuk-tuks**, for which heavy bargaining is expected – allow around B50 for getting from the train station to Tha Pae Gate. They're quick and useful on arrival and departure, and are quite reasonable if you're in a small group. The town still has a few **samlors**, which are cheap when used by locals to haul produce home from the market, but not so cheap when chartered by groups of upmarket tourists on sightseeing tours from their hotel.

Accommodation

Chiang Mai is well stocked with all kinds of **accommodation**; usually there are plenty of beds to go around, but many places fill up from December to February and at festival time, particularly during Songkhran (April) and Loy Krathong (November). At these times, you need to book to stay at one of the expensive hotels, and for guest houses it's a good idea to phone ahead – even if you can't book a place, you can save yourself a journey if the place is full.

Many touts at the bus and train stations offer a free ride if you stay at a particular guest house, but you'll probably find that the price of a room is bumped up to pay for your ride – try phoning guest houses, who may pick you up for free to avoid paying commission to the touts. For much of the year there's little need for air-con in Chiang Mai, though the more expensive air-conditioned rooms are usually more spacious and come with hot-water bathrooms, which is a plus in cooler weather. Some places can arrange to switch the air-con option off and charge you the fan-room rate.

Though many guest houses offer use of their safes as a free service, some charge up to B30 per day. Be sure that you can trust the proprietor before you leave valuables in one of the safes or excess baggage in one of the left-luggage rooms while you go off trekking. Choose one of the more well-established guest houses, as they're more conscious of the need to maintain their reputation, and make a detailed inventory to be signed by both parties – the hair-raising stories of theft and credit-card abuse are often true.

Inexpensive

The choice of **budget guest houses** is better in Chiang Mai than in Bangkok: they're generally friendlier, quieter and more atmospheric and comfortable, and often have their own outdoor cafés. In most you can get a hot shower – even if it's just in a shared bathroom – while a lot of the more successful places below have developed a few fancier rooms with air-con. Many of the least expensive places make their money from hill-tribe trekking, which can be convenient as a trek often needs a lot of organizing beforehand, but can equally be annoying if you're in Chiang Mai for other reasons and are put under pressure to trek, as can happen at some guest houses; most of the places listed below can arrange trekking, but at none of them should you get this kind of undue hassle.

Most low-cost places are gathered on the surprisingly quiet sois inside the old city and around the eastern side of the moat and Tha Pae Gate. This puts you in the middle of a larder of Thai and travellers' restaurants.

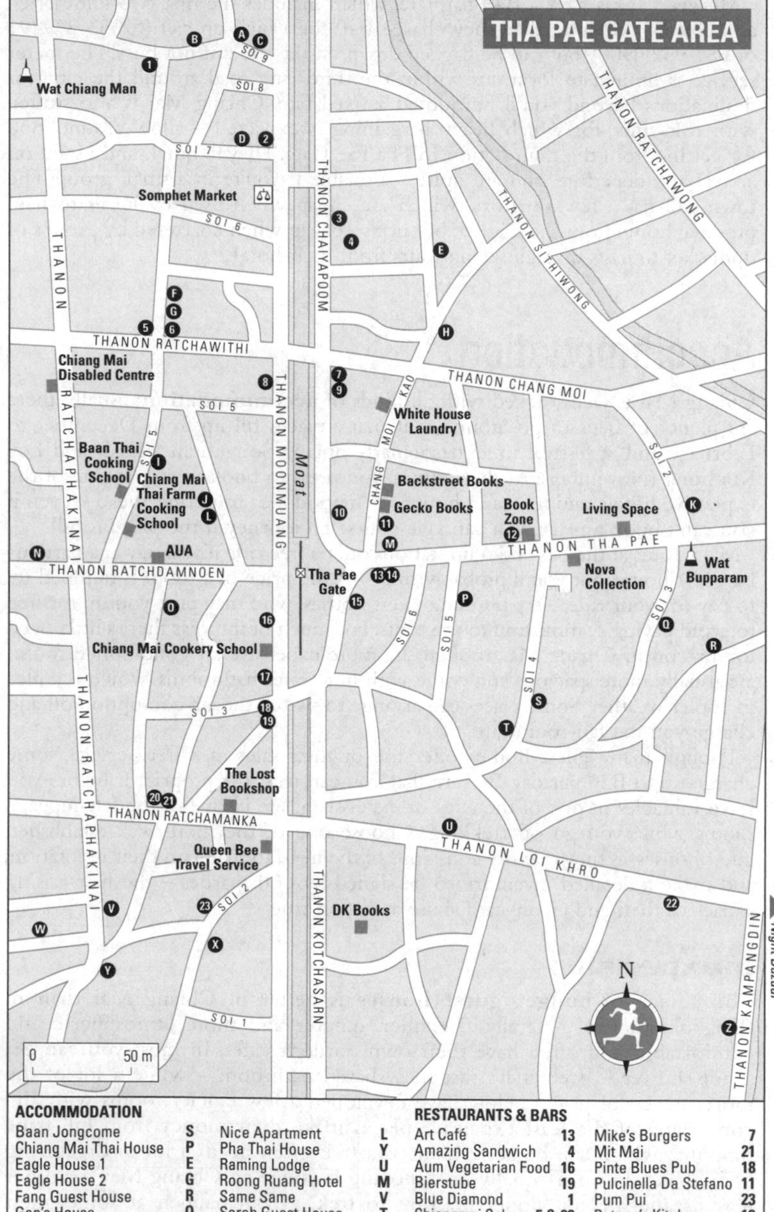

ACCOMMODATION

Baan Jongcome	S	Nice Apartment	L
Chiang Mai Thai House	P	Pha Thai House	Y
Eagle House 1	E	Raming Lodge	U
Eagle House 2	G	Roong Ruang Hotel	M
Fang Guest House	R	Same Same	V
Gap's House	O	Sarah Guest House	T
Imperial Mae Ping Hotel	Z	SK House	A
Julie Guest House	W	Sri Pat Guest House	D
Karinthip Village	H	Supreme Guest House	B
Kavil Guest House	I	Tamarind Village	N
Libra House	C	Top North Guest House	X
Manathai	Q	Veerachai Court	K
Mini Cost	J	Your House	F

RESTAURANTS & BARS

Art Café	13	Mike's Burgers	7
Amazing Sandwich	4	Mit Mai	21
Aum Vegetarian Food	16	Pinte Blues Pub	18
Bierstube	19	Pulcinella Da Stefano	11
Blue Diamond	1	Pum Pui	23
Chiangmai Saloon	5 & 22	Ratana's Kitchen	12
Daret's	10	Ruen Tamarind	N
The Hemp Collective	15	Spicy	3
The House	2	UN Irish Pub	6
Inter Bar	14	The Wok	20
Jerusalem Falafel	17		
Kafe	8		
Libernard Café	9		

Tha Pae Gate area

Baan Jongcome Guest House 47 Soi 4, Thanon Tha Pae ⓣ053 274823. This family-run place combines modern motel/hotel-style rooms – fan or air-con – with a guest-house atmosphere. The rooms, which are upstairs, are very clean and spacious, with cool tiled floors and big comfortable beds made up with sheets and blankets; bathrooms with hot shower are attached. Below there's a pleasant courtyard with a café. ❸

Eagle House 1 16 Soi 3, Thanon Chang Moi Kao ⓣ053 235387, and **Eagle House 2** 26 Soi 2, Thanon Ratchawithi ⓣ053 210620; ⓦwww.eaglehouse.com. Run by an Irishwoman and her Thai husband who are keen to promote ethical eco-tourism, these two friendly, relaxed, well-maintained guest houses have spacious garden terrace areas with good cafés and extensive information boards. Well-organized treks also on offer, as well as Thai cookery courses at The Chilli Club, based at *Eagle House 2*. Rooms in *Eagle House 1* all have their own bathroom, either with fan, cold water and access to a shared hot shower, or with air-con and hot water; the standard of rooms is higher at the newer *Eagle House 2*, a modern compound with clean, tiled en-suite rooms, all with hot water and some with air-con, as well as a dorm (B80, with shared hot showers). Phone for a free pick-up. Fan ❶, air-con ❸

Fang Guest House 46–48 Soi 1, Thanon Kampangdin ⓣ053 282940. Modern building, with cosy rooms, all with air-con. Very handy for the night bazaar, but on a fairly quiet lane. ❸

Gap's House 3 Soi 4, Thanon Ratchdamnoen ⓣ053 278140, and **Gap's House 2** 43/2-6 Thanon Arak ⓣ053 274277 (see Chiang Mai main map); ⓦwww.gaps-house.com. The main house is set around a relaxing, leafy compound strewn with antiques, containing plush air-con rooms with hot showers. The second place offers good value with fan or air-con rooms at a slightly cheaper price, with free use of bicycles. The room price at *Gap's 1* includes a simple breakfast, and a vegetarian buffet is served in the evening; one- or two-day cookery courses available. Fan ❷, air-con ❸–❺

Julie Guest House 7/1 Soi 5, Thanon Phra Pokklao ⓣ053 274355, ⓦwww.julieguesthouse.com. Relaxing, laid-way-back place with a variety of rooms with shared or en-suite hot showers and a dorm (B60), in a concrete block. Part-canopied roof terrace with hammocks for hanging out, and downstairs a shady garden café with a pool table. ❶–❷

Kavil Guest House 10/1 Soi 5, Thanon Ratchdamnoen ⓣ & ⓕ053 224740. Friendly place in a modern four-storey building on a quiet soi. All twelve rooms have en-suite hot-water bathrooms; the rooms with fans are small, plain and clean, while those with air-con are pleasantly decorated and more spacious (the air-con can be switched off to turn these into fan rooms). The downstairs café is at the front, which means there's no noisy courtyard effect. Fan ❶, air-con ❸

Libra House 28 Soi 9, Thanon Moonmuang ⓣ053 210687, ⓔlibra_guesthouse@hotmail.com. Excellent, modern, family-run, trekking-oriented guest house with a few traditional decorative trimmings and keen, helpful service. All rooms are en suite, some with hot water. Fan ❶, air-con ❸

Nice Apartment 15 Soi 1, Thanon Ratchdamnoen ⓣ053 210552, ⓕ053 419150. In a quiet lane in the old town, this is an excellent, popular choice for a longer stay, with weekly and monthly rates; for longer stays, you pay their daily rate minus B20–80. All rooms have hot showers, fridge and cable TV, and towels are supplied; there's a choice of air-con or fan. Very friendly. ❷

Pha Thai House 48/1 Thanon Ratchaphakinai ⓣ053 278013 or 081 998 6933, ⓕ053 274075. Set back from the road, this efficiently run, modern building has a quiet, pretty garden restaurant and hot water in all rooms (fan or air-con). Fan ❸, air-con ❺

Roong Ruang Hotel 398 Thanon Tha Pae ⓣ053 232017–8, ⓕ053 252409. Tucked away off the main road near Tha Pae Gate, this good-value place has attractive rooms, some with air-con and fridge, all with hot water and TV, snuggled around a pretty courtyard. ❸

Same Same 104 Thanon Ratchaphakinai ⓣ053 208056, ⓦwww.samesameguesthouse.com. Friendly place with helpful owner offering good-sized, clean rooms with shared bathroom in the main building and air-con rooms with all facilities in a second location in the lane opposite. There's a B80 dorm too, plus a congenial café downstairs. Fan ❶, air-con ❸

Sarah Guest House 20 Soi 4, Thanon Tapae ⓣ053 208271, ⓦwww.sarahguesthouse.com. A very clean, peaceful establishment, 200m from Tha Pae Gate, named for its English owner. Most rooms have ceiling fans and bathrooms, either with hot water or with access to shared hot showers; a few large, nicely furnished air-con rooms with hot-water bathrooms are available too. There's a pleasant garden with a daytime courtyard café serving Western breakfasts, Thai food, sandwiches and snacks, including plenty of veggie options. Fan ❷, air-con ❸

SK House 30 Soi 9, Thanon Moonmuang ⓣ053 210690, ⓦwww.sk-riverview.com. Efficient, brick-built high-rise with a ground-floor café and Internet access, a small, shaded swimming pool and a slightly institutional feel. Fan rooms come with hot-water bathrooms, while the air-con rooms are much more colourful and attractive, with cable TV. Fan ❷, air-con ❹

Supreme Guest House 44/1 Soi 9, Thanon Moonmuang ⓣ053 222480. Friendly Scottish-run guest house in a modern concrete block with a pleasant roof veranda. The rooms are comfortable and have fans and solar-heated showers. ❶

Top North Guest House 15 Soi 2, Thanon Moonmuang ⓣ053 278900 or 053 278684, ⓔtopnorth@hotmail.com. Large, modern, unpretentious place with a small swimming pool (B100 for non-guests), in a quiet enclave of guest houses. Fan-cooled and air-con rooms available, all with hot water, some with fridge and satellite TV. Fan ❸, air-con ❹

Your House 8 Soi 2, Thanon Ratchawithi ⓣ053 217492, ⓦwww.yourhouseguesthouse.com. A lovely old-town teak house with a suitably welcoming atmosphere. Big, airy, clean rooms share hot-water bathrooms; in the modern annexe across the road there are small rooms with their own hot-water bathrooms, some with air-con. The courtyard restaurant area serves good Thai and French food, with buffalo steak and chips a speciality. Free pick-ups from train, bus or airport. Fan ❶, air-con ❸

Rest of Chiang Mai

Chiang Mai Youth Hostel 54 Thanon Papaho ⓣ053 276737, ⓦwww.chiangmaiyha.org. On a side street to the west of Thanon Chang Klan about 1500m south of the night bazaar. Very clean, quiet and reliable; rooms have en-suite hot showers and fans or air-con. Small discounts for HI members. ❸

Hollanda Montri 365 Thanon Charoenrat ⓣ053 242450, ⓔhollandamontri@asia.com. North of the centre by Rama IX Bridge, in a spacious modern building by the river, this Dutch-run guest house has large, clean and attractive fan or air-con rooms with balconies and hot-water bathrooms and a very pleasant riverside bar-restaurant. Good value but a bit far from the action. Bus #2 from Nawarat Bridge. Fan ❷, air-con ❸

Pun Pun Guest House 321 Thanon Charoenrat ⓣ053 246180, ⓔpunpungh@gmail.com. This place has some of the cheapest riverside rooms in town, though it's a bit far from the centre; choose between wooden rooms in a house with hot-water bathrooms and bungalows with shared bath. Bus #2 from Nawarat Bridge. Fan ❷, air-con ❸

Riverside House 101 Thanon Chiang Mai–Lamphun ⓣ053 241860, ⓦwww.norththaitour.com. Welcoming place just east of the river, though just a short walk from the night bazaar, with small but clean and cosy air-con rooms with cable TV, and breakfast included. ❸

Souvenir Guest House 118 Thanon Charoen Prathet ⓣ053 818786, ⓦwww.souvenir-guesthouse.com. This spacious, friendly place is clean and well run, boasting modern rooms with air-con or fan (some with bathrooms) behind an overgrown garden and restaurant. Handy for the night bazaar and Anusarn Market. Fan ❷, air-con ❸

Wiriya House 10/4 Soi 1, Thanon Rajchiangsaen Kor ⓣ053 272948, ⓔwiriyah@loxinfo.co.th. Located in a quiet lane near the southeast corner of the old city, this friendly, four-storey establishment has cosy rooms with hot showers and fan or air-con, some with TV and fridge, as well as a pretty garden to relax in. Reductions for long-term stays. Fan ❷, air-con ❸

Moderate

For around B500 a double and upwards, you can buy yourself considerably more comfort than the bottom-bracket accommodation provides. By far the best of these **moderate** places are the upmarket guest houses and lodges, which as well as good facilities (hot water and air-con) often offer decent decor and atmosphere. Chiang Mai also has dozens of bland, no-frills hotels in the same price range.

Tha Pae Gate area

Chiang Mai Thai House 5/1 Soi 5, Thanon Tha Pae ⓣ053 904110, ⓔchiangmaithaihouse@hotmail.com. Choice of smallish but well-furnished rooms with fan or bigger ones with air-con in this new, centrally located place which also has a tiny pool. Fan ❹, air-con ❺

Mini Cost 19–19/4 Soi 1, Thanon Ratchadamnoen ⓣ053 418787–8 , f053 418787. Smart new place located just round the corner from Tha Pae Gate offering very spacious rooms, all tastefully furnished and with staff that are eager to please. ❹–❺

Sri Pat Guest House 16 Soi 7, Thanon Moonmuang ⓣ053 218716-7, F053 218718. Reasonable mid-range option offering attractive, clean rooms with air-con, cable TV and fridge in a convenient location. ❺

Veerachai Court 19 Soi 2, Thanon Tha Pae ⓣ053 251047–54, ⓕ053 252402. Conveniently located just off Thanon Tha Pae, this place has some small and some big rooms with air-con and cable TV, and is particularly popular among long-term visitors for its good monthly rates. ❹

Rest of Chiang Mai

Baan Kaew Guest House 142 Thanon Charoen Prathet ⓣ053 271606, ⓦwww.baankaew-guesthouse.com. Set back from the road in a quiet, pretty garden, this attractive modern building has large, simple but well-equipped and maintained rooms with hot water and air-con. ❹

Baan Orapin 150 Thanon Charoenrat ⓣ053 243677, ⓦwww.baanorapin.com. Delightful compound on trendy Thanon Charoenrat, containing just a dozen big, comfy and characterful rooms with teak and rattan furnishings and wooden floors. Some rooms come with four poster beds and balconies. ❻–❽

Buarawong Residence 129 /9 Thanon Rajang ⓣ053 273283, ⓕ053 820602. Located a short walk south of the night bazaar, this building is no beauty, but conceals smart rooms with all comforts at a very competitive price. Breakfast included. ❹

Chiang Mai Gate Hotel 11/10 Thanon Suriyawong ⓣ053 279085, ⓦwww.chiangmai-online.com/cmgate/. Located just to the south of the old city, this place has well-equipped rooms with Lanna touches in the design, plus a swimming pool and helpful staff. ❹–❺

Downtown Inn 172/1–11 Thanon Loi Khro ⓣ053 270662, ⓦwww.empresshotels.com. Western-style comforts like mini-bars and TVs without the extras of the big luxury hotels (such as its sister, the *Empress*); quiet considering its central location near the night bazaar. ❻

Galare Guest House 7 Soi 2, Thanon Charoen Prathet ⓣ053 818887 or 053 821011, ⓦwww.galare.com. Near Narawat Bridge, a long-standing, well-run upmarket guest house that's justly popular. Air-con rooms, each with hot-water bathroom, TV and fridge, overlook a shady lawn that gives way to a riverside terrace. ❻

Lai Thai 111/4–5 Thanon Kotchasarn ⓣ053 271725, 053 271414 or 053 271534, ⓦwww.laithai.com. On the southeast corner of the moat. Frenetic place, very popular with families, who are no doubt attracted by the (small) courtyard swimming pool around which the three floors of this 120-room modern Thai-style building are arranged. Besides hot-water, en-suite bathrooms, the small but clean rooms boast traditional wooden floors, bamboo walls and air-con. ❺

People Place 9 Soi 8, Thanon Charoen Prathet ⓣ053 282487, ⓦwww.people.infothai.com. A compact modern building, just a few steps from the night bazaar, whose spacious, comfy rooms come with en-suite hot-water bathrooms and air-con. ❹

Royal Peninsula Hotel 9/9 Thanon Assadatorn ⓣ053 252222, ⓦwww.royalpeninsulahotel.com. Smart new place located just outside the northeast corner of the old city; rooms are a decent size with attractive furnishings, air-con and cable TV, and some come with bathtubs and kitchen facilities. ❻

Expensive

There has been an explosion of top-line accommodation in Chiang Mai lately, with places ranging from small boutique hotels to massive projects like the Mandarin Oriental's *Dhara Devi*. The best hotels in this category lay on all the expected luxuries plus traditional Lanna architectural touches, and breakfast is included at most places. As well as those below, also worth considering in this price range is the *Four Seasons Resort*, out in the Mae Sa valley (see p.375); they'll collect you from the airport and lay on a shuttle bus service into Chiang Mai for guests.

Tha Pae Gate area

Imperial Mae Ping Hotel 153 Thanon Sri Dornchai ⓣ053 283900, ⓦwww.imperialmaeping.com. Central luxury hotel in a fifteen-storey high-rise, with two outdoor pools, a gym, Japanese and Chinese restaurants, and a pleasant beer garden; very convenient for the night bazaar. ❽

Karinthip Village 50/2 Thanon Chang Moi Kao ⓣ053 235414–8, ⓦwww.karinthipvillage.com. Peaceful compound located just east of the old city, with 62 rooms set around a decent-sized swimming pool, all nicely decorated in Lanna style and some with four-poster beds. ❽

Manathai 39/9 Soi 3, Thanon Tha Pae ⓣ053 281666–9, ⓦwww.manathai.com. Centrally located but set away from the main roads, this new boutique hotel consists of colonial-style buildings set around a small pool. The rooms are small but stylish and well-equipped with air-con, TV and mini-bar. ❾

Raming Lodge 17–19 Thanon Loi Kroh ⓣ053 271777, ⓦwww.raminglodge.com. Right in the heart of the downtown action, this new 6-storey place offers well-equipped air-con rooms with desks, armchairs and cable TV. Facilities include an on-site spa. ❼

Tamarind Village 50/1 Thanon Ratchadamnoen ⓣ053 418896–9, ⓦwww.tamarindvillage.com. Named for a huge tamarind tree that shades the compound, this boutique resort in the heart of Chiang Mai's old city is designed in Lanna style, though the extremely comfortable rooms have modern touches. The rooms all have lovely garden views and the place exudes tranquillity. Good sized pool and excellent restaurant too. ❾

Rest of Chiang Mai

Amari Rincome Hotel 1 Thanon Nimmanheimin ⓣ053 221130, ⓦwww.amari.com. Popular with tour groups, this hotel has an elegant lobby, tastefully furnished rooms, a tennis court and an excellent swimming pool; its *La Gritta* restaurant does a blow-out buffet lunch. Though it's a bit far from the centre, there are lots of restaurants and shops nearby. ❽

The Chedi 123 Thanon Charoen Prathet ⓣ053 253333, ⓦwww.ghmhotels.com. Occupying a prime riverside site (the grounds of the former British Consulate), this super-modern place, designed in what is termed a Lanna-Bali style, offers minimalist luxury in its spacious club suites and deluxe rooms, with sumptuous furnishings, balconies and river views. Extras include a spa, fitness centre, swimming pool and limitless use of the mini-bar. Rooms start at B10,400. ❾

Chiang Mai Orchid 23 Thanon Huai Kaeo ⓣ053 222099, ⓦwww.chiangmaiorchid.com. Grand, tasteful hotel with efficient service, a swimming pool and a health club, located on the northwest side of town. ❽

D2 Hotel 100 Chang Klan ⓣ053 999999, ⓦwww.d2hotels.com. With its muted orange theme, flat screen TVs and Internet connections in rooms, plus stunning lighting and minimalist furnishings, this new place in the heart of the night bazaar, run by the Dusit Group, is one of the city's trendiest places to stay. Two restaurants, a spa, fitness centre and rooftop pool are among the amenities. ❾

Dhara Devi 51/4 Thanon Chiang Mai–Sankamphaeng ⓣ053 888888, ⓦwww.mandarinoriental.com. Occupying 60 acres a few kilometres east of the city centre, the *Dhara Devi* transports its guests into another era – the heyday of the Lanna Kingdom, with traditional Lanna architecture complemented by modern touches such as air-con, dimmer switches and cable TV. The pavilions, villas and suites are equipped with every conceivable comfort and look out over rice fields and vegetable gardens. With its own breathtaking spa (modelled on the Royal Palace of Mandalay), craft village, shopping centre, swimming pools, tennis courts and three restaurants, guests need never leave the premises. Prices start at B14,000. ❾

Empress 199 Thanon Chang Klan ⓣ053 270240, ⓦwww.empresshotels.com. Grand international-class hotel with pool, sauna and health centre conveniently placed on the south side of town: within walking distance of the night bazaar, yet far enough removed to get some peace and quiet. ❼–❾

Ratchamanka 6 Soi 9, Thanon Ratchamanka ⓣ053 904111, ⓦwww.ratchamanka.com. Looking more like a temple than a hotel, this elegant property hidden in the backstreets of the old city is the perfect retreat from the hectic commerce of Chiang Mai's main streets. Plush rooms with sumptuous furnishings, and one of the city's best restaurants make this place a tempting option for a memorable stay. From B6500. ❾

River View Lodge 25 Soi 4, Thanon Charoen Prathet ⓣ053 271109–10, ⓦwww.riverviewlodgch.com. Tasteful, well-run and good-value alternative to international-class hotels, with a beautiful riverside garden, a small swimming pool and neat decorative touches in the rooms; the most expensive rooms have balconies overlooking the river. ❼

Royal Princess 111 Thanon Chang Klan ⓣ053 281033–43, ⓦwww.royalprincess.com. Tidy, centrally located hotel close to the night bazaar, with elegant rooms, a swimming pool and fitness centre, fine restaurants and impeccable service. ❽

Sheraton Chiangmai 318/1 Thanon Chiang Mai–Lamphun ⓣ053 275300, ⓦwww.starwood.com. Luxurious hotel with spacious, carpeted bedrooms and great views, located in one of Chiang Mai's tallest buildings, a few kilometres south of town by the river. Facilities include a pool, steam room, business centre and health club as well as two top-class restaurants. ❽

Tri Yaan Na Ros 156 Thanon Wualai ⓣ053 273174, ⓦwww.triyaannaros.com. Snuggled away to the south of the old city centre, this renovated colonial building oozes atmosphere, from the four-poster beds to the photos of ancient Lanna on the walls. A small library, Internet access and free bicycle use for guests. ❽

Yaang Come Village 90/3 Thanon Sridornchai ⓣ053 237222, ⓦwww.yaangcome.com. Yet another boutique hotel cleverly concealed just a few steps away from the night bazaar, this stylish "village" has a range of rooms, all with lots of character and Lanna art on the walls, plus a pool, spa and free Internet use. ❾

The City

Chiang Mai feels less claustrophobic than most cities in Thailand, being scattered over a wide plain and broken up by waterways. In addition to the moat and remnants of the defensive wall encircling the old town, the gentle Ping River brings a breath of fresh air to the eastern side of the pungent food markets above Nawarat Bridge, and the modern, hectic shopping area around Thanon Chang Klan. The most famous and fascinating **temples** in the city – Wat Phra Singh, Wat Chedi Luang and Wat Chiang Man – are clustered conveniently close to each other in the old town, though the main local place of pilgrimage, for Buddhists and tourists alike, is Wat Phra That Doi Suthep, which glitters in the sun from its perch some 1300 metres up the neighbouring mountain (see p.368). The city is also well-endowed with **museums**: the Arts and Cultural Centre in the old town for high-quality displays on Chiang Mai and Lanna culture, the National Museum to the north for the best of the region's historical artefacts, and, further north again, the Tribal Museum for a useful introduction to the hill-tribes of northern Thailand. And don't forget the diverse and impressive **zoo**, which occupies a huge area on the northwest side of town.

A pleasant way to get a feel for the city and its layout is to take a **boat trip** on the Ping River. Cruises operated by Mae Ping River Cruises (Ⓣ053 274822 or 081 884 4621) in a converted rice barge depart from the jetty beside the *Riverside* restaurant, on the east bank just north of Nawarat Bridge. Slow but sturdy, the boats offer a clear view of the surroundings as they take visitors through lush countryside north of town. Boats leave every couple of hours, currently at 10am, noon, 2pm, 4pm and 5.30pm, and the trip lasts around 1hr 40min and costs B250. They also run private boats (just call for a booking), leaving from Wat Chaimongkol on Thanon Charoen Prathet; the B350 per person charge (minimum two people) includes pick-up from your accommodation, a two-hour cruise – usually in a longtail boat – 8km upstream to a riverside farmhouse for a look around the fruit, herb and flower gardens, plus refreshments and fruit-tasting. Another alternative is to take a trip on a scorpion-tailed boat (Ⓣ081 960 9308, Ⓦwww.scorpiontailed.com), a reconstruction of vessels that plied the river a century ago. This cruise follows a similar route to the other two, but includes a commentary on historic places beside the river, and costs around B400 per person, depending on number of passengers. Departures are irregular, so call for information.

△ Wat Phra Singh

Wat Phra Singh

If you see only one temple in Chiang Mai it should be **Wat Phra Singh**, perhaps the single most impressive array of buildings in the city, at the far western end of Thanon Ratchdamnoen in the old town. Just inside

Courses in Chiang Mai

In recent years there's been a steady increase in the number of visitors who come to Chiang Mai looking to return home with a new skill by taking a self-improvement course. The most popular subject is how to cook Thai food, followed by Thai massage and meditation, but perhaps the most challenging of all, though vital for anyone planning to spend any length of time here, is the Thai language. Other skills to be tackled, besides rock-climbing (see p.339), include: **t'ai chi**, on a ten-day residential programme (twice monthly) at Naisuan House off Thanon Doi Saket Kao (ⓣ081 706 7406, ⓦwww.taichithailand.com); **yoga classes** at the Yoga Studio, 90/1 Thanon Ratchamanka (ⓣ086 192 7375, ⓦwww.yoga-chiangmai.com), or the Hathayoga Centre Chiangmai, 99/42 Thanon Huay Kaew (ⓣ085 864 0146, ⓦwww.hathayogachiangmai.com); joining in the training schedule of a **Thai boxing** camp at Lanna Muay Thai, 64/1 Soi 1, Thanon Huai Kaeo (ⓣ053 892102 or 081 951 3164, ⓦwww.lannamuaythai.com); and intensive workshops in **jewellery making** at Nova, 201 Thanon Tha Pae (ⓣ053 273058, ⓦwww.nova-collection.com).

Cookery

There has been an explosion of interest in preparing Thai food, and many Chiang Mai guest houses and cookery schools now offer lessons. The original – and still the best – is the Chiang Mai Thai Cookery School, 47/2 Thanon Moonmuang (ⓣ053 206388, ⓦwww.thaicookeryschool.com) run by Somphon and Elizabeth Nabnian. They offer courses of one to five days (B990–B4600), covering common Thai and one or two traditional Lanna dishes, including the use of substitute ingredients available in the West. Each day begins with either an introduction to Thai ingredients, shopping in the market, making curry pastes or vegetable carving. While the fees might seem expensive, the courses are well worth it, including a first-class lunch, seasonal fruit-tasting and a recipe book. Somphon, an experienced chef himself, also offers pricey evening masterclasses. Courses are held either at *The Wok* restaurant (see p.362) or at the Nabnians' house, a 15-minute drive out of town (transport provided). It's best to book in advance as the classes are very popular and the number of students is limited (the schedule of courses is given on the website), though it is sometimes possible to just turn up and secure a place. Another reliable school is at *Gap's House* (see "Accommodation"), which teaches the preparation of five main courses plus desserts and vegetable carving for B900 per day. Also centrally located and well-regarded is Baan Thai Cookery School, 11 Soi 5, Thanon Ratchdamnoen (ⓣ053 357339, ⓦwww.cookinthai.com), which offers daily couses at B800 and evening courses (5–8.30pm) for B700. On the same lane at no. 2/2 is the Chiang Mai Thai Farm Cooking School (ⓣ081 288 5958, ⓦwww.thaifarmcooking.com), which offers something slightly different, with the chance to pick your own organic vegetables, herbs and fruits for cooking on their farm, thirty minutes' drive from town (transport provided; B900/day).

Thai massage courses

The best place to study Thai massage in Thailand is considered to be Bangkok's Wat Pho (see p.141), which now has an affiliated school in Chiang Mai – the Chetawan Thai Traditional Massage School at 7/1–2 Soi Samud Lanna, Thanon Pracha Uthit (ⓣ053 410360–1), which offers thirty-hour courses (6hr/day for 5 days) in traditional Thai massage (B7000) or foot massage (B5500). Several other well-regarded schools make Chiang Mai a popular alternative to Bangkok as a more relaxing base for courses that can run for several weeks. The longest-established centre is the forty-year-old Old Medicine Hospital (aka *Shivagakomarpaj* after the Indian hermit who is said to have founded the discipline over two thousand years ago), off Thanon Wualai opposite the Old Chiang Mai Cultural Center (ⓣ053 275085 or 053 201663, ⓦwww.thaimassageschool.ac.th). Highly respected ten-day courses in English (B4000), under the supervision of the Ministry of Education, are held twice a month, though the group size can get a bit too big at popular times; two-day foot massage courses are held at weekends (B2000).

Also accredited by the Ministry of Education, and highly recommended by past pupils, is the Thai Massage School of Chiang Mai (Ⓣ053 854330, Ⓦwww.1thaimassage.com), located to the northeast of town on the Mae Jo road, 2km beyond the Superhighway. Three levels of Thai massage training are on offer, each taking five days, with the foundation course costing B5300. Thai foot reflexology is also taught (2 days; B3200). All courses include transportation and lunch.

Massage courses are also offered by the Sunshine Network (Ⓦwww.asokananda.com or Ⓦwww.thaiyogamassage.infothai.com), an international group of practitioners and teachers founded by the highly respected German teacher, Harald Brust, aka Asokananda, who died in June 2005. Asokananda emphasized the spiritual aspect of what he called Thai yoga massage or Ayurvedic bodywork. Led by one of Asokananda's followers, twelve-day beginners' courses (B9900, including extremely basic accommodation, simple vegetarian rice meals and transportation) are held at a rural retreat in a hill-tribe village between Chiang Mai and Chiang Rai, with optional yoga/t'ai chi classes, Vipassana meditation and discussions on Buddhism. There are also less frequent courses in Keralan Ayurvedic oil massage with hands and feet, the latter involving balancing from a rope (B12,000). For information about the courses in Chiang Mai, contact the Sunshine Massage School at 159/2 Thanon Kaew Nawarat (Ⓣ053 262574). Information about having a massage is given on p.367.

Meditation

Northern Insight Meditation Centre, at Wat Ram Poeng (aka Wat Tapotaram) on Thanon Canal near Wat Umong (Ⓣ053 278620, Ⓦwww.palikanon.com/vipassana/tapotaram/tapotaram.htm), holds disciplined Vipassana courses (with a rule of silence, days beginning at 4am, no food after noon and so on), taught by Thai monks with translators. The minimum stay is ten days, with a basic course lasting 26 days, and payment is by donation. The other well-known and respected monastery for meditation retreats in the area is Wat Phra That Chom Thong, 60km southwest of Chiang Mai (see p.397). Under the auspices of Wat Phra That Chom Thong, an International Buddhism Centre has recently been established at Wat Phra That Doi Suthep (Ⓣ053 295012, Ⓦwww.fivethousandyears.org or Ⓦwww.doisuthep.com; see p.368), which follows a very traditional Buddhist monastic way and offers a variety of Vipassana retreats for beginners and advanced meditators. For an introduction to meditation and Buddhist culture, go to a talk at Wat Umong on a Sunday afternoon (see p.355) or sign up for one of the free overnight courses run by Mahachulalongkorn Buddhist University, based at Wat Suan Dork (see p.356) on Thanon Suthep. These involve discussions about Buddhism, meditation, walking meditation, chanting and almsgiving, and begin at about 2pm on a Tuesday, before departure to the training centre on Doi Suthep, returning to Wat Suan Dork at 12.30pm the next day. As places are limited you should make contact in advance (Ⓣ053 278967 ext 11, Ⓦwww.monkchat.net).

Thai language

The longest-established and best place to learn Thai is the AUA (American University Alumni) Language Centre, 24 Thanon Ratchdamnoen (Ⓣ053 277951 or 053 278407, Ⓦwww.auathailand.org/chiangmai), which is certified by the Ministry of Education. Several levels of classes are offered, starting with spoken Thai for beginners (60hr over about 6 weeks; B3900), with class sizes limited to 5–12 students. Individual and small-group instruction can also be arranged, starting from B270 per hour for 1–2 students.

the gate to the right, the wooden scripture repository is the best example of its kind in the north, inlaid with glass mosaic and set high on a base decorated with stucco angels. The largest building in the compound, a colourful modern viharn fronted by naga balustrades, hides from view a rustic wooden bot, a chedi constructed in 1345 to house the ashes of King Kam Fu, and – the highlight of the whole complex – the beautiful **Viharn Lai Kam**. This wooden gem from the early nineteenth century is a textbook example of Lanna architecture, with its squat, multi-tiered roof and exquisitely carved and gilded pediment: if you feel you're being watched as you approach, it's the sinuous double arch between the porch's central columns, which represents the Buddha's eyebrows.

Inside sits one of Thailand's three **Phra Singh** (or Sihing) Buddha images (see p.687), a portly, radiant and much-revered bronze in a fifteenth-century Lanna style. Its setting is enhanced by the colourful **murals** of action-packed tableaux, which give a window on life in the north a hundred years ago. The murals illustrate two different stories: on the right-hand wall is an old folk tale, the *Sang Thong*, about a childless king and queen who are miraculously given a beautiful son, the "Golden Prince", in a conch shell. The murals on the left, which have been badly damaged by water, show the story of the mythical swan Suwannahong, who forms the magnificent prow of the principal royal barge in Bangkok. Incidentally, what look like Bermuda shorts on the men are in fact Buddhist **tattoos**: in the nineteenth century, all boys in the north were tattooed from navel to kneecap, an agonizing ordeal undertaken to show their courage and to enhance their appeal to women. On one side of the wat is a high school for young yellow-sashed novices and schoolboys in blue shorts, who all noisily throng the temple compound during the day. Dally long enough and you'll be sure to have to help them with their English homework.

Wat Chedi Luang

From Wat Phra Singh a ten-minute walk east along Thanon Ratchadamnoen brings you to **Wat Chedi Luang** on Thanon Phra Pokklao, where an enormous chedi, toppled from 90m to its present 60m by an earthquake in 1545, is the temple's most striking feature. You'll need a titanic leap of the imagination, however, to picture the beautifully faded pink-brick chedi, in all its crumbling grandeur, as it was in the fifteenth century, when it was covered in bronze plates and gold leaf, and housed the Emerald Buddha (see p.135) for eighty years. Recent attempts to rebuild the entire chedi to its former glory, now abandoned, have nevertheless led to modern replacements of the elephants at the base, the nagas that line the lengthy staircases, and the Buddha images in its four niches, including an oversized replica of the Emerald Buddha in its old spot on the eastern side. In an unprepossessing modern building (which women are not allowed to enter) by the main entrance stands the city's foundation pillar, the *Inthakin* post, here at the geographical centre of Chiang Mai, sheltered by a stately gum tree which, the story has it, will stand for as long as the city's fortunes prosper. On the north side of the chedi, **Monk Chat** is advertised (Mon–Sat noon–6.30pm), giving you a chance to meet and talk to the monks in English. While you're in the vicinity, pop in on **Wat Pan Tao** next door to see the wonderfully gnarled all-teak viharn, constructed of unpolished panels, supported on enormous pillars and protected by carved wooden bars on the windows, a classic of graceful Lanna architecture.

Chiang Mai City Arts and Cultural Centre

From Wat Chedi Luang, the old town's main commercial street, Thanon Phra Pokklao, heads north past a monument to King Mengrai, the founder of

Chiang Mai, set in its own small piazza on the corner of Thanon Ratchdamnoen and supposedly on the site where he was killed by lightning. On Sunday afternoons and evenings, Thanon Ratchdamnoen becomes a **walking street** (see box on p.359), a pedestrianized market with all kinds of shopping and eating, and live music.

A few minutes on up Thanon Phra Pokklao, Mengrai features again in the bronze Three Kings Monument, showing him discussing the auspicious layout of his "new city", Chiang Mai, with his allies, Ramkhamhaeng of Sukhothai and Ngam Muang of Phayao. Behind the monument, the elegant 1920s former provincial office has recently been turned into the **Chiang Mai City Arts and Cultural Centre** (Tues–Sun 8.30am–5pm; B90) by the municipality – essentially a museum with the aim of conveying the history, customs and culture of the city and the region. To this end, scale models and plenty of high-quality English-language audiovisuals are thoughtfully deployed, with some nice touches such as vivid reminiscences by Chiang Mai's older inhabitants about what the city was like in the early twentieth century. This was the site of Wat Sadeu Muang, home of the city pillar before it was moved to Wat Chedi Luang, and the symbolic significance of this is neatly explained on a see-through display board in front of a window, through which you can see one of the wat's restored thirteenth-century Haripunjaya-style chedis outside. Upstairs, the interest tails off, though there is an engaging audiovisual and exhibit on the hill tribes. The back half of the building shelters cultural activities such as weaving demonstrations, temporary exhibitions, a souvenir shop and a small café. At the time of writing, a new history museum was under construction behind the Arts and Cultural Centre, and another colonial-style building to the east of the Three Kings Monument was being converted into a museum focusing on Lanna culture.

Wat Chiang Man

Carry on up Thanon Phra Pokklao and turn right along Thanon Wiang Kaeo to reach the oldest temple in Chiang Mai, **Wat Chiang Man**, after about five minutes. Erected by Mengrai on the site where he first pitched camp, the wat is most notable for two dainty and very holy Buddha images housed in the viharn to the right of the entrance: the **Phra Sila**, a graceful stone work carved in northern India in the sixth century BC, stands in the typical *tribunga,* or hipshot stance; its partner, the **Phra Setangamani** (or Crystal Buddha), made four centuries later, probably in Lavo (modern Lopburi), is much revered by the inhabitants of Chiang Mai for its rain making powers and is carried through the streets during the Songkhran festival to help the rainy season on its way. Neither image is especially beautiful, but a powerful aura is created by making them difficult to see, high up behind three sets of iron bars. Check out the chedi at the back of the compound for the herd of stone elephants on whose backs it sits.

Wat Bupparam

On the east side of town at the midpoint of the main shopping drag, Thanon Tha Pae, **Wat Bupparam** makes for a mildly interesting stroll from the main guest-house area around Tha Pae Gate. Housed in the gleaming wedding-cake structure at the centre of the temple is a magnificent black Buddha, which was apparently made for King Naresuan of Ayutthaya over four hundred years ago from a single piece of teak. The **temple well** (off-limits for women) was used for watering the Buddha relics enshrined in the chedi and is also Chiang Mai's representative in the *murathaphisek* ceremony, when holy waters

Chiang Mai festivals

Chiang Mai is the best and busiest place in the country to see in the Thai New Year, **Songkhran**, which takes over the city between April 13 and 16. The most obvious role of the festival is as an extended "rain dance" in the driest part of the year, when huge volumes of canal water are thrown about in a communal water-fight that spares no one a drenching. The other elements of this complex festival are not as well known but no less important. In the temple compounds, communities get together to build sandcastles in the shape of chedis, which they cover with coloured flags – this bestows merit on any ancestors who happen to find themselves in hell and may eventually release them from their torments, and also shows an intent to help renovate the wat in the year to come. Houses are given a thorough spring-clean to see out the old year, while Buddha images from the city's main temples are cleaned, polished and sprinkled with lustral water, before being ceremonially carried through the middle of the water-fight to give everyone the chance to throw water on them and receive the blessing of renewal. Finally, younger family members formally visit their elders during the festival to ask for their blessings, while pouring scented water over their hands.

Loy Krathong, on and around the night of the full moon in November, has its most showy celebration at Sukhothai, but Chiang Mai – where it is also known as **Yipeng** – is not far behind (see the *Loy Krathong* colour section). While a spectacular but unnerving firework fiesta rages on the banks, thousands of candles are gently floated down the Ping River in beautiful lotus-leaf boats. People hope in this way to float away any sins or ill luck they have incurred, and give thanks for the rainy season to Mae Kong Kha, the ancient water goddess. As well as floating krathongs, people release **khom loy**, paper hot-air balloons that create a magical spectacle as they float heavenward with firecrackers trailing behind. As with krathongs, they are released to carry away problems and bad luck, as well as to honour the Buddha's top knot, which he cut off when he became an ascetic (according to legend, the top knot is looked after by the Buddha's mother in heaven).

Chiang Mai's brilliantly colourful **flower festival**, usually on the first weekend of February, also attracts huge crowds. The highlight is a procession of floats, modelled into animals, chedis and even scenes from the *Ramayana*, and covered in flowers. In early April, the **Poy Sang Long** festival (which has its most elaborate manifestation in Thailand in Mae Hong Son; see box on p.408), centred around Wat Pa Pao near the northeast corner of the old city, is an ordination ritual for young Shan men, who are paraded round town on the shoulders of relatives. The boys are dressed in extravagant, colourful clothing with huge floral headdresses, which they symbolically cast off at the end of the festival to don a saffron robe. In late May or early June, the **Inthakin** festival, a life-prolonging ceremony for the city of Chiang Mai, is focused around the city foundation pillar at Wat Chedi Luang, which throngs with locals making offerings.

are gathered from Thailand's most auspicious localities for the ritual bathing of a new king.

Chiang Mai National Museum

In telling the history of Lanna art and culture, the **National Museum**, on the northwestern outskirts of Chiang Mai (Wed–Sun 9am–4pm; B30; Ⓦwww.thailandmuseum.com), has far fewer bells and whistles than its rival, the Chiang Mai Arts and Cultural Centre, but in terms of the quality of artefacts on display, wins hands down. To get to the museum with your own transport, leave the old town through Chang Phuak Gate on the northern moat, then go 2km up Thanon Chotana, a crowded shopping street, before turning left along the Superhighway; here you must go past the museum, then make a U-turn along the road's central divider and head back towards your target along the eastbound lane. Alternatively, charter a tuk-tuk or songthaew from the centre of town (B40–50). The building is easy to identify by its soaring *kalae* motifs – elaborately carved extensions to the bargeboards that create a "V" shape over the apex of each roof and are a hallmark of Lanna architecture.

△ Loy Krathong

Inside, the airy rooms are cool enough for a long browse, and the collection is engrossing and liberally labelled in Thai and English. As you enter, you are greeted on the left by the head of a smiling bronze Buddha that is as tall as a man, but you need to go right to follow the displays, which are grouped into six sections. The first of these displays artefacts and skeletons unearthed by local archeological digs, as well as photographs of cave paintings found in the area. This leads into the the second section, which chronicles the golden age of the Lanna kingdom, from the fourteenth to the sixteenth centuries, including some lovely ceramics from San Kamphaeng, as well as subjugation by the Burmese from the sixteenth to eighteenth centuries. The third part recounts relations between Chiang Mai and the Siamese court at Bangkok from the late eighteenth century, while the fourth section (upstairs) focuses on the expansion of trade in the late nineteenth century, particularly due to the activities of logging companies. The fifth section shows how the process of modernization continued throughout the twentieth century with advances in educational opportunities, health facilities and the development of handicraft industries such as silverware.

The biggest section is given over to **Thai religious art**, with a particular focus on Lanna art. Hundreds of Buddha images are on display, ranging from a humble, warmly smiling sandstone head of the Haripunjaya (Lamphun) era, representing the earliest northern style, to gleaming images in the Ratanakosin (Bangkok) style. In the golden age of Lanna images were produced in two contrasting styles. One group, which resembles images from northern India, has been called the **lion-type**, after the Shakyamuni (Lion of the Shakyas) archetype at the great Buddhist temple at Bodh Gaya, the site of the Buddha's enlightenment. It's been conjectured that a delegation sent by King Tilok to Bodh Gaya in the 1450s brought back not only a plan of the temple to be used in the building of nearby Wat Jet Yot, but also a copy of the statue, which became the model for hundreds of Lanna images. These broad-shouldered, plump-bellied Buddhas are always seated with the right hand in the touching-the-earth gesture, while the face is well rounded with pursed lips and a serious, majestic demeanour. The second type is the **Thera Sumana** style named after the monk Mahathera Sumana, who came from Sukhothai in 1369 to establish his Sri Lankan sect in Lanna. The museum is well stocked with this type of image, which shows strong Sukhothai influence, with an oval face and a flame-like *ushnisha* on top of the head.

Wat Jet Yot

Set back from the Superhighway five minutes' walk west of the museum, the peaceful garden temple of **Wat Jet Yot** is named after the "seven spires" of its unusual chedi. The temple was built in 1455 by King Tilok, to represent the seven places around Bodh Gaya in India which the Buddha visited in the seven weeks following his enlightenment. Around the base of the chedi, delicate stuccos portray cross-legged deities serenely floating in the sky, a role model for all yogic fliers; their faces are said to be those of King Tilok's relatives.

The Tribal Museum and Ratchamangkla Park

One kilometre north of the Superhighway off Thanon Chotana, the **Tribal Museum** (bus #8 from Chang Phuak Gate or #2 from Nawarat Bridge; Mon–Fri 8.30am–4pm; free) enjoys a superb location behind the artfully landscaped **Ratchamangkla Park**. Originally established in 1965 as part of the Tribal Research Institute at Chiang Mai University, the museum was moved in 1997 to the present edifice, in the style of a Chinese pagoda. Overlooking a tree-lined lake, the very pretty and peaceful setting makes a visit worthwhile, as does the opportunity to learn something about the various hill tribes before heading off on a trek. It's about a ten-minute walk from the park gate on Thanon Chotana to the museum entrance, but, if you are getting here by songthaew, drivers can take their vehicles round the park directly to the museum. However, when it's time to leave you have to take the ten-minute walk to the gate to find transport back into town.

Set out on three floors, the museum has its main exhibition area on the ground floor, where displays about each of the main hill tribes are accompanied by concise information printed in both Thai and English. A useful wall chart shows the calendar of traditional village life, giving a month-by-month picture of the agricultural activities, ceremonies and festivals of the tribes featured; there are also photos and models of village dwellings, giving a good idea of the different styles of architecture, and a display of hill-tribe instruments accompanied by taped music. If you are especially interested, ask to see the slide show (B20; 15min) and video (B50; 55min). Despite the saccharine American narrator, the video is interesting, describing the six main tribes and showing a festival for each; by the end of it you should be able to distinguish between the modes of dress of the various tribes.

As you trawl through the exhibition, glimpses of the lake through the windows are very appealing, and it's worth taking a look at the reconstructions of hill-tribe houses erected along the lake's south side. The road around the lake is popular with joggers in the morning and evening, and snack stalls clustered around the lake attract groups of local people late in the day.

The zoo

About 1km beyond Wat Jet Yot, the Superhighway crosses Thanon Huai Kaeo, a broad avenue of posh residences and hotels that starts out from the northwest corner of the moat and ends at the foot of Doi Suthep. Heading out up Thanon Huai Kaeo, past the sprawling campus of Chiang Mai University (CMU), brings you to **Chiang Mai Zoo** (daily 8am–6pm, last tickets 4pm; B100 adults, B50 children; service car adults B20, children B10; see below for variations and extra charges), in an attractive 36-acre park at the base of the mountain. It's easy to get there and back from the centre by tuk-tuk or songthaew (B30–40 one way).

Originally a menagerie of a missionary family's pets, the zoo now houses an impressive collection of over seven thousand animals in modern, relatively comfortable conditions. There's a children's zoo, a colourful walk-through aviary and a tropical freshwater aquarium, housing the elusive giant Mekong catfish, while larger mammals include elephants, giraffes, Humboldt penguins and the current favourites, two **giant pandas** loaned by China for ten years in 2003 (adults B100. children B50). Despite a disorientating layout, it makes a diverting visit, especially for kids. Feeding times for animals are posted clearly, and refreshment stalls for humans are never far away. The grounds are too big to walk round, but "service cars", small open-sided buses, are available to take you around, soon to be replaced by a new monorail that was under construction at the time of writing. The zoo is better visited in the morning to avoid the afternoon heat, or in the evening (6–9pm), when a "**twilight zone**" features animals feeding, and the cost of B200 for adults and B100 for children includes use of the service car and a visit to the pandas. In an idyllic location in the upper reaches of the grounds there's a small campsite, mostly used for picnics by day-trippers, and a good restaurant, *Palaad Tawanron* (see "Eating"), with great views over the city.

Wat Umong

More of a park than a temple, **Wat Umong** makes an unusual, charming place for a stroll in the western suburbs, accessible by tuk-tuk or songthaew. If you're driving or biking from the zoo, you'll need to get through or round (on Thanon Chon Prathan) the extensive grounds of CMU. From the centre of town, head west along Thanon Suthep for about 2km and turn left after Wang Nam Gan (a royal agricultural produce project); then follow the signs to the wat for another kilometre along a winding lane.

According to legend the wat was built in the 1380s by King Ku Na for a brilliant but deranged monk called Jan, who was prone to wandering off into the forest to meditate. Because Ku Na wanted to be able to get Jan's advice at any time, he founded this wat and decorated the **tunnels** (*umong*) beneath the chedi with paintings of trees, flowers and birds to simulate the monk's favoured habitat. Some of the old tunnels can still be explored, where obscure fragments of paintings and one or two small modern shrines can be seen. Above the tunnels, frighteningly lavish nagas guard the staircase up to the overgrown **chedi** and a grassy platform supporting a grotesque black statue of the fasting Buddha, all ribs and veins: he is depicted as he was during his six years of self-mortification, before he realized that he should avoid extremes along the Middle Path to enlightenment. Behind the chedi, the ground slopes away to a **lake** inhabited by hungry carp, where locals come to relax and feed the fish. On a tiny island here, reached by a concrete bridge, stands a statue of the late Buddhadasa Bhikkhu (see p.635), a famous southern Thai monk who re-established the monastic community here in the 1960s. Informal discussions in English on Buddhism, and some meditation practice, are normally held in the Chinese pavilion on the lake's edge here on Sunday afternoons at 3pm, with one of the farang monks who are often in residence.

Throughout the tranquil wooded grounds, the temple's diverse education-focused philosophy comes vividly alive: as you enter the compound you pass through a shady grove where signs are pinned to nearly every tree, displaying simple Buddhist maxims in Thai and English and the botanical name of the species. At certain times of the day, your stroll is accompanied by a soothing Thai voice emanating from loudspeakers, expounding on Buddhism; the subject can be explored in more depth in the library, in the centre of the temple grounds, with some books in English, and at the adjacent bookshop – and outside at tables and covered seating areas local people read, study and conduct discussions. Up some nearby steps, the path leading to the chedi is lined with outrageous cartoons of sinning anthropomorphized dogs, moral maxims underneath each one, while colourful and surreal didactic paintings also cover the modern hall near the tunnel entrances. At the entrance gate, handicrafts are sold by the community of disabled people that has a house and workshop in the wat.

Chiang Mai University Art Museum

From the turn-off to Wat Umong, Thanon Suthep heads back towards town, eventually meeting the western moat at Suan Dork Gate. A short way along on the left, entered from just around the corner on Thanon Nimmanhemin, the modern **Chiang Mai University Art Museum** (Tues–Sun 9am–5pm; free; Ⓣ053 944833) is not only confirmation of the city's growing importance, but also a boon to the large local artistic community. The large, purpose-built exhibition areas are well designed and lit, and the exhibitions generally change each month, giving visitors an insight into modern Thai art, as well as anything from Japanese lacquerware sculpture to Iranian carpetry art. There's a café and shop, and films and concerts are regularly put on here.

Wat Suan Dork

A little further east along Thanon Suthep stands **Wat Suan Dork**, the "Flower Garden Temple", surrounded by walls as part of Chiang Mai's fortifications. Legend says that Mahathera Sumana, when he was invited to establish his Sri Lankan sect here in 1369, brought with him a miraculous glowing relic. Ku Na, the king of Chiang Mai, ordered a huge chedi – the one you see today – to be built in his flower garden, but as the pea-sized relic was being placed inside the chedi, it split into two parts: one half was buried here, the other found its way to Doi Suthep, after further adventures (see p.368).

The brilliantly whitewashed chedi now sits next to a garden of smaller, equally dazzling chedis containing the ashes of the Chiang Mai royal family; framed by Doi Suthep to the west, this makes an impressive and photogenic sight, especially at sunset. Standing in the way of a panoramic shot of all the chedis, the huge, open-sided viharn on the east side has been crudely restored, but the bot at the back of the dusty compound is more interesting – decorated with lively *Jataka* murals, it enshrines a beautifully illuminated, 500-year-old bronze Buddha image. Nearby signs point the way to **Monk Chat** (Mon, Wed & Fri 5–7pm; Ⓦwww.monkchat.net), organized by the Mahachulalongkorn Buddhist University (Chiang Mai Campus) based at the temple, which gives you the opportunity to talk to monks about anything from Buddhism to the weather (or about the university's overnight Buddhist culture and meditation courses – see p.349), and them the chance to meet foreigners and practise their English.

Museum of World Insects and Natural Wonders

This quirky and well-organized museum, located just around the corner from Wat Suan Dork at 72 Soi 13, Thanon Nimmanhemin (daily 9am–5pm; adults B300, children B100), presents a fascinating diversion, with dazzling displays of butterflies, hundreds of species of beetles, and insects that disguise themselves as leaves or twigs. The natural wonders include fossilized wood, beautiful stones, colourful seashells and fossils.

Sbun-Nga Textile Museum

Anyone with at least a passing interest in textiles and the great weaving traditions of northern Thailand should make time for the **Sbun-Nga Textile Museum** (bus #4 from Tha Pae Gate; daily except Wed 10.30am–6.30pm; B100) at the Old Chiangmai Cultural Centre – more famous for its *khan toke* dinners (see p.362) – on Thanon Wualai. Here over a thousand ancient and rare textiles are lovingly displayed and informatively labelled in English, classified according to which sub-group of Thais and which geographical area they come from. Thus you'll find among the patterns of the Thai Lue, who migrated from Sipsong Panna in southern China to various parts of northern Thailand, the brightly coloured and very intricate *lai nam lai* or "flowing water" design, signifying those who resettled by the Mekong River. Other highlights include a very beautiful royal headdress of the Thai Lao, who have migrated mainly from northeast Laos in the last two hundred years and are considered to have among the most sophisticated weaving techniques and designs in the world, and the swirling coronation dress of a Thai Yai crown prince, decorated with gems and precious metals.

Shopping

Shopping is an almost irresistible pastime in Chiang Mai, a hotbed of traditional cottage industries offering generally high standards of workmanship at low prices. Two main tourist shopping areas, the San Kamphaeng road and the night bazaar, conveniently operating at different times of the day, sell the full range of local handicrafts.

The **road to San Kamphaeng**, which extends due east from the end of Thanon Charoen Muang for 13km, is the main daytime strip; also known as the "Handicraft Highway", it's lined with every sort of shop and factory, where you can usually watch the craftsmen at work. The biggest concentrations are at Bo Sang, the "umbrella village", 9km from town, and at San Kamphaeng itself, once important for its kilns but now dedicated chiefly to silk-weaving. It's a worthwhile trip to watch age-old crafts in process, but the main problem is getting there. Frequent white songthaews to San Kamphaeng leave Chiang Mai from the central Lamyai market, but it's difficult to decide when to get off if you don't know the area. You could sign up for a tour or hire a tuk-tuk for a few hundred baht, but the catch here is that the drivers will want to take you to the shops where they'll pick up a commission. The best way to go is by bicycle or motorbike, which allows you to stop where and when you please, but take care with the fast-moving traffic on the narrow road.

The other main shopper's playground is the **night bazaar**, sprawling around the junction of Thanon Chang Klan and Thanon Loi Khro, where bumper-to-bumper street stalls and several indoor market areas and multi-storey arcades (including the original Chiang Mai Night Bazaar shopping centre on the west side of Thanon Chang Klan) sell just about anything produced in Chiang Mai, plus crafts from other parts of Thailand and southeast Asia, as well as counterfeit designer goods; the action starts up at around 5pm, and there are plenty of real bargains to be had here. Even if you're not into shopping, there's lots to see, including rock climbers in action at The Peak, a climbing wall (see p.339) surrounded by shops and cafés, and traditional dancing at the Kalare Food Centre (see p.363).

△ Warorot market

During the day, bustling **Warorot market**, along the river immediately north of Thanon Tha Pae, has lots of cheap and cheerful cotton, linen and ceramics for sale on the upper floors. In the heart of the market, you can watch locals buying chilli paste, sausage and sticky rice from their favourite stalls, and maybe even join the queue. There's also a flower market just east of here, on Thanon Praisani by the river, which is open late at night until the early hours of the morning.

The city's newest market is the **JJ market**, which sprawls over about 40 acres at the northern end of Thanon Assadatorn, near the Superhighway. The shops are gradually being occupied by leading producers of designer goods (fine furnishings, exclusive garments, art work and so on), and with coffee shops and refreshment kiosks scattered among them, this makes an interesting place for a stroll, especially in the evening. Check out the chunky bamboo furniture at Gerard Collection, or the original prints and photographs at Pictory. Run by the owners of Central Group, this is likely to become one of Chiang Mai's major shopping districts in the future. If you're settling into Chiang Mai for a while and want some potted plants or garden statues to feather your nest, head for the **Kamthieng Market**, just east of the JJ market, which has the city's biggest range of horticultural produce. Even if you're not buying, the stalls put on photogenic displays, especially during the cool season (Nov–Feb).

Another place worth knowing about is **Thanon Nimmanhemin**, the continuation of the western end of the Superhighway. Its northern end towards Thanon Huai Kaeo, which savvy locals sometimes tag Chiang Mai's Sukhumvit for its services to well-to-do expats, has a particular concentration of interesting shops and boutiques. Here, as well as upmarket clothes shops, you'll find some notable outlets for **contemporary Thai design**, fusing various of the crafts described below with modern, often minimalist elements. On Nimmanhemin's Soi 1, behind the *Amari Rincome Hotel*, Gong Dee is full of wood and lacquer vases, boxes, lamps and bowls, much of it gleaming gold and silver, while Ayodhya opposite sells stylish fabrics as well as funky bowls and boxes covered in dried water-hyacinth stalks, woven liana lampshades and lots of other novel

Chiang Mai's walking streets

If you're in Chiang Mai at the weekend it's worth heading down to Thanon Wualai, just south of the old city, on a Saturday between 3pm and midnight, or to Thanon Ratchdamnoen, which runs east–west through the centre of the old city, on a Sunday at the same time. Closed to traffic for the duration, these **walking streets** become crowded with vendors selling typical Northern Thai items such as clothes, musical instruments and snacks, and the atmosphere is enlivened by musicians busking and people thronging the street. The walking streets have become almost as popular as the night bazaar, as they are ideal places to pick up a souvenir and mingle with a very mixed crowd of Thais and farangs.

woven accessories and furniture. Over on the east side of the river at 35 Thanon Ratanakosin, Aka Gallery shelters thoroughly modern celadon, rich clothes and textiles and cutting-edge home furnishings. Also on the east side of the river, Thanon Charoenrat between Nawarat and Nakhon Ping bridges has several interesting outlets for clothes, furniture and artwork, including La Luna Gallery, at number 190, which displays and sells a striking range of paintings, posters, photos and pottery by local artists.

Fabrics and clothes

The **silk** produced out towards San Kamphaeng, to the east of Chiang Mai, is richly coloured and hard-wearing, with various attractive textures. Bought off a roll, the material is generally less costly than in Bangkok, though more expensive than in the northeast – prices are around B400–600 a metre for two-ply (for thin shirts and skirts) and B650–750 a metre for four-ply (suitable for suits). Ready-made silk clothes and made-to-measure tailoring, though inexpensive, are generally staid and more suited to formal wear. About 5km out from the centre of Chiang Mai on the right, Piankusol (daily 9am–5pm) is the best place to follow the silk-making process right from the cocoon. If you've got slightly more money to spend on better quality silk, head for Chiang Mai's oldest silk manufacturer, Shinawatra (7km out, with a shop at 18/1 Thanon Huai Kaeo; Ⓦwww.shinawatrathaisilk.com), which was once graced by no less a personage than Diana, Princess of Wales.

In Chiang Mai you'll find plenty of traditional, pastel-coloured **cotton**, which is nice for furnishings, most of it from the village of Pa Sang southwest of Lamphun. Outlets in the basement of the main Chiang Mai Night Bazaar shopping centre on Thanon Chang Klan have good, cheap selections of this sort of cloth at around B150 per metre, plus hand-painted and batik-printed lengths, and ready-made tablecloths and the like.

A shop worth a look around is Pa Ker Yaw (closed Sun), near the *Downtown Inn* at 180 Thanon Loi Khro, a weather-beaten wooden shophouse stuffed with a selection of rich **fabrics** from Thailand, Laos and Burma, as well as hill-tribe jewellery and basketware and other crafts. For the all-over ethnic look, Classic Lanna Thai, on the first floor of Chiang Mai Night Bazaar, sells classy ready-to-wear **clothes**, made from local fabrics by traditional northern methods. Also upmarket is Ginger, in the compound of *The House* restaurant at 199 Thanon Moon Muang, and at 6/21 Thanon Nimmanhemin, which has a striking range of original garments and accessories. Flower Earring, 6 Soi 1, Thanon Nimmanhemin, specializes in stylish, tastefully chosen women's clothes and traditional fabrics from northern Thailand, Burma and China, including some gorgeously coloured skirts. If you just need to replenish your backpack, try Ga-Boutique at 1/1 Thanon Kotchasarn (opposite Tha Pae Gate), which sells ordinary casual clothes of reasonable quality at low prices.

If you're interested in the whole process of traditional fabric production, particularly the use of **natural dyes**, Studio Naenna, 138/8 Soi Changkhian, Thanon Huai Kaeo at the base of Doi Suthep (Ⓦwww.infothai.com/naenna), is an excellent place to begin. If you phone for an appointment (Ⓣ053 226042) you can see a demonstration of dyeing, including the plants from which the dyes are extracted; you can then watch the weavers in action (Mon–Fri) and buy the finished products, which consist of top-quality ready-made garments and accessories, in their showroom. They also have an outlet for their products at 22 Soi 1, Thanon Nimmanhemin.

To make sure more of your money goes to those who make the goods, take your custom to one of the **non-profit-making shops** whose proceeds go to the hill tribes. These include the Hill Tribe Products Foundation, on Thanon Suthep in front of Wat Suan Dork, which sells beautiful lengths of cotton and silk, silverware and a variety of hill-tribe gear; Thai Tribal Crafts, 208 Thanon Bamrungrat off Thanon Kaeo Nawarat – *yaam*, the embroidered shoulder bags popular with Thai students, are particularly good here.

Woodcarving

Chiang Mai has a long tradition of **woodcarving**, which expresses itself in everything from salad bowls to half-size elephants. In the past the industry has relied on the cutting of Thailand's precious teak, but manufacturers are now beginning to use other imported hardwoods, while bemoaning their inferior quality. Carl Bock, who travelled through the region in 1882, observed a habit which is still common today: "The woodcarvers have a quaint taste for inlaying their work with odd bits of coloured glass, tinsel or other bright material: such work will not bear close inspection, but it has a remarkably striking effect when the sun shines on these glittering objects." Wooden objects are sold all over the city, but the most famous place for carving is **Ban Tawai**, a large village of shops and factories where prices are low and you can watch the woodworkers in action. One of Thailand's most important woodcarving centres, Ban Tawai relied on rice farming until thirty years ago, but today virtually every home here has carvings for sale outside and each backyard hosts its own cottage industry. To get there, you'll need your own transport: follow Highway 108 south from Chiang Mai 13km to Hang Dong, then head east for 2km.

Lacquerware

Lacquerware can be seen in nearly every museum in Thailand, most commonly in the form of **betel sets**, which used to be carried ceremonially by the slaves of grandees as an insignia of rank and wealth. Betel sets are still produced in Chiang Mai according to the traditional technique, whereby a woven bamboo frame is covered with layers of rich red lacquer and decorated with black details. A variety of other objects, such as trays and jewellery boxes, are also produced, some decorated with gold leaf on black gloss. Lacquerware makes an ideal choice for gifts, as it is both light to carry, and at the same time typically Thai. Just about every other shop in town sells lacquerware, but few places have such an appealing selection of original designs as Living Space, at 276–278 Thanon Tha Pae.

Celadon

Celadon, sometimes known as greenware, is a delicate variety of stoneware which was first made in China over two thousand years ago, and later produced in

Betel

Betel-chewing today is popular mainly with elderly Thais, particularly country women, but it used to be a much more widespread social custom, and a person's betel tray set was once a Thai's most prized possession and an indication of rank: royalty would have sets made in gold, the nobility's would be in silver or nielloware, and poorer folk wove theirs from rattan or carved them from wood. A set comprises at least three small covered receptacles, and sometimes a tray to hold these boxes and the knife or nutcracker used to split the fruit.

The three essential ingredients for a good chew are betel leaf, limestone ash and areca palm fruit. You chew the coarse red flesh of the narcotic fruit (best picked when small and green-skinned) first, before adding a large heart-shaped betel leaf, spread with limestone ash paste and folded into manageable size; for a stronger kick, you can include tobacco and/or marijuana at this point. An acquired and bitter taste, betel numbs the mouth and generates a warm feeling around the ears. Less pleasantly, constant spitting is necessary: in traditional houses you spit through any hole in the floorboards, while in more elegant households a spittoon is provided. It doesn't do much for your looks either: betel-chewers are easily spotted by their rotten teeth and lips stained scarlet from the habit.

Thailand, most famously at Sukhothai and Sawankhalok. Several kilns in Chiang Mai have revived the art, the best of them being Mengrai Kilns at 79/2 Soi 6, Thanon Samlarn (Ⓦwww.mengraikilns.com). Sticking to the traditional methods, Mengrai produces beautiful and reasonably priced vases, crockery and larger items, thrown in elegant shapes and covered with transparent green and blue glazes.

Umbrellas and paper

The village of **Bo Sang** bases its fame on souvenir **umbrellas** – made of silk, cotton or mulberry paper and decorated with bold, painted colours (from about B75 for a kid's parasol) – and celebrates its craft with a colourful **umbrella fair** every January. The artists who work here can paint a small motif on your bag or camera in two minutes flat. The grainy mulberry (*sa*) **paper**, which makes beautiful writing or sketching pads, is sold almost as an afterthought in many of Bo Sang's shops; it can also be bought from a few shops in the centre of the basement of the Chiang Mai Night Bazaar building, which sell a very wide range of *sa* paper in the form of albums, notepaper and so on (typically ten envelopes and ten pieces of paper for B85).

Silver and jewellery

Of the traditional craft quarters, only the **silversmiths'** area on Thanon Wualai remains in its original location. The oldest factory in Chiang Mai, Siam Silverware on Soi 3, a ramshackle and sulphurous compound loud with the hammering of hot metal, gives you a whiff of what this zone must have been like in its heyday. The end results are repoussé plates, bowls and cups, and attractive, chunky jewellery. Silver is often priced by the gram, with current rates at about B20 per gram, so a thin sterling-silver bracelet costs around B300–350 and a large, chunky bangle around B500–1000. If you want sterling silver, check for the stamp that shows the item is 92.5 percent pure; many items are only 80 percent pure and sell much more cheaply. A good general **jewellery** store is Nova Collection at 210 Thanon Tha Pae, which has some lovely rings and necklaces blending gold, silver and precious stones in striking and original designs, as well as running workshops in jewellery-making (see p.348).

Eating

The main difficulty with **eating** in Chiang Mai is knowing when to stop. All over town there are inexpensive and enticing restaurants serving typically northern food, which has been strongly influenced by Burmese cuisine, especially in curries such as the spicy *kaeng hang lay* (usually translated on menus as "Northern Thai curry"), made with pork, ginger, garlic and tamarind. Another favourite local dish is Chiang Mai *nem*, spicy pork sausage – although the uncooked, fermented varieties are usually too sour for Western palates. At lunchtime the thing to do is to join the local workers in one of the simple, inexpensive cafés that put all their efforts into producing just one or two special dishes – the traditional meal at this time of day is *khao soi*, a thick broth of curry and coconut cream, with egg noodles and a choice of meat. In the evenings, besides Anusarn market (reviewed below), the main **night markets** are in front of Somphet market on Thanon Moonmuang, along Thanon Bamrungburi by Chiang Mai Gate and on Thanon Suthep, between Thanon Chon Prathan and the back entrance to Chiang Mai University. Many of the **bars** listed below in "Drinking and nightlife" also have particularly good reputations for their food.

International food in Chiang Mai is generally more expensive than Thai, but there's plenty of it, particularly Italian-slanted, and sometimes it's hard to resist. Probably easier to refuse are the restaurants which lay on touristy **cultural shows** with *khan toke* dinners, a selection of northern dishes eaten on the floor off short-legged lacquer trays. If you are tempted, the Old Chiangmai Cultural Centre, 185/3 Thanon Wualai (Ⓣ053 275097, Ⓦwww.oldchiangmai.com; B320; bus #4 from Tha Pae Gate), with its show of northern Thai and hill-tribe dancing, has the best reputation – and be sure to make time for the attached Sbun-Nga Textile Museum beforehand (see p.357). **Dinner cruises** on the river are offered by Mae Ping River Cruises (see p.347), nightly at 7pm for B450 per person for a set menu, and by *The Riverside* (see p.366), at 8pm for an extra B70 per person on top of the cost of the meal, which you choose yourself from the menu.

Thai

Tha Pae Gate area

Aum Vegetarian Food 65 Thanon Moonmuang. Small and relaxing long-time favourite, with air-con and used books for sale. Interesting and cheap veggie dishes such as *khao soi* and Vietnamese spring rolls, Thai desserts and organic hill-tribe coffee. Closes 9pm.

Ratana's Kitchen 320–322 Thanon Tha Pae. A favourite among locals and visitors both for northern specialities like *kaeng hang lay* (B60) and *khao soi* (B30) and for tasty Western breakfasts (B90 for a big one), sandwiches and steaks. Wine (B60 per glass) and cocktails too.

Ruen Tamarind 50/1 Thanon Ratchdamnoen. Located at the *Tamarind Village* boutique hotel, this elegant restaurant serves up excellent Thai cuisine at surprisingly affordable prices. Try the *tom khaa kung* (coconut soup with shrimps; B130) or *kaeng phet linchee* (roast duck with lychees in red curry sauce; B150). Also a few Western dishes like burgers or chicken breast with broccoli and mushroom cream sauce (B180).

The Wok 44 Thanon Ratchamanka. Centrally located, with a relaxing ambience, and quality guaranteed as it's run by the Chiang Mai Cookery School. Main dishes around B50-80.

Rest of Chiang Mai

Anusarn Market Off Thanon Chang Klan. Happy night-time hunting ground of open-air stalls and restaurants. One-dish operators (serving up *hawy thawt*) square up to each other across a shared courtyard of tables; beyond lie halal restaurants specializing in barbecued chicken with honey, and several good seafood places, including the old favourite *Fatty's*. Prices are above average as this is the heart of tourist land.

Baanlansa 98/10 Thanon Ratchdamnoen. Just 50 metres east of Wat Phra Singh, this is a convenient place to grab a bite while exploring the downtown temples. It has a nice shady compound with converted sewing machines for tables, and serves standard Thai dishes like crispy pork and greens on rice (B45) and cheap shakes (B25), as well as burgers and sandwiches.

Chiang Mai Vegetarian Centre Thanon Mahidol. A cavernous traditional *sala* serving a wide range of good veggie dishes on rice, and desserts, with most selections costing under B30. Mon–Fri 6am–2pm.

The Gallery 25 Thanon Charoenrat. Refined restaurant on soothing riverside terraces, behind a gallery for local artists in a century-old teak house. Interesting selection of northern and central Thai food, big portions, slow service, and live traditional northern music nightly.

Hong Tauw Inn 95/17–18 Nantawan Arcade, Thanon Nimmanhemin. Comfortable air-con restaurant done out in "country inn" style, with antiques, plants and old clocks, making for a relaxing environment. The reliable menu ranges from rice and noodle dishes such as *khanom jiin*, to delicious central and northern Thai main dishes, such as a *phanaeng* curry for B90, and includes a wide range of Thai desserts.

Huen Phen 112 Thanon Ratchamanka. Probably Chiang Mai's most authentic northern restaurant, serving great *khao soi* amd other northern favourites from the simple front shop at lunchtime, and from the cosy, antique-laden house behind in the evenings. The selection of hors d'oeuvres at B85 gives a great taste of all the local specials.

Huen Sontharee 46 Thanon Wang Sing Kham. A convivial riverfront restaurant owned by the famous northern Thai folk-singer Sontharee Wechanon, who entertains diners from her balcony-level stage and serves up northern specialities, such as delicious fried Chiang Mai sausage with whole baby garlic. Split levels allow a choice of seating – on a riverside terrace, near the stage or on the floor at round low tables on a balcony overlooking the action. Evenings only.

Just Khao Soi 108/2 Thanon Charoen Prathet. If you get a taste for *khao soi*, you might like to check out this tourist-oriented spot where you can custom-build your own bowl of broth and noodles, adding condiments from a huge palette, for around B100. Aprons provided to prevent you staining your shirt with the sauce splashings.

Kalare Night Bazaar Food Centre Thanon Chang Klan. A coupon system operates at this open-air collection of northern and central Thai, Indian and veggie foodstalls and bars. It's a good lively place for a break from shopping, a budget meal and a beer, with free shows of traditional dancing on a stage between 8pm and 11pm, making a nice background accompaniment without being too loud or intrusive.

Khao Soi Samoe Jai Thanon Faham (no English sign). Thick and tasty *khao soi*, delicious satay and other noodle dishes pack the locals in each lunchtime. Bus #2 from Nawarat Bridge. Daily 9am–3pm.

Kiat Ocha 41–43 Thanon Inthrawarorot, off Thanon Phra Pokklao (no English sign). Delicious and very popular satay and *khao man kai* – boiled chicken breast served with dipping sauces, broth and rice, at around B30 a dish. This and the surrounding cafés are especially handy if you're looking round the old town. Daily 5am–2.30pm.

Krua Sabai Thanon Mahidol. Go into the car park for the golf driving range opposite Airport Plaza to find this little gem of a place that has a relaxing ambience and excellent, reasonably priced Thai food, including daily specials. Bus #4 from Tha Pae Gate.

Maha Naga 431 Thanon Charoenrat. Enjoying one of the best riverside locations in the city and with a choice of dining in elegant wooden *salas* or on a laterite terrace beneath huge banyan trees, this place offers top quality Thai and Thai fusion dishes (main courses around B400) in a romantic setting. Bus #2 from Nawarat Bridge.

New Lamduon Fahharm Khao Soi 352/22 Thanon Charoenrat. Excellent *khao soi* prepared to a secret recipe. Also satay, waffles and *som tam*. Daily 9am–3pm. Bus #2 from Nawarat Bridge.

Palaad Tawanron Above Chiang Mai Zoo. Go to the end of Thanon Suthep, then turn right and follow the signs to one of Chiang Mai's newest and most attractive restaurants, set beside a small waterfall with panoramic views of the city (don't forget the camera). Dishes like *tom yam kung* (B250) and fried sea bass in fish sauce (B270) keep the customers coming, and there's live music every evening.

Ratchamanka 6 Soi 9, Thanon Ratchamanka. In the grounds of the boutique hotel of the same name, this is one of Chiang Mai's classiest places to eat, with starched linen tablecloths and heavy cutlery, plus an unusual menu of Thai, Shan and fusion dishes. Try the Burmese-style beef (B170) or the Phuket lobster (B850) and finish off with the mango flambé in papaya bowl (B120). Evenings only.

Tha Nam 43/3 Moo 2, Thanon Chang Klan. Restaurant on the southern edge of town serving good traditional northern and central Thai food (northern hors d'oeuvres B130, *tom yam kung* B100) in a ramshackle teak house, where musicians play traditional music. Eat on the huge terrace, which has a romantic atmosphere, overlooking a quiet green stretch of the river.

Whole Earth 88 Thanon Sri Dornchai. Mostly veggie dishes from Thailand and India, plus a big fish and seafood selection, with main dishes costing B100-200; soothing atmosphere with occasional live mood music in a traditional Lanna house, with verandas overlooking a large garden.

International

Tha Pae Gate area

Art Café 291 Thanon Tha Pae. This Italian-run place is a popular farang hangout with a good ambience. All the café favourites (yoghurt and muesli as well as the usual American and continental breakfasts, sandwiches, soups, salads and ice cream) and full meals (pasta and pizza at B100–B150, Thai dishes and a big selection of vegetarian options – but avoid the Mexican menu) are served. A big selection of wines starts from B90 a glass.

Bierstube 33/6 Thanon Moonmuang. Friendly and efficient service combined with generous portions of German or Thai food at reasonable prices make this place a favourite among locals. The tables outside provide a good people-watching spot, too.

Blue Diamond Soi 9, Thanon Moon Muang. Popular travellers' haunt in a quiet neighbourhood of guest houses, serving very good Thai vegetarian food, Western breakfasts (B110), home-made bread, shakes (B20–30), herbal teas and hill-tribe coffee (B35). Mon–Sat 7am–9pm.

Chiangmai Saloon 80/1 Thanon Loi Kroh & 30 Thanon Ratchawithi. Huge T-bone steaks (B295), burgers and Tex-Mex dishes like tacos and nachos in two convenient locations. Plenty of beers, cocktails and shooters too.

Daret's 4 Thanon Chaiyapoom. The definitive budget travellers' hangout with outdoor trestles and a friendly buzz. Famous fruit shakes, good breakfasts and back-home staples, though the Thai food is rather bland.

The House 199 Thanon Moonmuang ⓣ 053 419011. In an imposing white mansion overlooking the moat, this stylish, upmarket restaurant serves very creative and successful fusion cuisine. The menu changes regularly but a typical main course, such as a lamb cutlet, costs around B650. For gourmets on a budget, the attached tapas bar might be more manageable. Evenings only.

Jerusalem Falafel 35/3 Thanon Moonmuang. Small and simple air-con café serving pitta bread, home-made cheeses and yoghurts, and Israeli food right near Tha Pae Gate.

Kafe 127–129 Soi 5, Thanon Moonmuang. Long-time favourite among locals, with tasty burgers, good Thai food at competitive prices and a wide range of drinks in a warm and welcoming atmosphere.

Libernard Café 36 Thanon Chaiyapoom. Small café with atmospheric garden serving very good coffee in any variety you can think of, made with freshly roasted local beans. Also English breakfast (B105), burgers, delicious pancakes and set Thai dinners , including three dishes, for B280.

Mike's Burgers Corner of Thanon Chaiyapoom and Thanon Chang Moi. Stools at the counter only, and the location is noisy and fumy, but that doesn't stop a steady stream of aficionados from turning up for the tasty home-made burgers and chilli dogs (B80–100).

Mit Mai 42/2 Thanon Ratchamanka. It looks like a simple Thai eatery from the street, but in fact *Mit Mai* serves up exotic food from Yunnan Province in China, such as *fong nom thawt* (fried cheese; B70) and white bamboo grubs (B100), as well as dishes like Yunnanese ham stir-fried with ginger and chilli (B80).

Pulcinella Da Stefano 2/1–2 Thanon Chiang Moi Kao. Just round the corner from Tha Pae Gate, this is one of Chiang Mai's most popular Italian restaurants, and it's easy to see why: it has a winning combination of tasteful ambience, efficient service and delicious food. The same family own *La Gondola*, with an attractive conservatory and garden by the river in the Rimping Condominium, 201/6 Thanon Charoenrat, by the Nakhon Ping Bridge (closed Mon).

Pum Pui 24 Soi 2, Thanon Moonmuang. Trattoria-style Italian-run place where you're guaranteed huge servings; the food is mostly pasta (including an excellent lasagna), but there's pizza too, lots of bruschetta and other antipasti, and the menu has a long vegetarian section. Seating is outside in a tree-filled courtyard off a quiet, fume-free lane.

Rest of Chiang Mai

Amazing Sandwich 252/3 Thanon Phra Pokklao, 20/2 Huai Kaew & 70/9 Thanon Chaiyapoom (see Tha Pae Gate area map). Now in three locations around the city, this is the place to go if you hanker for a sandwich, bagel or baguette made up to order, or fancy munching on a pie, quiche or salad. Mon–Sat 8.30am–7pm, Sun 10am–4pm.

Arcobaleno 60 Thanon Wat Ket. Tasty Italian food served in and around a spacious house on a quiet lane near the Nakhon Ping Bridge over the river. Try the *caprese* (tomato and mozzarella slices with basil and olive oil, B100) and the filling osso bucco with fettucine (B200). Desserts include a delicious tiramisu.

The Duke's 49/4–5 Thanon Chiang Mai–Lamphun. If you're looking for a decent steak house while in north Thailand, head on down to *The Duke's*, which serves up massive portions of steaks, ribs, seafood, plus enormous pizzas. Prices aren't cheap, but the meats are all imported and prepared to perfection.

Le Crystal 74/2 Thanon Paton ⓣ053 872890–1. If you're looking for somewhere to celebrate a special occasion in Chiang Mai, you won't do better than this classy French restaurant on the west bank of the River Ping north of the town centre. Try the rich and creamy lobster bisque (B250), followed by the succulent duck a l'orange (B420) or one of the many steaks on offer. Explore the wine cellar, and be serenaded by a cool jazz trio as you eat. Phone for reservation and free transportation.

Love at First Bite 28 Soi 1, Thanon Chiang Mai-Lamphun. Head south from the east side of Nawarat Bridge, then turn into the first lane on the left to discover this relaxing haven of home-baked cakes and pies, plus delicious coffee, served in a tiny café or on a neat lawn surrounded by flower beds. Tues-Sun 10.30am–6pm.

Drinking and nightlife

Although there's a clutch of hostess bars bordering the east moat and along Loi Khro, and several gay bars offering sex shows, Chiang Mai's **nightlife** generally avoids Bangkok's sexual excesses, but offers plenty of opportunities for a wholesome good time. If your heart's set on **dancing**, try the big hotels, some of which have predictable, westernized nightclubs (like *Space Bubble* at the *Porn Ping* on Thanon Charoen Prathet or *The Horizon Club* at the *Central Duangtawan Hotel* on Loi Kroh) which charge about B100 admission, including one drink; for something more adventurous, head for one of the more Thai-style nightclubs such as *Smooth*. Some of the places listed here are geared to a relaxing night out, while others get rocking as the night wears on.

Though there are **bars** scattered throughout the city, the main concentrations are on the east bank of the Ping River, around Tha Pae Gate and to the west of town along Thanon Nimmanhemin, which swarms with students from nearby Chiang Mai University. On a patch of open ground that runs from *Eagle House 2* to Thanon Ratchaphakinai, a string of laid-back, mostly open-air bars such as *Babylon, Heaven Beach* and *Utopia* have set up shop. Popular with backpackers and young, music-conscious locals, their playlists are more varied and interesting than their names might suggest.

For an introduction to the city's **gay scene**, check out the small roads off the west side of Thanon Chotana (aka Thanon Chang Phuak), where there is a clutch of gay bars, including *Adam's Apple*, north of the bus station at 1/21–22 Soi Viengbua (ⓣ053 220380–2), which styles itself as a one-stop entertainment venue for men, with a restaurant, karaoke, minimart, massage and a nightly cabaret show at 11pm.

Tha Pae Gate area

The Hemp Collective 19/4–5 Thanon Kotchasarn, opposite Tha Pae Gate. Laid-back crusty place, decorated with dayglo paint and paper lanterns, with live bands in the ground-floor bar and an eclectic music choice playing to the floor cushions in the rooftop bar.

Inter Bar 271–273 Thanon Tha Pae. Simple bar with pool table and live music every night – not always great, but it is just a few steps from Tha Pae Gate, the staff are friendly and the drinks are reasonably cheap.

Pinte Blues Pub 33/6 Thanon Moonmuang. The front of this simple bar is so small that you could miss it if you blink, but it's one of the city's longest-standing venues, and an ideal spot for a chat over cheap drinks with blues in the background.

Spicy 82 Thanon Chaiyapoom. Chiang Mai's favourite late-night spot – the place to go when everywhere else is closed – is conveniently located opposite Somphet market. DJs spin international music and food and drinks are in plentiful supply for the restless crowd of party animals. 9pm–late.

UN Irish Pub 24/1 Thanon Ratchawithi. Painted green and white, this place is as much a casual, moderately priced café-restaurant as a pub: home-made bread for satisfying breakfasts and sandwiches, jacket potatoes and Irish stew of course, plus pizzas and a good vegetarian selection. Guinness (bottled only), Carlsberg and Heineken (on tap) and reasonably priced wine. Live music Tues & Fri, quiz night Thurs, and sports on TV.

Rest of Chiang Mai

Brasserie 37 Thanon Charoenrat. Decent restaurant with pretty riverside terraces, but more famous as the venue for some of the city's best live blues and rock. Warms up around 11pm.

Drunken Flower (Mao Dok Mai) 295/1 Soi 1, Thanon Nimmanhemin. Tucked away in a lane beside the *Amari Rincome Hotel*, this quirky venue is a favourite among university students. Reasonable prices for Thai and Mexican food, cocktails and other drinks and an eclectic range of background music.

Fine Thanks 119 Thanon Nimmanhemin. Another spot that's popular among Thais, yet welcoming to farangs, an indoor-outdoor pub-restaurant, dimly lit and draped with plants. Thai bands play a mix of Thai and Western pop-rock.

Good View 13 Thanon Charoenrat. An upmarket clone of the neighbouring *Riverside*, this large venue appeals to fashionable Thais with its smart staff, extensive menu of Thai, Chinese, Japanese and Western food, and slick, competent musicians, who play anything from country to jazz.

Khan-asa 87 Thanon Siphum. Located inside the moat, just east of Chang Phuak Gate, this friendly bar has a cosy ambience and an eclectic range of music that makes it an ideal spot for a chat with friends. Good food at reasonable prices, too.

Modiwa 32 Soi 1, Thanon Nimmanhemin. Stylish new bar-restaurant set in and around a beautifully renovated building, featuring laid-back live jazz on Friday and Saturday evenings plus Sunday lunchtimes. Afternoon tea's served too, and there's a tempting range of dishes on the menu.

Monkey Club 7 Soi 9, Thanon Nimmanhemin. More sophisticated than your average Chiang Mai bar-restaurant, this place is usually heaving with twenty-something Thais and a few foreigners. DJs and live bands play Latin, reggae, jazz and pop, and the food is well received.

O'Malley's Anusarn Night Market. A taste of Ireland in Chiang Mai, with Guinness on tap, good pool table and sports on TV. Decent food too.

The Pub 189 Thanon Huai Kaeo. Homely, relaxing expat hangout, with the nearest thing to an English pub atmosphere to be found in Chiang Mai. Draught beer, separate sports bar, and items like bangers and mash (B135) and Sunday roast (B250) on the menu.

Riverside 9 Thanon Charoenrat ☎053 243239. An ideal location with candlelit terraces by the water, reliable Western and Thai food, extensive drinks list and reasonable draught beer. Various soloists and bands perform nightly on two stages, with the tempo increasing as the night wears on. For an extra B70, you can dine on their boat that cruises up the Ping River each evening at 8pm.

Smooth 68/2 Thanon Chiang Mai–Lamphun, 500m south of TAT and Narawat Bridge. The latest reincarnation of *Gigi's*, a fun, full-on, sweaty club, packed with young Thais dancing to techno on tables and around their bar stools. No admission charge but pricey drinks.

Tha Chang Gallery 29 Thanon Charoenrat. Squeezed between *The Gallery* and *Brasserie*, this is one of the best spots in town to catch a set of live jazz and blues, featuring some of the city's most competent musicians.

Warm Up 40 Thanon Nimmanhemin. Hugely popular venue with students and young locals, offering both live bands and DJs spinning the latest sounds in two different sections.

Writer's Club and Wine Bar 141/3 Thanon Ratchdamnoen. Welcoming bar near the centre of the old city, run by an English writer and popular among farang residents and visitors, serving a range of beers and wines, plus good Thai and Western food. Closed Sat.

Listings

Airlines Air Asia, Chiang Mai airport ☎053 922170; Air Mandalay, Room 107, Doi Ping Mansion, 148 Thanon Charoen Prathet ☎053 818049; Bangkok Airways, *Mae Ping Imperial Hotel* (use entrance on Thanon Sridornchai) ☎053 281519; Lao Airlines, Nakornping Condo, 115 Thanon Ratchapruek ☎053 223401; Nok Air, Chiang Mai airport ☎053 922183; Orient Thai, Chiang Mai airport ☎053 922197; Silk Air, *Central Duangtawan Hotel*, 132 Thanon Loi Kroh ☎053 243985–7; Thai Airways, 240 Thanon Phra Pokklao ☎053 920920 or 053 920999; Tiger Air, in Bangkok ☎02 351 8888.

Banks and exchange Dozens of banks are dotted around Thanon Tha Pae and Thanon Chang Klan, and many exchange booths here stay open for evening shoppers.

Books Book Zone at 318 Thanon Tha Pae stocks a wide range of English-language publications, including novels, books about Thailand and maps, while Bookazine in the Night Bazaar Pavilion on Chang Klan carries magazines and books. Two large book stores, Suriwong at 54/1 Thanon Sri Dornchai (closed Sun afternoons) and DK Books at 79/1 Thanon Kotchasarn, also have a wide selection; the former's display is the better organized, and it features a newspaper and magazine section, a large stationery shop and a nice little coffee shop downstairs. There are several second-hand bookshops in town, where you can buy or exchange books. The best of the bunch are Backstreet Books, 2/8 Thanon Chang Moi Kao, and Gecko Books, 2/6 Thanon Chang Moi Kao, conveniently located next to each other near Tha Pae Gate. The Lost Bookshop, 34/3 Thanon Ratchamanka, also has a reasonable selection.

Car rental Many outlets in the Tha Pae Gate area rent out cars and four-wheel drives, from as little as B800 a day: reliable companies offering insurance and breakdown recovery include Journey, 283 Thanon Tha Pae ⓣ053 208787, ⓦwww.journeycnx.com; North Wheels, 70/4–8 Thanon Chaiyapoom ⓣ053 874478, ⓦwww.northwheels.com; and Queen Bee, 5 Thanon Moonmuang ⓣ053 275525, ⓦwww.queen-bee.com. The more expensive international chains are represented by Avis, Chiang Mai airport ⓣ053 922130, or *Royal Princess Hotel*, 112 Thanon Chang Klan ⓣ053 281033–43; Budget, 201/2 Thanon Mahidol, opposite Airport Plaza ⓣ053 202871–2; and National, *Amari Rincome Hotel*, Thanon Huai Kaeo ⓣ053 210118.

Cinemas Go to ⓦwww.movieseer.com for details of which English-soundtrack or English-subtitled films are showing around town. Cineplexes include Vista (ⓣ053 224333 or 053 894415) at Kad Suan Kaew shopping plaza on Thanon Huai Kaeo, and Major (ⓣ053 283939) at Airport Plaza shopping centre. French-language films with English subtitles are screened at the Alliance Française, 138 Thanon Charoen Prathet on Fri at 8pm (ⓣ053 275277). Popular, mostly recent, arthouse films are shown at CMU Art Museum Theatre, near the corner of Suthep and Nimmanhemin roads, every Sat at 6.30pm (ⓣ053 218280).

Consulates China, 111 Thanon Chang Lo ⓣ053 276125 or 053 200424; India, 344 Thanon Charoenrat ⓣ053 243066; US, 387 Thanon Witchayanon ⓣ053 252629–31 or 053 252644. Honorary consulates include Canada, 151 Chiang Mai–Lampang Superhighway ⓣ053 850147; and UK, 198 Thanon Bamrungrat ⓣ053 263015.

Hospitals Lanna, at 103 Superhighway ⓣ053 357234–53, east of Thanon Chotana, has a 24hr emergency service and dentistry department; McCormick ⓣ053 241010 or 053 262200–19 is used to farangs and is nearer, on Thanon Kaeo Nawarat; Chiang Mai Ram at 8 Thanon Boonruangrit ⓣ053 224851–81 also has a very good reputation.

Immigration office On the southern leg of the Superhighway, 300m before the airport, on the left (Mon–Fri 8.30am–4.30pm; ⓣ053 277510 or 053 201756).

Internet access Most guest houses and hotels offer access to the Internet, and every second shop in town appears to be an Internet café, so you should have no problem getting online. Rates vary from as little as B15 per hour in locations near Chiang Mai University to as much as B120 in downtown areas; B1 a minute is the most typical rate, charged at *Click'n'Drink*, 147 Thanon Chang Klan opposite the *Royal Princess Hotel*, which stays open until 1am and offers a range of coffees. It's well worth taking your business to the Chiang Mai Disabled Centre, 133/1 Thanon Ratchaphakinai (ⓣ053 213941, ⓦwww.infothai.com/disabled), where for B20 per hour, among many other services, your custom will help to support the Foundation to Encourage the Potential of Disabled Persons.

Laundry Most guest houses and hotels have an efficient laundry service; otherwise, try the Chiang Mai Disabled Centre, which also offers sewing repairs and alterations (see "Internet access" above), or White House, 31–35 Thanon Chang Moi Kao (behind Thanon Chaiyapoom), which charges by the kilo and is affordable and dependable. More reliable again is Blue Elephant, which uses filtered water, at 8/5 Thanon Suthep.

Mail The GPO is on Thanon Charoen Muang near the train station (Mon–Fri 8.30am–4.30pm, Sat & Sun 9am–noon); private packing services operate outside on Thanon Charoen Muang. Poste restante should be addressed to: Chiang Mai Post and Telegraph Office, Thanon Charoen Muang, Chiang Mai 50000. There are also post offices at 43 Thanon Samlarn (Phra Singh PO), and on Thanon Phra Pokklao at the junction with Thanon Ratchawithi (Sri Phum PO), both in the old town, as well as on Thanon Wichayanon near Nawarat Bridge (Mae Ping PO), and at the airport.

Massages and spas The Old Medicine Hospital (see p.348) offers very good massages (B200 for 90min). Traditional massages by extremely competent, blind masseurs can be had (B150/hour) at the School for the Blind, 41 Thanon Arak (ⓣ053 278009), and by disabled masseurs for the same price at the Chiang Mai Disabled Centre (see "Internet access" above). Let's Relax (ⓦwww.bloomingspa.com), with a convenient location in the Night Bazaar Pavilion opposite the *Royal Princess Hotel* (ⓣ053 818498), is well run and reliable and lays on a wider range of treatments (B400 for a one-hour Thai massage up to B1000 for a facial treatment). Many of the top hotels now have full-service spas, and there are several upmarket stand-alones including: Ban Sabai, 17/7 Thanon Charoen Prathet in town (☎053 285204–6, ⓦwww.ban-sabai.com), with a village branch on the north side of town (☎053 854778–9); and Chiangmai Oasis Spa, which has three branches, including at 4 Thanon Samlan, just south of Wat Phra Singh (☎053 815000, ⓦwww.chiangmaioasis.com).

Motorbike rental Motorbikes of all shapes and sizes are available for rent around Tha Pae Gate, starting from about B150/day for a100cc step-through. Among reliable rental outlets, Queen Bee, 5 Thanon Moonmuang ☎053 275525, ⓦwww.queen-bee.com, and Mr Mechanic, 4 Soi 5, Thanon Moonmuang ☎053 214708, who has bikes of all sizes, can also offer limited insurance.

Pharmacy Boots, Thanon Chang Klan, in front of the Chiang Inn Plaza, and at Kad Suan Kaew and Airport Plaza shopping centres.

Swimming Pong Pot Swimming Pool, 73/22 Soi 4, Thanon Chotana (daily 9am–7pm; B20; ☎053 212812) has one big and one small pool.

Telephones The main office for calling abroad is the Chiang Mai Telecommunication Center (open 24hr), way out on the Superhighway, just south of the east end of Thanon Charoen Muang, but there are plenty of cardphones dotted around town. The GPO and the airport post office have overseas phone services.

Tourist police down a soi behind the *Lanna Palace Hotel*, off Thanon Chang Klan ☎053 248130 or nationwide helpline ☎1155.

Travel agents TransWorld Travel, 259–261 Thanon Tha Pae ☎053 272415, is affiliated with worldwide STA Travel and is reliable for plane tickets, as is Queen Bee, 5 Thanon Moonmuang ☎053 275525, ⓦwww.queen-bee.com, for train and bus tickets.

Around Chiang Mai

You'll never feel cooped up in Chiang Mai, as the surrounding countryside is dotted with day-trip options in all directions. Dominating the skyline to the west, **Doi Suthep** and its eagle's-nest temple are hard to ignore, and a wander around the pastoral ruins of **Wiang Kum Kam** on the southern periphery has the feel of fresh exploration. Much further south, the quiet town of **Lamphun** offers classic sightseeing in the form of historically and religiously significant temples and a museum. To the north, the **Mae Sa valley** may be full of tour buses, but its highlights, the elephant camp and the botanic gardens, as well as the nearby lake of **Huay Tung Tao**, merit an independent jaunt. For honest, unabashed commerce, head for the shopping strip which stretches east towards San Kamphaeng (see p.357); about 23km beyond the weaving village, you can relax at some **hot springs**. All the excursions described here can be done in half a day; longer trips, notably to Doi Inthanon National Park (see p.396) and to the Elephant Nature Park (see p.421), are dealt with later in the chapter.

Doi Suthep

A jaunt up **DOI SUTHEP**, the mountain which rises steeply at the city's western edge, is the most satisfying brief trip you can make from Chiang Mai, chiefly on account of beautiful **Wat Phra That Doi Suthep**, which dominates the hillside and gives a towering view over the goings-on in town. This is the north's holiest shrine, its pre-eminence deriving from a magic relic enshrined in its chedi and the miraculous legend of its founding. The original chedi here was built by King Ku Na at the end of the fourteenth century, after the glowing relic of Wat Suan Dork had self-multiplied just before being enshrined. A place had to be found for the clone, so Ku Na put it in a travelling shrine on the back of a white elephant and waited to see where the sacred animal would lead: it eventually climbed Doi Suthep, trumpeted three times, turned round three times, knelt down and died, thereby indicating that this was the spot. Ever since, it's been northern Thailand's most important place of pilgrimage, especially for the candlelit processions on **Maha Puja**, the anniversary of the sermon to the disciples, and **Visakha Puja**, the anniversary of the Buddha's birth, enlightenment and death.

Frequent **songthaews** leave from Thanon Huai Kaeo in front of Chiang Mai University for the sixteen-kilometre trip up to Wat Phra That (B50 to the wat, B100 return, B200 return to include Phuping Palace and Doi Pui village). The road, although steep in places, is paved and well suited for **motorbikes**. At the end of Thanon Huai Kaeo, a statue of Khruba Srivijaya, the monk who organized the gargantuan effort to build the road from here to the wat, points the way to the temple. Part of the plans for the city's future development include expanding the site around the statue into a leisure park and building a new road to loop around the park.

△ The chedi at Wat Phra That Doi Suthep

A signpost halfway up is about the only indication that Doi Suthep is a **national park** (B200), though an entry fee is not levied if you are only visiting

Khruba Srivijaya

Khruba Srivijaya, the most revered monk in northern Thailand, was born in 1877 in a small village 100km south of Chiang Mai. His birth coincided with a supernatural thunderstorm and earthquake, after which he was named In Fuan, "Great Jolt", until he joined the monkhood. A generous and tireless campaigner, he breathed life into Buddhist worship in the north by renovating over a hundred religious sites, including Wat Phra That Haripunjaya in Lamphun and Wat Phra That Doi Tung near Mae Sai. His greatest work, however, was the construction in 1935 of the paved road up to Wat Phra That Doi Suthep, which beforehand could only be reached after a climb of at least five hours. The road was constructed entirely by the voluntary labour of people from all over the north, using the most primitive tools. The project gained such fame that it attracted donations of B20 million, and on any one day as many as four thousand people were working on it. So that people didn't get in each other's way, Khruba Srivijaya declared that each village should contribute 15m of road, but as more volunteers flocked to Chiang Mai, this figure had to be reduced to 3m. The road was completed after just six months, and Khruba Srivijaya took the first ride to the temple in a donated car.

When Khruba Srivijaya died in 1938, Rama VIII was so moved that he sponsored a royal cremation ceremony, held in 1946 (a long wait until the auspicious day for a cremation signifies high respect for the deceased). The monk's relics were divided up and are now enshrined at Wat Suan Dork in Chiang Mai, Wat Phra Kaeo Don Tao in Lampang and at many other holy places throughout the north.

the wat, Phuping Palace and Doi Pui village. Despite the nearness of the city, its rich mixed forests support 330 species of birds, and the area is a favoured site for nature study, second in the north only to the larger and less disturbed Doi Inthanon National Park. On the higher slopes near park headquarters, about 1km beyond the wat (Ⓣ053 210244), there are national park **bungalows** (from B400 for two persons).

About 5km from the statue of Khruba Srivijaya, a road on the right leads 3km to **Mon Tha Than Falls**, a beautiful spot, believed by some to be home to evil spirits. Camping is possible beside the pretty lower cascade, where refreshment stalls are open during the day. The higher fall is an idyllic five-metre drop into a small bathing pool, completely overhung by thick, humming jungle.

Wat Phra That Doi Suthep

Opposite a car park and souvenir village, a flight of three hundred naga-flanked steps – or the adjacent funicular – is the last leg on the way to **Wat Phra That Doi Suthep** (Ⓦwww.doisuthep.com). From the temple's **lower terrace**, the magnificent views of Chiang Mai and the surrounding plain, 1000m below, are best in the early morning or late afternoon in the cool season, though peaceful contemplation of the view is frequently shattered by people sounding the heavy, dissonant bells around the terrace – they're supposed to bring good luck. At the northwestern corner is a two-metre-high statue of the elephant which, so the story goes, expired on this spot.

Before going to the **upper terrace** you have to remove your shoes – and if you're showing a bit of knee or shoulder, the temple provides wraps to cover your impoliteness. This terrace is possibly the most harmonious piece of temple architecture in Thailand, a dazzling combination of red, green and gold in the textures of carved wood, filigree and gleaming metal – even the tinkling of the miniature bells and the rattling of fortune sticks seem to keep the rhythm. A cloister, decorated with gaudy murals, tightly encloses the terrace, leaving room only for a couple of small minor viharns and the altars and ceremonial gold umbrellas which surround the central focus of attention, the **chedi**. This dazzling gold-plated beacon, a sixteenth-century extension of Ku Na's original, was modelled on the chedi at Wat Phra That Haripunjaya in Lamphun – which previously had been the region's most significant shrine – and has now become a venerated emblem of northern Thailand.

A small *hong*, or swan, on a wire stretching to the pinnacle is used to bless the chedi during major Buddhist festivals: a cup in the swan's beak is filled with water, and a pulley draws the swan to the spire where the water is tipped out over the sides of the chedi. Look out also for an old photograph opposite the northwestern corner of the chedi, showing a cockerel which used to peck the feet of visitors who entered with their shoes on.

Beyond the wat

Another 4km up the paved road from the wat, **Phuping Palace** (daily 8.30–11.30am & 1–3.30pm; B50) is the residence for the royals when they come to visit their village development projects in the north (usually Jan–March, when it is closed to the public). There is a viewpoint over the hills to the south, a rose garden and some pleasant trails through the forest, but the buildings themselves are off-limits. About 3km from the palace along a dirt side road and accessible by songthaew, **Ban Doi Pui** is a highly commercialized Hmong village, only worth visiting if you don't have time to get out into the countryside – seeing the Hmong is about all you get out of it.

Wiang Kum Kam

The well-preserved and rarely visited ruins of the ancient city of **WIANG KUM KAM** – traditionally regarded as the prototype for Chiang Mai – are hidden away in the picturesque, rural fringe of town, 5km south of the centre. According to folklore, Wiang Kum Kam was built by King Mengrai as his new capital of the north, but was soon abandoned because of inundation by the Ping River. Recent excavations, however, have put paid to that theory: Wiang Kum Kam was in fact established much earlier, as one of a cluster of fortified satellite towns that surrounded the Mon capital at Lamphun. After Mengrai had conquered Lamphun in 1281, he resided at Kum Kam for a while, raising a chedi, a viharn and several Buddha statues before moving on to build Chiang Mai. Wiang Kum Kam was abandoned sometime before 1750, probably as a result of a Burmese invasion.

About 3km square, the ancient city can be explored on a bicycle or a motorbike, though it's easy to get lost in the maze of lanes connecting the ruins. It's more enjoyable to rent a horse and cart from Chedi Si Liam (see below) for B200, which will take you on a leisurely ride round the main sites for about an hour. The best way to approach Wiang Kum Kam is from Route 1141, the southern leg of the Superhighway, which links the airport to Highway 11; immediately to the east of the Ping River bridge, take the signposted turning to the south.

About half of Wiang Kum Kam's 22 known temple sites have now been uncovered, along with a stone slab (now housed in the Chiang Mai National Museum) inscribed in a unique forerunner of the Thai script, and a hoard of terracotta Buddha images. Head first for **Chedi Si Liam**, reached 1km after the Ping River bridge, which provides a useful landmark: this much-restored Mon chedi, in the shape of a tall, squared-off pyramid with niched Buddha images, was built by Mengrai in memory of his dead wife. Modelled on Wat Kukut in Lamphun, it is still part of a working temple.

Backtracking along the road you've travelled down from Chiang Mai, take the first right turn, turn right again and keep left through a scattered farming settlement to reach, after about 2km, **Wat Kan Thom** (aka Chang Kham), the centre of the old city and still an important place of worship. Archeologists were only able to get at the site after much of it had been levelled by bulldozers building a playground for the adjacent school, but they have managed to uncover the brick foundations of Mengrai's viharn. The modern shrine next to it is where Mengrai's soul is said to reside. Also in the grounds are a white chedi and a small viharn, both much restored, and a large new viharn displaying fine craftsmanship.

If you have your own transport, from here you can head off along the trails through the thick foliage of the longan plantations to the northwest of Wat Kan Thom, back towards Chedi Si Liam. On this route, you come across surprisingly well-preserved chedis and the red-brick walls of Wiang Kum Kam's temples in a handful of shady clearings set between rural dwellings.

Chiang Mai Night Safari

Chiang Mai's newest tourist attraction, the **Night Safari** (Mon–Fri 1–4pm & 6pm–midnight; Sat & Sun 10am–4pm & 6pm–midnight; day ticket adults B100, children B50, night ticket adults B500, children B300; ⓣ053 999000, ⓦwww.chiangmainightsafari.com), located about 10km southwest of the city centre beside the canal road, got off to a bad start with environmentalists by encroaching on land belonging to Doi Suthep National Park, and then by announcing that the meat of all animals on display would also be available in its restaurant. The offer to dine on exotic meats has now been withdrawn, but this hasn't cleared the bad taste left by this white elephant of a project that cost over B1000 million of public money. For your entrance fee you get to sit on an open-sided bus for about twenty minutes to go round the "Savanna Safari" or the "Predator Prowl" (both evenings only), where you might spot the silhouettes of a few jungle animals in their dimly lit pens (no flash photography allowed). Probably more fun is to stroll round Swan Lake, which takes in a "Jaguar Trail" of about 1km, where you'll see hippos, tapirs, ring-tailed lemurs and flamingoes. Our advice is to give it a miss, and instead spend your money more wisely at the Chiang Mai Zoo, where you also have the option of watching animals feed at the "twilight zone" (see p.354).

Lamphun

Though capital of its own province, **LAMPHUN** lives in the shadow of the tourist attention (and baht) showered on Chiang Mai, 26km to the north. Yet for anyone interested in history, a visit to this former royal city is a must. The town's largely plain architecture is given some character by the surrounding waterways, beyond which stretch lush rice fields and plantations of *lamyai* (longan); the sweetness of the local variety is celebrated every year in early August at the **Ngan Lamyai** (Longan Festival), when the town comes alive with processions of fruity floats, a drum-beating competition and a Miss Lamyai beauty contest. Lamphun also offers a less frantic alternative to Chiang Mai during the Songkhran and Loy Krathong festivals (see box on p.352), the Khuang River being a far less congested place to float your krathong than Chiang Mai's Ping River. Though the streets of the town are usually sleepy, the ancient working **temples** of Wat Phra That Haripunjaya and Wat Kukut are lively and worth aiming for on a half-day trip from Chiang Mai. A full-day visit could include Wat Mahawan and the Chama Thevi monument, as well as a stroll round the town's market.

Lamphun claims to be the oldest continuously inhabited town in Thailand, and has a history dating back to the late eighth or early ninth century when the ruler of the major Dvaravati centre at Lopburi sent his daughter, Chama Thevi, to found the Theravada Buddhist state of **Haripunjaya** here. Under the dynasty she established, Haripunjaya flourished as a link in the trade route to Yunnan in southwest China, although it eventually came under the suzerainty of the Khmers at Angkor, probably in the early eleventh century. In 1281, after a decade of scheming, King Mengrai of Chiang Mai conquered Lamphun and integrated it once and for all into the Kingdom of Lanna, which by then covered all of the north country.

The Town

Chama Thevi's planners are said to have based their design for the town on the shape of an auspicious conch shell. The rough outcome is a rectangle, narrower at the north end than the south, with the Khuang River running down its kilometre-long east side, and moats around the north, west and south sides. The main street, Thanon Inthayongyot, bisects the conch from north to south, while the road to Wat Kukut (Thanon Chama Thevi) heads out from the middle of the west moat.

One of the north's grandest and most important temples, **Wat Phra That Haripunjaya** has its rear entrance on Thanon Inthayongyot and its bot and ornamental front entrance facing the river. The earliest guess at the date of its founding is 897, when the king of Haripunjaya is said to have built a chedi to enshrine a hair of the Buddha. More certain is the date of the main rebuilding of the temple, under King Tilokaraja of Chiang Mai in 1443, when the present ringed chedi was erected in the then-fashionable Sri Lankan style (later copied at Doi Suthep and Lampang). Clad in brilliant copper plates, it has since been raised to a height of about 50m, crowned by a gold umbrella.

The plain open courtyards around the chedi contain a compendium of religious structures in a wild mix of styles and colours. On the north side, the tiered Haripunjaya-style pyramid of **Chedi Suwanna** was built in 1418 as a replica of the chedi at nearby Wat Kukut. You get a whiff of southern Thailand in the open space beyond the Suwanna chedi, where the **Chedi Chiang Yan** owes its resemblance to a pile of flattened pumpkins to the Srivijayan style. On either side of the viharn (to the east of the main chedi) stand a dark red **belltower**, containing what's claimed to be the world's largest bronze gong, and a weather-beaten **library** on a raised base. Just to add to the temple's mystique, an open pavilion at the southwest corner of the chedi shelters a stone indented with four overlapping **footprints**, believed by fervent worshippers to confirm an ancient legend that the Buddha once passed this way. Next to the pavilion can be seen a small **museum** which houses bequests to the temple, including some beautiful Buddha images in the Lanna style. Finally, beside the back entrance, is the **Phra Chao Tan Jai**, a graceful standing Buddha, surrounded by graphic murals that depict a horrific version of Buddhist hell.

Across the main road from the wat's back entrance, the **Hariphunchai National Museum** (Wed–Sun 9am–4pm; B30) contains a well-organized but not quite compelling collection of religious finds, and occasionally stages some interesting temporary exhibitions. The terracotta and bronze Buddha images here give the best overview of the distinctive features of the Haripunjaya style: large curls above a wide, flat forehead, bulging eyes, incised moustache and enigmatic smile.

Art-history buffs will get a thrill out of **Wat Chama Thevi** (aka Wat Kukut), where two brick chedis, dated to 1218, are the only complete examples not just of Haripunjaya architecture, but of the whole Dvaravati style. Queen Chama Thevi is supposed to have chosen the site by ordering an archer to fire an arrow from the city's western gate – to retrace his epic shot, follow the road along the National Museum's southern wall to the west gate at the city moat, and keep going for nearly 1km along Thanon Chama Thevi. The main chedi – Suwan Chang Kot – is tiered and rectangular, the smaller Ratana Chedi octagonal, and both are inset with niches sheltering beautiful, wide-browed Buddha images in stucco, typical of the Haripunjaya style. Suwan Chang Kot, believed to enshrine Chama Thevi's ashes, lost its pinnacle at some stage, giving rise to the name Wat Kukut, the temple with the "topless" chedi.

On your way back to the town centre from Wat Chama Thevi, you might like to pop in at **Wat Mahawan**, famous for the Buddha image amulets on sale here and located just outside the west gate. The temple has been recently renovated and features some huge and fearsome nagas standing guard at the entrance to the viharn. Following the moat to the south from here brings you in about five minutes to the **Queen Chama Thevi monument**, situated in a large square by the moat in the southwest corner of the city; the monument receives a steady stream of locals making offerings to their heroine. Beside it is the town's main market, which mostly sells fresh produce and buzzes with activity in the morning.

Practicalities

The direct (and scenic) route from Chiang Mai to Lamphun is Highway 106, for much of the way a stately avenue lined by thirty-metre-tall *yang* trees that makes for a pleasant motorbike ride. Otherwise you could catch a blue **songthaew** from the Chiang Mai–Lamphun road, just south of Narawat Bridge and opposite the TAT office, or a white **bus** from Chang Puak bus station, via Lamyai flower market, either of which will put you off outside the back entrance of Wat Haripunjaya. If you turn up at Lamphun by **train**, it's a thirty-minute walk or a samlor ride southwest to the town centre.

Among the few **restaurants** in Lamphun with an English-language menu is *Lamphun Ice*, which serves tasty Thai food at reasonable prices; it's conveniently situated at 6 Thanon Chaimongkol, the road that runs along the south wall of Wat Haripunjaya. It's unlikely you'll want to stay overnight in Lamphun, as it makes a perfect day-trip from Chiang Mai and there's not a wide range of **accommodation**. The only decent choice in town is the *Supamit Holiday Inn* on Thanon Chama Thevi opposite Wat Kukut (Ⓣ053 534865–6; fan ❷, air-con ❸), a large modern building with an open-air restaurant on the fourth floor, where bedrooms boast en-suite, hot-water bathrooms and either fan or air-con.

San Kamphaeng hot springs

Thirty-five kilometres east of Chiang Mai, the **San Kamphaeng hot springs**, with their geysers, baths and gardens, as well as a resort, make for a wonderfully indulgent day-trip, easily accomplished by motorbike. The quickest way there is to take Highway 11 southeast of Chiang Mai, then turn left onto Route 1317, which heads eastwards as dual carriageway for much of the way before veering north towards Highway 118, the main Chiang Mai–Chiang Rai road (look for the turning on the left after about 35km, signposted "Hot Springs" in English). The slow route, heading east out of the city on Route 1008 through San Kamphaeng (see p.357) before turning north onto Route 1317, allows you to combine mineral bathing with some handicrafts shopping.

The government-run hot springs complex (B15) has pleasantly landscaped gardens and geysers that spout scalding water about 10m high. The best place to enjoy the springs, however, is next door at the *Rong Aroon Hot Springs Resort*, set in its own expansive gardens (Ⓣ053 248475, Ⓕ053 939128). It's perfect for a visit of a few hours, providing a soothing tonic to the general stresses of travel, though options do include staying in **bungalows** (❼), which have hot spring water piped into them. If you're not a guest, the main gate charges B20 admission to the property, and for another B70 you can take advantage of the bath house, which offers hot baths in a private room (towels provided). Massages, mud baths and facials are available at reasonable prices, and there are even Jacuzzi baths and a swimming pool. You can also have a restaurant lunch on the bougainvillea-draped terrace overlooking the hot spring geyser.

North of Chiang Mai

On the north side of Chiang Mai, Thanon Chotana turns into Highway 107, which heads off through a flat, featureless valley, past a golf course and an army camp, towards the small market town of **Mae Rim**, 16km away. With your own transport, you can head off down side roads to the west of Highway 107, either to **Huay Tung Tao** for a swim and chill out, or to the **Mae Sa valley**, which despite its theme-park atmosphere has sufficient attractions for an interesting day out, and some pretty resorts that might even tempt you to spend a night out of Chiang Mai. Without your own vehicle, it's best to visit as part of a tour group as public transport here is at best sporadic – Queen Bee, for example (see p.368), charge B500 for a half-day trip.

Huay Tung Tao

About 10km out of Chiang Mai, look for the signpost to the left to **Huay Tung Tao**, a large man-made lake at the base of Doi Suthep, 2km to the west of the turn-off along a dirt road which is easily driven. A great place to cool off during the hot season, the lake is safe to swim in, with canoes and pedaloes to rent, and is also used by anglers and windsurfers. Floating bamboo shelters along the water's edge provide shade from the sun, and you can order simple food such as sticky rice, grilled chicken and *som tam*.

Darapirom Palace

In Mae Rim itself, look out for a sign on the left just before the police station to the **Darapirom Palace** (Tues–Sun 9am–5pm; B20), a gorgeous colonial-style building from the early twentieth century. The palace was once the home of Princess Dara Rasamee (1873–1933), daughter of Chao Inthanon, the lord of Lanna, who became the favourite concubine of King Chulalongkorn of Siam in the days when Lanna was still a vassal state. Extremely proud of her northern heritage – and now something of a heroine to lovers of Lanna culture – the princess had this residence built in 1914, a few years after Chulalongkorn's death, when she returned from Bangkok to live out her later years in her homeland. Chulalongkorn University has recently opened the palace as a museum, featuring period furnishings and many items that once belonged to the princess. Photographs of her show her knee-length hair – which contrasted strongly with the fashion among Siamese women of the time to sport short-cropped hair – and the various rooms of the museum display her wardrobe and personal effects including musical instruments.

The Mae Sa valley

Turn left about 1km after Mae Rim to enter the **Mae Sa valley**, where a good sealed road, Route 1096, leads up into the hills. The main road through the valley passes a menagerie of snake farms, monkey shows, and orchid and butterfly farms, as well as the unspectacular **Mae Sa Waterfall** (B200 national park fee payable), where you can walk up a peaceful trail passing lots of little cascades along the way. Several elephant camps also lie along the route, of which the best is the **Mae Sa Elephant Camp**, 10km along the valley road (with an office at 119/9 Thanon Tha Pae, ⓣ053 206248). Mae Sa offers shows at 8am, 9.40am and 1.30pm daily (B120, children B80), in which the elephants paint pictures, play football, dance and stack logs. After the show you can take a short ride on an elephant (5 min, B120 per person) or a longer ride into the countryside (B800 for half an hour for two people, B1200 for an hour for two people).

Two kilometres beyond the Mae Sa Elephant Camp, the magnificent **Queen Sirikit Botanic Gardens** (B20, children B10, cars B30; no motorbikes or bicycles allowed) are well worth a look, and if you are at all botanically inclined, you could easily spend the whole day here as it covers such a large area, with several nature trails to explore. A car is certainly necessary to get to the upper area where glasshouses display a fantastic array of plants.

Among several **resorts** in the Mae Sa valley, the pick is the *Four Seasons* (ⓣ053 298181–9, ⓦwww.regenthotels.com; ⑨), down a side road on the left just 1km after the turning into the valley from Mae Rim. The last word in Lanna luxury, this award-winning resort has superbly appointed pavilions, plush apartments, a swimming pool, a gym and spa, set among beautifully landscaped grounds, and offers top-quality cooking courses among a long menu of activities. Even if you're not staying, it's a good spot to stop, especially in the late afternoon or early evening, to enjoy a meal or drink on a terrace with a lovely view across hills to the west. Other resorts in the valley are far simpler than the *Four Seasons*, but attractive nonetheless; among these the *Pong Yang Garden Resort* (Ⓣ & Ⓕ053 879151; fan ❼, air-con ❽) stands out, located a couple of kilometres beyond the botanic gardens on the south side of the road. It boasts well-equipped bungalows as well as a restaurant with a view of an attractive waterfall.

Once you've seen all you want to in the valley, you have the option of retracing your route to Chiang Mai, or continuing west for a scenic drive in the country. For the latter, turn left on to Route 121 before Samoeng, and follow this road as it swoops up and down over hills, skirting Doi Suthep to join Highway 108 8km south of Chiang Mai, a two-hour drive in all.

East of Chiang Mai

From Chiang Mai, visitors usually head northwest to Pai or Mae Hong Son, or north to Chiang Rai, but a trip eastwards to the ancient city-states of Lampang, Phrae and Nan can be just as rewarding, not only for the dividends of going against the usual flow, but also for the natural beauty of the region's upland ranges – seen to best effect from the well-marked trails of **Doi Khun Tan National Park** – and its eccentric variety of Thai, Burmese and Laotian art and architecture. Congenial **Lampang** contains Thai wats to rival those of Chiang Mai for beauty – in Wat Phra That Lampang Luang the town has the finest surviving example of traditional northern architecture anywhere – and is further endowed with pure Burmese temples and some fine old city architecture, while little-visited **Phrae**, to the southeast, is a step back in time to a simpler Thailand. Further away but a more intriguing target is **Nan**, with its heady artistic mix of Thai and Laotian styles and steep ring of scenic mountains.

A few major **roads**, served by regular through buses from Chiang Mai, cross the region: Highway 11 heads southeast through Lampang and the junction town of Den Chai before plummeting south to Phitsanulok; from Lampang Highway 1 heads north to Chiang Rai; and from Den Chai Highway 101 carries on northeast through Phrae to Nan, almost on the border with Laos. Route 1148 between Tha Wang Pha and Chiang Kham makes it tempting to continue north from Nan to Chiang Rai or Chiang Khong, through some spectacular scenery. The northern **rail line** follows a course roughly parallel with Highway 11 through the region, including a stop at Doi Khun Tan National Park, and although trains here are generally slower than buses, the Lampang and Den Chai stations are useful if you're coming up from Bangkok.

Doi Khun Tan National Park

One of three major national parks close to Chiang Mai, along with Suthep and Inthanon, **DOI KHUN TAN NATIONAL PARK** (Ⓣ053 519216–7; B200) is easily accessible by train from Chiang Mai: a 1352-metre-long rail tunnel, the longest in Thailand, and completed by German engineers in 1918, actually cuts through the mountain that gives the park its name. Even so, the park is the least spoilt of the three; a former hill station, it was not declared a national park until 1975 and a lack of tourist infrastructure until recently has meant that it's had few visitors. With food and accommodation now available, it is opening up to tourists: there is a restaurant beside the bungalows, which are spacious and well-appointed log cabins, and there are three campsites.

The park

Covering 255 square kilometres, the park's vegetation varies from bamboo forests at an altitude of 350m to tropical evergreen forests between 600 and 1000m; the 1373-metre summit of Doi Khun Tan is known for its wild flowers, including orchids. Most of the small mammal species in the park are squirrels, but you're more likely to see some birds, with over 182 species found here. A leaflet on the park's ecology can sometimes be obtained at the park **headquarters**.

The **trails** are clearly marked, running from short nature trails around the park headquarters (where maps are available) to three major trails that all eventually lead to the summit of **Doi Khun Tan**, the highest peak reachable on self-guided trails in the Chiang Mai area – with impressive views of the surrounding countryside, it's clear how it fulfilled its role as a World War II military lookout. The main 8.3-kilometre trail from the train station to the Doi Khun Tan summit, though steep, is very easy, divided into four quarters of approximately 2km each, with each quarter ending at a resting place. While you shouldn't have a problem reaching the summit and returning to the station in a day, a more rewarding option is to do the walk in two days, staying overnight in the bungalows or at one of the campsites along the trail. Alternatively, you can take a circular route to the summit and back, forsaking a large chunk of the main trail for the two subsidiary trails which curve around either side, taking in two **waterfalls**.

Practicalities

Though there are five daily **trains** from Chiang Mai (1hr 15min) which stop at the park, at least three of these arrive after dark, so day-trippers should make a very early start (leaving Chiang Mai at 6.55am and taking the last train back at 7.41pm; check current timetables). Get off at Khun Tan station, from where it's a 1300-metre walk along the summit trail to the park headquarters. A **car** or motorbike can also take you to the park headquarters, though no further: follow Highway 11 to the turn-off to Mae Tha and head northeast along a partly paved road, following signs for the park, a further 18km away.

The park is most popular on weekends, when groups of Thai schoolchildren visit, and during the cool season. Park **bungalows** (B1500 for four people, B2200 for six people, B2700 for nine people) plus a few small rooms (B400 for two people), are located just up the main trail from the headquarters, while tents can be hired (B150 sleeping 2 people) for the **campsites** (pitching your own costs B30). There's a small **restaurant** just up from the train ticket office, another beside the bungalows, and food is also available at a shop and café near the headquarters.

Lampang and around

A high road pass and a train tunnel breach the narrow, steep belt of mountains between Chiang Mai and **LAMPANG**, the north's second-largest town,

100km to the southeast. Lampang is an important transport hub – Highway 11, Highway 1 and the northern rail line all converge here – and given its undeniably low-key attractions, nearly all travellers sail through it on their way to the more trumpeted sights further north. But unlike most other provincial capitals, Lampang has the look of a place where history has not been completely wiped out: houses, shops and temples survive in the traditional style, and the town makes few concessions to tourism. Out of town, the beautiful complex of Wat Phra That Lampang Luang is the main attraction in these parts, but while you're in the neighbourhood you could also stop by to watch a show at the Elephant Conservation Centre, on the road from Chiang Mai.

Founded as Kelang Nakhon by the ninth-century Haripunjaya queen Chama Thevi, Lampang became important enough for one of her two sons to rule here after her death. After King Mengrai's conquest of Haripunjaya in 1281, Lampang suffered much the same ups and downs as the rest of Lanna, enjoying a burst of prosperity as a **timber** town at the end of the nineteenth century, when it supported a population of twenty thousand people and four thousand working elephants. Many of its temples are financially endowed by the waves of outsiders who have settled in Lampang: refugees from Chiang Saen (who were forcibly resettled here by Rama I at the beginning of the nineteenth century), Burmese teak-loggers and workers, and, more recently, rich Thai pensioners attracted by the town's sedate charm.

Arrival, information and transport

From Chiang Mai **buses** run to Lampang every thirty minutes from Thanon Chiang Mai–Lamphun, just south of Narawat Bridge, for most of the day, some of which then trundle on up Highway 1 to Phayao and Chiang Rai. Hourly buses also leave from Chiang Mai's Arcade station. Seven **trains** a day stop here in each direction; the **train and bus stations** lie less than 1km to the southwest of town, and many buses also stop on Thanon Phaholyothin in the centre. PB Air (Ⓣ054 226238 or 054 351102) run twice-daily **flights** from Bangkok

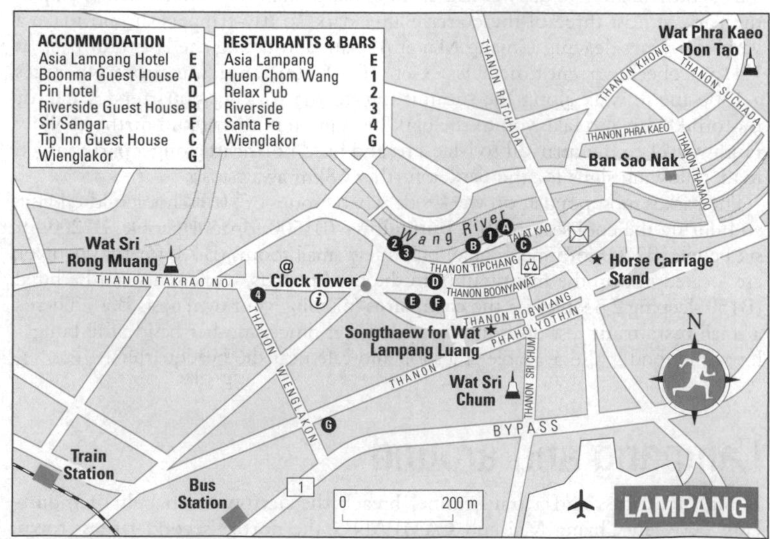

to the airport, just south of town, and songthaews are on hand for the short ride to the centre. The small, municipal **tourist information** centre (Mon–Fri 8am–noon & 1–4.30pm; ⓣ054 219300), just west of the clocktower and next to the fire station on Thanon Takrao Noi, can provide a decent map of the town and help with advice on excursions to the elephant conservation centre and the like. There's cheap and fast **Internet access** in many parts of town, including at an unnamed shop in the middle of Thanon Takrao Noi on the north side, just west of the *Tipchang Hotel*.

The whole town can be covered on foot, though to get out to Wat Phra Kaeo Don Tao you might want to employ the services of a **horse-drawn carriage**, which along with white chickens (see below) is a prevalent symbol of Lampang (in fact, Thais often refer to the city as *muang rot mah*, or "horse-cart city"). These colourfully decked-out carriages, complete with Stetson-wearing driver, can be hired near the big hotels in the centre of town or at the east end of Thanon Boonyawat. Standard routes around town cost B150 for about fifteen minutes, B200 for around thirty minutes or B300 for one hour, which includes a visit to Wat Phra Kaeo Don Tao and other points of interest. Apart from this quirky mode of transport, there are plenty of **songthaews** that cruise the streets looking for custom.

Accommodation

Lampang has several **guest houses** scattered along the quiet banks of the river, as well as a few reasonable mid-range and more expensive **hotels** located around the town centre.

Asia Lampang Hotel 229 Thanon Boonyawat ⓣ054 227844–7, ⓦwww.asialampang.com. Rooms here all have air-con, hot water bathrooms and TV and while they lack character, they are comfortable and represent good value. ③

Boonma Guest House 256 Thanon Talat Kao ⓣ054 218394. This gorgeous, stilted, wooden building offers a couple of spacious rooms upstairs and some cramped, less appealing rooms sharing bathrooms downstairs. ①–③

Pin Hotel 8 Thanon Suandok ⓣ054 221509, ⓔpinhotel@loxinfo.co.th. This place has a touch of class about it. The good-sized and attractively furnished rooms all have air-con, TV and hot water, and some have carpets and bathtubs. ③–⑤

Riverside Guest House 286 Thanon Talat Kao ⓣ054 227005. Peaceful traditional compound of elegantly decorated rooms, most with en-suite bathrooms and a few with air-con. Some rooms boast balconies overlooking the river and there's also a small, attractive garden and a relaxing communal veranda. The helpful Belgian owner is a good source of local information and she can rent out motorbikes. Fan ②, air-con ④

Sri Sangar 213–215 Thanon Boonyawat ⓣ054 217070. One of the cheapest hotels in town, where the small, en-suite fan rooms are reasonably clean, though traffic noise can be a problem. ①

Tip Inn Guest House 143 Thanon Talad Kao ⓣ054 221821. Rooms here are classic budget travellers' digs – small, cheap and without views, though a few have air-con. Fan ①, air-con ②

Wienglakor 138/35 Thanon Phaholyothin ⓣ054 316430–5, ⓕ054 316427. Of several big and expensive hotels in town, this one has the most tasteful decor and the cosiest rooms, as well as good views from some of the upper floors. ⑦

The Town

The modern centre of Lampang sprawls along the south side of the Wang River, with its most frenetic commercial activity taking place along Thanon Boonyawat and Thanon Robwiang near Ratchada Bridge. Here, you'll find stalls and shops selling the famous local pottery, a kitsch combination of whites, blues and browns, made from the area's rich kaolin clay. On all street signs around town, and in larger-than-life statues at key intersections, is a white chicken. This symbol of Lampang relates to a legend concerning the Buddha, who sent down angels from Heaven in the form of chickens to wake up the local inhabitants in time to offer alms to the monks at the end of Buddhist Lent. Perhaps the town's image as a laid-back, sleepy place is justified in the light of this tale.

Wat Phra Kaeo Don Tao and Ban Sao Nak

Lampang's few sights are well scattered; the best place to start is on the north side of the river (the site of the original Haripunjaya settlement), whose leafy suburbs today contain the town's most important and interesting temple, **Wat Phra Kaeo Don Tao** (B20). An imposing, rather forbidding complex on Thanon Phra Kaeo, 1km northeast of the Ratchada Bridge, the temple was founded in the fifteenth century to enshrine the Phra Kaeo Don Tao image, now residing at Wat Phra That Lampang Luang (see p.382). For 32 years it also housed the Emerald Buddha (local stories aver this to be a copy of Phra Kaeo Don Tao), a situation that came about when an elephant carrying the holy image from Chiang Rai to Chiang Mai made an unscheduled and therefore auspicious halt here in 1436. The clean, simple lines of the white, gold-capped **chedi**, which is reputed to contain a hair of the Buddha, form a shining backdrop to the wat's most interesting building, a Burmese **mondop** stacked up in extravagantly carved tiers; it was built in 1909 by craftsmen from the local Burmese community, employed for the task by a Thai prince (whose British-style coat of arms can be seen on the ceiling inside). All gilt and gaudy coloured glass, the interior decoration is a real fright, mixing Oriental and European influences, with some incongruously cute little cherubs on the ceiling. The mondop's boyish bronze centrepiece has the typical features of a Mandalay Buddha, with its jewelled headband, inset black and white eyes, and exaggerated, dangling ears, which denote the Buddha's supernatural ability to hear everything in the universe. In front of the Buddha is an image of Khruba Srivijaya, the north's most venerated monk (see box on p.367).

The small, gloomy **museum** diagonally opposite the mondop displays some dainty china among its exhibits, but its main focus is woodcarving, a craft at which Burmese artisans excel. To see a better, though still small, display of ceramics, lacquerware and teak furnishings, make your way to **Ban Sao Nak** ("many pillar house") at 6 Thanon Ratwattana, not far from Wat Phra Kaeo Don Tao (daily 10am–5pm; B50 with free soft drink). This sprawling wooden mansion is supported by a maze of teak pillars and contains some interesting fading photographs of its former occupants, who were local notables.

Wat Sri Chum and south of the river

The Burmese who worked on Wat Phra Kaeo Don Tao were brought to Lampang in the late nineteenth century when, after the British conquest of Upper Burma, timber companies expanded their operations as far as northern Thailand. Fearing that the homeless spirits of fallen trees would seek vengeance, the Burmese logging workers often sponsored the building of temples, most of which still stand, to try to appease the tree spirits and gain merit. Though the spirits had to wait nearly a century, they seem to have got their revenge: due to a short circuit in some dodgy wiring, the viharn of **Wat Sri Chum**, which is the biggest Burmese temple in Thailand as well as the most important and beautiful Burmese temple in town, burnt to the ground in 1992. Now restored to its former glory, with fresh carvings and murals by Burmese craftsmen, it's sited in a small grove of bodhi trees five minutes' walk south of Thanon Robwiang. None of the remaining wats is of outstanding architectural merit, but to get more of a flavour of Burma, try **Wat Sri Rong Muang**, towards the west end of Thanon Takrao Noi, which presents a dazzling ensemble: the crazy angles of its red and yellow roof shelter more Mandalay Buddhas and several extravagantly carved gilt sermon thrones, swimming in a glittering sea of coloured-glass wall tiles.

When you've had your fill of temples, **Thanon Talat Kao**, the "Old Market Street", running behind the south bank of the river, is good for a stroll in the early morning. It has some very old shophouses and mansions, showing a mixture of Burmese, Chinese and European influence, with intricate balconies, carved gables and unusual sunburst designs carved over some of the doors. Some of these lovely structures are now being restored to their former glory, while others, like the *Boonma Guest House*, offer visitors the chance to stay in an elaborately designed wooden house on stilts. Small lanes on the north side of Thanon Talat Kao lead down to the Wang River, whose waters are as green as some of its overgrown banks – what used to be the main thoroughfare for trading boats and huge rafts of felled timber has been reduced almost to stagnation by an upriver dam. Unfortunately a large section of the river bank through the main part of town is now stripped of its greenery, and the sandy soil and concrete tiers make for an ugly view.

△ Wat Sri Rong Muang

Lampang Medicinal Plants Conservation Assembly

Though the **Lampang Medicinal Plants Conservation Assembly** (177 Moo 12, Ban Kelangthong, Kanmuang Road ⓣ054 313128) sounds like the kind of place where botanists might hold seminars, it is in fact a traditional health centre set in a shady compound a few kilometres northeast of town. If you feel like pampering your body, head out here for a herbal sauna, traditional massage, face scrub, mud skin treatment or even a bare-footed health walk over a path of rounded pebbles designed to provide a natural foot massage. The facilities are spotless, the grounds are full of labelled herbs, and a huge range of medicinal plant products is on sale. To get there, a songthaew from the centre of Lampang costs around B60.

Eating and drinking

A popular place to **eat and drink** is the *Riverside* at 328 Thanon Tipchang, a cosy, relaxing spot on terraces overlooking the water. A wide variety of excellent Thai dishes like chicken sautéed with mushrooms (B70) and Western food, including pizza (around B110), is served here to the sounds of live music in the evenings. A quieter ambience prevails at *Huen Chom Wang*, 276 Thanon

Talat Kao (no English sign – look for the alley 100m east of the *Riverside Guest House*). The sprawling wooden building has fine views of the river and its menu features many northern specialities. Just west of the *Riverside*, *Relax Pub* also serves a range of good Thai and Western food, and features live music at night; the decor is more modern than the *Riverside* and it tends to be more lively. Among the hotels in town, the *Wienglakor* has a restaurant with an inviting ambience and a good choice of well-prepared dishes, while the one at the *Asia Lampang* has a wide menu of reasonably priced Thai dishes and a choice of dining on the open-air terrace or in a small, air-conditioned room. The stretch of Thanon Takrao Noi between the clocktower and Thanon Wienglakon is the liveliest part of town after dark with many simple restaurants and the Atsawin night market running off its side streets to the south. Also along Thanon Takrao Noi are a few Wild West **bars** – Lampang takes its Stetson-wearing image seriously – including *Santa Fe*, near the corner of Thanon Wienglakon. In this area, there are also pubs, discos and karaoke bars that attract the town's youth after dark.

Wat Phra That Lampang Luang

If you've made it as far as Lampang, a visit to **Wat Phra That Lampang Luang**, a grand and well-preserved capsule of beautiful Lanna art and design, is one of the architectural highlights of northern Thailand. Songthaews will take you to the temple direct from outside the savings bank on Thanon Robwiang (B40). On a motorbike (which can be rented in Lampang from the *Riverside Guest House*) or other transport, cross the bridge over the Mae Nam Wang at Kor Kha and turn right, heading north on a paved road.

The wat was built early in the Haripunjaya era as a *wiang* (fortress), one of a satellite group around Lampang – you can still see remains of the threefold ramparts in the farming village around the temple. A naga staircase leads you up to a wedding cake of a gatehouse, richly decorated with stucco, which is set in the original brick boundary walls. Just inside, the oversized **viharn** is open on all sides in classic Lanna fashion, and shelters a spectacular centrepiece: known as a *ku*, a feature found only in the viharns of northern Thailand, this gilded brick tower looks like a bonfire for the main Buddha image sitting inside, the Phra Chao Lan Thong. Tall visitors need to mind their heads on the panels hanging from the low eaves, which are decorated with attractive, though fading, early-nineteenth-century paintings of battles, palaces and nobles in traditional Burmese gear.

This central viharn is snugly flanked by three others. In front of the murky, beautifully decorated viharn to the left, look out for a wooden *tung chai* carved with flaming, coiled nagas, used as a heraldic banner for northern princes. The battered, cosy **Viharn Nam Tame**, second back on the right, dates to the early sixteenth century. Its drooping roof configuration is archetypal: divided into three tiers, each of which is divided again into two layers, it ends up almost scraping the ground. Under the eaves you can just make out fragments of panel paintings, as old as the viharn, illustrating a story of one of the exploits of the Hindu god Indra.

Hundreds of rainy seasons have turned the copper plates on the wat's huge
l **chedi** into an arresting patchwork of greens, blues and purples: safe
are supposed to be a hair of the Buddha and ashes from the right side
orehead and neck. By the chedi's northwest corner, a sign points to a
hole in the wat's boundary wall, once the scene of an unlikely act of
o: in 1736, local hero Thip Chang managed to wriggle through the

tiny hole and free the *wiang* from the occupying Burmese, before going on to liberate the whole of Lampang.

To the south of the chedi, the **Haw Phra Phuttabhat** (no entry for women) is a small chamber that acts as a camera obscura. If you close the door behind you, an image of the chedi is projected through a small hole in the door onto a sheet hung on a wall. A gate in the south side of the boundary wall leads to a spreading **bodhi tree** on crutches: merit-makers have donated hundreds of supports to prop up its drooping branches. The tree, with its own small shrine standing underneath, is believed to be inhabited by spirits, and the sick are sometimes brought here in search of a cure.

Don't miss the small, unimpressive viharn to the west of the main complex (go on round beyond the bodhi tree) – it's the home of **Phra Kaeo Don Tao**, the much-revered companion image to Bangkok's Emerald Buddha, and the wat's main focus of pilgrimage. Legend has it that the statuette first appeared in the form of an emerald found in a watermelon presented by a local woman to a venerated monk. The two of them tried to carve a Buddha out of the emerald, without much success, until the god Indra appeared and fashioned the marvellous image, at which point the ungrateful townsfolk accused the monk of having an affair with the woman and put her to death, thus bringing down upon the town a series of disasters which confirmed the image's awesome power. In all probability, the image was carved at the beginning of the fifteenth century, when its namesake wat in Lampang was founded. Peering through the dim light and the rows of protective bars inside the viharn, you can just make out the tiny meditating Buddha – it's actually made of jasper, not emerald – which on special occasions is publicly displayed wearing a headdress and necklace.

Cashing in on Phra Kaeo Don Tao's supernatural reputation, a shop in the viharn sells amulets and Buddha images. Outside the wat, simple snacks, handicrafts and antiques can be bought from market stalls; also available are the small china cows with which devotees make merit, inscribing the models first with their name and the date in black ink and then offering them to the shrine in front of the chedi, making a curious display.

The Thai Elephant Conservation Centre

The **Thai Elephant Conservation Centre** (admission B50; shows at 10am, 11am and 1.30pm; bathing at 9.45am and 1.15pm; ⓣ054 229042 or 054 228034, ⓦwww.thailandelephant.org), 37km west of Lampang on Highway 11, is the most authentic place in Thailand to see elephants displaying their skills and, being more out of the way, is less touristy than the elephant showgrounds to the north of Chiang Mai. **Shows** put the elephants through their paces, with plenty of amusing showmanship and loud trumpeting for their audience. After some photogenic bathing, they walk together in formation and go through a routine of pushing and dragging logs, then proceed to paint pictures and play custom-made instruments. You can buy bananas and sugar-cane to feed them after the show, and if you are impressed by their art or music you can buy a freshly painted picture or a CD by the Thai Elephant Orchestra. An interpretive centre has exhibits on the history of the elephant in Thailand and **elephant-rides** (B100/10min, B200/30min or B400/1hr) are cheaper here than anywhere else in the north. There is also a **home-stay programme**, on which you spend three days learning how to care for and control elephants for around B1500 a day. For more information, check out their website.

Run by the Forest Industry Organization, the conservation centre was originally set up in 1969 in another nearby location as a young elephant

The elephant in Thailand

To Thais the **Asian elephant** has profound **spiritual significance**, derived from both Hindu and Buddhist mythologies. Carvings and statues of **Ganesh**, the Hindu god with an elephant's head, feature on ancient temples all over the country and, as the god of knowledge and remover of obstacles, Ganesh has been adopted as the symbol of the Fine Arts Department – and is thus depicted on all entrance tickets to historical sights. The Hindu deity Indra rarely appears without his three-headed elephant mount **Erawan**, and miniature devotional elephant effigies are sold at major Brahmin shrines, such as Bangkok's Erawan shrine. In Buddhist legend, the future **Buddha's mother** was able to conceive only after she dreamt that a white elephant had entered her womb: that is why elephant balustrades encircle many of the Buddhist temples of Sukhothai, and why the rare white elephant is accorded royal status (see p.166) and regarded as a highly auspicious animal.

The **practical** role of the elephant in Thailand was once almost as great as its symbolic importance. The kings of Ayutthaya relied on elephants to take them into battle against the Burmese – one king assembled a trained elephant army of three hundred – and during the nineteenth century King Rama IV offered Abraham Lincoln a male and a female to "multiply in the forests of America" and to use in the Civil War. In times of peace, the phenomenal strength of the elephant has made it invaluable as a beast of burden: elephants hauled the stone from which the gargantuan Khmer temple complexes of the north and northeast were built, and for centuries they have been used to clear forests and carry timber.

The traditional cycle for domestic elephants is to be born in captivity, spending the first three years of their lives with their mothers (who get five years' maternity leave), before being separated and raised with other calves in training schools. From the age of three each elephant is assigned its own **mahout** – a trainer, keeper and driver rolled into one – who will stay with it for the rest of its working life. Training begins gently, with mahouts taking months to earn the trust of their charge; over the next thirteen years the elephant is taught about forty different commands, from simple "stop" and "go" orders to complex instructions for hooking and passing manoeuvres with the trunk. By the age of sixteen elephants are ready to be put to work and are expected to carry on working until they reach 50 or 60, after which they are retired and may live for another twenty years.

Ironically, the **timber industry** has been the animal's undoing. Mechanized logging has destroyed the wild elephant's preferred river-valley grassland and forest habitats, forcing them into isolated upland pockets. As a result, Thailand's population of wild elephants is now under two thousand. With the 1989 **ban on commercial logging** within Thai borders – after the 1988 catastrophe when the effects of deforestation killed a hundred people and wiped out villages in Surat Thani province, as mudslides swept down deforested slopes carrying cut timber with them – the domesticated population, numbering about three thousand, is becoming less useful. The biggest problem facing these elephants and their mahouts nowadays is **unemployment**. The estimated 250 elephants working on the illegal teak-logging trade are often abused and overworked, while mahouts who can no longer find work for their animals are forced to abandon them since they cannot afford the vast amount of food needed to sustain the creature – about 125kg a day. The discarded animals destroy forests and crops and are often hunted down and killed. In town streets and on beaches, you'll often see those mahouts who keep their elephants charging both tourists for the experience of hand-feeding them bananas, and Thais for the chance to stoop under their trunks for good luck. Training schools now concentrate as much on perfecting shows for tourists as on honing the elephants' practical skills, and another lucrative alternative tourist industry is elephant trekking. The Thai Elephant Conservation Centre near Lampang estimates that if drastic measures are not taken, in twenty years' time the elephant could be extinct in Thailand, where the population has dropped by over fifteen thousand since 1984.

training centre, the earliest of its kind in Thailand. However, with the high levels of elephant unemployment since the ban on logging, the new centre, opened in 1992, emphasizes the preservation of the elephant in Thailand. By promoting eco-tourism the centre is providing employment for the elephants and enabling Thai people to continue their historically fond relationship with these animals. Money raised from entrance fees helps to finance the **elephant hospital** here, which cares for sick, abused, ageing and abandoned elephants. Its yearly expenses are 12–14 million baht, with huge expenses incurred from looking after about sixty elephants; the enormous amounts of money the centre needs to feed and care for its elephants mean it is in a permanent funding crisis.

Practicalities

The Thai Elephant Conservation Centre is best visited en route between Chiang Mai and Lampang: ask the bus conductor to stop at the centre. On a day-trip from Lampang, a bus towards Lamphun or Chiang Mai should get you to the entrance gates in around forty minutes, from where there are regular shuttle buses to the centre a couple of kilometres away. If you have your own vehicle, the Thung Kwian **market**, 21km from Lampang on Highway 11, offers not only a useful stop for refreshments near the Elephant Centre, but also a chance to view the panoply of products on sale – rabbits and birds, honeycombs, bugs and creepy crawlies of every description. This is a favourite spot for city Thais to pick up some exotic taste to take back home with them.

Phrae and around

From Lampang, buses to Phrae follow Highway 11 to the junction town of Den Chai (Bangkok–Chiang Mai trains also stop here), 83km to the southeast, then veer northeastwards on Highway 101 through the tobacco-rich Yom valley, dotted with distinctive brick curing-houses. Frequent songthaews from Den Chai head for the small city of **PHRAE**, 20km further on, the capital of the province of the same name which is famous for woodcarving and the quality of its *seua maw hawm*, the deep-blue, baggy working shirt seen all over Thailand (produced in the village of Ban Thung Hong, 4km north of Phrae on Highway 101). If you're driving here from Lampang, turn left from Highway 11 at **Mae Khaem** onto Route 1023 and approach the town via Long and some lovely scenery.

The main reason to stop in Phrae is to explore the old city, delineated by an earthen moat, with its lanes filled with traditional teak houses – as in Lampang, the former logging industry attracted Burmese workers and the influence is evident – and to enjoy the old-fashioned and friendly nature of a place still virtually untouched by tourism. Out of town, 18km to the northeast off Highway 101, are the so-called ghost pillars at **Phae Muang Phi**, a geological quirk of soil and wind erosion, which are probably only worth visiting if you are going on through to Nan with your own transport.

The Town

Sited on the southeast bank of the Yom River, Phrae is clearly divided into old and new town; an earthen wall surrounds the roughly oval-shaped old town, with a moat on its southeastern side and the new town centre beyond that. At

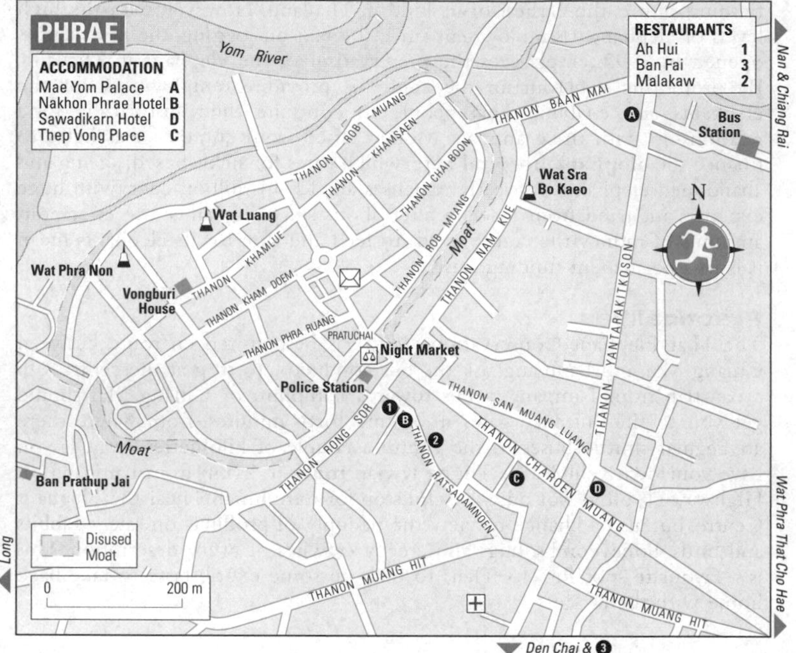

the centre of the **old town**, a large roundabout is the main orientation point; running northwest–southeast through the roundabout, through Pratuchai (the main gate on the southeastern side of the old town), and into the new town is Thanon Charoen Muang, where several shops sell the trademark deep indigo shirts. The main street in the new town, Thanon Yantarakitkoson, intersects Thanon Charoen Muang about 300m southeast of the old town, and leads northeast to the bus station.

Dotted around the old town, several wats are worth visiting and are easily reached on foot; in fact, a stroll through the area's quiet lanes is recommended, with traditional teak houses to gaze at and a glimpse of local life as extended families congregate sociably outside. The Thai smile is readily seen here: people are friendly and will probably try to talk to you with any English they have.

Vongburi House

The white and pink **Vongburi House** (daily 8.30am–5pm; B30) on Thanon Khamlue is a good place to begin an exploration of the old town. Built of teak between 1897 and 1907 in Thai-European style for a wealthy forest concessionary, it's smothered in elaborate, lace-like woodcarving, on all the eaves, gables and balconies, and around doors and windows. Inside the house, exhibits include a howdah, undershirts with magic spells written on them to ward off danger, and various documents such as elephant identity papers and artefacts that shed light on the history of the family, who still live in part of the complex. Fittingly, as this neighbourhood is a traditional silversmithing area, there's also plenty of fine silverware to admire; you can often watch a silversmith at work in the shady grounds, and buy the finished product from the ground-floor souvenir shop.

Wat Luang and Wat Phra Non

Around the corner from the Vongburi House, Phrae's oldest temple complex, **Wat Luang**, dates from the town's foundation around the twelfth century; it contains the only intact original brick entrance gate to the city, though unfortunately it has been closed up and turned into an ugly shrine to Chao Pu, an early Lanna ruler. Apart from the gate, the oldest component of the wat is the crumbling early Lanna-style **chedi** called Chang Kham after the four elephants – now mostly trunkless – which sit at its octagonal base; these alternate with four niches containing Buddha images and some haphazardly leaning gilded bronze parasols. Architectural experts have been called in from Bangkok to plan the restoration of the chedi and the overall complex: unfortunately, over the years, Wat Luang has been added to and parts of it have been quite spoilt in a gaudy modernization process. Until recently, a dishonest monk was even taking down parts of the temple to sell. Apart from the ruined entrance gate, this meddling is most evident in the **viharn** opposite, where an ugly and very out-of-place laterite brick facade has been placed in front of the original Lanna-style sixteenth-century entrance. Opposite the chedi on the north side of the compound, a **museum** on two floors houses some real treasures, the most important being a collection of sixteenth-century bronze Buddhas and several glass cases containing old manuscripts with beautifully gilded covers, which are located upstairs.

Still within the old city, about a block west of Wat Luang along the boundary road is **Wat Phra Non**, established three centuries ago, whose name comes from the reclining Buddha in a small viharn; look out for the bot's finely carved wooden pediment showing scenes from the *Ramayana*.

Ban Prathup Jai

Signposted among the peaceful lanes out beyond the old town's west gate lies the massive two-storey teak house of **Ban Prathup Jai** (daily 8am–5pm; B30), constructed out of nine old houses in the mid-1980s. A visit here allows you to appreciate the beauty and strength of the wood, even if the overall effect is just too ornate: the lower floor has an impressive interior of 130 pillars of solid teak carved with jungle scenes; huge wooden elephants wander among the columns set against solid teak walls and ornately carved furniture (plus a souvenir shop where you can buy all things wooden). Upstairs has the feel of a traditional house, and the furniture and objects are those that you might find in a well-to-do Thai home: ornately carved cabinets crammed with bowls and other ordinary household objects, tables displaying framed family portraits, wall carvings and even a teak bar.

Wat Sra Bo Kaeo

Just to the east of the old town, near the northern end of Thanon Nam Khue, **Wat Sra Bo Kaeo** is set in a peaceful, shady grove of trees. Its Burmese-style viharn is of no great age, but has an intriguing marble Buddha image and beautiful teak floorboards. The most striking aspect of the temple is the brightly painted Shan chedi with two unusually attractive guardian figures in flowing robes. Also note the intricate, decorative stucco work on the spire of the bot to the left of the viharn.

Practicalities

Phrae's **bus station**, off Thanon Yantarakitkoson, is 1km northeast of the modern centre. There are usually some **samlors** and **motorbike taxis**, the main forms of transport around town, congregating here, while **songthaews** head for out-of-town routes, including the train station at Den Chai.

Accommodation in Phrae comprises several **hotels** in the new town clustered around Thanon Charoen Muang, Thanon Yantarakitkoson and Thanon Ratsadamnoen. In the budget range, the best of these is the *Sawadikarn Hotel* at 72–74 Thanon Yantarakitkoson (Ⓣ054 511032; ❶), near the junction with Thanon Charoen Muang, a large three-storey hotel, with reasonably clean, simply furnished fan rooms and attached (cold-water) bathrooms. On an alley off the main road, *Thep Vong Place*, 346/2 Thanon Charoen Muang (Ⓣ054 521985; fan ❷, air-con ❸) offers considerably more comfort, with big rooms, cable TV and hot-water bathrooms. Another popular mid-range hotel, on Thanon Ratsadamnoen close to the Pratuchai gate and the old city, is the *Nakhon Phrae Hotel* (Ⓣ054 511122, Ⓕ054 521937; fan ❷, air-con ❷–❸). The fan rooms with parquet floors and hot-water en-suite bathrooms present very good value; extra baht on an incremental scale secure you air-con, cable TV and fridge. The city's best upmarket hotel is the *Mae Yom Palace* near the bus station at 181/6 Thanon Yantarakitkoson (Ⓣ054 521028–34, Ⓕ054 522904; ❺); a large swimming pool features among its amenities, and **bicycles** (with a suggested route map) can be rented for B100 per day.

For **eating**, you could start with the foodstalls at the lively night market by the Pratuchai gate on Thanon Charoen Muang. Nearby on Thanon Ratsadamnoen around the *Nakhon Phrae Hotel*, there are a few places to choose from including some simple Chinese cafés: the *Ah Hui*, right next to the *Nakhon Phrae Hotel*, serves several tasty rice dishes, though like most eateries in Phrae, it has no English menu. For this luxury, you have to pay slightly higher prices at *Malakaw*, on the opposite side of Thanon Ratsadamnoen about 50m down the road, a popular, rustic-style place serving everything from fried rice and noodles to salads, curries and soups. Phrae's best restaurant is *Ban Fai*, a couple of kilometres south out of town (about B30 by motorbike taxi) on the main road towards Den Chai, an open-sided barn-like place serving very good Thai food including northern specialities such as *nem* (spiced pork sausages) and the typical Lanna pork curry, *kaeng hang lay*.

Wat Phra That Cho Hae

Wat Phra That Cho Hae, 9km east of town (1km on from the village of Padang), is an important pilgrimage centre sited on a low hill, approached by two naga stairways through a grove of teak trees. One staircase leads to a shrine where a revered Buddha image, Phra Chao Tan Chai, is said to increase women's fertility. The small grounds also house a gilded 33-metre-high **chedi**, traditionally wrapped in the yellow satin-like cloth, *cho hae* (which gives the wat its name) in March or April, and a brightly decorated viharn with an unusual cruciform layout. To the north of the main compound, a new viharn houses a shiny Buddha and some well-crafted murals and window carvings. To get to the wat, take a shared songthaew (B15) from Thanon Charoen Muang near the Thanon Yantarakitkoson intersection.

Nan

After leaving the Yom, Highway 101 gently climbs through rolling hills of cotton fields and teak plantations to its highest point, framed by limestone cliffs, before descending into the high, isolated valley of the Nan River, the longest in Thailand (740km) and one of the tributaries of the Chao Phraya. Ringed by high mountains, the small but prosperous provincial capital of **NAN**, 225km east of Lampang, rests on the grassy west bank of the river. This stretch of water really comes alive during the **Lanna boat races**, usually held in late October or early November, when villages from around the province send teams of up to fifty oarsmen here to race in long, colourfully decorated canoes with dragon prows. The lush surrounding valley is noted for its cotton-weaving, sweet oranges and the attractive grainy paper made from the bark of local *sa* (mulberry) trees.

Although it has been kicked around by Burma, Laos and Thailand, Nan province has a history of being on the fringes, distanced by the encircling barrier of mountains. Rama V brought Nan into his centralization programme at the start of the twentieth century, but left the traditional ruling house in place, making it the last province in Thailand to be administered by a local ruler (it remained so until 1931). During the troubled 1970s, communist insurgents holed up in this twilight region and proclaimed Nan the future capital of the liberated zone, which only succeeding in bringing the full might of the Thai Army down on them; the insurgency faded after the government's 1982 offer of amnesty. Today, energies are focused on development, and the province has become less isolated with the building of several new roads. Nan still has a slight reputation for lawlessness, but most of the bandits nowadays are illegal loggers.

Arrival and information

The bus journey to Nan from Chiang Mai takes around six hours, so it might be worth catching one of the air-con or VIP vehicles that serve this route. The main **bus station** is in the southwest corner of town, off the main road to Phrae, and songthaews to the centre cost B10. The **airport** is located to the northwest of town; there are no flights at present to or from Chiang Mai, but PB Air (ⓣ054 771729, ⓦwww.pbair.com), with an office at the airport, operate five flights weekly from Bangkok. For **tourist information** about the town and the province, visit Fhu Travel (see "Around Nan"), while for exploring the area, Oversea, at 488 Thanon Sumondhevaraj, rents out decent **bicycles** (B50–80 a day) and **motorbikes** (B150). **Internet outlets** open and close regularly in Nan, but there is usually somewhere offering access near the centre of town, such as at 77/6 Thanon Mahawong.

Accommodation

Despite being a small town with few visitors, Nan has some attractive accommodation options, ranging from family-run guest houses to clean, reasonably priced hotels. The only time of year when finding somewhere to stay might be a problem is when the Lanna boat races take place in town (late Oct or early Nov).

Amazing Guest House 25/7 Thanon Rat Amnuay ⓣ054 710893. About 1km north of the centre, tucked away in a tiny lane to the west of Thanon Sumondhevaraj. Offers clean, simple rooms in a family-style, wooden house with shared bathroom, as well as five bungalows, some with air-con, in a shady garden. Gives considerable discounts for longer stays, and bicycles and motorbikes are available for rent. Fan ➊, air-con ➋

City Park 99 Thanon Yantarakitkoson ⓣ054 741343–52, ⓕ054 773135. About 2km from the centre on Highway 101 to Phrae, this smart place has tasteful rooms (all with cable TV) in low-rise buildings that give onto balconies overlooking a large swimming pool. ➎

Dhevaraj 466 Thanon Sumondhevaraj ⓣ054 710078 or 054 710212, ⓕ054 771365. Rooms at this centrally positioned hotel are quite plush, with fan or air-con, and cable TV; all are en suite. Though the fan rooms are good value, tour groups here can be noisy. Fan ➌, air-con ➎

Doi Phukha Guest House 94/5 Soi 1, Thanon Sumondhevaraj ⓣ054 751517. On the north side of town, this fine guest house occupies a beautiful wooden house in a quiet compound. The simple rooms share hot and cold showers, and there's an informative noticeboard and excellent maps of the province available. ➊

Fahthanin 303 Thanon Anantaworarichides ⓣ054 757321–4. The comfy and carpeted, air-con rooms here come with TV and mini-bar, and it's in a quiet part of town only a few minutes' walk from the centre. ➌

Nan Guest House 57/16 Thanon Mahaphom ⓣ054 771849. Adequate, if rather basic rooms in a wooden house down a quiet lane near the museum. ➊

PK Guest House 33/12 Thanon Prempracharaj ⓣ054 771999, ⓕ054 757099. This place offers a range of rooms with varying facilities, from simple fan rooms with shared bathrooms to air-con rooms with attached bathrooms, scattered around a large garden. Fan ➊, air-con ➌

SP Guest House 233 Thanon Sumondhevaraj ⓣ054 774897. Just half a dozen rooms in this well-maintained guest house, all with hot-water bathrooms and cable TV. Fan ➋, air-con ➌

The Town

Nan's centre comprises a disorientating grid of crooked streets, around a small core of shops and businesses where Thanon Mahawong and Thanon Anantaworarichides meet Thanon Sumondhevaraj. The best place to start an exploration is to the southwest at the **National Museum** (daily 9am–4pm; B30), located in a tidy, century-old palace with superb teak floors, which used to be home to the rulers of Nan. Its informative, user-friendly displays give you a bite-sized introduction to Nan, its history and its peoples, the prize exhibit being a talismanic elephant tusk with a bad case of brown tooth decay, which is claimed to be magic black ivory. The tusk was discovered over three hundred years ago and now sits on a colourful wooden *khut*, a mythological eagle. The museum also houses elegant pottery and woodcarving, gorgeously wrought silverware and some rare Lao Buddhas.

Nearby on Thanon Phakwang, **Wat Phumin** will grab even the most over-templed traveller. Its 500-year-old centrepiece is an unusual cruciform building, combining both the bot and the viharn, which balances some quirky features in a perfect symmetry. Two giant nagas pass through the base of the building, with their tails along the balustrades at the south entrance and their heads at the north, representing the sacred oceans at the base of the central mountain of the universe. The doors at the four entrances, which have been beautifully carved with a complex pattern of animals and flowers, lead straight to the four Buddha images arranged around a tall altar in the centre of the building – note the Buddhas' piercing onyx eyes and pointed ears, showing the influence of Laos, 50km away. What really sets the bot apart are the **murals**, whose bright, simple colours seem to jump off the walls. Executed in the late nineteenth century – though occasionally re-touched – the paintings take you on a whirlwind tour of heaven, hell, the Buddha's previous incarnations, local legends and incidents from Nan's history, and include stacks of vivacious, sometimes bawdy, detail, which provides a valuable pictorial record of that era. Diagonally opposite Wat Phumin, **Wat Chang Kham** is also over 500 years old, though the two viharns that stand side by side are unexceptional in design. The main feature here is a gorgeous, gold-capped chedi, supported by elephants on all sides; those on the corners are adorned with gold helmets. The temple is attached to a school, a reminder that temples were once the only source of education in the country.

Wat Phra That Chae Haeng, on the opposite side of the river 2km south-east of town, is another must, as much for its setting on a hill overlooking the Nan valley as anything else. The wat was founded in 1300, at a spot determined by the Buddha himself when he passed through this way – or so local legend would have it. The nagas here outdo even Wat Phumin's: the first you see of the wat across the fields is a wide driveway flanked by monumental serpents gliding down the slope from the temple. A magnificent gnarled bodhi tree with hundreds of spreading branches and roots guards the main gate, set in high boundary walls. Inside the walls, the highlight is a slender, 55-metre-high golden chedi, surrounded by four smaller chedis and four carved and gilded umbrellas, as well as small belfries and stucco lions. Close competition comes from the viharn roof, which has no fewer than fifteen Lao-style tiers, stacked up like a house of cards and supported on finely carved *kan tuei* (wood supports) under the eaves.

You can get another great overview of the Nan valley by turning right just after the bridge on Highway 101 to the south of town. Follow the lane a couple of kilometres, and go up the hill to **Wat Phra That Khao Noi**, where you can join a huge image of a standing Buddha in contemplating the lush panorama below.

Crafts and shops

Loyalty to local traditions ensures the survival of several good **handicrafts shops** in Nan, most of which are found on Thanon Sumondhevaraj north of the junction with Anantaworarichides. Traditional lengths of superb **cotton** (much of it *pha sin*, used as wraparound skirts) woven in local villages are sold at Pha Nan, 21/2 Thanon Sumondhevaraj; as the owner is a teacher, the shop has unusual hours (Mon–Fri 5–10pm, Sat & Sun 8am–10pm). The staff are friendly and you can happily browse the huge selection of cloths for hours without hard sell. Jangtragun, at nos. 304–306, also has a good selection of *seua maw hawm*, Phrae's famous blue working shirts, and a few notebooks made from *sa* paper. Hattasin, run by the Thai-Payap Development Association, a **non-profit-making organization** set up to bring extra income to local hill tribes, is a shop with some gorgeous textiles at 99/5 Mahawong Road, opposite the post office. On sale here are bags, basketware, woodcarving, honey and all manner of fabrics, even Hmong baby-carriers.

A large **silverware** showroom and workshop named Chom Phu Phukha is situated about 2km west of town along the road to Phayao (Route 1091), on the right opposite a petrol station. They stock a wide range of bracelets, necklaces, bowls and trays, priced according to design and weight, and are happy for visitors to look round the workshop, where young hill-tribe people fashion the items. A good variety of local cloth, hand-woven by the hill tribes, is also on sale here.

Eating and drinking

Plenty of **restaurants** line Thanon Anantaworarichides, among them ✱ *Poom Sam*, just next to the *Sukkasem Hotel*. It may look like any other street food outlet, but they prepare excellent Thai and Chinese food with great service at rock-bottom prices (try the tongue-tingling *tom yam kung* for B70), and there's now a comfy air-con room as well. Upstairs from *Poom Sam* is *Da Dario*, which serves up excellent pizzas and other Italian dishes. Right next door to both of these is *Tanaya Kitchen*, a tiny, homely café that serves good vegetarian food. The **night market**, on the same street, includes several good noodle stalls serving up staples like *phat thai* for B20, and for a taste of Isaan food, check out *Suan Issan* at 2/1 Thanon Anantaworarichides, which despite its address is actually in the narrow alley off Thanon Sumondhevaraj, just south of the junction with this road. Cheap and clean, with lots of plants out front, this restaurant has good service, and the fiery Isaan food will have your tongue flapping. Most shops and restaurants in Nan pull down their shutters by around 9pm, but if you're looking for **nightlife**, check out *Mai Muang* bar on Thanon Prempracharaj, to the north of the town centre, or *Channel X*, in a maze of lanes to the west of town, which both attract a fair crowd most nights.

Around Nan

The remote, mountainous countryside around Nan runs a close second to the precipitous scenery of Mae Hong Son province, but its remoteness means that Nan has even worse transport and is even more poorly mapped. This does, of course, make it an exciting region to explore, and one in which you may encounter the ethnic minorities of the area – the Thai Lue, the Htin and the little-known Phi Tong Luang.

With or without your own vehicle, your best option is to head for the reliable Fhu Travel, at 453/4 Thanon Sumondhevaraj (Ⓣ054 710636, Ⓔfhutravel@hotmail.com). Besides organizing popular and enjoyable guided **tours** and trekking trips, Fhu and Ung, his wife, can advise you where to go according to your interests or even arrange customized tours. One- to

Spirits of the yellow leaves

Inhabiting the remote hill country west of Nan, the **Phi Tong Luang** – "Spirits of the Yellow Leaves" – represent the last remnant of nomadic hunter-gatherers in Thailand, though their way of life, like that of so many other indigenous peoples, is rapidly passing. Believing that spirits will be angered if the tribe settles in one place, grows crops or keeps animals, the Phi Tong Luang build only temporary shelters of branches and wild banana leaves, moving on to another spot in the jungle as soon as the leaves turn yellow; thus they earned their poetic Thai name, though they call themselves Mrabri – "Forest People". Traditionally they eke out a hard livelihood from the forest, hunting with spears, trapping birds and small mammals, digging roots and collecting nuts, seeds and honey.

Recent deforestation by logging and slash-and-burn farming has eaten into the tribe's territory, however, and many of the Phi Tong Luang have been forced to sell their labour to Hmong and Mien farmers (the spirits apparently do not get angry if the tribe settles down and works the land for other people). They are paid only in food – because of their docility and their inability to understand and use money, they often get a raw deal for their hard work. They are also particularly ill-equipped to cope with curious and often insensitive tourists, although one of the American missionaries working with the tribe believes that occasional visits help the Phi Tong Luang to develop by teaching them about people in the outside world. The future doesn't look bright: they number only about 100–200 members; their susceptibility to disease (especially malaria) is high and life expectancy low.

three-day whitewater-rafting trips cost around B1000 per person a day, depending on group size, and go down the Nam Wa River near Mae Charim to the east of town. One-day tours to Wat Nong Bua, including a visit to the local weavers and views of Doi Phukha from nearby Pua, cost B2000 for two to three people or B600 per person for four to six people, including transport, driver/guide and lunch. Fhu can also arrange home-stays in Ban Don Moon, a small village near Ban Nong Bua, where you can learn more about local agricultural and weaving techniques. Treks (two days B1600/person, three days B2000/person; minimum four people) head west, through tough terrain of thick jungle and high mountains, visiting at least one Phi Tong Luang village (see box) and nearby Hmong and Mien villages where they work, as well as settlements of Htin, an upland Mon-Khmer people, most of whom migrated into Nan province after the Communist takeover of Laos in 1975. For those who want to go it alone, the bus service is sketchy, but Oversea (see p.390) rents out motorbikes.

There are plans to open the border at **Huai Kon**, in the extreme north of Nan Province, to foreigners in the near future. This will open up an intriguing alternative route to Louang Phabang in Laos (at present the only overland route is via Chiang Khong), since it would entail a short trip by road to the banks of the Mekong River, and from there just a couple of hours by boat. Check with Fhu Travel to find out the latest news on this.

Sao Din

One of several brief excursions from Nan possible with your own transport, **Sao Din** ("earth pillars"), 60km to the south, provides a more intriguing example of soil erosion than the better-known site at Phae Muang Phi near Phrae. Here the earth pillars cover a huge area and appear in fantastic shapes, the result of centuries of erosion by wind and rain. The site is almost impossible to reach by public transport, but if you have a motorbike or car, head south on Highway 101 to Wiang Sa, then turn left and follow Route 1026 to Na Noi; a turning on the right just after Na Noi leads into the site. If you visit, take care to wear long trousers and boots, especially in the cool season, as a thorny plant that grows in the region can cause discomfort.

Ban Nong Bua

The easiest and most varied day-trip out of Nan is to the north, heading first for **BAN NONG BUA**, site of a famous muralled temple of the same name. If you're on a bike, ride 40km up Route 1080 to the southern outskirts of the town of **Tha Wang Pha**, where signs in English point you left across the Nan River to Wat Nong Bua, 3km away. Buses from Nan's main bus station make the hour-long journey to Tha Wang Pha roughly hourly, then either hire a motorbike taxi in the centre of Tha Wang Pha, or walk the last 3km.

Wat Nong Bua stands behind the village green on the west side of the unpaved through road. Its beautifully gnarled viharn was built in 1862 in typical Lanna style, with low, drooping roof tiers surmounted by stucco finials – here you'll find horned nagas and tusked makaras (elephantine monsters), instead of the garuda finial which invariably crops up in central Thai temples. The viharn enshrines a pointy-eared Laotian Buddha, but its most outstanding features are the **murals** that cover all four walls. Executed between 1867 and 1888, probably by the Wat Phumin painters, they depict with much humour and vivid detail scenes from the *Chanthakhat Jataka* (the story of one of the Buddha's previous incarnations, as a hero called Chanthakhat). This is a particularly long and complex jataka (although a leaflet, available from the monks in return for a small donation to temple funds, outlines the story in English), wherein our hero gets into all kinds of scrapes, involving several wives, other sundry liaisons, some formidably nasty enemies and the god Indra transforming himself into a snake. The crux of the tale comes on the east wall (opposite the Buddha image): in the bottom left-hand corner, Chanthakhat and the love of his life, Thewathisangka, are shipwrecked and separated; distraught, Thewathisangka wanders through the jungle, diagonally up the wall, to the hermitage of an old woman, where she shaves her head and becomes a nun; Chanthakhat travels through the wilderness along the bottom of the wall, curing a wounded naga-king on the way, who out of gratitude gives him a magic crystal ball, which enables our hero to face another series of perils along the south wall, before finally rediscovering and embracing Thewathisangka in front of the old woman's hut, at the top right-hand corner of the east wall.

Ban Nong Bua and the surrounding area are largely inhabited by **Thai Lue** people, distant cousins of the Thais, who've migrated from China in the past 150 years. They produce beautiful cotton garments in richly coloured geometric patterns; walk 200m behind the wat and you'll find weavers at work under the stilted sky-blue house of Khun Janthasom Prompanya, who sells the opulent fabrics in the shop behind. The quality of design and workmanship is very high here, and prices, though not cheap, are reasonable for the quality.

Doi Phukha National Park

East of Tha Wang Pha, Route 1080 curves towards the town of **Pua**, on whose southern outskirts Route 1256, the spectacular access road for **Doi Phukha National Park** (ⓣ054 701000; B200), begins its journey eastwards and upwards. It's difficult to get into the park on public transport, and you'll have to stay the night. Hourly buses from Nan's main station run to Pua, from where infrequent songthaews (usually only one a day between 8am and 9am) serve the handful of villages along Route 1256. The trip is most exciting if tackled on a bike (though watch out for loose chippings on the bends). The paved road climbs up a sharp ridge, through occasional stands of elephant grass and bamboo, towards Doi Dong Ya Wai (1939m), providing one of the most jaw-droppingly scenic drives in Thailand. Across the valleys to north and south stand rows of improbably steep mountains (including the 1980-metre Doi Phukha itself, far to the south), covered in lush vegetation with scarcely a sign of human habitation.

At park headquarters, 24km up the road from Pua, **accommodation** ranges from a campsite (free, but you need to bring your own tent) to large bungalows sleeping six (B2000) and smaller ones sleeping four (B800) or two (B300). In case they are full, it's best to book in advance in Bangkok (see p.51). Another alternative is *Bamboo Hut* (Ⓣ081 883 7687; ❷), located at Ban Toei, a few kilometres beyond park headquarters towards the eastern edge of the national park, which has a dozen simple thatched bamboo huts with shared bathrooms and spectacular views. There are several trails within the park but they're not well marked, so it's best to hire a **guide** at headquarters (B300/day). The guides, who unfortunately don't speak English, lead visitors up the arduous slope to the nearest summit, Dong Khao (1305m). Depending on the season, you can arrange to have **meals** cooked for you at the headquarters, though the menu is limited and if you are part of a big group, it's best to call in advance and make sure they have enough supplies.

The Mae Hong Son loop

Two roads from Chiang Mai head over the western mountains into Mae Hong Son, Thailand's most remote province, offering the irresistible prospect of tying the highways together into a six-hundred-kilometre loop. The towns en route give a taste of Burma to the west, but the journey itself, winding over implausibly steep forested mountains and through tightly hemmed farming valleys, is what will stick in the mind.

The southern leg of the route, Highway 108, first passes **Doi Inthanon National Park**, with its lofty views over half of northern Thailand and enough waterfalls to last a lifetime, then **Mae Sariang**, an important town for trade across the Burmese border. The provincial capital, **Mae Hong Son**, roughly at the midpoint of the loop, makes a good base for exploring the area's mountains, rivers and waterfalls, though it can become frantic with tour groups in the cool season. The northern leg, Route 1095, heads northeast out of Mae Hong Son into an area of beautiful caves and stunning scenery around **Mae Suya** and **Soppong**: staying at one of the out-of-the-way guest houses here will enable you to trek independently around the countryside and the local hill-tribe villages. Halfway back towards Chiang Mai from Mae Hong Son is **Pai**, a cosy, cosmopolitan travellers' hangout with plenty of activities and some gentle walking trails in the surrounding valley.

We've taken the loop in a clockwise direction here, in part because Doi Inthanon is best reached direct from Chiang Mai and in part because this dispenses with the straight, fast and boring section of the journey (Chiang Mai–Hot) at the beginning. These considerations apart, you could just as easily go the other way round. Travelling the loop is straightforward, although the mountainous roads go through plenty of bends and jolts. Either way, Mae Hong Son is about eight hours' travelling time from Chiang Mai by air-con or ordinary **bus**, although services along the shorter but even more winding northern route are now augmented by faster **air-con minibuses**, which cover the ground via Pai four times a day in about six hours. The 35-minute Chiang Mai–Mae Hong Son **flight**, currently covered by Thai Airways and Nok Air, can work out surprisingly inexpensive, and is worth considering for one leg of the journey, especially if you're short on time. Above all, though, the loop is made for **motorbikes** and **jeeps**: the roads are generally quiet (but watch out for huge, speeding trucks) and you can satisfy the inevitable craving to stop every five minutes and admire the mountain scenery. A useful piece of equipment for this journey is the 1:375,000 **map** of the Mae Hong Son Loop, with useful insets of Pai's and Mae Hong Son's environs, published by Golden Triangle Rider (Ⓦwww.gt-rider.com) and available in local bookshops at B175.

Highway 108: Chiang Mai to Mae Hong Son

Bus drivers on **Highway 108** are expected to have highly sharpened powers of concentration and the landlubber's version of sea legs – the road negotiates almost two thousand curves in the 349km to Mae Hong Son, so if you're at all prone to travel sickness plan to take a breather in Mae Sariang. Buses to Mae Sariang and Mae Hong Son depart from Chiang Mai's Arcade bus station; services to Chom Thong (for Doi Inthanon National Park) leave from the southern end of Thanon Phra Pokklao (Chiang Mai Gate).

Just 29km south of Chiang Mai on H108, the *Kao Mai Lanna Resort* (Ⓣ053 834470–5, Ⓦwww.kaomailanna.com; ❽) makes a restful place to stay overnight, or even stop for refreshment in its attractive, open-sided restaurant. The ample grounds contain a large swimming pool, a spa and comfortable rooms ingeniously converted from tobacco-curing barns. Each room is decorated in an individual style, with teak furnishings and fittings, and bicycles are on hand for guests to ride around the grounds.

Doi Inthanon National Park

Covering a huge area to the southwest of Chiang Mai, **DOI INTHANON NATIONAL PARK**, with its hill-tribe villages, dramatic waterfalls and panoramas over rows of wild, green peaks to the west, gives a pleasant, if sanitized, whiff of northern countryside, its attractions and concrete access roads kept in good order by the Thai Forestry Department. The park, named after the highest mountain in the country and so dubbed the "Roof of Thailand", is geared mainly to wildlife conservation but also contains a hill-tribe agricultural project producing strawberries, apples and flowers for sale. Often shrouded in mist, Doi Inthanon's temperate forests shelter a huge variety of flora and fauna, which make this one of the major destinations for naturalists in Southeast Asia.

The park supports about 380 bird species, the largest number of any site in Thailand – among them the ashy-throated warbler and a species of the green-tailed sunbird, both unique to Doi Inthanon – as well as, near the summit, the only red rhododendrons in Thailand (in bloom Dec–Feb) and a wide variety of ground and epiphytic orchids. The waterfalls, birds and flowers are at their best in the cool season, but night-time temperatures sometimes drop below freezing, making warm clothing a must.

The gateway to the park is **CHOM THONG**, 58km southwest of Chiang Mai on Highway 108, a market town with little to offer apart from the attractive **Wat Phra That Si Chom Thong**, whose impressive brass-plated chedi dates from the fifteenth century. The nearby bo tree has become an equally noteworthy architectural feature: dozens of Dalí-esque supports for its sagging branches have been sponsored by the devoted in the hope of earning merit. Inside the renovated sixteenth-century viharn, a towering, gilded *ku* housing a Buddha relic just squeezes in beneath the ceiling, from which hangs a huge, sumptuous red and green umbrella. Weaponry, gongs, umbrellas, thrones and an elephant-tusk arch carved with delicate Buddha images all add to the welcoming clutter. The temple is now famous for its **meditation retreats**, based in the administration buildings at the back of the compound. With foreign monks and lay people teaching Vipassana meditation, a basic course here lasts around 21 days (donations to temple and teacher suggested); call as far as possible in advance to book a place (ⓣ053 826869, ⓦwww.fivethousandyears.org). Just beyond the wat and set back from the road, *Watjanee* is a simple but clean and well-run vegetarian **restaurant**.

The main road through the park turns west off Highway 108, 1km north of Chom Thong, winding generally northwestwards for 48km to the top of Doi Inthanon, passing the park headquarters about 30km in. A second paved road forks left 10km before the summit, reaching the riverside market of **Mae Chaem**, southwest of the park, after 20km. Several tour operators in Chiang Mai offer day-trips to the national park (around B1500 per person), but sticking to public transport, you can reach the park headquarters using one of the **songthaews** that shuttle between Chom Thong market (about 100m south of

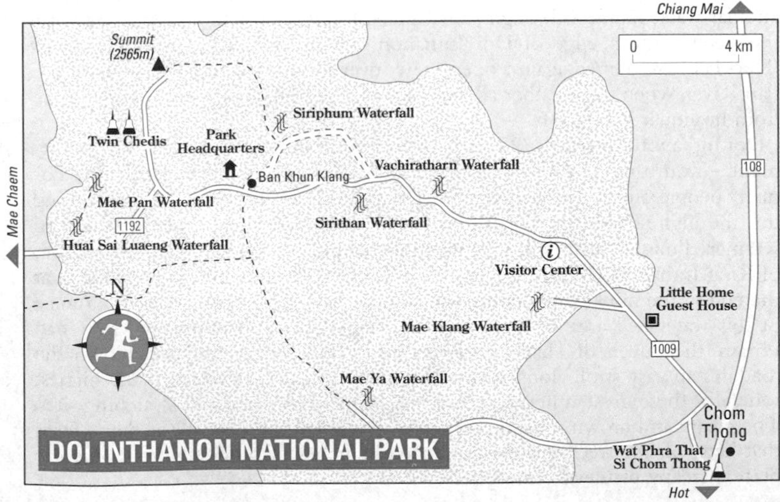

the temple) and Mae Chaem, along the mountain's lower slopes. To get to the summit, however, you'll have to hitch from the Mae Chaem turn-off (generally manageable), unless you want to charter a whole songthaew from Chom Thong's temple for around B1000 to the peak and back (about 4–5hr). By **motorbike** or **jeep**, you could do the park justice in a day-trip with an early start from Chiang Mai, or treat it as the first stage of a longer trip to Mae Hong Son, either following Route 1088 south from Mae Chaem to pick up Highway 108 again towards Mae Sariang or taking Route 1088 north then Route 1263 to Khun Yuam.

The park

Four sets of waterfalls provide the main roadside attractions on the way to the park headquarters: overrated **Mae Klang Falls**, 8km in, which with its picnic areas and food vendors gets overbearingly crowded at weekends; **Vachiratharn Falls**, the park's most dramatic, with a long, misty drop down a granite escarpment 11km beyond; **Sirithan Falls,** which looks like a smaller version of Vachiratharn and is just a couple of kilometres further up the hill; and finally the twin cascades of **Siriphum Falls**, backing the park headquarters a further 9km on. With your own wheels you could reach a fifth and much more beautiful cataract, **Mae Ya**, which is believed to be the highest in Thailand – the winding, fourteen-kilometre paved track to it heads west off the main park road 2km north of Highway 108. A rough unpaved side road offers a roundabout but culturally more enlightening route to the headquarters, leaving the main road 3km beyond Vachiratharn Falls, taking in three traditional and unspoilt Karen villages before rejoining the main road at the more developed Hmong village of **Ban Khun Klang**, 500m before the headquarters.

For the most spectacular views in the park, continue 11km beyond the headquarters along the summit road to the sleek, twin chedis looming incongruously over the misty green hillside: on a clear day you can see the mountains of Burma to the west from here. Built by the Royal Thai Air Force, the chedis commemorate the sixtieth birthdays of the Thai king and queen; the king's monument, **Napamaytanidol Chedi** (1987), is brown to the more feminine lilac of the queen's **Napapolphumsiri Chedi** (1992). Starting a short distance up the road from the chedis, the rewarding **Kew Mae Pan Trail**, a two-hour circular walk, wanders through sun-dappled forest and open savanna as it skirts the steep western edge of Doi Inthanon, where violent-red rhododendrons (Dec–Feb) are framed against open views over the canyoned headwaters of the Pan River, when the weather allows. To walk the trail, you have to hire a guide from headquarters (B200).

Doi Inthanon's **summit** (2565m), 6km beyond the chedi, is a big disappointment – from the car park you can see little beyond the radar installation. For many people, after a quick shiver and a snapshot in front of a board proclaiming this the highest point in Thailand, it's time to hop in the car and get back to warmer climes. A small, still-revered stupa behind this board contains the ashes of King Inthanon of Chiang Mai (after whom the mountain was renamed): at the end of the nineteenth century he was the first to recognize the importance of this watershed area in supplying the Ping River and ultimately the Chao Phraya, the queen of Thailand's rivers. One hundred metres back down the road, it's an easy stroll along a raised walkway to the bog which is the highest source of these great waterways, and one of the park's best bird-watching sites. The cream and brown sphagnum mosses that spread underfoot, the dense ferns that hang off the trees and the contorted branches of rhododendrons give the place a creepy, primeval atmosphere.

The paved **Mae Chaem road** skirts yet another set of waterfalls, 7km after the turning off the summit road: look for a steep, unpaved road to the right, leading down to a ranger station and, just to the east, the dramatic long drop of **Huai Sai Luaeng Falls**. A circular two-hour trail from the ranger station takes in creeks and small waterfalls as well as **Mae Pan Falls**, a series of short cascades in a peaceful, shady setting. Continuing southwest, the paved road affords breathtaking views as it helter-skelters down to the sleepy valley of **Mae Chaem**. With your own transport it's possible to take on a remote, paved route towards Mae Hong Son from here, heading north up Route 1088 then west along Route 1263, joining Highway 108 just north of Khun Yuam. To rejoin the classic Mae Hong Son loop, however, take the southern 45-kilometre stretch of Route 1088, which joins Highway 108 25km west of Hot.

Practicalities

A checkpoint by Mae Klang Falls collects **entrance fees** of B200 for foreigners, plus B20 per motorbike, and B30 per car. For information on the park, stop at the **visitor centre** (daily, roughly 8am–5pm), 1km beyond the checkpoint. Information is also available at the **park headquarters**, a further 22km on, where you need to stop if you plan to stay overnight or to pick up a guide to walk the Kew Mae Pan trail. Two hundred metres beyond the headquarters on the left, the **Birding Visitor Centre** has a useful logbook and information in English for birders to consult, and sells a primitive map of birding sites.

Accommodation and eating

Accommodation in the national park comes in the standard log-cabin or concrete varieties. Three- to ten-berth bungalows (B1000–6000; bookings at the park on ⓣ053 268550, or in Bangkok, see p.51), set among dense stands of pine near the headquarters, come with hot-water bathrooms, electricity, mattresses or beds and bedding. They are often fully booked at weekends and national holidays, but at other times you should be all right turning up on the day. Elsewhere, the *Little Home Guest House and Restaurant*, 7km from Chom Thong along the main park road (ⓣ053 267382 or 081 287 6242; fan ❹, air-con ❹–❺), has clean, breeze-block huts, with inside bathrooms, most with hot water. The *Navasoung Resort*, just before reaching Mae Chaem from Doi Inthanon (ⓣ & ⓕ053 828477; ❸) offers small, cosy chalets with hot water and fan, set in a colourful garden with pleasant views across the valley that are shared by its restaurant. In Mae Chaem itself, another appealing alternative is the *Pongsara Resort* (ⓣ053 485011; fan ❸, air-con ❹), which has spacious and well-equipped fan and air-con rooms in a big compound at the entrance to the town.

Camping, an often chilly alternative, is permitted on a site about 500m from the park headquarters and another site at Huai Sai Luaeng Falls (B30/person/night). Fully equipped two-person tents can be rented at headquarters for B250 per night.

Foodstalls operate in the daytime at Mae Klang, Vachiratharn and Mae Ya falls and also through the evening beside park headquarters. The Birding Visitor Centre serves up cheap but tasty dishes, and there's a popular canteen with a reasonable variety of food by the twin chedis. All these places will prepare food to take away if you need a packed lunch.

West to Mae Sariang and Mae Sam Laeb

South from Chom Thong, there are several weaving villages bordering Highway 108, and the **Pa-Da Cotton Textile Museum** (daily except Thurs

8.30am–4.30pm; free) at Ban Rai Pai Ngarm (on the east side of the road at kilometre-stone 68) is well worth a look. The museum is dedicated to the work of Saeng-da Bansiddhi, a local woman who started a co-operative practising traditional dyeing and weaving techniques using only natural products. Saeng-da died in the late 1980s, and the museum, which displays some of her personal effects as well as looms, fabrics and plants used in dyeing, was established to honour her efforts to revive these disappearing skills. It's situated on the upper floor of a large wooden building, while on the ground floor weavers can be seen busy at work. Bolts of cloth and a small range of clothes are on sale at reasonable prices.

Highway 108 parallels the Ping River downstream as far as **Hot**, a dusty, forgettable place 27km from Chom Thong, before bending west and weaving through pretty wooded hills up the valley of the Chaem River. Four kilometres west of town, the *Hod Resort* (Ⓣ & Ⓕ053 461070; fan ❸, air-con ❹) has well-appointed chalets and rooms with hot water, some air-conditioned, and a riverside restaurant which serves tasty food at moderate prices.

Another 13km brings you to **Ob Luang Gorge National Park** (B200), billed with wild hyperbole as "Thailand's Grand Canyon". A wooden bridge over the short, narrow channel lets you look down on the Chaem River bubbling along between sheer walls 50m below. The park is also tagged "Land of Prehistoric Human" because of the discovery of Bronze Age graves here, containing seashell bracelets and other decorative items, as well as rock paintings of elephants and human figures. Upstream from the bridge near park headquarters, you can relax at the roadside foodstalls and swim in the river when it's not too fast, and the shady river bank shelters a **campsite** (B30/person, plus B225 to hire a three-person tent and blankets). There are also a few large bungalows, sleeping eight people (B1800), and smaller rooms at B600. At headquarters you can arrange one-hour, five-kilometre **whitewater-rafting** trips on the river, which cost from B1400 for 4 people up to B1800 for 8 people, including guides, transport, life jackets and helmets. West of Ob Luang, the highway gradually climbs through pine forests, the road surface bad in patches and the countryside becoming steeper and wilder.

Mae Sariang

After its descent into the broad, smoky valley of the Yuam River, Highway 108's westward progress ends at **MAE SARIANG**, 191km from Chiang Mai, a quietly industrious market town showing a marked Burmese influence in its temples and rows of low wooden shophouses. Halfway along the southern route between Chiang Mai and Mae Hong Son, this is an obvious place for a stopover. From here you can make an intriguing day-trip to the trading post of Mae Sam Laeb on the border with Burma and out onto the Salween River, and it's also possible to strike off south on a bone-rattling journey to Mae Sot.

Apart from soaking up the atmosphere, there's nothing pressing to do in this border outpost, which is regularly visited by local hill tribes and dodgy traders from Burma. If you want something more concrete to do, stroll around a couple of temples off the north side of the main street, whose Burmese features provide a glaring contrast to most Thai temples. The first, **Wat Si Boonruang**, sports a fairy-tale bot with an intricate, tiered roof piled high above. Topped with lotus buds, the unusual *sema* stones, which delineate the bot's consecrated area, look like old-fashioned street bollards. The open viharns here and next door at **Wat Uthayarom** (aka Wat Jong Sung) are mounted on stilts, with broad teak floors that are a pleasure to get your feet onto. Both wats enshrine Burmese-style Buddhas, white and hard-faced.

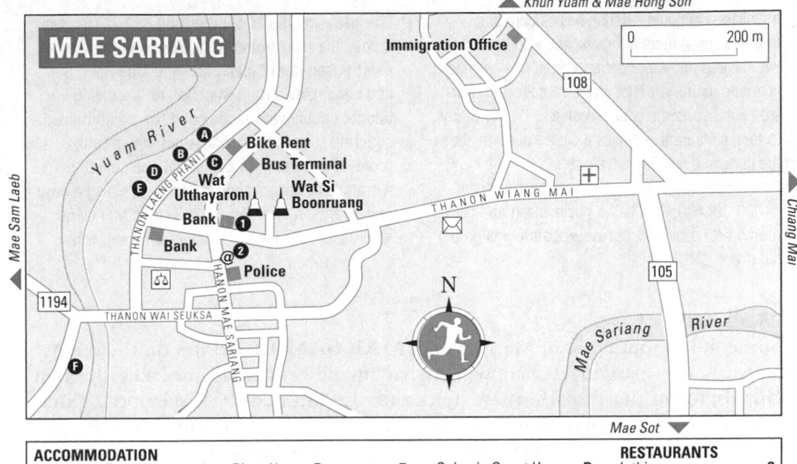

Practicalities

Buses enter Mae Sariang from the east along the town's main street, Thanon Wiang Mai, and pull in at the **terminal** on Thanon Mae Sariang, one of two north–south streets; the other, Thanon Laeng Phanit, parallels the Yuam River to the west. **Motorbikes** (B150/day) for exploring local temples and Karen villages can be hired from Pratin Kolakan, a small outlet opposite the bus terminal, or from the *See View* and *Northwest* guest houses (see below); these two guest houses also rent **bicycles** (B50). One- to three-day **treks** into the countryside northeast of Mae Sariang or along the border can be arranged at *River Side Guest House*, taking in Karen, Hmong, Lawa and Kuomintang villages, caves and waterfalls, and typically cost B2000 for three days including rafting and elephant-riding. As well as organizing **boat trips from Mae Sam Laeb** (see p.402), *See View Guest House* can offer one-day **jeep treks** to the southeast of town, visiting hill tribes, waterfalls and caves.

When it's time for **food**, don't be put off by the basic appearance of the *Inthira Restaurant* on Thanon Wiang Mai – it's the locals' favourite, and dishes up huge portions of excellent Thai food at give-away prices. *Renu Restaurant*, opposite, is less highly favoured but specializes in "wild food" such as nuthatch curry and wild boar. **Internet access** is available at Nam Waan Internet (no English sign), 263/1 Thanon Mae Sariang, just south of the crossroads with Thanon Wiang Mai. For such a tiny town, Mae Sariang has a good range of **accommodation**.

Northwest Guest House 81 Thanon Laeng Phanit ⓣ053 681956. Clean, friendly spot where you sleep on a mattress on the floor in a tidy, polished-wood room, and share smart hot-water bathrooms; good reductions for singles. ❷

River House Hotel 77 Thanon Laeng Phanit ⓣ053 621201, ⓔriverhouse@hotmail.com. Uncomplicatedly stylish rooms with fine river views, verandas, air-con, en-suite hot-water bathrooms and TVs. Fan ❹, air-con ❺

River House Resort 6/1 Moo 2 ⓣ053 683066, ⓦwww.riverhousehotels.com. Run by the owner of *River House Hotel*, this is Mae Sariang's fanciest place to stay. All rooms come with air-con and smart wood furnishings; some have bathtubs, and there's also an attractive restaurant overlooking the river. ❼

River Side Guest House 85 Thanon Laeng Phanit ⓣ053 681188, ⓕ053 681353. Along with the *See View*, this is one of Mae Sariang's long-standing travellers' hangouts, offering basic bedrooms (mattress only) in an old-fashioned wooden house with shared hot-water bathrooms, or low-ceilinged concrete rooms with hot water en-suite and riverside terraces, some with air-con and TV. The pretty terrace restaurant occupies a choice position above the curving river. Fan ❶, air-con ❺

Salawin Guest House 2 Thanon Laeng Phanit ☎053 681490. Just half a dozen clean and cosy rooms with attached, hot-water bathrooms on the riverfront. ❷

See View ☎053 681556 or 089 552 7616. Just across the river from the town centre, but they meet buses from Chiang Mai and Mae Hong Son and songthaews from Mae Sot. An appealing budget option, with a choice of big, comfortable, concrete rooms, each with a hot-water bathroom, two with air-con, or wood and concrete A-frames in the garden, where there's also a cosy restaurant. Their enthusiastic and helpful owner, Aekkasan, is a mine of local information. Fan ❶–❷, air-con ❸

Mae Sam Laeb

Some 46km southwest of Mae Sariang, **MAE SAM LAEB** lies on the mighty Salween (or Salawin) River, which, having descended from Tibet through Burma, forms the Thai–Burmese border for 120km here, before emptying into the Andaman Sea. Mae Sam Laeb is no more than a row of bamboo stores and restaurants, but with its Thai, Chinese, Karen and Burmese inhabitants, it has a classic frontier feel about it. Morning songthaews from Mae Sariang market are sporadic, but your best bet is to sign up for one of the highly recommended one-day **boat trips** organized and guided by Aekkasan at *See View Guest House*, which include transport out to Mae Sam Laeb. The boat (with life jackets provided) cruises down the Salween through idyllic countryside to the small unspoilt Karen village of Sop Moei, right on the confluence of the Moei River with the Salween, where lunch is taken before sailing back to Mae Sam Laeb; the cost is B600–1000 according to the number of people on the trip.

South from Mae Sariang: Highway 105 to Mae Sot

Highway 105, which drops south for 230km to Mae Sot (see p.313), makes a scenic and quiet link between the north and the central plains, though it has some major drawbacks. Setting off through the Yuam valley, the road winds over a range of hills to the Burmese border, formed here by the Moei River, which it then hugs all the way down to Mae Sot. Along the way, you'll pass through traditional Karen villages which still keep some working elephants, and dense forests with occasional forlorn stands of teak.

The major deterrent against travelling this way is the standard of public transport: though the route is paved, it's covered only by **songthaews** (5–6 daily), with a journey time of about six hours – really too much on a rattling bench seat – at a cost of B180 per person. This remote border area has been the scene of infrequent skirmishes between the Burmese army and opposition freedom fighters that have occasionally spilled over onto the Thai side of the border, though this hasn't happened for around ten years now.

North to Mae Hong Son

North of Mae Sariang, wide, lush valleys alternate with tiny, steep-sided glens – some too narrow for more than a single rice paddy – turning Highway 108 into a winding roller coaster. The market town of **KHUN YUAM**, 95km from Mae Sariang, is a popular resting spot, especially for those who've taken the direct route here (Route 1263) over the mountains from Mae Chaem. There's not much here in the way of attractions, though the **World War II Museum** (daily 8.30am–4pm; B10), on the left of the main thoroughfare, Thanon Rajaburana, opposite Wat Muai Tor at the north end of town, has a curious collection of rusting relics from the Japanese World War II occupation

– old trucks, rifles, water canisters and uniforms. Lining the walls, hundreds of black-and-white photos document this period, when after their retreat from Burma in 1944, some of the Japanese rested here with the sick and wounded for two years and longer.

The *Ban Farang* **guest house** (ⓣ053 622086 or 087 178 2496, ⓔbanfarang@hotmail.com; fan ❸, air-con ❻), north again from the museum and well signposted just off Thanon Rajaburana, can put you up in fine style. Each of its smart, very clean rooms has duvets and a hot-water bathroom; the restaurant serves up good Thai and Western food, at reasonable prices. Cheaper rooms can be had at the *Mithkhoonyoum Hotel*, 115 Thanon Rajaburana (ⓣ053 691057; fan ❶, air-con ❺), with large, airy and very simple rooms in the wooden building at the front, some with en-suite cold-water bathrooms, and more expensive rooms with hot-water bathrooms, some with air-con, in the comfy new building behind. There are a few bungalows too with hot water and air-con.

Just north of Khun Yuam, Route 1263 branches off to the east over the hills towards Mae Chaem; after about 20km, a side road leads north up to the **Buatong fields** on the slopes of Doi Mae U-Khor, where Mexican sunflowers make the hillsides glow butter-yellow in November and early December. Much of the roadside elsewhere is bordered by these same flowers at this time of year, but the sheer concentration of blooms at Mae U-Khor, combined with sweeping views over endless ridges to the west, make it worth sharing the experience with the inevitable tour groups. Around 15km further down the same road from the Hmong village of Ban Mae U-Khor, **Mae Surin Waterfall** in Nam Tok Mae Surin National Park (B200) is arguably the most spectacular waterfall in the whole country, the waters hurtling over a cliff and plunging almost 100m before crashing on huge boulders and foaming down a steep gorge. The kind topography of the region allows a great view of the falls from directly in front, but the best view, from below, requires a steep and at times precarious three-hour hike down and back from the well-appointed **campsite**. Basic food

△ Buatong fields, Mae Hong Son

is available from a stall at the campsite (Nov–Feb). To reach the park without your own transport, join a tour from Mae Hong Son.

Back on the main road, 35km north of Khun Yuam, a right turn leads up to **Mae Ko Vafe** – a Thai rendition of "microwave", referring to the transmitters that grace the mountain's peak; the paved road climbs for 10km to a Hmong village, where the fantastic view west stretches far into Burma. Around 15km beyond this turn-off Highway 108 climbs to a roadside **viewing area**, with fine vistas, this time to the east, of the sheer, wooded slopes and the Pha Bong Dam in the valley far below. Subsequently the road makes a dramatic, headlong descent towards Mae Hong Son, passing the **Ban Pha Bong** hot springs, 7km north of the viewing area (11km before Mae Hong Son). These have been turned into a small spa complex, with private rooms with hot spring-water baths, traditional masseurs and a restaurant.

Mae Hong Son and around

MAE HONG SON, capital of Thailand's northwesternmost province, sports more nicknames than a town of just under ten thousand people seems to deserve. In Thai, it's Muang Sam Mok, the "City of Three Mists": set deep in a mountain valley, Mae Hong Son is often swathed in mist, the quality of which differs according to the three seasons (in the hot season it's mostly composed of unpleasant smoke from burning fields). In former times, the town, which wasn't connected to the outside world by a paved road until 1968, was known as "Siberia" to the troublesome politicians and government officials who were exiled here from Bangkok. Nowadays, thanks to its mountainous surroundings, it's increasingly billed as the "Switzerland of Thailand": eighty percent of Mae Hong Son province is on a slope of more than 45 degrees.

To match the hype, Mae Hong Son has become one of the most popular tourist centres in the country, sporting, alongside dozens of backpacker guest houses, several luxury hotels for Thai and farang package tourists who like their city comforts. Most backpackers come here for **trekking** (see box opposite) and day-hiking in the beautiful countryside, others just for the cool climate and lazy upcountry atmosphere. The town is still small enough and sleepy enough to hole up in for a quiet week, though in the high season (Nov–Feb) swarms of minibuses disgorge tour groups who hunt in packs through the souvenir stalls and fill up the restaurants.

Mae Hong Son was founded in 1831 as a training camp for elephants captured from the surrounding jungle for the princes of Chiang Mai (Jong Kham Lake, in the southeastern part of the modern town, served as the elephants' bathing spot). The hard work of hunting and rearing the royal elephants was done by the **Thai Yai** (aka Shan), who account for half the population of the province and bring a strong Burmese flavour to Mae Hong Son's temples and festivals. The other half of the province's population is made up of various hill tribes (a large number of Karen, as well as Lisu, Hmong and Lawa), with a tiny minority of Thais concentrated in the provincial capital.

The latest immigrants to the province are **Burmese refugees**: as well as rural Karen, driven across the border when the Burmese army razed their villages (see box on p.312), many urban students and monks, who formed the hard core of the brutally repressed 1988 uprising, fled to this area to join the resistance forces. The refugee camps between Mae Hong Son and the border generally

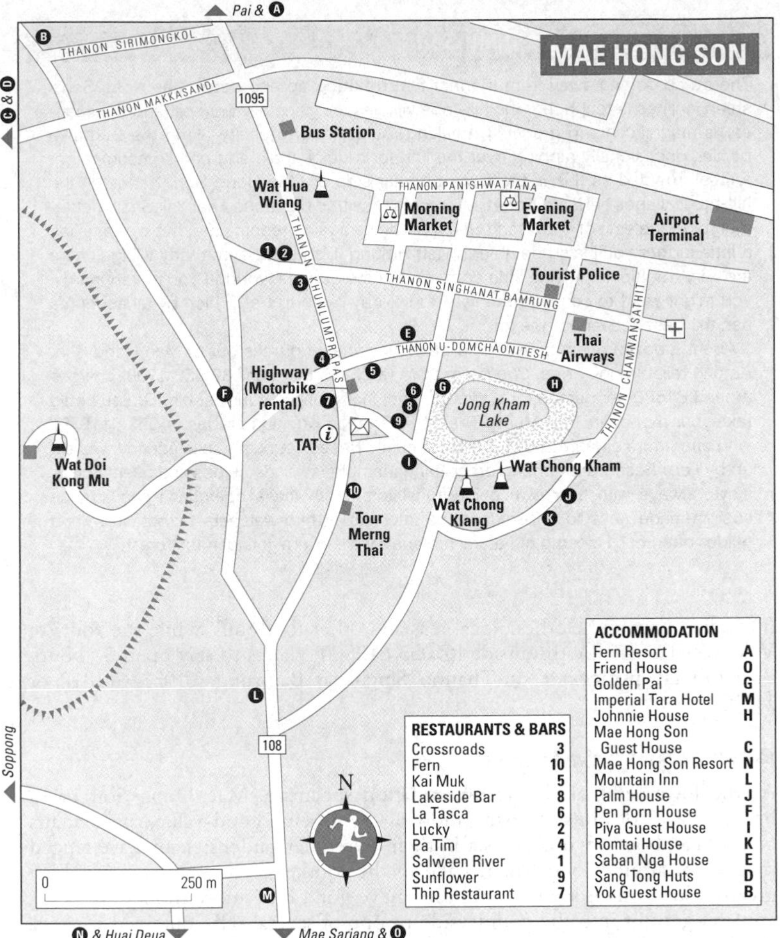

do not encourage visitors as they've got quite enough on their plates without having to entertain onlookers.

Arrival and information

Running north to south, Mae Hong Son's main drag, Thanon Khunlumprapas, is intersected by Thanon Singhanat Bamrung at the traffic lights in the centre of town. Arriving at Mae Hong Son's **bus station**, towards the north end of Thanon Khunlumprapas, puts you within walking distance of the central guest houses. Tuk-tuks (B50) run from the **airport** to the centre, though if you're already booked into a resort or hotel, a car or minibus should pick you up. Motorbike taxis also operate in and around the town: the local transport hub is the north side of the morning market.

TAT have a helpful office (daily 8.30am–4.30pm; ⓣ053 612982–3, ⓦwww.travelmaehongson.org) opposite the post office on Khunlumprapas. In the same building is a government-sponsored shop selling some attractive fabrics

Trekking around Mae Hong Son

There's no getting away from the fact that **trekking** up and down Mae Hong Son's steep inclines is tough, but the hill-tribe villages are generally unspoilt and the scenery is magnificent. To the west, trekking routes tend to snake along the Burmese border, occasionally nipping over the line for a quick thrill, and can sometimes get a little crowded as this is the more popular side of Mae Hong Son. Nearly all the hill-tribe villages here are Karen, interspersed with indigenous Thai Yai (Shan) settlements. To the east of Mae Hong Son the Karens again predominate, but by travelling a little further you'll also be able to visit Hmong, Lisu and Lahu; many villages here are very traditional, having little contact with the outside world. If you're very hardy, you might want to consider the five- to six-day route to Pai, which by all accounts has the best scenery of the lot.

About a dozen guest houses and travel agencies run treks out of Mae Hong Son. Among reliable operators, *Sunflower Café* (Ⓣ053 620549 or 089 950 1798) charges around B1500 per person for a two-day trek in a group of four people. Or you could take your money to Tour Merng Thai at 89 Thanon Khunlumprapas (Ⓣ053 611979), who offer tours organized by CBT (Community Based Tourism). This agency was set up by *Fern Resort* and among other things, employs village guides and offers homestays, always with their own guide-translators. Both these operations can arrange custom-made treks to encompass the interests of bird-watchers or botanists, and guides often build a camp of natural materials while overnighting in the forest.

(including bags and clothes), local teas and other foodstuffs, while the Tourism Volunteer Centre booth outside (Ⓣ053 612800) claims to stay open 24 hours. The **tourist police** are on Thanon Singhanat Bamrung (Ⓣ053 611812 or 1155).

Accommodation

At the lower end of the accommodation spectrum, Mae Hong Son has a healthy roster of **guest houses**, most of them being good-value, rustic affairs built of bamboo or wood and set in their own quiet gardens; many have ranged themselves around Jong Kham Lake in the southeast corner of town, which greatly adds to their scenic appeal. If you've got a little more money to spend, you can get out into the countryside to one of several self-contained **resorts**, though staying at one of these is not exactly a wilderness experience – they're really designed for weekending Thais travelling by car. Finally, several **luxury hotels**, notably the *Imperial Tara* on the southern edge of town, have latched onto the area's meteoric development, offering all the usual international-standard facilities.

Guest houses

Friend House 20 Thanon Pradit Jongkham Ⓣ053 620119. Smart and clean modern teak and concrete house with upstairs balcony giving views of the lake. Larger rooms have hot-water bathrooms, smaller ones share hot showers. ❶–❸

Johnnie House Thanon U-Domchaonitesh Ⓣ053 611667. In a small compound by the lake, this clean, friendly place has sturdy, airy wooden rooms which share hot showers, as well as bright, concrete affairs with en-suite hot-water bathrooms. ❶–❷

Mae Hong Son Guest House 295 Thanon Makkasandi Ⓣ053 612510 or 089 635 7045. Relaxing old-timer on the western outskirts of town with friendly staff. You'll get an en-suite hot-water bathroom, either in a large attractive bungalow or in one of the simpler rooms. ❶–❹

Palm House 22/1 Thanon Chamnansathit Ⓣ053 614022. Biggish, tiled rooms with cable TV set back behind the temples to the south of the lake. Fan ❷, air-con ❸

Pen Porn House 16/1 Thanon Padunomuaytaw Ⓣ & Ⓕ053 611577. Smart, clean, well-maintained, motel-like doubles with fans and hot showers, round a small, shady garden. ❷

Piya Guest House 1/1 Thanon Khunlumprapas ⓣ053 611260, ⓕ053 612308. Friendly, well-run, hotel-like guest house, boasting spacious rooms with hot-water bathrooms and air-con in a lush garden beside the lake. ❹

Romtai House 22 Thanon Chamnansathit ⓣ053 612437. Spacious, well-maintained rooms with friendly owner, rambling garden and lotus pond. Fan ❷, air-con ❸

Saban Nga House 14 Thanon U-Domchaonitesh ⓣ053 612280. Clean and central, with airy, rattan-walled rooms and shared hot showers. ❶

Sang Tong Huts Down a small lane opposite *Mae Hong Son Guest House* off Thanon Makkasandi ⓣ053 620680, ⓦwww.sangtonghuts.com. Upmarket, German-run guest house, offering tasteful rustic chic on a steep, jungly slope on the edge of town. Roofed with traditional, thatched *tong teung* leaves, and decorated with rugs and tapestries, the "huts" have verandas, mosquito nets on the beds and large, attractively tiled bathrooms with hot water. Home-baked bread and cakes are served in a simple, open-sided seating area around an open fire. ❸–❼

Yok Guest House Thanon Sirimongkol ⓣ053 611532 or 086 611 5819. Quiet and welcoming place in a small walled compound on the northwest side of town, offering functional but clean and good-value concrete rooms with fans and en-suite hot-water bathrooms. One air-con room too. Fan ❷, air-con ❸

Resorts

Fern Resort 6km south of town on Highway 108, then signposted 2km east on paved minor road ⓣ053 686110–1, ⓦwww.fernresort.info. The best resort around Mae Hong Son, an eco-friendly place employing local villagers as much as possible. In a peaceful, shady valley, a brook runs through the beautiful grounds, past stylish cottages with hot water, air-con and verandas (no phones or TV). There's an attractive swimming pool, and nature trails in the surrounding Mae Surin National Park; regular free shuttle bus to the *Fern Restaurant* in town. Book ahead through their website to be sure of a place. ❼

Golden Pai & Suite Resort 6km north of town, signposted to the left of the road towards Pai ⓣ053 612265–6, ⓦwww.goldenpai.com. Two compounds under the same ownership, with clean, well-appointed, air-con chalets arranged around smart swimming pools in pleasant grounds; mud treatments, mineral baths and saunas are available at the nearby Pooklon spa. ❻

Mae Hong Son Resort 6km south of town, on the road to Huai Deua ⓣ053 684138, ⓕ053 684137. In a relaxing spot by the Pai River, a friendly and quietly efficient place, with riverside chalets or rooms in the grounds behind. The room rate, at the lower end of this price code, includes cooked breakfast. ❼

Hotels

Imperial Tara Hotel 149 Moo 8, Tambon Pang Moo ⓣ053 684444–49, ⓦwww.imperialhotels.com. On the south side of the town by the turn-off for Huai Deua, this grand building is set in pretty landscaped gardens, overlooked by spacious rooms featuring satellite TV and mini-bar; there's a swimming pool, sauna and fitness centre, too. ❽

Mountain Inn 112 Thanon Khunlumprapas ⓣ053 611802-3, ⓦwww.mhsmountaininn.com. Large, neat and tasteful rooms with air-con, hot-water bathrooms, carpeting and TV, set round a flower-strewn garden. ❼

The Town

Beyond the typical concrete boxes in the centre, Mae Hong Son sprawls lazily across the valley floor and up the lower slopes of Doi Kong Mu to the west, trees and untidy vegetation poking through at every possible opportunity to remind you that open country is only a stone's throw away. Plenty of traditional Thai Yai buildings remain – wooden shophouses with balconies, shutters and corrugated-iron roof decorations, homes thatched with *tong teung* leaves and fitted with herringbone-patterned window panels – though they take a severe beating from the weather and may eventually be replaced by inexpensive, all-engulfing concrete.

Mae Hong Son's classic picture-postcard view is its twin nineteenth-century Burmese-style temples from the opposite, north shore of Jong Kham Lake, their gleaming white and gold chedis and the multi-tiered roofs and spires of their viharns reflected in the water. In the viharn of **Wat Chong Kham** is a huge, intricately carved sermon throne, decorated with the *dharmachakra* (Wheel of

Poy Sang Long

Mae Hong Son's most famous and colourful festival is **Poy Sang Long**, held over the first weekend of April, which celebrates the ordination into the monkhood, for the duration of the schools' long vacation, of Thai Yai boys between the ages of seven and fourteen. Similar rituals take place in other northern Thai towns at this time, but the Mae Hong Son version is given a unique flavour by its Thai Yai elements. On the first day of the festival, the boys have their heads shaved and are anointed with turmeric and dressed up in the colours of a Thai Yai prince, with traditional accessories: long white socks, plenty of jewellery, a headcloth decorated with fresh flowers, a golden umbrella and heavy face make-up. They are then announced to the guardian spirit of the town and taken around the temples. The second day brings general merry-making and a spectacular parade, headed by a drummer and a richly decorated riderless horse, which is believed to carry the town's guardian spirit. The boys, still in their finery, are each carried on the shoulders of a chaperone, accompanied by musicians and bearers of traditional offerings. In the evening, the novices tuck into a sumptuous meal, waited on by their parents and relatives, before the ordination ceremony in the temple on the third day.

Law) in coloured glass on gold; the building on the left has been built around the temple's most revered Buddha image, the benign, inscrutable Luang Pho To. Next door, **Wat Chong Klang** is famous for its paintings on glass, which are said to have been painted by artists from Mandalay over 100 years ago; they're displayed over three walls on the left-hand side of the viharn. The first two walls behind the monks' dais (on which women are not allowed to stand) depict *Jataka* stories from the Buddha's previous incarnations in their lower sections, and the life of the Buddha himself in their upper, while the third wall is devoted entirely to the Buddha's life. A room to the left houses an unforgettable collection of **teak statues**, brought over from Burma in the middle of the nineteenth century. The dynamically expressive, often humorous figures are characters from the *Vessantara Jataka*, but the woodcarvers have taken as their models people from all levels of traditional Burmese society, including toothless emaciated peasants, butch tattooed warriors and elegant upper-class ladies.

The town's vibrant, smelly **morning market**, just south of the bus station, is worth dragging your bones up at dawn to see. People from the local hill tribes often come down to buy and sell, and the range of produce is particularly weird and wonderful, including, in season, porcupine meat, displayed with quills to prove its authenticity. Next door, the many-gabled viharn of **Wat Hua Wiang** shelters, under a lace canopy, one of the most beautiful Buddha images in northern Thailand, the **Chao Palakeng**. Copied from a famous statue in Mandalay, the strong, serene bronze has the regal clothing and dangling ears typical of Burmese Buddhas. Though the town is generally quiet during the day while visitors are out exploring the hills, the main streets come alive in the evening as **handicraft stalls** display colourful bolts of cloth, lacquerware, Burmese puppets, ceramics and jewellery.

For a godlike overview of the area, drive or climb up to **Wat Doi Kong Mu** on the steep hill to the west. From the temple's two chedis, which enshrine the ashes of respected nineteenth-century Thai Yai monks, you can look down on the town and out across the sleepy farming valley north and south. Behind the chedis, the viharn contains an unusual and highly venerated white marble image of the Buddha, surrounded in gold flames. If you've got the energy, trek up to the bot on the summit, where the view extends over the Burmese mountains to the west.

Eating and drinking

Nobody comes to Mae Hong Son for the **food** – the available options are limited, although a few good restaurants have sprung up in order to cater specifically to foreigners. There's a small **evening market** on Thanon Panishwatana, along from the day market, that closes around 8pm, and several stalls selling tasty snacks cluster around Jong Kham Lake in the evening.

Crossroads 16 Singhanat Bamrung. Appropriately named as it is located at the junction of the town's two main roads, this welcoming place serves up American breakfasts (B90), great shakes, good coffee and draught Singha beer, and is a cool place to chill out in the evenings.

Fern 87 Thanon Khunlumprapas. A big, showy, tourist-oriented eating place, with a nice terrace and a good reputation for its Thai food, such as spicy coconut shoot salad (B65).

Kai Muk Thanon U-Domchaonitesh. Attractive, efficient and popular, with a huge variety of excellent Thai dishes on its menu.

Lakeside Bar 2/3 Thanon Khunlumprapas. A good place for a drink accompanied by some tasty Thai dishes. Here you can relax to the sounds of a live band playing Western and Thai pop and folk music, on a terrace overlooking Jong Kham Lake and the fairy lights on the temples behind. There's also a basic buffet in the evening for B69.

La Tasca Thanon Khunlumprapas. Reasonably authentic Italian restaurant with home-made pizzas and a long menu of familiar pasta dishes, including home-made gnocchi, fettuccini and lasagna (B125).

Lucky 5 Thanon Singhanat Bamrung. Next to *Salween River*, this place serves cheap rice dishes at B30, grilled fish sold by weight, and a good range of cocktails in a classic travellers' haunt.

Pa Tim Thanon Khunlumprapas. Cheap and cheerful place that packs in budget travellers with dishes like vegetable curry (B30) and chicken and cashew nuts (B60).

Salween River Just west of the main traffic lights off Thanon Khunlumprapas. English- and Thai-run restaurant and bar, dishing up a wide variety of Western faves, such as soups, baked potatoes, good burgers and chicken cordon bleu, as well as some delicious Thai food. Most dishes are around B40-80.

Sunflower 116/115 Soi 3, Thanon Khunlumprapas. A small, quiet, indoor-outdoor café with a relaxing fountain, serving a few Thai favourites and good Western food including excellent breakfasts with home-made bread and filter coffee.

Thip Restaurant Next to *Lakeside Bar*. Wide range of tasty Thai food, including northern specialities and local freshwater food. Great views of the lake, the temples and the mountains behind at lunchtime.

Listings

Airlines The Thai Airways office is at 71 Thanon Singhanat Bamrung ☎053 611367 or 053 612220. Nok Air can be contacted at their national call centre (☎1318 or 02 900 9955). PB Air, which flies non-stop Bangkok–Mae Hong Son, has an office at 46 Thanon Nives Pisarn (☎053 614369–70), just in front of the airport entrance.

Airport For flight information, call ☎053 612057.

Exchange The airport has a bank currency exchange (daily 10am–5pm). There are also several banks and exchange booths along Thanon Khunlumprapas.

Immigration office On Thanon Khunlumprapas north of the town centre (Mon–Fri 8.30am–4.30pm, plus some Sat & Sun; ☎053 612106).

Internet access Several nameless cybercafés cluster around the post office on Thanon Khunlumprapas.

Mail and telephones The post office is on Thanon Khunlumprapas, with cardphones outside and at the 7-11 supermarket across the road where you can buy the phonecards.

Around Mae Hong Son

Once you've exhausted the few obvious sights in town, the first decision you'll have to grapple with is whether to visit the **"long-neck" women**. Our advice is don't, though many travellers do. Less controversial, **boat and raft trips** on the babbling Pai River are fun, and the roaring **Pha Sua Falls** and the Kuomintang village of **Mae Aw** make a satisfying day out. If all that sounds too easy, Mae Hong Son is now Thailand's third-largest centre for **trekking**. Other feasible targets include the hot springs at Ban Pha Bong (see p.404) and, further out, Mae Surin Waterfall (see p.403) and Tham Lot (see p.413).

Local transport, in the form of songthaews from the morning market, is thinly spread and unreliable, so for all of these excursions it's best to rent your own vehicle or join an organized tour through your guest house or one of the many travel agents in town. Rose Garden Tours, for example, at 86/4 Thanon Khunlumprapas (Ⓣ053 611577, Ⓦwww.rosegarden-tours.com), offers a wide range of day-trips for B700–1500 per person, while CBT (Community Based Tourism; see p.406) make sure your money goes to local people. Highway at 67/2 Thanon Khunlumprapas rents out **motorbikes** for B150, and several places on the main street rent out **four-wheel drives**, as does Front & Fern (Ⓣ081 602 7558) at the airport, which has vehicles beginning at B1000 per day.

Nai Soi

The original and largest village of "long-neck" Padaung women in the Mae Hong Son area, **NAI SOI**, 28km northwest of town, has effectively been turned into a human zoo for snap-happy tourists, with an entrance fee of B250 per person. The "long necks" pose in front of their huts and looms, every now

"Long-neck" women

The most famous – and notorious – of the Mae Hong Son area's spectacles is its contingent of **"long-neck" women**, members of the tiny Padaung tribe of Burma who have come across to Thailand to escape Burmese repression. Though the women's necks appear to be stretched to 30cm and more by a column of brass rings, the "long-neck" tag is a technical misnomer: a *National Geographic* team once X-rayed one of the women and found that instead of stretching out her neck, the pressure of eleven pounds of brass had simply squashed her collarbones and ribs. Girls of the tribe start wearing the rings from about the age of six, adding one or two each year up to the age of sixteen or so. Once fastened, the rings are for life, for to remove a full stack would eventually cause the collapse of the neck and suffocation – in the past, removal was a punishment for adultery. Despite the obvious discomfort, and the laborious daily task of cleaning and drying the rings, the tribeswomen, when interviewed, say that they're used to their plight and are happy to be continuing the tradition of their people.

The **origin** of the ring-wearing ritual remains unclear, despite an embarrassment of plausible explanations. Padaung legend says that the mother of their tribe was a dragon with a long, beautiful neck, and that their unique custom is an imitation of her. Tour guides will tell you the practice is intended to enhance the women's beauty. In Burma, where it is now outlawed as barbaric, it's variously claimed that ring-wearing arose out of a need to protect women from tiger attacks or to deform the wearers so that the Burmese court would not kidnap them for concubines.

In spite of their handicap (they have to use straws to drink, for example), the women are able to carry out some kind of an ordinary life: they can marry and have children, and they're able to weave and sew, although these days they spend most of their time posing like circus freaks for photographs. Only half of the Padaung women now lengthen their necks; left to its own course, the custom would probably die out, but the influence of tourism may well keep it alive for some time yet. The villages in Mae Hong Son, and now also in Chiang Rai Province, where they live, are set up by Thai entrepreneurs as a money-making venture (all visitors are charged B150–250 to enter these villages), and though tour guides may tell you that the menfolk are "out working in the fields", in fact the women are separated from their husbands, whose short necks have no pulling power for tourists.

and then getting it together to stage a good-luck song – all a visitor can do is stand and stare in embarrassed silence or click away with a camera. All in all it's a disturbing spectacle, offering no opportunity to discover anything about Padaung culture. At least, contrary to many reports, the "long necks" are not held as slaves in the village: the entrance fee is handled by the Karenni National Progressive Party, a Kayah (Karenni) rebel group to whom the Padaung, in their precarious plight as refugees, have offered their services (the KNPP is fighting for the independence of Burma's Kayah state, where the Padaung come from). Part of the fee is used to support the KNPP, and some goes to help improve conditions in the village and the adjacent Kayah refugee settlement, while the "long necks" themselves are each paid a living wage of about B1500 per month. The main beneficiaries, however, are the tour operators.

Without your own transport, you have to hitch up with an expensive tour (about B800/person, including entrance fee) from a travel agent in town. By motorbike or jeep, head north along Route 1095 for 2km and turn left after the police box; cross the bridge over the Pai River, turn left at the next village, Ban Sop Soi, and continue for another 10km.

Trips on the Pai River

Scenic **boat trips** on the Pai River start from Huai Deua, 7km southwest of town near the *Mae Hong Son Resort*. There's no need to go on an organized tour: take a motorbike taxi, tuk-tuk or one of the infrequent songthaews from Mae Hong Son market to Huai Deua and approach the owners at the boat station. Twenty minutes downriver from Huai Deua (B500, plus B250 admission charge to the village) will get you to **Ban Nam Phiang Din**, where a dozen or so "long-neck" women display themselves in a setup similar to that at Nai Soi. You're better off enjoying the river for its own sake, as it scythes its way between cliffs and forests towards the nearby Burmese border, or travelling upriver to **Soppong** (B600), a pretty, quiet Thai Yai village 5km due west of Mae Hong Son (not to be confused with the Soppong on Route 1095, northeast of Mae Hong Son). **Elephant-rides** into the surrounding jungle, for B400–500 per hour for two people, can be arranged next to the boat station.

A small stretch of the Pai River between **Sop Soi**, 10km northwest of Mae Hong Son, and Soppong is clear enough of rocks to allow safe clearance for bamboo **rafts**. The journey takes two hours at the most, as the rafts glide down the gentle river, partly hemmed in by steep wooded hills. Most of Mae Hong Son's travel agents can fix this trip up for you, including travel to Sop Soi and from Soppong, charging around B800 per raft (two passengers).

Pha Sua Falls and Mae Aw

North of Mae Hong Son, a trip to Pha Sua Falls and the border village of Mae Aw takes in some spectacular and varied countryside. Your best options are to rent a motorbike or join a tour – agents typically charge around B600 per person for a one-day excursion, which includes a city tour and a visit to the highly overrated Fish Cave – as there are only occasional songthaews to Mae Aw from the market in the morning, and no guarantees for the return journey to Mae Hong Son. Under your own steam, the best route is to head north for 17km on Route 1095 (ignore the first signpost for Pha Sua, after 10km) and then, after a long, steep descent, turn left onto a side road, paved at first, which passes through an idyllic rice valley and the Thai Yai village of **Ban Bok Shampae**. About 9km from the turn-off you'll reach **Pha Sua Falls**, a wild, untidy affair, which crashes down in several cataracts through a dark, overhung cut in the limestone. The waterfall is in full roar in October after the rainy season, but has plenty of water all year round. Take care when swimming, as several people have been swept to their deaths here.

Above the falls the paved road climbs precipitously, giving glorious, broad vistas of both Thai and Burmese mountains, before reaching the unspectacular half-Hmong, half-Thai Yai village of **Naphapak** after 11km. A decent, largely flat stretch covers the last 7km to **MAE AW** (aka Ban Rak Thai), a settlement of Kuomintang anti-Communist Chinese refugees (see p.431), right on the Burmese border. In the past, this area saw fighting between the Kuomintang and the army of Khun Sa, the opium warlord who, having been kicked out of the Mae Salong area by the Thai army in 1983, set up base somewhere in the uncharted mountains across the border northeast of Mae Aw. The road up here was built by the Thai military to help the fight against the opium trade and all has been quiet for several years. Mae Aw is the highest point on the border that visitors can reach, and provides a fascinating window on Kuomintang life. The tight ring of hills around the village heightens the feeling of being in another country: delicate, bright-green tea bushes line the slopes, while Chinese ponies wander the streets of long, unstilted bamboo houses. In the central marketplace on the north side of the village reservoir, shops sell great bags of Oolong and Chian Chian teas, as well as dried mushrooms.

Route 1095: Mae Hong Son to Chiang Mai

Route 1095, the 243-kilometre northern route between Mae Hong Son and Chiang Mai, is every bit as wild and scenic as the southern route through Mae Sariang – if anything it has more mountains to negotiate, with a greater contrast between the sometimes straggly vegetation of the slopes and the thickly cultivated valleys. Much of the route was established by the Japanese army to move troops and supplies into Burma after its invasion of Thailand during World War II. The labour-intensive job of paving every hairpin bend was completed in the 1990s, but ongoing repair work can still give you a nasty surprise if you're riding a motorbike. If you're setting off along this route from Chiang Mai by public transport, catch one of the four daily buses to Mae Hong Son via Pai from the Arcade station.

Mae Suya

The first stretch north out of Mae Hong Son weaves up and down the west face of Doi Pai Kit (1082m), giving great views over the lush valley to the north of town. Beyond the turn-off for Mae Aw (see above) and the much-touted but unspectacular Fish Cave, the highway climbs eastward through many hairpin bends before levelling out to give tantalizing glimpses through the trees of the Burmese mountains to the north, then passes through a hushed valley of paddy fields, surrounded by echoing crags, to reach the Thai Yai/Kuomintang village of **MAE SUYA**, 40km from Mae Hong Son. Take the left turning by the police box, 3km east of the village to reach *Wilderness Lodge* after a further 1km of dirt road. Set in wild countryside, this friendly, laid-back guest house offers primitive bungalows (❷) and dorm beds (B70) in the barn-like main house, and does a wide range of vegetarian and meat-based Thai food. However, it often closes during the wet season.

The owner of the lodge can give you directions and maps for cave exploration and beautiful wilderness day walks through the mountains to hill-tribe villages. Two hours' walk to the north, **Tham Pha Daeng** is a pretty, 1600-metre-long cave (open Nov–May) with, like Tham Lot (see below), ancient coffins; apart from a few low crawls, the journey through the cave is relatively easy. To the south beyond Route 1095, **Tham Nam Lang**, one of the most capacious caves in the world, has a towering entrance chamber which anyone can appreciate, although the spectacular 9km beyond it demands full-on caving, again in the dry season only, and the proper equipment.

Soppong and Tham Lot

The small market town of **SOPPONG**, 68km from Mae Hong Son in the district of Pang Ma Pha (which is sometimes used on signposts), gives access to the area's most famous cave, **Tham Lot**, 9km north in **BAN THAM**. There's no public transport along the gentle paved forest road to the village, so if you haven't got your own wheels, you'll have to hitch, walk or rent a motorbike taxi (B60). Due to its proximity to Pai, Soppong has become popular for day-trippers, but note that there are no banks or ATMs in town.

Turn right in Ban Tham to find the entrance to the **Tham Lot Nature Education Station** set up to look after the cave, where you have to hire a local guide with lantern for B100 (1–4 people). A short walk through the forest brings you to the entrance of Tham Lot, where the Lang River begins a 600-metre subterranean journey through the cave. Access to the various parts of the cave depends on the time of year and how much rain there has been, and may involve hiring a bamboo raft for some or all of your journey: for most of the year you'll need to raft from Doll to Coffin Cave (B100/person), while at the driest times it may be possible to wade, and at the highest water levels it may be necessary to walk around to the exit and get to the last part, Coffin Cave, from there. Normally two hours should allow you enough time for travelling through the broad, airy tunnel, and for the main attraction, climbing up into the sweaty caverns in the roof – be sure not to touch any of the cave formations.

The first of these, **Column Cavern**, 100m from the entrance on the right, is dominated by a twenty-metre-high cave stalagmite snaking up towards the ceiling. Another 50m on the left, bamboo ladders lead up into **Doll Cave**, which has a glistening, pure white wall and a weird red and white formation shaped like a Wurlitzer organ; deep inside, stalagmites look like dolls. Just before the vast exit from the cave, wooden ladders on the left lead up into **Coffin Cave**, named after the remains of a dozen crude log coffins discovered here, one of them preserved to its full length of 5m. Hollowed out from tree trunks, they are similar to those found in many of the region's caves: some are raised 2m off the ground by wooden supporting poles, and some still contained bones, pottery and personal effects when they were discovered. These are now on display in a small museum by the main entrance. The coffins are between 1200 and 2200 years old, and local people attribute them to *phi man*, the cave spirits. A twenty-minute nature trail will bring you back to the main entrance, but it's worth hanging round the cave's exit at sunset, when hundreds of thousands of tiny black chirruping swifts pour into the cave in an almost solid column, to find their beds for the night.

Practicalities

Cave Lodge (Ⓣ053 617203, Ⓦwww.cavelodge.com; ❶–❺), on the other side of Ban Tham from the cave, makes an excellent and friendly base for exploring the area. The owners have plenty of useful information about Tham Lot and some of the two hundred other **caves** in the region, and organize **guided trips** through the more interesting ones when there's enough demand. They also offer **kayaking** trips through Tham Lot, plus 6km of fun rapids, at B490 for a couple of hours, and three-day trips on the Pai River in the dry season. Maps for self-guided walking from the lodge to local Karen, Lahu and Lisu villages are available, as well as four local licensed guides for full-on **trekking** (typically B1700 for 3 days, minimum 4 people). At a nearby Karen village, renowned for its traditional weaving, you can arrange elephant-riding or bamboo-rafting or hire a guide to take you to one of the local caves. There's a swimming hole right in front of the lodge, a funky communal area for eating and hanging out, and the kitchen bakes its own bread, pizza and cakes. Dorm beds here are B60, and the wooden rooms and bungalows, some with shared hot showers and others with their own bathrooms, are scattered over the overgrown hillside.

On the main road at the western end of Soppong, *Jungle Guest House* (Ⓣ053 617099; ❷–❸) is the most popular of several places in town, and can give advice on local walks to caves and Lisu villages or organize inexpensive trekking trips to Lisu, Lahu and Karen settlements further to the south. Accommodation here is in simple bamboo huts with shared bathrooms (hot showers in winter), or some sturdier teak bungalows with hot-water bathrooms attached; the food, including northern Thai and Western specialities and home-made bread and jam, is great. A short walk east of Soppong's bus stop and a little upmarket, *Little Eden Guest House* (Ⓣ053 617054, Ⓦwww.littleeden-guesthouse.com; ❸–❻) has neat, sturdy bungalows with their own hot-water bathrooms, in a pretty garden with a decent-sized swimming pool, sloping down to the Lang River and a relaxing riverside pavilion; plenty of services such as motorbike rental, Internet access and tours and treks are on offer. A further 500m east of Soppong on the main road, *Northern Hill Guest House* (Ⓣ053 617136, Ⓦwww.northernhillgh.com; ❸–❺) is another appealing alternative, with stylish furnishings and fittings in the good-sized rooms, which have great views from the hillside.

Pai

Beyond Soppong, the road climbs through the last of Mae Hong Son province's wild landscape before descending into the broad, gentle valley of **PAI**, 43km from Soppong. Once treated as a stopover on the tiring journey to Mae Hong Son, Pai is now a destination in its own right, and travellers settle into the town's laid-back, New-Agey feel for weeks or even months. There's nothing special to see in Pai, but you can partake of all manner of outdoor activities, courses and holistic therapies – even retail therapy at the art studios, bookstores, leather and jewellery shops – and the guest houses and restaurants have tailored themselves to the steady flow of travellers who make the four-hour bus journey out from Chiang Mai. The small town's traditional buildings spread themselves liberally over the west bank of the Pai River, but everything is within walking range of the bus station at the north end. On the town's main drag, Thanon Rungsiyanon, an odd mix of hill-tribe people, shrouded Thai Muslims and Westerners mingle together.

Arrival, information and getting around

There are currently no **flights** to Pai, but the disused airstrip to the north of town has recently been repaved and a small terminal has been built, so it is likely that planes will soon start going and coming to and from Bangkok (and possibly Chiang Mai), shattering the peace of the Pai Valley. Pai's **bus station** is near the junction of Thanon Rungsiyanon and Thanon Chaisongkhram;

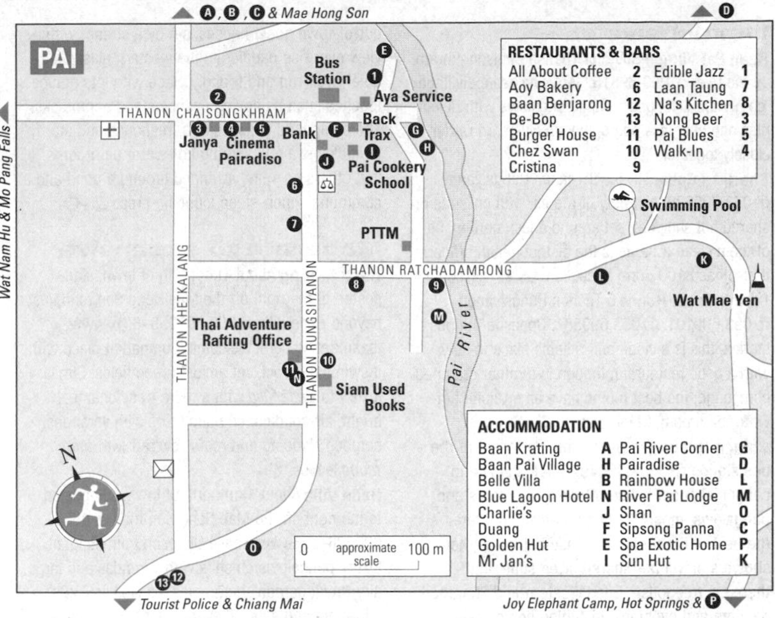

motorbike **taxis** are available at the junction itself, air-con minibus taxis on the east side of the bus station. As well as public buses, there are **air-con minibuses from Chiang Mai** (8 daily in high season, 4–6 daily low season; 3hr; B150, or B180 VIP with extra legroom), which will pick you up from your hotel or guest house; they're operated by Aya Service, a travel agency on Thanon Chaisongkhram (ⓣ053 699940 or 053 699888 in Pai; 053 820886–7 in Chiang Mai). The same company offers an overnight minibus service directly from Pai to Chiang Khong (B550), arriving in time to get a visa and take the morning boat to Louang Phabang. Aya Service is also the best place in town to **rent motorbikes**, charging from B80 a day, not including insurance, which is an extra B40–80. Several places in town rent out **mountain bikes** (B50–80), including *Duang Guest House*.

At the **post office** at the southern end of Thanon Khet Kalang, you can make international calls. Several shops near the intersection of Thanon Rungsiyanon and Thanon Ratchadamrong offer **Internet access**. The **tourist police** (ⓣ1155) are just south of town, on the road to Chiang Mai. Among several **bookshops** in Pai, the orderly Siam Used Books, on Thanon Rungsiyanon, has a good selection. If you plan to spend much time here, pick up a copy of *The Paioneer* (B190), a small but useful **guidebook** to the town compiled by Thomas Kasper, which is sold in many guest houses and restaurants. An informative **website** about the town is ⓦwww.paithailand.info.

Accommodation

Coinciding with the town's soaring popularity, **guest houses** are springing up all the time. There are now over fifty within town, as well as several options in the countryside around Pai, useful for escaping the growing bustle downtown. Upmarket **resorts** have also proliferated in town and in the countryside, catering largely for Thai weekenders with their own transport.

Inexpensive

Baan Pai Village South of Thanon Chaisongkhram by the river ⓣ053 698152, ⓦwww.baanpaivillage.com. Attractive, good-sized bungalows with balconies and big glass doors, though clustered rather closely together. ❸

Charlie's Guest House 9 Thanon Rungsiyanon ⓣ053 699039. A variety of rooms, with en-suite or shared hot showers, set around a lush garden, all of them clean (Charlie is the district health officer); it also has B100 dorm beds. Fan ❶–❷, air-con ❹

Duang Guest House 5 Thanon Rungsiyanon ⓣ053 699101, ⓕ053 699581. Opposite the bus station, this is a clean and reliable place to stay, with a good restaurant, though in a rather cramped compound; the best rooms have an en-suite hot-water bathroom, fridge and TV. ❶–❸

Golden Hut On the river bank, northeast of the bus station ⓣ053 699949. Quiet, shady and congenial guest house offering airy rooms and bungalows, mostly of bamboo-clad concrete, the best of them with riverside balconies; hot showers are either shared or en suite, and there's a treehouse. Good Western and Thai food daytime and evenings, including home-made pizzas, as well as home-made bread, jam and yoghurt for breakfast. ❶–❸

Mr Jan's Thanon Sukhaphibun 3 ⓣ053 699554. On one of a mess of small streets behind and to the east of *Charlie's*, these quiet, simple bamboo bungalows are set in a delightfully overgrown and fragrant medicinal herb garden. Recommended massages and saunas available too. ❶

Rainbow House A short way over the Pai River bridge on the right ⓣ086 921 3528, ⓔrainbowhousepai@hotmail.com. Homely and welcoming family-run place with lots of local info. The large, very clean bamboo-clad bungalows, with comfortable beds and en-suite or shared hot showers, stand round a small, pretty garden and pond. ❷

River Pai Lodge Down a lane on the south side of the main bridge. Helpful budget establishment, offering mostly bamboo stilted huts around a large lawn, priced according to distance from the river, with smart shared toilets and hot showers. ❶

Shan Guest House Thanon Rungsiyanon ⓣ053 699162. Almost in open countryside at the southern end of town, this is a friendly establishment in large pretty grounds, around a pond; old bamboo and wood bungalows with cold-water bathrooms are slowly being replaced by large, smart cottages with hot water en suite. ❶–❸

Sun Hut 10min out on the road heading east from town just before Wat Mae Yen on the right ⓣ053 699730, ⓔpai_thesunhut@yahoo.com. In one of the nicest locations of the out-of-town guest houses, set by a stream with a view over rice paddies to the western hills. It's a quiet, well-run and friendly place with lots of nice touches such as flowers, candles and hammocks. The compound consists of a treehouse and sturdy bungalows, a few sharing hot-water bathrooms and others en suite, arranged around a pond and a communal, open-sided lounging area. ❷–❻

Moderate to expensive

Baan Krating About 1km north of town, signposted to the right off the Mae Hong Son road, just beyond *Belle Villa* ⓣ053 698255–6, ⓦwww.baankrating.com. Welcoming upmarket place with a swimming pool, set amidst green fields. Similar luxury to *Belle Villa* with a more traditional feel: bright, air-conditioned bungalows with verandas, bamboo cladding and roofs covered with *tong teung* leaves. ❽

Belle Villa About 1km north of town, signposted to the right off the Mae Hong Son road ⓣ053 698226–7, ⓦwww.bellevillaresort.com. Elegant luxury bungalows on stilts with verandas and large, airy, "rock garden" bathrooms, as well as DVDs, mini-bars and safes. Traversed by a stream and decorated with ricefields, the grounds sport a stylish pool. Free transfers to town. ❼

Blue Lagoon Thanon Rungsiyanon ⓣ053 699998, ⓦwww.bluelagoon-pai.com. Conveniently situated in the middle of town, with good-sized and smart, hotel-style rooms that somehow lack character, but with the added bonus of a swimming pool to lounge beside. ❹

Pai River Corner Resort By the river at the western end of Thanon Chaisongkhram ⓣ053 699049, ⓦwww.pairivercorner.com. Elegant, new, Mediterranean-style resort with beautifully furnished rooms, some of which contain their own spas, set around an attractive garden. ❽

Pairadise About 10min walk out on the east side of town, across the Pai River, then first left (signposted) ⓣ089 838 7521, ⓦwww.pairadise.com. Smart and bright cabins, of brick and polished wood, with hot-water bathrooms en suite. Small artificial lake for swimming and lofty views over the valley. Home-baked bread for breakfast. Phone for free pick-up. ❹

Sipsong Panna Guest House On the Pai River north of town ⓣ053 698259, ⓔsipsongpanna33@hotmail.com. Head 1km north from town on the Mae Hong Son road, then turn right for another kilometre to the village of Wieng Neua and follow the signs. Airy Thai-style rooms with mosquito nets and stylish, hot-water bathrooms on the river, and a good vegetarian café offering Thai vegetarian cooking courses. ❺

Spa Exotic Home 6km south of Wat Mae Yen, off the minor road to the hot springs ⓣ081 917 9351. Cosy bungalows with polished-wood floors and airy spring-water bathrooms, and a pretty restaurant and sitting area, in a shady, attractive garden by the Pai River that features circular bathtubs filled with hot water piped from the nearby springs. ❺

Activities

Several undemanding **walks** can be made around Pai's broad, gently sloping valley. The easiest – one hour there and back – takes you across the river bridge on the east side of town and up the hill to Wat Mae Yen, which commands a great view over the whole district. On the way to the wat, you'll pass the town's large open-air **swimming pool** (daily 9am–7pm; adults B60, kids B20), with food and drink available, as well as fitness equipment and a pool table. To the west of town, an unpaved road (accessible by motorbike) heads out from Pai hospital, passing, after 3km, Wat Nam Hu, whose Buddha image has an unusual hinged top knot containing holy water, before gradually climbing through comparatively developed Kuomintang, Lisu and Lahu villages to **Mo Pang Falls**, with a pool for swimming, about 10km west of Pai.

Pai makes a good base for **trekking**, which can be arranged for around B700 per day (plus around B250 each for rafting and elephant-riding) through the guest houses or trekking agents, among which *Duang Guest House* and Back Trax at 17 Thanon Chaisongkhram (ⓣ053 699739, ⓔbacktraxinpai@yahoo.com) are reliable. Karen, Lisu and Lahu villages are within range, and the terrain has plenty of variety: jungles and bamboo forests, hills and flat valleys, caves and waterfalls. The area north of town, where trekking can be combined with bamboo-rafting and elephant-riding, can get a little touristy, but the countryside to the south is very quiet and unspoilt, with a wider range of hill tribes; hardened walkers could arrange a trek to Mae Hong Son, five days away to the southwest. If you just fancy a bit of **bamboo-rafting** without the trekking, Back Trax and plenty of other agents can arrange transport and a two-and-a-half-hour trip down the Pai River for around B500 for two people.

△ Elephants in the Pai River

Among several **elephant camps** around town, Joy, 5km from Wat Mae Yen on the minor road towards the hot springs, with an office at the western end of Thanon Chaisongkhram (ⓣ081 881 3923, ⓔcchiamchit@hotmail.com), offers something slightly different. You can go for an elephant ride (from B300/hour/person, minimum two people), which includes going into the river with the elephant and feeding it, as well as a free bathe in a hot spring pool, or you can volunteer to work at the camp, fetching the elephants from the jungle in the morning, cutting banana trees to feed them and swimming with them in the river.

With a little more cash to spare, you could strike up with the reliable and experienced French-run Thai Adventure Rafting (ⓣ053 699111, ⓦwww.activethailand.com/rafting; not to be confused with the imitative Pai Adventure Rafting), in an office opposite *Chez Swan* on Thanon Rungsiyanon, for a **rubber-raft trip** down the Pai River to Mae Hong Son, through gorges and class 3–4 rapids, and taking in waterfalls and hot springs. The journey takes two days, including a night at a comfortable jungle camp by the river, and costs B2000 per person; the season runs from July to the end of January, with the highest water from August to early September, and participants must be able to swim.

Accessible from the minor road south from Wat Mae Yen, 2km beyond Joy Elephant Camp, or by turning left off the main Chiang Mai road straight after the bridge over the Pai River, the **hot springs**, with one or two very hot, rough pools, aren't up to much, though there is an attractive valley campsite here. Better to go to one of the nearby **spas**, which put the piped hot water from the springs to much more productive use. Thapai Spa Camping (ⓣ089 557 6079), down a side road about 1km north of the springs, has a large and shady pool (B50) and offers massages, mud spas and various other accompanying treatments. They also offer rooms with spa-water bathrooms (as well as tents to rent), but for accommodation you're better off going to the more congenial and attractive *Spa Exotic Home* nearby (see opposite); the latter also has tiled outdoor spa tubs (B50) for non-guests.

Massages are available at several spots around town, including Janya on Thanon Chaisongkhram next to *Nong Beer* restaurant, while *Mr Jan's Guest House* is famous for its Thai and Burmese/Shan massages (B150/hour) and saunas (B50). Pai Traditional Thai Massage (PTTM), about 100m north of Thanon Ratchadamrong on a lane along the west bank of the river (ⓣ053 699121, ⓔpttm2001@hotmail.com), also has a good reputation for traditional massages (B150/hour), as well as foot, face, oil and hand massages (B200/hour) and saunas (B70), and runs three-day **massage courses** (B2500). The Pai Cookery School, near *Mr Jan's Guest House* on a backstreet parallel to Thanon Chaisongkhram (ⓣ081 706 3799), holds Thai **cooking courses** of one to three days, including a trip to the market to learn about ingredients, making six dishes, eating them and getting a free recipe book.

Eating, drinking and entertainment

As with the accommodation scene, new **restaurants** are opening practically every week, ever more sophisticated and cosmopolitan, as reflected in the recommendations below. In the evening, a popular spot for travellers to congregate is *Be-Bop*, at the south end of town opposite the landmark *View Pai Hotel*, a large, well-designed **bar** with a pool table which hosts live music. A mellower spot for a drink (with a limited food menu including sushi, which has to be ordered the day before) is *Edible Jazz*, a garden café and bar on a quiet, leafy lane off Chaisongkhram that plays "jazzy, funky, groovy music". Several other bars offer **open-mike sessions** to musicians, including *Walk In* on Thanon Chaisongkhram and the *Blue Lagoon* (see "Accommodation"). Some small restaurants along Thanon Chaisongkhram try to tempt customers in by showing **movies** in the evenings, while *Cinema Pairadiso*, on the same street, has a good selection of classic movies that you can choose from and watch in its three comfy rooms (opens midday, last show 10pm; B150 for 1 person, B200 for 2, B250 for 3–4, B300 for 5–6). Snacks and beers are also available.

All About Coffee Thanon Chaisongkhram. Superb coffee (from B35) in any variety you might want, in an atmospheric wooden shophouse hung with contemporary art (for sale). Also great breakfasts (B50–70) with home-made bread, a daily selection of home-made cakes, sandwiches and teas, hot chocolate and juices.

Aoy Bakery Thanon Rungsiyanon. It's not exactly a gourmet's paradise, but this place is very popular for a drink and a Thai or Western snack on the street outside in the evening. Its central location makes it a good spot for watching and meeting people.

Baan Benjarong South end of town, opposite the landmark *View Pai Hotel*. In a town where you can get everything from sushi to falafel, this place offers a wide variety of authentic Thai dishes – the banana flower salad (*yam hua pree*) is especially delicious (B80). The setting isn't bad either, open-sided and airy with a small terrace at the back.

Burger House Thanon Rungsiyanon. Surprisingly tasty burgers in various forms (B75–100), using imported beef, in a good central location. Closes around 9pm.

Chez Swan Thanon Rungsiyanon. Short menu of mostly international dishes such as fillet mignon (B150) and salads (B65–95) in an attractive old wooden shophouse.

Cristina Thanon Ratchadamrong, just west of the bridge over the river. Currently the best of Pai's few pizzerias, offering large, crispy pizzas at B120–140, plus great salads and pasta dishes.

Laan Taung 66/1 Thanon Rungsiyanon. If you're looking for somewhere a bit special to eat in Pai, this could be your spot. With gurgling fountains at the entrance and two inviting terraces on which to eat, this place serves up delicious Royal Thai cuisine, with daily specials and prices at around B130-400 a dish.

Na's Kitchen Thanon Ratchadamrong. One of a string of restaurants and bars near the junction with Thanon Rungsiyanon, this unpretentious place turns out tasty Thai dishes at very cheap prices.

Nong Beer Thanon Chaisongkhram. Great *khao soi* and a wide range of stir-fries, curries and salads (around B40–50) at one of Pai's longest-standing eateries.

Pai Blues Thanon Chaisongkhram. Easy-going, candlelit restaurant where, as well as a wide variety of pancakes and filling fried breakfasts, you can sample tasty Shan cuisine such as fried aubergine with tofu and pumpkin curry.

From Pai to Chiang Mai

Once out of the Pai valley, Route 1095 climbs for 35km of hairpin bends, with beautiful views north to 2175-metre Doi Chiang Dao near the top. In the cool season, with your own transport, you can witness – if you get started from Pai an hour before dawn – one of the country's most famous views of the sun rising over a sea of mist at **Huay Nam Dang National Park** (B200). The viewpoint is signposted on the left 30km out of Pai; take this turning and go on 6km to the park headquarters. Once over the 1300-metre pass, the road steeply descends the south-facing slopes in the shadow of Doi Mae Ya (2005m), before working its way along the narrow, more populous lower valleys. After 55km (at kilometre-stone 42), a left turn leads 6.5km over some roller-coaster hills to **Pong Duet hot springs**, where scalding water leaps up to four metres into the air, generating copious quantities of steam in the cool season. A few hundred metres downstream of the springs, a series of pools allow you to soak in the temperature of your choice. The last appealing detour of the route is to **Mokfa Falls** (part of Doi Suthep National Park; B200), where a cascade tumbles about 30m into a sand-fringed pool that is ideal for swimming, making an attractive setting for a break – it's 2km south of the main road, 76km from Pai. Finally, at

Mae Malai, turn right onto the busy Highway 107 and join the mad, speeding traffic for the last 34km across the wide plain of rice paddy to Chiang Mai.

Chiang Rai and the borders

The northernmost tip of Thailand, stretching from the Kok River and **Chiang Rai** to the border, is a schizophrenic place, split in two by Highway 1, Thailand's main north–south road. In the western half, rows of wild, shark's-tooth mountains jut into Burma, while to the east, low-lying rivers flow through Thailand's richest rice-farming land to the Mekong River, which forms the border with Laos here. In anticipation of Burma and Laos throwing open their frontiers to tourism, the region is well connected and has been thoroughly kitted out for visitors. Chiang Rai now has well over two thousand hotel rooms, catering mostly to upmarket fortnighters, who plough through the countryside in air-conditioned Scenicruisers in search of quaint, photogenic primitive life. What they get – fairground rides on boats and elephants, a sanitized presentation of the Golden Triangle's opium fields and colourfully dressed hill people performing artificial folkloric rituals – generally satisfies expectations, but has little to do with the harsh realities of life in the north.

Chiang Rai itself pays ever less attention to independent travellers, so although you will probably have to pass through the provincial capital, you should figure on spending most of your time in the border areas to the north, exploring the dizzy mountain heights, frenetic border towns and ancient ruins. If you're coming up **from Chiang Mai**, the quickest and most obvious route to Chiang Rai is Highway 118, a fast, 185-kilometre road that swoops through rolling hill country. A much more scenic approach, however, is to follow Highway 107 and Highway 1089 to **Tha Ton** and then complete the journey by longtail boat or bamboo raft down the **Kok River**.

To Chiang Rai via Tha Ton

Set aside two days if you're catching a bus from Chiang Mai, then a longtail along the **Kok River**, allowing for an overnight stay in **Tha Ton**. Buses between Chiang Mai's northern Chang Phuak bus station and Tha Ton take about four hours; it's best to leave the longtail-boat trip to Chiang Rai until the following afternoon. Several worthwhile diversions, notably the admirable **Elephant Nature Park** and a couple of guest houses that can arrange trekking in the countryside near **Chiang Dao**, may slow you down further on the journey north from Chiang Mai, and it's also possible to move on from Tha Ton by **songthaew** to Mae Salong or Chiang Rai.

En route to Tha Ton on public transport, you may have to change buses in the ugly frontier outpost of **Fang**, 153km from Chiang Mai, but you're far better off pushing on to Tha Ton for somewhere to stay. With your own transport, you can give Fang a miss altogether by branching west on a bypass signposted to Mae Ai.

Mae Taeng, Chiang Dao and Doi Angkhang

From Chiang Mai the route heads north along Highway 107, retracing the Mae Hong Son loop as far as Mae Malai, then continuing directly north, passing a couple of well-organized elephant camps along the way. About 3km after **Mae Taeng**, a signposted left turn leads about 10km to the **Elephant Nature Park**, which is essentially a hospital for sick and injured elephants, but hands-on educational – and recreational – visits by the public are encouraged. On a daytime visit, you'll get to feed, bathe and learn about the elephants close up, but it's also possible to stay for two or three days or sign up as a paying volunteer for a week or two. The park's owner, Sangduan ("Lek") Chailert, has become something of a celebrity in recent years, being featured on Discovery Channel and in *Time* magazine for her conservation efforts. You can find out more about the park at Ⓦwww.elephantnaturepark.org, and to visit the camp, contact Gem Travel at 6 Thanon Sridornchai (Ⓣ053 818932) in Chiang Mai.

After 56km, Highway 107 passes an **elephant-training centre** on the right (not to be confused with the elephant village a couple of kilometres before), which puts on logging shows daily at 9am and 10am (adults B60, kids under 10 B30); it's a more attractive setting than the Mae Sa Valley camps, especially good for elephant rides and bamboo-rafting. Beyond the elephant camp, the road squeezes through a narrow gorge, and at kilometre-stone 63, *Baan Krating* on the right offers a good spot for refreshment, serving a range of Thai and Western dishes in a pretty location by the River Ping.

Chiang Dao

Around kilometre-stone 72 **Chiang Dao**, an oversized market village, stretches on and on along the road as the dramatic crags and forests of Thailand's third-highest peak, Doi Chiang Dao (2240m), loom up on the left. A new ring road now sweeps round to the west of town, carrying traffic heading straight for Tha Ton.

In the town itself, a road served by yellow songthaews and motorbike taxis heads northwest of the village for 5km to an extensive complex of interconnected caverns, **Tham Chiang Dao**, with an attached monastery (the caves were given religious significance by the local legend of a hermit sage who is said to have dwelt in them for a millennium). Several of the caverns can be visited; a couple have electric light but others need the services of a guide with a lantern. Admission to the caves is B20 and guides ask around B100 to take a group of up to five people on a tour of about thirty minutes, during which they point out unusual rock formations. About 1500m further north along the road from the caves, the secluded *Malee's Nature Lovers Bungalows* (Ⓣ053 456426 or 081 961 8387, Ⓦwww.maleenature.com; ❷–❺) is a cosy compound delightfully set in the shadow of the mountain. Half a dozen comfy en-suite bungalows of varying size, some with shared hot showers and others with en-suite bathrooms, as well as camping facilities (B80/person) and good food, are available here. They can arrange treks, rafting, elephant-trekking and bird-watching trips, or just point birders in the right direction; bicycle and motorbike rental is available. On either side of *Malee's* is a branch of *Chiang Dao Nest* (Ⓣ053 456242, Ⓦwww.chiangdao.com; ❹); both have half a dozen bungalows with attached bathrooms and balconies. The one nearer to the caves serves Thai food, while the further one turns out gourmet Western dishes, with mains at around B300 each. Guided treks to the **summit of Chiang Dao** can be arranged by both *Malee's* and *Chiang Dao Nest* during the cool season, from November to March. It takes two to three days to go up and down and costs around B2000–3000 per person, depending on size of the group.

Doi Angkhang

Back on Highway 107, the road shimmies over a rocky ridge marking the watershed separating the catchment areas of the Chao Phraya River to the south and the Mekong River ahead, before descending into the flat plain around Fang and the Kok River. Branching off to the left some 60km from Chiang Dao, a steep and winding 25-kilometre road, Route 1249, leads up to **Doi Angkhang** (1928m). Besides a royal agricultural project here that produces peaches, raspberries and kiwis in the cool season, the mountain is home to the eco-friendly **Angkhang Nature Resort** (Ⓣ053 450110, Ⓦwww.amari.com/angkhang; ❽), where the luxurious teak pavilions have balconies with great views, and bird-watching or trekking, mule-riding or mountain-biking to nearby hill-tribe villages are the main activities.

Tha Ton and around

The tidy, leafy settlement of **THA TON**, nearly 180km north of Chiang Mai, huddles each side of a bridge over the Kok River, which flows out of Burma 4km to the west upstream. Life in Tha Ton revolves around the bridge – buses and boats pull up here, and most of the accommodation is clustered nearby. Opposite the boat landing you'll find a string of simple, cheap restaurants as well as Internet access.

The main attractions here are longtail-boat and bamboo-raft rides downstream to Chiang Rai, but on the south side of the bridge the over-the-top ornamental gardens of **Wat Tha Ton**, endowed with colossal golden and white Buddha images and an equally huge statue of Chao Mae Kuan Im, the Chinese goddess of mercy, are well worth the short climb. From any of the statues, the views up the narrow green valley towards Burma and downstream across the sun-glazed plain are heady stuff.

Accommodation

Kwan's Guest House (Ⓣ081 993 1267, Ⓔkwanguesthouse@hotmail.com; ❷), on the south side of the bridge, is a convenient and cheap **place to stay**, with decent en-suite rooms in a crowded compound, and good food. The owner can help arrange rafting trips and also rents out bicycles and motorbikes. Another good-value place is *Apple Guesthouse* (Ⓣ053 373144; fan ❸, air-con ❹), a smart, chalet-style hotel right in front of the boat landing, with attractive rooms, all with hot water, some with TV, above a good restaurant. On the north side of the river, *Garden Home Nature Resort* (Ⓣ053 373015, Ⓕ053 459325; fan ❷, air-con ❹), 300m west from the bridge, is a very appealing option, with attractive en-suite bungalows (some with hot water and air-con) sheltering under an orchard of lychees, and off-road motorbikes available for rent. About 200m beyond *Garden Home*, the *River View Resort* (Ⓣ053 373173–5, Ⓔthatonriverview@hotmail.com; ❼) enjoys the best location of all, on a bend in the river that is hemmed in by densely forested hillsides, of which the well-equipped, air-con rooms all have great views. The *River View Resort* also has an excellent restaurant that serves a wide range of tasty Thai dishes on a breezy, flower-strewn terrace. Try the *kaeng liang* (B60) – a peppery soup with vegetables and shrimp.

With its own gardens and a choice of three restaurants and two bars, about half a kilometre east of the bridge on the south bank of the river, the family-friendly *Mae Kok River Village Resort* (Ⓣ053 459355–6, Ⓦwww.maekok-river-village-resort.com; ⑧) is another good upmarket choice. Well-designed, air-con suites and family villas are set around a pool, and the owner, Shane Beary, also runs Track of the Tiger, which offers a wide variety of **soft adventure tours**, taking visitors off the well-trodden trekking trails in a measure of luxury. Tour options include a motorized river barge which can take people downstream to Chiang Rai via their riverfront jungle camp (with bamboo bungalows and hot showers), as well as (guided or self-guided) mountain-biking, canoeing and bamboo-rafting. At this multi-dimensional resort – which also includes an organic farming and vocational skills school for the disadvantaged – visitors can sign up for courses in Thai cooking or massage, meditation or rock-climbing.

Ban Lorcha

Beyond Tha Ton, Route 1089 heads east towards Mae Chan and Highway 1; about 20km out of town, at Ban Kew Satai, an exciting roller coaster of a side road leads north to Mae Salong (see p.431). To get to Mae Salong, take one of the yellow **songthaews** (B50) that leave a few hundred metres north of the bridge in Tha Ton. Songthaews direct to Chiang Rai charge B80. If you're heading for Mae Salong or Chiang Rai this way, it's worth breaking your journey about 1km west of Kew Satai on Route 1089 at **BAN LORCHA**. As part of a community-based tourism development project, owned and managed by the villagers, with technical assistance from the PDA in Chiang Rai (see p.430), this Akha settlement has been opened to visitors, who pay an entrance fee of B80 (income goes into a village development fund). A guide leads you on a one-kilometre walk through the village, which is strategically dotted with interesting display boards in English, and you'll get a chance to have a go on an Akha swing, see a welcome dance and watch people weaving and tool-making, for example.

Along the Kok River

Travelling down the hundred-kilometre stretch of the **Kok River** to Chiang Rai gives you a chance to soak up a rich diversity of typical northern landscapes, which you never get on a speeding bus. Heading out of Tha Ton, the river traverses a flat valley of rice fields and orchards, where it's flanked by high reeds inhabited by flitting swallows. After half an hour, you pass the 900-year-old **Wat Phra That Sop Fang**, with its small hilltop chedi and a slithering naga staircase leading up from the river bank. Beyond the large village of **Mae Salak**, 20km from Tha Ton, the river starts to meander between thickly forested slopes. From among the banana trees and giant wispy ferns, kids come out to play, adults to bathe and wash clothes, and water buffalo emerge simply to enjoy the river. About two hours out of Tha Ton the hills get steeper and the banks rockier, leading up to a half-hour stretch of small but feisty rapids, where you might well get a soaking. Beyond the rapids, crowds of boats suddenly appear, ferrying camcorder-toting tour groups from Chiang Rai to the Karen village of **Ruammid**, 20km upstream, for elephant-riding. From here on, the landscape deteriorates as the bare valley around Chiang Rai opens up.

The best time of year to make this trip is in the cool season (roughly Nov–Feb), when the vegetation is lushest and the rapids most exciting. Canopied **longtail boats** (B300/person) leave from the south side of the bridge in Tha

△ Longtail boats on the Kok River

Ton every day at 12.30pm for the trip to Chiang Rai, which takes around four rather noisy hours. The slower, less crowded journey upriver gives an even better chance of appreciating the scenery – the longtails leave Chiang Rai at 10.30am. If you can get a group of up to six people together (more in the rainy season), it's better to charter a longtail from the boat landing in Tha Ton (B2000; ⓣ053 459427), which will allow you to stop at the hill-tribe villages and hot springs en route.

If you have more time, the peaceful **bamboo rafts** which glide downriver to Chiang Rai in two days almost make you part of the scenery. Rafts, which leave at about 8–9am, generally take six paying passengers – there are usually plenty of travellers to hitch up with during the high season, when you shouldn't have to wait more than a day for a full complement; the price includes mats, sleeping bags, mosquito nets, soft drinks and food. Each party is accompanied by two steersmen who dismantle the rafts in Chiang Rai and bring the bamboo back to be recycled in Tha Ton. All the guest houses and resorts can organize the standard two-day, one-night raft trips (B2000/

person), with a night spent at the hot springs at Huai Mak Leam and a one-hour elephant ride at Ruammid.

Mae Kok River Village Resort (see p.423) offers upmarket rafting and barge trips on this stretch of river. Passengers departing from Tha Ton boat landing are required to sign the log book at the adjacent **tourist police** booth. Between Mae Salak and Ruammid, a couple of peaceful **guest houses** – from either of which you can go walking (guided or self-guided) – might tempt you to break your river journey. At *My Dream* in the Karen village of Ban Khaew Waaw Dam, on the north bank of the Kok (ⓣ081 672 0943; ❷), clean, comfortable bungalows with verandas are set among banana trees in a pretty garden and overlook the river; there are also dorm rooms in the house (B100). Downstream and on the opposite side of the Kok, 3km on foot from the riverside hot springs near Huai Kaeo waterfall, *Akha Hill House* (ⓣ089 997 5505 or 081 460 7450, ⓦwww.akhahill.com; ❶–❹) offers lofty views, comfortable rooms and bungalows, some with en-suite hot showers, and free transport daily to and from Chiang Rai.

Chiang Rai

Having lived in the shadow of Chiang Mai for all but thirty years of its existence, **CHIANG RAI** – sprawled untidily over the south bank of the Kok River – is now trying to make a challenge as an upmarket tourist centre, with all the hype and hustle that goes with it. The long arm of the package-tour industry has reached this northern outpost, bringing snap-happy bus-bound tourists and well-heeled honeymooners, who alight for a couple of days of excursions and then shoot off again. Paradoxically, this leaves the town to get on with its own business during the day, when the trippers are out on manoeuvres, but at night the neon lights flash on and souvenir shops and ersatz Western restaurants are thronged. Meanwhile, the town keeps up its reputation as a dirty-weekend destination for Thais, a game given away by just a few motels and carports – where you drive into the garage and pay for a discreet screen to be pulled across behind you. Budget travellers are now in the minority, but still turn up for the trekking, day-trips and other outdoor activities.

Chiang Rai is most famous for the things it had and lost. It was founded in 1263 by King Mengrai of Ngon Yang who, having recaptured a prize elephant he'd been chasing around the foot of Doi Tong, took this as an auspicious omen for a new city. Tradition has it that Chiang Rai prevailed as the capital of the north for thirty years, but historians now believe Mengrai moved his court directly from Ngon Yang to the Chiang Mai area in the 1290s. Thailand's two holiest images, the Emerald Buddha (now in Bangkok) and the Phra Singh Buddha (now perhaps in Bangkok, Chiang Mai or Nakhon Si Thammarat, depending on which story you believe), also once resided here before moving on – at least replicas of these can be seen at Wat Phra Kaeo and Wat Phra Singh.

Arrival, information and transport

Arriving at the **bus station** on Thanon Phaholyothin on Chiang Rai's south side leaves a long walk to some of the guest houses, so you might want to bundle into a tuk-tuk (around B30–50) or a songthaew, the two main forms of transport around town. Longtails from Tha Ton dock at the **boat station**, northwest of the centre on the north side of the Mae Fah Luang Bridge. Thai Airways (at

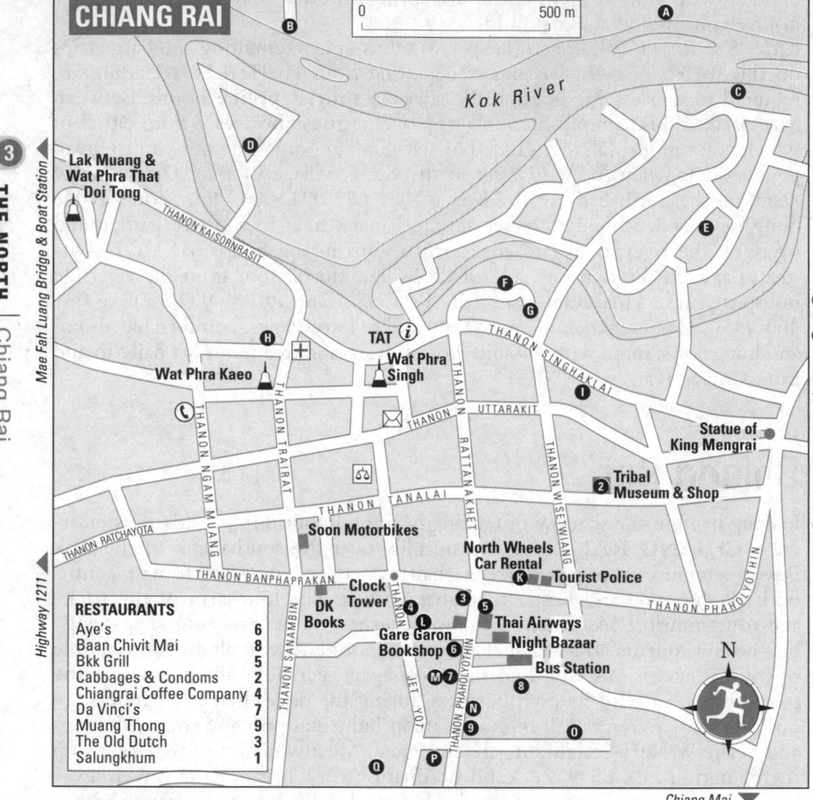

ACCOMMODATION

Baan Bua Guest House	M	Chian House	E	Jansom House	P	Moon & Sun	I	Wangcome	L
Baan Worabordee	O	Dusit Island Resort Hotel	D	The Legend	C	Rim Kok Resort	B	Wiang Inn	N
Bowling Guest House	F	Golden Triangle Inn	K	Mae Hong Son Guest House	G	River House	A	YMCA International Hotel	J
Chat House	H					Tourist Inn	Q		

the airport ⓣ053 798202–3, on Thanon Phaholyothin ⓣ053 711179) **fly** to Chiang Rai from Bangkok, while Air Asia (ⓣ053 798275–6) and Orient Thai (ⓣ053 793555) also operate flights on this route and have offices at the **airport**, from where **taxis** run into town (8km south), for about B300.

TAT has a helpful office at 448/16 Thanon Singhaklai near Wat Phra Singh (daily 8.30am–4.30pm; ⓣ053 717433 or 053 744674, ⓔtatcei@loxinfo.co.th) with some useful free maps and information brochures. From here they look after Chiang Rai, Nan, Phrae and Phayao provinces, as well as organizing the Mekong Challenge, a nine-day mountain-bike trip through China and Laos every October. Gare Garon, 869/18 Thanon Phaholyothin, has a small range of new and used **books** in English, as well as drinks for sale. DK Books has a branch on Thanon Banphaprakan near the clock tower that sells a small selection of newspapers, maps and guide books. The **tourist police** (ⓣ1155) are on Thanon Phaholyothin next to the *Golden Triangle Inn*.

Tours and trekking from Chiang Rai

Communities from all the hill tribes have settled around **Chiang Rai**, and the region offers the full range of terrain for **trekking**, from gentle walking trails near the Kok River to tough mountain slopes further north towards the Burmese border. The river is deep enough for rafts both to the west and the east of the town, and elephant-riding is included in most treks. However, this natural suitability has attracted too many tour and trekking agencies, and many of the hill-tribe villages, especially between Chiang Rai and Mae Salong, have become weary of the constant to-ing and fro-ing. Some of the trek agencies in Chiang Rai have recently widened their net to include the rest of the province, such as Chiang Khong, where there's a large population of Hmong and Mien. Sizes of group treks from Chiang Rai tend to be smaller than those from Chiang Mai, often with just two or three people, with a maximum of about seven in a group. The rate guidelines set by Chiang Rai TAT are rather high at the moment; an average three-day, two-night trek with an elephant ride typically costs B3000–4000 each for two to five people. Nearly all guest houses in Chiang Rai can fit you up with a trek – *Chat*, *Chian* and *Mae Hong Son* are responsible and reliable. Before you agree to sign up for a tour, check exactly what is covered by the fee, as some companies that advertise cheap rates do not offer all-inclusive tours. One place to avoid is the Union of Hilltribe Villages, just north of Chiang Rai's airport, where people from various ethnic groups are brought to live together in an artificial village for the convenience of tourists.

More expensive treks are offered by several non-profit foundations promoting community-based tourism that are based in Chiang Rai. The Hill Area and Community Development Foundation has set up Natural Focus, 129/1 Moo 4, Thanon Pa-Ngiw (ⓣ053 715696, ⓦwww.naturalfocusecotour.com), which offers one- to fifteen-day tours to learn about mountain life, as well as youth, workstay and volunteer skills programmes and craft workshops. The development agency PDA (ⓣ053 740088, ⓦwww.pda.or.th/chiangrai; see p.430) offers one- to three-day jungle treks, including elephant trekking and a longtail-boat ride. They also offer one-day **mountain-biking trips** up the Kok River, including fishing, meals and a guide/mechanic (B2200), as well as tours to Mae Salong and other places of interest.

Most of the guest houses can arrange sightseeing tours, boat trips and elephant rides; *Mae Hong Son Guest House* and *Chian* also offer motorbike trekking and the latter can lay on horse-riding.

Shared **songthaews**, which have no set routes, cost B10–20 for short hops. Most guest houses offer **motorbike rental** though **bicycles** can be a little more difficult to find. Both mountain bikes (B100/day) and motorbikes (B150–300) are for hire at the ever-reliable Soon Motorbikes, 197/2 Thanon Trairat (ⓣ053 714068). **Car rental** is available through North Wheels at 591 Thanon Phaholyothin, next to the tourist police office (ⓣ053 740585, ⓦwww.northwheels.com) or more expensively through Budget at the *Golden Triangle Inn* (ⓣ053 740442–3).

Accommodation

Chiang Rai is overstuffed with **accommodation** in all categories, but much of it offers poor quality for the price; that said, one or two guest houses compare with Chiang Mai's best, and in *The Legend* and *River House* it boasts two of the north's finest boutique hotels. Some places are located along the tranquil banks of the Mae Kok River, while others cluster around the town centre, from where the town's few sights are within walking distance.

Budget

Baan Bua Guest House 879/2 Thanon Jet Yot ⓣ053 718880, ⓔbaanbua@yahoo.com. Congenial and well-run establishment arrayed around a surprisingly large, quiet and shady garden, set back off the road. The very clean and attractive concrete rooms all come with hot-water en-suite bathrooms and some have air-con. Fan ❷, air-con ❸

Bowling Guest House Off Thanon Singhaklai ⓣ053 712704; near the *Mae Hong Son Guest House*. A cute, peaceful place in a residential soi with tiny, concrete rooms off a fragrant courtyard filled with pot plants. Run by a young family, this place is very friendly and homely. The five functional rooms all have their own cold-water bathrooms, and a shared hot shower is available. ❶

Chat House 3/2 Soi Sangkaew, Thanon Trairat ⓣ053 711481, ⓦwww.chathouse32.com. Located behind its own garden café on a quiet soi, this is Chiang Rai's longest-running travellers' hangout, with a very laid-back atmosphere. The rooms are modern, colourfully decorated and some have en-suite bathrooms with hot water. There's a B70 dorm too, and satellite TV is on nightly in the café. ❶–❷

Chian House 172 Thanon Koh Loy ⓣ & ⓕ053 713388. In a lively, ramshackle compound around a small swimming pool, the accommodation here includes pleasant en-suite rooms (all hot water, some with air-con) and spacious, clean and nicely furnished wooden bungalows with cool tiled floors. Internet access available. Fan ❶–❷, air-con ❷–❸

Jansom House 897/2 Thanon Jet Yot ⓣ053 714779. Smart rooms, all with air, hot water and cable TV in this new three-storey block set around a tiny courtyard. ❸

Mae Hong Son Guest House 126 Thanon Singhaklai ⓣ053 715367. This friendly establishment, in a quiet street, comprises wooden buildings arranged around a shady courtyard with neat bar and café. Very pleasant rooms – some en suite (hot water), others sharing hot showers. ❶–❷

Moon & Sun 632 Thanon Singhaklai ⓣ053 719279. Located northeast of the centre, this new place offers some of the best value in town, with good-sized, air-con rooms equipped with fridges and cable TV, plus attractive furnishings and fittings. ❸–❹

Tourist Inn 1004/4–6 Thanon Jet Yot ⓣ053 714682. Clean hotel-style guest house in a modern four-storey building run by a Japanese-Thai team. The reception area downstairs has a European-style bakery, a seating area with big comfy armchairs, TV area and library, while bright, light rooms all come with hot-water bathrooms and air-con or fan. There are cheaper rooms in an attached building, which are not as modern but have hot showers. Fan ❶–❷, air-con ❸

YMCA International Hotel 70 Thanon Phaholyothin ⓣ053 713785–6, ⓔymcawf@loxinfo.co.th. Ever reliable, with comfortable rooms, some with air-con, all with hot water, in a modern building 5km north of the town centre. Dorm beds (B90) are available, and there's a small swimming pool, a café-restaurant and a non-profit handicraft and organic products shop. Fan ❸, air-con ❹

Moderate

Baan Worabordee 59/1 Moo 18, Thanon Sanpanard ⓣ053 754488, ⓔbaan_warabordee@hotmail.com. Well-appointed, good-value place down a quiet lane off the main street. Comfortable, clean, attractively decorated rooms with small balconies, hot-water bathrooms and cable TV. Fan ❹, air-con ❺

Golden Triangle Inn 590 Thanon Phaholyothin ⓣ053 711339, ⓦwww.goldenchiangrai.com. Large, comfortable, tastefully decorated rooms with air-con and hot water in a garden compound in the heart of town. ❺

Expensive

Dusit Island Resort Hotel 1129 Thanon Kaisornrasit ⓣ053 715777, ⓦwww.dusit.com. Set on a ten-acre island in the Kok River offering unbeatable views of the valley, this is one of the swankiest places to stay in town, with high standards of service. The huge rooms are lavishly furnished, with fancy bathrooms, minibars and big TVs. Hotel facilities include a health club, tennis courts and swimming pool. ❾

The Legend 124/15 Thanon Kohloy ⓣ053 910400, ⓦwww.thelegend-chiangrai.com. Describing itself as a boutique resort, this new place offers luxury bungalows decorated in contemporary Lanna style with spacious verandas and bright, big bathrooms. Hugging the south bank of the River Kok, the compound also features Italian and Thai restaurants, a huge swimming pool, a top-class spa and impeccable service. ❾

Rim Kok Resort 6 Moo 4, Thanon Chiang Rai–Tha Ton ⓣ053 716445–60, ⓦwww.rimkokresort.com. Palatial luxury hotel in sprawling grounds with a swimming pool on the quiet north side of the river. ❼

River House 482 Moo 4, Thanon Mae Kok ⓣ053 750829–34, ⓦwww.riverhouse-chiangrai.com. Opposite *The Legend* on the north bank of the Kok River, this four-storey boutique resort has elegantly designed and sumptuously furnished rooms with lovely wooden floors, all overlooking the large swimming pool and landscaped riverside gardens. Extremely relaxing location and excellent service. ⑨

Wangcome 869/90 Thanon Pemavipat ⓣ053 711800, ⓔwangcome@loxinfo.co.th. Chintzy, ageing hotel with a swimming pool, not quite up to international five-star standards, but worth considering for its reasonable rates and convenient, central location. ⑦

Wiang Inn 893 Thanon Phaholyothin ⓣ053 711533, ⓦwww.wianginn.com. Located on the main road just a couple of blocks south of the Night Bazaar, this 260-room hotel has a bright and spacious lobby, comfortably furnished rooms with all facilities, and is popular among business people and tour groups. ⑦

The Town

A walk up to **Doi Tong**, the hummock to the northwest of the centre, is the best way to get your bearings and, especially at sunset, offers a fine view up the Kok River as it emerges from the mountains to the west. On the highest part of the hill stands the most interesting of Chiang Rai's few sights, a kind of phallic Stonehenge centred on the town's new **lak muang**, representing the Buddhist layout of the universe. Historically, the erection of a *lak muang* marks the official founding of a Thai city, precisely dated to January 26, 1263 in the case of Chiang Rai; the new *lak muang* and the elaborate stone model around it were erected 725 years later to the day, as part of the celebrations of King Bhumibol's sixtieth birthday. The *lak muang* itself represents Mount Sineru (or Meru), the axis of the universe, while the series of concentric terraces, moats and pillars represent the heavens and the earth, the great oceans and rivers, and the major features of the universe. Sprinkling water onto the garlanded *lak muang* and then dabbing your head with the water after it has flowed into the basin below brings good luck.

The old wooden *lak muang* can be seen in the viharn of **Wat Phra That Doi Tong**, the city's first temple, which sprawls shambolically over the eastern side of the hill. Look out for the small golden prang, the old-fashioned wooden spirit house and the Chinese shrine, with which the wat shares the hillside in a typically ecumenical spirit.

△ New *lak muang*, Chiang Rai

The Emerald Buddha, Thailand's most important image, was discovered when lightning cracked open the chedi (since restored) at **Wat Phra Kaeo** on Thanon Trairat. A beautiful replica, which was carved in China from 300kg of milky green jade and presented by a Chinese millionaire in 1991, can now be seen here in the Hor Phra Yok, a tiny, Lanna-style pavilion situated to the right behind the viharn. At 47.9cm wide and 65.9cm high, the replica is millimetres smaller than the Emerald Buddha, as religious protocol dictated that it could not be an exact copy of the original. The whole complex has recently been renovated and the decorative trimmings show a high level of craftsmanship, including those on the large wooden building to the left of the viharn, which houses ancient religious objects and texts.

The **Hill Tribe Museum and Handicrafts Shop** at 620/25 Thanon Tanalai stocks an authentic selection of tasteful and well-made hill-tribe **handicrafts**. The shop, on the second floor, was started by the country's leading development campaigner, Meechai Viravaidya, under the auspices of the PDA (Population and Community Development Association) and all proceeds go to village projects. The museum (Mon–Fri 9am–6pm, Sat & Sun 10am–6pm; B50) is a great place to learn about the hill tribes before going on a trek, and includes a slick, informative slide show (20min). You can donate old clothes or money for jumpers and blankets, and they also organize treks and tours themselves (see p.427). All sorts of handicrafts, some of good quality and competitively priced, are on sale at the **night bazaar** which is set up off Thanon Phaholyothin next to the bus station, and is usually buzzing with tour groups in the evening.

Eating and drinking

Chiang Rai's **restaurants**, including a growing number of Western places, congregate mostly along Phaholyothin road near the night bazaar, with some good Thai options in the moderate range scattered around. There's a **food centre** in the night bazaar with lots of delicious snacks and a beer garden too, where you can catch a free performance of transvestite cabaret, local folk-singers or traditional dancers.

Aye's 479 Thanon Phaholyothin. A spacious restaurant with a relaxing atmosphere and a wide menu of international and Thai dishes – try the *kaeng hang lay* (B125), a delicious pork and ginger curry. Its location near the night bazaar means it's often very busy.

Baan Chivit Mai 172 Thanon Pra Soop Sook, opposite the bus station. Scandinavian bakery run by a Swedish charity that helps children in Chiang Rai and Bangkok slums (see ⓦwww.thailandsbarn.com for more info). Very clean, air-con café serving excellent sandwiches, cakes, cinnamon buns, croissants, coffees and teas. Mon–Sat 7am–9pm, Sun 2–9pm.

Bkk Grill Thanon Phaholyothin. With bright lights and the feel of a fast-food restaurant, this place is very appealing for its competitive prices. Steaks, soups, salads, seafood and combination platters, such as a burger with sausage or steak, for just B99.

Cabbages and Condoms Hill Tribe Museum (see above). Proudly proclaiming "our food is guaranteed not to cause pregnancy", this restaurant covers its walls with paraphernalia devoted to birth control, including pictures of Meechai Viravaidya, who began this organization to promote family planning and HIV/AIDS prevention. The delicious menu of Thai food, including some traditional northern dishes, is well described in English, with a few dishes suitable for vegetarians. Daily 7am-midnight.

Chiangrai Coffee Company 1025/38 Thanon Jet Yot. Simple café-restaurant serving diverse styles of coffee made from local beans, as well as many teas, Belgian waffles, a variety of breakfasts and Western dishes such as chicken breast with orange sauce (B120).

Da Vinci's Thanon Phaholyothin. Stylish Italian restaurant serving huge pizzas (B175), lasagna (B150) and other pasta dishes.

Muang Thong On the corner of Thanon Phaholyothin, just south of the *Wiang Inn Hotel*. This no-frills and inexpensive place does a wide range of Thai and Chinese dishes supposedly 24hr a day, and displays a huge selection of ingredients outside its open-sided eating area. Popular with Thais and foreigners alike.

The Old Dutch 541 Moo 2, Thanon Phaholyothin. Looking like a classic European restaurant with solid furnishings and quirky memorabilia on the walls, this conveniently located place has a huge menu of international, Indonesian and Thai dishes. It's a bit pricey with steaks at around B300, but the high quality makes it worth it. Draught beer on tap as well.

Salungkhum 843 Thanon Phaholyothin, between King Mengrai's statue and the river. Justifiably rated by locals as serving the best Thai food in town, with a garden for evening dining; there's no sign in English, but look out for the Cosmo petrol station on the opposite side of the road.

North of Chiang Rai

At a push, any one of the places described in this section could be visited on a day-trip from Chiang Rai, but if you can devote three or four days, you'd be better off moving camp to make a circuit of **Mae Salong**, a mountain-top Chinese enclave, the intriguing border town of **Mae Sai**, and **Chiang Saen**, whose atmospheric ruins by the banks of the Mekong contrast sharply with the commercialism of nearby **Sop Ruak**. Given more time and patience, you could also stop over on the way to Mae Sai at **Doi Tung** to look down over Thailand, Laos and Burma, and continue beyond Chiang Saen to **Chiang Khong** on the banks of the Mekong, which is now a popular crossing point to Laos.

For hopping around the main towns here by **public transport**, the setup is straightforward enough: frequent buses to Mae Sai run due north up Highway 1; to Chiang Saen, they start off on the same road before forking right onto Highway 1016; for most other places, you have to make one change off these routes onto a songthaew.

Mae Salong (Santikhiri)

Perched 1300m up on a ridge with commanding views of sawtoothed hills, the Chinese Nationalist outpost of **MAE SALONG** lies 36km along a roller coaster of a road that ploughs into the harsh border country west of Highway 1. Songthaews make the dizzying ninety-minute journey when full, starting from **Ban Pasang**, 32km north of Chiang Rai on Highway 1. A few marginally interesting attractions might tempt you to hop off en route, notably the **Hill Tribe Culture Centre**, 12km from Ban Pasang, where there's a handicrafts shop, and a couple of Mien and Akha souvenir villages.

Mae Salong is the focal point for the area's fourteen thousand **Kuomintang**, who for two generations now have held fast to their cultural identity, if not their political cause. The ruling party of China for 21 years, the Kuomintang (Nationalists) were swept from power by the Communist revolution of 1949 and fled in two directions: one group, under party leader Chiang Kai-shek, made for Taiwan, where it founded the Republic of China; the other, led by General Li Zongren, settled in northern Thailand and Burma. The Nationalists' original plan to retake China from Mao Zedong in a two-pronged attack never came to fruition, and the remnants of the army in Thailand became major players in the heroin trade.

Over the last twenty years, the Thai government has worked hard to "pacify" the Kuomintang by a mixture of force and more peaceful methods, such as crop programmes to replace opium. Around Mae Salong at least, its work seems to have been successful, as evidenced by the slopes to the south of the settlement, which are covered with a carpet of rich green tea bushes. Since its rehabilitation, Mae Salong is now officially known as **Santikhiri** (Hill of Peace).

Drugs and the Golden Triangle

A variety of circumstances have led to North Thailand being notorious for the production of **illegal drugs**, especially **opium**, which comes from the resin that oozes from the seed heads of the opium poppy when slit. Though opium is associated with the Far East in the popular imagination, the opium poppy actually originated in the Mediterranean. It arrived in the East, however, over twelve centuries ago, and was later brought to Thailand from China with the hill tribes who migrated from Yunnan province.

Opium growing has been illegal in Thailand since 1959, but during the 1960s and 1970s rampant production and refining of the crop in the lawless region on the borders of Thailand, Burma and Laos earned the area the nickname **the Golden Triangle**. Two main "armies" operated most of the trade within this area. The **Shan United Army** (SUA), set up to fight the Burmese government for an independent state for the Shan people, funded itself from the production of **heroin** (a more refined form of opium). Led by the notorious warlord Khun Sa, the SUA attempted to extend their influence inside Thailand during the 1960s, where they came up against the troops of the **Kuomintang** (KMT). These refugees from China, who fled after the Communist takeover there, were at first befriended by the Thai and Western governments, who were pleased to have a fiercely anti-Communist force patrolling this border area. The Kuomintang were thus able to develop the heroin trade, while the authorities turned a blind eye.

Since the 1980s, the danger of Communist incursion into Thailand has largely disappeared, and the government has been able to concentrate on the elimination of the crop. The Kuomintang in the area around Mae Salong have been put on a determined "pacification" programme, though it appears they still play an important role as drugs middlemen. In 1983 the Shan United Army was pushed out of its stronghold at nearby Ban Hin Taek (now Ban Therd Thai), over the border into Burma, and in 1996, Khun Sa cut a deal with the corrupt Burmese military dictatorship. The man once dubbed the "Prince of Death" now lives under Burmese army protection in a comfortable villa in Rangoon and has turned his attention to supposedly legitimate business ventures.

The Thai government's concerted attempt to eliminate opium growing within its borders has succeeded in reducing the size of the crop to an insignificant amount. However, Thailand still has a vital role to play as a conduit for heroin; most of the production and refinement of opium has simply moved over the borders into Burma and Laos, where opium yields are second only to post-Taliban Afghanistan.

The destruction of huge areas of poppy fields has had far-reaching repercussions on the hill tribes. In many cases, with the raw product not available, opium addicts have turned to injecting heroin from shared needles, leading to a devastating outbreak of AIDS. It has been necessary for the Thai government to give the hill tribes an alternative livelihood through the introduction of more legitimate cash crops, yet these often demand the heavy use of pesticides, which later get washed down into the lowland valleys, incurring the wrath of Thai farmers.

The dangers of the heroin trade have in recent years been eclipsed by a flood tide of **methamphetamines** or *yaa baa* ("crazy medicine"), that is infiltrating all areas of Thai society, but most worryingly the schools. Produced in vast quantities in factories just across the Burmese border, mostly by former insurgents, the United Wa State Army, *yaa baa* is the main objective of vehicle searches in border areas, with perhaps a billion tablets smuggled into Thailand each year. The government estimates that three million Thais are methamphetamine users, prompting them into a fierce crackdown in the first half of 2003 which, much to the consternation of human rights watchers, led to 2000 extra-judicial deaths and 51,000 arrests. Things have quietened down since then, but the frequent busts of *yaa baa* dealers show that the problem has not gone away.

The Town and beyond

Though it has temples, a church and a mosque, it's the details of Chinese life in the back streets – the low-slung bamboo houses, the pictures of Chiang Kai-shek, ping-pong tables, the sounds of Yunnanese conversation – that make the village absorbing. Mae Salong gets plenty of Thai visitors, especially at weekends, who throng the main street's souvenir shops to buy such delicacies as sorghum whisky (pickled with ginseng, deer antler and centipedes) and locally grown Chinese tea, coffee and herbs. It's worth braving the dawn chill to get to the **morning market**, held in the middle of town near *Shin Sane Guest House* from around 5am to 7am, which pulls them in from the surrounding Akha, Lisu and Mien villages.

Towering above the town on top of the hill, the **Princess Mother Pagoda**, a huge, gilt-topped chedi, stands beside a small cruciform viharn and is so distinctive that it has quickly become the town's proud symbol. It is a long and steep climb to get there, but with a rented vehicle you can follow the road to the Tha Ton end of town, and branch right opposite the evening market on a road that carries you heavenward, revealing some breathtaking views on the way. At the western edge of town, and probably of interest only to history buffs, is the **Chinese Martyrs Memorial Museum** (daily 7am–6pm; B20). Housed in a huge building that looks like a Chinese temple, the exhibits (mostly photographs and text) recount the origins of the Kuomintang in Thailand, giving details of the battles fought against Chinese communists and depicting the Kuomintang as heroic protectors of the Kingdom of Thailand.

The Kuomintang live up to their Thai nickname – *jiin haw*, meaning "galloping Chinese" – by offering **treks on horses**, a rare sight in Thailand. Trips to Akha, Lahu and other Chinese villages can be arranged at the *Shin Sane Guest House* (see below) from B400 for four to five hours, but it's worth meeting your guide and checking out the itinerary and the horses before you hand over any money. Armed with a sketch map from one of the guest houses, it would be possible to walk to some of the same villages yourself.

Beyond Mae Salong, paved roads let you nip the back way to Tha Ton, past the interesting Akha village of Ban Lorcha (see p.423); songthaews cover the distance in an hour. North of Mae Salong lies **Ban Therd Thai**, although to get to it by road you'd have to backtrack down the main road 12km to Sam Yaek and then make your own way up a paved side road a further 13km into the hills. In its former incarnation as Ban Hin Taek, this mixed village was the opium capital of the notorious Khun Sa (see box above): the Thai army drove Khun Sa out after a pitched battle in 1983, and the village has now been renamed and "pacified" with the establishment of a market, school and hospital.

Practicalities

The best of Mae Salong's budget **accommodation** is *Shin Sane Guest House* (Ⓣ053 765026; ❶–❷), a friendly place on the west side of the main road, which has small bedrooms with shared bathrooms in a funky wooden building and smart bungalows (with hot showers) in the yard behind; motorbikes can be rented for B200 a day. Right next door are the simple but tidy and spacious rooms, with shared hot showers, of the *Akha Guest House* (Ⓣ053 765103; ❶), the polished-wood two-storey home of a Christianized Akha family. There are several upmarket places around town, among which the best is probably the *Mae Salong Flower Hills Resort* (Ⓣ053 765496–7, Ⓦwww.maesalongflowerhills.com; ❼), located about a kilometre east of town on Highway 1130. Well-appointed bungalows with comfortable rooms and fabulous views from the balconies sit amid a spectacularly landscaped hillside that gives the resort its name. Another alternative is *Mae Salong Villa* (☎053 765114–9; ⑤–⑦), on the main road towards the eastern end of the village, with a choice of functional rooms or comfy wooden bungalows with balconies facing the Princess Mother Pagoda and Burmese mountains, all with hot-water bathrooms, TVs and fridges. To the west of the town centre, the *Khum Nai Phol Resort* (☎053 765001–2; ④–⑧) presents a more rustic alternative, with simple but comfortable, wooden bungalows scattered in a tea plantation, and a pleasant, open-sided restaurant that specializes in Yunnanese food. In the centre of town, opposite the 7-11, is the *Mae Salong Central Hills Hotel* (☎053 765113, Ⓕ053 765349; ⑥), which also has expansive views, with small, functional rooms that are carpeted and reasonably clean, all with hot water and TV.

The terrace **restaurant** of *Mae Salong Villa* also has great views and cooks up some of the best food in town, including delicious but expensive Chinese specialities like *het hawm* (wild mushrooms) and *kai dam* (black chicken). A string of decent, cheaper eateries can be found on the main road beyond *Shin Sane Guest House*. *Salema* cooks up both Thai *khao soi* and Chinese noodle soup, while *Mini*, a little further on the same side, offers Chinese, Thai and Western food, including pancakes, fruit shakes and sandwiches.

Doi Tung

Steep, wooded hills rise abruptly from the plains west of Highway 1 as it approaches the Burmese border. Crowned by a thousand-year-old wat, the central peak here, 1322-metre **DOI TUNG**, makes a worthwhile outing just for the journey. A broad, new road runs up the mountainside, beginning 43km north of Chiang Rai on Highway 1, just before **Ban Huai Khrai**. It's best to have your own vehicle or go on a tour from Chiang Rai, though you will also find lilac songthaews in Ban Huai Khrai ferrying villagers up the mountain, usually in the morning and at weekends (about B60 one way). The only other options are to hitch (easy at weekends), hire a motorbike taxi (about B100 to the temple) or charter a whole songthaew for B720 (return).

The old road to the mountain from the centre of Ban Huai Khrai passes after a kilometre or so the **Cottage Industry Centre and Outlet**, where you can watch crafts such as paper making from the bark of the *sa* (mulberry) tree in progress. The centre was set up by the Princess Mother, who had her country seat at Doi Tung until her death in 1995 (the mother of the present king, she was never queen herself, but was affectionately known as *Mae Fa Luang*, "great mother of mankind"). The **Royal Villa**, the **Princess Mother Commemorative Hall** and **Mae Fa Luang Garden**, 12km up the main summit road past Thai Yai, Chinese, Akha and Lahu villages, then left up a side road, are well worth a visit (daily 7am–5/6pm, longer on busy days, villa closed if royals in residence; garden B80, villa B70, commemorative hall B30, all three B150). Regular guided tours take visitors round parts of the largely Swiss-style building that was the country home of the Princess Mother in her later years, passing the Grand Reception Hall, where constellations have been embedded in the ceiling, as well as the positions of the planets at the time of her birth in 1900, then her living room, bedroom and study, all left as when she lived there. The swanky commemorative hall is really for royal watchers, though it does include some of the intricate screens from her funeral *that* (tower). Below, the immaculate ornamental gardens throng with snap-happy day-trippers at weekends. The Princess Mother's hill-tribe project has helped to develop local villages by introducing new agricultural methods: the slopes which were formerly blackened by the fires of slash-and-burn farming are now used to grow teak and pine, and crops such as strawberries, macadamia nuts and coffee, which, along with pottery, *sa* paper, rugs and clothes, are sold in the shops by the entrance to the gardens. There's also a Doi Tung coffee shop, an excellent restaurant and self-service café, and in the woods below the royal villa, upmarket accommodation at *Doi Tung Lodge*, with air-con, hot water, balcony, TV and fridge (Ⓣ053 767015–7, Ⓦwww.doitung.org; ❽).

Beyond the turn-off for the royal villa, the main summit road climbs over a precarious saddle with some minor temple buildings 2km before the top, and finally climbs through a tuft of thick woods to **Wat Phra That Doi Tung**. Pilgrims to the wat earn themselves good fortune by clanging the rows of dissonant bells around the temple compound and by throwing coins into a well, which are collected for temple funds. For non-Buddhist travellers, the reward for getting this far is the stunning view out over the cultivated slopes and half of northern Thailand. The wat's most important structures are its twin **chedis**, erected to enshrine relics of the Buddha's collarbone in 911. When the building of the chedis was complete, King Achutaraj of Ngon Yang ordered a giant flag (*tung*), reputedly 2km long, to be flown from the peak, which gave the mountain its name.

A very steep, paved **back road** runs along the border with Burma to Mae Sai (22km), via the Akha village of Ban Pha Mee, beginning at the saddle beneath the peak. This area has been the scene of conflict among the Kuomintang, the hill tribes and others involved in the drugs trade, but is now safe to travel in with the development of Doi Tung under the Princess Mother's project, though it remains a little intimidating, with two checkpoints en route to Mae Sai. After about 4km of asphalt, you reach the delightful **arboretum** (B50) at the pinnacle of **Doi Chang Moob** (1509m), a landscaped garden planted with rhododendrons, azaleas, orchids and ferns and furnished with fantastic terrace viewpoints looking east to Chiang Saen, the Mekong and the hills of Laos beyond, and west to the mountains around Mae Salong. For the most awesome view, however, continue a short way up the Mae Sai road to the Thai military checkpoint, to gaze at the opposing Burmese camp and seemingly endless layers of Burmese mountain stacked up to the north.

Mae Sai and around

MAE SAI, with its bustling border crossing and hustling tourist trade, can be an intriguing place to watch the world go by, though most foreigners only come here on a quick visa run. Thailand's most northerly town lies 61km from Chiang Rai at the dead end of Highway 1, which forms the town's single north–south street. Wide enough for an armoured battalion, this ugly boulevard still has the same name – **Thanon Phaholyothin** – as at the start of its journey north in the suburbs of Bangkok. Buses, however, are no longer allowed to complete the journey, stopping 4km short of the frontier at the **bus station**, from where frequent songthaews shuttle into town.

Thanon Phaholyothin ends at a short but commercially important **bridge** over the Mae Sai River, which forms the border with Burma. During daylight hours (6am–6.30pm), Thais have long been allowed to cross over to **Thachileik**, the Burmese town opposite (though the frontier is sporadically closed during international disputes between the two countries), but this dubious pleasure is now also open to foreigners. You'll need first to get stamped out at the **Mae Sai immigration office** (Ⓣ053 733261), located at the entrance to the bridge. On the other side of the bridge, you pay $5 (payable in baht equivalent) to Burmese immigration for a one-day stay, or $10 for a two-week stay

△ Mae Sai

permit, which allows time for a trip to Kengtung and Mongla, on the border with China. On your return to Thailand, you'll be given a new thirty-day entry stamp (unless you have a multiple-entry visa or re-entry permit – see p.88) at the Thai immigration office at the bridge.

Thachileik's handful of temples has next to nothing of architectural interest, the town's big draw being – for foreigners and for the hundreds of Thai day-trippers who crowd the narrow streets – a frenzy of **shopping**. The huge market on the right after the bridge is an entrepôt for a bizarre diversity of goods from around the world – from Jacob's Cream Crackers, through CDs and DVDs, to bears' paws and tigers' intestines – but its main thrust is to cater to the everyday demands of Thai customers, with a selection of ordinary, cheap clothes and bedding. The array of Burmese handicrafts – tatty Pagan lacquerware and crude woodcarving – is disappointing.

Shopping is the main activity in Mae Sai, too: from the central morning market crowded with purposeful Burmese, to the stores around the bridge which hawk "Burmese" handicrafts – mostly made in the factories of Chiang Mai, though slightly better quality than in Thachileik – and coloured glass posing as gems. Village Product, 839 Thanon Phaholyothin, about a kilometre south of the bridge, offers more interesting stuff, such as hill-tribe fabric and clothes from both Thailand and Burma.

For a better perspective on the town, climb up to the chedi of **Wat Phra That Doi Wao**, five minutes' walk from the bridge (behind the *Top North Hotel*). As well as Doi Tung to the south and the hills of Laos in the east, you get a good view up the steep-sided valley and across the river to Thachileik. There is a market in the grounds with Burmese and Chinese stuff sold, running from about 5am to 6pm, or later if it's busy.

Practicalities

A handful of mostly ropey **guest houses** are strung out along the river bank west of the bridge. By far the best of these is the furthest away: *Mae Sai Guest House* (ⓣ053 732021; ❷–❹) is a pretty, relaxing place to stay with a wide variety of well-maintained bungalows, all with en-suite hot-water bathrooms, wedged between a steep hill and the river, a fifteen-minute walk from the main road. The only other guest house in Mae Sai currently worth recommending is *Chad Guest House* on Soi Wiangpan – look out for the signpost on the left, 1km before the bridge – which scores low for location but is the classic travellers' rest (ⓣ053 732054, ⓕ053 642496; ❶): the family is welcoming, with plenty of information and local maps for guests, the food is good, there are shared hot showers, and it's an easy place to meet people. Mae Sai's best **hotel** is *Piyaporn Place* at 77/1 Moo 1 Welangpangkhum (ⓣ053 734511–4, ⓦwww.piyapornplacehotel.com; ❻–❼). This swish new seven-storey block on the west side of the main road about 500m south of the bridge has well-equipped rooms with wooden floors, all with air-con and bathtubs, some with cable TV and fridge. An old standby is the *Wang Thong*, on the east side of the bridge at 299 Thanon Phaholyothin (ⓣ053 733388–95, ⓕ053 733399; ❺–❼), with a huge, ornate lobby and a pool, plus mini-bar, TV, hot water and air-con in every room. Much cheaper than both of these is the *Yee Sun* (ⓣ053 733455; ❸) at 816/13 Thanon Sailomjai, the road running west from the bridge; this newish place has good-value, carpeted rooms, with air-con, TV and fridge.

A popular **eating** place is *Rabieng Kaew*, a cosy, air-con restaurant opposite the Krung Thai Bank on Thanon Phaholyothin, serving a wide choice of excellent Thai cuisine. The terrace of the *Rim Nam* (*Riverside*), under the western side of the bridge, is crowded during the day with tourists watching the border action. For a bit more peace and quiet, check out the terrace at the *Mae Sai Riverside Resort*, located by the river just before the *Mae Sai Guest House*, which serves a good range of Thai dishes such as deep fried chicken with lemon grass (B89). There's a **tourist police** booth (ⓣ1155) hard by the frontier bridge. For getting around the local area, **motorbikes** can be rented from Pornchai, almost opposite the Bangkok Bank on Thanon Phaholyothin, for B150 a day. You can access the **Internet** on the second floor of the Wang Thong Shopping Center, located in front of the hotel of the same name.

Sop Ruak

The Golden Triangle, which was coined to denote a huge opium-producing area spreading across Burma, Laos and Thailand (see p.432), has, for the benefit of tourists, been artificially concentrated into the precise spot where the borders meet, 70km northeast of Chiang Rai. Don't come to the village of **SOP RUAK**, at the confluence of the Ruak and Mekong rivers, expecting to run into sinister drug-runners, addicts or even poppy fields – instead you'll find souvenir stalls, pay-toilets, two opium museums and lots of signs saying "Golden Triangle" which pop up in a million photo albums around the world.

Under the auspices of the Mae Fa Luang Foundation based at Doi Tung (see p.434), the ambitious **Hall of Opium** at the Mae Sai end of the village (Tues–Sun 8.30am–5pm, last ticket sale 4pm; B300; ⓦwww.goldentrianglepark.com) took B400 million and nine years to research and build, with technical assistance from the People's Republic of China. It provides a well-presented, largely balanced picture, in Thai and English, of the use and abuse of opium, and its history over five thousand years, including its spread from Europe to

Asia and focusing on the nineteenth-century Opium Wars between Britain and China. Dioramas, games and audiovisuals are put to imaginative use, notably in a reconstruction of a nineteenth-century Siamese opium den, playing the interactive "Find the Hidden Drugs", and, most movingly, watching the personal testimonies of former addicts and their families.

The Hall of Opium is worth the high admission fee, but if you baulk at the expense, you might be better off at the small **Opium Museum** in the centre of town (daily 7am–9pm; B50). All the paraphernalia of opium growing and smoking, accompanied by an English commentary, is housed in several display cases, including beautifully carved teak storage boxes, weights cast from bronze and brass in animal shapes and opium pipes.

The meeting of the waters is undeniably monumental, but to get an unobstructed view of it you need to climb up to **Wat Phra That Phu Khao**, a 1200-year-old temple perched on a small hill above the village: to the north, beyond the puny Ruak (Mae Sai) River, the mountains of Burma march off into infinity, while eastwards across the mighty Mekong spread the hills and villages of Laos. This pastoral scene has now been transformed, however, by the appearance of a Thai luxury hotel, the *Golden Triangle Paradise* (Ⓣ053 652111; ⑦) over on the uninhabited strip of Burmese land immediately upstream of the confluence. The attached casino bypasses Thai laws against gambling, and the usually strict border formalities are waived for visitors coming from Thailand. For B400, you can have the thrill of stepping on Lao soil. A longtail **boat** from the pier in the centre of the village will give you a kiss-me-quick tour of the "Golden Triangle", including a stop at a market on the Laos side (B20 admission).

Practicalities

From Mae Sai, blue songthaews make the 45-minute trip to Sop Ruak from the east side of Thanon Phaholyothin, about 400m south of the bridge (they leave when they're full). **From Chiang Saen** you can go by regular songthaew (departing from the west side of the T-junction) or rented bike (an easy 10-km ride on a paved road, though not much of it runs along the river bank).

There's nowhere decent to **stay** in Sop Ruak for budget travellers, but for those willing to splurge, one of the north's finest hotels, the *Anantara Resort and Spa* (Ⓣ053 784084, Ⓦwww.anantara.com; ⑨), tastefully designed in a blend of traditional and contemporary styles and set in extensive grounds, is located at the Mae Sai end of the village. The balconies of all its rooms – rates start at B7500 – and its swimming pool offer great views over the countryside to the Mekong, Burma and Laos. Bookings include two free tickets to the Hall of Opium. Among many amenities available to guests are a northern Thai cookery school and an elephant camp where you can take a basic three-day training course as a mahout. Somewhat cheaper rooms, furnished with fridge, TV, hot water and air-con, are also available at the *Greater Mekong Lodge* in the Golden Triangle Park, next to the Hall of Opium (Ⓣ053 784450; ⑦). Among the many riverfront **restaurants** in Sop Ruak, the *Sriwan* in front of the *Imperial Golden Triangle Hotel* offers a wide range of well-prepared Thai dishes, such as chicken fried rice (B30), and great views of the Mekong. If you need somewhere a bit cooler, try the smart, air-conditioned *Golden View*, a few steps further east along the river bank, which serves individual dishes at B80-100, plus a B120 lunch buffet.

Chiang Saen

Combining tumbledown ruins with sweeping Mekong River scenery, **CHIANG SAEN**, 60km northeast of Chiang Rai, is a rustic haven and a good base camp

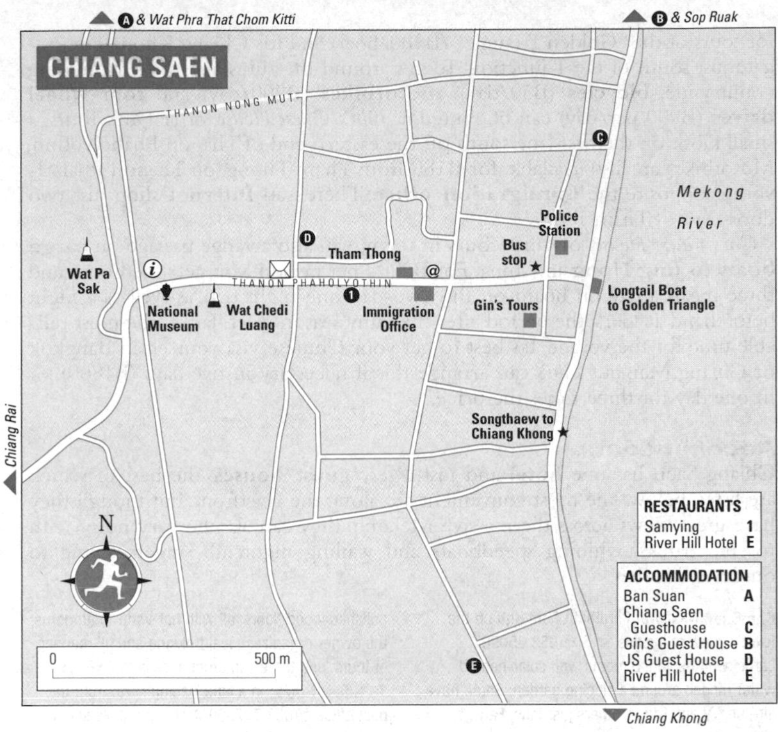

for the border region east of Mae Sai. The town's focal point, where the Chiang Rai road (Thanon Phaholyothin) meets the main road along the banks of the Mekong, is a lively junction thronged by buses, songthaews, longtails and cargo boats from Laos and China. Turning left at this junction soon brings you to Sop Ruak, and you may well share the road with the tour buses that sporadically thunder through. Very few tourists turn right in Chiang Saen along the road to Chiang Khong, even though this is the best way to appreciate the slow charms of the Mekong valley.

Originally known as Yonok, the region around Chiang Saen seems to have been an important Thai trading crossroads from some time after the seventh century. The city of Chiang Saen itself was founded around 1328 by the successor to the renowned King Mengrai of Chiang Mai, Saen Phu, who gave up his throne to retire here. Coveted for its strategic location guarding the Mekong, Chiang Saen passed back and forth between the kings of Burma and Thailand for nearly three hundred years until Rama I razed the place to the ground in 1804. The present village was established only in 1881, when Rama V ordered a northern prince to resettle the site with descendants of the old townspeople mustered from Lamphun, Chiang Mai and Lampang.

Arrival and information

Buses from Chiang Rai and **songthaews** from Sop Ruak stop just west of the T-junction of Thanon Phaholyothin and the river road, a short walk or a samlor ride from Chiang Saen's main guest houses, while songthaews from Chiang Khong stop on the river road to the south of the T-junction. **Longtail boats**

for tours of the "Golden Triangle" (B800/boat) and for Chiang Khong congregate just south of the T-junction. To get around the ruins and the surrounding countryside, **bicycles** (B50/day), **motorbikes** (B200/day) and **four-wheel drives** (B900 per/day) can be rented at *Gin's Guest House*, or at Gin's Tours, a small kiosk on the first lane south off the eastern end of Thanon Phaholyothin. Motorbikes are also available for B180 from Tham Thong, on Thanon Phaholyothin opposite the **immigration office**. There's an **Internet** shop just two doors east of Tham Tong.

Gin's Guest House, or Gin's Tours in town, can also arrange passage on **cargo boats to Jing Hong** in China. For B2700 per person, you get a bedroom and three meals a day on board on this two-day, one-night trip, as well as a night beforehand at *Gin's*; the period after the rainy season (Oct–Jan) is the most reliable time for the voyage. It's best to get your Chinese visa yourself in Bangkok or Chiang Mai, but *Gin's* can arrange this if necessary in five days (B1800), or in one day for three times the price.

Accommodation

Chiang Saen has one **hotel** and just a few **guest houses**, the best of which are listed below. The most convenient are along the riverfront, but though they have great views across the massive Mekong, they can also be very noisy with roaring trucks, whining speedboats and wailing nightclub singers trying to outdo each other.

Ban Suan Near Wat Phrathat Chom Kitti on the town's western bypass ⓣ & ⓕ 053 650907. Large, well-designed rooms with solar-heated water ranged around a sloping garden. Some have air-con, TV and fridge, others just fans. Fan ③, air-con ④

Chiang Saen Guesthouse Just a block north of the main junction ⓣ 053 650196. Basic, slightly tatty rooms, with shared cold-water bathrooms or en-suite hot showers. ①–②

Gin's Guest House Outside the ramparts, 2km north of the T-junction ⓣ 053 650847. At this attractive guest house – which also serves good food – there's a choice between large A-frame bungalows in a lychee orchard, or pricier spacious, well-furnished rooms in the main house, with polished wood floors, all with hot-water bathrooms; the owner organizes local trekking and all manner of tours, and there's Internet access too. ①–⑤

JS Guest House In a lane leading north from the post office ⓣ 053 777060. A cheap but clean option near the museum and main temples, where you'll get a hot shower, either shared or en suite. ①

River Hill South of the T-junction and a block back from the river road ⓣ 053 650826–7, ⓕ 053 650830. This hotel sets a high standard in a modern four-storey brick building with some traditional touches. Pleasant, friendly and well run, it's sited in a quiet rustic street; the rooms, all of which have air-con, TV, fridge and hot-water bathrooms, are very nicely done out right down to the axe cushion seats on the floor. ⑦

The Town

The layout of the old, ruined city is defined by the Mekong River running along its east flank; a tall rectangle, 2.5km from north to south, is formed by the addition of the ancient ramparts, now fetchingly overgrown, on the other three sides. The grid of leafy streets inside the ramparts is now too big for the modern town, which is generously scattered along the river road and across the middle on Thanon Phaholyothin. For serious temple explorers, the Fine Arts Department has an **information centre** (Mon–Sat 8.30am–4pm), opposite the National Museum, devoted to the architecture and conservation of the city.

The **National Museum** (Wed–Sun 8.30am–4.30pm; B30; ⓦ www.thailandmuseum.com) makes an informative starting point, housing some impressive Buddha images and architectural features rescued from the surrounding ruins, with good labelling in English. As in many of Thailand's museums, the back end is given over to exhibits on folk culture, one of many highlights being the beautiful wooden lintel carved with *hum yon* (floral swirls representing testicles), which would have been placed above the front door of a house to ward off evil. **Wat Phra That Chedi Luang**, originally the city's main temple, is worth looking in on next door for its imposing octagonal chedi, now decorated with weeds and a huge yellow ribbon, while handicraft stalls in the grounds sell Thai Lue cloths among their wares.

Beyond the ramparts to the west, **Wat Pa Sak**'s brick buildings and laterite columns have been excavated and restored by the Fine Arts Department, making it the most accessible and impressive of Chiang Saen's many temples (daily 8am–6pm; B30). The wat's name is an allusion to the hundreds of teak trees that Saen Phu planted in the grounds when he built the chedi in 1340 to house some Indian Buddha relics. The central chedi owes its eclectic shape largely to the grand temples of Pagan in Burma: the square base is inset with niches housing alternating Buddhas and *deva* (angels) with flowing skirts, and above rises the tower for the Buddha relic, topped by a circular spire. Beautiful carved stucco covers much of the structure, showing intricate floral scrolls and stylized lotus patterns as well as a whole zoo of mythical beasts.

The open space around modern Chiang Saen, which is dotted with trees and another 140 overgrown ruins (both inside and outside the ramparts), is great for a carefree wander. A spot worth aiming for is the gold-topped, crooked chedi of **Wat Phra That Chom Kitti**, which gives a good view of the town and the river from a small hill outside the northwest corner of the ramparts.

Eating

Food in Chiang Saen is nothing special; you could do worse than try the street stalls, which set up low pavement tables in the evening along the riverfront by the cargo pier. During the day (closes around 7pm), *Samying* on Thanon Phaholyothin opposite the Caltex petrol station is popular with locals, a clean, well-run restaurant serving river fish in various preparations and a good *tom yam*. For pleasant service and crisply clean and colourful surrounds, the moderate-to-expensive restaurant at the *River Hill Hotel* is worth a try.

East to Chiang Khong

Several routes lead **from Chiang Saen to Chiang Khong** (53km away by Highway 1129 or 65km by the picturesque, riverside route), the only other town of any size on the Mekong before it enters Laos. The most enjoyable way to get there is by **motorbike**, following the northward kink in the river for two hours along winding, scenic roads. There are plenty of **songthaews** (B50–60) between the two towns, though if you leave it until later in the day you may have to change songthaew at Ban Hat Bai.

Heading out of Chiang Saen by the river road, you pass through tobacco fields and, after 3km, the tall, brick gate of **Wat Phra That Pha Ngao** on the right. The temple, thought to have been built originally in the sixth century, contains a supposedly miraculous chedi perched on top of a large boulder, but the real attraction is the new chedi on the hillside above: take the one-kilometre track which starts at the back of the temple and you can't miss the gleaming, white-tiled Phra Borom That Nimit, designed by an American with attractive modern murals and built over and around a ruined brick chedi. From here, though you have to peer through the trees, the views take in Chiang Saen, the wide plain and the slow curve of the river. To the east, the Kok River, which looks so impressive at Chiang Rai, seems like a stream as it pours into the mighty Mekong. On the way down from the chedi, have a look at the new Lao-style

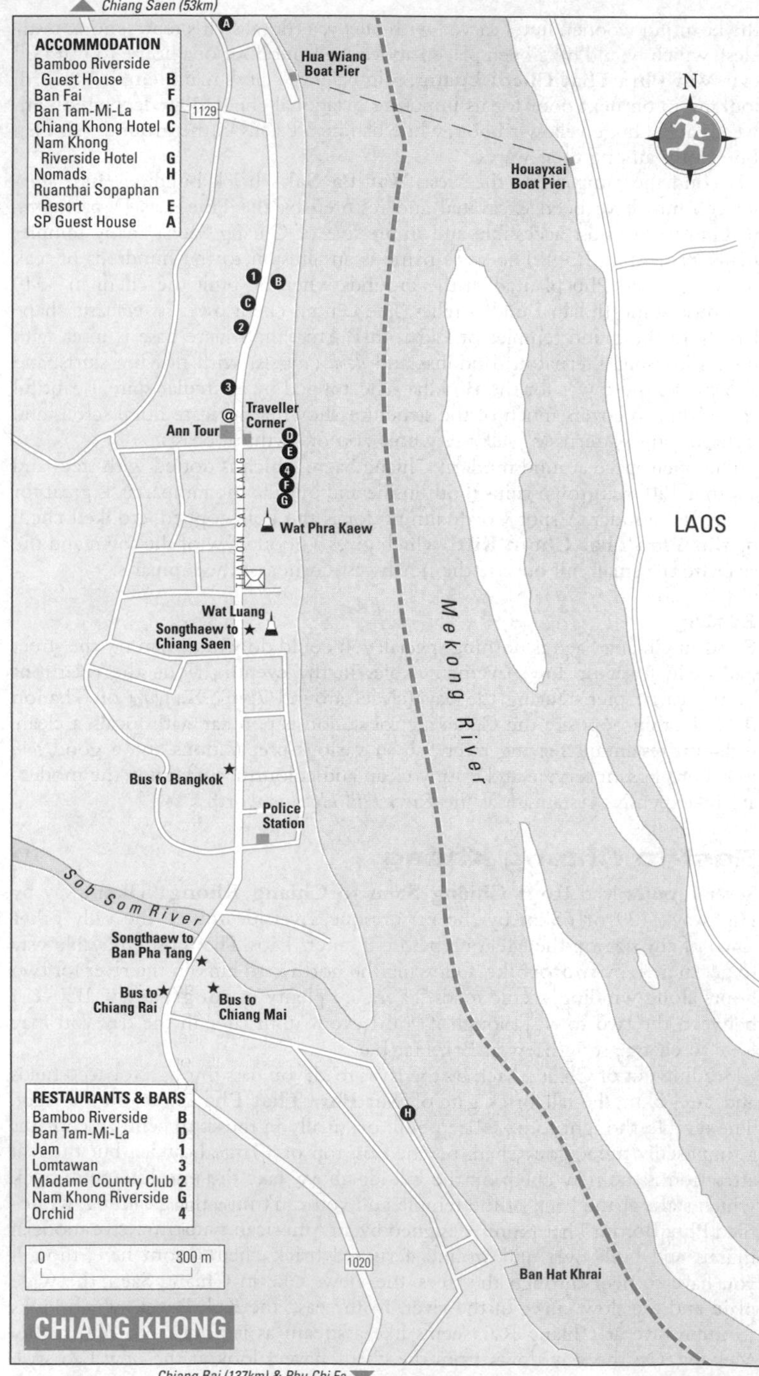
Chiang Saen (53km)
ACCOMMODATION
Bamboo Riverside Guest House B
Ban Fai F
Ban Tam-Mi-La D
Chiang Khong Hotel C
Nam Khong Riverside Hotel G
Nomads H
Ruanthai Sopaphan Resort E
SP Guest House A
Hua Wiang Boat Pier
Houayxai Boat Pier
N
1129
Traveller Corner
Ann Tour
THANON SAI KLANG
Wat Phra Kaew
LAOS
Mekong River
Wat Luang
Songthaew to Chiang Saen
Bus to Bangkok
Police Station
Sob Som River
Songthaew to Ban Pha Tang
Bus to Chiang Rai
Bus to Chiang Mai
RESTAURANTS & BARS
Bamboo Riverside B
Ban Tam-Mi-La D
Jam 1
Lomtawan 3
Madame Country Club 2
Nam Khong Riverside G
Orchid 4
0 300 m
1020
Ban Hat Khrai
CHIANG KHONG
Chiang Rai (137km) & Phu Chi Fa

bot, which was inaugurated by Princess Sirindhorn in 1999 and is covered from tip to toe in beautiful woodcarving.

Twenty-three kilometres from Chiang Saen at Ban Mae Ngoen, turn left off Route 1129 to follow the course of the Mekong, reaching the Thai Lue settlement of **Ban Hat Bai** after 9km. Turn left between the school and a temple to find an unnamed noodle shop serving cheap and tasty dishes on the river bank, as well as a weaving centre, where you can see examples of the beautifully coloured cotton for which the Thai Lue are famous. Beyond Hat Bai, the hills close in and the river enters a stretch of rocky rapids, forcing the road to climb up the valley side and making for some dramatic vantage points.

Chiang Khong and around

CHIANG KHONG is currently one of only five places in Thailand where it's possible for foreigners to **cross to Laos**, and word has clearly got around about the pleasures of the Mekong boat journey to Louang Phabang, and about the availability of fifteen-day **visas** on arrival (US$30 or B1500; see p.33 for information about other means of getting a Lao visa), as the small town these days is constantly bustling with foreigners. At the north end of town is Chiang Khong's main pier, **Hua Wiang**, the departure point for frequent passenger ferries (B20, plus B20 "overtime" payment to Lao immigration at lunchtime and after 4pm) to **Houayxai** across the border, from where the Louang Phabang boats leave. For fishing boats, the port is **Ban Hat Khrai**, just south of town. In between the two ports, Chiang Khong is strung out along a single, roughly north–south street, Thanon Sai Klang, on a high, steep bank above the river. Once you've admired the elevated view of the traffic on the Mekong and the turrets of the French-built Fort Carnot across in Houayxai, there's little to do in Chiang Khong (unless you're here on a Friday, when there's a bustling market around the bridge to the south of the centre) but relax and enjoy the fact that none of the hustle is directed at you.

If you do decide to cross the border, there are several possibilities for **onward travel in Laos**. From Houayxai, passenger boats leave at some time between 9 and 11am every morning, gliding down the scenic Mekong and taking two

Giant catfish

The **giant catfish** (*pla buk*), found only in the Mekong, is the largest scaleless freshwater fish in the world, measuring up to 3m and more in length and weighing in at 300kg. Chiang Khong has traditionally been the catfish capital of the north, attracting fish merchants and restaurateurs from Chiang Rai, Chiang Mai and Bangkok – the mild, tasty meat of the *pla buk* is prized for its fine, soft texture and can fetch more than B500 a kilo. The catfish season is officially opened at the port of Ban Hat Khrai on April 18 with much pomp, including an elaborate ceremony to appease Chao Por Pla Buk, the giant catfish god. The season's haul used to be between thirty and sixty fish all told, but recent years have been so disappointing (only four were caught in 2005) that Thailand's Fishery Department has begun an artificial spawning programme. Giant catfish are still caught on a regular basis in Cambodia, but it's now feared that they are going to disappear from Thailand completely, a fear heightened by the imminent blasting of the rapids and whirlpools between Chiang Saen and Chiang Khong – used as a spawning ground by the fish – to improve navigation. There was more bad news for giant catfish fans when a B10 million museum devoted to the species at Ban Hat Khrai collapsed a week before its scheduled opening, when water was put into its aquarium.

days – with an overnight and a change of boat at Pak Beng – to reach Louang Phabang (B700 or B850 if booked through an agent). Cramped and noisy speedboats cover the same stretch in six to seven hours for around B1200 per person, but these are not recommended as fatalities occur regularly despite the requirements for passengers to wear helmets and life jackets.

If you have time to spare and want to explore the area around Chiang Khong, try a trip to **Thung Na Noi**, a Hmong village 8km west where there is a market every Friday. You can get there by renting a bike from *Ban Tam-Mi-La* guest house, for example (get directions from the proprietor, who can also arrange home-stays there), or taking a songthaew (daily from about 9am; B20) from Soi 8, Thanon Sai Klang, opposite the navy building. First go to the village school, where you will be given a student guide and taken around the village; it's a good idea to make a donation to the school for lunch for the students. Ask the teacher for a guide to take you on the 3km walk to the attractive Huai Tong waterfall, or even about a two-day trek to Chiang Saen.

Chiang Khong practicalities

If you're coming straight to Chiang Khong **from Chiang Rai**, note that direct **buses** follow three different routes taking two hours, two and a half hours or three hours; be sure to ask for the quickest time, *sawng chua mohng*. Because of the popularity of the border crossing at Chiang Khong, there are now direct **air-con minibuses from Chiang Mai** (2 daily; 5hr; B220) available through guest houses and travel agents such as *Queen Bee* (see p.368), though they're rather cramped for a five-hour journey and passengers are dumped at a pre-arranged guest house – there's no obligation to stay there, and you're better off making your way to one of the better guest houses recommended below.

Most buses stop on the main road at the south end of town, though a few pull into the town centre itself. If you need to get from the bus to the ferry, or anywhere else about town, the local version of a **tuk-tuk**, a converted motorbike, should take you there for about B20. For exploring the local area, good **mountain bikes** (B150/day) can be rented from Wat at *Ban Tam-Mi-La*, who sometimes leads sunset cycling tours around Chiang Khong (otherwise he can provide sketch maps and info for touring); **motorbikes** (B200/day) can be hired through *Ban Tam-Mi-La* and other guest houses. Ann Tour, at 166 Thanon Sai Klang, organizes **kayaking** tours on the Mekong (B600), lasting 4–5 hours. This and other tour agents in town offer to arrange **visas** and **boat tickets** for Laos, but they charge an extra B200–300 for the privilege, and it's easy to do it yourself. **Internet** access is available next to Ann Tour, while Traveller Corner, at the corner of Thanon Sai Klang and Soi 2, has a small selection of new and used **books**.

Accommodation

Chiang Khong supports a high-quality batch of **guest houses**, as well as a couple of modest **resorts**, so finding a place to stay should not be difficult unless you arrive at the time of a national holiday or the catfish-season opening ceremony on April 18.

Bamboo Riverside Guest House 71/1 Moo 1, Hua Wiang ⓣ053 791621. Located on a jungly slope on the north side of town, with attractive, clean bamboo bungalows with shared hot showers or en-suite, wood and brick versions. ❶–❷

Ban Fai 27 Thanon Sai Klang ⓣ053 791394. Clean rooms, some with shared hot showers and others with attached bathrooms, in an attractive wooden house. ❶

Ban Tam-Mi-La 113 Thanon Sai Klang ⓣ053 791234, ⓔbaantammila@hotmail.com. Signposted down a lane in the middle of town among a cluster of shops, this place offers some of the best value in town. The staff are helpful and the shady, riverfront atmosphere is easy-going and restful; the place has tasteful, well-designed wooden bungalows and rooms with en-suite bathrooms, some with hot water, and sells good hammocks (Ⓦwww.siamhammock.com). ❷–❸

Chiang Khong Hotel 68/1 Thanon Sai Klang Ⓣ053 791182, Ⓕ053 655640. This motel-like place has large, good-value rooms set back off the street with hot showers and fan or air-con. Fan ❶, air-con ❷

Nam Khong Riverside Hotel On Thanon Sai Klang, just north of Wat Phra Kaew Ⓣ053 791796, Ⓔphayao@hotmail.com. Looking somewhat incongruous among the ramshackle houses of Chiang Khong, this fancy new hotel is the town's top spot to stay, with smartly furnished rooms, all with TV, fridge, balconies and river views, some with fan and others with air-con. Fan ❹, air-con ❺

Nomads 153/4 Moo 3 Baan Sopsom Ⓣ053 655537, Ⓦwww.nomadsgh.com. About 4km south of the ferry pier, but worth a mention for its cosy, spacious tiled rooms, some with river views and hot-water bathrooms. Internet access too. ❷–❹

Ruanthai Sopaphan Resort Ⓣ053 791023, Ⓔcomplicate2525@yahoo.com. Located right next to *Ban Tam-Mi-La*; most of the comfy, en-suite rooms within this large teak house have hot water and the best have good views of the river. Breakfast is included in the price, and there's Internet access. ❷–❹

SP Guest House Down the small lane opposite the ferry pier Ⓣ053 791767, Ⓦwww.spguesthouse.com. Simple but clean rooms in a quiet corner of town, convenient for the pier, with a B80 dorm and helpful staff. ❶

Eating and drinking

An increasing numbers of visitors means that eating options have improved in Chiang Khong, and with only one street in town, the restaurants and food stalls are not difficult to find. Nightlife is sporadic, but there is a **disco** on Thanon Sai Klang, strangely named *Madame Country Club,* and several low-key bars that cater for restless travellers.

Bamboo Riverside 71/1 Moo 1, Hua Wiang. This guest house has an attractive terrace by the river, which is popular for breakfast and dinner, with home-made wholewheat bread, pizzas and Mexican food.

Ban Tam-Mi-La 113 Thanon Sai Klang. This popular guest house has an excellent terrace restaurant with a sweeping view of the river, making it an ideal spot to while away the time, though it closes around 6pm in the low season. Lots of vegetarian options on the menu, as well as hearty breakfasts.

Jam (no English sign) almost opposite *Bamboo Riverside* on Thanon Sai Klang. This no-frills place turns out a mean *tom yam* (B50) plus several other Thai favourites.

Lomtawan 354 Thanon Sai Klang. Congenial bar/restaurant serving Thai dishes such as spicy salads (B60) and a few Western dishes such as spaghetti (B80) on a candlelit terrace, as well as drinks at the bar inside.

Nam Khong Riverside Thanon Sai Klang. The town's fanciest hotel also has a well-appointed restaurant overlooking the river, with reasonably priced Thai dishes like fried pork and asparagus (B80), plus a few Western dishes like burgers (B60) and spaghetti (B120).

Orchid Thanon Sai Klang. This place dishes up good-value Thai food such as fried rice, noodles, curries, soups and salads, as well as unpretentious Western main courses.

Doi Pha Tang and Phu Chi Fa

About 30km southeast of Chiang Khong, the Mekong River leaves Thailand and continues into Laos. From this point, the border between the two countries runs along a north–south ridge of precipitous mountains, which at some points drops away from the Thai border in a sheer cliff. Two mountain peaks in particular, **Doi Pha Tang** (1635m) and **Phu Chi Fa** (1628m), provide spectacular views over the lush and unpopulated hills of Laos, and in the cool season (Nov–Feb) the view is enhanced by a sea of mist sitting in the valley below. Both these summits are accessible via Highway 1093, one of Thailand's most scenic drives, which hugs the hillsides near the border.

It's possible to take a songthaew from Chiang Khong to Pha Tang village, leaving from the Esso station just south of the Sob Som River at 9.30am each morning and 3pm each afternoon, but it doesn't continue to Phu Chi Fa, and is a bumpy ride with very limited views. The journey is much better done by rented car, jeep or motorbike, and makes a thrilling route if you're heading on to Nan or Chiang Mai. Leave Chiang Khong heading south on Highway 1020 towards Thoen, then turn left after 15km on to H1155. This runs by the Mekong for a few kilometres before heading south. After 38km on this road, turn left again on to H1093, which climbs steeply for 12km to Pha Tang village. The road is sealed but frequently under repair, so take care. At the single fork along the road, keep to the left to pass through the hilltop village of **BAN PHA TANG**, populated mostly by Kuomintang. At the top of the hill on the right is some very basic **accommodation**, *Pha Tang Hills* (Ⓣ089 029 7755; ❷). Just beyond *Pha Tang Hills*, turn left at the junction – where there's an open-sided Yunnanese **restaurant** that serves up *kha moo* (pork leg) as its speciality – to continue on H1093 with, just fifty metres on, a left turn taking you up a kilometre or so to a viewpoint known as **Pratu Siam** (Siamese Gate). In clear weather, especially at dawn during the cool season, there are spectacular views from this lofty perch across the forested hills of Laos.

To get to **Phu Chi Fa**, continue south on H1093 for another 25km as it winds along the side of the mountains, with dizzying views back down into Thailand on the right. Phu Chi Fa, which has two separate, partly paved, approaches from H1093 (one from just north and the other from just south of the peak), has become an extremely popular place for Thais, so much so that it is worth avoiding at weekends in the cool season. You'll need to be up before 5am to walk up the steep, 1.8-kilometre path to the summit in order to be there for sunrise, but the effort is worth it. Phu Chi Fa means "the mountain that points at the sky", and at the top the reason is evident: a sheer wall drops away into Laos way down below, and distant peaks prod through the morning mist like islands floating on the clouds. There are plenty of **places to stay**, among which *Ruam Sansang* (Ⓣ081 993 3708; ❸–❺) is a reasonable choice, offering a range of cosy bungalows with hot-water bathrooms. It's located just beyond the second approach to the mountain as you come from the north; look for the yellow sign (no English) on the left opposite the *Phu Chi Fa Inn*. There's a somewhat smarter and more peaceful place a further 7km south along H1093. Turn left just north of the 58-kilometre marker to *Ukrit Farm Hill* (Ⓣ053 918100; ❽) where large A-frame bungalows with hot-water bathrooms have wonderful views, and breakfast and dinner is included in the price. If you continue southwards from Phu Chi Fa, when the road descends from the hills, you'll pass a pretty roadside waterfall at Pha Zang, 28km from Chiang Kham. At Chiang Kham, follow Highway 1021 via Phayao if you're heading for Chiang Mai, or Highway 1148, which is also very scenic, if you're heading for Nan.

Travel details

Trains

Chiang Mai to: Bangkok (7 daily; 12–14hr).
Den Chai to: Bangkok (9 daily; 9-10hr); Chiang Mai (7 daily; 4-5hr).
Doi Khun Tan to: Bangkok (5 daily; 12hr); Chiang Mai (5 daily; 1hr 15min).
Lampang to: Bangkok (7 daily; 10–12hr); Chiang Mai (7 daily; 2hr).
Lamphun to: Bangkok (6 daily; 12–14hr); Chiang Mai (6 daily; 20–30min).

Buses

Chiang Khong to: Bangkok (10 daily; 13–14hr); Chiang Mai (3 daily; 6hr); Chiang Rai (hourly; 2–3hr).
Chiang Mai to: Bangkok (19 daily; 10–11hr); Chiang Khong (3 daily; 6hr); Chiang Rai (every

30min; 3–6hr); Chiang Saen (2 daily; 5hr); Chom Thong (every 30min; 1hr); Fang (every 30min; 3hr 30min); Khon Kaen (13 daily; 12hr); Khorat (12 daily; 12hr); Lampang (every 20min; 1hr 30min); Lamphun (every 10min; 1hr); Mae Hong Son (5 daily via Mae Sariang, 8hr; 4 daily via Pai; 6hr); Mae Sai (8 daily; 4hr); Mae Sot (4 daily; 6hr); Nan (14 daily; 6-7hr); Pai (4 daily; 3hr); Phitsanulok (10 daily; 6hr); Phrae (17 daily; 4hr); Rayong (8 daily; 17hr); Sukhothai (12 daily; 5hr); Tha Ton (7 daily; 4hr); Ubon Ratchathani (6 daily; 17hr); Udon Thani (4 daily; 12hr).

Chiang Rai to: Bangkok (16 daily; 12hr); Chiang Khong (hourly; 2–3hr); Chiang Mai (every 30min; 3–6hr); Chiang Saen (every 15min; 1hr 30min); Khon Kaen (5 daily; 12hr); Khorat (5 daily; 13hr); Lampang (every 20min; 5hr); Mae Sai (every 15min; 1hr 30min); Mae Sot (2 daily; 11hr); Nakhon Phanom (4 daily; 16hr); Nan (1 daily; 6–7hr); Pattaya (4 daily; 16hr); Phitsanulok (4 daily; 7hr); Sukhothai (2 daily; 6hr); Udon Thani (3 daily; 13hr).

Lampang to: Bangkok (18 daily; 8hr); Chiang Mai (every 20min; 1hr 30min); Chiang Rai (every 20min; 5hr); Nan (10 daily; 4hr).

Mae Hong Son to: Bangkok (2 daily; 16hr); Chiang Mai via Mae Sariang (5 daily; 8hr); Chiang Mai via Pai (4 daily; 6hr).

Mae Sai to: Bangkok (8 daily; 13hr); Chiang Mai (8 daily; 4hr); Chiang Rai (every 15min; 1hr 30min); Fang, via Tha Ton (1 daily; 2hr).

Nan to: Bangkok (8 daily; 10hr); Chiang Mai (14 daily; 6–7hr); Chiang Rai (1 daily; 6–7hr); Den Chai (14 daily; 2hr 30min); Phrae (14 daily; 2hr).

Pai to: Chiang Mai (4 daily; 3hr); Mae Hong Son (4 daily; 3hr).

Phrae to: Chiang Mai (17 daily; 4hr); Nan (14 daily; 2hr).

Flights

Chiang Mai to: Bangkok (25–27 daily; 1hr); Jinghong (China; 3 weekly; 2hr 30min); Koh Samui (5 weekly; 2hr 30min); Kuala Lumpur (daily; 3hr 45min); Kunming (China; 2 weekly; 2hr 30min); Louang Phabang (Laos; 6 weekly; 1hr); Mae Hong Son (3 daily; 35min); Mandalay (Burma; 2 weekly; 50min); Phuket (daily; 2hr); Rangoon (Yangon in Burma; 1 weekly; 40min); Singapore (1–2 daily; 4hr); Sukhothai (1 daily; 40min); Vientiane (Laos; 3 weekly; 2hr 10min).

Chiang Rai to: Bangkok (5 daily; 1hr 15min).

Lampang to: Bangkok (2 daily; 1hr).

Mae Hong Son to: Bangkok (2 weekly; 1hr 20min).

Nan to: Bangkok (5 weekly; 1hr 40min).

4

The east coast

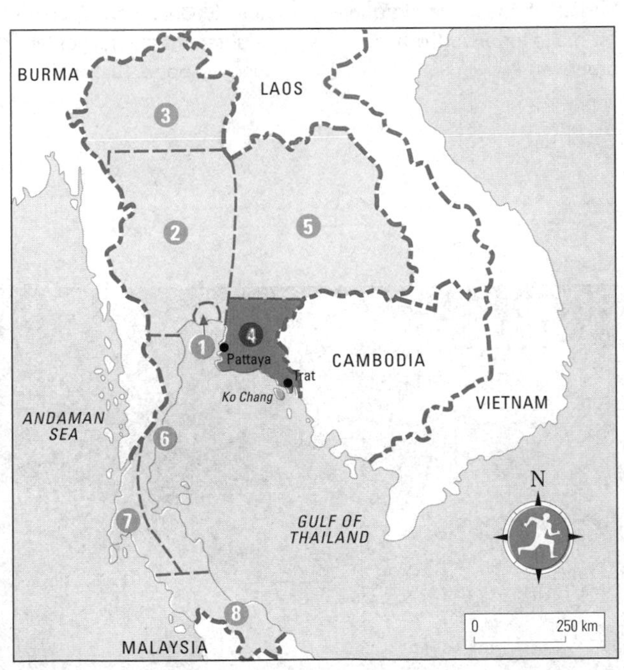

CHAPTER 4

Highlights

* **Ko Si Chang** Tiny, barely touristed island with craggy coastlines, glorious views, and an appealingly laid-back ambience. See p.454
* **Ko Samet** Pretty (and popular) little island fringed with dazzlingly white beaches. See p.471
* **Trat** Welcoming guest houses and an atmospheric old quarter make for a worthwhile stopover. See p.486
* **Ko Chang** Head for Lonely Beach if you're in the mood to party, or to Hat Khlong Phrao for a more tranquil scene. See p.491
* **Ko Mak** Lovely, lazy, palm-filled little island with peaceful white-sand beaches. See p.505
* **Ko Kood** The real beauty in the Ko Chang archipelago – untamed and as yet largely undeveloped. See p.509

△ Ko Si Chang

4

The east coast

Located within just a few hours' drive from the capital, the **east coast** resorts and islands attract a mixed crowd of weekending Bangkokians, pleasure-seeking expats and sybaritic tourists. Transport connections are good and, for overlanders, there are several Cambodian border crossings within easy reach. Beautiful beaches are not the whole picture, however, as the westernmost stretch of the east coast is also crucial to Thailand's industrial economy, its natural gas fields and deep-sea ports having spawned massive development along the first 200 kilometres of coastline, an area often dubbed the Eastern Seaboard. The initial landscape of refineries and depots shouldn't deter you though, as offshore it's an entirely different story, with island sands as glorious as many of those at the more celebrated southern retreats and enough peaceful havens to make it worth packing your hammock.

The first worthwhile stop comes 100km east of Bangkok at the town of **Si Racha**, which is the point of access for tiny **Ko Si Chang**, whose dramatically rugged coastlines and low-key atmosphere make it a restful haven. In complete contrast, nearby **Pattaya** is Thailand's number-one package-tour destination, its customers predominantly middle-aged Western and Chinese males enticed by the resort's sex-market reputation and undeterred by its lacklustre beach. Things soon look up, though, as the coast veers sharply eastwards towards Ban Phe, revealing the island of **Ko Samet**, the prettiest of all the beach resorts within comfortable bus-ride range of Bangkok.

East of Ban Phe, the landscape starts to get more lush and hilly as the coastal highway nears **Chanthaburi**, the dynamo of Thailand's gem trade and one of only two provincial capitals in the region worth visiting. The other is **Trat**, 68km further along the highway, and an important hub both for transport into **Cambodia** via Hat Lek – one of this region's two main border points, the other being Aranyaprathet – and for the islands of the Ko Chang archipelago. The star of this island group is large, forested **Ko Chang** itself, whose long, fine beaches have made it into Thailand's latest resort destination. A host of smaller, less-developed islands fill the sea between Ko Chang and the Cambodian coast, most notably the temptingly diverse trio of **Ko Whai**, **Ko Mak** and **Ko Kood**.

Highway 3 extends almost the entire length of the east coast – beginning in Bangkok as Thanon Sukhumvit, and known as such when it cuts through towns – and hundreds of **buses** ply the route, connecting all major mainland destinations. It's also possible to travel between the east coast and the northeast and north without doubling back through the capital: the most direct routes into **Isaan** start from Pattaya, Rayong and Chanthaburi. Bangkok's Suvarnabhumi Airport is less than 50km from Si Racha, and there are two **airports** along the east coast itself: at U-Tapao naval base, midway between Pattaya and Rayong,

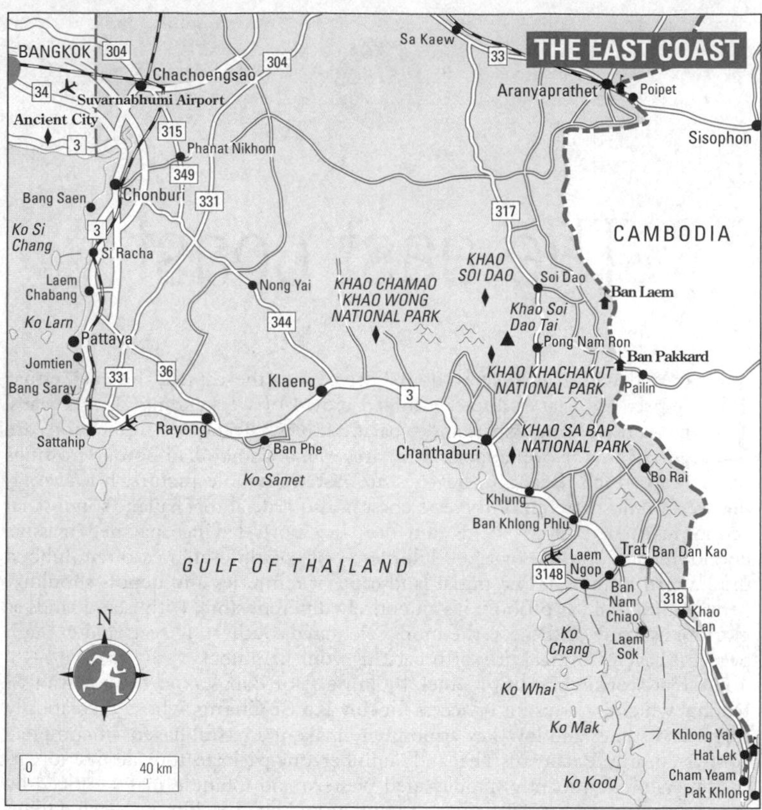

which is served by Bangkok Airways flights to and from Ko Samui and Phuket; and just outside Trat, for Bangkok Airways flights to Bangkok and Ko Samui. Though a rail line connects Bangkok with Si Racha and Pattaya, it is served by just one slow **train** a day in each direction; a branch line makes two journeys a day to Aranyaprathet near the Cambodian border.

Si Racha and Ko Si Chang

Almost 30km southeast of Bangkok, Highway 3 finally emerges from the urban sprawl at the fishing town of Samut Prakan, location of the impressive Muang Boran Ancient City open-air museum, described on p.183. It then continues via the provincial capital of **Chonburi**, whose only real attraction is its annual October bout of buffalo-racing, before reaching **Si Racha**, departure point for the island of **Ko Si Chang**.

Si Racha

Access to Ko Si Chang is from the fishing port and refinery town of **SI RACHA**, famous throughout Thailand as the home of *nam phrik Si Racha*, the orange-coloured, chilli-laced ketchup found on every restaurant and kitchen table in the country. You'll probably only find yourself staying here if you miss the last boat to the island, though the town is not without charm, especially at twilight, when the brightly painted fishing boats load up with ice and nets before setting off into the night. The "island temple" of **Wat Ko Loi**, at the end of the very long causeway 400m north of the Ko Si Chang pier, is the main sight in town.

Arrival and orientation

Buses to Si Racha leave frequently from both Bangkok's Eastern (Ekamai) Bus Terminal and the Northern (Mo Chit) Bus Terminal. Air-conditioned buses stop at various points along Thanon Sukhumvit in Si Racha's town centre; easiest landmarks for alighting are the huge Robinsons/Pacific Park shopping centre in the northern part of town, from where it's about 1km to the Ko Si Chang pier (B40 by tuk-tuk), or, about 300m further south, the sign for high-rise *The City Hotel,* across from which you should follow Thanon Surasakdi 1 (signed in English as Thanon Surasak) west to Thanon Chermchompon, and then south and almost immediately west again for the pier (about 10 minutes' walk in all). A few ordinary buses stop nearer the waterfront, on Thanon Chermchompon, close to the pier. There are also direct buses between Si Racha and Rayong (for Ban Phe and Ko Samet), Pattaya, and Trat (for Ko Chang): when moving on from Si Racha, all these buses can be flagged down at the above alighting points. White songthaews from Naklua, the northern suburb of Pattaya, run about twice an hour to Si Racha, dropping passengers near the clocktower, 200m south of the Si Racha pier soi. The one slow **train** a day from Bangkok – departing the capital at 6.55am – arrives at the **train station** on the eastern edge of the town, from where tuk-tuks are your easiest option for getting to the pier.

Most points of importance in Si Racha lie along either the main highway (Highway 3), **Thanon Sukhumvit**, which runs north-south along the eastern edge of the town centre, or its parallel artery, **Thanon Chermchompon** (also spelt **Thanon Jermjompol**). The **Ko Si Chang pier** is located at the end of Thanon Chermchompon's Soi 14, and signed off Thanon Chermchompon; the landmark **clocktower** and market are 200m south of Soi 14 and mark the southern edge of the town centre.

Accommodation and eating

Strung out along wooden jetties shooting off into the sea west of Thanon Chermchompon are the simple, cabin-like rooms of several waterfront **hotels**, the best of which is *Sri Wattana* (ⓣ038 311037; ❷), with a range of basic en-suite fan rooms and a pleasant sea-view terrace; it's on Soi Sri Wattana, directly across Thanon Chermchompon from Thanon Si Racha Nakhon 3, a few metres' walk to the left of the mouth of the Ko Si Chang pier. For flashier, air-con digs, head for the eleven-storey *The City Hotel* (ⓣ038 322700, ⓦwww.citysriracha.com; ❼–❽), near one of the bus drops at 6/126 Thanon Sukhumvit, where all rooms are large, comfortable and air-conditioned and there's a pool, fitness centre and several restaurants. For **eating**, *Jarin* (unsigned in English) on the Ko Si Chang pier is the obvious place to eat while you're waiting for a boat – its food is cheap and includes seafood curry and seafood fried rice. Elsewhere, Thanon Si Racha Nakhon 3 is a good place to browse, lined with restaurants and night-time foodstalls, or there's an official night market by the day market and clocktower further south down Thanon Chermchompon. Picha Bakery, just off Thanon Chermchompon on the corner of Thanon Surasakdi 1 (Thanon Surasak), is also good for snacks. The poshest seafood place in town is the rather elegant *Grand Seaside*, which occupies a contemporarily styled jetty restaurant at the end of Soi 18, Thanon Chermchompon, 100m south of the Ko Si Chang pier soi, or 100m north of the clocktower, and has large picture windows over the water. It serves a long menu of fish and seafood such as crab with chilli and cottonfish with green mango sauce (B125–225), and also does iced coffees.

Ko Si Chang

The unhurried pace and the absence of consumer pressures make tiny, rocky **KO SI CHANG** an engaging place to hang out for a few days. Unlike most other east-coast destinations, it offers no real beach life – though the water can be beautifully clear and there are opportunities to dive and snorkel – and there's little to do here but explore the craggy coastline by kayak or ramble up and down its steep contours on foot or by motorbike. The island is famous as the location of one of Rama V's summer palaces, parts of which have been prettily restored, and for its rare white squirrels, who live in the wooded patches inland.

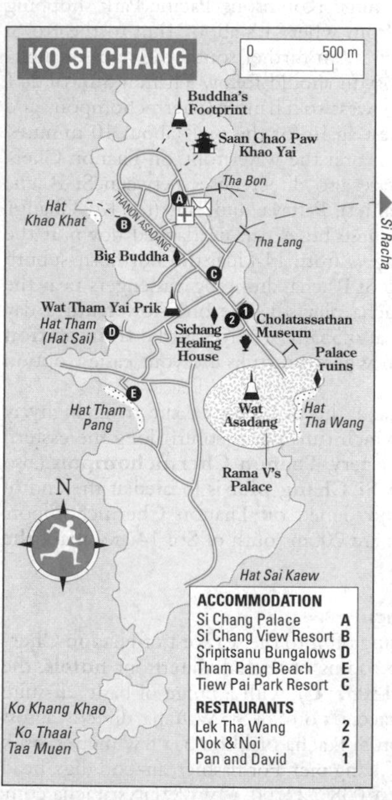

Arrival and information

Ferries to Ko Si Chang leave from the pier at the end of Si Racha's (unsigned) Soi 14, off Thanon Chermchompon, and run approximately hourly from 7am to 8pm (45min; B40). On **arrival**, you might dock at either one of Ko Si Chang's two piers, Tha Bon or Tha Lang, but in either case you will be met by samlors who charge B40 to most guest houses, or B80 to Hat Tham Pang; samlor drivers are paid commission by some guest houses and restaurants, so treat any disparaging remarks about your intended destination with caution. The first boat back to the mainland leaves Tha Lang at 6am and the last at 6pm – the same boats depart Tha Bon about fifteen minutes earlier. There's also a **speedboat** service (B1000 per boat; 15min) available from both Si Racha and Ko Si Chang, in theory round the clock: phone to request it on ⓣ038 216084.

Both piers connect with Thanon Asadang, a small ring road on which you'll find the market, shops and most of the island's houses. Much of the rest of the island is accessible only by paths and tracks. In town it's easy enough to walk from place to place, but to really enjoy what Ko Si Chang has to offer you'll need to either rent a **motorbike** – from *Tiew Pai Park Resort, Tham Pang Beach* or *Sripitsanu Bungalows*; B250–300/24hr – or psych yourself up for some challenging uphill cycling: **bicycles** can be rented through *Pan & David Restaurant* for B150/day. A popular alternative is to charter one of the island's trademark bizarrely elongated 1200cc motorbike **samlors** for the day. As there are hardly any private cars on Ko Si Chang, these contraptions virtually monopolize the roads, and a tour of the island will only set you back around B250, including time on one of the beaches or at a restaurant; some of the drivers speak good English and staff at any guest house or restaurant can contact one for you.

There are **exchange facilities** and an ATM at the bank between the two piers; the hospital is also near Tha Bon. For a fee of B50, non-guests can use the **swimming pool** at *Si Chang Palace* hotel. The exceptionally charming Sichang Healing House (daily except Wed 9am–6pm; ⓣ038 216467, ⓦwww.spa.ko-sichang.com) offers various **spa**, massage and herbal-healing treatments (from B500 for a 90-minute massage) at its stylishly designed little garden retreat; to get there follow the signs inland off the road to the old palace. Healing House also sells postcards of watercolour views of Ko Si Chang. For **information** on Ko Si Chang look for the locally produced brochure *Island Welcome*, available from some hotels and restaurants, which offers a good overview of the island's attractions and carries adverts for accommodation; the website ⓦwww.ko-sichang.com is another useful resource, as is its compiler, David, who can be found at *Pan and David Restaurant*.

Ko Si Chang celebrates three particularly interesting **festivals** which would be worth making a special effort to witness, but they're popular events so book accommodation in advance. **Songkhran** is celebrated here on April 17–19 with sandcastle-building, greasy-pole-climbing and a very special exorcist ritual for those islanders who have suffered unpleasant deaths over the previous year. At **Visakha Puja**, the full-moon day in May when Buddha's birth, death and enlightenment are honoured, islanders process to the old palace with their own hand-crafted Chinese lanterns, candlelit. And on September 20, Ko Si Chang marks its royal patron **King Chulalongkorn's birthday** with a *son et lumière* in the palace grounds and a beauty contest staged entirely in costumes from the Chulalongkorn era.

Accommodation

West-coast **accommodation** enjoys the best views, while Thanon Asadang and east-coast options are more convenient for restaurants and shops. Booking ahead is advisable for weekends and public holidays. For the very finest sea views, nothing can beat **camping** on your chosen spot: the cliffs at Hat Khao Khat are a particularly popular site, though quite exposed. You can rent tents for B100 from Uncle Juk on Hat Tham Pang (ⓣ081 822 5540), but phone ahead to reserve one for weekends.

Si Chang Palace Across from Tha Bon on Thanon Asadang ⓣ038 216276, ⓕ038 216030. The most upmarket place on the island and rather ostentatious, but facilities include a pool, and all rooms have air-con and TV. Price depends on whether or not you want a sea view. ❻–❼

Si Chang View Resort Hat Khao Khat ⓣ038 216210, ⓔjiyakiat@hotmail.com. Attractive fan and air-con accommodation in a pretty tropical garden set in a prime cliffside spot on the west coast, though sadly you can't see the rugged coastline clearly from the rooms. The air-con rooms are of a particularly high standard and there's a good restaurant here too. Fan ❹, air-con ❺–❻

Sripitsanu Bungalows Hat Tham ⓣ038 216336. From Tha Lang walk to *Tiew Pai*, cross Thanon Asadang and walk a few metres to the left, then take the first right, a narrow (unsigned) road heading uphill; follow this road up past the monastery Wat Tham Yai Prik, continuing straight ahead at the monastery junction; *Sripitsanu* is ten minutes' walk from *Tiew Pai*. Stunningly located place whose dozen large, if rather haphazardly maintained, fan and air-con rooms and bungalows sit almost right at the edge of the cliff – some are actually built into the rockface. It's a gorgeous spot, with unsurpassed views and the possibility of swimming at low tide, though the place is in need of some serious TLC, and there's not much English spoken. Some bungalows have their own cooking facilities. Rooms ④, bungalows ⑤

Tham Pang Beach Hat Tham Pang ⓣ038 216153, ⓕ038 216122. The busiest west-coast accommodation, whose twenty fairly rudimentary concrete bungalows – all with bathroom, fan, veranda and partial sea view – are stacked in tiers up the cliffside behind the eponymous strand, Ko Si Chang's only real beach. There's a restaurant here, too, and beach-equipment for hire. ③

Tiew Pai Park Resort Thanon Asadang ⓣ038 216084, ⓦwww.tiewpai.com. Very central and good value, and most backpackers' first choice. Bungalows are set in a wooded garden and include very good fan, en-suite bungalows (with TV and fridge); some slightly cheaper, simpler versions; plus deluxe air-con bungalows with separate living quarters and/or connecting rooms. Fan ③, air-con ④–⑤

Around the island

The main sights on the island are **Rama V's old palace** on the southeast coast and the popular Chinese pilgrimage temple **Saan Chao Paw Khao Yai** on the northeastern tip, with west-coast **Hat Tham Pang** the main beach. There's reasonable **diving** off diminutive **Ko Thaai Taa Muen**, an islet to the south of Ko Si Chang, best explored on a dive trip arranged through *Pan and David Restaurant* (B2500 including equipment and three tanks; minimum five people; book two days ahead). **Fishing** boats with a skipper can be chartered from the two Ko Si Chang piers for B1500 per day, or *Tiew Pai Park Resort* does half-day fishing trips with tackle, snorkelling gear and food for B2500 per ten-person boat.

Rama V's Palace and around

The most famous sight on the island is the partially ruined Rama V's Palace, which occupies a large chunk of gently sloping land midway down the east coast, behind pebbly **Hat Tha Wang**. It's an enjoyable place to explore and can be reached on foot from *Tiew Pai Park Resort* in about half an hour. En route, shortly before you reach the palace grounds, you'll pass the small and less than

△ Saphan Asadang pier at Rama V's Palace

riveting **Cholatassathan Museum** (Tues–Sun 9am–5pm; entry by donation), established by the resident Aquatic Resources Research Institute to provide an introduction to the coral and marine life around Ko Si Chang.

Built in the 1890s as a sort of health resort where sickly members of the royal family could recuperate in peace, **Rama V's Palace**, or Phra Judhadhut Ratchathan (daily 9am–5pm; free), formed the heart of a grand and extensive complex comprising homes for royal advisers, chalets for convalescents, quarters for royal concubines and administrative buildings. By the turn of the twentieth century, however, Rama V (King Chulalongkorn) had lost interest in his island project and so in 1901 his golden teak palace was moved piece by piece to Bangkok, and reconstructed there as Vimanmek Palace; its foundations are still visible just south of the palace's Saphan Asadang pier.

Following recent renovations, the elegant design of the **palace grounds** is apparent once more. It fans out around an elaborate labyrinth of fifty interlinked ponds, shaded by a semi-wild landscape of frangipani bushes and tropical shrubs – home to lots of millipedes and the odd snake – and connected via a maze of stone steps and balustrades that still cling to the shallow hillside. Close to the shore, four of the original Western-style **villas** have been reconstructed to house displays – of varying interest – on Chulalongkorn's relationship with Ko Si Chang; one of them also doubles as a coffee shop. There's enough to keep you ambling around here for a couple of hours, with signs directing you up the hillside to the palace's unusual whitewashed shrine, **Wat Asadang**, whose circular walls are punctuated with Gothic stained-glass windows and surmounted by a chedi. Beyond Wat Asadang a path leads you to a viewpoint, though there's little point following the signs for the information office beyond that as it's unstaffed.

Hat Tham Pang and around

The main beach on the west coast, and the most popular one on the island, is **Hat Tham Pang**, a B80 samlor ride from either pier. The kilometre-long stretch of sand here is lined with deckchairs and beach umbrellas and you can rent kayaks (B300/hour), inner tubes, snorkels (B100/hour) and fishing rods from Uncle Juk's watersports stall. The best **snorkelling** spots are further south, around the tiny islands off Ko Si Chang's southern tip, particularly off the north coast of **Ko Khang Khao** – forty minutes by kayak from Hat Tham Pang.

North of Hat Tham Pang, and also accessible via a fork off Thanon Asadang opposite *Tiew Pai* (a ten-minute walk), you'll find the **Wat Tham Yai Prik** temple and meditation centre, which is open to interested visitors and holds frequent retreats. Unusually, nuns as well as monks here wear brown (rather than white) and everyone participates in the upkeep of the monastery: you can see some of the fruits of their labour in the extensive roadside orchard. Just west of the wat, the dramatically situated *Sripitsanu Bungalows* offers glorious views over the pretty, rocky cove known as **Hat Tham** or **Hat Sai**, which is only really swimmable at low tide.

North to Saan Chao Paw Khao Yai

Back down on the ring road, continuing in a northwesterly direction, you'll pass beneath the gaze of a huge yellow Buddha before reaching the rocky northwest headland of **Khao Khat**, a few hundred metres further along Thanon Asadang. The uninterrupted panorama of open sea makes this a classic sunset spot, and there's a path along the cliffside.

From here the road heads east to reach the gaudy, multi-tiered Chinese temple, **Saan Chao Paw Khao Yai** (Shrine of the Father Spirit of the Great

Hill), stationed at the top of a steep flight of steps and commanding a good view of the harbour and the mainland coast. Established here long before Rama V arrived on the island, the shrine was dedicated by Chinese seamen who saw a strange light coming out of one of the **caves** behind the modern-day temple. The caves, now full of religious statues and related paraphernalia, are visited by boatloads of Chinese pilgrims, particularly over Chinese New Year. Continue on up the cliffside to reach the small pagoda built for Rama V and enshrining a **Buddha's Footprint**. Two very long, very steep flights of stairs give access to the footprint: the easternmost one starts at the main waterfront entrance to the Chinese temple and takes you past a cluster of monks' meditation cells, while the westerly one rises further west along the ring road and offers the finest lookouts. It's well worth the vertiginous ascent, not least for the views out over Thailand's east coast; looking down you'll see a congestion of river barges bringing tonnes of rice, sugar and tapioca flour from the central plains to the international cargo boats anchored off Ko Si Chang's lee shore, and behind them, the tiny island of Ko Khram.

Eating and drinking

One of the most enjoyable **places to eat** on the island is *Pan and David Restaurant* (closed Tues) on the east-coast road, 200m before the entrance to the old palace grounds, which is run by a sociable and well-informed American expat and his Thai wife. The long and delicious menu includes authentically fiery *som tam*, home-made fettuccine with black olives (B125), fillet steak (B245), Thai curries, a good vegetarian selection, brownies and home-made fresh strawberry ice cream (B55), as well as very good value Italian wine (from B65/glass). Other good options include *Nok and Noi,* across the road from *Pan and David*, and the locally famous *Lek Tha Wang*, slightly further down the road towards the palace, both of which are known for their seafood. *Tiew Pai* serves travellers' food, and *Si Chang View Resort's* speciality is its seafood served in one of several clifftop pavilions, especially popular at sunset, though be prepared for slow service and a fairly hefty bill; they do fresh coffee too.

Pattaya

With its streets full of high-rise hotels and touts on every corner, **PATTAYA** is the epitome of exploitative tourism gone mad, but most of Pattaya's two million annual visitors don't mind that the place looks like the Costa del Sol because what they are here for is sex. The city swarms with male and female **prostitutes**, spiced up by a sizeable population of transvestites (*katoey*), and plane-loads of Western men flock here to enjoy their services in the rash of hostess bar-beers, go-go clubs and massage parlours for which "Patpong-on-Sea" is notorious. The ubiquitous signs trumpeting "Viagra for Sale" say it all. Pattaya also has the largest **gay scene** in Thailand, with several exclusively gay hotels and a whole area given over to gay sex bars.

Pattaya's evolution into sin city began with the Vietnam War, when it got fat on selling sex to American servicemen. When the soldiers and sailors left in the mid-1970s, Western tourists were enticed to fill their places, and as the seaside Sodom and Gomorrah boomed, ex-servicemen returned to run the sort of joints they had once blown their dollars in. These days, almost half the bars and restaurants in Pattaya are Western-run. More recently, there has been an influx of criminal gangs from Germany, Russia and Japan, who reportedly find Pattaya

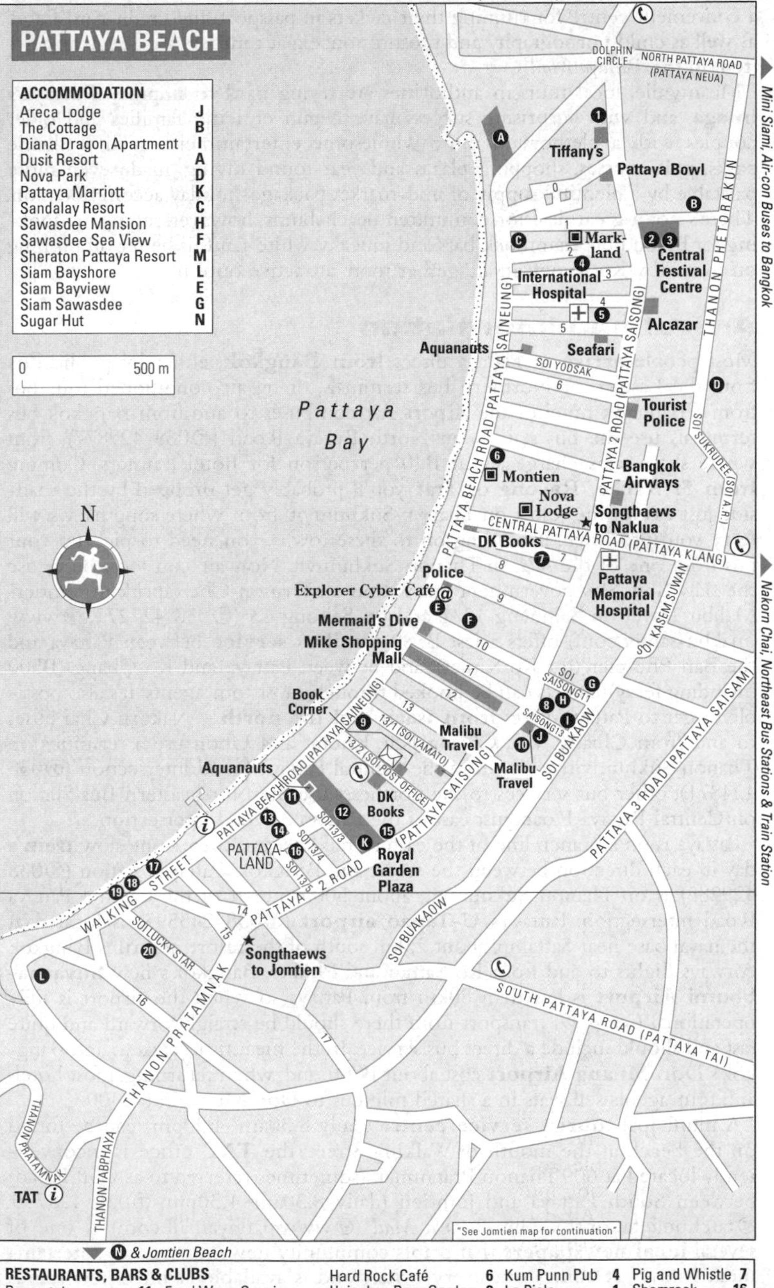

RESTAURANTS, BARS & CLUBS

Baywatch 11	Food Wave Seaview Food Court 12	Hard Rock Café 6	Kum Punn Pub 4
Bighorn Steakhouse 10	Fuji 3	Heineken Beer Garden 2	La Piola 1
The Blues Factory 20	Green Bottle 8	Hopf Brew House 9	Lucifer's 18
Café New Orleans 14		Jazz Pit 5	Marine Disco 19
		King Seafood 17	PIC Kitchen 5
Pig and Whistle 7	Shamrock 16	Shenanigans 15	Sugar Hut N
Tip's 13			

a convenient centre for running their rackets in passport and credit-card fraud, as well as child pornography and prostitution; expat murders are a regular news item in the *Pattaya Mail*.

Meanwhile, local tourism authorities are trying hard to improve **Pattaya's image**, and with surprising success have begun enticing families and older couples with a plethora of more wholesome entertainments such as theme parks, golf courses, shopping plazas and year-round diving, made even more palatable by a plentiful supply of mid-market package-holiday accommodation. There's not a great deal for committed beach-bums, however, so anyone looking for beach huts, hammock bars and squeaky white sands is better off pushing on to nearby Ko Samet, an altogether more attractive option.

Arrival and information

Most people **arrive** in Pattaya direct **from Bangkok**, either by public **bus** from the Eastern or Northern bus terminals, or by air-conditioned tour bus from a Bangkok hotel or the airport. Air-con buses to and from Bangkok bus terminals use the bus station on North Pattaya Road (Ⓣ038 429877), from where share-taxis charge about B40 per person for hotel transfers. Coming **from Si Racha**, **Rayong** or **Trat** you'll probably get dropped by the roadside just east of the resort on Thanon Sukhumvit, from where songthaews will ferry you into town; if heading on to these towns, you need to pick up your bus from one of the *sala* on Thanon Sukhumvit. Non-air-con local buses use the Baw Kaw Saw government bus station on Thanon Chaiyapruk in Jomtien. Malibu Travel on Sainueng 13/1 and on Saisong 13 (Ⓣ038 427277, Ⓦwww.malibu-samet.com) offers a fast B180 **minibus service** between Pattaya and the Ban Phe pier (for Ko Samet), and between Pattaya and Ko Chang (B500 including ferry); tickets can be booked through most tour agents. It's also possible to get to Pattaya direct **from Isaan and the north** – Nakorn Chai buses to and from Chiang Mai, Chiang Rai, Khorat and Ubon use a terminus on Thanon Sukhumvit, across from the Central Pattaya Road intersection (Ⓣ038 424871); other bus services to the northeast use the Northeastern Bus Station on Central Pattaya Road, just east of the Pattaya 3 Road intersection.

Pattaya is on a branch line of the eastern rail line, and there's one slow **train** a day in each direction between the resort and Bangkok. Pattaya's station (Ⓣ038 429285) is on Thanon Sukhumvit, about 500m north of the Central Pattaya Road intersection. Pattaya's **U-Tapao airport** (Ⓣ038 245595) is located at the naval base near Sattahip, about 25km south of the resort, and runs Bangkok Airways flights to and from Ko Samui and Phuket. Bangkok's new **Suvarnabhumi Airport** is less than 80km from Pattaya so when the airport is fully operational (see p.99) transport from there should be straightforward and quite fast and should include a direct bus service. In the meantime, taxis to and Bangkok's **Don Muang Airport** cost about B800, and, when returning, most hotels and tour agents sell seats in a shared minibus to Don Muang for B400.

A municipal **tourist service centre** (daily 8.30am–4.30pm) can be found on the beach at the mouth of Walking Street; the **TAT** office is inconveniently located at 609 Thanon Pratamnak (sometimes referred to as Cliff Road) between South Pattaya and Jomtien (daily 8.30am–4.30pm; Ⓣ038 428750, Ⓔtatchon@tat.or.th). The *Pattaya Mail* (Ⓦwww.pattayamail.com) is one of several **local newspapers** that prints community news stories and entertainment listings; it comes out every Friday and is available at most newsstands and bookstores. Most hotels and many restaurants hand out free monthly what's-on magazines.

Orientation

Pattaya comprises three separate bays. At the centre is the four-kilometre **Pattaya Beach**, the noisiest, most unsightly zone of the resort, crowded with yachts and tour boats and fringed by a sliver of sand and a paved beachfront walkway. Signed as Pattaya Sainueng, but known by its English name, **Pattaya Beach Road** runs the length of the beach and is connected to the parallel Pattaya 2 Road (Pattaya Saisong) by a string of sois numbered from 1 in the north to 17 in the south. The core of this block, between sois 6 and 13, is referred to as **Central Pattaya** (Pattaya Klang) and is packed with hotels, restaurants, bars, fast-food joints, souvenir shops and tour operators. During the day this is the busiest part of the resort, but after dark the neon zone south of Soi 13/2 – **South Pattaya** – takes over. Known locally as "the strip", this is what Pattaya is really about, with sex for sale in go-go bars, discos, massage parlours and open-sided bar-beers. The town's enclave of gay sex bars is here too, focused mainly on the interlinked network of small lanes known as **Pattayaland** sois 1, 2 and 3 (or Boyz Town), but actually signed as sois 13/3, 13/4 and 13/5, between the Royal Garden Plaza and Soi 14. Pattaya Beach Road continues south from its junction with South Pattaya Road (Thanon

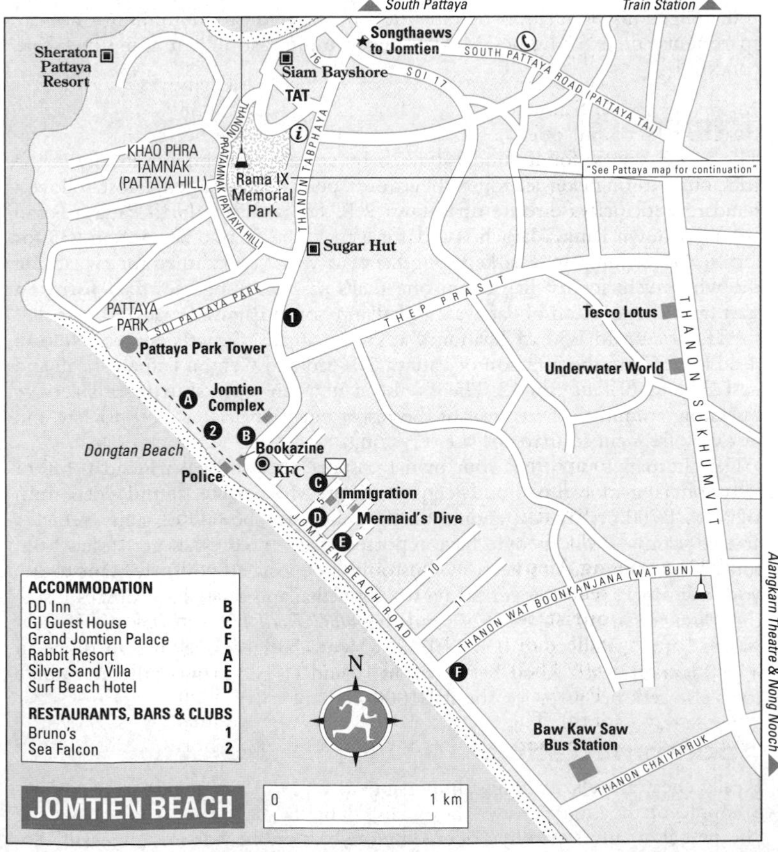

Pattaya Tai) all the way down to the *Siam Bayshore Hotel*; this stretch of road is also known as **Walking Street** because it's pedestrianized every evening from 7pm. **North Pattaya**, between Central Pattaya Road (Thanon Pattaya Klang) and North Pattaya Road (Thanon Hat Pattaya Neua), also has its bar-beers, but is a slightly calmer district.

The southerly bay, **Jomtien Beach** (sometimes spelt Chom Tian), is also fronted by enormous high-rises, many of which are condominiums, though there are some low-rise, mid-priced hotels along the beachfront road, Jomtien Beach Road (Thanon Hat Jomtien), as well. Fourteen kilometres long, it's considered Thailand's premier windsurfing spot. Though the atmosphere here is not as frantic as in Pattaya, Jomtien suffers from the same excess of bar-beers and shops peddling beachwear and tacky souvenirs and, like its neighbour, is also constantly under construction. The nicest stretch of sand is **Dongtan Beach**, beyond the northern end of the road: shady, and car-free between 10am and 5pm, it is Pattaya's main gay beach, though used by all. The bulge of land behind Dongtan Beach, separating Jomtien from Pattaya is Khao Phra Tamnak, variously translated as **Pattaya Hill** or Buddha Hill, site of several posh hotels and the Pattaya Park waterpark and funfair.

Naklua Bay, around the northerly headland from Pattaya Beach, is the quietest of the three enclaves, and has managed to retain its fishing harbour and indigenous population despite the onslaught of condominiums, holiday apartments and expat homes. Most of the accommodation here is in time-share condos.

Transport

The easiest way to get around Pattaya is by **songthaew**, known locally as the baht bus – though on all routes beware of being overcharged. Most follow a standard anticlockwise route up Pattaya 2 Road as far as North Pattaya Road and back down Pattaya Beach Road, for a fixed fee of B10 per person (B5 for locals). Never jump in a parked songthaew, as you'll be charged for chartering the whole vehicle: just flag down one that's passing. Songthaews **to Jomtien** start from the junction of Pattaya 2 Road and South Pattaya Road and cost B10 to *KFC* or up to B30 to Thanon Wat Boonkanjana. Songthaews **to Naklua** head north from the junction of Pattaya 2 Road and Central Pattaya Road and cost B10 to Naklua Soi 12. There's also a new **air-con shuttle-bus** service operating around all three areas of the resort but it's pricey at B30 flat fare and not very frequent so may not last very long.

The alternative is to rent your own transport: Pattaya Beach Road is full of touts offering motorbikes and jeeps for rent. **Motorbike rental** costs from B200 to B700 per day depending on the bike's size; beware of faulty vehicles, and of scams – some people have reported that rented bikes get stolen from tourists by touts keen to keep the customer's deposit, so you may want to use your own lock. Avis **car rental** (ⓦwww.avisthailand.com) have offices inside the *Dusit Resort* (ⓣ038 361627) and the *Hard Rock Hotel* (ⓣ038 428755) in North Pattaya, Budget (ⓣ038 710717, ⓦwww.budget.co.th) has an office in Tipp Plaza on Beach Road, between sois 10 and 11, and many of the motorbike touts also rent out jeeps for about B1000 per day.

Accommodation

Really cheap **hotels** are almost impossible to find in Pattaya and Jomtien. Only a couple of the "inexpensive" hotels listed below have rooms for B250; the cheapest alternatives are often offered by the bars on the side sois (especially Soi

6, Sois 13/2, 13/3 and 13/4) who keep rooms upstairs (4), both for short-term customers and for anyone else who doesn't mind the noise. Hotels in the next category up generally offer air-con rooms at least and often a swimming pool as well; prices in all categories plummet by up to fifty percent whenever demand is slack. Advance reservations are advisable to stay in the best-value hotels.

Bear in mind that the sex industry ensures that all rooms have beds large enough for at least two people; rates quoted here are for "single" rooms with one big double bed (a "double" room will have two big double beds and cost more). Another effect of the sex industry is that hotel guests are often assumed to be untrustworthy, so when checking in you're likely to be asked for a deposit against the loss of your room key and against the use of your mini-bar and phone.

Pattaya: inexpensive and moderate

Areca Lodge 198/21 Soi Saisong 13 (aka Soi Diana Inn), Central Pattaya ⓣ038 410123, ⓦwww.arecalodge.com. Unusually stylish place for Pattaya, with pleasantly furnished air-con rooms in two wings built around two swimming pools, all of them with balconies. 6–7

The Cottage Off Pattaya 2 Rd, North Pattaya ⓣ038 425650, ⓔthe_cottage2002@yahoo.com. Good-value, well-appointed brick bungalows, all with air-con, pleasantly located in a pretty garden compound a good distance off the main road. Convenient for the shops and restaurants in the Central Festival Centre complex. Facilities include two small swimming pools, a bar and a restaurant. 5

Diana Dragon Apartment 198/16 Soi Saisong 13 (aka Soi Diana Inn), Central Pattaya ⓣ038 423928, ⓦwww.dianapattaya.co.th. Enormous, low-budget fan and air-con rooms with fridge, and use of the pool at *Diana Inn*, 100m away; favoured by long-stay tourists. Fan 3, air-con 4

Nova Park Soi Sukrudee (aka Soi AR), off Thanon Phetdrakun, North Pattaya ⓣ038 415304, ⓦwww.novaparkpattaya.com. Plush, good-value serviced apartments with a pool on site and free ADSL Internet access and VCDs in every room. 7

Sandalay Resort Between sois 1 and 2, Pattaya Beach Rd, North Pattaya ⓣ038 422660, ⓦwww.sandalayresort.com. This medium-sized high-rise just across the road from the beach stands out because of its contemporary-style furnishings, giving it an unusually modish feel for a resort where image is rarely a priority. Standard rooms are small but well designed and deluxe versions are impressively big: both options are available with sea view and tiny balcony at extra cost. All rooms have air-con and TV and there's a swimming pool. 8–9

Sawasdee Mansion 502/1 Saisong 11 (aka Soi Honey Inn), Pattaya 2 Rd, Central Pattaya ⓣ038 425360, ⓦwww.sawasdee-hotels.com. The cheapest branch of the ubiquitous *Sawasdee* chain of budget hotels has some of the most inexpensive rooms in Pattaya and is friendlier than many. Rooms are shabby and spartan – and many have no external window – but are available with fan or air-con and there's a restaurant downstairs. Fan 2, air-con 3

Sawasdee Sea View 302/1 Soi 10, Central Pattaya ⓣ038 710566, ⓦwww.sawasdee-hotels.com. Occupying a great location in a still fairly quiet soi just a few dozen metres off the beachfront road, this place offers large and quite trendily decorated rooms, all with air-con and TV but none enjoying a real sea view. 5

Siam Sawasdee Corner of Soi Saisong 11 and Soi Buakaow, Central Pattaya ⓣ038 720330, ⓦwww.sawasdee-hotels.com. The swimming pool is the attraction here and draws a fairly rowdy crowd: the 206 rooms are on the scruffy side but all come with air-con, TV and fridge. 5

Pattaya: expensive

Dusit Resort 240/2 Pattaya Beach Road ⓣ038 425611, ⓦwww.dusit.com. This is one of only a few Beach Road hotels (the others are the southern end) to be actually on the beach, so many rooms have direct sea views – worth paying the extra for as some offer impressive panoramas of the whole bay – as do both swimming pools. Good facilities include spa, fitness club and several restaurants, and rooms are standard deluxe. 9

Pattaya Marriott 218 Pattaya Beach Rd, Central Pattaya ⓣ038 412120, ⓦwww.marriotthotels.com/pyxmc. Located right in the heart of the resort and across the road from the beach, but pleasingly secluded within a tropical garden, this well-equipped hotel has very comfortable top-notch rooms, a huge pool, a spa, floodlit tennis courts, mountain-bike rental and a kids' club. ⑨

Sheraton Pattaya Resort 437 Thanon Pratamnak (Cliff Rd), South Pattaya ⓣ038 259888, ⓦwww.starwoodhotels.com. Pattaya's best hotel is smaller and more intimate than most in its class and offers five-star rooms in its two hotel wings as well as in private pavilions. The beautiful series of freeform swimming pools is set within lush gardens – compensating for the minuscule private beach – and there's a spa and three restaurants, though it's built on a hill so be prepared for lots of steps, and you'll need transport to get to the shops and restaurants of downtown Pattaya. ⑨

Siam Bayshore 559 Pattaya Beach Rd ⓣ038 428678, ⓦwww.siamhotels.com. At the far southern end of the South Pattaya strip, overlooking the beach, this popular hotel comprises 270 rooms spread over twelve wings and is set in exceptionally lush tropical gardens. Many rooms have balconies offering uninterrupted sea views, and there are two pools as well as tennis courts and snooker, table-tennis and badminton facilities. ⑧

Siam Bayview Pattaya Beach Rd, on the corner of Soi 10, Central Pattaya ⓣ038 423871, ⓦwww.siamhotels.com. Large, very centrally located and well-priced 350-room hotel that has smart, good-sized rooms, many of them with sea views. Good value considering its location and facilities, which include two swimming pools, tennis courts, snooker and several restaurants. ⑧–⑨

Sugar Hut 391/18 Thanon Tabphaya, midway between South Pattaya and Jomtien ⓣ038 251686, ⓦwww.sugar-hut.com. The most characterful accommodation in Pattaya comprises a charming collection of 33 Ayutthaya-style traditional wooden bungalows set in a fabulously lush garden with three swimming pools. The bungalows are in tropical-chic style, with low beds, open-roofed shower rooms, mosquito nets and private verandas; the more expensive ones have a sitting room as well. You'll need your own transport as it's nowhere near the restaurants, shops or sea. ⑨

Jomtien Beach

DD Inn Just back from the beach, on a tiny soi opposite *KFC* at the far north end of Beach Rd ⓣ038 232995, ⓔddinn@hotmail.com. Friendly, good-value guest-house-style little hotel in an ideal spot just a few metres from the beach. Rooms with balconies are slightly pricier, but all rooms come with air-con and TV. ③–④

GI Guest House 75/14 Soi 5 (Soi Post Office), off Beach Rd ⓣ038 231581, ⓔgitravel@gmail.com. Small but cheap rooms in this little, Bangkok-style guest house. All rooms have TV and hot water; you pay more for air-con. Fan ②, air-con ③

Grand Jomtien Palace 365 Beach Rd, at the corner of Thanon Wat Boonkanjana (aka Wat Bun) ⓣ038 231405, ⓦwww.grandjomtienpalace.com. Welcoming, mid-market, package-oriented fourteen-storey hotel where many of the comfortable, air-con rooms have a decent sea view and even the cheapest have partial sight of the water. Facilities include three swimming pools, a beer garden and restaurant, and a small shopping arcade. ⑦

Rabbit Resort Dongtan beachfront, 400m north up the beach from Thep Prasit/Beach Road junction ⓣ038 303303, ⓦwww.rabbitresort.com. Beautiful place that's the most appealing option in Jomtien, and located on the nicest stretch of beach, the predominantly but not exclusively gay, Dongtan Beach. Comprising mainly teakwood cottages, elegantly furnished with Thai fabrics, artworks and antiques and many with garden-style bathrooms, plus some "forest rooms" in a two-storey block, all of them set around a tropical garden just a few metres off the beach. ⑨

Silver Sand Villa Next to Soi White House at the northern end of Beach Rd ⓣ038 231288, ⓦwww.silversandvilla.com. The huge, nicely furnished air-con rooms in the old wing here are good value (and most are wheelchair-accessible), but you need to book ahead to be sure of a pool view rather than a wall view. Rooms in the new wing are more expensive and, though plainly furnished, they all have balconies and pool views. The hotel also has two swimming pools and restaurant. Old wing ⑤, new wing ⑥

Surf Beach Hotel Between sois 5 and 7 at the north end of Beach Rd ⓣ038 231025, ⓕ038 231029. Popular mid-range place across from the beach. Rooms are old-fashioned and a bit faded, but all have air-con and TV, and some have a sea view. ⑤

The resort

Most tourists in Pattaya spend the days recovering from the night before: not much happens before midday, breakfasts are served until early afternoon, and the hotel pool generally seems more inviting than a tussle with water-skis. But the energetic are well catered for, with a decent range of dive centres, watersports facilities, golf courses and theme parks.

Snorkelling and scuba-diving

Snorkelling and scuba-diving are popular in Pattaya, though if you've got the choice between diving here or off the Andaman coast, go for the latter – the reefs there are a lot more spectacular. The big advantage of Pattaya is that it can be dived year-round, and underwater visibility is consistent. The main destinations for local **dive trips** are the group of "outer islands" about 25km from shore, which include Ko Rin, Ko Man Wichai and Ko Klung Badaan, where you have a good chance of seeing big schools of barracuda, jacks and tuna, as well as moray eels, blue-spotted stingrays, and hawksbill and green turtles. There are also three rewarding wreck dives in the Samae San/Sattahip area: the 21-metre-deep freighter *Phetchaburi Bremen*, which went down in the 1930s; the 64-metre-long cargo ship *Hardeep*, which was sunk during World War II and can be navigated along the entire length of its interior; and the HMS *Khram*, which was sunk deliberately by the Thai navy in 2003 to make a new artificial reef. A one-day dive trip with a reputable dive company, including two dives, equipment and lunch, generally costs around B3000, with accompanying snorkellers paying B800. Several companies along Pattaya Beach Road run **snorkelling** trips to nearby Ko Larn and Bamboo Island (B1500), though mass tourism has taken its toll on these two islands and their coral.

Pattaya is also an easy place to learn to dive: with the good dive companies, one-day Discover Scuba Diving courses start at about B4000, and four-day Openwater **courses** average B14,000. Be careful when signing up for a dive course or expedition: unqualified instructors and dodgy equipment are a fact of life in Pattaya, especially at those outfits offering cheap deals, and it's as well to question other divers about all operators, PADI-certified or not (see p.70 of Basics for more guidelines and for advice on dive insurance). See "Hospitals" on p.470 for details of recompression chambers in the Pattaya area. The following are well-respected **dive shops** that run diving expeditions and internationally certificated courses; both also offer technical diving (down to 85m in the Samae San area), and long-term instructor training/career-development courses (up to six months), and both sell imported dive gear.

Aquanauts Soi Yodsak (Soi 6), Central Pattaya ⓣ038 361724, ⓦwww.aquanautsdive.com; and Pattaya-land Soi 1, South Pattaya ⓣ038 710727. British-run PADI Five-Star Instructor Development Centre. Also does lots of specialist cave and cavern diving.

Mermaid's Dive Centre Soi White House, Jomtien ⓣ038 232219, ⓦwww.learn-in-asia.com; and at Tipp Plaza between sois 10 and 11 on Beach Rd, Central Pattaya. PADI Five-Star Instructor Development Centre. Also offers IAHD programmes for disabled divers and instructors.

Watersports and golf

Both Pattaya and Jomtien are full of beachfront stalls organizing **water-skiing** (B1000/hour), **jet-skiing** (B650/30min) and **parasailing** (B500/round), though for **windsurfing** you'll need to go to Jomtien (B500/hour).

There are over fifteen international-standard **golf courses** within easy reach of Pattaya (ⓦwww.thaigolfer.com), some of them designed by famous golfers. Visitors' green fees average B1000 on a weekday, B1800 on a weekend, plus B250 for a caddy, and a set of clubs can usually be rented for about B500. One popular option is to join a golf **package** to one of the top courses organized by East Coast Travel (ⓣ038 300927, ⓦwww.pattayagolfpackage.com). The following courses are all less than an hour's drive from Pattaya, with the closest listed first and the furthest last; for directions, either call the course or ask at your hotel. Phoenix Golf and Country Club (27 holes; ⓣ038 239391); Siam Country Club (18 holes; ⓣ038 249381); Laem Chabang International Country Club (27 holes; ⓣ038 372273, ⓦwww.laemchabanggolf.com); Eastern Star Golf Course (18 holes; ⓣ038 630410); St Andrew's 2000 (18 holes; ⓣ038 893838 ⓦwww.standrews2000golf.com).

Theme parks and other attractions

The family-oriented **Pattaya Park Water Park** (daily 11am–10pm; ⓣ038 251201, ⓦwww.pattayapark.com), whose gigantic 240-metre-high tower on Buddha Hill, at the far northern end of Jomtien, is visible from all over the resort, features water slides, a Viking ship, a 170-metre jump from said tower, and other funfair-style rides, as well as three panoramic revolving restaurants (on floors 52, 53 and 54). Easiest access is by taxi, though the Jomtien songthaew will drop you within about 750m.

One of the most enjoyable indoor attractions in the resort is **Ripley's Believe It Or Not** (daily 11am–11pm; B380, kids B280, joint tickets with other Ripley attractions from an extra B100), on the third floor of the Royal Garden Plaza on Pattaya Beach Road. It's part of a worldwide chain of curiosity museums inspired by the bizarre collections of the American cartoonist and adventurer Robert Leroy Ripley, and displays lots of outlandish objects and novelties from Thailand and further afield (such as models of the world's tallest, smallest and fattest men), as well as an exhibition on sharks. The Ripley's third-floor empire also includes Ripley's Haunted Adventure plus a 4D movie-screen simulator and an infinity maze.

Advertised as the only one of its kind in the world, the **Museum of Bottle Art** (daily 11am–8pm; B100), 100m south of the bus station on Thanon Sukhumvit, contains three hundred pieces of miniature art in bottles, including Dutch windmills, Thai temples, a Saudi mosque and a British coach and horses. To see them, take an eastbound songthaew along Central Pattaya Road, get off as soon as you reach Thanon Sukhumvit, and walk 200m south.

The hugely ambitious **Sanctuary of Truth**, also known as **Wang Boran** and **Prasat Mai** (daily 8am–5pm; B500, kids B250; ⓣ038 225407, ⓦwww.sanctuaryoftruth.com; daily dolphin shows at 11.30am and 3.30pm), is also a kind of replica, but on a 1:1 scale. Conceived by the man behind the Muang Boran Ancient City complex near Bangkok, it's a huge temple-palace designed to evoke the great ancient Khmer sanctuaries of Angkor and built entirely of wood. It was begun in 1981 and is still a work-in-progress. The sanctuary is located behind imposing crenellated walls off the west end of Naklua Soi 12, close to the *Garden Sea View* hotel; from Central Pattaya, take a Naklua-bound songthaew as far as Soi 12, then a motorbike taxi. Built in a fabulously dramatic spot beside the sea, the temple rises to 105m at its highest point and fans out into four gopura (entrance pavilions), each of which is covered in symbolic woodcarvings. The **carvings** on the north (seaside) gopura are inspired by Cambodian mythology, and include a tower above the gopura that's crowned with an image of the four-headed Hindu god Brahma; those on the east gopura refer to China, so the Mahayana Buddhist Bodhisattvas have Chinese faces; the carvings on the west gopura evoke India and include scenes from the Hindu epic the *Mahabarata*; and the southern entrance has images from Thailand, such as scenes from the Hindu tale, the *Ramayana*. For more on the symbolism of Hindu and Buddhist sculptures, see the piece on Art and Architecture in Contexts, p.873.

There are several theme parks, "culture villages" and wildlife parks on the outskirts of Pattaya, all well signed off the main roads. **Mini Siam** (daily 8am–10pm; B100, kids B50), just north of the North Pattaya Road/Thanon Sukhumvit intersection, is just what it sounds like: the cream of Thailand's most precious monuments reconstructed to 1:25 scale, plus miniature replicas of international icons such as the Sydney Opera House and the Statue of Liberty; call ⓣ038 421628 to arrange transport. **Nong Nooch Tropical Garden** (daily 8am-6pm; B550; ⓣ038 429321, ⓦwww.nongnoochtropicalgarden.com), 18km south of Pattaya off Thanon Sukhumvit, is a 600-acre botanical park that's said to have the world's largest **orchid garden**; in addition it puts on performances of traditional dancing and elephant-rides. The **Elephant Village**, 7km northeast of Pattaya, offers sixty-minute elephant "treks" round its park for B900, and there's also an elephant-training show every afternoon (2.30pm; B500). For details and transport, call ⓣ038 249818, or visit ⓦwww.elephant-village-pattaya.com. **Underwater World**, close to Tesco Lotus just south of the Thep Prasit junction with Thanon Sukhumvit (B360, kids B180 or free if under 90cm tall), is a small, expensive, but rather beautiful aquarium comprising a trio of long fibreglass tunnels that transport you through three different marine worlds; easiest access by songthaew would be to try and hail one travelling from Jomtien along Thanon Thep Prasit.

Eating

Overall, **food** in Pattaya and Jomtien is expensive and pretty dire, but there are some good spots. For the cheapest, most authentic Thai food, especially Isaan favourites such as *som tam* and fried chicken, just head for the nearest construction site (there's nearly always one within 500m) and you'll find stalls catering for the tastes and budgets of the construction-site workers, most of whom come from the northeast.

Baywatch Pattaya Beach Rd, between sois 13/3 and 13/4, Central Pattaya. Open 24hr, this is a good joint for your all-day breakfast (from B70), complete with sea view and sidewalk vantage point.

Bighorn Steakhouse Central Shopping Arcade, off Saisong 13 (Soi Diana Inn) ⓦwww.bighornsteakhouse.com. Famous for its tenderloin steaks – priced from B340 for 200g – if you are man or woman enough to down the one-kilo steak (B1350) you get into the restaurant's hall-of-fame and your name on the website. Daily noon–midnight.

Bruno's 306/63 Chateau Dale Plaza, Thanon Tabphaya, Jomtien ⓦwww.brunos-pattaya.com. A local institution that's a favourite with expats celebrating special occasions. The food is classy, expensive, European – Provençal-style rack of lamb, sirloin steak, dark-chocolate mousse – and there's a cellar of some 150 wines. Main dishes from B185. Daily noon–2.30pm & 6pm–late.

Café New Orleans Soi 13/4, Central Pattaya. Specializing in Cajun and Creole dishes, with especially recommended baby back ribs (B375), jambalaya (B235), and steaks. Mon–Fri 3pm–midnight, Sat &Sun noon–midnight.

Food Wave Seaview Food Court Top floor of the Royal Garden Plaza, Pattaya Beach Rd, Central Pattaya. Upscale food court with fine views of the bay and individual concessions serving Thai, Italian, Indian and European dishes averaging B85. Not exactly haute cuisine, but fast, hassle-free and fairly inexpensive for Pattaya.

Fuji Central Festival Centre, Pattaya 2 Road, North Pattaya. Phenomenally popular branch of the Japanese chain restaurant – and deservedly so. Authentic flavours and moderate prices for everything from sashimi (from B120) to teppanyaki, sushi sets and even chilled *zaru soba* noodles. Daily 11am–11pm.

King Seafood Opposite Soi 15, Walking St, South Pattaya. Considered to be the best of South Pattaya's three famously enormous seafront seafood restaurants, this place specializes in fresh seafood, in particular tiger prawns and giant lobsters for around B100–250. Daily 11am–1am.

Kitchen Soi 5, North Pattaya. One of Pattaya's finest traditional Thai restaurants, set in a stylish series of teak buildings with the option of Thai-style cushion seating. The mouth-watering menu (from B150) features elegantly presented curries, lots of different seafood platters (served grilled or fried, laced with chilli and/or coconut, or accompanied by asparagus and mushroom), spicy salads and some vegetarian dishes. Daily 8am–midnight.

La Piola Next to Tiffany's Cabaret on Pattaya 2 Rd, North Pattaya. A decent wine list and good Italian food including a ten-dish antipasto, wood-fired pizzas (from B220), Mediterranean-style fish with olives and tomatoes (from B200), and pasta with imported cheese (B300). Dine in the air-conditioned interior or outdoors with a prime view of Pattaya 2 Road's bar-beer enclave "Drinking Street". Daily 6pm–1am.

Sea Falcon Dongtan beachfront, Jomtien. Popular, mid-priced almost-on-the beach restaurant known for its lobster and steak. Daily 8am–11pm.

Sugar Hut 391/18 Thanon Tabphaya, midway between South Pattaya and Jomtien. Attached to the charming hotel described on p.464, this restaurant gives you the chance to soak up the ambience and enjoy the tropical gardens without shelling out for a bungalow. Food is served in an open-sided *sala* and is mainly classy (and expensive) traditional Thai; recommendations include fried catfish in coconut milk and chilli, and chicken baked with pineapple. Set menus from B500–750, but worth the splurge.

Tip's 22/10 Pattaya Beach Rd, between sois 13/4 and 13/5, South Pattaya. Long-running Pattaya institution offering over a dozen different set breakfasts (from B70). Daily 6.40am–midnight.

Drinking and nightlife

Entertainment is Pattaya's *raison d'être* and the **nightlife** is what most tourists come for, as do expats from Laem Chabang port, oilfield workers from the Arabian Gulf and shore-leave marines on R&R. Of the thousand plus **bars** in Pattaya, the majority are the so-called "bar-beers", open-air drinking spots staffed by hostesses who flirt, charm and banter their way through the afternoons and nights, encouraging punters to buy as much beer as possible and, ideally, to round off the night by taking one of them back to the hotel. Sex makes more money than booze in Pattaya – depending on who you believe, there are between six thousand and twenty thousand Thais working in Pattaya's sex industry; most depressing of all is the fact that this workforce includes children as young as 10, a disgusting iniquity that persists in spite of fairly frequent high-profile paedophile arrests. Sex-for-sale is an all-pervasive trade here: there are hundreds of go-go bars in town, and even the uninspiring discos – such as the huge and sleazy *Marine Disco* and *Lucifer's*, both towards the southern end of Walking Street, and the enormous *Palace*, just north of the intersection of Soi 1 and Pattaya 2 Road in North Pattaya – are just great big pick-up joints.

Bars

Pattaya's outdoor **bar-beers** group themselves in clusters all over North, Central and South Pattaya: there's barely a 500-metre stretch of road without its bar-beer enclave. The setup is the same in all of them: from mid-afternoon the punters – usually lone males – sit on stools around a brashly lit circular bar, behind which the hostesses keep the drinks, bawdy chat and well-worn jokes flowing. Beer is generally inexpensive at these places, the atmosphere low-key and good-humoured, and, though most of the hostesses are aiming to score for the night, couples as well as single women drinkers are almost always made welcome.

Drinks are a lot more expensive in the bouncer-guarded **go-go bars** on Walking Street in South Pattaya, where near-naked hostesses serve the beer and live sex shows keep the boozers hooked through the night. The scene follows much the same pattern as in Patpong, Nana and Soi Cowboy in Bangkok, with the women dancing on a small stage in the hope they might be bought for the night – or the week. Go-go dancers, shower shows and striptease are also the mainstays of the **gay scene**, centred on Pattayaland Soi 3 (Soi 13/5), South Pattaya.

There's not a great deal of demand for **bars** where the emphasis is on simple companionable drinking, but those listed below are comparatively low-key and welcoming.

The Blues Factory Soi Lucky Star, Walking Street, South Pattaya ⓦwww.thebluesfactorypattaya.com. Considered to be the best live-music venue in Pattaya, with nightly sets (except Mondays) from the famously charismatic rock guitarist Lam Morrison and his band, and (except on Wednesdays) from the house blues band as well. Happy hour 8.30–10pm.

Green Bottle Adjacent to *Diana Inn*, Pattaya 2 Rd, Central Pattaya. A cosy, air-con, pub-style bar that has forged a studiously unsleazy atmosphere and serves European food to keep you going just that little bit longer.

Hard Rock Café Just north of Central Pattaya Rd on Pattaya Beach Rd, Central Pattaya. Fairly standard franchise of the international chain, with nightly entertainment from a DJ and house band that do the usual classic pop and rock hits. Large cocktail menu plus a selection of burgers and salads to soak up the alcohol.

Heineken Beer Garden Central Festival Centre, Pattaya 2 Road, North Pattaya. Outdoor tables and live music nightly (from about 8pm) from Thai singers and bands, doing mostly Thai pop and country.

Hopf Brew House Between sois 13/1 (Yamato) and 13/2 (Post Office), Pattaya Beach Rd, Central Pattaya. Cavernous air-con pub, designed like a German beer hall around an internal courtyard, with a stage for the nightly live music. Attracts a youngish crowd, including vacationing couples, and serves bar snacks as well as beer.

Jazz Pit Soi 5, North Pattaya. Nightly live jazz (from 8pm) from the in-house trio in the cosy lounge-bar adjacent to the *PIC Kitchen* restaurant, and occasional high-profile celeb jamming sessions.

Kum Punn Pub Soi 2, North Pattaya. Typically Thai take on a country-and-western bar (lots of wood and the occasional buffalo head) that's known for its live bands who play nightly sets of authentic Thai folk music as well as soft rock.

Pig & Whistle Soi 7, Central Pattaya. Homely English-style pub that serves fish and chips, hosts twice-weekly quiz nights (Mon & Thurs) and shows all the major international sports events on its giant screen.

Shamrock Pattayaland 2 (Soi 13/4), South Pattaya. This British-run bar is a good place to catch local expat gossip. The manager sometimes entertains customers on his banjo, and his collection of folk-music tapes is also worth listening out for. On the edge of the gay district, but attracts a mixed crowd.

Shenanigans Next to the Royal Garden Plaza, Pattaya 2 Rd, Central Pattaya. Irish pub that keeps Guinness, Kilkenny Bitter and John Smith, serves UK-style pub food, and shows all major sports events on its big screen. Daily 9am till late.

Cabarets

Tour groups – and families – constitute the main audience at Pattaya's **transvestite cabarets**. Glamorous and highly professional, these shows are performed three times a night at Alcazar, opposite Soi 4 on Pattaya 2 Road in North Pattaya; and at Tiffany's, north of Soi 1 on Pattaya 2 Road in North Pattaya. Each theatre has a troupe of sixty or more transvestites who run through twenty musical-style numbers in fishnets and crinolines, ball gowns and leathers, against ever more lavish stage sets. All glitz and no sleaze, the shows cost from B400-600 per person. The even more ambitious Alangkarn (Tues–Sun from 6pm; B1400 including transport; ⓣ038 256000,

△ Tiffany's cabaret artiste

Ⓦwww.alangkarnthailand.com) is a Thai **cultural extravaganza** evening held at the Alangkarn Theatre in far southern Jomtien, featuring a highly theatrical medley of classical dance, martial arts, acrobatics and pyrotechnics; contact any tour agent for tickets and transport.

Shopping

Pattaya is not a bad place for **shopping**, especially at the two main shopping plazas – the Central Festival Centre on Pattaya 2 Road in North Pattaya, and Royal Garden Plaza in South Pattaya – which both have tempting arrays of fairly classy shops, ranging from designer clothes boutiques to smart gift and handicraft outlets, as well as branches of Boots the Chemist. Royal Garden Plaza 2nd floor also has a Jim Thompson Factory Sales outlet for silks and cottons.

Pattaya boasts some of Thailand's best English-language **bookshops** outside Bangkok. DK Books (daily 8am–11pm) on Soi 13/2 stocks a phenomenal range of books on Asia, and has a smaller branch north up Beach Road, on the corner of Central Pattaya Road. Bookazine, on the first floor of the Royal Garden Plaza in South Pattaya, and at Dongtan Beach in Jomtien, also has an impressive selection of titles, plus stacks of maps, but is best known for its unrivalled choice of international magazines. Book Corner on Soi 13/2 is another rewarding place to browse for Southeast Asian titles.

Listings

Airlines Bangkok Airways, 75/8 Pattaya 2 Rd, Central Pattaya Ⓣ038 412382; Thai Airways, inside the *Dusit Resort*, North Pattaya Ⓣ038 420995.

Cinemas Central Cineplex, on the top floor of the Central Festival Centre on Pattaya 2 Rd in North Pattaya, runs several English-language shows a day at each of its four screens. There's also a three-screen cinema on the top floor of Royal Garden Plaza in South Pattaya. See Ⓦwww.movieseer.com for programmes.

Dentists At the Bangkok-Pattaya Hospital Ⓣ038 259999 on Thanon Sukhumvit, about 400m north of the intersection with North Pattaya Rd; and at Pattaya International Hospital on Soi 4 Ⓣ038 428374–5.

Emergencies For all emergencies, call the tourist police on the free, 24hr phone line Ⓣ1155, contact them at their booth on Pattaya 2 Rd, just south of Soi 6, Central Pattaya Ⓣ038 429371, or call in at the more central police station on Beach Rd, just south of Soi 9.

Exchange There are numerous exchange counters and ATMs, particularly on Pattaya Beach Rd and Pattaya 2 Rd.

Hospitals The best-equipped hospital is the Bangkok-Pattaya Hospital Ⓣ038 259999, emergency Ⓣ038 259911 Ⓦwww.bangkokpattayahospital.com on Thanon Sukhumvit, about 400m north of the intersection with North Pattaya Rd. Other central private hospitals include the Pattaya International Hospital on Soi 4 Ⓣ038 428374–5, Ⓦwww.pih-inter.com, and Pattaya Memorial Hospital on Central Pattaya Rd Ⓣ038 429422–4. There are three recompression chambers in the area: at the Bangkok-Pattaya Hospital (see above); at the Apakorn Kiatiwong Naval Hospital in Sattahip, 26km south of Pattaya Ⓣ038 601185; and at the Queen Sirikit Hospital, also in Sattahip Ⓣ038 245926.

Immigration office Soi 5, off Jomtien Beach Road, Jomtien (Mon–Fri 8.30am–4.30pm; Ⓣ038 252750). Many travel agents offer cheap visa-renewal day-trips to Cambodia: check advertisements and local press for details.

Internet access There are dozens of Internet centres throughout the resort, including the efficient but pricey 24hr *Explorer Cyber Café*, between sois 9 and 10 on Pattaya Beach Rd.

Mail The post office is, not surprisingly, on Soi Post Office in Central Pattaya, though the road has now officially been re-signed as Soi 13/2.

Telephones The main CAT international telephone office is on South Pattaya Rd, just east of the junction with Pattaya 3 Rd. There are lots of private international call centres in the resort.

Rayong

Few farang travellers choose to stop for longer than they have to in the busy and fast-expanding provincial capital of **RAYONG**, 65km southeast of Pattaya, but it's a useful place for **bus connections**, particularly if you're travelling between the east coast and the northeast or north (see Travel details for destinations), or if you're trying to get to Ko Samet; Ban Phe, the ferry pier for Ko Samet, is about 17km east and served by frequent songthaews from Rayong bus station (every 30min; 30min). A direct bus service from Suvarnabhumi Airport is also planned. Rayong has long been famous for producing the condiment *nam plaa* – a sauce made from decomposed fish – as well as for the pineapples and durian grown in the provincial orchards, but these days it's the gas and oil-refining industries that are responsible for the city's breakneck growth.

The **TAT office** (Ⓣ038 655420, Ⓔtatryong@tat.or.th) for the Rayong region and Ko Samet is inconveniently located 7km east of Rayong town centre at 153/4 Thanon Sukhumvit (Highway 3), on the way to Ban Phe; any Ban Phe-bound bus or songthaew will drop you at its door. There's a bank with **exchange** counter opposite the access road to Rayong's bus station on Thanon Sukhumvit and the area's best **hospital**, the private Bangkok-Rayong Hospital (Ⓣ038 612999, Ⓦwww.rayonghospital.com) is just south off Thanon Sukhumvit on Soi Soi Saengchan Neramit. If you get stuck in town overnight, you can rent cheap, no-frills fan and air-con **rooms** at the *Asia Hotel,* just east of the bus station and north off Thanon Sukhumvit at no. 962/1 (Ⓣ038 611022; ❶–❸), or there's better, more comfortable accommodation at the *Burapa Palace*, 100m east of the bus station on the south side of Thanon Sukhumvit at no. 69 (Ⓣ038 622946; ❸–❺).

Ko Samet

Attracted by its proximity to Bangkok and its famously powdery white sand, backpackers, package tourists and Thai families flock to the island of **Ko Samet**, 80km southeast of Pattaya. Only 6km long, Ko Samet was declared a **national park** in 1981, but typically the ban on building has been ignored and there are now well over thirty bungalow operations here, with owners paying rent to the Royal Forestry Department. Inevitably, these developments have had a huge impact on the island's resources: waste water from many bungalows is dumped into the sea, you quite often stumble across piles of rotting rubbish, and the grounds of many bungalows are poorly landscaped and disfigured by construction detritus. The dazzling white beaches, however, remain breathtakingly beautiful and are still, for the moment at least, lapped by pale blue water.

As the island gets increasingly upmarket, it is becoming almost impossible to find a bungalow for under B500 in high season; the most backpacker-oriented **beaches** are Ao Hin Kok, Ao Phai and Ao Tub Tim; Ao Hin Kok and Ao Phai are also quite lively in the evenings. Ao Prao, Ao Wong Duan and Hat Sai Kaew are dominated by upmarket accommodation and attract families and package tourists as well as Bangkok trendies. In accordance with national park rules, **camping** is permissible on any of the beaches, despite what you might be told.

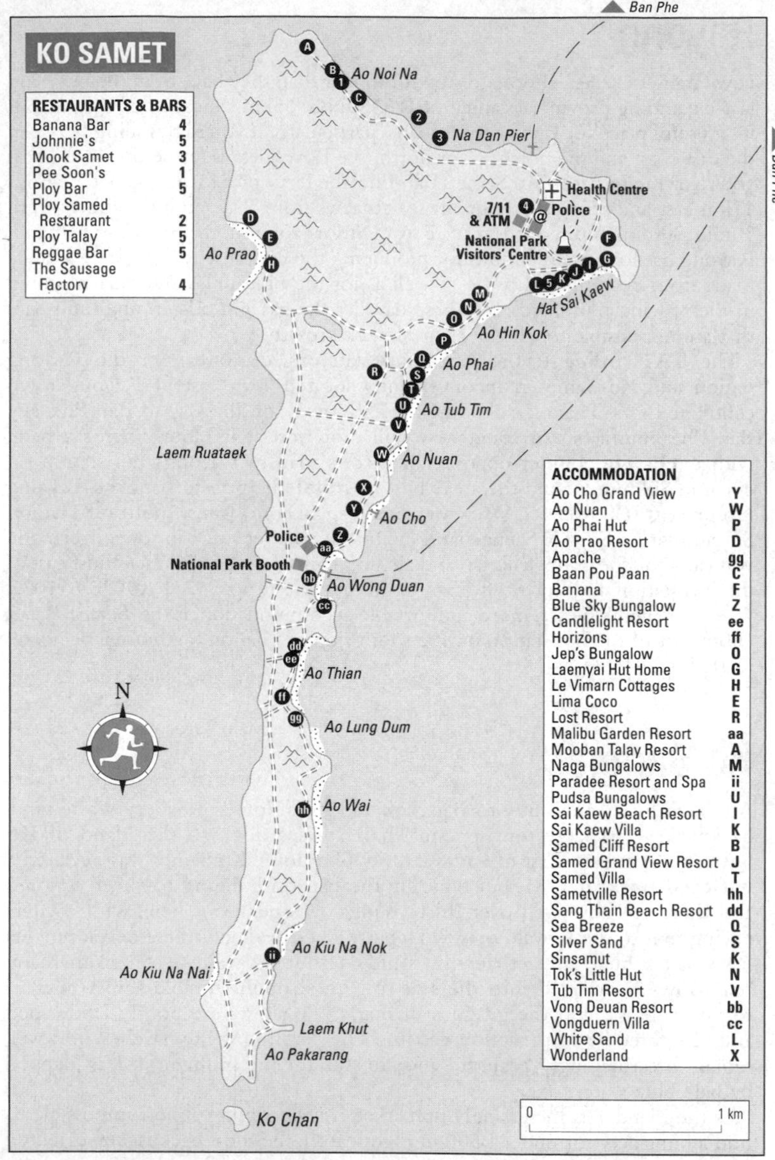

All beaches get packed on **weekends** and national holidays: you could try phoning ahead to reserve a room, though not every place accepts bookings. Many bungalow managers raise their rates by sixty percent during peak periods and sometimes for weekenders as well: the rates quoted here are typical high-season rates.

En route to the island: Ban Phe

The mainland departure-point for Ko Samet is the tiny fishing port of **BAN PHE**, about 17km east of Rayong and some 200km from Bangkok. There are hourly direct **buses** from Bangkok's Eastern (Ekamai) Bus Terminal to the Ban Phe pier, departing between 5am and 7pm, then at 8.30pm (3hr 10min), or you could take one of the more frequent buses to **Rayong** from either the Eastern Bus Terminal (every 40min; 2hr 40min) or the Northern Bus Terminal (every 30min; 2hr 30min–3hr 30min) and then change onto a songthaew to the pier as described on p.471. Alternatively, **tourist minibuses** run from Thanon Khao San to Ban Phe (B200–250; about 4hr); prices for these rarely include the boat fare and you should be prepared for some fairly crazed driving. A meter-taxi ride from **Bangkok** or the airport should cost around B2500. From **Pattaya**, there are hardly any direct Ban Phe buses so it's easier to take a bus to Rayong and then a songthaew. There are, however, tourist minibuses from Pattaya, which cost B180 – note that the B70 boat ticket available as an add-on to this fare is for Ao Wong Duan, so if you want to go to one of Samet's other beaches, don't buy your boat ticket until you get to Ban Phe. Coming by bus from points further east, such as **Chanthaburi** or **Trat**, you'll most likely be dropped at the Ban Phe junction on Highway 3, from where a songthaew or motorbike taxi will take you the remaining 5km to the pier.

If you get stuck with nothing to do between ferries, there are several places to check your **email** on and around Ban Phe's main pier-head, along with traveller-oriented restaurants, minimarkets and travel agents. You should also stock up on money here – the **bank** has currency exchange and an ATM – as the ATM on Ko Samet always runs out of money at weekends and during holidays, and island bungalows offer poor exchange rates. There are a few **accommodation** options around the piers: the *Diamond Hotel* (Ⓣ038 651757; fan ❸, air-con ❹), on the two-hundred-metre stretch of road between the main Taruaphe pier and the Ao Prao (Saphaan Sri Ban Phe) pier, is open 24hr, and has comfortable air-con rooms with TV, as well as cheaper fan options. The travellers' restaurant *Tan Tan Too*, on Soi 2 (where the minivans stop), across the road from the main Taruaphe pier, rents out a couple of large fan and air-con rooms with private bathrooms and DVD players (Ⓣ038 653671, Ⓔbwanabrad@yahoo.com.au; ❸–❹) and serves pizza, pies, falafels, veggie food and more at its two restaurants. It also has Internet terminals, rents bicycles (B50/day), sells minivan tickets to Bangkok's Khao San (B250) and Ko Chang (B250) and offers taxi services to Bangkok (B2000) and the airport (B2500). Next door, the **second-hand bookshop** Blue Sky Green Sea stocks a range of titles far superior to anything you'll find on Ko Samet.

Boats to Ko Samet

Once in Ban Phe, you need to decide which beach you want and then choose your **boat** accordingly. Some boats are owned by individual resorts and ferry both pre-paid package tourists and fare-paying independent travellers; others make the crossing as soon as they have enough passengers (minimum eighteen people) or sufficient cargo to make it worth their while. In theory, boats to the two main piers on Ko Samet run hourly from 8am to 5pm during high season (Nov–Feb) and on national holidays, and every two hours at other times. In practice, many of the boats leave at the same time, so you may end up waiting a couple of hours. Fares are standardized on each route. It's also increasingly common to charter a **speedboat** (carrying up to ten people) to the beach of your choice; prices start at B800 to Hat Sai Kaew.

Leaving Ko Samet

Several **scheduled boats** leave Ko Samet's Na Dan pier every day, currently at about 7am, 8am, 10am, noon and 5pm, and there are usually a few extra ones in between; times are posted at the pier, but if you have a plane to catch you should allow for boat no-shows and delays. There are also at least three departures from Ao Wong Duan (8.30am, 11.30am and 3.30pm) and in high season, you'll find at least one Ban Phe boat a day from Ao Cho and Ao Prao.

Arriving at Ban Phe, you can pick up **buses** to Bangkok, Chanthaburi or Trat, or a songthaew to Rayong, from where buses to all these destinations, plus Pattaya and Si Racha, are far more frequent (see p.471). The Ban Phe bus and songthaew stop is 400m east of the 7-11 shop, though most buses and songthaews pass the pier-head and will pick up passengers there. If you're heading straight back to Bangkok's Thanon Khao San or to Pattaya, your easiest (and most expensive) option is to buy a direct **tourist bus/minivan** ticket from one of Ko Samet's numerous tour operators; these tickets don't include the boat fare, but departure times from Ban Phe are arranged to coincide with boat arrivals. You can also book tourist buses at the tour operators' offices in Ban Phe on Soi 2 behind the 7-11, across from the main pier, though they may not always have room for last-minute bookings. Travelling to **Ko Chang**, it takes just two and a half hours by tourist bus/minivan from Ban Phe to the Laem Ngop pier, though it's expensive at B250 plus the boat fare and buses often "just miss" the 3pm outer-island ferry departures from Laem Ngop; the alternative route by ordinary bus can take all day and often entails changing buses at Chanthaburi and then getting onto a Laem Ngop-bound songthaew in Trat, though it works out at half the price.

The easiest place to get to on Ko Samet is **Na Dan pier** on the northeastern tip of the island, which is the most convenient arrival point for the beaches of Hat Sai Kaew, Ao Hin Kok, Ao Phai, Ao Tub Tim and Ao Nuan, and quite feasible for all the other beaches as well; songthaews meet the boats at Na Dan (see below) and will take you as far as Ao Wong Duan, or you can walk to your chosen beach – the whole island is little more than 6km long. Boats to Na Dan leave from Ban Phe's Taruabanphe pier, opposite the 7-11 shop; they take thirty minutes to get to Samet and charge B50 one way.

There are equally frequent boats to **Ao Wong Duan** (40min; B60), which is also convenient for the nearby beaches of Ao Cho and Ao Thian. Some of the bungalow resorts on the smaller beaches also run boats from Ban Phe direct to their beach – see the individual beach accounts for details.

Island practicalities

Foreign visitors are charged the B200 national-park **entrance fee** on arrival (B100 for children under 14 or free for the under-3s), payable either at the checkpoint between the Na Dan pier and Hat Sai Kaew (where there is a national park visitor centre, with displays on Ko Samet's marine life); or at one of the booths on the other beaches. A share-taxi **songthaew** service meets the Na Dan ferries and runs to the beaches: fares are posted at Na Dan pier and range from B10–100 to Hat Sai Kaew or B50–500 to Ao Kiu, depending on the number of passengers. There are **motorbikes** for rent at Na Dan pier, on the Na Dan-Hat Sai Kaew road, and on every beach (B100/hour or B300–400/day), but the tracks are very rough and riddled with deep potholes so not ideal for inexperienced riders. It would be even harder work on a **bicycle**, but you can rent bikes on the Na Dan-Hat Sai Kaew road for B100/day.

Small shops in Na Dan and on Hat Sai Kaew, Ao Phai, Tub Tim and Ao Wong Duan sell basic travellers' necessities at slightly higher prices than in Ban Phe and Rayong. There's an **ATM** at the 7-11 on the Na Dan-Hat Sai Kaew road (though it invariably runs out of cash on weekends and holidays) and the bigger bungalows also **change money**, albeit at less favourable rates than on the mainland. There are **international phone services** and **Internet centres** on the Na Dan-Hat Sai Kaew road and on almost every beach, and the island's **post office** is run by *Naga Bungalows* on Ao Hin Kok. CP Travel on Hat Sai Kaew (Ⓣ038 644136), among the beachfront shops near *Sinsamut*, sells domestic and international **air tickets** as well as train, bus and minibus tickets and package tours. Ko Samet's **health centre** and **police station** (Ⓣ038 644111) are on the Na Dan-Hat Sai Kaew road, but for anything serious you should make for the Bangkok-Rayong hospital in Rayong (see p.471).

Samet has no fresh **water**, so water is trucked in from the mainland and should be used sparingly; **electricity** in some places is rationed for evening consumption only. Many bungalows have **safety deposits** and it's well worth making use of them: theft is becoming an issue on Samet and there are occasional instances of drinks being spiked by freelance bar girls and punters waking next day without their valuables.

Around the island

Most islanders live in the **northeast** of the island, in ramshackle, badly drained Na Dan, which has small shops and foodstalls, as well as the island's only school, health centre and wat. Samet's best **beaches** are along the **east coast**, and this is where you'll find nearly all the bungalow resorts. A rough path connects some of them; otherwise it's a question of walking along the beach at low tide or over the low, rocky points at high water. The **north coast** has just one really beautiful stretch of beach but compensates with an appealing village atmosphere. Long stretches of the **west coast** are well-nigh inaccessible, though at intervals the coastal scrub has been cleared to make way for a track. The views from these clifftop clearings can be magnificent, particularly around sunset, but you can only safely descend to sea level at Ao Prao, near the northwest headland. A few narrow tracks – mostly signed at crucial junctions and generally straightforward to navigate – cross the island's forested central ridge to link the east and west coasts, but much of the **interior** is dense jungle, home of hornbills, gibbons and spectacular butterflies.

Samet has no decent coral reefs of its own, so you'll have to take a boat trip to the islands of Ko Kudi, Ko Thalu and Ko Mun, off the northeast coast, to get good **snorkelling** and **fishing**. Trips cost from B500 to B1000 including equipment, and depart from all the main beaches. Some places also offer full-day boat trips around Samet itself for about B400. Despite the lack of great reefs (it's hard coral only around here) there are a couple of **dive operators** on Samet: Ploy Scuba (Ⓣ038 644 212, Ⓦwww.ployscuba.com) on Hat Sai Kaew and Ao Noi Na, and Ao Prao Divers (Ⓣ038 644100, Ⓔaopraodivers@hotmail.com) on Hat Sai Kaew and Ao Prao. Four-day Openwater courses cost B14,000 and day-trips with two tanks cost about B3500. The bigger beaches offer jet skis, banana boat rides (B1000/30min) and water-skiing (B1500 for 30min), and *Naga* on Ao Hin Kok has a gym (daily 8am–9.30pm) and runs daily **muay Thai training** sessions (daily 3.30–8pm; B100-250).

Hat Sai Kaew

Arriving at **Na Dan** pier, a ten-minute walk south along the track brings you to **HAT SAI KAEW**, or Diamond Beach, named for its long and extraordinarily beautiful stretch of luxuriant sand, so soft and clean it squeaks underfoot – a result, apparently, of its unusually high silicon content, which also makes it an excellent raw material for glass-making. Songthaews from Na Dan to Hat Sai Kaew cost B10 per person, or B100 when chartered.

The most popular – and congested – beach on Samet, Hat Sai Kaew's shore is lined with bungalows, restaurants, beachwear stalls, deckchairs and parasols. Holidaying Thais and farangs flock here in pretty much equal numbers, especially at weekends, though the northern end is usually slightly more peaceful than the southern.

At night, you have a choice of fairly pricey seafront seafood **restaurants**, some of which, like *Ploy Talay*, set out mats and cushions for diners on the sand. For drinks under the stars, there are several beachside bars, among them *Johnnie's* and the *Reggae Bar*, as well as the air-con live-music *Ploy Bar*. Alternatively you could head down the Hat Sai Kaew-Na Dan road, where you'll find several congenial little restaurants, whose good food and reasonable prices mean that long-stay island farangs tend to congregate here. The tiny *Banana Bar*, not far from the police station, serves authentic Thai food, including yellow, green and massaman curries for B60, as well as *tom yums* and spicy salads, but closes by 10pm. British-run *The Sausage Factory*, a bit towards Hat Sai Kaew, is the place for authentic English breakfasts and meat pies.

There's **Internet access** at *Sai Kaew Villa* on the beach, and at several Internet cafés around the National Park office on the Hat Sai Kaew-Na Dan road. You can arrange **dive** trips through Ao Prao Divers and Ploy Scuba (see p.475) and make travel arrangements through CP Travel (see p.475).

Accommodation

Such is the popularity of this beach that much of the **accommodation** here is crammed uncomfortably close together and in high season it's impossible to find a room by the sea for under B500. However, if you ask at the little bars on the Na Dan-Hat Sai Kaew road, you should be able to rent one of their urban guest-house style rooms for a more affordable price (B150–300).

Banana ⓣ038 644193, ⓦwww.samedresorts.com. Although this is actually the deluxe cottage wing of the *Sai Kaew Beach Resort*, it's on its own secluded patch of coast and in a style class of its own. It's the most desirable accommodation on Hat Sai Kaew, if not the entire island. The vibe is funky-beach chic, with contemporary colour schemes, air-con and TV, garden bathrooms, and private decks. The bungalows occupy their own grassy haven with swimming pool, in front of a pretty but minute little patch of sandy shoreline and it's only a couple of minutes' walk to the beach in front of *Sai Kaew Beach*. ➒

Laemyai Hut Home ⓣ038 644282. These comfortable wooden bungalows with fan or air-con occupy one of the prettiest spots on the beach, under the Laem Yai headland at the nicest, far northern end of Hat Sai Kaew. Not to be confused with the decrepit *Nampet Ploy* bungalows on the (barely defined) adjacent plot to the south. Fan, ➎, air-con ➏

Sai Kaew Beach Resort ⓣ038 644193, ⓦwww.samedresorts.com. Distinctive and stylish blue-and-white bungalows, thoughtfully if quite simply designed, and a cut above everywhere else on this beach except sister outfit *Banana*. All bungalows have phones, TV and air-con and the priciest have uninterrupted sea views. ➒

Sai Kaew Villa ⓣ038 644144, ⓦwww.saikaew.com. Set in attractively landscaped gardens, this large and efficiently run place comprises over 100 rooms with fan or air-con, some in a hotel-like block, others in prettier, more expensive bungalows. The price drops a little for every night you stay. Fan room ➎, fan bungalow ➏, air-con ➐

Samed Grand View Resort ⓣ038 644220, ⓦwww.grandviewgroup.net. Bungalows here are built to an unimaginative standard concrete-and-tile design but are at least widely spaced around a garden that runs down to the beachfront. Fan ➎, air-con ➐

Sinsamut ⓣ038 644134, ⓦwww.sinsamut-kohsamed.com. Initial appearances aren't encouraging here, with various types of rooms stuffed into cheek-by-jowl little blocks behind the restaurant midway down the beach, but most rooms are very pleasant inside, with bright, contemporary decor, and many enjoying some outdoor space. There are even some quirky fan bungalows set around a little upstairs garden. Fan ❹, air-con ❻

White Sand Resort ⓣ038 644004. This huge complex of standard-issue bungalows in a garden behind the shorefront shops dominates the southern end of the beach. Rooms here are unexciting but relatively well priced for this beach, and there's a choice between fan or air-con. Fan ❹, air-con ❻

Ao Hin Kok

Separated from Hat Sai Kaew by a low promontory on which sits a mermaid statue – a reference to Sunthorn Phu's early nineteenth-century poem, *Phra Abhai Mani* (see box on p.478) – **AO HIN KOK** is smaller and less cluttered than its neighbour, and has more of a travellers' vibe, though it's still no bargain. There are three bungalow outfits here, overlooking the beach from the slope on the far side of the track. **Songthaews** from Na Dan will drop you at Ao Hin Kok for B20 per person (or B150 when chartered), or you can walk here in about fifteen minutes.

The English-run *Naga Bungalows* (ⓣ038 644167; ⓔsuewildnaga@gmail.com; fan ❸–❹, air-con ❹–❻) has some of the cheapest **accommodation** on Ko Samet. It offers simple bamboo and wood huts with decks, mosquito nets, platform beds and shared facilities as well as pricier concrete bungalows with their own adjacent bathroom and optional air-con. It's very popular, and has a library as well a gym and *muay Thai* ring. Next door, the blue-painted bungalows at *Tok's Little Hut* (ⓣ038 644072; fan ❷–❹, air-con ❺) are built high on stilts up the denuded slope and so nearly all enjoy some kind of view from their verandas; they're en suite and comfortable inside if a bit dilapidated and are pretty good value for Samet – price depends on distance from the seafront and whether you want fan or air-con. The efficiently managed *Jep's Bungalow* (ⓣ038 644112, ⓦwww.jepbungalow.com; ❻) has the most upmarket accommodation

△ Dinner on the beach, Ao Hin Kok

on Ao Hin Hok, in well-maintained smart wooden chalets and concrete bungalows, all with air-con and TV and again ranged up the slope.

Ao Hin Kok is a good beach for **restaurants**. *Naga* does lots of vegetarian dishes, and sells home-made bread, cakes and pizzas; it also has a pool table, a *muay Thai* boxing ring and puts on fire-juggling shows. *Tok's Little Hut* is known for its seafood, and has a nice little beach bar, but *Jep's* is the most popular of the three, serving up a great menu of authentic Thai curries, seafood, home-made pizzas, brownies and other travellers' fare at its tables on the beach, prettily decorated with lights in the trees and given extra atmosphere by mellow music. A nearby cappuccino stall does various fresh and liqueur coffees.

Ko Samet **post office** is run out of *Naga Bungalows* and offers a parcel-packing, phone, fax and **Internet** service as well as poste restante; letters are kept for three months and should be addressed c/o Poste Restante, Ko Samet, Ban Phe, Rayong 21160.

Sunthorn Phu and Phra Abhai Mani

Over thirty thousand lines long and written entirely in verse, the nineteenth-century romantic epic **Phra Abhai Mani** tells the story of a young prince and his adventures in a fantastical land peopled not only by giants and mermaids, but also by gorgeous women with whom he invariably falls in love. Seduced by an ogress who lives beneath the sea, and kept captive by her for several months, Phra Abhai Mani pines for dry land and eventually persuades a mermaid to help him escape. Naturally, the two fall in love, and decide to spend some time together on the nearby island of Ko Samet (hence the mermaid statue on Ao Hin Kok). But the prince soon tires of the mermaid's charms, and leaps aboard a passing ship in pursuit of another ill-fated affair, this time with a princess already engaged to someone else. And so it goes on.

Widely considered to be one of Thailand's greatest-ever poets, **Sunthorn Phu** (1786–1856) is said to have based much of his work on his own life, and the romantic escapades of *Phra Abhai Mani* are no exception. By all accounts, the man was a colourful character – a philandering commoner alternately in and out of favour at Bangkok's Grand Palace, where he lived and worked for much of his life. By the time Rama II ascended the throne in 1809, he was well established as the court poet, acting as literary aide to the king. However, he took to the bottle, was left by his wife and participated in a drunken fight that landed him in jail. It was during this stint inside (thought to have been around 1821) that he started work on *Phra Abhai Mani*. The poem took twenty years to complete and was rented out in instalments to provide the poet with a modest income – necessary as royal patronage was withdrawn during the reign of Rama III (1824–51), whose literary efforts Sunthorn Phu had once rashly criticized, and only revived when Rama IV was crowned in 1851.

Aside from authoring several timeless romances, Sunthorn Phu is remembered as a significant **poetic innovator**. Up until the end of the eighteenth century, Thai poetry had been the almost exclusive domain of high-born courtiers and kings, written in an elevated Thai incomprehensible to most of the population, and concerned mainly with the moral Hindu epics the *Mahabarata* and the *Ramayana* (see p.137). Sunthorn Phu changed all that by writing of love triangles, thwarted romances and heartbreaking departures; he also composed travel poems, or *nirat*, about his own journeys to well-known places in Thailand. Most crucially, he wrote them all in the common, easy-to-understand language of vernacular Thai. Not surprisingly, he's still much admired. In the province of Rayong, he's the focus of a special memorial park, constructed, complete with statues of his most famous fictional characters, on the site of his father's home in Klaeng.

Ao Phai

Narrow little **AO PHAI**, around the next headland, is Samet's party beach, with the shoreside *Silver Sand* bar and disco famous across the island for its late-night dance music and fire-juggling shows fuelled by cocktails and buckets of vodka red bull. Not everyone has to join in though, as the bungalows on the fringes of the bay are far enough away for a good night's sleep. There's a minimarket on the beach, and *Sea Breeze* has a small library, sells boat trips and minibus tickets, rents out windsurfing equipment and offers overseas telephone and money-exchange facilities. **Songthaews** from Na Dan cost B20 per person to Ao Phai (or B150 when chartered), or you can walk it in twenty minutes.

Ao Phai Hut (ⓣ038 644075; fan ❹, air-con ❻) sits on the rocky divide between Ao Phai and Hin Kok and offers a big range of rather variable split-bamboo and concrete **huts**, the more basic ones set in a scruffy area among the trees, the pricier options, some of them with air-con, occupying a more scenic spot overlooking the rocky end of the shore. *Sea Breeze* (ⓣ038 644124, ⓕ038 644125; ❹–❻) is the largest set of bungalows on the beach, offering simple wooden huts, more solid concrete row houses and bigger bungalows with air-con; as they're built up an unappealingly sparse wooded slope, none has a sea view. The adjacent *Silver Sand* (ⓣ038 644301, ⓦwww.silversandresort.com; ❼) has very nice, if small, white-plank air-con chalets with decent bathrooms and verandas ranged around a pretty garden plus some terraced rooms too. The huge villa-style bungalows at the Swiss-run *Samed Villa* (ⓣ038 644094, ⓦwww.samedvilla.com; ❼) are packed into a fairly small area along the rocks at the southern end of the bay and up the slope behind the restaurant, but interiors are pretty luxurious in a standard hotel-style way (complete with fitted wardrobes) and all have air-con and TV. Immediately behind *Sea Breeze*, on the road to Wong Duan, the two-storey block that is *Lost Resort* (ⓣ038 644041, ⓔlostresort-kosamet@yahhoo.com; fan ❹, air-con ❺) sits peacefully in a grove of tall trees, just a couple of minutes' walk from the beach but with no sea view. The twelve rooms here can be fan or air-con and are of a good standard and well priced, especially for air-con.

Ao Tub Tim

Also known as Ao Pudsa, **AO TUB TIM** is a small white-sand bay sandwiched between rocky points, partly shaded with palms and backed by a wooded slope. It has just two bungalow operations and feels secluded, if a bit crowded, but is only a short stroll from Ao Phai and the other beaches further north. **Songthaews** will bring you here from Na Dan pier for B20 per person (or B150 when chartered), or you can walk it in about thirty minutes.

The most popular of the two **places to stay** on Tub Tim is the sprawling, well-run *Tub Tim Resort* (ⓣ038 644025, ⓦwww.tubtimresort.com; fan ❹–❺, air-con ❻–❼) with around sixty bungalows of various sizes, designs and comfort including some very good wooden ones. Unusually, seafront positions are not all bagged by air-con bungalows so you could get a fairly cheap fan room with sea view (air-con is available only from 5pm–10am). The *Tub Tim Resort* restaurant is very good indeed, especially for north Thai cuisine such as *haw mok* (ground fish curry steamed in banana leaf). The smaller outfit on the beach is the adjacent *Pudsa Bungalows* (ⓣ038 644030; fan ❺, air-con ❼), which offers a range of large, sturdy huts, including some that sit alongside the track and enjoy direct sea views.

Ao Nuan

Clamber up over the next headland (which gives you a panoramic take on the expanse of Hat Sai Kaew) to reach Samet's smallest beach, the secluded **AO**

NUAN. Although not brilliant for swimming, the rocky shore reveals a good patch of sand when the tide withdraws, and the more consistent beach at Ao Tub Tim is only five minutes' walk away. The best way to get to Ao Nuan from the pier is to take a **songthaew** from Na Dan for B20 per person (B150 when chartered).

The atmosphere here is relaxed and far less commercial than the other beaches, and the mellow restaurant of the friendly *Ao Nuan* has some of the best veggie food on the island. Because it's some way off the main track, the beach gets hardly any through traffic and so feels quiet and private. The sturdy timber huts are idiosyncratic (❹–❺), each built to a slightly different design, and dotted across the slope that drops down to the bay; a few are built right over the beach. They're all spartanly furnished – the cheapest have just a mattress on the floor and a mosquito net, and all share bathrooms, but they all have fans and 24-hour electricity; price depends on the size and the location.

Ao Cho

A five-minute walk south along the track from Ao Nuan brings you to **AO CHO**, a fairly wide stretch of beach with just a few bungalow operations including one very large upmarket one, plus a pier, a minimarket and motorbikes for rent. Despite being long and partially shaded, this beach seems less popular than the others, so it may be a good place to try if you want a low-key atmosphere, or if the bungalows on other beaches are packed out. There's some coral off the end of the pier, and you can rent snorkelling gear on the beach. The easiest way to get to Ao Cho is to take a **boat** to Ao Wong Duan and then walk, or you could take the boat to Na Dan and then hang around for a songthaew (B30).

Wonderland (Ⓣ038 644162; fan ❷–❺, air-con ❻–❽) has some of the cheapest **bungalows** on Ko Samet, though many of them are small and grotty; its nicest bungalows are on the hill above the restaurant at the northern end of the beach. The southern end of the bay is entirely dominated by the imposing air-con villas of the upscale *Ao Cho Grand View* (Ⓣ038 644220, Ⓦwww.grandviewgroup.net; ❽), nearly all of which enjoy views north across the bay.

Ao Wong Duan

The horseshoe bay of **AO WONG DUAN**, round the next point, is Samet's second most popular beach after Hat Sai Kaew and though it's not as pretty and suffers even more from revving jet skis and hordes of day-trippers on organized tours, it does offer some attractive accommodation, much of it significantly better looked after than the Hat Sai Kaew equivalents. Rooms are not cheap here though, so most guests are either package tourists, Pattaya overnighters, or weekending Bangkokians – shoestring travellers aren't well catered for. Although the beach is fairly long and broad, the central shorefront is almost lost under a knot of bars and tourist shops, and the main stretch of beach nearly disappears at high tide. Facilities include minimarkets, motorbike rental, money exchange, Internet access, overseas telephone services and a police box. At least four direct **boats** a day should run from Na Dan to Wong Duan (see p.474 for details), and vice versa. Alternatively, take a boat to Na Dan, then a B30 ride in a songthaew (or a B200 taxi ride). Seven-person speedboats can be chartered from the Wong Duan pier to Ban Phe for B1000.

Accommodation

Blue Sky Bungalow Ⓣ081 509 0547. Just a handful of pretty good bamboo and wooden bungalows – the cheapest on this beach – set up on the hill above the *Blue Sky Restaurant* at the north, rocky, end of the bay, with some good views and a more old-style feel to the bungalows. Rooms have fans, bathrooms and verandas. ❺

Malibu Garden Resort ⓣ038 644020, ⓦwww.malibu-samet.com. Huge, rather soulless, package-oriented outfit which brings in many of its customers twice a day from Pattaya. The scores of white washed concrete bungalows are set round a shady tropical garden with a small swimming pool. Though uninspiring, the rooms are decent enough and all come with air-con and TV. ❼–❽

Vong Deuan Resort ⓣ038 651777, ⓦwww.vongdeuan.com. Attractive, upmarket bungalows in various designs, including nice cottages with stained dark-wood exteriors, contemporary styled interiors and garden bathrooms. Bungalows are set around a pretty tropical garden and all have air-con and TV. ❼–❽

Vongduern Villa ⓣ038 652300, ⓦwww.vongduernvilla.com. Occupying a big chunk of the bay's southern end, this place has character, even if it's not quite pristine. There are various types and standards of room, though they're all upscale and air-con, ranging from whitewashed timber huts built on stilts and with picture windows, decks and modern furnishings to more minimalist, versions kitted out with dark-wood floors and Japanese-style platform beds. There's an attractive restaurant deck jutting out over the water. ❻–❽

Ao Thian (Candlelight Beach) and Ao Lung Dum

AO THIAN ("Candlelight Beach"), and contiguous Ao Lung Dum display almost none of the commerce of Wong Duan, a couple of minutes' walk over the hill, though the lovely, scenic shorefront is fronted by an unbroken line of bungalows and little restaurants and the eponymous "candlelight" lighting is long gone. The narrow, white-sand bay is dotted with wave-smoothed rocks and partitioned by larger outcrops that create several distinct beaches; as it curves outwards to the south you get a great view of the island's east coast. The best way to get here is to take a boat from Ban Phe to Ao Wong Duan and then walk.

Towards the northern end, *Sang Thain Beach Resort* (ⓣ038 644255, ⓦwww.sangthain.com; ❼) has very tasteful air-con timber chalets built up the hillside on a series of decks and steps – decor is navy-and-white chic and views, mostly featuring the sea, are pretty; it also has compact brick **bungalows** with big glass windows (though no real view) and comfy interiors up the northern slope. Further down the shore, the plain but decent bungalows belonging to *Candlelight Resort* (ⓣ087 149 6139; fan ❺, air-con ❻) are strung out in a long line, with each one facing the water.

At its southern end, Ao Thian turns almost imperceptibly into **Ao Lung Dum**, where the laid-back *Apache* (ⓣ081 452 9472; ❹) offers basic fan huts all with sea view, mosquito nets and bathrooms. Nearby *Horizons* (ⓣ089 914 5585; ❺) has better, more modern bungalows staggered in a line up the hill, all with partial sea view: interiors are bright, bathrooms are attractive, there's 24-hour electricity and you get good discounts for stays of more than one night.

Ao Wai and Ao Kiu

A fifteen-minute walk along the coast path from Lung Dum brings you to **AO WAI**, a very pretty white-sand bay, partially shaded and a good size considering it supports just one (large) bungalow operation, *Sametville Resort* (ⓣ038 651681, ⓦwww.sametvilleresort.com; fan ❺–❻, air-con ❼–❾). Bungalows in all categories vary in quality, but you've plenty to choose from, especially during the week, when it's very quiet here; at weekends the place tends to fill up with Thai groups. There's a restaurant and Internet access on site. A chartered songthaew costs B400 from Na Dan or there's a daily boat here from Ban Phe (10am; B90) plus an extra one on Friday afternoons at 2pm, but call the resort to confirm. Over an hour's walk south of Ao Thian, via a track that begins behind *Vong Deuan Resort* on Ao Wong Duan and can be joined at the southern end of Ao Thian, the gorgeous little twin bays of **Ao Kiu** – Ao Kiu Na Nok on the east coast and Ao Kiu Na Nai on the west – are separated by just a few hundred metres of land. Both beaches are now the domain of the very posh, five-star, butler-service villa resort *Paradee Resort and Spa* (Ⓣ02 438 9771, Ⓦwww.samedresorts.com; published rates from B12,800, ⑨).

Ao Prao (Paradise Bay)

Across on the upper west coast, the rugged, rocky coastline only softens into beach once – at **AO PRAO**, also known as Paradise Bay, on the northwestern stretch, some 4km north of Ao Kiu Na Nai. This is Samet's most exclusive beach, dominated by two exceptionally elegant – and expensive – resorts, with only one slightly more affordable option available, though if you're spending top dollar, the beach in front of *Mooban Talay Resort* on Ao Noi Na has the edge. There's a dive centre on Ao Prao (see p.475) and activities also include boat tours and kayak rental. If you're only visiting for the day, the most direct route from the east-coast beaches is via the inland track from behind *Sea Breeze* on Ao Phai, which takes about twenty minutes on foot, though the track from the back of *Tub Tim* on Ao Tub Tim will also get you there. If staying on Ao Prao, your hotel will arrange **boat** transfers from Ban Phe's private Sri Ban Phe pier (4 daily at 8am, 11am, 1.30pm & 4pm), or you can come by songthaew from Na Dan for B30 per person, or B200 on charter.

Ao Prao Resort (Ⓣ038 644100, Ⓦwww.samedresorts.com; ⑨) boasts some of the most luxurious **accommodation** on the island, with comfortable wooden chalets set in a mature tropical garden that slopes down to the beach. All chalets have air-con, TVs and balconies overlooking the sea and there's also a serenely sited restaurant that juts out over the water. The even more indulgent *Le Vimarn Cottages* (Ⓣ038 644104, Ⓦwww.samedresorts.com; ⑨) is owned by the same company and comprises charming and gorgeously furnished cottages, a delightful spa and a swimming pool; prices start from B8800. *Lima Coco* (Ⓣ089 105 7080, Ⓦwww.limacoco.com; ⑧–⑨) is a younger, trendier, cheaper and altogether less snooty place, with a Bangkok contemporary chic look and lots of white walls, brightly coloured cushions, day beds and decks. Rooms are built up the side of the hill, with the priciest ones enjoying front-row sea views. Rates include transfer from Chok Kitsada pier in Ban Phe.

Ao Noi Na

West of Na Dan, the island's north coast – known simply as **Ao Noi Na** even though it's not strictly a single bay – has a refreshingly normal village feel about it compared to the rest of Samet. There are a few places to stay along here and several restaurants, but the road is quiet and shrub-lined, terminating at a beautiful beach at the far western end, and the views across the water to the hills behind Ban Phe are beautiful. The white-sand beach at the end has been hogged by the luxurious *Mooban Talay Resort* but it's not private and you can walk there from Na Dan pier in about 25 minutes. En route you'll pass several good **restaurants**, including two floating seafood places where diners have to ring a bell on the shore to alert the boatman to come over and pick them you; ★ *Ploy Samed Restaurant* is cheaper than *Mook Samet* and the food just as good: rock lobster is a speciality, and you eat on a deck at low tables with your feet dangling above the water. Another ten minutes walk further, just before *Samed Cliff Resort,* the unsigned but locally famous little *Pee Soon's* restaurant (daily till 8.30pm) is very popular in the neighbourhood, has an English menu and serves good, cheap Thai food, especially chicken with sweet basil.

Less than fifteen minutes' walk from Na Dan, Scottish-run *Baan Pou Paan* (Ⓣ038 644095, Ⓔlizziecj@hotmail.com; fan ⑤, air-con ⑥) is a chilled-out **guest house** offering three en-suite fan and air-con bungalows built on stilts in the sea, with large decks and great views, plus another three air-con rooms on shore, all furnished with cushions, lamps and lots of plants. There's a restaurant and large seating area here too, plus table tennis and tiny beaches to either side. Ten minutes walk further west, the good value *Samed Cliff Resort* (☎038 644044, Ⓦwww.samedcliff.com; ❼) has air-con chalets stepped up the hillside, all with sea view, overlooking a well-kept lawn and shrub-lined paths, plus a narrow beach out front. It also has a small pool. The poshest place on Ao Noi Na is *Mooban Talay Resort* (☎038 644251, Ⓦwww.moobantalay.com; ❾), a secluded haven at the end of the road set under the trees on a gorgeous – and quiet – white-sand beach. Accommodation is in large, attractive bungalows, all with platform beds, garden bathrooms and outdoor seating: the priciest, seafront ones have enormous decks, and there's a beachfront pool.

Chanthaburi

For over five hundred years, the seams of rock rich in sapphires and rubies that streak the hills of eastern Thailand have drawn prospectors and traders of all nationalities to the provincial capital of **CHANTHABURI**, 80km east of Ban

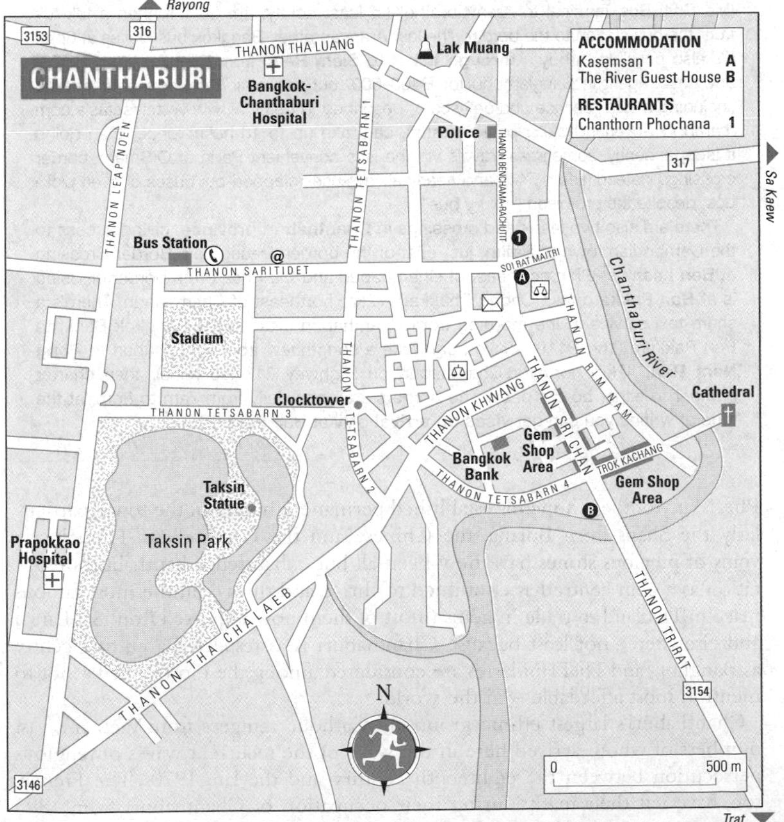

Overland into Cambodia via Aranyaprathet–Poipet and Chanthaburi province

The most commonly used **overland crossing into Cambodia** is at **Poipet**, which lies just across the border from the Thai town of **Aranyaprathet**. The border here is open daily from 7am to 8pm and officials will issue thirty-day Cambodian **visas on arrival** (see Basics p.33 for details, and Ⓦwww.talesofasia.com/cambodia-overland-bkksr-self.htm for a very detailed description of the crossing and for advice on onward transport into Cambodia). Because this border-crossing is so popular, formalities can take up to three hours, and once you're through, you face a gruelling journey of at least four hours in the back of a pick-up or, a much better but more expensive option, in a share-taxi, to cover the 150km of potholed road between Poipet and Siem Reap. If you need a **hotel** in Aranyaprathet, try either the comfortable fan and air-con rooms at *Inter Hotel* on Thanon Chatasingh (Ⓣ037 231291; fan ❸, air-con ❹), or the cheaper *Aran Garden II* at 110 Thanon Rat Uthit (fan ❷, air-con ❸).

Travelling to Poipet from east-coast towns, the easiest route is to take a bus **from Chanthaburi** to the town of **Sa Kaew**, 130km to the northeast, and then change to one of the frequent buses for the 55-kilometre ride east to Aranyaprathet. **From Bangkok**, you can travel to Aranyaprathet by **train** (2 daily; 6hr), though you'll need to catch the 5.55am to ensure reaching the border before 5pm; the other leaves at 1.05pm. Return trains depart Aranyaprathet at 6.35am and 1.35pm. Tuk-tuks will take you the 4km from the train station to the border post. Alternatively, take a **bus** from Bangkok's Northern (Mo Chit) Bus Terminal to Aranyaprathet (at least hourly; 4hr 30min), then a tuk-tuk from the bus station to the border. The last Aranyaprathet–Bangkok bus leaves at 6pm. It's also possible to buy a **through ticket to Siem Reap** from Bangkok from almost any travel agent in Banglamphu for B400–600, but this option is dogged by **scams** (including a visa "service charge" scam, described in detail at Ⓦwww.talesofasia.com/cambodia-overland-bkksr-package.htm), can take up to 10 hours longer than doing it independently, sometimes travels via the less convenient Pailin or O'Smach border crossings instead (see p.544), and nearly always uses clapped-out buses or even pick-ups, despite the promised "luxury bus".

There are also two less-used crossings in **Chanthaburi province**, giving access to the Cambodian town of **Pailin**, just east of the border. Daung Lem Border Crossing at **Ban Laem** is 88km northeast of Chanthaburi and the Phsa Prom border crossing is at **Ban Pakkard** (aka Chong Phakkat), 72km northeast of Chanthaburi. There's a share-taxi service in the morning from Chanthaburi (next to the Bangkok Bank) to Ban Pakkard (1hr; B110), or you can take a songthaew from Chanthaburi to **Pong Nam Ron**, 42km north of Chanthaburi on Highway 317 (90 mins), then charter another to either border pass. The borders are open daily from 7am to 8pm; at the time of writing you can get **visas on arrival** only at Ban Pakkard.

Phe. Many of these hopefuls established permanent homes in the town, particularly the Shans from Burma, the Chinese and the Cambodians. Though the veins of precious stones have now been all but exhausted, Chanthaburi's reputation as a gem centre has continued to thrive and this is still the most famous place in Thailand to trade in gems (most of them now imported from Sri Lanka and elsewhere), not least because Chanthaburi is as respected a cutting centre as Bangkok, and Thai lapidaries are considered among the most skilled – not to mention most affordable – in the world.

Chanthaburi's largest ethnic group are Catholic refugees from Vietnam, vast numbers of whom arrived here in the wake of the recurrent waves of religious persecution between the eighteenth century and the late 1970s. The French, too, have left their mark: during their occupation of Chanthaburi from 1893 to 1905, when they held the town hostage against the fulfilment of a territorial treaty on the Lao border, they undertook the restoration and enlargement of the town's Christian cathedral. This cultural diversity makes Chanthaburi an engaging place, even if there's less than a day's worth of sights here.

The Town

Built on the wiggly west bank of the Maenam Chanthaburi, the town fans out westwards for a couple of kilometres, though the most interesting parts are close to the river, in the district where there's most evidence of the **Vietnamese community**. Here, along Thanon Rim Nam, the narrow road running parallel to the river, the town presents a mixture of pastel-painted, colonial-style housefronts and traditional wooden shophouses, some with finely carved latticework.

Continuing south along this road, you'll reach a footbridge on the other side of which stands Thailand's largest **cathedral**: the Church of the Immaculate Conception. There's thought to have been a church on this site ever since the first Christians arrived in town in the eighteenth century, though the present structure was revamped in French style in the late nineteenth century. West of the bridge, the **gem dealers' quarter** begins, centred around Trok Kachang and Thanon Sri Chan (the latter signed in English as "Gem Street") and packed with dozens of gem shops. Most of the shops lie empty during the week, but on Fridays, Saturdays and Sunday mornings they come alive as local dealers arrive to sift through mounds of tiny coloured stones, peering at them through microscopes and classifying them for resale to the hundreds of buyers who drive down from Bangkok.

Chanthaburi has a reputation for high-grade fruit too, notably durian, rambutan and mangosteen, all grown in the orchards around the town and sold in the daily **market**, a couple of blocks northwest of the gem quarter. Basketware products made from woven reeds are also a good buy here, mostly made by the Vietnamese.

West of the market and gem quarter, the landscaped **Taksin Park** is the town's recreation area and memorial to King Taksin of Thonburi, the general who reunited Thailand between 1767 and 1782 after the sacking of Ayutthaya by the Burmese. Chanthaburi was the last Burmese bastion on the east coast – when Taksin took the town he effectively regained control of the whole country. The park's heroic bronze statue of Taksin is featured on the back of the B20 note.

Practicalities

Even if you're not planning a visit to Chanthaburi, you may find yourself stranded here for a couple of hours between **buses**, as this is a major transit point for east-coast services (including most Rayong–Trat buses) and a handy terminus for buses to and from the northeast. Eight daily buses make the scenic six-hour Chanthaburi–Sa Kaew–Khorat journey in both directions, with Sa Kaew being a useful interchange for buses to **Aranyaprathet and the Cambodian border** (see box opposite for details of this border-crossing and two other crossings in Chanthaburi province). Buses to and from all these places, as well as Bangkok's Eastern (Ekamai) and Northern (Mo Chit) stations, use the Chanthaburi **bus station** (Ⓣ039 311299) on Thanon Saritidet, about 750m northwest of the town centre and market. There are several **banks** with ATMs on Thanon Khwang, and **Internet** centres on Thanon Saritidet and Thanon Tetsabarn 2. The best **hospital** in town is the private Bangkok-Chanthaburi Hospital at 25/14 Thanon Tha

Luang (Ⓣ039 321222, Ⓦwww.bangkokchanthaburi.com) and the **police** are further east along the same road (Ⓣ039 311111).

The best-located **accommodation** options are near the river. First choice should be the fan and air-con rooms at the modern, hotel-style *The River Guest House,* which is ideally sited by the river and on the edge of the gems quarter at 3/5–8 Thanon Sri Chan (Ⓣ039 328211; ❸); it also serves very good food at its appealing waterside restaurant and has Internet access. Cheaper, but older and more faded is *Kasemsan 1* (Ⓣ & Ⓕ039 312340; fan ❷, air-con ❸), less than ten minutes' walk east of the bus station at 98/1 Thanon Benchama-Rachutit; choose between the sizeable, clean rooms with fan and bathroom on the noisy street side, and the similar but more expensive air-con ones in the quieter section. The most traveller-friendly **restaurant** in this area is *Chanthorn Phochana*, just north of the Saritidet intersection on Thanon Benchama-Rachutit, which has an English-language menu listing its mouthwatering range of spicy *yam* salads, curries and stir-fries; the restaurant also has a decent vegetarian section and features local Chateau de Klaeng wine. Otherwise, check out the foodstalls in the market and along the riverside soi for Vietnamese spring rolls (*cha gio*) served with sweet sauce, and for the locally made Chanthaburi rice noodles (*kway tiaw Chanthaburi*).

Trat and around

Most travellers who find themselves in or around the provincial capital of **Trat** are heading either for Ko Chang and the outer islands, via the nearby port at **Laem Ngop**, or for Cambodia, via the border at **Hat Lek**, 91km southeast of town. But Trat itself has a definite charm and lots of welcoming guest houses to tempt you into staying longer, so it's no great hardship to be stuck here between connections.

△ Wooden shophouses, Trat

Trat

The small and pleasantly unhurried market town of **TRAT**, 68km east of Chanthaburi, is the perfect place to stock up on essentials, extend your visa, or simply take a break, before striking out for Ko Chang, the outer islands, or Cambodia. Though there are no real sights in town, the historic neighbourhood down by Khlong Trat, where you'll find most of the guest houses and traveller-oriented restaurants, is full of characterful old wooden shophouses and

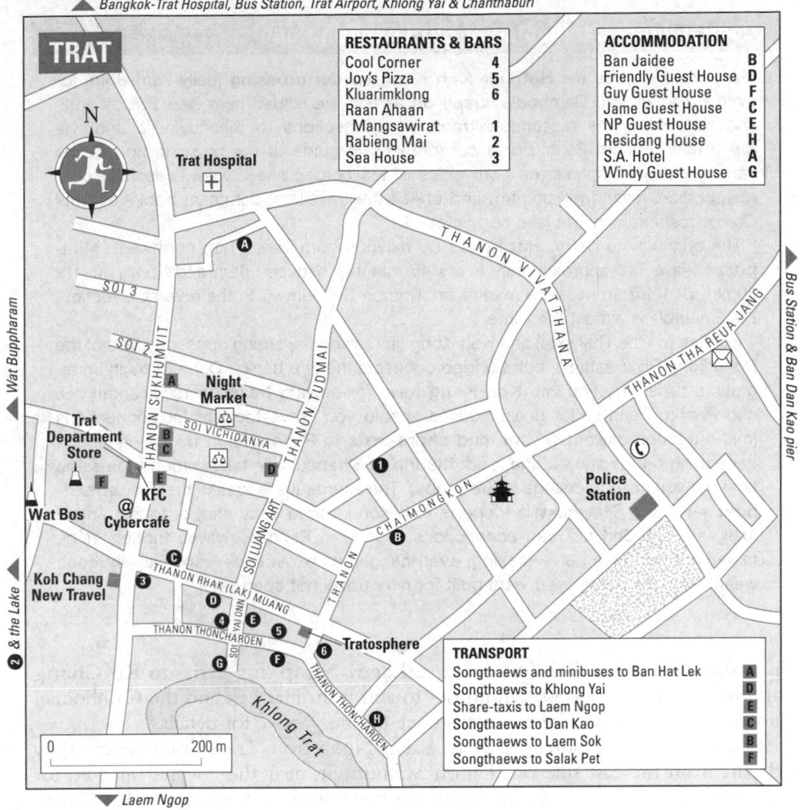

narrow, atmospheric sois. The covered market in the heart of town is another fun place to wander, though for focused explorations rent a bicycle and ride out to the attractively ornate seventeenth-century Wat Buppharam, 2km west of Trat Department Store, and the nearby lake.

Trat is famous across Thailand for the **yellow herbal oil** mixture, *yaa luang*, invented by one of its residents, Mae Ang Ki, and used by Thais to treat many ailments: sniff it for travel sickness or rub it on to relieve mosquito and sandfly bites, ease stomach cramps, or sterilize wounds. Ingredients include camphor and aloe vera. You can buy the oil in lip-gloss-size bottles at the market and at Tratosphere bookshop (B80–100); there are now several imitations, but Mae Ang Ki's original product has a tree logo to signify that it's made by royal appointment.

Arrival, transport and information

Trat is served by lots of **buses** from Bangkok's Eastern (Ekamai) Bus Terminal (5–6hr), and by some from Bangkok's Northern (Mo Chit) Bus Terminal as well (4hr 30min); a direct service from Suvarnabhumi Airport is also planned. Trat also has useful bus connections with Ban Phe (for Ko Samet), Chanthaburi, Pattaya and Si Racha. All buses use the bus station, 1.5km northeast of central Trat, on the Cambodia road (Highway 318), from where songthaews ferry passengers

Overland into Cambodia via Hat Lek–Koh Kong

Many travellers use the **Hat Lek–Koh Kong border crossing** (daily 7am–8pm) for overland travel into Cambodia: **visas on arrival** are issued here (see Basics p.32) and Koh Kong has reasonable transport connections to Sihanoukville and, via Sre Ambel, Phnom Penh. For a comprehensive guide to the crossing and to the various transport options on both sides of the border, see ⓦwww.talesofasia.com/cambodia-overland-bkkpp.htm, and check the travellers' comment books at *Cool Corner* restaurant in Trat (see opposite).

The only way to get to **Hat Lek** is by minibus from Trat, 91km northwest. **Minibuses** leave Trat approximately every 45 minutes between 6am and 5pm (1hr–1hr 30min; B110) from near the market on Thanon Sukhumvit. In the reverse direction, the timetable is almost the same.

Hat Lek (on the Thai side) and Koh Kong (in Cambodia) are on opposite sides of the Dong Tong River estuary, but a bridge connects the two banks. Once through immigration, taxis ferry you into **Koh Kong** town for onward transport to Sihanoukville and Phnom Penh or for guest houses should you arrive too late for connections (mid-afternoon onwards). **Vans and share-taxis** to Phnom Penh take 7–11 hours, depending on the state of the road; the trip to Sihanoukville takes around the same time but you need to change in Sre Ambel. The alternative is to take the daily **speedboat** service to Sihanoukville (departs Koh Kong pier at 8am; 4hr), or to Sre Ambel (daily at 7am; 3hr) for road connections to Phnom Penh. However, though much faster, this can be a nerve-racking, even dangerous experience, especially in rough weather, as the boats used were built for river travel not open seas.

into the town centre (B20) or direct to **Laem Ngop** (for ferries to **Ko Chang** and the outer islands; B50). Minibuses to and from Hat Lek and the Cambodian border also leave from the bus station: see the box above for details.

You can also catch songthaews to Laem Ngop from Trat's town centre: they depart from the east side of Thanon Sukhumvit, near the covered market; for full details on getting to Laem Ngop see p.490 and for transport to Ko Chang see p.491. Songthaews direct to **Salak Pet** on Ko Chang (for Hat Sai Yao/Long Beach, see p.504) leave from the temple compound behind *KFC* and Trat Department Store. Share-taxis to **Laem Sok** (30min; B40), 30km south of Trat and the departure for speedboats to Ko Mak and Ko Kood, leave from near the covered market on Thanon Sukhumvit, as do share-taxis to **Ban Dan Kao** (10min), on the river estuary about 6km northeast of Trat town and the departure point for the slow boat to Ko Kood.

Tiny Trat **airport** (ⓣ039 525767) is served by Bangkok Airways flights to and from Bangkok and Ko Samui. The airport is just 16km from the Ko Chang piers at Laem Ngop and there's an airport shuttle direct to Ko Chang hotels for B270 per person, including ferry ticket. Trat town is a thirty-minute, B300 taxi ride from the airport. Note that when flying out of Trat, there's a B200 domestic departure tax because it's a private airport. The Bangkok Airways office (ⓣ039 525299) is on the northern edge of town, just beyond the Highway 317 turn-off to Khlong Yai, across from the Bangkok-Trat Hospital but you can also buy tickets at the travel agent in the town centre (see p.490).

Trat's official **TAT** office is in Laem Ngop (see p.490), but any guest house will help you out with local **information**. Alternatively, drop by the Tratosphere bookshop at 23 Soi Kluarimklong for tips from the knowledgeable French owner and a copy of his free Trat guide, or visit *Cool Corner* restaurant (see opposite) for a browse through the travellers' comment books.

Accommodation

Most **guest houses** in Trat are small, friendly and run by well-informed local people who are used to providing up-to-date information on transport to the islands, and the Cambodian border crossings. All the guest houses listed here are within ten minutes' walk of the songthaew stops on Thanon Sukhumvit.

Ban Jaidee 67 Thanon Chaimongkon ⓣ039 520678, ⓔbanjaidee@yahoo.co.uk. Very calm, inviting and rather stylish guest house with a pleasant seating area downstairs and just seven simple bedrooms upstairs. The nicest rooms are in the original building and have polished wood floors, though those in the modern extension are further from the traffic noise. All rooms share bathrooms. Internet access and bicycles available for guests. ❶

Friendly Guest House 106–110 Thanon Rhak (Lak) Muang ⓣ039 524053. Simple rooms in the extended home of a friendly family; all have windows and share bathrooms. ❶

Guy Guest House 82 Thanon Thoncharoen ⓣ039 524556, ⓔguy.gh2001@gmail.com. Popular, commercial guest house that sweeps up a lot of travellers from the bus station. Rooms are well priced: many have private bathrooms and some have air-con. Internet access and a restaurant downstairs. Fan ❶, fan and bathroom ❷, air-con ❷–❸

Jame Guest House Thanon Rhak (Lak) Muang ⓣ039 530458. Just a few pleasant fan rooms in a traditional wooden house, with a lounge area downstairs. Bathrooms are shared. ❶

NP Guest House 10 Soi Yai Onn ⓣ039 512270. Welcoming place offering simple but decent enough rooms with shared bathrooms; not all of them have windows. ❶

Residang House 87/1–2 Thanon Thoncharoen ⓣ039 530103, ⓦwww.trat-guesthouse.com. Comfortably appointed three-storey German-managed place that's more of a small hotel than a guest house. Rooms are large and clean and all have thick mattresses and fans; most have en-suite bathrooms. Internet access downstairs. Shared bathroom ❶, en suite ❷, air-con ❸

S.A. Hotel Just off Thanon Sukhumvit ⓣ039 524572, ⓕ039 524411. Though hardly deluxe, the best hotel in town is set in a quiet spot and comprises large air-con rooms, all with bathrooms and French windows. ❹

Windy Guest House 63 Thanon Thoncharoen ⓣ089 707 9140. Tiny wooden house with a very laid-back atmosphere that's perfectly situated right on the khlong. There are just six simple rooms, all with windows and shared facilities. ❶

Eating

Two of the best **places to eat** in Trat are at the covered day market on Thanon Sukhumvit, and the night market (5–9pm), between Soi Vichidanya and Soi Kasemsan, east of Thanon Sukhumvit.

Cool Corner 21–23 Thanon Thoncharoen, on the corner of Soi Yai Onn. Run almost single-handedly by a local writer/artist, this funky place has lots of personality, both in its cute blue-and-white decor, and in its traveller-oriented menu of home-made bread, real coffee, veggie specials and great Thai curries (from B60). A good place to while away an extra hour, listening to the mellow music and perusing the travellers' comment books on the islands and Cambodia.

Joy's Pizza Thanon Thoncharoen. Great range of fairly pricey home-made pizzas (from B170) served in a chilled-out dining area furnished with low tables and groovy artwork.

Kluarimklong Soi Kluarimklong. More Bangkok than Trat in its style and menu, this unexpectedly classy little place has both an indoor and a court-yard dining area and serves delicious, upmarket Thai food (dishes from B60). The main focus is on seafood, along with lots of spicy *yam* salads and *tom yum* soups.

Raan Ahaan Mangsawirat No English sign, but follow the soi near *Ban Jaidee*, off Thanon Chaimongkon. Typical no-frills, very cheap Thai vegetarian place, where you choose two portions of veggie curry, stir-fry or stew from the trays laid out in the display cabinet, and pay about B25 including rice. Shuts about 2pm.

Rabieng Mai beside the lake, south of Wat Bos, on the southwest corner of town. Mid-priced Thai seafood place whose lake views make it a good focus for a hike or cycle trip out to Wat Buppharam.

Sea House On the corner of Thanon Rhak (Lak) Muang and Thanon Sukhumvit. Standard range of Thai and farang food (most dishes B60–80), fresh coffees and beer.

Listings

Banks and exchange There are several banks along the central stretch of Thanon Sukhumvit.
Bookshops The French-Thai run Tratosphere, at 23 Soi Kluarimklong, buys and sells second-hand books and is a very good source of local info; you can also buy curios from all over Thailand here, and hammocks.
Emergencies For all emergencies, call the tourist police on the free, 24hr phone line ⓣ1155, or contact the local police station off Thanon Vivatthana ⓣ039 511239.
Hospital The best hospital is the private Bangkok-Trat Hospital ⓣ039 532735, emergencies ⓣ039 522555, part of the Bangkok Hospital group, which also offers dental care services; it's on the Sukhumvit Highway, 1km north of Trat Department Store.
Immigration office Located on the Trat–Laem Ngop road, 3km northeast of Laem Ngop pier (Mon–Fri 8.30am–4.30pm; ⓣ039 597261).
Internet access At many guest houses, at the hi-tech cybercafé on Thanon Sukhumvit, and at the CAT overseas telephone office on Thanon Vivatthana.
Mail At the GPO on Thanon Tha Reua Jang.
Massage Ask at Tratosphere, *Cool Corner*, or any guest house for advice on where to go for a massage treatment or lesson.
Telephones The CAT overseas telephone office is on Thanon Vivatthana on the eastern edge of town (daily 8.30am–4.30pm).
Travel agencies International and domestic flights can be booked at Koh Chang New Travel on Thanon Sukhumvit ⓣ081 687 1112 (closed Sun).

Laem Ngop

Ferries to Ko Chang and some boat services to the outer islands currently leave from four different piers west along the coast from the port of **LAEM NGOP** (sometimes signed as Ngop Cape), 17km southwest of Trat. There are a couple of morning **buses** direct to Laem Ngop's Centrepoint pier from Bangkok's Eastern (Ekamai) bus terminal (5hr 15min), but the usual way to get to Laem Ngop by public transport is by share-taxi (songthaew) from Trat. **Songthaews** leave from Trat bus station and from the central stretch of Thanon Sukhumvit every half-hour or so, depending on boat departures and the time of day; rides can take anything from twenty to forty minutes, excluding the time taken to gather a full complement of passengers, so leave plenty of time to catch the boat. The usual songthaew fare is B30–50, depending on the number of passengers; if you board an empty songthaew you may find you've unwittingly chartered your own taxi for B100. Eight kilometres out of Trat, on the road to Laem Ngop, you'll pass though the village of **Ban Nam Chiao**, which is famous for its basketware items woven from bamboo and palm leaves, especially the emblematic conical rice-farmer's hat. Unless requested otherwise, songthaews will probably drop you at the tour agency near Laem Ngop's main passenger-ferry pier (for foot-passengers to Ko Chang, Ko Whai, Ko Mak and Ko Kham), which is known as the **Naval Monument Pier**, or **Tha Kromaluang Chumporn**. In addition to this pier there are two car-ferry piers for Ko Chang, **Tha Centrepoint** and **Tha Thammachat**, as well as the old **Harbour Pier**, near the TAT office, which is currently used by the Ko Kood Seatrans boats to Ko Mak and Ko Kood. For details of **boat services** from all these piers, see the relevant island accounts.

The Trat and Ko Chang **TAT office** (daily 8.30am–4.30pm; ⓣ039 597259, ⓔtattrat@tat.or.th) is close by the old Harbour Pier, a 15-minute walk from the Monument Pier or B20 by motorbike taxi. It provides independent advice on the islands as well as current boat times (staff will also email you the latest schedules on request). You can change money at the Thai Farmers' Bank (usual banking hours), five minutes' walk back down the main road from TAT.

Ko Chang

The focal point of a national marine park archipelago of 52 islands, **KO CHANG** is Thailand's second-largest island (after Phuket). Measuring 30km north to south and 8km across, it's mainly characterized by a chain of long, white-sand beaches and a broad central spine of jungle-clad hills, the highest of which, **Khao Salak Pet**, tops 740m. Until fairly recently the domain of just a few thousand fishing families and the odd adventurous tourist, Ko Chang has seen massive development since 2001, with real estate going through the roof and the government pouring mega-bucks into the island, financing road-building projects and giving the green-light to many new upmarket resorts. As a result Ko Chang is now very much a mainstream destination – with prices to match – even more popular with Thais than with foreign tourists, and in places still resembling a building site. Nonetheless, the hilly backbone and its waterfalls are protected as a national park, the island is very nearly encircled by a good road, and it is still just about possible to find accommodation to suit most budgets.

Ko Chang's west coast has the prettiest **beaches** and is the most developed, with **Hat Sai Khao** (White Sand Beach) drawing the biggest crowds to its mainly upmarket and increasingly overpriced mid-range accommodation; smaller **Hat Kai Bae** is also pretty congested. Most backpackers opt for **Hat Tha Nam**, known as **Lonely Beach**, with its choice of fairly inexpensive beach huts and established party scene, while travellers in search of quiet choose the more laid-back **Ao Bai Lan** or the long, attractive sweep at **Hat Khlong Phrao**, which caters to all budgets. During **peak season**, accommodation on every beach tends to fill up very quickly, so it's often worth booking ahead; the island gets a lot quieter (and cheaper) from May to October, when fierce storms batter the huts and can make the sea too rough for swimming.

Transport to Ko Chang

All **boats** to Ko Chang depart from the Laem Ngop coast, about 17km southwest of the provincial capital of Trat. If you're coming by public transport from Pattaya, Ko Samet, the northeast or Cambodia you'll need to travel via Trat first. Most buses from Bangkok also terminate in Trat, though a couple of morning ones from the Eastern Bus Terminal run direct to Laem Ngop's Centrepoint pier. If travelling via Trat airport, you can get a direct transfer to Laem Ngop, or across to your Ko Chang hotel; see p.488. Otherwise you could use one of the fast but cramped **tourist minibus** services that run direct to the Laem Ngop piers (most prices exclude ferry tickets) from Bangkok's Thanon Khao San (B180–350), Pattaya (B500 including ferry), and Ban Phe, near Ko Samet (B250).

Three different ferry services run from Laem Ngop to Ko Chang, each departing from a different pier. **Passenger-only ferries** (Ⓣ039 597434) depart from the **Naval Monument Pier** (aka Tha Kromaluang Chumporn), a fifteen-minute walk from the Laem Ngop TAT office, but if coming by songthaew from Trat or tourist bus from Bangkok, Ko Samet or Pattaya, you will get dropped at the correct departure point. In all but the worst weather, these boats start running at 5.30am and then leave every two hours between 9am and 7pm, with extra ones occasionally slotted in for busy periods (B80, or B120 return; 45min). In bad weather you can travel on one of the car ferries, described below. The boats arrive at Tha Dan Kao on Ko Chang's northeast coast, from where **songthaews** (B40–80/ person) transport passengers to the main beaches; to get

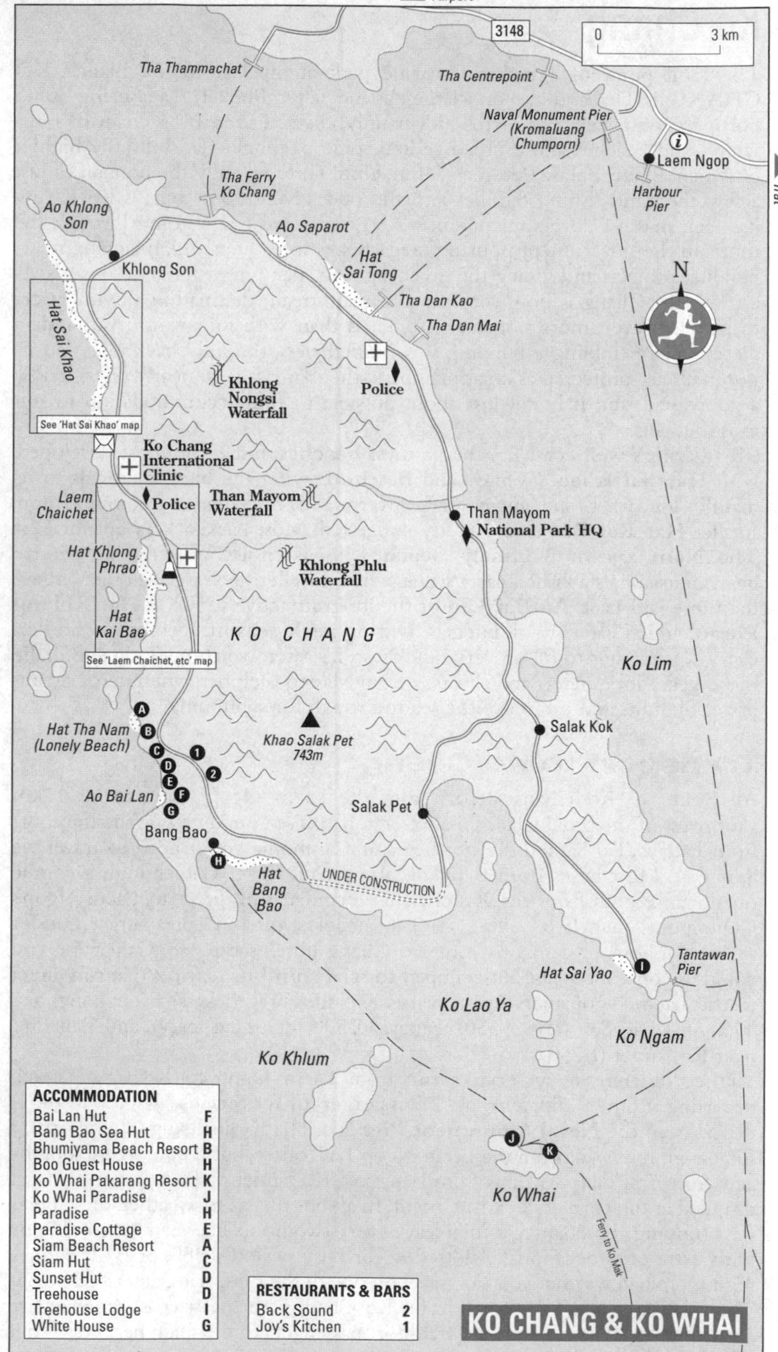

ACCOMMODATION	
Bai Lan Hut	F
Bang Bao Sea Hut	H
Bhumiyama Beach Resort	B
Boo Guest House	H
Ko Whai Pakarang Resort	K
Ko Whai Paradise	J
Paradise	H
Paradise Cottage	E
Siam Beach Resort	A
Siam Hut	C
Sunset Hut	D
Treehouse	D
Treehouse Lodge	I
White House	G

RESTAURANTS & BARS	
Back Sound	2
Joy's Kitchen	1

Moving on from Ko Chang

Leaving Ko Chang, passenger boats run from Tha Dan Kao at every two hours between 6am and 6pm, though songthaew drivers will drop you at one of the piers for the more frequent car ferry services (hourly, 6am–7pm) if appropriate. Tickets for the daily **tourist minibuses** from Laem Ngop to Bangkok's Thanon Khao San, Ban Phe (for Ko Samet) and Pattaya are best bought from bungalows and tour agents on Ko Chang, but you should also be able to buy them once you've landed in Laem Ngop. Alternatively, hop on one of the public songthaews that meet the boats and make your onward travel arrangements in Trat. The Bangkok Airways minibus charges B270 per person all-in for its transfer from Ko Chang hotels **to Trat airport**; buses are timed to fit with the planes and can be booked through any tour agent on the island. A taxi from Laem Ngop to the airport in Bangkok costs B3500.

From about mid-November to May there are several ways of travelling from Ko Chang direct to the **outer islands**, though as timetables vary according to how busy things are, you need to check locally first; see relevant island accounts for more details. Tickets can be bought through tour agencies on nearly every Ko Chang beach, and there's usually a fee of about B50 for transfers to the Bang Bao pier. Bang Bao Boat (Ⓣ087 054 4300) offers daily boats from Bang Bao to **Ko Mak** (2hr 15min; B300) via **Ko Whai** (1hr; B200) with the possibility of an extension ticket for a speedboat transfer from Ko Mak to **Ko Kood** (extra 30min and B300). There's also a daily **speedboat** service (Ⓣ081 377 4074) from Bang Bao to Ko Kood's Ao Prao (1hr 50min; B900) via Ko Whai (15min; B350), Ko Mak (45min; B600) and Ko Kood's Khlong Chao (1hr 30min; B900). Another option is to make use of the daily **Thai Fun** snorkelling boat (see p.494), which runs day-trips from Ko Chang (B999), picking up passengers at the main Ko Chang beaches and making snorkelling stops, and passenger drops, at Ko Whai (B350 one-way), Ko Kham (B550) and Ko Mak (B550), with island pick-ups possible several days later if requested.

to the more remote beaches you'll usually have to pay an extra fee, though some out-of-the-way bungalows send their own songthaew to meet the boats. If you are heading to Ko Chang's east coast, to Salak Pet, or to **Hat Sai Yao** (Long Beach), you can make use of the bargain B70 songthaew service that departs central Trat, behind the *KFC* (see map on p.487) and takes you all the way to Salak Pet, car-ferry passage included.

If you have your own car or motorbike, you need to use one of the **car ferries** that operate from two different piers further west along the Laem Ngop coast, both clearly signposted off the Trat–Laem Ngop road, but also accessible from Highway 3 should you want to bypass Trat. Because of fierce competition between the two ferry companies, timetables and prices change frequently, but from October to May there's at least one ferry an hour between 6am and 7pm in both directions; during the rest of the year there should be at least one every two hours. Expect to pay up to B150 per vehicle including driver, plus B30 per passenger. As the car ferries are more robust than the passenger ferries, they are a good option for foot-passengers during stormy weather: Trat songthaews will transport you to the car ferry piers on request and for an extra fee. Centrepoint Ferry (Ⓣ039 538196) runs ferries from Tha Centrepoint to Tha Dan Mai/Cabana (45min); and Ferry Ko Chang (Ⓣ039 597143) runs ferries from Tha Thammachat to Ao Saparot (25min).

Island practicalities

A wide road runs nearly all the way round the island, served by public **songthaews**, most frequent between Tha Dan Kao and Hat Kai Bae but often enough

Diving and snorkelling in the Ko Chang archipelago

The **reefs** of the Ko Chang archipelago are nowhere near as spectacular as Andaman coast dive sites, and can get very crowded, but they're rewarding enough to make a day-trip worthwhile. Local **dive sites** range from the beginners' reefs at the Southern Pinnacle, with lots of soft corals, anemones, myriad reef fish and the occasional moray eel at depths of 4–6m, to the more challenging 31-metre dive off **Ko Rang**, where you're likely to see snapper – as well as a lot of other divers and snorkellers, this being the favoured destination of boats from Ko Mak and Ko Kood as well as Ko Chang. The best coral is found around the islets off Ko Mak (see p.506): in particular at Ko Rayang, Ko Kra and Ko Rang; the coral around Ko Yuak, off Ko Chang's Hat Kai Bae, is mostly dead, though some operators still sell trips there.

Dive shops on Ko Chang

The biggest concentration of dive shops is on Ko Chang, though there are dive shops on Ko Whai, Ko Mak and Ko Kood (see relevant accounts for details). Some **Ko Chang dive shops** have their main office in Bang Bao, where most boats depart, as well as a branch office or agent elsewhere on the island; those listed below are the main, established operators. All dive shops will organize pick-ups from any beach. See p.70 in Basics for a general introduction to diving in Thailand and for advice on what to look for in a dive centre. The nearest **recompression chambers** are around Pattaya (see p.470).

BB Divers ⓣ086 155 6212, ⓦwww.bbdivers.com. On the road at Bailan and Bang Bao.

Ko Chang Dive Point ⓣ087 142 2948, ⓔarnhelm@gmx.de. On Lonely Beach.

Ploy Scuba Diving ⓣ039 558033 or 086 155 1331, ⓦwww.ployscuba.com. At Hat Sai Khao, Hat Khlong Prao, Hat Kai Bae, Lonely Beach and Bang Bao.

Scubadive Thailand ⓣ039 558028, ⓦwww.scubadive-thailand.com. At Bang Bao.

Sea Horse Diving ⓣ081 996 7147, ⓦwww.ede.ch/seahorse. On Hat Kai Bae.

Water World ⓣ086 139 1117, ⓦwww.waterworldkohchang.com. Ko Chang Plaza, on the road at northern Hat Khlong Prao.

Trips and courses

Waves permitting, the dive shops run trips to reefs off Ko Chang's more sheltered east coast during the **monsoon season** from June through September, though visibility is unlikely to be very rewarding during this period. Prices for dive trips should include two dives, transport and lunch, and be in the range of B2200 to B2700 depending on the operator and the destination; accompanying snorkellers generally pay B700–800 including lunch and equipment. All dive centres also offer PADI or other-internationally certificated **dive courses**: the introductory Discover Scuba averages B3200, the four-day Openwater B11,000, and the two-day Advanced B10,000.

Snorkelling and fishing

From about November to May, Thai Fun (ⓣ081 003 4800) runs popular one-day **snorkelling cruises** to the outer islands with stops at reefs en route as well as at Ko Whai and Ko Mak and often at Ko Kham as well. The B999 price includes snorkel gear and buffet lunch; tickets can be booked through tour agencies on all beaches. The boat collects passengers from the main Ko Chang beaches and can also be used as a one-way or return transfer service to the islands (see p.493). There are all sorts of other locally run snorkelling and fishing trips organized by tour operators and bungalows across the island, typically charging B400 per person, including equipment.

to be useful right down to Bang Bao; you can also rent cars and motorbikes on most beaches. The road can be dangerous in places, with steep hills and sharp, unexpected bends, so drive carefully – accidents are not uncommon.

Almost all the main beaches have roadside developments where you'll find **currency exchange** and ATMs, minimarkets, **Internet** access, clothes stalls and souvenir shops, as well as restaurants and bars. Most beaches have at least one dive shop (see opposite) as well as kayak rental (B100/hr), and there's **elephant trekking** at Chang Chutiman, opposite the temple in Khlong Phrao (ⓣ089 939 6676; B500/900 for a one/two-hour ride). Ko Chang Trekkers, who are based in Trat but pick up from Ko Chang beaches (ⓣ089 164 7490) lead full-day and overnight **treks** into Ko Chang National Park (from B690–1540 per person, plus B200 National Park entry fee, minimum two people). Hat Sai Khao and Hat Kai Bae have the densest concentrations of facilities, which at Hat Sai Khao include two **pharmacies** and, to the south of the main development, a **post office.** The private 24hr **Ko Chang International Clinic** (ⓣ039 551555 or ⓣ081 863 3609), part of the Bangkok Hospital Group, is located between Hat Sai Khao and Hat Kai Mook; it deals with minor injuries and has a dental service, and will transfer seriously ill patients to its parent Bangkok-Trat Hospital in Trat. Ko Chang's main **police station** is at Dan Mai on the northeast coast (ⓣ039 521657), and there are police boxes on Hat Sai Khao and at Hat Khlong Phrao's Ko Chang Plaza.

Though mosquitoes don't seem to be much in evidence, Ko Chang is one of the few areas of Thailand that's still considered to be **malarial**, so you may want to start taking your prophylactics before you get here, and bring repellent with you – refer to p.35 of Basics for more advice on this. Staff at the Ko Chang International Clinic, however, say that the risk to tourists is minimal and that cases are confined to those who work and stay overnight in the island's jungle interior. Sandflies can be more of a problem on the southern beaches and are best repelled by slathering yourself in coconut oil, though you can soothe your bites with locally made yellow oil (see p.487) or calamine. Watch out for **jellyfish**, which plague the west coast in April and May, and for **snakes**, including surprisingly common cobras, sunbathing on the overgrown paths into the interior. The other increasing hazard is **theft** from rooms and bungalows: use your own padlock on bags (and doors where possible) or, better still, make use of hotel safety boxes.

The free annual *Koh Chang Guidebook* and its website (ⓦwww.koh-chang.com) are a reasonable source of **information** and advertisements, and the website provides an accommodation-booking service, but for more intelligent insights and opinionated advice, check out ⓦwww.iamkohchang.com, compiled by a Ko Chang expat.

Hat Sai Khao (White Sand Beach)

Framed by a broad band of fine white sand at low tide, a fringe of casuarinas and palm trees and a backdrop of forested hills, **Hat Sai Khao** (White Sand Beach) is, at 2.5km long, the island's longest beach and its most commercial, with scores of upmarket hotel and bungalow operations squashed in between the road and the shore, plus dozens of shops, travel agents, bars and restaurants lining the inland side of the road. The vibe is more laid-back and traveller-oriented at the northern end of the beach, however, beyond *Yakah*, and this is where you'll find the most budget-priced accommodation, some of it pleasingly characterful and nearly all of it enjoying its own sea view. In addition, the road is well out of earshot of most of the bungalows up here, and there's hardly any passing

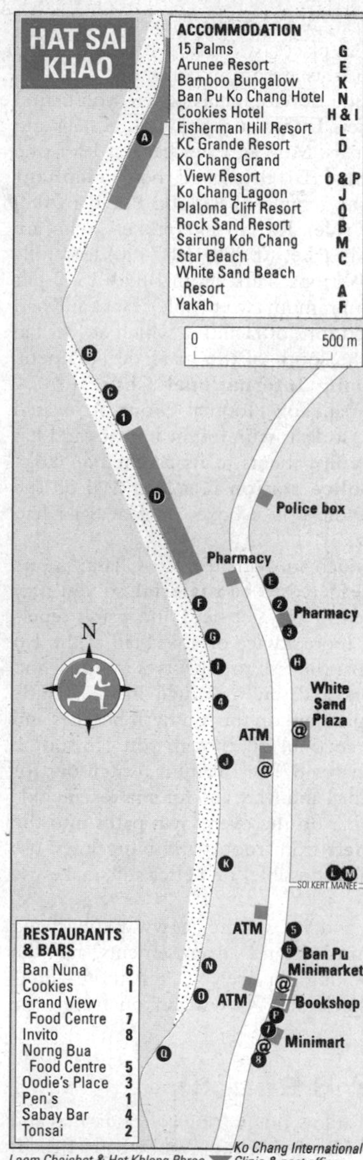

pedestrian traffic, so it can be quite peaceful. Wherever you stay on Hat Sai Khao, be careful when swimming as the **currents** are very strong here and there's no lifeguard service.

Practicalities

Songthaews take about 25 minutes to drive from Tha Dan Kao to Hat Sai Khao and cost B40. If you want the bungalows at *Star Beach*, *Rock Sand* or *White Sand Beach Resort*, the songthaew might take you down the side-road to *White Sand*, but if not, get off as soon as you see the sign for *KC Grande*, and then walk along the beach. For bungalows further south, the songthaew should drop you right outside. During daylight hours it's easy to get songthaews to other beaches, including Hat Khlong Phrao (B30) and Hat Kai Bae (B40).

The road through Hat Sai Khao is lined with (low-rise) resort **facilities**, including banks and ATMs, motorbike and car rental, minimarkets, pharmacies, tour operators, dive shops (see p.494 for details), Internet and international phone centres, souvenir shops and tailors' outlets. The Ban Pu minimarket complex sells new and second-hand books. The post office is about 1km south of *Plaloma*, and beyond that is the **Ko Chang International Clinic** (see p.495).

Accommodation

Central and southern Hat Sai Khao are mainly the province of mid-range and upmarket **accommodation**, a lot of which charges above the odds for decent but unexceptional rooms. Most of the cheaper, better-value options are in northern Hat Sai Khao, though even here it's hard to find anything under ❹ in high season.

Northern Hat Sai Khao

KC Grande Resort ⓣ081 833 1010, ⓦwww.kckohchang.com. One of the most popular "budget" places on Hat Sai Khao, *KC* has almost fifty very basic (though far from bargain-priced) bamboo huts that are strung out under the palm trees over a long stretch of beach so that each hut feels a little bit private and has a view of the sea. Huts all have mosquito nets and some have attached bathrooms. As well as the old-style huts, *KC* also offers much larger, more modern air-con bungalows set in landscaped gardens with a small pool. Huts, bungalows ❽–❾

The **wat**

Buddhist temple complexes, known as wats, are central to nearly every community in Thailand and, as the main expressions of public architecture and art over the centuries, are likely to loom large in many visitors' experience of the country. Wats are much more than museum pieces, however, and take on a surprising diversity of communal roles. Among Thailand's thirty thousand temples, which are home to a total of around a quarter of a million monks, you'll find classrooms, orphanages, drug rehab centres and hospitals. Some wats shelter massage clinics, playgrounds or even small nature reserves, and all come to life once a year for the *ngan wat* (temple fair) with food and market stalls, funfairs and a vibrant line-up of other entertainments.

▲ Phra Mondop, Wat Phra Kaeo, Bangkok

▲ Sema, Wat Phra Kaeo, Bangkok

The main religious principle guiding all this activity is merit-making (*tham bun*), by which monks and laity garner karmic points for their next reincarnation. For ordinary folk, **merit-making** can range from a simple donation (or even buying a ticket for the temple car park) to endowing a whole new building for the wat. The offerings you're most likely to see, however, consist of lotus buds, candles and three incense sticks (representing the three gems of Buddhism – the Buddha himself, the Dharma or doctrine, and the monkhood). The busiest days for merit-making are the *wan phra* (holy days), which occur four times a month according to the phases of the moon.

▼ Worshippers at Wat Phra That Doi Suthep, Chiang Mai

Architecture

Wat architecture has evolved in ways as various as its functions, but the names and purposes of the main buildings, as described below, have stayed constant in Thailand for some fifteen centuries. Some general design features of Thai temples are also distinctive. The **Khmers**, who had ruled much of the country long before the Thais came onto the scene, built their temples to a cosmological plan, with concentric layers representing earth, oceans and heavens, rising to a central high point (Phanom Rung near Surin is a stunning example of this). Remnants of this layout that persisted in Thai temples include boundary walls – which are sometimes combined with a moat – and the multi-tiered roofs of so many wat buildings. Furthermore, the Thais come from a tradition of building in wood rather than stone or brick, hence the leaning walls and long, curving roofs that give wats their elegant, tapering lines. On top of this, wat architects have long been preoccupied with light, symbol of Buddhist wisdom and clarity, covering their buildings with gilt, filigree and vividly coloured glass mosaics.

The bot

The most important wat building is the **bot** (sometimes known as the *ubosot*), where monks are ordained. It usually stands at the heart of the compound, but lay people are rarely allowed inside. There's only one bot in any wat complex, and often the only way you'll be able to distinguish it from other temple buildings is by the eight **sema** or boundary stones which always surround it. Positioned at the four corners of the bot and at the cardinal points of the compass, these *sema* define the consecrated ground and usually look something like upright gravestones, though they can take many forms. They are often carved all over with symbolic Buddhist scenes or ideograms, and sometimes are even protected within miniature shrines of their own. (One of the best *sema* collections is housed in the National Museum of Khon Kaen.)

▲ Wat Phra Singh, Chiang Mai, during Songkhran

The viharn

Often almost identical to the bot, the **viharn** or assembly hall is the building you are most likely to enter, as it usually contains the wat's principal **Buddha image**, and sometimes two or three minor images as well. Large wats may have several viharns, while strict meditation wats, which don't deal with the laity, may not have one at all.

▼ *Ho trai*, Wat Phra Singh, Chiang Mai

Other buildings

Less common wat buildings include the square **mondop**, usually built with a complex, cruciform roof, which houses either a Buddha statue or footprint or holy texts. One of the most spectacular examples, with an ornate green-and-gold roof and huge doors encrusted with mother-of-pearl, shelters Thailand's holiest footprint of the Buddha, at Wat Phra Phutthabat near Lopburi.

The **ho trai**, or scripture library, is generally constructed on stilts, sometimes over a pond, to protect against termites and fire. You can see particularly good examples of traditional *ho trai* at Wat Rakhang in Bangkok, at Wat Phra Singh in Chiang Mai and at Wat Yai Suwannaram in Phetchaburi.

Chedis

Upon the Buddha's death, disciples from all over Asia laid claim to his **relics**, enshrining many of them in specially constructed towers, known as **chedis** in Thailand. The temples containing such chedis were given the title **Wat Phra Mahathat** (Temple of the Great Relic), and each royal city had one; today you'll find a Wat Phra Mahathat in Ayutthaya, Lopburi, Phetchaburi, Phitsanulok, Sukhothai, Nakhon Si Thammarat and Bangkok, all enjoying a special status. In later centuries, chedis have also become repositories for the ashes of royalty or important monks – and anyone else who could afford to have one built.

Chedis are generally the most characteristic hallmarks of each architectural period in Thai history. The **Sukhothai** chedi (thirteenth to fifteenth centuries), for example, is an elegant reworking of the dagoba, the version found in Sri Lanka, from where Theravada Buddhism was imported to Thailand: early ones are bell-shaped (the bell symbolizing the ringing out of the Buddha's teachings), while the later, slimmer versions evoke the contours of a lotus bud. **Ayutthayan** architects (fourteenth to eighteenth centuries) owed more to the Khmers, elongating their chedis and resting them on a higher square platform, stepped and solid. Meanwhile, the independent **Lanna** kingdom (thirteenth to sixteenth centuries) of northern Thailand built some stupas to a squat pyramidal design that harked back to the seventh century, and other more rotund ones that drew on Burmese influences.

Contemporary chedi-builders have tended to combine historical features at will, but most still pay some heed to the traditional **symbolism** of the three main components. In theory, the base or platform of the chedi should be divided into three layers to represent hell, earth and heaven. Above this, the dome usually contains the cube-shaped reliquary, known as a *harmika* after the Sanskrit term for the Buddha's seat of meditation. Crowning the structure, the spire is graded into 33 rings, one for each of the 33 Buddhist heavens.

▼ Chedis at Wat Phra Si Sanphet, Ayutthaya

Rock Sand Resort ⓣ039 551456, ⓔrocksand .beachresort@planet.nl. In the heart of the backpackers' stretch of beach, this place has just a handful of simple timber huts perched on cliffside ledges, with fan or air-con, plus some better air-con rooms, some with good views. Also has a beautifully sited, if pricey, deck-restaurant jutting high over the water. Fan ❸, air-con ❺

Star Beach ⓣ081 940 2195, ⓔstarbeachbungalows@hotmail.com. A bit more basic than neighbouring sister-outfit *Rock Sand*, and squatting in similarly limpet-like fashion on the rock-face, above the sand, this place also fosters a chilled-out travellers' vibe. It has just ten basic, en-suite plywood huts built into the cliff-face, some of which enjoy nice high-level sea views. ❸

White Sand Beach Resort ⓣ081 863 7737. Ranged across a long, attractive stretch of uncommercialized beach at the far north end of the beach, *White Sand* offers a big range of nicely spaced huts, many of them lapping up uninterrupted sea views. Many of the huts are pretty basic affairs, though all have private bathrooms, but there are also some posher, sturdier ones. Fan ❺, air-con ❻–❼

Central and southern Hat Sai Khao

15 Palms ⓣ039 551095. Unusually nice, well designed and fairly stylish beachfront bungalows, all with air-con. Also has a great sea-view lounge-bar complete with leather sofas, pool table and cable TV. ❼

Arunee Resort ⓣ039 551075. Built in a row just across the road from the beach, the guest-house-style rooms here all have a small veranda, mattress, fan and en-suite bathroom and are a good price for Hat Sai Khao. ❸

Bamboo Bungalow ⓣ081 945 4106. Pretty smart but pricey air-con bungalows built in a staggered line on the beach, so there is at least a partial sea view from every one. ❼

Ban Pu Ko Chang Hotel ⓣ081 863 7314, ⓦwww.banpuresort.com. Upmarket accommodation comprising a low-rise hotel block and spacious wooden bungalows with unusual, open-roofed bathrooms built around a pretty tropical garden and a small swimming pool. All rooms have sea view, air-con, TV and a veranda. ❽

Cookies Hotel ⓣ081 861 4227. Large, plain but good "superior" rooms in an unexciting block on the seafront, plus similar "standard" ones across the road, with picture windows and big verandas but no sea views. ❼–❽

Fisherman Hill Resort Soi Kert Manee ⓣ081 429 3827. Friendly place ranged up the hillside about 200m off the road. It offers some of the cheapest rooms on Hat Sai Khao, in simple huts with fan and deck and shared bathroom, plus others with bathroom and some less good-value ones with air-con across the soi. A couple of huts have fabulous views of the jungle-encrusted mountains behind. Shared bathroom ❷ Fan and bathroom ❹ Air-con ❼–❽

Ko Chang Grand View Resort ⓣ081 863 7802, ⓦwww.grandviewthai.net. What sets this place apart from many others is the amount of space between most bungalows, many of which are set around either the shoreside garden, or, less scenically and more noisily, in a plot across the road. The beachfront garden drops down to a rocky part of the beach at the far southern end of the bay, but the sand is just a few steps away. The cheapest accommodation is in simple fan huts, with screens and thick mattresses and there are also concrete air-con bungalows and rooms. Fan ❺, air-con ❼–❽

Ko Chang Lagoon ⓣ039 551201, ⓦwww .kohchanglagoonresort.com. Large, resort-style, two-storey hotel complex with comfortably furnished air-con rooms and huge two-storey bungalows right on the sand. Hotel ❼, bungalows ❼–❽

Plaloma Cliff Resort ⓣ081 863 1305, ⓦwww .plaloma-cliff.thai.li. Though the interiors of the fan and air-con rooms and bungalows here are unexceptional, the landscaping is spacious and pleasant plus there's a nice pool. Some rooms also have panoramic coastal views. There's no beach right here, at the far southern end of Hat Sai Khao, just rocks, but you can still swim, or walk a couple of hundred metres down to the sand beyond *Ko Chang Grand View*. Fan room ❻, air-con ❼–❽

Sairung Koh Chang Soi Kert Manee ⓣ039 5511177. Half a dozen bamboo bungalows with attached bathrooms staggered up the hillside about 250m off the road. Cheap for Hat Sai Khao. ❸

Yakah ⓣ089 007 4326. Small collection of eleven teak-log bungalows right on the beach, all pretty nice inside and with air-con, TV, fridge and at least partial sea view. ❻–❼

Eating and drinking

All the bungalow operations on Hat Sai Khao have **restaurants**, most of which offer passable European food and standard Thai fare. As well as the listed beach **bars**, there's a more mellow cluster of little seafront options up on northern

Hat Sai Khao, around *Rock Sand* and *Star Bungalows*, and, at the other extreme, a knot of brash, Pattaya-style bar-beers inland from *Plaloma Cliff Resort* in southern Hat Sai Khao.

Ban Nuna Specializes in mid-priced German food, as well as pizzas.
Cookies The nightly seafood barbecues are the attraction here. Make your selection from the neat piles of barracuda, shark, tuna, king prawns, crab and squid laid out on ice trays on the beach, decide how you'd like it served, and take your seat at the candlelit tables on the sand.
Grand View Food Centre Collection of hot-food stalls serving soups, noodles and Isaan specialities that's a hit with local shop-workers as much for its authentic taste as for its very cheap prices.
Invito Expensive but highly rated, authentic Italian food (from B300) including wood-fired pizzas, pastas and imported wines.
Norng Bua Food Centre Very cheap night-market-style Thai food, including noodle soups, fried noodles and satays.
Oodie's Place Live music most nights, daily movies, and a Euro-Asian menu with a French accent; most main dishes cost B60–200.
Pen's Tiny beachfront restaurant that serves exceptionally good home-style Thai food at fairly cheap prices.
Sabay Bar One of Ko Chang's longest-running institutions, where you can choose to sit in the chic air-con bar and watch the nightly live sets from the decent in-house cover band (from 9pm), or lounge outside on mats and cushions on the sand and just listen to the music via the outdoor speakers. You pay for the pleasure, however, as drinks are pricey. Also stages fire-juggling shows on the beach and full moon beach parties.
Tonsai The atmosphere at this predominantly vegetarian restaurant is pleasingly mellow: seating is on Thai-style cushions scattered around a circular platform wedged between half a dozen trees and the menu (B50–150) includes Thai curries, pastas, Vietnamese sausage and around fifty cocktails.

Laem Chaichet and Hat Khlong Phrao

Four kilometres south of Hat Sai Khao, the scenic, rocky cape at **LAEM CHAICHET** curves round into sweeping, casuarina-fringed **HAT KHLONG PHRAO**, one of Ko Chang's nicest beaches, not least because it has yet to see the clutter and claustrophobic development of both its neighbours. For the moment at least, most of the restaurants, bars and shops are secreted way off the beach along the roadside, with the beachfront left mainly to a decent spread of differently priced accommodation. At the northern end, **Laem Chaichet** protects an inlet and tiny harbour and offers beautiful views south across the bay and inland to the densely forested mountains behind. **Northern Hat Khlong Phrao** is a nice kilometre-long run of beach that ends at a wide khlong, Khlong Phlu, whose estuary is the site of some characterful stilt homes and seafood restaurants. At low tide you can just about wade across to **southern Hat Khlong Phrao**; more reliably, during daylight hours, you can rent your own kayak from almost anywhere along the beach, or make use of the boatman who ferries guests at *Aana Resort* to and from the resort's private little patch of sand behind *Thalé* bungalows. The 2.5-kilometre-long southern stretch is partly shaded by casuarinas and backed in places by a huge coconut grove that screens the beach from the road; the central area in particular has retained an appealingly mellow atmosphere despite the presence of several upmarket resorts alongside the two long-running traveller-oriented options.

As well as dividing northern Hat Khlong Phrao from southern Hat Khlong Phrao, Khlong Phlu's waters tumble into the island's most famous cascade, **Khlong Phlu Falls** (Nam Tok Khlong Phlu), a couple of kilometres east off the main road. Signs lead you inland to a car park and some hot-food stalls, where you pay your national park entry fee (B200, kids B100) and walk the final 500m to the 20-metre-high waterfall (best in the rainy season) that plunges into an invitingly clear pool defined by a ring of smooth rocks.

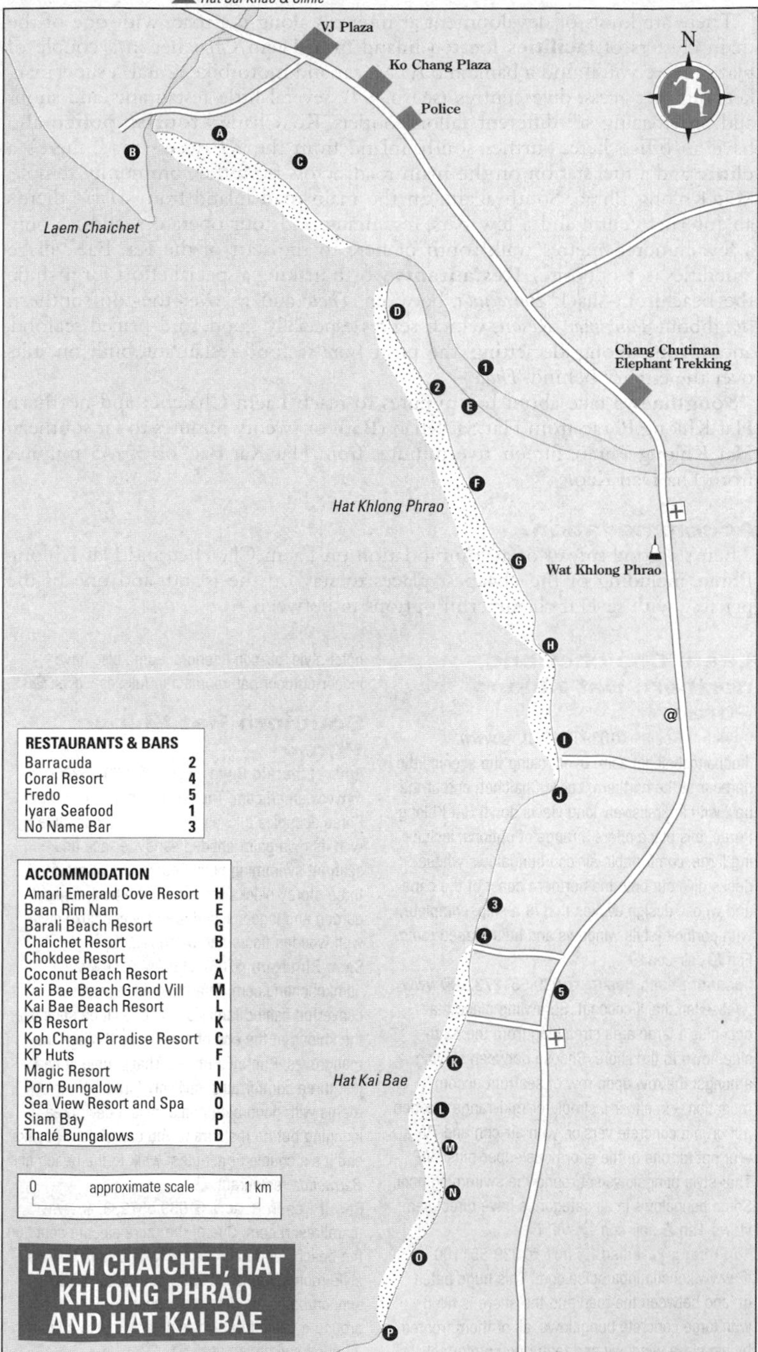

Hat Sai Khao & Clinic
VJ Plaza
Ko Chang Plaza
Police
N
Laem Chaichet
Khlong Phlu Falls
Chang Chutiman Elephant Trekking
Hat Khlong Phrao
Wat Khlong Phrao
Hat Kai Bae
Hat Tha Nam
RESTAURANTS & BARS
Barracuda 2
Coral Resort 4
Fredo 5
Iyara Seafood 1
No Name Bar 3
ACCOMMODATION
Amari Emerald Cove Resort H
Baan Rim Nam E
Barali Beach Resort G
Chaichet Resort B
Chokdee Resort J
Coconut Beach Resort A
Kai Bae Beach Grand Vill M
Kai Bae Beach Resort L
KB Resort K
Koh Chang Paradise Resort C
KP Huts F
Magic Resort I
Porn Bungalow N
Sea View Resort and Spa O
Siam Bay P
Thalé Bungalows D
0 approximate scale 1 km
LAEM CHAICHET, HAT KHLONG PHRAO AND HAT KAI BAE

There are knots of development at intervals along the road, with one of the main clusters of **facilities** located inland from Laem Chaichet in a couple of plazas. Here you'll find a bank and ATM, car and motorbike rental, a supermarket, Internet acess, dive centres (see p.494), several little restaurants and shops and an amazing six different tailors' outlets. Ko Chang's **tourist police** also have an office here. Further south, inland from the *KP* access road, there's a **clinic** and a fuel station on the main road, across from the community temple, Wat Khlong Phrao. South again, on the main road inland from *Magic*, there's an Internet centre and a few bars, restaurants and tour operators, and it's only a few hundred metres walk south of here to the start of the Kai Bae village amenities (see opposite). **Restaurants** worth making a special effort for include the beachfront-shack *Barracuda*, between *Thalé* and its over-the-top southern neighbour *Panviman Resort*, which serves especially good, mid-priced seafood; and, for its khlongside setting, the posh *Iyara* seafood restaurant, built on stilts over the estuary behind *Thalé*.

Songthaews take about ten minutes to reach Laem Chaichet and northern Hat Khlong Phrao from Hat Sai Khao (B30) or twenty minutes to far southern Hat Khlong Phrao, fifteen/five minutes from Hat Kai Bae, or 35/45 minutes from Tha Dan Kao.

Accommodation

There's a good spread of accommodation on Laem Chaichet and Hat Khlong Phrao, including of the cheapest places to stay on the island, and one of the priciest, with several characterful options in between.

Laem Chaichet and northern Hat Khlong Phrao

Chaichet Resort ⓣ039 551070, ⓦwww.kochangchaichet.com. Overlooking the scenic little harbour at the northern, Laem Chaichet, end of the bay, with impressively long views down Hat Khlong Phrao, this place offers a range of options, including large, comfortable air-con bungalows whose decks give out onto the northern coast of the cape and whose design evokes that of a ship, complete with porthole-style windows and hull-shaped roofs. Fan 5, air-con 6

Coconut Beach Resort ⓣ039 5512732, ⓦwww.webseiten.thai.li/coconut. Sprawling place that occupies a large area stretching from the roadside down to the shore. Choose between staying amongst the row upon row of seafront accommodation – in either a simple or mid-range wooden hut or in a concrete version with air-con and TV – or opt for one of the enormous super-plush VIP Thai-style bungalows set round the swimming pool. Some bungalows in all categories have direct sea views. Fan 5, air-con 7, VIP 8

Koh Chang Paradise Resort ⓣ039 551100 ⓦwww.kohchangparadise.com. This huge patch of land between the road and the shore is filled with large concrete bungalows, all of them fronted by big glass windows and featuring comfortable, hotel-style, air-con interiors. Some also have indoor-outdoor bathrooms and full sea views. 8

Southern Hat Khlong Phrao

Amari Emerald Cove Resort ⓣ039 552000 ⓦwww.amari.com. The poshest place on Khlong Phrao occupies a lovely tranquil spot, complete with its own palm-shaded sandy terrace and seafront swimming pool. Rooms are in low-rise three-storey blocks set around the pool, tropical garden and lagoons, and are typical deluxe style, with wooden floors and balconies. 9

Baan Rim Nam ⓣ087 005 8575, ⓦwww.iamkohchang.com. Charming, idiosyncratic converted fishing family's house, built on stilts over the khlong at the end of a walkway through the mangroves. Run by a British-Thai couple, it has just three comfortable, stylishly furnished air-con rooms with good bathrooms, plus a deck area for lounging but no restaurant. You can borrow kayaks and it's a couple of minutes' walk to the beach and *Barracuda* restaurant. 5

Barali Beach Resort ⓣ039 557238, ⓦwww.baraliresort.com. One of the more elegant spots on the beach, with forty tastefully designed, Balinese-style rooms, furnished with four-poster beds, sunken baths and lots of polished wood, and set around a beachfront tropical garden with an infinity-edge swimming pool. 9

Chokdee Resort ⓣ081 910 9052, ⓔchokdeeresort_kc@yahoo.com. Sitting astride the rocky promontory at the far southern end of Hat Khlong Phrao, but within a couple of hops of the sand around neighbouring *Magic* and next-door-but-one *Amari*, the concrete bungalows here are reasonable value if uninspired. Nearly all of them have a sea view and the price depends on whether or not you want air-con. Fan ❹, air-con ❻

KP Huts ⓣ084 099 5100. Very much traveller-oriented, this popular spot has fifty fairly simple wooden huts attractively scattered through a large shoreside coconut grove with plenty of sea views. Even some of the simplest versions (with shared bathrooms) are right on the shore, and a few are raised high on stilts for an extra-seductive panorama. There are also larger en-suite huts, some of which are designed for families. All rooms have fans and there's 24-hour electricity. The management rents out motorbikes and kayaks, and organizes snorkelling and fishing day-trips. Shared bathroom ❷–❸, en suite ❹

Magic Resort ⓣ039 557074. Bungalows here are widely spaced around a shorefront garden at the far southern end of the bay: choose between timber huts with fan, or air-con concrete versions. It also has a gorgeously sited restaurant that sits right over the water. Fan ❹, air-con ❻

Thalé Bungalows ⓣ081 926 3843. The entire northern stretch of southern Hat Khlong Phrao is occupied by the primitive wooden-plank huts of the determinedly old-style *Thalé*, whose land runs right up to the khlong. This is one of the cheapest places to stay on Ko Chang: none of the huts have private bathrooms, but all have mosquito nets and some have a deck too. ❷

Hat Kai Bae

South around the headland from *Chokdee*, narrow, pretty little **HAT KAI BAE** (see map on p.498) presents a classic picture of white sand, pale blue water and overhanging palms, but the shorefront is very slender indeed – and filled with bungalows – and the beach disappears entirely at high tide. The widest stretch of beach is in front of *KB Resort*, and there's also the option of kayaking across to the sandy shore at Ko Man Nai, the island that sits less than a thirty-minute paddle offshore from *Siam Bay*.

You should have no problem getting a **songthaew** to Kai Bae from Tha Dan Kao (50min; B60) or Hat Sai Khao (25min; B40). Several places on Hat Kai Bae rent out motorbikes, kayaks and boats and there are dive shops here (see p.494) as well as beachfront Internet access at *Kai Bae Beach Resort*. The roadside development is full of small shops, ATMs, currency exchange, second-hand book outlets, Internet access and restaurants, and there's also a **clinic/pharmacy** (evenings only).

Accommodation and eating

All the Kai Bae bungalows have restaurants, and some of the best **food** on the beach is served up by *Coral Resort*, whose restaurant occupies a gorgeous breezy spot on the coral rocks. The menu includes specialities from Isaan like *som tam* and minced pork *larb*, as well as Thai curries and consistently good barbecued seafood, not to mention decent pizzas. Away from the beach, on the main road, between the access road to *Kai Bae Hut* and the one to *Coral*, you'll find the recommended French restaurant *Fredo*, and a number of cheap Thai noodle restaurants and *som tam* shops. For a **beer** with a sea view, you could do worse than drop in at the ultra-laid-back *No Name Bar*, a few metres north along the shore from *Coral*.

Kai Bae Beach Grand Vill ⓣ081 940 9420, ⓦwww.kaibaegrandvill.com. All the accommodation here is plainly furnished, with the best value options being the fan-cooled timber bungalows on the shorefront, most of which enjoy direct sea views, and some of which sleep four people. Rooms in the small hotel block at the back have air-con and are quite a bit pricier. Fan ❹–❺, air-con ❼

Kai Bae Beach Resort ⓣ081 917 7704. This place has lots of bungalows stretching over a biggish patch of the seafront: choose between comfortable wooden ones with fan and bathroom, many with sea view, and elegant deluxe air-con versions, many set around the garden. Fan ❺, air-con ❼

KB Resort ⓣ039 557125, ⓦwww.kbresort.com. Attractive, upmarket place whose poshest bungalows, many of them on the seafront, have huge glass windows, air-con, TV and comfy interiors (though not much privacy). The cheaper fan versions are similar but don't have the big windows. Fan ❻, air-con ❼–❽

Porn Bungalow ⓣ089 099 8757. Laid-back, long-running travellers' hangout that's the main cheap place to stay on this beach. It has both old-style bamboo huts – many of them right on the seafront – with fans, mozzie nets and shared facilities, as well as a range of more comfortable en-suite wooden bungalows, also with nets and fans. There's also an attractive shoreside eating area full of cushions and low tables, and a bar. Shared bathroom ❷, en suite ❸–❺

Sea View Resort and Spa ⓣ039 551153, ⓦwww.seaviewkohchang.com. The most upmarket place on the beach, *Sea View* is set around a lawn and tropical flower garden and has a table-tennis table under the palm trees, a swimming pool and spa, and a currency exchange desk. The air-con hotel rooms and bungalows are large, light and airy, and fairly luxuriously furnished; all of them have decks or verandas and some have garden bathrooms. Price mainly depends on the view. ❼–❾

Siam Bay ⓣ081 859 5529. Set right at the southern end of the beach, *Siam Bay* has a beautifully sited restaurant and swimming pool overlooking the rocks, plus standard mid-range air-con bungalows on the hillside and pricier, more modern contemporary ones on the shore. Hillside ❻, shorefront ❼

Hat Tha Nam (Lonely Beach)

HAT THA NAM – dubbed **Lonely Beach** before it became the backpackers' choice spot, and still known as such – is one of the nicest beaches on the island. The kilometre-long curve of white-sand bay is broad even at high tide and bungalow developments are set at a decent distance from the shoreline. Be extremely careful when swimming here, however, especially around *Siam Beach* at the northern end, as the steep shelf and dangerous current result in a sobering number of **drownings** every year – twenty in 2003; do your swimming further south and don't go out at all when the waves are high.

Nearly all the accommodation on Hat Tha Nam is aimed at budget travellers, so prices are among the cheapest on Ko Chang. The youthful crowd means this

△ Lonely Beach: Hat Tha Nam

is also the island's main party beach: though there are just a handful of **bars**, they crank it up loud and late, so this is not the beach to head for if you want to be lulled to sleep by the sounds of the sea. Across the road from *Paradise Cottages*, *Back Sound* is the biggest bar, hosting regular red-bull-and-vodka-bucket parties and playing mainly house music. *Joy's Kitchen*, a short walk north up the road, near the *Treehouse* access road, is a good place to line your stomach first. There's a dive shop on the beach (see p.494), kayak and motorbike rental at most bungalows, and Internet access at *Siam Beach* and on the road. **Songthaews** from Tha Dan Kao take about an hour to Hat Tha Nam and cost B80.

Accommodation

Bhumiyama Beach Resort Central beach area ⓣ081 860 4623, ⓦwww.bhumiyama.com. The poshest place on the beach has just 45 attractively furnished rooms, in deluxe two-storey bungalows and cottage wings. The most expensive have sea views from their picture windows, and all have air-con and use of the pool. ❽–❾

Paradise Cottage Beyond the southernmost end of Lonely Beach, ⓣ039 558122. Though the 32 en-suite woven-bamboo and thatch huts here are fairly simple they are also in good condition, look almost chic, and all have fans, 24-hour electricity, and mozzie nets. The slightly more expensive ones have a sea view from their decks; the others are enveloped by banana trees in the jungle-garden. The huge communal wooden deck – for lounging, eating and horizon-gazing – is the focus of the place; there's no sand here, just rocks, though sandy Lonely Beach is just a few minutes' walk to the north. ❷–❸, sea view ❸–❹

Siam Beach Resort At the far north end of the beach ⓣ089 161 6664. Simple, decent enough bungalows with fan and bathroom, many of them on the beach, plus other air-con ones set back from the shore up the hillside. Fan ❹, air-con ❺

Siam Hut Central beach area ⓣ086 609 7772. Rows and rows of cheap, primitive, split-bamboo huts – ninety in total – all of them en suite and with mattresses and mozzie nets. It's first come, first served for the prime seafront locations. ❷

Sunset Hut Beyond *Treehouse* at the far southern end of the beach ⓣ081 818 7042. Posh concrete en-suite bungalows with proper beds and big glass windows – and some also have seafront decks – plus some old-style huts with shared bathrooms. It also has a good restaurant with lots of veggie options, and a bar. Shared bathroom ❷, en suite ❹

Treehouse Southern end of the beach ⓣ081 847 8215. Set on the rocky headland at the southern end of the bay, this German-Thai-managed place is the one that put this beach on the map and is the most chilled and characterful spot on Hat Tha Nam. However, the landowner is set to take the place back in the near future, so call to check first – or head straight for the genuinely lonely new branch of *Treehouse*, on Hat Sai Yao (see p.504). Until they're knocked down, accommodation here is in the cute, trademark, shaggy-thatched huts, each one simply furnished with a mattress, a mosquito net and a paraffin lamp (there's no electricity in the huts, so no fans either), and all of them with shared bathrooms. There's an inviting seaside deck-restaurant and bar, with hammocks and floor cushions. Also has a book exchange. ❶–❷

Ao Bai Lan

About one kilometre south of Hat Tha Nam (15 minutes' walk along the road and over the hill), **AO BAI LAN** accommodates the non-partying refugees from Lonely Beach – though *Bai Lan Hut* has its own chilled out jazz and blues bar set over the water, *Net n' Hook*, whose tag-line is "Jazz your mind, blues your soul". There's no beach here, just rocks, reef, and invitingly clear water, but you can still swim, snorkel and fish. The vibe at the longest-running place here, *Bai Lan Hut* (ⓣ087 028 0796, ⓔbailanhut2002@hotmail.com; ❶–❷), is ultra laid-back. It comprises 16 no-frills huts, many of them on stilts, some of them right beside the sea, others in the palm-filled garden, plus a lovely seating and eating area, decorated with shell-and-driftwood artwork, on a deck that extends right over the water; it's often closed between June and October, so phone first to check. The restaurant here, *Miss Naughty's*, is run by the owner-chef who studied Italian and Thai cuisine and will give cooking classes if asked. Sharing the rocky bay, the *White House* (Ⓣ039 558114; ❺–❻) has some dinky, quite stylish, contemporary all-white villas set round a swimming pool, all with partial sea view, plus rooms in a block at the back; all have air-con. The roadside village at Bai Lan has Internet access and a dive shop (see p.494). **Songthaews** from Tha Dan Kao take about an hour to Ao Bai Lan and cost B80.

Bang Bao village and Hat Bang Bao

Picturesque **BANG BAO VILLAGE**, about 4km south of Ao Bai Lan on Ko Chang's southern coast, is a popular and enjoyable focus for organized day-trips around Ko Chang, and is the departure point for snorkelling and diving trips and boat transfers to the outer islands. The village is built on stilts off one long jetty that extends out into the sheltered fishing harbour and is full of tourist-oriented seafood **restaurants**, including the highly regarded *The Bay*; dive shops (see box on p.494 for diving information); and tour operators like Jer Poo Dee Banyang, who run snorkelling trips (B600/person) and **night-fishing** expeditions (Nov–end April; 6pm–1am; B500 including barbecue). It also has a local health-care centre. Once the day-trippers have left, Bang Bao is quite an interesting **place to stay**, with several options on the main jetty, including the no-frills jetty huts with shared bathrooms at *Paradise* (❷); *Boo Guest House* (Ⓣ089 831 1874; ❸), where all the jetty rooms are en suite; and the very attractive *Bang Bao Sea Hut* (Ⓣ081 285 0570, Ⓦwww.bangbaoseahut.com; ❼), whose fourteen tasteful, octagonal stilted huts overlook the harbour and are connected to the main jetty by a series of walkways.

The nearest properly swimmable beach is the narrow sandy stretch at **Hat Bang Bao**, 2km east of the village; you can camp here and there's a small restaurant too. **Songthaews** from Hat Sai Khao take around 45 minutes to Bang Bao and cost about B70.

The east coast

The mangrove-fringed **east coast** is less inviting than the west, and there are hardly any places to stay here. South of the piers at Ao Saparot and Tha Dan Kao, the road runs through long swathes of rubber and palm plantations, with jungle-clad hills to the west and bronze-coloured beaches to the east, passing the national park office and bungalows at **Than Mayom** before reaching the little fishing port of **Salak Pet** on the south coast. Salak Pet is still a fairly quiet spot that's best known for its excellent seafood restaurants; **songthaews** from Trat come all the way here, departing from behind *KFC* in the temple yard in central Trat when full, driving on to the car ferry and then continuing all the way down to Salak Pet (B70). Just 12 kilometres separates Salak Pet from Bang Bao in the southwest, and although the road link between them is almost complete – bar about three kilometres – it is very narrow, gravel-surfaced, and full of dangerous hairpins and steep slopes.

If you fork off the Salak Pet road near the tiny fishing settlement of **Salak Kok**, you can drive down to the tip of the southeastern headland, to **Hat Sai Yao** (also known as **Long Beach**), the prettiest white-sand beach on this coast, which is good for swimming and has some coral close to shore. The famous *Treehouse* bungalows from Lonely Beach have set up a sister operation here, *Treehouse Lodge* (❷–❸; closed in low season), with a view to relocating entirely when the Lonely Beach bungalows are eventually closed down (see p.503); accommodation is in simple, characterful, thatched bamboo huts. To get here, either get a lift from the Lonely Beach branch, use the Trat–Salak Pet

songthaew service and wait for the *Treehouse* shuttle in Salak Pet, or take the 3pm Ko Whai **boat** from Laem Ngop (see below) and ask to be dropped at the Tantawan pier (1hr), where a *Treehouse* shuttle will pick you up.

The Ko Chang archipelago

South of Ko Chang lies an **archipelago** of 51 islands, a number of which support at least one set of tourist accommodation. None of the islands are especially appealing during the rainy season, when accommodation and transport options are much reduced, but from November through May the main islands of **Ko Whai**, **Ko Mak** and **Ko Kood** are served by regular boats from Laem Ngop and Ko Chang and by several inter-island speedboats too. There are also plans to build an air-strip on one of the uninhabited islands between Ko Mak and Ko Kood. For the latest information on boat times, weather conditions and the proposed air-strip, ask at any guest house in Trat or Ko Chang, or at the TAT office in Laem Ngop.

Ko Whai

Lovely, peaceful little **KO WHAI** (or Ko Wai), which lies about 10km off Ko Chang's southeastern headland, is the perfect place to escape the commercialism of Ko Chang. It's only about 3km long and 1.5km wide and has no facilities at all except for some rewardingly shallow reefs and a couple of **places to stay** (Oct–May only): the inviting, very laid-back *Ko Whai Paradise* (Ⓣ081 762 2548; ❷–❹), which has forty basic bamboo huts (no fans, electricity in the evenings only) in varying sizes right on the shore on the western end of the island; and the more comfortable though less atmospheric *Ko Whai Pakarang Resort* (Ⓣ081 945 4383; ❸–❹), which has forty en-suite bungalows with fans across on the next beach, towards the eastern headland. Ploy Scuba (Ⓣ039 558033, Ⓦwww.ployscuba.com) can arrange dive trips from the island. **Boats** to Ko Whai depart Laem Ngop's Naval Monument pier (Tha Kromaluang Chumporn; see p.490), once a day at 3pm (approx Nov–May; 2hr 30min; B180). Coming **from Ko Chang**, **Ko Mak or Ko Kood**, you can travel with Bang Bao Boat (Ⓣ087 054 4300), which runs daily boats from Ko Chang to Ko Whai (1hr; B200) and on to Ko Mak (1hr 15min), and back again; with the daily speedboat service (Ⓣ081 377 4074) from Ko Chang that stops at Ko Whai (15min; B350) and then continues to Ko Mak (30min) and Ko Kood's Khlong Chao (1hr 15min) and Ao Prao (1hr 35min); or with the daily Thai Fun snorkelling boat (see p.494), which runs day-trips from Ko Chang to the islands, making passenger drops and pick-ups at Ko Whai (B350 one-way), Ko Kham and Ko Mak.

Ko Mak and Ko Kham

Many travellers are so seduced by the peaceful pace of life on **KO MAK** (sometimes spelt "Maak"), 20km southeast of Ko Chang, that they wind up staying much longer than they intended. Home to no more than a few hundred people, most of whom either fish or live off the coconut and rubber plantations that dominate the island, Ko Mak measures just sixteen square kilometres and is traversed by a couple of narrow concrete roads and a network of red-earth tracks that cut through the trees. The island is shaped like a cross, with fine

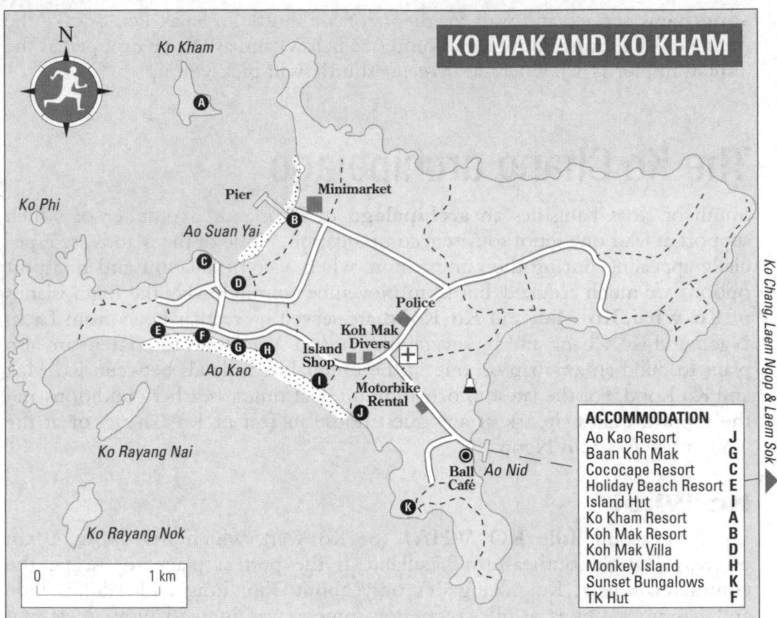

white-sand beaches along the southwest coast at **Ao Kao** and the northwest coast at **Ao Suan Yai**; the main pier is on the southeast coast, at the principal village of **Ao Nid**. The tiny island of **Ko Kham** lies just off Ao Suan Yai and supports only one small resort. Ko Mak gets lashed by wind and rain from early June through September so some bungalows close for the duration (call ahead to check) and there are no speedboat services or boats from Ko Chang during this period, though the daily slow boat from Laem Ngop still runs in all but the worst weather.

Lazing around is the main occupation of most island visitors but the three main centres of Ao Nid, Ao Kao and Ao Suan Yai are all within walking distance of each other, and other parts of the island are also fairly easy to explore on foot, mountain bike or kayak. There's decent **diving and snorkelling** at reefs within an hour's boat ride of Ko Mak, particular at Ko Yak, Hin Yak and No Name reef, which have up to thirty different species of hard and soft coral, and at the 28-metre-deep Hin Gor, where you've a good chance of encountering rays, black-tip sharks, white-tip sharks and leopard sharks. Island dive shops, which operate from October through May only, include Koh Mak Divers (Ⓣ085 922 5262), on the road behind *Island Hut*, and Ploy Scuba (Ⓣ081 862 7570, Ⓦwww.ployscuba.com), bookable through most accommodation. Both run dive trips and courses: prices average B2000 for two fun dives, B10,000 for the four-day Openwater course, and B500 for an accompanying snorkeller. During high season, *Baan Ko Maak* on Ao Kao runs a daily boat across to Ko Rayang Nok (B100/person; minimum six people), which lies less than a couple of kilometres off the western shore and has decent snorkelling; they also do all-day three-island trips to Ko Rang (see p.494), Ko Yak and Ko Kra (B550). *Koh Mak Resort* on Ao Suan Yai runs snorkel boats across to Ko Kham (B60 return, plus B60 visitors' tax).

Island practicalities

The best one-stop shop for **information** on Ko Mak and transport to Trat and the other islands is *Ball Café* at Ao Nid pier (daily 7am–7pm, year-round, ⓣ086 972 4918, ⓔkohmak@gmail.com), where you can also access the Internet, rent high-quality mountain bikes and quaff espressos, cappuccinos and lattes; it's a 20-minute walk from *Island Hut* on Ao Kao or about 30 minutes from *Koh Mak Resort*. There is as yet no major commercial development on the island and no bank, just a couple of local shops at Ao Nid, a tiny minimarket at *Ko Mak Resort* on Ao Suan Yai, and The Island Shop, on the road behind Ao Kao's *Island Hut*, which sells everything from sun-dresses to silver bangles and Rizzla papers. Bungalows on both beaches will **change money** and *Koh Mak Resort* does Visa card cash advances. As well as at *Ball Café*, there's **Internet access** (B2/minute) on Ao Kao at *Ao Kao Resort*, *TK Hut* and *Holiday Beach*, and on Ao Suan Yai at *Koh Mak Resort*; in addition, almost the whole island is wi-fi enabled, care of Ao Suan Yai's *Koh Mak Villa* (B300/day). Ko Mak **post office** is at *Koh Mak Resort*, and there's a small **clinic** on the cross-island road, though for anything serious a speedboat will whisk you back to the mainland). Bring some yellow oil with you from Trat (see p.487) to alleviate the inevitable sandfly bites, or prevent them altogether by embalming yourself in locally produced coconut oil, sold at most bungalows.

There's no public **transport** on the island and virtually no traffic of any sort, so most travellers either walk or rent a bicycle: *Ball Café* at Ao Nid Pier has ten excellent quality mountain bikes (B150/24 hr) and bikes are also available at some bungalows. Many bungalows also rent motorbikes (B350/day), as does a small restaurant just along the road from Ao Nid pier; apparently it's possible to walk, wade and swim around the entire perimeter of the island in ten hours.

There are a number of **boat services** to Ko Mak, from both the mainland and from Ko Chang and Ko Kood, but as many are seasonal and subject to visitor numbers as well as sea conditions you should phone ahead or ask locally to confirm schedules. Most boats arrive at Ao Nid on Ko Mak's southeastern coast, but wherever boats dock, bungalow staff are always there to meet potential guests. The most reliable service is the **slow boat from Laem Ngop**, which runs daily, year-round, in all but the worst weather, from the Naval Monument pier, Tha Kromaluang Chumporn (see p.490), to Ao Nid (departs 3pm; 3hr 30min; B250); the return boat leaves Ao Nid daily at 8am. From October–May there should also be daily services with **Ko Mak Speedboat** (2 daily to and from Laem Ngop's Naval Monument pier; 1hr; B450; ⓣ081 921 6591) and **Siriwhite Speedboat** (daily to and from Laem Sok, described on p.488; 40min; B400; ⓣ086 126 7860). Other operators that run two or three larger and less nerve-wracking boats a week during high season between the mainland and Ko Mak include **Ko Mak Express** (departs Laem Ngop's Naval Monument pier; 1hr 30min; B400; ⓣ039 59726) and **Ko Kud Seatrans** (departs Laem Ngop's Harbour Pier; 1hr 30min; B400; ⓣ081 444 9259).

Between November and May there's usually a daily Bang Bao boat (ⓣ087 054 4300) **from Ko Chang** (about 2hr 15min; B300) to Ko Mak, via **Ko Whai** (1hr 15; B200), or you can make use of Thai Fun snorkelling boat, described on p.494. For travel to or from **Ko Kood**, Nov–May only, there's the daily Siriwhite Speedboat (30min; B250; ⓣ086 126 7860); the daily speedboat service to Ko Kood's Ao Phrao (1hr; B350; ⓣ081 377 4074); and the 2–3 weekly Ko Kud Seatrans (1hr; B250; ⓣ081 444 9259).

Ao Kao

Ko Mak's longest and nicest beach is **AO KAO** on the southwest coast, a pretty arc of sand that's overhung with lots of stooping palm trees and backed in places by mangroves. The beach is divided towards its southern end by a low rocky outcrop that's straddled by *Ao Kao Resort*, with *Sunset Resort* occupying the southern headland beyond, while the long western beach is shared by half a dozen other sets of bungalows. All the bungalows have **restaurants**: *Monkey Shock* restaurant at *Monkey Island* does very good seafood; *TK Hut* does thrice-weekly seafood barbecues; the small beachfront restaurant between *TK* and *Holiday Beach* is famous across the island for its great *som tam*; and *Ao Kao Resort* serves fresh coffees and cappuccinos.

Accommodation

Ao Kao Resort ⓣ039 501001, ⓦwww.kohmak.com. This long-running and efficient if impersonal outfit drops down to the prettiest part of the beach and has a big range of accommodation including simple rattan huts with private bathrooms, and various large, comfortable en-suite timber and concrete bungalows, some with air-con and many with direct sea views. There's Internet access and kayaks, motorbikes and bicycles for rent. Open all year. Fan ❷–❹, air-con ❼

Baan Koh Mak ⓣ089 895 7592, ⓦwww.baan-koh-mak.com. The most bohemian accommodation on the island, with eighteen contemporary beach-chic-style bungalows, featuring rainbow-striped patio doors, comfortable beds, hammocks on the verandas and a good restaurant. It also does kayak rental and boat trips. Open all year; there's a surcharge over Christmas and New Year. Fan ❺, air-con ❻

Holiday Beach Resort ⓣ02 319 6714, ⓦwww.kohmakholiday.com. Located in a very peaceful spot at the far western end of the beach and the end of the road, within swimming distance of good reefs and on a stretch of quality sand. The fifteen fan-cooled en-suite bungalows are set round a grassy shorefront garden and nearly all enjoy unimpeded sea views. Price depends on the size, with the larger ones well designed to catch island breezes via narrow, screened windows on three sides. Internet access. ❹, VIP ❺

Island Hut ⓣ087 139 5537. Friendly, family-run little place with just a dozen en-suite rough-hewn timber huts with stripey doors, fans and their own deckchairs; they're thoughtfully designed and nearly all sit right on the narrow but pretty shore. ❷

Monkey Island ⓣ081 447 8448, ⓦwww.monkeyislandkohmak.com. There's a distinct whiff of the Bangkok sophisticate here, with club sounds played in the bar-restaurant and bachelor-chic decor in the bungalows – purple sheets on every bed, and huge glass windows and leather-style couches for the top end, air-con "Gorilla" huts. The cheapest "Baboon" huts share bathrooms, and the mid-range "Chimpanzee" huts have fans and huge private bathrooms, but rooms in all categories are very spacious. Shared bathroom ❷, fan and bathroom ❺, air-con ❼

Sunset Bungalows ⓣ081 875 4517, ⓔsunsetbungalow@yahoo.com. Built on a rocky point fifteen minutes' walk south along the track from *Ao Kao*, this is a laid-back if quite isolated place with some of the cheapest huts on the island. They range from pretty basic with fans, mosquito nets and shared bathrooms, to en-suite timber versions with thick mattresses. You'll need to walk to *Ao Kao* for the beach, but swimming is OK here and there's a pleasant deck extending out over the water. Sometimes stays open in low season, though the restaurant closes. ❶–❷

TK Hut ⓣ086 111 4378, ⓦwww.tk-hut.com. German-run place offering good standard, well-priced wood, stone and concrete bungalows set around a neat garden of casuarinas and little hedges. Rooms in all categories are en suite and have fans, with price depending on size and newness. Also has a good seafront bar and restaurant, Internet access, plus kayak and motorbike rental. ❸–❺

Ao Suan Yai

Long, curvy **Ao Suan Yai** is not as pretty a beach as Ao Kao, but the sand is fine enough and the outlook is beautiful, with Ko Chang's hilly profile filling the horizon and Ko Kham and other islets in between. The main **accommodation** option here is *Koh Mak Resort* (ⓣ039 501013, ⓦwww.kohmakresort.com; fan ❺, air-con ❼–❽), a big resort-style outfit with a good choice of large fan and air-con bungalows in all categories, most of them very well spaced around the shorefront garden and within view of the sea. It has lots of facilities, including an attractive bar-restaurant set on a waterfront deck, Internet access, currency exchange and Visa card cash advance, postal services, a taxi service, motorbike and kayak rental, and diving and windsurfing. Its *Cabana* restaurant does especially good *tom yam kung*.

Set high above *Cococape Resort* at the southern end of **Ao Suan Yai**, *Koh Mak Villa* (ⓣ084 659 7437, ⓦwww.kohmakvilla.com; ❼) enjoys outrageously glorious views over Ao Suan Yai and the islands from its hilltop position. It comprises just two very tasteful villas incorporating three fan and air-con rooms apiece, with the two-floored air-con suites bagging the premium views from their enormous glass windows. The villas are about ten minutes' walk uphill from the often non-existent beach at *Cococape,* or 20 minutes away from the better sands at either *Koh Mak Resort*, or *Holiday Beach* and the western end of Ao Kao.

Ko Kham

The miniature, private island of **KO KHAM** (measuring just 300m by 200m) lies almost within swimming distance of Ko Mak's Ao Suan Yai, and has room for just twenty simple bamboo bungalows and a restaurant at *Ko Kham Resort* (ⓣ081 303 1229, ⓦwww.kochanghotelsvr.com/kohkhamresort/hotelsthailand.htm; ❻–❼). The bungalows are set around the nicely tended garden and on the beach itself, and all have garden bathrooms and fans; the more expensive ones have two storeys. There's little to do here except swim, snorkel, sunbathe and enjoy the peace. From November through May a daily **boat** sails from Laem Ngop's Naval Monument pier (see p.490) to Ko Kham at 3pm (3hr; B250); the return boat leaves Ko Kham at around 8am daily. Or you can get a taxi-boat across from Ao Suan Yai on Ko Mak.

Ko Kood

The second-largest island in the archipelago after Ko Chang (and the fourth largest in Thailand), forested **KO KOOD** (also spelt Ko Kut and Ko Kud; ⓦwww.kokood.com) is still a wild and largely uncommercialized island. Though it's known for its sparkling white sand and exceptionally clear turquoise water, particularly along the west coast, Ko Kood is as much a nature-lover's destination as a beach-bum's. Swathes of its shoreline are fringed by grass and mangrove rather than broad sandy beaches and those parts of the island not still covered in virgin tropical rainforest are filled with palm groves and rubber plantations. Though the island is 25km long and 12km wide, it supports barely more than 20 kilometres of concrete road, with many areas penetrated only by the odd sandy track and, in places, by navigable canals, if at all. The highest point on the island, at just 315 metres, is Khao Phaenthi, towards the southeast. All of which makes Ko Kood a surprisingly pleasant place to explore on foot (or kayak), especially as the cool season brings refreshing breezes most days. The interior is also graced with several waterfalls, the most famous of which is Nam Tok Khlong Chao, inland from Ao Khlong Chao and the focus of day-trips from Ko Chang and Ko Mak.

Most of the 1500 islanders make their living from fishing and growing coconut palms and rubber trees. Many have Khmer blood in them as the island population mushroomed at the turn of the twentieth century when Thais and Cambodians resident in nearby Cambodian territory fled French control. The main settlements are **Ban Khlong Hin Dam**, just inland from the main Hin Dam pier and the attractive west-coast beach at **Ao Taphao**; **Ban Khlong Mat**, a very well protected natural harbour-inlet few kilometres further north up the coast; the stilted fishing village of **Ban Ao Salat** across on the north-east coast and the large fishing community of **Ban Ao Yai**, protected by a

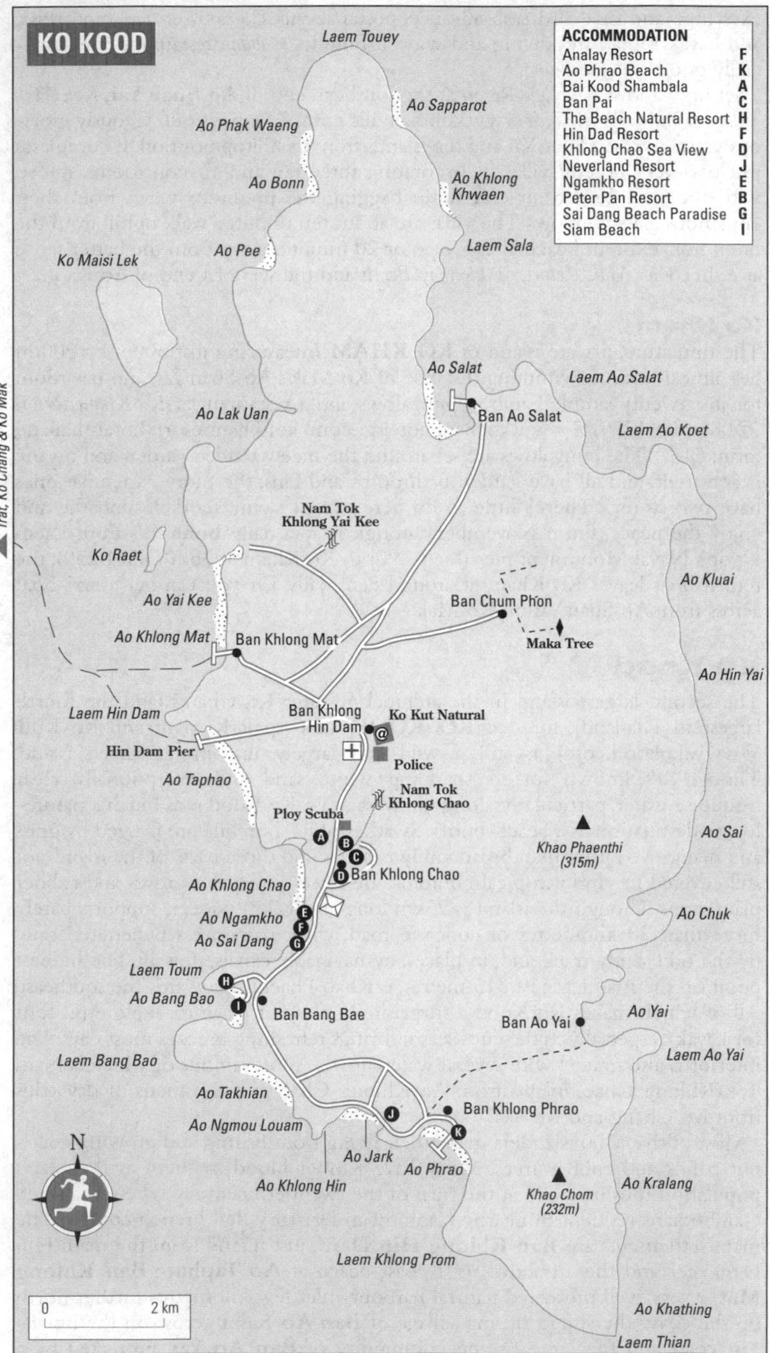

KO KOOD
ACCOMMODATION
Analay Resort F
Ao Phrao Beach K
Bai Kood Shambala A
Ban Pai C
The Beach Natural Resort H
Hin Dad Resort F
Khlong Chao Sea View D
Neverland Resort J
Ngamkho Resort E
Peter Pan Resort B
Sai Dang Beach Paradise G
Siam Beach I
Laem Touey
Ao Sapparot
Ao Phak Waeng
Ao Bonn
Ao Khlong Khwaen
Ao Pee
Laem Sala
Ko Maisi Lek
Ao Salat
Laem Ao Salat
Ban Ao Salat
Ao Lak Uan
Laem Ao Koet
Nam Tok Khlong Yai Kee
Ko Raet
Ao Kluai
Ao Yai Kee
Ban Chum Phon
Ao Khlong Mat
Ban Khlong Mat
Maka Tree
Ao Hin Yai
Laem Hin Dam
Ban Khlong Hin Dam
Ko Kut Natural
Hin Dam Pier
Police
Ao Taphao
Nam Tok Khlong Chao
Ploy Scuba
Ao Sai
Khao Phaenthi (315m)
Ban Khlong Chao
Ao Khlong Chao
Ao Ngamkho
Ao Chuk
Ao Sai Dang
Laem Toum
Ao Bang Bao
Ban Bang Bae
Ao Yai
Ban Ao Yai
Laem Ao Yai
Laem Bang Bao
Ao Takhian
Ban Khlong Phrao
Ao Ngmou Louam
Ao Jark
Ao Phrao
Ao Khlong Hin
Ao Kralang
Khao Chom (232m)
Laem Khlong Prom
Ao Khathing
Laem Thian
0
2 km
N

safe natural harbour on the southeast coast. On the southwest coast, the main beaches of **Ao Khlong Chao**, **Ao Bang Bao** and **Ao Phrao** also have small villages.

Because of its lack of development, and roads, Ko Kood has to date been the almost exclusive province of package-tourists booked in groups of at least ten, speeded on to the island by their resort boats, and kept busy with waterfall outings and snorkelling trips. Things are changing now, however, and the island is beginning to welcome independent travellers with new scheduled boat services from the mainland, as well as from Ko Chang and Ko Mak (and even plans for a possible run to Ban Hat Lek, on the Cambodian border, from Ban Ao Salat on the northeast coast), and the emergence of several small, cheap guest houses. The island is still very much a one-season destination, however, as nearly all the boat services only operate from November through May and much of the accommodation is closed outside that period.

Island practicalities

In all but the worst weather, there's a year-round **slow-boat service** from Ban Dan Kao, 6km northeast of central Trat (see p.488), to Ko Kood's Hin Dam pier, currently departing Trat every Tues, Wed, Fri and Sat at 10am and returning from Ko Kood every Tues, Thurs, Fri and Sun at 10am (4hr; B220; ⓣ089 511 3021). From November through May, **Siriwhite speedboat** (ⓣ086 126 7860) runs a daily service from Laem Sok, about 30km south of Trat (see p.488), to Ko Kood's Ban Khlong Mat (1hr 10min; B500), via Ko Mak (30 mins from Ko Kood; B250). Other operators running services to Ko Kood include **Ko Kud Seatrans** (departs Laem Ngop's Harbour Pier three times a week from Nov–May; 1hr 30min; B400; ⓣ081 444 9259), via Ko Mak (30min from Ko Kood; B250); and the **Ao Phrao speedboat** service between Ko Chang and Ko Kood's Ao Phrao (1hr 50min; B900; ⓣ086 133 0402), via Ko Whai (1hr 30min from Ko Kood; B600) Ko Mak (1hr; 350) and Ko Kood's Khlong Chao (20mins; B200). Arrival points vary according to weather conditions, but scheduled boats are always met by resort staff and share-taxis.

Getting around the island is mainly a question of walking or renting your own transport, though you should be able to charter a songthaew for the day for around B1000. You can rent **kayaks** on almost every beach, on Khlong Chao, and through Ko Kut Natural in Ban Khlong Hin Dam, who also have **mountain bikes** and motorbikes (see below). Several other places also rent **motorbikes** (B400/day), but be warned that the west-coast road is very narrow, concrete in parts, dirt and stone in others. Exploring the island **on foot** is both feasible and fun: south of Ao Khlong Chao there are no major hills and much of the route is shady. From Ao Khlong Chao to Ao Bang Bao takes about forty minutes; from Ao Bang Bao to Ao Jark is about an hour's walk, then another twenty minutes to Ao Phrao.

There's no bank on Ko Kood, and though you may be able to **change money** at the biggest resorts, it's best to bring cash with you. There's a **postal agent** behind *S Beach Resort*, beside the road at Ao Ngamkho. The **police** are in Ban Khlong Hin Dam (ⓣ039 521745), as is the **hospital** (ⓣ039 521852). One of the best sources of **information** about the island is Ko Kut Natural, opposite the hospital in Ban Khlong Hin Dam (Mon–Fri 5–9pm; Sat & Sun 9am–9pm; ⓣ089 594 4017 or ⓣ086 149 6028; ⓦwww.kokutnatural.com), which is staffed by the local English teacher and computer expert. It produces a good free **map** of the island (especially useful as road signs are sporadic) and rents imported **sea kayaks** (B600/day), **mountain bikes** (B300/2 days) and **motorbikes** (B300/day). You can access the **Internet** at Ko Kut Natural and on Ao Khlong Chao (see opposite). There is some **malaria** on Ko Kood so be especially assiduous with repellent and nets if you are not taking prophylactics.

The two **dive operators** on Ko Kood are based at Ao Khlong Chao: Ploy Scuba Diving (ⓣ081 983 2010, ⓦwww.ployscuba.com) is next to *Bai Kood Shambala*, and Paradise Divers is at *Khlong Chao Resort*, beside the khlong on the road to the falls (ⓣ087 144 5945). Two dives average B2500, with accompanying snorkellers paying B900. You might want to request a trip to somewhere other than Ko Rang (see p.494), which is always packed with dive boats from Ko Chang and Ko Mak. Openwater courses cost B11,500: Ploy does PADI courses and Paradise does CMAS courses.

Ao Khlong Chao

About five kilometres south of the main Hin Dam pier, **Ao Khlong Chao** (pronounced "Jao") is a fun place to stay because as well as a small sandy beach (no great beauty but a perfectly pleasant "village" beach, currently still without sunloungers or other commercial intrusions), you've got the pretty two-kilometre-long mangrove-lined Khlong Chao that runs down from the famous Khlong Chao Falls. Close by the road-bridge that spans the khlong, no more than 300m from the palm-fringed beach, is a cluster of little guest houses, some of them built partially on stilts over the river, which offer the cheapest accommodation on the island, as well as a number of package-tour resorts, complete with intrusive, late-night karaoke restaurants which unfortunately mar the atmosphere considerably at weekends.

Nam Tok Khlong Chao

The three-tiered **Nam Tok Khlong Chao** is a pretty if not exceptional waterfall, that tumbles down into a large, refreshing pool that's perfect for a dip. The falls are best visited in the morning as during the afternoons, especially on weekends, the constant arrival of groups in longtails and kayaks means you'll not find a spare slab of rock to sit on. It takes around twenty minutes to kayak upriver from the Khlong Chao bridge to the jetty near the falls, followed by a ten-minute walk – though you can also walk the whole thing in half an hour, or even take a car or motorbike to within 500m: just follow the signs from the bridge over the khlong in Khlong Chao. The track continues beyond the falls through unadulterated jungle for another few kilometres before terminating at a rubber plantation, making for a pleasant and very quiet four-hour walk there and back, though watch out for snakes, especially cobras.

Practicalities

Of the several cheap **guest houses** (only minimal English is spoken at all of them), *Ban Pai* (ⓣ089 931 5683; ❷) is the nicest of those on the khlong. It has just eight rooms, a couple of them en suite and all with fans, giving on to a huge deck seating area built right over the khlong, and the owner serves good food, especially fresh fish dishes. The drawback here is the noisy caterwauling at weekends from the karaoke resorts across and upstream. Away from the khlong – and the karaoke noise – friendly *Khlong Chao Sea View* (ⓣ087 908 3593; ❷) is set in a garden beside the road 200m beyond the bridge, from where you can indeed see the sea, 200m away, through the thinly planted palm grove. Its half-dozen bamboo bungalows each have a bathroom and a little veranda and there's good food here too, especially the Penang curries; the owners have a tiny store selling fruit, veg and whisky, which means that locals often congregate here for a drink or six. The most upmarket place to stay in Khlong Chao is *Bai Kood Shambala* (ⓣ087 147 7055, ⓦwww.kohkood.com; fan ❻, air-con ❽), whose gardens drop down to a rocky chunk of the shore; though there's no beach here you can swim off the jetty, laze in the garden, or take a free kayak across to Ao Khlong Chao beach proper, just a couple of minutes' paddle away. The split-bamboo fan bungalows here are way overpriced, though the air-con versions are quite appealing, if still pricey. There's Internet acess here too (B50/30min minimum) and the restaurant serves fresh coffee. Most of the other places to stay in Khlong Chao deal only in pre-booked **package tour deals**. *Peter Pan Resort* (ⓣ02 966 1800, ⓦwww.captainhookresort.com), accross the khlong from *Ban Pai*, is typical and charges B4000 for three days and two nights full-board, including boat transfers, trips to reefs and waterfalls, and use of kayaks and bicycles; accommodation is in fairly simple wooden chalets.

Every guest house lends or rents **kayaks**, and you can rent **motorbikes** (B400/day) at *Doy's Guest House,* beside the bridge, on the north side. Even without transport, it's quite easy to **walk** from Ao Khlong Chao to any of the beaches further south: it's forty minutes on foot to Ao Bang Bao or around two hours to Ao Phrao, with no real hills, barely any traffic and plenty of shade along the way.

There are two dive shops at Khlong Chao (see opposite). *Mark House*, near *Sea View* on the south side of the bridge, sells ice creams and a few other general supplies, gives info about boat times, and has **Internet** access.

Ao Ngamkho and Ao Sai Dang

South of Ao Khlong Chao the coastline offers up a handful of mostly tiny bays in between rocky points, accessed via the west-coast road and tracks that meander off it. Having climbed over the point at the south end of Ao Khlong Chao, the road dips down again to the beach at **Ao Ngamkho**. The nicest places to stay here are in two miniature bays between rocky points – with quite rewarding snorkelling and plenty of fish – at its southern end. Traveller-friendly *Ngamkho Resort* (ⓣ081 825 7076, ⓔngamkho@yahoo.com; ❹) has small but decent en-suite bamboo bungalows, with decks and hammocks, plus a restaurant in the secluded little shorefront garden; it's open year round. The point itself is shared by the sturdy fan and air-con chalets of *Hin Dad Resort* (ⓣ081 863 8776; ❻–❼) and by *Analay Resort* (ⓣ081 403 6174; fan ❻, air-con ❼), whose quaint Hansel-and-Gretel-style posh timber chalets (fan or air-con) are painted in pastel colours and nearly all enjoy panoramic sea views.

The next-door bay is **Ao Sai Dang**, named for its reddish sand and so secluded down a 400-metre-long track that it feels like a little private garden. Grassy and liberally planted with coconut palms, it's dotted with the half-dozen very basic en-suite bamboo huts and five-bed house of *Sai Dang Beach Paradise* (ⓣ086 329 2580; bungalows ❸, house ❾).

Ao Bang Bao

From Ao Sai Dang, follow signs for *The Beach* to reach **Ao Bang Bao**, about twenty minutes' walk further south (fifteen minutes west off the main road). This is one of Ko Kood's prettiest beaches, fronted by a longish sweep of bleach-white sand and deliciously clear turquoise water, plus the inevitable fringe of coconut palms. Though *The Beach Natural Resort* (ⓣ02 214 2149, ⓦwww.thebeachkohkood.com; fan and sea view ❺, air-con ❻) doesn't actually sit on the nicest part of the beach, but behind a rocky area at the northern end, its upmarket thatched bamboo bungalows are among the most tasteful on the island, built with a Balinese accent and featuring elegant furnishings, garden bathrooms and a lovely tropical flower garden. There's massage, kayaks, karaoke and a restaurant here and though it's package oriented it's happy to accept independent travellers. *Siam Beach* (☎081 829 7751; fan ❷–❸, air-con ❻; closed low season) occupies almost all of the best part of the beach and is the place to aim for if you're after a low-budget beach-centred stay on Ko Kood. Run by the people behind the various sets of *Siam* bungalows on Ko Chang's Lonely Beach and Hat Kai Bae, it offers huge, rustic, no-frills timber huts on the seafront with either fan or air-con, and slightly smaller cheaper ones further back. The restaurant cooks up regular seafood barbecues and serves travellers' food.

South to Ao Phrao and Ao Yai

Back on the main southbound road at the Ao Bang Bao turnoff, a 35-minute walk through coconut and rubber plantations brings you to **Ao Khlong Hin**, a wild little bay that's dominated mainly by a small coconut-processing centre and is not really great for swimming. Ten minutes further along the road, which hugs the coast so close here it gets washed by the waves at high tide, **Ao Jark**, sited at the mouth of a khlong, is another remote and pretty little bay, location of the package-oriented *Neverland Resort* and a good focus for a walk if nothing else (bring your own food and water as there's none here).

Continue twenty minutes further along the pretty coastal road to its current terminus and you reach the most southerly bay **Ao Phrao** (about 3km from Ao Khlong Hin), a long, stunning beach of white sand backed by densely planted palms and the slopes of Khao Chom. You can stay here at *Ao Phrao Beach* (☎039 525211, Ⓦwww.kokut.com; fan ❹, air-con ❻; 2-day 1-night packages from B2500–3300), a mainly but not exclusively package-oriented cluster of thatched fan and air-con bungalows. Behind Ao Phrao, the tiny fishing village of **Ban Khlong Phrao** occupies the mangrove-lined banks of Khlong Phrao (which extends another kilometre inland). You can get simple hot dishes in the village here and signs are that you may soon be able to spend the night as well, as fishing families are starting to sell their homes. A five-kilometre track that's very steep and rough in places connects Ban Khlong Phrao with **Ao Yai**, the southeast coast's main fishing village, full of traditional wooden houses and encased safely within a natural harbour.

Inland and the east coast

The administrative centre of the island is **Ban Khlong Hin Dam**, site of a few homes, the hospital, police station, school and main island temple but little else, other than the information centre and rental outlet at Ko Kut Natural (see p.511). It's about 2km east of the main pier at Laem Hin Dam, 3.5km north of Ao Khlong Chao, 9km north of Ao Khlong Hin and 9km south of Ban Ao Salat.

About five kilometres northwest of Ban Khlong Hin Dam, the small but appealing three-tiered waterfall **Nam Tok Khlong Yai Kee** is basically a smaller version of the famous Nam Tok Khlong Chao and rushes down into a good-sized pool that's ideal for swimming. It's accessible via a five-minute path that's very steep in places but there are ropes at the crucial points.

East off the road to the north coast, in the mature rainforest near Ban Chum Phon, is a locally famous **five-hundred-year old maka tree** (*Bridelia insulana*), known to islanders as the *dtohn maai yai*, that's an impressive 35 metres or more in height and drips with lianas and epiphytes. A one-kilometre path that runs though rubber trees and rainforest will get you there but you'll need to go with a local to stay on the right track. If nothing else it's a good excuse to go further into Ko Kood's extensive forest cover.

The road currently serves just one spot on the west coast and that's the tiny stilt-village and fishing community of **Ban Ao Salat**, 9km northeast of Ban Khlong Hin Dam. Several of the wooden stilt houses strung out along the jetty-promenade serve food so this is a great place for a fresh-seafood lunch, especially crab.

Travel details

Trains

Aranyaprathet to: Bangkok (2 daily; 5hr 15min–5hr 30min).
Pattaya to: Bangkok (1 daily; 3hr 20min); Si Racha (1 daily; 25min).
Si Racha to: Bangkok (1 daily; 3hr); Pattaya (1 daily; 25min).

Buses

Aranyaprathet to: Bangkok (10 daily; 4hr 30min).
Ban Phe to: Bangkok (12 daily; 3hr); Chanthaburi (6 daily; 1hr 30min); Rayong (every 30min; 30min); Trat (6 daily; 3hr).
Chanthaburi to: Bangkok (Eastern Bus Terminal; 18 daily; 4–5hr); Bangkok (Northern Bus Terminal; 5 daily; 3–4hr); Khorat (8 daily; 6hr); Rayong (8 daily; 2hr); Sa Kaew (for Aranyaprathet; 8 daily; 3hr); Trat (every 1hr 30min; 1hr 30min).
Pattaya to: Bangkok (Eastern Bus Terminal; every 30min; 2hr 30–3hr 30min); Bangkok (Northern Bus Terminal; every 30min; 2–3hr); Chanthaburi (6 daily; 3hr); Chiang Mai (6 daily; 14hr); Chiang Rai (4 daily; 15–17hr); Khorat (4 daily; 5–6hr); Nong Khai (7 daily; 12hr); Rayong (every 30min; 1hr 30min); Trat (6 daily; 4hr 30min); Ubon Ratchathani (7 daily; 12hr).
Rayong to: Bangkok (Eastern Bus Terminal; every 40min; 2hr 30min–3hr); Bangkok (Northern Bus Terminal; 5 daily; 3hr); Ban Phe (for Ko Samet; every 30min; 30 min); Chanthaburi (every 30min; 2hr); Chiang Mai (8 daily; 15–18hr); Khorat (18 daily; 4hr); Mae Sai (4 daily; 17–20hr); Ubon Ratchathani (10 daily; 11–14hr).
Si Racha to: Bangkok (Eastern Bus Terminal; every 30min; 2hr); Bangkok (Northern Bus Terminal; every 30min; 2hr); Chanthaburi (6 daily; 3hr 30min); Pattaya (every 20min; 30min); Rayong (for Ban Phe and Ko Samet; every 30min; 2hr); Trat (6 daily; 5hr).
Trat to: Bangkok (Eastern Bus Terminal; at least hourly; 5–6hr); Bangkok (Northern Bus Terminal; 5 daily; 4–5hr); Chanthaburi (hourly; 1hr 30min); Hat Lek (for the Cambodian border; every 45min; 1hr–1hr 30min); Pattaya (6 daily; 4hr 30min); Rayong (for Ko Samet; 6 daily; 3hr 30min); Si Racha (6 daily; 5hr).

Boats

Ban Phe to: Ko Samet (4–18 daily; 30min).
Ko Chang to: Ko Kood (Nov–May daily; 1hr 50min); Ko Mak (Nov–May 2 daily; 45min–2hr 15min); Ko Whai (Nov–May 2 daily; 15min–1hr 15min); Trat province (hourly; 25min–1hr).
Ko Kood to: Ko Chang (Nov–May daily; 1hr 50min); Ko Mak (Nov–May 2–3 daily; 30min–1hr); Trat province (4 weekly–3daily; 1hr 10min–4hr).
Ko Mak to: Ko Chang (Nov–May 2 daily; 45min–2hr 15min); Ko Kood (Nov–May 2–3 daily; 30min–1hr); Trat province (1–5 daily; 40min–3hr 30min).
Si Racha to: Ko Si Chang (hourly; 40min).
Trat province to: Ko Chang (hourly; 25min–1hr); Ko Kham (Nov–May 1 daily; 3hr); Ko Kood (4 weekly–3 daily; 1hr 10min–4hr); Ko Mak (1–5 daily; 40min–3hr 30min); Ko Whai (Nov–April 1 daily; 2hr 30min).

Flights

Pattaya (U-Tapao) to: Ko Samui (2 daily; 1hr); Phuket (1 daily; 1hr 40min).
Trat to: Bangkok (3 daily; 50min); Ko Samui (1 daily; 1hr).

5

The northeast: Isaan

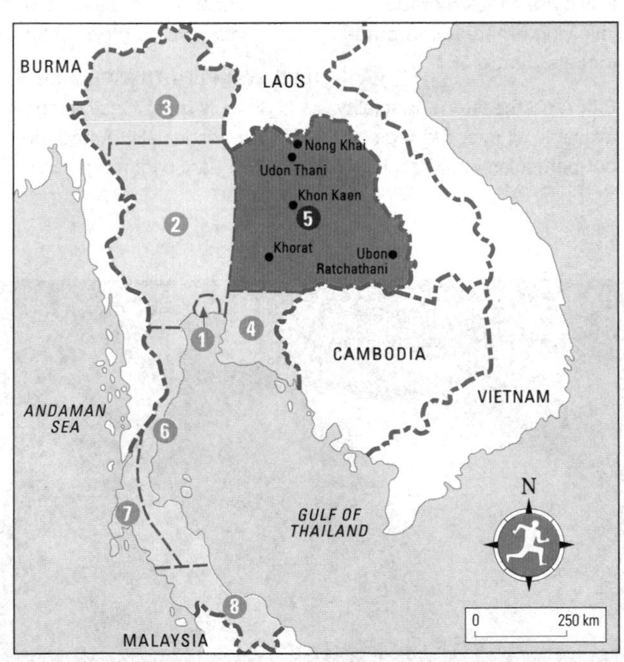

CHAPTER 5

Highlights

* **Khao Yai National Park** Fifteen trails, lots of birds, several waterfalls and night safaris. See p.522
* **Khmer ruins** Exquisite Angkor Wat-style temples at Phimai, Phanom Rung and Khao Phra Viharn. See p.537, p.540 & p.551
* **Yasothon Rocket Festival** Bawdy rain making ritual involving ornate home-made rockets. See p.564
* **Silk** A northeastern speciality, available all over the region but particularly in Khon Kaen. See p.570
* **Phu Kradung** Teeming table mountain, the most dramatic of the region's national parks. See p.579
* **The Mekong** The best stretch in Thailand for gentle exploration of the mighty riverscape is between Chiang Khan and Nong Khai. See p.582
* **Wat Phu Tok** Extraordinary meditation temple on a steep sandstone outcrop. See p.595
* **Wat Phra That Phanom** Isaan's most fascinating holy site, especially during the February pilgrimage. See p.597

△ Khao Yai National Park

5

The northeast: Isaan

Bordered by Laos and Cambodia on three sides, the tableland of **northeast Thailand** – known as **Isaan**, after the Hindu god of death and the northeast – comprises a third of the country's land area and is home to nearly a third of its population. This is the least-visited region of the kingdom, and the poorest: some seventy percent of Isaan villagers earn less than the regional minimum wage of B141 a day. Farming is the traditional livelihood here, despite appallingly infertile soil (the friable sandstone contains few nutrients and retains little water) and long periods of drought punctuated by downpours and intermittent bouts of flooding. In the 1960s, government schemes to introduce hardier crops set in motion a debt cycle that has forced farmers into monocultural cash-cropping to repay their loans for fertilizers, seeds and machinery. For many families, there's only one way off the treadmill: of the twenty million who live in Isaan, an average of two million economic refugees leave the area every year, most of them heading for Bangkok where northeasterners now make up the majority of the capital's lowest-paid workforce. Children and elderly parents remain in the villages, increasingly dependent on the money sent back every month from the metropolis and awaiting the annual visit in May when migrant family members often return for a couple of months to help with the rice planting.

Most northeasterners speak a dialect that's more comprehensible to residents of Vientiane than Bangkok, and Isaan's historic allegiances have tied it more closely to Laos and Cambodia than to Thailand. Between the eleventh and thirteenth centuries, the all-powerful **Khmers** covered the northeast in magnificent stone temple complexes, the remains of which constitute the region's most satisfying tourist attractions. During subsequent centuries the territories along the Mekong River changed hands numerous times, until the present border with Laos was set at the end of World War II. In the 1950s and 1960s, **Communist insurgents** played on the northeast's traditional ties with Laos; a movement to align Isaan with the Marxists of Laos gathered some force, and the Communist Party of Thailand, gaining sympathy among poverty-stricken northeastern farmers, established bases in the region. At about the same time, major US air bases for the **Vietnam War** were set up in Khorat, Ubon Ratchathani and Udon Thani, fuelling a sex industry that has plagued the region ever since. When the American military moved out, northeastern women turned to the tourist-orientated Bangkok flesh trade instead, and nowadays the majority of prostitutes in the capital come from Isaan.

Rather than the cities – which are chaotic, exhausting places, with little going for them apart from accommodation and onward transport – Isaan's prime destinations are its **Khmer ruins** and **Khao Yai National Park**. Four huge

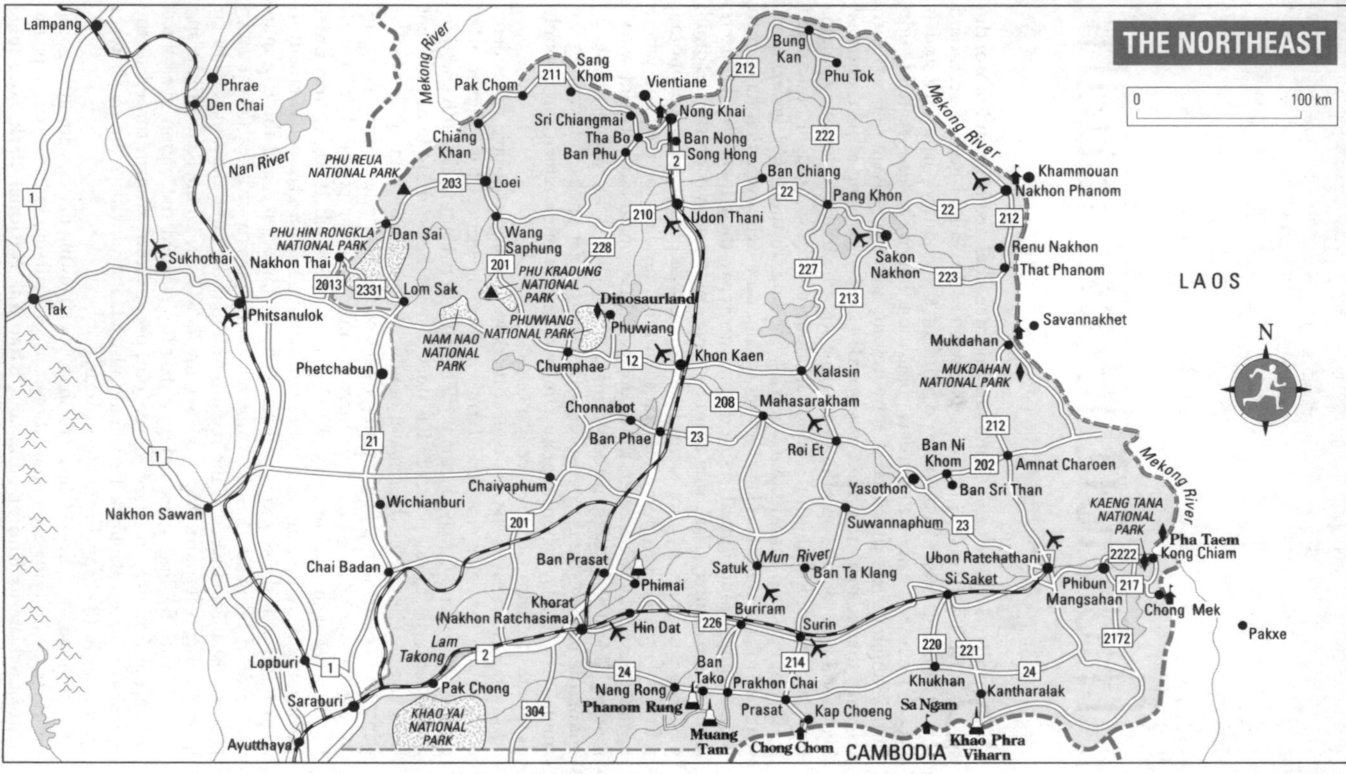
THE NORTHEAST
0 100 km
N
LAOS
CAMBODIA
Mekong River
Nan River
Mun River
Lampang
Phrae
Den Chai
Tak
Sukhothai
Phitsanulok
Nakhon Thai
Phetchabun
Nakhon Sawan
Chai Badan
Lopburi
Saraburi
Ayutthaya
Wichianburi
Chaiyaphum
Pak Chom
Sang Khom
Chiang Khan
Loei
Dan Sai
Lom Sak
Wang Saphung
Sri Chiangmai
Tha Bo
Ban Phu
Vientiane
Nong Khai
Ban Nong Song Hong
Udon Thani
Ban Chiang
Bung Kan
Phu Tok
Pang Khon
Sakon Nakhon
Khammouan
Nakhon Phanom
Renu Nakhon
That Phanom
Savannakhet
Mukdahan
Kalasin
Khon Kaen
Phuwiang
Dinosaurland
Chumphae
Chonnabot
Ban Phae
Mahasarakham
Roi Et
Yasothon
Ban Ni Khom
Ban Sri Than
Amnat Charoen
Suwannaphum
Ban Prasat
Phimai
Khorat (Nakhon Ratchasima)
Hin Dat
Satuk
Ban Ta Klang
Buriram
Surin
Si Saket
Ubon Ratchathani
Phibun Mangsahan
Kong Chiam
Pha Taem
Chong Mek
Pakxe
Lam Takong
Pak Chong
Nang Rong
Phanom Rung
Ban Tako
Muang Tam
Prakhon Chai
Prasat
Kap Choeng
Chong Chom
Khukhan
Sa Ngam
Kantharalak
Khao Phra Viharn
PHU REUA NATIONAL PARK
PHU HIN RONGKLA NATIONAL PARK
PHU KRADUNG NATIONAL PARK
PHUWIANG NATIONAL PARK
NAM NAO NATIONAL PARK
MUKDAHAN NATIONAL PARK
KAENG TANA NATIONAL PARK
KHAO YAI NATIONAL PARK
1
2
12
21
22
23
24
201
202
203
208
210
211
212
213
214
217
220
221
222
223
226
227
228
304
2013
2172
2222
2331

northeastern **festivals** also draw massive crowds: in May, Yasothon is the focus for the bawdy rocket festival; the end of June or beginning of July sees the equally raucous rain making festival of Phi Ta Kon in Dan Sai near Loei; in July, Ubon Ratchathani hosts the extravagant candle festival; while the flamboyant, though inevitably touristy, "elephant round-up" is staged in Surin in November.

Isaan's only mountain range of any significance divides the uninspiring town of **Loei** from the central plains and offers some stiff walking, awesome scenery and the possibility of spotting unusual birds and flowers in the **national parks** that spread across its heights. Due north of Loei at Chiang Khan, the **Mekong River** begins its leisurely course around Isaan with a lush stretch where a sprinkling of guest houses has opened up the river countryside to travellers. Marking the eastern end of this upper stretch, the border town of **Nong Khai** is surrounded by possibly the most outlandish temples in Thailand. The grandest and most important religious site in the northeast, however, is **Wat Phra That Phanom**, way downstream beyond **Nakhon Phanom**, a town which affords some of the finest Isaan vistas.

The other big draw for travellers are Isaan's four **border crossings into Laos**, at each of which you can now get a Lao visa on arrival. The most popular of these is at Nong Khai, a route that provides easy road access to the Lao capital, Vientiane; the others are Nakhon Phanom, Mukdahan and Chong Mek (see p.33 for a full run down on overland travel into Laos). You can get a Lao visa in advance from the consulate in the central Isaan town of Khon Kaen, where there's also a Vietnamese consulate issuing visas for Vietnam. It's now also possible to travel **overland between Isaan and Cambodia** through two different border crossings: via the Thai town of Kap Choeng, in Surin province, to O'Smach, which has transport to Anlong Veng and then on to Siem Reap (see p.544 for details); and via Sa Ngam in the Phusing district of Si Saket province to Choam in Anlong Veng. See p.32 for a roundup of overland crossings on the Thai-Cambodia border.

Many travellers approach Isaan from the north, either travelling directly from Chiang Mai to Loei, or going via Phitsanulok, in the northern reaches of the central plains, to Khon Kaen, but you can also take direct **buses** to Khorat from the east-coast towns of Pattaya, Rayong and Chanthaburi. All major northeastern centres have direct bus services from Bangkok. Two **rail** lines cut through Isaan, providing useful connections with Bangkok and Ayutthaya and there are also **flights** between Bangkok and several major northeastern cities. All major towns and cities in Isaan are connected by public transport, as are many of the larger villages, but compared to many other regions of the country, northeastern roads are fairly traffic-free, so renting your own vehicle is also a good option.

Southern Isaan

Southern Isaan more or less follows one of two branches of the northeastern rail line as it makes a beeline towards the eastern border, skirting the edge of **Khao Yai National Park** before entering Isaan proper to link the major provincial capitals of **Khorat**, **Surin** and **Ubon Ratchathani**. The rail line is handy enough for entering the region, but once here it's as well to follow a route that takes in smaller towns and villages wherever possible, which means switching to buses and songthaews. It is in these smaller places that you'll learn most about Isaan life, particularly if you head for the exceptionally welcoming **guest houses** in Surin, Nang Rong, Phimai and Kong Chiam. For even more of an immersion into a rural community, consider booking yourself onto the **home-stay** programme in the village of **Ban Prasat**.

Even if your time is limited, you shouldn't leave this part of Isaan without visiting at least one set of Khmer ruins: those at **Phimai** are the most accessible of the region's top three sites, but it's well worth making the effort to visit either **Phanom Rung** or **Khao Phra Viharn** as well, both of which occupy spectacular hilltop locations. Relics of an even earlier age, prehistoric cliff paintings also draw a few tourists eastwards to the town of **Kong Chiam**, which is prettily set between the Mekong and Mun rivers and is well worth a visit in its own right. Nearby **Chong Mek** is best known as a legal entry point into Laos, but is also the site of an enjoyable Thai–Lao border market.

Khao Yai National Park

About 120km northeast of Bangkok, the cultivated lushness of the central plains gives way to the thickly forested Phanom Dangkrek mountains. A 2168-square-kilometre chunk of this sculpted limestone range has been conserved as **KHAO YAI NATIONAL PARK**, one of Thailand's most popular. Spanning five distinct forest types and rising to a height of 1341m, the park sustains over three hundred bird and twenty large land-mammal species – hence its UNESCO accreditation in 2005 as a World Heritage Site – and offers a plethora of waterfalls and several undemanding walking trails.

For many Thais, especially Bangkokians, Khao Yai is not so much a place for wildlife spotting as an easily reachable weekend escape from the fumes. Many well-off city people have second homes in the Khao Yai area, while others come for the soft-adventure activities, especially horse-riding and off-road driving in ATVs, offered by the increasingly popular dude-ranch resorts. The cooler climate here has also made Khao Yai one of Thailand's most productive areas for viticulture and for dairy farming.

With your own transport, Khao Yai could just about be done as a long day-trip from Bangkok or Ayutthaya, but there's camping and basic accommodation in the park itself, and plenty of more comfortable options just beyond the perimeter and in the nearby town of **Pak Chong**. It's quite easy to trek around the park by yourself, as long as you stick to the official trails, but as some of Khao Yai's best features – its waterfalls, caves and viewpoints – are as much as 20km apart, you might get more satisfaction from joining a tour. Try to avoid visiting at weekends and holidays, when the trails and waterfalls get ridiculously crowded and the animals make themselves scarce. Even at quiet times, don't expect it to be like a safari park – patience, a soft tread and a keen-eyed guide are generally needed, and it's well worth bringing your own binoculars if you have them. Be prepared for patches of fairly rough terrain, and pack some warm clothes, as the air can get quite cool at the higher altitudes in the park, especially at night.

Should you tire of wildlife-spotting, there are a number of popular **golf courses** within easy reach of the park, including Mission Hills (Ⓣ044

426099, Ⓦwww.golfmissionhills.com), which is signed off the park road at kilometre-stone 20, and Kirimaya (Ⓣ044 249025, Ⓦwww.kirimaya.com), near kilometre-stone 23; hotels on the park road can arrange transport.

Practicalities

Whether you decide to see Khao Yai on your own or as part of a tour, your first port of call is likely to be the small market town of **PAK CHONG**, 37km north of Khao Yai's visitor centre and major trailheads, and served by trains and buses from lots of major towns. One of the three recommended Khao Yai tour leaders operates from Pak Chong, and there are a couple of places to stay in town too, should you decide to base yourself outside the park. If, on the other hand, you want to head straight up to Khao Yai, you need to get a songthaew from Pak Chong's town centre.

Thanon Tesaban cuts right through the middle of Pak Chong, and small sois shoot off it in parallel lines to the north and south; those to the north are odd-numbered in ascending order from west to east (Soi 13 to Soi 25) while those on the south side of the road have even numbers, from west to east (from Soi 8 to Soi 18). The heart of the town is on the north side, between the train station on Soi 15 and the footbridge a few hundred metres further east at Soi 21, and this is where you'll find the day market. Beyond the footbridge is the **post office**, on the corner of Soi 25, and the CAT international **phone office** on the other side of Thanon Tesaban. There are several **Internet centres** on the stretch of Thanon Tesaban near the train station, along with ATMs; on the south side of the main road you'll find a **currency-exchange** counter (bank hours) between the footbridge and Soi 18, a supermarket about 200m further west, and a **medical centre** between sois 8 and 10.

Getting to and from Khao Yai

Pak Chong **train station** is on Soi 15 (Ⓣ044 311534), one short block north of Thanon Tesaban. The **bus station** is towards the west end of town, one block south off the main road between sois 8 and 10, but some long-distance buses also stop in the town centre, beside the footbridge on the main road; private air-con buses to Bangkok and Khorat leave from an office on Thanon Tesaban just west of Soi 18.

The cheapest way to get **from Pak Chong to Khao Yai** is to take a public **songthaew** from outside the 7-11 shop, 200m west of the footbridge on the north side of the main road near Soi 21 (every 30min 6.30am–5pm, less frequently on Sun; 30min; B20–30). Public songthaews, however, are not allowed to enter the park itself, so you'll be dropped at the park checkpoint, about 14km short of the Khao Yai visitor centre, park headquarters and most popular trailheads. At the checkpoint (where you pay the B200 national-park entrance fee, or B100 for kids), park rangers will flag down passing cars and get them to give you a ride up to the visitor centre; this is common practice here. The whole journey from Pak Chong to Khao Yai visitor centre takes about an hour. Note that if you are not planning to stay the night inside the park but want to make two or more day-trips into the park, you'll have to pay the park entry fee every time you come through the checkpoint.

A less time-consuming but pricier option is to **charter a songthaew** from Pak Chong: chartered songthaews count as private vehicles and are allowed inside the park. They can be chartered from the corner of Soi 19, and cost around B700 for the ride from Pak Chong to Haew Suwat Falls, or about B1500 for a return trip, including several hours in the park.

Khao Yai tours and guides

Tours of Khao Yai are reasonably priced and cater primarily for independent tourists rather than big groups. Not only do you get to be accompanied by an expert wildlife spotter, but you also get transport around the park, so you don't have to backtrack along trails and can see the waterfalls without having to hitch a ride. On the downside, you probably won't be able to choose which trails you cover, and may find the amount of walking unsatisfactorily slight; in addition it's usual, though not compulsory, to stay in the tour operator's own accommodation. An alternative would be to hire a park ranger to be your personal **guide** on the more remote trails; you can arrange this at the park headquarters, but don't expect to get transport as well as a guide. There's no set fee, but a fair rate would be B300 for a few hours, or around B500 for the whole day; organize your guide the night before and be sure to specify a start time.

In recent years, Khao Yai has unfortunately been plagued with unscrupulous tour operators, and as it's not possible to keep track of all fly-by-night operators in Pak Chong and Khao Yai, we are recommending only three reputable tour outfits. If your time is limited, it's worth contacting your chosen tour operator in advance, especially if you're on your own, as prices quoted are for a minimum of two trekkers, and solo travellers will have to pay more if there's no one else to join up with. Advance booking is essential for overnight expeditions in the park.

In Pak Chong, the recommended tour operator is **Wildlife Safari** (ⓣ044 312922, mobile ⓣ089 628 8224, ⓔwildlifekhaoyai@yahoo.co.uk), which emphasizes plant-spotting and animal observation rather than hearty hikes. The standard one-and-a-half day programme features walks along one or two trails, depending on the season and on recent sightings, a swim in Haew Suwat Falls, and a late evening excursion for elephant-spotting rather than the usual night safari; it costs B1150 per person, including the B200 park entry fee. They also offer overnight expeditions with either one or two nights spent camping in the heart of the park (B4000/6000 per person in a group of two, less if there are more people). Wildlife Safari is based about 2km north of Pak Chong train station at 39 Thanon Pak Chong Subsanun, Nong Kaja (call ahead to arrange free transport from Pak Chong); their accommodation here features a range of spacious and comfortably furnished rooms in the garden of the family home, most with private bathrooms and many with the option of air-con (shared bathroom ❶, fan and bathroom ❷–❸, air-con ❸–❹); most people doing the one-and-a-half-day programme stay here on the middle night.

The large, efficient and long-established **Khao Yai Garden Lodge** (ⓣ044 365178, ⓦwww.khaoyai-garden-lodge.com) is based at kilometre-stone 7 on the road that runs from Pak Chong into the park. It runs a variety of programmes, including half-day visits (B350 plus B200 park entry fee) and one-day outings (B650 plus B200), as well as the one-and-a-half day programme (B950/person plus B200), in which the half day features a trip to the bat cave at dusk but no entry into the park proper, and the full day includes one or two trail hikes, a swim at one of the waterfalls and a night safari. It can also arrange tailor-made treks. For details of *Garden Lodge*'s accommodation, see below.

At family-run **Green Leaf Guest House and Tour** (ⓣ044 365073, mobile ⓣ089 424 8809, ⓦwww.greenleaftour.com), treks are mostly led by owner Nine, who gets good reviews, particularly as a bird-spotter. It's based at kilometre-stone 7.5 on the park road (B15 by songthaew from Pak Chong) and is not to be confused with Green Leaf Travel Service, which has an office in front of the train station in Pak Chong and mainly acts as an agent for *Garden Lodge*. *Green Leaf Guest House and Tour* offers the usual one-and-a-half-day programme of trails (with an emphasis on bird-watching), waterfalls and a night safari for the standard price of B1150 including park entry, and can do personalized tours as well. Accommodation is available at the family guest house (see opposite).

It's also possible to arrange an upmarket bicycle tour of Khao Yai and its wineries, departing from Bangkok, through **Spice Roads** (ⓣ02 712 5305, ⓦwww.spiceroads.com/thailand/khao_yai; 2 days, 1 night $155 per person all-inclusive).

Coming back from the park is often easier, as day-trippers will usually give lifts all the way back to Pak Chong. Otherwise, hitch a ride as far as the checkpoint, or walk to the checkpoint from the visitor centre – it's a pleasant three- to four-hour walk along the fairly shaded park road, and you'll probably spot lots of birds and some macaques, gibbons and deer as well. At the checkpoint you can pick up a songthaew to Pak Chong: the last one usually leaves here at about 5pm.

Accommodation and eating

You have several options when it comes to **accommodation** in and around Khao Yai, but if you decide to do a tour, it's usual to stay in the lodgings run by your tour guide.

In the park

If you're intending to do several days' independent exploring in the park, the most obvious places to stay are the **national park lodges and tents** in the heart of Khao Yai. Unfortunately, this usually involves making an advance reservation through the Royal Forestry Department office in Bangkok (Ⓣ02 562 0760, Ⓦwww.dnp.go.th/National_park.asp; see Basics p.51 for details) and bringing your receipt to the Khao Yai accommodation office (daily 6am–9pm; Ⓣ044 297406), next to the visitor centre, when you arrive. However, you could also try contacting the Khao Yai accommodation office direct, as they claim that it's often possible to get a bed on a walk-in basis Sunday–Thursday if there are just two or three of you. There are 25 two-person **lodges** (❺) in three locations around the park, and another 25 that cater for groups of four to thirty people. The much cheaper 35–50-bed **dorms** (B50/person) behind the visitor centre are only available to individuals if there are no groups booked in. The cheapest option is to rent one of the **tents**, with or without mats and bedding, pitched at the two park campsites, both of which have showers and toilets. *Pha Kluai Mai* campground (aka *Orchid Camp*) is about 4km east of the park headquarters, on the road to Haew Suwat Falls, and *Lam Takong* campsite is scenically set beside the river near the old golf course, about 5km from HQ, and has a restaurant. Fully equipped tents are only available at *Lam Takong* (from B250 inclusive), while unequipped tents are available at both sites (from B100); advance bookings are not essential for camping, but are advisable at weekends. You can pitch your own tent at either site for B30.

There's no need to bring all your food and water supplies with you as there are half a dozen **foodstalls** serving hot food from about 6am to 6pm in the cafeteria complex opposite the park headquarters, where you'll also find a small shop that sells drinking water, beer, snacks, and boil-in-the-bag camping food (the accommodation office rents out stoves). There are also **restaurants** at Haew Suwat Falls and *Lam Takong* campsite.

The park road

The 23-kilometre road that runs from Pak Chong up to the park checkpoint (Thanon Thanarat) is dotted with luxurious "lodges", whose predominantly Thai guests nearly always arrive by car, though most lodges can arrange transport from Pak Chong; the Pak Chong songthaew will also bring you here. Addresses are determined by the nearest kilometre-stone on Thanon Thanarat.

The cheapest place to stay on the park road is *Green Leaf Guest House and Tour* (Ⓣ044 365073, Ⓦwww.greenleaftour.com; ❷), a friendly, family-run outfit 12.5km out of Pak Chong, at kilometre-stone 7.5, with eighteen en-suite rooms behind the good, cheap restaurant and guided treks into the national park (see above). Half a kilometre south of *Green Leaf*, at kilometre-stone 7, *Khao Yai Garden Lodge* (Ⓣ044 365178, Ⓦwww.khaoyai-garden-lodge.com; shared bathroom ❷, en suite ❸, air-con ❺–❼) is a large, well-designed and popular bungalow resort set in a landscaped garden, complete with a swimming pool, ponds and an aviary. It offers a few simple rooms with shared facilities as well as various better-appointed en-suite ones, some of which have air-con and extra beds for kids. *Garden Lodge* runs tours of the park (see p.524) as well as day-trips to the Khmer temples and other sights of Isaan. There's a restaurant here, and Internet access. *Juldis Khao Yai Resort* (Ⓣ044 297297, Ⓦwww.khaoyai.com; ❼–❾; discounts on weekdays), at kilometre-stone 17, offers good-value upmarket accommodation in its large, comfortably furnished air-conditioned rooms and has three swimming pools, several tennis courts, mountain-bike rental, a restaurant and a pub.

Pak Chong

The obvious drawback to basing yourself in Pak Chong is that it's about an hour's journey from the Khao Yai trailheads, but if you make an early start you can make use of the cheap public songthaew service.

Pak Chong's most acceptable budget **hotel** is the *Phubade Hotel* (Ⓣ044 314964; fan ❷, air-con ❸), located just 50m south down Tesaban Soi 15 from the train station. Coming from the bus station, cross to the north side of the main road, walk 400m east and then turn left up Tesaban Soi 15. The hotel is spartan and shabby but fairly clean, and has both fan and air-conditioned rooms, all with bathrooms. Smarter and more appealing, if frayed around the edges, *Rim Tarn Inn* (Ⓣ044 313364, Ⓕ044 312933; ❹) is on the south side of the main road, handy for drivers and about 300m west of the bus station; it has large, pretty comfortable rooms, all with air-con, plus a swimming pool, restaurant and beer garden. You should be able to get a good discount on a week night.

The cheapest and most popular place to **eat** after dark is the night market, which sets up along the north edge of the main road, between Tesaban sois 17 and 19. *Be My Guest* restaurant, just west of the mouth of Soi 15, is a traveller-oriented place serving, among other more standard fare, blueberry pie. If you're looking for somewhere to have a beer, the *Riverside* **bar** and restaurant, signed off the southern end of Tesaban Soi 8, stages live music most nights.

The park

During the daytime you're bound to hear some of the local wildlife, even if you don't catch sight of it (see Contexts pp.894–7 for more on many of the following species). Noisiest of all are the **white-handed (lar) gibbons**, which hoot and whoop from the tops of the tallest trees, and the **pileated (capped) gibbons**, whose call is more of a bubbling trill. Gibbons generally avoid contact with the ground, but this is not the case with the hard-to-miss **pig-tailed macaques**, many of whom gather at favoured spots on the road through the park. **Hornbills** also create quite a racket, calling attention to themselves by flapping their enormous wings; Khao Yai harbours large flocks of four different hornbill species, which makes it one of the best places in Southeast Asia to observe these creatures. The great hornbill is particularly beautiful, with brilliant yellow and black undersides; the magnificent oriental pied hornbill boasts less striking black and white colouring, but is more commonly seen at close range because it swoops down to catch fish, rats and reptiles. You might also see red-headed trogons, orange-breasted trogons, silver pheasants, woodpeckers and Asian fairy-bluebirds and, if you're lucky, the fire-back pheasant, endemic only

△ Wrinkle-lipped bats, Khao Luuk Chang

to Thailand and western Cambodia. From November to March Khao Yai hosts several species of **migrant birds**, including the dramatically coloured Siberian thrush and the orange-headed thrush.

A herd of about two hundred Asian **elephants** lives in the park, and its members are often seen at night – it's the only place in Thailand where you have much likelihood of spotting wild elephants. Khao Yai is also home to an ever-dwindling number of **tigers**, currently estimated at fifteen, sightings of which are rare, though not mythical. You're almost certain to spot **civets**, and you might come across a **slow loris**, while barking **deer** and sambar deer are less nervous after dark. **Wrinkle-lipped bats** assemble en masse at sunset, especially at the cave entrance on Khao Luuk Chang (Baby Elephant Mountain), 6km north of the north (main) gate into the park, which every evening disgorges millions of them on their nightly forage.

Exploring the park

Fifteen well-worn **trails** – originally made by elephants and other park species, and still used by these animals – radiate from the area around the visitor centre and park headquarters at kilometre-stone 37, and a few more branch off from the roads that traverse the park. The main trails are numbered and should be easy to follow: a few are signposted en route and some are colour-coded. The **visitor centre** (daily 8am–6pm) sells B5 photocopied park sketch maps with brief trail descriptions, as well as a more detailed park guidebook (B150) that includes a so-so topographical map, trail outlines and descriptions of the main mammals and their tracks. Rangers sometimes alter the course of a trail and, confusingly, they also sometimes renumber them, so ask at headquarters before you set off. Wear good boots, be prepared for some wading through rivers, and take a hat and plenty of water. If you don't fancy walking, you can rent **mountain bikes** from outside the visitor centre (B50/hr or B300/day). Rangers discourage visitors from exploring the outer, non-waymarked reaches unguided, partly for environmental reasons, but also because of trigger-happy

sandalwood poachers, who tend to shoot on sight anyone who strays onto their collection patch. The highly prized sandalwood oil is extracted by making cuts in a mature aloewood tree and collecting chunks of oil-saturated wood several months later; this wood can earn poachers B20,000–40,000 per kg. Sandalwood trees are indigenous to Khao Yai and though oil-collection does not usually kill the tree it does weaken it.

Snacks, bottled water, hot meals and mosquito repellent are sold in the cafeteria complex opposite the visitor centre. You will probably be glad of a strong repellent to deter not just the usual insects but also **leeches**, which can be quite a problem during and just after the rainy season. If you've only got shorts, consider buying a pair of leech socks (canvas gaiters; B70) from the shop opposite the visitor centre. The most effective way to get leeches off your skin is to burn them with a lighted cigarette, or douse them in salt; oily suntan lotion or insect repellent sometimes makes them lose their grip and fall off.

The trails

The shortest and least taxing of the park's trails is the one-kilometre-long **Kong Kaew Nature Trail (trail 14)**, which starts just behind the visitor centre. It's paved all the way and takes just thirty minutes in each direction; if it's not too crowded, you could see gibbons, woodpeckers and kingfishers en route.

Of the more adventurous hikes that begin from the park headquarters, the most popular is **trail 5,** which runs from just uphill of the visitor centre restaurant to **Nong Pak Chee observation tower** in the west of the park. This is a fairly easy walk through forest and grassland that culminates at an observation tower built next to a lake. En route you'll hear (if not see) white-handed gibbons in the tallest trees, and might spot barking deer in the savanna. If you stay at the tower long enough you could see needletails dive-bombing the lake; elephants and gaurs sometimes come to drink here, too, and you may even glimpse a tiger. The walk takes about two and a half hours to the observation tower (4.5km), from where it's another 900m down a dirt track which meets the main road between kilometre-stones 35 and 36. From the road, you can walk or hitch back either to the headquarters (2km) or down to the checkpoint (12km) and then travel on to Pak Chong. If you just want to spend a few hours at the observation tower and forget the main part of the walk, stop beside the main road between kilometre-stones 35 and 36 (before reaching the park headquarters) and walk the kilometre down the access track to the tower.

Trails 6 and 7 both branch off trail 5 into slightly shorter alternatives. **Trail 6**, from the park headquarters to **Wong Cham Pi (Wang Jumpee)**, is a two- to three-hour 4.4-kilometre hike that ends on the main road just 1.5km north of the headquarters at kilometre-stone 36. **Trail 7**, from the headquarters to **Mo Sing To,** is about a two-hour 2.7-kilometre route and goes through a different stretch of grassland and past a small lake.

Another good focus for walks is the area around **Haew Suwat Falls**, east of the visitor centre. These 25-metre-high falls are a great place for an invigorating shower, and they featured in the 1999 film *The Beach*. To get to the falls from the park headquarters, either follow trail 1 (see below), or walk, drive or hitch the six-kilometre road beyond the headquarters to Haew Suwat – it's a popular spot, so there should be plenty of cars.

Trail 1 runs from the visitor centre (8km one way; 3–4hr), beginning on the Nature Trail (trail 14) behind the visitor centre, then veering off it, along a path marked with red flashes, to **Haew Suwat**. En route to Haew Suwat you'll pass a turn-off to **trail 2** (which goes to *Pha Kluai/Orchid* campsite and waterfall; 6.1km from the park headquarters; see below); about forty minutes before reaching Haew Suwat is a signed trail off to the left that leads to nearby Haew Pratun Falls; twenty minutes further down trail 1 you may hear Haew Sai Falls in the distance, though these are easier to reach from Haew Suwat itself.

Day-trippers often do the shorter walk from Haew Suwat waterfall to **Pha Kluai/Orchid campsite (trail 3)**, which is paved most of the way and takes two hours at most (3.1km). You've a good chance of spotting gibbons and macaques along this route, as well as kingfishers and hornbills. The area around nearby Pha Kluai Falls is famous for its impressive variety of orchids. **Trail 4**, from Haew Suwat Falls to the **Khao Laem ranger post**, is a more strenuous undertaking; its main attractions are the waterfall, the wide expanse of grassland near Khao Laem and the impressive view of Khao Laem hill itself. You should ask permission from the park headquarters before setting out on this trail, and don't attempt it in the rainy season, as the river gets too high to cross. The trail 4 walk starts just upstream of the falls, from where it's about two hours to Khao Laem (4km) and the same back (along the same route).

With access to transport, it might also be worth heading up to the clifftop viewpoint at **Khao Khiew**, one of the highest points in the park, where during the week you have a good chance of being there by yourself. The short-trail through forest to **Pha Deaw Dai** (literally "Very Lonely Cliff") starts across from the Khao Khiew car park and takes just ten minutes to reach a panoramic clearing with views over the dense southern part of Khao Yai and its neighbouring national park, Thap Larn. The Khao Khiew car park is 15km south of the visitor centre and signed all the way: it climbs quite steeply, and relentlessly, uphill and would be pretty challenging on a mountain bike.

Night safaris

A much-touted park attraction are the hour-long **night safaris** – officially known as "night-lightings" – which take truckloads of tourists round Khao Yai's main roads in the hope of catching some interesting wildlife in the glare of the specially fitted searchlights. Regular night-time sightings include deer and civets, and elephants and tigers are sometimes spotted as well. However, opinions differ on the quality of the night-lighting experience: some people find it thrilling just to be out on the edges of the jungle after dark, others see it as rather a crass method of wildlife observation, especially at weekends when the park can feel like a town centre, with four or five trucks following each other round and round the main roads. Whatever your conclusion, you will enjoy the outing a lot more if you take warm clothes with you – Khao Yai is quite high and gets very chilly after sunset.

The night-lighting trucks leave the park headquarters every night at 7pm and 8pm (they can pick you up from the campsite if requested). All night-lightings are run by the park rangers, so tour operators sometimes join forces to hire a truck with ranger and searchlights. If you're on your own, you'll probably need to accompany one of these groups, as the trucks cost B430 to rent and can take up to ten people: book your place at the national park accommodation office, next to the visitor centre.

Khorat (Nakhon Ratchasima) and around

Beyond Pak Chong, Highway 2 and the rail line diverge to run either side of picturesque Lam Takong Reservoir, offering a last taste of undulating, forested terrain before gaining the largely barren Khorat plateau. They rejoin

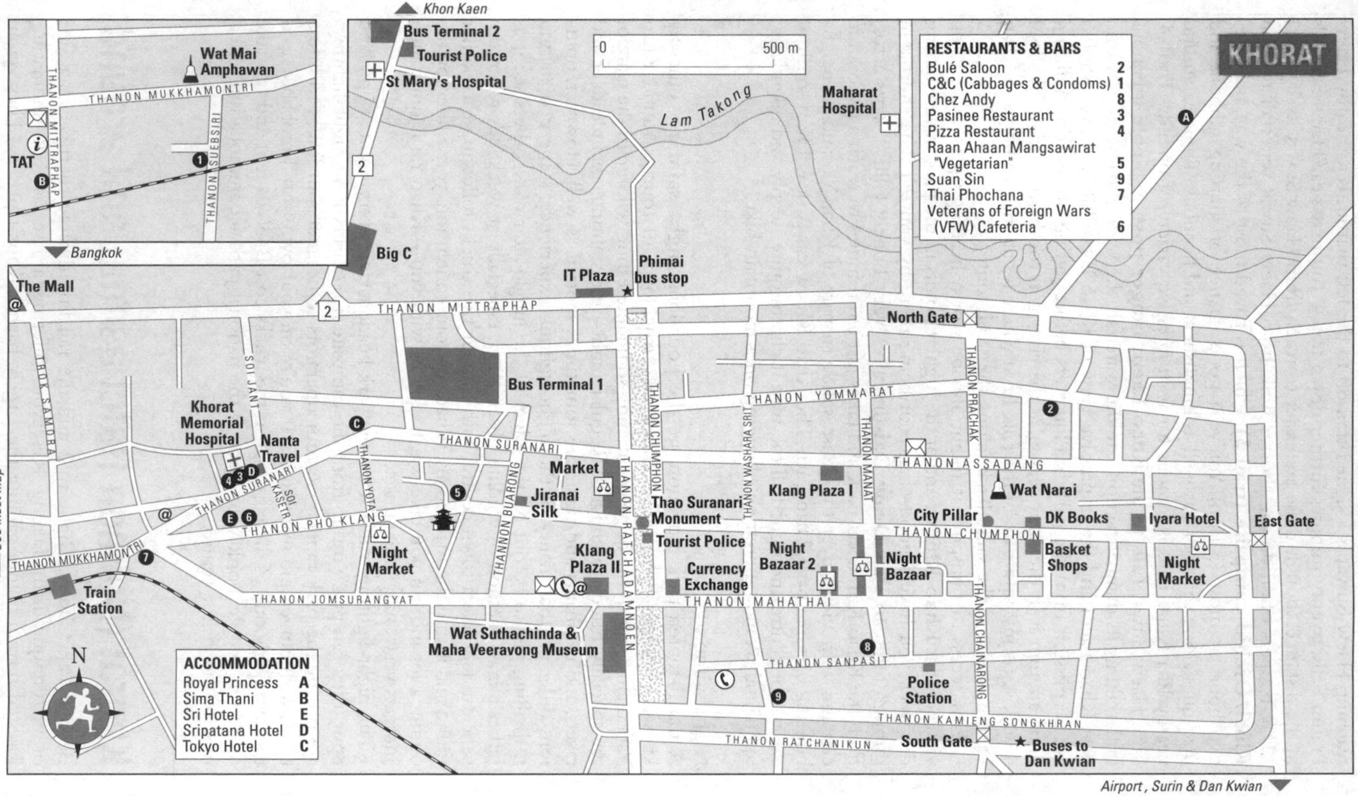

KHORAT

RESTAURANTS & BARS

Bulé Saloon	2
C&C (Cabbages & Condoms)	1
Chez Andy	8
Pasinee Restaurant	3
Pizza Restaurant	4
Raan Ahaan Mangsawirat "Vegetarian"	5
Suan Sin	9
Thai Phochana	7
Veterans of Foreign Wars (VFW) Cafeteria	6

ACCOMMODATION

Royal Princess	A
Sima Thani	B
Sri Hotel	E
Sripatana Hotel	D
Tokyo Hotel	C

Khon Kaen
Bangkok
See inset map
Airport, Surin & Dan Kwian
0 500 m
N
Bus Terminal 2
Tourist Police
St Mary's Hospital
Lam Takong
Maharat Hospital
Wat Mai Amphawan
THANON MUKKHAMONTRI
THANON MITTRAPHAP
THANON SUEBSIRI
TAT
Big C
IT Plaza
Phimai bus stop
The Mall
North Gate
Bus Terminal 1
TROK SAMORA
SOI JANT
Khorat Memorial Hospital
Nanta Travel
THANON SURANARI
THANON YOMMARAT
THANON PRACHAK
THANON CHUMPHON
THANON WASHARA SRIT
THANON MANAT
THANON ASSADANG
Market
Jiranai Silk
Klang Plaza I
Wat Narai
Thao Suranari Monument
Tourist Police
City Pillar
DK Books
Iyara Hotel
East Gate
SOI KASETR
THANON YOTA
THANNON BUARONG
THANON PHO KLANG
THANON RATCHADAMNOEN
Klang Plaza II
Night Bazaar 2
Night Bazaar
Basket Shops
Night Market
Currency Exchange
THANON MUKKHAMONTRI
Train Station
Night Market
THANON JOMSURANGYAT
THANON MAHATHAI
Wat Suthachinda & Maha Veeravong Museum
THANON SANPASIT
THANON CHAINARONG
Police Station
THANON KAMIENG SONGKHRAN
THANON RATCHANIKUN
South Gate
Buses to Dan Kwian

at **KHORAT** (officially known as **Nakhon Ratchasima**) – literally "Frontier Country" – which is still considered the gateway to the northeast.

If this is your first stop in Isaan, it's not a particularly pleasant introduction: Khorat is one of Thailand's most populous cities, its streets teem with traffic, and there's nothing here you could call a genuine tourist attraction. It can also be a confusing place to get to grips with: the **commercial centre** used to be contained within the old city moat, at the eastern end of town, but it has spilt over westwards and there are shops and markets as well as hotels and restaurants in both areas. But Khorat is at the centre of a good **transport network** and is within striking distance of the **Khmer ruins** at Phimai, Phanom Rung and Muang Tam, as well as the archeological remains of **Ban Prasat** and the pottery village at **Dan Kwian**. Aside from serving Bangkok and all the main centres within Isaan, Khorat's bus network extends south along Highway 304 to the east coast, enabling you to travel directly to Pattaya, Rayong and Chanthaburi without going through the capital.

Arrival, information and city transport

There are two bus terminals in town. **Bus Terminal 2** (Ⓣ044 256006–9), situated on the far northern edge of the city on Highway 2, is the main one and is the arrival and departure point for regular and air-con buses serving regional towns such as Pak Chong (for Khao Yai), Pak Tong Chai and Phimai, as well as long-distance destinations such as Bangkok (24-hr service), Ban Tako (for Phanom Rung), Chiang Mai, Khon Kaen, Nong Khai, Pattaya, Rayong (for Ko Samet) and Surin. The easiest way to get to and from Bus Terminal 2 is by tuk-tuk (B50 to the train station or nearby hotels), but city bus #15 also runs between Terminal 2 and the night bazaar area on Thanon Manat, from where city bus/songthaew #1 runs west along Thanon Chumphon to the train station and beyond (see below for details). **Bus Terminal 1** (Ⓣ044 268899) is more centrally located just off Thanon Suranari, and also operates both fan and air-con buses to Bangkok, via Pak Tong Chai and Pak Chong, but the service from Terminal 2 is more frequent. The **train station** on Thanon Mukkhamontri (Ⓣ044 242044) is served by city bus routes #1, #2 and #3, described below.

The **TAT office** (daily 8.30am–4.30pm; Ⓣ044 213666, Ⓔtatsima@tat.or.th) on the western edge of town gives out free maps of the convoluted city bus network and is reached from the city centre by city bus #2 or #3, as described below.

Flat-fare **songthaews** (B7) and **city buses** (B7) travel most of the main roads within town. The most useful routes – served by both songthaews and buses – are the yellow **#1**, which heads west along Thanon Chumphon, goes past the train station and then along Thanon Suebsiri to *Cabbages and Condoms* (on its return journey it travels east via Thanon Yommarat instead of Thanon Chumphon); **#2**, which runs between the main TAT office in the west, via the train station, along Thanon Suranari and Thanon Assadang to beyond the *lak muang* (city pillar) in the east; **#3**, which also runs right across the city, via Mahathai and Jomsurangyat roads, past the train station, to the TAT office in the west; and **#15**, which runs between Bus Terminal 2 and the night bazaar area on Thanon Manat.

Accommodation

The city's budget **hotels** are noisy and not that cheap (if visiting Phimai, consider staying in the atmospheric old guest house there instead), but there's a reasonable choice of air-con options.

Royal Princess 1137 Thanon Suranari ⓣ044 256629, ⓦkorat.royalprincess.com. Part of the Dusit group, this top-notch hotel is out on the northeastern fringes of town and has 186 comfortable air-con rooms and two restaurants, plus a large swimming pool, a jogging track and a business centre. ❼

Sima Thani Thanon Mittraphap ⓣ044 213100, ⓦwww.simathani.com. One of the city's best hotels, with smart air-con rooms, a swimming pool, three restaurants and a babysitting service. There's a relaxed feel to the place despite its popularity with businesspeople, and the rooms are good value. Its location beside Highway 2 (the Bangkok–Nong Khai road) makes it convenient for drivers, and buses from Bangkok or Khao Yai can drop you at the door en route to Bus Terminal 2, but it's too far to walk from the hotel to the town centre. ❻

Sri Hotel 688–690 Thanon Pho Klang ⓣ044 242831. Less than a 10min walk from the train station, the *Sri* has upgraded to become an all-air-con hotel, but it's still budget-traveller-oriented and remains a good-value option. Rooms are surprisingly quiet and spacious (though don't expect a view) and the management can arrange minibuses to Phimai (B900 for up to three people). ❸

Sripatana Hotel 346 Thanon Suranari ⓣ044 255349, ⓦsripatana.com. Huge hotel that's reasonably priced for the facilities, which include air-con in all rooms and a swimming pool and Internet on site. Rooms are a bit scruffy but feel large and bright. ❸–❹

Tokyo Hotel 256–258 Thanon Suranari ⓣ044 242788, ⓕ044 252335; a 5min walk from Bus Terminal 1, or #15 from the train station. Good value, conveniently located option with large, clean rooms and the choice of fan or air-con. Fan ❷, air-con ❸

The City

Sights are thin on the ground in Khorat, but if you spend more than a couple of hours in the city you're bound to come across the landmark statue at the western gate of the old city walls. This is the much-revered **Thao Suranari Monument**, erected to commemorate the heroic actions of the wife of the deputy governor of Khorat, during an attack by the kingdom of Vientiane – capital of modern-day Laos – in 1826. Some chronicles say she organized a feast for the Lao army and enticed them into bed, where they were then slaughtered by the Thais; another tells how she and the other women of Khorat were carted off as prisoners to Vientiane, whereupon they attacked and killed their guards with such ferocity that the Lao retreated out of fear that the whole Thai army had arrived. At any rate, Thao Suranari saved the day and is still feted by the citizens of Khorat, who lay flowers at her feet, light incense at her shrine and even dance around it. At the end of March, the town holds a week-long **festival** in her honour, with parades through the streets and the usual colourful trappings of Thai merry-making. The **Maha Veeravong Museum** (Wed–Sun 9am–4pm; B10; ⓦwww.thailandmuseum.com) houses a small and unexceptional collection of predominantly Dvaravati- and Lopburi-style Buddha statues found at nearby sites; it's in the grounds of Wat Suthachinda, on Thanon Ratchadamnoen.

Tourist shops and crafts outlets don't really feature in Khorat, but if you're not going further east to Surin, this is not a bad place to buy **silk**, much of which is produced in Pak Tong Chai, an uninteresting and over-exploited town 32km south of Khorat on Highway 304. The specialist shops along Thanon Chumphon sell lengths of silk at reasonable prices, but for the best and most exclusive selection visit Jiranai Silk, on the corner of Thanon Buarong and Pho Klang. Across the road from DK Books on Thanon Chumphon is a cluster of authentic **basketware** shops whose sticky-rice baskets, fish traps and rice winnowers make attractive souvenirs. The **night bazaar** that sets up at dusk every evening along Thanon Manat and nearby Thanon Mahathai deals mainly in bargain-priced fashions.

Eating and drinking

The night bazaar on and around Thanon Manat includes a few hot-food stalls, but there's a bigger selection of **night-market**-style foodstalls, with some streetside tables, about 800m further east near the *Iyara Hotel* on Thanon Chumphon. A smaller, more convenient grouping of night-time foodstalls sets up about 400m east of *Sri Hotel* on the corner of Thanon Yota. Because of its sizeable contingent of (mostly retired) expats, Khorat also offers the chance to satisfy foreign-food carvings, with a number of cuisines on offer, from Swiss to Lebanese.

Bulé Saloon Thanon Yommarat. Wild-West-style pub and beer garden that stages live music (mainly soft rock) every night. Evenings only.

C&C (Cabbages & Condoms) Next to the Soi 4 intersection at 86/1 Thanon Suebsiri. Typical Thai fare at this mid-priced restaurant (most dishes B60–120) managed along the same lines as its sister operation in Bangkok, with all proceeds going to the Population and Community Development Association of Thailand (PDA). Daily 10am–10pm.

Chez Andy 5–7 Thanon Manat. Swiss-run restaurant that's famous for its Australian steaks (up to B250), but which also does some seafood and Thai dishes. Kids under ten eat for free. Mon–Sat 11am–midnight, Sun 2pm–midnight.

Pasinee Restaurant 428 Thanon Suranari. The big draw at this farang-run restaurant is the Lebanese food, especially the huge chicken, pork and vegetable kebabs (from B75), and the fruit-scented-tobacco hookah pipes. Also serves delicious mixed fruit juices made with blueberries (B50). Daily 10am–10pm.

Pizza Restaurant 430 Thanon Suranari. One of a cluster of farang-run restaurants, this one specializes in pizzas but also does steaks, hamburgers and some Thai dishes. Mon–Sat 10am–10pm.

Raan Ahaan Mangsawirat "Vegetarian" Across the road from a Chinese temple on Thanon Pho Klang: no real English sign, but look for the yellow banner bearing Chinese characters and the word "Vegetarian"). Typical small, Chinese-style veggie café, with vegan curries and stews served buffet style for around B10 per portion. Daily 7am–6pm.

Suan Sin 163 Thanon Watcharasarit. Cheap place that's highly rated by locals for its tasty Isaan favourites, especially *som tam* and *kai yang* (from B50). Daily 10am–10pm.

Thai Phochana 142 Thanon Jomsurangyat. Centrally located air-con restaurant known for its duck curries (*kaeng pet*) and Khorat-style noodles cooked with coconut cream (*mii khorat*). Also has several vegetarian options. Most dishes cost from B50–120. Daily 7am–2am.

Veterans of Foreign Wars (VFW) Cafeteria Next to the *Sri Hotel* on Thanon Pho Klang. No-frills diner, complete with booths, which was set up by and for the GIs who've settled in the city. A handy if not particularly welcoming place for US and European breakfasts, served from 8am, it also does steak and fries (from B70), Polish sausage and pizzas. Daily 8am–9pm; drinks only after about 7pm.

Listings

Bookshops DK Books, east of the *lak muang* on Thanon Chumphon, sells a few cheap Penguin Popular Classics upstairs and a couple of English-language books about Thailand.

Car and motorbike rental From Nanta Travel on Thanon Suranari (see below).

Cinema 3rd floor, The Mall, Thanon Mittraphap. Shows mostly Thai soundtracks, but see Ⓦ www.movieseer.com for programmes.

Hospitals Expats tend to favour the private St Mary's Hospital at 307 Thanon Mittraphap (Highway 2), near Bus Terminal 2 ⓣ 044 261261; the government Maharat Hospital is on the northeast edge of town ⓣ 044 254990–1.

Internet access At T-Net (daily 10am–10pm) in The Mall shopping centre, Thanon Mittraphap, about 750m north of the train station; at the Games Centre west of the *Pizza Restaurant* on Thanon Suranari (24hr); Catnet terminals in the CAT overseas phone office on Thanon Jomsurangyat (Mon–Fri 8.30am–4.30pm; Sat 8.30am–noon); and (expensively) at the *Sima Thani* and *Royal Princess* hotels.

Mail There are post offices next to TAT on Thanon Mittraphap, inside the city walls on Thanon Assadang, and just west of the city walls on Thanon Jomsurangyat.

Telephones The CAT overseas telephone office is on Thanon Jomsurangyat (Mon–Fri 8.30am–4.30pm; Sat 8.30am–noon).

Tourist police For all emergencies, call the tourist police on the free, 24hr phone line ⓣ 1155, or contact them at one of their booths in town: their main office is opposite Bus Terminal 2 on Highway 2 ⓣ 044 341777–9, and there's a more central booth beside the Thao Suranari Monument on Thanon Chumphon.

Tours and travel agents The clued-up Nanta Travel Service, located a couple of doors east of the *Sripatana Hotel* at 334 Thanon Suranari (daily 8am–8pm; ⓣ 044 251339, ⓔ nantatravel@yahoo.com), sells domestic and international air tickets, rents motorbikes (B200/day) and cars (from B1000/day or B1600 with driver), is also an outlet for Budget car rental, and offers day-trips to local sights, including to Phimai and Ban Prasat (Mon, Wed & Fri; B690), to Phanom Rung, Muang Tam and Dan Kwian (Tues, Thurs, Sat & Sun; B890 per person), and to Khao Yai (on request; B1860 per person). *Siri Hotel* organizes car plus driver for up to three people to Phimai (B900/minibus) or Phanom Rung (B1400).

Dan Kwian

Some of the most sought-after modern pottery in Thailand is produced by the potters of **DAN KWIAN**, a tiny village 15km south of Khorat on Route 224. To get there, take local bus #1307 (destination Chok Chai; every 30min; 30min) from Bus Terminal 2, or pick it up at Khorat's southern city gate; get off as soon as you see the roadside pottery stalls, which display the whole range of goods, from inexpensive sunbaked clay necklaces to traditional urn-shaped water jars.

The local clay, dug from the banks of the Mun River, has a high iron content, which when fired in wood-burning kilns combines with ash to create the unglazed metallic finish that is characteristic of **Dan Kwian pottery**. The geometrical latticework pattern is also typical, and is incorporated into everything from incense burners and ashtrays to vases and storage jars. Dan Kwian potters also produce ceramic tiles and large-scale religious and secular murals, which make popular decorations in modern wats and city homes.

First settled by Mon in the mid-eighteenth century, Dan Kwian has always been a convenient rest spot for travellers journeying between the Khorat plateau and Cambodia – hence its name, which means "Cart Place" or "Wagon Station". The tag still applies, as the village is now home to a **cart museum** (always open; free), a ramshackle outdoor collection of traditional vehicles and farming implements assembled at the back of the pottery stalls. Look out for the monster with two-metre wheels, designed to carry two tons of rice, and the covered passenger wagons with their intricately carved shafts. The exhibits aren't all as archaic as they look – Isaan farmers still use some of the sugar-cane presses on display, and the fish traps are a common sight in this part of the country, where any body of fresh water, no mater how small or seasonal, offers the prospect of a vital protein supplement to the daily rice.

Ban Prasat

The quintessentially northeastern village of **Ban Prasat** has become a source of great interest to archeologists following the discovery in the 1990s of a series of **burial grounds** within its boundaries, some of which date back 3000 years. The skeletons and attendant artefacts have been well preserved in the mud, and many of the finds are now on public display in Ban Prasat; the village has made extra efforts to entice tourists with low-key craft demonstrations and a home-stay programme. It's also a pleasant village in its own right, a traditional community of stilt houses set beside the Tarn Prasat River, which rises in Khao Yai National Park; water from Tarn Prasat, one of the nine most sacred rivers in Thailand, was used in the religious ceremonies for the king's 72nd (sixth-cycle) birthday celebrations in 1999.

There are currently three **excavation pits** open to the public, each clearly signed from the centre of the village and informatively labelled. From these pits archeologists have surmised that Ban Prasat was first inhabited about 1000

BC and that its resident rice farmers traded their wares with coastal people, from whom they received shell jewellery, among other goods. Each pit contains bones and objects from different eras, buried at different depths but also with the head pointing in different directions, suggesting a change in religious or superstitious precepts. **Artefacts** found and displayed alongside them include stone discs, or *chakra,* believed to date back to 1000 BC, lots of wide-lipped or "trumpet-rim" earthenware vessels decorated with patterns applied in red slip, glazed Khmer-style pottery, and glass and bronze bangles. There are additional exhibits at the **Ban Prasat Museum** beside the car park, though its opening hours seem rather erratic.

Signs in the village direct you to local family-run projects, such as the household of **silk-weavers**, where you should be able to see several stages of the sericulture process (see box on p.547 for more on the Thai silk industry) and buy some cloth. Other village crafts include the weaving of floor mats from locally grown bulrushes, and the making of household brooms.

Practicalities

Ban Prasat is located just off Highway 2, 46km north of Khorat and 17km southwest of Phimai. Any Khorat–Phimai bus (#1305 from Khorat's Bus Terminal 2; every 30min; about 1hr from Khorat or 20min from Phimai) will drop you at the Highway 2 junction, from where motorbike taxis will ferry you the 2km to the village. There are no hotels or restaurants in the village, but there is a **home-stay** programme, which is a great opportunity to savour typical village life. Home-stays cost B400 per person per night, including two meals, and should be arranged at least a week in advance by contacting the village headman, Khun Teim Laongkarn, of the Eco-tourism Society, 282 Mu 7, Tambon Tarn Prasat, Amphoe Non Sung, Nakhon Ratchasima 30420 (Ⓣ044 367075). Alternatively, staff at the Khorat TAT office may be able to help (Ⓣ044 213666, Ⓔtatsima@tat.or.th).

Phimai

Hemmed in by its rectangular old city walls and encircled by tributaries of the Mun River, the small modern town of **PHIMAI**, 60km northeast of Khorat, is completely dominated by the charmingly restored Khmer temple complex of **Prasat Hin Phimai**. No one knows for sure when the prasat was built or for whom, but as a religious site it probably dates back to the reign of the Khmer king Suriyavarman I (1002–49); the complex was connected by a direct road to Angkor and orientated southeast, towards the Khmer capital. Over the next couple of centuries Khmer rulers made substantial modifications, and by the end of Jayavarman VII's reign (1181–1220), Phimai had been officially dedicated to Mahayana Buddhism. Phimai's other claim to fame is **Sai Ngam** (Beautiful Banyan), reputedly the largest banyan tree in Thailand, still growing a couple of kilometres beyond the temple walls.

Phimai's biggest event of the year is the annual festival of **boat races**, held on the Mun's tributaries over a weekend in early November, in a tradition that's endured for over a century. In common with many other riverside towns, Phimai marks the end of the rainy season by holding fiercely competitive longboat races on the well-filled waterways, and putting on lavish parades of ornate barges done up to emulate the Royal Barges of Bangkok. As part of the boat-race festival, a **son-et-lumière show** is staged at the temple ruins for five

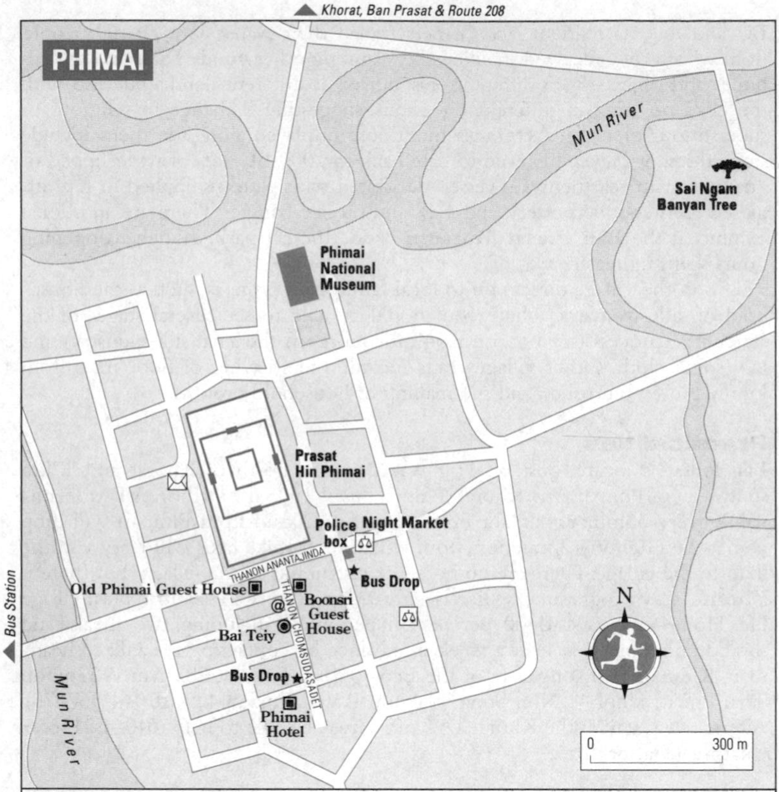

Khorat, Ban Prasat & Route 208
PHIMAI
Mun River
Sai Ngam Banyan Tree
Phimai National Museum
Prasat Hin Phimai
Police box
Night Market
THANON ANANTAJINDA
Bus Drop
Old Phimai Guest House
THANON CHOMSUDASADET
Boonsri Guest House
Bai Teiy
Bus Drop
Phimai Hotel
Bus Station
Mun River
N
0
300 m

PRASAT HIN PHIMAI

Gopura
Gopura
Main Prang
Gopura
Gallery
Gopura
Gopura
N
4
3
Main Prang
5
2
1

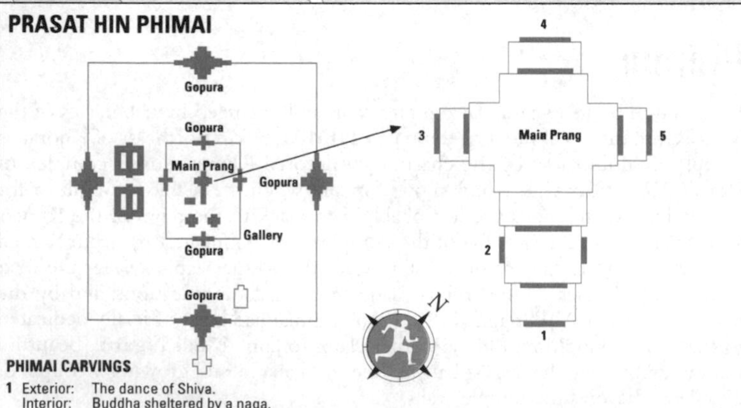

PHIMAI CARVINGS

1 Exterior: The dance of Shiva.
Interior: Buddha sheltered by a naga.

2 Exterior: Krishna lifting Mount Govadhana. Rama and his brother Lakshaman bound with serpentine ropes.

3 Exterior: Battle scene from the *Ramayana*; Rama and his monkeys build a bridge by hurling mountains into the sea.
Interior: Buddha beneath trees; dancers and musicians embellish Buddha's sermons.

4 Exterior: *Ramayana* battle; Vishnu holding conch shell, lotus, club and chakri disc.
Interior: Five Vajarasatvas, each with six hands and three faces.

5 Exterior: The God of Justice pronounces on the Rama/Ravana dispute; Rama kills the giant Viradha.
Interior: Boddhisatva Trailokayavicha with his left foot suspended over Ignorance.

Khmer temples

To make sense of the **Khmer ruins** of Thailand, it's essential to identify their common architectural features. At the centre of the rectangular temple compound is always the main prang, a pyramidal or corn cob-shaped tower built to house the temple's most sacred image. Each prang has four entrance chambers or gopura, the most important of which (usually the eastern one, facing the dawn) is often extended into a large antechamber. The lintels and pediments above the gopura are carved with subjects from relevant mythology: typical Hindu reliefs show incidents from the *Ramayana* epic (see box on p.137) and lively portraits of the Hindu deities Shiva and Vishnu, while Buddhist scenes come from the lives of the Buddha and other Bodhisattvas. Antefixes on the roof of the prang are often carved with the Hindu gods of direction, some of the most common being Indra on the three-headed elephant (east); Yama on a buffalo (south); Varuna on a naga or a *hamsa*, a sacred goose (west); Brahma on a *hamsa* (north); and Isaana on a bull (northeast).

Originally, the prang would have sheltered a **shiva lingam** (a phallic sculpture representing the god Shiva), continuously bathed by lustral water dripping from a pot suspended over it; the water then flowed out of the inner chamber by means of a stone channel, a process which symbolized the water of the Ganges flowing from the Himalayan home of Shiva. In most prasats, however, the lingam has disappeared or been replaced with Hindu or Buddhist statues.

One or two **minor prangs** usually flank the main prang: often these were added at a later date to house images of less important gods, though in some cases they pre-date the main structure. Concentric sets of walls shield these shrines within an inner courtyard. In many temples, the innermost wall – the **gallery** – was roofed, either with wood (none of these roofs has survived) or stone. Many of the stone blocks used to build the temple walls have **small round holes** in them; these were either fitted with pegs that enabled blocks to be moved with ropes, or were used to fit poles for leverage. At their cardinal points some galleries have gopuras with carved lintels and pediments, which are usually approached by staircases flanked with **naga balustrades**; in Khmer temples, nagas generally appear as symbolic bridges between the human world and that of the gods. Most prangs enclose ponds between their outer and inner walls, and many are surrounded by a network of moats and **reservoirs**: historians attribute the Khmers' political success in part to their skill in designing highly efficient irrigation systems (see p.856 for the history of the Khmers in Thailand).

nights in a row; check with the Khorat TAT office for details (Ⓣ044 213666, Ⓔtatsima@tat.or.th).

The ruins

Built mainly of dusky pink and greyish white sandstone, **Prasat Hin Phimai** (daily 7.30am–6pm; B40) is a seductive sight for so solemn a set of buildings. Even from a distance, the muted colours give off a far from austere glow; closer inspection reveals a mass of intricate carvings.

From the main southeastern gate, a staircase ornamented with classic naga balustrades leads to a gopura in the **outer walls**, which are punctuated on either side by false balustraded windows – a bit of sculptural sleight-of-hand to jazz up the solid stonework without piercing the defences. A raised pathway bridges the space between these walls and the inner gallery that protects the prangs of the **inner sanctuary**. The minor prang to the right, made of laterite, is attributed to the twelfth-century Buddhist king Jayavarman VII, who engaged in a massive temple-building campaign during his reign. Enshrined within is a statue of him; it's a copy of the much more impressive original, which was found in the same location and is now housed in the Phimai National Museum. The pink sandstone prang to the left, which is connected to a Brahmin shrine where seven stone linga were found, was probably built around the same time.

After more than twenty years of archeological detective work and painstaking reassembly, the magnificent white sandstone **main prang** has now been restored to its original cruciform groundplan and conical shape, complete with an almost full set of carved lintels, pediments and antefixes, and capped with a stone lotus bud. The **carvings** around the outside of the prang depict predominantly Hindu themes. Shiva the Destroyer dances above the main entrance to the southeast antechamber: his destruction dance heralds the end of the world and the creation of a new order, a supremely potent image that warranted this position over the most important doorway. For more on these legends, see "Art and Architecture" in Contexts (p.875). Most of the other external carvings pick out momentous episodes from the *Ramayana* (see box on p.137), starring heroic Rama, his brother Lakshaman and their band of faithful monkeys in endless battles of strength, wits and magical powers against Ravana, the embodiment of evil. Inside, more sedate Buddhist scenes give evidence of the conversion from Hindu to Buddhist faith, and the prasat's most important image, the Buddha sheltered by a seven-headed naga, sits atop a base that once supported a Hindu Shiva lingam.

Phimai National Museum

Much of the ancient carved stonework discovered at Phimai but not fitted back into the renovated structure can be seen at the **Phimai National Museum** (daily 9am–4pm; B30; Ⓦwww.thailandmuseum.com), where it's easier to appreciate, being at eye-level, well labelled and contextualized. The museum stands between one of the old Khmer reservoirs and the Mun River, just inside the old city walls to the northeast of the ruins. It's an easy walk from the ruins, but if you're here for the day from Khorat, you can save your legs a bit as the Khorat–Phimai bus will stop outside the museum if requested. The museum's *pièce de résistance* is the exceptionally fine sandstone statue of Jayavarman VII that was found in Phimai's laterite prang; seated and leaning slightly forward, he's lost his arms and part of his nose, but none of his grace and serenity. Elsewhere in the galleries, displays take you through the religious and cultural history of the Phimai region, featuring prehistoric items from Ban Prasat (see p.534) as well as some exquisite Buddha statues from more recent times.

△ Hindu carvings, Prasat Hin Phimai

Sai Ngam

Two kilometres northeast of the museum – get there by bicycle (see below) or samlor – **Sai Ngam** is a banyan tree so enormous that it's reputed to cover an area about half the size of a soccer pitch (approximately 2300 square metres). It might look like a grove of small banyans, but Sai Ngam is in fact a single *Ficus bengalensis* whose branches have dropped vertically into the ground, taken root and spawned other branches, so growing further and further out from its central trunk. Banyan trees are believed to harbour animist spirits, and you can make merit here by releasing fish into the artificial lake that surrounds Sai Ngam. The tree is a popular recreation spot, and several restaurants have sprung up alongside it.

Practicalities

Phimai's **bus station** is inconveniently located 1.5km southwest of the ruins, on the bypass, but nearly everybody gets on and off in the town centre, either near the night-market area or in front of the *Phimai Hotel*. Regular **bus** #1305 runs direct to Phimai from Khorat's Bus Terminal 2, with a pick-up point near the Thanon Mittraphap/Ratchadamnoen junction (every 30min until 6.30pm, then sporadically until 10pm; 1hr 30min); the last return bus departs for Khorat at 7pm. The bus passes the turn-off to Ban Prasat (see p.535), so if you get up early you can combine the two places on a day-trip from Khorat. If travelling from Khon Kaen, Udon Thani or Nong Khai, take any Khorat-bound bus along Highway 2 as far as the Phimai turn-off (Highway 208), then change onto the Khorat–Phimai service for the last 10km; the same strategy works in reverse. It's also feasible, if a bit of an effort, to visit Phimai en route to points east or west without having to pass through Khorat. You can do this by taking a **train** to the tiny station of **Hin Dat**, which is about an hour and forty minutes' train ride west of Surin, or about 55 minutes' ride east of Khorat. Hin Dat is 25km south of Phimai, so from here you should either wait for one of the infrequent songthaews to Phimai, splash out on an expensive motorbike taxi or try hitching. Songthaews back to Hin Dat from Phimai are generally timed to link up with east-bound trains; check with the *Old Phimai Guest House*, for current timetables.

Once in Phimai, the best way to get about is by **bicycle**, although this isn't permitted inside the ruins. *Bai Teiy* restaurant has bicycles for rent and issues free maps of cycling routes around town, while *Old Phimai Guest House* has bicycles for guests only. Aside from the ride out to Sai Ngam, the area just west of the ruins, beyond the post office, is especially atmospheric – many of the traditional wooden houses here double as workshops, and you'll often see householders weaving cane chairs in the shade beneath the buildings. There's **Internet** access inside the Agfa photo shop on Thanon Chomsudasadet, and the post office has a Catnet terminal.

Accommodation and eating

Though most people visit the ruins as a day-trip, Phimai has two inexpensive **places to stay** as well as an unpretentious hotel, and makes a more attractive and peaceful overnight stop than Khorat. Your first choice should be the laid-back *Old Phimai Guest House* (Ⓣ & Ⓕ044 471918; dorm beds B100, fan ❶, air-con ❸), an old wooden house with a roof terrace, just off Thanon Chomsudasadet and only a couple of minutes' walk from the ruins. The rooms are large and some are air-conditioned, but they all share bathrooms. The *Old Phimai* is an excellent source of information and also runs day-trips to Phanom Rung at B400 per person (minimum four people). Equally central, and offering huge, immaculate rooms, *Boonsri Guest House* (Ⓣ044 471159; ❸–❹) occupies the upper floors of the proprietor's home, above her duck restaurant on Thanon Chomsudasadet; doubles here are en suite and very spruce, or a dorm mattress costs B150. More upmarket, the friendly *Phimai Hotel*, next to the bus drop (Ⓣ044 471306; ❸–❹), has large, good-quality rooms with fan or air-con.

Bai Teiy on Thanon Chomsudasadet, the town's most popular **restaurant**, serves tasty Thai dishes, including fresh fish from the river; it also acts as an informal tourist information service and can help with bus and train timetables. If you prefer a meal with a view, head out to the string of pricier restaurants alongside Sai Ngam. The night market sets up at dusk on the eastern stretch of Thanon Anantajinda, just southeast of the ruins, and is a good place to sample genuine local fare at genuine local prices.

Phanom Rung and Muang Tam

East of Khorat the bleached plains roll on, broken only by the occasional small town and, if you're travelling along Highway 24, the odd tantalizing glimpse of the smoky Phanom Dangkrek mountain range above the southern horizon. That said, it's well worth jumping off the Surin-bound bus for a detour to the fine Khmer ruins of **Prasat Hin Khao Phanom Rung** and **Prasat Muang Tam**. Built during the same period as Phimai, and for the same purpose, the temple complexes form two more links in the chain that once connected the Khmer capital with the limits of its empire. Sited dramatically atop an extinct volcano, Phanom Rung has been beautifully restored, and the more recently renovated Muang Tam lies on the plains below.

Prasat Hin Khao Phanom Rung

Prasat Hin Khao Phanom Rung stands as the finest example of Khmer architecture in Thailand, graced with innumerable exquisite carvings and with its sandstone and laterite buildings so perfectly aligned that on the morning of the fifteenth day of the waxing moon in the fifth month of the lunar calendar you can stand at the westernmost gopura and see the rising sun through all fifteen doors. This day (usually in April: check dates at Ⓦwww.thailandgrandfestival.com or contact Buriram municipality at Ⓣ044 613315) is celebrated with a day-long **festival** of huge parades all the way up the hill to the prasat – a tradition believed to go back eight hundred years. As at most Khmer prasats, **building** at Phanom Rung was a continuous process that spanned several reigns: the earliest structures are thought to date to the beginning of the tenth century and final additions were probably made three hundred years later, not long before it was abandoned. The heart of the temple was constructed in the mid-twelfth century, in early Angkorian style, and is attributed to local ruler Narendraditya and his son Hiranya. A lintel inside the temple is thought to depict Narendraditya's investiture as ruler. Narendraditya was a follower of the Shivaite cult, a sect which practised yoga and fire worship and used alcohol and sex in its rituals, and carved depictions of all these practices decorate the temple. Restoration work at Phanom Rung was begun in 1971 and lasted seventeen years: the results are impressive and give the most complete picture of Khmer architecture in Thailand.

There are two car parks and two **entrances** to the Phanom Rung complex; if you have your own transport, ignore the Gate 2 (west) entrance, signed off the access road, and carry on to the main, Gate 1 (east), entrance and car park – the drama of the site is lost if you explore it back-to-front. Motorbike taxis should take you to the main entrance. There are cheap foodstalls outside the Gate 1 entrance, and a restaurant in its car park area.

Awesome as the temple complex is, its appeal is greatly enhanced if you can make sense of the layout and symbolism, so it's well worth spending twenty minutes in the excellent, museum-like **Phanom Rung Tourist Information Centre** inside the Gate 1 car park (daily 9am–4pm; free) before entering. A series of clear display boards provide an outstanding introduction to the temple's construction, iconography and restoration. The exhibition also includes small displays on Muang Tam and other nearby Khmer ruins, and there's a separate children's room with related puzzles and activity ideas.

Exploring the temple

The approach to **Prasat Hin Khao Phanom Rung** (daily 6am–6pm; B40) is one of the most dramatic of its kind. Symbolic of the journey from earth to the heavenly palace of the gods, the ascent to the inner compound is imbued with metaphorical import: by following the 200-metre-long avenue, paved in laterite and sandstone and flanked with lotus-bud pillars, you are walking to the ends of the earth. Ahead, the main prang, representing Mount Meru, home of the gods, looms large above the gallery walls, and is accessible only via the first of three **naga bridges**, a raised cruciform structure with sixteen naga balustrades, each naga having five heads. Once across the bridge you have traversed the abyss between earth and heaven. A series of stairways ascends to the eastern entrance of the celestial home, first passing four small ponds, thought to have been used for ritual purification. A second naga bridge crosses to the **east gopura**, entrance to the inner sanctuary, which is topped by a lintel carved with Indra (god of the east) sitting on a lion throne. The gopura is the main gateway through the **gallery**, which runs right round the inner compound and has one main and two minor entranceways on each side. Part of the gallery has been restored to its original covered design, with arched stone roofs, small chambers inside and **false windows**; real windows wouldn't have been strong enough to support such a heavy stone roof, so false ones, which retained the delicate pilasters but backed them with stone blocks, were an aesthetically acceptable compromise. The chambers may have been used for exhibiting as well as storing artefacts.

The main prang

Phanom Rung is surprisingly compact, so the east gopura leads almost directly into the **main prang**, separated from it only by a final naga bridge. A dancing Shiva, nine of his ten arms intact, and a lintel carved with a relief of a **reclining Vishnu** preside over the eastern entrance to the prang. The Vishnu image has a restless history: stolen from the site in the early 1960s, it mysteriously reappeared as a donated exhibit in the Art Institute of Chicago; for over ten years the curators refused to return it to Thailand, but as restoration work on Phanom Rung neared completion in 1988, the Thai media took up the cause and the Institute finally relented. The relief depicts a common Hindu creation myth, known as "Reclining Vishnu Asleep on the Milky Sea of Eternity", in which Vishnu dreams up a new universe, and Brahma (the four-faced god perched on the lotus blossom that springs from Vishnu's navel) puts the dream into practice. On the pediment above this famous relief is a lively carving of **Shiva Nataraja**, or Shiva's Dance of Destruction, which shows him dancing on Mount Kailash in front of several others gods, including Ganesh, Brahma and Vishnu (see p.875 for more on the Hindu legends). Labels highlight the most interesting narrative lintels in the prang, one of which is the supposed investiture of Phanom Rung builder Narendraditya, above the second (inside) southern doorway. Of the other recurring figures decorating the prang, one of the most important is the lion head of Kala, also known as Kirtimukha, symbolic of both the lunar and the solar eclipse and – because he's able to "swallow" the sun – considered far superior to other planetary gods. Inside the prang kneels an almost life-size statue of Shiva's vehicle, the bull Nandi, behind which stands the all-powerful **Shiva lingam**, for which the prang was originally built; the stone channel that runs off the lingam and out of the north side of the prang was designed to catch the lustral water with which the sacred stone was bathed.

Two rough-hewn laterite libraries stand alongside the main prang, in the northeast and southeast corners, and there are also remains of two early-tenth-century brick prangs just northeast of the main prang. The unfinished **prang noi** (little prang) in the southwest corner now contains a stone Buddha footprint, which has become the focus of the merit-making that underlies the annual April festivities, thus neatly linking ancient and modern religious practices.

Prasat Muang Tam

Down on the well-watered plains 8km to the southeast of Phanom Rung and accessed via a scenic minor road that cuts through a swathe of ricefields, the small but elegant temple complex of **Prasat Muang Tam** (daily 7.30am–6pm; B30) is sited behind a huge kilometre-long *baray* (Khmer reservoir), which was probably constructed at the same time as the main part of the temple, in the early eleventh century. Like Phanom Rung, Muang Tam was probably built in stages between the tenth and thirteenth centuries, and is based on the classic Khmer design of a central prang flanked by minor prangs and encircled by a gallery and four gopura. Muang Tam's history is presented in brief at the **tourist information centre** (daily 9am–4pm; free) in the temple car park, where a short English-language video gives a reasonable introduction to the complex, backed up by a few photographic displays.

The ruins

The approach to Muang Tam is nothing like as grand as at Phanom Rung but, once through the main, eastern gopura in the outside wall, it's a pretty scene, with the central gallery encircled by four **L-shaped ponds** – such important features that they are referred to in a contemporary inscription that states "this sanctuary is preserved by sacred water". The shape of the ponds gives the impression that the prasat is set within a moat that's been severed by the four entrance pathways at the cardinal points. Each pond is lined with laterite brick steps designed to enable easy access for priests drawing sacred water, and possibly also for devotees to cleanse themselves before entering the central sanctuary. The rims are constructed from sandstone blocks that form naga, the sacred water serpents.

The rectangular central **gallery** was probably roofed with timber (long since rotted away) and so could be punctuated with real windows, rather than the more load-bearing false versions that had to be used at Phanom Rung. Inside, the **five red-brick towers** of the inner sanctuary are arranged on a laterite platform, with three prangs in the front (eastern) row, and two behind. The main, central, prang has collapsed, leaving only its base, but the four other towers are merely decapitated and some have carved **lintels** intact. The lintel above the doorway of the front right tower is particularly lively in its depiction of the popular scene known as Ume Mahesvara (Uma and her consort Shiva riding the bull Nandi). There are interesting details in the temple complex, including recurrent motifs of foliage designs and Kala lion-faces, and figures of ascetics carved into the base of the doorway pillars on the eastern gopura of the outer wall.

Practicalities

Most people do the ruins as a day-trip from Khorat or Surin, though it's also possible to stay closer to the sights, in **Nang Rong** or **Buriram**. There's public transport from Khorat, Surin, Nang Rong and Buriram as far as the little town of **Ban Tako**, from where you'll need to take a motorbike taxi for the final few kilometres to the ruins. Alternatively, rent your own motorbike from Nang Rong, or join one of the inexpensive **day-tours** from Phimai (see p.539) or Khorat (see p.534).

Ban Tako

Served by frequent **buses** from Khorat (via Nang Rong) and Surin, the town of **BAN TAKO** is located on Highway 24 about 115km southeast of Khorat or 83km southwest of Surin. Bus #274 travels between the two provincial capitals, leaving every thirty minutes around the clock and taking 2 hours 25 minutes from Khorat or 1 hour 45 minutes from Surin.

From Ban Tako it's 12km south to Phanom Rung and another 8km southeast along a side road to Muang Tam, and as there's no public transport direct to the ruins most people rent an expensive **motorbike taxi** here, which usually costs B300–400 per person for the round-trip to Phanom Rung, Muang Tam and back to Ban Tako. Alternatively you could try **hitching** – a time-consuming option during the week (so you should take a very early bus from Khorat or Surin), but a lot easier at weekends. The best place to hitch from is a small village south of Ban Tako called **Ban Don Nong Nae**, which you can reach from Ban Tako by taking a ten-minute songthaew ride.

Nang Rong

The nearest **accommodation** to Phanom Rung is in the town of **Nang Rong**, on the #274 bus route, 14km west of Ban Tako on Highway 24. Here, the welcoming guest house *Honey Inn* (Ⓣ044 622825, Ⓦhoneyinn.com; shared bathroom ❶, en suite ❷), at 8/1 Soi Sri Koon, offers rooms with and without bathroom, motorbike rental, meals with the family and Internet access. To get to *Honey Inn* from the Nang Rong bus terminal, either take a B20 samlor ride or walk north about 100m onto Highway 24, cross the highway, turn right and walk east along the highway for about 300m, passing a PTT petrol station after about 200m. Turn left at the *Honey Inn* sign and it's about 100m further on.

For onward **transport to the ruins**, either take the #274 bus to Ban Tako, then a motorbike taxi as described above; hire a motorbike taxi all the way from Nang Rong (slightly pricier than from Ban Tako) or charter a songthaew instead (the cheaper option for two or more people); or, cheapest of all, rent your own motorbike.

Buriram

If arriving direct from Bangkok, it may be easier to stay in the provincial capital of **Buriram**, 40km north of Ban Tako, which is served by all Bangkok–Ubon **trains**, and (currently) by PB Air **flights** (Ⓣ044 680132, Ⓦwww.pbair.com) between Bangkok and Buriram Airport, 30km from town. Buses connect Buriram with Ban Tako (about 1hr). About 200m south of Buriram train station along the main drag, Thanon Romburi, the *Thai Hotel* (ⓣ044 611112, ⓕ044 612461; ❷–❸), at 38/1, has decent air-con **rooms**, or there's slightly more upmarket accommodation at the *Vongthong Hotel* (ⓣ044 612540, ⓦwww.awadee.com/isan/vongthong; ❺–❻), a few minutes' walk west of the bus terminal, off Thanon Buladmuan at 512/1 Thanon Jira, which offers large rooms with air-con and TV.

Surin and around

Best known for its much-hyped annual elephant round-up, the provincial capital of **Surin**, around 150km east of Khorat, is an otherwise typical northeastern town, a good place to absorb the easy-going pace of Isaan life, with the bonus of some atmospheric Khmer ruins nearby. The elephant tie-in comes from the local Suay people, whose prowess with pachyderms is well known and can sometimes be seen first-hand in the nearby villages of **Ban Ta Klang**. Thais, Lao and Khmers make up the remainder of the population of Surin province – the Khmers have lived and worked in the region for over a thousand years, and their architectural legacy is still in evidence at the ruined temples of Ta Muean and Ban Pluang. The local Khmer population was boosted during the Khmer Rouge takeover of Cambodia in the 1970s, when many upper-class Cambodians fled here. Three decades on and, with a slightly more stable political situation in Cambodia, it is now possible for foreigners **to cross overland between Thailand and Cambodia** via Surin province's Chong Chom checkpoint near Kap Choeng.

Arrival and information

Several services a day make the Bangkok–Surin connection, stopping at the **train station** (ⓣ044 511295) on the northern edge of town. The **bus terminal** (ⓣ044 511756) off Thanon Jitbumrung runs frequent services to and from Bangkok, to major northeastern towns, and to Pattaya, Rayong, Phitsanulok, Lampang and Chiang Mai There's an **airstrip** on the southeastern edge of Surin, which sometimes runs flights to and from Bangkok: contact Saren Travel (ⓣ044 713828, ⓔsarentour@yahoo.com) for details.

There's no tourist **information** in town, but the provincial government has quite a useful website (ⓦwww.surin.go.th) or you can ask at *Pirom & Aree's House 2*, *Farang Connection* or Saren Travel (see p.549).

Overland into Cambodia via Chong Chom

If you're planning to cross **overland into Cambodia**, there are air-con buses (about every 90min 6.40am–3.30pm; 1hr 30min; B50) and non-air-con buses (approximately hourly 5.50am–5.30pm; B35; 2hr) via Prasat to the Chong Chom border pass, 70km south of Surin; or you can arrange a taxi through *Farang Connection*, located behind Surin bus station (ⓣ044 511509, ⓦwww.farangconnection.com). Cambodian visas are issued on arrival at the Chong Chom–O'Smach checkpoint (daily 7am–8pm; US$20 or B1000), from where you can get transport to Anlong Veng and then on to Siem Reap, which is 150km from the border crossing. Arriving from Cambodia, songthaews and motorbike taxis ferry travellers from the border checkpoint to the bus stop for Prasat and Surin. For travellers' accounts of the border crossing, see ⓦtalesofasia.com/cambodia-overland-osm-reports.htm; for details on other overland routes into Cambodia, see p.32.

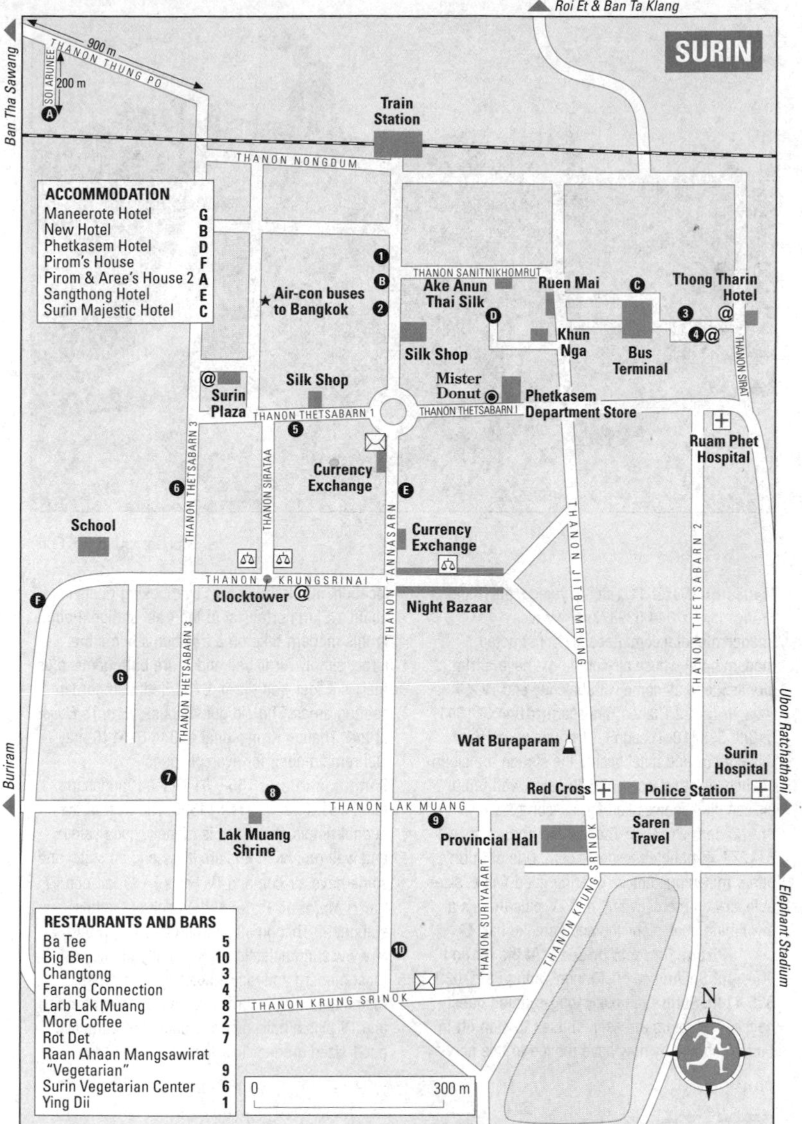

Accommodation

During the elephant round-up, room rates in Surin double and **accommodation** is booked out weeks in advance, so you may want to make use of the accommodation-booking websites listed in Basics on p.50. During the rest of the year you'll have no trouble finding a place to stay.

△ Elephant round-up, Surin

Maneerote Hotel 11/1 Soi Poytango, off Thanon Krungsrinai ⓣ 044 539477, ⓦ www.maneerotehotel.com. Recently constructed, modern hotel whose air-con rooms have a trim, airy look and all come with balcony and TV. ❺

New Hotel 22 Thanon Tannasarn ⓣ 044 511341, ⓕ 044 538410. Though far from new, rooms at this bottom-end hotel beside the station are clean enough, if rather worn, and all come with fan or air-con plus shower. Fan ❶, air-con ❷

Phetkasem Hotel off Thanon Jitbumrung ⓣ 044 511274, ⓔ pkhotel@cscoms.com. One of Surin's better mid-range hotels, offering good-value, sizeable air-con rooms with (Thai) TV, plus there's a swimming pool, nightclub and karaoke bar. ❹

Pirom & Aree's House 2 At the far end of Soi Arunee off Thanon Thung Po ⓣ 089 355 4140. Surin's famously long-running guest-house – for years a reason in itself to stop off in Surin – should by now have moved to this new location, in a tranquil spot overlooking ricefields about 1.5km northwest of the train station. Rooms in this modern take on a traditional home are large, simply furnished and share bathrooms, plus there's a four-bed dorm (B100/bed) and garden seating areas. The old guest house, *Pirom's House*, at 242 Thanon Krungsrinai ⓣ 044 515140 may still remain open for overspill guests. ❷

Sangthong Hotel 155–161 Thanon Tannasarn ⓣ 044 512099, ⓕ 044 514329. The best of the budget hotels, this place is friendly, good value and well run. All rooms are large and en suite, and some have air-con and TV. Fan ❶–❷, air-con ❷

Surin Majestic Hotel At the back of the bus station, 99 Thanon Jitbumrung ⓣ 044 713980, ⓦ www.surinmajestic.net. Currently the newest, most modern and nicest hotel in town, where rooms are smartly furnished and all have air-con and TV plus a balcony overlooking the attractive, good-sized ground-floor swimming pool. ❺

The Town

Surin has no special sights of its own, but the **Surin National Museum** (Wed–Sun 9am–4pm; B30; ⓦ www.thailandmuseum.com), inconveniently located 4km south of town on Highway 214 (any Khorat-bound bus will drop you outside), is the place to get a handle on the province's diverse cultural roots and its major attractions, including the Suay elephant-handlers, nearby Khmer ruins and the local silk industry.

Surin's **silk** weave is famous for its variety: seven hundred designs are produced in Surin province alone, many of them of Cambodian origin, including the locally popular rhomboid pattern. Not surprisingly, Surin is one of the best places in the country to buy silk: in high season, there are usually several women selling their cloth around the Tannasarn-Krungsrinai intersection, or you can try Khun Nga's **shop** just outside the *Phetkasem Hotel* off Thanon Jitbumrung; nearby Ruen Mai, at 52 Thanon Jitbumrung, which has a superb selection of silks as well as ready-made silk jackets, bags and accessories, silver jewellery and axe pillows; or Ake Anun Thai Silk at 126 Sanitnikhomrut. For details on visiting local silk-weaving villages, see p.549.

Surin's **elephant round-up**, held every year on the third weekend of November, draws some forty thousand spectators to watch 400 elephants play football, engage in tugs of war and parade in full battle garb. These

Silk production

Most hand-woven **Thai silk** is produced by Isaan village women, some of whom oversee every aspect of sericulture, from the breeding of the silkworm through to the dyeing of the fabric. A principal reason for Isaan's pre-eminence in the silk industry is that its soils are particularly suitable for the growth of mulberry trees, the leaves of which are the **silkworms'** favoured diet. The cycle of production begins with the female silk-moth, which lives just a few days but lays around 300–500 microscopic eggs in that time. The eggs take about nine days to hatch into tiny silkworms, which are then kept in covered rattan trays and fed on mulberry leaves three or four times a day. The silkworms are such enthusiastic eaters that after three or four weeks they will have grown to about 6cm in length (around ten thousand times their original size), ready for the cocoon-building **pupal** stage.

The silkworm constructs its **cocoon** from a single white or yellow fibre that it secretes from its mouth at a rate of 12 centimetres a minute, sealing the filaments with a gummy substance called sericin. The metamorphosis of the pupa into a moth may take as few as two days or as many as seven, but the sericulturist must anticipate the moment at which the new moth is about to break out of the cocoon in order to prevent the destruction of the precious fibre – which at this stage is often 900m long. At the crucial point the cocoon is dropped into boiling water, killing the moth (which is often eaten as a snack) and softening the sericin, so that the unbroken filament can be unravelled. The fibres from several cocoons are "reeled" into a single thread, and two or three threads are subsequently twisted or "thrown" into the yarn known as **raw silk** (broken threads from damaged cocoons are worked into a second-rate yarn called "spun silk"). In most cases, the next stage is the "de-gumming process", in which the raw silk is soaked in soapy water to dissolve the sericin entirely, reducing the weight of the thread by as much as thirty percent and leaving it soft and lustrously semi-transparent. Extremely absorbent and finely textured, reeled silk is the perfect material for **dyeing**; most silk producers now use chemical dyes, though traditional vegetable dyes are making a bit of a comeback. These days, it's not worth the bother for those women who live near town to raise their own silkworms and spin their own thread as they can easily buy Japanese ready-to-weave silk in the market. **Japanese silk** is smoother than Thai silk but lasts only about seven years when woven into a sarong; hand-raised, raw Thai silk is rougher but lasts around forty years, and so is still favoured by women living in remote villages.

Once dyed (or bought), the silk is ready for **weaving**. This is generally done during slack agricultural periods, for example just after the rice is planted and again just after it's harvested. Looms are usually set up in the space under the house, in the sheltered area between the piles, and most are designed to produce a sarong length of around 1m x 2m. Isaan weavers have many different weaving techniques and can create countless patterns, ranging from the simplest single-coloured plain weave for work shirts to exquisitely complex wedding sarongs that may take up to six weeks to complete.

shows last about three hours and give both trainers and animals the chance to practise their skills, but if you arrive early (about 7.30am) you can watch the preliminary street processions when locals set out long trestle tables filled with pineapples, bananas and sugar cane so the elephants munch their way into town. Note that however well controlled the elephants appear, you should always approach them with caution – in the past, frightened and taunted elephants have killed tourists. Tickets cost B200 (for unnumbered seats) or B500 (for numbered VIP seats), and the easiest way to book them is through Saren Travel (see opposite), who can also arrange accommodation and transport if you contact them three months ahead; the Bangkok TAT office should also be able to help, or you could join one of the overnight packages organized by Bangkok travel agencies. If you miss the Surin show, you might catch the lesser round-up in Ayutthaya (see p.268) – or take a trip out to Ban Ta Klang (see p.550).

One of the best reasons for coming to Surin aside from the elephant round-up is to take one of the excellent **local tours** organized from *Pirom & Aree's House 2* (see p.546). Pirom is a highly informed former social worker whose day- and overnight trips give tourists an unusual chance to see glimpses of rural northeastern life as it's really lived. Tours cost from B1200 per person, with prices depending on the destination and the number of people. The village tours feature visits to local silk-weavers and basket-makers, as well as to Ban Ta Klang elephant trainers' village, and it's also possible to do overnight village trips, including one that takes in Khao Phra Viharn, Kong Chiam and Pha Taem. Tours to ancient Khmer ruins cover prasats at Ban Pluang and in the Ta Muean group in a remote area close to the Cambodian border.

Eating and drinking

Aside from a reasonable range of local **restaurants**, Surin boasts a good-sized **night bazaar**, which occupies the eastern end of Thanon Krungsrinai and offers a tasty selection of local food (including roasted crickets and barbecued locusts when in season), as well as stalls selling fashions and toys.

Ba Tee (Pae Ti) 40–42 Thanon Thetsabarn 1 (no English sign, but enter via the shopfront with all the Jack Daniels posters). Huge place that serves the best, and priciest, Chinese food in Surin, including lots of seafood.

Big Ben Southern end of Thanon Tannasarn (no English sign, but easily recognizable from its barbecue-hot-plate tables). A Korean barbecue restaurant, where you select your meat and cook it at your own table. Prices are reasonable and include vegetable dishes and rice. Nightly 4–11pm.

Changtong At the back of the bus terminal, off Thanon Sirat. Despite its unprepossessing location, this is a rather snooty air-con restaurant, serving good Thai food, including *tom yam* and various sea bass dishes, from B60.

Farang Connection At the back of the bus terminal, off Thanon Sirat. The place to come for imported beer, big-screen TV sports, pool, Internet access and the chance to meet local expats. It serves a big menu of everything from fry-ups with baked beans to *som tam* with crab; most mains cost around B70.

Larb Lak Muang A couple of shops west of *Memorial Hotel* on Thanon Lak Muang (no English sign). The best place in town for cheap and tasty servings of the northeastern speciality, *larb* – a spicy salad made with minced meat or fish, dry-roasted rice and lots of lime and chilli.

More Coffee Thanon Tannasarn. Real coffee, milk shakes, a few cakes and white-bread sandwiches. Daily until 9pm.

Raan Ahaan Mangsawirat "Vegetarian" Thanon Lak Muang; no English sign, but look for "Vegetarian" on the glass cabinet and for the trademark small yellow pennant flag. Cheap, canteen-style pre-cooked veggie curries, spicy salads and the like, served over rice for about B30/set. Daily 7am–5pm.

Rot Det Thanon Thetsabarn, the last restaurant on the west side before the junction with Thanon Lak Muang (no English sign but look for the overhanging wooden balcony). Cheap place that's locally renowned for its trademark dish, pork noodle soup. Lunch only.

Surin Vegetarian Center (Raan Ahaan Mangsawirat) 130/5 Thanon Thetsabarn 3. Very similar in style and price to Surin's other veggie restaurant (above) and serving cheap, nutritious vegan meals for around B30 per plate. Daily 7am–3pm.

Ying Dii next to *New Hotel* at 4 Thanon Tannasarn (no English sign). Inexpensive, decent-sized portions of Thai standards (from B40) served with or over rice, right by the train station. Lunch only.

Listings

Banks and exchange Several banks along Thanon Tannasarn have ATMs and currency exchange.

Car and motorcycle rental Saren Travel, 202/1-4 Thanon Thetsabarn 2 (Mon–Sat 8am–7pm; ⓣ044 713828, ⓔsarentour@yahoo.com; outside office hours ⓣ089 949 1185) does car rental with/without driver (from B1500/day), and is an agent for Budget car rental. Ask at *Farang Connection* restaurant, at the back of the bus station (ⓣ044 511509, ⓦwww.farangconnection.com) for help with motorcycle rental.

Hospitals Ruam Phet Hospital, on the eastern arm of Thanon Thetsabarn 1 ⓣ044 513638 & 044 513192; and the government-run Surin Hospital on Thanon Lak Muang ⓣ044 511006 & 044 511757.

Immigration For visa extensions you need to go to the immigration office in Kap Choeng (Mon–Fri 8.30am–4.30pm; ⓣ044 559166), the town nearest Cambodia's Chong Chom border bass, about 50km south of Surin; see p.544 for transport details.

Internet access At *Farang Connection* at the back of the bus station; at Focus Comnet next to Surin Plaza off the north end of Thanon Thetsabarn; opposite *Thong Tarin Hotel* on Thanon Sirat (24hr); and at several other small games centres around town (see map for locations).

Mail The post office is at the Thanon Tannasarn roundabout.

Tours and travel agents Saren Travel 202/1-4 Thanon Thetsabarn 2 (Mon–Sat 8am–7pm; ⓣ044 713828, ⓔsarentour@yahoo.com; outside office hours ⓣ089 949 1185), sells air and train tickets, does car rental (see above), arranges day-trips (from B950 per person), runs transfers to Champasak (Laos) and Siem Reap (Cambodia) and is an outlet for elephant-show tickets. Also offers elephant riding at the village of Ban Ta Thid, from B200–400 per person (see p.551).

Ban Tha Sawang and other silk-weaving villages

Though it is possible to visit the nearby **villages** where women weave most of Surin's silk and cotton, you'll need to go with a guide to get a more behind-the-scenes look at the process, like how the silkworms are bred and how thread is extracted (see p.547 for a summary of the process); you can arrange a guide through *Pirom & Aree's House 2* guest house or Saren Travel. The best months to visit are between November and June, when the women aren't required to work day and night in the fields.

Some of Thailand's most exclusive silk is produced in the village of **Ban Tha Sawang**, 7km west of Surin, which shot to fame when its weavers were chosen to make the fabric for the shirts presented to a Bangkok conference of Asia-Pacific leaders in 2003. The Tha Sawang fabric is gold-brocade silk whose ancient designs are so intricate that it takes four weavers working simultaneously on a single loom a whole day to produce just 6cm. And while a standard everyday *mut mee* sarong might use five heddles (vertical frames of threads that determine the pattern) in its design, a Ban Tha Sawang sarong will use more than 800; not surprisingly, Ban Tha Sawang sarongs cost B30,000 and must be ordered several months in advance. The Ban Tha Sawang weaving centre houses around twenty looms and visitors are welcome to observe the weavers at close quarters. There's a display area across the road, down the asphalt chipping path, where you can see a picture of the APEC leaders in their famous shirts, alongside some fine examples of brocade cloth. Several stalls in the village sell local silk, but not the Ban Tha Sawang brocades. It's possible to get to Ban Tha Sawang by **bus** from Surin, but as there is no English signage or information you'll have a more rewarding experience on a tour. If doing it on your own, flag down any bus from the corner of Thanon Thung Po, just north of the railway tracks in Surin, and get off at the sign "Wat Sameka 300m"; follow the side road on the opposite side of the road from the wat sign for about 1km to reach the weaving centre.

Ban Ta Klang

Fifty-eight kilometres north of Surin, the "elephant village" of **BAN TA KLANG** is the main settlement of the Suay people and training centre for their elephants. One out of every two Ta Klang families owns its own elephant, occasionally using it as a Western farmer would a tractor, but otherwise treating it as a much-loved pet (see box on p.384 for an introduction to the role of the elephant in Thailand). Traditionally regarded as the most expert hunters and trainers of elephants in Thailand, the **Suay** tribe (also known as the Kui people) migrated to the region from Central Asia before the rise of the Khmers in the ninth century. It was the Suay who masterminded the use of elephants in the construction of the great Khmer temples, and a Suay chief who in 1760 helped recapture a runaway white elephant belonging to the king of Ayutthaya, earning the hereditary title "Lord of Surin". Surin was governed by members of the Suay tribe until Rama V's administrative reforms of 1907.

Now that elephants have been replaced almost entirely by modern machinery in the agricultural and logging industries, there's little demand for the Suay mahouts' skills as captors and trainers of wild elephants, but they do occasionally still get called upon by foreign governments with elephant trouble, giving them the chance to observe some of their traditional pre-hunting rituals, including the use of sacred ropes and magic clothing and the keeping of certain taboos. There's some insight into this mysterious aspect of Suay life at the rather desultory **Centre for Elephant Studies** in Ban Ta Klang (daily 8.30am–4.30pm; free), which also covers the zoology of a wild elephant, its anatomy, its historical relationship with humans and the traditional dress and rituals used in sacred elephant ceremonies.

There are currently around sixty **elephants** registered as living in Ban Ta Klang, but because there's not much for them to do around Surin they spend a lot of the year travelling through Thailand with their mahouts, charging curious urbanites for the pleasure of feeding them or even walking under their trunk or belly for good luck (pregnant women who do this are supposedly guaranteed an easy birth). It's not unheard of for a Suay mahout to walk his elephant the 450km from Surin to Bangkok, charging around B20 per limbo en route and earning up to B20,000 a month for his troubles. This doesn't always go down well: town officials view them as a traffic menace, and animal rights' activists see it as cruel.

All of which means you're unlikely to turn up and find Ban Ta Klang teeming with elephants. Mahouts and their elephants do, however, return to Ban Ta Klang every November to help with the rice harvest and to prepare for the annual elephant show in Surin. In addition, every year on the first weekend of November, the elephants compete in **swimming races**, held further up the Mun River in the town of Satuk, 30km west of Ta Klang. A more authentic local elephant spectacle is the annual **monks' ordination ceremony**, held in Ban Ta Klang as part of the preparations for the beginning of Khao Pansa (Buddhist Lent, which usually takes place in May), when young men ride to the temple on ceremonially clad elephants. At other times of the year you might turn up at Ban Ta Klang and not find a single elephant, though you have a better chance if you come on a tour from Surin. Local **buses** to Ban Ta Klang depart approximately hourly from the Surin terminal and take about two hours. If driving yourself, head north along Highway 214 for 36km, turn left at the village of Ban Nong Tad and continue for 22km until you reach Ban Ta Klang.

Five kilometres beyond Ta Klang, the village of **Ban Ta Thid** is also starting to try and entice tourists to ride its resident elephants, a project that is being promoted by Saren Travel in Surin, whose office you should contact for details and tickets (B200–400); the village is accessible on the same bus as the one to Ta Klang.

Khao Phra Viharn, Kantharalak and Si Saket

Perched atop a 547-metre-high spur of the Dangkrek mountains right on the Thai–Cambodian border, about 140km southwest of Ubon Ratchathani and 220km southeast of Surin, the ninth- to twelfth-century Khmer ruins of **KHAO PHRA VIHARN** (also known as Preah Vihear) surpass even the spectacularly set Phanom Rung. A magnificent avenue over 500m long rises to the clifftop sanctuary, from where you get breathtaking views over the jungle-clad hills of Cambodia. The temple buildings themselves, built of grey and yellow sandstone, retain some fine original carvings and have been sufficiently restored to give a good idea of their original structure. Constructed over a three-hundred-year period, Khao Phra Viharn was dedicated to the Hindu god Shiva and is thought to have served both as a retreat for Hindu priests – hence the isolated site – and an object of pilgrimage, with the difficulty of getting there an extra challenge for devotees. The large complex would have also been inhabited by a big cast of supporting villagers who took care of the priests and the pilgrims, and this explains the presence of several large reservoirs on the site.

An added attraction for modern-day tourists is that the whole complex was only reopened to visitors in 1998, following almost a century of **territorial dispute** between Thailand and Cambodia over who owned the site. The situation was further complicated by Cambodia's civil war, with the Khmer Rouge taking control of the temple in 1975 and laying mines around it, making the temple far too dangerous to visit. Although the ruins have now been de-mined, there are skull-and-cross-bones signs in the vicinity, which should be heeded. It's now accepted that the central sanctuary of the Khao Phra Viharn complex stands on Cambodian land (though that didn't prevent another recent neighbourly spat, resulting in the site being closed to everyone from 2001 to 2003), but the temple is very difficult to reach from the Cambodian side of the border, so most visitors arrive via the northern cliffside-staircase, which starts just inside Thailand's southern border. For the tourist, this dual ownership means having to pay both parties to get into the ruins: there's a B200 National Park **entry fee** payable to the Thai authorities about 12km north of the temple car park, at the barrier near the Ban Phum Saron junction (where you have to relinquish your passport); a B5 fee for an "ID check"; and another B200 entry fee at the base of the temple steps, which goes to the Cambodians. In addition to the expense involved, Khao Phra Viharn is very difficult to get to without your own **transport** (see "Practicalities", p.553), often involving an overnight stop in either **Kantharalak** or **Si Saket** – and when you do get there you have to contend with large crowds of tourists and a big gaggle of very persistent hawkers. But, if you can ignore the hassle, the ruins are worth the effort.

The temple car park is lined with souvenir stalls and a score of cheap restaurant shacks. From here it's about 1km to the base of the temple steps – if you can't face the walk, wait for the **shuttle-bus** which ferries people to and fro continuously throughout the day for B5. En route you'll pass the beginning of the path up to the **Pha Mo I Daeng viewpoint**, from where you get a good view of the temple cliff and can just about make out the Khao Phra Viharn complex on its summit. There's not much information on the temple available at the site, so if you have a serious interest in the ruins, buy a copy of the excellent *Preah Vihear* **guidebook** before you come; published by River Books, it's available from most Bangkok bookshops. For a brief guide to the main architectural features and symbolism of Khmer ruins in Thailand see the box on p.537.

The ruins

The approach to the **temple complex** (daily from 8.30am; last entry 3.30pm; total entry fee B405) begins with a steep stairway and continues up the cliff-face via a series of pillared causeways, small terraces with naga balustrades and four cruciform-shaped **gopura** (pavilions), each built with doorways at the cardinal points, and decorated with carved reliefs of tales from Hindu mythology. Beyond the first gopura, as you walk along the first of the pillared causeways, you'll see to the left (east) one of the temple's biggest **reservoirs**, a large stone-lined tank sunk into the cliff and guarded by statues of lions.

As you pass through the last, southernmost, doorway of the second gopura, look back at the door to admire the pediment carving, which depicts the Hindu creation myth, the **Churning of the Sea of Milk**, in which Vishnu appears in his tortoise incarnation and, along with a naga and a sacred mountain (here symbolized by the churning stick), helps churn the cosmic ocean and thereby create the universes, as well as the sacred nectar of immortality; see p.875 for the full story. The third gopura is much larger than the others and is extended by east and west wings. Its central doorways are all decorated with clearly discernible carvings; a particularly eye-catching one above the outside of the northern doorway shows an episode from the Hindu epic the *Mahabarata*, in which the god **Shiva fights with the heroic Arjuna** over who gets the credit for the killing of a wild boar – in fact the carving here looks as if they are enjoying an affectionate embrace. A causeway flanked with two naga balustrades links the third gopura to the fourth; the buildings on either side of the fourth gopura are thought to have been libraries.

The ascent of the cliff-face finally reaches its climax at the **central sanctuary**, built on the summit and enclosed within a courtyard whose impressive colonnaded galleries are punctuated by windows to the east and west. Cambodian monks tend the modern Buddha image inside the sanctuary, keeping a fire burning and selling offertory garlands and incense to tourists. The pediment above the northern entrance to this shrine is carved with an image of the multi-armed **dancing Shiva**, whose ecstatic dance brings about the destruction of the existing world and the beginning of a new epoch (see p.875). Climb through one of the gallery windows to walk across to the cliff edge, from where you get far-reaching views of Cambodia, and can appreciate just how isolated the temple must have been. A look back at the temple complex shows that though the sanctuary's southernmost wall is punctuated by a couple of beautifully carved false doors, there are no genuine south-facing doors or windows – experts assume that this was a deliberate design feature to stop priests being distracted by the clifftop panorama.

Practicalities: Kantharalak and Si Saket

Khao Phra Viharn is not served by public **transport**, so by far the easiest way of getting to the ruins is to rent a car (with or without driver) or motorbike from Ubon Ratchathani, Surin or Si Saket, all of which have a range of hotels and good long-distance transport connections. Alternatively, you could take a motorbike taxi to the temple from the nearest sizeable town to Khao Phra Viharn, **Kantharalak**, or from the road junction and national park barriers at Ban Phum Saron.

Kantharalak

KANTHARALAK is located just off the Khao Phra Viharn-Si Saket road (Highway 221), 36km north of the temple. There's an hourly **bus** service here from Ubon Ratchathani (1hr 30min), which departs from a terminus just across the Mun River in Ubon's Warinchamrab suburb, and a half-hourly bus service from Si Saket; buses arrive at Kantharalak **bus station** (ⓣ045 661486), 50m from the market on the main street, Thanon Sinpradit.

There is no **songthaew** service from Kantharalak to the temple, but occasional songthaews do connect Kantharalak with **Ban Phum Saron**, the junction near the national-park barrier 12km north of Khao Phra Viharn, from where you can get a **motorbike taxi** to the temple; you can also get a motorbike taxi all the way from Kantharalak to Khao Phra Viharn (about B100 each way).

Kantharalak is a two-street town, with the best of the budget **hotels**, the friendly, English-speaking *Kantharalak Hotel* (ⓣ045 661085; ❸–❹), on the main street at 131/35–36 Thanon Sinpradit, about 1km off Highway 221; its rooms, scruffy but serviceable (the better ones are upstairs), are set back off the road, all with en-suite bathrooms and TV, and some with air-con.

Si Saket

The quiet provincial capital of **SI SAKET** is a more enjoyable place to base yourself than Kantharalak, with a better choice of hotels, a good night market and decent transport connections; however, it is 98km from Khao Phra Viharn. Si Saket **train station** (ⓣ045 611525) is in the centre of the town; the **bus station** (ⓣ045 612500) is in the southern part of town and connects Si Saket with Ubon Ratchathani, Phibun Mangsahan, Chong Mek, Surin and Bangkok, but there are no buses from here to Khao Phra Viharn, so you have to get the #523 to Kantharalak (hourly; 2hr) and make onward arrangements from there. You should also be able to get buses from here to **Sa Ngam** for access to the **Cambodian border crossing** to Choam (for Anlong Veng and Siem Reap).

For **hotels** within easy walking distance of the train station, try the passable *Phrompinan* (ⓣ045 612677, ⓕ045 612696; fan ❷, air-con ❷–❸), at 849/1 Thanon Lak Muang (about 200m west of the train station on the road that parallels the rail line to the south), whose ground-floor fan rooms are grotty and to be avoided, though the upstairs air-con ones are much more comfortable and reasonable value. Or there's the *Kessiri Hotel*, at 1102–5 Thanon Khukan (ⓣ045 614007, ⓕ045 614008; ❺), which is the most comfortable place in town, with good (frequently discounted) rooms, all furnished with TV and air-con, and there's a restaurant downstairs; Thanon Khukan runs south from the rail line from a point some 150m east of the train station.

The best place to **eat** in town is the lip-smackingly diverse night market, which sets up around a small plaza along the southern edge of the rail line. Otherwise there are half a dozen small Thai-Chinese restaurants on Thanon Khukan, between the *Kessiri Hotel* and the rail line; along this road you'll also find several handicraft shops selling locally produced lengths of silk and triangular axe pillows.

Ubon Ratchathani

East of Si Saket, the sprawling provincial capital of **UBON RATCHATHANI** (almost always referred to simply as Ubon – not to be confused with Udon, aka Udon Thani, to the north) holds little in the way of attractions beyond a couple of wats and a decent museum. It's only really worth visiting in order to make trips out: east to Kong Chiam beside the Mekong River (see p.560) and the Lao border market at Chong Mek (see p.562), or southwest to the Khmer ruins of Khao Phra Viharn (see p.551), astride the Cambodian border.

If you're near Ubon in early July, however, you should definitely consider coming into town for the local **Asanha Puja** festivities, an auspicious Buddhist holiday celebrated all over Thailand to mark the beginning of Khao Pansa, the annual three-month Buddhist retreat. Ubon's version of this festival is the most spectacular in the country: each of the city's temples makes a huge wooden or plaster sculpture, coats it in orange beeswax and then carves intricate decorations in the wax. The sculptures are mounted on floats around enormous candles and paraded through the town – hence the tourist name for the celebrations, the **Ubon Candle Festival** – before being judged and then returned to

City bus and songthaew routes

Ubon is fairly well served by a fleet of numbered and differently coloured **city buses and songthaews**, which charge a flat fare of B8. They are especially useful for getting to the train station and regional bus depots in Warinchamrab. The following are some of the most useful routes for hotels, sights and transport terminals – not all pass the front door, but should leave you with no more than a five-minute walk; buses cover the same routes in reverse.

#1 (grey/white): Ban Nong Kae–Thanon Jaengsanit–Thanon Sumpasit–Thanon Buraphanai–Thanon Phromthep–Thanon Upparat–Nakorn Chai Bus Terminal–Talat Warinchamrab (for Kong Chiam and Chong Mek buses)–Ubon University.

#2 (white): Main Bus Terminal–Thanon Chayangkun (for a 600-metre-walk to Wat Nong Bua; *Tokyo Hotel*)–Thanon Phichitrangsarn–Thanon Luang (for post office)–Thanon Khuenthani (for TAT, hotels and museum)–Thanon Upparat–Nakorn Chai Bus Terminal–Talat Warinchamrab (for Kong Chiam and Chong Mek buses)–*River Moon Guest House* –Warinchamrab train station.

#3 (pink): Main Bus Terminal–Thanon Chayangkun (for a 600-metre-walk to Wat Nong Bua)–Thanon Sumpasit–Thanon Luang (for post office)–Thanon Khuenthani (for TAT, hotels and museum)–Thanon Phrommathep (for *Sri Isan* hotel–Nakorn Chai Bus Terminal–Talat Warinchamrab (for Kong Chiam and Chong Mek buses)–Wat Nong Pha Phum.

#6 (pink): Thanon Sumpasit west–Thanon Phichitrangsam west–Thanon Chayangkun (for *Tokyo Hotel*)–Thanon Upparat (for museum, Thanon Khuenthani hotels and TAT)–Nakorn Chai Bus Terminal–Talat Warinchamrab (for Kong Chiam and Chong Mek buses)–Warin army base.

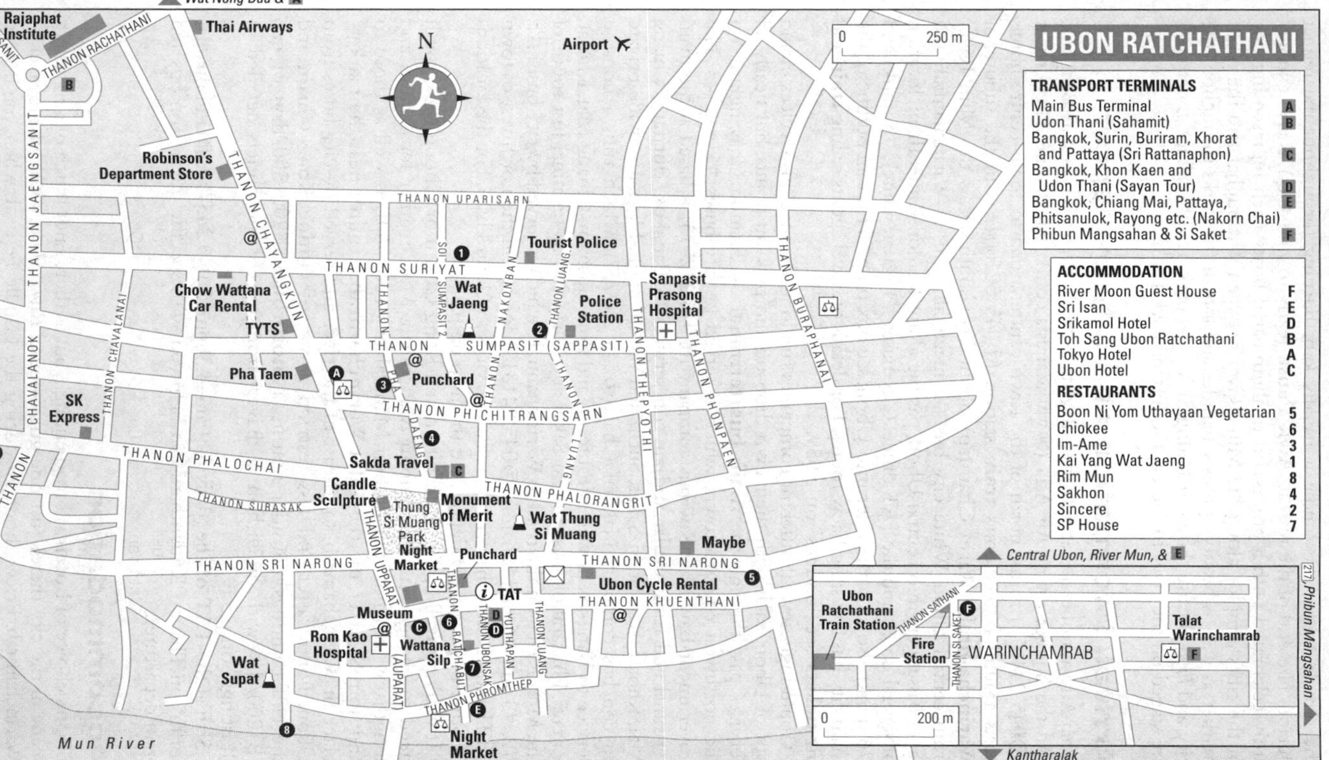
UBON RATCHATHANI
TRANSPORT TERMINALS
Main Bus Terminal A
Udon Thani (Sahamit) B
Bangkok, Surin, Buriram, Khorat and Pattaya (Sri Rattanaphon) C
Bangkok, Khon Kaen and Udon Thani (Sayan Tour) D
Bangkok, Chiang Mai, Pattaya, Phitsanulok, Rayong etc. (Nakorn Chai) E
Phibun Mangsahan & Si Saket F
ACCOMMODATION
River Moon Guest House F
Sri Isan E
Srikamol Hotel D
Toh Sang Ubon Ratchathani B
Tokyo Hotel A
Ubon Hotel C
RESTAURANTS
Boon Ni Yom Uthayaan Vegetarian 5
Chiokee 6
Im-Ame 3
Kai Yang Wat Jaeng 1
Rim Mun 8
Sakhon 4
Sincere 2
SP House 7
0 250 m
N
Wat Nong Bua & A
Rajaphat Institute
Thai Airways
Airport
JAENGSANIT
THANON RACHATHANI
Robinson's Department Store
THANON JAENGSANIT
THANON CHAYANGKUN
THANON UPARISARN
Tourist Police
THANON SURIYAT
SOI SUMPASIT 2
Wat Jaeng
THANON NAKONBAN
THANON LUANG
Police Station
Sanpasit Prasong Hospital
THANON BURAPHANAI
Chow Wattana Car Rental
TYTS
THANON CHAVALANAI
THANON SUMPASIT (SAPPASIT)
Pha Taem
Punchard
THANON PHA DAENG
THANON PHICHITRANGSARN
THANON THEPYOTHI
THANON PHONPAEN
SK Express
THANON CHAVALANOK
THANON PHALOCHAI
Sakda Travel
Candle Sculpture
THANON SURASAK
Thung Si Muang Park
Monument of Merit
Wat Thung Si Muang
THANON PHALORANGRIT
Maybe
THANON SRI NARONG
Night Market
Punchard
THANON UPPARAT
TAT
Ubon Cycle Rental
THANON KHUENTHANI
Museum
Rom Kao Hospital
Wattana Silp
(AUPARAT)
THANON RATCHABUT
THANON UBONSAK
YUTTHAPAN
THANON LUANG
THANON PHROMTHEP
Wat Supat
Night Market
Mun River
F, E, F (See Inset) & Train Station
Central Ubon, River Mun, & E
Ubon Ratchathani Train Station
THANON SATHANI
Fire Station
THANON SI SAKET
WARINCHAMRAB
Talat Warinchamrab
217 Phibun Mangsahan
0 200 m
Kantharalak

the temple, where the candle is usually kept burning throughout the retreat period. The end of the retreat, **Awk Pansa** (early to mid-Oct), is also exuberantly celebrated with a procession of illuminated boats, each representing one of the city's temples, along the Mun River between Wat Suphat and the night market, as well as beauty contests, parades and lots of fireworks throughout the city, and *likay* theatre shows in Thung Si Muang park. Traditional longboat races are staged on the river in the days following Awk Pansa.

Arrival, information and city transport

Thai Airways operates at least two **flights** a day between Ubon and Bangkok, and the budget airline Air Asia (Ⓦwww.airasia.com) at least one. The airport (Ⓣ045 244073) is just north of the town centre; a taxi to town-centre hotels costs around B70. Ubon's **train** station (Ⓣ045 321004) is in the suburb of **Warinchamrab** (Warin Chamrap), about 2km south across the Mun River from central Ubon. White city bus #2 meets all trains at Warinchamrab and takes passengers into central Ubon, passing along Thanon Khuenthani, location of several hotels and the TAT office. City buses #1 (grey/white), #3 (pink) and #6 (pink) also cross the river into Ubon; see box on p.554 for an outline of the main city bus and songthaew routes. For details of travel agents selling **train** and **air tickets**, see "Listings" on p.559.

Confusingly, several different companies run long-distance bus services in and out of Ubon, each with their own drop-off and pick-up points, but nearly all services pass through the **main bus terminal** on Thanon Chayangkun, on the northwest edge of town, which is served by city buses #2 and #3. The government Baw Kaw Saw bus company (Ⓣ045 312773) is based at the main terminal and runs regular and air-con services to Bangkok, Buriram, Chiang Mai, Khorat, Roi Et, Si Saket, Surin and Yasothon; the big, nationwide private air-con bus company Nakorn Chai (Ⓣ045 269777), which runs a nonstop service to Bangkok as well as routes to and from Buriram, Chiang Mai, Khorat, Pattaya, Phitsanulok, Rayong, Si Saket and Surin, has its terminal just south of the Mun River, on the road to Warinchamrab, which is served by city buses #1, #2, #3 and #6; and Sahamit (Ⓣ045 241319), located in the northwest of town off Thanon Ratchathani, runs air-con services to Udon Thani. For the locations of other bus company depots, see the map on p.554.

If you're travelling between Ubon and Kong Chiam or Chong Mek you'll need to change buses at Phibun Mangsahan. Most regular local buses and songthaews to and from Phibun Mangsahan (see p.560), as well as those to and from Si Saket, use the **Talat Warinchamrab** terminal near the marketplace in Warinchamrab, southeast of the river and served by city buses from Ubon. For a faster and less restrictive way of visiting Kong Chiam and the cliff paintings, consider renting a **motorbike** (B200–500/day) or **car** (B1200/day with or without a driver) from one of the outlets detailed in "Listings" on p.559.

Staff at the **TAT office** (daily 8.30am–4.30pm; Ⓣ045 243770, Ⓔtatubon@tat.or.th) on Thanon Khuenthani can help you with specific queries on bus and train departures.

Accommodation

Ubon's choice of **hotels** is broad enough, but as there's not much of a travellers' scene in the city there's just one guest house, *River Moon*, south of the river in Warinchamrab. Prices shoot up during the Candle Festival, when you'll need to book a room as far ahead as possible.

River Moon Guest House 21 Thanon Si Saket 2, Warinchamrab ⓣ045 286093, ⓔPhanth_Boonjob@yahoo.com. Ubon's only guest house comprises a group of five old wooden houses, each with a couple of very basic fan rooms upstairs and shared bathrooms downstairs. It's cheap but pretty dilapidated. It's about 300m from the train station or 500m from the Talat Warinchamrab bus terminal. From the main bus terminal in Ubon, take city bus #2 across the Mun River to the guest house or train station in Warinchamrab. ❶

Sri Isan 62 Thanon Ratchabut ⓣ045 261011, ⓦwww.sriisanhotel.com. This small, quite classy hotel enjoys a good location in Ubon's old quarter, just across from the market and night market, and a mere 100 metres from the river. Its forty rooms are set around an open-roofed atrium and all have air-con and cable TV. ❹

Srikamol Hotel 26 Thanon Ubonsak ⓣ045 241136, ⓕ045 243792. To make the most of the expansive city views ask for a room on the top, seventh, floor of this good-value mid-range hotel in the heart of downtown Ubon. Rooms are comfortable, unusually large and air-conditioned. ❹

Toh Sang Ubon Ratchathani 251 Thanon Phalochai ⓣ045 245531, ⓦwww.tohsang.com. The poshest hotel in town, with comfortable air-con rooms in a peaceful but rather inconvenient location 1km west of Thanon Chayangkun or about 2km from TAT. City songthaews #4 and #8 pass the door. ❻–❽

Tokyo Hotel 178 Thanon Chayangkun ⓣ045 241739, ⓕ045 241262. About a 5min walk north of the museum, this is most budget travellers' first choice in central Ubon. Although you can choose between fan and air-con rooms in either the old block or the new wing, they are mostly pretty shabby though decent enough, and nearly all come with cable. Old wing ❷, new wing ❸

Ubon Hotel 333 Thanon Khuenthani ⓣ045 241045, ⓕ045 209020. Centrally located place offering fan rooms that are almost as cheap as the old ones at *Tokyo*, and in better condition, as well as basic air-con versions. Fan ❷, air-con ❸

The City

Central Ubon is easy enough to negotiate, with the main accommodation and eating area confined to a fairly compact rectangle between Thanon Sumpasit (Sappasit) in the north and the Mun River in the south. The centrepiece of this area is **Thung Si Muang Park** and its unmissable landmark, the 22-metre-high **Candle Sculpture**, an enormous yellow-painted replica of the wax sculptures that star in the annual Candle Festival. This particular sculpture was inspired by a story written by the King and features a boat with an enormous garuda figurehead that's ploughing past various figures who are apparently being devoured by sea monsters. In the northeast corner of the park stands a much more unassuming memorial in the shape of a three-metre-high obelisk. Known as the **Monument of Merit**, it was erected by a group of POWs who wanted to show their gratitude to the people of Ubon for their support during

△ Temple roof, Ubon Ratchathani

World War II. Despite the real threat of punishment by the Japanese occupiers, between 1941 and 1943 Ubon citizens secretly donated food and clothes to the POWs imprisoned in a nearby camp.

South from the park across Thanon Sri Narong and also accessible from Thanon Khuenthani, **Ubon Ratchathani National Museum** (Wed–Sun 9am–4pm; B30; ⓦwww.thailandmuseum.com) is airily designed around a central courtyard and offers a good overview of the history, geology and culture of southern Isaan, with well-labelled displays on everything from rock formations to folk crafts and musical instruments. Especially notable are a couple of very fine Khmer sculptures: a ninth-century statue of Ganesh and, in the same room, an eleventh-century lintel carved with nine little archways containing nine Hindu deities astride their nine different vehicles, each figure just 20cm high. Elsewhere you'll find examples of the star-embroidered fabric that is a speciality of Ubon, and a pre-fourth-century bronze bell and ceremonial drum found in the vicinity.

Of the city's eight main wats, **Wat Thung Si Muang**, a few hundred metres east of Thung Si Muang Park, along Thanon Sri Narong, is the most noteworthy, mainly for its unusually well-preserved teak library – or *ho trai* – which is raised on stilts over an artificial pond to keep book-devouring insects at bay. The murals in the bot, to the left of the library, have also survived remarkably well: the lively scenes of everyday life in the nineteenth century include musicians playing *khaen* pipes and devotees performing characteristic Isaan merit-making dances, as well as conventional portraits of city life in Bangkok.

Off Thanon Chayangkun near the main bus terminal at the northern edge of town, the much more modern **Wat Nong Bua** (city bus #2 or #3) is modelled on the stupa at Bodh Gaya in India, scene of the Buddha's enlightenment; the whitewashed replica is carved with scenes from the *Jataka* and contains a scaled-down version of the stupa covered in gold leaf. Of more interest, especially if you don't happen to be here during the Candle Festival, is the wax float kept in a small building behind the chedi.

Silk, cotton and silverware are all good buys in Ubon. The biggest selection of clothes made from the stripey rough **cotton** weaves peculiar to the Ubon area is at Maybe, on the eastern end of Thanon Sri Narong. You'll find cotton tableware and clothes made to local designs, as well as Ubon's best collection of **northeastern crafts**, at Punchard, which has one branch at 128–130 Thanon Ratchabut, 50m east of the museum, and another on Thanon Pha Daeng. Both shops specialize in fine-quality regional goods, like triangular axe pillows (*mawn khwaan*) and lengths of **silk**, and also deal in antique farm and household implements.

Eating

Ubon is a good place for sampling local Isaan specialities, you can enjoy either in air-conditioned comfort at the restaurants listed below, or at one of the city's night markets: behind the day market on the north bank of the Mun River; on Thanon Ratchabut (north off Thanon Khuenthani); and on the sidewalk next to the *Tokyo Hotel*.

Boon Ni Yom Uthayaan Vegetarian Restaurant and Centre Thanon Sri Narong; no English sign but its barn-like, open-sided wooden structure is unmistakeable. Famous, canteen-style veggie place that's run by members of a Buddhist organization who grow, sell and cook their own produce. All sorts of meat substitutes and tasty veg and tofu dishes are on offer here at very cheap per-plate prices (B15–30). Tues–Sun 6am–2pm.

Chiokee Thanon Khuenthani. Café-style place serving a large menu of Thai and Western staples (B20–60). Especially popular at breakfast time, when Westerners come for the ham and eggs, local office workers for rice gruel. Daily 5am–10pm.

Im-Ame Thanon Pha Daeng (no English sign). Air-con place that's renowned for its Isaan specialities, but also serves dishes from other parts of Thailand. Main dishes from B60. Daily 10am–10pm.

Kai Yang Wat Jaeng Thanon Suriyat, close to the junction with Soi Sumpasit (Sappasit) 2. This simple streetside restaurant is famous across town for its signature barbecued chicken (*kai yang*), which it serves at lunchtime only, for B20–40. Daily 9am–3pm.

Rim Mun On the river bank near Wat Supat. Floating restaurant that makes the most of the breeze from the river and specializes in fish dishes (B60–130). Daily 10am–10pm.

Sakhon 66–70 Thanon Pha Daeng. Another of Ubon's top northeastern restaurants, particularly recommended for its more unusual dishes, like *tom yam* with fish eggs and red ant eggs. Most dishes B60–150. Daily 11am–10pm.

Sincere 126/1 Thanon Sumpasit. Highly regarded, predominantly French menu (most dishes B60–130), with an emphasis on steaks and classic sauces. Mon–Sat 11am–10pm.

SP House Thanon Ratchabut. Local outlet of the chain of bakery and ice-cream shops that's a reliable source of coffee, cakes and sundaes and is usually packed out with schoolkids. Daily 8am–9pm.

Listings

Airline The Thai Airways office is at 364 Thanon Chayangkun ⓣ045 263916, in the north part of town.

Car, motorbike and bicycle rental Bicycle rental from Ubon Cycle Rental, 115 Thanon Sri Narong, east of the post office (ⓣ045 242813; B100/24hr); motorbikes and cars from Chow Wattana at 39/8 Thanon Suriyat, opposite Nikko Massage ⓣ045 242202, and at the airport; Budget car rental at the airport (ⓣ045 240507, ⓦwww.budget.co.th), through SK Express, near the *Toh Sang* hotel on Thanon Phalochai ⓣ045 264712, and the *Sri Isan* hotel; car plus driver (B1500) through Sakda Travel World offices at 234 Thanon Phalorangrit, central Ubon ⓣ045 243560, ⓦwww.sakda.com and 150/1 Thanon Kantharalak in Warinchamrab ⓣ045 32151.

Exchange At several banks and ATMs, including next to TAT on Thanon Khuenthani and on Thanon Ratchabut.

Hospitals Rom Kao Hospital, near the museum on Thanon Upparat (ⓣ045 244658), is well regarded and has English-speaking staff and a dental clinic.

Immigration office In the town of Phibun Mangsahan (see below), 45km east of Ubon (Mon–Fri 8.30am–4.30pm; ⓣ045 441108).

Internet access At the community library across from the Khuenthani/Upparat junction and at various small Internet centres around town (see map on p.555).

Mail The GPO is centrally located at the Thanon Sri Narong/Thanon Luang intersection.

Telephones The TOT telephone office is next to the GPO on the Thanon Sri Narong/Thanon Luang intersection.

Tourist police For all emergencies, call the tourist police on the free, 24hr phone line ⓣ1155, or contact them at their office on Thanon Suriyat ⓣ045 244941.

Travel agents Sakda Travel World, at 234 Thanon Phalorangrit, central Ubon ⓣ045 243560, ⓦwww.sakda.com and at 150/1 Thanon Kantharalak in Warinchamrab ⓣ045 32151, sells air tickets, does guided tours around Isaan and into Laos, and offers car plus driver from B1500 per day; SK Express, near the *Toh Sang* hotel on Thanon Phalochai ⓣ045 264712, also sells air tickets and is an agent for Budget car rental.

Around Ubon

On the whole, the area **around Ubon** is a good deal more interesting than the metropolitan hub, particularly if you venture eastwards towards the appealing Mekong riverside town of **Kong Chiam**, the prehistoric paintings at **Pha Taem** and the Lao border market at **Chong Mek**. Nearly all the routes detailed on the following pages can be done as a day-trip from Ubon – most comfortably with your own transport, but manageable on buses and songthaews if you set off very early in the morning – though there's a lot to be said for taking things more slowly and spending a night or two in the rural reaches of Ubon Ratchathani province.

Phibun Mangsahan

There are several routes east out of Ubon, but they nearly all begin with Highway 217, which starts in Ubon's southern suburb of Warinchamrab and then follows the Mun River east for 45km before splitting into two at the town of **Phibun Mangsahan**. From here, Highway 217 continues southeast to the border at Chong Mek, while the northeasterly fork out of Phibun, called Route 2222, follows the course of the Mun to its confluence with the Mekong at Kong Chiam.

Sited at a turbulent point of the Mun called Kaeng Saphue (*kaeng* means rapids), Phibun Mangsahan (known locally as Phibun) has little more to it than a central bus station and a sprawling market, but for travellers it's an inevitable interchange on any eastbound journey. In April, Phibun celebrates the Thai New Year festival of Songkhran by staging performances of Isaan folk music and dance beside the Kaeng Saphue rapids; these **Maha Songkhran** festivities run from April 12 to 15. Phibun's one exceptional sight, **Wat Phokakaew**, stands on the western outskirts of town, 1km before you get to the town limit, and is signposted off Highway 217. An unusually attractive modern temple, it's worth a look for its elegant proportions, eye-catchingly tiled exterior and fine naga-encircled platform from where you can see the hills of Laos on the horizon. The wat's interior walls are decorated with reliefs of twelve of Thailand's most revered temples, including Wat Saket's Golden Mount in Bangkok and Nakhon Pathom's monumental chedi. The space under the temple has been converted into a serene meditation hall.

To get to Phibun from Ubon, take a city bus across the river to the Talat Warinchamrab bus station and change on to a Phibun-bound bus, which depart several times an hour until 4.30pm. In Phibun, buses terminate at the **bus station** behind the market in the town centre, where you can change onto the songthaews that run to Chong Mek. Kong Chiam songthaews leave from **Kaeng Saphue bridge**, a short tuk-tuk ride or ten-minute walk from Phibun's bus station: exit the bus station through the market to the main road, turn right and walk the few hundred metres to the main highway (passing currency exchange and Internet facilities on the way), then turn left to reach the river and the songthaew stop.

Kong Chiam and the Pha Taem paintings

The riverside village of **KONG CHIAM** (pronounced Kong Jiem) is a popular destination for day-tripping Thais, who drive out here to see the somewhat fancifully named "two-coloured river" for which the village is nationally renowned. Created by the merging of the muddy brown Mun with the muddy brown Mekong at "the easternmost point of Thailand", the water is hardly an irresistible attraction, but the village has a certain tranquil appeal. Comprising little more than a collection of wooden houses, the requisite post office, school and police station, a few guest houses, several restaurants and two wats, Kong Chiam feels like an island, with the Mun defining its southern limit and the Mekong its northern one. A paved walkway runs several hundred metres along the banks of the Mekong, passing the district office and running down to the large *sala* that's built right over the confluence and affords uninterrupted views. Behind the *sala*, **Wat Kong Chiam** is the more charming of the village's two temples and has an old wooden bell tower in its compound; the cliffside **Wat Tham Khu Ha Sawan**, located near the point where Route 2222 turns into Kong Chiam, is unprepossessing, with a huge modern Buddha image staring down on the villagers below.

Kong Chiam's sights are thin on the ground, but you can rent motorbikes from *Apple Guest House* and explore the area, or charter a **longtail boat** for a trip up the Mekong River, taking in the Pha Taem cliff-paintings on the way (B800/boat). Even though Laos is just a few hundred metres away from Kong Chiam, on the other bank of the Mekong, foreigners are not supposed to cross the border here, though if you're keen to step on to Lao soil you can usually persuade boatmen to take you there and back for B400 per boat, with a quick stop at the bankside village of Ban Mai; the official border crossing is further downstream at Chong Mek (see p.563).

Pha Taem cliff-paintings

The most popular outing from Kong Chiam is a visit to the **Pha Taem cliff-paintings**, contained within Pha Taem National Park (daily 5am–6pm; B200, kids B100), which cover a 170-metre stretch of cliff-face 18km up the Mekong. Clear proof of the antiquity of the fertile Mekong valley, these bold, childlike paintings are believed to be between 3000 and 4000 years old, the work of rice-cultivating settlers who lived in huts rather than caves. Protected from the elements by an overhang, the red paint – a mixture of soil, tree gum and fat – has kept its colour so well that the shapes and figures are still clearly discernible; human forms, handprints and geometric designs appear in groups alongside massive depictions of animals and enormous fish – possibly the prized catfish still caught in the Mekong.

Pha Taem (Taem Cliff) is clearly signposted from Kong Chiam, but try to avoid coming here on a weekend when the place gets swamped with scores of tour buses. It's an especially popular spot at sunrise, this being the first place in Thailand to see the sun in the morning – a full eighteen minutes ahead of Phuket, the westernmost point. Unless you rent a motorbike, you'll have to hitch all the way or charter a tuk-tuk or taxi from the village – ask at *Apple Guest House* for advice. The road passes a group of weird, mushroom-shaped sandstone rock formations known as **Sao Chaliang** before reaching the Pha Taem car park, site of several foodstalls and the visitor centre, on top of the cliff. From the car park, follow the path that's signed "Pha Taem Loop 3km", which runs down the cliff-face and along the shelf in the rock to the paintings. If you continue along the path past the paintings, you'll eventually climb back up to the top of the cliff again, via the **viewpoint** at Pha Mon, taking in fine views of the fertile Mekong valley floor and glimpses of hilly western Laos. It's about 1700m from Pha Mon back to the car park, along a signed trail across the rocky scrub. Should you feel inclined to stay and catch the sunrise, you can rent national park **bungalows** (B1200 for up to ten people) and large 2-person tents (B150) near the national-park checkpoint at Sao Chaliang, about 2km before the car park; these must be booked in advance through the Pha Taem office (Ⓣ045 249780, ⒺPHATAEM_3@hotmail.com, or via Ⓦwww.dnp.go.th/National_park.asp).

Practicalities

Kong Chiam is 30km northeast of Phibun, along Route 2222, or 75km from Ubon. Kong Chiam-bound **songthaews** leave Phibun Mangsahan's Kaeng Saphue bridge every half-hour throughout the morning and then hourly until 3.30pm, and take an hour to an hour and a half. Four daily buses run between Kong Chiam and Bangkok in both directions. Songthaews and buses terminate at the Kong Chiam **bus station** at the west end of Thanon Kaewpradit, Kong Chiam's main drag. If you have your own transport, Kong Chiam combines well with visits to Chong Mek (just 27km away) and Kaeng Tana National Park;

Apple Guest House rents motorbikes for B200 per day. There's a small **minimarket** and a **pharmacy** on Thanon Kaewpradit, along with a bank that has an **exchange** facility, but no ATM.

Accommodation

Kong Chiam has a nice range of reasonably priced guest houses and "resorts", which is a good incentive to stay over in this pleasant, slow-paced village.

Apple Guest House Opposite the post office on Thanon Kaewpradit, but also accessible from Thanon Phukamchai, about a 5min walk from the bus station and the Mekong ⓣ045 351160. The most traveller-oriented place in Kong Chiam, this is a convivial setup with decent en-suite rooms around a yard, as well as a restaurant, motorbike rental and a useful noticeboard. The pricier rooms have air-con. Fan ❶, air-con ❷

Araya Resort Towards the eastern end of Thanon Phukamchai, 10min walk from the bus station ⓣ045 351191. Good-value set of steeply roofed, whitewashed, chalet-style bungalows, built around a garden with several ponds; the rooms are comfortable and have air-con, hot water and TV. Price depends on the view, as the best look straight ahead over trees to distant Lao hilltops. ❸–❹

Ban Kiang Nam Resort Towards the eastern end of Thanon Kaewpradit ⓣ045 351374. Immaculate, prettily painted set of nine terraced rooms and detached chalet-style bungalows, all furnished in cosy fashion and featuring air-con and TV. ❹–❼

Ban Rim Khong Resort 37 Thanon Kaewpradit ⓣ045 351101. Also has another entrance one block north on the road in front of the Mekong River, between the district office and the wat. Great-looking little resort with half a dozen timbered chalets wreathed in bougainvillea and ranged round a lawn, plus a couple of fabulous riverside ones (#1 and #2, worth phoning ahead to reserve) with huge verandas overlooking the Mekong. The interiors are nothing special but all are spacious and have air-con, TV and fridge, and there are discounts for stays of more than one night. ❻

Toh Sang Kong Chiam On the south bank of the Mun ⓣ045 351174, ⓦwww.tohsang.com. Romantically located upmarket resort where all rooms have balconies overlooking the river and are very comfortably, if a little kitschly, furnished. There's a swimming pool, table-tennis room, spa, Internet access and bicycle and kayak rental, plus a couple of restaurants and boat trips to Pha Taem and other riverside sights. Well-priced (discounts are often available), but inaccessible by public transport and about 10km from Kong Chiam; with your own wheels, follow Highway 2134 south past Kong Chiam bus station, cross the river, take the first left and then continue for 7km, following signs for Ban Woen Buk. ❽–❾

Eating

The most popular places to eat are, not surprisingly, the two **floating restaurants**, *Araya* and *Nam Poon*, moored on the Mekong in front of the district office. Neither is signed in English, but there's little to choose between them as both serve fairly pricey menus of Thai-Chinese dishes and, of course, plenty of fish. Be sure to ask if they have any *pla buk*, the giant catfish that is very much a local speciality (see box on p.443). There are a string of cheaper, less flashy little restaurants on the river bank behind the floating restaurants, including the friendly *Rim Khong*, next to the two riverside *Rim Khong* bungalows, along with a few food vendors. Away from the river, about 10m east of the bus station on Thanon Kaewpradit, the (unsigned) restaurant-shack *Tuk Tik Tham Mua* serves up good local dishes at good cheap prices: spicy papaya (*som tam*), green bean salads (*yam thua fak yao*), grilled fish (*ping plaa*) and chicken (*ping kai*), all served with individual baskets of sticky rice.

To Chong Mek and the Lao border

Nine kilometres east out of Phibun, Route 2172 forks south off the main Highway 217 and heads straight to the so-called **Emerald Triangle**, the spot where Thailand, Laos and Cambodia meet (the name echoes the more famous border area in north Thailand, the Golden Triangle, where Thailand, Laos and

Burma meet). A further 10km along Highway 217, the road begins to run alongside one of the largest reservoirs in Isaan (measuring some 43km north to south), held back by the **Sirindhorn dam**, and dotted with permanent fishing-net platforms. Thirteen kilometres later, Route 2296 veers north off Highway 217 to take traffic across the Mun River via the **Pak Mun dam** (whose construction and ill-thought-out design continues to cause controversy more than a decade after its completion in 1994) and on to Kong Chiam. **Kaeng Tana National Park** (B200; kids B100) is signed just off the dam road, but offers only a couple of short trails through predominantly scrubby vegetation to waterfalls and caves.

Chong Mek and crossing into Laos

Disregarding all deviations, Highway 217 finally ends at the village of **CHONG MEK** on the Lao border, 44km east of Phibun Mangsahan and site of a busy Thai-Lao market and one of the legal border crossings for foreigners. Large pale-blue **songthaews** leave approximately hourly between 7am and 3.30pm from Phibun Mangsahan bus station, taking about an hour and a half to reach Chong Mek. There is also a daily **bus** between Chong Mek and Bangkok, departing Chong Mek market at 4pm, arriving at Mo Chit Northern Bus terminal about eleven hours later.

It's now possible to get a Lao **visa** on arrival at Chong Mek **border crossing**, but you'll be charged US$30 and will only receive a fifteen-day visa – half the time-period of the cheaper visas issued at the Lao consulate in Khon Kaen (see p.571); you'll also need two passport photos. If you get an advance visa from Khon Kaen or elsewhere, it must specify Chong Mek as the entry point (see p.33 for more information). Whichever option you choose, once at Chong Mek you first need to get the Thai exit stamp from the office hidden behind the market on the Thai side (daily 8.30am–noon & 1–4.30pm; ⓣ045 485107); having crossed over to the Lao side of the market, Vangtao, you pass via the Lao immigration office (official hours: Mon–Fri 8am–4pm; "surcharge" hours, Mon–Fri 4–6pm, Sat, Sun & hols 8.30am–6pm), where you need to pay US$1 if you arrive during "surcharge" hours and an extra B20 (B50 during "surcharge" hours) for an entry stamp. A songthaew service runs from Vangtao to the city of Pakxe, 40km away (until about 5pm). In reverse, you simply pay the Lao exit tax (B20/50) and get your Thai visa on arrival for free (but note the shorter hours on the Thai side).

Even if you're not planning to cross into Laos, the **border market** at Chong Mek is good for a browse, especially at weekends when it's at its liveliest. The market on the Thai side of the border is full of stuff brought from Bangkok for Lao shoppers, especially fashions, jeans and sarongs, but you'll also find traditional herbalists flogging bits of dried vegetable and animal matter, lots of basketware sellers and plenty of restaurant shacks serving both Thai and Lao dishes. Foreign shoppers can cross over to the Lao-side market in Vangtao simply by paying B5 at the checkpoint across from the duty-free shop (no visa required). Descend into the market area beside the café selling fresh Lao coffee for a huge selection of sarongs, as well as cheap VCDs and foreign whisky.

Yasothon, Ban Sri Than and Roi Et

By the beginning of May, Isaan is desperate for rain; there may not have been significant rainfall for six months and the rice crops need to be planted. In northeastern folklore, rain is the fruit of sexual encounters between the gods, so at this time villagers all over Isaan hold the bawdy **Bun Bang Fai** – a merit-making **rocket festival** – to encourage the gods to get on with it. The largest and most public of these festivals takes place in the provincial capital of **YASOTHON**, 98km northwest of Ubon, on a weekend in mid-May (check Ⓦwww.thailandgrandfestival.com for dates). Not only is the fireworks display a spectacular affair, but the rockets built to launch them are superbly crafted machines in themselves, beautifully decorated and carried proudly through the streets before blast-off. Up to 25 kilograms of gunpowder may be packed into the nine-metre-long rockets and, in keeping with the fertility theme of the festivities, performance is everything. Sexual innuendo, general flirtation and dirty jokes are essential components of Bun Bang Fai; rocket-builders compete to shoot their rockets the highest, and anyone whose missile fails to leave the ground gets coated in mud as a punishment. At other times of the year, Yasothon has little to tempt tourists other than a handful of unremarkable wats and a few evocative old colonial-style shopfronts near **Wat Singh Tha** at the west end of Thanon Srisonthoon.

The most interesting attraction in the surrounding area is the village of **BAN SRI THAN**, 21km east of Yasothon, where nearly every household is employed in the making of the famous *mawn khwaan* triangular **axe pillows**. These pillows (*mawn*), so named because their shape supposedly resembles an axe-head (*khwaan*), have been used in traditional Thai homes for centuries, where it's normal to sit on the floor and lean against a densely stuffed *mawn khwaan*. The design has been slightly adapted so it's now also possible to get *mawn khwaan* with up to four flat cushions attached, making lying out more comfortable. The price depends on the number of triangular pods that make up the pillow: in Ban Sri Than, a stand-alone ten-triangle pillow costs B100, or B370 with three attached cushions – around a third of what it'll cost in Bangkok or Chiang Mai. A good place to see villagers at work, often in the space under their stilted houses, is on Thanon Koson Thammarat, though you're unlikely to find any English-speakers here. If you're driving to Ban Sri Than from Yasothon, follow Route 202 northeast towards Amnat Charoen as far as kilometre-stone 18.5km, then turn south (right) off the highway for 3km to reach the village. Coming by public transport, take a **songthaew** (half-hourly until noon) or **bus** (approximately hourly throughout the day) from Yasothon bus station to **Ban Ni Khom** on Route 202, then a motorbike taxi to cover the last 3km to the village.

Practicalities

All Khon Kaen-bound **buses** from Ubon stop in Yasothon, at the bus station on Thanon Rattanakhet. The nearest airports are in Ubon Ratchathani and Roi Et (see opposite). If you want to stay here during festival time, book your **hotel** well in advance and be prepared to pay double the normal prices quoted here. *Yot Nakhon*, one block north then west of the market and two blocks north then west of the bus station at 141–143 Thanon Uthai-Ramrit (Ⓣ045 711481, Ⓕ045 711476; ❷–❸) has plenty of decent fan and air-conditioned rooms, all of them en suite. The best hotel in town is the comfortable and good-value *JP Emerald*, which has large, attractive air-con rooms close to the provincial hall on the far north perimeter at 36 Thanon Pha Pa (Ⓣ045 724848, Ⓕ045 724655; ❺–❻). The most rewarding place to **eat** is at the covered **night bazaar**, which runs east off the central section of Thanon Chaeng Sanit; some of the stalls here also open during the day, including a vegetarian one (6am–2pm only). Thanon Chaeng Sanit is where you'll find all the main **banks**, with ATMs and currency exchange, plus the **post office**, a couple of blocks north of the night bazaar. The **travel agent** inside the *JP Emerald* hotel sells domestic and international air tickets.

If Yasothon's booked out, you might want to commute there from either Ubon Ratchathani or **ROI ET**, a pleasant if unarresting town 71km further northwest and also on the Ubon-Khon Kaen bus route. Roi Et's **bus station** (ⓣ043 511939) is way out beyond the western fringes of town on Thanon Chaeng Sanit, so you need to take a samlor or tuk-tuk to the town centre hotels. Roi Et **airport** (ⓣ043 518246), 13.5km out of town on the way to Khon Kaen, is currently served by PB Air (ⓣ043 518572, ⓦwww.pbair.com) in conjunction with Thai Airways (ⓦwww.thaiairways.com), which runs daily flights to and from Bangkok. Just off the eastern shore of Roi Et's artificial lake, Beung Phlan Chai, the centrally located *Saithip* at 133 Thanon Suriyadet Bamrung (ⓣ043 514028; ❷–❸) is convenient and has both fan and air-con rooms. On the northern edge of town at 404 Thanon Kolchapalayuk, *Petcharat Garden Hotel* is a quite stylish mid- to upper-range option with air-con rooms, a swimming pool and restaurant (ⓣ043 519000, ⓕ043 519008; ❹–❼), or there's more luxurious accommodation at the *Roi Et City Hotel* (ⓣ043 520387, ⓦwww.sawasdee.com/hotel/643104; ❻) at 78 Thanon Ploenchit, on the eastern edge of town, which offers a swimming pool, business centre and gym as well as large, comfortable air-con rooms. The night market sets up two blocks east of the *Banchong* hotel and is an enjoyable **place to eat**, or there's more upmarket dining at the restaurants around the edge of the lake.

Central Isaan

The more northerly branch of the northeastern rail line bypasses Khorat, heading straight up through **central Isaan** to the Lao border town of Nong Khai via Khon Kaen and Udon Thani, paralleling Highway 2 most of the way. West of these arteries, the smaller Highway 201 is shadowed by the thickly wooded Phetchabun hills and Dong Phaya Yen mountain range, the westernmost limits of Isaan, chunks of which have been turned into the **national parks** of Phu Kradung, Phu Reua, Phu Hin Rongkla and Nam Nao. But hills play only a minor part in central Isaan's landscape, most of which suffers from poor-quality soil that sustains little in the way of profitable crops and, quite apart from what it does to the farmers who work it, makes for drab views from the bus or train window.

Nevertheless, there are a handful of towns worth stopping off at: **Khon Kaen**, for its museum of local history, its textiles and its handicraft shops; **Udon Thani**, a departure point for the Bronze Age settlement of **Ban Chiang**; and **Loei**, for its access to the mountainous national parks. Trains connect only the larger towns, but **buses** link all the above centres, also conveniently serving the town of Phitsanulok – the springboard for a tour of the ruins of Sukhothai and a junction for onward travel to Chiang Mai – via a spectacularly hilly route through the rounded contours of Phetchabun province.

Khon Kaen and around

Geographically at the virtual centre of Isaan, **KHON KAEN** is the wealthiest and most sophisticated city in the northeast, seat of a highly respected university as well as Channel 5 and Channel 11 television studios. Considering its size and importance, the city is surprisingly uncongested and spacious, and there's a noticeably upbeat feel to the place, underlined by its apparently harmonious combination of traditional Isaan culture – huge markets and hordes of street vendors – and flashy shopping plazas and world-class hotels. Its location, 188km northeast of Khorat on the Bangkok–Nong Khai rail line and Highway 2, makes it a convenient resting point, even though a startling modern temple and

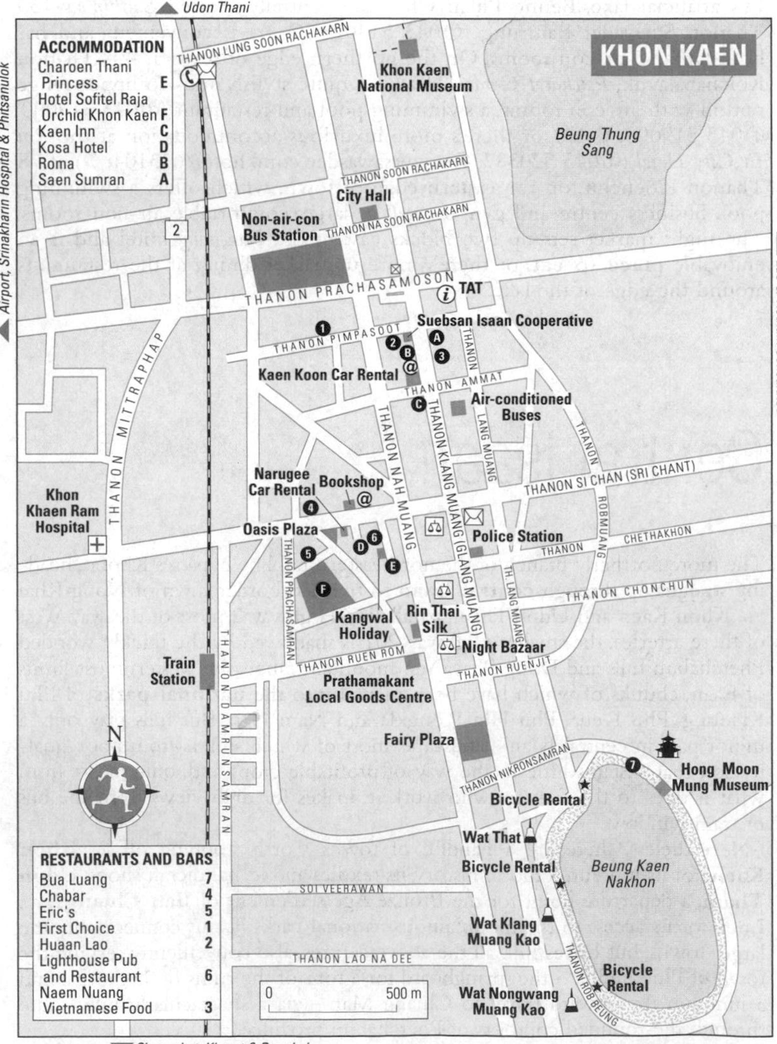

the provincial museum are just about the only sights in town; municipal authorities do, however, make a big deal of the province's prehistoric credentials – the **dinosaur graveyard** at Phuwiang is within day-tripping distance of the city, so you can hardly round a corner in town without coming across a cute statue of a tyrannosaurus. Local silk is another draw, available year round at outlets across the city, it gets special focus during the annual **Silk and Phuk Siao Festival** (Nov 29–Dec 10; Ⓦwww.thailandgrandfestival.com) when weavers from across the province congregate at the City Hall on Thanon Na Soon Rachakarn to display and sell their fabrics; this is also the chance to witness the moving *phuk siao* ceremony, a traditional friendship-deepening ritual involving the exchange of symbolic wrist strings. During the rest of the year, the foreigners staying in the city tend to be expat husbands of local women, businesspeople or university teachers rather than tourists, though an increasing number of travellers are stopping here for **Lao and Vietnamese visas**, now that both nations have consulates in Khon Kaen.

Arrival, information and city transport

Khon Kaen is well served as a transport hub: the **train station** (Ⓣ043 221112) is on the southwestern edge of town, about fifteen minutes' walk from the main hotel area; the non-air-conditioned **bus station** (Ⓣ043 237300) is a five-minute walk northwest of the Thanon Klang Muang hotels; and the air-con bus terminal (Ⓣ043 239910) is right in the town centre. Khon Kaen **airport** (Ⓣ043 246305), 10km northwest of the city centre, runs daily Thai Airways **flights** to and from Bangkok and has Avis and Budget car-rental desks (see p.571 for details); hotel minibuses meet all flights and while some hotels provide this service for free, others charge B50–70. The **TAT** office (daily 8.30am–4.30pm; Ⓣ043 244498, Ⓔtatkhkn@tat.or.th) is on Thanon Prachasamoson, about five minutes' walk east of the non-air-con bus station.

Local buses and songthaews ply Khon Kaen's streets from 5am to 8pm, charging a fixed fare of B7, or B10 for air-con journeys. Khon Kaen TAT publishes a handy map showing the colour-coded routes of all 22 city routes, of which the most useful include: **#3** (yellow), which connects the train station and the regular bus terminal; **#11** (red), which connects the train station, the air-con bus terminal, via Thanon Si Chan, and TAT; **#8** (light blue) and **#9** (light blue), which both connect the regular bus terminal with the air-con bus terminal and continue south down Thanon Klang Muang; and **#15** (yellow) and **#21** (orange), which both run up and down Thanon Klang Muang at least as far as Thanon Chonchun. A short **tuk-tuk** ride within the city should cost you B40, while the minimum fare in a **samlor** is B20. For **car, motorbike and bicycle rental** outlets see "Listings" on p.571.

Accommodation

Accommodation in Khon Kaen is plentiful and reasonably priced, particularly in the mid-price range.

Charoen Thani Princess 260 Thanon Si Chan Ⓣ043 220400, Ⓦkhonkaen.royalprincess.com. Dated but comfortable enough and well-priced upper-mid-range hotel with a pool, several bars and restaurants, a nightclub and a women-only floor. ❼

Hotel Sofitel Raja Orchid Khon Kaen 9/9 Thanon Prachasamran Ⓣ043 322155, Ⓦwww.sofitel.com. One of the nicest hotels in the northeast, this gorgeously appointed, luxury high-rise hotel has extremely comfortable rooms, a swimming pool and spa, and plenty of bars and restaurants. Significant discounts are often available, which makes it well worth splashing out on. ❼–❾

Kaen Inn 56 Thanon Klang Muang Ⓣ043 245420, Ⓔkaeninnhotel@yahoo.com. Reasonable value if slightly shabby mid-range place, where all rooms are en suite and have air-con, TV and fridge. ❹

Kosa Hotel 250 Thanon Si Chan ⓣ043 320320. Seventeen-storey hotel offering reasonably priced, standard issue upmarket rooms, all with air-con and TV, plus a beer garden and snooker hall. ❻

Roma 50/2 Thanon Klang Muang ⓣ043 334444, ⓕ043 242458. All rooms in this old, sizeable hotel are fairly basic, but if you're after cheap air-con then it's worth considering, and they also have cable TV. Fan ❷, air-con ❸

Saen Sumran 55 Thanon Klang Muang ⓣ043 239611, ⓔsaensamran@gmail.com. One of the oldest hotels in Khon Kaen, this is also the most traveller-friendly place in town (though most of its customers are Thai salesmen), with a useful noticeboard and genial, clued-up managers. All rooms are basic but en suite: the price depends on the size of the room and thickness of the mattress. The large, wooden-floored rooms upstairs are nicest. ❷–❸

The Town

Khon Kaen's most arresting sight is the enormous nine-tiered pagoda at **Wat Nongwang Muang Kao**, located at the far southern end of Thanon Klang Muang and served by city songthaews #8 (light blue) from the central stretch of Thanon Klang Muang and #14 (blue) from the train station, Thanon Sri Chan and south-central Thanon Klang Muang. Unmissable in its glittering livery of red, white and gold, this breathtakingly grand structure was the brainchild of the temple's famously charismatic and well-travelled abbot, Phra Wisuttikittisan, and took seven years and a huge amount of foreign donations before it was completed in 1997. The nine-tiered design is said to have been inspired by Burma's most sacred stupa, Shwedagon, but the gallery running around each tier is more Lao in style, and the crowning *that* (tower) is typically Thai. Nine is an auspicious number in Thailand, triply so in this case as the current king is Rama IX and the current abbot of the temple is the ninth since the wat's foundation in 1789. Inside the pagoda, the walls of the first tier are painted with modern murals that depict the founding of Khon Kaen. Each tier has its different purpose, with the first used for assemblies, the second for monks' residences, the third for a scripture library and so on. Climb the staircase all the way up to the ninth tier for views north across the city and east to the lake, Beung Kaen Nakhon.

△ Wat Nongwang, Muang Kao

A walk or cycle round **Beung Kaen Nakhon** and its perimeter park is a pleasant way to spend a few hours. It's the main recreation area for Khon Kaen residents who jog or cycle around it, fish in its waters or make use of the several kids' playparks. You can rent bicycles (B20) at three different spots, close to each of the lakeside temples (see map), there are table-tennis tables near the Wat Klang Muang Kao entrance, and foodstalls all over, as well as restaurants, the most famous of which is *Bua Luang* (see below), where you can also rent pedalos. Just east of *Bua Luang*, the utilitarian building beneath the outdoor amphitheatre houses the **Hong Moon Mung Khon Kaen City Museum** (Mon–Sat 9am–5pm; B90), which presents the history of Khon Kaen province in a series of tableaux and includes a fair amount of explanation in English. The most direct route to the lake is by **city bus or songthaew** #13, which runs east along Thanon Si Chan and then south down Thanon Nah Muang, or #21 (brown), which runs the length of Thanon Klang Muang, to the Hong Moon Mung Khon Kaen City Museum, most easily recognized by the very ornate Chinese temple directly across the road.

Across on the other, northern, edge of town, **Khon Kaen National Museum** on Thanon Lung Soon Rachakarn (daily 9am–4pm; B30; ⓦwww.thailandmuseum.com) presents a digestible introduction to the region through an assortment of locally found artefacts some of which date back to the bronze age. It's about 600m from Thanon Prachasamoson (1km from TAT) or you can catch city bus or songthaew #21 (brown) from anywhere on Thanon Klang Muang, #12 (green) or #45012 (yellow) from anywhere on Thanon Nah Muang, or #17 (blue) from Thanon Lang Muang, and you'll be dropped outside the museum. The star **exhibit** on the ground floor of the museum is a ninth-century Dvaravati-era *sema* (boundary stone) carved with a sensuous depiction of Princess Bhimba wiping the Buddha's feet with her hair on his return to Kabilabasad after years of absence in search of enlightenment. Also on this floor is an interesting reconstruction of a local musical ensemble centred around the *pong lang*, a wooden xylophone that's particular to the region. The highlights of the upstairs gallery are a fine collection of ninth- and tenth-century votive tablets in clay and embossed silver, plus some exquisite little Khmer-influenced Lopburi-style bronze Buddha images.

Eating, drinking and entertainment

Khon Kaen has a reputation for very **spicy food**, particularly sausages, *sai krog isaan*, which are served with cubes of raw ginger, onion, lime and plenty of chilli sauce, at stalls along Thanon Klang Muang to the north of the *Kaen Inn*. These and other local favourites – such as pigs' trotters, roast duck and shellfish – can also be sampled at the stalls along the northern edge of the lake Bueng Kaen Nakhon. Foodstalls pop up all over other parts of town at dusk, with a particular concentration at the **night bazaar** on the eastern end of Thanon Ruen Rom. **Nightlife** in Khon Kaen is mainly focused in and around the *Charoen Thani*, *Kosa* and *Sofitel* hotels.

Restaurants

Baker's Basket Lobby of the *Hotel Sofitel*. Can't be beaten for its delicious, if pricey, selection of cakes and pastries.

Bua Luang North shore of Beung Kaen Nakhon, off Thanon Rob Beung. The largest and most popular of the lakeside restaurants, where you can choose to dine right on a terrace over the water. The cuisine is classy Thai, with plenty of seafood (B60–180).

First Choice 18/8 Thanon Pimpasoot. Another tourist-friendly restaurant, featuring an English-language menu offering Thai, Western and Japanese options (from B40–120), plus a sizeable vegetarian selection and decent breakfasts. Daily 7am–11pm.

Huaan Lao 39 Thanon Pimpasoot (no English sign). Located inside an elegant modern wooden home decorated with crafts and antiques, this is a conducive place in which to enjoy tasty Thai and Lao dishes (B40–120).

Lighthouse Pub and Restaurant In the car park of *Charoen Thani Princess* hotel, just off Thanon Si Chan. A favourite with Thais and expats for its cheap eats (*phat thai* for B35), spicy Shanghai

hai fun noodles and American breakfasts. You can choose to dine out front or in the air-con interior, and there are copies of the *Bangkok Post* to keep you occupied between mouthfuls.

Naem Nuang Vietnamese Food Next door but one to the *Saen Sumran* hotel at 87/14–15 Thanon Klang Muang. Very popular air-con place that serves mainly Vietnamese food from its pictorial menu (no English translations), plus some north-eastern standards. Their eponymous speciality is *naem nuang*, Vietnamese spring rolls made with barbecued fermented pork sausage, which you assemble yourself from half a dozen or more ingredients of your choice, including lots of fresh coriander, mint, ginger, lemon rind, thin noodles and beansprouts. Spring roll sets from B50 and all-you-can-eat buffets from B99. Daily 6am–9.30pm.

Underground In the basement of the *Hotel Sofitel*. Basement food and drink complex which includes a sushi bar and an expensive Chinese restaurant.

Bars and clubs

Chabar 47/8-10 Thanon Si Chan. Appealing, funkily decorated neighbourhood bar-restaurant which serves pitchers of draft Beer Chang under the pavementside trees or inside in front of sports TV.

Eric's Across from the *Hotel Sofitel* driveway, off Thanon Prachasamran. Popular expat-run and expat-oriented bar-restaurant; one of several in the area.

Gik Club Inside the *Hotel Sofitel*, 9/9 Thanon Prachasamran. Typical hotel nightclub where DJs hold the floor every night and there's live music most evenings. Nightly 9pm–2am.

Krönen Brauhaus In the basement of the *Hotel Sofitel*. Cosy, dimly lit microbrewery bar where the German-style beer flows strong and dark. Daily 6pm–1am.

Zolid Inside the *Charoen Thani Princess* hotel, 260 Thanon Si Chan. This three-floor nightclub hosts live bands and cabarets nightly, has enormous music-video screens, and is said to be the biggest disco in the northeast. Nightly 9pm–2am.

Shopping

Khon Kaen is great for **shopping**, its stores boasting a wide range of regional **arts and crafts**, particularly high-quality Isaan **silk** of all designs and weaves. One of the best outlets is the cavernous Prathamakant Local Goods Centre (Mon–Sat 9am–8pm) at the southern end of town, about 500m from the *Kosa Hotel*, at 81 Thanon Ruen Rom. The selection here is quite phenomenal (much better than the disappointing government-sanctioned OTOP (One Tambon One Product) shop beside the *Kosa Hotel* on Soi Kosa), with hundreds of gorgeous *mut mee* cotton and silk weaves, as well as clothes, furnishings, triangular axe pillows (B350 for an unstuffed three-seater), *khaen* pipes and silver jewellery. Though it feels touristy, locals buy their home furnishings and dress fabrics here too. To get to Prathamakant from the north part of town, take almost any local bus down Thanon Nah Muang to the Ruen Rom junction. Rin Thai Silk at 410–412 Thanon Nah Muang stocks a smaller range of Isaan silk, but will tailor clothes too. Itinerant vendors, who wander the main streets with panniers stuffed full of silk and cotton lengths, also offer competitive prices, and you can be sure most of the money will go to the weavers; they often gather on the steps of the *Kaen Inn* and along the stretch of Thanon Klang Muang just north of the hotel. Another fair-trade outlet for local craftspeople is the Suebsan Isaan Cooperative shop at 16 Thanon Klang Muang, which sells textiles fabricated from bamboo fibre and water hyacinth, as well as more usual *mut mee* silks and cottons, basketware, herbal cosmetics and other traditional products. Nearby on this stretch of Thanon Klang Muang, just north of *Roma Hotel*, Naem Lap Lae is the place to buy local food specialities such as spicy sausages, sugar-coated beans and other Khon Kaen delicacies.

For everything else you should either head to the huge, modern Fairy Plaza, between Nah Muang and Klang Muang, which has the usual clothes, accessories and mobiles concessions, plus *Pizza Co*, *McDonald's* and

Swensen's and a cinema, or to the smaller, more central Oasis Plaza in front of the *Kosa Hotel*.

Listings

Airline The Thai Airways office is inside the *Hotel Sofitel* on Thanon Prachasamran ⓣ043 245001 (Mon–Fri 8am–5pm).

Banks and exchange There are several banks with currency-exchange facilities on Thanon Si Chan, between the *Charoen Thani* and *Kosa* hotels (daily 9am–5pm), plus plenty of ATMs on southern Thanon Nah Muang and north-central Thanon Klang Muang.

Bookshop The bookshop opposite the *Charoen Thani* on Thanon Si Chan stocks a reasonable selection of English-language titles published by Asia Books, plus some novels, Thai maps and road atlases.

Car and motorbike rental Avis ⓣ043 344313, ⓦwww.avis.com and Budget ⓣ043 345460, ⓦwww.budget.co.th both have desks at the airport, and Budget also has a desk inside the *Kaen Inn* (ⓣ043 234 573). Cars, with or without driver (B1350/1200), and motorbikes (B200) are also available from: Narujee Car Rent, next to Oasis Plaza department store at 178 Soi Kosa off Thanon Si Chan ⓣ043 224220, ⓦwww.narujeecarrent.com; cars only from Kaen Koon Car Rental at 54/1–2 Thanon Klang Muang ⓣ043 239458.

Cinema Fairy Cineplex inside Fairy Plaza, between southern Thanon Nah Muang and Klang Muang (B80–120).

Consulates The Lao consulate is located some way east of TAT at 171 Thanon Prachasamoson (Mon–Fri 8am–noon & 1–4pm; ⓣ043 242856–8); city songthaew #11 (red) runs right past the consulate from the train station, via Thanon Si Chan and the Thanon Klang Muang air-con bus terminal, as does city songthaew #10 (blue), en route from the non-air-con bus station and TAT, then continuing all the way down Thanon Klang Muang via the air-con bus station. Thirty-day visas usually take three working days to process or can be done in 15min for an extra fee; see ⓦwww.bkklaoembassy.com for a list of the charges. For more details on travel into Laos, see p.33. There's also a Vietnamese consulate in Khon Kaen (Mon–Fri 8.30–11.30am & 1.30–4.30pm; ⓣ043 242190 and ⓣ043 241586), south of the Lao consulate and about 1.5km from the TAT office, off Thanon Prachasamoson at 65/6 Thanon Chaiaphadung; city songthaew #10 (blue) runs right past it: see above for details. Thirty-day Vietnamese visas are issued here within 24hr; see ⓦwww.vietnamembassy.or.th for details.

Hospitals Khon Kaen Ram Hospital, on the far western end of Thanon Si Chan, is the main private hospital in town ⓣ043 333900–3, or there's the government Srinakarin Hospital, attached to Khon Kaen University, north of town on Highway 2 ⓣ043 348360-9.

Internet access The cheapest and most hi-tech Internet centre is TNet, run by the TOT phone company, on the ground floor of the Oasis Plaza off Thanon Si Chan (B30/hr; daily 10am–8.30pm). Otherwise there are several Internet/computer games centres around the *Roma Hotel* on Thanon Klang Muang and between the *Charoen Thani* and *Kosa Hotel* on Thanon Si Chan.

Mail The most centrally located post office is on Thanon Si Chan, and there's another branch next to the phone centre on Thanon Lung Soon Rachakarn.

Pharmacies Several along north-central Thanon Klang Muang, plus a Boots the Chemist outlet on the ground floor of Oasis Plaza on Thanon Si Chan.

Telephones The CAT international telephone centre is in the north of town on Thanon Lung Soon Rachakarn.

Tourist police For all emergencies, call the tourist police on the free, 24hr phone line ⓣ1155, or contact them at the TAT office on Thanon Prachasamoson ⓣ043 236937.

Travel agents Domestic and international air tickets are available from Kaen Koon Car Rent at 54/1–2 Thanon Klang Muang ⓣ043 239458, ⓔkaenkoontravel@yahoo.co.uk; and Kangwal Holiday, on the *Charoen Thani* approach road on Thanon Si Chan ⓣ043 227777, ⓦwww.kangwal.com.

Around Khon Kaen

The outer reaches of Khon Kaen province hold a couple of places that are worth exploring on **day-trips**. If you're looking for other things to occupy yourself, don't be duped by the TAT brochure on the "tortoise village" in the village of Ban Kok, about 5km west of Chonnabot, which is both duller and more depressing than the tourist literature implies.

Chonnabot

Khon Kaen makes a reasonable base from which to explore the local silk-weaving centre of **Chonnabot**, about 54km southwest of the city. Traditionally a cottage industry, this small town's **silk production** has become centralized over the last few years, and weavers now gather in small workshops in town, each specializing in just one aspect of the process. You can walk in and watch the women (it's still exclusively women's work) at their wheels, looms or dye vats, and then buy from the vendors in the street out front. For more details on silk-weaving processes, see the box on p.547. To get to Chonnabot from Khon Kaen, take any ordinary Khorat-bound bus to **Ban Phae** (every 30min), then a songthaew for the final 10km to Chonnabot.

Phuwiang National Park: Dinosaurland

Khon Kaen hit the international headlines in 1996 when the oldest-ever fossil of a tyrannosaur **dinosaur** was unearthed in Phuwiang National Park, about 90km northwest of Khon Kaen. Estimated to be 120 million years old, it measures just 6m from nose to tail and has been named *Siamotyrannus isanensis* – Siam for Thailand, and Isaan after the northeastern region of Thailand. Before this find at Phuwiang, the oldest tyrannosaur fossils were the 65-million- to 80-million-year-old specimens from China, Mongolia and North America. These younger fossils are twice the size of the *Siamotyrannus*; the latter's age and size have therefore established the *Siamotyrannus* as the ancestor of the *Tyrannosaurus rex*, and confirmed Asia as the place of origin of the tyrannosaur genus, which later evolved into various different species.

The fossil of this extraordinary dinosaur – together with eight moderately interesting paleontological finds – is on show to the public at Dinosaurland in **Phuwiang National Park** (daily 8.30am–4.30pm; B200; ⓣ043 249052, ⓦwww.dnp.go.th/National_park.asp). The **Dinosaurland** tag is a little misleading as there are no theme-park attractions here, just nine dig sites and a **museum** (Thurs–Tues 9am–5pm; free). Nearly all the information is in Thai, so it's worth picking up the informative English-language brochure on Dinosaurland from Khon Kaen's TAT office before you come.

The *Siamotyrannus isanensis* is displayed at **Site 9**, which is accessible via the 1.5-kilometre track that starts across the road from the visitor centre; from the car park at the end of the track, it's a five-hundred-metre walk to the quarry. The fossil is an impressive sight, with large sections of the rib cage almost completely intact. **Site 1**, 900m south along a track from Site 9, contains the cream of the other finds, including two previously undiscovered species. The theropod *Siamosaurus sutheethorni* (named after the paleontologist Warawut Suteehorn) is set apart from the other, carnivorous, theropods by its teeth, which seem as if they are unable to tear flesh; the fifteen- to twenty-metre-long *Phuwiangosaurus sirindhornae* (named in honour of Thailand's Princess Royal) is thought to be a new species of sauropod.

Though it's possible to take a non-air-con **bus** from Khon Kaen to Phuwiang town (every 30min; about 1hr), you then need to hire a motorbike taxi to continue to Dinosaurland and back (about B200 return), so it's easier to rent your own wheels in Khon Kaen. To **get to the park**, head west out of Khon Kaen on Highway 12, following the signs for Chumpae as far as kilometre-stone 48, marked by a dinosaur statue. Turn right off the main road here, and continue for another 38km along Highway 2038, passing through the small town of Phuwiang and following signs all the way for Dinosaurland. There's a **food** and drink stall at the car park in front of Quarry #3, which is about one kilometre's drive north of the visitor centre.

Udon Thani and Ban Chiang

Economically important but charmless, **UDON THANI** looms for most travellers as a misty, early-morning sprawl of grey cement seen from the window of the overnight train to Nong Khai. The capital of an arid sugar-cane and rice-growing province, 137km north of Khon Kaen, Udon was given an

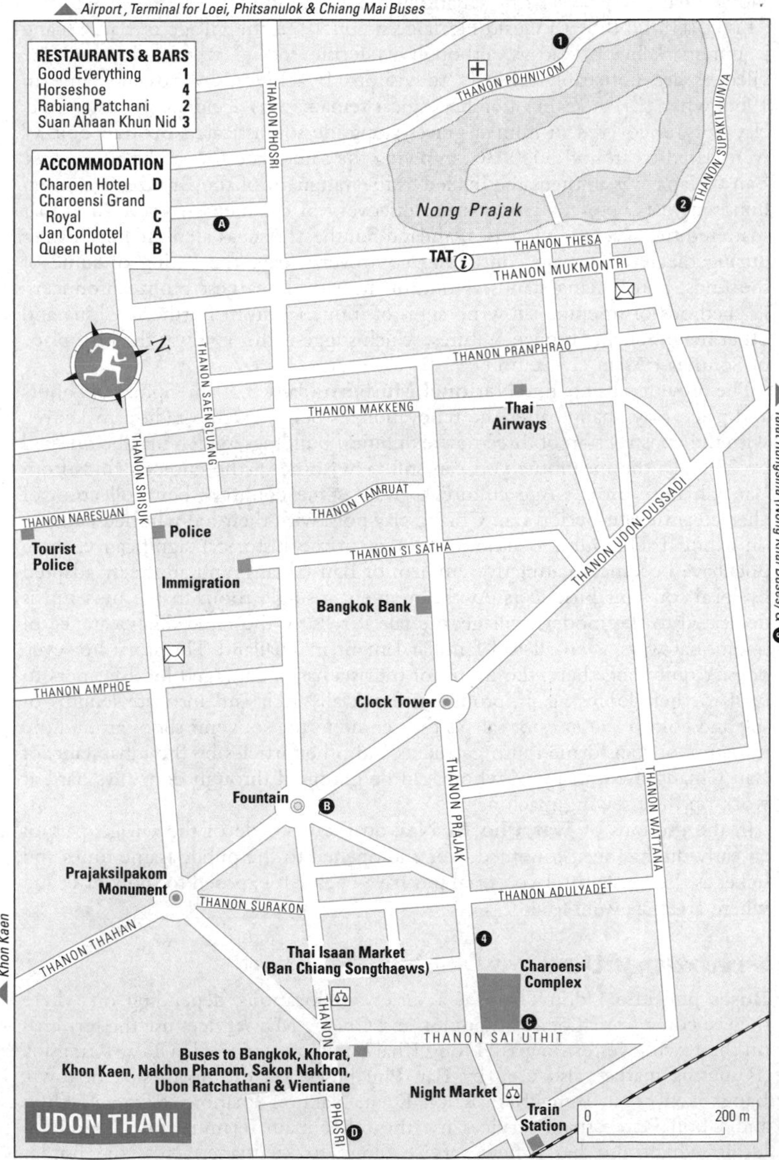

economic shot in the arm during the Vietnam War with the siting of a huge American military base nearby, and despite the American withdrawal in 1976, the town has maintained its rapid industrial and commercial development. The only conceivable reason to alight here would be to satisfy a lust for archeology at the excavated Bronze Age settlement of **BAN CHIANG**, 50km to the east in sleepy farming country, though plenty of travellers avoid spending time in Udon by visiting Ban Chiang on a day-trip from the much preferable base of Nong Khai (see p.587) or by staying in the village itself.

Listed as a UNESCO World Heritage site in 1992, the village of Ban Chiang is unremarkable nowadays, although its fertile setting is attractive and the villagers are noticeably friendly to visitors. It achieved worldwide fame in 1966, when a rich seam of archeological remains was accidentally discovered: clay pots, uncovered in human graves alongside sophisticated **bronze** objects, were dated to around 3000 BC, implying the same date for the bronze pieces. Ban Chiang was immediately hailed as the vanguard of the Bronze Age, seven hundred years before Mesopotamia's discovery of the metal – a revelation that shattered the accepted view of mainland Southeast Asia as a cultural backwater during that era. Despite continuing controversy over the dating of some of the finds, Ban Chiang stands as one of the world's earliest bronze producers; its methods of smelting show no signs of influence from northern China and other neighbouring bronze cultures, which suggests the area was the birthplace of Southeast Asian civilization.

The present village's fine **National Museum** (daily 8.30am–5pm; B30; hours and price may change after the renovation) is being given a radical makeover, with the construction of three new exhibition buildings, which may be finished by 2007. In the meantime you can still view some of the choicest finds from Ban Chiang's Bronze Age culture, as well as the country's best collection of characteristic late-period Ban Chiang clay pots, with their red whorled patterns on a buff background – although not of prime historical significance, these pots have become an attractive emblem of Ban Chiang, and are freely adapted by local souvenir producers. At the moment a single room in the museum is dedicated to the modern village; the tale it tells, of the rapid disappearance of traditional ways, is an all-too-familiar lament in Thailand. The story, however, doesn't quite end there: the influx of tourists has encouraged local farmers to turn to their looms again, producing especially rich and intricate lengths of silk and cotton *mut mee*, for sale as they come in the souvenir shops around the museum, or transformed into garments and other articles by the inhabitants of Ban Chiang itself, many of whom can be glimpsed through doorways hard at work on their sewing machines.

In the grounds of **Wat Pho Si Nai**, on the east side of the village, part of an early dig has been canopied over and opened to the public (same times and ticket as the museum). Two burial pits have been left exposed to show how and where artefacts were found.

Practicalities

Buses pull into Udon Thani at a variety of locations, depending on where they've come from: Loei, Phitsanulok and Chiang Mai services use the terminal on the town's western bypass; Nong Khai buses are stationed at Talat Rungsina (Rungsina market, also used by Ban Phu buses) on the north side of town; Bangkok, Khorat, Bung Kan, Khon Kaen, Nakhon Phanom, Sakon Nakhon and Ubon Ratchathani services use the other main terminal on Thanon Sai Uthit, which also has a new service direct to Vientiane, across the border in Laos; nearby, Ban Chiang-bound songthaews (big, multi-coloured truck versions) base themselves at the morning market, Talat Thai Isaan. The **train station** is on the east side of town, a ten-minute walk from the Thanon Sai Uthit bus terminal. Thai Airways, Air Asia and Nok Air all operate several **flights** a day from Bangkok to Udon Thani; air-con minibuses meet incoming flights at the airport, 3km southwest of the centre, charging B100 per person to drop off anywhere in town. Alternatively, both Avis (Ⓣ042 244770) and Budget (Ⓣ042 246805) have **car-rental** desks at the airport.

Udon's **TAT office** (daily 8.30am–4.30pm; Ⓣ042 325406–7, Ⓔtatudon@tat.or.th) also covers Nong Khai, Nong Bua Lamphu and Loei provinces; it's housed at 16/5 Thanon Mukmontri on the south side of Nong Prajak, a landscaped lake and park to the northwest of the centre. Numbered **songthaews** ply set routes around town for B8 per person (a rough map is available from TAT); among the more useful routes, #15 connects the Thanon Sai Uthit bus terminal with the terminal on the western bypass, while #6 runs the length of Thanon Udon-Dussadi to Talat Rungsina. Alternatively, there are plenty of **skylabs**, Udon's version of tuk-tuks, for hire (from B30 for a short journey). You can access the **Internet** at dozens of places in and around the Charoensi Complex shopping centre on Thanon Prajak.

To **get to Ban Chiang** from Udon, either take a direct songthaew from Talat Thai Isaan (Mon–Sat every 30min or so until about noon) or catch a Sakon Nakhon-bound bus (every 20min) to Ban Palu and then a motorized samlor (B50 for one person, B60 for two) for the last 5km or so from the main road to the village. Heading back to Udon the same day by songthaew is not possible as the service runs only until about 9am, so you'll have to make do with a samlor and bus combination.

Accommodation and eating

It's possible to **stay overnight in Ban Chiang** at the excellent *Lakeside Sunrise Guesthouse* (Ⓣ042 208167, Ⓦwww.banchianglakeside.com; ❷), and in fact many guests linger for a few days; rates, which are at the lower end of this price code, can be reduced for longer stays. The guest house is just a few minutes' walk from the museum, where the friendly owner, Tong, works: during opening hours, ask for her at the museum; otherwise, facing the museum, head left then turn right at the first intersection and look for a large Western-style wooden two-storey house. Guests here sleep in clean first-floor rooms with fans, mosquito screens and shared hot showers and can relax on a huge balcony – equipped with a helpful noticeboard and small library – overlooking an artificial lake. Bicycles are available for exploring the surrounding countryside, or Tong can arrange motorbike rental; there's a bird and animal sanctuary 6km away, and a couple of interesting forest wats closer to the village, all marked on a useful hand-drawn map of the area. There are half a dozen simple **restaurants** in the village – the place directly opposite the museum does an excellent *raht nah* (noodles in a thick gravy).

Among **Udon's accommodation** options, the centrally located *Queen Hotel* at 6–8 Thanon Udon-Dussadi (Ⓣ042 221451; fan ❶, air-con ❷) is a decent budget option, though you'd be far better off heading to the guest house in Ban Chiang if you can. Moving up the scale, *Jan Condotel*, 102/17 Soi Sansuk, between Srisuk and Phosri roads (Ⓣ042 329223–7, Ⓔjan_condo2005@hotmail.com; ❸), offers excellent value: in a beautifully appointed new condo, rooms are equipped with air-con, hot water, cable TV, fridges and duvets. Towards the top end, the smart, well-run *Charoen Hotel*, 549 Thanon Phosri (Ⓣ042 248155, Ⓔcharoenhotel@hotmail.com; ❺), has 250 air-con rooms with hot showers, fridges and satellite TV, and an attractive swimming pool outside, but better still is the luxury *Charoensri Grand Royal*, next to the Charoensi Complex at 277/1 Thanon Prajak (Ⓣ042 343555, Ⓦwwwcharoensrigrand.com; ❼), with health club, spa, sauna, pool and karaoke bar among its offerings.

For evening **eats**, you could do a lot worse than the night market, which offers a wide variety of low-priced comestibles – Thai, Chinese and Vietnamese – on the west side of the train station. At lunchtime, probably the best deal in Udon is the buffet at the *Charoensri Grand Royal*, a huge, all-you-can-eat selection of Thai and Western food, with salads, desserts and coffee, for B180 per person. One of Udon's most popular restaurants is the *Rabiang Phatchani*, northeast of the centre in Nong Prajak Park, with a large menu of Thai and Chinese dishes and outdoor seating on a leafy terrace overlooking the lake. On the opposite side of the lake, *Good Everything* offers a range of teas, coffees and cakes, as well as Thai, Japanese and Western lunches and dinners in a civilized garden setting. For a real culinary treat, head out into the northern suburbs to the very clean and friendly *Suan Ahaan Khun Nid*, which is famous among Thai gourmets for its carefully prepared Isaan food, such as spiced, salted and grilled snakehead fish, deep-fried land crab, deep-fried sun-dried beef and a wide variety of northeastern salads. It's on Soi 9 (Soi Nonniwate), Thanon Udon-Dussadi (Ⓣ042 246128): to get there, take a skylab or catch songthaew #6 up Udon-Dussadi, then walk ten minutes west along the soi past the temple and it's on the left at the end of a short alley (no English sign). Around the Charoensri Complex, there's a cluster of decent **bars**, including the *Horseshoe*, an English-run pub and restaurant round the corner at 254/26 Thanon Prajak.

Loei and around

Most people carry on from Udon Thani due north to Nong Khai (see p.587), but making a detour via **LOEI**, 147km to the west, takes you within range of several towering national parks and sets you up for a lazy tour along the Mekong River. The capital of a province renowned for the unusual shapes of its stark, craggy mountains, Loei is, more significantly, the crossroads of one of Thailand's least-tamed border regions, with all manner of illegal goods coming across from Laos. This trade may be reined in – or perhaps spurred on – by the recent opening of a 3km-long bridge (not open to foreigners, unless on a package tour) across the Heuang River, a tributary of the Mekong, to Xainyabouli province in Laos. Despite its frontier feel, the town, lying along the west bank of the small Loei River, is friendly and offers legitimate products of its own, such as sweet tamarind paste and pork sausages, which are for sale along Thanon Charoenrat, Loei's main street, and the adjacent Thanon Oua Aree.

One reason to make a special trip to this region is to attend the unique rain-making **festival of Phi Ta Kon**, or Bun Phra Wet, held over three days either at the end of June or the beginning of July in the small town of **Dan Sai**, 80km southwest of Loei. In order to encourage the heavens to open, townsfolk dress up as spirits in colourful patchwork rags and fierce, brightly painted masks (made from coconut palm fronds and the baskets used for steaming sticky rice), then rowdily parade the town's most sacred Buddha image round the streets while making fun of as many onlookers as they can, waving wooden phalluses about and generally having themselves a whale of a time. Top folk and country musicians from around Isaan are attracted to perform in the evenings during Phi Ta Kon; the afternoon of the second day of the festival sees the firing off

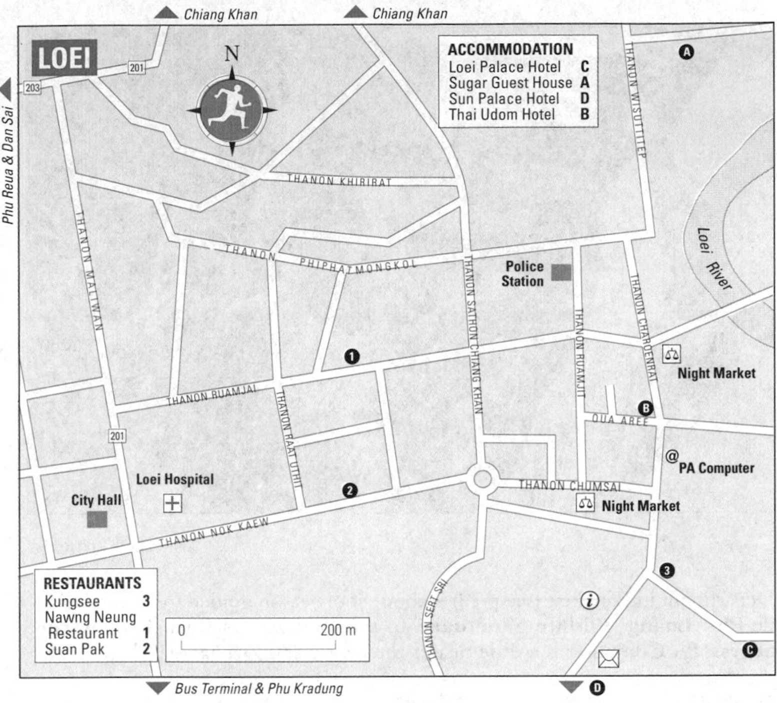

of dozens of bamboo rockets, while the third day is a much more solemn affair, with Buddhist sermons and a purification ceremony at Wat Phon Chai. The carnival can be visited in a day from Loei, though rooms are hard to come by at this time.

Practicalities

Beyond its meagre attractions, Loei is really only useful as a transport hub and a base for the nearby national parks. **Buses** run here from Udon Thani every twenty minutes and from Khon Kaen every thirty minutes, from Phitsanulok in the central plains three times a day and from Bangkok (via Chaiyaphum) around twenty times a day. Nine buses a day, supplemented by slower, roughly half-hourly songthaews, link the town to Chiang Khan, 55km to the north at the start of the Mekong River route, while buses run hourly in the mornings to Sang Khom (3hr, bypassing Chiang Khan) and all the way to Nong Khai (6–7hr); if you come this way in the afternoon, you'll have to change buses in Pak Chom. If you're going straight from Loei to Nong Khai, it's quicker but far less scenic to catch a bus to Udon and change. All of these arrive at and depart from the **bus terminal** on Thanon Maliwan, the main through north–south road (Highway 201), about 2.5km south of the centre. Nok Air (Ⓣ1318 or 02 900 9955) currently runs **flights** to Loei twice weekly from both Bangkok and Udon Thani.

The TAT **tourist office** (daily 8.30am–4.30pm; Ⓣ042 812812, Ⓔtatloei@tat.or.th) is in the old district office on Thanon Charoenrat on the south side of the centre. Keen nature-lovers might want to ask here – or through the Parks

△ Phi Ta Kon festival

Department in Bangkok (see p.72) – about cool-season guided treks in the fragile **Phu Luang Wildlife Sanctuary**, to the southwest of Loei. For **Internet access**, PA Computer is a little nearer the centre at 139 Thanon Charoenrat.

Accommodation and eating

Unless it's festival time, finding a decent **place to stay** in Loei shouldn't be a problem. In a quiet residential area, five minutes' walk from the top of Thanon Charoenrat on the north side of the centre, lies *Sugar Guest House*, 4/1 Soi 2, Thanon Wisuttitep (Ⓣ042 812982, Ⓔsugarnamtan@hotmail.com; fan ❷, air-con ❸). Bright, colourful rooms are either fan-cooled with shared hot-water bathrooms, or air-con with cable TV and en-suite hot-water bathrooms. Bicycles (B30) and motorbikes (B200) can be rented, and the owners can arrange day-trips in a car with driver (from B1600) to, for example, Phu Reua or the relaxing Huay Krating, where bamboo rafts are towed out onto the reservoir and you can eat lunch delivered to you by longtail boat. Comfortable and centrally placed, *Thai Udom Hotel*, at 122/1 Thanon Charoenrat (Ⓣ042 811763, Ⓕ042 811789; ❷), has rooms with fan or air-con, all with hot-water bathrooms and TVs. The quieter and smarter *Sun Palace Hotel*, south of the centre at 191/5 Thanon Charoenrat (Ⓣ042 815714, Ⓦwww.sunpalacehotel.com; ❸), offers air-con, hot water, TVs and fridges throughout, and some of the rooms on the higher floors offer good mountain views. Out on its own at the top of the range is the *Loei Palace Hotel*, 167/4 Thanon Charoenrat (Ⓣ042 815668–74, Ⓦwww.amari.com; ❽), a shining white landmark in the city park on the southeast side of the centre. Attractive, international-standard rooms enjoy fine garden views, and there's a large swimming pool, Jacuzzi and fitness centre.

The **food** at the *Nawng Neung Restaurant*, by the TMB Bank at 8/22 Thanon Ruamjai, is delicious and very economical – *khao man kai*, *khao muu daeng* and noodle soup with duck or pork are the specialities – but it's only open until 3pm. *Suan Pak*, 17/26 Thanon Nok Kaew, is an excellent little daytime vegetarian place (closed Sun), dishing up everything from *phat thai* and *som tam* to trays of curries and daily specials such as Vietnamese spring rolls. During the evening the old night market, a bustling, smoky, enclosed affair on the east side of Thanon Charoenrat, serves up the usual budget eats, as well as Isaan specialities such as *larb*, *som tam* and *kai yaang* and the distinctly uncommon local delicacy, *khai ping* – barbecued eggs on skewers, which taste like coarse, salty soufflés. Similar fare is on offer at a new night market on a broad, pedestrianized street off Thanon Chumsai, which wears its "Clean Food, Good Taste" signs with pride. At the simple, open-air *Kungsee*, 167/1 Thanon Charoenrat, you can tuck into noodles or fried rice on a terrace with pretty views over the river and the thickly forested hills beyond.

Phu Kradung National Park

The most accessible and popular of the parks in Loei province, **PHU KRADUNG NATIONAL PARK**, about 80km south of Loei, protects a grassy 1300-metre plateau whose temperate climate supports a number of tree, flower and bird species not normally found in tropical Thailand. Walking trails crisscross much of sixty-square-kilometre Phu Kradung (Bell Mountain), and you ought to reckon on spending three days here if you want to explore them fully – at a minimum you have to spend one night, as the trip from Loei to the top of the plateau and back can't be done comfortably in a day. The park is closed during the rainy season (June–Sept), owing to the increased risk of mud-slides and land-slips, and is at its busiest during weekends in December and January, when the summit headquarters is surrounded by a sea of tents.

Access and accommodation

To get to the park, take any **bus** between Loei and Khon Kaen and get off at the village of Phu Kradung (1hr 30min), then hop on a **songthaew** for the remaining 5km to the well-organized **Sri Taan Visitor Centre** (Oct–May daily 8.30am–4.30pm) at the base of the plateau, where you can pick up a trail map and pay the B200 admission fee. You can also leave your gear at the visitor centre, or hire a porter to tote it to the top for you. Three national park **bungalows** at Sri Taan (B1200, sleeping 4 people), with the added bonus of hot water, take the overflow when accommodation on the mountain itself is full. Up on the plateau at the **Wang Kwang Visitor Centre** (☎042 871333), 8km from the Sri Taan Visitor Centre, there are over twenty **bungalows** sleeping four–twelve people (B900–2400); at busy times it's best to reserve in advance through the Parks Department in Bangkok (see p.51). There are also fully equipped tents for rent (B150 per person) or you can pitch your own for B30 per person. Simple **restaurants** at park headquarters compete with several at the rim of the plateau, all of which can rustle up inexpensive, tasty food from limited ingredients, so there's no need to bring your own provisions. On the plain beneath the plateau (2–3km from the Sri Taan Visitor Centre towards Phu Kradung village), *Phu Kradung Resort* has en-suite bungalows, with either fan and cold water or air-con and hot water, and a restaurant (☎042 871076; fan ❸, air-con ❺).

The park

The challenging main **trail** leads from the visitor centre 5.5km up the eastern side of Phu Kradung, passing occasional refreshment stalls, and becoming steeper and rockier on the last 1km, with wooden steps over the most difficult parts; most people take at least three hours, including rest stops. The main trail is occasionally closed for maintenance, when a parallel 4.5-kilometre trail is opened up in its place. At the end of the climb, the unbelievable view as your head peeps over the rim more than rewards the effort: flat as a playing field, the broad plateau is dotted with odd clumps of pine trees thinned by periodic lightning fires, which give it the appearance of a country park. Several feeder trails fan out from here, including a 9.5-kilometre path along the precipitous southern edge that offers sweeping views of Dong Phaya Yen, the untidy range of mountains to the southwest that forms the unofficial border between the northeast and the central plains. Another trail heads along the eastern rim for 2.5km to Pha Nok An – also reached by a two-kilometre path east from the Wang Kwang Visitor Centre – which looks down on neat rice fields and matchbox-like houses in the valley below, an outlook that's especially breathtaking at sunrise.

The attractions of the mountain come and go with the **seasons**. October is muddy after the rains, but the waterfalls that tumble off the northwestern edge of the plateau are in full cascade and the main trail is green and shady. December brings out the maple leaves; by February the waterfalls have disappeared and the vegetation on the lower slopes has been burnt away. April is good for rhododendrons and wild roses, which in Thailand are only found at such high altitudes as this.

Among the park's **wildlife**, mammals such as elephants, sambar deer and gibbons can be seen very occasionally, but they generally confine themselves to the evergreen forest on the northern part of the plateau, which is out of bounds to visitors. In the temperate pines, oaks and beeches that dot the rest of the plateau you're more likely to spot resident **birds** such as jays, sultan tits and snowy-browed flycatchers if you're out walking in the early morning and evening.

Nam Nao National Park

Amongst the undulating sandstone hills of the Phetchabun range, the flat-topped summit of Phu Phajit (1271m), **Nam Nao National Park**'s highest peak, can be seen to the southwest from nearby Phu Kradung National Park. At just under a thousand square kilometres, Nam Nao is larger and more ecologically valuable than its neighbour, with a healthy population of possibly over a hundred mammal species, including large animals such as forest elephant, banteng and a handful of tigers, and more-often-seen barking deer, gibbons and leaf monkeys, as well as over two hundred bird species. These creatures thrive in habitats ranging from tropical bamboo and banana stands to the dominant features of dry evergreen forest, grasslands, open forest and pine stands that look almost European. Though the park was established in 1972, it was regarded as unsafe for visitors, remaining a stronghold for guerillas of the Communist Party of Thailand until the early 1980s; still much less visited than Phu Kradung, it can provide a sense of real solitude. The range of wildlife here also benefited from a physical isolation that stopped abruptly in 1975, when Highway 12 was cut through the park and poachers could gain access more easily. However, as the park adjoins the **Phu Khieo Wildlife Sanctuary**, there is beneficial movement by some species between the two areas.

The turn-off to the park headquarters is on Highway 12; look out for the sign at kilometre-stone 50, 147km west of Khon Kaen and 160km by road from Loei. Several **buses** a day run through at irregular times from Khon Kaen, Phitsanulok and Loei – all about two- to three-hour journeys. Once you've paid the B200 admission fee, walk or hitch the 2km down the potholed road past the park HQ to the **visitor centre** (☎056 729002), where you can pick up an English-language brochure that contains a rough sketch map of the park.

There are a dozen or so **bungalows** here (from B1000 for a four-person unit), a **campsite** (B30 per person) and stalls near headquarters sell simple **meals**.

A good network of clearly marked circular forest **trails** begins near the park headquarters, ranging from a one-kilometre nature trail teeming with butterflies to a six-kilometre track known for occasional elephant sightings; another 3.5-kilometre trail climbs through mixed deciduous forest to the Phu Kor outlook, with its sweeping views across to Phu Phajit. Other trails can be accessed directly from Highway 12, most of them clearly signposted from the road: at kilometre-stone 39, a steep climb up 260 roughly hewn steps leads to the Tham Pha Hong viewpoint, a rocky outcrop offering stunning panoramas of the park; at kilometre-stone 49, there's a four-kilometre nature trail taking in Suan Son Dang Bak viewpoint; and at kilometre-stone 67, a seven-hundred-metre trail leads to the beautiful Haew Sai waterfall, best seen during or immediately after the rainy season. Experienced walkers can reach the top of Phu Phajit along a rugged trail which begins from kilometre-stone 69; you need to hire a guide from the visitor centre (best booked in advance) for the steep six-hour climb. Most people camp on top, bringing their own gear and supplies, before making the descent the next day.

Phu Reua National Park

About 50km west of Loei, the 120-square-kilometre **Phu Reua National Park** gets the name "Boat Mountain" from its resemblance to an upturned sampan, with the sharp ridge of its hull running southeast to northwest. The highest point of the ridge, Yod Phu Reua (1365m), offers one of the most spectacular panoramas in Thailand: the land drops away sharply on the Laos side, allowing views over toy-town villages to countless green-ridged mountains spreading towards Louang Phabang. To the northwest rises Phu Soai Dao (2102m) on Laos' western border; to the south are the Phetchabun mountains. If you happen to be driving yourself here from the west along Highway 203, it might be worth breaking your journey 10km from the Phu Reua turn-off at the **Château de Loei vineyard**, for the novelty value if nothing else: you can drive for 6km around the vast, seemingly incongruous fields of vines, taste a variety of wines and brandy, and get something to eat at the simple restaurant.

Access and accommodation

The nine-kilometre paved road north from Ban Pachan Tom on Highway 203 to the summit means the park can get crowded at weekends, though during the week you'll probably have the place to yourself. The snag is that there's no organized **public transport** up the steep summit road – regular Lom Sak and Phitsanulok buses from Loei can drop you at the turn-off to the park on Highway 203, but then you'll have to walk/hitch or charter a songthaew (B400–700, depending on how far up the mountain you want to be taken). The easiest option would be to **rent a motorbike** at the *Sugar Guest House* in Loei (see p.578). Once on the summit road, you have to pay B200 admission at a checkpoint, before reaching the **headquarters** and **visitor centre 1** (Ⓣ042 801716 or 884144) after 4km, which has a trail map, two simple restaurants, and, in the pretty, pine-shaded grounds, six four- to six-berth national park **bungalows** with hot showers (B2000–3000/bungalow). **Visitor centre 2** (Phuson), a three-kilometre walk or 5.5-kilometre drive further up the mountain near Hin Sam Chan waterfall, boasts several restaurants and is at the heart of the mountain's network of paths. At both visitor centres, a variety of **tents** can be rented and pitched: all with bedrolls and pillows, they cost B270–810 for two to six people; there's a B30 charge per person if you bring your own tent. Warm clothes are essential on cool-season nights – the lowest temperature in Thailand (-4°C) was recorded here in 1981 – and even by day the mountain is usually cool and breezy.

There are also plenty of **private accommodation** options, both on Highway 203 around Ban Pachan Tom and on the summit road itself. *Chachadaa Resort* (Ⓣ042 899399 or 081 841 4111; fan ④, air-con ⑦), at the east end of the village, 1km towards Loei from the turn-off to the national park, offers decent, spacious chalets, some with hot water and air-con, or you could stay 800m up the summit road at *Phupet Hill Resort* (Ⓣ042 899157 or 081 320 2874, Ⓦwww.phuphet.com; ④), in one of their large, attractive rooms with hot water, air-con and TV.

The park

A day's worth of well-marked trails fan out over the meadows and pine and broad-leaved evergreen forests of Phu Reua, taking in gardens of strange rock formations, the best sunrise viewpoint, Loan Noi, and, during and just after the rainy season, several waterfalls. The most spectacular **viewpoint**, Yod Phu Reua (Phu Reua Peak), is an easy one-kilometre stroll from the top of the summit road where the songthaews drop you. The park's population of barking deer, wild pigs and pheasants has declined over recent years – rangers' attempts to stop poaching by local villagers have been largely unsuccessful and have resulted in occasional armed clashes – but you may be lucky enough to spot one of 26 bird species, which include the crested serpent-eagle, green-billed malkoha, greater coucal, Asian fairy-bluebird, rufescent prinia and white-rumped munia, as well as several species of babbler, barbet, bulbul and drongo.

Along the Mekong

The **Mekong** is the one of the great rivers of the world and the third longest in Asia, after the Yangtse and the Yellow River. From its source 4920m up on the east Tibetan plateau it roars down through China's Yunnan province – where it's known as Lancang Jiang, the "Turbulent River" – before snaking its way a little more peaceably between Burma and Laos, and then, by way of the so-called "Golden Triangle", as the border between Thailand and Laos. After a brief shimmy into rural Laos via Louang Phabang, the river reappears in Isaan to form 750km of the border between Thailand and Laos. From Laos it crosses Cambodia and continues south to Vietnam, where it splinters into the many arms of the Mekong delta before flowing into the South China Sea, 4184km from where its journey began.

This dramatic stretch around Isaan is one of the more accessible places to observe the mighty river, and as Laos opens further border crossings to visitors, the Mekong is slowly becoming more of a transport link and less of a forbidding barrier. The guest houses along the upper part of this stretch, east from **Chiang Khan**, are geared towards relaxation and gentle exploration of the rural way of life along the river bank. **Nong Khai**, the terminus of the rail line from

Bangkok and the principal jumping-off point for trips to the Lao capital of Vientiane, is the pivotal town on the river, but has lost some of its restful charm since the building of the massive Thai-Australian Friendship Bridge and the ensuing increase in cross-border trade. East of Nong Khai you're into wild country; here the unique natural beauty of **Wat Phu Tok** is well worth the hefty detour, and your Mekong journey wouldn't be complete without seeing **Wat Phra That Phanom**, a place of pilgrimage for 2500 years. Sights get sparse beyond that, although by continuing south through **Mukdahan** you can join up with the southern Isaan route at Ubon Ratchathani (see p.554).

A road, served by very slow **buses** and **songthaews**, runs beside or at least parallel to the river as far as Mukdahan. If you've got the time (allow at least a week to do it any sort of justice) you could make the entire marathon journey described in this section, although realistically you'll probably start in Nong Khai and work your way either upstream or downstream from there. **Motorbike rental** may provide another incentive to base yourself in Nong Khai (though they're also available, on a smaller scale, in Chiang Khan): having your own transport will give you more freedom of movement, and the roads are quiet and easy to negotiate, though often in a state of disrepair. There's no official long-distance **boat** transport along this stretch of the river, at least from the Thai side, though several interesting river trips are available from Chiang Khan.

Chiang Khan to Nong Khai

Rustic "backpackers' resorts" – and the travelling between them – are the chief draw along the reach of the Mekong between **Chiang Khan** and Nong Khai. Highway 211 covers this whole course: songthaews take you from Chiang Khan to **Pak Chom**, from where buses complete the journey, stopping at all towns en route.

Chiang Khan

The Mekong route starts promisingly at **CHIANG KHAN**, a friendly town that happily hasn't been entirely converted to concrete yet. Rows of shuttered wooden shophouses stretch out in a two-kilometre ribbon parallel to the river, which for much of the year runs red with what locals call "the blood of the trees": rampant deforestation on the Lao side causes the rust-coloured topsoil to erode into the river. The town has only two streets – the main through route (Highway 211, also known as Thanon Sri Chiang Khan) and the quieter Thanon Chai Khong on the waterfront – with a line of sois connecting them, numbered from west to east.

Arguably the most enjoyable thing you can do here is to hitch up with other travellers for a **boat-trip** on the river, organized through one of the guest houses. If you opt to go **upstream**, you'll head west towards the lofty mountains of Khao Laem and Khao Ngu on the Thai side and Phu Lane and Phu Hat Song in Laos, gliding round a long, slow bend in the Mekong to the mouth of the Heuang River tributary, 20km from Chiang Khan, which forms the border to the west of this point; stops can be arranged to share the fine views with Phra Yai, a twenty-metre-tall golden Buddha standing on a hilltop at the confluence, and at Hat Sai Kaew, a sandy beach for swimming, fishing and picnicking. Upstream trips, costing around B250 per person, take three hours or so and are best undertaken in the afternoon, returning at sunset. A ride **downstream to**

△ The Mekong River

Pak Chom will take you through some of the most beautiful scenery on the Thai Mekong: hills and cliffs of all shapes and sizes advance and recede around the winding flow, and outside the rainy season, the rapids are dramatic without being dangerous (best between December and April), and the shores and islands are enlivened by neat grids of market gardens. This jaunt costs around B2000 for the boat, and takes around six hours, including an hour in Pak Chom, if you go both ways. Most guest houses also offer a one-hour **sunset on the Mekong** cruise for about B150 per person.

It's also worth taking a walk towards the eastern end of the river road to **Wat Tha Khok**, by Soi 20, for its unobstructed view across the majestic Mekong. The Lao viharn shows some odd French influences in its balustrades, rounded arches and elegantly coloured ceiling. Continuing another 2km east along the main highway, a left turn back towards the river will bring you to **Wat Tha Khaek**, a formerly ramshackle forest temple which, on the back of millions of bahts' worth of donations from Thai tourists, has embarked on an ambitious but slow-moving building programme in a bizarre mix of traditional and modern styles. One kilometre further along this side road lies the reason for the influx of visitors: at this point, the river runs over rocks at a wide bend to form the modest rapids of **Kaeng Kut Khu**. Set against the forested hillside of imaginatively named Phu Yai (Big Mountain), it's a pretty enough spot, with small restaurants and souvenir shops shaded by trees on the river bank. If you're feeling brave, try the local speciality *kung ten*, or "dancing shrimp" – fresh shrimp served live with a lime juice and chilli sauce. Boats can be hired at Kaeng Kut Khu, costing from B300 for a half-hour pootle around the rapids. With your own transport you could continue your explorations to **Phu Thok**, an isolated hill topped by a communications mast to the south of here. On Highway 211 just east of the turn-off to Wat Tha Khaek and Kaeng Kut Khu, a small signpost will point you down 3km of rough paved road, before you fork right and climb steeply for nearly 2km to the summit. From there, you'll be rewarded with splendid views of Chiang Khan, the Mekong and the striking patchwork of fields in the broad valley to the south, especially at sunset.

Practicalities

Songthaews from Loei (roughly every 30min) and Pak Chom (hourly in the morning, twice only in the afternoon) and **buses** from Loei (roughly hourly) stop at the west end of town near the junction of Highway 201 (the road from Loei) and Highway 211. The three guest houses recommended below all rent out **bicycles** (B50/day) and **motorbikes** (B200/day), and can arrange herbal steam baths and traditional massages. There's **Internet access** on Soi 10, near the junction with Highway 211, but currently there are **no banks** nor ATMs in Chiang Khan – the nearest are in Loei. You can extend your visa at the **immigration office** (Mon–Fri 8.30am–4.30pm; ⓣ042 821911 or 042 821175), a ten-minute walk east along Thanon Chai Khong from the *Rabieng* restaurant.

Accommodation

When it comes to **accommodation**, there are several appealing guest houses strung out along the riverside Thanon Chai Khong. The night market is on Thanon Chiang Khan, between sois 17 and 18, while the best **restaurant** in town, with peaceful water views and inexpensive Chinese and Thai dishes, is *Rabieng*, at the T-junction of Soi 9 and the river road.

Chiang Khan Hill Resort at Kaeng Kut Khu ⓣ042 821285, ⓦwww.chiangkhanhill.com. Upmarket resort with a swimming pool and a variety of air-con bungalows, all with hot-water bathroom, TV and fridge, in a pretty garden overlooking the river. ❺

Loogmai Guesthouse 112 Thanon Chai Khong, near Soi 5 ⓣ042 822334 or 086 234 0011, ⓔloogmaiguest@thaimail.com. Spacious, colonial-style, white mansion, adorned with green shutters and hung with modern art. Some of the lovely, airy rooms are en suite (sharing hot showers), and there's a pretty garden terrace overlooking the river. ❷–❸

Rimkong Pub and Guesthouse 294 Thanon Chai Khong, opposite Soi 8 ⓣ042 821125. A wide variety of wooden rooms with fans and mosquito screens here share clean hot-water bathrooms, and there's a small terrace on the top floor. The helpful Thai-French owners, who have lived in Chiang Khan for over ten years, are a great source of information on the area and offer a range of local tours. ❶

Souksomboon Thanon Chai Khong, between sois 8 and 9 ⓣ042 821064, ⓕ042 822482. Traditional hotel in an old-fashioned wooden building around a courtyard; choose between simple rooms with attached cold-water bathrooms and TVs, and smart, refurbished air-con rooms with hot showers. Fan ❷, air-con ❹

Tonkhong Guest House 299/3 Thanon Chai Khong, between sois 9 and 10 ⓣ042 821547, ⓔtonkhong@hotmail.com. Easy-going place run by a welcoming Thai couple, with slightly scrappy but clean rooms – some en suite (with shared hot showers), some with air-con – and a first-floor terrace overlooking the river, perfect for lounging. The popular Thai restaurant downstairs offers veggie options, as well as Western breakfasts. Extras on offer include occasional local day-trips and cooking courses. Fan ❷, air-con ❸

Pak Chom, Sang Khom and on towards Nong Khai

Hourly songthaews from Chiang Khan cover the beautiful, winding route to **PAK CHOM**, 41km downriver, where you can pick up a bus from Loei (7 daily) to continue your journey towards Nong Khai via Sang Khom. Pak Chom used to be the site of a refugee camp for fifteen thousand Lao Hmong, who were later dispersed to all parts of the globe, and although it remains a busy market town, its array of largely redundant administrative buildings lends something of the air of a ghost town. There's little incentive to stay apart from the *Pak Chom Guest House* (ⓣ042 881332 or 085 220 4263; ❶–❷), on Soi 1 at the west end of town, which is set in leafy grounds with peerless views of the Mekong. Bungalows are either primitive affairs on stilts, or smart and wooden with verandas, fans and en-suite cold-water bathrooms, and the owners can rustle up Western breakfasts, vegetarian food and communal Thai-Lao dinners; also on offer are boat trips (B80/person/hour) and massages.

Beyond Pak Chom, the road through the Mekong Valley becomes flatter and straighter. After 50km, a sign in English points down a side road to **Than Tip Falls**, 3km south, which is well worth seeking out. The ten-metre-high waterfall splashes down into a rock pool overhung by jungle on three sides; higher up, a bigger waterfall has a good pool for swimming, and if you can face the climb you can explore three higher levels.

Staying in **SANG KHOM**, which straggles along the tree-shaded south bank of the Mekong about 60km east of Pak Chom, puts you in the heart of an especially lush stretch of the river within easy biking distance of several backroad villages and temples. *Bouy Guest House* (ⓣ042 441065 or 086 356 5319; ❶) is the best of the accommodation here, enjoying a particularly choice location: decent bamboo huts, with beautiful views out over the river, are set in a spacious, flower-strewn compound on a spit of land that's reached by a wooden bridge over a small tributary. The welcoming owners can arrange day-trips to Ban Phu, or if that sounds too strenuous, you can settle for a massage or just relax in the hammocks strung from the veranda of each hut. Good Thai and Western food is available on a deck overlooking the stream (most of it also in vegetarian versions), and you can access the Internet, make international phone calls and rent bicycles (B40/day) and motorbikes (B200/day). On the Pak Chom side of town, just west of the bridge, the tidy, concrete bungalows of *Bungalow Cake Resort* shelter in a small, shady garden, with a large, attractive riverside terrace (ⓣ042 441440 or 087 219 9184; fan ❷, air-con ❹); some have air-con, hot water and TVs, but the best of them, with fans and cold-water bathrooms, overlook the Mekong.

Another 19km east on Route 211, midway between Sang Khom and Sri Chiangmai, **Wat Hin Maak Peng** is a famous meditation temple, popular with Thai pilgrims and rich donors. The long white boundary wall and huge modern buildings are evidence of the temple's prosperity, but its reputation is in fact based on the asceticism of the monks of the Thammayut sect, who keep themselves in strict poverty and allow only one meal a day to interrupt their meditation. The flood of merit-makers, however, proved too distracting for the founder of the wat, Luang Phu Thet, who before his death in 1994 decamped to the peace and quiet of Wat Tham Kham near Sakon Nakhon. Visitors have the opportunity to stroll around the immaculate gardens and to revere no fewer than three effigies of the great monk, one in his chedi-like mausoleum, another in a *sala* overlooking a lake, and the third in a lifelike attitude of meditating near the river.

Nong Khai and around

The major border town in these parts is **NONG KHAI**, still a relative backwater but developing fast since the construction of the huge **Thai-Australian Friendship Bridge** over the Mekong on the west side of town in 1994. Occupying a strategic position at the end of Highway 2 and the northeastern rail line, and just 24km from Vientiane, Nong Khai acts as a conduit for goods bought and sold by Thais and Lao, who are allowed to pass between the two cities freely for day-trips. Consequently, the souvenir markets that sprawl extensively around the main pier, **Tha Sadet**, carry Lao silver, wood and cane items, as well as local basketware and woven goods.

As with most of the towns along this part of the Mekong, the thing to do in Nong Khai is just to take it easy, enjoying the riverside atmosphere and the peaceful settings of its guest houses, which offer good value. Before you lapse into a relaxation-induced coma though, try joining an evening river tour, or make a day-trip out to see the sculptures and rock formations in the surrounding countryside.

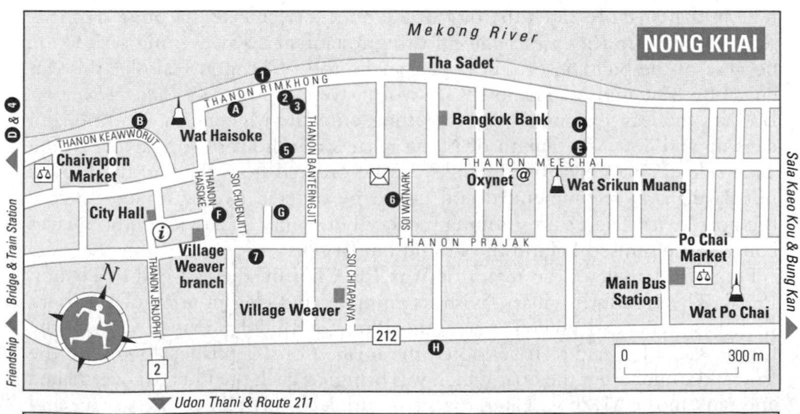

ACCOMMODATION				RESTAURANTS			
Friendship Guest House	C	Pantawee Hotel	F	The Danish Baker	5	Nobbi's Restaurant	2
Janhorm Apartment	G	Royal Mekong Nongkhai	D	Deang Namnuang	3	OJ's	6
Mut Mee Guest House	B	Ruan Thai Guest House	A	Mut Mee Guest House	B	Thai Thai Restaurant	7
Nongkhai Grand Thani Hotel	H	Sawasdee Guest House	E	Nam Tok Rim Khong	1	Zodiac	4

Nong Khai celebrates the generic Thai and Isaan festivals with due gusto, but in recent years a peculiarity of this stretch of the Mekong River has begun to attract celebrants from Bangkok and beyond. Every year in or around October, silent and vapourless **naga fireballs** appear from the river, small, pink, fiery balls that float vertically up to heights of as much as 150m, then disappear. This strange occurrence has now been consolidated into the festival of **Bang Fai Phaya Nak**, held over two days around the fifteenth day of the waxing moon in the eleventh lunar month. A tentative scientific theory proposes that the balls are methane gas from the mud on the bottom of the river, which reaches a certain temperature at that time of the year and is released; romantics will prefer the local belief that the nagas or *naks* (serpents) of the river breathe out the fireballs to celebrate the Buddha's return to earth at the end of Buddhist Lent.

The Town

Nong Khai lays itself out along the south bank of the Mekong in a four-kilometre band which is never more than 500m deep. Running from east to west, Thanon Meechai dominates activity: the main shops and businesses are plumb in the middle around the post office and Tha Sadet, with more frenetic commerce to the east at the Po Chai morning market by the bus station, and to the west at Chaiyaporn market in the afternoons. Although most of the old buildings have been replaced by concrete boxes, one or two weather-beaten wooden houses remain, their attractive balconies, porticoes and slatted shutters showing the influence of colonial architecture, which was imported from across the river before the French were forced out of Laos in 1954.

The most pleasant place for a stroll is the riverside area. Although built-up in the centre around Tha Sadet, it becomes rustic and leafy around the fringes, which are often busy with people bathing, washing their clothes and fishing, especially in the early morning and evening. If you're lucky, you might also catch sight of a sunken chedi at the far eastern end of town, **Phra That Nong Khai**, which slipped into the river in 1847 and has since subsided so far that it's only visible in the dry season; this is thought to be a particularly good spot to see naga fireballs (see above), said to be produced by the naga that guards the relic in the chedi. To catch the best of life on the river, take the **boat trip** that sets out from the *Ruenpae Haisoke* floating restaurant every evening at 5.30pm; because of the building of a new pier at the top of Thanon Haisoke, this can currently be found off Thanon Keawworut, west of *Mut Mee Guest House*. At B30, it's the least expensive way of getting onto the Mekong in Thailand, and runs up and down the length of Nong Khai for an hour or so, sticking to the Thai side. Reasonably priced drinks can be ordered from the bar; the food is not particularly recommended and has to be ordered twenty minutes before the boat leaves. There's no stunning scenery, but plenty of activity on both river banks as the sun sets behind the Friendship Bridge.

The main temple of the region is **Wat Po Chai** off the east end of Thanon Prajak. The cruciform viharn, with its complex and elegant array of Lao tiers, shelters a venerated golden image, the Phra Sai Buddha. Prince Chakri, the future Rama I, is said to have looted the image from Vientiane, along with the Emerald Buddha, but the boat which was bringing back the Phra Sai overturned and sank in the Mekong. Later, the statue miraculously rose to the surface and the grateful people of Nong Khai built this great hangar of a viharn to house it, decorating the walls with murals of its miraculous journey; the present king, Chakri's descendant, still comes every year to pay his respects. It's worth a visit for the Buddha's stagy setting, in front of a steep, flame-covered altar, dazzlingly

Crossing to Laos from Nong Khai

When crossing to Laos, you can now get a fifteen-day tourist **visa on arrival** at Nong Khai's **Thai-Australian Friendship Bridge** for US$30, plus two photos (full details of the visa options for Laos are given on p.33). It's possible to pay in baht at the bridge, though it's over the odds at B1500; Monday to Friday at lunchtime and after 4pm, and all day at weekends, there's an "overtime" surcharge of US$1/B50. Foreigners have to use the bridge here (daily 6am–10pm), as the ferry service from Tha Sadet is reserved for Thais and Lao. From downtown Nong Khai, your best bet is to take one of the four daily **buses** that run all the way through to Vientiane from the bus station (B35). Otherwise, it's a question of taking a tuk-tuk to the foot of the bridge (about B40–50), then a minibus (every 10min until 10pm; B20) across the span itself; on the other side you can catch a taxi (about B200 one-way, B600 for a one-day tour), tuk-tuk (about B100 one-way, B300 for a one-day tour) or infrequent bus (B20) to Vientiane, 24km away.

lit from above and below. The solid gold head is so highly polished that you have to peer carefully to make out the Sukhothai influence in its haughty expression and beaked nose.

Fifteen minutes' walk west of Wat Po Chai at 1151 Soi Chitapanya, just off Thanon Prajak, **Village Weaver Handicrafts** (daily 8am–5pm; ⓣ042 411236 or 042 421000, ⓦwww.villageweaver.net) specializes in **mut mee** (literally "tied strings"), the northeastern method of tie-dyeing bundles of cotton thread before hand-weaving, which produces geometrical patterns on a coloured base; Village Weaver also has a branch shop (daily 9am–7pm) slightly nearer the centre at 1020–1020/1 Thanon Prajak, on the corner of Thanon Haisoke. Through a self-help project initiated in 1982 to help local rural women earn cash, the work is produced in nearby villages and in the yard behind the main shop, where you can watch the weaving process (daily except Sun). White on indigo is the simplest, most traditional form, but the shop also carries a wide range of more richly patterned lengths of silk and cotton (tailoring available), as well as ready-made clothes, wall hangings, bags and axe pillows; they offer a very reasonable and professional posting and packing service back to your home country, and it's also possible to order through the website. Seven kilometres south of Nong Khai on the road to Udon Thani, the **Village Vocational Training Centre** is another self-help initiative by the Good Shepherd Sisters, producing **pottery** and weaving sold at the Isan Shop, 3km back towards Nong Khai on the same road; you're welcome to visit the centre to see the artisans at work (centre and shop both open Mon–Sat 8am–5pm, centre closes for lunch noon–1pm).

Practicalities

From Bangkok, you'll most likely be coming to Nong Khai by night **train**, arriving just after dawn at the station 3km southwest of the centre near the Friendship Bridge. Day **buses** from all points in Isaan and night buses from further afield pull in at the bus station on the east side of town off Thanon Prajak. There are also Thai Airways' **air-con minibuses** from Udon Thani airport (B100), which meet incoming flights from Bangkok.

As everything in Nong Khai is so spread out, you might want to consider hopping on a **tuk-tuk** for getting around (from B15 for a short journey such as bus station to Tha Sadet, up to B45 for bus station to train station). To get around under your own steam, **bicycles** (B30/day) and **motorbikes** can be rented (around B200/day) on Thanon Keawworut in front of the *Mut Mee*

Guest House, and from *Ruan Thai Guest House*; motorbikes are also available at *Friendship Guest House*, along with **mountain bikes** (B40/day).

There's a **TAT office** in front of the City Hall on Thanon Prajak (daily 8.30am–4.30pm; ⓣ042 421326). If time's running out on your Thai visa, you can get an extension at the **immigration office** (Mon–Fri 8.30am–4.30pm; ⓣ042 420242) on the road leading up to the Friendship Bridge – though at current prices for extensions, you might as well treat yourself to a day in Vientiane and get a free thirty-day Thai entry stamp on your way back.

There are plenty of places offering **Internet access**, including Oxynet, 569/2 Thanon Meechai, the *Mekong Guest House* on Thanon Rimkong just west of Tha Sadet, and the Hornbill Bookshop, on the funky little lane leading to *Mut Mee Guest House*. The shop stocks an excellent selection of new and second-hand **books** in English, as well as postcards and batik hangings. Good, strong **massages** and foot massages can be had at Suan Sukapab, 623 Thanon Banterngjit (daily 9am–9pm; ⓣ042 423323).

Accommodation

As well as several good-value luxury **hotels**, Nong Khai has an excellent choice of inexpensive **guest houses**, the best and most reliable among which are *Mut Mee* and *Sawasdee*.

Friendship Guest House 538 Soi Srikunmuang, Thanon Meechai ⓣ085 747 7298, ⓔinfo@friendshipguesthouse.com. Welcoming, Thai-Australian place with some pretty, decorative touches, in a quiet spot near the river and just round the corner from *Sawasdee*. Clean, well-kept rooms with fans and shared hot-water bathrooms occupy a traditional wooden house looking onto a neat ornamental garden and shady bar-restaurant. ❷

Janhorm Apartment 479 Soi Srichumchuen, Thanon Prajak ⓣ042 460293, ⓕ042 460415. A modern, lime-green block on a quiet soi, set against the wall of Wat Sri Chum Chuen and with a pleasant, shady sitting area at the front. Not really apartments (though they are available by the month, with substantial discounts), but large, clean rooms with armchairs, fridges, TVs and hot-water bathrooms. Fan ❷, air-con ❸

Mut Mee Guest House 1111 Thanon Keawworut ⓣ042 460717, ⓦwww.mutmee.net. A magnet for travellers, where well-kept rooms sprawl around an attractive riverside terrace. Bathrooms with cold or hot water are either shared or en suite, and three-bed dorms are available (dorm bed B90). With helpful, well-informed staff and a good riverside restaurant, it also offers yoga, meditation and massage sessions. Fan ❶, air-con ❹

Nongkhai Grand Thani Hotel 589 Moo 5, Nongkhai–Phonpisai road ⓣ042 420033, ⓦwww.nongkhaigrand.com. On the southern bypass, this luxury hotel has high standards of service, a swimming pool and a rooftop terrace restaurant offering Isaan specialities and panoramic views over Nong Khai and Laos. ❻

Pantawee Hotel 1049 Thanon Haisoke ⓣ042 411568–9, ⓦwww.nongkhaihotel.com. A good, well-run mid-range choice that's surprisingly comfortable for the price: immaculately clean fan or air-con rooms all come with hot-water bathroom, TV, DVD player and fridge, and some have free Internet access and computers. There's also a small pool and spa. Fan ❺, air-con ❻

Royal Mekong Nongkhai 222 Thanon Panungchonprathan ⓣ042 465777–81, ⓦwww.welcome.to/royal_mekong. In riverside grounds west of town, 200m past the Friendship Bridge and next to the dry-season beach at Hat Jommanee, an international-standard hotel with a large swimming pool where all two hundred bedrooms have views of the Mekong and Laos. ❻

Ruan Thai Guest House 1126 Thanon Rimkhong ⓣ042 412519. Recently renovated wooden houses in a quiet garden compound with attractive, well-maintained rooms, which run the gamut of facilities from shared hot-water bathrooms to air-con, hot-water en suites with TVs. Internet access available. Fan ❶, air-con ❷

Sawasdee Guest House 402 Thanon Meechai ⓣ042 412502, ⓕ042 420259. A well-restored, grand old wooden shophouse round a pleasant courtyard, with helpful and meticulous management: free luggage storage and showers available for those catching a night train or bus. Fan-cooled rooms sharing bathrooms (try to avoid those overlooking the noisy main road), with hot showers available, and air-con rooms with en-suite hot-water bathrooms. Fan ❶, air-con ❷

Eating

With so many travellers of different nationalities passing through this border town, it's not surprising that a few have hung around to purvey their national cuisine. *Deang Namnuang*, Nong Khai's most famous restaurant, for example, is Vietnamese, but good Thai restaurants are harder to come by.

The Danish Baker Thanon Meechai. Sociable bar-restaurant with a few pavement tables on the busy main road for people-watching. Decent Thai food, good Western breakfast buffets, pizzas and Scandinavian specials such as Swedish caviar and Danish meatballs with potato salad.

Deang Namnuang Thanon Rimkong. Delicious, inexpensive Vietnamese food at this immaculately clean and popular place, with an air-con room and a lovely riverside terrace. Specialities include *nam nuang* (Vietnamese sausages), fresh spring rolls and deep-fried prawns on sugarcane skewers. Closes at 8pm.

Mut Mee Guest House 1111 Thanon Keawworut. This relaxed, inexpensive riverfront eatery under bamboo shelters is deservedly popular: good Thai and Isaan dishes, particularly vegetarian versions, vie with tasty Western efforts including quiche lorraine and home-made apple pie.

Nam Tok Rim Khong Thanon Rimkhong. Simple but popular and cheap restaurant with an attractive balcony overlooking the river, specializing in *nam tok*, spicy hot beef salad, as well as other Isaan delicacies such as *som tam*, dried beef, sausages and hot-and-sour soups. Closes at 8.30pm.

Nobbi's Restaurant 997 Thanon Rimkhong. Run by a German-Thai couple, this relaxing bar-restaurant, hung with plants and fairy lights, is popular with expats for its all-day Western breakfasts, delicious home-made German sausages, smoked ham, tasty pizzas and wide variety of German beer on tap and in bottles. All manner of German produce available to take away.

OJ's Soi Watnark, Thanon Meechai. Congenial and relaxing bar-café with plenty of outdoor tables, run by a friendly Anglo-Thai couple. Tasty Thai food and English favourites such as roasts and pies, as well as all-day Western breakfasts and fresh juices.

Thai Thai Restaurant 1155/8 Thanon Prajak. The place to come for an honest, inexpensive Thai dinner; the menu in English is limited, but will get you as far as fried rice or noodles, soups and curries, or you can point out anything else you fancy on the colourful display counter. The similar *Dee Dee Pochana Restaurant* next door is also very popular.

Zodiac Thanon Keawworut, about 2km west of *Mut Mee Guest House*. Go through the grounds of Wat Meechaitha on the north side of Thanon Keawworut and descend the steps to this very good floating restaurant, which catches any breezes going on the river. The menu features Isaan specialities, including a taster plate of local appetizers (B150), as well as plenty of fish and vegetarian dishes.

Around Nong Khai

By far the easiest and most popular day-trip out of Nong Khai takes in **Sala Kaeo Kou**, with its surreal sculptures, a short songthaew hop to the east. To the southwest of town and also fairly easy to get to, **Wat Phra That Bang Phuan** offers classic temple sightseeing, while the natural rock formations at **Ban Phu** require much more effort and a full day out. Some of the sights upstream along the Mekong described on the previous pages, as well as Wat Phu Tok described below, are also within day-tripping distance, and it's quite possible to get to **Ban Chiang** (see p.573) and back in a day, changing buses at Udon Thani.

Sala Kaeo Kou

Just off the main highway 5km east of Nong Khai, **Sala Kaeo Kou** (aka Wat Khaek; daily 8.30am–6pm; B10) is best known for its bizarre sculpture garden, which looks like the work of a giant artist on acid. The temple was founded by the late **Luang Phu Boonlua Surirat**, an unconventional Thai holy man who studied under a Hindu guru in Vietnam and preached in Laos until he was thrown out by the Communists in the late 1970s. His charisma – those who drank water offered by him would, it was rumoured, give up all they owned to the temple – and heavy emphasis on morality attracted many followers among

△ Sala Kaeo Kou

the farmers of Nong Khai. Luang Phu's popularity suffered, however, after his eleven-month spell in prison for insulting King Bhumibol, a crime alleged by jealous neighbours and probably without foundation; he died aged 72 in August 1996, a year after his release.

Arrayed with pretty flowers and plants, the **sculpture garden** bristles with Buddhist, Hindu and secular figures, all executed in concrete with imaginative abandon by unskilled followers under Luang Phu's direction. The religious statues, in particular, are radically modern. Characteristics that marked the Buddha out as a supernatural being – tight curls and a bump on the crown of the head called the *ushnisha* – are here transformed into beehives, and the *rashmis* on top (flames depicting the Buddha's fiery intellect) are depicted as long, sharp spikes. The largest statue in the garden shows the familiar story of the kindly naga king, Muchalinda, sheltering the Buddha, who is lost in meditation, from the heavy rain and floods: here the Buddha has shrunk in significance and the seven-headed snake has grown to 25m, with fierce, gaping fangs and long tongues.

Many of the statues illustrate **Thai proverbs**. Near the entrance, an elephant surrounded by a pack of dogs symbolizes integrity, "as the elephant is indifferent to the barking dogs". The nearby serpent-tailed monster with the moon in his mouth – Rahoo, the cause of eclipses – serves as an injunction to oppose all obstacles, just as the people of Isaan and Laos used to ward off eclipses by banging drums and firing guns. In the corner furthest from the entrance, you enter the complex Circle of Life through a huge mouth representing the womb, inside which a hermit, a policeman, a monk, a rich man and a beggar, among others, represent different paths in life. A man with two wives is shown beating the older one because he is ensnared by the wishes of the younger one, and an old couple who have made the mistake of not having children now find they have only each other for comfort.

The disturbingly vacant, smiling faces of the garden Buddhas bear more than a passing resemblance to Luang Phu himself, photos of whom adorn the **temple building**, a huge white edifice with mosque-like domes. On the second floor, his corpse is preserved on a domed palanquin, which is decorated with fairy lights and a virtual fish tank. If you're heading over to Laos, the **Xiang Khouan** sculpture garden – Sala Kaeo Kou's precursor, 25km from downtown Vientiane on the Mekong River – shouldn't be missed; Luang Phu spent twenty years working on the sculptures there before his expulsion.

Wat Phra That Bang Phuan

More famous as the site of a now concealed 2000-year-old Indian chedi than for its modern replacement, rural **Wat Phra That Bang Phuan** remains a highly revered place of pilgrimage. The wat is in the hamlet of **Ban Bang Phuan**, southwest of Nong Khai on Highway 211; buses from Nong Khai to Pak Chom and Loei pass this way (though not buses to Tha Bo, which use the minor road west along the river bank from Nong Khai), or it might be quicker to take an Udon-bound service 12km down Highway 2 to Ban Nong Song Hong, then change onto an Udon–Sri Chiangmai bus for the remaining 12km. On the way to or from Wat Phra That Bang Phuan, it would be well worth breaking your journey at the Village Vocational Training Centre and shop, between Nong Khai and Ban Nong Song Hong on Highway 2 (see p.589).

The original **chedi** is supposed to have been built by disciples of the Buddha to hold 29 relics – pieces of breastbone – brought from India. A sixteenth-century king of Vientiane piously earned himself merit by building a tall Lao-style chedi over the top of the previous stupa; rain damage toppled this in 1970, but it was restored in 1977 to the fine, gleaming white edifice seen today. The unkempt compound also contains a small museum, crumbling brick chedis and some large open-air Buddhas.

Ban Phu

Deep in the countryside 61km southwest of Nong Khai, the wooded slopes around **BAN PHU** are dotted with strangely eroded sandstone formations, which have long exerted a mystical hold over people in the surrounding area. Local wisdom has it that the outcrops, many of which were converted into small temples from around the ninth century onwards, are either meteorites – believed to account for their burnt appearance – or, more likely, were caused by glacial erosion. Together with a stupa enshrining a Buddha footprint that is now an important pilgrimage site (especially during its annual festival in March), the rock formations have been linked up under the auspices of fifty-square-kilometre **Phu Phra Bat Historical Park** (daily dawn–dusk; B30). The **information centre** (daily 8am–4.30pm) by the park entrance contains fairly interesting displays on the red prehistoric paintings of animals, humans, hands and geometric patterns that are found on the rock formations, and on the tale of Ussa and Barot (see below). Around the information centre, a well-signposted network of **paths** has been cleared from the thin forest to connect 25 of the outcrops, each of which has a helpful English-language information board attached. It would take a good five hours to explore the whole park, but the most popular circuit, covering all the sights listed below, can be completed in an ambling two hours.

On **public transport**, the easiest way of getting there from Nong Khai is to take the 7.15am bus to Ban Phu; if you leave any later you won't have time to see the park properly, as the whole journey takes a couple of hours and the last bus back to Nong Khai leaves at around 3.30pm. From Ban Phu, it's another 14km west to the historical park; take a songthaew for the first 10km to the Ban Tiu intersection; from here a motorbike taxi will bring you the final 4km up to the main park entrance and information centre. If you happen to be coming from Udon Thani, it's best to catch a bus from Talat Rungsina towards either Nam Som or Na Yung, which will drop you off at Ban Tiu.

Among the most interesting of the outcrops are **Tham Wua** and **Tham Khon**, two natural shelters whose paintings of oxen and human stick figures suggest that the area was first settled by hunter-gatherers two to three thousand years ago. A legend that's well known in this part of Thailand and Laos accounts for the name of nearby **Kok Ma Thao Barot** (Prince Barot's Stable), a broad platform overhung by a huge slab of sandstone. A certain Princess Ussa, banished by her father to these slopes to be educated by a hermit, sent out an SOS that was answered by a dashing prince, Barot. The two fell in love and were married against the wishes of Ussa's father, prompting the king to challenge Barot to a distinctly oriental sort of duel: each would build a temple, and the last to finish would be beheaded. The king lost. Kok Ma Thao Barot is celebrated as the place where Barot kept his horse when he visited Ussa.

The furthest point of the circuit is the viewpoint at **Pha Sadej**, where the cliff drops away to give a lovely view across green fields and forest to the distant mountains. More spectacular is **Hor Nang Ussa** (Ussa's Tower), a mushroom formed by a flat slab capping a five-metre-high rock pillar. Under the cap of the mushroom, a shelter has been carved out and walled in on two sides. The *sema* found scattered around the site, and the square holes in which others would have been embedded, indicate that this was a shrine, probably during the ninth to eleventh centuries in the Dvaravati period. Nearby, a huge rock on a flimsy pivot miraculously balances itself against a tree at **Wat Por Ta** (The Father-in-Law's Temple); the walls and floor have been evenly carved out to form a vaguely rectangular shrine, with Dvaravati Buddha images dotted around.

The left fork on the way to the park entrance leads to **Wat Phra Bat Bua Bok**: a crude *that* built in imitation of Wat Phra That Phanom (see p.597), it's decorated with naive bas-reliefs of divinities and boggle-eyed monsters, which add to the atmosphere of simple, rustic piety. In a gloomy chamber in the tower's base, the only visible markings on the sandstone **Buddha footprint** show the Wheel of Law. Legend has it that the Buddha made the footprint here for a serpent that had asked to be ordained as a monk, but had been refused because it was not human. Higher up the slope, a smaller *that* perches on a hanging rock that seems to defy gravity.

Downstream to Mukdahan

East of Nong Khai, the land on the Thai side of the Mekong becomes gradually more arid, while jagged forest-covered mountains loom on the Laos side. Not many visitors make it this far, to the northeast's northeast, though the few attractions are surprisingly varied, ranging from painterly riverscapes to Isaan's major religious site, **Wat Phra That Phanom**. **Transport** along Highway 212 out of Nong Khai is fairly straightforward: hourly buses from Nong Khai run to Bung Kan, 137km away, which four daily continue to Nakhon Phanom, where you have to change onto one of the hourly buses to get to That Phanom and Mukdahan.

Wat Phu Tok

The most compelling destination in the area to the east of Nong Khai is the extraordinary hilltop retreat of **Wat Phu Tok**. One of two sandstone outcrops that jut steeply out of the plain 35km southeast of Bung Kan, Phu Tok has been transformed in the past few years into a meditation wat, its fifty or so monks building their scattered huts on perches high above breathtaking cliffs. The outcrop comes into sight long before you get there, its sheer red face sandwiched between green vegetation on the lower slopes and tufts of trees on the narrow plateau above. As you get closer, the horizontal white lines across the cliffs reveal themselves to be painted wooden walkways, built to give the temple seven levels to represent the seven stages of enlightenment.

In an ornamental garden at the base, reflected in a small lake, an elegant, incongruously modern marble chedi commemorates **Phra Ajaan Juen**, the famous meditation master who founded the wat in 1968 and died in a plane crash ten years later. Within the chedi, the monk's books and other belongings, and diamond-like fragments of his bones, are preserved in a small shrine.

The first part of the ascent of the outcrop takes you to the third level up a series of long, sometimes slippery, wooden staircases, the first of many for which you'll need something more sturdy than flip-flops on your feet. A choice of two routes – the left fork is more interesting – leads to the fifth and most important level, where the **Sala Yai** houses the temple's main Buddha image in an airy, dimly lit cavern. The artificial ledges that cut across the northeast face are not for the fainthearted, but they are one way of getting to the dramatic northwest tip here on level five: on the other side of a deep crevice spanned by a wooden bridge, the monks have built an open-sided Buddha viharn under a huge anvil rock (though the gate to the viharn is usually locked). This spot affords stunning **views** over a broad sweep of countryside and across to the second, uninhabited outcrop. The flat top of the hill forms the seventh level, where you can wander along overgrown paths through thick forest.

Practicalities

Getting to Wat Phu Tok isn't easy – the location was chosen for its isolation, after all – but the journey out gives you a slice of life in remote countryside.

The best option is to hire a motorbike in Nong Khai, as it's a real slog by public transport: change buses at Bung Kan, catching one of the half-hourly buses south along Route 222 towards Pang Khon; get off after 25km at **Ban Siwilai** from where songthaews make the hour-long, twenty-kilometre trip east to Phu Tok either when they gather a full complement of passengers (more likely in the morning) or under charter (around B200).

It's not possible to **stay** at Wat Phu Tok or in the attached village (Ban Siwilai has a couple of very basic hotels if you get really stuck), though **food** is available: just outside the grounds, a collection of foodstalls and a simple restaurant dish up the usual noodles and grilled chicken.

Nakhon Phanom

Beyond Bung Kan, the river road rounds the hilly northeastern tip of Thailand before heading south through remote country where you're apt to find yourself stopping for water buffalo as often as for vehicles. The Mekong can only be glimpsed occasionally until you reach **NAKHON PHANOM** (meaning "City of Mountains"), 313km from Nong Khai, a clean and prosperous town, which affords the finest view of the river in northern Isaan, framed against the giant ant hills of the Lao mountains opposite.

The town makes a pleasant place to hang out, its quiet broad streets lined with some grand old public buildings, colonial-style houses and creaking wooden shophouses. During the Indochina wars, Nakhon Phanom was an important gateway for thousands of Vietnamese refugees, who built a landmark clock tower to thank the Thais for their hospitality, just north of the main pier for Laos. The passenger **ferry** from this pier crosses to **Khammouan (Tha Khaek) in Laos** usually every half-hour or so between 8.30am and 4pm (depending on demand; B50 one-way), and fifteen-day **Lao visas** can be bought on arrival for US$30 (see p.33). If you're not crossing the border, you can still appreciate the beautiful riverscape by joining one of the daily **boat trips** that depart from just south of the main pier at 5pm (B50; drinks available). Walking around town, you'll see several lit-up boat shapes around the place, a reminder of Nakhon Phanom's best-known festival, the **illuminated boat procession**, which is held on the river every year at the end of the rainy season, usually in late October. Around fifty boats of up to ten metres in length, adorned with elaborate lights and carrying offerings of food and flowers, are launched on the river in a spectacular display. The week-long celebrations – marking the end of the annual three-month Buddhist Rains Retreat – also feature colourful dragon-boat races along the Mekong, pitting Thai and Lao teams against each other.

Practicalities

The main **bus station** is about 2km west of the centre on Highway 22. You can fly to Nakhon Phanom from Bangkok with PB Air (Ⓦwww.pbair.com); air-con minibuses from the **airport** cost B70 per person. **TAT** has an office in an impressive old mansion at 184/1 Thanon Suntorn Vichit, corner of Thanon Salaklang (daily 8.30am–4.30pm; Ⓣ042 513490–2, Ⓔtatphnom@tat.or.th), 500m north of the pier for Laos; they also cover Sakon Nakhon and Mukdahan provinces. Ask here for directions if you're interested in visiting the house where the Vietnamese national hero, Ho Chi Minh, lived in the late 1920s, when he was forced to go underground during the struggle for independence from France; around 5km away on the southwestern edge of Nakhon Phanom at Ban Na Joke, the Vietnamese-style wooden house – terracotta roof tiles and no stilts – has recently been reconstructed, but is really only for Uncle Ho devotees.

There's cheap **Internet access** at an unnamed place opposite the *Grand Hotel* (see below) on Thanon Sri Thep.

Accommodation and eating

The best of Nakhon Phanom's budget **hotels** is the friendly four-storey *Grand Hotel* at 210 Thanon Sri Thep (Ⓣ042 511526, Ⓕ042 511283; fan ❶, air-con ❷), a block back from the river just south of the passenger ferry and market. It has bright, modern, en-suite rooms, some with fan and cold-water bathrooms (with access to a shared hot shower), others with hot water, TV and air-con. Less central, but good value in the moderate range is the friendly *Mae Nam Kong Grand View*, on Highway 212 towards the southern edge of town (Ⓣ042 513564, Ⓕ042 511037; ❺); the large, colourfully decorated, marble-floored rooms here come with air-con, en-suite hot-water bathrooms and TVs, and the nicest have balconies with river views. More luxurious and expensive is the eight-storey *Nakhonphanom River View* (Ⓣ042 522333–40, Ⓔriverview@cscoms.com; ❺), a few hundred metres south of the *Mae Nam Kong Grand View*, with tasteful rooms boasting facilities ranging from cable TV to bathtubs, as well as an outdoor swimming pool overlooking the river.

Among several riverside **restaurants**, friendly *Satang*, a couple of hundred metres north of the *Mae Nam Kong Grand View Hotel*, stands out: here you can sit at the pleasant tables out front, on an open balcony or across the road on the promenade, tucking into specialities such as *thawt man kung* (deep-fried prawn cakes), *hor mok* (seafood curry soufflé) and *gataa rawn* (a sizzling hot-plate of seafood). The popular terrace restaurant attached to the *Mae Nam Kong Grand View Hotel* also serves up excellent Thai food, notably fresh fish, in a lovely riverside setting. Thanon Fueng Nakhon, running west from the old clock tower, has a choice of several simple eateries and is a lively spot at night, while several simple Isaan restaurants on stilts line the river bank to the south of the *Nakhonphanom River View Hotel*.

That Phanom and around

Fifty kilometres south of Nakhon Phanom, **THAT PHANOM**, a small, friendly, riverside town of weather-beaten wooden buildings, sprawls around Isaan's most important shrine. Popularly held to be one of the four sacred pillars of Thai religion (the other three are Chiang Mai's Wat Phra That Doi Suthep, Wat Mahathat in Nakhon Si Thammarat, and Wat Phra Phutthabat near Lopburi), **Wat Phra That Phanom** is a fascinating place of pilgrimage, especially at the time of the ten-day Phra That Phanom festival, usually in February, when thousands of people come to pay homage and enjoy themselves in the traditional holiday between harvesting and sowing; pilgrims believe that they must make the trip seven times during a full moon before they die.

This far-northeastern corner of Thailand may seem like a strange location for one of the country's holiest sites, but the wat used to serve both Thais and Lao, as evidenced by the ample boat landing in the village, now largely disused; since the Pathet Lao took over in 1975, Lao have only been allowed to cross the river for the Ngan Phra That Phanom and the fascinating Monday and Thursday morning waterfront **market**, where Lao people offer for sale such items as wild animal skins, black pigs and herbal medicines, alongside the usual fruit and veg. The temple reputedly dates back to the eighth year after the death of the Buddha (535 BC), when five local princes built a simple brick chedi to house bits of his breastbone. It's been restored or rebuilt seven times, most recently after it collapsed during a rainstorm in 1975; the latest incarnation is in the form of a Lao *that*, 57m high, modelled on the That Luang in Vientiane.

The best approach to the temple is from the river: a short ceremonial way leads directly from the pier, under a Disneyesque victory arch erected by the Lao, through the temple gates to the **chedi** itself, which, as is the custom, faces water and the rising sun. A brick-and-plaster structure covered with white paint and gold floral decorations, the chedi looks like nothing so much as a giant, ornate table leg turned upside down. From each of the four sides, an eye forming part of the traditional flame pattern stares down, and the whole thing is surmounted by an umbrella made of 16kg of gold, with precious gems and gold rings embedded in each tier. The chedi sits on a gleaming white marble platform, on which pilgrims say their prayers and leave every imaginable kind of offering to the relics. Look out for the brick reliefs in the shape of four-leaf clovers above three of the doorways in the base: on the northern side, Vishnu mounted on a garuda; on the western side, the four guardians of the earth putting offerings in the Buddha's alms bowl; and above the south door, a carving of the Buddha entering nirvana. At the corners of the chedi, brick plaques, carved in the tenth century but now heavily restored, tell the stories of the wat's princely founders.

Practicalities

The bus station, just off Thanon Chayangkun, south of the wat, is served by frequent **buses** from Nakhon Phanom, Sakon Nakhon and Mukdahan; the Nakhon Phanom route is also covered by frequent songthaews, which gather to the north of the wat.

That Phanom's outstanding **accommodation** choice is the welcoming *Niyana Guest House* on Soi Weethee Sawrachon, which runs between the riverfront road and Thanon Phanom Phanarak, a block north of the victory arch and the pier (Ⓣ042 540880; ❶). The effusive owner, Niyana, is a fund of information and rents out bicycles for local exploration (B40/day). The pleasant rooms in her quiet, two-storey house are decorated with her own paintings and share hot-water bathrooms. Niyana has a sideline selling unstuffed axe pillows, rarely available unfilled elsewhere in Thailand, and much cheaper to post home. If Niyana can't put you up, try the *Chaivon Hotel*, a basic but characterful old place on Thanon Phanom Phanarak on the north side of the victory arch (Ⓣ042 541391; ❶).

For somewhere to **eat**, there are a few simple restaurants around the victory arch, the best of these being *That Phanom Pochana*, on the north side of the arch, a big, clean, airy place which is good for a *phat thai* or a choice of Isaan, Thai and Chinese dishes. There are several **banks** with ATMs on Thanon Chayangkun near the wat, and a few **Internet** places scattered around town, including an unnamed shop opposite the *That Phanom Pochana* restaurant.

Around That Phanom

From That Phanom the weaving village of **Renu Nakhon**, 15km northwest, can be reached by regular songthaews to the Renu junction, then 8km north by tuk-tuk. The wat at the centre of the village has a smaller, stubbier imitation of the Phra That Phanom, crudely decorated with stucco carvings and brown paint, and an attached cultural centre where local dance performances are sometimes held. Around the wat, shops sell a wide variety of local crafts, including reasonable cotton and silk, much of it in simple, colourful *mut mee* styles.

An interesting cycle ride from That Phanom (bikes can be rented from *Niyana Guest House*; see above) takes the road following the river – a mixture of deteriorating paved road and red dirt – through green countryside and a couple of villages 18km south to the **Kaeng Kabao rapids**. Here Thai tourists gather to watch the white water; their numbers are catered for with bamboo *sala*s overlooking the river where they can picnic, and many stalls and restaurants selling simple food such as barbecued chicken or pork.

Continuing 3km south of the rapids along the river road (it's also signposted off Highway 212), you'll be met with the incongruous sight of a very lavish Catholic church, **Our Lady of the Martyrs of Thailand Shrine** (called Wat Songkhon in Thai), which was blessed and dedicated in December 1995. It's situated on an idyllic stretch of the Mekong, with manicured lawns looking across a few river islands and some longtail-boat activity to Laos. Many of the people who live along the stretch of the river between That Phanom and Mukdahan are Catholic, and in the 1950s some were accused of being Communist sympathisers and were killed by the Thai authorities; at the rear of the church, seven glass coffins hold models of the bodies of the Thais who have been declared martyrs by the Catholic Church. The minimalist modern complex is surrounded by a terracotta-coloured laterite circular wall with Stations of the Cross, and the square glass-walled church comes complete with a gold-coloured floating Jesus; note that, just as with Buddhist temples in Thailand, it's customary to take off your shoes before going inside.

Mukdahan and beyond

Fifty kilometres downriver of That Phanom, **MUKDAHAN** is the last stop on the Mekong trail before Highway 212 heads off inland to Ubon Ratchathani, 170km to the south. You may feel as if you're in the Wild East out here, but this is one of the fastest-developing Thai provinces, owing to increasing friendship between Laos and Thailand and the proximity of **Savannakhet**, the second-biggest Lao city, just across the water. Though the Mekong is particularly wide here, at nearly 2km, a bridge across the river, 7km north of Mukdahan, is being built (scheduled to open at the end of 2007); further into the future, a new train line linking Mukdahan with the existing Thai rail network at Ubon Ratchathani has also been discussed. Very few farang visitors make it this far, though Mukdahan–Savannakhet is an officially sanctioned crossing to Laos, with fifteen-day tourist visas available for US$30 on arrival (see p.33 for further details).

In the heart of town, the main river **pier** serves the cross-border trade, which accounts for a large part of the local economy. By the pier, the promenade overlooking Savannakhet is swamped by the daily **Indochina Market**, which is especially busy at weekends. On sale here are household goods and inexpensive ornaments, such as Vietnamese mother-of-pearl and Chinese ceramics, brought over from Laos; the market is also good for local fabrics like lengths of coarsely woven cotton in lovely muted colours, and expensive but very classy silks. At the southern edge of town rises the 65-metre-high **Mukdahan Tower** (*Ho Kaeo Mukdahan*; daily 8am–6pm; B20), a modern white edifice that looks somewhat out of place in the low-rise outskirts. Built in 1996 to commemorate the fiftieth anniversary of the king's accession to the throne, the tower houses an interesting array of historic artefacts from the Mukdahan area, including traditional Isaan costumes, pottery, coins, amulets, vicious-looking weaponry and fossils. The highlight, however, is the expansive view from the sixth floor – 50m high to reflect fifty years of Rama IX – over Mukdahan and the Mekong into Laos. On the smaller floor above is a much-revered, Sukhothai-style silver Buddha image, the Phra Phuttha Nawaming Mongkhon Mukdahan, fronted by the bone relics of famous monks in small glass containers.

Practicalities

Half-hourly buses from That Phanom and Ubon Ratchathani stop at the **bus terminal** about 2km northwest of the centre on Highway 212. **Ferry** services for Savannakhet leave Mukdahan between six and nine times a day (B50).

The best budget **accommodation** option is the friendly, well-run *Huanum Hotel*, 36 Thanon Samut Sakdarak at the corner of Thanon Song Nang Sathit, a block back from the pier (ⓣ042 611137, ⓕ042 611197; fan ❶, air-con ❷). Set back from the road overlooking a courtyard are simple, cheap rooms with shared cold-water bathrooms and smarter affairs with air-con, en-suite hot showers, TVs and fridges, while the lobby shelters a modern café, serving Western breakfasts, sandwiches and great expressos. **Internet** access and **motorbike rental** (B100/day) are also available. At 40 Thanon Pitakpanomkhet, the main east–west street, *Ploy Palace Hotel* (ⓣ042 631111, ⓦwww.ploypalace.com; ❻), a grand pink edifice with an overblown marbled lobby and tasteful bedrooms, is the best of Mukdahan's upmarket options, with good service and a rooftop swimming pool, sauna and gym.

Of the **restaurants** that dot the riverside promenade, Thanon Somranchaikhong, the best – and priciest – is the popular *Riverside*, 1km south of the pier, which serves excellent food on a pretty bougainvillea-covered terrace built out over the Mekong. En route you'll pass a couple of cheaper places on the same street, including the friendly *Wine, Wild, Why*, a small restaurant-bar in a cute wooden house, with a terrace overlooking the river and a good range of Thai meals, notably salads. There's also a good night market, where you'll find Vietnamese spring rolls and plenty of Isaan specialities, four blocks back from the pier along Thanon Song Nang Sathit.

Mukdahan National Park

If you're tired of concrete Isaan towns, stretch your legs exploring the strange rock formations and beautiful waterfalls of **Mukdahan National Park** (aka Phu Pha Terp; ⓣ042 601753; B200), down a minor road along the Mekong southeast of Mukdahan. Regular songthaews pass the turning for the park 14km out of town, and from there it's just over a one-kilometre walk uphill to the park headquarters. Just above the headquarters is a hillside of bizarre rocks, eroded into the shapes of toadstools, camels and crocodiles, which is great for scrambling around. The hillside also bears two remnants of the area's prehistory: the red finger-painting under one of the sandstone slabs is reckoned to be 4000 years old, while a small cage on the ground protects a 75-million-year-old fossil. Further up, the bare sandstone ridge seems to have been cut out of the surrounding forest by a giant lawnmower, but from October to December it's brought to life with a covering of grasses and wildflowers. A series of ladders leads up a cliff to the highest point, on a ridge at the western end of the park (a two-kilometre walk from the park headquarters), which affords a sweeping view over the rocks to the forests and paddies of Laos. Nearby, at least from July to November, is the park's most spectacular waterfall, a thirty-metre drop through thick vegetation, and a cave in which villagers have enshrined scores of Buddha images.

The park has just one standard-issue **bungalow** (sleeps six; B1800), and you can camp with your own gear free of charge. The simple **foodstalls** near headquarters will keep you going with fried rice and noodles.

Travel details

Trains

Buriram to: Ayutthaya (10 daily; 4hr 30min–7hr 45min); Bangkok (10 daily; 6hr–9hr 30min); Khorat (10 daily; 1hr 30min–2hr 40min); Pak Chong (10 daily; 2hr 30min–5hr); Si Saket (8 daily; 1hr 45min–3hr 20min); Surin (10 daily; 35–65min); Ubon Ratchathani (7 daily; 2hr 30min–4hr 15min).
Khon Kaen to: Ayutthaya (5 daily; 6hr–8hr 20min); Bangkok (5 daily; 7hr 30min–10hr 20min); Khorat (1 daily; 2hr 30min); Nong Khai (5 daily; 2hr 25min–3hr); Udon Thani (7 daily; 1hr 35min–2hr 15min).
Khorat (Nakhon Ratchasima) to: Ayutthaya (11 daily; 3hr 30min); Bangkok (11 daily; 4–5hr); Khon Kaen (1 daily; 2hr 30min); Pak Chong (11 daily; 1hr 30min–2hr); Si Saket (8 daily; 4hr–5hr 30min); Surin (10 daily; 2hr 5min–3hr 40min); Ubon Ratchathani (7 daily; 5hr–6hr 40min); Udon Thani (1 daily; 4hr).
Nong Khai to: Ayutthaya (4 daily; 9–11hr); Bangkok (4 daily; 10hr 30min–12hr 30min); Khon Kaen (4 daily; 2hr 25min); Udon Thani (5 daily; 1hr).
Pak Chong (for Khao Yai) to: Ayutthaya (11 daily; 2hr–2hr 45min); Bangkok (11 daily; 3hr 30min–4hr 45min); Khorat (11 daily; 1hr 30min–2hr); Si Saket (8 daily; 4hr 20min–7hr 30min); Surin (10 daily; 3hr 10min–5hr 15min); Ubon Ratchathani (7 daily; 6hr 50min–8hr 40min); Udon Thani (1 daily; 6hr).
Surin to: Ayutthaya (10 daily; 5hr 10min–9hr); Bangkok (10 daily; 7–10hr); Buriram (10 daily; 35–65min); Khorat (10 daily; 2hr–3hr 15min); Pak Chong (10 daily; 3hr 30min–5hr 30min); Si Saket (8 daily; 1hr 35min–2hr 10min); Ubon Ratchathani (7 daily; 2hr 30min–3hr 30min).
Ubon Ratchathani to: Ayutthaya (7 daily; 7–12hr); Bangkok (7 daily; 8hr 30min–14hr); Buriram (7 daily; 2hr 30min–4hr 15min); Khorat (7 daily; 5hr–6hr 40min); Si Saket (7 daily; 1hr 10min); Surin (7 daily; 2hr 30min–3hr 30min).
Udon Thani to: Ayutthaya (5 daily; 8–10hr); Bangkok (5 daily; 10–12hr); Khon Kaen (7 daily; 1hr 35min–2hr 15min); Khorat (1 daily; 4hr); Nong Khai (5 daily; 1hr); Pak Chong (1 daily; 6hr).

Buses

Bung Kan to: Bangkok (4 daily; 8hr); Nakhon Phanom (6 daily; 4hr); Nong Khai (14 daily; 2hr); Sakon Nakhon (hourly; 3hr); Udon Thani (hourly; 4hr).
Chiang Khan to: Bangkok (5 daily; 9–11hr); Khorat (2 daily; 7hr); Loei (9 daily, plus frequent songthaews; 1hr); Pak Chom (by songthaew, hourly in the morning, 2 in the afternoon; 1hr).
Chong Mek to: Bangkok (1 daily; 11hr); Phibun Mangsahan (every 30min; 90min).
Khon Kaen to: Bangkok (29 daily; 6–7hr); Chiang Mai (11 daily; 11–12hr); Khorat (hourly; 2hr 30min–3hr); Loei (every 30min; 4hr); Nong Khai (10 daily; 2–3hr); Phitsanulok (6 daily; 5–6hr); Rayong (13 daily; 10–12hr); Sri Chiangmai (6 daily; 3hr); Surin (hourly; 4hr 30min–6hr); Ubon Ratchathani (15 daily; 4–6hr); Udon Thani (every 30min; 1hr 30min–2hr).
Khorat to: Bangkok (every 20min; 4–5hr); Ban Tako (for Phanom Rung; every 30min; 2hr); Buriram (every 30min; 3hr); Chanthaburi (10 daily; 6–8hr); Chiang Khan (2 daily; 7hr); Chiang Mai (9 daily; 12–14hr); Chiang Rai (5 daily; 14–16hr); Dan Kwian (every 30min; 30min); Khon Kaen (hourly; 2hr 30min–3hr); Lopburi (10 daily; 3hr 30min); Nakhon Phanom (3 daily; 8hr); Nong Khai (11 daily; 6–8hr); Pak Tong Chai (every 30min; 45min); Pattaya (8 daily; 6–8hr); Phimai (every 30min; 1hr–1hr 30min); Phitsanulok (7 daily; 7–9hr); Rayong (for Ko Samet; 15 daily; 6–8hr); Si Racha (7 daily; 5hr); Sri Chiangmai (6 daily; 6hr 30min); Surin (every 30min; 4–5hr); Ubon Ratchathani (9 daily; 5–7hr); Udon Thani (11 daily; 3hr 30min–5hr).
Kong Chiam to: Bangkok (4 daily; 11hr).
Loei to: Bangkok (20 daily; 10hr); Chiang Khan (9 daily, plus frequent songthaews; 1hr); Chiang Mai (5 daily; 9–12hr); Chiang Rai (4 daily; 9–11hr); Khon Kaen (every 30min; 4hr); Nong Khai (hourly via Pak Chom; 6–7hr); Pak Chom (every 30min; 2hr 30min); Phitsanulok (3 daily; 4hr); Sang Khom (hourly; 3hr); Udon Thani (every 20min; 3–4hr).
Mukdahan to: Bangkok (13 daily; 11hr); Nakhon Phanom (hourly; 2hr); That Phanom (every 30min; 1hr 20min); Ubon Ratchathani (every 30min; 2–3hr); Udon Thani (5 daily; 4hr–4hr 30min).
Nakhon Phanom to: Bangkok (17 daily; 12hr); Bung Kan (4 daily; 4hr); Mukdahan (hourly; 2hr); Nong Khai (4 daily; 6hr); That Phanom (hourly; 1hr); Ubon Ratchathani (7 daily; 4hr); Udon Thani (9 daily; 5–7hr).
Nong Khai to: Bangkok (13 daily; 10hr); Bung Kan (hourly; 2hr); Loei (hourly via Pak Chom; 6–7hr); Nakhon Phanom (4 daily; 6hr); Rayong (19 daily; 12hr); Sang Khom (hourly; 3–4hr); Udon Thani (every 25min; 1hr); Vientiane, Laos (4 daily; 1hr).
Pak Chom to: Chiang Khan (hourly by songthaew; 1hr); Loei (every 30min; 2hr 30min); Nong Khai (hourly; 5hr).
Sang Khom to: Loei (hourly via Pak Chom; 3hr); Nong Khai (hourly; 3–4hr).

That Phanom to: Bangkok (4 daily; 12hr); Mukdahan (every 30min; 1hr 20min); Nakhon Phanom (hourly; 1hr); Ubon Ratchathani (7 daily; 3–4hr); Udon Thani (4 daily; 4–5 hr).
Ubon Ratchathani to: Bangkok (19 daily; 10–12hr); Chiang Mai (6 daily; 17–18hr); Kantharalak (8 daily; 1hr 30min); Khon Kaen (16 daily; 4–6hr); Khorat (17 daily; 5–7hr); Mukdahan (every 30min; 2–3hr); Pattaya (10 daily; 12hr–13hr 30min); Phibun Mangsahan (every 25min; 1hr); Rayong (10 daily; 14hr); Roi Et (16 daily; 3hr); Si Saket (at least 12 daily; 45min–1hr); Surin (at least 12 daily; 2hr 30min–3hr); Udon Thani (11 daily; 5–7hr); Yasothon (18 daily; 1hr 30min–2hr).
Udon Thani to: Ban Chiang (every 30min until around noon, by songthaew; 1hr 30min); Bangkok (every 15min; 9hr); Ban Phu (every 45min; 1hr); Chiang Mai (4 daily; 11–13hr); Chiang Rai (4 daily; 12–14hr); Khon Kaen (every 30min; 1hr 30min–2hr); Khorat (hourly; 3hr 30min–5hr); Loei (every 20min; 3–4hr); Mukdahan (5 daily; 4hr–4hr 30min); Nakhon Phanom (9 daily; 5–7hr); Nong Khai (every 20min; 1hr); Phitsanulok (2 daily; 7hr); Rayong (7 daily; 12hr); Sakon Nakhon (every 30min; 3hr); That Phanom (4 daily; 4–5hr); Ubon Ratchathani (7 daily; 5–7hr); Vientiane, Laos (5 daily; 1hr 30min).
Yasothon to: Khon Kaen (hourly; 3hr–3hr 30min); Roi Et (hourly; 1hr).

Flights

Buriram to: Bangkok (3 weekly; 55min).
Khon Kaen to: Bangkok (3 daily; 55min).
Loei to: Bangkok (2 weekly; 1hr 25min).
Nakhon Phanom to: Bangkok (1–2 daily; 1hr 5min).
Roi Et to: Bangkok (daily; 1hr).
Ubon Ratchathani to: Bangkok (5 daily; 1hr 5min).
Udon Thani to: Bangkok (9 daily; 1hr); Loei (2 weekly; 35min).

6

Southern Thailand: the Gulf coast

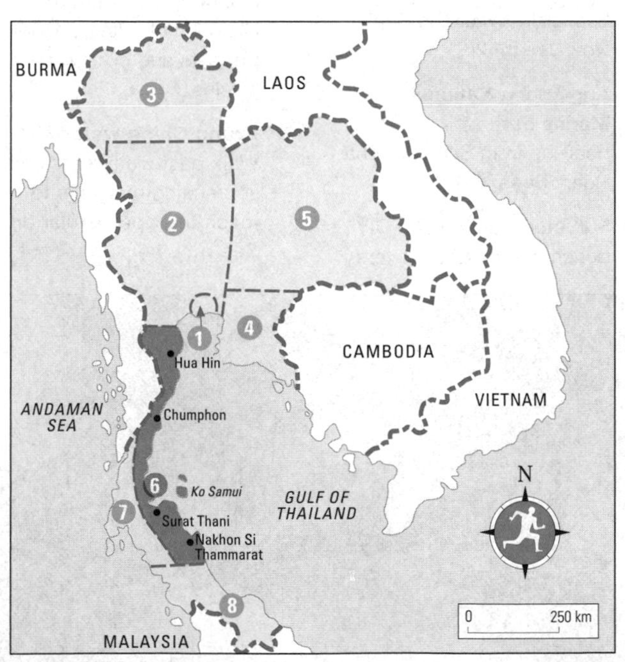

CHAPTER 6

Highlights

* **Phetchaburi** Charming historic town, boasting several fine old working temples. See p.607

* **Leisurely seafood lunches** At the squid-pier restaurants in Hua Hin or under the trees at Ban Krud. See pp.619 & 628

* **Bird-watching in Khao Sam Roi Yot National Park** Especially rewarding Sept–Nov. See p.624

* **Ang Thong National Marine Park** A dramatic boat-trip from Samui or Pha Ngan. See p.644

* **Full moon at Hat Rin** DIY beach parties draw ravers in their thousands. See p.663

* **Ao Thong Nai Pan on Ko Pha Ngan** Beautiful, secluded bay with good accommodation. See p.669

* **A boat-trip round Ko Tao** Satisfying exploration and great snorkelling. See p.677

* **Nakhon Si Thammarat** Historic holy sites, shadow puppets and excellent cuisine. See p.682

* **Krung Ching waterfall** Walk past giant ferns and screeching monkeys to reach this spectacular drop. See p.689

△ Wat Yai Suwannaram, Phetchaburi

6

Southern Thailand: the Gulf coast

The major part of southern Thailand's **Gulf coast**, gently undulating from Bangkok to Nakhon Si Thammarat, 750km away, is famed above all for the Samui archipelago, three small idyllic islands lying off the most prominent hump of the coastline. This is the country's most popular seaside venue for independent travellers, and a lazy stay in a Samui beachfront bungalow is so seductive a prospect that most people overlook the attractions of the mainland, where the sheltered sandy beaches and warm clear water rival the top sunspots in most countries. Added to that you'll find scenery dominated by forested mountains that rise abruptly behind the coastal strip, especially impressive in **Khao Sam Roi Yot National Park**, which is one of Thailand's most rewarding bird-watching spots, and a sprinkling of historic sights – notably the crumbling temples of ancient **Phetchaburi**. Though not a patch on the islands further south, the stretch of coast around **Cha-am** and **Hua Hin** is popular with weekending Thais escaping the capital and is crammed with condos, high-rise hotels, bars and restaurants, not to mention a large population of foreign tourists. The scene at the sophisticated little beach resort of **Pak Nam Pran**, just a short distance further south, is much quieter, and there's only slightly more development at **Ban Krud**. Though the provincial capital of **Chumphon**, 150km further down the coast, has little to offer in its own right, it's the convenient departure point for direct boats to Ko Tao.

Southeast of Chumphon lies **Ko Samui**, by far the most naturally beautiful of the islands, with its long white-sand beaches and arching fringes of palm trees. The island's beauty has not gone unnoticed by tourist developers of course, and its varied spread of accommodation these days draws as many package tourists and second-homers as backpackers. In recent years the next island out, **Ko Pha Ngan**, has drawn increasing numbers of backpackers away from its neighbour: its bungalows are generally simpler and cost less than Ko Samui's, and it offers a few stunning beaches with a more laid-back atmosphere. The island's southeastern headland, **Hat Rin**, has no less than three white-sand beaches to choose from, but now provides all the amenities the demanding traveller could want and after durk swings into action as Thailand's dance capital, a reputation cemented by its farang-thronged full moon parties. The furthest inhabited island of the archipelago, **Ko Tao**, has taken off as a **scuba-diving** centre, but despite a growing nightlife and restaurant scene, still has the feel of a small, rugged and isolated outcrop.

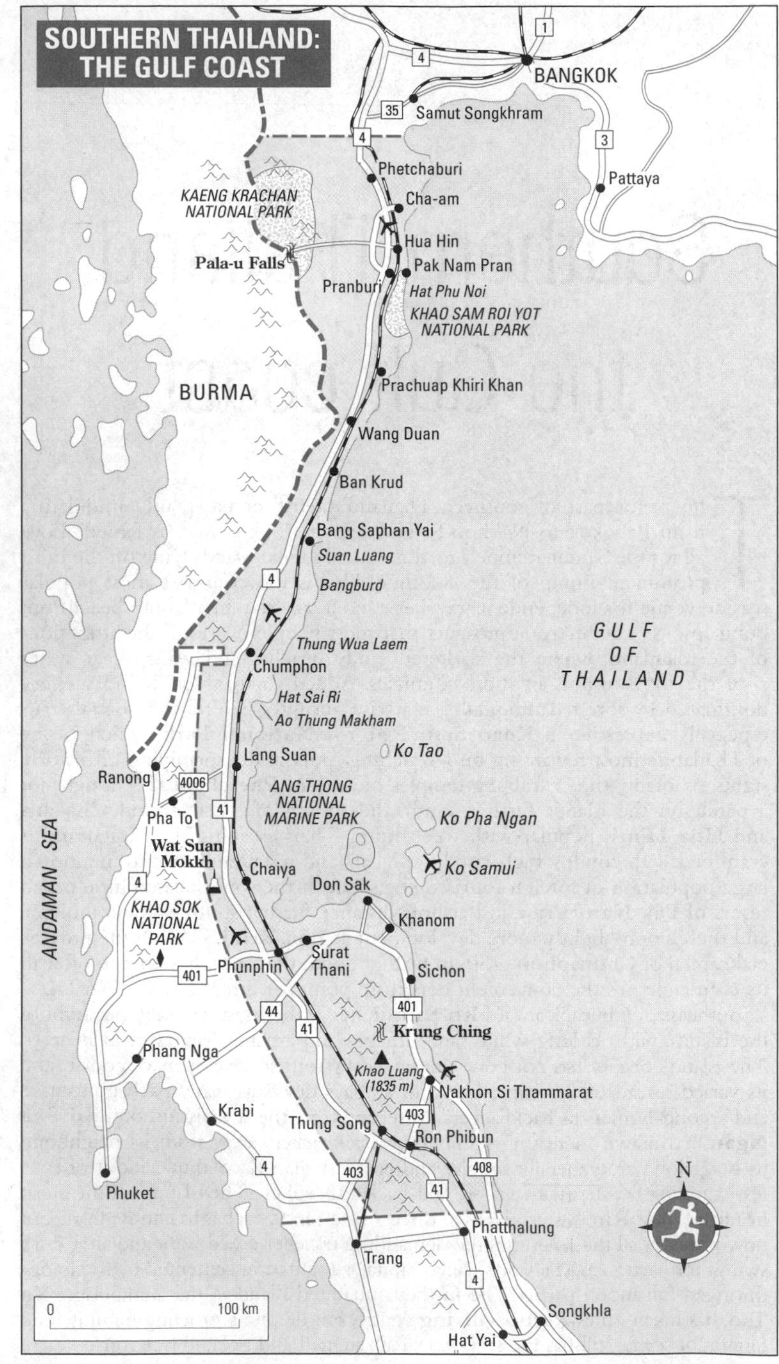
SOUTHERN THAILAND: THE GULF COAST
BANGKOK
Samut Songkhram
Pattaya
Phetchaburi
Cha-am
KAENG KRACHAN NATIONAL PARK
Hua Hin
Pala-u Falls
Pak Nam Pran
Pranburi
Hat Phu Noi
KHAO SAM ROI YOT NATIONAL PARK
BURMA
Prachuap Khiri Khan
Wang Duan
Ban Krud
Bang Saphan Yai
Suan Luang
Bangburd
GULF OF THAILAND
Thung Wua Laem
Chumphon
Hat Sai Ri
Ao Thung Makham
Ko Tao
Lang Suan
Ranong
ANG THONG NATIONAL MARINE PARK
Pha To
Ko Pha Ngan
ANDAMAN SEA
Wat Suan Mokkh
Ko Samui
Chaiya
Don Sak
KHAO SOK NATIONAL PARK
Khanom
Surat Thani
Phunphin
Sichon
Krung Ching
Phang Nga
Khao Luang (1835 m)
Nakhon Si Thammarat
Krabi
Thung Song
Ron Phibun
Phuket
N
Phatthalung
Trang
Songkhla
Hat Yai
0
100 km

Tucked away beneath the islands, **Nakhon Si Thammarat**, the cultural capital of the south, is well worth a short detour from the main routes through the centre of the peninsula – it's a sophisticated city of grand old temples, delicious cuisine and distinctive handicrafts. With its small but significant Muslim population, and machine-gun dialect, Nakhon begins the transition into Thailand's deep south.

The **train** from Bangkok connects all the mainland towns, including a branch line to Nakhon, and **bus** services, along highways 4 (also known as the Phetkasem Highway, or, usually, Thanon Phetkasem when passing through towns) and 41, are frequent. From Bangkok, Thai Airways. Air Asia and Orient Thai **fly** to Surat Thani, PB air and Nok Air to Nakhon Si Thammarat while Bangkok Airways operates a variety of popular routes to Ko Samui's airport. Daily boats run to the islands from two jumping-off points: **Surat Thani**, 650km from Bangkok, has the best choice of routes, but the alternatives from **Chumphon** get you straight to the tranquillity of Ko Tao.

The Gulf coast has a slightly different **climate** to the Andaman coast and much of the rest of Thailand, being hit heavily by the northeast monsoon's rains, especially in November, when it's best to avoid this part of the country altogether. Most times during the rest of the year should see pleasant, if changeable, weather, with some mild effects of the southwest monsoon felt on the islands between May and October. Late December to April is the driest period, and is therefore the region's high season, which also includes July and August. **Jellyfish** can be a problem on the Gulf coast, particularly just after a storm. Fatalities are very rare, but two travellers on Ko Pha Ngan died from (unidentified) jellyfish stings in August 2002. Ask for local advice before swimming, and scour the shore for dead jellyfish, which are a sign that they're in the area; see p.36 for more on jellyfish and how to deal with stings.

Phetchaburi

Straddling the Phet River about 120km south of Bangkok, the provincial capital of **PHETCHABURI** has been settled ever since the eleventh century, when the Khmers ruled the region, but only really got going six hundred years later, when it began to flourish as a trading post between the Andaman Sea ports and Burma and Ayutthaya. Despite periodic incursions from the Burmese, the town gained a reputation as a cultural centre – as the ornamentation of its older temples testifies – and after the new capital was established in Bangkok it became a favourite country retreat of Rama IV, who had a hilltop palace built here in the 1850s, at Khao Wang ("Palace Hill"). Modern Phetchaburi's main claim to fame is as one of Thailand's finest sweet-making centres, the essential ingredient for its assortment of *khanom* being the sugar extracted from the sweet-sapped palms that cover the province. This being very much a cottage industry, twenty-first-century downtown Phetchaburi has lost relatively little of the ambience that so attracted Rama IV: the central riverside area is hemmed in by historic wats in varying states of disrepair, and wooden rather than concrete shophouses still line the river bank.

Despite the attractions of its old quarter, Phetchaburi gets few overnight visitors as most people do it on a day-trip from Bangkok, Hua Hin or Cha-am. It's also possible to combine a day in Phetchaburi with an early-morning expedition from Bangkok to the floating markets of Damnoen Saduak, 40km north; budget tour operators in Bangkok's Thanon Khao San area offer this option as a day-trip package for about B600 per person.

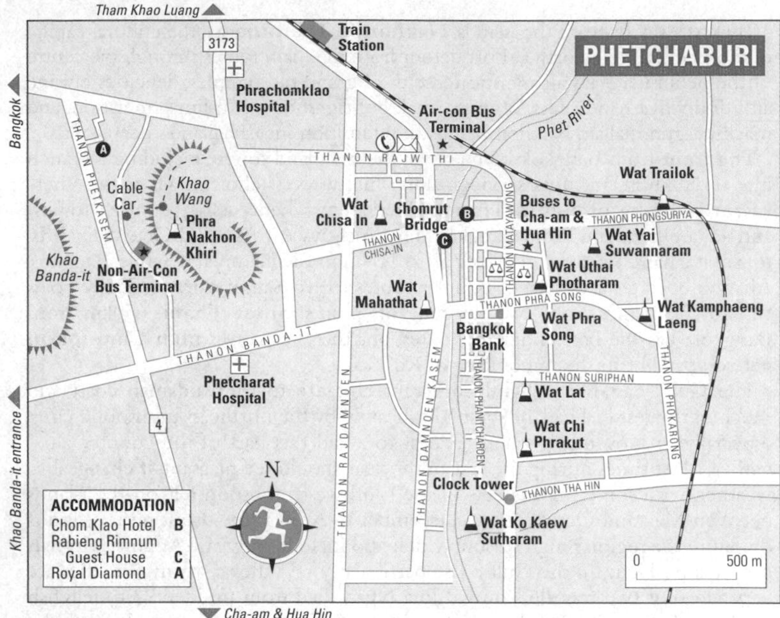

Arrival, information and transport

Arriving by **bus**, you're likely to be dropped in one of three places. The main station for **non-air-con buses** is on the southwest edge of Khao Wang, about thirty minutes' walk or a ten-minute songthaew ride from the town centre. However, non-air-con buses to and from **Cha-am and Hua Hin** use the small terminal in the town centre, less than ten minutes' walk from the Chomrut Bridge accommodation. The **air-con bus terminal** is also about ten minutes' walk from Chomrut Bridge, just off Thanon Rajwithi. Phetchaburi **train station** is on the northern outskirts of town, about 1500m from the main sights.

There's no TAT office in town, but *Rabieng Rimnum Guest House* is a good source of local **information**; there's Internet access at the CAT **phone office** (daily 8.30am–4.30pm), which is next to the **GPO** on Thanon Rajwithi. The branch of Bangkok Bank 150m east of Wat Mahathat on Thanon Phra Song does **currency exchange** and has an ATM. Phetcharat Hospital is on Thanon Banda-It (Ⓣ032 417070).

To see the major temples in a day and have sufficient energy left for climbing Khao Wang, you might want to hire a **samlor** for a couple of hours, at about B100 per hour. Alternatively make use of the public **songthaews** that circulate round the town, or **rent** a bicycle or motorbike from *Rabieng Rimnum Guest House*.

Accommodation

Most travellers **stay** at the *Rabieng Rimnum (Rim Nam) Guest House*, centrally located at 1 Thanon Chisa-in, on the southwest corner of Chomrut Bridge (Ⓣ032 425707; ❷). Occupying a century-old house next to the Phet River and, less appealingly, a noisy main road, the guest house offers nine simple rooms with shared bathrooms, lots of local info and the best restaurant in town; it also rents out bicycles and motorbikes and organizes day-trips and overnight visits to Kaeng Krachan National Park for bird-watching and hiking. Less traveller-oriented, but quieter and cheaper, is the friendly *Chom Klao* hotel across on the northeast corner of Chomrut Bridge at 1–3 Thanon Phongsuriya (ⓣ032 425398; ❶); it's not signed in English, but is easily recognized by its pale-blue doors and riverside location. Some of the rooms give out onto the riverside walkway and you can choose whether or not you want an en-suite bathroom; all rooms have fans. West of Khao Wang, on the outskirts of town, is Phetchaburi's most upmarket option, the *Royal Diamond* (ⓣ032 411061, ⓦwww.royaldiamondhotel.com; ❺), which has comfortable air-con rooms and is located on Soi Sam Chao Phet, just off the Phetkasem Highway.

The Town

The pinnacles and rooftops of the town's thirty-odd **wats** are visible in every direction, but only a few are worth stopping off to investigate; the following description takes in the top three, and can be done as a leisurely two-hour circular walk beginning from Chomrut Bridge. Phetchaburi's other significant sight, the palace-museum at Phra Nakhon Khiri, is on a hill on the northwestern edge of town, and can be reached both on foot and by public transport.

Wat Yai Suwannaram

Of all Phetchaburi's temples, the most attractive is the still-functioning seventeenth-century **Wat Yai Suwannaram** on Thanon Phongsuriya, about 700m east of Chomrut Bridge. The temple's fine old teak **sala** has elaborately carved doors, bearing a gash said to have been made by the Burmese in 1760 as they plundered their way towards Ayutthaya. Across from the *sala* and hidden behind high whitewashed walls stands the windowless Ayutthaya-style bot. The bot compound overlooks a pond, in the middle of which stands a small but well-preserved scripture library, or **ho trai**: such structures were built on stilts over

△ Khao Wang

water to prevent ants and other insects destroying the precious documents. Enter the walled compound from the south and make a clockwise tour of the cloisters filled with Buddha statutes before entering the bot itself via the eastern doorway (if the door is locked, one of the monks will get the key for you). The **bot** is supported by intricately patterned red and gold pillars and contains a remarkable, if rather faded, set of murals, depicting Indra, Brahma and other lower-ranking divinities ranged in five rows of ascending importance. Once you've admired the interior, walk to the back of the bot, passing behind the central cluster of Buddha images, to find another Buddha image seated against the back wall: climb the steps in front of this image to get a close-up of the left foot, which for some reason was cast with six toes.

Wat Kamphaeng Laeng

Fifteen minutes' walk east and then south of Wat Yai, the five tumbledown prangs of **Wat Kamphaeng Laeng** on Thanon Phra Song mark out Phetchaburi as the probable southernmost outpost of the Khmer empire. Built to enshrine Hindu deities and set out in a cruciform arrangement facing east, the laterite corncob-style prangs were later adapted for Buddhist use, as can be seen from the two that now house Buddha images. There has been some attempt to restore a few of the carvings and false balustraded windows, but these days worshippers congregate in the modern whitewashed wat behind these shrines, leaving the atmospheric and appealingly quaint collection of decaying prangs and casuarina topiary to chickens, stray dogs and the occasional tourist.

Wat Mahathat and the market

Continuing west along Thanon Phra Song from Wat Kamphaeng Laeng, across the river you can see the prangs of Phetchaburi's most fully restored and important temple, **Wat Mahathat** long before you reach them. Boasting the "Mahathat" title only since 1954 – when the requisite Buddha relics were donated by the king – it was probably founded in the fourteenth century, but suffered badly at the hands of the Burmese. The five landmark prangs at its heart are adorned with stucco figures of mythical creatures, though these are nothing compared with those on the roofs of the main viharn and the bot. Instead of tapering off into the usual serpentine *chofa*, the gables are studded with miniature *thep* and *deva* figures (angels and gods), which add an almost mischievous vitality to the place. In a similar vein, a couple of gold-embossed crocodiles snarl above the entrance to the bot, and a caricature carving of a bespectacled man rubs shoulders with mythical giants in a relief around the base of the gold Buddha, housed in a separate mondop nearby.

Leaving Wat Mahathat, it's a five-minute walk north up Thanon Damnoen Kasem to Thanon Phongsuriya and another few minutes east to Chomrut Bridge, but if you have the time, backtrack a little and return via the **market**, which lines Thanon Matayawong and spills over into the alleyways on either side – there are enough stalls selling the locally famous *khanom* to make it worth your while.

Khao Wang and Khao Banda-It

Dominating the western outskirts, about thirty minutes' walk from Wat Mahathat, stands Rama IV's palace, a stew of mid-nineteenth-century Thai and European styles scattered over the crest of the hill known as **Khao Wang**. During his day, the royal entourage would struggle its way up the steep brick path to the summit, but now there's a **cable car** (daily 8.15am–5.15pm; B50, kids under 90cm tall go free), which starts from the western flank of the hill off Highway

4, quite near the non-air-con bus terminal. To get to the base of the hill from the town centre, take a white local **songthaew** from Thanon Phongsuriya and ask for Khao Wang. If you want to walk to the summit, get off as soon as you see the pathway on the eastern flank of the hill, just across from the junction with Thanon Rajwithi; for the cable car, stay put until you've passed the last of the souvenir stalls on Highway 4, then walk south about 700m. If you do walk up the hill, be warned that hundreds of quite aggressive monkeys hang out at its base and on the path to the top.

Up top, the wooded hill is littered with wats, prangs, chedis, whitewashed gazebos and lots more, in an ill-assorted combination of architectural idioms – the prang-topped viharn, washed all over in burnt sienna, is particularly ungainly. Whenever the king came on an excursion here, he stayed in the airy summer house, **Phra Nakhon Khiri** (daily 9am–4pm; B40, kids B10; Ⓦwww.thailandmuseum.com), with its Mediterranean-style shutters and verandas. Now a museum, it houses a moderately interesting collection of ceramics, furniture and other artefacts given to the royal family by foreign friends. Besides being cool and breezy, Khao Wang also proved to be a good star-gazing spot, so Rama IV had an open-sided, glass-domed observatory built close to his sleeping quarters. The king's amateur astronomy was not an inconsequential recreation: in August 1868 he predicted a solar eclipse almost to the second, thereby quashing the centuries-old Thai fear that the sun was periodically swallowed by an omnipotent lion god. The spot where he observed the eclipse, further down the Gulf coast just south of Prachuap Khiri Khan, is now the site of a commemorative science museum (see p.627), and Rama IV is internationally recognized as the father of Thai science.

If you've got energy to spare, the two cave wats out on the western edges of town make good time-fillers. **Khao Banda-it**, a couple of kilometres west of Khao Wang, comprises a series of stalactite caves filled with Buddha statues and a 200-year-old Ayutthaya-style meditation temple. Five kilometres north of Khao Wang, the dramatic, partially roofless cave **Tham Khao Luang** is filled with assorted Buddha images and chedis, including a huge reclining Buddha statue.

Eating

Phetchaburi's best **restaurant** is the *Rabieng Rimnum* (*Rim Nam*; daily 8am–1am), which is attached to the guest house of the same name and occupies a traditional wooden house beside the Chomrut Bridge, overlooking the Phet River. It offers a long and interesting menu of inexpensive Thai dishes, from banana-blossom salad to spicy crab soup, and is deservedly popular with local diners.

Almost half the shops in the town centre stock Phetchaburi's famous **sweet snacks**, as do many of the souvenir stalls crowding the base of Khao Wang, vendors at the day market on Thanon Matayawong, and the shophouses on the soi behind the Bangkok Bank. The most famous local speciality is *khanom maw kaeng*, a baked sweet egg custard made with mung beans and coconut and sometimes flavoured with lotus seeds, durian or taro. *Khanom taan* is another Phetchaburi classic: small, steamed, saffron-coloured cakes made with local palm sugar, coconut and rice flour, and wrapped in banana-leaf cases.

Cha-am and around

Forever in the shadow of its more famous neighbour, Hua Hin, the beach resort of **CHA-AM**, 41km south of Phetchaburi, picks up the overspill from

Hua Hin, 25km further south, and positions itself as a more sedate alternative. It used to be a typically Thai resort, with accommodation catering mainly to families and student groups from Bangkok and an emphasis on shorefront picnics rather than swimming and sunbathing, but that's beginning to change as the Europeans and expats move in, bringing with them package-holiday high-rises and Western-style restaurants. The most developed bit of Cha-am's coastal strip stretches about 3km along Thanon Ruamchit (sometimes spelt Ruamjit), from the *Golden Beach Cha-am Hotel* in the north to the *Santisuk* bungalows in the south. The beach here is pleasantly shaded, though rather gritty and very narrow at high tide, and the water is perfectly swimmable, if not pristine. During the week the pace of life in Cha-am is slow, and it's easy to find a solitary spot under the casuarinas, particularly at the northerly end of the beach, but that's rarely possible at weekends, when prices shoot up and traffic thickens considerably. Away from the seafront there's not much to do here, but there are several **golf courses** within striking distance (see p.619) and buses shuttle between Cha-am and Hua Hin (25km south) every half-hour, taking just 35 minutes.

Practicalities

Nearly all ordinary and air-con **buses** use the bus station (☎032 425307) in the town centre on Thanon Phetkasem (Highway 4), close to the junction with Thanon Narathip, 1km west of the beach. Some private air-con buses to and from Bangkok use the depot at the little plaza on the beachfront Thanon Ruamchit, just south of the Ruamchit/Narathip junction. The **train station** (☎032 861222) is a few short blocks west of this junction. Thanon Narathip is the most useful of the side roads linking Thanon Phetkasem and the beachfront, and ends at a small seaside promenade and **tourist police** booth (☎032 471000) on Thanon Ruamchit, roughly halfway down the three-kilometre strip of beachfront development. To get down to the beach from Thanon Phetkasem, either walk or take a B30 motorbike taxi.

Thanon Ruamchit is where you'll find most of the hotels and restaurants, as well as a few tourist-oriented businesses. **Addresses** on Thanon Ruamchit are determined by whether they are north or south of the Thanon Narathip junction, and the sois running off the beachfront road are labelled accordingly, eg Soi Cha-am North 1 is the first lane off Ruamchit to the north of the Narathip junction, while Soi Cha-am South 1 is the first minor road to the south. The landmark *Golden Beach Cha-am Hotel* at the northern end of the main beachfront sits alongside Soi Cha-am North 8, while *Santisuk* bungalows near the southern end of the beach is next to Soi Cha-am South 4.

The small Thanon Ruamchit **post office** is just north of Soi Cha-am North 5 and has one Internet terminal; there are more terminals inside the CAT **phone office**, which is 200m north up Thanon Narathip from the seafront and several private **Internet** centres along Thanon Ruamchit. A number of shops along the beachfront rent **motorbikes** as well as **tandems** and three-person **pushbikes**. Cha-am's main business district occupies the small grid of streets west of Thanon Phetkasem, between the bus drop and the train station, and this is where you'll find the market, most of the shops, the **police station** (☎032 471323), the **GPO** and banks with **exchange** facilities and ATMs. The local **TAT** office (daily 8.30am–4.30pm; ☎032 471005, Ⓔtatphet@tat.or.th) is on Highway 4, about 1km south of the centre.

Accommodation

Most of the cheaper accommodation is concentrated on **central Cha-am Beach**, set along the west side of beachfront Thanon Ruamchit. There are no obvious backpacker-oriented guest houses in Cha-am; instead you'll find mainly small, mid-range hotels. The more expensive accommodation occupies the 25km of coastline **between Cha-am and Hua Hin**, where resorts are able to enjoy what are in effect private beaches, though guests without transport have to rely on hotel shuttles or public buses to get to the shops and restaurants of Cha-am or Hua Hin. Many Cha-am hotels give a fifteen- to thirty-percent discount from Sunday to Thursday.

Central Cha-am Beach

Golden Beach Cha-am Hotel Just south of Soi Cha-am North 8 at 208/14 Thanon Ruamchit ⓣ032 433830. Good-value high-rise where the nicely appointed deluxe rooms all have a balcony, most of which afford a partial, long-distance, sea-view. All rooms are equipped with air-con, and TV, and there's a swimming pool. Fifty-percent discounts during the week. ⑥

Kaenchan Beach Hotel North of Soi Cha-am North 7 241/3 Thanon Ruamchit ⓣ032 471314, ⓦkaenchan-beach-hotel.th66.com. Characterful and stylish mid-sized hotel, with a papaya-coloured facade, a sixth-floor swimming pool and appealing, sleekly furnished rooms, all with air-con, TV and sea view. Also has some terraced bungalows in the garden behind. ⑥

Nirandorn 3 Just south of the Narathip junction on Thanon Ruamchit ⓣ032 470300, ⓕ032 470303. Clean, well-maintained hotel rooms with air-con and TV – the best ones are on the upper floors and have sea views. ⑥

Between Cha-am and Hua Hin

Beach Garden Hotel and Spa About 7km south of Cha-am at 949/21 Soi Suan Loi, off Thanon Phetkasem ⓣ032 508234, ⓦwww.beachgardenchaam.com. Set in a lush tropical garden that runs down to the sea, accommodation in this good-value resort is in either attractive, comfortably furnished cottages or a less characterful but smart hotel block with sea views. There's a swimming pool, games room, tennis courts, windsurfing and other watersports facilities. ⑦–⑧

Dusit Resort Hua Hin 14km south of Cha-am and 9km north of Hua Hin at 1349 Thanon Phetkasem ⓣ032 520009, ⓦhuahin.dusit.com. One of the most luxurious spots on this stretch of coast, with 300 large, elegant rooms set around a tropical garden and lotus-filled lagoon. Facilities include four restaurants, a huge pool and children's pool, a spa, horse-riding, and tennis and squash courts. It runs frequent shuttles into Hua Hin and has an Avis car rental desk. ⑨

Regent Cha-am About 8km south of Cha-am at 849/21 Thanon Phetkasem ⓣ032 451240, ⓦwww.regent-chaam.com. Well-regarded upmarket chain resort set in appealing gardens that run down to a nice stretch of beach. Choose between rooms in differently appointed wings: old-style or more modern; with or without sea view; hotel wing or chalet style. Facilities include three swimming pools, squash and tennis courts, a fitness centre and horse-riding on the beach. ⑦–⑨

Eating and drinking

The choice of **restaurants** in Cha-am is not a patch on the range you get in Hua Hin, but for a change from hotel food you might want to drop by the *Tipdharee* on Thanon Ruamchit, north of Soi Cha-am North 5, which has a huge menu of mid-priced Thai dishes, including lots of seafood, curries and one-plate dishes. *Poom*, about 150m north of Soi Cha-am North 5 at 274/1 Thanon Ruamchit, serves a good, if pricey selection of Thai-style seafood dishes (B80–200), including recommended shrimps with garlic, on its sea-view terrace. *Baan Plang Pub and Restaurant* on Thanon Narathip opens nightly from 7pm to 2am and stages live music.

Phra Ratchaniwet Marukhathaiyawan

Ten kilometres south of Cha-am, on the way to Hua Hin, stands the lustrous seaside palace of Rama VI, **Phra Ratchaniwet Marukhathaiyawan** (daily 8am–4pm; B90), a rarely visited place, despite the easy access; the half-hourly Cha-am–Hua Hin buses stop within a couple of kilometres' walk of the palace at the sign for Rama VI Camp – just follow the road through the army compound.

Designed by an Italian architect and completed in just sixteen days in 1923, the golden teak building was abandoned to the corrosive sea air after Rama VI's death in 1925. Restoration work began in the 1970s, and today most of the structure looks as it once did, a stylish composition of verandas and latticework painted in pastel shades of beige and blue, with an emphasis on cool simplicity. The spacious open hall in the north wing, hung with chandeliers and encircled by a first-floor balcony, was once used as a theatre, and the upstairs rooms, now furnished only with a few black-and-white portraits from the royal family photo album, were given over to royal attendants. The king stayed in the centre room, with the best sea view and access to the promenade, while the south wing contained the queen's apartments.

Hua Hin

Thailand's oldest beach resort, **HUA HIN** used to be little more than an overgrown fishing village with one exceptionally grand hotel, but the arrival of mass tourism, high-rise hotels and farang-managed hostess bars has made a serious dent in its once idiosyncratic charm. With the far superior beaches of Ko Samui, Krabi and Ko Samet so close at hand, there's little here to draw the dedicated sunseeker, but it's nonetheless a convivial place in which to drink and enjoy fine seafood and, if you can afford it, stay in the atmospheric former *Railway Hotel*. In addition, the town makes a convenient base for day-trips to Khao Sam Roi Yot National Park, 63km south, and there are half a dozen golf courses in the area, plus a couple of exceptionally indulgent hotel spas. If none of that appeals, you might consider stopping by for Hua Hin's well-respected **jazz festival** in June (check Ⓦwww.thailandgrandfestival.com for details), or for the rather more unusual **elephant polo tournament**, held every September (Ⓦwww.thaielepolo.com).

The **royal family** were Hua Hin's main visitors at the start of the twentieth century, but the place became more widely popular in the 1920s, when the opening of the Bangkok–Malaysia rail line made short excursions to the beach much more viable. The Victorian-style *Railway Hotel* was built soon after to cater for the leisured classes, and in 1926 Rama VII had his own summer palace, Klai Klangwon (Far from Worries), erected at the northern end of the beach. It was here, ironically, that Rama VII was staying in 1932 when the coup was launched in Bangkok against the system of absolute monarchy. The current king lives here most of the time now, apparently preferring the sea breezes to the traffic fumes of the capital, which means that the navy is on constant guard duty in the resort and the police are also on their best behaviour; consequently both Thais and expats consider Hua Hin an especially safe place to live and do business – hence the number of farang-oriented real estate agencies in the area. But the town is not without its controversies, most pressing of which is the local government's plan to bulldoze the Thanon Naretdamri **neighbourhood of squid-pier restaurants and guest houses** – Hua Hin's most distinctive attraction – and replace it with a privately financed promenade and shopping plaza. The squid piers are the hub of the original fishing village, which dates back to the early nineteenth-century; as the fishing industry declined, local families looked to tourism as an alternative source of income, converting their jetties into the restaurants and guest houses that are still in situ today. But despite successive generations having lived on the same spot for 170 years, they have no land-ownership papers, and so the authorities consider their piers an

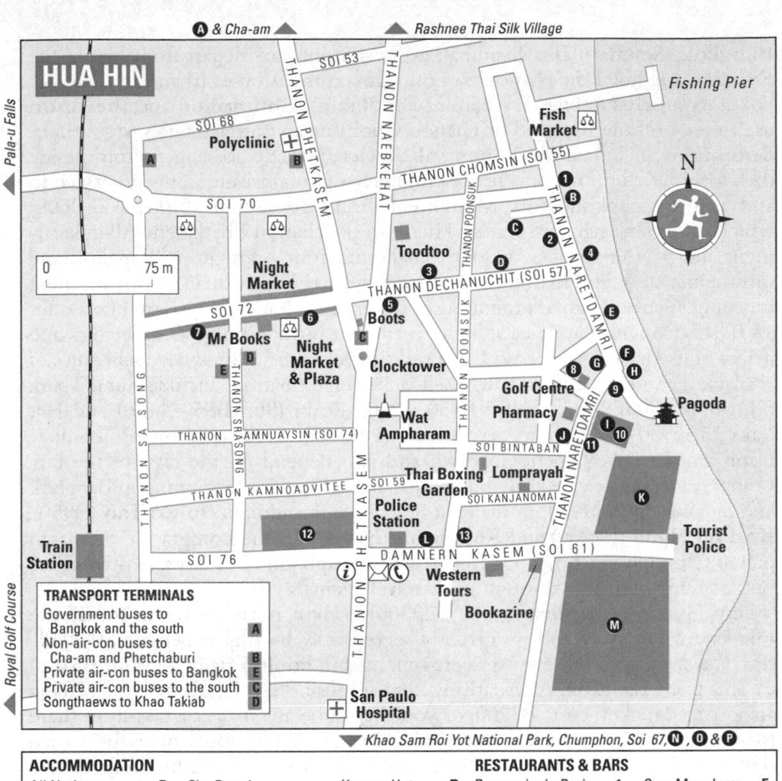

ACCOMMODATION

All Nations	D	City Beach Resort	L	Karoon Hut	B
Anantara Resort & Spa	A	Fresh Inn	J	Mod Guest House	F
Bird	H	Fu-Lay Guest House & Hotel	E	Pattana Guest Home	C
Central Village Hua Hin	K	Hilton Hua Hin	I	Sofitel Central Hua Hin	M
Chiva-Som International Health Resort	N	Jinning Beach Guest House	P	Veranda Lodge	O
		K Place	G		

RESTAURANTS & BARS

Brasserie de Paris	1	Som Moo Joom	5
Chao Lay	4	A Taste of Asia	3
Hua Hin Brewing Company	11	Tarachan Restaurant	6
Jasmine's	8	La Villa	13
Lung Ja	7	White Lotus	10
Monsoon	2	World News Coffee	9
Satukarn Square	12		

encroachment on public land (the sea). At the time of writing, the community was taking legal action to try and save their neighbourhood.

Arrival, information and transport

Hua Hin is on the Bangkok–Surat Thani rail line, but journeys tend to be slow (3hr 30min–4hr from Bangkok), and inconveniently timetabled. You can also get from Kanchanaburi to Hua Hin by train, but you need to change trains at Ban Pho (not listed on English-language timetables). Famously photogenic Hua Hin **train station** (ⓣ032 511073), which has changed little since it was built in the 1920s, is at the west end of Thanon Damnern Kasem, about ten minutes' walk from the seafront.

Hua Hin's **bus** service is more useful, though there are a confusing number of bus arrival and departure points (see map for locations). Non-air-con **Cha-am and Phetchaburi** buses arrive and depart from a spot just north of the junction of Thanon Phetkasem and Thanon Chomsin; private air-con buses to and from

Bangkok (Southern Bus Terminal; every 40min; 3hr) depart from beside the *Sri Phetkasem* hotel on Thanon Sa Song; government buses to and from Bangkok (second class only; every 25min; 3hr 30min), **Chumphon** and **the south** use a depot off the west end of Thanon Chomsin; and private buses to southern destinations, including the Lomprayah service, pick up passengers from beside the clocktower on Thanon Phetkasem. There's also a private minivan service to and from Bangkok's Victory Monument (every 30min; 3hr; ⓣ081 633 0609) which drops passengers in central Hua Hin on Thanon Phetkasem. All government and private services to southern destinations originate in Bangkok and most come through Hua Hin in the evening, arriving at their destination next morning. Generally government buses are cheaper but some private buses offer a VIP service with fewer seats; the government bus station posts timetables and prices of its services on the wall, and most travel agents should have schedules of available private services and will sell tickets. Destinations include Surat Thani (7hr; B700–900), Phuket (9hr; B850–1250), Krabi (9hr; B850–1120) and Hat Yai (10hr; 930–1250); note that prices are flexible because of intense competition among tickets agents in town and also depend on the class of the bus. Lomprayah runs a twice-daily bus and catamaran service, beginning in Bangkok and picking up in Hua Hin (daily at 8.30am and midnight) to **Ko Tao** (B850), **Ko Pha Ngan** (B1250) and **Ko Samui** (B1400) via the Lomprayah catamaran pier at Chumphon (ⓣ032 553739, ⓦwww.lomprayah.com; book at their office on Soi Kanjanomai or through most travel agents).

Tiny Hua Hin **airport** (ⓣ032 522300) is 6km north of town, beside the Phetkasem Highway, and is currently served only by tiny, expensive SGA 12-seat Cessna planes (ⓦwww.sga.aero/en/huahin.html; 3 daily; 40min; B3100) to and from Bangkok. Alternatively, the limousine service from Don Muang airport in Bangkok costs B3200, or you should be able to get a taxi from there for around B2500, which is the price Hua Hin's taxi touts offer for return transfers (about 3hr). Prices for Suvamabhumi Airport should be similar, and a direct bus service is also planned.

Information and city transport

The rudimentary **tourist information** desk at the local government office (daily 8.30am–8pm; ⓣ032 532433), on the corner of Thanon Damnern Kasem and Thanon Phetkasem, can supply town maps and limited info.

For getting around, Hua Hin has plenty of **samlors** and **motorbike taxis**, but many tourists rent cars and motorbikes to explore the area by themselves.

Accommodation

A night or two at the former *Railway Hotel* (now the *Sofitel*) is reason in itself to visit Hua Hin, but there are plenty of other **places to stay**. The most unusual guest houses are those built on the squid piers (now under threat of destruction), with rooms strung out along wooden jetties so you can hear, feel – and smell – the sea beneath you, even if you can't afford a room with an actual sea view. Rooms at jetty guest houses are no bargain – they tend to be a bit pokey and there's a rather strong aroma of seashore debris at low tide – but they are characterful. Room rates at many places can drop significantly from Mondays to Thursdays, so don't be afraid to ask for a discount.

About 15 minutes' walk south down the beach from the *Sofitel*, or 2km by road down the Phetkasem Highway, there's a little knot of accommodation on **Soi 67,** just south of the *Marriott Hotel*. Here, facing each other across the short, narrow soi about 200m back from the beach, are about a dozen little guest houses, mainly Scandinavian-Thai run; none comprise more than 20 rooms and most charge B900. They're very popular with older European couples, many of whom return for several months every winter, so booking is essential. Resorts beyond the northern fringes of Hua Hin, on the stretch of coast **between Hua Hin and Cha-am**, are described on p.613, and those in Pranburi/Pak Nam Pran, south of Hua Hin, are covered on p.623.

Inexpensive and moderate

All Nations 10 Thanon Dechanuchit ⓣ032 512747, ⓔcybercafehuahin@hotmail.com. A range of comfortable rooms in varying sizes, many of them with balconies, a few with distant sea views, some with air-con, and most with bathrooms shared between two rooms. Also has a roof terrace. Good value for Hua Hin. Fan ❸, air-con ❹

Bird 31/2 Thanon Naretdamri ⓣ032 511630, ⓔbirdguesthousehuahin@hotmail.com. A classic friendly little jetty guest house, with smallish and fairly basic en-suite rooms set over the water (those with air-con occupy the prime end-of-pier position), plus a nice breezy sea-view terrace at the end. Reserve ahead as it's very popular. Fan ❸, air-con ❹

Fresh Inn 132 Thanon Naretdamri ⓣ032 511389, ⓕ032 532166. Small Italian-run hotel with a friendly, cosy atmosphere and a swimming pool. Rooms are quite stylishly furnished and all have air-con and TV. ❼

Fu-Lay Guest House and Hotel 110/1 Thanon Naretdamri, guest house ⓣ032 513145, hotel ⓣ032 513670, ⓦfulay-huahin.com. *Fu-Lay* is in two halves, with guest-house rooms strung along a jetty and hotel accommodation in a low-rise block across the street. The jetty guest-house rooms are the most stylish of their kind in Hua Hin, offering attractively appointed air-con rooms with nice en-suite bathrooms and TV, plus some cheap cell-like en-suite fan rooms too and a breezy seating area set right over the water. Air-con rooms in the small hotel wing across the road are more upmarket, with the pricier ones on the upper floors offering sea views from their shared verandas. Jetty fan ❸, jetty air-con ❺, hotel ❺–❼

Jinning Beach Guest House East end of Soi 67, off Thanon Phetkasem ⓣ032 532597, ⓦwww.jinningbeachguesthouse.com. Typical Soi 67 guest house under welcoming Danish-Thai management, with just 16 good-sized air-con rooms, some with verandas, and all with TV and fridge. ❺–❻

Karoon Hut 80 Thanon Naretdamri ⓣ032 530242, ⓕ032 530737. Friendly jetty guest house, with decent fan- and air-con rooms (no cells) and a nice big open-air seating area at the end of the pier. Well priced for Hua Hin. Fan ❸, air-con ❹–❺

K Place 116 Thanon Naretdamri ⓣ032 511396, ⓔkplaceus@yahoo.com. Just ten large, comfortable and well-appointed rooms behind the mini market, all with air-con and TV, make this small place a good-value mid-range option. There's a roof terrace too. ❺–❻

Mod Guest House 116 Thanon Naretdamri ⓣ032 512296. Jetty guest house with some good rooms (a few with air-con), others fairly basic but very cheap (for Hua Hin), plus a seafront seating area. Call ahead to secure a room. Fan ❷, air-con ❸–❹

Pattana Guest Home 52 Thanon Naretdamri ⓣ032 513393, ⓔhuahinpattana@hotmail.com. Cosy, comfortable rooms with character in an appealingly traditional and attractively furnished teakwood house, quietly located at the end of a small soi. Some rooms have private bathrooms. ❸

Expensive

Anantara Resort and Spa 5km north of Hua Hin at 43/1 Thanon Phetkasem ⓣ032 520250, ⓦwww.anantara.com. Set in effusive, beautifully designed tropical gardens that run right down to the shore, this is a lovely resort-style idyll, just out of town. Accommodation is in a series of Thai-style pavilions, whose stylishly appointed rooms use plenty of wood. It has three restaurants, two free-form pools, a charming spa and its own stretch of beach. ❾

Central Village Hua Hin Thanon Damnern Kasem ⓣ032 512036, ⓦwww.centralhotelsresorts.com. Like its sister operation, the adjacent *Sofitel*, the *Central Village*, comprised of 41 cream-painted wooden villas set in a seafront garden, has a distinctive old-fashioned charm, though it's less swanky and more homely than its neighbour. All the villas have large verandas, and some have two rooms and an uninterrupted sea view. There's a pool and a restaurant on the premises, and guests can also use the facilities at the *Sofitel* over the road. ❾

Chiva-Som International Health Resort About 3km south of the *Sofitel* at 73/4 Thanon Phetkasem ⓣ032 536536, ⓦwww.chivasom.com. Super-deluxe beachfront spa and health resort that's a favourite with A-list celebs and is famous for its personalized holistic health treatments, detox programmes, fitness plans and psycho-spiritual consultations. Accommodation is in 57 exclusive bungalows and hotel rooms set in tropical beachfront gardens. Published rates for full board with treatments start at US$1140 per person for the minimum three-day stay. ⑨

City Beach Resort 16 Thanon Damnern Kasem ⓣ032 512870, ⓦwww.citybeach.co.th. A good upper-mid-range option that's reasonably priced, centrally located and has a swimming pool, a nightclub and a couple of restaurants. Air-con rooms in the high-rise block are comfortable, if old-fashioned, with most enjoying a sea view from the balcony. ⑦

Hilton Hua Hin 33 Thanon Naretdamri ⓣ032 512888, ⓦwww.huahin.hilton.com. Set bang in the centre of Hua Hin's beachfront, the *Hilton's* high-rise profile disfigures the local skyline, but the facilities are extensive and the views excellent. There's a large, inviting lagoon-like swimming pool right on the seafront, a spa, a kids' club, a panoramic Chinese restaurant (see p.621) and an impressive indoor-outdoor water garden in the lobby. All 300 rooms are large and comfortable and have sea-view balconies; published rates start at US$189. ⑨

Sofitel Central Hua Hin 1 Thanon Damnern Kasem ⓣ032 512021, ⓦwww.sofitel.com. The former *Railway Hotel* remains a classic of colonial-style architecture, with high ceilings, polished wood panelling, period furniture, wide sea-view balconies and a garden full of topiary animals. All is much as it was in 1923, except for the swimming pools and tennis courts, which were built especially for the filming of *The Killing Fields* – the *Railway Hotel* stood in as Phnom Penh's plushest hotel. The hotel also has a spa. Internet rates start at B6840; weekends get booked out several weeks in advance. ⑨

Veranda Lodge Beachfront end of Soi 67, off Thanon Phetkasem ⓣ032 533678, ⓦwww.verandalodge.com. Chic 18-room boutique hotel set a little apart from the Soi 67 guest houses in its own beachfront garden. Deluxe rooms have a contemporary look (lime green, pink or china-blue walls) and petite balconies; suites have separate living rooms and sea-view balconies. All rooms have air-con and cable TV and there's a small pool and seafront terrace restaurant. ⑧–⑨

The resort

The prettiest part of Hua Hin's five-kilometre-long **beach** is the patch in front of and to the south of the *Sofitel*, where the sand is at its softest and whitest. North of here the shore is crowded with tables and chairs belonging to a string of small restaurant shacks, beyond which the beach ends at a Chinese temple atop a flight of steps running down to Thanon Naretdamri. The coast to the north of the pagoda is dominated by the jetties and terraces of the squid-pier guest houses and seafood restaurants.

South of the *Sofitel*, holiday homes and high-rise condos overshadow nearly the whole run of beach down to the promontory known as Khao Takiab (Chopstick Hill), 6km further south, but during the week it's fairly quiet along here, with just a few widely spaced food stalls along the broad, squeakily soft beach. Kiteboarding Asia (ⓦwww.kiteboardingasia.com) runs **kiteboarding** courses from a spot off the end of Soi 75/1, about 2.5km south of the *Sofitel* (B11,000 for a three-day course; best conditions from March to May). **Khao Takiab** itself is a wooded outcrop surmounted by a temple and home to a troupe of monkeys; the road to the top is guarded by a tall, golden, standing Buddha and affords good coastal views. Green songthaews run to Khao Takiab from central Hua Hin, departing from Thanon Sa Song, just south of the junction with Soi 72 (at least every 30min; B10; 15min).

Pala-u Falls and other excursions

Hua Hin is well placed for **excursions** to Khao Sam Roi Yot National Park, Phetchaburi, Damnoen Saduak floating markets and the old summer palace of Phra Ratchaniwet Marukhathaiyawan (see p.613). The fifteen-tiered **Pala-u Waterfall** is another popular destination within day-tripping distance and, though the falls themselves are hardly exceptional, the route there takes you through lush, hilly landscape and past innumerable pineapple plantations. The falls are 63km west of Hua Hin, close to the Burmese border and within **Kaeng Krachan National Park** (daily 8am–4.30pm; B200; Ⓦwww.dnp.go.th/National_park.asp). There's no public transport to the falls, but every tour operator features them in its programme (about B1300/person). To get there under your own steam, follow the signs from the west end of Thanon Chomsin along Highway 3218. Once inside the park you'll see hundreds of butterflies and may also catch sight of monitor lizards and hornbills. A slippery and occasionally steep path follows the river through the fairly dense jungle up to the falls, passing the (numbered) tiers en route to the remote fifteenth level, though most people opt to stop at the third level, which has the first pool of any decent depth (full of fish but not that clear) and is a half-hour walk from the car park.

Golf courses

The Thai enthusiasm for **golf** began in Hua Hin in 1924, with the opening of the Royal Hua Hin Golf Course behind the train station, and now there are another five courses of international standard in the Hua Hin/Cha-am area. Visitors' green fees range from B1300 to B2500 on a weekday, B1600 to B2500 on a weekend, plus about B200 for a caddy. Some clubhouses also rent sets of clubs for B500, or you can ask at the Hua Hin Golf Centre (daily noon–10pm; Ⓣ032 530119, Ⓦwww.huahingolf.com) on Thanon Naretdamri across from the *Hilton*, which also sells and repairs clubs and organizes trips to local courses. Many other general tour operators also offer golf packages, which include transfers and green fees.

The historic eighteen-hole Royal Hua Hin Golf Course (Ⓣ032 512475) is the most centrally located of the **courses**, easily reached on foot by simply crossing the railway tracks to the west side of Hua Hin Railway Station. All the others are outside town and all have eighteen holes except where noted: Bangkok Golf Milford (Ⓣ032 572441; 15km south of Hua Hin near Pak Nam Pran); Imperial Lake View (27 holes; Ⓣ032 456233; 15km north of Hua Hin); Majestic Creek Country Club (Ⓣ032 520162; 20km west of Hua Hin); Palm Hills Golf Resort (Ⓣ032 520800, Ⓦwww.palmhills-golf.com; 8km north of Hua Hin); Springfield Royal Country Club, designed by Jack Nicklaus (Ⓣ032 593223, Ⓦwww.springfieldresort.com; 22km north of Hua Hin, just to the south of Cha-am).

Eating, drinking and entertainment

Hua Hin is renowned for its **seafood**, and some of the best places to enjoy the local catch are the seafront and squid-pier restaurants along Thanon Naretdamri. Fish also features heavily at the large and lively **night market**, which sets up at sunset along Soi 72 (the western end of Thanon Dechanuchit). The biggest concentration of **bars** is in the network of sois between the *Hilton Hotel* and Wat Hua Hin, particularly along Soi Bintaban, Soi Kanjanomai and Thanon Poonsuk; many of these places are so-called "bar-beers", with lots of seating round the bar and hostesses dispensing beer and flirtation through the night.

Tarachan Restaurant, located in amongst the night-market stalls at 67/2 Thanon Dechanuchit, hosts The Hua Hin Thai Show, a changing programme of **Thai dance**, cabaret and music (Mon, Wed & Fri 8–9pm; B350 including set dinner or B200 with one free drink; Ⓦwww.huahinthaishow.com). The more upmarket Sasi Garden Theatre, near the *Hyatt Regency*, about 4km south of the *Sofitel*, stages a classical Thai dance performance with dinner nightly at 7pm (vegetarians catered for); book through any travel agent (B750 including set dinner and

△ Jetty restaurant, Hua Hin

transfer; ⓣ032 512488, ⓦwww.sasi-restaurant.com). Tuesdays and Fridays are fight nights at the **Thai Boxing Garden** off Thanon Poonsuk (ⓣ032 515269), with programmes starting at 9pm and featuring five different fights (B300); it's owned by local *muay Thai* champion Khun Chop, who also runs Thai boxing classes most days at 5pm.

A Taste of Asia 42 Thanon Dechanuchit. Cosy, German-run Thai restaurant decorated with Thai folk paintings and artefacts and serving good quality Thai food and seafood, including grilled white snapper, seafood salad, frogs legs, and locally famous desserts from nearby Phetchaburi. Also has a good selection of imported wines and a few from Thailand. Most dishes from B150. Nightly 5–11pm.

Brasserie de Paris 3 Thanon Naretdamri. Refined French restaurant that's known for its seafood and has an appealing terrace over the water. Specialities include crab Hua Hin, *coquilles St Jacques* and *filet à la Provençal*. Mains come in at about B350, the seafood set menu is B595. Daily 11am–11pm.

Chao Lay 15 Thanon Naretdamri. Hua Hin's most famous jetty restaurant is deservedly popular, serving up a simple menu of high-quality seafood, including rock lobster, blue crab, scallops, cottonfish and mixed seafood platters. Most main dishes cost B100–200. Daily 11am–11pm.

Hua Hin Brewing Company In front of the *Hilton* on Thanon Naretdamri. Cavernous, half-timbered pub-restaurant that attempts to re-create the feel of a fisherman's tavern. There's live music nightly, plus a fairly pricey seafood-dominated menu, but the real attractions are the special beers produced by the in-house microbrewery: Sabai Sabai wheat beer, Elephant Tusk dark ale and Dancing Monkey lager. Nightly 5pm–2am.

Jasmine's 17/2 Soi Selakam. Classy but unpretentious restaurant serving good Thai food (most mains B150), lots of seafood, including especially good sea bass, as well as pizzas and steaks. Daily 11am–11pm.

La Villa 12/2 Thanon Poonsuk. Long-established and highly regarded Italian place that serves famously delicious home-made ice creams as well as a typical selection of mid-priced pizzas and pastas. Daily 11am–11pm.

Lung Ja Soi 72. One of several food-stall restaurants in the nightmarket that's so popular that its tables extend way back off the street. Cheap seafood is its big attraction. Nightly from 5pm.

Monsoon 62 Thanon Naretdamri. Atmospheric teakwood house, with brass fans, mellow lighting and a garden patio, that serves Thai and Vietnamese food, including Vietnamese *pho* (noodle soup), fresh spring rolls and *luc lac* (warm beef and watercress salad), as well as duck curry and seafood. Average price B150. Also serves afternoon tea. Daily from 3pm.

Satukarn Square At the Thanon Phetkasem/ Damnern Kasem junction. Though it's not so much fun as the night market, nor as cheap, you can take your pick from twenty or so mid-priced little restaurants in this partially open-air plaza, where the choice includes Italian, Indian, German and seafood outlets. Nightly from around 4pm.

Som Moo Joom 51/6 Thanon Dechanuchit (corner of Thanon Naebkehat); no English sign. Exceptionally good seafood at very cheap prices has made this place extremely popular with Thai holidaymakers. The trademark dish is shrimp and seafood soups, but the menu also covers the range of standard seafood dishes. Decor is bare bones and indoor seating is available only from 6pm to 9pm nightly, after which it's pavement tables only.

Thanachote 11 Thanon Naretdamri. Atmospheric seafood restaurant, set on its own pier over the sea and serving great fish dishes from B250; shrimps from B60. Daily 10am–11pm.

White Lotus 17th Floor, *Hilton Hua Hin*, Thanon Naretdamri. Contemporary Chinese cuisine with unsurpassed seventeenth-floor views over the Hua Hin jetty restaurants and surrounding coastline. Highlights include wok-fried snow fish in black-bean sauce (B360) and New Zealand lamb with garlic and shaonsing sauce (B420), or you could splash out on a *degustation* menu (B900–1800). Nightly from 5.30pm (come early to make most of views) and also open for dim sum lunches at weekends 11.30am–2.30pm.

World News Coffee Thanon Naretdamri. The place to come for skinny lattes, sun-dried tomato bagels, cheesecakes, fresh vegetable juices, UK and US newspapers, Internet access – and a very large bill. Daily 8am–11pm.

Shopping

The most enjoyable places to shop for clothes and souvenirs (after 6pm only) are the stalls at the night market on the west end of Thanon Dechanuchit, the more upmarket little shops in the Night Plaza that runs off it, and the handful of stalls selling handicrafts and clothes among the restaurants in Satukarn Square at the Thanon Phetkasem/Thanon Damnern Kasem crossroads. There's a small outlet for the high-quality Jim Thompson silk and clothing franchise in the lobby area of the *Hilton* hotel on Thanon Naretdamri, but a more rewarding place to start any serious silk shopping is the **Rashnee Thai Silk Village** (daily 9am–6pm; ⓣ032 531155, ⓦwww.mikecompany.com) at 18 Thanon Naebkehat, about ten minutes' walk north from the town-centre clocktower, or phone for a free pick-up. Every visitor to the "village" (actually a series of open-air workshop pavilions and an air-conditioned shop) is given a free and well-explained guided tour of the entire silk production process, after which you are encouraged to pop in to the Rashnee tailors' shop and get yourself suited up.

Listings

Banks and exchange There are currency-exchange counters all over the resort, especially on Thanon Damnern Kasem and Thanon Naretdamri; most of the main bank branches with ATMs are on Thanon Phetkasem.

Books English-language books at the excellent Bookazine, on the corner of Damnern Kasem and Naretdamri; at several branches of Book Corner, on Thanon Phetkasem, Thanon Damnern Kasem and Thanon Dechanuchit; and in some minimarkets.

Car and motorbike rental Avis (ⓣ032 520009, ⓦwww.avis.com) has desks inside the *Hotel Sofitel* and the *Hilton*, and at the *Dusit Resort Hua Hin*, north of town (see p.613); several Hua Hin tour agencies also act as agents for Budget (ⓣ032 514220, ⓦwww.budget.co.th). The transport touts outside the *Hotel Sofitel* and across from the telephone office rent out 150cc bikes for around B200 a day.

Emergencies For all emergencies, call the tourist police on the free, 24hr phoneline (ⓣ1155), or contact them at their office opposite the *Sofitel* at the beachfront end of Thanon Damnern Kasem (ⓣ032 515995). The Hua Hin police station is further west on Damnern Kasem (ⓣ032 511027).

Hospitals The best private hospital in Hua Hin is the San Paulo, 222 Thanon Phetkasem (ⓣ032 532576–80), south of the tourist office, but for minor ailments there's also the reputable Hua Hin International Polyclinic (daily 8am–9pm; ⓣ032

516424) beside the Thai Farmers Bank on Thanon Phetkasem, which also offers dental services.
Internet access Available at several outlets in the resort, including on Thanon Phetkasem and, cheapest of all, at the CAT international phone office on Thanon Damnern Kasem (daily 8.30am–11pm).
Mail The GPO is on Thanon Damnern Kasem.
Pharmacy Several in the resort, including the very well-stocked Medihouse (daily 9.30am–10pm) opposite the *Hilton* on Thanon Naretdamri.
Spas Plenty of options, from the numerous cheap day-spa shops that offer foot massages and Thai massages in several town-centre locations on Thanon Naretdamri and Thanon Phetkasem, to the artfully designed luxury havens at Hua Hin's top hotels, notably the *Chiva-Som* (see p.617) and the *Anantara* (see p.617).
Telephones The CAT overseas telephone office (daily 8.30am–11pm) is on Thanon Damnern Kasem, next to the GPO.
Tour operators Western Tours, at 11 Thanon Damnern Kasem (Ⓣ032 533303, Ⓦwww.westerntourshuahin.com) sells air tickets, golf packages, and day-trips to Khao Sam Roi Yot National Park (B1300/person), Pala-u Falls (B1300), Damnoen Saduak Floating Market (B1800) and the rest. Toodtoo Tours, at 9/2 Soi Pharephan, off Thanon Naebkehat (Ⓣ032 530553, Ⓦwww.toodtoo.com), offers similarly priced day-trips as well as local elephant rides (from B640/30min). Sunseeker Tours, based inside Bookazine at 166 Thanon Naretdamri (Ⓣ032 533666, Ⓦwww.sunseekertours.com), offers cruises to local beaches on its yacht for around B2000 per person as well as fishing and snorkelling trips and a local sunset cruise around Khao Takiab.

Pak Nam Pran

The stretch of coast between Hua Hin and Chumphon barely registers on most foreign tourists' radar, but many better-off Bangkokians have favourite beaches in this area, the nicest of which is sophisticated **PAK NAM PRAN**. Just 33km south of Hua Hin, Pak Nam Pran used to cater only for families who owned beach villas here, but in the last few years the shorefront homes have been joined by a growing number of enticing, if pricey, boutique hotels, and signs are there's more development to come. For now, facilities consist of just a few minimarkets, car-rental outlets and independent restaurants, plus the possibility of organizing day-trips to nearby Khao Sam Roi Yot National Park through hotel staff. As along much of the Gulf coast, the beach itself is not exceptional (it has hardly any shade and is suffering from erosion in parts), but it is long and sandy, and nearly always empty, and you're quite likely to see dolphins playing within sight of the shore.

Practicalities

Pak Nam Pran beach (also known as Hat Naresuan) begins just south of the Pran River estuary and its eponymous town and runs south for around five kilometres to Khao Kalok headland and the tiny Thao Kosa Forest Park. Easiest **access** is via the town of **PRANBURI**, which straddles Highway 4 some 23km south of Hua Hin and is served by air-con buses from Bangkok's Southern Bus Terminal (every 40min; 3hr 30min) as well as local buses from Hua Hin (every 20min; 40min), which drop passengers close by the town centre's main intersection. There's no public transport from Pranburi to Pak Nam Pran beach, 10km away, but hotels can arrange transfers, any Pranburi songthaew driver will taxi you there, or you could rent your own car or motorbike from Hua Hin. If making your own way, turn east off Highway 4 at Pranburi's town-centre traffic lights and then take minor road 3168 down to the sea (about 10km in all), picking up the relevant sign for your hotel. All the hotels are south of the little town of Pak Nam Pran.

Accommodation

Pak Nam Pran's charmingly characterful **accommodation** is its biggest draw: for once, "boutique" is the appropriate term, as many of the hotels here offer a dozen or fewer rooms, and the style tends to be more arty than five-star, though you will certainly be comfortable. Some hotels aren't suitable for kids owing to their multiple levels and unfenced flights of steps. Breakfast is generally included in the price of the room. During weekends in high season (Nov–May) you'll need to book ahead.

The *Evason* is the northernmost of the hotels (about 2km southeast of Pak Nam Pran town); the others are spread over a two-kilometre stretch of the beachfront road, starting about 2km south of the *Evason*.

Aleenta Central Pak Nam Pran beach ⓣ032 618333, ⓦwww.aleenta.com. This stunningly designed tiny hotel is the sleekest outfit on the beach, comprising three gorgeous circular bungalows, each with an uninterrupted sea view, a deck and personal plunge pool, plus half a dozen other very tasteful villa-style rooms. The feel is modernist chic, with elegantly understated local furnishings and huge glass windows, and iPods and wi-fi capability rather than TVs in every room. There's a small rooftop pool, a spa and restaurant, plus a couple of family villas available for rent. ⑨

Evason Hua Hin Resort and Spa Far northern Pak Nam Pran beach, ⓣ032 632111, ⓦwww.evasonresorts.com. With 185 rooms and a distinct resort atmosphere, the *Evason* is the biggest, best-known and most expensive hotel in Pak Nam Pran, but as accommodation is divided into discrete village areas and screened by graceful gardens, the feel is quite private and small-scale. For extra privacy you could check in to the *Hideaway* complex of super-luxe private-pool villas, the favourite choice of Thai film stars. All rooms are attractively cool and contemporary and have big balconies, TV and air-con. Facilities include a huge beachfront pool, two spa complexes, three restaurants, tennis courts, a kids' club and Internet access. Internet rates start at B6420, or B15,560 for *Hideaway* villas. ⑨

Huaplee Lazy Beach Central Pak Nam Pran beach ⓣ032 630555, ⓦwww.huapleelazybeach.com. This exceptionally cute collection of eight idiosyncratic white-cube beachfront rooms is the work of the architect-interior designer owners. It's a characterful place of whimsical interiors done out with white-painted wood floors, blue-and-white colour schemes and funky shell and driftwood decor. All rooms are air-con and all but one has a sea view from its terrace/balcony. ⑧

Jamsawang Resort Northern Pak Nam Pran beach ⓣ032 570050, ⓦwww.jamsawang.com. Currently the cheapest place to stay in the area, with just seventeen rooms in bungalows widely spaced around a neatly trimmed garden across the road from the beach. All rooms have air-con and TV, with half of them in comfortable if not especially sophisticated pale-blue concrete bungalows and the other half in pricier, more stylishly furnished yellow-painted bungalows, some with garden-style bathrooms. ⑥–⑧

Pran Havana Central Pak Nam Pran beach ⓣ032 570077, ⓦwww.pranhavana.net. More white-cube architecture right next to *Huaplee* at this slightly bigger but equally charming beachfront accommodation, where the warren of individually furnished rooms is accessed by a series of whitewashed steps and sea-view terraces. Interiors are idiosyncratic seaside-chic, personalized with hand-crafted furnishings and artworks. The price depends on the view. ⑧–⑨

Eating

The shorefront **restaurant** *Khao Kalok* (unsigned in English), at the far southern end of Pak Nam Pran beach, about 1km south of *Huaplee*, *Pran Havana* and *Aleenta*, has an extensive menu of very good seafood dishes; mosquitoes are a problem here though, so take repellent. On the edge of Pak Nam Pran town, about 2km north of the *Evason*, *Krua Jao* (daily 9am–9pm) offers an enormous, mid-priced menu of 120 mostly fish and seafood dishes, including very good crab curry and pork with garlic. The restaurant is on the seafront road but accessible only via Pak Nam Pran town: from the main road through Pak Nam Pran head east down (signed) Soi Pasukvanich 16, which is opposite a gate in a large walled temple compound; when the soi emerges at the sea you'll find the restaurant immediately to your left – it's unsigned in English but you can't miss it. The *Evason*'s *The Other Restaurant* does posh Asian fusion cuisine (dinner only) and its wine list features 220 different bottles.

Khao Sam Roi Yot National Park

With a name that translates as "The Mountain with Three Hundred Peaks", **KHAO SAM ROI YOT NATIONAL PARK** (daily 6am–6pm; B200; Ⓦwww.dnp.go.th/National_park.asp), 28km south of Pak Nam Pran beach or 63km south of Hua Hin, encompasses a small but varied coastal zone of just 98 square kilometres. The dramatic limestone crags after which it is named are the dominant feature, looming up to 650m above the Gulf waters and the forested interior, but perhaps more significant are the mud flats and freshwater marsh which attract and provide a breeding ground for thousands of migratory birds. **Bird-watching** at Thung Khao Sam Roi Yot swamp is a major draw, but the famously photogenic Phraya Nakhon Khiri cave is the focus of most day-trips, while a few decent trails and a couple of secluded beaches provide added interest.

The park

Khao Sam Roi Yot's most-visited attraction is the surprisingly worthwhile **Tham Phraya Nakhon** cave system, hidden high up on a cliffside above **Hat Laem Sala**, an unremarkable sandy bay at the base of a headland that's inaccessible to vehicles but has a park checkpoint, a restaurant and some national park bungalows. The usual way to get to Hat Laem Sala is by a five-minute boat-ride from the knot of food stalls behind Wat Bang Pu on the edge of **Ban Bang Pu** fishing village (6km from the park's northern checkpoint). Boat prices are fixed at B200 per boat for the round-trip visit to Hat Laem Sala. It's also possible to walk over the headland from behind Wat Bang Pu to Hat Laem Sala, along a signed, but at times steep, five-hundred-metre-long trail. From Hat Laem Sala, another taxing though shaded trail runs up the hillside to the Tham Phraya Nakhon caves and takes around thirty minutes.

The huge twin **caves** are filled with stalactites and stalagmites and wreathed in lianas and gnarly trees, but their most dramatic features are the partially collapsed roofs, which allow the sunlight to stream in and illuminate the interiors, in particular beaming down on the famous royal pavilion, Phra Thi Nang Khua Kharunhad, which was built in the second cave in 1890 in honour of Rama V. A three-hour trek south from Tham Phraya Nakhon brings you to **Tham Sai**, a genuinely dark and dank limestone cave, complete with stalactites, stalagmites and petrified waterfalls. The trek offers some fine coastal views, but a shorter alternative is the twenty-minute trail from **Ban Khung Tanot** village (accessible by road, 8km on from the Ban Bang Pu turn-off), where you can hire an essential flashlight and rent private bungalows (see opposite).

Another enjoyable activity is to charter a boat (B300/hour for up to ten people) from beside Wat Khao Daeng in the southern part of the park (1.5km from park HQ) and take a trip along the mangrove-fringed **Khao Daeng canal**; some Hua Hin and Hat Phu Noi tour companies also offer kayaking excursions here. You can scramble up **Khao Daeng** itself, a 322-metre-high outcrop that offers good summit views over the coast, from a thirty-minute trail that begins close by the park headquarters. The park's two official **nature trails** also start from close by HQ – the "Horseshoe Trail" takes in the forest habitats of monkeys, squirrels and songbirds, while the "Mangrove Trail" leads through the swampy domiciles of monitor lizards and egrets, with the chance of encountering long tailed (crab-eating) macaques.

The park hosts up to three hundred species of **bird** and between September and November the mud flats are thick with migratory flocks from Siberia, China and northern Europe. Khao Sam Roi Yot also contains Thailand's largest freshwater marsh, **Thung Khao Sam Roi Yot**, which is near the village of **Rong Jai** (Rong Che) in the north of the park, and accessed not from the main park road, but by turning east off Highway 4 200m north of kilometre-stone 276 and continuing 9km to the wetlands (it's outside the park boundary and not subject to the park entry fee). This is an excellent place for observing **waders** and **songbirds**, and is one of only two places in the country where the **purple heron** breeds; rangers rent out boats here for bird-watching excursions (B200/boat).

Practicalities

Like most of Thailand's national parks, Khao Sam Roi Yot is very hard to explore by public transport. The nearest **bus** drop is in Pranburi (see p.622), which is served by air-con buses from Bangkok's Southern Bus Terminal (every 40min; 3hr 30min) and by local buses from Hua Hin (every 20min; 40min). Once in Pranburi, either charter a songthaew or motorbike taxi (B200–300) into the park, or use the limited local **songthaew** service, which runs hourly from 6am to noon from Pranburi market to the village of **Ban Bang Phu**, the access point for boats to Hat Laem Sala and the Phraya Nakhon Khiri cave – but note that the last return songthaew leaves Ban Bang Phu at 1pm and this option is only feasible if you're not interested in visiting any of the other sights in the park, all of which are spread too far apart to walk between. It's much easier either to join a one-day **tour** from Hua Hin, Pak Nam Pran or Hat Phu Noi (see p.626) or to rent your own transport from Hua Hin. With your own wheels, take Highway 4 south to Pranburi, turn east at Pranburi's main intersection (kilometre-stone 254) and then follow the national-park signs to the **northern park checkpoint** 23km further south. All the main attractions are well signed from the main road through the park: it's 6km from the northern checkpoint to the departure point for boats to Hat Laem Sala and Phra Nakhon Khiri, and 14km to the **park headquarters** (Ⓣ032 619078), **trailheads**, **visitor centre** and **southern park checkpoint** near the village of Khao Daeng. If coming from the south, turn off Highway 4 into the park at kilometre-stone 286.5, following signs to the southern park checkpoint, HQ and so on, 13km further east. Rangers hand out rather sketchy **park maps** when you pay your entrance fee at the checkpoint.

Accommodation

The park's **accommodation** sites are near the headquarters at Khao Daeng, at Sam Phraya Beach, and at Laem Sala; at Laem Sala it's a choice between camping, at B125–250 per tent, or staying in one of the national park bungalows (from B1200), which sleep up to twenty people; at Sam Phraya it's camping only and at Khao Daeng it's bungalows only. Tents can be rented from the park headquarters but bungalows must be booked ahead through the central National Park office in Bangkok (Ⓣ02 562 0760, Ⓦwww.dnp.go.th/National_park.asp; see Basics p.51 for booking advice), though they can be paid for at Khao Sam Roi Yot. It's also possible to stay in the privately run fan bungalows of *Kathom Tongsuk* (Ⓣ089 533 8664; ④), near Tham Sai in the village of Ban Khung Tanot.

Most people prefer to stay a few kilometres outside the park entrance at the more appealing, family-friendly hotels on the long, quiet, pleasingly shaded golden-sand beach of **HAT PHU NOI**, where dolphins are a daily sight from October to March – you may even spot the very rare, pink Indo-Pacific humpback dolphin – and there are plenty of opportunities to explore nearby islands and national park attractions. Hat Phu Noi is clearly signed off the road into the park, 4km before the northern checkpoint, and is at the end of a two-kilometre side road; hotels can arrange transfers from Pranburi or Hua Hin. At the northern end of Hat Phu Noi, the long-running *Dolphin Bay Resort* (Ⓣ032 559333, Ⓦwww.dolphinbayresort.com; ❻) has about sixty comfortable air-con rooms and bungalows ranged around a couple of swimming pools, plus a big restaurant with a bar, pool table and Internet access. The adjacent Dutch-run *Terra Selisa Bungalows* (Ⓣ032 559359, Ⓦwww.terraselisa.com; ❻) is much smaller, with just twenty attractively furnished air-con bungalows set around a pool and garden, also just across the road from the beach. Both these hotels organize lots of **excursions** into the park, as well as dolphin-watching, sailing, snorkelling and squid-fishing trips, plus outings by boat or kayak to Monkey Island, just offshore. *Terra Selisa* also offers a dry-season trip to track wild elephants in nearby Kuiburi National Park (B600 per person, minimum four people), and *Dolphin Bay* rents out Hobie Cat sailboats, speedboats, motorbikes and bicycles.

South to Chumphon

Most foreign tourists zip through the region immediately south of Khao Sam Roi Yot en route to the more obvious delights of the Ko Samui archipelago, but the unexpectedly charming seaside town of **Prachuap Khiri Khan** and the small beach resorts at **Ban Krud** and **Suan Luang** are worth investigating if you're happy to substitute good seafood and laid-back Thai hospitality for full-on resort facilities. Twenty-two kilometres south of Prachuap, Highway 4 passes through Wang Duan, where a sign announces the fact that this is the narrowest part of Thailand: just 10.96km of Thai land separates the Gulf of Thailand from the Burmese border at this point.

Prachuap Khiri Khan

Despite lacking any must-see attractions, the tiny provincial capital of **PRACHUAP KHIRI KHAN**, 67km south of Pranburi and 90km from Hua Hin, exudes a certain small-town charm and makes a pleasant place to break any journey up or down the coast; if nothing else, it's a great spot for a seafood lunch with a view. The town is contained in a small grid of streets that runs just 250m east to west, between the sea and the train station, and around 500m north to south, from the Khao Chong Krajok hill at the northern end to the air-force base in the south.

Monkey-infested **Khao Chong Krajok** is Prachuap's main sight: if you climb the 417 steps from Thanon Salacheep to the golden-spired chedi at the summit you get a great perspective on the scalloped coast below and west to the mountainous Burmese border, just 12km away. At the far southern end of town, the long sandy beach at **Ao Manao** is the best place in the area for swimming and sunbathing. The bay is inside the air-force base, so you usually need to sign in at the checkpoint two kilometres north of the beach itself. To get there, just head south down the town centre's Thanon Salacheep for about 4km until you get to the base sign and checkpoint. A tuk-tuk to the beach should cost around B50, or about B25 for a motorbike taxi. On weekdays you're likely to have the sand almost to yourself, but it's a very popular spot with Thai families on weekends when the stalls at the beachfront food centre do a roaring trade in the locally famous *som tam poo* (spicy papaya salad with fresh crab). At low tide you can walk out from Ao Manao along a sandy spit to an outcrop known as **Khao Lommuak**, where a memorial commemorates the battle that took place here between Thai and Japanese forces in World War II.

About 12m south of town in **Wa Ko** (Waghor), east off Highway 4 at kilometre-marker 335, the **King Mongkut Memorial Park of Science and Technology** (also signed as Phra Chomklao Science Park; daily 8.30am–4.30pm; currently free but tickets are due to be introduced) features the pretty well stocked **Waghhor Aquarium** as well as some exhibits on astronomy, presented here to honour the scientifically minded Rama IV, who accurately predicted the total solar eclipse of August 1868 and came here to observe it.

Practicalities

Prachuap **train station** (Ⓣ032 611175) is on the edge of town at the western end of Thanon Kongkiat, which runs east down to the sea and the main pier. The **non-air-con bus stop**, for services (most frequent in the morning) to Chumphon, Pranburi and Hua Hin, is one block east of the train station and two blocks north, on Thanon Phitak Chat. Second-class **air-con buses** to Bangkok via Hua Hin and Phetchaburi (every 30min) and first-class services direct to Bangkok (hourly) leave from two offices 100m further south down Thanon Phitak Chat (one block south of Thanon Kongkiat). For the fastest service to Chumphon and Surat Thani you need to wait on Highway 4 at the Highway Police office, about 1km north of the access road into town, for the air-con buses that whizz down from Bangkok; several southbound services pick up passengers here between 8.30am and 11.30am (and many more around midnight).

There's a small, clued-up **tourist information** office (daily 8.30am–4.30pm; Ⓣ032 611491) at the far northern end of town in a little compound of municipal offices that sits between Thanon Susuek (Sooseuk) and beachfront Thanon Chai Thaleh; it's housed in the white Thai-style building with a blue roof, about 200m northeast of the non-air-con bus terminal, or 350m from the train station. The **post and telephone office**, directly behind the *Hadthong Hotel* on Thanon Susuek has a couple of Catnet **Internet** terminals upstairs (Mon–Fri 8.30am–4.30pm, Sat & Sun 9am–noon), or there's a private Internet place one block west and around the corner to the left on Thanon Salacheep, which keeps longer hours. There's **currency exchange** on Thanon Kongkiat, between the train station and the sea, and several ATMs on the main stretch of Thanon Phitak Chat. Prachuap Government **hospital** (Ⓣ032 601060-4) is a couple of blocks south of the air-con bus offices on Thanon Phitak Chat.

Accommodation

The cheapest and most traveller-oriented **place to stay** in town is the friendly *Prachuapsuk Hotel* at 69 Thanon Susuek (Ⓣ032 611019, Ⓕ032 601711; fan ❷, air-con ❸), where the en-suite rooms are simple but large and come with either fan or air-con. It's 50m south of the post office or about 300m southeast of the train station. Fan and air-con rooms at the larger *Suksant Hotel*, located at 11 Thanon Susuek, but also accessible from the beachfront road (Ⓣ032 611145, Ⓕ032 601208; ❸), are more expensive but not as inviting, though the upper floors do have very nice sea views. Nearby *Hadthong Hotel*, at 21 Thanon

Susuek, but also with an entrance on the beachfront road (Ⓣ032 601050, Ⓦwww.hadthong.com; ❹–❺), is a better maintained and more comfortable variation on the same theme, with bigger balconies and equally nice sea views in the more expensive rooms, air-con all round – and a swimming pool. For more of a real beach scene, the air-force hotel *Akan Ti Pak Sawatdikan* (Ⓣ032 661088; ❺) has air-con rooms all with sea view on the seafront in Ao Manao.

Eating

Prachuap's famously good seafood is most cheaply sampled at the town's two main **night markets**. The cheaper, more varied stalls set up in the empty lot around the junction of the pier road, Thanon Kongkiat, and Thanon Phitak Chat; the more upscale versions, with sit-down seafood stalls, menus in English and a couple of makeshift bars alongside, occupies the stretch of Thanon Susuek that runs alongside the small park, just north of Thanon Kongkiat and the pier. Otherwise there are several well-regarded seafood **restaurants** along Thanon Chai Thaleh, including *Pan Pochana*, south of the pier and next to the *Suksant Hotel*, where dishes range from shrimp and crab salads to fried sea asparagus and plenty of squid, and the shady terrace commands a perfect bay view. Almost next door, alongside the *Hadthong Hotel*, *Plern Smut* (English-sign at the Thanon Suseuk entrance only, not on the beachfront road) has famously delicious pan-fried oysters on its seafood-dominated menu.

Ban Krud

Graced with a tranquil, five-kilometre sweep of white sand, pale-blue sea and swaying casuarinas, **BAN KRUD** (Ban Krut), 70km south of Prachuap, is scenic and quite popular. A dozen or so fairly upmarket bungalow outfits and seafood restaurants line the central stretch of beachfront road, whose northern headland, **Khao Thongchai**, is dominated by the fourteen-metre-high Phra Phut Kitti Sirichai Buddha image and its sparkling modern temple, Wat Phra Mahathat Phraphat. Crowned with nine golden chedis, the temple displays an impressive fusion of traditional and contemporary features, including a series of charming modern stained-glass windows depicting Buddhist stories; reach it via a 1500-metre-long road that spirals up from the beachfront. Other than a visit to the temple and possibly a snorkelling trip to nearby Ko Lamla (about B400/person), the main pastime in Ban Krud is sitting under the trees and enjoying a long seafood lunch or dinner (the casuarinas are lit with fairylights at night).

Most southbound **buses** drop passengers at the Ban Krud junction on Highway 4, from where motorbike taxis cover the twelve kilometres down to the beach. Ban Krud **train** station is about 3km from the beach. *Bann Kruit Youth Hostel* (Ⓣ032 619103, Ⓦwww.thailandbeach.com; ❸–❹), north of the Big Buddha headland, about 2.5km from the central area, is one of the best, and priciest, youth hostels in the country. It occupies an effectively private chunk of very good beach, and offers air-con, two-person **bungalows** right on the shore, a range of other garden-view, fan bungalows and air-con dorms (B200/bed), wheelchair accessible accommodation, plus a swimming pool and bicycle rental. More central is the friendly and clued-up *Sala Thai* (Ⓣ032 695182, Ⓦwww.resortinthai.com; ❹–❻) in the main beach area, whose wooden bungalows with air-con and TV are spread under the coconut trees just across the road from the beach. Another popular option is the German-run *Baanklangaow Beach Resort* (Ⓣ032 695123, Ⓦwww.baanklangaowresort.com; ❼), a big compound of air-conditioned wooden chalets set in a mature tropical garden across the road from the sea and located 2km south of the central resort area. Facilities include two swimming pools, table tennis, a restaurant, Internet access, bicycle and kayak rental and the **dive company** Absolut Wreck (Ⓣ081 316 6009, Ⓦwww.absolutwreck.com).

Suan Luang

Thirty kilometres south down the coast from Ban Krud, the beach at **SUAN LUANG** is scruffy and has a slight air of abandonment, but for some this is part of its appeal, and there are a couple of pleasant places to stay here. About 750m before you hit the coast, laid-back, traveller-oriented *Suan Luang Resort* (Ⓣ032 691663; ❸–❹) has fourteen fan and air-con bungalows widely spaced around a peaceful garden, a very good restaurant, pool and table-tennis tables, motorbike rental, and masses of information on the local area. Down on the beach, the French-run mini-resort *Coral Hotel* (Ⓣ032 691667, Ⓦwww.coral-hotel.com; ❻–❽) also offers very good facilities, including a huge pool, sauna, games room and fitness centre, Internet access, two restaurants and a range of rooms and bungalows, all with air-con and TV. *Coral* runs a big programme of day-trips, adventure-sports activities and diving excursions. Access to Suan Luang is by **train** or bus to Bang Saphan Yai, about 7km from Suan Luang; hotels will collect guests on request.

Chumphon and around

South Thailand officially starts at **CHUMPHON**, where the main highway splits into west- and east-coast branches, and inevitably the provincial capital saddles itself with the title "gateway to the south". Most tourists take this tag literally and use the town as nothing more than a transport interchange between the Bangkok train and **boats to Ko Tao** (see p.631), so the town is well equipped to serve these passers-through, offering clued-up travel agents, efficient transport links and plenty of Internet cafés. As for reasons to stick around, there are average **beaches** north and south of town and a few offshore reefs worth diving and snorkelling, but perhaps the most rewarding direction for day-trippers is inland, through Chumphon province's famously abundant fruit orchards to **Pha To** and the **Lang Suan River**. If you're looking for something to do on a rainy day (of which Chumphon has quite a high number), you could visit the moderately interesting **Chumphon National Museum** (Wed–Sun 9am–4pm; B30; Ⓦwww.thailandmuseum.com), 3km north of town, in a compound of municipal buildings on the road to Thung Wua Laem beach and served by the same yellow songthaews from Thanon Pracha Uthit. Its displays summarize the history of the province from prehistoric times through to the modern day and include a "before-and after" diorama presentation (shown only at 10am and 2pm) on the devastation wreaked on Chumphon in 1989 by Typhoon Gay, and a feature on the arrival of invading Japanese forces at Chumphon and several other places on December 8, 1941 (see p.867).

Arrival, information and transport

Chumphon **train station** (Ⓣ077 511103) is on the northwest edge of town, less than ten minutes' walk from most guest houses and hotels. The government **bus station** (Ⓣ077 576796) is currently temporarily located just south of the river, though some bus drivers drop passengers on Thanon Tha Tapao first. There are also several private **air-con bus and minibus** services that leave from other

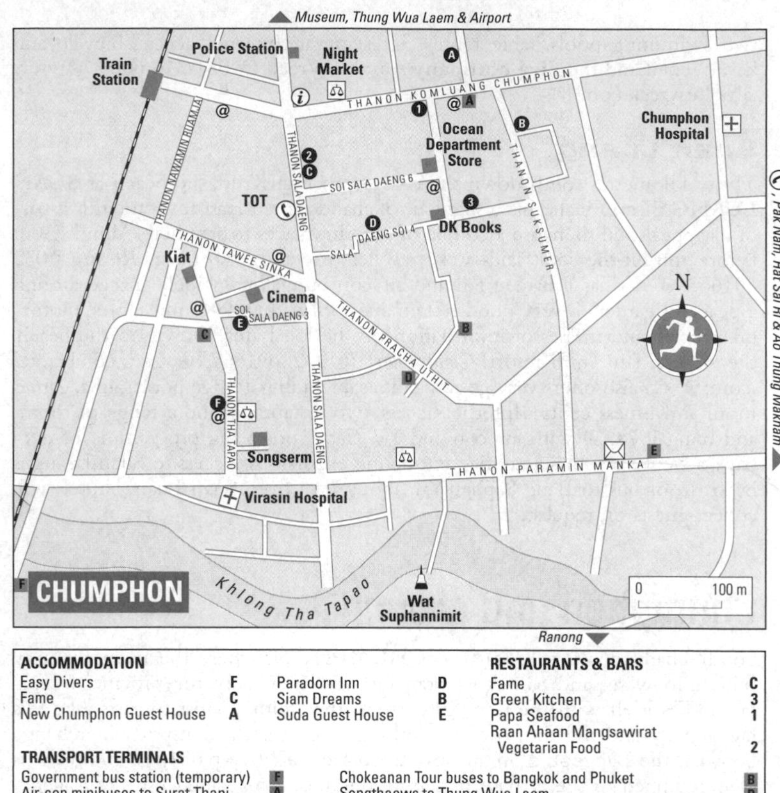

parts of town (see map for locations), including air-con minibuses to Surat Thani (every 30min); air-con minibuses to Ranong (hourly); and Chokeanan Tour air-con buses to Bangkok (4 daily; ⓣ077 511757). There are currently no scheduled flights in and out of Chumphon **airport**, 35km north of town; taking the overnight train to or from Bangkok is the most comfortable alternative.

The municipal **tourist information** centre is conveniently located about 175m east of the train station, at the junction of Thanon Komluang Chumphon and Thanon Sala Daeng (Mon–Fri 8.30am–7.30pm; ⓣ077 511730, ⓔchumphon@mots.go.th), though staff here are rarely as clued-up on the essentials as the town's league of **travel agents,** most of whom have offices on Thanon Tha Tapao. As well as flogging Ko Tao boat tickets, these places all sell bus tickets, and many also book accommodation on Ko Phayam, near Ranong off the Andaman coast, offer day-trip programmes including rafting at Pha To (B800, minimum 5 people), do visa runs to Burma via Ranong (B600 excluding B300 visa), and will store luggage free of charge; some also offer free showers to travellers who've bought tickets from them and are awaiting onward connections. Agents on Thanon Tha Tapao include Ko Tao ferry operator Songserm Travel (24hr; ⓣ077 506205), whose staff let travellers nap on the office floor while waiting for the boat; Easy Divers (ⓣ077 570085), which has

Boats to Ko Tao

There are several different **boat services from Chumphon to Ko Tao**, tickets for all of which are sold by all travel agents and most guest houses in town. The fastest service is **Lomprayah Catamaran** (daily at 7am and 1pm; 1hr 30min–2hr; B550 including transport to the pier; ⓣ077 558212, ⓦwww.lomprayah.com), which departs from the pier beside *MT Resort* at Ao Thung Makham Noi (see p.632), 25km south of Chumphon, but cannot sail in windy weather. All other services depart from Pak Nam port, 14km southeast of Chumphon, including **Songserm express** (7am; 2hr 30min; B400, also does through-tickets to Ko Pha Ngan for an extra B250 and Ko Samui for an extra B400; ⓣ077 506205). A Songserm bus meets all the morning trains from Bangkok and takes passengers to their office in town, from where there's onward transport to the Pak Nam ferry port at about 6.20am; Songserm will pick up from guest houses in town as well. There are also two late-night services from Pak Nam, both of which do pick-ups from town guest houses at around 10pm (B50 per person) and which run in all but the very worst weather. Of these, the slightly pricier **Ko Jaroen car ferry** (daily at 11pm; 6hr; B300 plus B50 for transport to the pier; ⓣ077 580030) is more comfortable and has blankets and pillows for passengers; cheapest of all is the smaller **midnight boat** (daily at midnight; 6hr; B200 plus B50 for transport to the pier; ⓣ077 521615).

a cheap accommodation above its office (see below); and Kiat (ⓣ077 502127, ⓔsomkia_t@hotmail.com).

Accommodation

Chumphon's **guest houses** are well used to accommodating Ko Tao-bound travellers, so most are happy to store luggage until the night boat leaves and offer shower services to non-guests for B20–30.

Easy Divers ⓣ077 570085, ⓦwww.chumphoneasydivers.com. Exceptionally cheap, mostly windowless rooms above the tour agency and dive centre, all with shared bathrooms. ❶

Fame 188/20-21 Thanon Sala Daeng ⓣ077 51077, ⓔakeychumphon@hotmail.com. Above the restaurant and tour agency of the same name, this place has good sized and very clean rooms with mattresses on the floor and fans; some have attached bathrooms. Share bathroom ❶, en suite ❷

New Chumphon Guest House (aka *Miao*) Soi 1, Thanon Komluang Chumphon ⓣ077 502900. Popular place (especially with Germans) on a quiet, residential soi with a pleasant outdoor seating area and an interesting programme of treks and day-trips. Rooms all share facilities and the price depends on the size of the room. ❶

Paradorn Inn 180/12 Thanon Paradorn, east off Thanon Sala Daeng ⓣ077 511598, ⓦwww.chumphon-paradorn.com. The best value of the town's mid-range hotels: all rooms have air-con and TV, and the VIP ones are refurbished and the poshest in town. There's a restaurant too. Air-con ❸, VIP ❹

Siam Dreams 116/31 Thanon Suksumer ⓣ077 571790. Variously sized rooms with fans and shared bathrooms. Phone the owner's mobile ⓣ087 269 3668 for free transfer from bus or train station. ❶–❷

Suda Guest House Thanon Sala Daeng Soi 3 (aka Soi Bangkok Bank), 30m off Thanon Tha Tapao ⓣ077 504366. Chumphon's most genuine and welcoming home-stay, offering just four clean and well-maintained fan and air-con rooms with shared bathroom in the owner's own modern house. Plenty of info available, B20 showers for passers-through, motorbikes for rent, jungle treks, boat tickets and day-trips. Phone ⓣ089 970 0304 for free transport from train or bus station. Fan ❷, air-con ❷

Around Chumphon: beaches and islands

Chumphon's best beach is **THUNG WUA LAEM**, 12km north of town and served by frequent yellow songthaews (B25–30) from halfway down Thanon

Pracha Uthit. The long sandy stretch has a few bungalow resorts and a handful of fairly pricey seafood restaurants with beachfront tables. A shop close to *Clean Wave* bungalows rents out sea canoes, bicycles and motorbikes and *Chumphon Cabana* also rents bicycles (B50/hr). The biggest and most popular **place to stay** on Thung Wua Laem is the ecologically conscious *Chumphon Cabana* (Ⓣ077 560245, Ⓦwww.cabana.co.th; ❻–❼), whose low-rise buildings are energy-efficient and comfortable, if not exactly stylish. Rooms all have air-con, TV and balcony, and there are some cheaper fan bungalows too. The resort has a big pool, two restaurants and an excellent programme of day-trips, including Lang Suan river-rafting at Pha To (see below), squid-trapping and firefly-watching. There's also a **dive centre** (late April–Sept only) here, which does trips to nearby islands for B1950 per diver and B680 per snorkeller, Openwater courses for B13,500 including four nights' accommodation and full board, and live-aboards to Ko Tao and Ang Thong. *Chumphon Cabana* runs shuttle buses between the resort and Chumphon. Cheaper places to stay include the (slightly musty) fan rooms and large, more airy air-con bungalows set round a garden at *Clean Wave* (Ⓣ077 560151; fan ❷, air-con ❺), halfway down the beach, and towards the far northern, quietest, end of the beach, fairly basic fan and slightly better air-con bungalows just 30m across the road from the sea at *Sea Beach* (Ⓣ07 560115; fan ❷, air-con ❹). *New Chumphon Guest House* in town also rents rooms in their *New Miao House* a few hundred metres inland from the beach, for travellers staying three days or more (❷–❸).

About 25km south of town, peaceful, palm-fringed **AO THUNG MAKHAM NOI** is one half of a double bay, with its larger twin, Ao Thung Makham Yai (site of Wat Pong Pang and its cave containing a large Buddha image), visible just over the headland to the south. There's hardly any development save for *MT Resort*, sometimes known as *Mother Hut* (Ⓣ077 558153, Ⓦwww.mtresort-chumphon.com; ❼), which has just nine attractive air-con chalets set around a beachside garden and restaurant; rooms have cable TV and rates include free use of kayaks. There's plenty of local info available, plus motorbike rental, snorkelling trips and fishing outings. The Lomprayah catamaran pier for the fastest service to Ko Tao is just a few metres from *MT*. To get to Ao Thung Makham Noi from Chumphon, either take one of the songthaews from Thanon Paramin Manka or call *MT* for a pickup.

Nearly all Chumphon's guest houses and tour agencies offer snorkelling trips to nearby **islands** (most of which lie within Mu Ko Chumphon National Park, so you may have to pay the B200 national park fee on top of the tour price). *Chumphon Cabana* on Thung Wua Laem also organizes diving trips. The reefs and underwater caves around **Ko Ngam Yai** and **Ko Ngam Noi**, about 18km offshore, are particularly good for divers, who are likely to see hawksbill turtles, large rays and nudibranchs. More rewarding for snorkellers is the shallower kilometre-long reef at **Ko Lawa**, about half an hour by longtail from Ao Thung Makham Noi.

Inland to Pha To

Though Chumphon province may not be renowned for its beaches and islands, its reputation as a major **fruit-growing** region is well established, and a great way to appreciate this is to head inland for some gentle **rafting on the Lang Suan River** near Pha To, and perhaps a stay at a lodge in a nearby village. All tour agencies and most guest houses offer rafting for around B1000 per person, depending on the size of the group. Or you can do it with your own transport by heading south down Highway 41 for 71km and then continuing west along Highway 4006 for 26km until you reach Pha To. Highway 4006 winds its exceptionally scenic way through endless plantations of trees bearing papayas, mangosteens, durians, bananas, rambutans, pomelos and coconuts, plus the occasional *robusta* coffee field as well (over fifty percent of Thailand's *robusta* coffee crop is grown in Chumphon).

At **PHA TO**, about 300m west of the roadside Pha To post office, a left turn takes you into the tiny town centre, where Malin Rafting (Ⓣ077 539053), easily spotted from the dozens of lifejackets outside, offers rafting trips, including transport, local lunch at a fruit farm, and a couple of hours' floating down the pretty if not spectacular Lang Suan River, for B500 per person (minimum six people, book the day before). There are plenty of chances to swim in the river, and it's good fun for kids too. Also based near Pha To is the Thai-Dutch eco-tourism outfit Runs 'N Roses (Ⓣ086 172 1090, Ⓦwww.runsnroses.com), which, as well as offering bamboo and wildwater rafting, treks and mountain-bike rental, also has **accommodation** in its tiny lodge 9km from Pha To (B850 for two people including all meals), runs a home-stay programme (B250 per person all-inclusive), and does half-day and one-day Thai cooking, cultural and language **workshops** for adults and kids (B300–500). Profits support the **Thai Child Development Foundation** (Ⓦwww.thaichilddevelopment.org), which helps house and educate needy local children; the foundation welcomes donations and volunteers – see Basics p.78 for more details.

Eating and drinking

The cheapest place to eat is the **night market**, which sets up along both sides of Thanon Komluang Chumphon and is an enjoyable place to munch your way through a selection of fried noodles, barbecued chicken and sticky, coconut-laced sweets. For live music with your beer, head down to the wood-fronted, country-style pub *Montana*, at the north end of Thanon Suksumer (nightly 6pm–1am).

Fame 188/20-21 Thanon Sala Daeng. Travellers' restaurant (plus guest house, boat tickets, tours and Internet access) serving pizzas topped with imported cheeses (B170), Indian dhal, loads of sandwiches, and huge American and veggie breakfasts (B90–120).

Green Kitchen Behind *Jansom Chumphon Hotel*, off Thanon Suksumer/Thanon Sala Daeng. Upscale Thai and Vietnamese food served daily 10am–10pm.

Papa Seafood Thanon Komluang Chumphon, One of the liveliest places to eat dinner is this huge, open-sided restaurant, which has an extensive menu of fresh seafood priced by weight, plenty of Western standards – and singers most evenings.

Puen Jai Across from the train station on Thanon Komluang Chumphon. An upmarket garden restaurant that also caters to hungry backpackers, serving pizza and home-baked bread as well as Thai food, and offering Internet access, free showers and left-luggage storage for diners passing through.

Raan Ahaan Mangsawirat Vegetarian Food Right next to *Fame* on Thanon Sala Daeng. Tiny place offering ready-cooked Thai-Chinese vegetarian food at B10–15 per serving. Daily 7am to about 3pm.

Listings

Airline tickets International and domestic tickets through travel agents Kiat Travel and Songserm, both on Thanon Tha Tapao (see p.630); some international tickets take 48 hours to issue from Bangkok.

Banks and exchange The main banks, with exchange counters and ATMs, are on Thanon Sala Daeng and Thanon Pracha Uthit.

Books DK Books, opposite the *Jansom Chumphon* hotel, has a stand of English-language books upstairs, and sells the *Bangkok Post*.

Car and motorbike rental Jeeps (B1200/24hr) and minibus plus driver (B1500/day) from Kiat, 115 Thanon Thatapao (Ⓣ077 502127, Ⓦwww.chumphonguide.com). Motorbikes from any travel agency and most guest houses (B200/day).

Emergencies For all emergencies, call the tourist police on the free, 24hr phoneline Ⓣ1155, or contact the Chumphon police station on the north end of Thanon Sala Daeng (☎077 511300).

Hospitals The private Virasin Hospital (☎077 503238–40) is off the southern end of Thanon Tha Tapao, and the government Chumphon Hospital (☎077 503672–4) is on the northeast edge of town.

Internet access Available all over town: see map for locations.

Mail The GPO is on the southeastern edge of town, on Thanon Paramin Manka (Mon–Fri 8.30am–4.30pm, Sat 9am–noon).

Pharmacy On Thanon Sala Daeng.

Telephones The TOT overseas phone centre and card phones is near the *Suriwong Chumphon* hotel on Thanon Sala Daeng (Mon–Fri 8.30am–4.30pm).

Chaiya and around

About 140km south of Chumphon, **CHAIYA** was the capital of southern Thailand under the Srivijayan empire, which fanned out from Sumatra between the eighth and thirteenth centuries. Today there's little to mark the passing of the Srivijayan civilization, but this small, sleepy town has gained new fame as the site of **Wat Suan Mokkh**, a progressively minded temple whose meditation retreats account for the bulk of Chaiya's foreign visitors. Unless you're interested in one of the retreats, the town is best visited on a day-trip, either as a break in the journey south, or as an excursion from Surat Thani.

Chaiya is 3km east of Highway 41, the main road down this section of the Gulf coast: **buses** running between Chumphon and Surat Thani will drop you off on the highway, from where you can catch a motorbike taxi or walk into town; from Surat Thani's Talat Kaset II bus station, hourly air-con minibuses and more frequent but slower songthaews take around an hour to reach Chaiya. The town also lies on the main Southern Rail Line, though many **trains** from Bangkok arrive in the middle of the night.

The Town

The main sight in Chaiya is **Wat Phra Boromathat** on the western side of town, where the ninth-century chedi – one of very few surviving examples of Srivijayan architecture – is said to contain relics of the Buddha himself. Hidden away behind the viharn in a pretty, red-tiled cloister, the chedi looks like an oversized wedding cake surrounded by an ornamental moat. Its unusual square tiers are spiked with smaller chedis and decorated with gilt, in a style similar to the temples of central Java.

The **National Museum** (Wed–Sun 9am–4pm; B30; ⓦwww.thailandmuseum.com), on the eastern side of the temple, is a bit of a disappointment. Although the Srivijaya period produced some of Thailand's finest sculpture, much of it discovered at Chaiya, the best pieces have been carted off to the National Museum in Bangkok. Replicas have been left in their stead, which are shown alongside fragments of some original statues, two intricately worked 2000-year-old bronze drums, found at Chaiya and Ko Samui, and various examples of Thai handicrafts. The best remaining pieces are a calm and elegant sixth- to seventh-century stone image of the Buddha meditating from Wat Phra Boromathat, and an equally serene head of a Buddha image, Ayutthayan-style in pink sandstone, from **Wat Kaeo**, an imposing ninth- or tenth-century brick chedi on the south side of town. Heading towards the centre from Wat Phra Boromathat, you can reach this chedi by taking the first paved road on the right, which brings you first to the restored base of the chedi at Wat Long, and then after 1km to Wat Kaeo, enclosed by a thick ring of trees. Here you can poke around the murky antechambers of the chedi, three of which house images of the Buddha subduing Mara.

Wat Suan Mokkh

The forest temple of **Wat Suan Mokkh** (Garden of Liberation), 6km south of Chaiya on Highway 41, was founded by **Buddhadasa Bhikkhu**, southern Thailand's most revered monk until his death in 1993 at the age of 87. His back-to-basics philosophy, encompassing Christian, Zen and Taoist influences, lives on and continues to draw Thais from all over the country to the temple, as well as hundreds of foreigners. It's not necessary to sign up for one of the wat's retreats to enjoy the temple, however – all buses from Surat Thani to Chaiya and Chumphon pass the wat, so it's easy to drop by for a quiet stroll through the wooded grounds.

The layout of the wat is centred on the Golden Hill: scrambling up between trees and monks' huts, past the cremation site of Buddhadasa Bhikkhu, you'll reach a hushed clearing on top of the hill, which is the temple's holiest meeting-place, a simple open-air platform decorated with images of Buddha and the Wheel of Law. At the base of the hill, the outer walls of the Spiritual Theatre are lined with bas-reliefs, replicas of originals in India, which depict scenes from the life of the Buddha. Inside, every centimetre is covered with colourful didactic painting, executed by resident monks and visitors in a jumble of realistic and surrealistic styles.

Meditation retreats

Meditation retreats are led by Western and Thai teachers over the first ten days of every month at the International Dharma Heritage, a purpose-built compound 1km from the main temple at Wat Suan Mokkh. Large numbers of foreign travellers, both novices and experienced meditators, turn up for the retreats, which are intended as a challenging exercise in mental development – it's not an opportunity to relax and live at low cost for a few days. Conditions imitate the rigorous lifestyle of a *bhikkhu* (monk) as far as possible, each day beginning before dawn with meditation according to the Anapanasati method, which aims to achieve mindfulness by focusing on the breathing process. Although talks are given on Dharma (the doctrines of the Buddha – as interpreted by Buddhadasa Bhikkhu) and meditation technique, most of each day is spent practising Anapanasati in solitude. To aid concentration, participants maintain a rule of silence, broken only by daily chanting sessions, although supervisors are available for individual interviews if there are any questions or problems. Men and women are segregated into separate dormitory blocks and, like monks, are expected to help out with chores.

Each course has space for about one hundred people – turn up at the information desk in Wat Suan Mokkh as early as possible on the last day of the month to enrol. The fee is B1500 per person, which includes two vegetarian meals a day and accommodation in simple cells. Bring a flashlight (or buy one outside the temple gates) and any other supplies you'll need for the ten days – participants are encouraged not to leave the premises during the retreat. For further information, go to Ⓦwww.suanmokkh.org or telephone Ⓣ077 431597.

Surat Thani

Uninspiring **SURAT THANI** ("City of the Good People"), 60km south of Chaiya, is generally worth visiting only as the jumping-off point for the Samui archipelago. Strung along the south bank of the Tapi River, with a busy port for rubber and coconuts near the river mouth, the town is experiencing rapid

> **The Chak Phra Festival**
>
> At the start of the eleventh lunar month (usually in October) the people of Surat Thani celebrate the end of Buddhist Lent with the **Chak Phra Festival** (Pulling the Buddha), which symbolizes the Buddha's return to earth after a monsoon season spent preaching to his mother in heaven. On the Tapi River, tugboats pull the town's principal Buddha image on a raft decorated with huge nagas, while on land sleigh-like floats bearing Buddha images and colourful flags and parasols are hauled across the countryside and through the streets. As the monks have been confined to their monasteries for three months, the end of Lent is also the time to give them generous offerings in the *kathin* ceremony, of which Surat Thani has its own version, called Thot Pha Pa, when the offerings are hung on tree branches planted in front of the houses before dawn. Longboat races, between teams from all over the south, are also held during the festival.

economic growth and paralysing traffic jams. It might be worth a stay, however, when the Chak Phra Festival (see box) is on, or as a base for seeing the nearby historic town of Chaiya.

Practicalities

Buses to Surat Thani arrive at three different locations, two of which are on Thanon Taladmai in the centre of town, at Talat Kaset I on the north side of the road (Phunphin and one or two other local buses) and opposite at Talat Kaset II (many long-distance buses, including those from Krabi, Phang Nga, Phuket, Ranong, Nakhon Si Thammarat and Hat Yai). The new bus terminal, 2km southwest of the centre on the road towards Phunphin, handles mostly services from Bangkok; Talat Kaset II buses going to or from places to the west such as Krabi, Phang Nga and Phuket also make a stop here. Arriving by **train** means arriving at **Phunphin**, 13km to the west, from where buses run into Surat Thani every ten minutes or so between around 5.30am and 7.30pm, while share-taxis (based in Surat at Talat Kaset II) charge B100 to charter the whole car into town; many buses heading west out of Surat also make a stop at Phunphin station, which might save you a journey into town and out again. It's also possible to buy through-tickets to Ko Samui and Ko Pha Ngan from the train station for the same price as they would be from Surat Thani town, including a connecting bus to the relevant pier. If you're planning to leave by train, booking tickets at Phantip Travel, in front of Talat Kaset I at 293/6–8 Thanon Taladmai (Ⓣ077 272230 or 077 272906), will save an extra trip to Phunphin.

Details of **boats** to **Ko Samui**, **Ko Pha Ngan** and **Ko Tao** are given in the account of each island – see p.641, p.661 and p.677. Phunphin and the bus stations are teeming with touts, with transport waiting to escort you to their employer's boat service to the islands – they're generally reliable, but make sure you don't get talked onto the wrong boat. If you manage to avoid getting hustled, you can buy tickets direct from the boat operators: Seatran, on Thanon Ban Don near the night-boat pier (Ⓣ077 215555, Ⓦwww.seatranferry.com), has vehicle ferries to Samui and Pha Ngan (with connecting buses), from Don Sak, 68km east of Surat; Samui Tour, 326/12 Thanon Taladmai (Ⓣ077 282352), handles buses to Ko Samui via the Raja vehicle ferries from Don Sak; Phangan Tour, also on Thanon Taladmai (Ⓣ077 205799), handles buses to Ko Pha Ngan via the Raja vehicle ferries from Don Sak; tickets for Songserm Express Boats to Samui, Pha Ngan and Tao (and from there to Chumphon) from the pier at Pak Nam Tapi, on the east side of Surat town itself, can be bought at ADV on

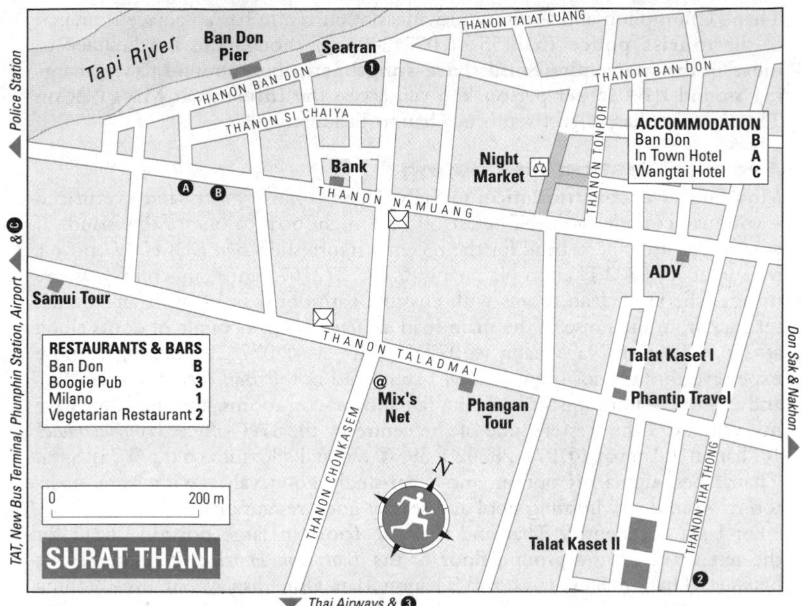

Thanon Namuang (☎077 205419). The night boats to Ko Samui, Ko Pha Ngan and Ko Tao line up during the day at Ban Don Pier in the centre of Surat; as they're barely glorified cargo boats, it's worth going along there as early as you can, as the first to buy tickets get the more comfortable upstairs mattresses.

Arriving by **air**, you can take a B75 Phantip minibus for the 27-kilometre journey south from the airport into Surat Thani, or a combination ticket to Ko Samui (B280) or Ko Pha Ngan (B450); if you're flying out of Surat, you can catch the minibus from town to the airport at the Phantip Travel office in front of Talat Kaset I (see opposite). Budget (☎077 441166) have an outlet at the airport for **car rental**. Two of the **airlines** currently serving Surat airport have offices in town: Thai Airways at 3/27–28 Thanon Karoonrat, off Thanon Chonkasem (☎077 272610), and Orient Thai (One-Two-Go) on Thanon Taladmai opposite the *Wangtai Hotel* (☎077 222780–1); Air Asia can be contacted at their Bangkok call centre (☎02 515 9999).

If you're coming from points south by **air-conditioned minibus** or **share-taxi**, you should be deposited at the door of your destination. For **moving on** to the rest of the mainland, share-taxis and air-con minibuses tend to congregate around Talat Kaset II. Be aware, however, that there have been many reports of overcharging and **scams**, especially involving any kind of combination ticket, on the private, tourist-oriented minibus and bus services out of Surat, including those heading for Khao Sok National Park (see p.714) and Malaysia. Generally, as in most places in Thailand, you're better off making your own way to the public bus terminal, which, for most journeys from Surat, is bang in the centre of town. Certainly, avoid the unregistered travel agents at Talat Kaset II itself in favour of walking the short distance to the reliable Phantip Travel (see opposite); otherwise get in touch with TAT, who will recommend a registered travel agent.

TAT's office at the western end of town at 5 Thanon Taladmai (daily 8.30am–noon & 1–4.30pm; ☎077 288817–9, Ⓦwww.tat.or.th/south5) covers Surat

Thani, Chumphon and Ranong provinces; it currently has an adjacent branch of the **tourist police** (ⓣ1155 or 077 200133), though this is scheduled to move in the near future. Small **share-songthaews** buzz around town, charging around B10–15 per person. You can access the **Internet** at Mix's Net on Thanon Chonkasem, just south of Thanon Taladmai.

Accommodation and eating

Most budget **accommodation** in Surat Thani is noisy, grotty and overpriced – you may consider yourself better off on a night boat to one of the islands. If you do get stuck here, head for the recently refurbished *Ban Don Hotel*, above a restaurant at 268/2 Thanon Namuang (ⓣ077 272167; fan ❷, air-con ❸), where most of the very clean rooms with en-suite bathrooms and fans or air-con are set back from the noise of the main road. *In Town Hotel*, a couple of doors along at 276/1 Thanon Na Muang (ⓣ077 210145–50, ⓕ077 210422; ❸), is more expensive though not quite as well maintained as the *Ban Don*; there are TVs and en-suite bathrooms in both the fan and air-con rooms, and the latter have hot water. On the western side of the centre by the TAT office, *Wangtai Hotel*, 1 Thanon Taladmai (ⓣ077 283020–39, ⓔwangtai@loxinfo.co.th; ❺), is Surat Thani's best upmarket option, and surprisingly good value, with large, smart rooms around a swimming pool and several good restaurants.

For tasty, inexpensive Thai and Chinese **food** in large portions, head for the restaurant on the ground floor of the *Ban Don Hotel*. The night market between Thanon Si Chaiya and Thanon Ban Don displays an eye-catching range of dishes; a smaller offshoot by Ban Don pier offers less choice but is handy if you're taking a night boat. Also near the night-boat piers on Thanon Ban Don, *Milano* has an authentic oven turning out very tasty and reasonably priced pizza, and serves panini, home-made pasta and a few Italian fish and meat main courses. During the day, simple restaurants around Talat Kaset II bus station serve noodles, dim sum and Thai-style fast food, while one block east on Thanon Tha Thong, an unnamed vegetarian restaurant offers a wide selection of cheap and delicious tray food or fried noodles, (look for the yellow flags outside and a sign saying "vegetarian food"; closes 4pm). If you're stranded in Surat for the night, your best bet for a **drink** is the *Boogie Pub*, a typical Wild West-style bar-restaurant with regular live music; it's a ten-minute walk from Thanon Taladmai down Thanon Chonkasem, then take the first road on the left and it's on your left.

Ko Samui

A wide cross-section of visitors, from globetrotting backpackers to suitcase-toting fortnighters, come to southern Thailand just for the beautiful beaches of **KO SAMUI**, 80km from Surat. At 15km across and down, Samui is generally large enough to cope with this diversity – except during the rush at Christmas and New Year – and the paradisal sands and clear blue seas have to a surprising extent kept their good looks, enhanced by a thick fringe of palm trees that gives a harvest of three million coconuts each month. However, development behind the beaches – which has brought the islanders far greater prosperity than the crop could ever provide – speeds along in a messy, haphazard fashion with little concern for the environment. At least there's a local bye-law limiting new construction to the height of a coconut palm (usually about three storeys), though this has not deterred either the luxury hotel groups or the real-estate developers who have recently been throwing up estates of second homes for Thais and foreigners.

For most visitors, the days are spent indulging in a few watersports or just lying on the beach waiting for the next drinks' seller, hair-braider or masseur to come along; some even have the energy to make it to one of Samui's many **spas**, whether independent or attached to one of the posh hotels, for further pampering. Night-time entertainment is provided by a huge number of beach bars, tawdry bar-beers and several nightclubs on Chaweng and Lamai. For something more active, you should not miss the almost supernatural beauty of the **Ang Thong National Marine Park** (see p.644), which comprises many of the eighty islands in the Samui archipelago (speedboat day-trips to Ko Tao

△ Ang Thong National Marine Park

are also available all over the island, but they cost a lot of money – around B1800 – for a matter of hours on the island). A day-trip by rented car or motorbike on the fifty-kilometre round-island road will throw up plenty more fine beaches – though it's hard to recommend a motorbike, as Samui has the highest rate of driving fatalities in Thailand, most of them involving bikes. Otherwise you could hook up with a **round-island tour**, such as those organized by Mr Ung's Magical Safari Tours (bookable through travel agents or your accommodation or contact ⓣ077 230114 or 081 895 5657, ⓦwww.ungsafari.com; from B1200), which will at least get you up the rough tracks of the mountainous interior to some spectacular viewpoints.

The island's most appealing beach, **Chaweng**, has seen the heaviest, most crowded development and is now the most expensive place to stay, though it does offer by far the best range of amenities and nightlife. Its slightly smaller neighbour, **Lamai**, lags a little behind in terms of looks and top-end development, but retains large pockets of backpacker bungalow resorts. The other favourite for backpackers is **Maenam**, which though less attractive again, is markedly quiet, with plenty of room to breathe between the beach and the round-island road. Adjacent **Bophut** is similar in appearance, but generally more sophisticated, with a cluster of boutique resorts, fine restaurants and a distinct Mediterranean feel in its congenial beachfront village. **Choeng Mon**, set apart in Samui's northeast corner, offers something different again: the small, part-sandy, part-rocky bay is tranquil and pretty, the seafront between the handful of upmarket hotels is comparatively undeveloped, and Chaweng's nightlife is within easy striking distance.

Accommodation on the island is generally in bungalow resorts, from the basic, through the comforts of the ever-growing mid-range, to the very swish: at the lower end of the scale, there are very few places left for under B350, but nearly all bottom-end bungalows now have en-suite bathrooms, constant electricity and fans; for the most upmarket places you can pay well over B4000 for the highest international standards. The price codes on the following pages are based on high-season rates, but out of season (roughly April–June, Oct & Nov) dramatic reductions are possible.

No particular **season** is best for coming to Ko Samui. The northeast monsoon blows heaviest in November, but can bring rain at any time between October and January, and sometimes causes high waves and strong currents, especially on the east coast. January is often breezy, March and April are very hot, and between May and October the southwest monsoon blows mildly onto Samui's west coast and causes some rain.

TAT runs a small but helpful office (daily 8.30am–noon & 1–4.30pm; ⓣ077 420504 or 077 420720–2, ⓔtatsamui@tat.or.th), tucked away on an unnamed side road in Na Thon (north of the pier and inland from the post office). Another useful source of **information** is ⓦwww.samui.sawadee.com, a website set up by a German based at Lamai, which handles, among other things, direct bookings at a range of hotels on the island.

Ko Samui has around a dozen **scuba-diving** companies, offering trips for qualified divers and a wide variety of courses throughout the year, and there's a **recompression chamber** at Bangrak (ⓣ081 084 8485, ⓦwww.sssnetwork.com). Although the coral gardens at the north end of Ang Thong National Marine Park offer good diving between October and April, most trips for experienced divers head for the waters around Ko Tao (see p.674), which contain the best sites in the region; a day's outing costs around B3000, though if you can make your own way to Ko Tao, you'll save money and have more time in the water. The range of courses is comparable to what's on offer at Ko Tao,

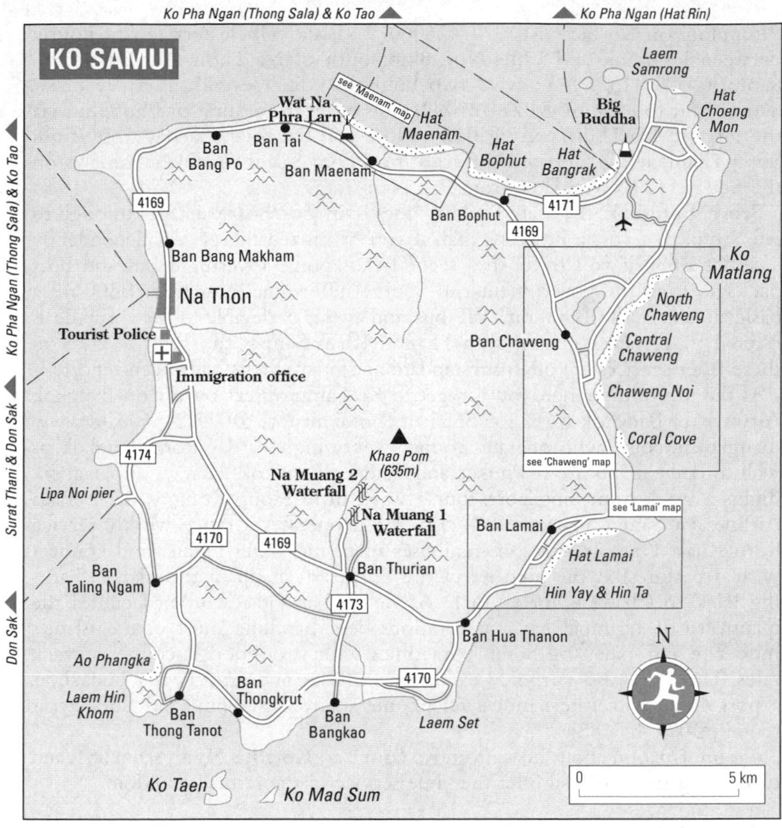

though prices are generally higher. Established and reliable PADI Five-Star Dive Centres include, each with several branches around the island, Samui International Diving School (Ⓦ www.planet-scuba.net), which has its head office at the *Malibu Resort* towards the north end of Central Chaweng (Ⓣ 077 422386); and Easy Divers (Ⓦ www.easydivers-thailand.com), which has its head office next to *Sandsea Resort*, towards the north end of Lamai (Ⓣ 077 231190).

Getting to the island

The most obvious way of getting to Ko Samui is on a **boat** from the **Surat Thani** area; for contact details of transport companies in Surat, see p.636. Services may fluctuate according to demand, but the longest-established ferry is the night boat that leaves **Ban Don** pier in Surat Thani itself for **Na Thon** – the main port on Samui – at 11pm every night (6hr); tickets (B150) are sold at the pier on the day of departure. From **Pak Nam Tapi** pier, on the east side of Surat town, one so-called Express Boat a day, handled by Songserm Travel (on Ko Samui Ⓣ 077 420157), runs to Na Thon (2hr 30min; B180 including transport from Surat or Phunphin train station to the pier).

From **Don Sak**, 68km east of Surat, Seatran vehicle ferries run every hour to the new pier at Na Thon (1hr 30min; B180 including bus from Surat or

Phunphin; on Ko Samui ⓣ077 426000–2). Raja vehicle ferries run hourly between Don Sak and **Lipa Noi**, 8km south of Na Thon (1hr 30min; on Samui ⓣ077 415230–3); every two hours to coincide with alternate boats, Samui Tour (on Samui ⓣ077 421092) runs buses from Surat or Phunphin via the ferry to Na Thon, costing B180. Note that the total journey time (from Surat Thani) using the vehicle ferries from Don Sak is much the same as on the Songserm Express Boat from Pak Nam Tapi.

From Bangkok, the State Railway does train/bus/boat packages through to Ko Samui that cost a little less than if you organized the parts independently – about B680 if you travel in a second-class bunk. Overnight bus and boat packages from the government-run Southern Terminal cost from B600 on a basic air-con bus to B900 on a VIP bus, and are far preferable to the cheap deals offered by private companies on Thanon Khao San, as the vehicles used on these latter services are often substandard and many thefts have been reported.

At the top of the range, you can get to Ko Samui direct **by air** on Bangkok Airways (in Bangkok ⓣ02 265 5555; at Samui airport ⓣ077 245600, ⓦwww.bangkokair.com), who operate around twenty flights a day from Bangkok, as well as daily flights from Phuket and Pattaya. Bangkok Airways also run six flights a week from Singapore, four a week from Hong Kong, while Berjaya Airlines (at Samui airport ⓣ084 053 2353) operates a twice-weekly service from Kuala Lumpur. Air-con minibuses meet incoming flights (and connect with departures) at the **airport** in the northeastern tip of the island, charging B100 to Chaweng for example. As well as bar and restaurant facilities, the quaint, rustic terminal has a reservations desk handling most of the island's moderate and expensive hotels, sometimes with very good discounts on rack rates. There are also currency-exchange facilities and an ATM, a bookshop, a post office with international telephones (daily 8am–8pm) and Budget car rental (ⓣ077 427188).

For information about boats from Ko Samui to **Ko Pha Ngan** see p.661, and to **Ko Tao** see p.677; all offer the same service in the return direction.

Island transport

Songthaews, which congregate at the car park between the two piers in Na Thon, cover a variety of set routes during the daytime, either heading off clockwise or anti-clockwise on Route 4169, to serve all the beaches; destinations are marked in English and fares for most journeys range from B30 to B60. In the evening, they tend to operate more like taxis and you'll have to negotiate a fare to get them to take you exactly where you want to go. Ko Samui now also sports dozens of **air-con taxis**. By law, they're required to use their meters (on top of which they're allowed to add a B50 service charge), but you'll have a hard job persuading any driver to do so; you might be lucky enough to settle on a flat fare of B300 from Maenam to Chaweng, for example, after some hard bargaining. You'll also see some **motorbike taxis** buzzing about the island, which charge from B30 for a local drop, up to B150 from Na Thon to Chaweng. You can **rent a motorbike** from B150 in Na Thon and on the main beaches. Dozens are killed on Samui's roads each year, so proceed with great caution, and wear a helmet – apart from any other considerations, you can be landed with an on-the-spot B500 fine by police for not wearing one.

Na Thon

The island capital, **NA THON**, at the top of the long western coast, is a frenetic half-built town which most travellers use only as a service station before hitting the sand: although most of the main beaches now have post offices, currency-exchange facilities, ATMs, supermarkets, travel agents and clinics, the biggest and best concentration of amenities is to be found here. The town's layout is simple: the two piers come to land at the promenade, Thanon Chonvithi, which is paralleled first by narrow Thanon Ang Thong, then by Thanon Taweeratpakdee, aka Route 4169, the round-island road; the main cross-street is Thanon Na Amphoe, by the more northerly of the piers.

Accommodation and eating

If you really need a **place to stay** in Na Thon, your best bets are the *Nathon Residence* (Ⓣ077 236058; ❹), on Thanon Taweeratpakdee next to Siam City Bank and near the market, a well-run place with a café downstairs and large, plain but spotless tiled rooms with air-con, cable TV and en-suite bathrooms, some with hot water, upstairs; and *Jinta Hotel* towards the south end of Thanon Chonvithi (Ⓣ077 420630, Ⓦwww.tapee.com; fan ❸, air-con ❹), with smart, bright, en-suite ground-floor rooms in a pleasant garden (some with air-con and hot water, all with cable TV) and its own **Internet café**.

Several stalls and small cafés purvey inexpensive Thai **food** around the market on Thanon Taweeratpakdee and on Thanon Chonvithi (including a lively night market by the piers), and there are plenty of Western-orientated places clustered around the piers. Justifiably popular, especially for breakfast, is cheerful and inexpensive *RT (Roung Thong) Bakery*, with one branch opposite the piers and another on Thanon Taweeratpakdee, which serves sandwiches, pancakes and pizzas, as well as Thai food and a wide variety of coffees. For lunch, head for the modern block of shops behind the large Samui Mart department store towards the south end of Thanon Taweeratpakdee: here you can choose between *Vegetarian Food*, a neat and simple veggie restaurant (closed Sun), and *Hia Meng (Starfish)*, a popular, well-run café serving duck or pork on rice.

Listings

Bookshop Nathon Book Store, on Thanon Na Amphoe, is a good second-hand place.
Hospital The state hospital (Ⓣ077 421230–2) is 3km south of town off Route 4169.
Immigration office 2km south of town down Route 4169 (Mon–Fri 8.30am–4.30pm; Ⓣ077 421069).
Massage The Garden Home Health Center, 2km north along Route 4169 in Ban Bang Makham (Ⓣ077 421311), dispenses some of the best traditional Thai massages (B350/hr) on the island, though note that it closes at 5pm.
Post office At the northern end of the promenade (Mon–Fri 8.30am–4.30pm, Sat & Sun 9am–noon). Poste-restante and packing services downstairs, international telephone service upstairs, including Catnet Internet access.
Tourist police 1km south of the town centre on Route 4169 Ⓣ1155, 077 421281 or 077 421360.
Travel agent The reliable Phantip is on Thanon Taweeratpakdee (north of Thanon Na Amphoe; Ⓣ077 421221–2). Services include through-buses all the way to Bangkok, Krabi, Phuket and Hat Yai from Na Thon.

Maenam

The most westerly of the bays on the north coast is **MAENAM**, 13km from Na Thon and Samui's most popular destination for shoestring travellers. The exposed four-kilometre bay is not the island's prettiest, being more of a broad dent in the coastline, and the sloping, white-sand beach is relatively narrow and slightly coarse by Samui's high standards. But Maenam features the cheapest bungalows on the island, unspoilt views of fishing boats and Ko Pha Ngan, and good swimming. Despite the recent opening of some upmarket developments on the shoreline and a golf course in the hills behind, this is still the

Ang Thong National Marine Park

Even if you don't get your buns off the beach for the rest of your stay, it's worth taking at least a day out to visit the beautiful **Ang Thong National Marine Park**, a lush, dense group of 42 small islands strewn like dragon's teeth over the deep-blue Gulf of Thailand, 31km west of Samui. Once a haven for pirate junks, then a Royal Thai Navy training base, the islands and their coral reefs, white-sand beaches and virgin rainforest are now preserved under the aegis of the National Parks Department. Erosion of the soft limestone has dug caves and chiselled out fantastic shapes that are variously said to resemble seals, a rhinoceros, a Buddha image and even the temple complex at Angkor.

The surrounding waters are home to dolphins, wary of humans because local fishermen catch them for their meat, and *pla thu* (short-bodied mackerel), part of the national staple diet, which gather in huge numbers between February and April to spawn around the islands. On land, long-tailed macaques, leopard cats, common wild pig, sea otters, squirrels, monitor lizards and pythons are found, as well as dusky langurs, which, because they have no natural enemies here, are unusually friendly and easy to spot. Around forty bird species have had confirmed sightings, including the white-rumped shama, noted for its singing, the brahminy kite, black baza, little heron, Eurasian woodcock, several species of pigeon, kingfisher and wagtail, as well as common and hill mynah; island caves shelter swiftlets, whose homes are stolen for bird's nest soup (see box on p.802). The largest land mass in the group is **Ko Wua Talab** (Sleeping Cow Island) where the park headquarters shelter in a hollow behind the small beach. From there it's a steep 430-metre climb (about 1hr return; bring walking sandals or shoes) to the island's peak to gawp at the panorama, which is especially fine at sunrise and sunset: in the distance, Ko Samui, Ko Pha Ngan and the mainland; nearer at hand, the jagged edges of the surrounding archipelago; and below the peak, a secret cove on the western side and an almost sheer drop to the clear blue sea to the east. Another climb from the beach at headquarters, only 200m but even harder going (allow 40min return), leads to Tham Buabok, a cave set high in the cliff-face. Some of the stalactites and stalagmites are said to resemble lotuses, hence the cave's appellation, "Waving Lotus". If you're visiting in September, look out for the white, violet-dotted petals of **lady's slipper orchids**, which grow on the rocks and cliffs.

The feature that gives the park the name Ang Thong, meaning "Golden Bowl", and that was the inspiration for the setting of cult bestselling novel, *The Beach*, is a landlocked saltwater lake, 250m in diameter, on **Ko Mae Ko** to the north of Ko Wua Talab. A well-made path (allow 30min return) leads from the beach through natural rock tunnels to the rim of the cliff wall that encircles the lake, affording another stunning view of the archipelago and the shallow, blue-green water far below, which is connected to the sea by a natural underground tunnel.

quietest and most laid-back of the major beaches, with little in the way of nightlife – though if you want to go on the razzle, there are late-night songthaews to and from Chaweng and Lamai. Though now heavily developed with multi-storey concrete shophouses, the main road is set back far from the sea, connected to the beachside bungalows by an intricate maze of minor roads through the trees. At the midpoint of the bay, **Ban Maenam** is centred on a low-key road down to the fishing pier, which is flanked by several Internet shops and small boutiques.

Practicalities

Most visitors to Maenam **eat** in their hotel or resort restaurant, though a couple of unaffiliated places stand out. At the west end of the bay,

Practicalities

There are no scheduled **boats to Ang Thong**, only organized day-trips, which can be easily booked through your accommodation or a travel agent. The main operator is Highway Travel and Highsea Tour, Thanon Taweeratpakdee (north of Thanon Na Amphoe; ⓣ077 421290, ⓦwww.highseatour.com) whose boats leave Na Thon every day at 8.30am, returning at around 5pm. In between, there's a two-hour stop to explore Ko Wua Talab (just enough time to visit the viewpoint, the cave and have a quick swim, so don't dally), lunch, some cruising through the archipelago, a visit to the viewpoint over the lake on Ko Mae Ko and a snorkelling stop. Tickets cost B1150 per person, including pick-up from your accommodation and the B200 national park fee. Similar trips run from Ban Bophut on Ko Samui (organized by Air Sea Tour, ⓣ077 422262–3) and less frequently from Ko Pha Ngan and Ko Tao; *Seaflower*, at Ao Chaophao on Ko Pha Ngan's west coast, does three-day "treks" (see p.671). Several companies in Maenam and Bophut on Samui do pricey speedboat day-trips to Ang Thong, and the luxury yacht *Seatran Discovery* does the trip twice a week for B2800, including hotel pick-up, national park fee and kayaking (ⓣ077 426000–2, ⓦwww.seatrandiscovery.com).

If you want to make the most of the park's beautiful scenery of strange rock formations and hidden caves, take a dedicated **kayaking** trip with Blue Stars, based at Gallery Lafayette near the *Green Mango* nightclub on Chaweng (ⓣ077 413231, ⓦwww.bluestars.info). For a one-day trip, taking in the lake at Ko Mae Ko and kayaking and snorkelling among the islands in the northern part of the park, they charge B2000, including pick-up from your accommodation and boat over to the park, buffet lunch, snorkelling gear and national-park entrance fee. A two-day trip, which also comprises camping on a beach at Ko Sam Sao and kayaking to Ko Wua Talab, costs B4750.

If you want to **stay at Ko Wua Talab**, the National Parks Department maintains simple two- to eight-berth bungalows (B500–1500) at the headquarters. To book accommodation, contact the Ang Thong National Marine Park Headquarters (ⓣ077 280222 or 077 286025), or the Parks Department in Bangkok (see p.51). Camping is also possible in certain specified areas: if you bring your own tent, the charge is B30 per person per night, or two-person tents can be rented for around B100 a night. If you do want to stay, you can go over on a boat-trip ticket – it's valid for a return on a later day. For getting around the archipelago from Ko Wua Talab, it's possible to charter a motorboat from the fishermen who live in the park; the best snorkelling is off Ko Thai Plao. At the daytime canteen at park headquarters, you can pre-order dinner for the evening.

signposted on a lane that runs east from Wat Na Phra Larn, *Sunshine Gourmet* is worth hunting down for its warm welcome and keen prices; it does a bit of everything, from cappuccino and home-made yoghurt for all-day breakfast, through own-baked pies, sandwiches and cakes, to international, especially German, main courses, seafood and other Thai dishes. *Angela's Bakery*, opposite the police station on the main through-road to the east of the pier, is a popular, daytime-only expat hangout, offering great breakfasts and a wide choice of sandwiches, salads, soups and Western main courses, as well as cakes, pies and home-made chocolates.

If you need a **travel agent** on Maenam, head for the reliable Nice Tour and Travel, on the main road 200m east of the police station (ⓣ077 247198).

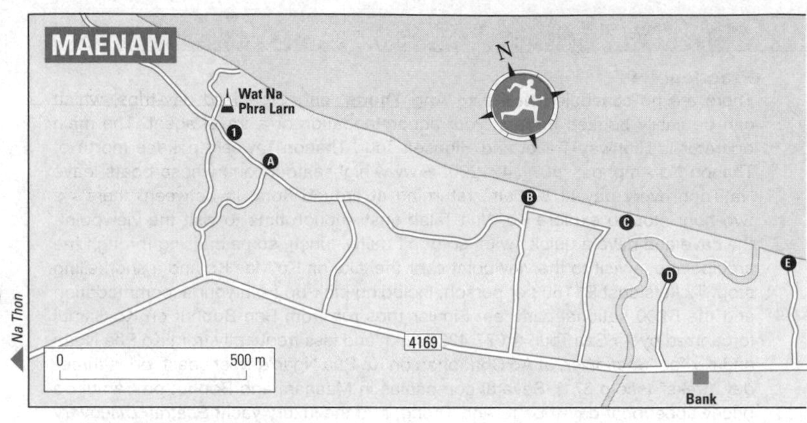

Accommodation

As well as one or two luxury resorts, Maenam has around thirty inexpensive and moderately priced bungalow complexes, most offering a spread of accommodation; the cheapest of these are at the far eastern end of the bay.

Cleopatra Palace At the eastern end of the bay, 1km from the village ⓣ077 425486, ⓦwww.cleopatra.freehomepage.com. In an unshaded, sandy but flower-strewn compound, this quiet, friendly place has a variety of clean, en-suite concrete bungalows, some with air-con and hot water. The Thai and Western food is recommended. Fan ③, air-con ⑤

Friendly About 500m east of *Cleopatra's Palace* ⓣ077 245736–7. Easy-going, fairly spacious place with helpful staff. All the bungalows are very clean and have their own bathrooms, though the place feels a little exposed, with few trees to provide shade. Internet access. ②

Harry's At the far western end, near Wat Na Phra Larn ⓣ077 425447, ⓦwww.harrys-samui.com. Set back about 150m from the beach amidst a secluded and shady tropical garden complete with a decent-sized swimming pool and waterfall, this popular, well-run place offers clean, spacious en-suite bungalows, with air-con, fridge and cable TV, as well as a small spa and Internet access. ⑥

Lolita On the east side of *Santiburi Resort* ⓣ077 425134, ⓔlolitakohsamui@yahoo.com. Quiet, efficiently run resort in a colourful, grassy garden on a long stretch of beach. Large, wooden, fan-cooled bungalows, some with hot water, and much smarter air-con rooms cluster around a kitsch, circular bar-restaurant adorned with pink Corinthian columns. Fan ④, air-con ⑦

Maenam Beach Huts At the eastern end of the bay ⓣ07 273 0226. Mellow, easy-going place offering old-style, thatched, rattan bungalows, with fans, en-suite bathrooms and mosquito screens, under the coconut palms on an extensive, sandy plot. There's also a massage sala and a popular beachside restaurant with a pool table. ②

Maenam Resort 500m west of the village, just beyond *Santiburi Resort* ⓣ077 247286–7, ⓦwww.maenamresort.com. A welcoming, tranquil resort (no TVs) in tidy, shady grounds, with an especially long stretch of beach. The rooms and large bungalows, with verandas, hot water and fans or air-con, offer good-value comfort. ⑥

Moonhut On the east side of the village ⓣ077 425247, ⓦwww.kohsamui.com/moonhut. Welcoming farang-run place on a large, sandy plot, with a busy restaurant and beach bar and colourful, substantial and very clean bungalows; all have verandas, mosquito screens, wall fans and en-suite bathrooms, some have hot water and air-con. Fan ③, air-con ⑥

Morning Glory Next door to *Friendly* at the eastern end of the bay (no phone). Laid-back, farang-run old-timer that has resisted the urge to upgrade: in a shady compound, basic thatched-roofed wooden huts, either en suite or sharing, with mosquito nets and fans. All-you-can-eat seafood buffets in the evenings (B250) and live rock bands two nights a week. ①–②

Santiburi Resort 500m west of the village ⓣ077 425031–8, ⓦwww.santiburi.com. Luxury hotel in beautifully landscaped grounds spread around a huge freshwater swimming pool and stream. Accommodation is mostly in Thai-style villas, inspired by Rama IV's summer palace at

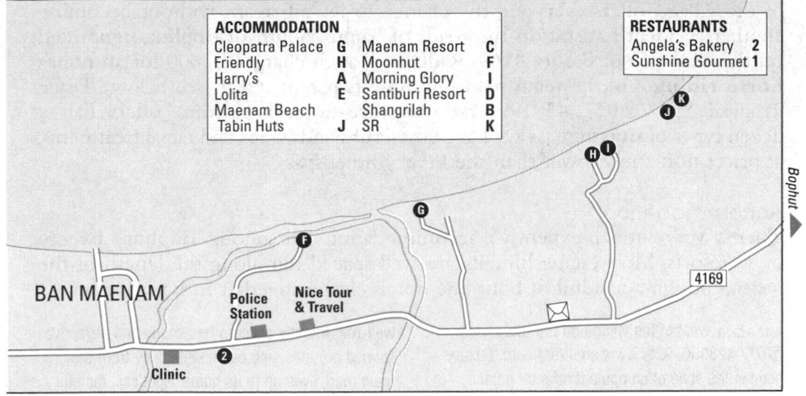

Phetchaburi, each with a large bathroom and separate sitting area, furnished in luxurious traditional design; some also have a private outdoor Jacuzzi. Facilities include watersports on the private stretch of beach, tennis courts, squash court and golf course, a spa, car rental, and an excellent "royal" cuisine restaurant, the *Sala Thai*. ⑨

Shangrilah West of *Maenam Resort*, served by the same access road ⓣ077 425189, ⓦwww.geocities.com/pk_shangrilah. In a flower-strewn compound that sprawls onto the nicest, widest stretch of sand along Maenam, these smart, well-maintained though tightly packed, en-suite bungalows come with verandas, ceiling fans, decent furniture and mosquito screens. The restaurant serves good Thai food. ④

SR At the far eastern end of the bay ⓣ077 427530, ⓔsr_bungalow@hotmail.com. A quiet, welcoming, good-value place, set in a flower garden, with a very good restaurant. Accommodation is in large, smart, concrete bungalows with bathrooms, verandas and chairs, those on the beachfront having air-con. Fan ③, air-con ⑥

Bophut

The next bay east is **BOPHUT**, which has a similar look to Maenam but shows a marked difference in atmosphere and facilities, with a noticeable French influence. The quiet, two-kilometre beach attracts a mix of young and old travellers, as well as families, and **Ban Bophut**, now tagged "Fisherman's Village", at the east end of the bay, is well geared to meet their needs, with a sprinkling of small, comfortable hotels, and a bank currency-exchange booth, ATMs, scuba-diving outlets, a small second-hand bookstore, travel agents, Internet cafés and supermarkets. While through traffic sticks to Route 4169 to Chaweng and Route 4171 towards the airport, development of the village has been reasonably sensitive, preserving many of its old wooden shophouses on the two narrow, largely car-free streets that meet at a T-junction by the pier. At night, in sharp contrast to Chaweng's frenetic beach road, it's a fine place for a promenade, with a concentration of good upmarket restaurants and low-key farang-run bars. The nicest part of the beach itself is at the west end of the bay, between *Peace* and *Zazen* resorts, but again the sand is slightly coarse by Samui's standards.

Practicalities

Watersports are amply catered for, with jet-skis available just to the west of the village, and a little further along, next to *Anantara*, kayaks, water-skiing and windsurfing at The Dive Academy. Samui Go-kart, a **go-karting** track (daily 9am–9pm; ⓣ077 425097; from B500 for 10min) on the main road 1km west of the village, offers everyone the chance to let off steam without becoming another accident statistic on the roads of Samui. South of Bophut, signposted off the west side of Route 4169, Ride on Ranch charges B1000 for an hour's **horse riding**. On the main road opposite its parent resort (see below), Peace Tropical Spa (ⓣ077 430199, ⓦwww.peace-tropical-spa.com) offers half a dozen types of **massage**, as well as body scrubs and wraps and facial treatments, at prices noticeably lower than the luxury hotel spas.

Accommodation

There's very little inexpensive accommodation left among Bophut's twenty or so resorts. Most establishments are well spaced out along the length of the beach, though a handful of boutique hotels cluster together in Ban Bophut.

Anantara west of the village on the main road ⓣ077 428300–9, ⓦwww.anantara.com. Luxury hotel in the style of an opulent oriental palace, with blocks of balconied rooms arrayed round lush gardens, ponds, an attractive swimming pool and a central bar and restaurant. Thoughtful touches in the rooms include cafetieres and a choice of bath salts, and service is attentive. There's also a very attractive spa and a wide range of activities, from yoga to watersports. 9

Cactus Towards the west end of the beach between *Peace* and *Samui Palm Beach Resort* ⓣ077 245565, ⓔcactusbung@hotmail.com. Welcoming place where ochre cottages with attractive bed platforms, small verandas and well-equipped bathrooms stand in two leafy rows running down to the beachside bar-restaurant; the cheapest have fans and cold water, the most expensive hot water, air-con and TV. Pool table, Internet access. Fan 5, air-con 6

Eden West of the village T-junction ⓣ077 427645, ⓦwww.edenbungalows.com. Congenial, French-run place with very well appointed and maintained rooms and bungalows, all sporting air-con, hot water and cable TV. It's not on the beach, but in a garden setting around a pretty little pool. 6

Juzz'a Pizza 2 East of the village T-junction ⓣ077 245662–3, ⓦwww.juzzapizza.com. Above the recommended restaurant (see below), four small but smart rooms, well equipped with comfy beds, air-con, hot showers, fridges and cable TV. Two rooms look onto the road, while the other two have beachside terraces with great views. 6–7

The Lodge Towards the western end of the village ⓣ077 425337, ⓦwww.lodgesamui.com. Apartment-style block with immaculately clean and tastefully decorated modern rooms, all with balconies looking over the water, and boasting air-con, ceiling fan, mini-bar, satellite TV, plus spacious bathrooms with tubs to soak in. There's a seafront bar downstairs where you can get breakfast. 7

Peace At the mid-point of the beach ⓣ077 425357, ⓦwww.peaceresort.com. This large, well-run, friendly concern has shady and attractive lawned grounds, and being well away from the main road, lives up to its name. Spotless, tasteful bungalows, all with air-con, mini-bars, hot water and verandas, are brightly decorated and thoughtfully equipped. There's a beautiful pool with Jacuzzi and children's pool, a children's playground, a spa, Internet access, and a beachside restaurant serving good Thai and European food. Breakfast included. 8

Samui Palm Beach Resort West of *Peace*, from which it's next door-but-two ⓣ077 425494–5, ⓦwww.samuipalmbeach.com. Expensive but with frequent large discounts, especially at the airport (it's owned by Bangkok Airways). Spacious cottages and hotel rooms with air-con, satellite TV and fridges are in a Mediterranean style with hints of southern Thai architecture, and there are two attractive swimming pools, a gym and a giant chessboard in the spacious grounds. 9

Smile House Across the road from *The Lodge*, at the western end of the village ⓣ077 425361, ⓦwww.smilehouse-samuinet.com. Despite a slightly institutional feel, *Smile* has a reliable set of chalets adorned with silk cushions and some other nice decorative touches, grouped around a decent-sized, clean swimming pool and Jacuzzi. Hot water, minibar, TV and air-con in each room, with breakfast buffet included. 7

The Waterfront East of the village T-junction ⓣ077 427165, ⓦwww.thewaterfrontbophut.com. English-run boutique hotel, sociable and family-friendly, with a small swimming pool in a grassy garden. All sixteen simply but tastefully decorated rooms and bungalows have air-con, hot water, mini-bars, safes, cable TV, DVD players and views of the sea. Free pick-ups, Internet access and babysitting; breakfast included in the price. 7

Zazen At the far west end of the beach ⓣ077 425085, ⓦwww.samuizazen.com. Stylish bungalows clustered round a cute pool and lotus pond, furnished with traditional Thai tables, wardrobes and cabinets, as well as satellite TV, DVD and music station, free Internet connection and mini-bar; many sport a tropical-style open-air bathroom with rockery and fountain. Other facilities include a spa, a recommended international restaurant, cooking classes, table-tennis, pool table and the like. Breakfast included. ❽

Eating

A stroll through the village will turn up a wide choice of good restaurants for dinner, though at a couple of the smaller places recommended below you might be advised to book in advance. *Siam Classic*, on the pier road (ⓣ077 430065 or 087 111 1646, ⓦwww.samuiclassic.com), stages a well-regarded show of **classical dance-drama** every night at 9.30pm (plus a 7.30pm show Mon, Tues, Fri & Sun). With a four-course Thai meal, it costs B580 if booked in advance, B680 on the door, or you can just watch the late show for B250 (including one drink).

Happy Elephant West of the village T-junction. Good choice of mostly Thai food, including a few unusual dishes and reasonably priced seafood, and friendly service. There's an attractive beachside terrace and a contemporary-style annexe, *On the Beach*, next door.

Healthy and Fun Yoga Café East of the village T-junction. Tasty, healthy lunches such as sandwiches, pomelo and other salads, and Thai desserts, as well as a wide range of juices, teas and coffees. Mon–Sat 11.30am–4pm.

Juzz'a Pizza 2 East of the village T-junction ⓣ077 245662–3. Friendly, small, elegant restaurant with a beachside terrace, serving excellent, authentic pizzas, with vegetarian and seafood options and a wide choice of extra toppings, as well as pastas and Thai and Western main courses. Evenings only.

La Boulangerie (Samui French Bakery) East of the village T-junction. The real deal: delicious, inexpensive croissants, breads, quiches, pizzas and patisserie. Also offers simple, very reasonably priced French brasserie fare, such as chicken breast with mustard sauce, sandwiches and salads. Around behind the ovens is a small terrace on the beach with fine views.

The Shack Grill West of the village T-junction ⓣ077 246041. Small, pricey spot, run by an ebullient New Yorker, and focused on the large, open grill at the front of the restaurant: here all manner of local seafood and imported meats, such as Australian beef and New Zealand lamb, are cooked to your liking. Delicious apple pie and decent house wine.

Bangrak

Beyond the sharp headland with its sweep of coral reefs lies **BANGRAK**, sometimes called **Big Buddha Beach** after the colossus that gazes sternly down on the sun worshippers from its island in the bay. The beach is no great shakes, especially during the northeast monsoon, when the sea retreats and leaves a slippery mud flat, but Bangrak still manages to attract the watersports crowd, and every Sunday it sees the family-friendly **Secret Garden Festival**, with barbecues, drink and live music from around 5 to 11pm.

The **Big Buddha** (*Phra Yai*) is certainly big and works hard at being a tourist attraction, but is no beauty. A short causeway at the eastern end of the bay leads across to a messy clump of souvenir shops and foodstalls in front of the temple, catering to day-tripping Thais as well as foreigners. Here you can at least get a decent cup of coffee or tea, or a sandwich at *Big Buddha Coffee*. Ceremonial dragon-steps then bring you up to the covered terrace around the Big Buddha, from where there's a fine view of the sweeping north coast. Look out for the B10 rice-dispensing machine, which allows you symbolically to give alms to the monks at any time of the day.

Bangrak's **bungalows** are squeezed together in a narrow, noisy strip between busy Route 4171 and the shore, underneath the airport flight path. By far the best of a disappointing bunch is *Shambala* (ⓣ077 425330, ⓦwww.samui-shambala.com; ❹), an English-run place that's well spread out in a lush garden;

the large, smart bungalows all have verandas, en-suite bathrooms and fans, and most have hot water; good Thai and Western food and massages are also on offer, as well as diving, sailing and other activities through in-house travel agent, One Hundred Degrees East (Ⓦwww.100degreeseast.com). Bangrak also supports one noteworthy **restaurant**, *The Mangrove*, a short way down the airport access road (Ⓣ077 427584; daily from 5.30pm; closed last three days of month), serving pricey but high-quality French-influenced food in a quiet, friendly and informal alternative to big hotel restaurants.

The northeastern cape

After Bangrak comes the high-kicking boot of Samui's **northeastern cape**, with its small, rocky coves overlooking Ko Pha Ngan and connected by sandy lanes. Songthaews run along Route 4171 to the largest and most beautiful bay, **Choeng Mon**. Its white sandy beach is lined with casuarina trees that provide shade for the bungalows and upmarket resorts, though on the whole it remains comparatively underdeveloped and laid-back.

Accommodation

Boat House Hotel Choeng Mon Ⓣ077 425041–52, Ⓦwww.imperialhotels.com. Run by the reliable Imperial group, *Boat House* is named after the two-storey rice barges that have been converted into suites in the grounds. It also offers luxury rooms in more prosaic modern buildings, often filled by package tours. Beyond the garden pool and the beachside boat-shaped pool, the full gamut of watersports is drawn up on the sands, plus there's a spa and a fitness room. ⑨

Island View Tucked in on the east side of Choeng Mon's *Boat House Hotel* Ⓣ077 245031, Ⓕ077 425583. Smart, good-value chalets with either fan and en-suite cold-water bathroom or air-con, hot water, TV and fridge, in a lively compound with a supermarket, a dive shop offering kayaks and snorkelling, a small bookshop and a beachfront bar. Fan ③, air-con ⑦

Ô Soleil West of the *Boat House Hotel* on Choeng Mon Ⓣ077 425232, Ⓔosoleil@loxinfo.co.th. A lovely, orderly, Belgian-run place in a pretty garden dotted with ponds. The good-value, pristine bungalows all have hot water, fridges and air-con and some have TVs. ⑤

Sila Evason Hideaway On Samui's northernmost headland, Laem Samrong Ⓣ077 245678, Ⓦwww.six-senses.com. Ultra-luxury resort, with an informal, congenial air, where chic villas with large, open-style bathrooms are secluded by bamboo fences and served by butlers; many also have their own private, infinity-edge swimming pool. There's an attractive main pool too, of course, with fine hilltop views, plus a seductive spa, a superb fusion restaurant, *Dining on the Rocks*, and access to the beach where watersports are available. ⑨

The Tongsai Bay Cottages and Hotel North side of Choeng Mon Ⓣ077 425015–28, Ⓦwww.tongsaibay.co.th. The island's finest hotel, an easy-going establishment with the unhurried air of a country club and excellent service. The luxurious hotel rooms, red-tiled cottages and palatial villas command beautiful views over the spacious, picturesque grounds, the private beach (with plenty of non-motorized watersports), a freshwater and a vast saltwater swimming pool and the whole bay. They all also sport second bathtubs on their secluded open-air terraces, so you don't miss out on the scenery while splashing about. There's an array of very fine restaurants and a delightful health spa, as well as a tennis court and gym. ⑨

Chaweng

For looks alone, none of the other beaches can match **CHAWENG**, with its broad, gently sloping strip of white sand sandwiched between the limpid blue sea and a line of palm trees. Such beauty has not escaped attention of course, which means, on the plus side, that Chaweng can provide just about anything the active beach bum demands, from thumping nightlife to ubiquitous and diverse watersports. The negative angle is that the new developments are ever

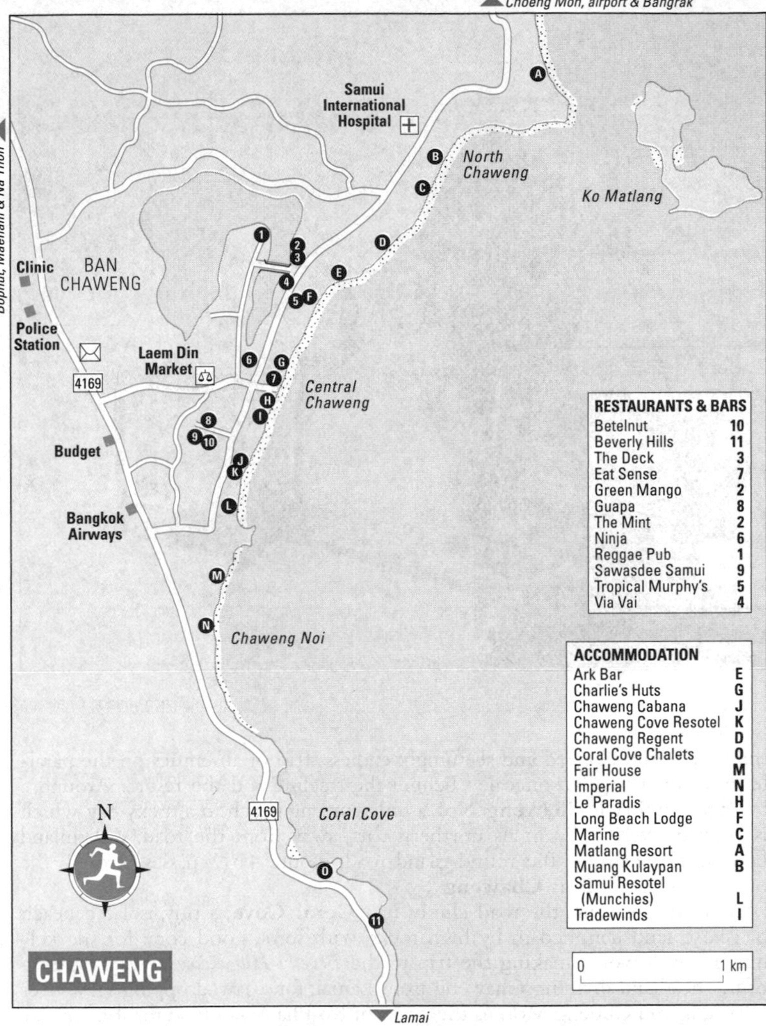

more cramped and expensive, building work behind the palm trees and repairs to the over-commercialized main beach road are always in progress – and there's no certainty that it will look lovely when the bulldozers retreat.

The six-kilometre bay is framed between the small island of Ko Matlang at the north end and the 300-metre-high headland above Coral Cove in the south. From **Ko Matlang**, where the waters provide some decent snorkelling, an often exposed coral reef slices southwest across to the mainland, marking out a shallow lagoon and **North Chaweng**. This S-shaped part of the beach is comparatively peaceful, though it has some ugly pockets of development; at low tide it becomes a wide, inviting playground, and from October to January the reef shelters it from the worst of the northeast winds. South of the reef, the idyllic shoreline of **Central Chaweng** stretches for 2km in a dead-straight line,

△ Beach vendor, Chaweng

the ugly, traffic-clogged and seemingly endless strip of amenities on the parallel main drag largely concealed behind the treeline and the resorts. Around a low promontory is **Chaweng Noi**, a little curving beach in a rocky bay, which is comparatively quiet in its northern part, away from the road. Well inland of Central Chaweng, the round-island road, Route 4169, passes through the original village of **Ban Chaweng**.

South of Chaweng, the road climbs past **Coral Cove**, a tiny, isolated beach of coarse sand hemmed in by high rocks, with some good coral for snorkelling. It's well worth making the trip to the *Beverly Hills Café*, towards the tip of the headland dividing Chaweng from Lamai, for a jaw-dropping view over Chaweng and Choeng Mon to the peaks of Ko Pha Ngan (and for some good, moderately priced food, notably seafood).

Accommodation

Over fifty **bungalow resorts** and **hotels** at Chaweng are squeezed into thin strips running back from the beachfront at right angles. In the ever-diminishing moderate range, prices are generally over the odds, while more and more expensive places are sprouting up all the time, offering sumptuous accommodation at top-whack prices.

Moderate

Charlie's Huts In the heart of Central Chaweng Ⓣ077 422343, Ⓕ077 414194. The cheapest accommodation options left on Central Chaweng are the thatched wooden huts in *Charlie's* grassy compound, but you'll have to get in quick – a luxury hotel is scheduled to move in some time in 2007. Fan ❹, air-con ❺

Long Beach Lodge Towards the north end of Central Chaweng Ⓣ & Ⓕ077 422372. An unusually spacious and shady sandy compound. All the orderly, clean bungalows and rooms are a decent size and have hot water, fridge, TV and air-con. Service is friendly, and breakfast is included in the price. ⑥

Marine North Chaweng Ⓣ077 422416, Ⓦwww.samuimarineresort.com. On a quieter part of North Chaweng, with a little bit of elbow room amidst the flowers, the large bungalows here are decent enough for the price; all have hot water, some have air-con and fridge. Internet access. Fan ⑤, air-con ⑥

Matlang Resort At the far north end of North Chaweng Ⓣ077 230468–9, Ⓔmatlang@loxinfo.coth. Tranquil, friendly place facing a broad stretch of beach with nice views of Ko Matlang. The en-suite wooden bungalows, all with verandas and mosquito screens, some with air-con, are a little bit battered, but are spread around a very pleasant, shady flower garden. Fan ④, air-con ⑥

Samui Resotel (Munchies) At the south end of Central Chaweng Ⓣ077 422374, Ⓦwww.samuiresotel.com. Under the same ownership as *Chaweng Cove Resotel*, with a similar concept of no-frills luxury, but marginally cheaper and with a smaller pool. All rooms with hot water, air-con, mini-bar and TV: choose between hotel rooms at the back by the road, and squat chalets increasing in price towards the beach. ⑥

Expensive

Ark Bar (Garden-Beach Resort) North end of Central Chaweng Ⓣ077 422047, Ⓦwww.ark-bar.com. For party people who want to be near the heart of Chaweng's nightlife: decent, no-frills rooms with air-con, TV, fridge and hot water flank a long, narrow strip stuffed with flowers, which runs down to a popular beach bar and a small pool and Jacuzzi. ⑦

Chaweng Cabana South end of Central Chaweng Ⓣ077 422377, Ⓦwww.chawengcabana.com. Reliable, well-run option, popular with families, with a smallish swimming pool; tightly packed bungalows in a lush garden with bland but tasteful decor, come with air-con, hot water, satellite TV and mini-bar. ⑧

Chaweng Cove Resotel South end of Central Chaweng Ⓣ077 422509–10, Ⓦwww.chawengcove.com. Welcoming, reliable place that offers all mod cons (air-con, hot water, mini-bar, TV), though little character, at reasonable prices. At the back towards the road the hotel rooms come with balconies, while towards the beach, there's a good-sized pool and tightly packed wooden bungalows with thatched roofs and verandas. Breakfast included. ⑦

Chaweng Regent At the bottom end of North Chaweng Ⓣ077 422389–90, Ⓦwww.chawengregent.com. Reliable, well-run place offering elegant bungalows and rooms with private terraces and all mod cons around lotus ponds, two pools, a fitness centre, sauna and spa. ⑨

Coral Cove Chalets Above Coral Cove Ⓣ077 422260–1, Ⓦwww.coralcovechalet.com. Good-value and stylish place with bright, tasteful bungalows and rooms, each with air-con, balcony, TV and mini-bar, grouped around an attractive pool and Jacuzzi. ⑦

Fair House North end of Chaweng Noi Ⓣ077 422255–6, Ⓦwww.fairhousesamui.com. A great location on a lovely stretch of beach, with extensive, lush gardens and two pools. The colourfully decorated bungalows are preferable to the large hotel rooms, which have good facilities but lack style. ⑧

Imperial Chaweng Noi Ⓣ077 422020–36, Ⓦwww.imperialhotels.com. The longest-established luxury hotel on Samui is a grand but lively establishment with a Mediterranean feel, set in sloping, landscaped gardens; features include two pools (one sea water, one fresh with a Jacuzzi), a spa, tennis court and all kinds of watersports. ⑨

Le Paradis Central Chaweng Ⓣ077 239041–3, Ⓦwww.leparadisresort.com. Set in lush, spacious gardens, twelve traditional Ayutthaya-style houses on stilts, decorated with traditional silk and cotton fabrics, blended stylishly with the Western-style bathrooms, mini-bars and air-con. Attractive beachside swimming pool and health spa. ⑨

Muang Kulaypan North Chaweng Ⓣ077 230036, Ⓦwww.kulaypan.com. Original, stylish boutique hotel arrayed around a large, immaculate garden with a black-tiled swimming pool and an excellent beachside restaurant (see below). Rooms – each with their own private balcony or garden – combine contemporary design with traditional Thai-style comforts. ⑧

Tradewinds Central Chaweng Ⓣ077 414294, Ⓦwww.tradewinds-samui.com. A cheerful, well-run place of characterful bungalows and rooms (all with air-con, hot water, mini-bar, cable TV and balcony) with plenty of room to breathe in colourful tropical gardens. The resort specializes in sailing, with its own catamarans (instruction available), as well as offering kayaks and croquet. ⑧

Eating

Chaweng offers all manner of foreign **cuisines**, from Italian to Korean, much of it of dubious quality. Amongst all this, it's quite hard to find good, reasonably priced Thai food – setting aside the places recommended below, it would be worth exploring the cheap and cheerful night-time food stalls at Laem Din market, which are popular with local workers, on the middle road between Central Chaweng and Highway 4169.

Betelnut Soi Colibri, a small lane at the south end of Central Chaweng opposite the landmark *Central Samui Beach Resort* ⓣ077 413370. By far Samui's best restaurant, serving exceptional Californian-Thai fusion food, with prices to match. Few tables, so reservations highly recommended.

Budsaba Restaurant At the *Muang Kulaypan Hotel* ⓣ077 230036. This charming, upmarket beachfront restaurant fully justifies the journey up to North Chaweng: you get to recline in your own seaside *sala* or open-sided hut on stilts while tucking into unusual and excellent Thai dishes such as banana-flower and shrimp salad. Live traditional music and dance Tues, Thurs, Sat & Sun evenings.

The Deck Central Chaweng, just north of the *Full Circle* club. Good, reasonably priced all-rounder where you're bound to find something to satisfy from the wide-roaming menu: Western and Thai main courses with good vegetarian and vegan options, hearty baguettes, very good espresso coffees, Thai desserts and all-day set breakfasts for B99.

Eat Sense Central Chaweng, next to *Charlie's Huts* ⓣ077 414242. Spacious, relaxing, mostly open-air restaurant on the beachfront, serving expensive but delicious Thai food – try the deep-fried prawns with cashew nuts and tamarind sauce.

Guapa Soi Colibri, Central Chaweng. Small, elegant "tropical tapas" bar under the same ownership as *Betelnut* opposite. Sangria and delicious Spanish and Asian tapas for around B120 each, such as beautifully presented paella and delicious Andalucian sausages fried with apples.

Ninja Near *Charlie's Huts* in Central Chaweng. Popular, well-run, very basic and cheap restaurant, serving simple Thai faves such as *tom yam*, *som tam* and *phat thai*, as well as crepes, breakfasts and other Western food. Open 24hr.

Sawasdee Samui Soi Colibri, next to *Betelnut*. Small, popular, welcoming restaurant, run by the former manager of the SITCA cooking school, serving, as you'd expect, delicious, attractively presented Thai food at around B120 a dish.

Via Vai Near *Swensen's*, Central Chaweng. Two Neapolitan brothers have built an authentic wood-fired brick oven here to produce great thin-crust pizzas such as Delicata with asparagus and blue cheese. The pasta menu includes several home-made varieties and sauces such as smoked salmon and mascarpone, and there are twenty varieties of home-made ice cream to look forward to as well.

Drinking and nightlife

Avoiding the raucous bar-beers and English theme pubs on the main through road, the best place to **drink** is on the beach: at night dozens of resorts and dedicated bars lay out small tables and candles on the sand, especially towards the north end of Central Chaweng and on North Chaweng. On Wednesdays, from 2pm until well into the evening, the *Ark Bar* (see p.653) hosts a popular beach party, with house and funk DJs and a free barbecue. One of the main drag's theme pubs is worth singling out: with draught Guinness and Kilkenny, big-screen sports, quiz nights, live music and decent food, Irish-run *Tropical Murphy's*, opposite *McDonald's* in Central Chaweng, has turned itself into a popular landmark and meeting place.

Bang in the middle of Central Chaweng but set well back from the beach across a small lake, *The Reggae Pub* is Chaweng's oldest **nightclub**, a venerable Samui institution with a memorabilia shop to prove it. It does time now as an unpretentious, good-time, party venue, with plenty of drinking games, but shows its roots with a rasta party on Wednesday and a dancehall party on Saturday. The area's other long-standing dance venue, *Green Mango* at the north end of Central Chaweng, occupies a similarly huge shed combining an industrial look with that of a tropical greenhouse. The alley leading up to it, Soi Green Mango, is now lined with vibrant bars and clubs, including

Samui's current hippest venue, *The Mint*, which brings in the best local and international DJs.

Listings

Airline Bangkok Airways, south end of Ban Chaweng on Route 4169 ⓣ 077 422512–9.
Bookshop Bookazine, next to *Tropical Murphy's* in Central Chaweng, sells English-language books, newspapers and magazines.
Cookery courses The highly recommended Samui Institute of Thai Culinary Arts (SITCA; ⓣ 077 413172, ⓦ www.sitca.net), on Soi Colibri, a small lane at the south end of Central Chaweng opposite the landmark *Central Samui Beach Resort*, runs two-and-a-half-hour classes in the morning and afternoon (B1600), and you get to eat what you've cooked with a friend afterwards. They also run fruit- and vegetable-carving courses (2hr/day for 3 days; B3500), and have a culinary shop selling Thai cooking accessories, ingredients and cookbooks.
Hospital The private Samui International Hospital in North Chaweng (ⓣ 077 230781, ⓦ www.sih.co.th) provides, among other things, 24-hour emergency services, house calls and a dental clinic.
Language courses Mind Your Language, on Route 4169 towards the south end of Ban Chaweng near Budget (ⓣ 077 230314, ⓦ www.mindyourlanguage.net), offers Thai language courses from beginners to advanced, including five-day courses for tourists and private tutoring.
Laundry English-run Bubbles, Soi Colibri (ⓣ 077 230715), is dependable.
Pharmacy Boots has a convenient branch in the middle of Central Chaweng, just up the road from *Tropical Murphy's* pub.
Police station Route 4169, Ban Chaweng. The tourist police (ⓣ 1155) are planning to open a branch behind *McDonald's* in Central Chaweng.
Post office Route 4169, Ban Chaweng; poste-restante and packing service.
Spas Among stand-alone spas, which are generally cheaper than the luxury hotel versions, Living Senses, above *McDonald's* in the Living Square shopping plaza in Central Chaweng (ⓣ 077 230917, ⓦ www.livingsensesspa.com), has a good reputation for its massages, reflexology, body wraps and scrubs; Four Seasons, a short way south on the opposite side of the main drag, next to Bookazine (ⓣ 077 414141–3, ⓦ www.spafourseasons.com), offers a wider range of treatments and a little more style, at higher prices.
Travel agent English-run Travel Solutions, just off the main road opposite *Tropical Murphy's* (ⓣ 077 239007, ⓦ www.travelsolutionsthailand.com), is a reliable and knowledgeable all-round agent, offering worldwide air-ticketing, Thai train and bus tickets and local services.
Vehicle rental Motorbikes (from B150/day) and four-wheel drives (from B800/day) can be rented from many locations along the main drag; if reliability is your main priority, contact Budget in Ban Chaweng (ⓣ 077 413384, ⓦ www.budget.co.th; from B1300 a day).
Watersports Samui Ocean Sports, on the beach in front of the *Chaweng Regent* at the bottom end of North Chaweng (ⓣ 081 940 1999, ⓦ www.sailing-in-samui.com), rents windsurfers (B450–550/hr) and kayaks (one-person B150/hr; two-person B200/hr), as well as offering sailing lessons, trips and charters.

Lamai

Samui's nightlife is most tawdry at **LAMAI** (though Chaweng is fast catching up): planeloads of European package tourists are kept happy here at dozens of open-air hostess bars, sinking buckets of booze while slumped in front of music videos. The action is concentrated into a farang toytown of bars and Western restaurants that has grown up behind the centre of the beach, interspersed with supermarkets, clinics, banks, ATMs, dive shops and travel agents. Running roughly north to south for 4km, the white palm-fringed beach itself is, fortunately, still a picture, and generally quieter than Chaweng, with far less in the way of watersports and a lighter concentration of development – it's quite easy to avoid the boozy mayhem by staying at the peaceful extremities of the bay, where the backpackers' resorts have a definite edge over Chaweng's. At the northern end, the spur of land that hooks eastward into the sea is perhaps the prettiest spot, though it's beginning to attract some upmarket development: it has more rocks than sand, but the shallow sea

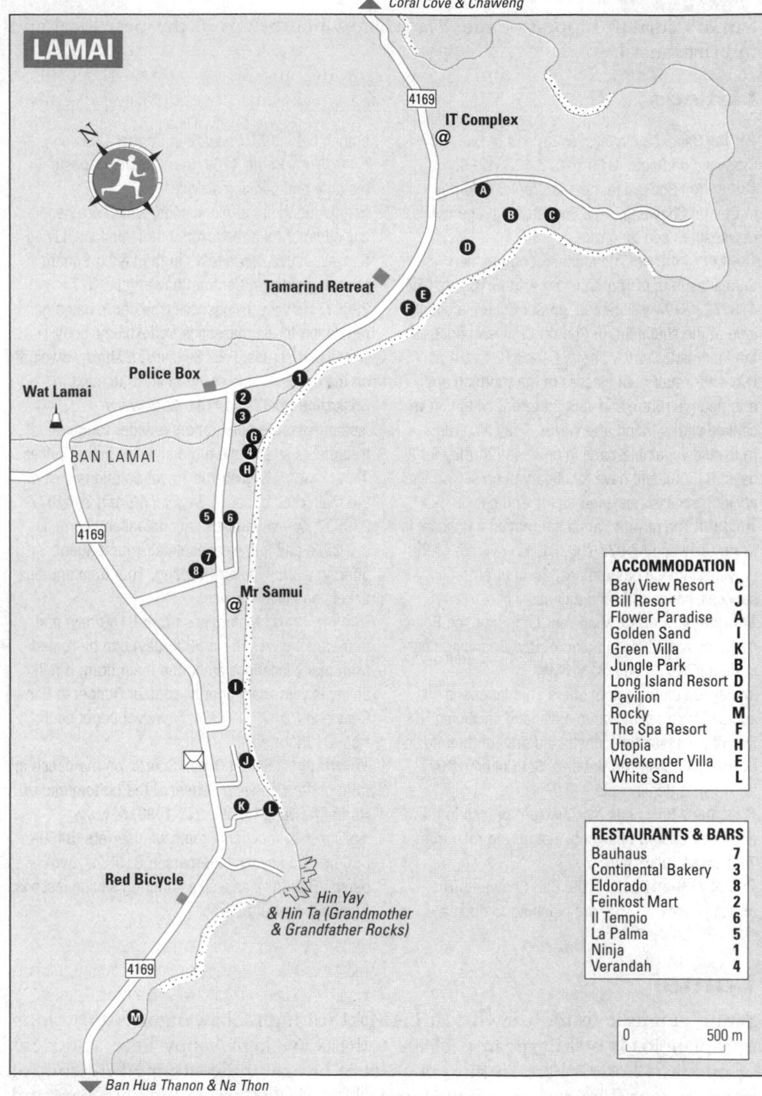

behind the coral reef is protected from the high seas of November, December and January.

The original village of **Ban Lamai**, set well back on Route 4169, remains surprisingly aloof, and its wat contains a small museum of ceramics, agricultural tools and other everyday objects. Most visitors get more of a buzz from **Hin Yay** (Grandmother Rock) and **Hin Ta** (Grandfather Rock), small rock formations on the bay's southern promontory, which never fail to raise a giggle with their resemblance to the male and female sexual organs. On the main road, 300m south of the rocks, Red Bicycle (☎077 232136 or 087 278 8818,

Ⓦwww.redbicycle.org) rents out **mountain bikes** (B350/day) and runs daily, four-hour **guided rides** (B1500), as well as a variety of longer trips.

Lamai boasts two of Samui's longer-standing and better **spas**. The oldest, *The Spa Resort* (Ⓣ077 230976, Ⓦwww.spasamui.com) covers everything from fasting programmes (US$300/week) to Thai massage (B300/hour) and herbal saunas (B300/hour). Also on offer are a wide range of other massages, body and facial wraps, and yoga, meditation, massage and cooking classes. *The Spa* now has two locations, the main one at the far north end of the beach next to *Weekender Villa*, the other, more upmarket branch 3km away in the hills above Lamai, each with a swimming pool and a wide variety of accommodation (❹–❽; minimum 4-night stay). With less of an emphasis on clean living, and more on pampering, Tamarind Retreat (Ⓣ077 230571 or 077 424436, Ⓦwww.tamarindretreat.com) is set in a beautiful, secluded coconut grove just north of *Spa Resort's* beachside branch off the main road. Here a session in their unique herbal steam room, set between two boulders by a waterfall-fed plunge pool, and a two-hour Thai massage, for example, costs B1900. Other massages, such as head, foot and face, are also available, activities include yoga and t'ai chi classes, and there are luxury villas on the site to rent.

Practicalities

Several places on the main beachside drag offer **rental motorbikes** (from B150/day) and **four-wheel drives** (from B800/day). A couple of **Internet cafés**, among dozens of options on Lamai, stand out. *Mr Samui's* art gallery and café, just south of the central crossroads, is a congenial choice offering good espresso coffee, or you could head for the unmissable, shiny IT Complex at the north end of the bay, which contains a smart Internet café.

Accommodation

Lamai's **accommodation** is generally less cramped and slightly better value than Chaweng's, though it presents far fewer choices at the top end of the market. The far southern end of the bay towards the Grandparent Rocks has the tightest concentration of budget bungalows.

Bay View Resort On the bay's northern headland Ⓣ077 418429, Ⓦwww.bayviewsamui.com. Neat, stylish bungalows with verandas and en-suite hot-water bathrooms in an extensive, flower-bedecked compound; the poshest come with air-con, mini-bar and cable TV. Offers a friendly welcome and great sunset views of the beach from the attractive restaurant. Fan ❺, air-con ❻

Bill Resort At the far southern end of the bay Ⓣ077 424403, Ⓦwww.thebillresort.com. A friendly, efficient and orderly setup, crammed into a fragrant, overgrown garden with a decent-sized pool and Jacuzzi, on a pleasant stretch of beach and up the hill behind. Its clean, en-suite rooms and bungalows, most with air-con and hot water, offer very good value if you don't need much elbow room. Fan ❹, air-con ❺

Flower Paradise Northern end of the bay, on the headland above *Jungle Park* Ⓣ089 288 8326, Ⓦwww.samui.ch. Just a short walk from the beach, a friendly, well-run, German-Swiss place in a small, lush garden. All the clean, well-tended bungalows have hot water and there's a good restaurant. ❸

Golden Sand Towards the southern end of the beach Ⓣ077 424031–2, Ⓦwww.goldensand-resort.com. Smart, well-equipped rooms and bungalows – air-con, TV, fridge and hot water, a few with bathtubs – on a broad, grassy plot studded with coconut palms, with a small, elegant pool. ❼

Green Villa On the access road to *White Sand*, at the far southern end of the bay Ⓣ077 424296, Ⓔresagreenvilla@hotmail.com. Quiet, spacious, French-run operation set back from the beach among the palm trees, with a small swimming pool, clean, simple, en-suite bungalows with fans and grand, air-con villas with TVs, fridges and bathtubs. Fan ❸, air-con ❼

Jungle Park On the bay's northern headland Ⓣ077 418034–7, Ⓦwww.jungle-park.com. Next door to *Bay View Resort*. Lives up to its name with spacious grounds full of shady trees. Notable here are the large swimming pool and the attractive bar-restaurant sandwiched between it and the beach; there's also a small spa. All the reliable, well-maintained rooms and bungalows have air-con, minibar and hot water; buffet breakfast included. ❼

Long Island Resort At the far north end of the beach ⓣ077 424202 or 077 418456, ⓦwww.longislandresort.com. Fashionable boutique resort with elegant but cosy bungalows (all with hot water, the cheapest with fans, the priciest with air-con, satellite TV, DVD players and minibars), an attractive pool, a small, rustic spa and a good Thai and Western bar-restaurant. Fan ❺, air-con ❼

Pavilion On the central stretch of Lamai, north of the crossroads ⓣ077 424030, ⓦwww.pavilionsamui.com. Lamai's best upmarket choice, just far enough from the pubs and clubs to get some peace; the atmosphere is friendly and lively, and there's a spa and a good beachside pool and restaurant. Most of the accommodation is in attractive, contemporary Thai-style rooms, but if your purse will stretch that far, go for one of the spa junior suites, each boasting a private courtyard with Jacuzzi and day bed. ❾

Rocky Beyond the headland, at the far southern end of the bay ⓣ077 418367, ⓦwww.rockyresort.com. Recently upgraded to a boutique resort, though the service doesn't quite match the high prices. On a plot thick with vegetation that gives access to three beaches, elegant, Thai-style bungalows with air-con and hot water, an attractive swimming pool fed by an artificial waterfall, a good restaurant and an appealing beach bar with tables on the eponymous rocks. ❽

Utopia On the central stretch of Lamai, north of the crossroads ⓣ077 233113, ⓔjim_utopia@hotmail.com. Well-run, welcoming place on a narrow strip of land teeming with flowers, good value and reasonably quiet considering its central location. The cheapest bungalows have mosquito screens, fans and en-suite bathrooms, while those at the top of the price range boast air-con, hot water, TV and fridge. Fan ❹, air-con ❼

Weekender Villa Between the main road and the beach to the east of Ban Lamai ⓣ077 424116, ⓦwww.weekender-villa.com. Despite its location, this very well-maintained, German-run establishment is quiet enough; the staff are friendly and the large, smart bungalows, equipped with en-suite hot showers and decorated with contemporary art, shelter under the coconut trees in a spacious compound. There's a small swimming pool, an air-con massage room and an attractive beachside bar-restaurant that sports a pool table and hosts bridge, chess and draughts nights. Fan ❻, air-con ❼

White Sand At the far southern end of the bay ⓣ077 424298. Long-established and laid-back budget place in a large, shady, sandy compound, with around two dozen simple beachside huts, some en suite, which attract plenty of long-term travellers. ❶–❸

Eating and drinking

There are far fewer eating options on Lamai than on Chaweng to tempt you away from your guest-house kitchen. Besides the **restaurants** recommended below, you could try any one of several decent Italian places, such as *Il Tempio* and *La Palma*, a short way north of the tourist village's main crossroads. Lamai's **nightlife** is all within spitting distance of the central crossroads. Apart from the hostess bars, *Bauhaus* is the main draw, a barn-like entertainment complex with a bistro, pool tables, big screens showing satellite sport and a dance floor (foam parties Mondays and Fridays).

Continental Bakery North of the central crossroads, near Highway 4169. Friendly, Swiss-run place serving good breads, cakes, burgers, sandwiches and espressos, as well as all-day breakfasts ranging from French and American to Belgian (with pork steak, apparently).

Eldorado Just west of the central crossroads. Highly recommended, good-value Swedish restaurant, serving a few Thai favourites, salads, steaks and other international main courses, plus one or two indigenous specialities such as Swedish meatballs. All-you-can-eat barbecue Wed evening for B230.

Feinkost Mart next to *Continental Bakery*. Wide selection of Western, mostly German food, including plenty of sausages and good pizzas, with German beer to wash it all down and apple pie to finish you off.

Ninja On Highway 4169, east of Ban Lamai. A branch of Chaweng's backpacker hotspot, a dependable, simple, cheap café serving basic Thai favourites, as well as crepes and other Western food.

The Spa Resort At the far north end of the beach. Excellent, casual, moderately priced beachside restaurant, serving a huge range of mostly vegetarian Thai and Western (including Mexican) dishes, as well as raw food. The veggie "ginger nuts" stir-fry is excellent, omelettes and salads are specialities, but there are also plenty of meat and marine offerings. A long menu of juices, smoothies and shakes includes a delicious lime juice with honey.

Verandah At *Mui Bungalows*, a few hundred metres north of the central crossroads. Reliable, German-run place, which serves excellent, well-presented, moderately priced international and Thai food.

The south and west coasts

Lacking the long, attractive beaches of the more famous resorts, the **south and west coasts** rely on a few charming, isolated spots with peaceful accommodation, which can usually only be reached by renting a motorbike or four-wheel drive. Heading south from Lamai, you come first to the Muslim fishing village at **Ban Hua Thanon** and then, about a kilometre or so south and well signposted off Route 4170, the spacious gardens of *Samui Marina Cottage* (ⓣ077 233394–6, ⓦwww.samuimarina.com; ❻), a well-run, welcoming place with a large swimming pool and air-con, hot water, satellite TV and mini-bar in all the bungalows. Off Route 4170 a kilometre or so further down the coast, Kiteboarding Asia (ⓣ081 591 4592–4, ⓦwww.kiteboardingasia.com), based at *Samui Orchid Resort*, offer instruction in **kiteboarding**, which is at its best here between December and February. Don't be tempted by the pitiful aquarium at the same resort, where the tanks are barely bigger than the fish.

A kilometre further on is one of the island's most secluded hotels: originally founded as a private club on a quiet south-facing promontory, the *Laem Set Inn* (ⓣ077 424393, ⓦwww.laemset.com; fan ❻, air-con ❾) offers a wide range of elegant rooms and suites – some of them reassembled village houses – as well as an excellent restaurant, cookery courses, a spa, plenty of watersports and a scenically positioned swimming pool. The access road to the *Laem Set Inn* takes you past the nearby **Samui Butterfly Garden** (daily 9am–5pm; B150, children B100), opposite *Central Samui Village*, where you can wander the hillside overlooking the sea surrounded by dozens of brilliantly coloured lepidopterans.

The gentle but unspectacular coast beyond is lined with a good reef for snorkelling, which can be explored most easily from the fishing village of **Ban Bangkao**. There's also good snorkelling around **Ko Taen**, a short way offshore to the south: an all-day tour from, for example, TK Tour (ⓣ077 423117) in the next village to the west, **Ban Thongkrut**, including pick-up from your accommodation, snorkelling equipment and lunch on the neighbouring island of Ko Mad Sum, will set you back B700 per person.

About 5km inland, near **Ban Thurian**, the **Na Muang Falls** make a popular outing as they're not far off the round-island road (each of the two main falls has its own signposted kilometre-long paved access road off Route 4169). The lower fall splashes and sprays down a twenty-metre wall of rock into a large pool, while Na Muang 2, upstream, is a more spectacular, shaded cascade that requires a bit of foot-slogging from the car park (about 15min uphill); alternatively you can walk up there from Na Muang 1, by taking the 1500-metre trail that begins 300m back along the access road from the lower fall. The self-styled "safari camp" at the Na Muang 1 entrance (ⓣ077 424098, ⓦwww.namuang-safaripark.com) offers thirty-minute **elephant-rides** for B700 per person.

At the base of the west coast, **Ao Phangka** (Emerald Cove) is a pretty horseshoe bay, sheltered by **Laem Hin Khom**, the high headland that forms Samui's southwestern tip. On the south-facing shore of Laem Hin Khom, the quiet *Coconut Villa* (ⓣ & ⓕ077 423151, ⓔcoconutvilla@sawadee.com; fan ❸, air-con ⑤) commands stunning views of Ko Mad Sum and its neighbouring islands; the fan-cooled or air-con bungalows all have en-suite bathrooms, the food is recommended, and there's an excellent swimming pool set in attractive gardens by the sea.

Further up the coast, the flat beaches are unexceptional but make a calm alternative when the northeast winds hit the other side of the island. In a gorgeous, elevated setting near **Ban Taling Ngam** village, *Le Royal Meridien Baan Taling Ngam* (Ⓣ077 429100, Ⓦwww.meridien-samui.com; ⑨) boasts a dramatic, hilltop swimming pool with a negative edge, as well as another pool beachside. The accommodation is in villas – some with their own pools – or balconied rooms on the resort's steep slopes, luxuriously decorated in traditional style. There's a spa and a Thai cookery school, and the hotel lays on the largest array of sports and watersports facilities on the island.

Ko Pha Ngan

In recent years, backpackers have tended to move over to Ko Samui's fun-loving little sibling, **KO PHA NGAN**, 20km to the north, but the island still has a simple atmosphere, mostly because the lousy road system is an impediment to the developers. With a dense jungle covering its inland mountains and rugged granite outcrops along the coast, Pha Ngan lacks the huge, gently sweeping beaches for which Samui is famous, but it does have plenty of coral to explore and some beautiful, sheltered bays: if you're seeking total isolation, trek out to **Hat Khuat** (**Bottle Beach**) on the north coast or the half-dozen pristine beaches on the east coast; **Thong Nai Pan** at the top of the east coast is not quite as remote, and offers a decent range of amenities and accommodation; while on the long neck of land at the southeast corner, **Hat Rin**, a pilgrimage site for ravers, is a thoroughly commercialized backpackers' resort in a gorgeous setting. Much of Pha Ngan's development has plonked itself on the south and west sides along the only coastal roads on the island, which fan out from **Thong Sala**, the capital; the unattractive south coast is hard to recommend, but the west coast offers several handsome sandy bays with great sunset views, notably **Hat Yao** and **Hat Salad**.

Pha Ngan's **bungalows** all have running water and electricity (on the remotest beaches, only in the evenings and from individual generators), and nearly all come with en-suite bathrooms. There are only a handful of luxury resorts, though plenty of places now offer air-con, especially on Hat Rin. The three hundred or so resorts generally have more space to spread out than on Ko Samui, and the cost of living is lower; the prices given on the following pages are standard for most of the year, but in slack periods you'll be offered discounts, and at the very busiest times (especially Dec and Jan) Pha Ngan's bungalow owners are canny enough to raise the stakes. As on Ko Samui, nearly all the bungalow resorts have inexpensive, traveller-orientated **restaurants**, supplemented on Hat Rin and at one or two other spots around the island by a variety of stand-alone eateries. **Nightlife** is concentrated at Hat Rin, climaxing every month in a wild **full moon party** on the beach; a couple of smaller outdoor **parties** have now got in on the act, the Half Moon Festival at Ban Tai (twice monthly, about a week before and after the full moon; Ⓦwww.halfmoonfestival.com) and the monthly Black Moon Party at Ban Khai.

There's no TAT office on Ko Pha Ngan, but a couple of free, widely available booklets provide regularly updated **information** about the island, *Phangan Info* (which has a particularly good website at Ⓦwww.phangan.info) and *Phangan Explorer* (Ⓦwww.phanganexplorer.com). If you're going to be exploring, well worth picking up from supermarkets on the island is Visid Hongsombud's excellent, annually updated **map** of Ko Pha Ngan and Ko Tao (B100). The island isn't a great base for **scuba-diving**: getting to the best sites around Ko Tao involves time-consuming and expensive voyages, and there aren't as many dive companies here as on Ko Samui or Ko Tao – of those that exist, Phangan Divers on Hat Rin, Thong Nai Pan, Ao Mae Hat and Hat Yao (Ⓣ077 375117, Ⓦwww.phangandivers.com) is a PADI Five-Star Centre, which offers frequent trips to Sail Rock and the Ang Thong National Marine Park.

Getting to Ko Pha Ngan

The most obvious way of getting to Ko Pha Ngan is on a **boat** from the **Surat Thani** area; for contact details of transport companies in Surat, see p.636. Boat services fluctuate according to demand, but the longest-established ferry is the night boat from Ban Don pier in Surat Thani to Thong Sala, which leaves at 11pm every night (Ⓣ077 284928 or 081 326 8973; 6hr; B250); tickets are available from the pier on the day of departure. From Don Sak to Thong Sala, there are four Raja vehicle ferries a day (2hr 30min; B290; on Ko Pha Ngan Ⓣ077 377452–3) and one Seatran vehicle ferry (via Na Thon on Ko Samui; 2hr 30min; B280; on Ko Pha Ngan Ⓣ077 238129); from Pak Nam Tapi, there's one Songserm Express Boat service a day (3hr 30min; B250; on Ko Pha Ngan Ⓣ077 377046); all the above include bus transport to the pier from Surat Thani. Note that the total journey time (from Surat Thani) using the vehicle ferries from Don Sak is much the same as on the Songserm Express Boat from Pak Nam Tapi. **From Bangkok**, bus and train packages similar to those for getting to Ko Samui are available (see p.642).

One Songserm Express Boat a day does the 45-minute trip from Na Thon on **Ko Samui** to Thong Sala (B130), while a Seatran vehicle ferry does the same voyage once a day in an hour (B110). Two Seatran express boats a day from Bangrak and the Lomprayah catamaran from Wat Na Phra Larn on Maenam (twice a day; sometimes from Bangrak in rough seas; Ko Samui Ⓣ077 427765–6, Ko Pha Ngan Ⓣ077 238412, Ⓦwww.lomprayah.com) call in at Thong Sala after thirty minutes (B250), on their way to Ko Tao. There's also a daily Phangan Cruises boat from Bangrak to Thong Sala (45min; B150; on Pha Ngan Ⓣ077 377274, Samui Ⓣ089 473 4836), which continues to Ko Tao. From Bangrak, four passenger boats a day take an hour to cross to Hat Rin (B120; Ⓣ077 484668 or 077 427650). If there are enough takers and the weather's good enough – generally reliable between January and September – one small boat a day crosses from the pier in Ban Maenam to Hat Rin (B120), before sailing up Ko Pha Ngan's east coast, via Hat Sadet and anywhere else upon demand, to Thong Nai Pan (B300).

For information about boats from **Ko Tao** to Ko Pha Ngan see p.677; all offer the same service in the return direction.

Thong Sala and the south coast

Like the capital of Samui, **THONG SALA** is a port of entrance and little more, where the incoming ferries are met by touts sent to escort travellers to bungalows elsewhere on the island. In front of the piers, transport to the rest of the island (songthaews, jeeps and motorbike taxis) congregates by a dusty row of banks, supermarkets, Internet cafés, scuba-diving outfits and motorbike (B150–200/day) and jeep (B800–1000) rental places. Among many

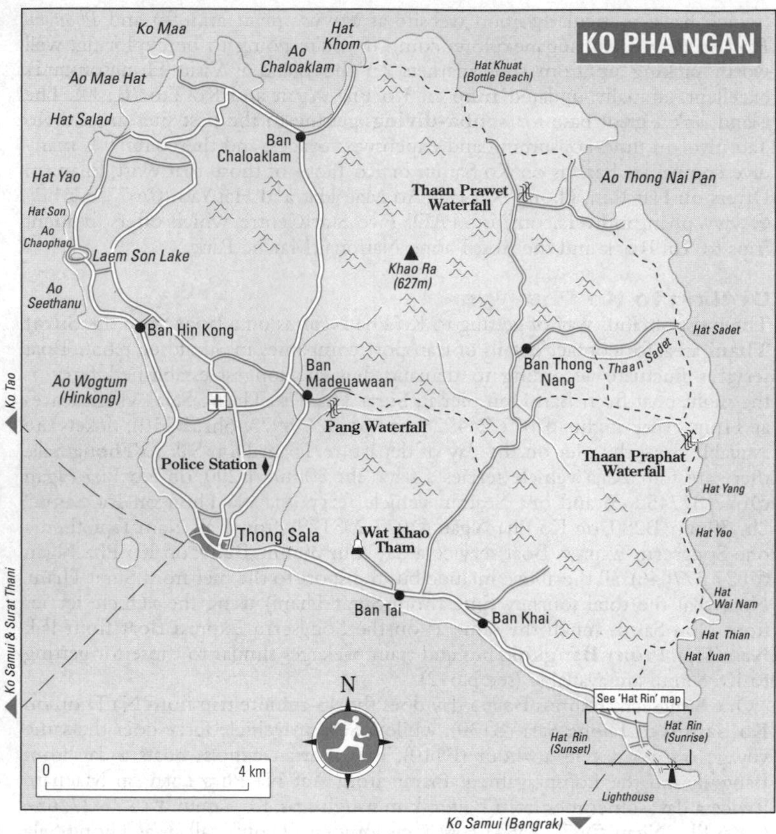

travellers' **restaurants** here, *Yellow Café*, on the corner in front of the main pier, a few doors up from *Pha Ngan Chai Hotel*, is a good, friendly choice, serving tasty coffee, baguettes, baked potatoes and other Western meals. If you go straight ahead from the main pier, you can turn right onto the town's old high street, a leafy mix of shops and houses that's ghostly and windswept at night. A short way down here you'll find Hammock Home, which makes and sells a colourful selection of home-made hammocks, shoulder bags and sarongs, and, set back on the west side of the street, Phangan Batik (daily 10am–10pm), which offers cheap Internet access. Further on are a couple of clinics and, about 500m from the pier after a dog-leg left, the **post office** (Mon–Fri 8.30am–noon & 1–4.30pm, Sat 9am–noon). Thong Sala's sprinkling of travel agents can organize train, bus and plane tickets, and visa extensions, and they sometimes put together speedboat trips to Ang Thong National Marine Park for around B1600 a head (see p.644). The island's main **hospital** (ⓣ077 377034) lies 3km north of town, on the inland road towards Mae Hat, while the **police station** (ⓣ077 377114) is nearly 2km up the Ban Chaloaklam road. Cuttlebone (ⓣ081 940 1902, ⓦwww.cuttlebone.net), based at *Golden Light Resort*, about 1km from Thong Sala on the Hat Rin road, runs **kitesurfing** courses.

In the vicinity of Thong Sala, an easy excursion can be made to the grandiosely termed Than Sadet–Ko Pha Ngan National Park, which contains **Pang Waterfall**, Pha Ngan's biggest drop, and a stunning viewpoint overlooking the south and west of the island. The park lies 4km northeast of Thong Sala off the road to Chaloaklam – if you don't have a bike, take a Chaloaklam-bound songthaew as far as Ban Madeuawaan, and then it's a one-kilometre signposted walk east. A roughly circular trail has been laid out through the park, as mapped out by the signboard in the car park. The main fall – bouncing down in stages over the hard, grey stone – is a steep 250-metre walk up a forest path. The trail then continues for over 1km upriver beyond the falls, before skirting through thick rainforest to the viewpoint and back to the car park in a couple of hours.

The long, straight **south coast** is well served by songthaews and motorbike taxis from Thong Sala, and is lined with bungalows, especially around **Ban Khai**, to take the overspill from nearby Hat Rin. It's hard to recommend staying here, however: the beaches are mediocre by Thai standards, and the coral reef that hugs the length of the shoreline gets in the way of swimming.

On a quiet hillside above **Ban Tai**, 4km from Thong Sala, **Wat Khao Tham** holds ten-day **meditation retreats** most months of the year (B4000/person to cover food; minimum age 20, with further requirements for under-26s during the high season); the American and Australian teachers emphasize compassionate understanding as the basis of mental development. Space is limited (retreats are especially heavily subscribed Dec–March), so it's best to pre-register either in person or through Ⓦwww.watkowtahm.org, which gives full details of rules and requirements and the schedule of retreats.

If you need to **stay** around Thong Sala, walk 800m north out of town to *Siripun* (Ⓣ077 377140, Ⓦwww.siripunbungalow.com; fan ❸, air-con ❺). The owner is helpful, the food very good and kayaks and Internet access are available. The bungalows are clean and well positioned along the beach; all have showers and mosquito screens on the windows, and an extra wad of baht buys air-con, hot water, fridge, TV and one of the island's few bathtubs. Alternatively, *Charm Beach Resort*, a friendly, easy-going place in a sprawling, rag-tag plot on the beach only 1500m southeast of Thong Sala (Ⓣ077 377165, Ⓦwww.triptrekkers.com/charmbeach; fan ❸, air-con ❺), has a wide variety of decent bungalows (some with air-con and hot water) and good Thai food. The incongruous white high-rise overshadowing Thong Sala's pier is the *Pha Ngan Chai Hotel* (Ⓣ & Ⓕ077 377068–9; ❹), which makes a fair stab at international-standard features for visiting businessmen and government officials, with air-con, hot water, TVs, fridges and, in some rooms, sea-view balconies.

Hat Rin

HAT RIN is now firmly established as the major party venue in Southeast Asia, especially in the peak season of December and January, but every month of the year people flock in for the **full moon party** – something like *Apocalypse Now* without the war. The atmosphere created by thousands of folk mashing it up on a beautiful, moon-bathed beach, lit up by fireworks and fire-jugglers, ought to be enough of a buzz in itself, but unfortunately drug-related horror stories are common currency here, and many of them are true: dodgy Ecstasy, *ya baa* (Burmese-manufactured methamphetamines) and all manner of other concoctions put an average of two farangs a month into hospital for psychiatric treatment. The local authorities have started clamping down on the trade in earnest, setting up a permanent police box at Hat Rin, instigating regular roadblocks

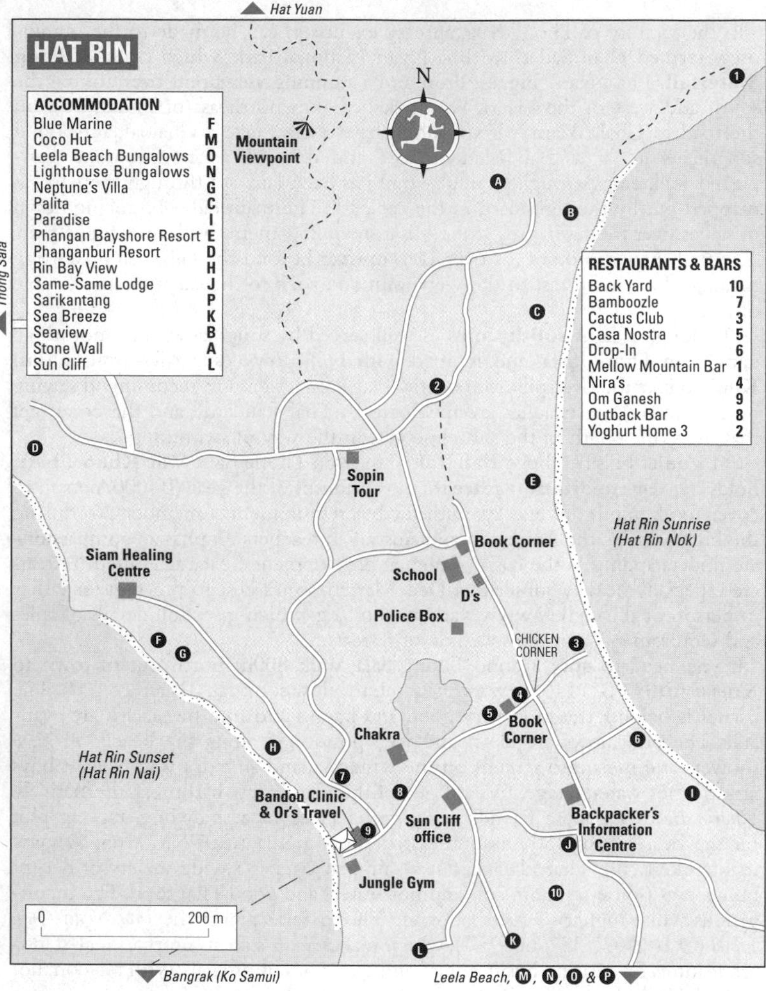

and bungalow searches, and drafting in scores of police (both uniformed and plain-clothes) on full moon nights. It doesn't seem to have dampened the fun, only made travellers a lot more circumspect. Other **tips** for surviving the full moon are mostly common sense: leave your valuables in your resort's safe – it's a bad night for bungalow break-ins – and don't take a bag out with you; watch out for broken bottles on the beach; and do not go swimming while under the influence – there have been several deaths by drowning at previous full moon parties. Note that when the full moon coincides with an important **Buddhist festival**, the party is moved one night away to avoid a clash; check out Ⓦwww.fullmoon-party.com for details.

Hat Rin occupies the flat neck of Pha Ngan's southeast headland, which is so narrow that the resort comprises two back-to-back beaches, joined by transverse roads at the north and south ends. The eastern beach, usually referred

△ Ko Pha Ngan

to as **Sunrise**, or Hat Rin Nok (Outer Hat Rin), is what originally drew visitors here, a classic curve of fine white sand between two rocky slopes; there's still some coral off the southern slope to explore, though the water is far from limpid these days. This beach is the centre of Hat Rin's action, with a solid line of bars, restaurants and bungalows tucked under the palm trees. **Sunset** beach, or Hat Rin Nai (Inner Hat Rin), which for much of the year is littered with flotsam, looks ordinary by comparison but has plenty of quieter accommodation. Unfortunately, development between the beaches does no justice to the setting: it's ugly, cramped and chaotic, with new low-rise concrete shophouses thrown up at any old angle. Half-hearted attempts to tart up the large body of water in the middle of the headland with a few park benches and lights have been undermined by all-too-accurate signposts pointing to "Hat Rin Swamp".

Practicalities

The awkwardness of **getting to Hat Rin** in the past helped to maintain its individuality, but this has changed now that the road in from Ban Khai has been paved. All the same, it's a winding, precipitous roller coaster of a route, covered by songthaews and motorbike taxis from Thong Sala – take care if you're driving your own motorbike. The easiest approach of all, however, if you're coming from Ko Samui, or even Surat Thani, is by direct boat from Bangrak on Samui's north coast (see p.661): four boats a day cross to the pier on Sunset beach in under an hour.

The area behind and between the beaches – especially around what's known as Chicken Corner, where the southern transverse road meets the road along the back of Sunrise – is crammed with shops and businesses, including supermarkets, overseas phone facilities, dozens of Internet outlets, plenty of ATMs and bank currency-exchange booths.

Accommodation

For most of the year, Hat Rin has enough bungalows to cope, but on **full moon nights** over ten thousand revellers may turn up. Your options are either to arrive at least a day early (especially during the Dec–Jan peak season), to forget about sleep altogether, or to hitch up with one of the many **party boats** (about B400 return/person) organized through guest houses and restaurants on Ko Samui, especially at Bangrak and Bophut, which usually leave between 9pm and midnight and return after dawn; there's also generally transport by boat or car from other beaches on Pha Ngan. Even at other times, staying on **Sunrise** is often expensive and noisy, though a few places can be recommended. On **Sunset**, the twenty or more resorts are laid out in orderly rows, and are especially quiet and inexpensive between April and June and in October. Many visitors choose to stay on the **headland** to the south of the main beaches, especially at white-sand, palm-fringed **Leela Beach**, which is a twenty-minute walk along a well-signposted route from Chicken Corner, on the west side of the headland. At any of the places out here your bungalow is likely to have more peace and space and better views, leaving you a torchlit walk to the night-time action.

Blue Marine Next to *Neptune's Villa* on Sunset ⓣ077 375079–80, ⓕ077 375407. In a broad, grassy compound, cheap, en-suite bungalows made of white clapboard and concrete, all with mosquito screens and hammocks, some with hot water, and large, tiled cottages with air-con and hot showers. Fan ❷, air-con ❻

Coco Hut Leela Beach ⓣ077 375368, ⓦwww.cocohut.com. On a clean, quiet stretch of beach, this lively, efficiently run place is smart and attractive, painted ochre and with some traditional southern Thai elements in the architecture. On offer is a huge variety of accommodation, from rooms with fans and cold water to bungalows with air-con and hot water, an attractive pool and Internet access. Fan ❹, air-con ❼

Leela Beach Bungalows Leela Beach ⓣ077 375094 or 081 995 1304, ⓦwww.leelabeach.com. A good, friendly and reliable budget choice with plenty of space under the palm trees and almost half of the white-sand beach to itself. The no-frills bungalows are sturdy and well built and all have fans and en-suite bathrooms; air-con cottages with hot water are planned. ❷

Lighthouse Bungalows On the far southwestern tip of the headland ⓣ077 375075, ⓦwww.lighthousebungalows.com. Free boat-taxi from Sunset pier thrice daily, or a 30min walk from Chicken Corner, the last section along a wooden walkway over the rocky shoreline. At this friendly haven, wooden and concrete bungalows, sturdily built to withstand the wind and backed by trail-filled jungle, either share bathrooms or have their own. The restaurant food is varied and tasty. The owners have plans to upgrade the bungalows, so rates may rise. ❷–❺

Neptune's Villa Near the small promontory at the centre of Sunset ⓣ077 375251. Popular, well-run place, in a narrow but lovingly tended garden giving onto the beach. The wide variety of smart accommodation ranges from fan-cooled cottages with their own hot-water bathrooms, to air-con rooms with hot showers and fridges. Fan ❸, air-con ❼

Palita At the northern end of Sunrise ⓣ077 375170–1 or 081 917 7455, ⓔpalitas9@hotmail.com. Clean, well-run place on a broad plot that stretches a long way back from the beach. Building was ongoing at the time of writing, but most of the accommodation is in smart, white-clapboard bungalows with either fans and cold showers or air-con and hot water. The food gets rave reviews. Fan ❸, air-con ❻

Paradise Spread over the far southern end of Sunrise and up the slope behind ⓣ077 375244–5, ⓦwww.paradisebungalow.com. Well-established place, with plenty of room and a good restaurant – the original full moon party began here, and it's still a party focus once a month. There's a range of rooms and bungalows of different sizes, but all are en suite with fans and some have air-con and hot water; those further up the hillside offer fine views over the bay from their verandas. Fan ❷, air-con ❺

Phangan Bayshore Resort In the middle of Sunrise ⓣ077 375227, ⓦwww.phanganbayshore.com. Hat Rin's first upmarket resort, a well-ordered place, though staff seem somewhat jaded. Big, en-suite bungalows with spacious verandas, some with hot water and air-con, are set on a broad, green lawn, shaded with palms. Fan ❹, air-con ❻

Phanganburi Resort Towards the north end of Sunset beach ⓣ077 375481, ⓦwww.phanganburiresort.net. Welcoming, new luxury complex that encompasses three hotel blocks, dozens of bungalows, a small spa and two very attractive pools in its extensive, beachside grounds. Decorated in a simple but smart Thai style, all the rooms have air-con, hot water, fridge and satellite TV. Internet access and wi-fi. ❼

Rin Bay View Near the pier on Sunset ⓣ077 375188. A good-value, friendly option in a central location, occupying a narrow strip of land – though not too tightly squeezed – and ornamented with flowers and trees. The en-suite bungalows with mosquito screens and balconies are a decent size and generally well maintained and clean. Price varies according to size and distance from the beach, and whether they are fan-cooled or air-con, with hot or cold water. Fan ❷, air-con ❺

Same-Same Lodge Above Sunrise at the start of the road to Leela Beach ⓣ077 375200, ⓦwww.same-same.com. Well-run, welcoming and sociable Thai-Scandinavian spot. Above a popular restaurant, clean, well-maintained and decent-sized rooms come with fan and cold showers or air-con and hot water. Unusually for Hat Rin, cheaper rates for single occupation. Fan ❸, air-con ❹

Sarikantang Leela Beach ⓣ077 375055–6, ⓦwww.sarikantang.com. Boutique resort with a swimming pool, a beachside spa and a good measure of style, though housekeeping could be better. Accommodation ranges from rooms with fans, verandas and cold-water bathrooms to chic, white-painted "superior" rooms with air-con, hot showers, TVs and separate outdoor sunken baths. Internet access and kayaks for rent (B100/hr). Fan ❺, air-con ❻

Sea Breeze Next to and above *Sun Cliff* ⓣ077 375162. Sprawling untidily over the ridge from near the southern transverse all the way to the north end of Leela Beach (with steps down to the sand), this place has plenty of space and views out to the west. Choose between older en-suite bungalows with fans, and large, smart, new villas on stilts, with air-con, hot water, fridges, big decks and great sunset vistas. A swimming pool is planned, so expect rates to go up. Fan ❸, air-con ❻

Seaview At the quieter northern end of Sunrise ⓣ077 375160. On a big plot of shady land, this clean, orderly place offers simple, en-suite huts at the back, posher bungalows with air-con and cold showers beachside. Fan ❸, air-con ❺

Stone Wall ⓣ077 375460 or 081 080 5924, ⓔstonewallbungalow1@hotmail.com. Friendly resort recently opened by a family who were forced to leave Ko Lanta after the 2004 tsunami. The stiff, 5min walk up behind *Seaview* – there is a primitive lift – is rewarded with great views of the Hat Rin peninsula and Samui. On the steeply sloping, lush plot are simple, cheap en-suite bungalows with verandas and hammocks to catch the breeze, and a quiet restaurant serving good Thai and Western food. ❷

Sun Cliff High up on the tree-lined slope above the south end of Sunset ⓣ077 375134. Friendly place with great views of the south coast and Ko Samui, and a wide range of bright, well-maintained bungalows, some with large balconies, fridges, hot water and air-con. Fan ❷, air-con ❺

Eating

As well as good simple Thai fare at some of the bungalows, Hat Rin sports an unnerving choice of world **foods** for somewhere so remote, and vegetarians are unusually well provided for.

Bamboozle Off the southern transverse, near Sunset pier. Among a wide variety of tasty Mexican food here, the chicken fajitas with all the trimmings are especially good.

Casa Nostra On the southern transverse, opposite 7-11. Excellent, small, Italian café-restaurant which prepares great pastas – try the spaghetti bolognese – pizzas (whole or by the slice), espresso coffee, salads and plenty of other dishes for vegetarians, such as cannelloni with ricotta and spinach, and a chocolate mousse to die for. Daily 2pm–midnight.

Nira's Near Chicken Corner. Justly popular restaurant, bar and 24hr bakery offering great all-day breakfasts of croissants, cakes and good coffees and teas, as well as sandwiches, quiches and more substantial Western main courses.

Om Ganesh On the southern transverse near the pier. Excellent, relaxing Indian restaurant with good vegetarian and non-vegetarian thalis, cheerful service and outdoor tables that are good for people-watching.

Yoghurt Home 3 Behind the north end of Sunrise, on the northern transverse. Although this establishment is now mostly devoted to a travel agency, it still offers home-made yoghurt in many combinations, including tzatziki, a wide range of coffees, teas and shakes, and cheap, generous servings of Thai and Western veggie and non-veggie food, including a tasty vegetable tempura.

Nightlife

Nightlife normally begins at the south end of Sunrise at open-air dance halls such as the *Cactus Club* and *Drop-In*, which pump out mostly radio-friendly dance music onto low-slung candlelit tables and mats on the beach. Inland on the southern transverse, *Outback Bar* is a lively meeting place with pool tables, big-screen sports and well-received steak pies and the like. For somewhere to chill, head for *Mellow Mountain Bar*, which occupies a great position up in the rocks on the north side of Sunrise, with peerless views of the beach. Up the hill behind the southern end of Sunrise, off the path to Leela Beach, *Back Yard*, with a large balcony area overlooking the beach, hosts a progressive set on Sundays.

On **full moon night**, *Paradise* is the main party host, sometimes bringing in big-name international DJs. However, the mayhem spreads along most of Sunrise, fuelled by hastily erected drinks stalls and around a dozen major sound systems – listen out for psy-trance and driving techno at *Zoom* and *The Vinyl Club*, and drum'n'bass at *Orchid* further up the beach. Next day, as the beach party winds down, *Back Yard* kicks off its afterparty at around eleven in the morning, with the best of the previous night's DJs.

Listings

Boat trips Several places on Hat Rin, such as Sopin Tour on the northern transverse (ⓣ077 375092), organize day-trips up the east coast and back, typically charging B500 (including simple lunch and snorkelling equipment) and taking in Mae Hat, Thong Nai Pan, Hat Khuat and Thaan Sadet. Or's Travel on the southern transverse (ⓣ081 719 6057) organizes speedboat tours to Ang Thong National Marine Park (see p.644) for B1600 per person.

Bookshops Two branches of Book Corner, behind Sunrise beach near the school and on the southern transverse, carry a decent line of new fiction, guides and books about Thailand and Southeast Asia. D's, also near the school behind Sunrise, is good for second-hand books.

Clinic Bandon International Hospital, a large private hospital on Ko Samui, run a clinic on the southern transverse near the pier (ⓣ077 375471–2, ⓦwww.bandonhospital.com).

Cookery courses *Same-Same Lodge* (see p.667) runs Thai cooking classes lasting one (B900), three (B2500) or five (B4200) days.

Gym Jungle Gym (ⓦwww.junglegym.co.th), near the pier, offers Thai boxing classes, a steam room, yoga and a juice bar.

Massages Chakra, in an alley off the southern transverse (ⓣ077 375401, ⓦwww.islandwebs.com/thailand/chakra.htm), does the best massages in Hat Rin, and also runs massage courses. Siam Healing Centre, on the small promontory at the centre of Sunset (ⓣ077 375450–1), offers the same, plus yoga, meditation and t'ai chi.

Post office On the southern transverse, near the pier on Sunset.

Travel agent The excellent, English-Thai Backpackers Information Centre, based to the south of Chicken Corner (ⓣ077 375535, ⓦwww.backpackersthailand.com), is a very reliable and clued-up full-service travel agency, which can make bookings and give advice on local tours and travel throughout Thailand and Asia; in the shop, you can consult a large database of advice and comments from previous customers. Also agents for Lotus Diving.

Vehicle rental Plenty of places on Hat Rin rent jeeps (B1000/day) and motorbikes (from B150/day). There have been lots of reports, however, of travellers being charged exorbitant amounts if they bring the vehicle back with even the most minor damage – at the very least, check the vehicle over very carefully before renting. *Sun Cliff* (see p.667), who have an office just off the southern transverse, is a reliable place for motorbikes, and won't try this scam.

The east coast

North of Hat Rin, the rocky, exposed **east coast** stretches as far as Ao Thong Nai Pan, the only substantial centre of development. No roads run along this coast, only a rough, steep, fifteen-kilometre trail, which starts from Hat Rin's northern transverse road (near *La Luna Bungalows*, waymarked with green painted dots as far as Hat Yuan) and runs reasonably close to the shore, occasionally dipping down into pristine sandy coves with a smattering of bungalows. From roughly January to September, one small boat a day runs via the east coast beaches from Hat Rin to Thong Nai Pan (see opposite), having started its voyage across at Maenam on Ko Samui. Otherwise there are ample longtails on Sunrise that will taxi you up the coast – around B150 to Hat Thian, for example. See opposite for information about organized day-trips by boat up this coast from Hat Rin.

Hat Yuan, Hat Thian and Hat Wai Nam

About ninety minutes up the trail, the adjoining small, sandy bays of **HAT YUAN**, **HAT THIAN** and **HAT WAI NAM** have established a reputation as a quieter alternative to Hat Rin and now sport about a dozen bungalow outfits between them. On Hat Yuan, *Barcelona* (ⓣ077 375113; ❷–❹) is a good choice, with plenty of space, great views and well-built accommodation either in en-suite huts or white bungalows with large verandas. Accommodation on Hat Thian is available at the friendly *Haad Tien Resort* (ⓣ081 229 3919; ❶), with en-suite wood or concrete bungalows in a large coconut grove on the slope above the beach; and at the *Sanctuary* (ⓣ081 271 3614, ⓦwww.thesanctuary-kpg.com; ❸–❻), which offers a huge range of basic and luxury en-suite bungalows and family houses, as well as dorm accommodation (B80), kayaking and good vegetarian fare, seafood and home-made bread and cakes. It also hosts courses in yoga, meditation and the like, and provides two diverse kinds of treatment: the Spa does massage, facials and beauty treatments, while the Wellness Centre goes in for fasting and cleansing. *Why Nam Huts* (❷; for information, contact *Yoghurt Home 3* in Hat Rin, see p.667) has Hat Wai Nam to itself, in a rocky, stream-fed bay that's good for snorkelling; the large, en-suite bungalows come with fans and hammocks, and the restaurant offers home-baked bread and plenty of vegetarian dishes.

Hat Sadet

Steep, remote **HAT SADET**, 12km up the trail from Hat Rin, has a handful of bungalow operations, sited here because of their proximity to **Thaan Sadet**, a boulder-strewn brook that runs out into the sea. The spot was popularized by various kings of Thailand who came here to walk, swim and vandalize the huge boulders by carving their initials on them. A rough track has been bull-dozed through the woods above and parallel to Thaan Sadet to connect with the unpaved road from Thong Sala to Ao Thong Nai Pan. Best of the bungalows is the welcoming *Mai Pen Rai* (ⓣ077 445090, ⓦwww.thansadet.com; ❷–❺), which has a variety of attractive, characterful accommodation with airy bathrooms (some with big upstairs terraces), either on the beach at the stream mouth or scattered around the rocks for good views; a jeep taxi leaves Thong Sala for the resort every day at 1pm (B100).

Ao Thong Nai Pan

AO THONG NAI PAN is a beautiful, semicircular bay backed by steep, green hills, which looks as if it's been bitten out of the island's northeast corner by a gap-toothed giant, leaving a tall hump of land dividing the bay into two parts, Thong Nai Pan Noi to the north, Thong Nai Pan Yai to the south. With lovely, fine, white sand, the longer, more indented Thong Nai Pan Yai has marginally the better beach, but both halves are sheltered and deep enough for swimming. The bay is now developed enough for tourism to support a few Internet shops, travel agents, dive outfits, bars, stand-alone restaurants and an ATM (on Thong Nai Pan Yai). A bumpy nightmare of a road, partly paved though mostly dirt, winds its way for 13km over the steep mountains from Ban Tai on the south coast to Thong Nai Pan: jeeps (B100/person) connect with incoming and outgoing boats at Thong Sala every day.

A dozen or so resorts line the southern half of the bay, **Thong Nai Pan Yai**. Near its centre, the friendly *Pingjun* (ⓣ077 299004; ❷) has a range of battered, old-style, wooden bungalows with fans, mosquito nets, en-suite bathrooms, verandas and hammocks, set in a large, grassy compound on a broad stretch of beach. At the quieter southern end, *Dolphin* (no phone; ❷) is a popular, tranquil spot, overgrown with lush vegetation and with lots of comfortable salas to recline in. The large, very clean bungalows come with fans, mosquito nets and en-suite bathrooms, and the beachfront restaurant, which serves good Western breakfasts and lunches and great coffee, turns into a mellow bar at night. In a colourful garden next door, friendly *White Sand* (ⓣ077 445125, ⓔthailasse@msn.com; ❸) offers smart, comfortable bungalows with en-suite bathrooms. **Boat trips** are available here, taking in Ao Mae Hat, Hat Khuat and Thaan Sadet.

The steep slopes of the central outcrop make a beautiful setting for *Panviman* (ⓣ077 445101–9, ⓦwww.panviman.com; ❽–❾), one of Ko Pha Ngan's few attempts at a luxury resort, comprising a swimming pool, a small massage spa, and air-conditioned cottages and hotel-style rooms with verandas, hot water, satellite TV and mini-bars. For non-guests it's worth making the climb up here for the view from the restaurant perched over the cliff edge.

On the northern beach, **Thong Nai Pan Noi**, *Star Huts* (ⓣ077 445085, ⓔstar_hut@hotmail.com; fan ❸, air-con ❺) is probably the best choice: very clean, well-maintained bungalows, with en-suite hot or cold showers, line the sand, and the friendly owners dish up good food and offer Internet access. Styling itself as "upmarket budget accommodation", nearby *Baan Panburi* (ⓣ077 238599, ⓦwww.baanpanburi.bigstep.com; ❸–❽) has a slightly institutional feel. Attractive, well-designed huts and bungalows, some of them a little cramped together, are set among flowers and come in a variety of sizes and styles, either with ceiling fans and cold showers or with air-con and hot water. The food is good, there's a massage house and small spa, and cooking classes and kayaks are available. Set back from the beach near *Star Huts*, *Mr Handsome* rustles up decent sandwiches, except when he's leading **day-trips to Ang Thong National Marine Park** in a big longtail boat (ⓣ086 278 8119, ⓔhandsomesandwiches @hotmail.com; B900 including snorkelling and lunch; minimum eight people).

The north coast

The village of **BAN CHALOAKLAM**, on Ao Chaloaklam, the largest bay on the **north coast**, has long been a famous R&R spot for fishermen from all over the Gulf of Thailand, with sometimes as many as a hundred trawlers littering the broad and sheltered bay. As a tourist destination, it has little to recommend it save that it can easily be reached from Thong Sala, 10km away, by songthaew or motorbike taxi along a paved road. **Hat Khom** has more to offer, a tiny cove dramatically tucked in under the headland to the east, with a secluded strip of white sand and good coral for snorkelling. Here, friendly *Coral Bay* (ⓣ077 374245; ❶–❹) has plenty of space and great views on the grassy promontory dividing Hat Khom from Ao Chaloaklam. The sturdy bungalows range from simple affairs with mosquito nets and shared bathrooms to large pads with funky bathrooms built into the rock; snorkelling equipment is available to make the most of Hat Khom's reef. Phangan Adventure, based at *Lotus Dive Resort* in Ban Chaloaklam (ⓣ077 374142, ⓦwww.phanganadventure.com), offers all manner of **adventure activities** on land and sea: an array of boat trips, including Ang Thong National Marine Park (kayaking optional), kayak rental, wakeboarding and mountain-bike tours and rental.

If the sea is not too rough, longtail boats run three times a day for most of the year from Ban Chaloaklam to isolated **HAT KHUAT** (**Bottle Beach**), the best of the beaches on the north coast, sitting between steep hills in a perfect cup of a bay; you could also walk there along a testing trail from Hat Khom in around ninety minutes. Among a handful of resorts here, the best is *Smile Resort* (❷), which has a pleasant, quiet setting for its en-suite, fan-cooled bungalows, on a pretty flower-strewn hillside at the western end of the beach.

The west coast

Pha Ngan's **west coast** has attracted about the same amount of development as the forgettable south coast, but the landscape here is more attractive and varied, broken up into a series of long sandy inlets with good sunset views over the islands of the Ang Thong National Marine Park to the west; most of the bays, however, are sheltered by reefs which can keep the sea too shallow for a decent swim, especially between May and October. The coast road from Thong Sala as far up as Hat Yao is in decent condition, as is the inland road via the hospital, which loops round, with a paved side road down to Hat Salad, past Ao Mae Hat to Ban Chaloaklam. However, the road between Hat Yao and Hat Salad has not as yet been similarly upgraded, and can be testing if you're on a bike. Taxis, motorbike taxis and sometimes boats cover the whole coast.

The first bay north of Thong Sala, Ao Wogtum (aka Hinkong), yawns wide across a featureless expanse that turns into a mud flat when the sea retreats behind the reef barrier at low tide. The nondescript bay of **AO SEETHANU** beyond is home to the excellent *Loy Fa* (ⓣ077 377319, ⓔloyfa@yahoo.com; fan ❹, air-con ❼), a well-run place that commands good views from its perch on top of Seethanu's steep southern cape, and offers decent snorkelling and swimming from its private beach below; bungalows are either on the hilltop or down on the beach, and come with fan and cold showers or air-con, hot water and minibar; Internet access is available.

Ao Chaophao

Continuing north, there's a surprise in store in the shape of **Laem Son Lake**, a beautiful, tranquil stretch of clear water cordoned by pines. However, as with any freshwater lake in Thailand, you should avoid swimming here; furthermore, there have been unconfirmed reports that this lake is toxic. To the west of the lake by the beach, Agama (ⓣ089 233 0217, ⓦwww.agamayoga.com), based at the otherwise unremarkable *Bovy Resort*, offers **yoga** classes and certificate courses, from beginners to advanced. *Seethanu Bungalows* (ⓣ077 349113, ⓕ077 349112; fan ❷, air-con ❺), actually round the next headland on the small, pretty bay of **AO CHAOPHAO**, is a lively spot with a popular restaurant; sturdy, characterful wooden and concrete bungalows (all en suite) are arrayed around a colourful garden, with the more expensive options, with air-con and hot water, by the beach. Next door, *Seaflower* (ⓣ077 349090, ⓕ077 349091; ❷–❺) is quieter and more congenial, set in a well-tended garden, and the veggie and non-veggie food is excellent. En-suite bungalows with their own bathrooms vary in price according to their size and age: the newer ones – more like cottages – have marble open-air bathrooms and big balcony seating areas. If you're feeling adventurous, ask the owner about the occasional three-day, two-night longtail-boat treks to Ang Thong National Marine Park (see p.644), which involve snorkelling, caving, catching your own seafood, and sleeping in tents on the beach (B3000/person, including food and soft drinks; minimum ten people). The adjacent, English-run *Village Green* pub-restaurant keeps the punters happy with a wide variety of breakfasts, great sandwiches (including the raid-the-pantry DIY option), and Thai and Western (including Mexican) main courses, washed down with a big choice of drinks and cocktails; on Sunday evenings there's a traditional English roast dinner and a live band. Three doors away, behind a travel agent that has second-hand books for sale and Internet access, stands friendly *Haad Chao Phao Resort* (ⓣ077 349273, ⓔpermanachart@yahoo.com; ❷): in a small shady garden, the simple but clean and well-kept en-suite bungalows (all with mosquito nets and verandas) lead down to an attractive patch of beach.

Hat Son and Hat Yao

North of Chaophao, *Haad Son Resort* (ⓣ077 349104, ⓦwww.haadson.com; fan ❹, air-con ❻) has the small, sandy beach of **HAT SON** to itself. They're spaciously laid out among pretty flowers on a terraced hillside, and vary from the simple (though fan-cooled and en suite), to the deluxe (air-con, hot water and mini-bar). This popular, family-oriented place also has a very attractive swimming pool with a separate children's pool, Internet access and kayaks for rent.

Beyond the next headland, the long, attractive, gently curved beach of **HAT YAO** is gradually and justifiably becoming livelier and more popular, with several stand-alone bars and restaurants, diving outfits, supermarkets, a bank currency-exchange booth, an ATM and jeep and bike rental. Among a nonstop line of bungalows here, good budget bets are *Ibiza* (ⓣ077 349121, ⓦwww.ibizabungalows.com; fan ❶, air-con ❻), a lively, central spot in a spacious garden with airy bungalows that run the full gamut, whether you're happy to share a bathroom or want air-con and hot water, as well as Internet access and kayaks for rent; and the friendly *Bay View* (ⓣ077 374148; ❸), which offers good food and views from a variety of en-suite bungalows on the quiet northern headland. Hat Yao's plushest spot is *Long Bay Resort*, with a long stretch of beach and spacious gardens towards the north end of the bay (ⓣ077 349057–9, ⓦwww.geocities.com/lbresort; fan ❺, air-con ❼). Choose between small but smart fan bungalows with cold showers, and large, air-con cottages with hot water, fridge and TV. There's an attractive swimming pool and kayaks to rent, and you can book a **boat trip** on the longtail *Luna Sea*, taking in Ao Mae Hat, Hat Khuat, Ao Thong Nai Pan and Thaan Sadet.

Hat Salad and Ao Mae Hat

To the north of Hat Yao, **HAT SALAD** is another pretty bay, sheltered and sandy, with good snorkelling off the northern tip. On the access road behind the beach is a rather untidy service village of shops, travel agents, bike and jeep rental outlets and Internet offices. Among the dozen or so bungalow outfits, the laid-back and well-run old-timer, *Salad Hut*, stands out (ⓣ077 349246, ⓦwww.saladhut.com; ❸–❻). Arrayed along the beachfront in a shady, colourful garden are bamboo bungalows with cold showers, and large, airy, wooden affairs with hot water; all come with fans, big verandas, hammocks and mosquito nets. The owners have plans to upgrade, including possibly a swimming pool, so rates may go up.

On the island's northwest corner, **AO MAE HAT** is good for swimming and snorkelling among the coral that lines the sand causeway to the tiny islet of Ko Maa. The bay supports several bungalow resorts, notably the popular, friendly *Wang Sai Resort* at its south end (ⓣ077 374238; fan ❷, air-con ❻). On a huge plot of land, most of the en-suite bungalows are set back from the beach – the best of them are up the slope behind, with great sunset views.

Ko Tao

KO TAO (Turtle Island) is so named because its outline resembles a turtle nose-diving towards Ko Pha Ngan, 40km to the south. The rugged shell of the turtle, to the east, is crenellated with secluded coves where one or two bungalows hide among the rocks. On the western side, the turtle's underbelly is a long curve of classic beach, **Hat Sai Ree**, facing **Ko Nang Yuan**, a beautiful Y-shaped group of islands offshore, also known as Ko Hang Tao (Turtle's Tail Island). The 21 square kilometres of granite in between is topped by dense forest on the higher slopes and dotted with huge boulders that look as if they await some Easter Island sculptor. It's fun to spend a couple of days exploring the network of rough trails, after which you'll probably know all 1100 of the island's inhabitants. Ko Tao is now best known as a venue for **scuba-diving**, with a wide variety of dive sites in close proximity; see the box on p.674 for further details. The island is also a good spot for bouldering: Zen Gecko runs **rock-climbing** courses, starting at B800 for half a day (make contact on Ⓔzengecko5@hotmail.com; Ⓦwww.zengecko.com).

The island is the last and most remote of the archipelago that continues the line of Surat Thani's mountains into the sea. There were around 120 sets of **bungalows** at the latest count (still sometimes not enough during the peak season from December to March, when travellers occasionally have to sleep on the beach until a hut becomes free) concentrated along the west and south sides. Some still provide the bare minimum, with plain mattresses for beds, mosquito nets and shared bathrooms, but nearly all places can now offer en-suite bathrooms and a few comforts, and there are a growing number of upmarket resorts around with such luxuries as air-con, hot water and swimming pools. There's a limited government supply of electricity, so much of it still comes from private generators, and it's usually evenings only, with few places providing 24-hour service. Ko Tao suffers from a scarcity of water, especially during the hot season, so visitors are asked to conserve water whenever possible.

If you're just arriving and want to stay on one of the less accessible beaches, it might be a good idea to go with one of the touts who meet the ferries at Mae Hat, with pick-up or boat on hand, since at least you'll know their bungalows aren't full, which is possible from December to March; otherwise call ahead, as even the

△ Scuba-diving off Ko Tao

Scuba-diving off Ko Tao

Some of the best **dive sites** in Thailand are found off Ko Tao, which is blessed with outstandingly clear (visibility up to 35m) and deep water close in to shore. On top of that, there's a kaleidoscopic array of coral species and other marine life, and you may be lucky enough to encounter whale sharks, barracudas, leatherback turtles and pilot whales. Diving is possible at any time of the year, with sheltered sites on one or other side of the island in any season – the changeover from southwest to northeast monsoon in November is the worst time, while visibility is best from April to July, in September (usually best of all) and October. Ko Tao now supports a small, one-person recompression chamber, evacuation centre and general diving medicine centre at Badalveda in Mae Hat (Ⓣ077 456664 or 086 272 4618, Ⓦwww.badalveda.com), and there's a bigger chamber on Ko Samui, only ninety minutes away by speedboat (see p.640).

To meet demand, Ko Tao has about fifty **dive companies**, making this the largest dive-training centre in Southeast Asia; most of them are staffed by Westerners and based at Mae Hat, Hat Sai Ree or Ao Chaloke Ban Kao. Twenty or so of the more reputable companies have organized themselves into the **Koh Tao Dive Operators Club** (DOC), to maintain standards and to undertake important environmental initiatives. Be sure to dive with a member of the DOC – they have an office in Mae Hat just north of the main pier and a website, Ⓦwww.kohtaodoc.com, with a list of members. Beyond that, when choosing a company, talk to other travellers about their experiences and check out the kind of instruction, the size of group on each course, and whether you get on with the instructors. Companies generally offer discounted accommodation for the duration of an Openwater course, but ask exactly how long it's for (3 or 4 nights), where it is and what it's like. Among members of the DOC, PADI Five-Star (or higher) Dive Centres, all of which are committed to looking after the environment and maintaining high standards of service, include: *Ban's Diving Resort* on Hat Sai Ree Ⓣ077 456446, Ⓦwww.amazingkohtao.com; Big Fish at Ao Chaloke Ban Kao Ⓣ077 456290, Ⓦwww.bigfishresort.com; Black Tip at Ao Ta Note Ⓣ077 456488 and Mae Hat Ⓣ077 456204, Ⓦwww.blacktipdiving.com; Coral Grand Divers (Ⓦwww.coralgranddivers.com) at the *Koh Tao Coral Grand Resort* on Hat Sai Ree (see p.680); *Ko Tao Resort* on Ao Chaloke Ban Kao (see p.682); Planet Scuba at Mae Hat Ⓣ077 456110, Ⓦwww.planet-scuba.net; and Scuba Junction on Hat Sai Ree Ⓣ077 456164, Ⓦwww.scuba-junction.com.

By far the most popular **course**, PADI's four-day "Openwater" for beginners costs a minimum of B9000 with a member of the Dive Operators' Club. One-day introductions to diving are also available for a minimum of B2000, as is the full menu of PADI courses, up to "Instructor". Discounted accommodation during courses is also usually offered, costing from B200 for a fan room per night, from B500 for an air-con room, with a DOC member.

For **qualified divers**, one dive typically costs B1000, a ten-dive package B7000, with fifteen percent discounts if you bring your own gear. Among the more unusual offerings available are luxury live-aboards with Coral Grand Divers (Ⓦwww.coralgranddivers.com) at the *Koh Tao Coral Grand Resort* (see p.680), and three-day trips to Ang Thong National Marine Park through Koh Tao Divers at Ban Hat Sai Ree (Ⓣ086 069 9244, Ⓦwww.kohtaodivers.com). *Ban's Diving Resort* (see

remotest bungalows now have landlines or mobile phones. Some resorts with attached scuba-diving operations have been known to refuse guests who don't sign up for diving trips or courses; on the other hand, many of the dive companies now have their own lodgings, available at a discounted price to divers. With a year-round customer base of divers – and resident dive above) maintains a speciality in underwater photography. Some of the companies will take **snorkellers** along on their dive trips; Dive Point, based between the piers in Mae Hat (Ⓣ077 456231, Ⓦwww.divepoint-kohtao.com), for example, charge B500 for a long afternoon (B400 if you bring your own snorkelling equipment).

Main dive sites

Ko Nang Yuan Surrounded by a variety of sites, with assorted hard and soft corals and an abundance of fish, which between them cater for just about everyone: the **Nang Yuan Pinnacle**, a granite pinnacle with boulder swim-throughs, morays and reef sharks; **Green Rock**, a maze of boulder swim-throughs, caves and canyons, featuring stingrays and occasional reef sharks; **Twins**, two rock formations covered in corals and sponges, with a colourful coral garden as a backdrop; and the **Japanese Gardens**, on the east side of the sand causeway, which get their name from the hundreds of hard and soft coral formations here and are good for beginners and popular among snorkellers.

White Rock (Hin Khao) Between Hat Sai Ree and Ko Nang Yuan, where sarcophyton leather coral turns the granite boulders white when seen from the surface; also wire, antipatharian and colourful soft corals, and gorgonian sea fans. Plenty of fish, including titan triggerfish, butterfly fish, angelfish, clown fish and morays.

Shark Island Large granite boulders with acropora, wire and bushy antipatharian corals, sea whips, gorgonian sea fans and barrel sponges. Reef fish include angelfish, triggerfish and barracuda; there's a resident turtle, and leopard and reef sharks may be found as well as occasional whale sharks.

Hinwong Pinnacle At Ao Hinwong; generally for experienced divers, often with strong currents. Similar scenery to White Rock, over a larger area, with beautiful soft coral at 30m depth. A wide range of fish, including blue-spotted fantail stingrays, sweetlips pufferfish and boxfish, as well as hawksbill turtles.

Chumphon or **Northwest Pinnacle** A granite pinnacle for experienced divers, starting 14m underwater and dropping off to over 36m, its top covered in anemones; surrounded by several smaller formations and offering the possibility of exceptional visibility. Barrel sponges, tree and antipatharian corals at deeper levels; a wide variety of fish, in large numbers, attract local fishermen; barracudas, batfish, whale sharks (seasonal) and huge groupers.

Southwest Pinnacle One of the top sites in terms of visibility, scenery and marine life for experienced divers. A huge pyramid-like pinnacle rising to 6m below the surface, its upper part covered in anemones, with smaller pinnacles around; at lower levels, granite boulders, barrel sponges, sea whips, bushy antipatharian and tree corals. Big groupers, snappers and barracudas; occasionally, large rays, leopard and sand sharks, swordfish, finback whales and whale sharks.

Sail Rock (Hin Bai) Midway between Ko Tao and Ko Pha Ngan, emerging from the sand at a depth of 40m and rising 15m above the sea's surface. Visibility of up to 30m, and an amazing ten-metre underwater chimney (vertical swim-through). Antipatharian corals, both bushes and whips, and carpets of anemones. Large groupers, snappers and fusiliers, blue-ringed angelfish, batfish, kingfish and juvenile clown sweetlips; a likely spot for sighting whale sharks and mantas.

instructors – more and more sophisticated Western **restaurants** and **bars** are springing up all the time, notably in Mae Hat and on Hat Sai Ree.

The **weather** is much the same as on Pha Ngan and Samui, but being that bit further off the mainland, Ko Tao feels the effect of the southwest monsoon more: June to October can have strong winds and rain, with a lot

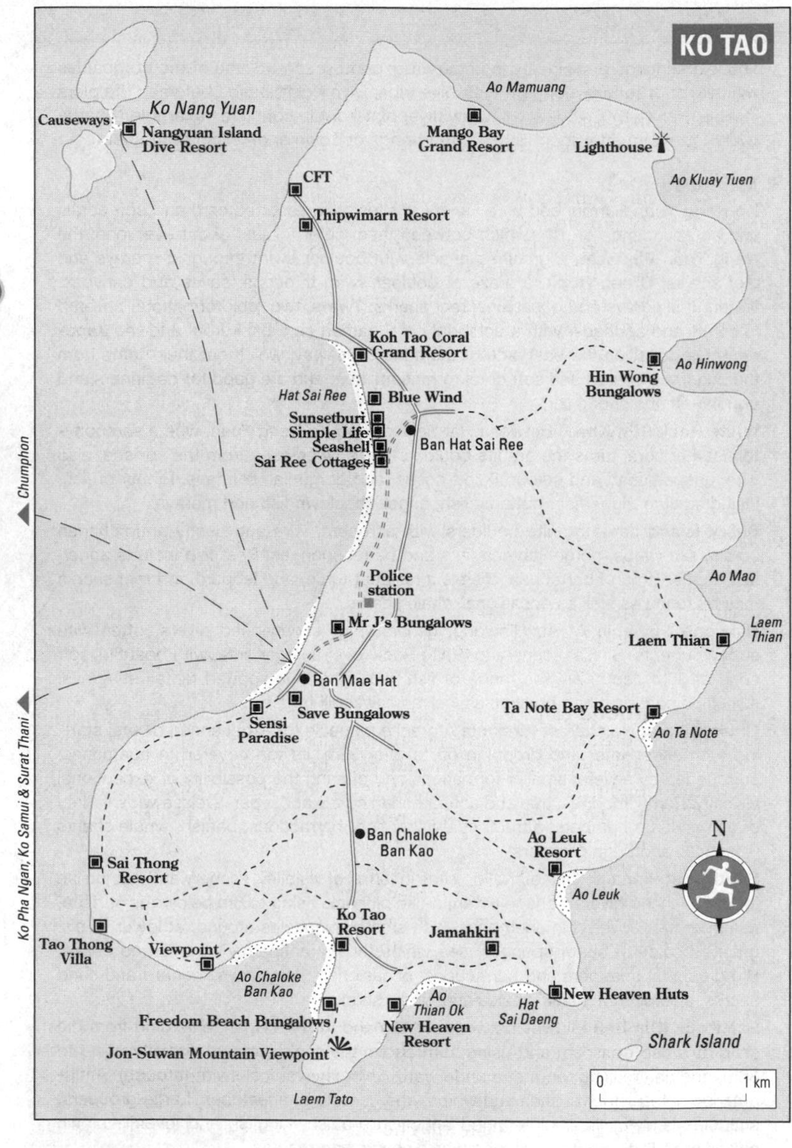

of debris blown onto the windward coasts. There isn't a TAT office on Ko Tao, but the regularly updated and widely available free booklet, *Koh Tao Info*, is a useful source of **information**, along with its associated **website**, Ⓦwww.kohtao-online.com, which allows online accommodation booking. If you're going to be exploring, well worth picking up from supermarkets on Ko Tao or Ko Pha Ngan is Visid Hongsombud's excellent, annually updated **map** of Ko Pha Ngan and Ko Tao (B100).

Getting to Ko Tao

For details of the night boat and morning boats **from Chumphon**, which is connected to Bangkok by train and bus, see p.631. Among the Chumphon–Ko Tao boat companies, Lomprayah (on Ko Tao ⓣ077 456176; ⓦwww.lomprayah.com), for example, organizes VIP bus and boat packages for B850 from Thanon Khao San in **Bangkok** (ⓣ02 629 2569–70), via **Hua Hin** (ⓣ032 533738–9).

Four companies currently operate daily scheduled boats between Thong Sala on **Ko Pha Ngan** and Ko Tao. Songserm (on Ko Tao ⓣ077 456274) and Phangan Cruises (on Ko Tao ⓣ077 456012 or 089 871 2939) do the voyage in 1hr 30min (both 1 daily; B250). Lomprayah (see above) and Seatran (on Ko Tao ⓣ077 456263–4) cover the ground in an hour (both 2 daily; B350) – though in heavier seas, all four companies' boats take about the same time. The Lomprayah catamaran originates at Maenam, Seatran at Bangrak, on **Ko Samui** (total journey time to Ko Tao on either 1hr 30min; B550), while Phangan Cruises originate at Bangrak and the Songserm Express Boat docks at Na Thon (journey time to Ko Tao on either 2hr-plus; B350). This Songserm boat originates at **Surat Thani** (5hr-plus to Ko Tao; B500); there's also a night boat from Surat Thani, departing at 11pm (ⓣ077 284928 or 081 326 8973; 9hr; B500).

These services fluctuate according to demand, and in high season extra boats may appear. Voyages to and from Ko Tao may also be at the mercy of the weather at any time between June and January. Boat ticket prices fluctuate, too – for example, with so much competition between operators and routes, you'll currently find that leaving the island is a lot cheaper than the prices quoted above for getting there.

Island transport

You can **get around** easily enough on foot, but there are roads of sorts now to most of the resorts, though many are still very rough tracks, suitable for four-wheel drive only; motorbike **taxis** and pick-ups (roughly B50–100/person, more late at night, and more for a 4WD to somewhere more remote) are available in Mae Hat. There are also **rental** mopeds (B100–150/day), ATVs (all-terrain vehicles or quad bikes; B450/day) and even a few jeeps (B1000/day). As on Ko Phangan, however, there have been lots of reports of travellers being charged exorbitant amounts if they bring the vehicle back with even the most minor damage – for motorbikes, avoid the outfits in front of the main pier in Mae Hat, and rent from your bungalow or someone reliable like Mr J (see p.679).

Longtail-boat taxis are available at Mae Hat or through your bungalow, or you could splash out on your own **round-island boat tour**, allowing you to explore the coastline fully, with stops for snorkelling and swimming (about B1500 for the boat for the day, depending on the number of passengers); alternatively you could hook up with a group tour, again through your resort or at Mae Hat (usually about B500/head). The *Mango Bay Resort* office in Mae Hat (see p.680) organizes occasional **speed-boat trips** to Ang Thong National Marine Park for the day (B3200/person).

Mae Hat and around

All boats to Ko Tao dock at **MAE HAT**, a small, lively village in a pleasant, beachfront setting, which boasts the lion's share of the island's amenities, including a few supermarkets, pharmacies and clinics. A paved high street heads straight up the hill from the main pier (eventually ending up in Ao Chaloke

Ban Kao), with narrower front streets running at right angles, parallel to the seafront. The Lomprayah and Songserm boats each have their own pier, to the south of the main one.

Accommodation

If you just want functional, reliable, good-value **accommodation**, head for either *Save Bungalows*, next to Mr J's supermarket just south of the piers (ⓣ077 456656; fan ❷, air-con ❺), or *Mr J's Bungalows*, behind Mr J's other supermarket, five minutes' walk north of the village (ⓣ077 456066–7; fan ❷, air-con ❺). They're both part of Mr J's trusty network of businesses (see opposite), and offer large, clean, mostly en-suite rooms.

For somewhere more characterful to stay near Mae Hat, head for the charming, well-run *Sensi Paradise Resort* (ⓣ077 456244, ⓦwww.kohtaoparadise.com; ❻–❾), whose pretty, flower-covered grounds sprawl over the lower slopes of the headland just to the south of the village. It offers a pretty beachside restaurant and some of the best upmarket accommodation on the island, in well-designed wooden cottages and villas with en-suite cold-water bathrooms and mini-bars, some with air-con and some with large terraces and open-air bathrooms.

A good way further down the coast (40min walk from Mae Hat or around B100 in a taxi-boat) is *Sai Thong Resort*, whose shady grounds spread between its own, private Sai Nual beach and the next small bay to the south (ⓣ077 456476, ⓦwww.sai-thong.com; ❶–❻). Efficiently run and popular with families, it provides a wide variety of bungalows (some with shared bathrooms), which have few frills but are decently maintained. There's a small, basic spa with a seawater pool, and kayaks and snorkels are available.

About ten minutes' walk further south again, *Tao Thong Villa* (ⓣ077 456224; ❶–❺) offers plenty of shady seclusion and good snorkelling and swimming. Accommodation, ranging from very cheap huts with no electricity and shared bathrooms to sturdy, en-suite bungalows with fans and fridges, are dotted around a rocky outcrop and the slope behind, with a breezy restaurant on the small, sandy isthmus in between.

Eating and drinking

Not surprisingly, Mae Hat boasts the pick of the island's **eating and drinking** options. French-run *Cappuccino*, 100m from the pier up the high street, does a mean *pain au chocolat* and coffee, plus gourmet sandwiches and salads. Further up the street, *La Matta* turns out delicious pizzas in scores of varieties, tasty home-made pastas, and a few Italian meat and fish dishes and desserts, as well as espresso coffees and home-made *limoncello*. Off the north side of the high street near the pier, on what's sometimes known as Mae Hat Square, *Café del Sol* probably has the biggest choice of expensive Western goodies on the island – this is the place to come if you fancy breadcrumbed fish'n'chips or beef carpaccio with parmesan.

Whitening, a congenial and chic bar, restaurant and club 200m south of the main pier down the front street, has a great deck and relaxing beach tables overlooking the bay. It dishes up some very tasty and creative Thai and Western food, as well as mean cocktails, and is famous for its Friday night parties. Other popular bars include *Dragon Bar*, a stylish place on the high street, painted ochre and decorated with elegant bamboo fronds, with regular DJ sessions; and *Dirty Nelly's*, an Irish-managed pub near the pier on Mae Hat Square, which has decent Guinness on tap, a pool table and big-screen sports.

Listings

Banks Mae Hat now supports several banks, including Siam City Bank, up the high street on the left, with an ATM and Western Union facilities; and at the crossroads hard by the pier, a Krung Thai Bank currency-exchange booth, with an ATM on the corner opposite.

Books B-Books up the high street on the right sells second-hand and new books and international newspapers.

Internet access Prasit Service, up the high street on the left, has a good reputation both as a travel agent and for Internet access.

Police station Five minutes' walk north of Mat Hat, on the narrow paved road towards Hat Sai Ree (ⓣ077 456631).

Post office At the top of the village (turn left), near the start of the paved road to Ban Hat Sai Ree, with ATM, phone and poste-restante facilities.

Supermarket and travel agency Five minutes' walk north of Mae Hat, at the top of a small rise opposite the primary school, you'll find the head office of Ko Tao's all-purpose fixer, and all-round character, Mr J. Here – and at Mr J's other two shops, south of the piers in Mae Hat (Save Shop) and at Ao Chaloke Ban Kao (Mr D's) – you can rent motorbikes, organize a visa extension, exchange several currencies, recycle batteries, buy and sell second-hand books, even borrow money.

Watersports MV Watersports (ⓣ077 456065 or 087 264 2633), south of the piers on the front street at *Kallaphanga Resort*, is one of several places on the island that rents kayaks (two-person B150/hr, B800/day), as well as offering sailing rental and tuition, windsurfer rental, wakeboarding and water-skiing.

Hat Sai Ree and Ko Nang Yuan

To the north of Mae Hat, beyond a small promontory, you'll find **Hat Sai Ree**, Ko Tao's only long beach. The strip of white sand stretches for 2km in a gentle curve, backed by a smattering of coconut palms and around twenty bungalow resorts. A narrow paved track runs along the back of the beach to the village of Ban Hat Sai Ree, parallelled by the main road further inland. Opposite the Bank of Ayudhya and its ATM at the south end of Hat Sai Ree, *Pure Lounge* is a stylish beach **bar**, with regular party nights, striking crimson beanbag seats and tables to recline at on the sand framed by dramatic boulders.

Towards the midpoint of the beach, twenty minutes' walk from Mae Hat, *Sai Ree Cottages* (ⓣ077 456126; ❷–❸) has primitive huts and sturdy **bungalows**, all en suite and well maintained, in a large, beautiful, flower-strewn garden, and serves excellent grub. The spacious, tidy compound next door belongs to *Seashell Resort* (ⓣ077 456271, ⓦwww.kohtaoseashell.com; fan ❹, air-con ❼), a friendly, well-run place, with a DOC dive school; it offers traditional massage, as well as very smart, sturdy bungalows, with en-suite cold showers and mosquito screens, either with fans or with air-con, fridge and TV. A hundred metres or so further up the beach, *Simple Life* (ⓣ077 456142, ⓦwww.simplelifedivers.com; ❹) is another good choice with a DOC dive school, offering comfortable, en-suite, fan-cooled bungalows, great food and a lively beach bar. On a narrow but tree-lined strip of land next door is the upmarket *Sunsetburi Resort* (ⓣ077 456266, ⓕ077 456101, fan ❺, air-con ❻–❽), with its own large swimming pool and modern, concrete cottages, many with air-con and some with the luxury of hot water. *Blue Wind* (ⓣ077 456116, ⓔbluewindwadear@hotmail.com; fan ❷, air-con ❻), next door but one, offers a variety of smart, well-kept, en-suite rooms and bungalows, many with hot water and some with air-con and TV, scattered about a shady compound. The very good beachside restaurant serves up home-made breads, croissants, cakes and espresso coffee, as well as Indian and Thai food, home-made pasta and other Western meals; yoga courses (ⓔshambhalayogaa@yahoo.co.nz) are also held here.

Around and inland from *Simple Life* and *Sunsetburi* spreads **BAN HAT SAI REE**, a burgeoning village of supermarkets, clinics, pharmacies, travel agents,

Internet outlets, a branch of Siam City Bank with an ATM and Western Union facilities, **restaurants** and **bars**. On the south side of the village, the stylish *New Heaven Deli & Bakery* serves up great, home-baked breads and cakes, as well as sandwiches, pies, salads, shakes and booster juices. Nearby on the beach, *Suthep* is an expat favourite, serving all kinds of Western food, including pasta, pizza and a very good vegetarian selection, as well as tasty Thai food. The beach tables at the adjacent *Dry Bar* are a great spot to chill over a sundowner and come alive for a Friday night beach party. Inland, there's a branch of B-Books (see p.679) in Sairee Plaza on the main road from Mae Hat, while at the east end of the village, on the road towards Ao Hinwong, is Monsoon **gym** (ⓣ086 271 2212, ⓦwww.monsoongym.com), which offers *muay Thai* classes.

The main paved road continues **north of the village** past a luxury beach-front development, the welcoming *Koh Tao Coral Grand Resort* (ⓣ077 456431–4, ⓦwww.kohtaocoral.com; ❽). Sandstone-pink octagonal cottages with hardwood floors and large, attractive bathrooms gather – some a little tightly – around a pretty, Y-shaped pool; all have hot water, TV and air-con. North again beyond the end of Hat Sai Ree, another upscale spot, *Thipwimarn Resort* (ⓣ077 456409, ⓦwww.thipwimarnresort.com; fan ❼, air-con ❽), tumbles down a steep slope, past an elevated, infinity-edge swimming pool, to its own small beach. Dotted around the hillside, smart, thatched, whitewashed villas, most with hot water and mini-bar, enjoy a fair measure of seclusion, satellite TV and fine sunset views. The road ends at isolated *CFT* (ⓣ077 456730; ❶–❺) on the rocky northwest flank of the island, which offers cheap shacks or en-suite bungalows, and excellent food; there's no beach here, but you can swim off the rocks and the views over to Ko Nang Yuan are something else. Based at *CFT* is Here and Now (ⓦwww.hereandnow.be), a respected centre for traditional massages, as well as t'ai chi/chi gong courses.

Ko Nang Yuan

One kilometre off the northwest of Ko Tao, **KO NANG YUAN**, a close-knit group of three tiny islands, provides the most spectacular beach scenery in these parts, thanks to the causeway of fine white sand that joins up the islands. You can easily swim off the east side of the causeway to snorkel over the Japanese Gardens, which feature hundreds of hard and soft coral formations. Boats from the Lomprayah pier in Mae Hat, just south of the main pier, run back and forth three times a day (B100 return), but note that rules to protect the environment here include banning visitors from bringing cans, plastic bottles and fins with them, and day-trippers are charged B100 to land on the island; alternatively, it's B300 for an all-in day-trip, including boat transfers, lunch and snorkelling. Transfers from and to Mae Hat are free for people staying at the *Nangyuan Island Dive Resort* (ⓣ077 456088–93, ⓦwww.nangyuan.com; fan ❻, air-con ❼), which makes the most of its beautiful location, its pricey fan and air-con bungalows, with en-suite bathrooms and fridges, spreading over all three islands.

The north and east coasts

The lone bay on the north coast, **Ao Mamuang** (Mango Bay), is a beautiful, tree-clad bowl, whose shallow reef is a popular stop on snorkelling day-trips. There's little in the way of a beach here, but the well-appointed, new wooden bungalows and attractive bar-restaurant of *Mango Bay Grand Resort* perch on stilts on the rocks (ⓣ077 456097 or 087 893 6998, ⓦwww.mangobaygrandresortkohtaothailand.com; office in Mae Hat just south of the main pier; fan ❻, air-con ❽).

The sheltered inlets of the east coast, most of them containing one or two sets of bungalows, can be reached by boat, pick-up or four-wheel-drive. The

Thai cuisine

Thai food is now hugely popular in the West, but nothing, of course, beats coming to Thailand to experience the full range of subtle and fiery flavours, constructed from the freshest ingredients. Four fundamental tastes are identified in Thai cuisine – spiciness, sourness, saltiness and sweetness – and diners aim to share a variety of dishes that impart a balance of these flavours, along with complementary textures. Lemon grass, basil, coriander, galangal, chilli, garlic, lime juice, coconut milk and fermented fish sauce (used instead of salt) are some of the distinctive components that bring these tastes to life. The repertoire of main dishes described below – along with Chinese-style stir-fries such as sweet-and-sour and chicken with cashew nuts – is pretty much standard throughout Thailand, but when you get out into the provinces, you'll have the chance to sample a few local specialities, too.

▲ Kaeng som

Curries

Thai **curries** (*kaeng*) have as their foundation a variety of curry pastes, elaborate and subtle blends of herbs, spices, garlic, shallots and chilli peppers that are traditionally ground together with pestle and mortar. The use of some of these spices, as well as of coconut cream, was imported from India long ago; curries that don't use coconut cream are naturally less sweet and thinner, with the consistency of soups.

While some curries, such as *kaeng karii* (mild and yellow) and *kaeng matsaman* (literally "Muslim curry", with potatoes, peanuts and usually beef), still show their roots, others have been adapted into quintessentially Thai dishes, notably *kaeng khiaw wan* (sweet and green), *kaeng phet* (red and hot) and *kaeng phanaeng* (thick and savoury, with peanuts). *Kaeng som* generally contains vegetables and fish and takes its distinctive sourness from the addition of tamarind or, in the northeast, okra leaves. Traditionally eaten during the cool season, *kaeng liang* uses up gourds or other bland vegetables, but is made aromatic by the heat of peppercorns and shallots and the fragrance of basil leaves.

Soups

Thai **soups**, an essential component of most shared meals, are eaten simultaneously with other dishes, not as a starter. They are often flavoured with the distinctive tang of lemon grass, kaffir lime leaves and galangal, and garnished with fresh coriander, and can be extremely hot if the cook adds liberal handfuls of chillies to the pot. Two favourites are *tom kha kai*, a creamy coconut chicken soup; and *tom yam kung*, a hot and sour prawn soup without coconut milk. *Khao tom*, a starchy rice soup that's generally eaten for breakfast, meets the approval of few Westerners, except as a traditional hangover cure.

Salads

One of the lesser-known delights of Thai cuisine is the *yam* or **salad**, which can often impart all four of the fundamental flavours in an unusual and refreshing harmony. *Yam* can be made in many permutations – with noodles, meat, seafood or vegetables, for example – but at the heart of every variety is a liberal squirt of fresh lime juice and a fiery sprinkling of chopped chillies. As well as *som tam*, *laap* and *nam tok* described in the box on regional cuisine, salads to look out for include *yam som oh* (pomelo), *yam hua plee* (banana flowers) and *yam plaa duk foo* (crispy fried catfish).

▼ Chillies at Warorot market, Chiang Mai

Noodle and rice dishes

Thais eat **noodles** when Westerners would dig into a sandwich – for lunch, as a late-night snack or just to pass the time. Sold on street stalls everywhere, they come in assorted varieties – including *kway tiaw* (made with rice flour) and *ba mii* (egg noodles), *sen yai* (wide) and *sen lek* (thin) – and get boiled up as soups (*nam*), doused in gravy (*rat na*) or stir-fried (*haeng*, "dry", or *phat*, "fried"). Most famous of noodle dishes is *kway tiaw phat thai* (usually abbreviated to *phat thai*, meaning "Thai fry-up"), a delicious combination of fried noodles, beansprouts, egg, tofu and spring onions, sprinkled with ground peanuts and the juice of half a lime, and often spiked with tiny dried shrimps.

▲ Preparing *som tam* at a street stall

Fried **rice** (*khao phat*) is the other faithful standby that's guaranteed to feature on menus right across the country. Also popular are cheap, one-dish meals served on a bed of steamed rice, notably *khao kaeng* (with curry), *khao na pet* (with roast duck) and *khao muu daeng* (with red-roasted pork).

▲ Bottles of fish sauce

Desserts

Desserts (*khanom*) don't really figure on most restaurant menus, but a few places offer bowls of *luk taan cheum*, a jellied concoction of lotus or palm seeds floating in a syrup scented with jasmine or other aromatic flowers. Coconut milk is a feature of most other desserts, notably delicious coconut ice cream, *khao niaw mamuang* (sticky rice with mango), and a royal Thai cuisine special of coconut custard (*sangkhayaa*) cooked inside a small pumpkin, whose flesh you can also eat.

▼ Desserts laid out in the Mah Boon Krong Food Centre, Bangkok

Regional dishes

Many of the specialities of **northern Thailand** originated over the border in Burma. One such is *khao soi*, in which both boiled and crispy egg noodles are served with beef, chicken or pork in a curried coconut soup. Also popular around Chiang Mai are thick spicy sausages (*nem*), which are made from minced pork, rice and garlic, left to cure for a few days and then sometimes eaten raw with spicy salad. Somewhat more palatable is the local curry *kaeng hang lay*, made from pork, ginger, garlic, turmeric and tamarind, and a delicious spicy dipping sauce, *nam phrik ong*, made with minced pork, roast tomatoes and lemon grass, and served with crisp cucumber slices.

The crop most suited to the infertile lands of **Isaan** is **sticky rice** (*khao niaw*), which replaces the standard grain as the staple diet for northeasterners. Served in its own special rattan "sticky rice basket" (the Isaan equivalent of the Tupperware lunchbox), it's usually eaten with the fingers, rolled up into small balls and dipped once (double-dipping looks crass to Thai people) into chilli sauces. It's perfect with such spicy local delicacies as *som tam*, a green-papaya salad with garlic, raw chillies, green beans, tomatoes, peanuts and dried shrimps (or fresh crab). Although you'll find basted barbecued chicken on a stick (*kai yaang*) all over Thailand, it originated in Isaan and is especially tasty in its home region. Raw minced pork, beef or chicken is the basis of another popular Isaan and northern dish, *laap*, a salad that's subtly flavoured with mint and lime. A similar northeastern salad is *nam tok*, featuring grilled beef or pork and roasted rice powder, which takes its name, "waterfall", from its refreshing blend of complex tastes.

Aside from putting a greater emphasis on seafood, **southern Thai** cuisine displays a marked Malaysian and Muslim aspect as you near the border. Satays feature more down here, and in Muslim areas you're likely to come across *khao mok kai*, the local version of a biryani: chicken and rice cooked with turmeric and other Indian spices, and served with clear chicken soup. In the south you'll also find many types of *roti*, a kind of pancake sold hot from pushcart griddles and, in its plain form, rolled with sickly sweet condensed milk and sugar. Other versions include savoury *mataba* (with minced chicken or beef) and, served with curry sauce for breakfast, *roti kaeng*. A huge variety of curries are also dished up in the south, many of them substituting shrimp paste for fish sauce. Two of the most distinctive are *kaeng luang*, "yellow curry", featuring fish, turmeric, pineapple, squash, beans and green papaya; and *kaeng tai plaa*, a powerful combination of fish stomach with potatoes, beans, pickled bamboo shoots and more turmeric.

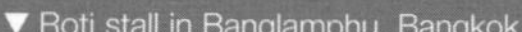

▼ Roti stall in Banglamphu, Bangkok

most northerly inhabitation here is at **Ao Hinwong**, a deeply recessed bay strewn with large boulders and coral reefs, which has a particularly remote, almost desolate air. Nevertheless, *Hin Wong Bungalows* (ⓣ077 456006 or 081 229 4810; ❷–❺) is welcoming and provides good, en-suite accommodation on a steep, grassy slope above the rocks, either in small, older bungalows or attractive, new, wooden affairs with large bathrooms. In the middle of the coast, the dramatic tiered promontory of **Laem Thian** shelters a tiny beach and a colourful reef on its south side. With the headland to itself, *Laem Thian* (ⓣ077 456477 or 081 083 5186, ⓔpingpong_laemthian@hotmail.com; fan ❸, air-con ❻) offers comfy bungalows and cheaper hotel-style rooms, decent food and a secluded, castaway feel.

Laem Thian's coral reef stretches down towards **Ao Ta Note**, a horseshoe inlet sprinkled with boulders and plenty of coarse sand, with excellent snorkelling just north of the bay's mouth. The pick of the half-dozen resorts here is *Ta Note Bay Dive Resort* (ⓣ077 456757–8, ⓔtanotebay@hotmail.com; fan ❹, air-con ❼), with well-designed, en-suite wooden bungalows, set among thick bougainvillea, some enjoying large verandas and views out towards Ko Pha Ngan and Ko Samui. Snorkelling equipment is available at the resort, while the *Black Tip Dive Resort* (ⓣ077 456488, ⓦwww.blacktipdiving.com) offers kayaking, water-skiing and wakeboarding. The last bay carved out of the turtle's shell, **Ao Leuk**, has a well-recessed beach and is serviced by the en-suite bungalows at *Ao Leuk Resort* (ⓣ077 456692; ❷), which enjoy plenty of space and shade, either in the palm grove behind the beach or up the hill to the south. The water is deep enough for good swimming and snorkelling, featuring hard and soft coral gardens.

The south coast

The southeast corner of the island sticks out in a long, thin mole of land, which points towards Shark Island, a colourful diving and snorkelling site just offshore; the headland shelters the sandy beach of **Hat Sai Daeng** on one side if the wind's coming from the northeast, or the rocky cove on the other side if it's blowing from the southwest. Straddling the headland is *New Heaven Huts* (ⓣ087 933 1329, ⓔnewheavenhut@yahoo.com; ❸), a laid-back, well-equipped place with a good kitchen, whose pleasantly idiosyncratic en-suite bungalows enjoy plenty of elbow room and good views. Overlooking **Ao Thian Ok**, the next bay along on the **south coast**, is the same family's *New Heaven Resort*, a scenic restaurant with attractive bungalows and an affiliated, DOC dive school in Ao Chaloke Ban Kao (ⓣ077 456462, ⓦwww.newheavenresort.com). On a beautiful deck perched high on the eastern flank of the Laem Tato headland, classic Thai dishes, including seafood specialities, are dished up in the evening, simpler fare at lunch-time, and yoga classes are held in the morning; the bungalows (❻–❽), on a tree-covered slope running down to a private sandy beach, feature large, cold-water bathrooms and verandas with great views, and include family and air-con rooms. The remote hills between Hat Sai Daeng and Ao Thian Ok provide the spectacular location for a luxurious **spa resort**, *Jamahkiri* (call ⓣ077 456400–1 for reservation and pick-up; free hourly shuttle from their Mae Hat office, next to *Café del Sol* on Mae Hat Square; ⓦwww.jamahkiri.com), which offers saunas, body wraps, facials and massages. There's also a panoramic bar-restaurant and opulent, secluded rooms, a chic mix of Thai and Western design, with red silk furnishings, sunken Jacuzzi baths, air-con, LCD satellite TVs and mini-bars (❾); a swimming pool and fitness centre are planned.

The deep indent of **Ao Chaloke Ban Kao** is protected from the worst of both monsoons, and consequently has seen a fair amount of development, with several dive resorts taking advantage of the large, sheltered, shallow bay. Behind the beach are clinics, ATMs, bike rental shops, stand-alone bars and restaurants, and a branch of Mr J's supermarket and travel agency (see p.679), Mr D's.

Three accommodation options stand out from the crowd here. Run by a friendly bunch, *Viewpoint Bungalows* (Ⓣ077 456666 or 077 456777, Ⓦwww.kohtaoviewpoint.com; ❺) sprawl along the western side of the bay and around the headland beyond, with great sunset views; architect-designed in chic Balinese style, they boast rock bathrooms, mosquito nets and attractive verandas. *Ko Tao Resort* (Ⓣ077 456133–4, Ⓦwww.kotaoresort.com; fan ❼, air-con ❼–❾) makes a fair stab at institutionalized luxury and is worth a splurge, especially if you're considering scuba-diving with its diving school. The cottages and rooms, which have verandas and plain, smart decor (all with TV, some with air-con, hot water, sea views and mini-bars), are ranged around a decent-sized pool and restaurant by the beach, or up the hillside above.

On the east side of the bay, *Freedom Beach Bungalows* (Ⓣ077 456596; fan ❸, air-con ❼) offers a mix of old-style, blue-painted, en-suite huts with sturdy corrugated roofs and small verandas, and smart, new bungalows with air-con and hot water; they dot a spacious slope that leads down to the idyllic white sand of Freedom Beach, a secluded palm-lined spot carved out of the **Laem Tato** headland. Rough signposts will lead you beyond the bungalows for a fifteen-minute walk, the last stretch up a steep hillside to **Jon-Suwan Mountain Viewpoint**, which affords fantastic views, especially at sunset, over the neighbouring bays of Chaloke Ban Kao and Thian Ok and across to Ko Pha Ngan and Ko Samui.

Nakhon Si Thammarat and around

NAKHON SI THAMMARAT, the south's second-largest town, occupies a blind spot in the eyes of most tourists, whose focus is fixed on Ko Samui, 100km to the north. Nakhon's neglect is unfortunate, for it's an absorbing place: the south's major pilgrimage site and home to a huge military base, it's relaxed, self-confident and sophisticated, well known for its excellent cuisine and traditional handicrafts. The stores on Thanon Thachang are especially good for local nielloware (*kruang tom*), household items and jewellery, elegantly patterned in gold or silver often on black, and *yan lipao*, sturdy basketware made from intricately woven fern stems of different colours. Nakhon is also the best place in the country to see how Thai shadow plays work, at Suchart Subsin's workshop.

The town is recorded under the name of Ligor (or Lakhon), the capital of the kingdom of Lankasuka, as early as the second century, and classical dance-drama, *lakhon*, is supposed to have been developed here. Well placed for trade with China and southern India (via an overland route from the port of Trang, on the Andaman Sea), Nakhon was the point through which the Theravada form of Buddhism was imported from Sri Lanka and spread to Sukhothai, the capital of the new Thai state, in the thirteenth century.

Known as *muang phra*, the "city of monks", Nakhon is still the religious capital of the south, and the main centre for **festivals**. The most important of these are the **Tamboon Deuan Sip**, held during the waning of the moon in the tenth lunar month (either September or October), and the **Hae Pha Khun That**, which is held several times a year, but most importantly on Maha Puja (February full moon – see also p.59) and on Visakha Puja (May full moon – see p.59). The purpose of the former is to pay homage to dead relatives and friends; it is believed that during this fifteen-day period all *pret* – ancestors who have been damned to hell – are allowed out to visit the world, and so their relatives perform a merit-making ceremony in the temples, presenting offerings from the first harvest to ease their suffering. A huge ten-day fair takes place at Sanam Na Muang at this time, as well as processions, shadow plays and other theatrical performances. The Hae Pha Khun That also attracts people from all over the south, to pay homage to the relics of the Buddha at Wat Mahathat. The centrepiece of this ceremony is the Pha Phra Bot, a strip of yellow cloth many hundreds of metres long, which is carried in a spectacular procession around the chedi.

Arrival, information and accommodation

Nakhon's **bus terminal** and **train station** are both fairly centrally placed, though the **airport**, served daily by PB Air (at the airport, ⓣ075 313030) and Nok Air (ⓣ1318 or 02 900 9955), is way out to the northwest of the city off the Surat Thani road; air-con minibuses meet arriving flights to ferry passengers to the centre of town. **Share-taxis** congregate towards the south end of Thanon Yomarat, while **air-con minibus** offices around town include one for Sichon, Surat Thani and Ko Samui (via the Don Sak ferry) at the top of Thanon Chamroenwithi, and those for Trang and Hat Yai on Thanon Boh-Ang. On arrival, both share taxis and air-con minibuses should drop you off right at your destination. For getting around Nakhon, small blue **share-songthaews** ply up and down Thanon Ratchadamnoen for B8 a ride.

TAT has an office in a restored 1920s government officers' club on Sanam Na Muang (daily 8.30am–4.30pm; ⓣ075 346515–6, ⓔtatnksri@tat.or.th), which also covers the provinces of Trang and Phatthalung. The main **post office** (Mon–Fri 8.30am–4.30pm, Sat & Sun 8.30am–noon) is nearby on Thanon Ratchadamnoen, opposite the police station, and has international phones upstairs. Klickzone in Bovorn Bazaar on Thanon Ratchadamnoen is a good place to access the **Internet**.

Accommodation

Nakhon has no guest houses or traveller-oriented **accommodation**, but the best of its hotels offer very good value in all price ranges.

Bue Loung Hotel 1487/19 Soi Luang Muang, Thanon Chamroenwithi ⓣ075 341518, ⓕ075 343418. Friendly and central but reasonably quiet; gets the thumbs-up from visiting reps and businessmen, with a choice of fan and cold water or air-con and hot water in basic double or twin rooms with cable TV. ❷

Grand Park Hotel 1204/79 Thanon Pak Nakhon ⓣ075 317666–75, ⓦwww.grandparknakhon.com. If you're looking for something more upmarket in the centre of town, this recently established place is worth considering – it's large, stylish and bright, with air-con, hot water, TV and fridge in every room, and staff are cheery and attentive. ❹

Nakorn Garden Inn 1/4 Thanon Pak Nakhon ⓣ075 313333, ⓕ075 342926. A rustic but sophisticated haven in a three-storey, red-brick building overlooking a tree-shaded yard. Large, attractive rooms come with air-con, hot water, cable TV and mini-bars. ❸

Thai Hotel 1375 Thanon Ratchadamnoen ⓣ075 341509, ⓦwww.thaihotel-nakorn.com. Formerly top of the range in Nakhon – and still boasting some of the trappings, such as liveried doorman – this large institutional high-rise is now offering very good value on its clean, reliable rooms, with fans and cold water or air-con and cold or hot water, all with cable TV. ❷

Thai Lee Hotel 1130 Thanon Ratchadamnoen ⓣ075 356948. For rock-bottom accommodation, the large, plain and reasonably clean rooms here aren't a bad deal (it's worth asking for a room at the back of the hotel to escape the noise of the main street). ❶

Twin Lotus About 3km southeast of the centre at 97/8 Thanon Patanakarn Kukwang ⓣ075 323777, ⓕ075 323821. Gets pride of place in Nakhon – though not for its location; sports five restaurants, a large, attractive outdoor swimming pool and a health club. ❻

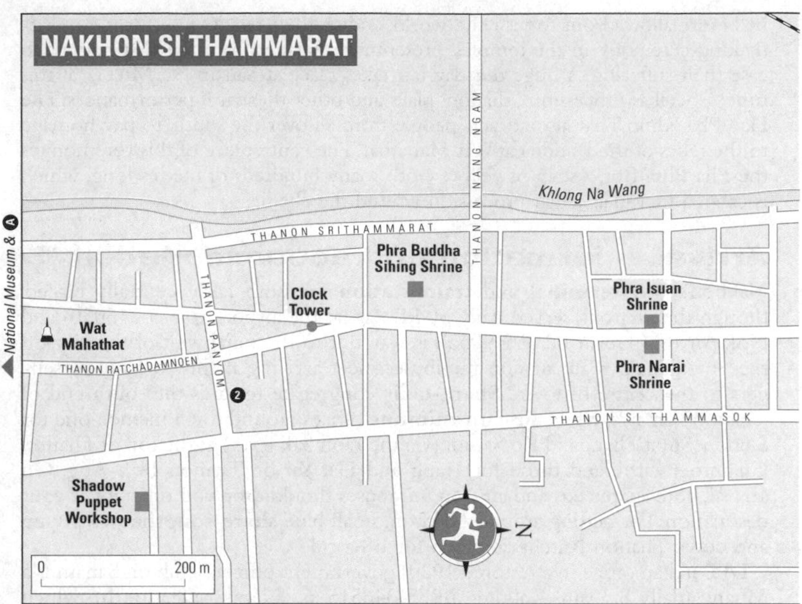

The Town

The **town plan** is simple, but puzzling at first sight: it runs in a straight line for 7km from north to south and is rarely more than a few hundred metres wide, a layout originally dictated by the availability of fresh water. The modern centre for businesses and shops sits at the north end around the train station, with the main day market (to the east of the station on Thanon Pak Nakhon) in this food-conscious city displaying a particularly fascinating array of produce that's best around 8 or 9am. To the south, centred on the elegant, traditional mosque on Thanon Karom, lies the old Muslim quarter; south again is the start of the old city walls, of which few remains can be seen, and the historic centre, with the town's main places of interest now set in a leafy residential area.

Wat Mahathat

Missing out **Wat Mahathat** would be like going to Rome and not visiting St Peter's, for the Buddha relics in the vast chedi make this the south's most important shrine. In the courtyard inside the temple cloisters, which have their main entrance facing Thanon Ratchadamnoen, about 2km south of the modern centre, row upon row of smaller chedis, spiked like bayonets, surround the main chedi, the **Phra Boromathat**. This huge, stubby Sri Lankan bell supports a slender, ringed spire, which is in turn topped by a shiny pinnacle said to be covered in 600kg of gold leaf. According to the chronicles, relics of the Buddha were brought here from Sri Lanka two thousand years ago by an Indian prince and princess and enshrined in a chedi. It's undergone plenty of face-lifts since: an earlier Srivijayan version, a model of which stands at one corner, is encased in the present twelfth-century chedi. The most recent restoration work, funded by donations from all over Thailand, rescued it from collapse, although it still seems to be leaning dangerously to the southeast. Worshippers head for the north side's

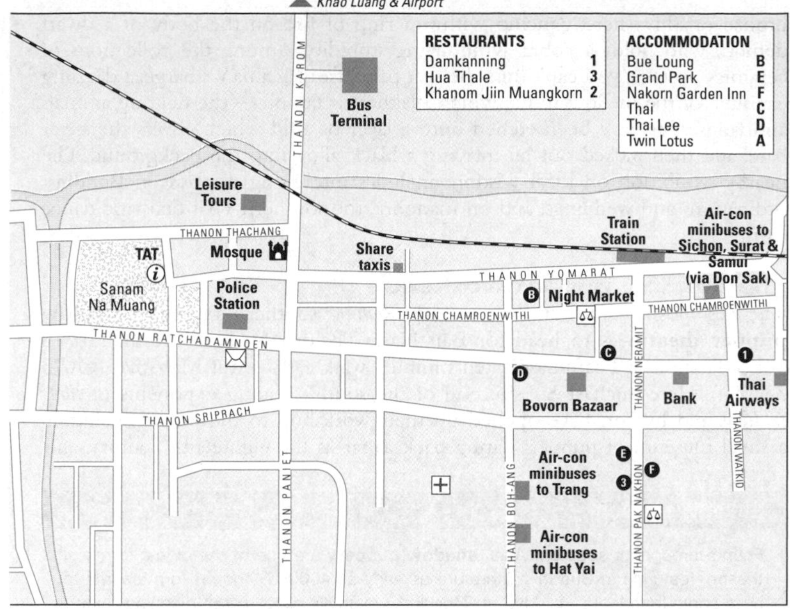

vast enclosed stairway, framed by lions and giants, which they liberally decorate with gold leaf to add to the shrine's radiance and gain some merit.

The **Viharn Kien Museum** (hours irregular, but usually daily 8am–4pm), which extends north from the chedi, is an Aladdin's cave of bric-a-brac, said to house fifty thousand artefacts donated by worshippers, ranging from ships made out of seashells to gold and silver models of the Bodhi Tree. At the entrance to the museum, you'll pass the Phra Puay, an image of the Buddha giving a gesture of reassurance. Women pray to the image when they want to have children, and the lucky ones return to give thanks and to leave photos of their chubby progeny.

Outside the cloister to the south is the eighteenth-century **Viharn Luang**, raised on elegant slanting columns, a beautiful example of Ayutthayan architecture. The interior is austere at ground level, but the red coffered ceiling shines with carved and gilded stars and lotus blooms. In the spacious grounds on the viharn's south side, cheerful, inexpensive stalls peddle local handicrafts such as shadow puppets, bronze and basketware.

The National Museum

Ten minutes' walk south again from Wat Mahathat, the **National Museum** (Wed–Sun 9am–4pm; B30) houses a small but diverse collection, mostly of artefacts from southern Thailand. In the prehistory room downstairs, look out for the two impressive ceremonial bronze kettledrums dating from the fifth century BC, one of them topped with chunky frogs (the local frogs are said to be the biggest in Thailand and a prized delicacy). Also on the ground floor are some interesting Hindu finds, including several stone lingams from the seventh to ninth centuries AD and later bronze statues of Ganesh, the elephant-headed god of wisdom and the arts. Look out especially for a vivacious, well-preserved bronze of Shiva here, dancing within a ring of fire on the body of a dwarf demon, who holds a cobra symbolizing stupidity. Among the collections of ceramics upstairs, you can't miss the seat panel from Rama V's barge, a dazzling example of the nielloware for which Nakhon is famous – the delicate animals and landscapes have been etched onto a layer of gold which covers the silver base, and then picked out by inlaying a black alloy into the background. The nearby exhibition on local wisdom includes interesting displays on Buddhist ordinations and weddings, and on manohra, the southern Thai dramatic dance form.

The shadow puppet workshop

The best possible introduction to *nang thalung*, southern Thailand's **shadow puppet theatre**, is to head for Ban Nang Thalung Suchart Subsin, 110/18 Soi 3, Thanon Si Thammasok, ten minutes' walk east of Wat Mahathat (ⓣ075 346394). Here Suchart Subsin, one of the south's leading exponents of *nang thalung*, and his son have opened up their workshop to the public, including a small museum of puppets dating back as far as the eighteenth century, and,

Shadow puppets

Found throughout southern Asia, **shadow puppets** are one of the oldest forms of theatre, featuring in Buddhist literature as early as 400 BC. The art form seems to have come from India, via Java, to Thailand, where it's called *nang*, meaning "hide": the puppets are made from the skins of water buffalo or cows, which are softened in water, then pounded until almost transparent, before being carved and painted to represent the characters of the play. The puppets are then manipulated on bamboo rods in front of a bright light, to project their image onto a large white screen, while the story is narrated to the audience.

The grander version of the art, **nang yai** – "big hide", so called because the figures are life-size – deals only with the *Ramayana* story (see box on p.61). It's known to have been part of the entertainment at official ceremonies in the Ayutthayan period, but has now almost died out. The more populist version, **nang thalung** – *thalung* is probably a shortening of the town name, Phatthalung (which is just down the road from Nakhon), where this version of the art form is said to have originated – is also in decline now: performances are generally limited to temple festivals, marriages, funerals and ordinations, lasting usually from 9pm to dawn. As well as working the sixty-centimetre-high *nang thalung* puppets, the puppet master narrates the story, impersonates the characters, chants and cracks jokes to the accompaniment of flutes, fiddles and percussion instruments. Not surprisingly, in view of this virtuoso semi-improvised display, puppet masters are esteemed as possessed geniuses by their public.

At big festivals, companies often perform the *Ramayana*, sometimes in competition with each other; at smaller events they put on more down-to-earth stories, with stock characters such as the jokers Yor Thong, an angry man with a pot belly and a sword, and Kaew Kop, a man with a frog's head. Yogi, a wizard and teacher, is thought to protect the puppet master and his company from evil spirits with his magic, so he is always the first puppet on at the beginning of every performance.

In an attempt to halt their decline as a form of popular entertainment, the puppet companies are now incorporating modern instruments and characters in modern dress into their shows, and are boosting the love element in their stories. They're fighting a battle they can't win against television and cinemas, although at least the debt owed to shadow puppets has been acknowledged – *nang* has become the Thai word for "movie".

△The Phra Buddha Sihing

for a small fee (usually around B100 per person), they'll show you a few scenes from a shadow play in the small open-air theatre. You can also see the intricate process of making the leather puppets and can buy the finished products as souvenirs: puppets sold here are of much better quality and design than those usually found on southern Thailand's souvenir stalls.

The Phra Buddha Sihing shrine

In the chapel of the provincial administration complex on Thanon Ratchadamnoen sits the **Phra Buddha Sihing** statue (Mon–Fri 9am–noon & 1–4pm), which according to legend was magically created in Sri Lanka in the second century. In the thirteenth century it was sent by ship to the king of Sukhothai, but the vessel sank and the image miraculously floated on a plank to Nakhon. Two other images, one in the National Museum in Bangkok, one in Wat Phra Singh in Chiang Mai, claim to be the authentic Phra Buddha Sihing, but none of the three is in the Sri Lankan style, so they are all probably derived from a lost original. Although similar to the other two in size and shape, the image in Nakhon has a style unique to this area, distinguished by the heavily pleated flap of its robe over the left shoulder, a beaky nose and harsh features, which sit uneasily on the short, corpulent body. The image's plumpness has given the style the name *khanom tom* – "banana and rice pudding".

Eating and drinking

Nakhon is a great place for inexpensive **food**, not least at the busy, colourful night market on Thanon Chamroenwithi near the *Bue Loung Hotel*. If you're looking for somewhere to **drink**, head for *Rock 99*, a bar-restaurant with outdoor tables in the Bovorn Bazaar that's popular with Nakhon's sprinkling of expats.

Damkanning On the corner of Thanon Watkid and Thanon Ratchadamnoen. A decent Thai-Chinese fallback in the evening, one of several affordable, popular restaurants with pavement tables in the area.

Hao Coffee In the Bovorn Bazaar, Thanon Ratchadamnoen. Popular place modelled on an old Chinese-style coffee shop, packed full of ageing violins, clocks and other antiques. Offers a wide selection of Thai dishes, cakes teas and coffees, including Thai filter coffee and delicious iced capuccinos. Daytime only.

Hua Thale Thanon Pak Nakhon, opposite the *Nakorn Garden Inn*. Nakhon's best restaurant, renowned among locals for its excellent, varied and inexpensive seafood. Plain and very clean, with an open kitchen and the day's catch displayed out front and relaxing patio tables and an air-con room at the back. Recommended dishes include whole baked fish, *yam het ku nu*, white mushroom salad with prawns and cashews, and *hoy meng pho op mordin*, large green mussels in a delicious herb soup containing lemon grass, basil and mint. Daily 4–10pm.

Khanom Jiin Muangkorn Thanon Panyom, near Wat Mahathat. Justly famous, inexpensive outdoor restaurant dishing up one of the local specialities, *khanom jiin*, noodles topped with hot, sweet or fishy sauce served with *pak ruam*, a platter of crispy raw vegetables. Lunchtimes only.

Krua Nakhon In the Bovorn Bazaar, Thanon Ratchadamnoen. A big, rustic pavilion with good *khanom jiin* and other cheap local dishes: *kaeng som*, a mild yellow curry; *kaeng tai plaa*, fish stomach curry; *khao yam*, a delicious southern salad of rice and vegetables; and various *khanom wan*, coconut milk puddings. Lunchtimes only.

Khao Luang National Park

Rising to the west of Nakhon Si Thammarat and temptingly visible from all over town, is 1835-metre-high **Khao Luang**, southern Thailand's highest mountain. A huge national park encompasses Khao Luang's jagged green peaks, beautiful streams with numerous waterfalls, tropical rainforest and fruit orchards, as well as the source of the Tapi River, one of the peninsula's main waterways, which flows into the Gulf of Thailand at Surat Thani. **Fauna** here include macaques, musk deer, civets, binturongs, as well as more difficult to see Malayan tapirs and serows, plus over two hundred bird species. There's an astonishing diversity of **flora** too, notably rhododendrons and begonias, dense mosses, ferns and lichens, plus more than three hundred species of both ground-growing and epiphytic orchids, some of which are unique to the park. The best time to visit is after the rainy season, from January onwards, when there should still be a decent flow in the waterfalls, but the trails will be dry and the leeches not so bad. However, the park's most distinguishing feature for visitors is probably its difficulty of access: main roads run around the 570-square-kilometre park with spurs into some of the waterfalls, but there are no roads across the park and very sparse public transport along the spur roads. Only **Krung Ching Waterfall**, one of Thailand's most spectacular, really justifies the hassle of getting there.

Before heading off to Khao Luang, be sure to drop into Nakhon's TAT office for a useful park **brochure**, with a sketch map and sketchy details of the walking routes to Krung Ching waterfall and to the peak itself. For the latter, which begins at Ban Khiriwong on the southeast side of the park and involves at least one night camping on the mountain, contact the Ban Khiriwong Ecotourism Club (Ⓣ075 533113), who can arrange a trek to the peak, including meals and guides. Irregular **songthaews** on the main roads around the park and to Ban Khiriwong congregate on and around Thanon Chamroenwithi south of the *Bue Loung Hotel* in Nakhon. Leisure Tours, 921/10 Thanon Thachang (Ⓣ075 356829 or 086 940 6400), rents **motorbikes** (B150/day), and pricey air-conditioned **minibuses with drivers** are available from Muang Korn Travel, 1242/67 Thanon Boh-Ang (Ⓣ075 356574; B1800/day plus petrol); otherwise you might try doing a deal with a share-taxi driver at the bottom of Thanon Yomarat to take you to the park.

Krung Ching

A trip to **Krung Ching**, a nine-tier waterfall on the north side of the park, makes for a highly satisfying day out, with a mostly paved nature trail taking you through dense, steamy jungle to the most beautiful, third tier. The easiest way to **get there** from Nakhon with your own transport is to head north on Highway 401 towards Surat Thani, turning west at Tha Sala on to Highway 4140, then north again at Ban Nopphitam on to Highway 4186, before heading south from Ban Huai Phan on Highway 4188, the spur road to Ban Phitham and the Krung Ching park office, a total journey of about 70km. Songthaews will get you from Nakhon to Ban Huai Phan in about an hour, but you'd then have to hitch the last 13km. Two- to six-person bungalows, most with hot water, are available at the park office (B200–1800); camping is free if you bring your own tent. There's a sporadically open canteen, and an informal shop selling snacks and drinks.

The shady four-kilometre **trail** to the dramatic main fall is very steep in parts, so you should allow four hours at least there and back. On the way you'll pass giant ferns, including a variety known as *maha sadam*, the largest fern in the world, gnarled banyan trees, forests of mangosteen and beautiful, thick stands of bamboo. You're bound to see colourful birds and insects, but you may well only hear macaques and other mammals. At the end, a long, stepped descent brings you to a perfectly positioned wooden platform with fantastic views of the forty-metre fall; here you can see how, shrouded in thick spray, it earns its Thai name, Fon Saen Ha, meaning "thousands of rainfalls".

Sichon

The coast north from Nakhon is dotted with small, Thai-orientated beach resorts, none of which can match the Ko Samui archipelago, in the Gulf beyond, for looks or facilities. However, if you're searching for a quiet, low-key antidote to Samui's Western-style commercialism, the most interesting of these resorts, **SICHON**, might be just the place.

Buses, air-con minibuses and share-taxis make the 65-kilometre journey north from Nakhon along the Surat Thani road to Talat Sichon, as the town's unpromising modern centre, with a few facilities such as banks and plenty of motorbike taxis, is known. This half-hearted, built-up area sprawls lazily eastwards for 3km to Pak Nam Sichon, a lively and scenic fishing port at the mouth of the eponymous river. Here, when they're not fishing in the bay, brightly coloured boats of all sizes draw up at the docks, backed by low-slung traditional wooden shophouses, the angular hills around Khanom beyond and, in the far distance, Ko Samui. About 1km south of the river mouth, **Hat Sichon** (aka Hat Hin Ngarm) begins, a pretty crescent bay of shelving white sand ending in a tree-tufted, rocky promontory. The beach is home to the best-value accommodation option in the area, *Prasarnsuk Villa* (ⓣ075 335562, ⓦwww.pssresort.com; fan ❹, air-con ❺), a neatly organized, welcoming place with a good, popular restaurant that stretches to a few tables and umbrellas on the beach. Amid spacious lawns, trees and flowers, bungalows range from decent, fan-cooled, en-suite affairs with verandas to suites with air-con, hot water, fridge and TV. The next beach south, **Hat Piti**, is not quite so attractive, a long, straight, deserted stretch of white sand backed by palm trees. But if you want a few more facilities, this is where to come: *Piti Resort* (ⓣ075 335301–4, ⓦwww.pitiresort.com; ❼), 2km south of *Prasarnsuk*, can offer a small swimming pool, a fitness room and a tastefully designed beachside restaurant, as well as hot water, air-con, fridge and cable TV in all bungalows and rooms.

Travel details

Trains

Ban Krud to: Bangkok (2 daily; 6hr–7hr 30min); Hua Hin (2 daily; 3hr 30min); Nakhon Pathom (2 daily; 5hr 30min); Phetchaburi (2 daily; 6hr); Prachuap Khiri Khan (2 daily; 30min).
Bang Saphan Yai to: Bangkok (4 daily; 6hr 30min–8hr); Hua Hin (4 daily; 3–4hr); Nakhon Pathom (4 daily; 4hr 35min–6hr); Phetchaburi (3 daily; 4hr–4hr 30min); Prachuap Khiri Khan (4 daily; 20min–1hr).
Cha-am to: Bangkok (12 daily; 3hr 10min–3hr 50min); Chumphon (10 daily; 4–5hr); Hua Hin (11 daily; 25min); Surat Thani (7 daily; 7hr 10min–8hr 25min).
Chumphon to: Bangkok (11 daily; 7hr–9hr 30min); Hua Hin (11 daily; 3hr 30min–5hr); Surat Thani (11 daily; 2hr 5min–4hr).
Hua Hin to: Bangkok (12 daily; 3hr 30min–4hr); Chumphon (11 daily; 3hr 30min–5hr 20min); Prachuap Khiri Khan (9 daily; 2hr 40min–3hr 40min); Surat Thani (11 daily; 5hr 40min–8hr).
Nakhon Si Thammarat to: Bangkok (2 daily; 15–16hr); Chumphon (2 daily; 6hr–6hr 30min); Hua Hin (2 daily; 11hr 30min); Nakhon Pathom (2 daily; 14hr); Surat Thani (Phunphin; 2 daily; 3hr 30min).
Phetchaburi to: Bangkok (8 daily; 2hr 45min–3hr 45min); Cha-am (12 daily; 35min); Chumphon (9 daily; 4hr 30min–6hr 30min); Hua Hin (10 daily; 1hr); Prachuap Khiri Khan (9 daily; 3hr 40min–4hr 10min); Surat Thani (9 daily; 6hr 45min–9hr).
Prachuap Khiri Khan to: Bangkok (9 daily; 4hr 15min–7hr 40min); Nakhon Pathom (9 daily; 4hr 15min–5hr 40min).
Surat Thani (Phunphin) to: Bangkok (11 daily; 9–12hr); Butterworth (Malaysia; 1 daily; 10hr 30min); Chumphon (11 daily; 2–3hr); Hat Yai (5 daily; 4–5hr); Hua Hin (11 daily; 5–8hr); Nakhon Pathom (11 daily; 9hr–10hr 30min); Nakhon Si Thammarat (2 daily; 3hr 30min); Phatthalung (5 daily; 3–4hr); Trang (2 daily; 4hr).

Buses

Cha-am to: Bangkok (every 40min; 2hr 45min–3hr 15min).
Chumphon to: Bangkok (12 daily; 7–9hr); Hat Yai (4 daily; 7hr 30min); Hua Hin (every 40min; 3hr 30min–4hr 30min); Phuket (3 daily; 7hr); Ranong (hourly; 2hr); Surat Thani (every 30min; 2hr 45min).
Hua Hin to: Bangkok (every 40min; 3–4hr); Cha-am (every 30min; 35min); Chumphon (every 40min; 3hr 30min–4hr 30min); Hat Yai (4 daily; 10hr); Krabi (3 daily; 9hr); Phetchaburi (every 30min; 1hr 30min); Phuket (7 daily; 9hr); Pranburi (every 20min; 40min); Surat Thani (4 daily; 7hr).
Ko Samui to: Bangkok (Southern Terminal; 8 daily; 12–13hr); Nakhon Si Thammarat (1 daily; 5hr).
Nakhon Si Thammarat to: Bangkok (Southern Terminal; 11 daily; 12hr); Hat Yai (16 daily; 3hr); Ko Samui (1 daily; 5hr); Krabi (2 daily; 3hr); Phatthalung (7 daily; 3hr); Phuket (7 daily; 8hr); Ranong (1 daily; 6hr); Surat Thani (21 daily; 2hr 30min); Trang (3 daily; 2–3hr).
Phetchaburi to: Bangkok (every 30min; 2hr); Cha-am (every 30 min; 50min); Chumphon (about every 2hr; 5hr–6hr); Hua Hin (every 30 min; 1hr 30min).
Prachuap Khiri Khan to: Bangkok (every 30min; 4–5hr); Chumphon (6 daily; 2–3hr); Hua Hin (every 30min; 1hr 30min–2hr); Phetchaburi (every 30min; 3hr–3hr 30min).
Pranburi to: Bangkok (every 40min; 3hr 30min); Hua Hin (every 20min; 40min).
Surat Thani to: Bangkok (Southern Terminal; 10 daily; 10–11hr); Chumphon (hourly; 3hr 30min); Hat Yai (11 daily; 5hr); Krabi (23 daily; 3–4hr); Nakhon Si Thammarat (21 daily; 2hr 30min); Phang Nga (10 daily; 3hr 30min); Phatthalung (10 daily; 5hr); Phuket (14 daily; 5–6hr); Phunphin (every 10min; 40min); Ranong (9 daily; 4–5hr).

Flights

Hua Hin to: Bangkok (3 daily; 40min).
Ko Samui to: Bangkok (20 daily; 1hr–1hr 30min); Hong Kong (4 weekly; 3hr); Kuala Lumpur, Malaysia (2 weekly; 2hr); Pattaya (2 daily; 1hr); Phuket (2 daily; 50min); Singapore (daily except Tues; 1hr 40min).
Nakhon Si Thammarat to: Bangkok (3–5 daily; 1hr 15min).
Surat Thani to: Bangkok (4 daily; 1hr 10min).

7

Southern Thailand: the Andaman coast

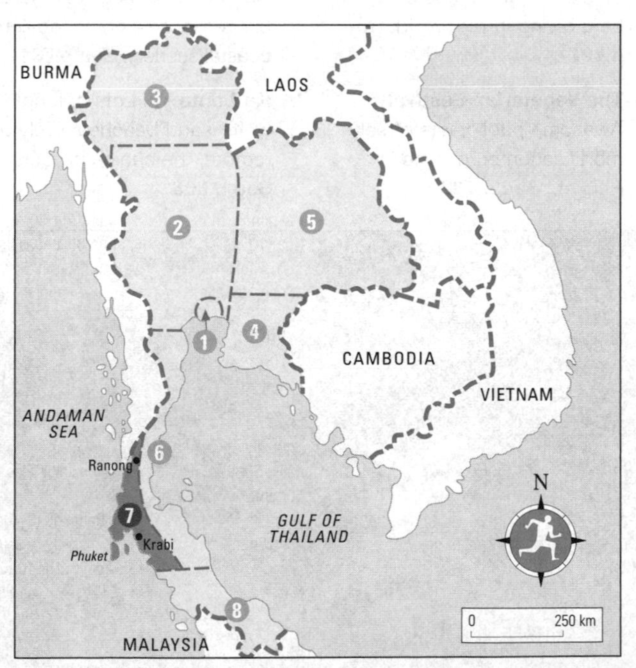

CHAPTER 7

Highlights

* **Island idylls** Tranquillity rules on the uncommercial islands of Ko Phayam, Ko Yao Noi and Ko Jum. See p.706, 761 and 802

* **Khao Sok National Park** Sleep in a treehouse or on a lake, and wake to the sound of hooting gibbons. See p.714

* **Ko Similan** Remote chain of islands with some of the best diving in the world. See p.727

* **The Vegetarian Festival** Awesome public acts of self-mortification on parade in Phuket. See p.738

* **Reefs and wrecks** Dive Thailand's finest underwater sights from Phuket, Ko Phi Phi, Ao Nang or Ko Lanta. See p.750, 794, 789 and 808

* **Sea-canoeing in Ao Phang Nga** The perfect way to explore the limestone karsts and hidden lagoons of this spectacular bay. See p.766

* **Rock-climbing on Laem Phra Nang** Even novices can get a bird's-eye view of the fabulous coastal scenery. See p.781

* **Ko Lanta Yai** Lots of long white-sand beaches: lively or remote, the choice is yours. See p.806

△ Sea-canoeing in Ao Phang Nga

7

Southern Thailand: the Andaman coast

As Highway 4 switches from the east flank of the Thailand peninsula to the **Andaman coast** it enters a markedly different country: nourished by rain nearly all the year round, the vegetation down here is lushly tropical, with forests reaching up to 80m in height, and massive rubber and coconut plantations replacing the rice and sugar-cane fields of central Thailand. Sheer limestone crags spike every horizon and the translucent Andaman Sea harbours the largest **coral reefs** and most rewarding dive spots in the country. This is of course the same sea whose terrifyingly powerful **tsunami** waves battered the coastline in December 2004, killing thousands not only in Thailand but around Asia and even East Africa, and changing countless lives and communities forever. The waves have left many wounds along Thailand's Andaman coast, for more on which see p.722, but with one partial exception all its affected tourist resorts have re-emerged as enjoyable holiday destinations. Now more than ever, locals depend on tourists for their economic survival, and holidaymakers have been returning in their hundreds of thousands to honour that bond.

There's plenty to tempt them. The attractions of the northern Andaman shores are often ignored by those keen to race down to the high-profile honeypots around Phuket and Krabi, but gems up here include the idyllic islands of **Ko Chang** (not to be confused with its larger, more famous namesake off the east coast) and **Ko Phayam**; the awesome, world-class reefs of the **Ko Surin** and **Ko Similan** island chains; and the enjoyable **Khao Sok National Park**, where you can stay on a raft or in a treehouse beneath looming limestone outcrops. Tourism begins in earnest on **Phuket**, Thailand's largest island and a popular place to learn to dive, though the high-rises and consumerist gloss that characterize many of the beaches here don't appeal to everyone. Those in search of a quieter island retreat head across to rural **Ko Yao Noi**, scenically located on the periphery of spectacular **Ao Phang Nga**, whose artfully scattered karst islets make it one of the country's top natural wonders, best appreciated from a sea-canoe. The Andaman coast's second hub is at **Krabi**, springboard for the hugely popular mainland beaches of unexceptional **Ao Nang**, upmarket **Klong Muang** and spectacular **Laem Phra Nang**, and departure point for boats to picturesque but overcrowded **Ko Phi Phi**, low-key **Ko Jum** and long and still lovely **Ko Lanta Yai**.

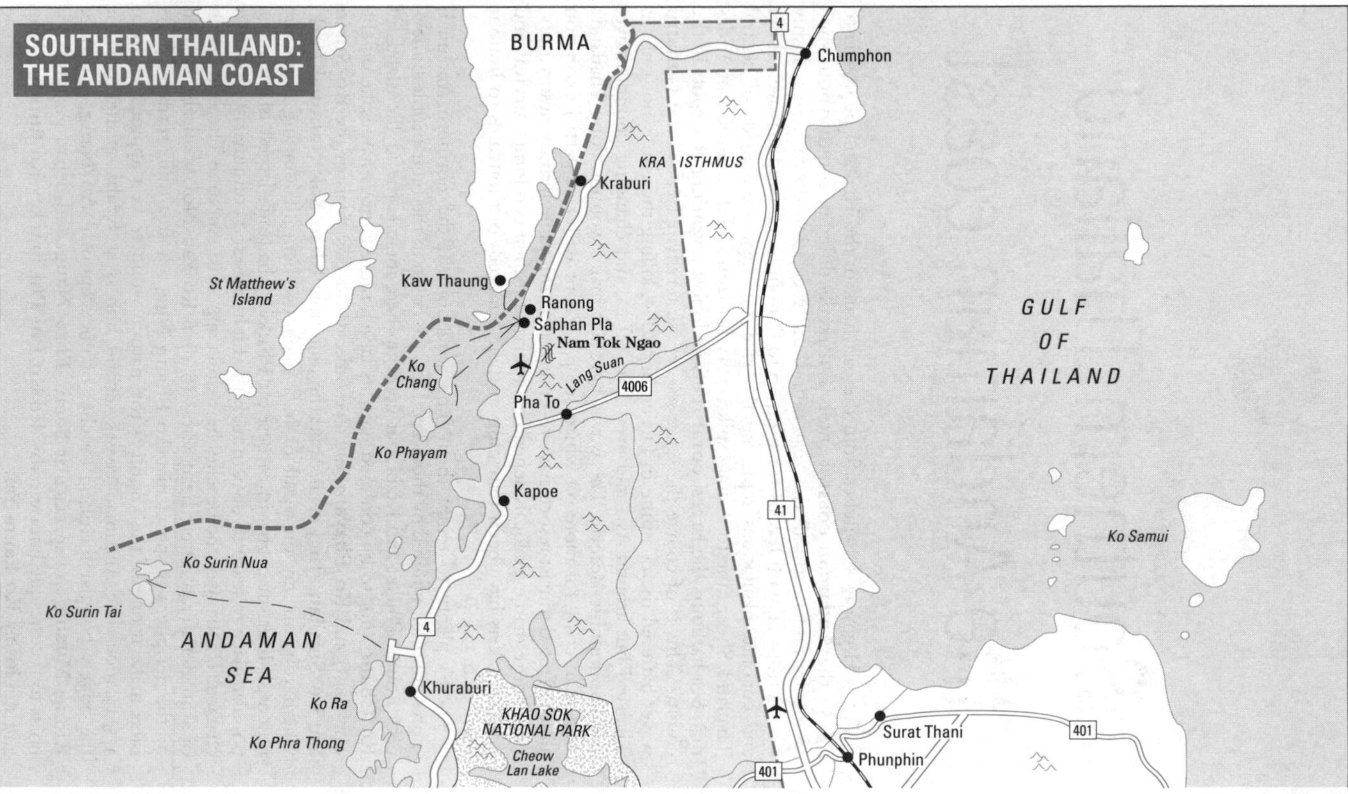
SOUTHERN THAILAND: THE ANDAMAN COAST
BURMA
4
Chumphon
KRA ISTHMUS
Kraburi
St Matthew's Island
Kaw Thaung
Ranong
Saphan Pla
Nam Tok Ngao
GULF OF THAILAND
Ko Chang
Lang Suan
4006
Pha To
Ko Phayam
Kapoe
41
Ko Samui
Ko Surin Nua
Ko Surin Tai
ANDAMAN SEA
Khuraburi
Ko Ra
KHAO SOK NATIONAL PARK
Ko Phra Thong
Cheow Lan Lake
Surat Thani
401
Phunphin

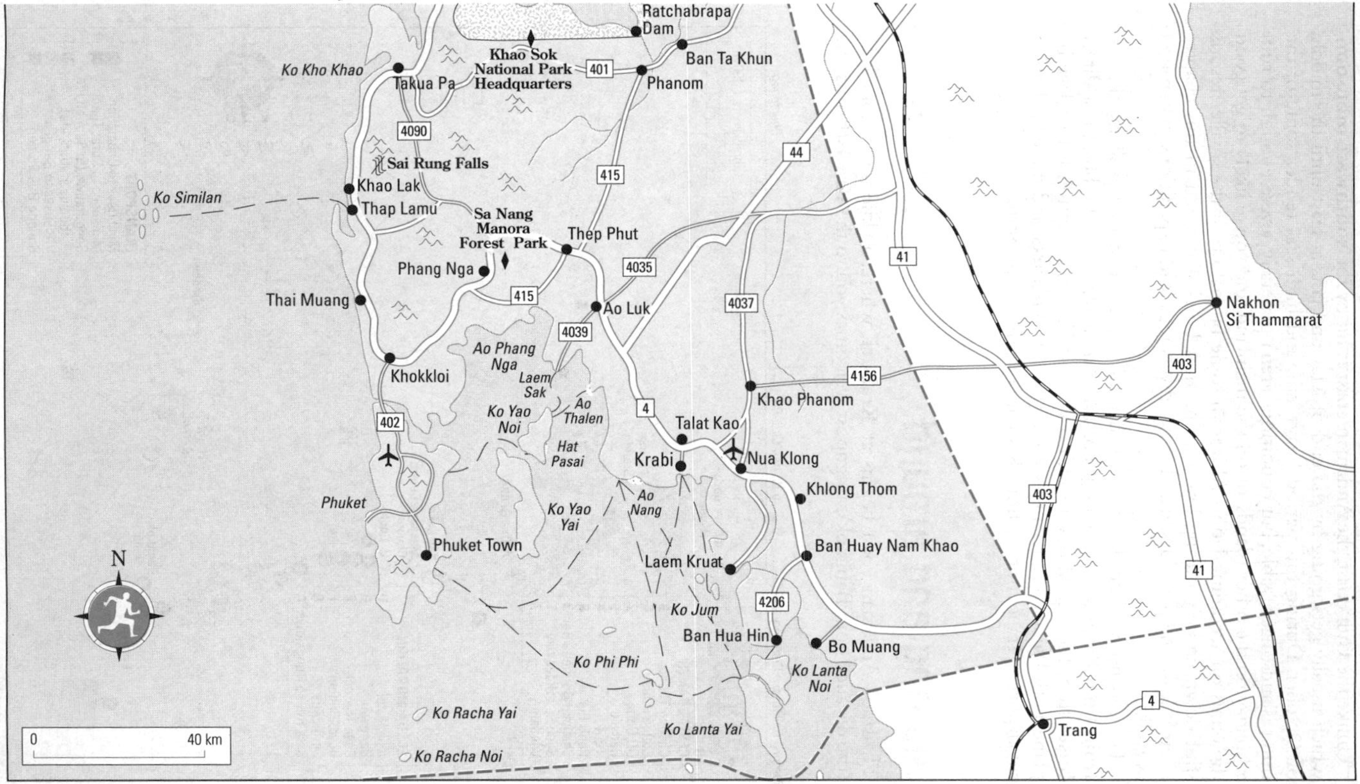

Ratchabrapa Dam
Ban Ta Khun
Khao Sok National Park Headquarters
401
Phanom
Ko Kho Khao
Takua Pa
4090
Sai Rung Falls
415
44
Khao Lak
Ko Similan
Thap Lamu
Sa Nang Manora Forest Park
Thep Phut
4035
41
Phang Nga
Thai Muang
415
Ao Luk
4037
Nakhon Si Thammarat
4039
Ao Phang Nga
Laem Sak
Khokkloi
4156
403
Ao Thalen
Ko Yao Noi
4
Khao Phanom
402
Talat Kao
Hat Pasai
Krabi
Nua Klong
Khlong Thom
Phuket
Ao Nang
Ko Yao Yai
403
Phuket Town
Ban Huay Nam Khao
Laem Kruat
41
N
4206
Ko Jum
Ban Hua Hin
Bo Muang
Ko Phi Phi
Ko Lanta Noi
Ko Racha Yai
4
0 40 km
Ko Lanta Yai
Trang
Ko Racha Noi

Unlike the Gulf coast, the Andaman coast is hit by the **southwest monsoon**, which usually gets going by the end of May and lasts at least until the middle of October. During this period heavy rain and high seas render some of the outer islands inaccessible, but conditions aren't generally severe enough to ruin a holiday on the other islands, or on the mainland, and you're likely to get good discounts on accommodation. Although some bungalows at the smaller resorts shut down entirely during low season, most beaches covered in this chapter keep at least one place open, and many dive shops lead expeditions year-round as well.

There is no rail line down the Andaman coast, but many travellers take the **train** from Bangkok to the Gulf coast and then nip across by bus; most direct **buses** from the capital travel south overnight. The faster option is to arrive by plane: both Phuket and Krabi have international **airports**, and there's a domestic airport at Trang, not far from Ko Lanta in the deep south.

Ranong and around

Thailand's Andaman coast begins at **Kraburi**, where, at kilometre-stone 545 (the distance from Bangkok), a signpost welcomes you to the **Kra Isthmus**, the

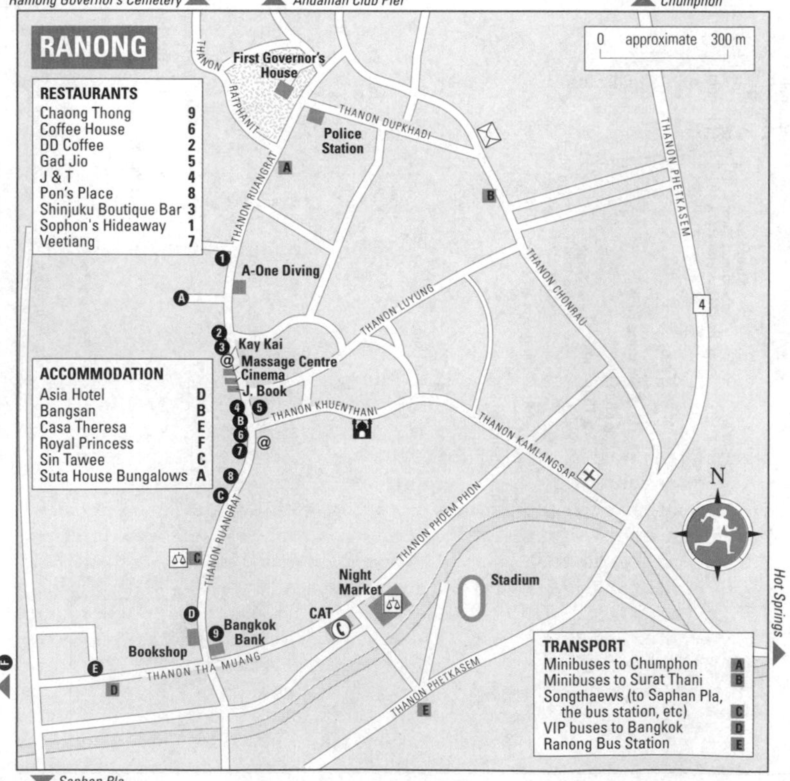

narrowest part of peninsular Thailand. At this point just 22km separates the Gulf of Thailand from the mangrove-fringed inlet where the Chan River flows into the Andaman Sea, west of which lies the southernmost tip of mainland Burma, Kaw Thaung (aka Victoria Point). Ever since the seventeenth century, Thai governments and foreign investors have been keenly interested in this slender strip of land, envisaging the creation of an Asian Suez canal that would cut some 1500km off shipping routes between the Indian Ocean (Andaman Sea) and the South China Sea (the Gulf of Thailand). Despite a number of detailed proposals, no agreement has yet been reached, not least because of the political implications of such a waterway: quite apart from accentuating the divide between prosperous southern Thailand and the rest of the country, it would vastly reduce Singapore's role in the international shipping industry.

Seventy kilometres south of the isthmus, the channel widens out at the provincial capital of **Ranong**, which thrives on its proximity to Burma. Thai tourists have been coming here for years, to savour the health-giving properties of the local spring water, but foreign holidaymakers have only recently discovered that Ranong is a useful departure-point for the delightful nearby islands of **Ko Chang**, which appeals to those who prefer paraffin lamps and early nights, and **Ko Phayam**, which attracts a more sociable crowd. The other reason to stop off in Ranong is to make a day-trip to the Burmese town of **Kaw Thaung** and acquire a new thirty-day Thai tourist **visa** into the bargain – an option that's popular with Phuket expats.

Ranong is the capital of Thailand's wettest province, which soaks up over 5000mm of rain every year – a fact you'll undoubtedly experience first hand if you linger in the region. The landscape to the south of Ranong town is particularly lush, and any journey along Highway 4 will whizz you between waterfall-streaked hills to the east and mangrove swamps, rubber plantations and casuarina groves to the west; much of this coastal strip is preserved as **Laem Son National Park**.

Ranong Town

Despite being the wettest town in the country, **Ranong** (Ⓦ www.ranong.go.th) has a pleasing buzz about it, fuelled by the mix of Burmese, Thai, Chinese and Malay inhabitants. As with most border areas, however, there's also a flourishing illegal trade operating out of Ranong – in amphetamines, guns and labour, allegedly – not to mention the inevitable tensions over international fishing rights, which sometimes end in shoot-outs, though the closest you're likely to get to any of these activities is reading about them in the *Bangkok Post*.

Ranong's history is closely associated with its most famous son, **Khaw Soo Cheang**, a poor Chinese emigrant who was to become the first governor of Ranong province and a man so respected that politicians continue to pay public homage at his grave more than a century after his death. Khaw Soo Cheang emigrated from China in 1810 a penniless peasant. After six years in Penang he moved to southern Thailand, where he became enormously successful both in trading with Penang, and in tin-mining. By the 1840s he had been granted the sole right to operate tin mines in the Ranong area and, admired by the government and Rama IV for his ruthlessness and commercial acuity, was appointed the first governor of Ranong province in 1854. He proved his mettle once more in Rama V's reign, when in 1876 he quashed a violent rebellion by maltreated immigrant tin-miners, and was duly rewarded with a title equivalent to Raja of Ranong. Following Khaw Soo Cheang's death in 1882, his sons were also ennobled by the king and made governors of Ranong and other southern provinces. The family was honoured again in 1916 when Rama VI decreed that all descendants of Khaw Soo Cheang living in Thailand should have the surname "na Ranong" ("of Ranong"), an aristocratic title that still commands respect today. Little now remains of Khaw Soo Cheang's house, but in its grounds, west off Thanon Ruangrat on the northern edge of town, descendants have established a shrine and small museum, the **First Governor's House** (Nai Khai Ranong; daily 9am–4.30pm; free), to the Khaw clan, with photos, newspaper cuttings and other memorabilia on display. Follow either road running north from near the First Governor's House, in the direction of the Andaman Club pier, for about 4km to reach his burial site at the **Ranong Governor's Cemetery**, where Chinese-style horseshoe-shaped graves and a series of symbolic stone statues stand proud at the foot of the expansive, tree-lined, grassy hill donated to Khaw Soo Cheang for this purpose by a grateful Rama V; songthaews from the Thanon Ruangrat market should get you there in about 15 minutes.

The **geothermal springs** (daily 8am–5pm; B10) so favoured by Thai tourists are the focus of Raksawarin Park, about 3km east of the central Thanon Ruangrat market and accessible on songthaew #2 or by motorbike taxi. At the park, you can buy eggs to boil in the sulphurous 65°C water, or paddle in the cooler pools that have been siphoned off from the main springs. To properly appreciate the springs you need to soak in the mineral water, either at the Jacuzzis in the Siam Hot Spa Ranong complex just across the road (daily 6.30am–10pm), which also offers spa, massage and steam treatments, or in the Jacuzzis at *Royal Princess Hotel* on the western edge of town (daily 4–9pm; B60 for non-guests).

If you haven't had enough of water features, you could make a trip out of town to the impressive **Nam Tok Ngao**, an enormous waterfall 12km south of Ranong, which cascades almost all the way down the eastern hillside in full view of Highway 4. It's part of Nam Tok Ngao National Park (Ⓦwww.dnp.go.th/National_park.asp; B200). Any south-bound bus will drop you there. Another enjoyable day out would be to head into the interior for a day's organized rafting at **Pha To**, 51km east of Ranong, off Route 4006 to Chumphon (see p.632 for details); Runs n' Roses tours and accommodation at Pha To (Ⓦwww.runsroses.com) can be booked through Ranong tour agencies.

Arrival, transport and information

All Andaman-coast **buses** travelling between Bangkok or Chumphon and Khuraburi, Takua Pa, Phuket or Krabi stop briefly at Ranong's **bus station** on Highway 4 (Thanon Phetkasem), 1500m southeast of the central market. Coming from Khao Sok or Surat Thani, you'll usually need to change buses at Takua Pa, though there is also a private minibus service to and from Surat Thani (4 daily; 3hr; B130), which uses a depot on Thanon Chonrau. There is a direct government bus service from **Chumphon** (2–3hr), as well as a faster private minibus service (hourly 6am–5pm; 2hr; B100) that operates from a terminal at the northern end of Thanon Ruangrat, so from Bangkok it's often more comfortable to take a night **train** to Chumphon and then change on to a bus or minibus. There are currently no scheduled **flights** in or out of Ranong airport, which is 20km south of Ranong on Highway 4, but Phuket Airlines (Ⓣ077 824591, Ⓦwww.phutairlines.com) may resume its Bangkok–Ranong operations.

City songthaews serve major destinations in and around Ranong and most of them start from and terminate in front of the Thanon Ruangrat market, close to town-centre hotels. Many songthaews have their destinations written in English on the side, and most charge B10–15 per ride. Several songthaews pass

Ranong bus station, including one that runs to the Thanon Ruangrat hotels and day market, and another that shuttles between the bus station and the port area at Saphan Pla, 5km to the southwest, where you pick up boats to Kaw Thaung, Ko Chang and Ko Phayam; another songthaew runs direct from the market on Thanon Ruangrat to the Saphan Pla port area.

The best source of **tourist information** in town is the ever helpful Pon at *Pon's Place* restaurant and tour agency at 129 Thanon Ruangrat (daily 7.30am–9pm; ⓣ081 597 4549, ⓔponplace@hotmail.com), where you can also book a visa run to Burma and back (B650, including the visa), arrange tours of the local area (weekends only), book accommodation on Ko Chang and Ko Phayam, rent bicycles (B80/day), motorbikes (B200/day) and cars (B1200–1500/day), and buy air, bus and (Chumphon) train tickets. Kay Kai Internet centre and restaurant further north on Thanon Ruangrat also rents out motorbikes for B200 per day.

Accommodation

Most travellers linger in Ranong for just one night, but there's a reasonable spread of accommodation to choose from.

Asia Hotel 39/9 Thanon Ruangrat ⓣ077 811113. Painted pale blue inside and out, this very central, typical Thai-Chinese hotel has large and mostly quite spruce fan and air-con rooms, all of them en suite. Fan ❷, air-con ❹

Bangsan 225 Thanon Ruangrat ⓣ089 727 4334, ⓔbangsanbar@chaiyo.com. Cheap and funky guest house occupying the floor above the sixties-styled *TV Bar*. Rooms share bathrooms and are simple but cheerful despite mostly having no windows. It's a popular spot so call ahead. ❶

Casa Theresa 119/18 Thanon Tha Muang ⓣ077 811135, ⓦwww.casatheresa.com. Set around a small garden and open-sided lobby area, this is a quiet guest house, located behind a streetfront bakery shop (which also serves fresh coffee). It's a bit of a walk from the market, but handy for transport to Saphan Pla. All but the cheapest rooms have bathrooms, though not all the cheaper air-con rooms have windows; the very comfortable VIP options, huge and with air-con and TV, are the best value. Fan ❷, air-con without window ❸, VIP ❺

Royal Princess 41/144 Thanon Tha Muang ⓣ077 835240, ⓦranong.royalprincess.com. Modern chain hotel that's the most luxurious in town. As well as typical upmarket air-con rooms, the hotel has an outdoor Jacuzzi pool filled with local spa water, a swimming pool and massage centre. ❻–❽

Sin Tawee 81/1 Thanon Ruangrat ⓣ077 811213. Central place, of a similar style to the *Asia Hotel* but cheaper and shabbier. There's a choice of en-suite accommodation ranging from small fan rooms to larger versions with TV, and air-con options at the top end. Fan ❶, air-con ❷

Suta House Bungalows Thanon Ruangrat ⓣ077 832707. Set 100m off the main road this is an unusual find in a city as it comprises a row of small but well-maintained air-con bungalows, all of them with TV. It also has some fan rooms in a low-rise building, all of which have private bathrooms though they are not en suite. Fills up fast so reserve ahead. Fan rooms ❷, air-con bungalows ❸

Eating and drinking

Ranong's ethnic diversity ensures an ample range of **eating** options, and a stroll up Thanon Ruangrat will take you past Muslim foodstalls and Chinese pastry shops as well as a small but typically Thai night market. A bigger night market convenes at dusk just east of the CAT phone office off Thanon Phoem Phon. There's a small nightlife zone of bars on Thanon Ruangrat around the Thanon Luyung junction.

Chaong Thong 8–10 Thanon Ruangrat. Choose from a long and varied selection of inexpensive dishes that includes Spanish omelette, shrimp curry and lemon-grass tea, as well as lots of veggie options and hearty breakfasts. Closed Sun.

Coffee House 173 Thanon Ruangrat. Managed by the same French-Thai family who run *Aow Yai Bungalows* on Ko Phayam, this is the place for filled baguettes (from B50), pancakes, cheap fried rice (B30) – and coffee. You can also book accommodation at *Aow Yai Bungalows* and speedboats to Ko Phayam here.

DD Coffee 299 Thanon Ruangrat. Despite the name, this place only gets going in the evening when locals pack the outdoor, streetside terrace for an evening of whisky-drinking and chat.

Gad Jio Thanon Ruangrat. Expat-oriented bar-restaurant serving mid-priced burgers, steaks and pizzas.

J & T Thanon Ruangrat. Very popular family café serving cheap Thai fare (B20–50), including stir-fries, soups, salads and over-rice dishes.

Pon's Place Thanon Ruangrat. Opens at 7.30am for breakfast and continues dishing out cheap farang-oriented food and travel advice until 9pm.

Shinjuku Boutique Bar 297 Thanon Ruangrat. Another local favourite drinking spot, also with sports TV.

Sophon's Hideaway Thanon Ruangrat. Relaxed place wreathed in greenery that's a favourite with local expats both for its good food, including sour'n spicy fish curry (B65) and fried pork spare ribs (B80), and cheap beer, as well as for its lounge area, which shows international sports on its TV and has a pool table.

Veetiang 159 Thanon Ruangrat. Boasts an extensive and inexpensive menu covering all manner of seafood cooked to Thai and Chinese recipes, as well as standard over-rice dishes.

Listings

Banks and exchange There's a Bangkok Bank with an ATM and an exchange counter at the southern end of Thanon Ruangrat, and several other banks with ATMs within a few hundred metres' walk, west of the junction with Thanon Tha Muang.

Bookshops English-language books and newspapers from the bookstore at 35-37 Thanon Ruangrat. J Book opposite the Thanon Luyung junction on Thanon Ruangrat (daily noon-9pm) has a few second-hand English books for rent and sale.

Dive centre Ko Phayam's A-One Diving has an office at 256 Thanon Ruangrat ⓣ 077 832984, ⓦ www.a-one-diving.com.

Emergencies The police station is Dupkhadi ⓣ 077 811173.

Hospital The Thonburi-Ranong hospital is at 41/142 Thanon Tha Muang ⓣ 077 834214.

Immigration office 5km out of town in Saphan Pla; for details on how to extend or renew your visa here see opposite.

Internet access At several places north of the *Sin Tawee* hotel on Thanon Ruangrat, including Kay Kai, and Catnet at the CAT international phone office (Mon–Fri 8.30am–4.30pm) on Thanon Tha Muang.

Mail At the GPO on Thanon Chonrau, 1.5km northeast of the central market. You can buy stamps more centrally, at the pharmacy at 31 Thanon Ruangrat, south of the *Asia Hotel*.

Massage The massage centre next to the cinema on Thanon Ruangrat offers everything from Thai massage to hot-stone massage (B250–1100).

Telephones The CAT international phone office is on Thanon Tha Muang (Mon–Fri 8.30am–4.30pm).

Into Burma: visa runs and Kaw Thaung (Ko Song)

The southernmost tip of Burma – known as **Kaw Thaung** in Burmese, Ko Song in Thai, and Victoria Point when it was a British colony – lies just a few kilometres west of Ranong across the Chan River estuary, and is easily reached by longtail boat from Saphan Pla fishing port, 5km southwest of Ranong town centre on the Thai side of the border. It's quite straightforward for foreign tourists to **enter Burma** at this point, and nipping across the border and back is a popular way of getting a new thirty-day Thai tourist visa – though it does mean you're giving your money to the Burmese military regime. You can either do it independently, as described below, or you can make use of one of the numerous "**visa run**" **services** advertised all over town, including at *Pon's Place*; this might cost you a bit more (B650 including visa) but will save you time. Most visa-run operators use the Saphan Pla route into Burma, but there is a more luxurious alternative which entails using the fast **Andaman Club boat** (ⓣ 077 830461; 15 daily from 7am–11.50pm; 20 min; B650 return including visa, but you must have at least 3 days remaining on your current Thai visa), which departs from the Andaman Club pier 5km north of Ranong's town centre and travels to and from the swanky *Andaman Club* hotel (Ⓣ081 894 2583, Ⓦwww.andamanclub.com; ⑨), casino and duty-free complex, located on a tiny island in Burmese waters just south of Kaw Thaung. The *Andaman Club* has its own immigration facilities, so the whole process is much faster than going via Saphan Pla, and you can also have lunch, stay over if you want to and check out the duty free shopping. Phone ahead for *Andaman Club* transport from Ranong town to the pier (B100 per person), or take a songthaew there from the Thanon Ruangrat market (B20).

Visa-run practicalities

All non-Thais must first get a Thai exit stamp before boarding a boat to Kaw Thaung, so take a songthaew from Ranong bound for **Saphan Pla** – the fastest and most direct songthaew from the market is the red #3 (20min; B10–15) – and get out of the songthaew at the Thai **immigration office** (daily 8.30am–6pm), across the road from the Thai Farmers Bank on the outskirts of Saphan Pla. Once you've got your stamp you can either accompany the hovering boat boys (who charge B300 per person return) or continue walking down the road for about fifteen minutes until you reach the PTT petrol station, where you should turn down to the right to find a quayside thick with longtails. There's another small quay a few hundred metres further up the quayside, but the PTT one is busier.

Longtails leave for Kaw Thaung when they have enough custom: the fare should be B50 one-way per person. The crossing takes about thirty minutes, but en route you will stop at tiny Snake Island where you buy your Burmese visa from the **Burmese immigration** office: US$5 (or B300) gets you a one- to three-day pass, which entitles you to stay up to two nights in Kaw Thaung but not to travel anywhere beyond. Next stop is Kaw Thaung itself, a few minutes' boat ride further on, where you will need to get stamped out of Burma at the immigration office up the hill from the pier. Once you've had enough of Kaw Thaung, you may or may not be taken via Snake Island again on your boat ride back to Saphan Pla. Once back on Thai soil you must return to the Thai immigration office to get your new Thai thirty-day tourist visa before catching a songthaew back to Ranong. Note that Burma time is 30 minutes behind Thailand time, and that to get back into Thailand you'll have to be at the immigration office in Saphan Pla before it closes at 6pm.

Kaw Thaung

Although there's nothing much to do in **Kaw Thaung** itself, it's an enjoyable focus for a trip out of Ranong, and sufficiently different from Thai towns to merit an hour or two's visit. Alighting at the quay, the market, immigration office, and tiny town centre lie before you, while over to your right, about twenty minutes' walk away, you can't miss the hilltop **Pyi Taw Aye Pagoda**, surmounted by a huge reclining Buddha and a ring of smaller ones. Once you've explored the covered market behind the quay and picked your way through the piles of tin trunks and sacks of rice that crowd the surrounding streets, it's fun to take a coffee break in one of the typically Burmese quayside pastry shops before negotiating a ride in a boat back to Saphan Pla; Thai money is perfectly acceptable in Kaw Thaung.

Ko Chang

Not to be confused with the much larger island of Ko Chang on Thailand's east coast (see p.491), Ranong's **Ko Chang** (Ⓦwww.kohchang-ranong.com) is

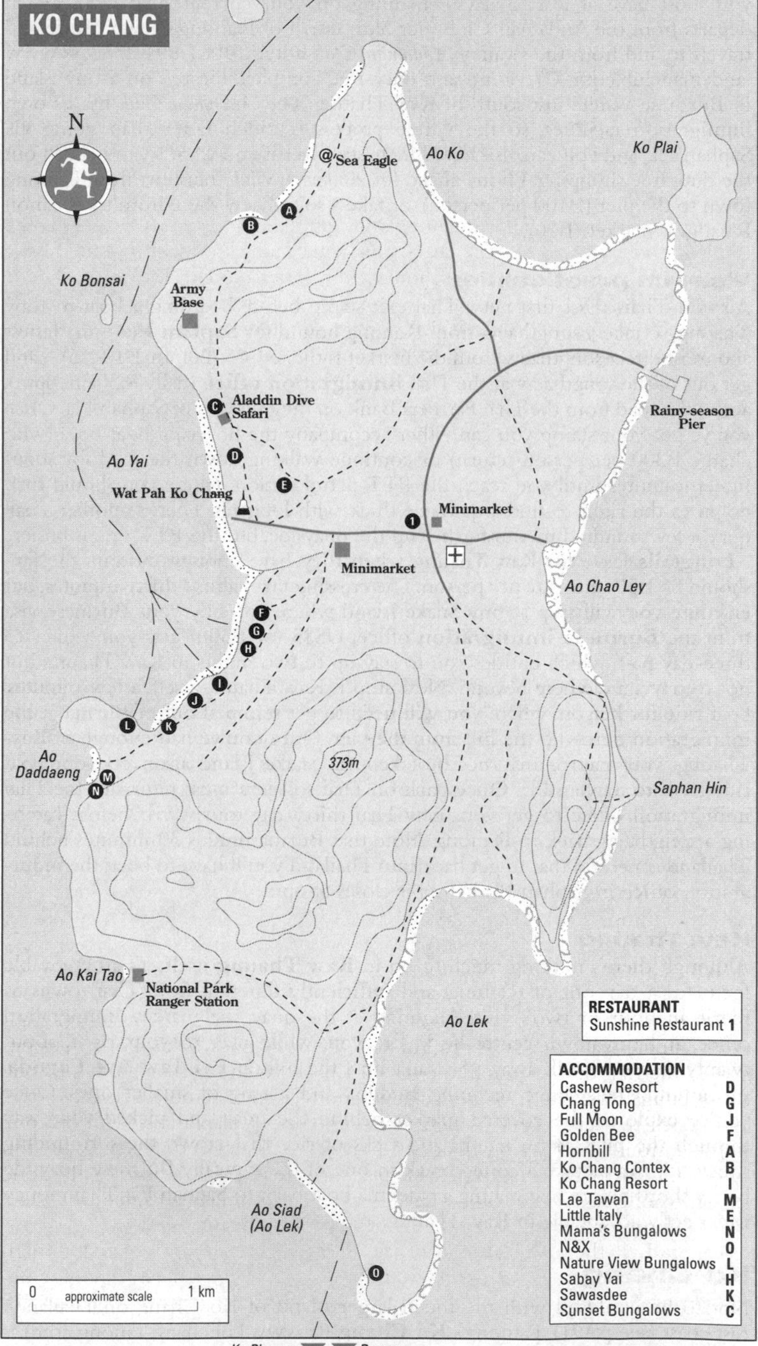
Ranong
KO CHANG
N
Sea Eagle
Ao Ko
Ko Plai
Ko Bonsai
Army Base
Aladdin Dive Safari
Rainy-season Pier
Ao Yai
Wat Pah Ko Chang
Minimarket
Minimarket
Ao Chao Ley
Ao Daddaeng
373m
Saphan Hin
Ao Kai Tao
National Park Ranger Station
Ao Lek
Ao Siad (Ao Lek)
RESTAURANT
Sunshine Restaurant 1
ACCOMMODATION
Cashew Resort D
Chang Tong G
Full Moon J
Golden Bee F
Hornbill A
Ko Chang Contex B
Ko Chang Resort I
Lae Tawan M
Little Italy E
Mama's Bungalows N
N&X O
Nature View Bungalows L
Sabay Yai H
Sawasdee K
Sunset Bungalows C
0 approximate scale 1 km
Ko Phayam
Ranong

a forested little island about 5km offshore, with less than perfect greyish-yellow-sand beaches but a charmingly low-key atmosphere. The beaches are connected by tracks through the trees; there are no cars (just a few motorbikes) and, for the moment at least, only sporadic, self-generated supplies of electricity. Most islanders make their living from fishing and from the rubber, palm and cashew-nut plantations that dominate the flatter patches of the interior. The pace of life on Ko Chang is very slow, and for the relatively small number of tourists who make it here the emphasis is strongly on kicking back and chilling out – bring your own hammock and you'll fit right in. Nearly all the bungalows on Ko Chang **close** down from about mid-May until mid- or late October, when the island is subjected to very heavy rain; many bungalow staff relocate to the mainland for this period, so you should phone ahead to check first.

The best of Ko Chang's beaches are on the west coast, and of these the longest, nicest and most popular is **Ao Yai**. A narrow concrete road connects central Ao Yai with a mangrove-filled little harbour on the east coast, a distance of around 1700m that can be walked in under half an hour. The western end of the road begins beside the island's only temple, **Wat Pah Ko Chang**, whose bot and monks' quarters are partially hidden amongst the trees beside the beach, with a sign that asks tourists to dress modestly when in the area and not to swim or sunbathe in front of it. About halfway between the two coasts, a crossroads bisects Ko Chang's only **village**, a tiny settlement that is home to most of the islanders and holds just a few shops, restaurants and a clinic. Signs at the *Sunshine Restaurant* crossroads direct you south to Saphan Hin (3km) and Ao Lek (5km); follow the unsigned northern route for a concrete path to the northern pier (used by boats during the wet season).

Ao Yai and Ao Daddaeng

Effectively divided in two by a khlong, the main cross-island track, and the stumps of a long wooden pier, **Ao Yai** enjoys a fine view of the brooding silhouette of Burma's St Matthew's Island, which dominates the western horizon. The 800-metre-long stretch of Ao Yai that runs north from the khlong is the most attractive on the island, nice and wide even at high tide, and especially popular with kids. South of the khlong, the beach is very narrow at high tide, but when the water goes out you have to walk a longish distance to find any depth. Southern Ao Yai, which begins just beyond the rocky divide occupied by *Ko Chang Resort*, has greyish sand but is fine for swimming. Further south still, around an impassable rocky headland, tiny secluded gold-sand **Ao Daddaeng** (Tadang) is sandwiched between massive boulders and holds just a few bungalows: reach it via a five-minute footpath from behind *Tadang Bay*.

The rest of the island

A 25-minute walk **north of Ao Yai**, following the track behind *Sunset*, brings you to the first of a series of little bays, each of which is occupied by just one set of bungalows. The bays are secluded and feel quite remote, accessible only via a track that takes you through forest and rubber plantations with just one house en route. On the way, about 10 minutes' walk north of *Sunset*, at the top of the hill (currently the most reliable place on the island to get a mobile phone signal), you'll pass the barbed-wire perimeters of a military camp, established here to monitor activity along the (maritime) Thai-Burma border.

Ao Siad, at the southern end of the island, is even more isolated, though there are several bungalow outfits fronting the sandy shore here. It's sometimes known as Ao Lek, though the real **Ao Lek** is the mangrove-lined bay 15 minutes' walk to the northeast, on the other coast. The Ranong–Ko Phayam boat service makes a stop off Ao Siad (Ranong–Ko Chang boats do not; see below for details), but to get anywhere else you'll need to negotiate a ride in a longtail if staying here. The alternative is to walk, either from Ao Daddaeng or from the village. From Ao Daddaeng, a clear path takes you south, in about an hour, to **Ao Kai Tao**, a pretty beach and site of the national park ranger station. From Ao Kai Tao the route then follows an indistinct path across the saddle between two hills and along a creek bed to reach eastcoast Ao Lek (this takes another hour), after which it's 15 minutes south to Ao Siad. Coming from the village, you follow the signed track from the *Sunshine Restaurant* crossroads south to Ao Lek and then on to Ao Siad; it's 5km and should take about two hours.

Practicalities

Boats to Ko Chang leave from the Ko Phayam Pier in **Saphan Pla**, 5km south of Ranong's town centre. Several different **songthaew** services connect Ranong and Saphan Pla: from the town centre's Thanon Ruangrat market, the fastest and most direct songthaew is the red #3 (20min; B10–15); the unnumbered blue ones, which also serve the bus station, follow a circuitous route that can take up to 45mins and usually charge B20. You'll probably be dropped on the main road through Saphan Pla, from where it's about 500m to the pier and its coffee shop, minimarket and Internet access. Some accommodation-booking agents in Ranong offer free transport to the pier for their customers.

At the time of writing there were scheduled daily **boat departures** to Ko Chang's Ao Yai beach at 9.30am, noon and 2pm, with an occasional 3.30pm service added in peak season; ask at Ranong information centres for the latest info. If there are more than six in your party, you can probably charter your own boat almost immediately. The journey takes about an hour and costs B140 per person; you'll be dropped as close as possible to your intended bungalow. If heading for Saphan Hin or Ao Siad, you'll probably be put on the Ko Phayam boat (see above), which stops off at both those beaches en route. If you're travelling to Ko Chang **from Ko Phayam** and want to stay on Ao Yai, it's generally simpler, though more expensive, to take the boat back to Saphan Pla on the mainland and start again, as it's a long hot walk to Ao Yai from Ao Lek and Saphan Hin. The alternative would be to charter a boat from Ko Phayam to Ko Chang (about B800–1000). Very few boats travel to Ko Chang during the **rainy months** of June through October, and those that do drop passengers on the island's east coast, a three-kilometre walk from Ao Yai. During the tourist season, there's at least one boat a day from Ko Chang **back to Saphan Pla**, generally in the morning between about 7am and 9am, and another one at 2pm – ask at your bungalows the day before.

To date there is very little commercial activity on Ko Chang, save for a few local **minimarkets** selling basic necessities: at *Golden Bee* and behind the khlong on Ao Yai, and at *Sunshine Restaurant*, beside the crossroads in the heart of the island. The crossroads is also where you'll find the island **clinic**. **Overseas phone calls** can be made at *Cashew Resort* and they can also arrange bus tickets, Ranong–Bangkok flights, and speedboat charters to Ranong (20min; B3000 for up to six people). There is **Internet** access at *Sea Eagle*, north of Ao Yai.

The German-Dutch-run **dive shop** Aladdin Dive Safari (ⓣ077 820472, and at Ko Chang boat pier in Ranong ⓣ077 813698, ⓦwww.aladdindivesafari.com) is based next to *Cashew Resort* and from late October through mid-May teaches PADI dive courses and runs live-aboards to Ko Similan, Richlieu Rock, Ko Bon and Ko Tachai (4 days; B14,900), to Ko Surin and Ko Tachai (3 days; B13,900), and to the Mergui Archipelago.

Accommodation and eating

Most of the **bungalow** operations are simple wooden-plank or woven bamboo constructions, comprising just a dozen huts and a small restaurant each. Though they nearly all have their own generators (which usually only operate in the evenings), it's a good idea to bring a torch as some bungalow managers bow to customers' preference to stick to candles and paraffin lamps. Due to limited Internet access on the island, few bungalow owners check their email more than once a fortnight during high season, more frequently in low season. Except where stated, all bungalows listed here **close** down from about mid-May until early or mid-October.

Bungalow restaurants tend to serve a broadly similar menu of travellers' **food**. Those that stand out include *Cashew Resort* for its fresh bread; *Sawasdee* for its fish with tamarind sauce and its massaman curries; and *Mama's* for its huge breakfasts and home-cooked south-German specialities. Italian-run *Little Italy* serves authentic sauces with its spaghetti dishes.

Ao Yai

Cashew Resort ⓣ077 820116. The longest-running set of bungalows on the island, and also the largest, with 35 bungalows along 700m of beachfront land, this place is nicely spread out among the cashew trees, giving all bungalows both a sea view and some privacy. Bungalows come in various styles, in either wood or brick, and some have proper glass windows. The resort offers the most facilities on the island, including foreign exchange, Visa and MasterCard capability, an overseas phone service (with Internet service planned), and a pool table. ❷–❸

Chang Tong ⓣ077 820178. Simple, clean wood and bamboo bungalows, well spaced in two rows. All have mosquito nets. ❶–❷

Full Moon ⓣ077 820130, ⓔfamilymoon99@hotmail.com. Offers very cheap huts with shared bathrooms at the back of the shore, plus a range of bamboo and wooden en-suite bungalows on the beachfront, and some larger bungalows for up to five people. Bungalows are lamp-lit at night. ❶–❹

Golden Bee ⓣ087 889 9613. Set among the palm trees, the wooden huts here come in various styles; though interiors are simply designed, they are en suite. Open all year. ❶–❷

Ko Chang Resort ⓣ077 820176, ⓔsound_of_sea@lycos.com. Occupying a fabulous spot high on the rocks right over the water, the en-suite wooden bungalows here have fine sea views from their balconies and are simply but intelligently designed inside. The bamboo ones are set further back beside the path. The swimmable beach is just a couple of minutes' scramble to south or north. ❷

Little Italy ⓔdaniel060863@yahoo.it. A tiny outfit of just two attractive bungalows set in a secluded spot amongst the trees 300m inland from the temple, behind the Italian restaurant. Bungalows are two storeys, with exceptionally clean, smartly tiled and well-appointed bathrooms downstairs and Thai-style wooden-walled sleeping quarters upstairs, with big decks. ❸–❹

Nature View Bungalows ⓔkornelis@mail.com. Occupying a fine elevated position, with views right up the beach, this Canadian-Thai-run place comprises just four huge bungalows, all of them with big glass windows and en-suite bathrooms. The bungalows are lit by paraffin lamps, but elsewhere everything's run on solar and wind-powered energy. ❷

Sabay Yai ⓣ 086 278 4112.Sturdy, spacious wooden bungalows, widely spaced among shorefront trees, some of them big enough for families. ❶–❸

Sawasdee ⓣ077 820177, ⓔsawasdeekohchang@yahoo.com. Welcoming place with nine nicely designed wooden bungalows, in various styles and sizes but all of them with exceptionally good bathrooms (tiled floors, colour-washed walls, sinks and showers). Also has a couple of quite elegant seating and eating areas out front. ❷–❸

Sunset Bungalows ⓣ077 820171. Very popular, laid-back, cosy outfit that's set in a rather dark grove of cashew-nut trees on the edge of the beach, comprising16 huts with or without attached bathrooms, the priciest with beach view. ❶–❸

The rest of the island

Hornbill North around two headlands from Ao Yai, about 45 minutes' walk through forest and rubber plantation ⓣ077 820134. Tiny place of just eight unobtrusive en-suite bungalows constructed to different designs and set amongst the trees behind their own little gold-sand bay. Lives up to its name, as majestic black-and-white hornbills are a common sight here. ❶–❷

Koh Chang Contex About a 25min walk over the hill from *Sunset* and northern Ao Yai ☎077 820118, ✉contexkohchang@hotmail.com. Located in its own peaceful little bay, which is good for snorkelling and fine for swimming except at low tide, this place has fifteen huts, both with and without private bathrooms, scattered across the rocks in a garden just above the beach. ❶–❷

Lae Tawan Five minutes' walk south over the headland from Ao Yai, on Ao Daddaeng ☎077 820179. The fifteen simple en-suite bungalows here share the small bay with just a couple of other bungalow outfits and enjoy good sunset views. It's open all year but you should expect "family-style" (rudimentary) service and food during the rainy season. ❶–❷

Mama's Bungalows South over the headland from Ao Yai, on Ao Daddaeng ☎077 820180, ✉mamasbungalows@yahoo.com. The ten attractive, well-maintained bungalows here come in two sizes, all of them with decent bathrooms. They're built in a pretty flower garden atop a rocky outcrop that overlooks the bay and affords fine views of St Matthew's Island. The restaurant serves generous portions of good food, including many German specialities. ❷

N&X Ten minutes' walk south of Ao Siad and at least a two-hour walk from either Ao Daddaeng or from the inland village ☎077 825752. Occupying its own tiny bay, isolated even from remote Ao Siad, this place offers ten good bungalows ranged up the shorefront hillside. ❶–❷

Ko Phayam

The diminutive kangaroo-shaped island of **KO PHAYAM** offers fine white-sand beaches and coral reefs and is home to around five hundred people, most of whom either make their living from prawn, squid and crab fishing, or from growing cashew nuts, *sator* beans, coconut palms and rubber trees. Many islanders live in Ko Phayam's only **village**, on the northeast coast, which comprises a pier, a temple and about two dozen shops and businesses and connects to other corners of the island by a network of concrete roads and muddy tracks. A motorbike taxi service plies the more popular routes, including to the main beaches and accommodation centres of **Ao Yai** and **Ao Kao Kwai**, but no journey is very great as the island measures just four by seven kilometres at its widest points. Because of the roads, Ko Phayam has a slightly more developed feel to it than neighbouring Ko Chang, underlined by a fledgling though still very low-key bar scene, and the presence of a significant number of foreigners who choose to spend six or more months here every year. Some expats even take up the rainy-season challenge, staying on through the downpours and rough seas that lash the island from June to October, but a number of bungalows close down during this time. As the island gets more popular, residents and expats are beginning to try and forestall the inevitable negative impact on the island's **environment**. In particular they are urging visitors not to accept plastic bags from the few shops on the island, to take non-degradable rubbish such as batteries and plastic items back to the mainland, and to minimize plastic water-bottle usage by buying the biggest possible bottles or better still creating a demand for a water-refill service.

Around the island

Ko Phayam's nicest beach is the three-kilometre-long **Ao Yai** on the southwest coast, a beautiful long sweep of soft white sand that curves quite deeply at its northern and southern ends into rocky outcrops that offer some snorkelling possibilities. The shore is pounded by decent waves that are fun for boogie-boarding and pretty safe; the sunsets are quite spectacular here too. For the moment Ao Yai's bungalow operations are still widely spaced along the shoreline, and much of the forest behind the beach is still intact. You're more than likely to see – and hear – some of the resident black-and-white hornbills at dawn and dusk, and sightings of crab-eating macaques and white-bellied sea eagles are also very possible. The main seven-kilometre-long route from Ao Yai to the village, which starts from behind *Smile Hut*, is very pleasant, whether done on foot, by

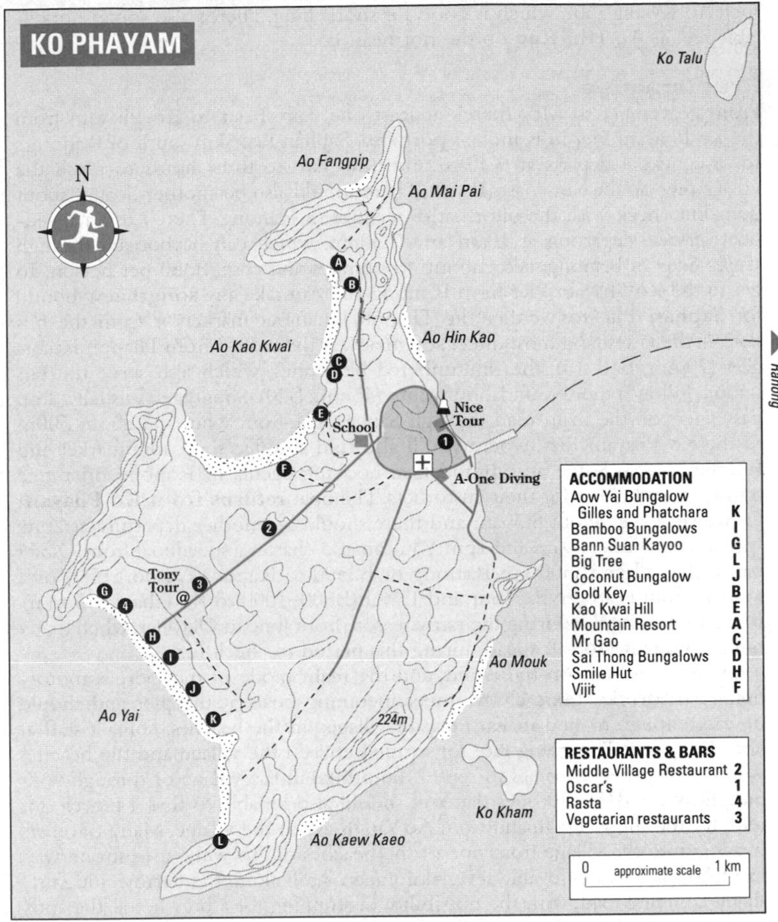

bicycle (the concrete road undulates a lot but there are no insurmountable hills so it takes around 30 minutes), or motorbike; it runs through almost unadulterated cashew plantations, dotted with the occasional house.

The northwest coast is scalloped into **Ao Kao Kwai**, a name that's pronounced locally as **Ao Kao Fai** and translates as **Buffalo Bay**; if you stand on the cliffside midway along the bay you'll appreciate how it got its name, as the two halves of the beach curve out into buffalo-like horns. The southern half of Ao Kao Kwai is subject to both very low and very high tides, which makes it unreliable for swimming, but the northern stretch, from *Sai Thong* and *Mr Gao* bungalows and beyond, is pretty, with appealing golden sand, decent swimming at any tide, and none of the big waves that characterize Ao Yai. The entire beach affords impressive views of the enormous hilly profile of Burma's St Matthew's Island.

North of *Mountain Resort* at the northern end of Ao Kao Kwai, a thirty-minute walk brings you to the pretty little sandy beach at **Ao Fangpip** (also spelt Ao Kwang Pib), which is good for snorkelling. There's also some snorkellable reef at **Ao Hin Kao** on the northeast coast.

Practicalities

From November to May there's at least one daily **boat** to Ko Phayam from the Ko Phayam Pier in Ranong's port area, Saphan Pla, 5km south of Ranong's town centre; it departs at 9.30am and takes two to three hours to reach the village pier on the east coast (B150). There should also be another boat at about 2pm, but check with the information centres in Ranong. There's also a speedboat service, departing at 10am and 2.30pm, which can be booked through *Coffee Shop* in Ranong, takes about 40 minutes and costs B350 per person. To get to the Ko Phayam Pier from Ranong you can take any **songthaew** bound for **Saphan Pla** from either the Thanon Ruangrat market or from the bus station: the fastest and most direct songthaew is the red #3 from Thanon Ruangrat (20min; B10–15); the unnumbered blue ones, which also serve the bus station, follow a more roundabout route (45min; B20). Songthaews usually drop passengers on the main road through Saphan Pla, from where it's about 500m to the Ko Phayam Pier, where you'll also find a coffee shop, minimarket and Internet access. Some accommodation-booking agents in Ranong offer free transport to the pier for their customers. The boat **returns from Ko Phayam** to Saphan Pla at about 8.30am and there should be another departure at 2pm; speedboats return at 9am and 1pm. You can also charter a speedboat from *Oscar's* bar in the village (B3000 to Ranong or B2500 to Ranong's airport pier) or a longtail from nearby Nice Tour and Travel (B800–1000 to Ko Chang; 45 min). Boats are less regular during the rainy season, from June to October, when many bungalows close, so call ahead during this period to check first.

There are no cars on the island, and the main mode of transport is motorbikes. **Motorbike taxis** always meet incoming boats at the pier and should be easy enough to find in Ko Phayam village; on the beaches, contact staff at your bungalow. The going rate for a ride between the village and the beaches is B80. The other option is to rent a motorbike in the village or through your bungalow for B150–200 per day. You should also be able to find a bicycle for rent, try the shops just inland from Ao Yai, or ask in the village. Many travellers heading into the village from one of the beaches opt to **walk** at least one way: from Ao Yai it's an enjoyable seven-kilometre stroll along the narrow and fairly shady concrete road, with the possibility of stopping for a breather at the aptly named *Middle Village Restaurant*; from southern Ao Kao Kwai to the village takes less than an hour.

The **village** has just enough to cater to travellers' needs, including a few tiny general stores, a 24-hour minimarket, a couple of small restaurants and a **clinic**. Most mobile phones can get a signal in the village but not elsewhere on the island. *Oscar's* bar (see opposite), which is just north of the pier-head, is a good source of island **information**, rents motorbikes and takes people wakeboarding in the village bay. A couple of doors further along, the **tour agent** Nice Tour and Travel (Ⓣ077 828093, Ⓦwww.koyphayamisland.com) changes money and does Visa cash advance, has large-scale maps of the island, sells bus, train and airline tickets, can arrange boat hire and fishing tours from the island (B2500), and offers Internet access (B3/minute) and an **international phone** service; it also sells creative Nepalese clothing and handicrafts. A-One Diving (Ⓣ077 824303, Ⓦwww.a-one-diving.com), on the road to the pier, teaches PADI **dive** courses and runs live-aboards to Ko Surin, Richelieu Rock, Ko Tachai, Ko Bon and Ko Similan (from B12000 for three days) and to Burma Banks and the Mergui archipelago (from B34,000 for five days). *Mr Gao* on Ao Kao

Kwai (☎077 823995) runs two-day **snorkelling** trips to Ko Surin at B3500 per person: transport is by speedboat and the price includes food, a round-archipelago tour, and accommodation in national park tents.

Elsewhere on the island, there is **Internet access** at some bungalows on both beaches, as well as at Tony Tour, 200m inland from Ao Yai's *Smile Hut*, which also sells bus and train tickets (☎077 820082, ⓔtonytour_kohpayam@yahoo.com); there's a minimarket nearby too.

Accommodation, eating and drinking

The best of Ko Phayam's **accommodation** is found on the two main beaches, Ao Yai and Ao Kao Kwai. Unless otherwise stated all bungalows close down during the wet season, from June to October. Every set of bungalows has a **restaurant**, and there are several others away from the two beaches, including, 200m inland along the road from Ao Yai's *Smile Hut*, a couple of laid-back vegetarian restaurants (Mon–Sat 8am–5pm), serving home-made bread, cakes, daily specials and pastas; and *Middle Village Restaurant*, on the Ao Yai–village road, which serves very cheap Thai food and drink. *Oscar's* (daily 7am–9pm), in the village, has no menu, serving anything from breakfasts to shepherds' pie, seafood to Indian curries, depending on availability, but it's most famous for its (mostly open-air) **bar**, which is the focal point of the expat social scene and makes an enjoyable place to while away an afternoon, as well as being a useful source of island information. Customers who stay late and can't get home are invited to crash out at the adjacent *Hangover Hut*. Several bungalow operations on Ao Yai, including the long-running *Rasta*, also run **beach bars** during high season (Dec–Feb).

Ao Yai

Aow Yai Bungalow Gilles and Phatchara ☎077 821753, ⓔgilles_phatchara@hotmail.com. Established by a French-Thai couple, this was the first set of bungalows on the island and remains one of the most popular, especially with return guests. The bungalows are dotted around an extensive garden of flowers, fruit trees and palms; each has its own washbasin inside, and only the very cheapest share bathrooms. Otherwise you're looking at a range of wood and concrete options, with price depending on size (some sleep four). During the rainy season it's best to email to check whether it's open. Shared bathroom ❶, en suite ❷–❹

Bamboo Bungalows ☎077 820012. The liveliest place to stay on the beach and many travellers' first port of call, with 28 bungalows set under the trees in a well-tended flower garden in the middle of the beach. They've been built with imaginative use of local materials and all but the cheapest have bathrooms and mosquito nets. At the top of the range, the appealing shell-studded concrete bungalows have verandas and characterful open-air bathrooms; other options include a choice of bamboo and wood huts, with price depending on size. *Bamboo* rents out boogie boards and offers Internet access, exchange and overseas phone services. It's run by an Israeli-Thai couple and stays opens year-round. Shared bathroom ❶, en suite bamboo ❷–❸, shell bungalow ❹

Bann Suan Kayoo ☎077 820133, ⓦwww.gopayam.com. Though the bungalows here are not the best value on the beach, there's a genuinely warm welcome from the island-family owners and the peaceful location at the far northern end of the bay appeals particularly to solo travellers looking for quiet. Choose between simple en-suite thatched bamboo huts or slightly sturdier ones with tin roofs and bigger decks, all of them set within a grassy shorefront garden with floral hedges. Closed May–Oct. ❷–❹

Big Tree ☎077 820504. Another quiet spot, removed from the main action at the far southern end of the bay, and set near the eponymous tree and above a rocky point that offers some snorkelling. The seven bamboo and wood bungalows are a good size, with price depending on size and location, though nearly all of them have a direct sea view. It's popular with long stayers so phone ahead. ❷–❸

Coconut Bungalow ☎077 820011, ⓔcoconut_phayamisland@thaimail.com. Occupying a great spot in the centre of the bay and run by a Ko Phayam family, this good-value place offers a range of 25 high standard bungalows, from small bamboo en-suite huts through larger wood or bamboo versions to big concrete bungalows at the top end. ❷–❹

Smile Hut ⓣ077 820335, ⓦwww.designparty.com/member/4615710/smile_hut.html. Like *Bamboo*, this is a lively place and very popular with travellers. It comprises around 30 simple en-suite bamboo huts, many of them spread among the shorefront trees, with the slightly cheaper versions set one row behind. Phone to check whether they are open during the rainy season. ❷–❸

Ao Kao Kwai (Buffalo Bay)

Gold Key ⓣ077 812202. Just a handful of nice, en-suite wooden bungalows in the central part of the northern bay, some of them with sea view, others located further back, behind the restaurant. ❷–❸

Kao Kwai Hill ⓣ081 847 6285, ⓦwww.kaokwaihill.com. Nine simple bamboo, wood and concrete bungalows set amongst the cashew and *sator* trees high up on the rocks, with easy access to the southern half of the beach but a rocky walk (possible at low-tide only) to the northern stretch. The attractively sited restaurant overlooks a pair of eye-catchingly eroded outcrops and affords perfect views of Ao Kao Kwai's eponymous "buffalo horn" layout; you can also access the Internet here. ❷

Mountain Resort ⓣ077 820098. Managed by a welcoming family, the five bungalows here are small but comfortable, and all are en suite and have screened doors. They're set in a pretty garden at the peaceful, northernmost end of the beach, under palms and among bougainvillea and hibiscus. The concrete road runs out about 1km south of *Mountain Resort*, so the last stretch is via a potholed dirt track (or you can walk that bit via the beach instead). Open all year. ❸

Mr Gao ⓣ077 823995, ⓦwww.mr-gao-phayam.com. Located on the best stretch of the beach, this is one of the most famous and popular spots, a well-established operation comprising just eight well-designed bungalows, in assorted sizes and luxury, set in a lovingly tended garden of shrubs and bamboos. All have bathrooms and most have polished wood floors, screened windows and thoughtfully furnished interiors. Mr Gao runs overnight trips to the Surin islands (see p.712) as well as fishing and snorkelling outings to other parts of Ko Phayam. There is Internet access here and the place is open all year. It's popular, so reserve ahead. ❷–❹

Sai Thong Bungalows ⓣ077 820466, ⓔjutharat_1980@yahoo.com. Friendly, local setup that shares the same pretty stretch of beach with *Mr Gao* and has just five good-quality rattan huts, each furnished with a thick mattress, a mosquito net and its own well-appointed bathroom. ❷–❸

Vijit ⓣ077 834082, ⓔvijitbungalows@hotmail.com. This long-running outfit is the most commercial on Ao Kao Kwai and very popular, despite occupying the part of the beach whose tides make it the least reliable for swimming. It's bungalows are spacious and en suite and the price mainly depends on the proximity to the shorefront. Open all year. ❷–❹

Khuraburi and Ko Surin

The small town of **Khuraburi**, 110km south of Ranong on Highway 4, is the main departure point for the magnificent national park island chain of **Ko Surin**, a group of five small islands around 60km offshore, just inside Thai waters. Much closer to Khuraburi are the islands of **Ko Ra** and **Ko Phra Thong**, which offer empty beaches and decent snorkelling and bird-watching.

Khuraburi and around

Most travellers use the town of **Khuraburi** as a staging post en route to or from the Surin islands: the main pier for boats to the islands is just 7.5km away, and Khuraburi's tour agents sell boat tickets and offer transport to the pier, plus there is accommodation in town. Though lacking in famous attractions, the local area is nonetheless scenic, both offshore and inland: with an afternoon or more to spare, you could either rent a motorbike, mountain bike or kayak to explore it independently, or charter a motorbike taxi or longtail boat. There is also a community-based tourism initiative in the area, Andaman Discoveries (ⓦwww.andamandiscoveries.com), which runs a **homestay programme**. It was founded after the tsunami by the NGO North Andaman Tsunami Relief (NATR, ⓣ087 917 7165, ⓦwww.northandamantsunamirelief.com) to help the area's many devastated fishing communities get back on their feet. A typical three-day package, including accommodation, home-cooked meals, and fishing, trekking and cultural tours, costs B3000: check the website for detailed info or, locally, ask Jaeb at the bus station.

Chief among nearby maritime attractions are the **islands** of Ko Ra and Ko Phra Thong, both of them reached from the Khuraburi pier, either by chartered longtail (B2500 per day including snorkel gear and transfers from Khuraburi town) or, if you're feeling energetic, by self-powered kayak. Hilly, forested **Ko Ra** (measuring about 10km north to south and about 3km wide) sits just off Khuraburi pier's mangrove-lined estuary and has no permanent residents. Graced with intact rainforest full of towering trees, resident hornbills and empty gold-sand beaches, it makes an enticing prospect for a day's boat trip, with especially pretty beaches and reefs along its west-facing coasts (about 1hr by longtail), though you'll need a guide to explore the interior. You can also kayak around to its western coast in about two hours from Khuraburi pier (ask at the bus station for a map), but check tide conditions locally first, and be warned that currents in the channel between southern Ko Ra and Ko Phra Thong are treacherous, so it's risky to attempt an entire circuit. Immediately to the south of Ko Ra, about one kilometre off the Khuraburi coast, **KO PHRA THONG** (Golden Buddha Island) also has some lovely beaches, the nicest of which, on the west coast, is 10km long and blessed with fine gold sand. This is the site of the *Golden Buddha Beach Resort* (ⓣ081 894 7195, ⓦwww.goldenbuddhaisland.com; ❼–❽), an ecologically minded resort 90 minutes' boat ride from the pier that comprises nineteen idiosyncratic, two-storey wooden houses, all of them with fans, mosquito nets and open-air bathrooms as well as downstairs kitchens. Food is served buffet-style in the dining area (B490/person/day). The resort hosts yoga retreats and a turtle conservation project run by the Italian Naucrates (ⓦwww.naucrates.org) and is open year-round. Ko Phra Thong used also to be home to three thriving fishing villages, but the island was very badly hit by the 2004 tsunami, as a result of which many lives were lost and the settlements decimated. Rebuilding will take some years, and in the meantime most villagers have been relocated to the Khuraburi mainland.

Inland Khuraburi offers several possibilities for a scenic ride on a bicycle (or motorbike). Jaeb at the bus station can supply sketch-maps of a 20-kilometre circular **cycle route** along rural, mildly undulating backroads to a small dam and swimming spot in the river, with optional off-road cycle tracks through the surrounding forest. The route begins by heading east towards the Khao Phra Mee hills, along the side road that starts north of the town-centre bridge and *Tararin* bungalows, taking you through rubber and oil-palm plantations, past fields of watermelon (Nov–Jan), and to the Khura River dam; backtracking a little you then return via some small hamlets and the prettiest, residential part of Khuraburi itself, arriving back in the town centre 100m south of the bus station.

Practicalities

The commercial heart of Khuraburi is a 500-metre strip of shops and businesses either side of Highway 4. Most **buses** travelling along Highway 4 between Bangkok/Chumphon/Ranong and Takua Pa/Khao Lak/Phuket stop here, either outside or across from the tiny bus-station office on the east side of the road. The bus station's helpful English-speaking manager, Jaeb, is a great source of **information** on the area and can supply a **map** showing local mountain-biking, kayaking and hiking routes. Tom Tour, across the road (Ⓣ086 272 0588, Ⓔtom_tammarat@yahoo.co.th), rents bicycles (B80) and motorbikes (B200), as well as **tents** (B100/day), sleeping bags (B50/day) and snorkel sets (B50/day). *Boon Piya Resort* (see below) rents **kayaks** as well as motorbikes and mountain bikes and can arrange snorkelling trips to Ko Ra and Ko Phra Thong. Many places in town sell **boat tickets to Ko Surin**, including all the above-listed outlets; see p.714 for boat times and prices.

There are several **places to stay** in and around Khuraburi. Set alongside the river at the northern end of town, about 250m north of the bus station, *Tararin* (Ⓣ076 491 789; fan ❷, air-con ❹) is a cute, rustic-style place with just a handful of simple but characterful en-suite wooden and concrete bungalows overlooking the water, plus an attractive riverside restaurant and eating deck. The pristine concrete bungalows at the motel-style *Boon Piya Resort* (Ⓣ081 752 5457; ❹), 150m north of the bus station, are better appointed, if rather tightly packed, and all have air-con and powerful showers; they're the usual choice of sales reps and NGOs. The poshest accommodation in the area is at *Khuraburi Greenview Resort* (Ⓣ076 421360, Ⓦwww.kuraburigreenview.co.th ❼), 12km south of Khuraburi, beneath a range of forested hills alongside Highway 4, at kilometre-stone 739. The attractively designed wooden chalets all have air-con, TV and use of the swimming pool, and the hotel sells tickets for speedboats to Ko Surin and can provide transfers to the pier. You can also stay with a family in a traditional fishing village near Khuraburi as part of the NATR **homestay programme** described on p.710, on a bed and breakfast basis (❷ excluding meals); Jaeb at the bus station is the contact point for arranging this, though dates need to be booked at least two days in advance.

At night, most people **eat** at the night market next to bus station, where the roti stall is a particular favourite, flipping out a constant pile of sizzling *roti mataba* (chicken) and *roti kluay* (banana). The morning market (daily from 5am) across from *Boon Piya* is the place to stock up on food for the Surin Islands but the best place for fresh coffee is next door but one to *Boon Piya* at the *Friends de Sea* **Internet** café (daily 8am–9pm).

Ko Surin

The spectacular shallow reefs around **KO SURIN** National Park (open from 16 Nov to 16 May; Ⓦwww.dnp.go.th/National_park.asp; B200 entry) offer some of the best snorkelling and diving on the Andaman coast. The most beautiful and easily explored of the reefs are those surrounding the two main islands in the group, Ko Surin Nua (north) and Ko Surin Tai (south), which are separated only by a narrow channel. **SURIN NUA**, slightly the larger at about 5km across, holds the national park headquarters, visitor centre and park accommodation, as well as an interpretative trail and a turtle hatchery. The water is so clear here, and the reefs so close to the surface, that you can make out a forest of sea anemones while sitting in a boat just 10m from the park headquarters' beach. Visibility off the east and west coasts of both islands stretches to a depth of 40m.

Across the channel, **SURIN TAI** is the long-established home of a community of Moken *chao ley* (see opposite) who divide their time between boat-building and fishing. Although their settlements were destroyed in the 2004 tsunami, they have since built new homes on the island. Every April, as part of the Songkhran New Year festivities, *chao ley* from nearby islands (including those in Burmese waters) congregate here to celebrate with a ceremony involving, among other rites, the release into the sea of several hundred turtles, which are a symbol of longevity and especially precious to Thai and Chinese people.

The chao ley: Moken and Urak Lawoy

Sometimes called sea gypsies, the **chao ley** or *chao nam* ("people of the sea" or "water people") have been living off the seas around the west coast of the Malay peninsula for hundreds of years. Some still pursue a traditional nomadic existence, living in self-contained houseboats known as **kabang**, but many have now made permanent homes in Andaman coast settlements in Thailand, Burma and Malaysia. Dark-skinned and sometimes with an auburn tinge to their hair, the *chao ley* of the Andaman Sea are thought to number around five thousand, divided into five groups, with distinct lifestyles and dialects.

Of the different groups, the **Urak Lawoy**, who have settled on the islands of Ko Lanta (see p.821), Ko Jum (see p.803), Ko Phi Phi (see p.792), Phuket (see p.759) and Ko Lipe (see p.849), are the most integrated into Thai society. They came north to Thailand from Malaysia around 200 years ago (having possibly migrated from the Nicobar Islands in the Indian Ocean some two centuries prior) and are known as *Mai Thai*, or "New Thai". Thailand's Urak Lawoy have been recognized as Thai citizens since the 1960s, when the Queen Mother granted them five family names, thereby enabling them to posses ID cards and go to school. Many work on coconut plantations or as fishermen, while others continue in the more traditional *chao ley* **occupations** of hunting for pearls and seashells on the ocean floor, attaching stones to their waists to dive to depths of 60m with only an air-hose connecting them to the surface; sometimes they fish in this way too, taking down enormous nets into which they herd the fish as they walk along the sea bed. Their agility and courage make them good bird's-nesters as well (see box on p.801).

The **Moken** of Thailand's Ko Surin islands and Burma's Mergui archipelago probably came originally from Burma and are the most traditional of the *chao ley* communities. They still lead remote, itinerant lives, are mostly unregistered as Thai citizens, and own no land or property, but are dependent on fresh water and beaches to collect shells and sea slugs to sell to Thai traders. They have extensive knowledge of the plants that grow in the remaining jungles on Thailand's west-coast islands, using eighty different species for food alone, and thirty for medicinal purposes.

The *chao ley* are **animists**, with a strong connection both to the natural spirits of island and sea and to their own ancestral spirits. On some beaches they set up totem poles as a contact point between the spirits, their ancestors and their shaman. The sea gypsies have a rich **musical heritage** too. The Moken do not use any instruments as such, making do with found objects for percussion; the Urak Lawoy on the other hand, due to their closer proximity to the Thai and Malay cultures, are excellent violin- and drum-players. During community entertainments such as the Urak Lawoy's twice-yearly full-moon **festivals** on Ko Lanta (see p.821), the male musicians form a semicircle around the old women, who dance and sing about the sea, the jungle and their families. See the discography on p.906 for details of *chao ley* music on CD.

Building a new boat is the ultimate expression of what it is to be a *chao ley*, and tradition holds that every newly married couple has a *kabang* built for them. But the complex art of constructing a seaworthy home from a single tree trunk, and the way of life it represents, is disappearing. In Thailand, where **assimilation** is actively promoted by the government, the truly nomadic flotillas have become increasingly marginalized, and the number of undeveloped islands they can visit unhindered gets smaller year by year. The 2004 tsunami further threatened their cultural integrity: when the waves destroyed the Moken's boats and homes on Ko Surin, they were obliged to take refuge on the mainland, where certain missionary NGOs blackmailed some into converting from their animist religion. Though the Moken have since returned to the Surin islands, inappropriate donations and the merging of two villages have exacerbated family rivalries and caused divisions that may prove lethal to their traditional way of life. For more information on Thailand's *chao ley* peoples, see the website of the Unesco-supported Andaman Pilot Project (ⓦwww.cusri.chula.ac.th/andaman/en).

Practicalities

Because the islands are so far out at sea, Ko Surin is closed to visitors from May 17–Nov 16, when monsoon weather renders the sixty-kilometre trip a potentially suicidal undertaking. During the rest of the year, the majority of visitors either join **snorkelling day-trips** to the islands from Khuraburi, Phuket, or Phang Nga, or opt for live-aboard **dive trips** out of Khao Lak (see p.725), Phuket (see p.750), Ranong (see p.700), Ko Chang (see p.704) or Ko Phayam (see p.708). Many of these trips also feature other remote reefs such as Richelieu Rock or the Burma Banks and cost from B12,000 for three days; *Mr Gao* on Ko Phayam runs overnight snorkelling trips to Ko Surin at B3500 per person (see p.710).

For independent travellers, the usual way to reach the islands is on one of the **boat services from Khuraburi**. Several agencies in Khuraburi (see p.712) sell tickets for both these boats and the price should include transport from Khuraburi to the pier, 7.5km northwest (private transport from town to the pier costs B100 by motorbike or B150 by taxi). Between mid-May and mid-November, there should be at least one **slow boat** a day (departs Khuraburi pier 9am; 2–3hr; B1100 rtn; returns from Ko Surin at 1pm) and, weather permitting, between January and April there's generally at least one **fast boat** service as well (departs Khuraburi pier 9am; 1hr; B1700 rtn; returns from Ko Surin at 2.30pm).

For **accommodation on Ko Surin**, you have the choice of renting one of the expensive national park **bungalows** on Surin Nua (❼), renting a national park tent (B200–300/day), or bringing your own tent (available for hire from Khuraburi) and pitching it for B80 per day. Bungalows need to be booked in advance through the National Parks website at Ⓦwww.dnp.go.th/National_park.asp, and tents should be reserved ahead by phoning the Ko Surin National Park office at either their Khuraburi pier office Ⓣ076 491378 or their Ko Surin office Ⓣ076 419028. Unless you take your own **food** to the islands (Khuraburi has a market and general stores), you'll be restricted to the meals served at the restaurant on Surin Nua.

Khao Sok National Park

Most of the Andaman coast's attractions are found, unsurprisingly enough, along the shoreline, but the stunning jungle-clad karsts of **KHAO SOK NATIONAL PARK** (Ⓦwww.dnp.go.th/National_park.asp) are well worth heading inland for. Located about halfway between the southern peninsula's two coasts and easily accessible from Khao Lak, Phuket and Surat Thani, the park has become a popular stop on the travellers' route, offering a number of easy jungle **trails** as well as the chance to explore the enormous **Cheow Lan Lake** and its shoreside caves. Much of the park is carpeted in impenetrable rainforest, home to gaurs, leopard cats and tigers among others – and up to 155 species of bird. It protects the watershed of the Sok River, is dotted with dozens of waterfalls, and rises to a peak of nearly 1000m. The limestone crags that dominate almost every vista both on and off the lake are breathtaking, never more so than in the early morning: waking up to the sound of hooting gibbons and the sight of thick white mist curling around the karst formations is an experience not quickly forgotten.

Practicalities

The park has two centres: the **tourist village** that has grown up around the park visitor centre and trailheads, and the dam, 65km further east, at the head of

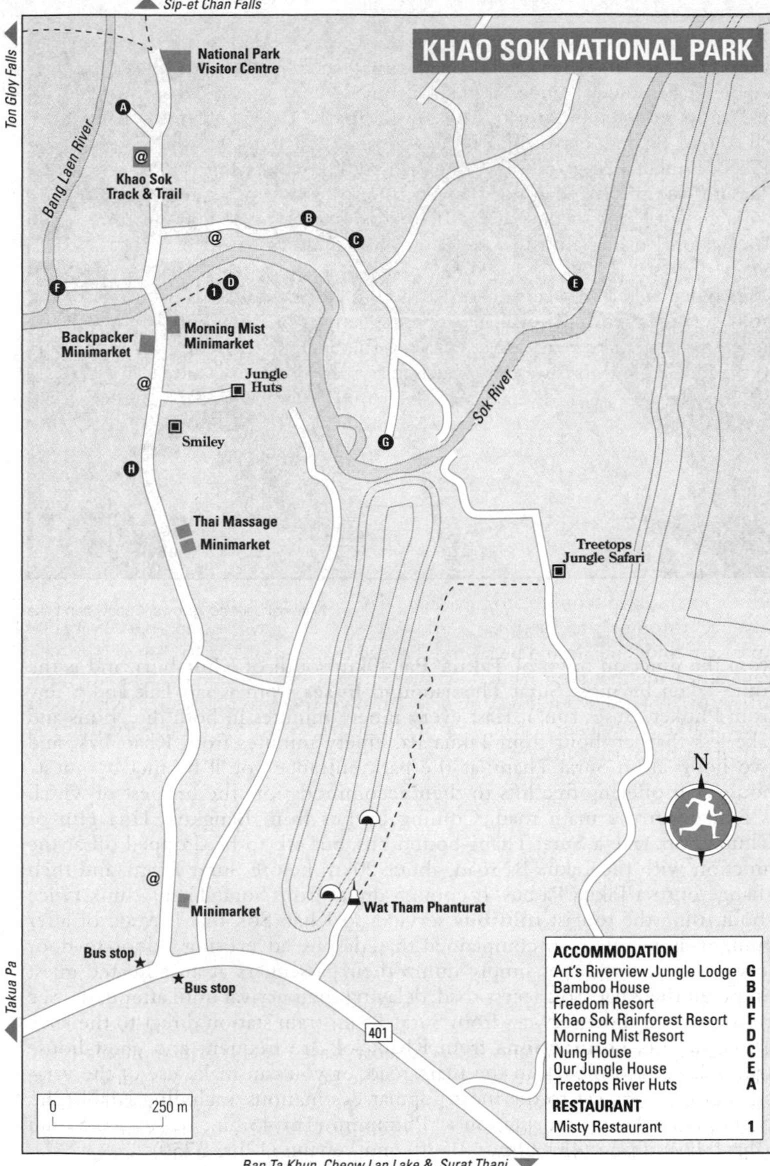

Cheow Lan Lake. Most visitors stay in the tourist village and organize their lake trips from there, but it's also feasible to do one or more nights at the lake first.

Arrival and information

The main access road into the park takes you to the tourist village and trailheads. It starts at kilometre-stone 109 on Highway 401, which cuts east

△ National park bungalows, Cheow Lan Lake

from the junction town of **Takua Pa**, 40km south of Khuraburi, and is the route taken by most Surat Thani-bound **buses** from Khao Lak and a few from Phuket. Buses run at least every ninety minutes in both directions and take less than an hour from Takua Pa, ninety minutes from Khao Lak, and two hours from Surat Thani; at the park entrance you'll be met by guest-house staff offering free lifts to their accommodation, the furthest of which is 3km from the main road. Coming by bus from Bangkok, Hua Hin or Chumphon, take a Surat Thani-bound bus, but ask to be dropped off at the junction with the Takua Pa road, about 20km before Surat Thani, and then change onto a Takua Pa bus. If coming direct from Surat Thani, think twice about using the tourist **minibus** services to Khao Sok that leave at or after 3pm: many people have complained that, despite advertising a door-to-door service, these minibuses simply dump their passengers at an affiliated guest house on the Khao Sok access road, delaying their arrival until after dark. See below for transport services from Surat Thani train station direct to the lake. **Onward bus connections** from Khao Sok are frequent and guest-house staff will ferry you back to the main road, or you can make use of the various minibus services to the most popular destinations, including Krabi (2hr; B300), Surat Thani train station at Phunphin (1hr 45min; B250); Ko Samui (3hr; B430), Trang (4hr 30min; B520) and Penang (12hr; B750).

At the **tourist village** there are around twenty sets of bungalows, along with half a dozen minimarkets and email centres, laundry services and the all-important massage centres – a life-saver after a challenging jungle trek. Khao Sok Track & Trail does currency exchange (there's no ATM in Khao Sok), offers an international phone service and sells bus, boat, plane and train tickets. Several minimarkets and guest houses rent out **motorbikes** (B200/day)and Morning Mist minimarket also has a few **bicycles** for rent (B60/day).

Accommodation and eating

The longest-running and most peaceful of **guest houses** in the tourist village are situated down the side road that runs alongside the river; the newer ones are located along the road to the park checkpoint. For lake accommodation, see p.719. Nearly all the guest houses serve **food**: *Misty Restaurant* at *Morning Mist Resort* serves exceptionally tasty Thai dishes, including inventive spicy *yam* salads and fresh juices such as sapodilla and tamarind; they grow much of their own produce in the guest-house garden and the manager also runs cooking classes (B800).

Art's Riverview Jungle Lodge ⓣ086 282 2677, ⓦkrabidir.com /artsriverviewlodge/index.htm. One of the longest-running and most popular places to stay in Khao Sok, with 20 bungalows nicely located away from the main fray, surrounded by jungle and mostly enjoying lovely river views. The cheaper bungalows are spacious, tastefully designed wooden affairs, with shutters and a deck; the deluxe versions are even bigger and attractively furnished, and there are treehouse-style ones as well, plus family sized options. All rooms have fans and mosquito nets. Because of the location you really do fall asleep and wake to an orchestra of countless insect, birds, monkeys and other unidentifiable creatures. ❹–❻

Bamboo House ⓣ081 787 7484, ⓦkrabidir .com/bamboohouse/index.htm. One of the first guest houses in the park and run by members of the park warden's family, this place offers a range of options, from simple bamboo huts with attached bathrooms to stilted wooden huts, concrete versions, and a couple of treehouses. Also has a swimming platform in the river. ❷–❺

Freedom Resort ⓣ081 370 1620, ⓔfreedomresort@yahoo.com. Australian-managed place comprising ten sizeable bamboo and wooden houses on stilts, with verandas, most of which look straight into a patch of jungle. Rooms are simply furnished but all have en-suite bathrooms. The adjacent restaurant hosts regular barbecues. ❷

Khao Sok Rainforest Resort ⓣ077 395135, ⓦkrabidir.com/khaosokrainforest/index.htm. This welcoming place has five spectacularly sited "mountain view" bungalows – set high on a jungle slope and affording unsurpassed karst views – plus eight other bungalows at ground level, overlooking the river. Interiors are decent enough if a bit faded and all rooms are en suite. ❸–❹

Morning Mist Resort ⓣ089 971 8794, ⓦwww .morningmistresort.com. Built within a gorgeously profuse riverside garden that's filled with carefully tended tropical blooms and a big herb garden whose produce is used in the restaurant and cooking school, this place offers ten large, immaculate rooms in variously styled bungalows, all with hot water and either river or garden view. It's well set up for families, with several rooms sleeping up to four people plus lots of space for kids to play in. ❸–❹, family rooms ❺

Nung House ⓣ077 395147 ⓦwww.nunghouse .com. Friendly place run by the park warden's son and his family with fourteen huts set around a garden full of rambutan trees. Choose between simple bamboo constructions with en-suite facilities, brick and concrete bungalows, and treehouses. ❷–❸

Our Jungle House ⓣ089 909 6814, ⓦwww .ourjunglehouse.com. The most romantically located of Khao Sok's guest houses occupies a secluded riverside spot beneath the limestone cliffs, about a 15min walk beyond *Nung House*. You can choose between beautifully situated treehouses and private cabins by the river, or garden versions with equally great views. All of them are simply but elegantly designed wooden constructions, furnished with fans, mosquito nets and bathrooms. ❹–❺

Treetops River Huts ⓣ077 395143, ⓦkrabidir .com/treetopsriverhuts/index.htm. Located beside the river, very close to the visitor centre and trailheads, with a choice of 30 comfortable rooms ranging from simple bamboo huts with bathrooms through to en-suite wood or stone ones. ❷–❺

Guided treks and tours

Even though the signed park trails are straightforward and easy to navigate, it's well worth making at least one **guided trek** into the jungle, preferably one that goes off-trail. The best jungle guides will educate you in rudimentary jungle craft and open your eyes to a wealth of detail that you'd miss on your own, such as the claw marks left by a sun-bear scaling a tree in search of honey, and the medicinal plants used for malarial fevers and stomach upsets. If you're lucky you might even see the **rafflesia kerrii** in bloom. Officially classified as having the second-biggest flowers in the world, with a diameter of up to 80cm, this rather unprepossessing brown, cabbage-like plant unfurls its enormous russet-coloured petals at some point between December and March, having emitted a disgusting stink in order to attract its pollinator, the green-headed housefly.

Guided treks into the jungle interior can be arranged through most of Khao Sok's guest houses, but the most reputable and long-serving **guides** are to be booked via *Bamboo House*, *Nung House*, *Khao Sok Rainforest Resort* and *Treetops River Huts*. For between B400 and B600 per person (excluding national park entry), you can join a trek along the main park trails, usually to Ton Gloy waterfall or Sip-et Chan falls, or to a nearby cave; a tailor-made off-trail hike costs around B1000. A good quality guide will also enhance the Cheow Lan Lake experience, described opposite.

Most guest houses also do **night safaris** along the main park trails, when you're fairly certain to see civets and might be lucky enough to see some of the park's rarer inhabitants, like elephants, tigers, clouded leopards and pony-sized black-and-white tapirs (B350–500 for 2hr or B600 for 4hr).

The **Sok River** that runs through the park and alongside many of the guest houses is fun for swimming in and inner-tubing down; tubing and canoeing trips (with tube/canoe and pick-up or drop included) cost around B375/B700. Many guest houses can also arrange **elephant-rides** (2hr; B800).

The park trails

Several trails radiate from the park headquarters and visitor centre, some of them more popular and easier to follow than others, but all quite feasible as day-trips. Take plenty of water as Khao Sok is notoriously humid. The B200 national park **entrance fee** (B100 for kids) is payable at the checkpoint (6am–6pm) close to the visitor centre and is valid for 24 hours – you'll need to pay this in addition to the fees for any guided treks or tours and you'll have to pay again at the lake if you arrive more than 24 hours later. The checkpoint office and **visitor centre** (daily 8am–6pm, ⓣ077 395155) both supply a small sketch map of the park and trails, but the best introduction to Khao Sok is the recommended **guidebook**, *Waterfalls and Gibbon Calls* by Thom Henley, which includes lots of information on flora and fauna as well as a full description of the interpretative trail (see p.929); it's available at some Khao Sok minimarkets and bungalows. If you don't buy the book, you might want to spend a few minutes looking at the exhibition on Khao Sok's highlights inside the visitor centre.

Seven of the park's nine current **trails** branch off the same clearly signed route, which heads directly west of the park headquarters and follows the course of the Sok River. Its first 3.5km constitute the **interpretative trail** described in *Waterfalls and Gibbon Calls* – a ninety-minute one-way trail along a broad, road-like track that's not terribly interesting in its own right but is greatly enhanced by the descriptions in the book. Most people carry on after the end of the interpretative trail, following signs for **Ton Gloy waterfall**, 7km from headquarters (allow 3hr each way), which flows year-round and tumbles into a pool that's good for swimming. En route to Ton Gloy, you'll pass signs for other attractions including **Bang Leap Nam waterfall** (4.5km from headquarters), which is a straightforward hike; and **Tan Sawan waterfall** (6km from headquarters), a more difficult route that includes a wade along the river bed for the final kilometre and should not be attempted during the rainy season.

The other very popular trail is the one to **Sip-et Chan waterfall**, which shoots off north from the park headquarters and follows the course of the Bang Laen River. Though these falls are only 4km from headquarters, the trail can be difficult to follow and involves a fair bit of climbing plus half a dozen river crossings. You should allow three hours each way, and take plenty of water and some food. With eleven tiers, the falls are a quite spectacular sight; on the way you should hear the hooting calls of white-handed gibbons at the tops of the tallest trees, and may get to see a helmeted hornbill flying overhead.

Cheow Lan Lake

Dubbed Thailand's Guilin because of its photogenic karst islands, forested inlets and mist-clad mountains encircling jade-coloured waters, the enormous 28-kilometre-long **Cheow Lan Lake** (also known as **Ratchabrapa Dam** reservoir; B200 national park entry fee) is Khao Sok's most famous feature and the most popular destination for guided tours. It was created in the 1980s when the Khlong Saeng river was dammed to power a new hydro-electricity plant, and its forested shores and hundred or more islands now harbour abundant birdlife, as well as some primates, most easily spotted in the very early morning. Tours generally combine a trip on the lake with a wade through the nearby flooded cave system and a night on a floating raft house. The lake is 65km from Khao Sok's accommodation area, and can only be explored by longtail boat tour, arranged either from Khao Sok or from Ratchabrapa Dam.

For many people, the highlight of their lake excursion is the adventurous three-hour trek to and through the 800-metre-long horseshoe-shaped **Nam Talu cave**, a five-minute boat ride from the national park raft houses, or about an hour's boat ride from the dam. The **trek** is not for everyone, however, as the cave section entails an hour-long wade through the river that hollowed out this tunnel: it's slippery underfoot and pitch black and there will be at least one 20-metre section where you have to swim. When the river level is high there will be longer swims, but on no account agree to go into the cave during the rainy season, whatever your guide says, as it's just too dangerous with high water levels and strong currents – there has been a fatality in these conditions. Wear sandals with decent grip and request (or take) your own torch.

Lake practicalities

Access to the lake is via the town of **BAN TA KHUN**, 50km east of Khao Sok on the Takua Pa–Surat Thani bus route, Route 401, from where it's 12km north to the dam. Many travellers book their tour of the lake from their Khao Sok accommodation, in which case all transport is included, but if coming from Surat Thani or Phang Nga, you could do the lake first before pushing on to the Khao Sok tourist village and trails. There's a regular **minibus service** from Surat Thani's Phunphin train station to and from the dam (every 2hr; 1hr; B70) or you could take the normal Surat Thani–Takua Pa bus service, as described on p.716, alight at Ban Ta Khun and either get a motorbike taxi to the dam or arrange for a tour operator to transfer you. The Australian-Thai-run Limestone Lake Rainforest Tours (Ⓣ078 954476, Ⓦwww.limestonelaketours.com) offers a big range of **lake-based tours**, including a two-hour trip (from B1500 per boat) and a full-day trip with optional overnight in a raft house (from B1500/2800 per person for up to 3 people, excluding park entry fee, or cheaper with larger groups). Khao Sok guest houses charge similar prices and all tours follow broadly the same itinerary. It's also possible to simply turn up at the dam and hire a boat for around B1800–2000.

On overnight trips to the lake, **accommodation** is either in tents in the jungle or at raft houses on the lake. There are both private and national park raft houses moored at various scenic spots around the lake shore, mostly around an hour's boat ride from the dam. All raft house huts are rudimentary bamboo structures with nets and mattresses, offering fabulous lake views from your pillow. If you've arranged your own boat transport, you can fix accommodation at any of the lake's raft houses for B500 per person including three meals. Part of the appeal of a night in a raft house is the **dawn safari** the next morning, when you've a good chance of seeing langurs, macaques and gibbons on the lakeshore; some tours include this option, or you can usually borrow a kayak from your accommodation and paddle around the shore yourself.

Khao Lak

The scenic strip of bronze-coloured beach at **KHAO LAK**, some 30km south of Takua Pa, became a household name for all the worst reasons in December 2004 when the tsunami devastated its shores, killing thousands and vaporizing almost every shorefront home and hotel (see p.722 for more on how the tsunami affected south Thailand). It may be years before the resort regains its pre-tsunami buzz but, at the time of research, sixteen months after the disaster, a great deal of the central, Nang Thong, area had been rebuilt, and tourists were once again enjoying the beach there and using local companies for snorkelling and **diving trips** to Ko Similan and Ko Surin.

The area usually referred to as Khao Lak is in fact three separate beaches. The real **Khao Lak** is the southernmost and least developed part, isolated from the heart of the resort by a rocky headland and five-kilometre run of Highway 4, and with just a few places to stay. In the area around its longest-running accommodation, *Poseidon Bungalows*, there is minimal obvious tsunami damage. **Nang Thong** occupies the central stretch and contains the bulk of the accommodation and tourist-oriented businesses. An ever-growing number of the hotels and bungalows down on Nang Thong beach, about 500m west of Highway 4, have re-established themselves, and there are still more under reconstruction, while the main road through Nang Thong is packed with small restaurants, dive operators, shops and a few guest houses. A 45-minute walk north up the beach brings you to **Bang Niang**, whose lovely long stretch of golden sand is for the most part free of rocks and good for swimming between November and April. It is also very empty – because of its flat topography, Bang Niang was the worst hit of the three areas and rebuilding has been a lot slower. By April 2006 only a few hotels and restaurants had reopened and there were still many forlorn "Land for Sale" signs on derelict plots, some with abandoned hotel buildings displaying big holes where their guts had been punched out by the waves. Inland from the highway at Bang Niang, a beached police boat has become an informal memorial to the extraordinary power of the tsunami waves – it was propelled up here, 2km inland, while patrolling the waters in front of *La Flora* resort. An official memorial is to be erected on government land near the national park headquarters just north of Khao Lak beach. Post-tsunami reconstruction is also ongoing within nearby communities that are off the tourist radar, so many NGOs still maintain offices in and around Bang Niang; among these, the Tsunami Volunteer Center, next to *Phu Khao Lak* resort in Nang Thong (Ⓣ089 882 8840, Ⓦwww.tsunamivolunteer.net), continues to welcome donations and volunteers.

Aside from Ko Similan, there are several other attractions within day-tripping distance of Khao Lak, including a number of local **waterfalls**. Of these, Sai Rung (Rainbow Falls) about 16km north of Nang Thong in Bang Sak, is

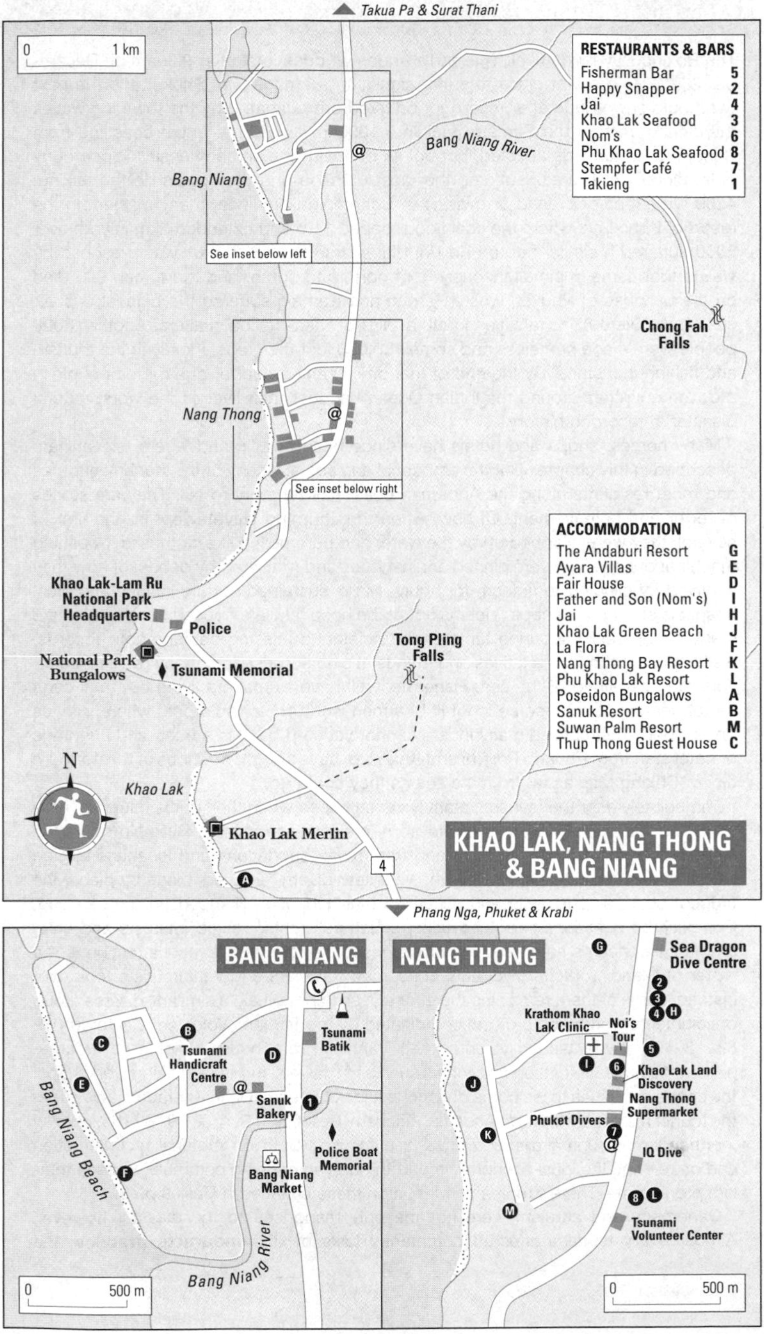

Takua Pa & Surat Thani
0 1 km
RESTAURANTS & BARS
Fisherman Bar 5
Happy Snapper 2
Jai 4
Khao Lak Seafood 3
Nom's 6
Phu Khao Lak Seafood 8
Stempfer Café 7
Takieng 1
Bang Niang River
Bang Niang
See inset below left
Chong Fah Falls
Nang Thong
See inset below right
ACCOMMODATION
The Andaburi Resort G
Ayara Villas E
Fair House D
Father and Son (Nom's) I
Jai H
Khao Lak Green Beach J
La Flora F
Nang Thong Bay Resort K
Phu Khao Lak Resort L
Poseidon Bungalows A
Sanuk Resort B
Suwan Palm Resort M
Thup Thong Guest House C
Khao Lak-Lam Ru National Park Headquarters
Police
National Park Bungalows
Tsunami Memorial
Tong Pling Falls
N
Khao Lak
Khao Lak Merlin
4
KHAO LAK, NANG THONG & BANG NIANG
Phang Nga, Phuket & Krabi
BANG NIANG
Tsunami Batik
Tsunami Handicraft Centre
Sanuk Bakery
Police Boat Memorial
Bang Niang Market
Bang Niang Beach
Bang Niang River
0 500 m
NANG THONG
Sea Dragon Dive Centre
Krathom Khao Lak Clinic
Noi's Tour
Khao Lak Land Discovery
Nang Thong Supermarket
Phuket Divers
IQ Dive
Tsunami Volunteer Center
0 500 m

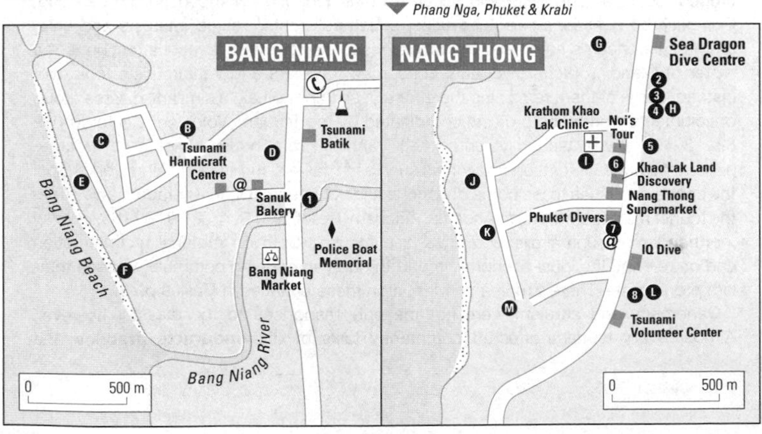

After the tsunami

The Boxing Day tsunami hit Thailand's Andaman coast just after 9.30am on December 26 2004. The first place to suffer significant damage was Phuket and the next two hours saw village after resort get battered or decimated by the towering waves thundering in from the Sumatra faultline, 1000km away. The entire coastline from Ranong to Satun was affected, but not all of it with the same intensity. Topography determined which areas suffered the most damage and the figures do the talking: 4200 were recorded dead or missing in Phang Nga province, many of them in the resort of Khao Lak, where the tidal flood topped 11m and extended 3km inland; over 2000 suffered a similar fate on Ko Phi Phi, whose sandy isthmus was breached by waves that came in simultaneously from north and south; and more than 900 died on the beaches of Phuket, where Patong and Kamala suffered the biggest casualties. There were 8212 fatalities in all, a third of them holidaymakers. Another 6000 people were made homeless and some 150,000 lost their jobs, mostly in the tourism and fishing industries. By the end of that day, nearly a quarter of a million people in a dozen countries around the Indian Ocean had lost their lives in the worst natural disaster in recorded history.

Many homes, shops and hotels have since been rebuilt, and where relevant are described in this chapter. But the emotional and social legacy of the tsunami endures and most residents along the Andaman coast have a story to tell. They are stories of terror and bereavement. Of how, when the churning wave swept in, the first of several, they were whipped up by the water and pummelled like clothes in a washing machine; of how they were pinned against trees and mutilated by debris; of how they survived by clinging to flotsam for hours. Many sustained horrific injuries and local hospitals struggled to cope. Victims not at the hospital were housed in camps, where many spent weeks scouring temple mortuaries and missing-persons noticeboards, waiting for sightings of relatives and friends. It's no surprise that many tsunami survivors are now afraid of the sea. Fishermen still have to make a living but they can't forget: fearing ghosts, some longtail boatmen won't motor solo past where villages once stood. Traumatized mainlanders cannot yet step back in a boat, and hundreds of hotel staff from Phuket, Phi Phi and Khao Lak have sought new jobs in the northern city of Chiang Mai, as far from the sea as they could go.

Immediately after the tsunami, many were surprised when then prime minister Thaksin Shinawatra declined offers of **aid** from foreign governments. But help poured in instead from the Thai government and from royal foundations and local and foreign NGOs and individuals. On Ko Phi Phi, volunteer divers removed, piece by piece, the fridges, beds, air-con units and suitcases that had been dumped on the sea bed. Complicated questions over land titles, squatters' rights, vested interests and environmental concerns hampered the official response to Phi Phi's reconstruction, but a roster of island workers, dive staff, concerned travellers and voluntourists took over instead, some of them remaining there for a year. In Khao Lak, a similarly diverse group of volunteers worked on projects coordinated by the Tsunami Volunteer Center (Ⓣ089 882 8840, Ⓦwww.tsunamivolunteer.net), ranging from house-building to income-generating projects for tsunami victims such as "Thaikea" furniture-making workshops; the centre continues to welcome donations and volunteers. Up in Khuraburi, away from the tourist mainstream, North Andaman Tsunami Relief (NATR, Ⓣ087 917 7165, Ⓦwww.northandamantsunamirelief.com) has also focused both on material reconstruction and on reviving the local economy, in part through an ongoing community-based tourism programme. There's more information on these charities in Basics p.78.

Generosity and altruism were not the only responses to the disaster however. Almost every tsunami-affected community talks of **dishonourable practice** and

corruption, experiences which have caused bitterness and rifts. Many allegations concern donated money and goods being held back by the community leaders charged with distributing them, with favouritism determining who got what. In other cases, well-intentioned privately established funds were so hamstrung by jealousies and lack of consensus that the money remained unspent or at best unused as it was intended. Many NGO projects were dedicated to building replacement houses for those made homeless by the tsunami – often in new locations, away from the devastated area, sometimes inland – but there is resentment over the number of non-victims who claimed new homes and some scammers are even said to have migrated hundreds of kilometres south from north and northeast Thailand. Some religious NGOs reportedly used blackmail: a villager could receive a new house or building materials if they denied their Buddhist or animist faith and proved, by attending church every Sunday, that they had espoused Christianity instead. Meanwhile, other genuinely homeless locals were subjected to impossible requests for documents now lost to the waves, only to find, in some cases, that big business interests subsequently muscled in on their officially "ownerless" plots.

Most small businesses had no insurance. Government **compensation** was offered but varied and was not, according to some, always fairly distributed. In Khao Lak, for example, an incomer might have lived and worked there for ten years but was only entitled to B17,000, or less (about US$400, or three months' wages for someone on minimum wage), because they had not been born in the neighbourhood – a tiny fraction of the B1 million a typical Khao Lak restaurant would have cost to establish, furnish and run. The banks did their bit by offering interest-free loans for three years (and Siam Commercial Bank donated thousands of sunloungers to the big resorts, whose beachfronts have now turned purple under the welter of SCB parasols), but in a country where most family enterprises scrape by season to season, it's sobering to contemplate the number of tsunami victims who simply picked up and started again. It's been especially difficult for those in the **tourist industry**: in the year following the tsunami, visitor numbers dropped to less than 50 percent of recent averages and many small tourist businesses simply couldn't continue. In places such as Ao Nang, where actual damage to property was relatively minor, the post-tsunami impact was far greater: when the local economy plummeted, beleaguered smallholders were obliged to sell their land at bargain rates, usually to bigger guns who could afford to wait for better times.

In the weeks that followed the tsunami, aftershocks were on many people's minds and serious warnings were issued at least twice, prompting everyone to scramble up the nearest high ground. Since then, even the vaguest news of tremors in the region cause panic. The government has responded by creating a **tsunami early-warning system** that relays public announcements from special towers constructed at intervals all the way down the Andaman coast. They have also mapped out evacuation routes, highlighted by innumerable "Tsunami Hazard Zone" signs in all the big resorts. For their part, Phuket authorities have remodelled stretches of Ao Patong's beachfront as a building-free zone, creating a park that doubles as a tsunami memorial. Krabi officials now require all new buildings to be constructed at least 30m inland from a high-tide boundary, and they even forbid the use of sunloungers below that point. In Khao Lak, an official **memorial** to the victims has been commissioned, and a museum may also be established there, though in the meantime it is the beached police boat that serves as the more palpable Khao Lak memorial: it rests where it was hurtled by the wave, two kilometres inland, on the other side of the highway.

considered the best. Others include Tong Pling, across from the *Merlin* resort in Khao Lak; Nam Tok Lumphi, about 20km south of Khao Lak; and Chong Fah Falls, located less than 5km east of Bang Niang, which is subject to a B200 entry fee because it's part of Khao Lak–Lam Ru National Park (Ⓦwww.dnp.go.th/National_park.asp), whose headquarters is on the headland between Nang Thong and Khao Lak beaches.

Arrival, transport and information

Khao Lak is just 70km north of **Phuket airport** (1hr, B1500 by taxi; see p.731). All **buses** running from Phuket to Takua Pa and Ranong (and vice versa), as well as some of its Surat Thani services, pass through Khao Lak and can drop you anywhere along Highway 4; if you're coming from Krabi or Phang Nga you should take a Phuket-bound bus as far as **Khokkloi** bus terminal and switch to a Takua Pa or Ranong bus. When it comes to moving on, many guest houses and all tour operators can arrange **taxi services** for up to four people to Krabi (B450 per person), Phuket airport or beaches (B1200–1800 per taxi) and Don Sak pier for Ko Samui (B3500).

It's sometimes also feasible to use the Highway 4 buses for **local transport** between the three beaches, particularly if staying at *Poseidon* down in Khao Lak, from where they charge about B10 to Nang Thong or Bang Niang. A fleet of blue songthaews also shuttles up and down Highway 4, running north from Nang Tong Supermarket to Takua Pa (B40), via Bang Niang (B20); the drivers also act as taxi drivers, so be careful you don't end up unintentionally chartering a whole songthaew (eg B200 to *Poseidon*). Alternatively, you can rent **motorbikes** (B200) through many hotels, and **cars** (B1200) through several tour operators, including Khao Lak Land Discovery in Nang Thong, who include insurance in all their car rentals; Budget also has an agent on the soi down to *Nang Thong Resort* (Ⓦwww.budget.co.th). Noi's Tour near Nang Thong Supermarket rents **bicycles** (B100–150).

Nang Thong has **minimarkets** stocked with all the essentials, plus **banks** with ATMs and exchange counters, **Internet** access, and a **clinic** at *Krathom Khao Lak* bungalows north of Nang Thong Supermarket (every evening during high season from about 3–9pm; the doctor is on call 24hr; Ⓣ089 868 2034). There are several tailors' shops here too. Most Nang Thong tour agents sell international and domestic air tickets and some can arrange train tickets. The biggest local **tour operator** is Khao Lak Land Discovery (Ⓣ076 420411, Ⓦwww.khaolaklanddiscovery.com). They offer lots of trips (most for a minimum of two people), including one that features elephant riding and a visit to Chong Fah Falls (B1650, kids B1200); a longtail boat tour around the karst islands of Ao Phang Nga (B1500/B1000); trekking, canoeing and elephant-riding in Khao Sok National Park (B2500/B1500); and day trips to Ko Similan (B2500/B1800) and Ko Phi Phi (B3150/B1950). For dive operators and details of diving and snorkelling trips to Ko Similan see the box opposite. Bang Niang has fewer shops and businesses, but there is Internet access and essential supplies on the main road to the beach, and a number of outlets for **crafts** made by and in aid of tsunami victims, including the Tsunami Handicraft Centre (closed Sun) on the road to the beach, and a batik centre on the highway, where you can also learn batik-making on request. The twice-weekly **Bang Niang market** convenes every Wednesday and Saturday afternoon beside the highway and is a fun spot for a browse through stalls selling everything from hot food and fresh vegetables to clothes and household items.

Dive operators in Khao Lak

Khao Lak is the closest and most convenient departure point for **diving and snorkelling trips** to the Similan islands and beyond. These trips are extremely popular and don't necessarily leave every day, so you should try to book them in advance. Normal live-aboard boats take around four or five hours to reach the Similans from Khao Lak, but some dive operators also use speedboats for day-trippers – these take less than two hours, but aren't recommended for anyone prone to seasickness (the high-speed catamarans are less bumpy). The diving season runs from November through April, though some dive shops do run trips year-round, weather permitting. All Khao Lak dive shops also teach PADI **dive courses**, and most offer learners the option of doing the last two days of their Openwater course on location in the Similans; for advice on choosing a dive shop see Basics p.70; for more on the Similans, see p.727 and for more on Ko Surin see p.713.

IQ Dive Central Nang Thong ⓣ076 423614, ⓦwww.iq-dive.com. Swiss–Thai-run PADI Five-Star Instructor Development Centre. They use both big boats and high-speed catamarans for their one-day dive trips to the Similans (B4100 plus equipment), but also do overnight trips, using national park accommodation on the islands (around B10,000 plus equipment); accompanying snorkellers get a forty percent discount. Openwater courses from B11,000, or B13,500 with two days in the Similans.

Phuket Divers Central Nang Thong ⓣ076 420628, ⓦwww.phuketdivers.com. Four-day trips on a comfortable live-aboard boat to the Similans, Surin islands and Richelieu Rock for B17,500; two days to the Similans for B10,000. Snorkellers are welcome on both for a reduced price. A PADI Five-Star dive centre.

Poseidon At *Poseidon Bungalows*, 7km south of central Nang Thong, in Khao Lak (see p.726) ⓣ076 443258, ⓦwww.similantour.com. Highly recommended three-day live-aboard snorkelling trips to the Similans (B6500); can arrange dives for accompanying divers if requested (B1400/dive). Current departures are twice weekly on Tuesdays and Fridays, from the end of October to the end of April.

Sea Dragon Dive Center Northern Nang Thong ⓣ076 420420, ⓦwww.seadragondivecenter.com. The longest-running Khao Lak dive operator is managed by experienced and safety-conscious farangs, is a PADI Five-Star IDC dive centre, has a good reputation and is highly recommended. They have three live-aboard boats – including a budget traveller-oriented boat, and a deluxe boat – and prices (which all include equipment) range from B10,800 for a three-day trip to the Similans with nine dives (available year-round), to B17,800 for a four-day expedition with thirteen dives on the Similans, Surin islands, Ko Bon, Ko Tachai and Richelieu Rock. Snorkellers can accompany some trips at one-third off the price. Aside from live-aboards you can also do one-day local dives for B1300–1800. All their Padi dive courses can be done in Khao Lak, where they have their own pool – one-day Discover Scuba from B1700, or four-day Openwater for B7800 – and some can be also be done while on one of the above dive trips.

Accommodation

The standard of **accommodation** in Khao Lak is high, with the vast majority of hotels benefiting from extensive post-tsunami refurbishment. The trend is upmarket, so you'll find very little under ❹, but, because of slow take-up following the tsunami, you may find decent discounts are offered on the below-listed rates, even during high season. Another reason for cut-price rates, however, might be in compensation for noisy construction work nearby, so double-check with your hotel first.

Bang Niang

Ayara Villas ⓣ076 423108, ⓦwww.ayara-villas.com. An attractive upper-range option, where the 57 air-con rooms, most of them in terraced bungalows just a few metres from the sea, are smartly furnished in dark wood and all have kitchenettes. ❼–❽

Fair House ⓣ089 473 7985. Currently the cheapest place to stay in Bang Niang, with its handful of neat, fan-cooled concrete bungalows and rooms widely spaced around a garden set back from the highway, about a kilometre's walk from the beach. Contact the *Fair House* office right beside Highway 4 to check in. ❹

La Flora ⓣ076 428000, ⓦwww.lafloraresort.com. The 77 rooms at this upscale beachfront hotel are all furnished in elegant contemporary Asian style, with day beds, stylish bathrooms and balconies. The cheaper ones are in three-storey hotel wings, and you pay extra for stand-alone villas, many of which enjoy direct sea views. There's a pool and spa, Internet access, and mountain bike and kayak rental. ❾

Sanuk Resort ⓣ076 420800 ⓦwww.sanukresort.com. This little complex of five brick bungalows occupies a small grassy garden compound, with tiny pool, just 100m from the beach. Rooms come with either fan or air-con and all have fridges and coffee-making facilities. Check in via the office next to the Sanuk Bakery on the main access road from the highway. ❺–❻

Thup Thong Guest House ⓣ076 420722, ⓔthupthong@gmail.com. The dozen large fan rooms here occupy a small three-storey block just back from the beach and all have a balcony offering either a sea view or an inland one. ❺–❻

Nang Thong

The Andaburi Resort ⓣ076 443388, ⓦwww.theandaburiresort.com. A good value upper-mid-range resort comprising sleek, modern air-con rooms in bungalows and two-storey terraced blocks set around a garden with a decent-sized swimming pool. There's no direct beach access, but it's about a 500-metre walk to the sea. ❼–❽

Father and Son (Nom's) ⓣ076 420277. This tiny haven of a place occupies a lovely, unexpectedly spacious tropical garden, a good distance behind *Nom's* restaurant and away from the highway. It offers just ten bungalows, the cheapest of which are made of bamboo and are the least expensive rooms in Khao Lak; sturdier concrete options are also available. All bungalows are en suite and have fans. The on-site Father and Son massage service has a great reputation. Phone ahead as it's very popular. ❷–❺

Jai ⓣ076 420390. A busy, family-run place that fills up fast not least because it offers some of the cheapest accommodation in Khao Lak. The 15 good-quality en–suite concrete bungalows are fan cooled and are dotted around a small garden behind the excellent restaurant, quite close to the highway and about 600m from the beach. ❸–❹

Khao Lak Green Beach ⓣ081 952 0917, ⓔgreenbeach_th@yahoo.com. The attractive design and shorefront location of the bungalows here make this a good-value option. The cream-painted chalet-style bungalows come with fan or air-con chalets and all have polished wood floors, pretty furnishings, garden showers and a fridge. Some are right on the shore. Fan ❻, air-con ❻–❼

Nang Thong Bay Resort ⓣ076 420088, ⓔnangthong1@hotmail.com. Efficiently run, popular, good quality beachfront place that offers a range of smartly maintained air-con bungalows and hotel-style rooms in small blocks. Interiors have contemporary furnishings and some have garden bathrooms. The bungalows are well spaced around the shorefront garden, so many have sea views, and there's a sea-view swimming pool as well. Prices drop by 50 percent from Oct–May. ❼–❽

Phu Khao Lak Resort ⓣ076 420141, ⓔphukhaolak@hotmail.com. There is a luxurious amount of space at this well-run place, where the two-dozen large, spotlessly clean brick and concrete bungalows sit prettily amid a grassy lawned park-style coconut plantation. Rooms have fans and bathrooms and are among the cheapest in the resort, about 500m walk from the beach. Price depends on the size of the bungalow. ❹

Suwan Palm Resort ⓣ076 423170, ⓦwww.suwanpalm.com. Occupying a prime beachfront location, with sea views enjoyed by most of its 44 rooms, this place offers comfortably furnished upper-bracket air-con rooms in a three-storey block, plus a pool, on-site pub, spa and shop. ❽–❾

Khao Lak

Poseidon Bungalows ⓣ076 443258, ⓦwww.similantour.com. Seven kilometres south of central Nang Thong, above a wild and rocky shore surrounded by rubber plantations, this Swedish-Thai-run guest house is a lovely place to hang out for a few days and it's also a long-established organizer of snorkelling expeditions to the Similan islands (see opposite). All 15 bungalows are en suite and fan cooled, and some can sleep four; there's a restaurant too, plus Internet access and motorbike rental. To get here, either ask to be dropped off the bus at the *Poseidon* access road between kilometre-stones 53 and 54, from where it's a walk of 1km; or get off at the bus station in nearby Lam Kaen village (between kilometre-stones 50 and 51), from where it's easy to get a B40 motorbike taxi ride to the bungalows. Motorbikes are available for rent. ❺–❻

Eating and drinking

Except where stated, all listed restaurants and bars are located alongside the highway in Nang Thong.

Fisherman Bar A lively bar that's popular with young NGO workers, serves cocktails very cheap from 5–8pm, holds regular barbecues and sometimes has live music. Nightly 5pm–1am.

Happy Snapper This very chilled-out bar and restaurant is popular with dive instructors and makes a pleasant place to while away an evening. Upstairs, it's mainly floor seating in the open-sided *sala* among the Thai and Burmese artefacts, while downstairs there's live music most nights from 10.30pm except Sundays (usually blues), and the occasional open-mike session for would-be entertainers. The food menu is fairly limited but tasty enough, featuring mid-priced tacos, pasta and red snapper; the drinks menu runs to 140 different cocktails. Nightly 6pm–1am.

Jai Deservedly popular restaurant that serves lots of different curries (from B60), including penang and *matsaman* versions, as well as plenty of seafood, *tom yam* and the like.

Khao Lak Seafood Very popular, unpretentious place to sample the local catch; most dishes B60–200.

Nom's Nang Thong. Home-style cooking: mainly noodle and rice dishes (from B40) as well as plenty of fresh seafood.

Phu Khao Lak Seafood Well-known and good-value restaurant attached to the bungalows of the same name serving exceptionally good Thai food from a menu that stretches to over 100 dishes. Everything from red, yellow and green curries (from B60) to seafood platters (B200).

Stempfer Café European-run café serving eight different set breakfasts (B50–100), fresh coffees, hot chocolate, lots of cakes and bread, plus salads and a few hot dishes.

Takieng Next to the police-boat tsunami memorial in Bang Niang. Authentic Thai food, including good *tom yum kung* and seafood, at authentic Thai prices (B40–100).

Ko Similan

Rated by *Skin Diver* magazine as one of the world's top ten spots for both above-water and underwater beauty, the eleven islands at the heart of the **KO SIMILAN** National Park (Ⓦwww.dnp.go.th/National_park.asp) are among the most exciting **diving** destinations in Thailand. Massive granite boulders set magnificently against turquoise waters give the islands their distinctive character, but it's the thirty-metre visibility that draws the divers. The underwater scenery is nothing short of overwhelming here: the reefs teem with a host of coral fish, from the long-nosed butterfly fish to the black-, yellow-and-white-striped angel fish, and the ubiquitous purple and turquoise parrot fish, which nibble so incessantly at the coral. A little further offshore, magnificent mauve and burgundy crown-of-thorns starfish stalk the sea bed, gobbling chunks of coral as they go – and out here you'll also see turtles, manta rays, moray eels, jacks, reef sharks, sea snakes, red grouper and quite possibly white-tip sharks, barracuda, giant lobster and enormous tuna.

The **islands** lie 64km off the mainland and include the eponymous Ko Similan chain of nine islands as well as two more northerly islands, Ko Bon and Ko Tachai, which are both favoured haunts of manta rays and whale sharks and are half way between the Similan chain and the islands of Ko Surin. The nine islands of the Similan chain are numbered north–south from nine to one and often referred to by number. In descending order, they are: Ko Ba Ngu (number nine), Ko Similan, Ko Hin Posar (aka Hin Huwagralok), Ko Payoo, Ko

Ha, Ko Miang (number four), Ko Pahyan, Ko Pahyang and Ko Hu Yong. Only Ko Ba Ngu and Ko Miang are inhabited, with the national park headquarters and accommodation located on the latter; some tour groups are also allowed to camp on Ko Similan. Ko Similan is the largest island in the chain, blessed with a beautiful, fine white-sand bay and impressive boulders; Ko Miang has two pretty beaches, twenty minutes' walk apart; Ko Hu Yong has an exceptionally long white-sand bay and is used by **turtles** for egg-laying (see box on p.846) from November to February.

Such beauty has not gone unnoticed and the islands are extremely popular with day-trippers from Phuket and Khao Lak, as well as with divers and snorkellers on longer live-aboard trips. This has caused the inevitable congestion and environmental problems and the Similan reefs have been damaged in places by anchors and by the local practice of using dynamite in fishing. National parks authorities have responded by taking drastic action to protect this precious region, banning fishermen from the island chain (to vociferous and at times violent protest), imposing a three-kilometre ban on sport fishing and enforcing strict regulations for tourist boats. Although Ko Similan is open all year, during the **monsoon season** between mid-May and mid-November only dive boats visit the islands as high seas make it too dangerous for day-trippers' fast boats.

Practicalities

Most travel agents in Khao Lak, Phuket and Phang Nga sell one-day (B2500–3000) and overnight (from B4500) snorkelling **packages** to Ko Similan (usually mid-Nov–mid-May only), which feature at least four island stops. The majority of these trips carry quite large groups and use fast boats that depart from **Thap Lamu pier**, about 8km south of central Khao Lak, 90 km north of Phuket town, at 8.30am and get to their first island stop, Ko Ba Ngu, in under two hours. They depart the islands at around 3pm. Independent travellers wanting to stay on the island for a few days can usually use these **boats** for transfers, with the chance of a discount if joining the boat at Thap Lamu pier rather than being picked up from one of the resorts. Companies offering this service include Jack Similan (Ⓣ076 443205, Ⓦwww.jacksimilan.com) and Met Sine Travel and Tours (Ⓣ076 443276, Ⓦwww.similanthailand.com), both of which have offices at the Thap Lamu pier. If travelling independently, you'll need to use Ko Similan longtail boats to travel **between the islands** and to explore different reefs: prices are fixed and cost B150–300 per person, depending on the distance.

Limited **accommodation** is available on Ko Miang, in the shape of national park bungalows sleeping 4–8 people (B600–2000) and tents (B200–400), and there's an expensive restaurant. You should book your accommodation in advance, either with the national parks office near Thap Lamu pier (Ⓣ076 595045) or online (Ⓦwww.dnp.go.th/National_park.asp), as facilities can get crowded with tour groups, especially on weekends and holidays. There's no drinking-water available outside Ko Miang, and campfires are prohibited on all the islands.

Overcrowding is a growing problem at the Similans and the best way to escape this is to join a small-scale **live-aboard** diving or snorkelling trip to the islands, which means you can visit the best spots before or after the package-tour groups. The best and cheapest of these run out of Khao Lak, the closest mainland resort to the Similans; Phuket is another popular springboard and you can also start live-aboard trips from Ko Chang (see p.704) and Ko Phayam (see p.708). Khao Lak prices start at B10,000 for a two-day live-aboard **diving** trip, with about a forty percent discount for accompanying snorkellers, while a three-day dedicated **snorkelling** live-aboard costs B6500; for full details see p.725. Most of the Phuket-based dive operators (see p.750) only offer three- or four-day live-aboards to the Similans (also featuring Richelieu Rock and a couple of other sites) for B20,000–30,000 (excluding equipment); some trips are open to accompanying snorkellers at a slight discount. IQ Dive in Khao Lak (see box on p.725) also does one-day dive and snorkel trips to the Similans (B4100/2300 excluding equipment), and Santana on Phuket does one-day dives (B4600; see p.751).

Phuket

Thailand's largest island and a province in its own right, **Phuket** (pronounced "Poo-ket") has been a prosperous region since the nineteenth century, when Chinese merchants got in on its tin-mining and sea-borne trade, before turning to the rubber industry. It remains the wealthiest province in Thailand, with the highest per-capita income, but what mints the money nowadays is **tourism**: with an annual influx of foreign visitors that tops one million, Phuket ranks second in popularity only to Pattaya, and the package-tour traffic has wrought its usual transformations. Thoughtless tourist developments have scarred much of the island, and the trend on all the beaches is upmarket, with very few budget possibilities, though some of Phuket's tiny offshore islands offer a calmer and often better value alternative. Remoter parts of Phuket itself are also still attractive, however, particularly the interior, whose fertile, hilly expanse is dominated by rubber and pineapple plantations. Many inland neighbourhoods are clustered round the local mosque – 35 percent of Phuketians are **Muslim**, and there are said to be more mosques on the island than Buddhist temples – and, though the atmosphere is generally as easy-going as elsewhere in Thailand, it's especially important to dress with some modesty outside the main resorts, and to not sunbathe topless on any of the beaches. Phuket's watersports and diving facilities are among the best in the country, but as with the rest of the Andaman coast, the sea is at its least inviting during the **monsoon**, from June to October, when Phuket's west-coast beaches in particular become quite rough and windswept. Some stretches of Phuket's coast were very badly damaged by the December 2004 tsunami, which caused significant loss of life and destroyed a lot of property. Reconstruction was swift, however, and a first-time visitor to the island is now unlikely to notice any major post-tsunami effect. For more on the tsunami and its legacy, see the box on p.722.

Phuket's capital, Muang Phuket or **Phuket town**, is on the southeast coast, 42km south of the Sarasin Bridge linking the island to the mainland. Most people pass straight through the town on their way to the **west coast**, where three resorts corner the bulk of the trade: high-rise **Ao Patong**, the most developed and expensive, with an increasingly seedy nightlife; the slightly nicer, if unexceptional, **Ao Karon**; and adjacent **Ao Kata**, the smallest of the trio. If you're after a more peaceful spot, aim for the seventeen-kilometre-long national park beach of **Hat Mai Khao**, its more developed neighbour **Hat Nai Yang**, or one of the smaller alternatives at **Hat Nai Thon**, or **Hat Kamala**. Most of the other west-coast beaches are dominated by just a few upmarket hotels, specifically **Hat Nai Harn**, **Ao Pansea** and **Ao Bang Tao**, while the south and east coasts have unswimmable beaches and are used mainly for access to other islands, including **Ko Racha Yai** or **Ko Kaeo Pisadan**.

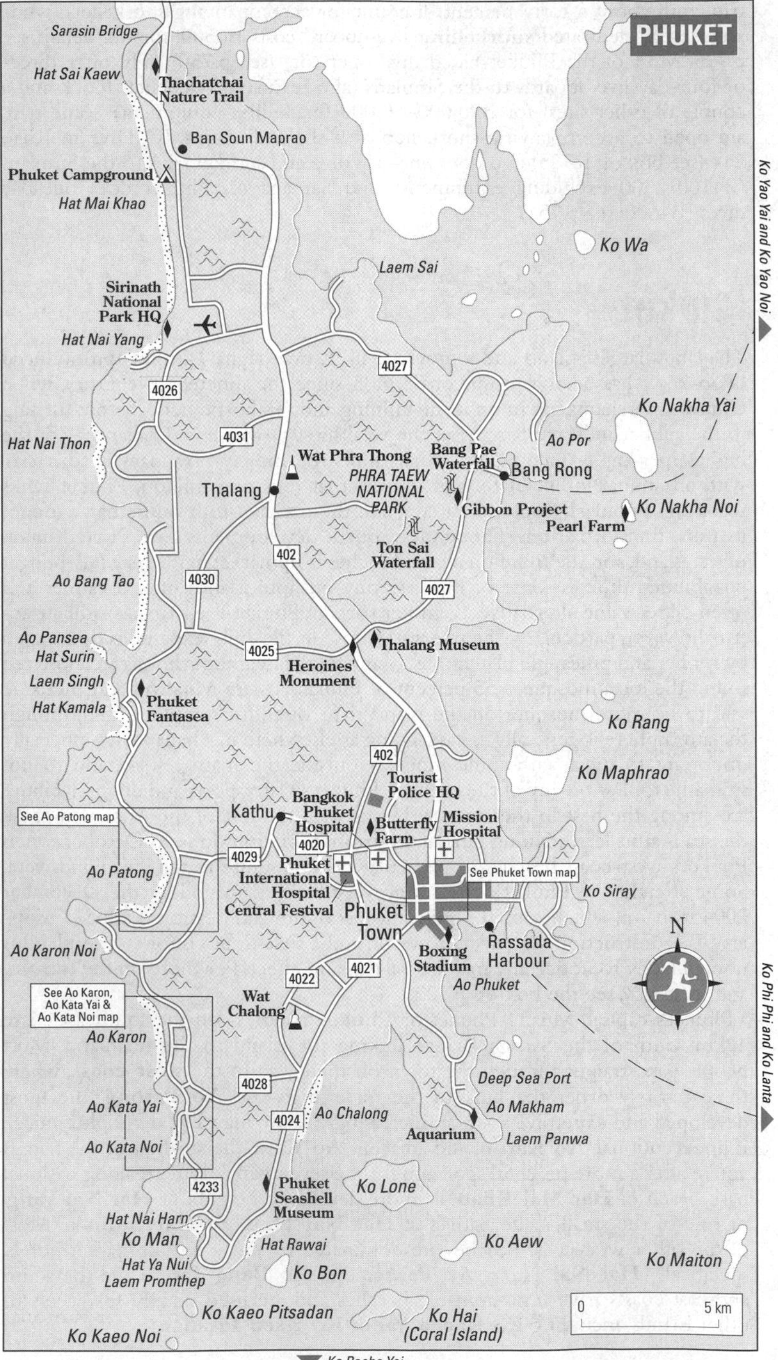
PHUKET
Ranong & Krabi
Sarasin Bridge
Hat Sai Kaew
Thachatchai Nature Trail
Ban Soun Maprao
Phuket Campground
Hat Mai Khao
Ko Yao Yai and Ko Yao Noi
Ko Wa
Laem Sai
Sirinath National Park HQ
Hat Nai Yang
4027
4026
Ko Nakha Yai
4031
Hat Nai Thon
Ao Por
Wat Phra Thong
Bang Pae Waterfall
Bang Rong
Thalang
PHRA TAEW NATIONAL PARK
Gibbon Project
Ko Nakha Noi
Pearl Farm
Ton Sai Waterfall
402
4030
4027
Ao Bang Tao
Ao Pansea
Hat Surin
Laem Singh
Hat Kamala
4025
Thalang Museum
Heroines' Monument
Phuket Fantasea
Ko Rang
402
Ko Maphrao
Tourist Police HQ
See Ao Patong map
Kathu
Bangkok Phuket Hospital
Butterfly Farm
Mission Hospital
4020
4029
Ao Patong
Phuket International Hospital
See Phuket Town map
Ko Siray
Central Festival
Phuket Town
Boxing Stadium
Rassada Harbour
N
Ao Karon Noi
4021
4022
Ao Phuket
See Ao Karon, Ao Kata Yai & Ao Kata Noi map
Wat Chalong
Ko Phi Phi and Ko Lanta
Ao Karon
4028
Deep Sea Port
Ao Kata Yai
Ao Makham
4024
Ao Chalong
Aquarium
Laem Panwa
Ao Kata Noi
4233
Phuket Seashell Museum
Ko Lone
Hat Nai Harn
Ko Man
Ko Aew
Hat Rawai
Ko Maiton
Hat Ya Nui
Ko Bon
Laem Promthep
0
5 km
Ko Kaeo Pitsadan
Ko Hai (Coral Island)
Ko Kaeo Noi
Ko Racha Yai

There's a wide-ranging **website** about Phuket, Ⓦwww.phuket.com, which is particularly good for discounted accommodation on the island.

Getting to the island

There's no shortage of transport to Phuket, with plenty of flights from Bangkok, a good bus service from major southern towns, and ferries running in from nearby islands.

By air

Quite a few airlines operate direct **international flights** to Phuket, so if you're starting your Thailand trip in the south, it may be worth flying straight here or via another Asian city rather than having to make connections via Bangkok. Between them, Thai Airways, Bangkok Airways, Air Asia and Nok Air run fifteen **domestic flights** a day between Bangkok and Phuket (1hr 20min), while Bangkok Airways also runs daily flights to Phuket from Pattaya (1hr 40min) and Ko Samui (50min).

Phuket International Airport (Ⓣ076 327230) is located on the north-west coast of the island, 32km northwest of Phuket town. There is an hourly **airport bus** that runs as far as the bus station in Phuket town but does not serve the beaches (you'll need to change on to the songthaews in town to reach those); buses run from the airport from 6.30am–5.30pm and cost B52 to the bus terminal, taking about an hour. In the reverse direction they depart approximately hourly from 5am–6.30pm. There's also an **airport minibus**, which will drop you at your hotel and charges B100 per person for the ride into town, B150 to Ao Patong and B180 to Ao Kata or Ao Karon. **Taxis** cost about B400–600 to the main west-coast beaches of Ao Patong, Ao Karon and Ao Kata, or about B300 to Phuket town. **Rental car** companies Avis (Ⓣ076 351244, Ⓦwww.avisthailand.com) and Budget (Ⓣ076 205397, Ⓦwww.budget.co.th) both have desks in the arrivals area, and there's a **left-luggage** service (daily 6am–10pm; B40/item/day).

The cheapest way for solo travellers to **get to the airport** is by the airport bus, described above, but from the resorts, most people use taxis instead, a service offered by nearly all hotels on Patong, Karon and Kata for B400–600; the trip takes about an hour. One company on Patong offers a cheaper hourly minibus service, described on p.746. The domestic **departure tax** is included in the price of the air ticket, but for international departures you will be charged at check-in: until January 2007 the tax is B500, but from February 1 2007 it rises to B700. Contact details for the Phuket offices of international and domestic airlines are given on p.738.

By bus

Direct **air-con buses** from Bangkok to Phuket leave from the Southern Bus Terminal and take about 14 hours to reach Phuket town's bus station; most make the journey overnight, departing from mid-afternoon onwards. Most return buses also travel overnight. There is no train service to Phuket, but you could book an overnight sleeper train to Surat Thani, about 290km east of Phuket, and take a bus from there to Phuket (about six hours). There are plenty of ordinary and air-con buses between **Surat Thani** and Phuket, some of which run via **Khao Sok**, **Takua Pa** and **Khao Lak**, and a fast private minibus service also runs from Phuket's *Montri Hotel* on Thanon Montri to Surat Thani (every 2hr; 4hr 30min; B220). Takua Pa is a useful interchange for local services to Khuraburi and Ranong, though there are a few direct buses between **Ranong** and Phuket. As for points further south: numerous buses travel between **Krabi** and Phuket, via **Phang Nga**, and there are also frequent services to and from **Trang**, **Hat Yai** and **Nakhon Si Thammarat**; a private minibus service also runs between Phuket town and Nakhon Si Thammarat, departing from the Thanon Deebuk/Thanon Suthat junction (hourly; 7hr; B220). The TAT office in Phuket town (see p.739) keeps up-to-date bus timetables.

Nearly all buses to and from Phuket use the **bus station** (☎076 211977) at the eastern end of Thanon Phang Nga in Phuket town, from where it's a ten-minute walk or a short tuk-tuk ride to the town's central hotel area, and slightly further to the Thanon Ranong departure-point for songthaews to the beaches. The hourly airport bus also serves the bus terminal.

By boat

If you're coming to Phuket from Ko Phi Phi, Ko Lanta or Ao Nang, the quickest and most scenic option is to take the **boat**. During peak season, up to three ferries a day make the trip to and from **Ko Phi Phi** (1hr 30min–2hr 30min), usually docking at Rassada Harbour on Phuket's east coast; during low season, there's at least one ferry a day in both directions. Travellers from **Ko Lanta** (service available Nov–May only; 1 daily; 4hr 30min) may have to change boats at **Ao Nang** (Nov–May only; 1 daily; 2hr 30min) or Ko Phi Phi. Minibuses meet the ferries in Phuket and charge B70 per person for transfers to Phuket

Day-trips and other activities

There are heaps of things to do on Phuket, and tour agents on all the main beaches will be only too happy to fix you up with your activity of choice, or you can arrange it yourself by calling the relevant numbers. Transport from your hotel is usually included in the price of a day-trip. For details of dive operators in Phuket, see p.750.

Activities and days out

Bicycle touring Full- and half-day guided mountain-bike rides into Phuket's peaceful, scenic interior with Action Holidays Phuket (☎076 263575, ⓦwww.biketoursthailand.com; full day from B1950/kids B1600).

Deep-sea fishing Day-trips and overnight charters in custom-built boats from Andaman Hooker ☎076 282036, ⓦwww.phuket.com/fishing/andaman.htm; Harry's Fishing Adventures ☎076 340418, ⓦwww.harrysfishing-phuket.com; and Phuket Sportfishing Centre ☎076 214713.

Elephant trekking Many companies offer the chance to ride an elephant, including the award-winning, conservation-conscious Siam Safari, whose tour also includes a visit to their elephant camp in the hills behind Chalong (☎076 280116, ⓦwww.siamsafari.com; from B1350, kids B700).

Golf Phuket has four eighteen-hole courses open to the public, costing B3100 to B5300, with club rental B400–850 and caddies about B200: the Blue Canyon Country Club near Hat Nai Yang ☎076 328088, ⓦwww.bluecanyonclub.com; the Laguna Phuket Club on Hat Bang Tao ☎076 270991, ⓦwww.lagunaphuket.com/golfclub; the Loch Palm Golf Club in Kathu ☎076 321929, ⓦwww.lochpalm.com; and the Phuket Country Club, also in Kathu ☎076 321038, ⓦwww.phuketcountryclub.com. You can arrange golf packages through Phuket Golf Tours ☎076 244893, ⓦwww.phuketgolftours.com.

Horse-riding Ride along jungle trails and sandy beaches with Phuket Laguna Riding Club on Hat Bang Tao ☎076 324199 ⓦwww.phuket-bangtao-horseriding.com, or Phuket Riding Club in Rawai ☎076 288213.

Sea-canoeing Sunset, one- and two-day expeditions in sea kayaks around the spectacular limestone karsts of Ao Phang Nga, or in Khao Sok National Park for town hotels, B150 to the major west-coast beaches, or B200 to the airport (leave plenty of extra time if you have a flight to catch as boats are notoriously tardy); some ferry agents include the transfer price in their tickets. Taxis to the main beaches usually cost B500.

Island transport

Although the best west-coast beaches are connected by road, to get from one beach to another by **public transport** you nearly always have to go back into Phuket town; songthaews run regularly throughout the day from Thanon Ranong in the town centre and cost between B20 and B40 from town to the coast. **Tuk-tuks and taxis** do travel directly between major beaches, but charge around B100 from Kata to Karon, B200 between Patong and Karon, and B300 for Karon to Kamala. For transport within resorts, the cheapest option is to make use of the public songthaews where possible, and to hail **motorbike taxis** elsewhere (from B20). However, many tourists on Phuket ride **motorbikes** or mopeds, available for rent on all the main beaches for B200–250 per day (be sure to ask for a helmet, as the compulsory helmet law is strictly enforced in most areas of Phuket, fines of B500 for not wearing them); alternatively, rent a **jeep** for B800–1200. Be aware though that traffic accidents are legion on Phuket, especially for bikers: some reports put the number of motorbike

around B3000–3500 per person per day. Contact John Gray's Sea Canoe ⓣ076 254505, ⓦwww.johngray-seacanoe.com.

Thai cookery courses Different daily classes at Phuket Thai Cookery School east of Phuket town (ⓣ076 252354, ⓦwww.phuket-thaicookeryschool.com; B1900 incl transfer from main beaches); and at many hotels, including, most famously, every Saturday and Sunday at *Mom Tri's Boathouse* hotel on Ao Kata Yai (ⓣ076 330015, ⓦwww.boathousephuket.com; B2000 for one day, or B3200 for both days).

Nights out

Phuket Fantasea ⓣ076 385000, ⓦwww.phuket-fantasea.com. Enjoyable spectacular that's staged at the Fantasea entertainments complex just inland of Hat Kamala. The 75-minute show is a slick, hi-tech fusion of high-wire trapeze acts, acrobatics, pyrotechnics, illusionists, comedy and traditional dance – plus a depressing baby elephant circus. Transport should be included in the steep ticket price (B1100/800 adults/children), with an optional, unexciting pre-show dinner (B500). The show starts at 9pm every night except Thursday; tickets can be bought through any tour operator.

Phuket Simon Cabaret ⓣ076 342011, ⓦwww.phuket-simoncabaret.com. Famous extravaganza in which a troupe of outrageously flamboyant transvestites perform song-and-dance numbers. It's all very Hollywood – a little bit risqué but not at all sleazy – so the show is popular with tour groups and families. The cabarets are staged two or three times a night, and tickets can be bought from any tour agent for B500–600 (kids B300/400); agents should provide free transport to the theatre, which is south of Patong, on the road to Karon.

Thai Boxing Bouts at the Saphan Hin stadium, located at the southern end of Thanon Phuket in Saphan Hin, just south of Phuket town (ⓣ076 214690; Tues & Fri 8–11pm; B700–1000), and at Bangla Boxing Stadium, Thanon Bangla, Ao Patong (ⓣ076 345578; 5–11pm; B700–10000). The Saphan Hin stadium also offers *muay Thai* training at their Suwit Gym (ⓣ076 381167, ⓦwww.bestmuaythai.com; B500/day or B2000/6-day course).

fatalities on Phuket as high as three hundred per year, many of which could allegedly have been prevented if the rider had been wearing a helmet.

Phuket town

Though it has plenty of hotels and restaurants, **PHUKET TOWN** (Muang Phuket) stands distinct from the tailor-made tourist settlements along the beaches as a place geared primarily towards its residents. Most visitors hang about just long enough to jump on a beach-bound songthaew, but you may find yourself returning for a welcome dose of real life; Phuket town has an enjoyably

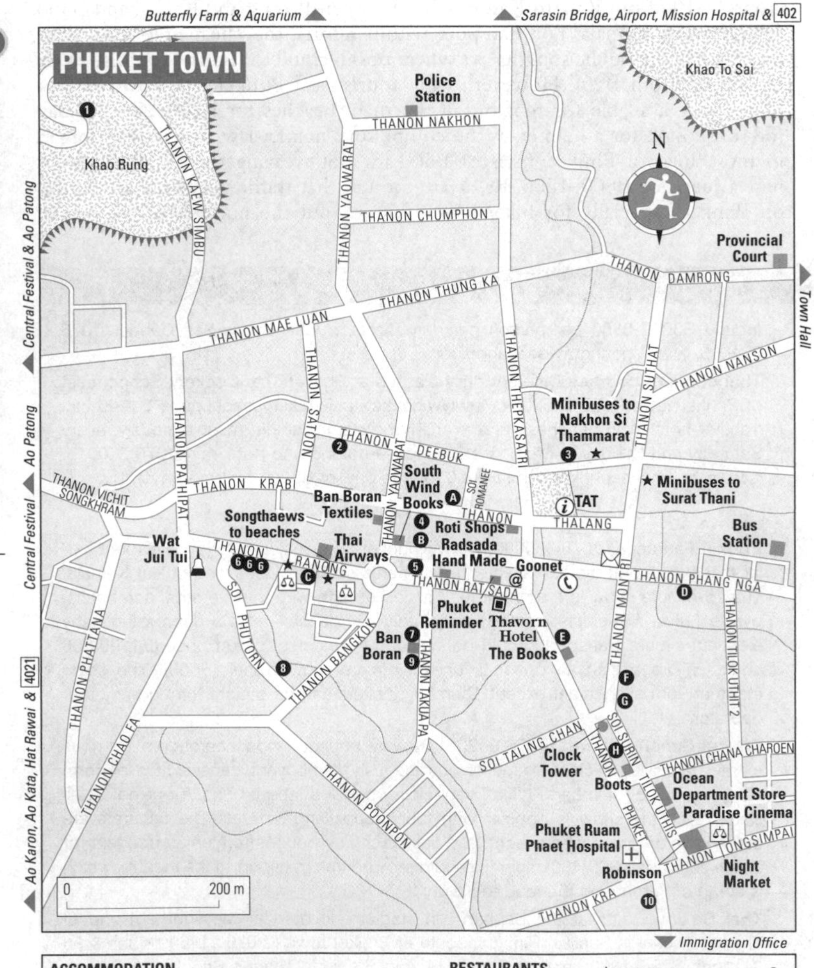

ACCOMMODATION			
Crystal Guest House	F	On On Hotel	B
Crystal Inn	H	Phuket Backpacker Hostel	C
Imperial Hotel	E	Royal Phuket City	D
The Metropole Phuket	G	Talang Guest House	A

RESTAURANTS			
China Inn Café	4	Lemongrass	3
Dibuk Restaurant	2	Natural Restaurant (Thammachat)	8
Ka Jok See	9	Phuket View Restaurant	1
Kanasutra	7	Salavatore's Restaurant	5
La Gaetana	10	Vegetarian Restaurants	6

authentic market on Thanon Ranong, great restaurants and some of the best handicraft shops on the island. If you're on a tight budget, the town is worth considering as a base, as accommodation and food come a little less expensive, and you can get out to all the beaches with relative ease. Bear in mind, though, that the town offers limited nightlife, and as public transport to and from the more lively beaches stops at dusk, you'll have to either rent your own wheels or spend a lot of money on tuk-tuks.

The town's most interesting sights are its historic colonial-style **Sino-Portuguese shophouses**, which were built by Chinese merchants who emigrated from Penang in the late nineteenth century. A string of these elegant old buildings lines the still charmingly traditional western arm of **Thanon Thalang**, where signs at a dozen shops highlight the special features worth an upward glance, including pastel-coloured doors and shutters, elaborate stucco mouldings and ornate wooden doors. The Thanon Yaowarat end of the road is dominated by Chinese shops and businesses including *Talang Guest House* at no. 37 (see p.736), and the delightful *China Inn Café* at no. 20 (see p.736); 100m further east along Thanon Thalang there's more of an Islamic emphasis, with many old-style shops selling fabric and dressmaking accessories, including lots of good-value sarongs from Malaysia and Indonesia, and several Muslim roti shops. Restoration work at buildings along **Thanon Romanee**, the tiny soi north off Thalang that was once a red-light alley, means that this road is also worth a stroll, as is the western arm of nearby **Thanon Deebuk** (Dibuk), around *Dibuk Restaurant* at no. 69, where doors and window shutters display intricate wooden fretwork. You'll find other renovated Sino-Portuguese buildings on Thanon Yaowarat, and on Thanon Ranong (where the Thai Airways office is a fine example), Thanon Phang Nga (the *On On Hotel*) and Thanon Damrong, where the town hall, just east of the Provincial Court, stood in for the US embassy in Phnom Penh in the film *The Killing Fields*. There's a much quainter, mustier whiff of the past contained within the wood-panelled lobby of Thanon Rat Sada's *Thavorn Hotel*, whose museum-like reception area and adjacent rooms, signed as the **Phuket History Corner**, are filled with faded photos of historic Phuket, plus

△ Songthaew stop, Thanon Ranong

a jumble of posters, typewriters and other everyday objects dating from the late nineteenth and early twentieth century, most of it amassed by the Thavorn family. Entry is free and non-guests are welcome to admire the eclectic collection, some of which also spills over into the hotel's streetside *Collector Pub*.

Kids usually enjoy the **Phuket Butterfly Farm and Aquarium** (*Faam Phi Seua*; daily 9am–5pm; B200, kids B100), located a couple of kilometres beyond the northern end of Thanon Yaowarat at 71/6 Soi Paneang in Ban Sam Kong, but though there are heaps of butterflies of various species, and a few reef fish, there's a lack of specific information. There's no public **transport** to the butterfly farm, but a tuk-tuk from the town centre should cost around B100 return. If you have your own vehicle, follow Thanon Yaowarat as far north as you can and then pick up the signs for the farm.

Accommodation

Few tourists choose to stay in Phuket town, but there's a reasonable spread of accommodation to choose from and it's a much better place to meet other travellers than at the beaches.

Crystal Guest House 41/16 Thanon Montri ⓣ076 222774. Old-fashioned, hotel-style downtown guest house where all rooms are en suite, though some of the cheapest have no window; the most expensive have air-con, hot water and TV. Fan 2, air con 3

Crystal Inn 2/1-10 Soi Surin, Thanon Montri ⓣ076 256789. Surprisingly stylish and contemporary bedroom decor make this small 54-room downtown hotel an inviting and good-value option. All rooms have air-con. 5

Imperial Hotel 51 Thanon Phuket, ⓣ076 212311. This small, all-air-con hotel is a handily central standby if preferred options are full. Rooms are old style and shabby but comfortable and all have TV. 5

The Metropole Phuket 1 Thanon Montri ⓣ076 215050, ⓦwww.metropolephuket.com. Grand, conservative high-rise hotel that's popular with domestic tourists and businesspeople. The air-con rooms are comfortably outfitted if not especially elegant; some are wheelchair accessible. There's also a fourth-floor outdoor pool and traditional massage service. 8

On On Hotel 19 Thanon Phang Nga ⓣ076 211154. This attractive, colonial-style 1920s building is a long-running travellers' favourite, mainly because the rooms are so cheap. They're pretty basic, with very thin walls, holes in the floorboards and ancient plumbing, but they're adequate; the cheapest share bathrooms, the most expensive have air-con. There's Internet access and a tour agent in the lobby. Shared bathroom 1, en suite 2, air-con 3

Phuket Backpacker Hostel 167 Thanon Ranong, ⓣ 076 256680, ⓦwww.phuketbackapacker.com. Right in the fresh market a couple of steps from the songthaew stop for the beaches, this place has made a big effort to look modern and upbeat, with bright colour schemes, abstract art on the walls, a DVD lounge and a communal kitchen. It offers B250 dorm bunk beds in four-bed train-like cubicles within a mixed-sex 16-bed fan dorm, or B350 beds in smaller air-con dorms. It also has some cheerful fan and air-con singles and doubles, though most of these just have windows on to a passageway. 4

Royal Phuket City 154 Thanon Phang Nga ⓣ076 233333, ⓦwww.royalphuketcity.com. Large, high-rise business hotel, with swimming pool, spa, gym, business centre and comfortable air-con rooms, most of them with fine views over the city. 7

Talang Guest House 37 Thanon Thalang ⓣ076 214225, ⓦwww.thalangguesthouse.com. Housed in a 1940s, Sino-Portuguese, wood-floored former shophouse in one of Phuket's most attractive traditional streets, this place is a little faded but full of character, traveller-friendly and good value. The dozen fan and air-con rooms are large and en suite – the best of them are up on the rooftop, affording unusual panoramic views. It's very popular, so you need to book ahead. Rates include breakfast. 2–3

Eating

Phuket town has much the largest concentration of good Thai food on the island, well worth making the effort for.

China Inn Café 20 Thanon Thalang. This Sino-Portuguese house has been stunningly renovated inside and out. The interior serves as a gallery and shop displaying Asian antiques, textiles and one-off artefacts, while the café occupies the tranquil enclosed garden and colonnade at the back, filled with tropical blooms and marble-top tables. The menu features classy Thai and Mediterranean food, including delicious mozzarella salads (B220), spicy Thai salads (from B120), and innovative juice mixes with tamarind and rambutan among others (B85). Mon–Sat 9am–6pm.

Dibuk Restaurant 69 Thanon Deebuk. Posh, expensive French food – including steaks, beef bourgignon and *moules* (mussels) – plus some Thai dishes, served in an attractive old Sino-Portuguese building. Daily 11am–11pm.

Ka Jok See 26 Thanon Takuapa ☎076 217903. A Phuket institution, housed in a beautiful restored traditional shophouse (unsigned), next to Ban Boran antiques shop, this place serves fabulous food and fosters a fun, sociable atmosphere. The menu is sophisticated, beautifully presented Thai food – their *goong sarong*, individual shrimps bound in a crisp-noodle wrap, is famous island-wide – and although nearly all main dishes cost B280, every diner also gets a free starter and dessert. By about 10pm there is jiving between courses as staff take the lead and encourage locals and expats to have a boogie. Reservations are essential. Tues–Sun 6pm–1am.

Kanasutra 18 Thanon Takuapa. Contemporary Indian restaurant with a tandoori oven, serving everything from sheesh kebab to prawn vindaloo. Most dishes cost around B220. Nightly from 6pm.

La Gaetana 352 Thanon Phuket ☎076 250523. Welcoming Italian-Thai eatery whose menu includes home-made pasta with some great sauces, a special house fish stew, outstanding home-made ice creams – the durian ice cream is an acquired taste but worth the effort – and good-value wine by the glass (B90). Most mains cost B180. Mon, Tues & Fri noon–2pm & 6pm–late, Thurs, Sat & Sun 6pm–late.

Lemongrass 2/9 Thanon Dibuk. This popular, unpretentious, open-air plaza-garden restaurant, serves good, authentic, mid-priced Thai food – mountain fern salad, wing bean and banana-flower salad, lots of fish dishes and numerous curries – at reasonable prices (most are B80). Daily 5pm–1am.

Natural Restaurant (Thammachat) 62/5 Soi Putorn (Phoo Thon). Very popular with Phuket residents, this is a rambling, informal eatery whose open-sided dining rooms are wreathed in trailing plants. The well-priced food (B60–180) is great and includes fried sea bass with chilli paste, fried chicken with Muslim herbs, soft-shelled crab with garlic and pepper, and spicy Phuket bean salad. Tues–Sun 9am–midnight.

Phuket View Restaurant On Thanon Kaew Simbu near the top of Khao Rung, the wooded hill on the northwestern outskirts of town. Middle-class Phuketians drive up to this slightly formal restaurant for mid-priced outdoor seafood with a view. Bring mosquito repellent.

Salavatore's Restaurant 15 Thanon Rat Sada. Cosy Sardinian trattoria that's popular with expats. The authentic Italian menu (prices from B150–650) includes crab-meat tagliatelle, spaghetti with bottarga (Mediterranean) caviar, various steaks and daily specials, plus around 60 different wines. Tues–Sun noon–3pm & 6.30–11pm.

Vegetarian Restaurants 207, 209 and 215 Thanon Ranong. A trio of cheap and simple vegan canteens, located almost side by side near Wat Jui Tui Chinese temple. For B20-30 you get two main-course servings and a plate of brown rice: choose from the trays of stir-fries and curries, many of them made with soya-based meat substitutes. Daily 7am to about 8pm.

Shopping

Phuket town has the best **bookshop** on the island: The Books (daily 9am–9pm) on Thanon Phuket stocks a phenomenal range of English-language volumes about Thailand plus some modern novels. South Wind Books on Thanon Phang Nga (Mon–Sat 9am–7pm, Sun 10am–3pm) has a big range of second-hand books. Ban Boran Textiles, at 51 Thanon Yaowarat, specializes in clothes made from the handspun cotton of north and northeast Thailand, while for high-street **fashions**, there's Robinson department store on Thanon Tilok Utis 1, and Ocean Department Store nearby. For the biggest brand names, however, including Esprit, Lacoste and Jim Thompson silk, you need to head out to the cavernous **Central Festival shopping plaza** on the bypass at the western fringes of town, at the big intersection of roads to Phuket town, Ao Patong, and Ao Chalong; Patong- and Chalong-bound songthaews can drop you within a few hundred metres. Downtown, the two most fruitful shopping roads for **handicrafts** and **antiques** are Thanon Yaowarat and Thanon Rat Sada. On Thanon Rat Sada, Radsada Hand Made at no. 29 sells textiles, carved wooden

Ngan Kin Jeh: the Vegetarian Festival

For nine days every October or November, at the start of the ninth lunar month (see www.thailandgrandfestival.com for exact dates), the streets of Phuket are enlivened by **Ngan Kin Jeh** – the Vegetarian Festival – which culminates in the unnerving spectacle of men and women parading about with steel rods through their cheeks and tongues. The festival marks the beginning of **Taoist Lent**, a month-long period of purification observed by devout Chinese all over the world, but celebrated most ostentatiously in Phuket, by devotees of the island's five Chinese temples. After six days' abstention from meat (hence the festival's name), alcohol and sex, the white-clad worshippers flock to their local temple, where drum rhythms help induce a trance state in which they become possessed by spirits. As proof of their new-found transcendence of the physical world they skewer themselves with any available sharp instrument – fishing rods and car wing-mirrors have done service in the past – before walking over red-hot coals or up ladders of swords as further testament to their otherworldliness. In the meantime there's singing and dancing and almost continuous firework displays, with the grandest festivities held at Wat Jui Tui on Thanon Ranong in Phuket town.

The ceremony dates back to the mid-nineteenth century, when a travelling Chinese opera company turned up on the island to entertain emigrant Chinese working in the tin mines. They had been there almost a year when suddenly the whole troupe – together with a number of the miners – came down with a life-endangering fever. Realizing that they'd neglected their gods somewhat, the actors performed expiatory rites, which soon effected a cure for most of the sufferers. The festival has been held ever since, though the self-mortification rites are a later modification, possibly of Hindu origin.

textile hangers, mango-wood vases and silver jewellery, while both Soul of Asia at no. 37 and Touch Wood at no. 14 specialize in quality Southeast Asian antiques, fine art and furniture. Ocean Department Store's more mass-market souvenir stalls are also worth a browse.

Note that if you're planning to buy antiques or religious artefacts and take or send them home, you need to have an **export licence** granted by the Fine Arts Department, which can be obtained through Thalang Museum, located 12km north of Phuket town in Thalang (see p.760; ☎076 311426); see Basics p.82 for more information.

Listings

Airlines Bangkok Airways, 158/2–3 Thanon Yaowarat ☎076 225033; China Airlines, at the airport ☎076 327099; Dragon Air, 156/14 Thanon Phang Nga ☎076 215734; Korean Air, at the airport ☎076 328540; Malaysia Airlines, 1/8 Thanon Thungka ☎076 213749; Silk Air/Singapore Airlines, 1 Soi Surin ☎076 213895; Thai Airways, 78 Thanon Ranong, international ☎076 212499, domestic ☎076 211195.

Banks and exchange All the main banks have branches on Thanon Phang Nga or Thanon Rat Sada, with adjacent exchange facilities open till at least 7pm and ATMs dispensing cash around the clock.

Cinemas English-language blockbusters are shown throughout the day and evening at the Paradise Multiplex next to Ocean Department Store on Thanon Tilok Uthis 1 and the SF Coliseum inside the Central Festival shopping plaza on the bypass road.

Dentists At Phuket International Hospital (☎076 249400, www.phuket-inter-hospital.co.th), on the airport bypass road just west of Phuket town, and at Bangkok Hospital Phuket, on the north-western edge of town at 2/1 Thanon Hongyok Utis ☎076 245425; see map on p.730 for locations.

Hospitals Phuket International Hospital (☎076 249400, emergencies ☎076 210935, www.phuket-inter-hospital.co.th), north of Central Festival shopping centre on the airport bypass road just west of Phuket town, at 44 Thanon Chalermprakiat

Ror 9, is considered to have Phuket's best facilities, including an emergency department, an ambulance service and private rooms. Other reputable alternatives include Bangkok Hospital Phuket, on the northwestern edge of town just off Thanon Yaowarat at 2/1 Thanon Hongyok Utis ⓣ1719 or ⓣ076 245425, ⓦwww.phukethospital.com, and the Mission Hospital (aka Phuket Adventist Hospital), on the northern outskirts at 4/1 Thanon Thepkasatri ⓣ076 237220–5, emergencies ⓣ076 237227, ⓦphuketdir.com/missionhospital. See map on p.730 for locations.
Immigration office At the southern end of Thanon Phuket, in the suburb of Saphan Hin ⓣ076 221905; Mon–Fri 8.30am–4.30pm, Sat 8.30–noon.
Internet access At several places on Thanon Thepkasatri, include cheap and fast at Goonet (Daily 10am-1am), at *On On Hotel*, 19 Thanon Phang Nga, and Catnet at the CAT phone office on Thanon Phang Nga (daily 8am–11pm).
Mail The GPO is on Thanon Montri. Poste restante should be addressed c/o GPO Thanon Montri, Phuket 83000 and can be collected Mon–Fri 8.30am–4.30pm, Sat 8.30am–3.30pm.
Pharmacy There are branches of Boots on Soi Surin and in the Central Festival shopping centre, plus plenty of local pharmacies all over town.
TAT 191 Thanon Thalang (daily 8.30am–4.30pm ⓣ076 212213, ⓔtatphket@tat.or.th).
Telephones For international calls use the CAT phone office on Thanon Phang Nga (daily 8am–11pm).
Tourist Police For all emergencies, call the tourist police on the free, 24hr phone line ⓣ1155, or contact them at their office just north of Tesco Lotus on the northwest edge of town, on Route 402 ⓣ076 355015.

Hat Mai Khao

Phuket's northwest coast kicks off with the island's longest and least-visited beach, the seventeen-kilometre **HAT MAI KHAO**, which starts a couple of kilometres north of the airport and 34km northwest of Phuket town, and remains almost completely unsullied by any touristic enticements, with to date just a couple of discreet budget accommodations hidden behind a sandbank at the back of the shore, plus one deluxe development. Parts of Hat Mai Khao, and of Hat Nai Yang immediately to the south, are protected as **Sirinath National Park** (ⓦwww.dnp.go.th/National_park.asp), chiefly because a few giant marine turtles still come ashore here between October and February to lay their eggs (see box on p.846). Mai Khao is also a prime habitat of a much-revered but non-protected species – the sea grasshopper or sea louse, a tiny crustacean that's considered a great delicacy. Also within the national park is the **Thachatchai Nature Trail**, about 8km north from the Hat Mai Khao accommodation.

If you're looking for peace, solitude and 17km of soft sand to yourself, then the Hat Mai Khao **accommodation** is for you. At the far northern end of the beach, just 3km south of Sarasin Bridge, the five-star *JW Marriott Phuket Resort and Spa* (ⓣ076 338000, ⓦwww.marriotthotels.com; ⑨) comprises an enormous low-rise complex of tasteful, upmarket rooms, three pools, a spa complex and several restaurants. It's popular with families not least because kids love the water slide; there's also a kids' centre with pool table and Internet, and the hotel rents out mountain bikes for local expeditions. Several kilometres further south along the beach, the other two options are much cheaper and more traveller-oriented and are by far the most uncommercialized places to stay on Phuket. Run by members of the same family, they occupy adjacent plots in their own little shorefront enclave, surrounded by coconut plantations 1.5km off the road, with easy access to nearby wetlands and their large bird populations. *Phuket Campground* (ⓣ081 676 4318, ⓦwww.phuketcampground.com) rents out tents with bedding (B150/person), which you can either set up near their small restaurant or move down onto the beach a few metres away beyond the sandbank. On the other side of a small shrimp-breeding pond, *Mai Khao Beach Bungalows* (ⓣ081 895 1233; ⑤) has just a few bungalows with fan and en-suite bathrooms. Both places offer an exceptionally warm, homestay-like welcome, both serve food and can arrange motorbike rental, and both close during the monsoon season (from May–Oct) when wind and rain make it dangerous to swim.

The easiest way to get to Hat Mai Khao is by long-distance **bus**. All buses travelling between Phuket town bus station and any mainland town (eg Krabi, Phang Nga, Khao Lak or Surat Thani) use Highway 402: just ask to be dropped in **BAN SOUN MAPRAO**, a road junction just north of kilometre-stone 37. (If coming directly here from the mainland you'll waste a good couple of hours if you go into town and then come back out again.) Five songthaews a day also travel this far up Highway 402, but buses are faster and more frequent. The owner of *Phuket Campground* has an office at the bus drop on the east side of the road in Ban Soun Maprao, from where you can arrange transfers to the accommodation, but if the office isn't open you can either phone for a pick-up or walk. From the bus drop, walk 1km west down the minor road until you reach a signed track off to the west, which you should follow for 1.5km to reach the accommodation and the beach. Travelling to Hat Mai Khao from the airport, 15km away, is best done by taxi.

Thachatchai Nature Trail

Snaking through the mangroves at Phuket's northern tip, 700m south of the Sarasin Bridge exit to the mainland, the **Thachatchai Nature Trail** (dawn to dusk; free) aims to introduce visitors to life in a mangrove swamp (for more on which, see p.776). It's run by the Sirinath National Park and is located east off Highway 402, across the road from the old national park headquarters (now relocated to Hat Nai Yang); any bus travelling between Phuket town and the mainland should drop you at the sign. There's a visitor centre at the trailhead, where you can pick up a leaflet, and a drinks stall next door. The six-hundred-metre **trail** follows a raised wooden walkway that loops through a patch of coastal mangrove swamp. Informative English-language boards describe the flora and fauna: you can't fail to spot the swarms of fiddler crabs scuttling around the roots of the mangrove trees, and the "bok-bok" sound that you can hear above the roar of the distant highway is the noise the mangrove-dwelling shrimps make when they snap their pincers as they feed – they're the ones that give the distinctive taste to the green papaya salad, *som tam*.

Hat Nai Yang

The long curved sweep of **HAT NAI YANG**, 5km south of Hat Mai Khao and 30km north of Phuket town, is partly under the protection of Sirinath National Park and has only fairly low-key development, with plentiful shade from the feathery casuarina trees that run the length of the bay, and a tiny, low-rise tourist village of transport rental outlets, minimarkets, a few accommodation options, an Internet centre and the inevitable tailors' shops. Nai Yang is locally famous for its two-dozen little open-air restaurant-shacks that serve mostly barbecued seafood (and the odd wood-fired pizza) at tables on the sand: eating out here is a hugely popular weekend pastime with Phuket families. There are also a few little beach bars, including the strikingly style-conscious beachfront bar, *The Beach Club*, along the shoreside track at the southern end of the bay, which plays live music nightly from 8pm and hosts weekly parties. The beach is clean and good for swimming at the southern end, and there's a reasonable, shallow **reef** about 1km offshore (10min by longtail boat) from the national park headquarters, which are a fifteen-minute walk north of the tourist village. If you're staying here and have your own transport, you could make a trip to the Thachatchai Nature Trail (see above).

Practicalities

Accommodation is pleasingly limited on Hat Nai Yang. The cheapest and most peaceful place to stay is at the national park bungalows (Ⓣ076 328226, Ⓦwww.dnp.go.th/National_park.asp; ③–⑤), prettily set out under the trees on a very quiet stretch of beach (unswimmable at low tide) fifteen minutes' walk north from the tourist village. Two-person fan and air-con rooms and bungalows are basic but en suite, and must be booked in advance. Tents are also available for B200 and can be pitched anywhere you like; if you bring your own you must first get permission from the park headquarters or visitor centre (both daily 8.30am–4.30pm). *Nai Yang Beach Resort* (Ⓣ076 328300, Ⓦwww.naiyangbeachresort.com; fan ⑥, air-con ⑥–⑧) in the heart of the tourist village has a range of neat, white-tiled, white-walled mid-market bungalows set in a dry but shady garden on the inland side of the beachfront road, and offers a choice between fan and air-con. Best of the lot is the elegant and luxurious *Indigo Pearl* (Ⓣ076 327006, Ⓦwww.indigo-pearl.com; ⑨) where hotel rooms and villas furnished in chic modern-Thai style look on to gorgeously landscaped tropical gardens that run down to the southern end of the beachfront road; facilities here include three swimming pools and a kids' playground.

Hat Nai Yang is just 2km south of the **airport**, B150 by taxi. An infrequent **songthaew** service (B35; 1hr 45min) runs between Phuket town and Hat Nai Yang via the airport, or a taxi costs around B600.

Hat Nai Thon

The next bay south down the coast from Hat Nai Yang is the small but perfectly formed **Hat Nai Thon**, currently one of the least commercialized beaches on the island. The five-hundred-metre-long gold-sand bay is shaded by casuarinas and surrounded by fields and plantations of coconut, banana, pineapple and rubber trees, all set against a dazzling backdrop of lush green hills. The access road off Highway 402 winds through this landscape, passing a few villages en route before reaching the shore, and to date there are just a handful of formal places to stay at the beach, plus a couple of businesses with rooms for rent, a dive operator, tour agent, several restaurants and bars. There's good snorkelling at reefs that are easily reached by longtail, but otherwise you'll have to make your own entertainment. All this might change quite soon, however, as land speculation south along the coast from Nai Thon has been feverish and development is likely to follow. There's no public transport to Nai Thon, but half-hourly **songthaews** (B25; 1hr 30min) run from Phuket town to Ao Bang Tao, the next resort south down the coast, from where a taxi which will cost at least B150.

At the northern end of the shorefront road, across the road from the sea, the three-storeyed *Naithonburi Beach Resort* (Ⓣ076 318700, Ⓦwww.naithonburi.com; ⑨) is the largest **hotel** in Nai Thon, with 79 posh air-con rooms in a U-shaped complex enclosing a decent-sized pool. Next door, *Phuket Naithon Resort* (Ⓣ076 205233, Ⓦwww.phuketnaithonresort.com; fan ⑥, air-con ⑥–⑧) offers big, apartment-style rooms in terraced bungalows with the choice between (genuine) mountain views or (less interesting) across-the-road sea views, and the option of air-con, balcony and TV; the resort also has a small spa. About 100m south down the road, *Naithon Beach Resort* (Ⓣ076 205379, Ⓔnaithon_beach_resort@yahoo.com; ⑥), set in a small garden across the road from the beach, has just 16 compact wooden fan and air-con bungalows with more character but lesser views and a teeny swimming pool squeezed alongside. The nearby *Tienseng* restaurant (Ⓣ081 535 0512; ⑥) has about ten fan and air-con rooms upstairs, some with sea view. About two kilometres south over the

△ Ao Patong

southern headland, occupying cliffside land that runs down to its own gorgeous wee bay of white sand and turquoise water, *Andaman White Beach Resort* (Ⓣ076 316300, Ⓦwww.andamanwhitebeach.com; B5500) offers a range of attractive, upmarket rooms and villas with surpassing views, including some designed for families, plus a swimming pool.

Ao Bang Tao

The eight-kilometre-long **Ao Bang Tao** is dominated by the upscale *Laguna Resort*, an "integrated resort" comprising five luxury hotels set in extensive landscaped grounds around a series of lagoons. There's free transport between the hotels, and for a small fee all *Laguna* guests can use facilities at any one of the five hotels – which include fifteen swimming pools, thirty restaurants, several children's clubs, a couple of spas and countless sporting facilities ranging from tennis courts to riding stables, windsurfers, and hobie-cats to badminton courts. There's also the eighteen-hole Laguna Phuket golf course, the Quest Laguna outdoor sports centre and a kids' activity centre called Camp Laguna, with entertainments for 8- to 18-year-olds ranging from abseiling and rock-climbing to team games and arts and crafts workshops. Not surprisingly the *Laguna* hotels are exceptionally popular with families, though beware of the undertow off the coast here, which confines many guests to the hotel pools. South and mainly out of sight of the enormous *Laguna* complex, an unsightly jumble of development has been squashed into every remaining inch of Bang Tao's beachfront land. Half-hourly **songthaews** (B25; 1hr 15min) cover the 24km from Phuket town to Ao Bang Tao; taxis cost about B250 for the same journey. There are reputable **car-rental** desks at all the hotels, as well as small shopping arcades.

Accommodation

All *Laguna Phuket* **hotels** are in the top price bracket: the *Allamanda* and *Laguna Beach* have the cheapest rooms and the *Banyan Tree Phuket* is the most exclusive option on the beach (and the whole island). The below quoted rates are generally discounted a little if you book via the *Laguna Phuket* website (Ⓦwww.lagunaphuket.com), and rates drop by up to fifty percent during the low season, from May to October.

Allamanda Ⓣ076 324359, Ⓦwww.allamanda.com. Consciously family-oriented hotel comprising 235 apartment-style suites – all with a kitchenette and separate living area at the very least – set round the edge of a lagoon and the fringes of the golf course. There are some special children's suites, children's pools, a kids' club and a babysitting service. ⑧

Banyan Tree Phuket Ⓣ076 324374, Ⓦwww.banyantree.phuket.com. The most sumptuous and exclusive of the *Laguna* hotels, and considered among the best hotels in the whole of Phuket, with a select 108 villas, all gorgeously furnished and kitted out with private gardens and outdoor sunken baths. Also on site are the award-winning, and glorious indulgent, Banyan Tree spa and an eighteen-hole golf course. Rates from US$700. ⑨

Dusit Laguna Ⓣ076 324324, Ⓦphuket.dusit.com. Located between two lagoons and set amidst lush tropical gardens fronting the beach, all rooms in this relaxed, low-rise complex have private balconies with pleasant views. Many rooms have broadband access and even the beach is wi-fi enabled. Other facilities include a spa, a pool and a kids' club. ⑨

Laguna Beach Resort Ⓣ076 324352, Ⓦwww.lagunabeach-resort.com. Another family-oriented hotel, with a big waterpark, lots of sports facilities, Camp Laguna activities for 8–18-year-olds, plus a spa and luxury five-star rooms in the low-rise hotel wings. ⑨

Sheraton Grande Laguna Ⓣ076 324101, Ⓦwww.sheraton.phuket.com. Built on its own island in the middle of one of the lagoons, with exceptionally nice five-star rooms, a long, serpentine pool featuring a waterfall and children's pool, a Very Important Kids club, and nine bars and restaurants. Some rooms are designed for wheelchair access. Rates from US$245. ⑨

Hat Surin and Ao Pansea

South of Ao Bang Tao, **HAT SURIN** proper is packed with ugly condominium developments, but its small northern bay, secluded from the riff-raff and sometimes referred to as **AO PANSEA**, is a favourite haunt of royalty and Hollywood stars, who stay here at one of Phuket's most indulgent resorts, the *Amanpuri* (Ⓣ076 324333, Ⓦwww.amanresorts.com; ⑨; rates start at US$700). Part of the super-exclusive, Hong Kong-based Aman chain, the *Amanpuri* comprises a series of private, elegantly understated, Thai-style pavilions, each of which is staffed by a personal attendant, plus a spa and black marble swimming pool. Also on pretty, white-sand Ao Pansea is the delightful, and slightly more reasonably priced, *The Chedi Phuket* (Ⓣ076 324017, Ⓦwww.ghmhotels.com; ⑨; rates from B14,700), whose traditional-style thatched villas are set within a lushly planted hillside palm grove that drops down to the shore. There's also a spa and shorefront pool.

Songthaews travel the 24km between Phuket town and Hat Surin, via Hat Kamala, approximately every half-hour and cost B25.

Hat Kamala and Laem Singh

With its cheerfully painted houses and absence of high-rises, the small, village-like tourist development along the shorefront of **HAT KAMALA** is an appealingly low-key spot, sandwiched between the beach and the predominantly Muslim little town of Ban Kamala, about 300m west of the main Patong-Surin road and 26km northwest of Phuket town. Although Kamala was very badly hit by the tsunami – which killed many residents and wiped out the school, the temple and countless homes and businesses – extensive rebuilding (still a work in progress at the southern end) has enabled it to resurface as an enticing tourist destination once more. Aside from the accommodation, the little tourist village, which is mostly clustered either side of Thanon Rim Had (also spelt Rim Hat), has several restaurants and bars, transport rental, Internet access, a couple of minimarkets, dive shops and several tour operators. For anything else you'll need to head inland to the faceless shophouse developments on the main road, or continue south around the headland to Ao Patong, 6km away. The Phuket Fantasea entertainments complex (see box on p.733) is about 1km northeast of Hat Kamala on the main Patong-Surin road. A few hundred metres north of Fantasea, a couple of steep paths lead west off the main road and down to **Laem Singh** cape, a pretty little sandy cove whose picturesque combination of turquoise water and smooth granite boulders makes it one of Phuket's finest. It's good for swimming and very secluded, plus it's great for kids as there's a decent patch of shade throughout the day. The easiest way to get to Hat Kamala is by **songthaew** from Phuket town (every 30min, 1hr 15min; B30). Tuk tuks charge B200 between Patong and Kamala or motorbike taxis will take you there for B150.

Accommodation and eating

Hat Kamala is popular with long-stay tourists, and several **hotels** offer rooms with kitchenettes; on the whole prices here are reasonable for Phuket, and there's a preponderance of small-scale places. The most famous **restaurant** in Kamala is Australian-run *Rockfish*, which enjoys an island-wide reputation for great food – mostly Asian fusion and seafood, with dishes averaging B200 – and lovely views from its headland location attached to *Kamala Beach Estate*. Down in the heart of the tourist village, there are several other seafood-oriented restaurants to try out, while the breezy rood terrace and fresh coffee make *Kamala Coffee House* a good spot for breakfast.

Benjamin Resort 83 Thanon Rim Had, at the southerly end of the beachfront road ⓣ076 385147, ⓦwww.phuketdir.com/benjaminresort. Set right on the beach, this block of 35 air-con rooms lacks character but couldn't be closer to the sea. Although views are occluded from all but the most expensive rooms, the spacious interiors are almost identical and no more than a few footsteps from the sand. 4–7

Kamala Beach Estate ⓣ076 279756, ⓦwww.kamalabeachestate.com. Stunningly located on Hat Kamala's far southern headland (above a stretch of bay that's unswimmable at low tide, though just five minutes' walk from the more serviceable shore) and set around a swimming pool in tropical gardens, this place comprises serviced one-, two- and three-bedroom apartments – garden- or sea-view – each furnished with a well-equipped kitchen, dining area and balcony or terrace. 9

Kamala Dreams 74/1 Thanon Rim Had ⓣ076 279131, ⓦwww.kamaladreams.net. Epitomising all the best things about Kamala, this is a really nice, small hotel set right on the shore, in the middle of the tourist village. Its 18 rooms are large, stylishly furnished in contemporary mode, and all have air-con, TV, a kitchenette and a large balcony overlooking the pool and the sea. 8

Malinee House 75/4 Thanon Rim Had ⓣ086 600 4616, ⓦwww.malineehouse.com. Very friendly, traveller-oriented guest house in the middle of the tourist village, with Internet access and the Jackie Lee travel agency downstairs, and large, comfortably furnished air-con rooms upstairs, all of them with balconies. 5

Print Kamala Resort 74/8 Thanon Rim Had ⓣ076 385396, ⓦprint-kamala-resort.th66.com. The best accommodation here is in a village-like complex of very generously sized bungalows, connected via stilted walkways that wend around a tropical Bali-style garden. The bungalows all have prettily furnished air-con bedrooms plus separate living rooms, with TV, and capacious, shaded decks. The pricier ones are detached. The hotel also has some less interesting rooms in a hotel wing, and a large pool. 8

Ao Patong

The busiest and most popular of all Phuket's beaches, **AO PATONG** – 5km south of Ao Kamala and 15km west of Phuket town – is vastly over-developed and hard to recommend. A congestion of high-rise hotels, tour agents and

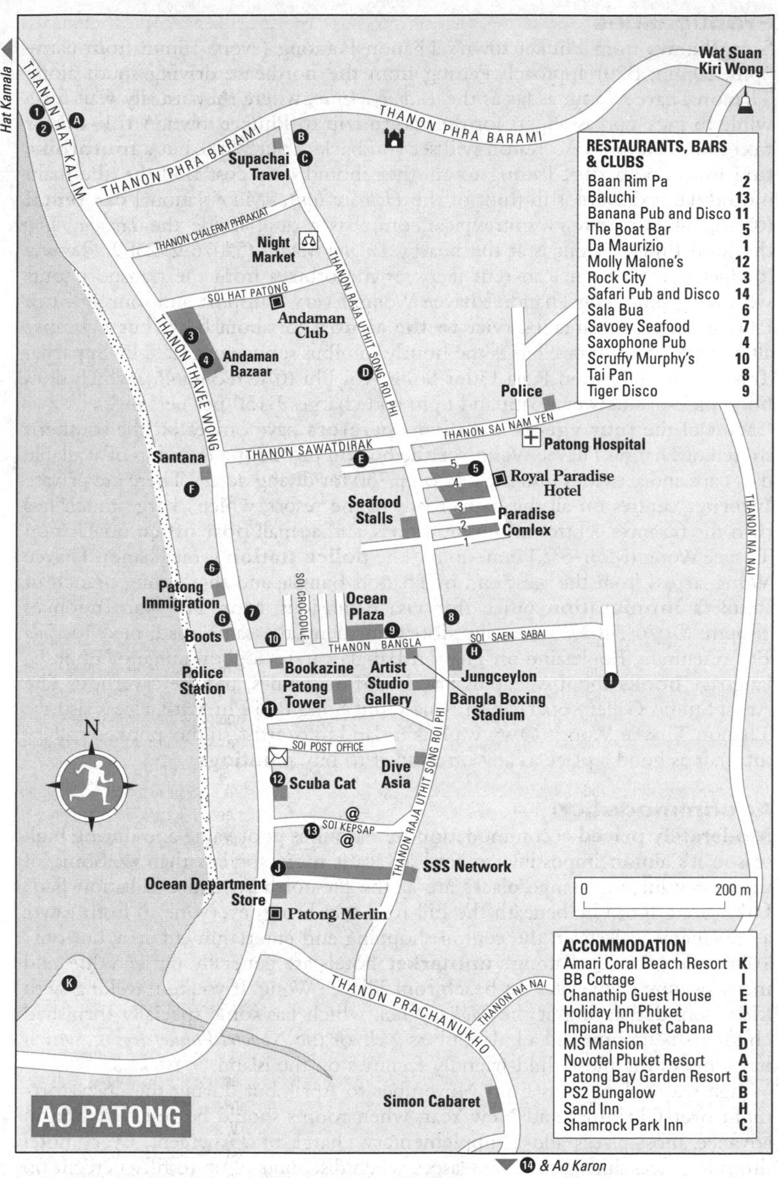

souvenir shops disfigures the beachfront road, tireless touts are everywhere, and hostess bars and strip joints dominate the resort's nightlife, attracting an increasing number of single Western men to what is now the most active scene between Bangkok and Hat Yai. On the plus side, the broad, three-kilometre-long beach offers good sand and plenty of shade beneath the parasols and there are hundreds of shops and bars to keep you busy after dark.

Practicalities

Songthaews from Phuket town's Thanon Ranong (every 15min from 6am–6pm; 20min; B20) approach Patong from the northeast, driving south along Thanon Thavee Wong as far as the *Patong Merlin*, where they usually wait for a while to pick up passengers for the return trip to Phuket town. A **tuk-tuk** or **taxi** from Patong to Ao Karon will set you back about B200, but a **motorbike taxi** from one part of Patong to another should only cost B30–40 (the main motorbike taxi stand is in front of the *Holiday Inn*). SMT/National **car rental** (ⓣ076 340608, ⓦwww.smtrentacar.com) has a desk inside the *Holiday Inn*; the local Budget agent is at the nearby *Patong Merlin* (ⓣ076 292389, ⓦwww.budget.co.th); or you can rent jeeps or motorbikes from the transport touts who hang out along Thanon Thavee Wong. Every transport and tour agent in Patong can provide a taxi service **to the airport** for about B400, but a cheaper alternative for solo travellers is the hourly minibus service operated by Supachai Travel at 26/1 Thanon Raja Uthit Song Roi Phi (ⓣ076 340046), which does hotel pick-ups between 6am and 6pm and charges B150 per person.

Most of the **tour agents** and **dive operators** have offices on the southern stretch of Thanon Thavee Wong: see the box on p.732 for a roundup of available day-trips and activities, and the box on p.750 for diving details. There are private **Internet** centres on all the main roads in the resort, which charge much less than the business centres in the top hotels, and a small **post office** on Thanon Thavee Wong (Mon–Sat 11am–6pm). The **police station** is on Thanon Thavee Wong, across from the west end of Thanon Bangla, and the Patong branch of Phuket's **Immigration** office (for visa extensions; Mon–Fri 10am–noon & 1–3pm; ⓣ076 340477) is a few doors north up the same road, next to *Sala Bua* restaurant. Bookazine on Thanon Bangla carries a good range of English-language **books** about Asia, plus novels and magazines, and the cavernous The Artist Studio Gallery on Thanon Raja Uthit Song Roi Phi, with access also via Thanon Thavee Wong (ⓦwww.phuketisland.info/artist-studio-phuket/gallery.htm), is as good a place as any on Phuket to buy **paintings**.

Accommodation

Moderately priced accommodation on Patong is poor value and during high season it's almost impossible to find a vacant room for less than ❺. Some of the best-value, mid-range places are at the far northern end of Thanon Raja Uthit Song Roi Phi, beneath the hill road that brings everyone in from town, a 750-metre walk from the central shopping and entertainment area, but only 100m from the sea. Patong's **upmarket** hotels are generally better value, and many occupy prime sites on beachfront Thavee Wong. If you're travelling with **kids**, consider staying at the *Holiday Inn*, which has some specially furnished children's bedrooms and a kids' club as well, or the *Novotel Phuket Resort*, which has some of the most child-friendly facilities on the island.

High season here runs from November to April, but during the crazy fortnight over Christmas and New Year, when rooms should be reserved well in advance, most places add a supplementary charge of 25 percent. Every hotel drops its prices during the low season, when discounts of up to fifty percent on the rates listed are on offer.

Inexpensive and moderate

BB Cottage 17/21 Soi Saen Sabai ⓣ076 342948, ⓔppropt@loxinfo.co.th. A rare thing indeed in Patong: 29 lowish-budget bungalows dotted around a peaceful green oasis of a garden. Admittedly, interiors are plain – though they are large, and some have kitchens – and there are no verandas, but there's a sense of space and you're close to the nightlife yet a little bit secluded. For a fee, guests can also use a nearby swimming pool. Fan ❹, air-con ❺–❻

Chanathip Guest House Thanon Raja Uthit Song Roi Phi Soi Neung ⓣ081 787 2537, ⓔbaby-ingfar@hotmail.com. This tiny mansion block contains just a handful of good, modern rooms, all with air-con, stylish furnishings and a balcony. Rooms on the upper floors get more light. ❺
MS Mansion 132 Thanon Raja Uthit Song Roi Phi ⓣ076 344394, ⓔmsinnphuket@hotmail.com. A small hotel above a restaurant, offering large, clean, air-con rooms, the best of them with balconies. ❺
PS2 Bungalow 78/54 Thanon Raja Uthit Song Roi Phi ⓣ076 342207, ⓦwww.ps2bungalow.com. This well-managed mini-hotel has sizeable and well-priced if slightly scruffy fan and air-con bungalows set around a swimming pool and garden area. It's at the far northern end of the resort, so a fair walk from the main shopping and bar areas. Fan ❹, air-con ❺
Sand Inn 171 Soi Saen Sabai ⓣ076 340275, ⓦwww.sandinnphuket.com. Clean, well-appointed air-con rooms, a little on the compact side, but maintained to a good standard in the ideal location for nightlife, just east off bar-packed Thanon Bangla. There's TV in all rooms, a Euro Café bakery downstairs, and use of the small swimming pool just a few metres up the soi. ❼
Shamrock Park Inn 31 Thanon Raja Uthit Song Roi Phi ⓣ076 340991. Friendly, reasonable-value three-storey hotel at the northern end of the resort with 28 pleasant, well-maintained, air-con rooms, most of them with balconies. Unlike many places it doesn't raise its rates for Christmas and New Year. ❺

Expensive

Amari Coral Beach Resort 104 Thanon Traitrang ⓣ076 340106, ⓦwww.amari.com. Occupying its own secluded little beach on a headland at the southernmost end of the bay, the Phuket branch of Thailand's upmarket Amari chain offers contemporary-chic rooms, all with generous sea-view balconies, plus two swimming pools, gorgeously romantic spa facilities, a fitness centre and tennis courts, as well as several restaurants. The views are exceptional and the location peaceful but convenient; as it's ranged up a slope it's not ideal for guests with mobility problems. ❾
Holiday Inn Phuket 86/11 Thanon Thavee Wong ⓣ076 340608, ⓦwww.phuket.holiday-inn.com. Reliable, upmarket chain hotel that offers smart, contemporary rooms just across the road from the beach, in two differently styled wings, and fosters a relaxed and informal atmosphere. The poshest Busakorn villa rooms have their own interconnected plunge-pools and there are also large pools for each wing, plus several restaurants and an interesting programme of daily activities. The hotel makes a big effort to be family-friendly, with special "kidsuites" (bedrooms designed for children) and both an all-day kids' club and a teens' club, with two children's pools. Also offers non-smoking and wheelchair-accessible rooms. ❾
Impiana Phuket Cabana 94 Thanon Thavee Wong ⓣ076 340138, ⓦwww.impiana.com. Located right on the beach and in the heart of the resort, this is a gorgeous collection of very tastefully designed air-con cabanas, set around a garden swimming pool; also has a kids' pool and a spa. ❾
Novotel Phuket Resort Thanon Phra Barami / Thanon Hat Kalim ⓣ076 342777, ⓦwww.novotelphuket.com. Luxurious and relaxing chain hotel built on the hillside above the quieter, northern end of the beach. Occupying landscaped tropical gardens and offering fine sea views, it's especially popular with families as it offers heaps of activities as well as a kids' club with games, videos and craft-making. Other facilities include three restaurants and a multi-level swimming pool. ❾
Patong Bay Garden Resort 33/1 Thanon Thavee Wong ⓣ076 340297, ⓦwww.patongbaygarden.com. Small hotel set right on the beach, with the top "studio" rooms having uninterrupted sea views, quite unusual in central Patong. Other rooms look out on the small shorefront pool or have no view at all. Rooms are quite elegantly furnished and all have air-con and TV. ❽–❾

Eating

Much of the **food** on Patong is dire – low-grade microwaved slop sold at inflated prices. But in among the disastrous little cafés advertising everything from Hungarian to Swedish "home cooking" you'll find a few genuinely reputable, long-running favourites. Phone numbers are given where reservations are advisable. For cheap Thai food, try the night market that sets up around 5pm towards the northern end of Thanon Raja Uthit Song Roi Phi, just south of Thanon Chalerm Phrakiat, or the row of seafood stall-restaurants further south, opposite the *Royal Paradise Hotel* complex.

Baan Rim Pa Across from the *Novotel* at 223 Thanon Phra Barami/Thanon Hat Kalim ⓣ076 340789 ⓦwww.baanrimpa.com. One of Phuket's most famous fine-dining restaurants, this is an elegant spot that's beautifully set in a teak building on a clifftop overlooking the bay, with tables also on its sea-view terrace. Known for its, classic, expensive, "Royal Thai" cuisine (mains from B250–500), including banana blossom salad, creamy duck curry and fried tiger prawns with tamarind sauce, as well as for its cellar of more than 270 wines. Live jazz-piano nightly except Mondays. Advance booking advised.

Baluchi Inside the *Horizon Beach Hotel* on Soi Kepsap. One of the better Indian restaurants in the resort, specializing in North Indian cuisine and tandoori dishes – roganjosh kashmiri lamb (B220), tandoori prawns (B375) – with fixed-price menus for B300 and B500.

Da Maurizio Across from the *Novotel* at 223 Thanon Phra Barami/ Thanon Hat Kalim ⓣ076 344079, ⓦwww.damaurizio.com. Superior, expensive, Italian restaurant in a stunning location set over the rocks beside the sea. Serves authentic home-made pasta and antipastos (bacon-wrapped goats cheese, rock lobster salad), fabulous seafood (Phuket lobsters and black crabs from Phang Nga), and a good wine list. Recipes are now collected in a book sold on the island. Main dishes from B450. Reservations advisable.

Sala Bua Thanon Thavee Wong. Fabulously stylish, breezy, beach-view restaurant attached to the equally glamorous *Impiana Phuket Cabana* hotel. The innovative, pricey, Pacific Rim menu (from B200–1400) includes ravioli stuffed with mud crabs, local rock-lobster omelette, New Zealand tenderloin steaks – and sweet sushi rolls filled with mango and coconut cream. Expensive, but worth it.

Savoey Seafood On the central stretch of Thanon Thavee Wong, just north of Thanon Bangla. Cavernous, unatmospheric but very popular open-sided restaurant that serves all manner of locally caught fish and seafood (dishes from B180), particularly Phuket lobster, cooked to Thai, Chinese and Western recipes.

Nightlife and entertainment

After dark, everyone heads to pedestrianized Thanon Bangla for their own taste of Patong's notorious **nightlife** and the road teems with a cross-section of Phuket tourists, from elderly couples and young parents with strollers, to glammed-up girlfriends and groups of lads. The big draw for the more innocent onlookers is Thanon Bangla's Soi Crocodile, better known as Soi Katoey, or "Trannie Alley", where pouting, barely clad transvestites jiggle their implants on podiums at the mouth of the soi and pose for photos with giggling tourists (B200 a shot). But the real action happens further down the many bar-filled sois shooting off Thanon Bangla, where open-air bar-beers and neon-lit go-go clubs packed with strippers and goggle-eyed punters pulsate through the night. The pick-up trade pervades most bars in Patong, and though many of these joints are welcoming enough to couples and female tourists, there are a few alternatives, listed below, for anyone not in that kind of mood.

The **gay** entertainment district is concentrated around the Paradise Complex, a network of small sois and dozens of bar-beers in front of *Royal Paradise Hotel* on Thanon Raja Uthit Song Roi Phi: see ⓦwww.gaypatong.com.com for events listings and details of the annual Gay Pride festival, which is usually held in early February.

If you're looking for something else to do with yourself (or your kids) in the evening, check out the nearby transvestite Simon Cabaret, the spectacular show at Phuket Fantasea, or the Thai boxing stadium on Thanon Bangla; see the box on p.732 for details.

Banana Pub and Disco Inside the *Patong Beach Hotel* complex at 124 Thanon Thavee Wong. The upstairs disco and street-level bar attract a mixed clientele of Thais, expats, tourists and the inevitable freelance bar girls. The B100 entry fee includes one free drink. Nightly from 9pm.

The Boat Bar Soi 5, Paradise Complex, off Thanon Raja Uthit Song Roi Phi. Long-running, very popular gay bar and disco, with two cabaret shows nightly. Opens daily from 8pm.

Molly Malone's Next to McDonalds on Thanon Thavee Wong. As you'd expect, the resort's original Irish pub serves draught Guinness and Kilkenny beer

(B250 a pint), dishes out bar food and all-day breakfasts, and entertains drinkers with live Celtic music every night from 9pm; also shows live TV coverage of international sports. There's a nice beer garden and no overt hostess presence. Daily from 10am.

Rock City Andaman Bazaar complex Thanon Thavee Wong. A roster of heavy-metal bands – including Metallica and AC-DC tribute acts – entertain drinkers and diners here nightly. Daily from 5pm.

Safari Pub and Disco Just beyond the southern edge of Patong, between Simon Cabaret and the *Le Meridien* hotel at 28 Thanon Siriat. Decked out to look like a jungle theme park, complete with waterfalls and five different bars, this is one of the most popular dance venues on Phuket, with two bands playing nightly from around 9pm; the music fuses disco beats from the 1980s with more recent techno sets. Nightly from 8pm.

Saxophone Pub 188/2 Andaman Bazaar complex Thanon Thavee Wong. The Phuket branch of Bangkok's famous long-running jazz pub fosters a similar ambience with lots of rough timber interior, portraits of chilled musicians and nightly live jazz blues, funk and soul from 9pm–2am. Nightly from 6pm.

Scruffy Murphy's Thanon Bangla. Like *Molly Malone's* around the corner, this is one of the few bars in Patong where you stand a decent chance of not being hassled by hostesses. Here too there's Guinness and Kilkenny on tap, nightly live music from 9pm, sports TV, and some outdoor seating from which to enjoy the Bangla parade. Also does pub-style food. Daily from 11am.

Tai Pan Thanon Raja Uthit Song Roi Phi. Crowded disco-bar playing loud techno and disco hits to a dance-floor packed with typical Patong party animals. Nightly from 9pm.

Tiger Disco Thanon Bangla. By midnight, the upstairs disco in this complex of bar-beers and go-go bars is packed with a mixed crowd of tourists, freelancers and punters. You can't miss the entrance, with its huge moulded jungle trees and rocks, plus the trademark larger-than-life tiger sculptures. B100 entry includes one free drink. Nightly from 9pm.

Ao Karon

AO KARON, Phuket's second resort, after Patong, is very much a middle-of-the-road destination. Far less lively, or congested, than Patong, but more commercial – and less characterful – than the smaller beaches further north, it's the domain of affordable guest houses and package-tour hotels and appeals chiefly to mid-budget tourists, many of them from Scandinavia. The 2.5-kilometre-long **beach** (see map on p.754) is graced with squeaky soft golden sand and is completely free of developments, though there's very little natural shade; an embankment screens most of the southern half of the beach from the road running alongside, but north of the *Hilton* the road is more often in view and parts of the shore back on to lagoons and wasteland. The **undertow** off Ao Karon is treacherously strong during the monsoon season from June to October, so you should heed the warning signs and flags and ask for local advice – fatalities are not uncommon. The tiny bay just north of Ao Karon – known as Karon Noi or Relax Bay – is almost exclusively patronized by guests of the swanky *Le Meridien* hotel, but non-guests are quite welcome to swim and sunbathe here.

For inland entertainment, there's the Dino Park **mini-golf** (daily 10am–midnight; B240, kids B180, or B120/90 without the golf), next to *Marina Phuket Resort* on the Kata/Karon headland, which is part of a pseudo-prehistoric theme park comprising a dinosaur restaurant and an erupting "volcano". For theatrical entertainment, try an evening at the nearby transvestite Simon Cabaret or the spectacular show at Phuket Fantasea, both of which are described in the box on p.732. Some of the posher hotels on Phuket's other beaches offer expensive **spa treatments** to their guests, but on Karon anyone is welcome to the Kata Spa, near *Peach Hill* at 95 Thanon Pakbang (Ⓣ086 541 3629, Ⓦwww.katabeachsparesort.com), where local herbs are used in all steam baths and massage treatments and multi-treatment packages cost from B1400; Kata Spa also teaches **courses in Thai massage**.

Diving and snorkelling off Phuket

The reefs and islands within sailing distance of Phuket rate among the most spectacular in the world, and this is where you'll find Thailand's largest concentration of **dive shops**, offering some of the best-value certificated courses and trips in the country. All the dive centres listed below offer PADI-certificated diving courses and have qualified instructors and dive-masters; we have highlighted those that are accredited PADI Five-Star Centres (the Instructor Development Centres are one step higher than the Five-Star Centres); see p.71 for details. Nonetheless, you should still try to get first-hand recommendations from other divers before signing up with any dive shop, however highly starred, and always check the equipment and staff credentials carefully.

You should also check that the dive shop has membership for one of Phuket's three **recompression chambers**; if yours doesn't, you could take out your own membership with Badalveda (ⓦwww.badalveda.com; B300), which entitles you to sixty percent discounts on the hourly rate for use of the chamber (down from US$350 to $115/hour), though the best dive shops should ensure that their customers never get into a situation that requires recompression. Phuket's recompression centres are: SSS Network (HST), 233 Thanon Raja Uthit Song Roi Phi on Ao Patong (ⓣ076 342518, ⓦwww.sssnetwork.com); Badalveda Diving Medicine Centre at Bangkok Hospital Phuket, 2/1 Thanon Hongyok Utis, in Phuket town (ⓣ076 254425, ⓦwww.badalveda.com); and at Wachira Hospital, Soi Wachira, Thanon Yaowarat, Phuket town (ⓣ076 211114). All dive shops rent **equipment**, and many of them sell essential items too.

A one-day introductory **diving course** averages B2000–3900, and a four-day Openwater course costs between B8000 and B12,500, usually including equipment. The price of **day-trips** to local reefs depends on the distance to the dive site, and the operator, but generally falls between B3000 and B4000, including at least two dives, all equipment and food. Nearly all dive centres also offer **live-aboard** cruises: four-day live-aboard trips to Hin Daeng and Hin Muang (see p.808), and to Ko Similan (see p.727) plus either Ko Surin (see p.712) or the Mergui archipelago in Burmese waters; such trips cost B20,000–30,000, including at least 12 dives and full board but excluding equipment and national park/visa fees.

Snorkellers are usually welcome to join divers' day-trips (for a discount of about B1000) and can sometimes go on live-aboard cruises at slightly reduced rates. In addition, all travel agents sell mass-market day-trips to Ko Phi Phi, which include snorkelling stops at Phi Phi Leh and Phi Phi Don, an hour's snorkelling (mask, fins and snorkel provided) and a seafood lunch. Transport is on large boats belonging to the main local ferry companies, with prices from B1000, or B700 for children. Some companies also offer day-trips to Ko Similan, for about B3000, depending on the speed of the boat; some companies use boats from Phuket, which take three hours, while other companies bus passengers to Thap Lamu and then use speedboats, which also takes around three hours in total. A more exclusive experience is offered by Coralseekers (ⓣ076 354074, ⓦwww.coralseekers.com), who specialize in tailor-made private snorkel speedboat charters to local reefs and islands (from B8000/boat).

Dive shops

All the dive shops listed below offer a variety of itineraries and cruises, with schedules depending on weather conditions and the number of divers; most operate year-round.

Ao Patong

Dive Asia 204 Thanon Raja Uthit Song Roi Phi ⓣ076 292517, ⓦwww.diveasia.com. Five-Star PADI Career Development Centre.

Santana 49 Thanon Thavee Wong ⓣ076 294220, ⓦwww.santanaphuket.com. Five-Star PADI Instructor Development Centre.
Scuba Cat 94 Thanon Thavee Wong ⓣ076 293120, ⓦwww.scubacat.com. Five-Star PADI Instructor Development Centre.

Ao Karon/Ao Kata

Dive Asia Kata/Karon headland ⓣ076 330598, ⓦwww.diveasia.com. Five-Star PADI Career Development Centre.
Marina Divers Next to *Marina Phuket Resort* at 45 Thanon Karon ⓣ076 330272, ⓦwww.marinadivers.com. Five-Star PADI Instructor Development Centre.

Andaman coast dive and snorkel sites

The major **dive and snorkel sites** visited from Andaman coast resorts are listed below. Here you'll find a stunning variety of coral and a multitude of fish species, including sharks, oysters, puffer fish, stingrays, groupers, lion fish, moray eels and more. For more information on marine life see "Flora, fauna and environmental issues" in Contexts, p.891.

Anemone Reef About 22km east of Phuket. Submerged reef of soft coral and sea anemones starting about 5m deep. Lots of fish, including leopard sharks, tuna and barracuda. Usually combined with a dive at nearby Shark Point. Unsuitable for snorkellers.

Burma Banks About 250km northwest of Phuket; only accessible on live-aboards from Khao Lak and Phuket. A series of submerged "banks", well away from any land mass and very close to the Burmese border. Visibility up to 25m.

Hin Daeng and **Hin Muang** 26km southwest of Ko Rok Nok, near Ko Lanta (see box on p.808). Hin Daeng is a highly recommended reef wall, with visibility up to 30m. One hundred metres away, Hin Muang also drops to 50m and is a good place for encountering stingrays, manta rays, whale sharks and silvertip sharks. Visibility up to 50m. Because of the depth and the current, both spots are considered too risky for novice divers who have logged fewer than 20 dives. Unsuitable for snorkellers.

King Cruiser Near Shark Point, between Phuket and Ko Phi Phi. Dubbed the *Thai Tanic*, this became a wreck dive in May 1997, when a tourist ferry sank on its way to Ko Phi Phi. Visibility up to 20m, but hopeless for snorkellers because of the depth.

Ko Phi Phi 48km east of Phuket's Ao Chalong. Visibility up to 30m. Spectacular drop-offs; good chance of seeing whale sharks. See p.794.

Ko Racha Noi and **Ko Racha Yai** About 33km and 28km south of Phuket's Ao Chalong respectively. Visibility up to 40m. Racha Yai is good for beginners and for snorkellers; at the more challenging Racha Noi there's a good chance of seeing manta rays, eagle rays and whale sharks. See p.758.

Ko Rok Nok and **Ko Rok Nai** 100km southeast of Phuket, south of Ko Lanta (see box on p.808). Visibility up to 18m. Shallow reefs that are excellent for snorkelling.

Ko Similan 96km northwest of Phuket; easiest access from Khao Lak. One of the world's top ten diving spots. Visibility up to 30m. Leopard sharks, whale sharks and manta rays, plus caves and gorges. See p.727.

Ko Surin 174km northwest of Phuket; easiest access from Khuraburi, or from Ko Chang and Ko Phayam. Shallow reefs particularly good for snorkelling. See p.712.

Richelieu Rock Just east of Ko Surin (see p.712), close to Burmese waters. A sunken pinnacle that's famous for its manta rays and whale sharks.

Shark Point (Hin Mu Sang) 24km east of Phuket's Laem Panwa. Protected as a marine sanctuary. Visibility up to 10m. Notable for soft corals, sea fans and leopard sharks. Often combined with the *King Cruiser* dive and/or Anemone Reef; unrewarding for snorkellers.

Practicalities

Ao Karon is 20km southwest of Phuket town and served by **songthaews** from the Thanon Ranong terminal (every 20min; 30min; B25). They arrive in Karon via Thanon Patak, hitting the beach at the northern end of Ao Karon and then driving south along beachfront Thanon Karon, continuing over the headland as far as *Kata Beach Resort* on Ao Kata Yai. To catch a songthaew back into town, just stand on the other side of the road and flag one down. If you're aiming for accommodation on Thanon Taina, you can save yourself at least ten minutes by getting off at the songthaew drop signed "Kata Beach", just north of the post office on Thanon Patak; for Thanon Luang Pho Chuain accommodation, alight just after the *Baan Karon* hotel on Thanon Patak. Transport touts throughout the resort rent motorbikes and jeeps; it's 5km from northern Karon to Patong.

Karon's main **shopping** and eating areas are grouped around the *Islandia Hotel* on the northern curve of Thanon Patak, along and around Thanon Luang Pho Chuain, and along Thanon Taina (sometimes referred to as Kata Centre). In all these places you'll find **currency exchange** facilities, with ATMs, **Internet centres**, minimarkets, tour agents, tailors' shops, beachwear outlets, craft shops, restaurants and bars. The local branch of Bookazine, with plenty of books about Thailand, foreign newspapers and magazines and novels, is across from the Thanon Taina junction on the Kata-Karon headland. There's a **clinic** on Thanon Luang Pho Chuain and a **police box** on central Thanon Karon.

Accommodation

Karon **accommodation** (marked on the map on p.754) is less pricey than Patong, but there's still just one lone ❷ option in the resort. High season here runs from November to March/April, but you'll almost certainly be charged an extra 25 percent over the Christmas and New Year fortnight when everything gets booked up weeks in advance. During the low season, expect to get discounts of up to fifty percent on the rates given below.

Inexpensive and moderate

Bazoom Hostel Off Thanon Luang Pho Chuain ⓣ076 396914. Korean-oriented backpackers' centre, offering the cheapest beds in this area at B150 per curtained-off bunk bed in a mixed-sex dorm, plus doubles with fan and shared bathroom or en suites with air-con. The cheap prices, boldly painted walls and downstairs Internet café together generate a very traveller-friendly vibe – and it's less than 300m from the sea. Fan and shared bathroom ❷, en-suite air-con ❹

Casa Brazil 9 Soi 1, Thanon Luang Pho Chuain ⓣ076 396317, ⓦwww.phukethomestay.com. Unusually arty, characterful little hotel, designed in Santa Fe style, with adobe-look walls, earth-toned paintwork, and funky decor and furnishings. The 21 rooms are comfortable and nearly all have air-con. Choose rooms at the back for a rare green and peaceful view of Karon's hilly backdrop, best enjoyed from the French windows and private balconies. Rates include breakfast. ❻

Happy Inn Soi 1, Thanon Luang Pho Chuain ⓣ076 396260. Decent bungalows in a small garden that occupies a surprisingly peaceful spot. Price depends on the size of the bungalow and whether it has air-con. Fan ❸, air-con ❺

The Little Mermaid 94/25 Thanon Taina, Kata Centre ⓣ076 330730, ⓦwww.littlemermaidphuket.net. Scandinavian-owned place with city-style fan and air-con rooms in a guest-house block, plus bungalow-style rooms, all with air-con and TV, set tightly round a small swimming pool. Advance booking essential. Fan rooms ❸, air-con rooms ❹, air-con bungalows ❺–❼

Lucky Guest House 110/44–45 Thanon Taina, Kata Centre ⓣ076 330572, ⓔluckyguesthouseka ta@hotmail.com. Reasonable-value place offering unusually large, bright en-suite rooms in a low-rise block (the best ones have balconies) and some rather plain semi-detached bungalows on land further back. Choose between fan and air-con. Fan ❸, air-con ❺

Merit Hill Bungalow 28 Soi 2, Thanon Karon ⓣ076 333300, ⓔmhb@bluehorizons.de. Located up a slope across the road from the beach, this is an appealing spot with a range of different accommodation options. The nicest are the apartment-style bungalows, all with air-con, kitchen, living room and a restful view over an adjacent palm grove. Cheapest are the terraced fan rooms with no views. Fan ❸, air-con ❻

Prayoon Bungalows Behind the stadium, off Thanon Karon; access via *Andaman Seaview* ☎076 396196. Long-established family-run place with just seven large, comfortable old-style fan bungalows, all with verandas and good bathrooms, widely spaced around a big, sloping garden just 150m or so off the beach. ❺

Expensive

Golden Sand Inn Northern end of Ao Karon ☎076 396493, ⓦwww.phuket-goldensand.com. Popular, medium-sized, mid-priced hotel, one of the least costly of its kind, with good-value, old-style air-con bungalows set around a tropical garden and swimming pool, plus pricier rooms in the central block. Bungalows ❼, hotel ❽

Le Meridien On Ao Karon Noi (also known as Relax Bay), north of Ao Karon ☎076 340480, ⓦwww.lemeridien.com. This huge hotel complex has the tiny bay all to itself and boasts an amazing breadth of facilities, including nine restaurants, two lake-style swimming pool (with islands), a spa, squash and tennis courts, a climbing wall and private woods. It's a good choice for kids, with reliable babysitting services, a kids' club and lessons in everything from windsurfing and water polo to Thai cookery. ❾

Marina Phuket Resort 47 Thanon Karon, far southern end of Ao Karon, on the Karon/Kata headland ☎076 330625, ⓦwww.marinaphuket.com. The 92 cottages here are dotted around an effusive and secluded tropical garden that leads right down to the beach. All the bungalows air-con and some kind of outdoor space from which to enjoy the garden; the top-end options have ocean views. The resort is known for its charming service and has good facilities, including a pool and the prettily located restaurant, *On the Rock*, plus it's convenient for Karon's other bars and restaurants. ❾

The Old Phuket Soi Aroona Karon, 192/36 Thanon Karon ☎076 6353, ⓦwww.theoldphuket.com. Designed to evoke early twentieth-century Sino-Portuguese shophouse architecture from Malacca (and Phuket town), rooms here manage to be both pretty and modern. Coloured glass window panels and East Indies-style wooden doors are complemented by contemporary furnishings and air-conditioning, with the "terrace rooms" enjoying garden shower rooms plus their own little streetside garden out front. The hotel has a rooftop pool, a sauna and a kids' area. It's located 100m from the beach down a soi oriented towards Scandinavian tourists. ❾

Eating and drinking

Karon's choice of **restaurants** is underwhelming, lacking either the big-name restaurants of Patong or the authentic eateries of Phuket town. Places worth trying out are listed below, in addition to which is the string of seven open-fronted streetside restaurants just north of the stadium on Thanon Karon, whose inexpensive offerings range from king prawns to burgers, and *matsaman* curries to spaghetti.

Most of the Thanon Taina **bars** are small, genial places: *Café del Mar* is an inviting, hip little joint serving margaritas and daiquiris as well as other drinks, while *Blue Fin* has happy hours from 3–7pm daily and *Anchor Bar* serves Blackthorn cider. Though there are as yet no go-go bars on Karon, the Patong bar scene has made significant inroads, and there are clusters of bar-beers with hostess service in the Karon Centre and on sois off Thanon Luang Pho Chuain, and around the *Islandia Hotel* on Thanon Patak.

Kampong-Kata Hill Restaurant Access via a steep ramp off Thanon Karon. Quality Thai and seafood dishes and fancy Thai-style decor set this place apart and ensure it always gets a good crowd. Its curries – red, green, dry and country-style – are especially good and come in all permutations (B120–180). Also serves reasonably priced imported wine by the glass. Nightly 5pm–midnight.

Kwong Seafood Shop Thanon Taina. Very popular for its array of freshly caught fish and seafood which can be barbecued or cooked to order; most dishes B120. Daily 11am–11pm.

Noo Noi Restaurant Soi 1, Thanon Luang Pho Chuain. Small, simple, family-run café, in front of the family home, that deserves a mention for determinedly continuing to dish out Thai standards (mainly fried rice and noodle dishes, from B35) at exceptionally cheap prices, despite the inflated rates charged by most other similar places. Daily 8am–10pm.

On the Rock In the grounds of *Marina Phuket Resort*, Kata/Karon headland. Occupying a fine spot above the rocks at the southern end of Ao Karon, this open-air restaurant serves especially good mixed baskets of grilled and deep-fried seafood. Main dishes cost from B150–600. Daily 8am–11pm.

Wildfire Thanon Karon. This strikingly designed four-in-one dining experience includes an outdoor, sea-view deck-bar, the *Sandbar*, and a restaurant on the top-floor, serving Thai "tapas" at B50 a dish, good wood-fired pizzas, and all-you-can-eat barbecue specials (B750). Daily 11am–11pm.

Ao Kata Yai and Ao Kata Noi

Broad, curving **AO KATA YAI** (Big Kata Bay) is only a few minutes' drive around the headland from Karon (17km from Phuket town), but both prettier and safer for swimming, thanks to the protective rocky promontories at either end. It's also a good distance from the road. The northern stretch of Kata Yai is given over to the unobtrusive buildings of the *Club Med* resort, and the southern to *Kata Beach Resort*: in between the soft sand is busy with sunloungers and the occasional drink and fruit stall. The rest of the accommodation and the bulk

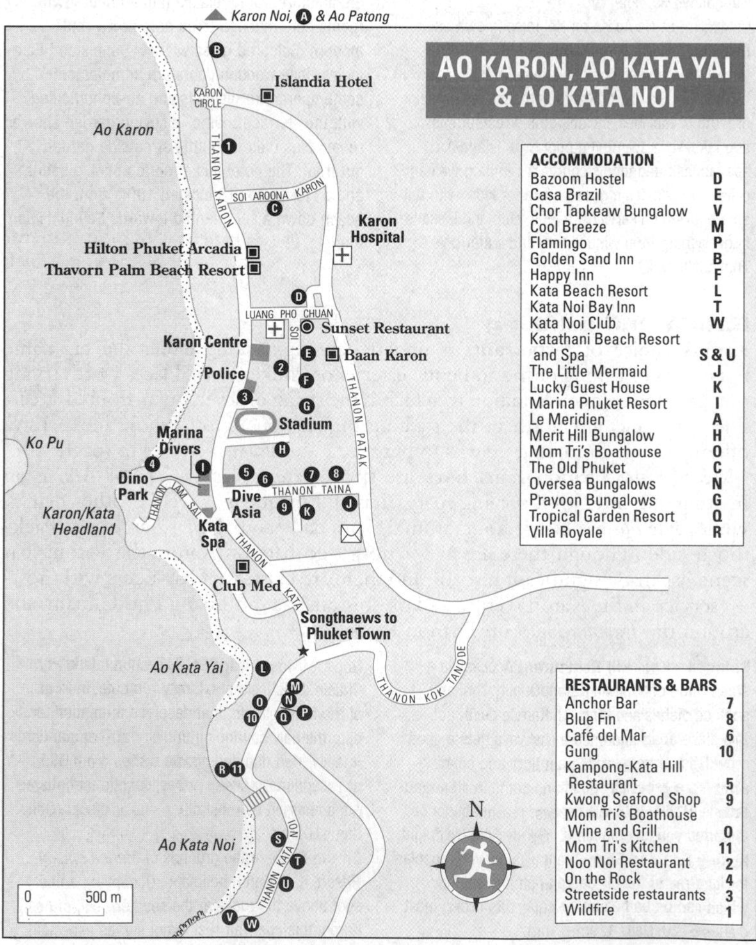

of the tourist village, is at the southern end, where you'll also find the restaurants, bars, minimarkets, tour operators and transport rental outlets. A headland at the southernmost point divides Ao Kata Yai from the smaller **AO KATA NOI** (Little Kata Bay), whose gold-sand bay feels secluded, being at the end of a dead-end road, but is very popular and so gets quite crowded with loungers. Kata Noi has its own low-key but rather charmless cluster of businesses, including a minimarket, several restaurants, transport rental and a tailor's shop, though it's dominated by the enormous two-site complex of the *Katathani* hotel.

Most **songthaews** from Phuket go first to Karon (B25), then drive south past *Club Med* and terminate at *Kata Beach Resort* on the headland between Kata Yai and Kata Noi (B30); returning songthaews depart approx every 20min from 5.30am–4.30pm. To get to Kata Noi, continue walking over the hill for about ten minutes, or take a tuk-tuk for about B100. A tuk-tuk from Kata Yai to Karon will cost you about B150.

Accommodation and eating

There is no really cheap **accommodation** on Kata Noi or Kata Yai. Most of the hotels along Kata Yai's Thanon Kok Tanode (also spelt Kok Tanot) are built up the hillside, which means guests face a steep climb to get to their rooms, but are then rewarded with expansive bay views.

The best and most famous **restaurant** here is *Mom Tri's Boathouse Wine and Grill* on Kata Yai, which has a famously extensive wine list and an exquisite and extremely expensive menu (B300–900) of Thai and Western delicacies; it runs Thai cooking classes every weekend (see below). Mom Tri also has two other highly rated restaurants in the Kata area: the less formal but still fairly pricey *Gung*, almost next door to the *Boathouse*, with beachfront seating and a menu that includes a range of Thai dishes as well as seafood and rock lobster (*gung*); and the exclusive *Mom Tri's Kitchen*, part of the *Villa Royale* hotel complex, which overlooks Kata Noi from the rocks at its northern point.

Kata Yai

Cool Breeze 225 Thanon Kok Tanode ⓣ076 330484, ⓦwww.phuketindex.com/coolbreezebungalows. The sixteen good-sized fan and air-con bungalows here are set at different levels within the hillside garden, above the street-side restaurant, and the best of them have partial sea views from their terraces. Fan ⑤, air-con ⑥

Flamingo Thanon Kok Tanode ⓣ076 330776. Dozens of prettily positioned air-con bungalows built among the trees on a steep incline above the flamingo-coloured restaurant and bar. Most have verandas and some have sea views. Also has a tiny swimming pool and a small spa. ⑥–⑦

Kata Beach Resort Thanon Kata ⓣ076 330530, ⓦwww.katagroup.com. This huge, high-rise hotel occupies a great spot right on the edge of the white-sand beach. It has a big, shorefront swimming pool, a kids' pool and lots of watersports facilities, so it's popular with families; also runs Thai cooking and fruit-carving classes. ⑨

Mom Tri's Boathouse Thanon Kok Tanode ⓣ076 330015, ⓦwww.boathousephuket.com. Exclusive and very pricey beachfront boutique hotel with just 36 elegantly furnished sea-view rooms, a reputation for classy service, and a famously top-notch restaurant. Also has some even more luxurious suites and studios at *Villa Royale*, a "gourmet hotel" set in landscaped tropical gardens above Kata Noi. Advance booking essential. Published rates from B8200. ⑨

Oversea Bungalows Thanon Kok Tanode ⓣ076 284155, ⓦwww.twochefs-phuket.com. Nine huge bungalows ranged up the hillside and accessed by a series of steep stairways. Many offer fine sea views from their wraparound balconies and all have air-con. Closed May–Oct. ⑦

Tropical Garden Resort 247 Thanon Kok Tanode ⓣ076 285211, ⓦwww.tropicalphuketresort.com. Good value mid-range hotel just one minute's walk from the beach, with comfortable air-con rooms in half a dozen buildings stacked up the hillside and some excellent bay-view panoramas from the balconies of pricier options. Has two pools and a kids area. Popular with package tourists. ⑧

Kata Noi

Chor Tapkeaw Bungalow 18 Thanon Kata Noi ⓣ076 330433, ⓦwww.phuketdir.com/ctabkaew.

The spacious and fairly comfortably furnished fan and air-con bungalows here are ranged up the hillside at the far southern end of the road; the verandas give good sea views and the restaurant is right on the beach. Book ahead as there are only 24 rooms and it's popular. Fan ❻, air-con ❼

Kata Noi Bay Inn Thanon Kata Noi ⓣ076 333308, ⓦwww.phuket.com/katanoibayinn. Small, friendly little hotel attached to a seafood restaurant, offering the cheapest accommodation on this beach. Most of the 28 fan and air-con rooms have balconies and, in some cases, a distant sea view. Fan ❺, air-con ❻–❼

Kata Noi Club Thanon Kata Noi ⓣ076 284025, ⓔkatanoi_club@yahoo.com. Set in among lots of trees at the far southern end of the beachfront road, this small, 25-room operation has some rather spartan bungalows as well as a few better, pricier air-con ones. Fan ❻, air-con ❼

Katathani Beach Resort and Spa 14 Thanon Kata Noi ⓣ076 330124, ⓦwww.katathani.com. Occupying about half the beachfront, and a big chunk of land across the narrow road, this is the biggest and poshest outfit on Kata Noi. The shorefront all-suite *Katathani* wing is pricier and all its rooms have sea-view balconies, though rooms at the inland, garden-view *Bhuri* wing are also very deluxe. The hotel has five swimming pools and a spa, plus tennis courts, a games room, a dive shop and a kids' playground. Published rates from US$200. ❾

Hat Nai Harn, Hat Ya Nui and Laem Promthep

Around the next headland south from Kata Noi, **HAT NAI HARN**, 18km southwest of Phuket town, is a beautiful curved bay of white sand backed by a stand of casuarinas and plenty of foodstalls but only minimal development. It's a popular spot for day-trippers, so the beach soon gets crowded with parasols and loungers, but you can escape the throng by hiring a kayak (B100–150/hr or B500–700/day) and paddling off to the Laem Promthep headland or to the nearby island of Ko Kaeo Pisadan (see opposite). Be warned though that during the monsoon the waves here are huge. The beach is dominated by the luxurious **hotel**, *Le Royal Meridien Phuket Yacht Club* (ⓣ076 380200, ⓦphuketyachtclub.lemeridien.com; ❾), whose attractive rooms are raked up the hill and all have capacious balconies to make the most of the fine sea views. There's slightly cheaper accommodation next door at the well-sited though architecturally unappealing *Sabana Resort* (ⓣ076 289327, ⓦwww.sabana-resort.com; ❽–❾), which offers plain concrete row rooms and a decent sized pool and is just over the narrow road from the shore.

Follow the coastal road 2km south around the lumpy headland and you reach the tiny roadside beach of **Hat Ya Nui**, which gets a surprising number of visitors despite being so small and right next to the admittedly quiet road. There are coral reefs very close to the shore, though the currents are strong, and kayaks and sunloungers for rent. Just across the road from the beach the family-run *Ya Nui Beach Bungalows* offers simple bamboo **huts** with fan and bath in a pretty garden (ⓣ076 288278, ⓦwww.yanuibungalow.com; ❹), while 200m uphill from the beach there are larger, better and more stylish en-suite fan-cooled bamboo bungalows, also in an attractively shaded garden with higher-level sea views, at *Nai Ya Beach Bungalow* (ⓣ076 288817, closed May–Oct; ❺–❻).

A further 1km on, you reach the southernmost tip of Phuket at the sheer headland of **Laem Promthep**. Wild and rugged, jutting out into the deep blue of the Andaman Sea, the cape is one of the island's top beauty spots: at sunset, busloads of tour groups get shipped in to admire the scenery – and just to ensure you don't miss the spectacle, a list of year-round sunset times is posted both at the viewpoint and in the middle of Phuket town. Several reefs lie just off the cape, and anglers often try their luck from the boulders around the shoreline.

Songthaews from Phuket town (every 30min; 45 min; B30) go to Nai Harn, via Rawai, but for Hat Ya Nui and Laem Promthep you have to do the lengthy climb round the promontory on foot. Taxis from this area to Patong cost B500.

The southeast coast and its islands

Shadowed by the mainland, Phuket's **southeast coast** lacks the fine sandy beaches and resorts of the west coast, and is chiefly the province of harbours for boats to other islands, though Phuketians come for the numerous seafood restaurants along the shore. Some of these smaller satellite islands, in particular **Ko Kaeo Pisadan** and **Ko Racha Yai**, offer a beach experience now lost on "mainland" Phuket, of turquoise waters and near-empty shores.

Hat Rawai

Phuket's southernmost beach, **HAT RAWAI**, was the first to be exploited for tourist purposes, but, forty years on, the hoteliers have moved to the softer sands of Kata and Karon, leaving Rawai to its former inhabitants, the Urak Lawoy *chao ley* ("sea gypsies", for more on whom, see p.713), and to an expanding expat population. Most visitors are here for the seafood – served both at the many open-air restaurants on the beachfront, and Thai-style on mats under the shorefront casuarinas – or for the expat-run bars, while others barely linger as they hire a longtail or speedboat out to the islands offshore. Aside from the food, the chief local attraction is the **Phuket Seashell Museum** (daily 8am–6pm; B100), on the main road inland from the beach, which displays some two thousand species of shell, including 380 million-year-old fossils, giant clams, and a 140-carat gold pearl. **Songthaews** from Phuket town's Thanon Ranong market pass through Rawai (B25, 35min) on their way to and from Nai Harn.

Ko Kaeo Pisadan

The tiny islet of **Ko Kaeo Pisadan** (also known as Ko Kaeo Yai and sometimes spelt Ko Kaew Phitsadan) makes an idyllic escape from the big resorts and works either as a day-trip or as an ultra-peaceful overnight getaway. It lies just 1km off Laem Promthep cape and takes only 15–20 minutes to reach by longtail from either Hat Rawai or Hat Nai Harn (B800 return for the whole boat), or about half an hour by kayak from Nai Harn.

The island is known locally for its Buddhist monastery, Wat Ko Kaeo Pisadan, which receives a steady stream of devotees keen to pay their respects and to chat with the coterie of resident monks, the island's only permanent inhabitants. Ko Kaeo is so small it takes mere minutes to cross on foot, or two hours to circumnavigate in a kayak (available for rent on the island). Its principal beach is only 200-metres long but graced with dazzling white sand and turquoise water and with enough reefs to be worth putting on a mask and snorkel. You can make the most of this exclusive spot by staying at *Ko Kaeo Pisadan* (Ⓣ084 745 5907, Ⓦwww.kokaeopisadan.com; ❻), whose three large, nicely designed timber **bungalows** are sited in a breathtakingly beautiful location above the water and have French windows opening on to huge sea-view decks; it's a strictly no-smoking resort. Alternatively you could a rent a tent for B300 and pitch it among the palms and flowering shrubs in the shorefront garden. The restaurant, *Bistro Havana*, also enjoys fine vistas; it makes an effort to use wholesome ingredients and serves seafood and some veggie dishes (from B100).

Ko Hai

Despite the name, the reefs around **KO HAI** (aka Ko Hey or **Coral Island**), 9km southeast off Hat Rawai, are not as rewarding as those at Ko Racha, and the waters get very crowded with visiting tour boats. But the island is blessed with several beautiful white-sand beaches that are good for swimming year-round. Organized day-trips to the island are sold by all travel agents and cost B600. You can also stay on the island, at *Coral Island Resort* (Ⓣ076 281060, Ⓦwww.phuket.com/coralisland; ❼–❽), which has 64 bungalows and a pool and dive centre set in lush tropical gardens.

Ko Racha Yai

Tiny **Ko Racha Yai**, measuring approximately three kilometres long by three kilometres wide, boasts a couple of awesome white-sand beaches with crystal-clear turquoise water, several reefs with prolific and varied fish life, and a range of places to stay. The beaches are small, however, so if you're here independently you'll likely share each one of them with day-trippers for an hour or two, though the best looking, Ao Siam, is big enough to cope. Exploring the interior is also fun – tracks crisscross through palm groves and a couple of hamlets, with plenty of wilderness still in evidence and occasional stands of cashew and jackfruit, mango and tamarind tree, even a few water buffaloes and some resident metre-long iguanas. There's Internet access at *The Racha* and *Ban Raya*, plus on Ao Batok, where there's also a minimarket and several small bars and restaurants. Both these hotels also have dive shops, open to all for trips and courses. Ko Racha Yai is 23 km south of Phuket and **access** is via longtail from Hat Rawai (1hr 30min; about B2500 to charter for the day) or by speedboat from Ao Chalong (about 30min). From November through April several speedboats, including those run by *Bungalow Raya Resort* and by *Ban Raya* (see opposite), leave Ao Chalong every morning at about 9am and return from the island at 3pm (B500–600 one way or B1200 day trip, including transfers, lunch and snorkelling equipment plus usually three stops in different spots around the island). *The Racha* has its own guest boat.

The main docking point, and the focus for day-trippers, is tiny, deep cut **Ao Batok** (Patok), whose 400-metre-long shorefront is dominated by the elegant white-cube and slate-roof buildings of the ultra-luxurious **hotel**, *The Racha* (Ⓣ076 355455, Ⓦwww.theracha.com; rates from US$200; ❾). Guests here can choose between sleekly designed superior and deluxe villas, some with their own plunge pool and direct sea view. There's a gorgeous infinity pool, three restaurants and a spa plus free cycle, kayak and snorkel rental for guests. The much more affordable en-suite fan-cooled bamboo bungalows at *Bungalow Raya Resort* (Ⓣ076 288271, Ⓦwww.bgracharesort.com, Ⓔrayaresort@phuketinternet.co.th; ❺) share the bay, sitting atop the northern headland, with a couple offering unbeatable views over the sparkling sea; there's a nicely sited, if pricey, restaurant here too, with a similar view.

The next beach around the headland, two minutes' walk over the hill from beside *Bungalow Raya Resort*, is north-facing **Ao Siam**, the longest and prettiest on the island and still largely backed by coconut palms. A couple of **places to stay** sit atop its western cliff, both offering en-suite bamboo bungalows, with fan, mosquito net and some sort of view: *Raya Seaview Bungalow* (Ⓣ081 397 5141; closed May–Oct; ❺) has the better accommodation, while *Jungle View* (Ⓣ081 396 0887; closed May–Oct; ❺) has a gloriously sited high-level restaurant deck with panoramas that take in the whole bay. The *Jungle Bar* at the eastern end of the bay does barbecues and occasional live music and there are a couple of small food and drink stalls too.

About 15 minutes' walk due east of Ao Batok, **Ao Ter** is a scruffy little bay, full of flotsam (though this may change if signs of construction work come to fruition), but its chief attraction is its good snorkelling both on the shoreline, where the reef is uninteresting but the fish quite spectacular in range and number, and about 100m offshore, where there are two dive sites, including a small wreck. Further down the east coast, there's even less of a beach at **Ao Kon Kare**, though you can swim here, and its reefs are rewarding for snorkelling and diving. It's also the site of *Ban Raya* (Ⓣ076 355563, Ⓦwww.banraya.com; fan ❼, air-con ❼), a mid-market place of fan and air-con wooden chalets set in carefully landscaped flower gardens beneath palm trees; the resort has bicycles for rent, and a spa and library and is about 15 minutes' walk from Ao Batok or Ao Siam.

Ao Chalong, Laem Panwa and Ko Siray

East of Rawai, the sizeable offshore island of Ko Lone protects the broad sweep of **AO CHALONG**, where many a Chinese fortune was made from the huge quantities of tin mined in the bay. These days, Ao Chalong is the main departure point for dive excursions and fishing trips, and for speedboats to other islands, including Ko Racha Yai and Ko Hai. For islanders, however, Chalong is important as the site of **Wat Chalong** (8km southwest of Phuket town, on Thanon Chao Fa Nok, aka Route 4022; the Phuket–Karon songthaew passes the entrance), Phuket's loveliest and most famous temple, which enshrines the statue of revered monk Luang Pho Cham, who helped quash a violent rebellion by migrant Chinese tin-miners in 1876. Elsewhere in the temple compound, the Phra Mahathat chedi is believed to contain a relic of the Buddha. Though there's no special reason to **stay** in this part of the island, you might make an exception for the sister branch of Bangkok's famously laid-back backpacker haven, *Shanti Lodge* (Ⓣ076 280233, Ⓦwww.shantilodge.com/phuket; ❸–❺), just a few hundred metres south down Thanon Chao Fa Nok on Soi Bangrae (the Phuket-Karon songthaew should drop you close by). It's set in a relaxing garden, with herbal sauna, and has B150 dorms as well as fan and air-con doubles with or without private bathroom.

Ao Chalong tapers off eastwards into **LAEM PANWA**, at the tip of which you'll find the **Phuket Aquarium** (daily 8.30am–4pm; B100, kids B50), 10km south of Phuket town and accessible by frequent songthaews from the market. Run by the island's Marine Research Centre, it's not a bad primer for what you might see on a reef and has walk-through tunnels and a touch pool where you can interact with sea cucumbers and sea stars.

Around the other side of Laem Panwa, the island's deep-sea port of **Ao Makham** is dominated by a smelting and refining plant, bordered to the north by **Ao Phuket** and **KO SIRAY** (aka Ko Sire), which just about qualifies as an island because of the narrow channel that separates it from Phuket. Tour buses stop off at Ko Siray (5km due east of Phuket town) to spy on Phuket's largest and longest-established *chao ley* community; for more on the *chao ley* see p.713. The Ko Siray channel is the departure point for many scheduled **ferries to Ko Phi Phi**, most of which use **Rassada Harbour**; transfers to and from the port are fixed price and sometimes included in the price of the boat ticket.

Songthaews to Ao Chalong (B20) and the aquarium (B25) leave approximately every thirty minutes from Thanon Ranong in Phuket town.

The interior

If you have your own transport, exploring the lush, verdant **interior** makes a good antidote to lying on scorched beaches. All the tiny backroads – some too small to figure on tourist maps – eventually link up with the arteries connecting Phuket town with the beaches, and the minor routes south of Hat Nai Yang are especially picturesque, passing through monsoon forest that once in a while opens out into spiky pineapple fields or regimentally ordered **rubber plantations**. Thailand's first rubber trees were planted in Trang in 1901, and Phuket's sandy soil proved to be especially well suited to the crop. All over the island you'll see cream-coloured sheets of latex hanging out to dry on bamboo racks in front of villagers' houses.

Thalang and around

North of Ao Karon, Phuket's minor roads eventually swing back to the central Highway 402, also known as Thanon Thepkasatri after the landmark monument that stands on a roundabout 12km north of Phuket town. This **Heroines' Monument** commemorates the repulse of the Burmese army by the widow of the governor of Phuket and her sister in 1785: the two women rallied the island's womenfolk who, legend has it, cut their hair short and rolled up banana leaves to look like musket barrels to frighten the Burmese away. All songthaews to Hat Surin and Hat Nai Yang pass the monument (as does all mainland-bound traffic), and this is where you should alight for the **Thalang Museum** (Ⓦwww.thailandmuseum.com; daily 9am–4pm; B30), five minutes' walk east of here on Route 4027. Phuket's only museum, it has a few interesting exhibits on the local tin and rubber industries, as well as some colourful folkloric history and photos of the masochistic feats of the Vegetarian Festival (see box on p.738). If you continue along Route 4027 you'll eventually reach the Gibbon Rehabilitation Project, described below.

Eight kilometres north of the Heroines' Monument, just beyond the crossroads in the small town of **THALANG**, stands **Wat Phra Thong**, one of Phuket's most revered temples on account of the power of the Buddha statue it enshrines. The solid gold image is half-buried and no one dares dig it up for fear of a curse that has struck down excavators in the past. After the wat was built around the statue, the image was encased in plaster to deter would-be robbers.

Phra Taew National Park

The road east of the Thalang intersection takes you to the visitor centre of **PHRA TAEW NATIONAL PARK**, 3km away. Several paths cross this small hilly enclave, leading you through the forest habitat of macaques and wild boar, but the most popular features of the park are the Gibbon Rehabilitation Project and the Ton Sai and Bang Pae waterfalls, which combine well as a day-trip. The Gibbon Project is located about 10km northeast of the Heroines' Monument, off Route 4027. **Songthaews** from Phuket town, more frequent in the morning, will take you most of the way: ask to dropped off at Bang Pae (a 40min drive from town) and then follow the signed track for about 1km to get to the project centre. You can get drinks and snacks at the foodstall next to the Rehabilitation Centre, and the route to the waterfalls is signed from here. The **Bang Rong pier** for boats to Ko Yao Noi is a few kilometres northeast of the national park; see p.762 for details.

The Gibbon Rehabilitation Project

Phuket's forests used once to resound with the whooping calls of indigenous white-handed lar gibbons, but because these primates make such charismatic pets there is now not a single wild gibbon at large on the island. The situation has become so dire that the lar is now an endangered species, and in 1992 it became illegal in Thailand to keep them as pets, to sell them or to kill them.

Despite this, you'll come across a good number of pet gibbons on Phuket, kept in chains by bar and hotel owners as entertainment for their customers or as pavement photo opportunities for foolish tourists. The **Gibbon Rehabilitation Centre** (daily 9am–4pm, last tour at 3.15pm; B200, kids 100; Ⓦwww.gibbonproject.org) aims to reverse this state of affairs, first by rescuing as many pet gibbons as they can, and then by resocializing and re-educating them for the wild before finally releasing them back into the forests. It is apparently not unusual for gibbons to be severely traumatized by their experience as pets: not only will they have been taken forcibly from their mothers, but they may also have been abused by their owners.

Visitors are welcome at the project, which is centred in the forests of Phra Taew National Park, close to Bang Pae waterfall, but because the whole point of the rehab project is to minimize the gibbons' contact with humans, you can only admire the creatures from afar. There's a small exhibition here on the aims of the project, and the well-informed volunteer guides will fill you in on the details of each case and on the idiosyncratic habits of the lar gibbon (see "Flora, fauna and environmental issues" in Contexts, p.891, for more about Thailand's primates). Should you want to become a project volunteer yourself, or make a donation, you can email the project centre.

Bang Pae and Ton Sai waterfalls

If you follow the track along the river from the Gibbon Project, you'll soon arrive at **Bang Pae Falls**, a popular picnic and bathing spot, ten to fifteen minutes' walk away. Continue on the track for another 2.8km (about 1hr 30min on foot) and you should reach **Ton Sai Falls**: though not a difficult climb, it is quite steep in places and can be rough underfoot. There are plenty of opportunities for cool dips in the river en route. Once at Ton Sai you can either walk back down to the Phra Taew National Park access road and try to hitch a ride back home, or return the way you came.

Ko Yao Noi

Located in an idyllic spot on the edge of Phang Nga bay, almost equidistant from Phuket, Phang Nga and Krabi, the island of **KO YAO NOI** enjoys magnificent maritime views from almost every angle and makes a refreshingly tranquil getaway. Measuring about 12km at its longest point, it's home to some 3200 islanders, the vast majority of them Muslim, who earn their living from rubber and coconut plantations, fishing and shrimp-farming. Tourism here is low key, not least because the beaches lack the wow factor of more sparkling nearby sands, and visitors are drawn instead by the rural ambience and lack of commercial pressures. Nonetheless, there's decent swimming off the east coast at high tide, and at low tide too in a few places, and plenty of potential kayaking destinations. Exploring the interior is a particular pleasure, either via the barely trafficked round-island road as it runs through tiny villages and past the occasional ricefield, or via the trails that crisscross the forested interior, where you've a good chance of encountering monkeys as well as cobras and even pythons, not to mention plenty of birds, including majestic oriental pied hornbills.

Island practicalities

There are three mainland departure points for **boats** to Ko Yao Noi: from Phuket, Krabi's Ao Thalen, and Phang Nga. The most common route is from

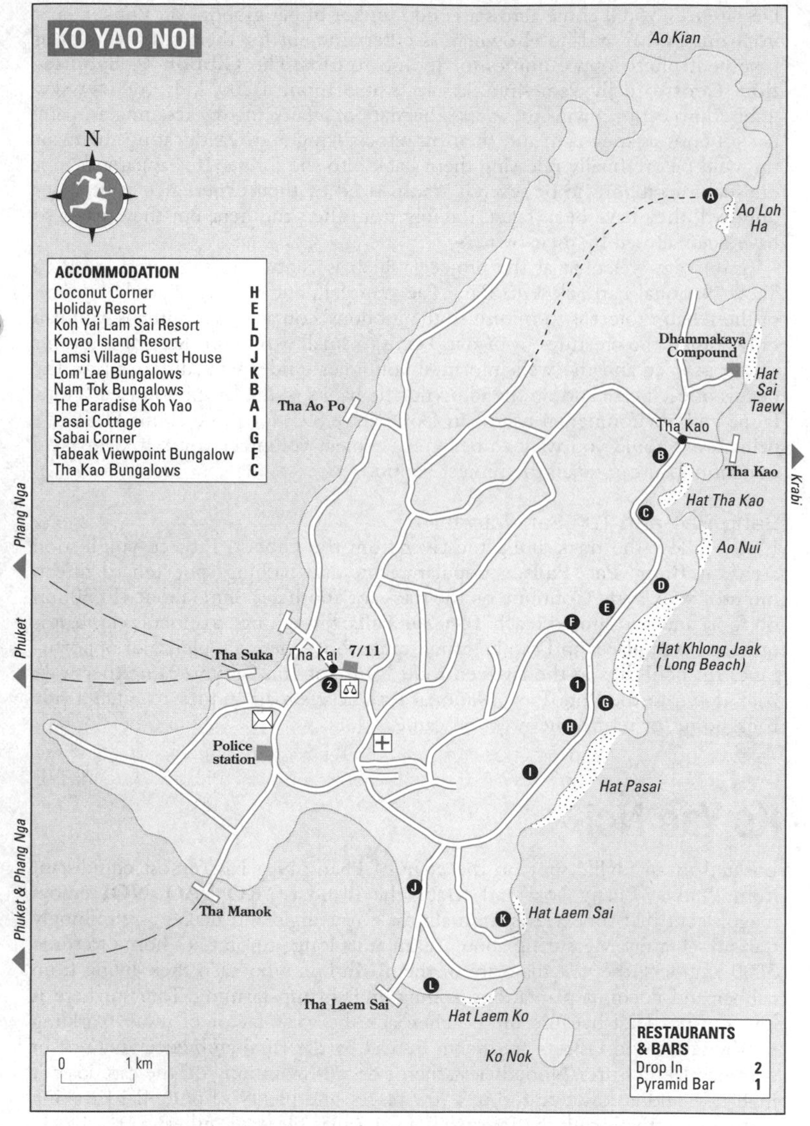

Bang Rong on **Phuket's** northeast coast (1hr; B80). Boats depart Bang Rong at 9.30am, 11am, 12.30pm, 2.30pm and 5pm, and return from Ko Yao Noi at 7.30am, 10am, 1.30pm and 3.30pm; a songthaew service from Phuket town's Thanon Ranong market runs to Bang Rong approximately hourly from 9am–1pm (90min; B25). The Phuket boats use either of two piers on Ko Yao Noi's southwest coast, Tha Manok or Tha Suka, depending on the tide; taxi drivers always know which to head for and charge B50–70 per person for transfers to accommodation. The **Krabi** option entails taking a boat from Ao Thalen, about 30km northwest of Krabi. Boats depart Ao Thalen at 11am and 1pm (1hr; B80) and songthaews from Krabi town connect with them (depart from near the Vogue Department Store at 10am and noon). Boats return from Ko Yao Noi at 7.30am. The Krabi boats use the Tha Kao pier on Ko Yao Noi's northeast coast. Boats also run to Ko Yao Noi from **Phang Nga** bay pier at Tha Dan, 9km south of Phang Nga town, departing at 1pm, returning from Ko Yao Noi at 7.30am (90min; B120); songthaews connect Phang Nga town with the pier. On Ko Yao Noi, the Phang Nga boats use the same pier as the Phuket boats, depending on the tide. The Ko Yao Noi–Phang Nga ride is especially scenic as it takes you through the heart of Ao Phang Nga, passing close by the stilt-house island of Ko Panyi (see p.767).

A paved 17-kilometre-long ring road runs around the southern two-thirds of the island, and to explore it you need either to ask your accommodation to phone for a **taxi**, or to rent your own transport. Most hotels can arrange **motorbike** rental (B200–250/day) and **bicycles** can be rented from *Coconut Corner*, *Lom'Lae* and *Holiday Resort* for B150/day: a circuit of the ring road takes a couple of hours by bicycle, with just one significant hill west of Tha Khao, though there are many enticing side branches too. **Kayaking** around the coast is also possible, and the dozens of tiny islands visible from the east coast make enticing destinations for experienced paddlers; kayaks can be rented through Ko Yao Noi hotels for about B150/hour, or you can join an overnight kayaking trip here from Phuket (see p.732) or Krabi (see p.776).

Nearly all island hotels can arrange **excursions**. *Sabai Corner* offers longtail charters to Ko Hong and other islands in the bay for B2000–3000 (maximum seven people, excluding lunch, with kayaks an optional extra) and *Lom'Lae* does all-inclusive snorkelling trips for B1600 per person (kids B800) as well as guided self-paddle kayak outings for B2600/1300 per person. They also run rock-climbing courses (B1800/half-day) and cooking classes (B1600/800) and have the only **dive** shop on the island, Ko Yao Dive and Marine Sports (Ⓦwww.kohyaodive.com), which leads dives trips to sites around Phuket and Phi Phi for B2500–3500, and teaches Openwater courses for B12,000.

Around the island

Most tourists stay on the **east coast**, which has the main beaches and the bulk of the accommodation. But the rest of the island is well worth a day's outing by motorbike or bicycle, which also gives you the chance for a roti and even an email check in the island's tiny town, **Tha Khai**.

Hat Tha Khao and Hat Sai Taew

The most northerly of the main eastern beaches is **Hat Tha Kao**, site of a small village, with a couple of shops and a restaurant, the pier for boats to and from Krabi, and a few tourist bungalows. It's also the closest point to Ko Yao's nicest beach, so-called **Temple Beach** or **Hat Sai Taew**, 2km away, whose pretty, gold-sand shore is great for swimming at any tide. It's accessed via land that belongs to the Dhammakaya Foundation, a popular Buddhist sect, and is unsigned and so a bit tricky to find. From Tha Khao pier head inland and take the first right, then go right again, via the khlong and its sheltered marina, and through rubber plantations; you will need to go through the gated Dhammakaya compound to reach the beach – there's no temple, just a group of *kuti* (meditation cells) around a pond and some other meditators' accommodation.

A five-minute walk south from the Tha Kao ferry pier brings you to the ultra laid-back *Nam Tok Bungalows* (Ⓣ087 292 1102; ③), one of the cheapest

places to stay on the island. Its eight bungalows are set back from Hat Tha Khao beach, beside a khlong, in a small garden full of flowers and a fishpond; they're simple but comfortable and all have cute garden bathrooms. The owner, an island fisherman, lets you cook your own meals in his kitchen and takes his guests on camping trips to Ko Pak Bia (B3000 per boat); he also rents motorbikes. At the southern end of Hat Tha Kao, *Tha Kao Bungalows* (ⓣ076 596564; ④) has five rudimentary beachfront huts with fans and nets.

Hat Klong Jaak (Long Beach)

South of Hat Tha Kao, **Hat Klong Jaak**, more commonly referred to as **Long Beach**, is the site of the longest-running and best-known tourist accommodation. It's also where you'll find the genial, Scottish-Thai-run *Pyramid Bar* (daily 5pm–1am), which plays chilled music, serves **cocktails** and beer, and is a good spot to meet islanders and expats; it's about 200m north of *Sabai Corner* at the southern end of the beach. To date there are no shops or other amenities on Long Beach.

The most stylish and exclusive of the Long Beach **bungalows** is *Koyao Island Resort* (ⓣ076 597474, ⓦwww.koyao.com; ⑨; high-season rates from B8000), which also happens to occupy the nicest stretch of the beach, the only bit that's reliable for swimming at any tide. The resort comprises just 15 chic Baliesque fan-cooled cottage compounds, all of them with separate living areas, huge bathrooms, and sliding doors that give access to the spacious garden and its fine bay views. There's Internet access here and a spa, and the restaurant serves expensive European food. Heading south, you can't miss the blue roofs of *Holiday Resort* (ⓣ081 607 7912, ⓦwww.holidayresort.co.th; ⑧, but frequently discounted and one night in seven is thrown in for free), a mid-market place that's one of only a handful on the island to offer both fan and air-con. Though they look uninspiring from the outside, the bungalow and room interiors are attractive and comfortable and the bay views from the roadside garden and many verandas are superlative. The resort rents motorbikes, bicycles and kayaks. Two hundred metres inland, on a cross-island track, the Japanese-Thai-run *Tabeak Viewpoint Bungalows* (ⓣ089 590 4182, ⓦwww.kohyaobungalowgroup.com; ④–⑤) has just four large, well outfitted fan-cooled wood-and-bamboo bungalows all offering commanding views of the islands; the Thai owner is a community policeman and an excellent source of island info. Long Beach's far southern headland, about 3.5km south of the Tha Kao pier, is occupied by the long-established *Sabai Corner* (ⓣ076 597497, ⓔsabaicorner@yahoo.com; ④–⑤), a laid-back little outfit of ten thoughtfully designed wooden bungalows, all with fans, nets and bathrooms, plus decks and hammocks, set on a rise between the road and the beach, under cashew and jackfruit trees.

Hat Pasai and Laem Sai

South around the headland from Long Beach is **Hat Pasai,** at the top end of which, just one minute's walk from Long Beach's *Sabai Corner*, sits the traveller-friendly *Coconut Corner*, (ⓣ076 597134, ⓔthaimrbean@hotmail.com; ③–④), among the cheapest **places to stay** on the island. Its simple en-suite bungalows are set around a small garden just across the road from the beach and there's Internet access here as well as bicycle and motorbike rental. Further south is *Pasai Cottage* (ⓣ076 597478; B600), whose six bamboo cottages have unexpectedly tasteful interiors, folding glass doors and prettily tiled bathrooms.

Beyond Hat Pasai, tiny **Hat Laem Sai** is often known simply as **Hat Lom'Lae**, after the appealing Thai-Canadian-run *Lom'Lae Bungalows* (ⓣ076 597486, ⓦwww.lomlae.com; ⑥, family houses ⑧–⑨) which sits on the shore.

It's a beautiful, secluded haven, 500m down a track off the round-island road, backed by ricefields and rubber plantations and enjoying stunning bay views from its palm-fringed beach and grassy garden. The eight attractive, wooden, fan-cooled bungalows are widely spaced and have sliding doors, decks and hammocks to capitalize on the vistas. Some have additional upstairs loft beds, and there are two-bedroom family houses with kitchens available as well. Kayaks, bikes, motorbikes and windsurfers are available for rent and there's a dive shop here.

A few hundred metres west from the *Lom'Lae* turn-off, about 3km from Tha Kai, another side-road takes you down towards **Laem Sai pier**, along a coast that has no real beach but is scenically dotted with houses on stilts, fishing platforms, dozens of longtails and some inviting views of Ko Yao Noi's larger twin, Ko Yao Yai, just across the channel. There are many **homestays** around here, participants in the REST community-based tourism initiative (Ⓦwww.rest.or.th; see Basics p.51 for more on this), as well as a couple of **guest houses**. The British-Thai run *Lamsi Village Guest House* is a two-storey block of just eight good-quality tiled rooms, all with fan, TV and balcony (Ⓣ081 978 4257; ❺). About 1.5km further down the road, beyond where the paving stops, *Koh Yai Lam Sai Resort and Seafood* (Ⓣ076 597345; ❹) enjoys fine view across the water to Ko Yao Yai – it's a great place for a seafood lunch even if you're not staying in one of its six little en-suite fan huts located up the rise behind; the resort has bicycles for rent and there's a nice little beach 300m east around the rocks.

Tha Kai and north

The island's commercial and administrative centre is **Tha Kai**, inland from the main piers on the southwest coast. This is where you'll find the post office, the hospital, the police station (Ⓣ076 593123), the obligatory 7-11 shop, with ATM, as well as a couple of Internet centres, the main market, several roti stalls and a few simple Thai-food restaurants, including the welcoming *Drop In*, diagonally across the from 7-11.

The road running **north from Tha Kai**'s 7-11 is particularly scenic, taking you through several hamlets with their mosques and latex-pressing mangles, and past ricefields and their resident buffaloes, with mangroves in the middle distance, sea eagles hovering overhead, and the rounded hills of nearby sister island Ko Yao Yai in the background. At a junction about 3km from Thai Khai, the northbound road soon turns into a horrible track leading to Ao Loh Ha, while veering right will take you over the hill and down to Tha Khao on the east coast, about 4km away.

Within a couple of kilometres, the northbound road to **Ao Loh Ha**, Ko Yao Noi's northernmost beach, turns into rough, four-wheel-drive-only track which finally ends the deluxe thatched villas of *The Paradise Koh Yao* (Ⓣ081 892 4878, Ⓦwww.theparadise.biz; ❾).

Ao Phang Nga

Protected from the ravages of the Andaman Sea by Phuket, **AO PHANG NGA** has a seascape both bizarre and beautiful. Covering some four hundred square kilometres of coast between Phuket and Krabi, the mangrove-edged bay is spiked with limestone karst formations up to 300m in height, jungle-clad and craggily profiled. It's Thailand's own version ofVietnam's world-famous Ha Long

△ Ao Phang Nga

bay, reminiscent too of Guilin's scenery in China, and much of it is now preserved as **national park** (entry B200; Ⓦ www.dnp.go.th/National_park.asp). The bay is thought to have been formed about twelve thousand years ago when a dramatic rise in sea level flooded the summits of mountain ranges, which over millions of years had been eroded by an acidic mixture of atmospheric carbon dioxide and rainwater. Some of these karst islands have been further eroded in such a way that they are now hollow, secreting hidden lagoons or *hongs* that can only be accessed at certain tides and only by kayak. The main *hong* islands are in the **western** and **eastern** bay areas – to the west or east of Ko Yao Noi, which sits roughly mid-way between Phuket and Krabi. But the most famous scenery is in the **central bay** area, which boasts the biggest concentration of karst islands, and the most weirdly shaped formations.

Exploring the bay

There are several **departure points** for tours of the bay and several ways of seeing its many attractions. The most rewarding, and generally the most expensive option is to join a **sea-canoeing** trip (either guided or self-paddle), which enables you both to explore inside the *hongs* and to see at close quarters the extraordinary ecosystems around and inside the karst islands. Most sea-canoeing tours use large support boats carrying groups of up to 30 people; they can be arranged from any resort in Phuket, at Khao Lak, at all Krabi beaches and islands, and on Ko Yao Noi (see relevant resort accounts for details and prices), but the itinerary is usually determined by your departure point, with Phuket trips focusing on the western bay and Krabi tours concentrating on the eastern half. Most tours of the central bay are either in large **tour boats** booked out of Phuket or Krabi, which generally feature snorkelling and beach stops rather than kayaking, or in inexpensive, small-group **longtail boats** that depart from Phang Nga town, Phuket and Ko Yao Noi. All the main areas of the bay are extremely popular so don't expect a solitary experience.

The central bay

On tours of the **central bay**, the standard itinerary follows a circular or figure-of-eight route, passing extraordinary karst silhouettes that change character with the shifting light – in the eerie glow of an early-morning mist it can be a

The hongs

Hongs are the *pièce de résistance* of Ao Phang Nga: invisible to any passing vessel, these secret tidal lagoons are enclosed within the core of seemingly impenetrable limestone outcrops, accessible via murky tunnels that can only be navigated at certain tides in kayaks small enough to slip beneath and between low-lying rocky overhangs. Like the karsts themselves, the *hong*s have taken millions of years to form, with the softer limestone hollowed out from above by the wind and the rain, and from the side by the pounding waves. Eventually, when the two hollows met, the heart of the karst was able to fill with water via the wave-eroded passageway at sea level, creating a lagoon. The world inside these roofless hollows is an extraordinary one, protected from the open bay by a ring of cliff faces hung with vertiginous prehistoric-looking gardens of upside-down cycads, twisted bonsai palms and tangled ferns. And as the tide withdraws, the *hong's* resident creatures emerge to forage on the muddy floor, among them fiddler crabs, mudskippers, dusky langurs and crab-eating macaques, with white-bellied sea eagles often hovering overhead.

breathtaking experience. Some of the formations have nicknames suggested by their weird outlines – like **Khao Machu (Marju)**, which translates as "Pekinese Rock". Others have titles derived from other attributes – **Tham Nak** (or Nark, meaning Naga Cave) gets its name from the serpentine stalagmites inside; **Ko Thalu** (Pierced cave) has a tunnel through it; and a close inspection of **Khao Kien** (Painting Rock) reveals a cliff wall decorated with paintings of elephants, monkeys, fish, crabs and hunting weapons, believed to be between three thousand and five thousand years old.

Ao Phang Nga's most celebrated features, however, earned their tag from a movie: the cleft **Khao Ping Gan** (Leaning Rock) and its tapered outcrop **Khao Tapu** (Nail Rock) are better known as **James Bond Island**, having starred as Scaramanga's hideaway in *The Man With the Golden Gun*. Every boat stops off here so tourists can pose in front of the iconic rock (whose narrowing base is a good example of how wave action is shaping the bay) and the island crawls with seashell and trinket vendors.

The central bay's other must-see attraction is **Ko Panyi**, a Muslim village built almost entirely on stilts around the rock that supports the mosque. Nearly all boat tours stop here for lunch, so you're best off avoiding the pricey seafood restaurants around the jetty, and heading instead towards the islanders' foodstalls near the mosque. You can enjoy a more tranquil experience of Ko Panyi by joining one of the overnight tours from Phang Nga town (see p.769), which include an evening meal and guest-house accommodation on the island – and the chance to watch the sun set and rise over the bay; you can also rent a kayak from the jetty (B300/hr) and go exploring yourself.

At some point on your central-bay tour you should pass several small brick **kilns** on the edge of a mangrove swamp, which were once used for producing charcoal from mangrove wood. You'll also be ferried beneath **Tham Lod**, a photogenic archway roofed with stalactites and opening onto spectacular limestone and mangrove vistas.

The western bay: Ko Panak and Ko Hong

The main attraction of **the western bay** is **Ko Panak**, whose limestone cliffs hide secret tunnels to no less than five different **hongs** within its hollowed heart. These are probably Ao Phang Nga's most spectacular hidden worlds, the pitch-black tunnel approaches infested by bats and the bright, roofless *hongs* an entire other world, draped in hanging gardens of lianas, miniature screw pines and pandanus palms and busy with cicadas and the occasional family of crab-eating macaques. Western-bay tours also usually take in nearby **Ko Hong** (different from the Ko Hong in the eastern bay), whose exterior walls are coated with red, yellow and orange encrusting sponges, oyster shells and chitons (560 million-year-old slipper-shaped shells), which all make good camouflage for the scuttling red, blue and black crabs. Ko Hong's interior passageways light up with bioluminescent plankton in the dark and lead to a series of cave-lagoons.

The eastern bay: Ko Hong, Ao Thalen and Ao Luk

The principal *hong* island in the **eastern bay**, known both as **Ko Hong** and **Ko Lao Bileh**, lies about mid-way between Krabi's Hat Klong Muang beach and the southeast coast of Ko Yao Noi. The island is fringed by white-sand beaches and is a popular snorkelling destination as its aquamarine waters are so clear that the surrounding reef and its plentiful fish are clearly visible from the surface. The island's actual *hong* lacks the drama of Ao Phang Nga's best *hongs* because it's not fully enclosed or accessed via dark tunnels as at Ko Panak, but it is pretty, full of starfish, and tidal, so can only be explored at certain times.

The eastern bay's other big attractions are the mangrove-fringed inlets along the mainland coast between Krabi and Phang Nga, particularly around **Ao Thalen** (aka Ao Talin or Talane) and **Ao Luk**. Trips around here take you through complex networks of channels that weave through the mangrove swamps, between fissures in the limestone cliffs, beneath karst outcrops and into the occasional cave. Many of these passageways are *hongs*, isolated havens that might be up to 2km long, all but cut off from the main bay and accessible only at certain tides. The **Ban Bor Tor** (aka Ban Bho Tho) area of Ao Luk bay is especially known for **Tham Lod**, a long tunnel hung with stalagmites and stalactites whose entrance is obscured by vines, and for nearby **Tham Phi Hua Toe,** whose walls display around a hundred prehistoric cave-paintings, as well as some interestingly twisted stalactite formations.

Phang Nga town and around

Friendly if unexciting little **PHANG NGA TOWN**, approximately mid-way between Phuket and Krabi, serves mainly as a point from which to organize budget longtail trips around the spectacular karst islands of Ao Phang Nga. But there are also several caves and waterfalls nearby, accessible either on cheap tours run by every Phang Nga tour operator, or by motorbike. It's also possible to arrange trips from Phang Nga agencies to Ko Similan (B2900 for a day-trip or B3900 overnight), and Ko Surin (B3000/4900). The pier for boats to Ao Phang Nga is at Tha Dan, 9km south of town and served by songthaews, though transport to the pier is included in the tour price. For a description of the bay, see p.765.

Practicalities

All **buses** from Phuket and Takua Pa to Krabi pass through Phang Nga town about midway along their routes, dropping passengers at the bus station (Ⓣ076 412014) on Thanon Phetkasem, located towards the northern end of this long, thin town. Phang Nga runs half-hourly buses to and from Phuket, Krabi and Trang, and there are five air-con departures a day to Surat Thani, with the 9.30am and 11.30am services timed to link up with the Ko Samui boats. If you're heading to or from Khao Lak or Khao Sok, it's faster to get a bus to Khokkloi (40min) and then change for Khao Lak (1hr). Taxis from Phang Nga to Khao Lak cost about B1000 and to Khao Sok about B1200.If you want to go straight to the bay, change onto a songthaew bound for **Tha Dan** (B20); the pier is 9km to the south.

There's no official **tourist information**, but the several tour operators inside the bus station compound are helpful and will store your baggage for a few hours; they also sell bus and boat tickets for onward journeys to Krabi, Trang, Ko Phi Phi, Ko Lanta and Ko Samui.

Turning right (north) out of the bus station onto Thanon Phetkasem, you'll find **banks**, with exchange counters and ATMs and several **Internet** centres. Most other municipal facilities are further south down Thanon Phetkasem: the **police station** (Ⓣ076 430390) and immigration office (Ⓣ076 412011) are about 500m south of the bus station, off Soi Thungchedi, the **telephone office** is another 100m south of them, and Phang Nga Hospital (Ⓣ076 412034) and the **post office** are over 2km south of the bus station.

Accommodation and eating

Phang Nga's best budget **hotels** are all within 250m of each other and the bus station, on the bus station side of Thanon Phetkasem. First up, on the right-hand side as you turn right out of the bus station, is the welcoming *Ratanapong Hotel* at no. 111 (Ⓣ076 411247; fan ❷, air-con ❸), which gets the most custom, offering en-suite fan and air-con rooms and a roof terrace. A few doors further on, the modern, well-liked *Phang Nga Guest House* (Ⓣ076 411358; fan ❷, air ❸) has clean and comfortable en-suite rooms, though few have anything but a brick-wall view, while the old-style *Thawisuk Hotel* at no. 77 (Ⓣ076 412100; ❶) has large, slightly cheaper fan rooms and a rooftop terrace. The most upmarket accommodation in town is at *Phang Nga Inn* (Ⓣ076 411963; ❹–❻), which is clearly signed to the left of the bus station, about 250m away, at 2/2 Soi Lohakji, just off the town's main road. It's the former family home of the people who also own the *Phang Nga Guest House*, and the seventeen rooms here are all attractively furnished and equipped with air-con and TV, the price depending on the size of the room. Down at Tha Dan pier, the *Phang Nga Bay Resort* (Ⓣ076 412067, Ⓕ076 412070; ❺–❻) has a swimming pool and all rooms have balcony views of the mangrove-lined estuary.

For **eating**, the *Vorapin*, diagonally across from the *Ratanapong Hotel*, offers cheapish Thai and Chinese standards, or there's pizza, sandwiches and other western dishes at *Ivy*, further along the road at no. 38. There's a also a tiny vegetarian canteen (*raan ahaan jeh*; daily 6.30am until about 2pm) on Thanon Phetkasem, about 100m walk left out of the bus station, which serves the usual array of exceptionally cheap veggie curries and stir-fries over brown rice.

Tours of Ao Phang Nga

The most popular budget tours of Ao Phang Nga are the **longtail-boat trips** run by tour operators based inside Phang Nga bus station. Competition between these outfits is fierce and the itineraries they offer are almost identical (see p.766 for a description), so it's best to get recommendations from other tourists fresh from a bay trip, especially as reputations fluctuate with every change of staff. To date the one that's remained most constant is Mr Kean Tour (Ⓣ076 430619); next door but one is Sayan Tour (Ⓣ076 430348, Ⓦwww.sayantour.com). Both offer half-day tours of the bay (daily at about 8am & 2pm; 3–4hr) costing B450 per person (minimum four people), as well as full-day extensions, which last until 4pm and cost B750, including lunch; take the 8am tour to avoid seeing the bay at its most crowded. These prices exclude the B200 national park entry fee. All tours include a chance to swim in the bay, and most offer the option of an hour's canoeing around Ko Thalu as well, for an extra B300. The tours leave from the tour operators' offices, but will pick up from the town's hotels if booked in advance; people staying at Tha Dan, the departure-point for trips around Ao Phang Nga, can join the tours at the pier.

All tour operators also offer the chance to **stay** overnight at a guest house on **Ko Panyi**. This can be tacked onto the half- or full-day tour for an extra B250 (departures at 8am, 2pm & 4pm); dinner, accommodation, and morning coffee are included in the price. Mr Kean also offers an interesting alternative overnight programme on his home island of **Ban Mai Phai**, a much less commercial version of Ko Panyi; the B1100 fee includes all food, accommodation, plus cycle and kayak use and the chance to trek and go rock-climbing.

Around Phang Nga town

One of the most famous caves near Phang Nga town is **Tham Phung Chang**, or **Elephant Belly Cave**, a natural 1200-metre-long tunnel through the massive 800-metre-high wooded cliff that towers over the Provincial Hall, about 4km west of the town centre. With a bit of imagination, the cliff's outline resembles a kneeling elephant, and the hollow interior is, of course, its belly. It's possible to travel through the elephant's belly to the other side of the cliff and back on organized two-hour excursions that involve wading, rafting and canoeing along the freshwater stream, Khlong Tham, that has eroded the channel. Any Phang Nga tour operator can arrange this for you, or you can organize it yourself at the desk in the car park in front of the cliff (afternoons are quieter) for B500. To get to the cave entrance yourself, exit Phang Nga along the Phuket–Krabi highway and watch for signs – and a large statue of an elephant – on the north side of the road, before the highway forks right for Phuket and left for Krabi.

Another quite popular local attraction is **Sa Nang Manora Forest Park** (free entry), 9km north of the bus station, where there are ten hiking trails to explore plus several waterfalls with swimmable pools. Tour agencies will take you there for about B250; with your own transport, continue north through town along Thanon Phetkasem for about 5km, until you pick up signs for the park.

Krabi town and around

The compact little fishing town of **KRABI** is both provincial capital and major hub for onward travel to some of the region's most popular islands and beaches, including Ko Phi Phi, Ko Lanta, Ao Nang, Klong Muang and Laem Phra Nang (Railay). So efficient are the transport links that you don't really need to stop here, but it's an attractive, refreshingly green spot, strung out along the west bank of the Krabi estuary, with mangrove-lined shorelines to the east, looming limestone outcrops on every horizon, and plenty of welcoming guest houses, so it's both possible and enjoyable to base yourself here and make day-trips to the Krabi beaches (see p.778), 45 minutes' ride away by boat or songthaew. A good way to appreciate the town's setting is to follow the paved **riverside walkway** down to the fishing port, about 800m south of Tha Chao Fa; several hotels capitalize on the views here, across the estuary to mangrove-ringed Ko Klang, and towards the southern end the walkway borders the pleasant municipal Thara Park. Inland, in the centre of town, you can't miss the bizarre sculptures of hulking **anthropoid apes** clutching two sets of traffic lights apiece at the Thanon Maharat/Soi 10 crossroads. They are meant to represent Krabi's hugely

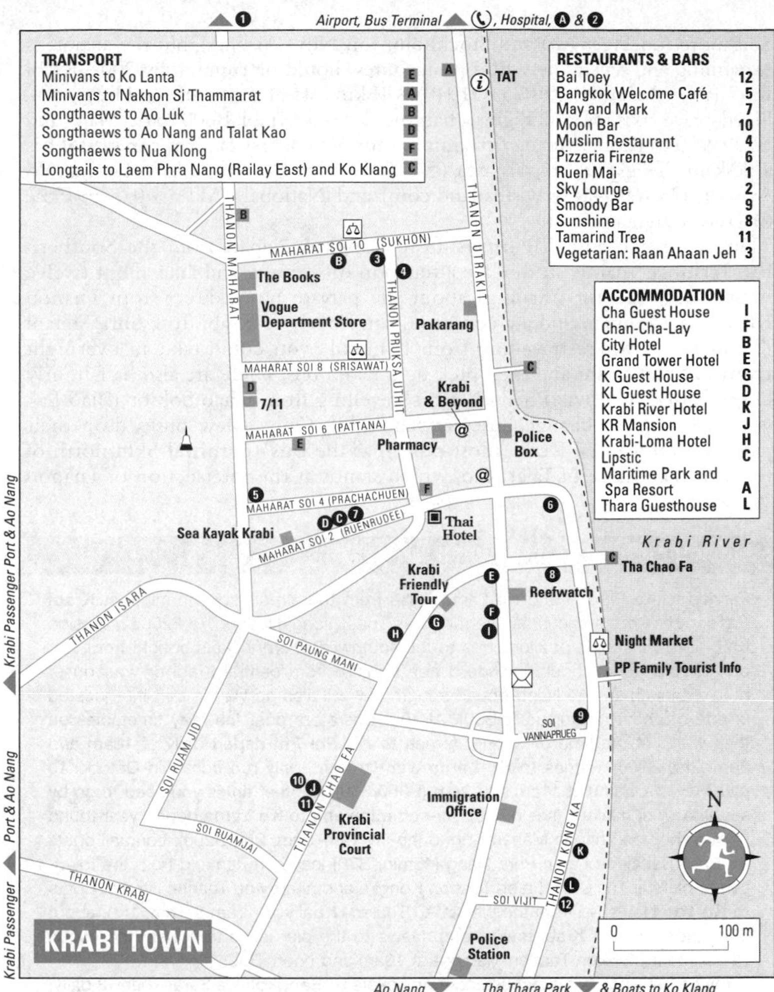

significant ancestors, the tailless *Siamopithecus oceanus*, whose 40-million-year-old remains were found in a lignite mine in the south of the province and are believed by scientists to be among the earliest examples worldwide of the ape-human evolutionary process.

Krabi is at its busiest during high season, from November through February, a period which officially begins with the annual **Krabi Berk Fah Andaman festival**, a week of festivities featuring parades, outdoor concerts, fishing contests, a funfair and lots of street stalls and climaxes at Loy Krathong, the nationwide festival celebrated in late October or early November (see colour insert).

Arrival, transport and information

Thai Airways and Air Asia operate several daily domestic **flights** between Bangkok and Krabi. International routes are currently limited to flights from

Singapore (on Tiger Air) and Stockholm (on Nova Airlines), but the airport is expanding and several new European routes should be running by 2007. Krabi International **airport** (ⓣ075 691940) is 18km east of town, just off Highway 4. Fixed-price taxis meet all flights, charging B350 to Krabi, B600 to Ao Nang and B700–900 to Klong Muang (maximum four passengers). Budget **car rental** has a desk in the airport arrivals area (ⓣ075 691938, ⓦwww.budget.co.th), as do Avis (ⓣ075 691941; ⓦavisthailand.com) and National/SMT (ⓣ075 691939, ⓦwww.smtrentacar.com).

Direct air-con and VIP **buses** from Bangkok depart from the Southern Bus Terminal, mainly in the late afternoon or evening and take about twelve hours; see p.213 for warnings about the private buses direct from Thanon Khao San. Ordinary and air-con buses run hourly to Krabi from Surat Thani (2–3hr), so if you're travelling from Bangkok, you could take an overnight **train** to Surat Thani and then pick up a Krabi bus. There are also half-hourly buses from Phuket via Phang Nga; if travelling from Khao Sok or Khao Lak you may have to change buses at Khokkloi. Only a few buses drop their passengers in central Krabi: most pull in at the **bus terminal** 5km north of town in the village of Talat Kao, which stands at the intersection of Thanon

Moving on from Krabi town

Ferries to Ko Phi Phi and Ko Lanta leave from the airport-style terminal at **Krabi Passenger Port** (sometimes referred to as Tha Khlong Jilad; ⓣ075 620052) outside Krabi town, a couple of kilometres to the southwest. Ferry tickets bought from tour operators in town should include a free transfer from central Krabi or your guest house, though any Ao Nang-bound songthaew will also go via the port if requested (a ride of about ten minutes; B30). All tour operators post the ferry timetables on their walls: at the time of writing, ferries **to Ko Phi Phi** depart daily at 10am and 3pm (2hr; B300). Ferries **to Ko Lanta**, via **Ko Jum**, only run from mid-October to mid-May, departing at 11am and 2pm (B350/300); at other times you need to go by songthaew or minibus (see p.810). Air-con **minivans to Ko Lanta** depart year-round from a shop on Thanon Maharat Soi 6 (hourly 7am–5pm; 2hr; B200). Longtail boats for **East Railay** on Laem Phra Nang (45min; B70) leave on demand from the town-centre piers at Tha Chao Fa on Thanon Kongka and nearby on Thanon Utrakit. Boats **to Ko Yao Noi** leave from the pier at Ao Thalen (2 daily at 11am & 1pm; 1hr), about 30km northwest of Krabi town; songthaews to the pier leave from near the Vogue Department Store on Thanon Maharat at 10am and noon (B50).

You can buy combination bus and train tickets **to Bangkok** via Surat Thani (2 daily; 16hr; B600–850) from any travel agent; these firms also sell tickets on private tourist buses, minibuses and/or boats to **Phuket beaches** (daily; 4hr; B250–300), **Ko Samui** (2 daily; 6hr; B350–450), **Ko Pha Ngan** (2 daily; 6hr; B500), Bangkok's **Thanon Khao San** (daily; 14hr; B600; see warnings on p.213), **Penang** (2 daily; 9hr; B650) and **Langkawi** (daily; 10hr; B700). Note that despite the advertising, nearly all these privately operated tourist buses are minibuses and they are often quite dilapidated. Private minivans to Nakhon Si Thammarat (approximately hourly 7.30am–4pm; 3hr) leave from Thanon Utrakit, across from the TAT office. **Government buses** run to all major destinations – including Bangkok, Phuket, Phang Nga, Surat Thani and Trang (see Travel Details on p.821 for info on frequencies and duration) – from Krabi's Talat Kao bus terminal (ⓣ075 611804), which is 5km from town and served by frequent songthaews from the town centre. If travelling to Khao Sok or Khao Lak you may have to change buses at Khokkloi.

Any hotel or travel agent can arrange transport **to the airport** at rates equivalent to those charged by the airport taxis at Arrivals.

Utrakit and Highway 4. From here there's a frequent songthaew service to Krabi's Thanon Maharat.

Most of the public **songthaew** services to local beaches, towns and attractions leave from outside the 7-11 just south of the Soi 8 intersection on Thanon Maharat; they usually circulate around town and along Thanon Utrakit before heading out; unless otherwise stated, most run at least twice an hour from dawn till noon, and then less frequently until dusk. Useful destinations include **Ao Nang** (6am–6.30pm, B30; 6.30–10.30pm, B50), via Krabi Passenger Port and Hat Nopparat Thara (6am–about 6.30pm only; B30) and Wat Tham Seua. The Ao Luk service departs from just north of the Soi 10 intersection (every 30min; B40).

Information

Krabi's **TAT office** (daily 8.30am–4.30pm ⓣ075 622163, ⓔtatkrabi.or.th) is housed in a lone whitewashed hut on Thanon Utrakit at the northern edge of the town centre. Don't confuse this with the tourist information office run by the ferry operator PP Family, which is down on Thanon Kongka; you can get information here, but it may be partisan. The town has no shortage of **tour agents**, all of whom will be only too happy to sell you bus, boat and train tickets, and to fix you up with a room on one of the islands – a service that may be worth using for your first night's island or beach accommodation, as Ko Phi Phi especially gets packed out during peak season.

The monthly free, independent, **tourist magazine**, *Flyer* (ⓦwww.yourkrabi.com), carries features on local sights and activities and rounds up general transport information in the Krabi, Laem Phra Nang and Ao Nang area; it's available at some restaurants and guest houses. If you're spending some time in this region, it's worth buying a copy of *Krabi: Caught in the Spell – A Guide to Thailand's Enchanted Province*, expat environmentalist Thom Henley's lively and opinionated **book** about Krabi people, islands and traditions, which is packed with enticing photographs and ideas for exploratory day-trips; see "Books" on p.929 for details.

Accommodation

The guest houses and small hotels in Krabi offer a good range of **accommodation** that's mostly a lot better value than equivalent options on nearby beaches.

Cha Guest House 45 Thanon Utrakit ⓣ075 611141, ⓔchaguesthouse@hotmail.com. Busy, long-standing travellers' hangout, with basic rooms in bungalows set round a garden compound behind an Internet centre. Room rates depend on size and whether you want a private bathroom. Also has very cheap, cell-like singles. Shared bathroom ❶, en suite ❷–❸

Chan-Cha-Lay 55 Thanon Utrakit ⓣ075 620952. With its stylish blue-and white-theme throughout, funky bathrooms, white-painted wooden furniture and blue shutters, this is the most charming and arty place to stay in Krabi. The en suites in the garden come with fan or air-con and are by far the nicest option; rooms in the main building share bathrooms and some don't have windows. Shared bathroom ❷, en suite fan ❸, air-con ❹

City Hotel 15/2-4 Maharat Soi 10 ⓣ075 611961, ⓦwww.citykrabi.com. Good quality if not exactly stylish air-con rooms, all with TV and hot water. Rooms in the new wing are more modern and pricier. Old wing ❹, new wing ❺

Grand Tower Hotel 9 Thanon Chao Fa, on the corner of Thanon Utrakit ⓣ075 621456. Central, fairly comfortable five-storey travellers' hotel with well-furnished if scruffy rooms, all of them en suite and some with TV and air-con. Some rooms can be noisy because of the bar next door. Internet access and a travel agency downstairs. Fan ❷, air-con ❹

K Guest House 15–25 Thanon Chao Fa ⓣ075 623166, ⓦwww.krabidir.com/kguesthouse. Deservedly popular option, in a peaceful but central spot, contained within a long, timber-clad log-cabin-look rowhouse, partially screened by a row of towering pot plants. The attractive upstairs rooms have wooden floors and panelled walls and mostly have streetside balconies. Also offers some cheaper, less interesting rooms with shared bathroom downstairs and at the back. Shared bathroom ❷, en suite ❸

KL Guest House 28 Soi 2, Thanon Maharat ⓣ075 612511. No frills, budget option; all rooms have a fan and shared bathroom, but the cheapest have no window. ❶

KR Mansion 52 Thanon Chao Fa ⓣ075 612761, ⓦwww.kr-mansion.com. Traveller-oriented five-storey hotel with a range of pretty decent fan and air-con rooms, with or without private bathroom, pleasingly enlivened by chic touches (photos, vases, designer lamps); the uppermost ones offer fine panoramic views. Staff are a good source of local information, and there's a nice rooftop bar, Internet access, nightly movies and motorbike rental. Fan ❷, air-con ❸

Krabi-Loma Hotel 20 Thanon Chao Fa ⓣ075 611168. Small hotel offering uninspired though perfectly comfortable mid-market air-con rooms, with the main attraction being the small swimming pool and garden. ❹

Krabi River Hotel 73/1 Thanon Kongka ⓣ075 612321, ⓔkrabiriver@hotmail.com. In a little cluster of accommodation occupying a scenic spot beside the estuary on the southern edge of Krabi town, a few minutes' walk south of Tha Chao Fa pier, this place offers high-standard air-con rooms: the best have big balconies overlooking the river; the smaller, cheaper ones look onto the wall of the adjacent hotel. ❹, river-view ❻

Lipstic 20–22 Soi 2, Thanon Maharat ⓣ075 612392, ⓔkayanchalee@hotmail.com. Good budget choice tucked away off the street with simple, well-priced rooms; some have windows and others have private bathrooms, but none have both. Shared bathroom ❶, en suite ❷

Maritime Park and Spa Resort 2km north of town off Thanon Utrakit ⓣ075 620028, ⓦwww.maritimeparkandspa.com. Beautifully located luxury hotel, set beside the limestone karsts and mangroves of the Krabi River. Rooms are attractive and have fine views. There's a big pool, a spa, a kids' games room and babysitting service. Free scheduled shuttles to Krabi town and the beach at Ao Nang. ❽–❾

Thara Guesthouse 79/3 Thanon Kongka ⓣ075 630499 ⓔmilkgirl@.hotmail.com. Small hotel, prettily set beside the estuary on the southern edge of Krabi town, a few minutes' walk south of Tha Chao Fa pier, with clean, well-maintained fan and air-con rooms, the best of which enjoy partial river views. Fan ❷, air-con ❹

Eating and drinking

Krabi has plenty of traveller-oriented restaurants, the best of which are detailed below, but for a truly inexpensive Thai meal, either go to the riverside **night market**, which sets up around the pier-head on Thanon Kongka every evening from about 6pm, try the inland market on Maharat Soi 10, or walk south down the riverside walkway, past *Krabi River Hotel* to reach an-open-air riverside food court.

Bai Toey Next to *Thara Guesthouse* on Thanon Kongka. Good place for a sundowner with pleasing river views and great seafood, especially spicy mussels salad. Most dishes B60–180.

Bangkok Welcome Café On the corner of Thanon Maharat Soi 4 and Thanon Maharat itself. Fried rice, *phat thai* and noodle soups for B25 a serving. Daily 6am–4pm.

May and Mark Early hours, home-baked bread, including sourdough loaves, and full-English fry-ups (B100) make this a popular spot for breakfast. Also does tacos, Thai standards and pizzas. Daily 6.30am–9.30pm.

Moon Bar Top floor of KR Mansion, Thanon Chao Fa. It's well worth climbing the stairs to this breezy rooftop bar before sunset to soak up the distant mountain and estuary views while you work your way through the cocktail menu. Also serves some food. Daily 4pm–1am.

Muslim Restaurant Thanon Pruksa Uthit. Filling rotis (flat fried breads) served with a choice of curry sauces, from B10. Daily 7am–7pm.

Pizzeria Firenze Thanon Kongka. Authentic Italian dishes, including 20 different pizzas (from B150), pastas, ice creams, tiramisu (B75) and imported wines. Daily 11am–10pm.

Ruen Mai About 2km north of the town centre on Thanon Maharat. Popular with locals and well regarded, this inviting, artfully planted garden restaurant is worth making the effort to get to, not least for the change from the more touristed options in the town centre. It serves quality Thai dishes (B60–180), including lots of seafood and *tom yam*. Run by the same man behind *Same*

Same But Different restaurant on Ko Lanta. Daily 11am–9pm.

Sky Lounge *Maritime Park and Spa Resort*, 2km north of the town centre off Thanon Utrakit. Fabulous views from the eighth floor bar at Krabi's poshest hotel – a great place for a sunset beer as you're admiring the riverine landscape of karsts and mangrove swamps. Nightly 6pm–midnight.

Smoody Bar Thanon Kongka. Nightly live music and reasonably priced beer at this funky, atmospheric bar just back from the waterfront at the edge of the night market. Nightly from 5pm.

Sunshine Thanon Kongka. Travellers' restaurant, serving standard Thai and Western dishes (B40–60) and set breakfasts, including some with croissants, real coffee, curries and burgers. Daily 8am–10pm.

Tamarind Tree Next to *KR Mansion* at 52 Thanon Chao Fa. Housed in a pleasant plant-filled wooden building, this is one of the few restaurants in Krabi that appeals both to travellers and locals – its spicy *yam* salads and curries, especially the piquant *matsaman* curries (B60) are authentically flavoured, plus there are plenty of sandwiches and fish dishes. Daily 10am–10pm.

Vegetarian: Raan Ahaan Jeh Thanon Pruksa Uthit. Typical unpretentious Thai veggie café serving meat-substitute curries and stir-fries at B20 for two servings over rice. Mon–Sat 9am–5pm.

Listings

Airlines Any Krabi tour operator can book you a flight, or contact the airlines direct: Air Asia, at the airport (☎075 623554); Thai Airways, beside *Maritime Park Resort Krabi* on Thanon Utrakit ☎075 622440.

Banks and exchange All major banks have branches on Thanon Utrakit with exchange counters and ATMs.

Bookshops The Books, next to Vogue Department Store on Thanon Maharat, carries a range of new English-language books about Thailand, plus maps and some novels. Pakarang on Thanon Utrakit buys and sells second-hand books and has lots in stock.

Car rental At Krabi airport (see p.772), and through some guest houses and tour companies, including Krabi Friendly Tour at 13/6 Thanon Chao Fa (☎075 612558, Ⓦwww.krabifriendly.com), which rents jeeps for B1200 per 24hr and cars for B1500, including full insurance.

Cookery classes Available at the Krabi Thai Cookery School, just off the Krabi–Ao Nang road (9am–1pm & 2–6pm; B1000 including transport; ☎075 695133, Ⓦwww.krabidir.com/krthaicookery).

Dive centre Although there are dive centres at all the Krabi beaches, it's possible to organize trips and courses from Krabi town through the British-run Reefwatch Worldwide Dive Operator, 48 Thanon Utrakit (☎075 632650, Ⓦwww.reefwatchworldwide.com), a PADI Five-Star Instructor Development Centre. They charge B13,900 for the four-day Openwater course and run dive trips to local sites (see p.750) from B2900, generally in a longtail boat.

Hospitals Krabi Hospital is about 1km north of the town centre at 325 Thanon Utrakit (☎075 611202) and also has dental facilities, but the better hospital is considered to be the private Muslim hospital, Jariyatham Ruampaet Hospital (☎075 611223), which is about 3km north of town and has English-speaking staff.

Immigration office On Thanon Utrakit (Mon–Fri 8.30am–4.30pm; ☎075 611097).

Internet access Available at nearly every Krabi guest house and, fast and efficiently at Krabi and Beyond on Maharat Soi 6. Catnet Internet terminals at the phone office on Thanon Utrakit.

Mail The GPO is on Thanon Utrakit. Poste restante should be addressed c/o GPO and can be collected Mon–Fri 8.30am–4.30pm, Sat 9am–noon.

Motorbike rental Through some guest houses and tour companies for about B250 per day.

Pharmacies There are several pharmacies, including on Thanon Utrakit and Maharat Soi 6, and a branch of Boots the Chemist inside Vogue Department Store on Thanon Maharat.

Police For all emergencies, call the tourist police on the free, 24hr phone line ☎1155, or contact the local branch of the tourist police in Ao Nang on ☎075 637208. Krabi police station is at the southern end of Thanon Utrakit ☎075 611222.

Telephones For international calls use the CAT phone office about 2km north of the town centre on Thanon Utrakit (Mon–Fri 8am–8pm, Sat & Sun 8.30am–4.30pm), which is easily reached on any songthaew heading up that road, or on foot.

Day-trips from Krabi town

With time on your hands you'll soon exhaust the possibilities in Krabi, but there are several trips to make out of town, in addition to the nearby beaches at Laem Phra Nang (Railay), Hat Nopparat Thara, Ao Phang Nga and Ko Phi

Phi. Alternatively, you could join one of the numerous **organized tours** sold by every Krabi travel agent, for example a tour of four or five islands, which take in the reefs and beaches around Laem Phra Nang (about B700); a hike through the national park near Khlong Thom, home of the turquoise-feathered Gurney's pitta, a rare bird that's endemic to southern Thailand and southern Burma; a kayaking trip around Ao Luk or Ao Thalen in Phang Nga bay (B800–2000; see p.768); or a visit to the botanical gardens of **Than Bokkharani**, near Ao Luk, whose grottoes and waterfalls are enclosed in a ring of lush forest (you can also visit these independently, by catching an Ao Luk songthaew from Krabi, which takes an hour, and then walking down to the gardens). Tour agencies sell the same basic itineraries, so prices are kept competitive. You can also arrange private tours with the longtail boatmen at Tha Chao Fa, who charge B1000 per boat for a day-trip to Ko Poda or to Chicken Island, though you'll need your own snorkel.

The mangroves and Ko Klang

Longtail-boat tours of the **mangrove swamps** that clog the Krabi River estuary can be organized directly with the boatmen who hang around Krabi's two piers (B100 per person per hour, minimum 3 people) or through most tour operators (average B500/person for three hours). All mangrove tours give you a chance to get a close-up view of typical mangrove flora and fauna (see box below), and most will stop off at a couple of riverside caves on the way. The most famous features on the usual mangrove itinerary are the twin limestone outcrops known as **Khao Kanab Nam**, which rise a hundred metres above the water from opposite sides of the Krabi River near the *Maritime Park and Spa Resort* and are so distinctive that they've become the symbol of Krabi. One of the twin karsts hides caves, which can be easily explored – many skeletons have been found here over the centuries, thought to be those of immigrants who got stranded by a flood before reaching the mainland.

Life in a mangrove swamp

Mangrove swamps are at their creepiest at low tide, when their aerial roots are fully exposed to form gnarled and knotted archways above the muddy banks. Not only are these roots essential parts of the tree's breathing apparatus, they also reclaim land for future mangroves, trapping and accumulating water-borne debris into which the metre-long mangrove seedlings can fall. In this way, mangrove swamps also fulfil a vital ecological function: stabilizing shifting mud and protecting coastlines from erosion and the impact of tropical storms.

Mangrove swamp mud harbours some interesting creatures too, like the instantly recognizable **fiddler crab**, named after the male's single outsized reddish claw, which it brandishes for communication and defence purposes – the claw is so powerful it could open a can of baked beans. If you keep your eyes peeled you should be able to make out a few **mudskippers**. These specially adapted fish can absorb atmospheric oxygen through their skins as long as they keep their outsides damp, which is why they spend so much time slithering around in the sludge; they move in tiny hops by flicking their tails, aided by their extra-strong pectoral fins. You might well also come across **kingfishers** and white-bellied **sea eagles**, but you'd be very lucky indeed to encounter the rare crab-eating macaque.

Though the Krabi mangroves have not escaped the **environmentally damaging** attentions of invasive industry, or the cutting down of the bigger trees to make commercial charcoal, around fifteen percent of the Andaman coastline is still fringed with mangrove forest, the healthiest concentration of this rich, complex ecosystem in Thailand.

Most of Krabi's longtail boatmen come from **Ko Klang**, the mangrove-encircled island that's clearly visible across the estuary from Tha Chao Fa and Tha Thara Park. On a two-hour mangrove tour you can choose to stop off on the island for a visit, or you can go there yourself, on one of the public longtail boats that shuttle across throughout the day, both from Tha Chao Fa (B10, or B50 to charter; 10min) and Tha Thara Park (B10, or B20 to charter; 3min). You can also stay there in Ban Ko Klang, as part of a **homestay** programme, which features batik-making, rice-farming and trips to local islands, and can be booked locally through the English-speaking co-ordinator Khun Supranee (Ⓣ089 475 0495) or in advance as part of a package with Tell Tale Travel (Ⓦwww.telltaletravel.co.uk). The predominantly Muslim island (in reality a peninsula but accessible only by water) is home to three small villages housing a total of around 4000 people, most of whom earn their living from tourism and fishing. The island is no great beauty but therein lies its charm, for it's entirely untouristed and offers the chance to experience typical southern-Thai life. The homestays have bicycles and motorbikes for rent or you can take your own over on the Tha Thara Park longtail; there's about 12 km of paved road on the island. You can swim off Ko Klang's long southwestern beach, though the shorefront is wild rather than picturesque; from this beach you also get an excellent view of the distinctive profiles all the famous local islands – Laem Phra Nang (30 minutes' boat ride away), Ko Poda (45min), Bamboo Island, Ko Phi Phi (2hr) and Ko Jum – and any island boatman will take you out there for the same price as from Krabi town.

Wat Tham Seua and Khao Phanom Bencha

Beautifully set amid limestone cliffs about 10km northeast of Krabi, the tropical forest of **Wat Tham Seua** (Tiger Cave Temple) can be reached by taking one of the infrequent red songthaews from Thanon Maharat or Thanon Utrakit (20min; about B25) and then walking 2km down the signed track, or chartering one from town to the temple gates (B150). As Wat Tham Seua is a working monastery, visitors must wear respectable dress (no shorts or singlets for men or women), so bear this in mind before you leave town.

Wat Tham Seua's main **bot** – on the left under the cliff overhang – might come as a bit of a shock: alongside portraits of the abbot, a renowned teacher of Vipassana meditation, close-up photos of human entrails and internal organs are on display – reminders of the impermanence of the body. Any skulls and skeletons you might come across in the compound serve the same educational purpose. The most interesting part of Wat Tham Seua lies beyond the bot, reached by following the path past the nuns' quarters until you get to a couple of steep **staircases** up the 600-metre-high cliffside. The first staircase is long (1272 steps) and very steep, and takes about an hour to climb, but the vista from the summit is quite spectacular, affording fabulous views over the limestone outcrops and out to the islands beyond. There's a small shrine and a few monks' cells hidden among the trees at the top. The second staircase, next to the large statue of the Chinese fertility goddess Kuan Im, takes you on a less arduous route down into a deep dell encircled by high limestone walls. Here the monks have built themselves self-sufficient meditation cells, linked by paths through the lush ravine: if you continue along the main path you'll eventually find yourself back where you began, at the foot of the staircase. The valley is home to squirrels and monkeys as well as a pair of remarkable trees with overground **buttress roots** over 10m high.

With your own transport, you could combine a visit to Wat Tham Seua with a meander around the scenic backroads and a plunge into **Huay Toh Falls**, a five-tiered cascade that lies within **Khao Phanom Bencha National Park** (Ⓦwww.dnp.go.th/National_park.asp; dawn till dusk; B200 entry), 25km north of Krabi. You can also **stay** in the Phanom Bencha area, about 10km north of Wat Tham Seua, in the tranquil garden cabins and tents of *Phanom Bencha Mountain Resort* (Ⓣ081 958 0742, Ⓦwww.phanombenchamountainresort.com; cabins ❹–❺, tents ❷).

Susaan Hoi

Thais make a big deal out of **Susaan Hoi** (Shell Cemetery), 17km west around the coast from Krabi, but it's hard to get very excited about a shoreline of metre-long forty-centimetre-thick beige-coloured rocks that could easily be mistaken for concrete slabs. Nevertheless, the facts of their formation are impressive: these stones are 75 million years old and made entirely from compressed shell fossils. You get a distant view of them from any longtail boat travelling between Krabi and Ao Phra Nang; for a closer look take any of the frequent Ao Nang-bound songthaews from Thanon Maharat or Thanon Utrakit (B40).

Krabi beaches

Although the mainland beach areas west of Krabi can't compete with the local islands for underwater life, the stunning headland of **Laem Phra Nang** is accessible only by boat, so staying on one of its four beaches (**Ao Phra Nang, West and East Railay and Ao Ton Sai**) can feel like being on an island,

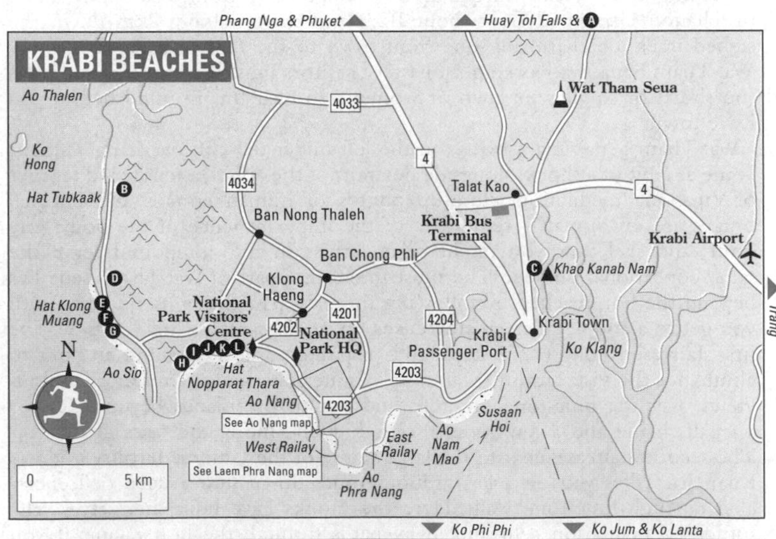

ACCOMMODATION

Andaman Holiday Resort	F	Long Beach Bungalow and Camp	I	Phanom Bencha Mountain Resort	A
Andaman Inn	L	Maritime Park and Spa Resort	C	Private Beach Resort	J
Emerald Bungalows	K	Nakamanda	E	Sheraton Krabi Beach Resort	G
Krabi Sands	D	PAN Beach	H	The Tubkaak Krabi	B

△ Ao Nang

albeit a crowded and potentially rather claustrophobic one. In contrast, a road runs right along the **Ao Nang** beachfront, which has enabled a burgeoning resort to thrive around its rather unexceptional beach, while the next bay to the west, **Hat Nopparat Thara**, is long and unadulterated and has some appealingly solitary places to stay at its western end. **Klong Muang** is different again, secluded and quiet and catering almost exclusively to the guests of its top-end hotels. Swimming and snorkelling conditions deteriorate at all Krabi beaches during the rainy season from May to October, so prices at all accommodation drops by up to fifty percent for this period, and a few places close down for the duration.

Laem Phra Nang (Railay)

Seen from the close quarters of a longtail boat, the combination of sheer limestone cliffs, pure white sand and emerald waters at **LAEM PHRA NANG** is spectacular – and would be even more so without the hundreds of other admirers gathered on its beaches. Almost every centimetre of buildable land on the cape's two main beaches, East and West **Railay**, has now been taken over by bungalows, and development is creeping up the cliffsides and into the forest behind. But at least high-rises don't feature, and much of the construction is hidden among trees or set amid prettily landscaped gardens. The headland has four beaches within ten minutes' walk of each other: **Ao Phra Nang** graces the southwestern edge, and is flanked by **East and West Railay**; **Ao Ton Sai** is beyond West Railay, on the other side of a rocky promontory. The scene at Laem Phra Nang is laidback, but by no means comatose; it's as popular with backpackers as it is with couples on short breaks, and the accommodation and entertainment facilities reflect this. It's also a major rock-climbing centre, both for beginners and experienced climbers. Even if you don't want to stay, it's worth coming for the day to gawp at the scenery and scramble down into the lushly vegetated area around the cape's enclosed lagoon.

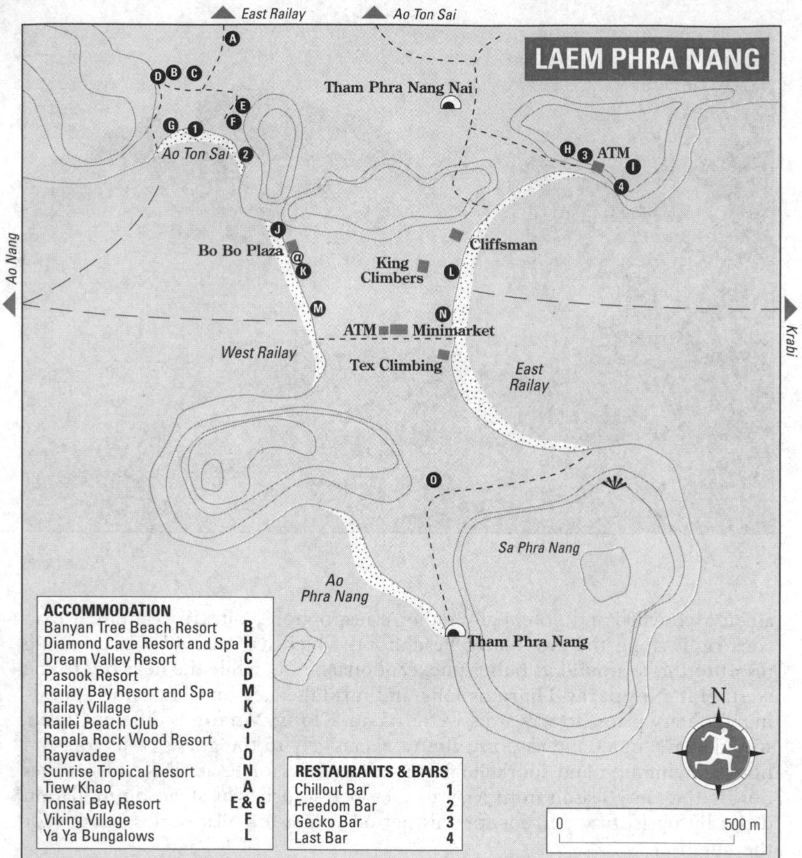

The beaches

Set against a magnificent backdrop of cliffs and palms, diminutive **AO PHRA NANG** (aka **Hat Tham Phra Nang**) is the loveliest spot on the cape, attracting sunbathers to its luxuriously soft sand and snorkellers to the reefs some 200m offshore. Screened from the beach is just one luxury resort, the *Rayavadee*, with the sole means of direct access to Ao Phra Nang, but non-guests can walk there from East Railay in under ten minutes, following the walkway that winds alongside the resort's boundary, under the lip of the karst, to the beach.

The beach and cape are named after a princess (*phra nang* means "revered lady"), whom the local fisherfolk believe lives here and controls the fertility of the sea. If you walk past the entrance to **Tham Phra Nang** (Princess Cave), hollowed out of the huge karst outcrop at the eastern edge of the bay, you'll see a host of red-tipped wooden phalluses stacked as offerings to her, by way of insurance for large catches. The numerous passageways and rocks around the cave are fun to clamber over, but getting down into **Sa Phra Nang** (Princess Lagoon) is more of a challenge. Buried deep inside the same rock, the lagoon is accessible only via a steep 45-minute descent that starts at the "resting spot" halfway along the walkway connecting the east edge of Ao Phra Nang with

East Railay. After an initial ten-minute clamber, negotiated with the help of ropes, the path forks: go left for a panoramic view over the east and west bays of Railay, or right for the lagoon. (For the strong-armed, there's the third option of hauling yourself up ropes to the top of the cliff for a bird's-eye view.) Taking the right-hand fork, you'll pass through the tropical dell dubbed "big tree valley" before eventually descending to the murky lagoon.

Sometimes known as Sunset Beach, **WEST RAILAY** comes a close second to Ao Phra Nang, with similarly impressive karst scenery, crystal-clear water and a longer stretch of good sand. There's some shade here too, and you only have to walk a few hundred metres to get beyond the longtails and the beachfront diners' line of vision. It gets crowded though, with day-trippers from Ao Nang as well as beach-hungry refugees from East Railay and Ao Ton Sai.

The least attractive of the cape's beaches, **EAST RAILAY** (also sometimes known as Nam Mao, but not to be confused with the Ao Nam Mao proper, immediately to the east) is not suitable for swimming because of its fairly dense mangrove growth, a tide that goes out for miles and a bay that's busy with incoming longtails. Still, there's a greater concentration of less expensive bungalows here, and none is more than ten minutes' walk from the much cleaner sands of West Railay and Ao Phra Nang. To get to East Railay from Ao Phra Nang, follow the walkway from the eastern edge; from West Railay walk through the *Railay Bay*, or *Railay Village* bungalow compounds.

At low tide you can pick your way over the razor-sharp oyster rocks at the northern end of West Railay (beyond the *Railei Beach Club* compound) to reach **AO TON SAI**; at high tide you either need to swim or get a longtail. If coming by boat direct from Krabi, be prepared for a very muddy walk to shore at low tide, or a wade at high water. There's also an inland route between Ao Ton Sai and East Railay: simply follow the track past *Tiew Khao* bungalows, through the forest, over the hill and, about 20 minutes later it will bring you down to the northern end of East Railay. Ao Ton Sai is the travellers' beach, with a bigger choice of fairly low-budget accommodation than Railay and regular all-night beach parties hosted by some of the shorefront bars. Hardly any of the accommodation here has direct beach access as most of it is well hidden several hundred metres back from the shore, scattered within the remains of a forest. The beach itself is not one of Krabi's prettiest, prone to murk and littered with rocks that make it impossible to swim at low tide. But the karst-filled outlook is awesome and Ao Ton Sai's own orange-and-ochre-striped cliffs are equally fabulous confections, dripping with rocky curlicues, pennants and turrets that attract a lot of rock-climbers.

Climbing, kayaking and snorkelling

Given the topography, there's huge potential for **rock-climbing**, abseiling and caving at Laem Phra Nang. There are some seven hundred bolted sport-climbing routes on the cape, ranging in difficulty from 5a–8c, and no shortage of places where you can rent equipment and hire guides and instructors. Some of the longest-established climbing outfits include: Cliffsman (Ⓣ075 621768), on East Railay; King Climbers (Ⓣ075 637125, Ⓦwww.railay.com/railay/climbing/climbing_king_climbers.shtml), at *Ya Ya* on East Railay, Hot Rock (Ⓣ075 621771, Ⓦwww.railayadventure.com), in Bobo Plaza on West Railay, as well as on Ao Ton Sai; and Tex Climbing (Ⓣ081 891 1528, Ⓦwww.texrock.com), beyond *Sunrise Tropical* on East Railay. it's a good idea to check with other tourists before choosing a climbing guide, as operators' safety standards vary. All the climbing centres rent out equipment (B1000/day for two people) and offer a range of climbing **courses** and expeditions. A typical half-day introduction for novice climbers costs B800, a one-day climbing outing is B1500, and for B5000 you get a three-day course which should leave you experienced enough to strike out on your own. If you're already self-sufficient, you might want to get hold of the *Route Guide* to the Laem Phra Nang climbs, written by the guys at King Climbers and available from most of the climbing shops. For more information check out Ⓦwww.simonfoley.com/climbing/krabi.htm and see Basics p.73.

Limestone cliffs and mangrove swamps also make great **kayaking** environments, and there are kayak rental outlets on all the beaches (B100–200 per hour). All the tour agents also offer kayaking tours of spectacular Ao Luk and Ko Hong in Phang Nga bay (see p.768) for B1200–1500, as well as **snorkelling trips** (from B450 including equipment) to the nearby islands of Ko Poda and Chicken Island (Hua Kwan); the boatmen do private four-island snorkelling trips for B1000/half day or B1800/full day, and Railay Diving, in Bo Bo Plaza on West Railay and on Ao Ton Sai (Ⓣ075 622592) do sunset snorkelling and dinner trips as well as **dive trips** to local reefs (see p.750) from B3600.

Practicalities

Laem Phra Nang is only accessible by **boat** from Krabi town, Ao Nang and Ko Phi Phi. Longtail boats to Laem Phra Nang depart from various spots along the **Krabi** riverfront (45min; B70 per person, minimum 8 people, or B700 when chartered), leaving throughout the day as soon as they fill up. Depending on the tide, all Krabi boats land on or off East Railay, so you'll probably have to wade; from East Railay it's easy to cut across to West Railay along any of the through-tracks. Krabi boats do run during the rainy season, but the waves make it a nerve-wracking experience, so you're advised to go via Ao Nang instead. **Ao Nang** is much closer to Laem Phra Nang, and longtails run from the beachfront here to West Railay and Ao Ton Sai (10min; B60, or B100 after 7pm) all year round. Boats between Ao Ton Sai and West Railay cost B30. During high season there should also be daily services from Ao Nang via West Railay to **Ko Phi Phi** (2hr 30min), **Ko Lanta** (2hr 30min) and **Phuket** (3hr); if not, you'll need to transfer to Ao Nang yourself.

There are tour agencies and shops selling beach essentials on each beach, and you can **change money** at many bungalow operations, though rates can be up to ten percent lower than at the Krabi banks; you'll find ATMS at *Viewpoint Bungalows* on East Railay and at the minimarket behind *Railay Bay*. There's **Internet access** and overseas phone services at *Railay Village*, *Ya Ya* and *Ton Sai Bay Resort*, and **bookshops** stocked with new and second-hand books in BoBo Plaza on West Railay and behind *Viking Village* on Ao Ton Sai.

Accommodation, eating and drinking

Accommodation on the Railay beaches tends to be more expensive and less good value than equivalent options on the mainland. Despite this, it's often hard to get a room on spec at East or West Railay, though you should have more luck on Ao Ton Sai. Prices listed below are for high season, but rates can drop up to fifty percent from May to October and are often subject to a surcharge for the Christmas-New Year fortnight.

Nearly all the bungalow operations have **restaurants**, but don't expect haute cuisine – or bargain prices. There's no shortage of relaxed beachfront **bars** – think mellow tunes, cushions on the beach and fire juggling – including *Gecko Bar* and the famously chilled-out *Last Bar*, both near *Diamond Cave Bungalows* on East Railay, but the main party beach is Ao Ton Sai, where the shoreside *Freedom Bar* and *Chillout Bar* both hold regular all-night events, plus monthly full moon **parties.** Though not as hectic, or large, as the famous Ko Pha Ngan versions, these draw lively crowds and there's boat transport from West Railay and Ao Nang through the night.

Ao Phra Nang

Rayavadee ⓣ075 620740, ⓦwww.rayavadee.com. Set in an extensive, beautifully landscaped compound – with resident monkeys – bordering three beaches, this is the only place with direct access to Ao Phra Nang. It's an exclusive resort comprising an unobtrusively designed small village of supremely elegant two-storey spiral-shaped pavilions costing a staggering B22,000 a night. The lack of beachfront accommodation is more than compensated for by a swimming pool with sea view. ❾

West Railay

Railay Bay Resort and Spa ⓣ 075 622570, ⓦwww.krabi-railaybay.com. A huge range of accommodation on a stretch of land that runs down to both East and West Railay, with a swimming pool and spa centre on site. All rooms have air-con, TV, mini-bar and hot water: the cheapest are in small, old-style but spruce bungalow and there are also some comfortable, more modern rooms in a two-storey hotel block. Bungalows ❼–❽, hotel ❽

Railay Village ⓣ075 622578, ⓦwww.railay.com/railay/accommodation/railay_village.shtml. Attractive fan and air-con bungalows occupying very pretty tropical gardens in between the two beaches, with nowhere more than 300m from the West Railay shore. Fills up fast as it's good value considering the competition. Fan ❺, air-con ❼–❽

Railei Beach Club ⓣ075 622582, ⓦwww.raileibeachclub.com. Exclusive, secluded, garden-haven compound of nineteen charming fan-cooled private houses, built of wood in idiosyncratic Thai style and rented out by their owners. One- two- and three-bed houses are available, but must be booked several months in advance. Nearly all houses have kitchen facilities and offer a housekeeping service, and there's also a club house in the compound. ❻–❾

East Railay

Diamond Cave Resort and Spa ⓣ075 622589, ⓦwww.diamondcave-railay.com. Set up high above the beach, impressively located beside several karsts, including Diamond Cave itself, this place has 95 rooms in all, so there's plenty of choice, even if it's all quite tightly packed. Rooms are plainly but comfortably furnished, and come in various permutations, most of them fan or air-con bungalows, with the poshest being in low-rise hotel-style buildings. Also has a small swimming pool. Fan ❺–❻, air-con ❼–❽

Rapala Rock Wood Resort ⓣ075 622586. A popular place, with a travellers' vibe, this is the best of the cheaper options on Railay. Climb a steep flight of stairs to reach the 31 nice, rough-hewn timber huts, set in rows around a scruffy garden high above the beach, with some enjoying dramatic karsts views from their verandas. All bungalows have mattress-beds, screens or mosquito nets, and decent bathrooms; the pricier ones are a bit bigger and nearer the front. There's also a tiny hot-tub-sized pool up here, a lounging area on a deck that juts out into the treetops, and a restaurant that serves Indian food. ❸–❹

Sunrise Tropical Resort ⓣ075 622599, ⓦwww.sunrisetropical.com. The most stylish of the affordable hotels on the cape offers just 28 elegantly designed air-con bungalows, all with Thai furnishings and generously spacious living areas, set around a landscaped tropical garden with a small pool. The only drawback is its location – on the lesser, mangrove-filled, eastern beach. ❽–❾

Ya Ya Bungalows ⓣ075 622593. This idiosyncratic place is built almost entirely of wood, with most of the 70 fan and air-con rooms contained in a series of sturdy, quite well-designed, three-storey wooden towers, and all of them having verandas and en-suite bathrooms. Soundproofing is not great however. The price mainly depends on room size. Fan ❹–❻, air-con ❼

Ao Ton Sai

Banyan Tree Beach Resort ⓣ075 621684. Built in a line under the trees, the 35 bungalows come in two types: standard bamboo and wooden versions with mosquito nets and bathrooms, or nicer mint-green clapboard chalets with comfortable beds and good bathrooms. ❷–❹

Dream Valley Resort ⓣ075 622583, ⓦwww.krabidir.com/dreamvalresort/index.htm. The close-on sixty bungalows here are ranged discreetly amongst the trees, offering a range of accommodation from split-bamboo huts with fan and bathroom through to air-conditioned cabins. Fan ❹–❺ Air-con ❺

Pasook Resort ⓣ089 649 8491. This little place, squeezed right under the karst at a peaceful corner near the western end of the path, offers two styles of bungalow, all of them with fan and bathroom. Cheapest are the orange-painted breezeblock bungalows, but the wooden ones are more appealing and quite spacious. ❸–❹

Tiew Khao ⓣ075 621664. Veer off the main inland path to venture deeper into the forest and after about 250m you reach *Tiew Khao*'s collection of rudimentary bamboo huts ranged up the hillside beside the track. They're the cheapest on Ao Ton Sai: all of them share bathrooms and facilities comprise nothing more than a mattress and a veranda. ❷

Tonsai Bay Resort ⓣ075 622584 ⓦwww.tonsaibayresort.com. With its large, widely spaced and beautifully appointed air-con bungalows, each one boasting huge glass windows and big decks from which to soak up the pretty location in a grove of trees about 200m back from the shore, this is the plushest and most stylish place on Ao Ton Sai. The fan options nearer the beach are overpriced and within earshot of the all-night *Freedom Bar*. Fan ❻, air-con ❼

Viking Village ⓣ081 970 4037. Popular, laid-back option very close to the shore, with a dozen primitive bamboo huts, with fan and mozzie nets, and with or without private bathrooms. Shared bathroom ❸, en suite ❹

Ao Nang and Hat Nopparat Thara

AO NANG (sometimes confusingly signed as Ao Phra Nang), a couple of bays further north up the coast from Laem Phra Nang, is a busy, continually expanding, rather faceless mainland resort that mainly caters for mid-market and package-holiday tourists, the majority of whom come from Scandinavia. Although it lacks Laem Phra Nang's fine beaches, some people find Ao Nang a less claustrophobic place than the cape, and there's a much greater choice of restaurants and bars, plus a wealth of dive shops, tour operators and other typical resort facilities. The best stretch of shore for swimming and sunbathing is about 1km southeast of the commercial centre, accessed via a walkway from *Phra Nang Inn*. Walk past the circular villas at *Golden Beach* and along the paved walkway to *The Last Café*, where the beach is backed by a towering karst and is sufficiently removed from the roar of incoming longtails. En route you can take your pick of two-dozen massage huts set out under the trees, several of which advertise themselves as Wat Pho-trained, or as specialists in remedial treatments; the standard price is B200 per hour. Around a small headland beyond *The Last*

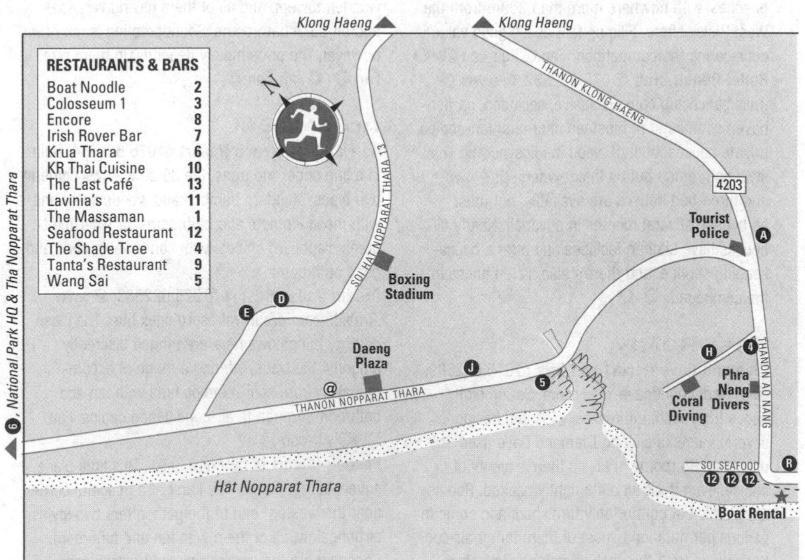

Café lies **Ao Phai Plong**, another small bay that's accessible by swimming, wading or kayak but is dominated by a single posh hotel. Alternatively, it's an impressive ten-minute boat ride from the Ao Nang shore to the beaches of Laem Phra Nang.

Adjacent **Hat Nopparat Thara**, part of which comes under the protection of the national marine park that also encompasses Ko Phi Phi, is effectively two beaches, divide by a khlong. With inland development moving fast, the **eastern beach,** a two-kilometre-long stretch of sand that begins about 1km northwest of *Krabi Resort*, is fast becoming Ao Nang's western suburb. Transport into Ao Nang is frequent, and it's easily reached on foot, so the restaurants, bars and shops of Ao Nang are shared between the two accommodation centres. The eastern beach itself is long and uncrowded, though the road runs unscreened alongside. At low tide it's almost impossible to swim here, but the sands are enlivened by thousands of starfish and hermit crabs, and from near the khlong you can walk out to the small offshore island. The **National Park visitor centre** is located beside the khlong and its sheltered marina and jetty, Tha Nopparat Thara, which is the departure point for Ao Nang ferry services to Phuket, Phi Phi and Ko Lanta, as well as for longtails across the khlong to Hat Nopparat Thara's western beach. The visitor centre's car park has several locally popular seafood restaurants, and Krabi residents also like to picnic under the shorefront trees here. The National Park headquarters and accommodation are a few hundred metres away at the western end of the eastern beach's beachfront road.

Sometimes known as **Hat Ton Son**, the **western beach**, across on the other side of the khlong and accessible only via longtail from Tha Nopparat Thara, has a quite different atmosphere from its eastern counterpart: just five bungalow operations share its long swathe of peaceful casuarina- and palm-shaded shoreline, making it a great place to escape the crowds and commerce of other Krabi beaches. The views of the karst islands are magnificent – and you can walk to some of the nearer ones at low tide, though swimming here is just as

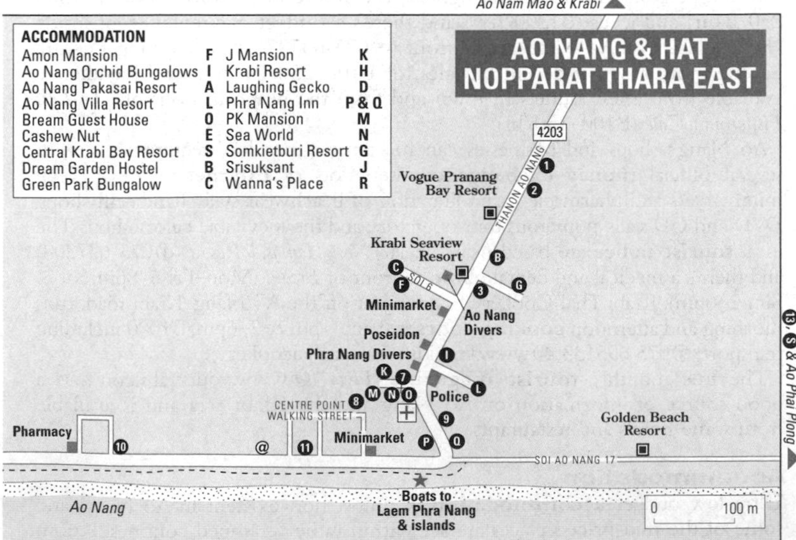

tide-dependent as on central and eastern Hat Nopparat Thara. Some of the bungalow outfits can arrange snorkelling trips to nearby islands.

Arrival, transport and information

For details on arriving at **Krabi airport**, about 35km from Ao Nang, see p.771; taxis from the airport to Ao Nang and Hat Nopparat Thara take about 30 minutes and cost B600. All other long-distance journeys to Ao Nang involve going via Krabi, 22km east, from where **songthaews** to Ao Nang run regularly throughout the day, taking about 45 minutes (every 10min 6am–6.30pm; B30; every 30min 6.30pm–10.30pm; B50); some of these songthaews start at Krabi bus terminal. During the day, all Krabi–Ao Nang songthaews go via the national park visitor centre (for the harbour and boats to the western beach) and all travel the length of eastern Hat Nopparat Thara as well. The fare is B30 from Krabi (30min) or B10–20 from Ao Nang (10–15min); the 6.30–10.30pm Krabi–Ao Nang service takes a different route and doesn't pass any part of Hat Nopparat Thara. Taxis between Krabi and Ao Nang cost about B400.

Longtails from Tha Hat Nopparat Thara leave for the **western beach** when full and will drop you beside the closest set of bungalows, *Andaman Inn* (B20), from where you can walk to the accommodation of your choice; at high tide they'll take you further up the beach if asked (B40). Although there is a 4WD track to the western beach, it's only used by experienced bikers and pick-up trucks. Frequent longtail boats shuttle back and forth from Ao Nang to West Railay and Ao Ton Sai on **Laem Phra Nang** (10min; B60, or B100 after dark), while from November to May daily boats run to **Ko Phi Phi Don** (2hr 30min), **Ko Lanta** (2hr 30min) and **Phuket** (3hr) from the harbour at Hat Nopparat Thara; transfers from Ao Nang hotels are included in the ticket price.

There's still a lack of **street-signing** and numbering in this continually evolving resort, but the main road through Ao Nang is officially known as Thanon Ao Nang, with a few of its sideroads distinguished as numbered sois. Similarly, the main beachfront road along eastern Hat Nopparat Thara is Thanon Nopparat Thara, with some numbered sois.

Tour operators and touts throughout the resort hire **motorbikes** (B150–250/24hr) and jeeps (B1200/day) and there's a Budget **car** rental agent inside *Ao Nang Villa* on Ao Nang's beachfront (ⓣ075 637270, ⓦwww.budget.co.th). Several shops rent out decent bicycles for B100–250/24 hour and **kayaks** are available from a few outlets in town and from the beach in front of *The Last Fisherman Café* (B100–150/hr).

Ao Nang's shops and businesses can meet most travellers' requirements, with several official **money exchange** counters, lots of **Internet** centres, several minimarkets and pharmacies, a proliferation of beachwear stalls, handicraft shops, DVD and CD stalls, numerous tour operators, and the inevitable tailors' shops. The local **tourist police** are based near the *Ao Nang Pakasai Resort* (ⓣ075 637208) and there's a medical and dental **clinic** in front of *Bream* (Mon–Fri 5–8pm, Sat & Sun 2–6pm). Krabi Thai Cookery School, just off the Ao Nang–Krabi road, runs morning and afternoon **cooking courses** (9am–1pm & 2–6pm; B1000 including transport; ⓣ075 695133, ⓦwww.krabidir.com/krthaicookery).

The free monthly **tourist magazine**, *Flyer* (ⓦwww.yourkrabi.com), is a good source of information on Ao Nang and the Krabi area and is available from some hotels and restaurants.

Accommodation

Ultra-low budget **accommodation** is almost non-existent in Ao Nang, and some of the mid-priced places are set within rather cramped confines. Room standards are good, however, and there are decent deals to be had at the upper end of the market if you book online (see Basics p.50 for some online booking agents). Hat Nopparat Thara east has a couple of enticing budget options, but you'll have to head out to Hat Nopparat Thara west to find the archetypal beach bungalow, most of which have electricity in the evenings only and some of which close up for the rainy season from May to October. For locations of accommodation on Hat Nopparat Thara west, see the map on p.778. It's also possible to stay at **national park bungalows** at the west end of Thanon Nopparat Thara beside the National Park headquarters (Ⓣ075 637200, Ⓦwww.dnp.go.th/National_park.asp); these are mostly designed for groups of eight (B4000), though there are a couple of doubles (❺); you can also rent tents (❷–❸), but the campsite is close to the road.

Ao Nang

Inexpensive and moderate

Amon Mansion Soi Ao Nang 6 Ⓣ075 637695. All 20 rooms in this small, four-storey, family-run hotel have air con, TV, hot water and a balcony, making the cheapest ones especially good value. Price depends on the size of the room. Fills up fast so call ahead. ❺–❻

Ao Nang Orchid Bungalows Off Thanon Ao Nang Ⓣ075 637697, Ⓦwww.krabidir.com/orchidbungalows. A reasonable, lower-mid-range place whose 20 or so bungalows are ranged around an attractive garden full of birds that's set back from the main road, a few minutes' walk from the sea. Interiors are plain but practically appointed and verandas enable you to make the most of the garden. Fan ❺, air-con ❻–❼

Bream Guest House Off Thanon Ao Nang Ⓣ075 637555. Much sought-after urban-style guest house offering some of the cheapest rooms in the resort, all with shared bathroom. ❷

Dream Garden Hostel Off Thanon Ao Nang Ⓣ075 637338, Ⓦwww.krabidir.com/dreamgardenhostel. Squashed into a narrow strip behind a shopfront, this place offers two storeys of very good fan and air-con rooms, all with TV and hot water, the only drawback being the wall view (partly obscured by plants). Upstairs rooms are brighter. ❻

Green Park Bungalow Soi Ao Nang 6 Ⓣ075 637300. Friendly, family-run place offering a range of well-furnished, en-suite fan bungalows within a shady grove of trees just off the main drag. ❹

J Mansion Off Thanon Ao Nang Ⓣ075 695128, Ⓦwww.krabidir.com/j_mansion. Four-storey travellers' hotel whose very good rooms are extremely popular and must be booked ahead. They're all large, air-con and have satellite TV and high-level views, some of which extend to the green-clad karsts behind. The rooftop terrace also has a panoramic outlook. ❻

PK Mansion Off Thanon Ao Nang Ⓣ075 637431, Ⓦkrabidir.com/pkmansion. Even cheaper than its neighbours on the backpackers' soi, this place has fairly grim bottom-range cell-like rooms with shared bathrooms and windows on to a passageway wall, but also offers much better en-suite options in the main building, some of them with balconies, karst views and air-con. ❷–❻

Sea World Off Thanon Ao Nang Ⓣ075 637388, Ⓔseaworld_aonang@hotmail.com. Considering the competition, rooms here are well-priced as they all have a bathroom, a balcony and the choice of fan or air-con; some also enjoy good views, mostly green ones to the karsts inland, though a few look towards the sea. There's Internet access downstairs. It's very popular, so try to reserve ahead. Fan ❺, air-con ❻

Expensive

Ao Nang Pakasai Resort Thanon Klong Haeng Ⓣ075 637777, Ⓦwww.pakasai.com. The low-rise accommodation wings at this smallish, 74-room, upmarket hotel are staggered steeply up the hillside amidst profuse tropical gardens, though views of the bay are mostly blocked by neighbouring developments. The rooms are beautifully furnished and there's a scenically located rooftop swimming pool, a kids' pool, an attractive spa, and bicycle hire. ❾

Ao Nang Villa Resort 113 Thanon Ao Nang Ⓣ075 637270, Ⓦwww.aonangvilla.com. A very popular hotel whose grounds run down to the beachfront walkway. The 157 upscale, air-con rooms are contained within several low-rise wings, a few of them enjoying a sea view, but most overlooking the garden or the bigger of the resort's two pools. ❽–❾

Central Krabi Bay Resort Ao Phai Plong Ⓣ075 637789, Ⓦwww.centralhotelsresorts.com. With the sandy bay of Ao Phai Plong all to itself, this is a secluded option just a few minutes by longtail boat from the facilities of Ao Nang proper. All rooms in the multi-storeyed hotel buildings and stand-alone villas have sea views, interiors are modern and there's a big pool and a spa. ❾

Krabi Resort Ao Nang ⓣ075 637030, ⓦwww.krabiresort.net. Set in a huge tropical garden that runs right down to the nicest, western end of Ao Nang beach, this is the oldest resort in Ao Nang, and one of the more old-fashioned. Air-con cottages are staggered in rows back from the shoreline and are plain and very old-style considering the price, though it's about the only place in central Ao Nang where you have the sea right on your doorstep. Rooms in the main, low-rise building are a little more modern. Also has a big pool and the Coral Diving Centre (see opposite) on site. ❽–❾

Phra Nang Inn Thanon Ao Nang ⓣ075 637130, ⓦwww.phranangInn.com. This timber-clad hotel, built in two wings on either side of the road and within a few metres of the sea, looks quaint from the outside, but the interiors have a contemporary feel and plenty of character. The comfortable air-con rooms are painted in bold, modern colours, tastefully furnished and attached to funky bathrooms. The best rooms overlook one of the hotel's three pools (one of which is for kids); there's also a spa and a recreation room. ❽–❾

Somkietburi Resort Thanon Thanon Ao Nang ⓣ075 637990, ⓦwww.somkietburi.com. Guests here enjoy one of the most delightful settings in Ao Nang, with rooms and swimming pools surrounded by a feral, jungle-style garden that's full of hanging vines and lotus ponds. Rooms are perfectly pleasant but nothing special; all have air-con and TV, and there's a spa. ❽

Wanna's Place and Andaman Sunset Resort 31 Thanon Ao Nang ⓣ075 637484, ⓦwww.wannasplace.com. This two-in-one operation is the most affordable of the few beachfront places, with 47 air-con rooms in a low-rise sea-view hotel block and in bungalows ranged up the steep hill behind. The rooms are all of a good standard, the place is well run, and there's a small swimming pool. It's very popular so reserve ahead. ❼

Hat Nopparat Thara east

Cashew Nut Soi Hat Nopparat Thara 13 ⓣ075 637560. Twenty-two good, sturdy en-suite brick and concrete bungalows with fan or air-con ranged around a peaceful garden full of cashew trees. Price depends on the size. Fan ❷–❸, air-con ❺

Laughing Gecko Soi Hat Nopparat Thara 13 ⓣ075 695115 ⓦwww.laughinggeckothailand.com. Perhaps the last of the old-style bungalows left in the Ao Nang area, this is an exceptionally traveller-friendly haven that's run by a Thai-Canadian couple who cultivate an atmosphere of easy-going hospitality. Choose from a range of simple bamboo huts set around a garden dotted with cashew trees: the cheapest beds are in a nine-person dorm (B120), or there are private rooms with shared bathrooms, en-suite huts with platform beds and mosquito nets, and en-suite family bamboo houses comprising three rooms for five people plus a seating area. Also has Internet access and hosts nightly all-you-can-eat Thai buffets for B120–150, with live music. Shared bathroom ❷, en suite ❷–❸, family house ❹

Srisuksant 145 Thanon Nopparat Thara, near the Ao Nang end ⓣ075 638002, ⓦwww.srisuksantresort.com. Despite being right beside the road, with the priciest rooms having traffic-view balconies, this place is very popular, both because the price is good for such well-furnished air-con rooms – and because it's also just over the road from the beach and a five minute walk to the edge of central Ao Nang. It also has two small pools. ❼

Hat Nopparat Thara west

Andaman Inn 100m west of the khlong ⓣ081 956 1173 ⓔmildbungalow@yahoo.com. The most commercial option on the western beach, with a range of old- and new-style huts, all of them en-suite and with fans. Does day-trips and snorkelling tours. Closes May to early Sept. ❷–❹

Emerald Bungalows Next to *Andaman Inn* ⓣ081 956 2566, ⓦder-workshop.de/emerald/emeraldhomepage.html. There's some very comfortable accommodation here, in big, brightly painted and stylishly furnished en-suite wooden bungalows, all with sea views, large decks, and either fan or air-con. Also has a good restaurant and a bar. Usually closed May–Aug, but phone to check. Fan ❺, air-con ❼

Long Beach Bungalow and Camp ⓣ087 275 0949. Laid-back outfit (so laid back that it's sometimes staffed, sometimes not) whose simple bamboo huts all come with platform bed and mosquito net; some also have private bathrooms. You can also rent tents here. The owner organizes three-day fishing camps to Bamboo Island. Should be open all year. Tents ❶, bungalows ❷

PAN Beach At the westernmost end of the beach, about 700m walk from the khlong ⓣ081 803 4849, ⓦwww.panbeach.com. Ten sturdy, simply furnished wooden bungalows, each with screened windows and bathroom, set just back from the shore. Also has kayaks for rent. In low season, call to check whether it's open. ❸

Private Beach Resort Next to *Emerald* ⓣ081 425 9686 ⓦwww.privatebeachresort.net. There are just nine bungalows in a row here, each one tastefully furnished with elegant lamps, cushions and drapes, and designed with big windows and verandas. Choose to activate the air-con or not. Fan ❻, air-con ❼

Diving, snorkelling and kayaking

Ao Nang is Krabi's main centre for **dive shops**, with a dozen or more outlets, the most reputable of which include Ao Nang Divers at *Krabi Seaview* (Ⓣ075 637242, Ⓦwww.aonang-divers.com), German-UK run Coral Diving at *Krabi Resort* (Ⓣ075 637662, Ⓦwww.coral-diving.com), Phra Nang Divers (Ⓣ075 637064, Ⓦwww.pndivers.com), and Poseidon (Ⓣ075 637263, Ⓦwww.poseidon-krabi.com). All these dive operators stick to a price agreement and charge the same rates, and most offer the same programmes. Diving with Ao Nang operators is possible year-round, with some dive staff claiming that off-season diving is more rewarding, not least because the sites are much less crowded. Most one-day **dive trips** head for the area round Ko Phi Phi and include dives at Shark Point and the "King Cruiser" wreck dive (see p.751 for descriptions) for B2900 including two tanks; the Ko Ha island group, near Ko Lanta, is also popular and costs about the same (see p.808). Two dives in the Ao Nang area – at Ko Poda and Ko Yawasam – average B2500, or B2200 (B1400 for snorkellers) if you opt to go in a longtail rather than a dive boat. PADI dive courses start at B4500 for the introductory Discover Scuba day, or B13,900 for the Openwater. The nearest **recompression chambers** are on Phuket (see p.750); check to see that your dive operator is insured to use one of them. See Basics p.70 for general information on diving in Thailand.

It's quite common to arrange your own **snorkelling trips** with the longtail boatmen who congregate on the Ao Nang beachfront: a typical price would be B300 per person (minimum five people) for a four- or five-hour snorkelling trip to either Ko Poda or Chicken Island, or B2000 for a whole boat to Ko Hong. Alternatively, all Ao Nang tour agents sell snorkelling and swimming day-trips such as those advertised as "four-island" tours. Most dive shops rent mask, snorkel and fins for about B150 the set. It's also possible to arrange an all-inclusive **longtail boat tour** around Krabi's islands and beaches: Australian-Thai run Krabi Island Tours offers various tailor-made programmes that take in local islands as well as Ko Phi Phi, Ko Jum and Ao Luk and feature snorkelling, kayaking, fishing and camping or local accommodation (Ⓣ087 885 1125, Ⓦwww.krabi-island-tours.com; ten-day trips for B18,000 per person).

All tour agents in Ao Nang sell **kayaking** expeditions around the spectacular limestone karsts, mangrove swamps and caves of Ko Hong, Ao Luk and Ao Thalen in Phang Nga bay (described on p.765). Some outlets also rent kayaks at B100–150 per hour. Alternatively, you can simply paddle yourself across to West Railay on Laem Phra Nang, which takes about an hour: outlets all along Ao Nang beach rent kayaks for B100–200 per hour.

Eating, drinking and entertainment

Seafood is Ao Nang's best suit, and one of the best places to enjoy it is on so-called Soi Seafood, off the western end of Ao Nang's beachfront road, where a string of half a dozen **restaurants** serve well-priced fish dishes and fresh seafood by weight and offer uninterrupted views of the waves from their tables on decks above the sand; sunset is an especially popular time to dine here. Locals prefer less formal sea-view dining: buying fried chicken from the streetside stalls on Hat Nopparat Tara and eating it on **mats** under the shorefront trees. Ao Nang has a big Muslim population and as dusk falls handcarts selling the Muslim **roti** pancakes pop up all over the resort, particularly on the stretch of road between *Phra Nang Inn* and *Bream*: choose from a selection of sweet fillings including condensed milk, banana or chocolate.

The **bar** scene in Ao Nang is mainly focused around the **Ao Nang Centerpoint Walking Street**, a U-shaped passageway that runs behind the beachfront shops and is packed with tiny bars, each of them comprising just a few tables, a flirty bartender or two, plus sports TV and perhaps a pool table.

The *muay Thai* **boxing** stadium behind Hat Nopparat Thara, 2km west out of Ao Nang, near the *Laughing Gecko* guest house on Soi Nopparat Thara 13, stages regular bouts in high season (tickets B600–1000); check local flyers for details.

Boat Noodle Thanon Ao Nang. Locals eat here because food is very cheap: the boat noodle soups (*kway tiaw reua*) – so called because these dark, pungent broths were originally served from hawker boats that paddled around the canals of central Thailand – are made with beef, chicken or pork and cost a bargain (for Ao Nang at least) B10–30. Daily 10am–5pm.

Colosseum 1 Thanon Ao Nang. The attraction here is that dishes are made with organic produce grown in the nearby Phanom Bencha hills and in northern Thailand. The menu features Thai curries (B70–100) and soups – served with a choice of jasmine, brown or black rice – as well as lasagnes (B240), pasta dishes, pizzas and ice creams, plus specials and imported wines. Daily 6–11pm.

Encore Ao Nang Centerpoint Walking Street. Nightly live music from 10pm – and the pool table – draws decent-sized crowds to this bar decorated with pictures of rock stars. Daily 11am–1am.

Irish Rover Bar Off Thanon Ao Nang. A little piece of home In the backpackers' soi – bangers and mash, roast dinners, draught Guinness and sports TV – so it's hugely popular with travellers. Daily 10am–1am.

KR Thai Cuisine Beachfront road, Ao Nang. Low-key but popular tourist café that serves a huge, well-priced menu (B60–180) of everything from stir-fries to yellow, green and *matsaman* curries, plus seafood, a decent vegetarian selection and cocktails. Daily 10am–10pm.

Krua Thara National Park visitors' centre car park, near the barrier, Hat Nopparat Thara. Hugely popular with locals and visiting Thais for its fresh seafood and shellfish (B60–180). Daily 11am–9pm.

The Last Café Soi Ao Nang 17. Situated beneath a towering karst at the far eastern end of the beach, this is a perfect, peaceful spot on Ao Nang's prettiest sands. Tables are set under the trees just back from the shore and the menu runs from rice-based dishes (B60) and soups through fruit shakes and home-made cakes. To get there, simply follow Soi Ao Nang 17 from *Phra Nang Inn* as far as you can go, passing *The Last Fisherman Bar* and massage huts en route – about 1km in all. Daily7am–7pm.

Lavinia's Beachfront road, Ao Nang. Choose from over twenty thin-crust pizzas (B160-200) or a variety of sandwiches made with ciabatta or dark bread. Also specializes in pasta and home-made ice cream, and has a decent selection of imported wines. Daily 11am–11pm.

The Massaman Thanon Ao Nang. Tiny Thai-food place whose signature dish is chicken fillet *matsaman*, a Muslim-style curry (B120). Most of their other curries cost B40–60. Daily 5–11pm.

The Shade Tree Next to *Krabi Resort* on Thanon Ao Nang. Despite being by the road, this is a therapeutic place for lunch or a snack as you can sit outside, streetside – under the shade tree – or inside, on loungers with axe pillows, among the paintings and handicrafts for sale. The deli-style menu includes brown bread, baguettes, Greek salads, imported cheese (sandwiches B140), chai, herbal teas and lots of fresh coffees. Daily 9am–6pm.

Tanta's Restaurant Thanon Ao Nang. Large, open-sided restaurant that attracts capacity crowds of diners eager to enjoy the exceptionally tasty, Thai and seafood dishes (B40–200), not to mention the Penang and *matsaman* curries. Daily 11am–11pm.

Wang Sai Beside the bridge at the eastern end of Thanon Nopparat Thara. Pricey but scenic seafront seafood restaurant that overlooks the shore; most dishes cost from B80–200.

Hat Klong Muang

Fifteen kilometres drive north of Ao Nang, an enclave of four- and five-star hotels is emerging at **Hat Klong Muang**. The beach here is pleasant rather than perfect – it's rocky in places, and there's exposed reef at low tide, but it's also long and very quiet, plus the sand is soft and there are plenty of casuarinas for shade. The *Sheraton* occupies the nicest bit. It's also refreshingly uncluttered, as a local bye-law ensures that sunloungers are restricted to hotels' shorefront gardens. The outlook over the eastern reaches of Phang Nga bay is also attractive, with several islands beckoning enticingly from the horizon, including the popular sea-kayaking destination of Ko Hong, famous for its clear waters, decent snorkelling and secret tidal lagoons (see p.768). The dusty, noisy presence of a gypsum mine between Hat Klong Muang and Hat Tubkaak, 4km further north, has stifled development in this area, but the concession ends in 2007 and the area is set to take off, with a Hilton and a Sofitel both already under construction. For the moment however, the biggest hotel here is the *Sheraton* and this is the focus of a cluster of tour operators, taxi services, small restaurants and bars, tailors and minimarkets; there's another little knot of commercial outlets around the *Andaman Beach Resort* further up the road. All the hotels have pools and can arrange excursions to attractions in the Krabi area and local longtail boatmen run snorkelling trips to nearby islands for B1200–1500. An occasional songthaew runs from Krabi town to Klong Muang (45min; B40), but there is as yet no regular public **transport**, so you're usually dependent on taxi touts and hotel shuttles; most hotels offer scheduled transport to Ao Nang or Krabi town for around B200 round-trip. Taxis from Krabi airport charge B700–900; see p.771 for airport information.

Accommodation and eating

Accommodation on Hat Klong Muang is currently all in the ⑧ category and above; for locations, see the map on p.778. All the hotels have **restaurants**, most of which charge correspondingly high prices, but there are alternatives, including *Ruean Mai*, a casual, sociable café that's right next to the *Sheraton*, on the beach, and serves tasty curries, fresh seafood and western standards for less than half the price of its neighbour. *Pan Sea*, diagonally opposite the *Sheraton* entrance, is another good bet for seafood, while there are several cheap noodle shops in and around the Klong Muang Plaza a few metres south down the road.

Andaman Holiday Resort 300m along the beach from the *Sheraton*, just south of the promontory ⓣ075 628300 ⓦwww.andamanholiday.com. Good value mid-market place that's currently the cheapest of the Klong Muang beachfront hotels and so is popular with package tourists. It's set in lush, pleasantly landscaped, tropical gardens that drop down to the sea, and has three pools, a beachfront restaurant and 116 rooms. Choose between slightly dated rooms in the main building, cheaper, more appealing, semi-detached cottages, and top-end villas. ⑧–⑨

Krabi Sands About 300m north of the *Nakamanda* ⓣ075 600 027, ⓦwww.krabisands.com. Located beside a khlong just across the road from a rocky patch of beach, this is an attractively designed little resort, comprising just 26 tastefully designed bungalows set around a garden with a serpentine swimming pool and a kids' pool. Bungalows are spacious and comfortable and all of them have air-con, TV and French windows on to the veranda. ⑧

Nakamanda On the promontory, 500m north up beach from the *Sheraton* ⓣ075 628200, ⓦwww.nakamanda.com. This exceptionally stylish but very expensive boutique hotel – all done out in slate, whitewash and dark wood – has just 39 sophisticated villa rooms set in stepped, terraced grounds full of clipped hedges and sleek lines. Rooms are elegant and capacious, with separate living areas, and bathtubs beneath skylight windows. There's a gorgeous sea-view pool with the grounds run down to the rocky point. High season rates from B12,000. ⑨

Sheraton Krabi Beach Resort ⓣ075 628000 ⓦwww.sheraton.com/krabi. Unusually for a top-notch beachfront hotel, the *Sheraton* Krabi does not boast of its sea views because the entire low-rise resort has been built amongst the mangroves and alongside a khlong; the result is refreshingly green and cool – and full of birdsong. The sea is anyway just a few steps away, accessed via a series of wooden walkways, and there's a seafront lawn for lounging. Rooms are large, sleek and very comfortable; there's a big pool, a spa and watersports centre, plus, weather permitting, nightly films on the outdoor movie screen. ⑨

The Tubkaak Krabi Hat Tubkaak, 4km north of *Krabi Sands* ⓣ075 628400 ⓦwww.tubkaakresort.com. Indulgent and very secluded little spot on Hat Tubkaak, 4km north of Klong Muang beach, with just 44 chic (and pricey) villas set among the beachfront trees around a freeform pool. Views from the shoreside beanbags across to Ko Hong and other islands are stunning. Facilities include a spa and a couple of restaurants, plus free kayak rental, though there are currently no other bars or restaurants between here and Hat Klong Muang, which is reached via the old gypsum mine. High-season rates from B14,000. ⑨

Ko Phi Phi Don

About 40km south of Krabi, the island of **Ko Phi Phi Don** looks breathtakingly handsome as you approach from the sea, its classic arcs of pure white sand framed by dramatic cliffs and lapped by turquoise water so clear that the banks of cabbage coral and yellow-striped tiger fish are clearly visible from the surface. Phi Phi Don would actually be two islands were it not for the tenuous sandy isthmus that connects the hilly expanses to east and west, scalloped into the stunningly symmetrical double bays of Ao Ton Sai to the south and Ao Loh Dalum to the north. So steep is the smaller western half that the island's tiny population lives in isolated clusters across the slopes of the densely vegetated eastern stretch, while the tourist accommodation is mainly confined to the intervening sandy flats, with a few developments on the beaches beneath the cliffs east and north of the isthmus.

Such beauty, however, belies the island's turbulent recent history. By the early 1990s, the island's reputation as a tropical idyll was bringing huge crowds of backpackers to its shores, and these began to lose their looks under the weight of unrestricted development and non-existent infrastructure. The problem worsened after uninhabited little sister island **Ko Phi Phi Leh** – under national marine park protection on account of its lucrative bird's-nest business (see box on p.802) – gained worldwide attention as the location for the movie *The Beach* in 1999, adding day-trippers, package-tourists and big hotels to the mix on Phi Phi Don. Then, in December 2004, the **tsunami** struck. As a five-metre-high wave crashed in from the north, over the hotels, restaurants and hundreds of sunbathers on Ao Loh Dalum, a three-metre-high wave from the south hurtled in across the ferry dock and tourist village at Ao Ton Sai. The waves met in the middle, obliterating seventy percent of all buildings on the sandy isthmus, uprooting scores of trees, and killing 2000. The rest of the island was barely affected. Volunteers and donations flooded in to help the island back on its feet, but the response from the authorities was less straightforward – partly, it was said, out of a desire to start afresh with a more sustainable environmental approach, and partly, it was rumoured, because influential bigwigs were keen to develop the island for their own profit.

Despite the continued stalling by officials, large swathes of the affected area have been rebuilt and visitors are pouring on to the island again. **Ton Sai village** has re-emerged as the island's commercial heart and its legendary nightlife is kicking once more. All boats dock in its bay, **Ao Ton Sai**, from where it's a short walk to accommodation in the village and at **Laem Hin**, the next little stretch of sand to the east, or to **Ao Loh Dalum**, the still gorgeous, deeply curved bay across the isthmus. These areas attract the bulk of Phi Phi's day-trippers and overnight guests and get pretty congested, so those in search of a quieter life head elsewhere, either to **Hat Yao**, another fine beach a short boat ride away or, more peaceful still, to one of the bays further north, at **Hat Toh Ko**, **Ao Rantee**, **Hat Pak Nam**, **Ao Loh Bakao** or **Laem Tong**.

Island practicalities

Ferries to Ko Phi Phi Don all dock at Ao Ton Sai. They run at least twice daily year-round **from Krabi**, 40km to the north (currently departing Krabi at 10am & 3pm and returning from Phi Phi at 9am & 1.30pm; 2hr; B300); and **from Phuket**, 48km to the west (departing Phuket at 8.30am & 1pm and returning from Phi Phi at 9am & 2.30pm; 1hr 30min–2hr 30min; B350). From November to May, daily ferries run to Phi Phi Don from **Ao Nang**, via **Laem**

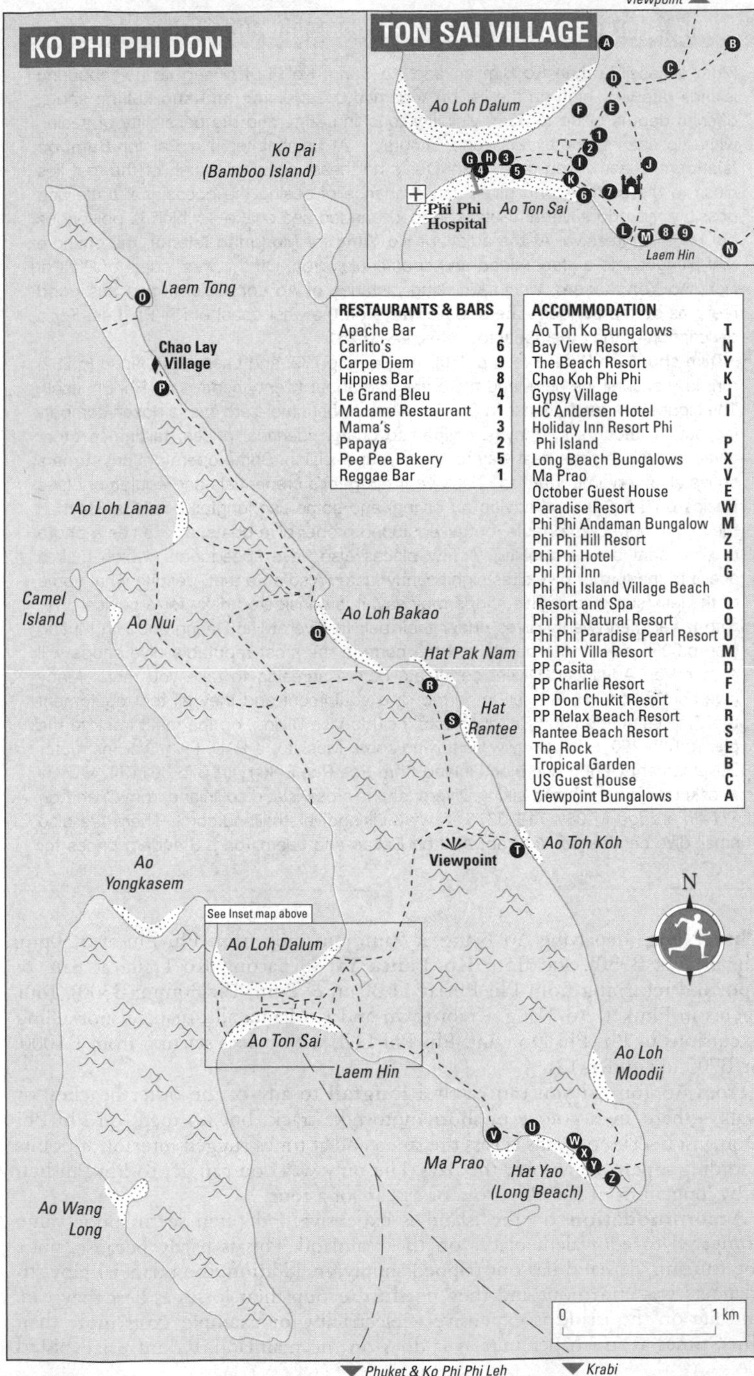
KO PHI PHI DON
TON SAI VILLAGE
Viewpoint
Ao Loh Dalum
Phi Phi Hospital
Ao Ton Sai
Laem Hin
Ko Pai (Bamboo Island)
Laem Tong
Chao Lay Village
Ao Loh Lanaa
Camel Island
Ao Nui
Ao Loh Bakao
Hat Pak Nam
Hat Rantee
Ao Toh Koh
Viewpoint
Ao Yongkasem
See Inset map above
Ao Loh Dalum
Ao Ton Sai
Laem Hin
Ao Loh Moodii
Ma Prao
Hat Yao (Long Beach)
Ao Wang Long
N
0
1 km
Phuket & Ko Phi Phi Leh
Krabi
RESTAURANTS & BARS
Apache Bar 7
Carlito's 6
Carpe Diem 9
Hippies Bar 8
Le Grand Bleu 4
Madame Restaurant 1
Mama's 3
Papaya 2
Pee Pee Bakery 5
Reggae Bar 1
ACCOMMODATION
Ao Toh Ko Bungalows T
Bay View Resort N
The Beach Resort Y
Chao Koh Phi Phi K
Gypsy Village J
HC Andersen Hotel I
Holiday Inn Resort Phi Phi Island P
Long Beach Bungalows X
Ma Prao V
October Guest House E
Paradise Resort W
Phi Phi Andaman Bungalow M
Phi Phi Hill Resort Z
Phi Phi Hotel H
Phi Phi Inn G
Phi Phi Island Village Beach Resort and Spa Q
Phi Phi Natural Resort O
Phi Phi Paradise Pearl Resort U
Phi Phi Villa Resort M
PP Casita D
PP Charlie Resort F
PP Don Chukit Resort L
PP Relax Beach Resort R
Rantee Beach Resort S
The Rock E
Tropical Garden B
US Guest House C
Viewpoint Bungalows A

Diving, snorkelling, kayaking and rock-climbing off Ko Phi Phi

More accessible than Ko Similan and Ko Surin, Ko Phi Phi and its neighbouring islands rate very high on the list of Andaman coast **diving and snorkelling** spots, offering depths of up to 35m, visibility touching 30m, and the possibility of seeing white-tip sharks, moray eels and stingrays. At uninhabited **Ko Pai** (or **Bamboo Island**), off Laem Tong on Phi Phi Don's northeast coast of, much of the reef lies close to the surface, and gives you a chance of seeing the occasional turtle and possibly the odd silver-and-black-striped banded sea snake – which is poisonous but rarely aggressive. At the adjacent **Ko Yung** (or **Mosquito Island**), the offshore reef plunges into a steep-sided and spectacular drop. Off the west coast of Phi Phi Don, **Ao Yongkasem**, within kayaking distance of Ao Loh Dalum, also has good reefs, as do the tranquil waters at **Ao Maya** on the west coast of Phi Phi Leh. For a description of the other local top sites, see p.751.

Dive shops on Phuket (see p.750), Ao Nang (p.789) and Laem Phra Nang (p.782) run daily excursions here, and there are also about twenty centres on Phi Phi itself. The biggest concentration is in Ton Sai village, where there are over a dozen competing outfits, though, as they're obliged to charge identical prices, talking to other divers is probably the best way to make your decision. Some operators cut corners so it's also very important to check your operator's credentials and equipment (see Basics p.70 for general advice on diving) and some use longtail boats rather than the much more comfortable, better-equipped proper dive boats: ask to see a photo of your boat before booking. A few places also have speedboats, which makes acess to the further dive sites significantly faster. Also note that, despite what some of the less scrupulous dive shops may say, it is considered risky for a novice diver with fewer than twenty dives under their belt to dive at Hin Daeng and Hin Muang (see p.808), due to the depth and the current; the most reputable dive shops will demand an Advanced Divers certificate before agreeing to take you there. Many dive centres on Phi Phi sell imported dive equipment and they all rent equipment too. Recommended Ton Sai operators include Visa Diving, on the main track to the pier (ⓣ087 280 1721, ⓦwww.visadiving.com); Moskito, a PADI Five-Star Instructor Development Centre one block inland from Pee Pee Bakery (ⓣ075 601154, ⓦwww.moskitodiving.com); and Viking Divers, on the cross-island soi inland from *Chao Koh Phi Phi Lodge* (ⓣ081 719 3375, ⓦwww.vikingdiversthailand.com). There are also small dive centres on Hat Yao, Ao Loh Bakao and Laem Tong. Standard prices for

Phra Nang (departing Ao Nang at 9am, returning from Phi Phi at 3.30pm; 2hr 30min; B350); and from **Ko Lanta Yai** (departing Ko Lanta at 8am & 1pm and returning from Phi Phi at 11.30am & 2pm; 1hr 30min; B300). Tour agents in Phuket, Ao Nang, Krabi town and Ko Lanta all organize snorkelling excursions to Phi Phi Don and Phi Phi Leh, with prices starting from B1000, or B700 for under-12s.

From Ao Ton Sai you can catch a **longtail** to any of the other beaches, or walk – there are a couple of short motorbike tracks but no roads on Phi Phi Don, just a series of paths across the steep and at times rugged interior, at points affording superb views over the bays. The only way you can get to Phi Phi Leh is by longtail from Phi Phi Don, or as part of a tour.

Accommodation on the island is expensive and often seems poor value compared to equivalent places on the mainland. This is partly because, since the tsunami, demand has outstripped supply; in addition, the financial blow to islanders was enormous and they need to recoup their losses as best they can, and life on the island is expensive – electricity, for example, costs more than three times as much per unit as it does on the mainland. Room prices listed

day-trips including two tanks, equipment and lunch are: B2200 for local reefs off Phi Phi Leh; B3200 for the *King Cruiser* wreck; and B4500 for Hin Daeng and Hin Muang (by speedboat). Excalibur Liveaboards (Ⓦwww.thailand-liveaboard.com), which runs out of Moskito, organizes live-aboard trips direct from Phi Phi to the Similan and Surin islands (US$680 for four days). **Dive courses** on Phi Phi cost B3100 for the introductory Discover Scuba day, B11,900 for the certificated four-day Openwater course, and B9500 for a two-day Advanced course. If you're short on time, email ahead to reserve a place on a dive course or live-aboard trip. The nearest **recompression chambers** are on Phuket (see p.750); check to see that your dive operator is insured to use one of them.

Nearly all the tour operators and bungalow operations on Phi Phi Don organize day and half-day **snorkelling** trips. Prices average B600 for a day-trip, including lunch and snorkelling gear, with the price depending on the size of the boat and number of participants; dive boats charge the same. Longtail boatmen charge around B1200 per boat for private two-person half-day snorkel trips including equipment. In the case of snorkelling, the longtails that run from Ko Phi Phi are better than the larger fishing boats and the Phuket cruise ships, which are so popular that you can rarely see the fish for the swimmers. Many dive operators will take accompanying snorkellers on their one-day dives for B600.

The limestone cliffs and secluded bays of the Phi Phi islands make perfect **kayaking** territory, as the lagoons and palm-fringed coasts are much better appreciated in silence than accompanied by the roar of a longtail or cruise ship. If you rent a kayak for a whole day you can incorporate sunbathing and snorkelling breaks on small, unpopulated bays nearby. Tour operators in the village and on all beaches rent out kayaks at around B200 per hour or B800 per day, depending on size and quality. Kayak/snorkel tours of Phi Phi Leh and Phi Phil Don cost B600.

Phi Phi's topography is also a gift for **rock-climbers** and several places in the village offer climbing instruction and equipment rental. Prices average B500 for a two-hour beginners' introduction, and B1300 for a one-day course with full instruction and equipment. The main climbing area is a small beach just to the west of Ao Ton Sai, and includes the Ton Sai Tower and the Drinking Wall, with heights of 15m and 30m respectively. A newer attraction is **cliff-jumping**, offered by several tour agencies and featuring jumps of up to 18m off a Phi Phi Don cliff.

below are for high season, which runs from November to April, but most bungalow operators slap on a thirty to fifty percent surcharge during Christmas and New Year; reservations are essential over that fortnight, and are strongly recommended throughout high season. From May to October you should be able to negotiate up to fifty percent off the prices quoted below.

Ton Sai village has all the island shops and **services**, though there is also Internet access at some hotels on Hat Yao, Ao Loh Bakao and Laem Tong.

Ton Sai village, Ao Loh Dalum and Laem Hin

Ton Sai village is the commercial and nightlife centre of the island, a hectic warren of narrow streets packed with day-trippers and lined with dive shops, tour agents, restaurants, bars and minimarkets. Nearly every visitor arrives at the pier here, and few escape the attentions of the army of touts trying to steer you towards a guest house, boat tour or diving trip. **Ao Ton Sai** beach itself used to be most attractive at the western end, under the limestone karsts, but with so much damage to its hinterland it's nowhere near the beauty it once was and the eerie presence of the still unrenovated *PP Island Cabana* hotel doesn't help. The central part of the bay is too busy with ferries and longtails for swimming, so most people simply head for **Ao Loh Dalum**, less than 300m north across the narrow isthmus, which looks astonishingly pretty at high tide, with its glorious curve of powder-white sand beautifully set off by pale blue water, though it's a different story at low-water, as the tide goes out for miles. The **viewpoint** that overlooks the far eastern edge of Ao Loh Dalum affords a magnificent panorama over the twin bays of Ao Loh Dalum and Ao Ton Sai: every evening crowds of people make the steep 15-minute climb up the clearly signposted concrete steps for sunset shots, but early morning is an equally good time, and the shop at the summit, whose owners have created a pretty tropical garden around it, serves coffee as swell as cold drinks. From the viewpoint you can descend the rocky and at times almost sheer paths to the trio of little east coast bays at Ao Toh Ko, Ao Rantee (Lanti), and Hat Pak Nam. East along the coast from the Ton Sai pier, about ten minutes' walk down the main track, is the promontory known as **Laem Hin**, beyond which lies a small stretch of beach that's quieter than Ao Ton Sai and better for swimming. Bungalows cover the Laem Hin promontory and beachfront, and they're popular places to stay, being in easy reach of the restaurants and nightlife at Ao Ton Sai but feeling a little less claustrophobic and hectic.

Much of the village has been seamlessly rebuilt so in places the only reminders are the before-and-after photos posted on the walls of some of the surviving Ton Sai shops and restaurants. A small Tsunami Memorial Park of carefully tended shrubs and garden benches, just inland from east end of Loh Dalum near *Viewpoint Bungalows*, commemorates some of the victims, and the smilewith-pum.com foundation, based at *Pum* restaurant in the village, sells books of kids' tsunami art and stories, as well as sarongs and jewellery, in aid of the 104 island children who lost one or both parents in the waves.

Ton Sai village has all the essential services, including **ATMs** and **exchange** counters run by national banks (daily 7am–10pm), international telephone call centres and scores of little places offering **Internet access**. The island's only health centre, **Phi Phi Hospital** (ⓣ081 270 4481) is at the western end of Ton Sai, and there's a **police** box (ⓣ081 536 2427) next to the *Apache Bar* on the track to Laem Hin. A number of outlets offer **bicycle rental** for B200/day, but outside the village there aren't really any cyclable tracks.

Accommodation

Most of Ton Sai's **accommodation** is packed between the Ao Ton Sai pier and the base of the viewpoint hill to the east. Rooms are snapped up fast in this area, so prices are high and standards vary; to save you dragging your pack fruitlessly from place to place you can make use of the tour agents close by the pier who will ring round for vacancies for you. The cheapest options are often business premises that have simply stuck up a sign announcing "room for rent", though even at these places you're unlikely to get much under ❹ in high season and for that may have to share a bathroom. Alternatively, ask at any of the dive shops along the main drag as they often know who is currently offering the best deal.

Ton Sai village and Ao Loh Dalum

HC Andersen Hotel ⓣ089 287 7980, ⓦwww.phiphisteakhouse.com. Small, all-air-con hotel where standards are pretty good, though views are nil as it's jammed behind several street business and the cheapest rooms are not much bigger than a double bed. Every room has a TV and DVD player. ❻–❼

October Guest House ⓣ075 601193. Rooms here are all built on higher ground, so you get some kind of a view from most balconies. The cheapest en-suite fan rooms are cell-like but decent enough; the better versions have longer views and the option of air-con. Fan ❺, air ❻

Phi Phi Hotel ⓣ075 611233 ⓦwww.phiphi-hotel.com. One of the biggest hotels in Ton Sai, with a range of mid-market air-con rooms in low-rise buildings just inland from the pier. The top-end rooms have sea views, while the cheapest have neither window, view or TV. There's a small pool on site. ❼–❽

Phi Phi Inn ⓣ081 910 4622, ⓔphiphi_inn@yahoo.com. Small, sparklingly clean, all-air-con little hotel, where all rooms have TV and a balcony, though only the upstairs ones have the chance of a view and anyway enjoy more privacy. ❼

PP Casita ⓣ075 601215. On the northeast edge of the village, just inland from Ao Loh Dalum, this place is designed as its own little village, comprising some 50 dinky whitewashed cabanas built on stilts and connected by wooden walkways that sit above an embryonic garden that should be pretty in time (tsunami salt water ruined the soil). Interiors are good considering the competition, with fans, platform beds, satellite TV and nice tiled bathrooms. The drawback is that the cabanas are tightly packed and outdoor seating is on the walkway, making it a sociable place, but not very private or quiet. ❺

PP Charlie Resort ⓣ075 620615, ⓦwww.ppcharlie.com. While it waits to rebuild its seafront properties on Ao Loh Dalum, *PP Charlie Resort* is meantime offering some of the best value and most popular rooms in the Ton Sai-Loh Dalum areas. It has 40 rooms in a two-storey block, 150m inland from Ao Loh Dalum, with the choice of small or large, fan or air con. All rooms have sea views and are well maintained. There's also a swimming pool but you need to pay to use it. Fan ❹–❺, air-con ❻

The Rock ⓣ084 052 8270. Traveller-oriented hangout offering the cheapest beds on the island, in a mixed-sex four-bed dorm (B200/bed) and similar sixteen-bed dorm (B200/bed). Also has a few singles and doubles with shared bathrooms. ❸

Tropical Garden ⓣ081 968 1436, ⓔtimeandtide101@hotmail.com. The good sized rough-timber fan and air-con huts here are mostly built on stilts up the side of an outcrop, beyond the turn-off for the path to the viewpoint. The better ones have a breezy veranda (though not much of a view) and there's a refreshing amount of greenery around, plus a tiny pool, despite being surrounded by other accommodation. Fan ❺, air-con ❼

US Guest House ⓣ089 728 1509. This two-storey block of functional en-suite fan and air-con rooms has the look and feel of an urban guest house, and offers some of the cheaper rooms in the area. It's close by the base of the viewpoint access steps. Fan ❺, air-con ❼

Viewpoint Bungalows ⓣ075 622351, ⓦwww.phiphiviewpoint.com. Strung out across and up the cliffside at the far eastern end of Ao Loh Dalum, these attractive and comfortable, if pricey, bungalows enjoy great views out over the bay. The most expensive have air-con and TV and full-on edge-of-the-hill bay vistas. It's a popular, well-managed place and facilities include a scenically sited restaurant, a couple of bars and a small pool. Fan ❻, air-con ❽

Laem Hin

Bay View Resort Yao ⓣ075 621223, ⓦwww.phiphibayview.com. The nicely furnished air-con bungalows here have massive windows affording great views and occupy a superb position high on the cliffside, at the far eastern end of Laem Hin beach and stretching east along the hillside almost as far as *Ma Prao* on Hat Yao. ❽

Gypsy Village ⓣ075 601044. The 25 shabby but relatively cheap concrete bungalows, all with fan and attached bathroom, are set round an unusually spacious lawn about 150m down the track between the mosque and *Phi Phi Villa*. ❹

Phi Phi Andaman Bungalow ⓣ081 124 5547, ⓦwww.krabidir.com/ppandamanresort. Set in secluded enclosure just a few metres back from the beach, the bungalows here are arranged in a square around a large lawn and small central swimming pool. There are low-quality terraced fan rooms at the back, and better, freestanding bungalows with either fan or air-con around the sides. There's also a public gym on site. Fan rooms ❺, fan bungalows ❻, air-con bungalows ❼

Phi Phi Villa Resort ⓣ075 601100, ⓦwww.phiphivillaresort.com. The best of the many options at this outfit are the huge, deluxe, thatched air-con family cottages occupying the front section of the prettily landscaped garden, near the small pool. Also available are smaller air-con bungalows, some pretty scruffy fan bungalows and a few cheap fan rooms right at the back. Fan rooms ❺, fan bungalows ❻, air-con bungalows ❽, family bungalows ❾

PP Don Chukit Resort ⓣ075 618126. Choose between small, mid-range, air-con bungalows, reasonably well spaced around a pretty garden, and similar but pricier (and probably noisier) versions beside the seafront walkway, with uninterrupted sea views. Also has some fan rooms in single-storey blocks at the back of the compound. Handily located just east of the promontory, not far beyond *Carlito's* bar. Fan rooms ❻, air-con bungalows ❼

Eating

Ton Sai is the best place to eat on the island, offering everything from bakery cafés to seafood **restaurants**, though don't expect haute cuisine. Less expensive but arguably more tasty are the typically Thai curry-and-rice stalls in the heart of the village, and there are always lots of hawkers flogging rotis and fried bananas from their hand-carts.

Le Grand Bleu Classy place close to *Phi Phi Hotel* serving French-inspired food, including lots of fresh seafood, duck fillet with mango (B270), sirloin steak (B340) and changing menus of the day. Nightly from 6pm.

Madame Restaurant Deservedly popular spot almost next door to *Reggae Bar* which serves good curries – penang, *matsaman* green and red – for around B70, plus plenty of thin-crust pizzas from about B180. Also has a decent vegetarian selection, cheap glasses of wine (B60) and nightly movies. Daily from 4pm.

Mama's Known for its fresh seafood (from B80) and tempting cakes. Also does a reasonable selection of tapas for B30 a dish. Daily 11am–3pm & 6–11pm.

Papaya One of the best of several village-style kitchens whose authentic and reasonably cheap Thai standards, including noodle soups, *phat thai* (B60), fried rice dishes and fiery curries, makes it very popular with locals and dive staff. Daily 11am–10pm.

Pee Pee Bakery The usual venue for breakfast, with its different blends of real coffee (B35–50), set breakfasts (B75) and big selection of freshly baked croissants, Danish pastries, home-made breads, cakes and cookies. Daily 7am–8pm.

Drinking

Ton Sai nightlife is young and drunken, involving endless buckets of Sansom and red bull, dance music played into the early hours, and fire-juggling shows on the beach. All the bars offer a pretty similar formula, so it's often the one-off events and happy hours that determine which one gets the biggest crowds.

Apache Bar At the eastern end of the village, just beyond *Chao Ko Phi Phi*, on the track to Laem Hin. Big, multi-tiered bar and dance floor that hosts regular parties (check locally posted flyers), stages ladyboy cabaret shows and has a long happy hour.

Carlito's At the eastern end of the village, next to *Chao Ko Phi Phi*, on the track to Laem Hin. Popular seafront joint with a long cocktails menu, an easy-going vibe, plus DJs and a dance floor.

Carpe Diem Opposite *PP Villa* at Laem Hin. There's cushion seating on the upper terrace here, and nightly fire shows from around 10pm.

Hippies Bar Across from *PP Andaman* on Laem Hin. Hugely popular place with a chilled-out sea-view bar and restaurant that shows nightly movies at 8pm, followed by fire shows at 10pm and hosts regular half-moon parties. You can learn fire-juggling here yourself every afternoon.

Reggae Bar In the heart of the village, on the soi that runs north beside *Chao Koh Phi Phi Lodge*. A Phi Phi institution that's been running for years in various incarnations. These days it arranges regular amateur *muay Thai* bouts in its boxing ring and has pool tables and a bar around the sides.

Hat Yao

With its deluxe sand and large reefs packed with polychromatic marine life just 20m offshore, **HAT YAO** (Long Beach) is considered the best of Phi Phi's main beaches, but that can be hard to appreciate, with hundreds of sunbathers pitching up on the gorgeous sand every day and throngs of day-trippers making things even worse at lunchtime. Unperturbed by all the attention, shoals of golden butterfly fish, turquoise and purple parrot fish and hooped angel fish continue to scour what remains of Hat Yao's coral for food, escorted by brigades of small cleaner fish who live off the parasites trapped in the scales of larger species. Long Beach Divers (Ⓦwww.leisure-dive.com) at *Long Beach* offers all the same **dive** facilities as shops in the village and offers discounts on accommodation at *Long Beach* bungalows to anyone doing a dive course.

Longtail **boats** do the ten-minute shuttle between Hat Yao and Ao Ton Sai (B80 per person, or B100 after dark), but it's also possible to **walk** between the two in half an hour. At low tide you can get to Hat Yao along the shore, though this involves quite a bit of clambering over smooth wet rocks – not ideal when wearing a heavy rucksack, nor after a night spent trawling the bars of Ton Sai village (take a torch). The alternative route takes you over the hillside via the steps up from *Bay View Resort* and through neighbouring *Arayaburi Resort* on Laem Hin – with a side track running down to *Ma Prao*'s little bay – and then finally dropping down to Hat Yao. A different path connects Hat Yao to the as yet undeveloped bay of **Ao Loh Moodii**, ten minutes' walk to the north: the trail starts between *The Beach Resort* and *Phi Phi Hill*'s restaurant and can also be accessed from *Phi Phi Hill* itself.

Accommodation

The Beach Resort ⓣ075 618267, ⓔphi-phi-the-beach-resort@hotmail.com. Currently the poshest option on Hat Yao, this place has just 19 large, timber-clad chalets built on stilts up the hillside. Each one enjoys attractive sea views from its generous balcony (albeit partially occluded by the tin roofs of the adjacent *Long Beach*) and has a fairly upscale interior, with air-con and liberal use of wood for flooring and wall panels. The price depends on the view. The resort also has a small beachfront pool. ❽

Long Beach Bungalows ⓣ075 612217. The first choice of most budget travellers, this fairly cheap, well-located and long-running option has dozens of tightly packed huts for rent. At the bottom end you get ultra-simple bamboo huts, many of which contain nothing more than a bed, a fan and a mosquito net, though some also have their own bathrooms. The better ones are sturdier wooden huts and many of these are right on the shorefront. Shared bathroom ❷, en suite ❹, beachfront ❺

Ma Prao ⓣ075 622486, ⓦwww.maprao.com. Tucked away in a little cove just west of Hat Yao itself, with easy access via a rocky path, this small, secluded and friendly Belgian-run place has 30 characterful wood and bamboo bungalows ranged across the hillside overlooking the sea, and a pleasant eating area out front. The cheapest A-frame huts have nothing more than a mattress, a fan and a mozzie net and share bathrooms, but some have a terrace; among the more expensive en-suite options, you can choose to have a boat-shaped deck, a rooftop sun-terrace or a bamboo villa set high among the trees. There's a small dive operation here, you can rent kayaks, and the kitchen produces a long menu that includes eighty different cocktails, and home-made yoghurt. Phone the day before to secure a room. Shared bathroom ❸, en suite ❺–❼

Paradise Resort ⓣ081 968 3982, ⓦwww.paradiseresort.co.th. The 25 fan and air-con bungalows here are all huge and well furnished, and are located either right on the shorefront or just a few metres back from it. Fan ❻, air-con ❼

Phi Phi Hill Resort ⓣ075 618203, ⓦwww.phiphihill.com. The fifty mint-green wooden cabins here occupy a glorious spot high above the beach, overlooking the far eastern end of Hat Yao. With fine sunrise or sunset views, depending on your location, and plenty of breeze, the only off-putting factor here are the one hundred steps that connect the resort with the beach below (though there is a pulley system for luggage). Rooms are simply furnished and come with fan and air-con; the cheapest share bathrooms. Shared bathroom ❸, en suite with fan ❹–❻, air-con ❼

Phi Phi Paradise Pearl Resort ⓣ075 622100. The 30 bungalows at this efficiently run place are fairly well spaced along the western half of the beach, with none more than a few steps from the shore. Interiors are unremarkable but perfectly comfortable and come with fan or air-con. There's Internet access and an international phone service here, plus a tour counter and book exchange. Fan ❺, air-con ❼

Ao Toh Ko, Hat Rantee and Hat Pak Nam

Travellers wanting to escape the crowds around Ton Sai and Hat Yao without spending a fortune head for the trio of little bays mid-way along the east coast: Ao Toh Ko, Hat Rantee (Lanti) and Hat Pak Nam. The bays are quiet and support just a few bungalows each. Longtail transfers cost about B100 per person from Ao Ton Sai, or you can reach the bays inland, via trails that run from the Viewpoint above Ao Loh Dalum (see p.796) and take at least half an hour to walk. At **Ao Toh Ko**, the range of huts at the well-liked *Ao Toh Ko Bungalows* (Ⓣ081 731 9470, Ⓔdreaminfijian@hotmail.com; ❷–❸) encompasses basic ones with shared bathrooms, plus better en-suite options including some that are set right over the rocks. On **Hat Rantee**, *Rantee Beach Resort* (Ⓣ086 746 3297, Ⓔranteebeach@hotmail.com; ❶–❺) has rudimentary bamboo huts, some of which have private bathrooms; the priciest enjoy direct sea views. *PP Relax Beach Resort* (Ⓣ081 083 0194, Ⓔsuteejanson@yahoo.com; ❺–❻) on **Hat Pak Nam** offers the most comfortable, and expensive, accommodation, in 16 en-suite thatched bamboo bungalows.

Ao Loh Bakao and Laem Tong

Far removed from the hustle of Ao Ton Sai and its environs, the beautiful, secluded northern beaches at **Ao Loh Bakao** and **Laem Tong** are the domain of just a few upscale resorts. If travelling from Phuket, you can get direct transport to Laem Tong on the Andaman Wave Master boat (Ⓣ076 232561, Ⓦwww.andamanwavemaster.com; departs Phuket at 8.30am & 1.30pm and departs Laem Tong at 9am and 2.30pm; B500). From anywhere else, you'll need to take a ferry to Ao Ton Sai and then transfer from there. There are no scheduled boats to Loh Bakao or Laem Tong from Ao Ton Sai, but pre-booked guests should be entitled to a reasonably priced transfer by longtail or speedboat. Chartering your own longtail from Ao Ton Sai will cost about B400–500; the trip takes around 40 minutes to Ao Loh Bakao and a further 15 minutes north to Laem Tong.

Ao Loh Bakao and Ao Lanaa

Just over halfway up the coast, the 104 plush, air-conditioned chalets at ✱ *Phi Phi Island Village Beach Resort and Spa* (Ⓣ075 628900, Ⓦwww.ppisland.com; ❾; rates start at B6100 and rise if you want a sea view) have the gorgeous eight-hundred-metre-long white-sand beach and turquoise waters of **AO LOH BAKAO** all to themselves. It's a popular honeymoon spot, and a lovely location for anyone looking for a quiet, comfortable break. The thatched, split-bamboo bungalows are designed in traditional Thai style and furnished with character and elegance. There's a good-sized pool and spa centre in the prettily landscaped tropical gardens, as well as a dive centre, tennis courts and kayak rental. If you tire of these sands, just follow the clearly signed track to **AO LANAA** across on the west coast: it's a 10-minute walk away, via a cheap Thai food restaurant and through the remnants of a palm grove. Wilder and more natural than Ao Loh Bakao, and prone to flotsam, Ao Lanaa's long, semicircular white-sand bay has no facilities other than a stall that sells drinks and rents kayak and longtail boats. Following the track in the other direction, north along the coast, will bring you to Laem Tong in half an hour.

Laem Tong

Almost right at Phi Phi's northernmost tip, **LAEM TONG** is busier and significantly more commercial than Loh Bakao, with several upmarket resorts along its also very inviting white-sand shores, many of them enjoying views across to nearby Bamboo Island and Mosquito Island. The beach is home to a group of Urak Lawoy *chao ley* "sea gypsies" (see p.713 for more information on them), whose village is next to the *Holiday Inn*; all longtail boat tours and transfers are run by Laem Tong's *chao ley* co-operative.

At the southern end of the beach, *Holiday Inn Resort Phi Phi Island* (Ⓣ075 261334, Ⓦwww.phiphi-palmbeach.com; ❾; published rates from B6200) offers 76 luxurious air-conditioned bungalows set in graceful gardens of tidy lawns and flowering shrubs plus a swimming pool, dive centre and tennis courts, as well as batik and cookery courses. Up at the northern end, the old-style air-con rooms and wooden chalets at *Phi Phi Natural Resort* (Ⓣ075 613010, Ⓦwww.phiphinatural.com; ❽–❾) are scattered around an extensive tropical shorefront garden that stretches along the coast to the next tiny uninhabited bay. Facilities here include a swimming pool and a terrace restaurant offering fine sea views, plus snorkelling, fishing and dive trips.

Ko Phi Phi Leh

More rugged than its twin, Ko Phi Phi Don, and a quarter the size, **KO PHI PHI LEH** is home only to the **sea swift**, whose valuable nests are gathered by intrepid *chao ley* for export to specialist Chinese restaurants all over the world. Tourists descend on the island not only to see the nest-collecting caves but also to snorkel off its sheltered bays and to admire the very spot where *The Beach* was filmed; the anchoring of tourist and fishing boats has damaged much of the coral in the most beautiful reefs. Most snorkelling trips out of Phi Phi Don include Phi Phi Leh, which is only twenty minutes south of Ao Ton Sai, but you can also get there by hiring a longtail from Ao Ton Sai or Hat Yao (about B1200/six-person boat). If you do charter your own boat, go either very early or very late in the day, to beat the tour-group rush. Alternatively, why not try paddling yourself in and out of the quiet bays in a kayak – see box on p.795 for details.

Most idyllic of all the bays in the area is **Ao Maya** on the southwest coast, where the water is still and very clear and the coral extremely varied – a perfect snorkelling spot and a feature of most day-trips. Visit after 4pm to see it at its peaceful best. Unfortunately the discarded lunch boxes and water bottles of day-trippers threaten the health of the marine life in **Ao Phi Leh**, an almost

Bird's-nesting

Prized for its aphrodisiac and energizing qualities, **bird's-nest soup** is such a delicacy in Taiwan, Singapore and Hong Kong that ludicrous sums of money change hands for a dish whose basic ingredients are tiny twigs glued together with bird's spit. Collecting these nests is a lucrative but life-endangering business: sea swifts (known as edible nest swiftlets) build their nests in rock crevices hundreds of metres above sea level, often on sheer cliff-faces or in cavernous hollowed-out karst. **Nest-building** begins in January and the harvesting season usually lasts from February to May, during which time the female swiftlet builds three nests on the same spot, none of them more than 12cm across, by secreting an unbroken thread of saliva, which she winds round as if making a coil pot. **Gatherers** will only steal the first two nests made by each bird, prising them off the cave walls with special metal forks. Gathering the nests demands faultless agility and balance, skills that seem to come naturally to the *chao ley*, whose six-man teams bring about four hundred nests down the perilous bamboo scaffolds each day, weighing about 4kg in total. At a market rate of up to B120,000 per kilo, so much money is at stake that a government franchise must be granted before any collecting commences, and armed guards often protect the sites at night. The *chao ley* seek spiritual protection from the dangers of the job by making offerings to the spirits of the cliff or cave at the beginning of the season; in the Viking Cave, they place buffalo flesh, horns and tails at the foot of one of the stalagmites.

completely enclosed east-coast lagoon of breathtakingly turquoise water. Not far from the cove, the **Viking Cave** gets its misleading name from the scratchy wall-paintings of Chinese junks inside, but more interesting than these 400-year-old graffiti is the **bird's-nesting** that goes on here: rickety bamboo scaffolding extends hundreds of metres up to the roof of the cave, where the harvesters spend the day scraping the tiny sea-swift nests off the rockface.

Ko Jum

Situated halfway between Krabi and Ko Lanta Yai, **KO JUM** (also known as **Ko Pu**) is the sort of laid-back spot that people come to for a couple of days, then can't bring themselves to leave. Though there's plenty of accommodation on the island, there's nothing more than a couple of beach bars for evening entertainment, and little to do during the day except try out the half-dozen west-coast beaches and read your book under a tree. The beaches may not be pristine, and are in some places unswimmably rocky at low tide, but they're mostly long and

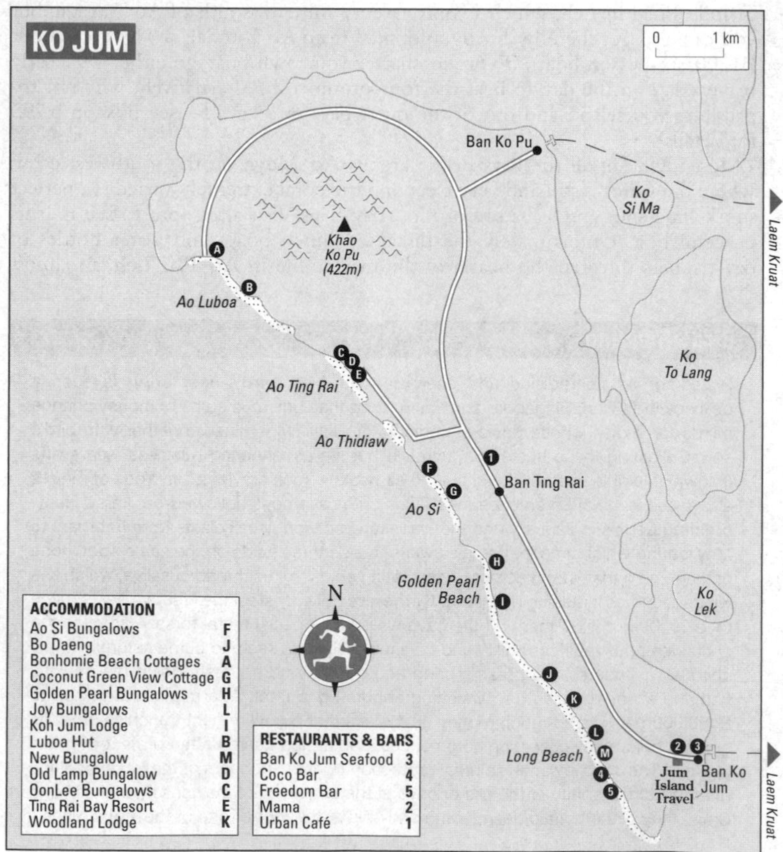

wild, fronted only by the occasional discreet set of bungalows, and all but empty of people. Nights are also low key: the bungalow generators mostly get turned off by 11pm, after which it's paraffin lamps and starlight.

The island is home to around 3000 people, the majority of them Muslim, though there are also communities of *chao ley* sea gypsies on Ko Jum (for more on the *chao ley* see p.713), as well as Buddhists. The main village is **Ban Ko Jum,** on the island's southeastern tip, comprising a few local shops and small restaurants, one of the island's two piers for boats to and from Laem Kruat on the mainland, and a beachfront school. It's about 1km from the southern end of the longest and most popular beach, called... **Long Beach**. Long Beach is connected to **Golden Pearl Beach**, which sits just south of **Ban Ting Rai**, the middle-island village that's about half way down the east coast. North of Ban Ting Rai, a trio of smaller, increasingly remote beaches at **Ao Si**, **Ao Ting Rai**, and **Ao Luboa** complete the picture. The island's third village, **Ban Ko Pu,** occupies the northeastern tip, about 5km beyond Ban Ting Rai, and has the other Laem Kruat ferry pier. Some islanders refer to the north of the island, from Ban Ting Rai upwards, as Ko Pu, and define only the south as Ko Jum. Much of the north is made inaccessible by the breastbone of forested hills, whose highest peak (422m) is Khao Ko Pu; the ten-kilometre road that connects the north and south of the island runs around its northeastern flank.

Very high winds and heavy seas mean that Ko Jum becomes an acquired taste from May through October, so most tourist accommodation **closes** for that period: exceptions are highlighted in the text. Many west-coast homes and bungalows were destroyed by the 2004 tsunami and the waves pelted the beaches with rocks and broken reef, but no lives were lost. The majority of property has since been rebuilt or relocated, and first-time visitors to the island are now unlikely to notice any major damage.

Island practicalities

During high season, access to Ko Jum is via the Krabi–Ko Lanta **ferries** (1hr 30min–2hr from Krabi, B300; or about 45min from Ko Lanta, B250; see p.809 for times); Ko Jum bungalows send longtails out to meet the ferries as they pass the west coast. When it comes to moving on, you can charter a longtail from Ko Jum to Ko Phi Phi for about B1300: the trip takes a couple of hours. In the **rainy season** you have to travel to Ko Jum overland, and this route is also a useful all-year alternative, for example if getting an early morning flight out of Krabi. Coming from Krabi town, you will first need to take a **songthaew** to **Nua Klong**, either direct from opposite *Viva* restaurant on Thanon Pruksa Uthit, or first to the Talat Kao bus station (to catch the last boat you need to leave Krabi by 1pm); at Nua Klong you get another songthaew to **Laem Kruat**; the total distance from Krabi is about 40km and can take nearly 2 hours. Three **boats** run daily from Laem Kruat **to Ban Ko Jum** in the southern part of the island, departing between noon and 3pm and returning from Ko Jum between 7am and 7.45am (1hr; B60); from Ban Ko Jum it's an easy 20- to 30-minute walk to the southern bungalows on Long Beach, or a motorbike taxi (with sidecar) will cost you B40–50. You can also get boats from Laem Kruat to **Ban Ko Pu** in the north (depart Laem Kruat when full between 8am and 4pm, returning from Ban Ko Pu between 7am and 8.30am; 45min; B20), from where you'll need a motorbike taxi to where you're staying.

Most bungalows can arrange **kayak** and **motorbike** rental (B250–350), and *Joy Bungalows* on Long Beach has bicycles. Many also organize **day-trips**, as do several tour agencies in the village, for example to Ko Phi Phi Don and Ko Phi

Phi Leh for B2000 per boat. Or you can enlist a longtail boatmen to take you out to Bamboo Island for a day's snorkelling (about B1500).

There's no ATM on the island, but you can **change money** at Jum Island Travel next to the pier in Ban Ko Jum. The island **medical centre** is on the road just south of *Golden Pearl* bungalows, beyond the southern edge of Ban Ting Rai. For a comprehensive **guide** to life on the island and pictures of all the bungalow operations, see ⓦ www.kohjumonline.com.

Long Beach and Ban Ko Jum

Long Beach (sometimes known as **Andaman Beach**), is the main backpackers' beach and was the first to offer tourist accommodation in the 1990s. It is indeed long – at least 1.5km – and large chunks of the shoreline are still uncultivated, backed with trees and wilderness, and well beyond sight of the island road. From *New Bungalow* at the southern end it's a 20-minute walk into Ban Ko Jum village.

There are two main clusters of **accommodation** on the beach. The southernmost place to stay is *New Bungalow* (ⓣ 075 618116; ❷–❹), which has 20 differently styled bungalows including a few cheapie bamboo ones with and without private bathrooms, a couple of treehouses with idyllic sea views and shared bathrooms, plus some plain, en-suite wooden huts. Next door, *Joy Bungalows* (ⓣ 075 618199, ⓦ www.kohjum.com/joy; ❷–❽) is the longest running and most popular spot on the island, though not necessarily the friendliest. It has a huge range of bungalows – around forty in all – set in a peaceful stand of trees behind the shorefront, from ultra-basic bamboo huts with shared bathrooms through smart wood and concrete bungalows to deluxe two-storey villas. Only a few of the bungalows have electricity, so most rely on paraffin lanterns. Staff rent out kayaks (B600/day) and mountain bikes (B200/day).

North up the beach about 750m (a 15-minute walk), UK-Thai run *Woodland Lodge* (ⓣ 081 893 5330, ⓦ www.woodland-koh-jum.tk; ❹–❻) is a welcoming, peaceful spot and one of the few places on the island to stay open year round. Its large, attractive bungalows are widely set beneath the trees of its shorefront garden and all have good bathrooms; the cheaper options have platform beds, varnished wooden floors and deep shady decks, while the pricier ones are more deluxe. Nearly all of them enjoy sea views between the trees. Next door to *Woodland*, the funky, ultra cheap and ultra basic *Bo Daeng* (ⓣ 081 494 8760; ❶–❷) is run by an effervescent family and appeals to long-stayers on a tiny budget. It offers bamboo huts with and without private bathrooms, plus some treehouses.

All the bungalows serve **food**: *Joy* does pizzas and fresh coffee, *Woodland* makes great curries, and *New* has newspapers to read while you wait for your meal. In **Ban Ko Jum**, there's cheap village food at *Mama*, and seafood at *Ban Ko Jum seafood* beside the pier at the far end of the village road. On the beach south of *New*, the tiny driftwood beach-shack **bar** *Coco Bar* is run by the island postman, who plays good music and serves drinks till late, as does *Freedom Bar*, south a bit further down the beach.

Golden Pearl Beach

At its northern end, Long Beach segues into **Golden Pearl Beach**, which is about 750m/15 minutes' walk north up the beach from *Bo Daeng*, 5km by road from Ban Ko Jum and 1km south of Ban Ting Rai. Like Long Beach, it also has only a few bungalow outfits along its curving shoreline, though these are close by the island road.

Golden Pearl Beach is the site of the poshest **accommodation** on the island, the French-run *Koh Jum Lodge* (ⓣ089 921 1621, ⓦwww.kohjumlodge.com; ❾, open all year), whose 15 thatched wooden rustic-chic chalets are both stylish and charming. Thoughtfully designed to make the most of the island breezes, they have doors onto the veranda to avoid the need for air-con, low beds and stylishly simple furniture. All the bungalows can sleep up to four kids as well as two adults. The resort has a small pool, Internet access, a TV and DVD area, a massage service and a restaurant. A few hundred metres further north up the beach, the 19 simple bamboo huts of eponymous *Golden Pearl Bungalows* (ⓣ075 618131, ❶–❹) are set within a coconut grove across the road from the shore; the cheapest shared bathrooms.

Ao Si

Around the rocky headland from Golden Pearl Beach, accessible in ten minutes at low tide or quite a bit further by road, **Ao Si** is good for swimming. In the middle of the beach is *Coconut Green View Cottage* (ⓣ084 088 8300; ❷) whose 20 simple en-suite bamboo huts are pleasingly shaded beneath a coconut grove. Ao Si's northern headland is occupied by *Ao Si Bungalows* (ⓣ081 747 2664; ⓔreena.aosi@hotmail.com; ❷–❹), whose nine woven-bamboo, en-suite bungalows are built on piles up the side of the cliff and from their wraparound verandahs offer commanding views of the bay and the southern half of the island.

Ban Ting Rai, Khao Ko Pu and Ao Ting Rai

The road begins to climb as soon as you leave Golden Pearl Beach, taking you up through the ribbon-like village of **Ban Ting Rai**, pretty with bougainvillea and wooden houses, and location of a few small restaurants and noodle shops, including the humorously named *Urban Café*. **Khao Ko Pu** which rises in the distance is, at 422m, the island's highest mountain and home to macaques who sometimes come down to forage on the rocks around the northern beaches; outside the rainy season, *OonLee* bungalows on Ao Ting Rai (see below) organizes treks up the eastern flank to the summit (about 1hr), from where the 360-degree panoramas encompass the entire island, the mainland and the outer islands (B500 including picnic lunch).

The little bay of **Ao Ting Rai**, sometimes known as **Hat Kidon**, has some nice places to stay, and good snorkelling off its shore, with reef to explore and plenty of fish. At low tide it's too rocky for swimming though, when you'll need instead to rent a kayak, or walk south 500m along the coastal track, to get to the isolated little sandy crescent known both as **Ao Thidiaw** and Magic Beach, which is swimmable at any tide. Ao Ting Rai is accessible via a **track** that runs off the main island road, a very pleasant half-hour walk (or 20 minutes from Ao Si) that mostly runs high above the shoreline, through forest and rubber plantations, offering pretty coastal views and long-range vistas that take in the distinctive outlines of Ko Phi Phi Leh, Ko Phi Phi Don and Bamboo Island.

The southernmost **accommodation** on Ao Ting Rai is at *Ting Rai Bay Resort* (ⓣ087 277 7379; ⓦwww.tingraibayresort.com; ❸–❹), where fourteen smallish bungalows are ranged up the sloping shorefront. Interiors are beautifully presented, with pretty floral bedspreads, four-poster style beds, and plenty of attention to detail. The food here is also good. Next door, *Old Lamp Bungalow* (ⓣ089 876 8572, ⓦwww.oldlampbungalows.com; ❸–❺; open all year) has a dozen surprisingly large and spacious bungalows made from coconut wood, secreted among the trees, and designed with thoughtful, practical touches; the pricier ones have nice garden bathrooms and all of them have big wooden beds. North again, the French-Thai-run *OonLee Bungalows* (Ⓣ087 200 8053, Ⓔ OonLee@hotmail.com; ❷–❹; phone ahead for a pick-up from your landing point; open all year) is a small, enthusiastically run place with seven bungalows in various styles, plus a four-bed family bungalow and a three-bedroom house with kitchen and living area (❽). The wooden bungalows are especially well designed with plenty of storage, appealing bathrooms and sea-view verandas. Bungalows are stacked up the cliffside here, so there are quite a lot of steps; there's a stylish upper-level lounge area and restaurant and a bar and massage area at beach level, plus free kayaks and snorkels for guests. *OonLee* offers lots of organized **activities** and tours, including guided treks up Khao Ko Pu (see p.805), fishing trips, day trips to Ko Lola, the islet that lies just off the southern end of Long Beach, round-island tours and trips to Ko Phi Phi.

Ao Luboa

Ko Jum's northernmost beach, **Ao Luboa**, is for the time being remote and peaceful, accessed chiefly by a loop in the main island road that circles the northeastern slopes of Khao Ko Pu and terminates at the north end of the bay, though at low tide you can also trudge here over the rocks from Ao Ting Rai in about half an hour (better to take a kayak). However, there are plans to extend the coastal road from Ao Ting Rai, which will make things easier. Like Ao Ting Rai, Ao Luboa's shorefront reef gets exposed at low tide, making it impossible to swim, though at high water things are fine and it's anyway a supremely quiet, laid-back beach with just has a few **bungalows**. The friendly *Luboa Hut* (Ⓣ081 388 9241, Ⓦwww.toensberg.com/luboahut; ❷–❸, family huts ❺) has just half a dozen simple en-suite bamboo bungalows with sea view, a couple of which can sleep four; the owners do kayak and motorbike rental and their restaurant has a reputation for good food. At the far northern end of the beach, *Bonhomie Beach Cottages* (Ⓣ081 844 9069, Ⓦwww.geocities.com/bonhomiebeach; ❷–❺) has attractively designed en-suite wooden chalets, many with sea view.

Ko Lanta Yai

Although **Ko Lanta Yai** can't compete with Phi Phi's stupendous scenery, the thickly forested 25-kilometre-long island is graced with plenty of fine sandy beaches and safe seas and offers an ever increasing number of places to stay. Encouragingly, development has been more considered and regulated here than on many other fast-growing island destinations (Ko Chang being a case in point), and local laws prohibiting jet-skis, beachfront parasols and girlie bars have had positive effect. Add to that a growing number of day-trip options offered by the island's ubiquitous tour agents and it's no surprise that many tourists are now basing themselves on Ko Lanta for their entire holiday fortnight.

The majority of Ko Lanta Yai's ten thousand indigenous residents are mixed-blood Muslim descendants of Chinese-Malay and *chao ley* peoples and most have traditionally supported themselves by fishing and cultivating the land, though the recent tourist boom has had a big impact on island job opportunities. The local *chao ley* name for the island is *Pulao Satak*, "Island of Long Beaches", an apt description of the string of silken **beaches** along the western coast, each separated by rocky points and strung out at quite wide intervals. All the bungalow outfits advertise snorkelling trips to the reefs off Ko Lanta's

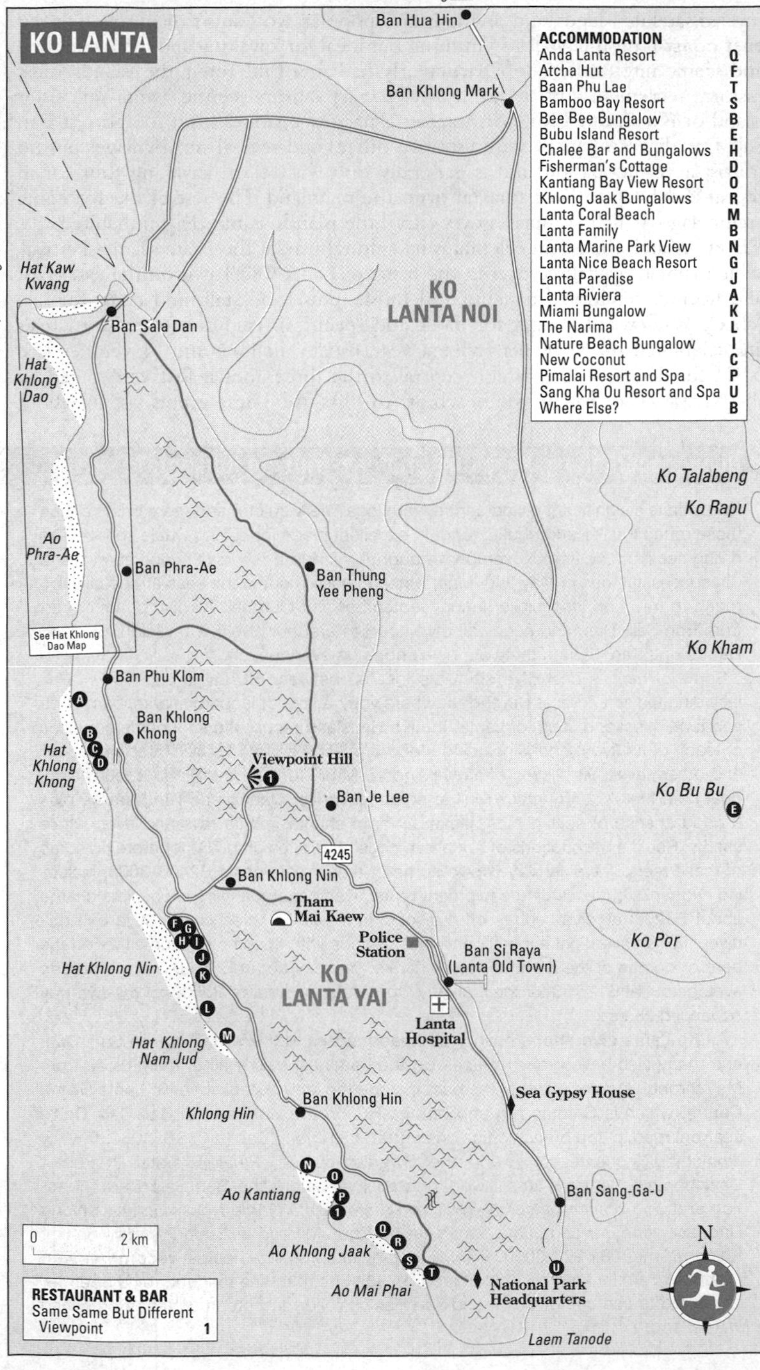

SOUTHERN THAILAND: THE ANDAMAN COAST | Ko Lanta Yai

myriad satellite islands, and diving is also popular. Ko Lanta's mangrove-fringed **east coast** is unsuitable for swimming but ideal for kayaking and there's cultural and scenic interest here too, particularly in Lanta Old Town, the island's most historic settlement and at the nearby *chao ley* cultural centre. Lanta Yai's sister island of **Ko Lanta Noi**, north across a narrow channel from the port at Ban Sala Dan, has Ko Lanta's administrative offices and several small villages but no tourist accommodation, and is generally only visited on kayaking tours or in transit if driving to Ko Lanta Yai from the mainland. The rest of the Ko Lanta archipelago, which comprises over fifty little islands, is mostly uninhabited.

Every March the island celebrates its cultural mix at the Laanta Lanta Festival, which is held over three days in the heart of Lanta Old Town on the east coast and features traditional dancing and music, plus food stalls and crafts for sale (check Ⓦwww.kolanta.net for dates and specifics). Traditional *chao ley* rituals are celebrated on Ko Lanta twice a year, usually in June and November (see p.821 for details). Music is also central to the three annual **festivals** staged by the *Reggae House* bar on the beach at Ao Phra-Ae. These events last for about

Diving, snorkelling, kayaking and day-trips on Ko Lanta

Ko Lanta is a significant diving centre, with local reefs quieter and more pristine than those round Phi Phi and Phuket, and an excellent place for seeing whale sharks. The diving season runs from November through April, and a few dive shops continue to run successful trips in May and June; outside these months the seas are usually too rough to travel on, especially during September and October. All dive boats depart from Ban Sala Dan, and nearly all dive courses are taught either in Sala Dan or on Hat Khlong Dao, though there are dive shops on every beach.

Some of Lanta's best **dive sites** are located between Ko Lanta and Ko Phi Phi, including the soft coral at **Hin Bidah**, where you get lots of leopard sharks, barracuda and tuna. West and south of Lanta, the **Ko Ha** island group offers four different dives on each of its five islands, including steep drop-offs and an "underwater cathedral" and other caves; visibility is often very good. Much further south, about four hours' boat ride, there's a fifty-metre wall at spectacular **Hin Daeng** and **Hin Muang**, plus a good chance of seeing tuna, jacks, silvertip sharks, manta rays and even whale sharks. See the descriptions of Andaman coast dive sites on p.750 for more on some of these reefs. A typical **day-trip** to some of these reefs costs B2400–3000, including two tanks but excluding equipment rental, with accompanying snorkellers charge about B1200; all dive centres offer discounts if you do three consecutive one-day dives. For an overnight expedition to local islands with accommodation either on the boat or on one of the islands, and six tanks, you pay about B7500. Diving **courses** average out at B12,750 for the four-day Openwater course, or B9500 for the two-day Advanced course.

All Ko Lanta **dive shops** have their headquarters in the village of Ban Sala Dan, and many also have branch offices on the beaches; nearly all of them close from May through October. Two of the best include the long-established Ko Lanta Diving Centre, which is German-run and has its HQ on the west arm of Ban Sala Dan's seafront road, plus a branch office on central Hat Khlong Dao (Ⓣ075 684065, Ⓦwww.kohlantadivingcenter.com); and the Swedish-owned, PADI Five-star Instructor Development Centre, Lanta Diver, located just before the Ban Sala Dan T-junction and with branch offices at *Twin Lotus* and *Lanta Noble House* on Hat Khlong Dao, at *Ozone Bar* and *Lanta Sands* on Ao Phra-Ae, and at *Lanta Paradise* on Hat Khlong Nin (Ⓣ081 271 9050, Ⓦwww.lantadiver.com). The nearest **recompression chambers** are located on Phuket (see p.750); check to see that your dive operator is insured to use one of them, and see Basics p.70 for more information on diving in Thailand.

three days each and are as laid-back, alternative and organic as the bar that sponsors them (for more on which, see p.816). Their season of events begins in December with a World Music festival featuring musicians from all over; in early February there's more music of a similar bent at the Ko Lanta Peace and Love Festival; and in early March the highlight of the Country Music Festival is performances by *chao ley* musicians. For dates and details, you'll need to ask at *Reggae House*.

Transport to Ko Lanta Yai

The principal mainland gateways to Ko Lanta are Krabi, Phuket and Trang, all of which have airports; Trang also has a train station (see relevant accounts for travel information). From mid-October to mid-May there are **ferries** to Ban Sala Dan on the northern tip of Ko Lanta Yai from **Krabi** (2 daily; 2hr 30min; B300; return from Ko Lanta Yai at 8am & 1pm), via Ko Jum (B250, about 45min). From November to May ferries also run to Sala Dan from **Ko Phi Phi**

Snorkelling, kayaking and other day-trips

The best and most popular snorkelling outing is to the islands of **Ko Rok Nai** and **Ko Rok Nok**, forested twins that are graced with stunning white-sand beaches and accessible waterfalls and separated by a narrow channel full of fabulous shallow reefs. The islands are 47km south of Ko Lanta and served by speedboats (1hr; B1400) that can be booked through most tour agents, or direct with Lanta Garden Hill Speed Boat (Ⓣ075 684042, Ⓦwww.lantaislandtours.com). The other very popular day-trip is to four islands off the Trang coast (see p.835 for island descriptions): the enclosed emerald lagoon on the island of **Ko Mook** (aka Ko Muk), nearby **Ko Hai** (Ko Ngai), **Ko Cheuak** (Ko Chuk) and **Ko Kradan**. Though the islands are beautiful, and the coral passable, these trips are large-scale outings in boats that can hold around a hundred passengers, so the sites get very crowded: tickets cost about B850 per person, including snorkelling gear, lunch and national park entry fee. You may find it more rewarding to organize a private long-tail-boat tour to the better reefs off the **Ko Ha** island group, described under "diving", above (about two hours' boat ride southwest of Lanta), with snorkelling or fishing as requested: enthusiastic angler Jack, of Ko Lanta Tour at *Lanta Villa* on Hat Khlong Dao (Ⓣ081 538 4099, Ⓔlantajack2000@yahoo.com), charges B4000 per boat carrying up to four people, or he also arranges speedboat trips there which cost B10,000 for up to eight people. Another option is a day-trip by speedboat to Phi Phi Don, Phi Phi Leh and Bamboo Island, for snorkelling, sunbathing and shopping (B1400, kids B700).

There are several rewarding **kayaking** destinations, rich in mangroves and caves, around Ko Lanta Yai's east coast and around Ko Lanta Noi and its eastern islands, including **Ko Talabeng** and **Ko Bubu**; a few companies also offer kayak-snorkel trips to the four islands described above. Trips can be arranged through tour operators in Ban Sala Dan, and on most beaches, for B750–1200 per person (kids B550–600): Seaborn Ventures (Ⓣ075 684696) is considered one of the best operators.

Day-trips inland

Ko Lanta's biggest inland attraction is the **Tham Mai Kaew caves**, described on p.819. Though it's not much more than a trickle, the **waterfall** inland from Ao Khlong Jaak is another fairly popular spot, and can be reached from the bay by walking along the course of the stream for about two hours. Alternatively join one of the tours that combine visits to the caves and the waterfall in a half-day trip for about B500, or B950 with an **elephant-ride** thrown in. Mr Yat's Lanta On Beach Travel and Tour on Ao Phra-Ae (Ⓣ089 021 1924) does **horse-riding lesso**ns on the beach for B650/hr.

(2 daily; 1hr 30min; B300; return from Ko Lanta Yai at 8am & 1pm), with journeys from **Phuket** also using this service and connecting on Phi Phi (2 daily; 4hr 30min; B650–700; return from Ko Lanta Yai at 8 & 1pm). Boats from **Ao Nang** also operate from November to May (1 daily; 2hr 30min; B380; return from Ko Lanta Yai at 1.30pm) and run via West Railay on **Laem Phra Nang** (2hr; B380). Bungalow touts always meet the boats at Ban Sala Dan and transport you to the beach of your choice. There is also an **overland route**, which is used year-round by minivans from **Trang** (4 daily; 3hr; return vans depart Ban Sala Dan at 8am and noon; B250), minivans from **Krabi town** (hourly; 2hr; B200; these vans should drop you at your requested accommodation anywhere between Ban Sala Dan and the Klong Nin junction en route to the terminus in Lanta Old Town) and by anyone bringing their own vehicle. It's also the only route open during the **rainy season**. Overland access is via Ban Hua Hin on the mainland, 75km east of Krabi, from where a small ferry crosses to Ban Khlong Mark on Ko Lanta Noi, after which there's a seven-kilometre drive across to Lanta Noi's southwest tip, then another ferry over the narrow channel to Ban Sala Dan on Ko Lanta Yai; both ferries run approximately every twenty minutes from about 7am to 10pm and cost B50 per car per leg. Most Ko Lanta travel agents can fix you up with an onward bus or air ticket **to Bangkok** or elsewhere and some can also organize train tickets, though this will take several days and cost quite a bit extra. Several also offer **visa-run** day-trips to Satun for about B1000.

Island practicalities

A decent road runs almost the entire length of Ko Lanta Yai's west coast, as far as the *Pimalai Resort* on Ao Kantiang, beyond which it degenerates into a potholed track. There's no public **transport** on the island, so many people hire a motorbike, available in Ban Sala Dan and from most accommodation (about B40/hour, B250/day; B500/day for a big trailbike); a few Ban Sala Dan agents also rent jeeps (B1200/day). An organized **motorbike taxi** plus sidecar service operates out of Ban Sala Dan, from a stand opposite the 7–11: its per-passenger rates are B30 to Hat Khlong Dao, B40–50 to Ao Phra-Ae, B70 to Hat Khlong Kong, or B120 for a trip to Hat Khlong Nin and B250 to Ao Kantiang. Most bungalows charge similar rates. If you're staying on Hat Khlong Dao it's an easy half-hour walk to the village.

Most bungalows will **change money**, though you'll get the best rates at the bank in Ban Sala Dan, where there are also a couple of **ATMs**; there are also ATMs beside the road at most of the beaches. Many bungalows offer international telephone services for guests, and there are **Internet** centres in Ban Sala Dan, and on Hat Khlong Dao and Ao Phra-Ae (B2/min). The post office is in Lanta Old Town. Nearly every beach has a **clinic** in among its roadside development, there's a health centre in Ban Sala Dan (variable hours, often Mon–Fri 4.30–8.30pm, and Sat & Sun 8.30am–4.30pm) and the island hospital is in Lanta Old Town (Ⓣ075 697017), though for anything serious you'll need to go to Phuket. The **police** station is also in Lanta Old Town (Ⓣ075 697085), though there's a police box in Sala Dan (Ⓣ075 684657). *Time for Lime* bungalows on Hat Khlong Dao runs a **cookery school**, described on p.813.

Ko Lanta Yai is extremely popular during **high season** (Nov–Feb), when it's well worth either booking your first night's accommodation in advance or taking up the suggestions of the bungalow touts who ride the boats from the mainland. **Accommodation pricing** on Ko Lanta is extremely flexible and alters according to the number of tourists on the island: bungalow rates can triple between mid-December and mid-January, while during the **rainy season** between May and October rates are vastly discounted and the seas become too rough for boats to get here from Krabi (some places close for this period and these are highlighted in the reviews). The price range shown in our Ko Lanta accommodation listings are for the beginning and end of high season (generally Nov to early Dec & late-Jan to April).

Ban Sala Dan

During high season, direct boats from Krabi and Phi Phi arrive at the fishing port and village of **BAN SALA DAN**, located on the northernmost tip of Ko Lanta Yai. It's essentially a T-junction village, with about fifty shops and businesses, including banks with currency **exchange** and ATMs, minimarkets that sell all the essentials, and half a dozen tour operators offering day-trips (see box on p.808 for a guide to destinations), as well as boat, bus, train and air tickets, and bike and jeep rental. A shop near *Seaside* restaurant has a couple of bicycles for rent.

While you're in the village, it's well worth stopping for a breezy meal at one of the **restaurants** whose dining area juts out on a shaded jetty right over the water, giving enjoyable views of the fishing boats and Ko Lanta Noi. *Ko Lanta Seafood* on the left-hand arm of the T is the oldest restaurant in town and the most highly rated – its seafood is great, worth braving the service which is lackadaisical at best. Also near here are wood-fired pizzas at *Ko Lanta Pizzeria*, next to the police box. Along the right-hand arm of the T, both *Seaside* and the nearby *Sea View* have good, very inexpensive menus offering authentic Thai dishes from chicken with cashew nuts to fish fried with chilli or garlic. Also here are the similar *Catfish*, which sells art cards and second-hand books categorized by genre, as well as food; *Green Bay*, which sells bagels, pastries and the like; and *Bai Fern*, which does noodles.

Hat Khlong Dao

Lanta Yai's longest and most popular beach is **HAT KHLONG DAO**, the northernmost of the west-coast beaches, about half an hour's walk from Ban Sala Dan, or 2–3km by road. The sand here is soft and golden, the sunsets can be magnificent, and the whole is framed by a dramatic hilly backdrop. Despite being developed to capacity, the beach is long and broad enough never to feel overcrowded and as it's flat and safe for swimming it's very popular with families. The northern curve of Hat Khlong Dao juts out into a rocky promontory known as **Laem Kaw Kwang** (Deer Neck Cape), whose north-facing shore, **Hat Kaw Kwang**, is mainly characterized by mud flats and mangroves and is home to a *chao ley* settlement.

There are a few small minimarts and tour agencies on the beach and dive shops at several of the bungalows. Ko Lanta Tour at *Lanta Villa* does recommended fishing trips as well as other boat tours (see box on p.808). You can rent motorbikes at several places along the road, including at the bike showroom on the road behind *Andaman Lanta Resort*; they also have a couple of bicycles for rent (B100/day).

Accommodation

Accommodation on Khlong Dao (see map on p.813) is predominantly mid-market, with just a couple of options in the ❷–❹ brackets and a few notable top-end places; none is more than 100m from the sea.

Cha-Ba Bungalows ⓣ075 684118, ⓦwww.krabidir.com/chababungalows/index.htm. Just fifteen cute, brightly painted fan and air-con bungalows in a compound that's enlivened by creatively kitsch concrete sculptures and bright blue Flintstone walls and archways. Interiors are pretty simple and flimsy but all are en suite and each bungalow has its own little shrub-garden screen out front. Fan ❺, air-con ❻

Costa Lanta ⓣ075 684630, ⓦwww.costalanta.com. You're either going to love or hate this ultra-brutal minimalist grouping of 22 polished-grey concrete boxes, each module containing an unadorned bedroom all in grey and white and a similarly-styled bathroom. The setting is less than magnificent – a dry, plain garden bisected by greenish khlongs – but there's a biggish pool, a striking bar-restaurant and DVD players in every room. ❾

Hans ⓣ075 684152, ⓦwww.krabidir.com/hansrestaurant. Small, inexpensive outfit that's the cheapest on this beach, where the thirteen huts are ranged in a little strip garden behind the shorefront restaurant. Choose between simple, rickety bamboo bungalows with mosquito nets, and better-furnished wooden versions with screened windows. Closed from early April to October. ❷–❹

Kaw Kwang Beach Resort At the northernmost end of Khlong Dao on the deer neck itself ⓣ075 684462, ⓦwww.kawkwangbeachresort.com. Welcoming, family-run outfit of 55 rooms occupying a beachfront garden in a nice secluded position beneath the still-wooded nose of the headland, on land between the deer neck's two shores. There's a big range of options here, from decent en-suite wood and concrete huts among the trees above the shore, through bigger, more comfortable air-con bungalows on the shorefront, plus some deluxe air-con ones with uninterrupted sea views. Also has family bungalows and a pool. Open all year with fifty percent discounts from June to Oct. Fan ❷–❹, air-con ❻–❽

Laguna Beach Club ⓣ075 684172, ⓦwww.laguna-beach-club.com. European-managed place that has half a dozen different types of accommodation, all of it thoughtfully designed and tastefully kitted out with northern Thai furniture. The cheapest options are fan-cooled bungalows, the priciest are air-con rooms in a three-storey block, where there's even a two-roomed penthouse suite. Also has a swimming pool and dive centre. Closed June–Sept. Fan ❻, air-con ❼, penthouse ❾

Lanta Noble House ⓣ075 684096, ⓦwww.lantanoblehouse.com. Quite small, Swiss-run place where the 23 inviting fan and air-con bungalows have big glass windows and bathtubs. They're set in facing rows, mostly around the little swimming pool. Also has a dive centre. Fan ❻, air-con ❼

Lanta Villa ⓣ075 684129, ⓦwww.lantavillaresort.com. A big collection of comfortably furnished, decent-sized wooden bungalows, set in a garden running back from the shore, many with air-con and TV, and some with sea view. Also has a swimming pool, Internet access and a good restaurant. ❻–❽

Southern Lanta Resort ⓣ075 684175, ⓦwww.southernlanta.com. One of the biggest hotels on the beach, offering dozens of very spacious air-con bungalows set at decent intervals around a garden of shrubs, clipped hedges and shady trees. There's a good-sized swimming pool too. Good value considering the competition, and popular with families and package tourists. ❼

Time for Lime ⓣ075 684590, ⓦwww.timeforlime.net. Just eight peacefully located, understated, fan-cooled, en-suite bungalows attached to a cooking school at the rocky, far southern end of the beach. The style is plain but comfortable, there are hammocks on every veranda and a pretty, narrow garden to gaze at, though there are no views. Closed mid-June–early Nov. ❹–❺

Twin Lotus Resort and Spa ⓣ075 60700 ⓦwww.twinlotusresort.com. An upscale collection of 78 chic, single-storey bungalows set quite closely together around a grassy garden between the shore and the road. Though the restaurant design is strikingly contemporary, it's all softer than its uncompromising neighbour *Costa Lanta* and there's a tempting pool (which is sometimes open to non-guests who eat at the restaurant), spa and fitness centre. ❾

Eating and drinking

All the bungalows have **restaurants** serving tourist fare and standard Thai dishes, and at night they're lit up with fairy lights and low lanterns, which lends a nice mellow atmosphere to the evenings. Many offer fresh seafood barbecues at night: those at *Lanta Villa* are popular and good. *Hans* is known for its German-style fillet steaks, creamy coconut curries and barbecued meats, while *Banana Beach* also serves good curries, as well as cocktails and ice creams. Further south, *Don's Restaurant and Bar* does a tasty line in steaks and pizzas, as well as Thai soups, and plays an eclectic mix of tunes, from funk to house. The Norwegian-run *Time* *for Lime* serves breakfasts and imaginative lunchtime sandwiches, and plans to open for night-time meals, with changing menus nightly, but is mainly known for its highly rated **cookery school** (ⓣ075 684590, ⓦwww.timeforlime.net), whose workshops take place in the modern open-plan kitchen behind the bar (Tues–Sun afternoons and evenings; from B1400 including meal).

Clusters of little beach **bars** dot the shoreline. In the centre of the beach, behind *Cha-Ba Bungalows*, there's *Picasso Bar and Easy Bar*, while further south, near *Lanta Garden Home*, you'll find the pleasingly chilled-out *Bomp Bar*, with cushions, deckchairs and low tables spread out on the sand, a campfire, and decent music. Several hundred metres further south, beyond *Don's*, *Time for Lime* stirs a mean mojito at its chic beach-front bar.

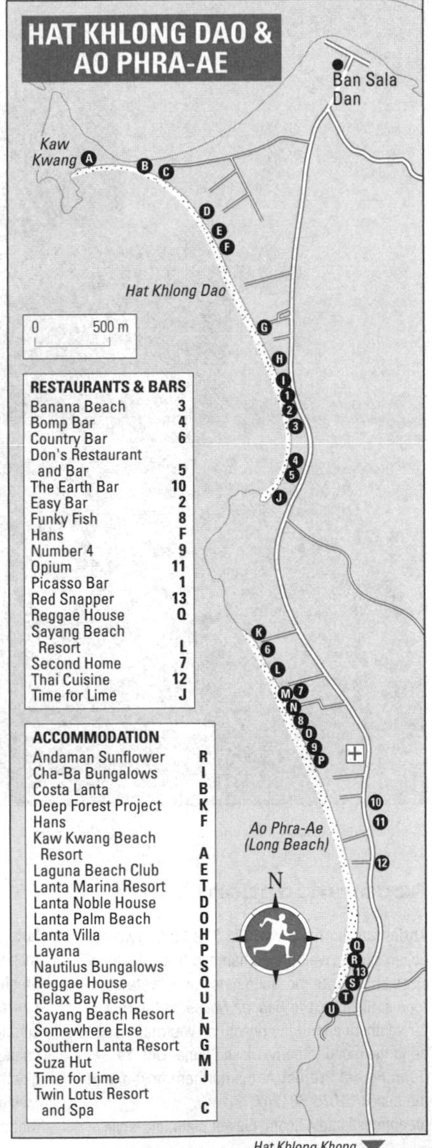

Ao Phra-Ae (Long Beach)

A couple of kilometres south of Khlong Dao, **AO PHRA-AE** (also known as **Long Beach**) boasts a beautiful long strip of soft white sand, with calm, crystal-clear water that's good for swimming, some shady casuarinas, and some clusters of little bars, in particular the famous *Reggae House*, which holds regular parties with live music and also stages three big music festivals a year. Traveller-oriented bamboo huts are available, but the trend is upmarket, with a growing number of quite swanky hotels occupying the central beach. The main stretch of the beach is divided from the southern rocky extremity by a shallow, easily wadeable khlong; *Lanta Marina Resort* marks the far southern end of the beach. All bungalows on Ao Phra-Ae rent out **motorbikes** for around B250 a day and organize boat trips for snorkelling and fishing. There's a roadside clinic and ATM near *Red Snapper* restaurant.

△ Ao Phra-Ae

Accommodation

Andaman Sunflower ⑦085 222 1027. Two-dozen simple, well-priced bamboo huts of varying sizes but all with mosquito nets and private bathrooms. Right next to *Reggae House*, at the rocky, far southern end of the beach, so you may need to be in the mood to party. Closed June–Oct. ❷

Deep Forest Project At the northernmost end of the beach ⑦075 684247, ⓦwww.deepforestlanta.4T.com. Eleven plain, old-style huts, sold at old-style prices, and all equipped with mosquito net, fan and en-suite bathroom but not much else. Closed during low season. ❷

Lanta Marina Resort ⑦075 684168. At the far southern end of Ao Phra-Ae, inland from a rocky point, this friendly little place has just 13 shaggily thatched wood-and-split-bamboo bungalows facing the sea, connected by a wooden walkway that circles a little patch of wilderness. Huts vary in size but all have nice beds, and many have well-designed bathrooms. ❷–❸

Lanta Palm Beach ⓣ075 684406, ⓦwww.lantapalmbeachresort.com. A busy and popular spot that has a range of different bungalows, plus Internet access, and is within stumbling distance of several beach bars. Cheapest are the bamboo huts with bathrooms, good beds and mosquito nets – they're set on the edge of a dry shorefront lawn in the scant remains of a coconut grove and enjoy a full view of the sea. The pricier concrete bungalows sit back from the shore, within a garden of neat clipped hedges, and come with fan or air-con. Bamboo ❸, concrete ❺, air-con ❻

Layana ⓣ075 607100, ⓦwww.layanaresort.com. Located plumb in the middle of the beach, this is currently the top spot on Ao Phra-Ae. Its fifty posh air-con rooms occupy chunky, two-storey villas designed in modern-Thai style and are set around a tidy beachfront garden of lawns and shrubs; the priciest have sea views. There's a gorgeous shorefront salt-water infinity pool and a spa. Published rates from B9000. ❾

Nautilus Bungalows ⓣ084 994 9848, ⓔnautiluslanta@hotmail.com. A cute spot at the far southern, rocky, end of the bay, where the dozen attractive wooden chalets all have big glass windows, thick mattresses and open-roofed bathrooms and come with either air-con or fan. Also has a small spa and massage service. Fan ❹, air-con ❺

Reggae House One of Lanta's funkiest institutions, the *Reggae House* live music bar and jamming centre (see p.816) attracts laid-back musos and chilled travellers to its half a dozen primitive, almost circular, en-suite brick huts. Interiors are bare bones, but it's one of the cheapest spots on the island. ❶

Relax Bay Resort ⓣ075 684194, ⓦwww.relaxbay.com. Set in its own tiny bay south around the next rocky point (and quite a hike) from *Lanta Marina*, the style of this French-managed place is affordable rustic chic. The nicest accommodation is in tastefully simple bamboo and wood bungalows, all of which have large sea-view decks, fans and open-air bathrooms. Also has a few less-interesting concrete air-con bungalows. ❺–❽

Sayang Beach Resort ⓣ075 684156, ⓔsayangbeach@hotmail.com. Very welcoming, family-run mid-range boutique-style operation occupying expansive shorefront grounds with bungalows nicely spaced among the palm trees. All 30 bungalows are stylishly decorated with batik furnishings, Thai-chic accessories, and a tasteful wood and bamboo finish. Price depends on location and size, and whether or not you want air-con. Also has some family bungalows and a beachfront suite. Prices include large breakfasts. Fan ❻, air-con ❽

Somewhere Else ⓣ081 536 0858. Located in the heart of the liveliest part of Ao Phra-Ae, with beach bars left, right and seaward, this little outfit has just sixteen spacious, unusually designed hexagonal bungalows made of tightly woven bamboo and with pretty bathrooms. Price depends on the size. The drawback is that most are close together and lack a sense of privacy, though many have sea views. Run by the same family as *Where Else?* bungalows on Hat Khlong Khong. ❷–❺

Suza Hut ⓣ081 577 2210, ⓔsuzahutlanta@gmail.com. Some of the cheapest accommodation on the beach, in a handful of rudimentary bamboo huts furnished with nothing more than a mattress and a mosquito net, though some have their owns bathrooms. Closed during low season. ❷–❹

Eating and drinking

Ao Phra-Ae's best **restaurants** are along the road, and this is also where you'll find some of the bigger, high-profile **bars**, favourite haunts of expats. Down on the beach you get small, mellow drinking spots.

Country Bar On the beach in front of *Sayang Beach* bungalows. Mellow little bar at the far northern end of the beach, with Thai-style cushion seating, and chairs, set around a bar hung with fairy lights. Nightly from about 6pm.

The Earth Bar On the road, inland from inland from *Layana Resort*. Sophisticated, open-sided bar and club with ambient lighting, lounging mats and cushions, and a long list of DJs and regular parties. Very popular with expats and dive-shop staff. Nightly from 6pm.

Funky Fish On the beach, next to *Somewhere Else* bungalows. One of the most famous bars on the beach: renowned for pizzas, cocktails and a quality sound system. You can get massages here too.

Number 4 On the beach just south of *Lanta Palm* bungalows. Small, laid-back spot that serves food and drink, best enjoyed from the cushions scattered around the roof terrace.

Opium On the road, inland from *Layana*. Next door to *Earth Bar* and run along similar lines, this long-established bar and club plays lots of dance music, holds regular special events and is a popular meeting place for island expats. It has a good-sized dance floor – and a long bar overlooking it for watching the moves – plus an outdoor pool table and garden seating. Nightly from 6pm.

Red Snapper On the road, inland from *Andaman Sunflower* bungalows at the southern end of Phra-Ae. Tapas and creative European cuisine are the hallmarks of this highly rated Dutch-run restaurant and bar, where the mid-priced menu changes every couple of months. Nightly from 6pm.

Reggae House On the shorefront, next to *Andaman Sunflower* bungalows. An island institution, this place is the brainchild of Thai selecta DJ Pirate, whose wacky imagination is behind the grown-up treehouse of a bar-building, cobbled together from driftwood and timber and continually evolving. It stages parties around twice a week and frequent live music events, including three big music festivals every year (see p.808) featuring local famous musicians such as southern Thai reggae band Job to Do, as well as *chao ley* musicians. On quieter nights DJs play mainly reggae and dub. Closed every September. Nightly from about 6pm.

Sayang Beach Resort On the beach, at *Sayang Beach Resort*. This is a lovely spot for dinner, with tables set out under shoreside casuarinas strung with fairylights. The kitchen here has a tandoori oven and serves a long, mid-priced menu of authentic Indian dishes, including sheesh and dhal, as well as Thai and western food, plus fresh seafood nightly (seafood hotplate B160) and a big veggie menu.

Second Home On the beach, next to *Suza Hut*. A good choice for fresh fish – barbecued or fried; the fried red snapper with three styles of Thai sauce is especially tasty (from B100).

Thai Cuisine On the road, inland from inland from *Layana*, towards the southern end of Phra-Ae. Very popular, outdoor place that serves some of the most authentic Thai food on the island (B60–150), from thick *matsaman* curries to fiery *kway tiaw phat kii maew* (drunkard's fried noodles, so called because the liberal use of chilli is meant to sober you up). Also has plenty of seafood plus some more unusual choices including a surprisingly delicious rice fried with banana. Nightly from 6pm.

Hat Khlong Khong

The lovely long beach at **HAT KHLONG KHONG**, 2km south of Ao Phra-Ae's *Relax Bay Resort*, is peppered with rocks and only really swimmable at high tide, though the snorkelling is good. The shore is lined with predominantly traveller-oriented bungalows, including some of the most creatively designed and characterful spots on the island. Many of them are reasonably priced, and there are quite a number of funky little beach-bars too, including the laid-back *Feeling Bar* at *Where Else?* bungalows, which is decorated with driftwood sculptures and has a pool table, the more sophisticated Bangkok-by-the-beach *FMCK Beach Club* bar at *Fisherman's Cottage*, with leather-look sofas and occasional DJ parties, and the beachfront *Monkey Bar at New Coconut* bungalows.

Accommodation

Bee Bee Bungalow Ⓣ081 537 9932, Ⓔbeebeepiya02@hotmail.com. A great spot that stands out from other places on the beach because of its eleven highly individual huts, each of which is a charmingly idiosyncratic experiment in bamboo architecture. All the bungalows are comfortably furnished and have fans, mosquito nets and open-air bathrooms; some have an upstairs room as well. Closed mid-May–early Oct. ❷–❹

Fisherman's Cottage Ⓣ081 476 1529, Ⓦwww.fishermanscottage.biz. This quiet, low-key place at the southern end of the beach has just ten bungalows, each with big glass windows, idiosyncratic if mostly quite spartan furnishings, mosquito nets and decent bathrooms. Closed July–Oct. ❷–❺

Lanta Family Ⓣ075 648310, Ⓔdumsupaporn@yahoo.com.sg. Commercially minded place whose seventeen en-suite fan-cooled bungalows are ranged in rows under the palm trees. The cheapest options are split-bamboo huts at the back of the compound; larger, pricier bamboo and brick versions sit nearer the sea. ❷–❹

Lanta Riviera Ⓣ075 684 300 Ⓦwww.lantariviera.com. There are rows and rows of good, standard-issue, comfortably furnished fan and air-con concrete bungalows here, set in a among shady beds of shrubs and flowers at the far northern end of the beach. Many of the rooms sleep three so it's popular with families. Also has a small pool near the shore. Fan ❺, air-con ❼

New Coconut ⓣ081 537 7590, ⓔlantamaster@hotmail.com. Twenty simple, en-suite, split-bamboo fan-cooled bungalows in a garden. ❷

Where Else? ⓣ081 536 4870, ⓔwhereelse_lanta@yahoo.com. As you might expect from the name, this charming collection of 22 bungalows has a relaxed, laid-back atmosphere and lots of personality. The individually designed bamboo and coconut-wood bungalows all have fans, mosquito nets and open-air bathrooms filled with plants, and there are shell mobiles, driftwood sculptures and pot plants all over the place. The pricier bungalows are larger and nearer the sea, and some even have sunroofs and turrets. The restaurant is also a work of art, hung with banners, shells, textile art and more. ❹–❺

South to Hat Khlong Nin

About four kilometres south of Hat Khlong Khong the road forks at kilometre-stone 13, at the edge of the village of **Ban Khlong Nin**. The left-hand, east-bound arm runs across to Ko Lanta Yai's east coast, via the caves and viewpoint, and is covered on p.819. The right-hand fork is the route to the southern beaches and continues southwards along the west coast for 14km to the southern tip.

Just beyond the junction, the little enclave of bungalows, restaurants, bars – and strangely plentiful tattoo shops – at **HAT KHLONG NIN** lend this beach more of a village atmosphere than the northern beaches. The (quiet) west-coast road runs close alongside the shore and is still lined with trees and greenery, while the beach itself is lovely: long and sandy and good for swimming. The burgeoning if fairly low-key nightlife revolves around a dozen little beach bars and there are quite a few places to stay here – rather tightly packed at the centre of the beach, more spaced at the northerly end; some places have bungalows both on the shore and across the road. The large, beach-view **restaurant** *Otto Bar and Grill*, serves seafood and Thai and European dishes and *Cook Kai* restaurant, across from *Chalee Bar* bungalows, teaches Thai cooking.

Nearly all the bungalows rent **motorbikes** for B250 per day and many also offer email and international phone services; there's a **minimarket**, **ATM** and **clinic** at the Ban Khlong Nin junction. Taxis to Sala Dan should cost about B50 per person and you can walk the 3km to the Tham Mai Kaew caves from Khlong Nin in about an hour.

Accommodation

Atcha Hut ⓣ09 470 4607, ⓦwww.atchahut.com, ⓔjuneto14@hotmail.com. A truly individual, alternative spot at the northern end of the beach, where a couple of adobe caravanserai-style dormitory buildings have B150 beds, each in their own little concrete, open-sided cubbyhole, screened by a curtain. Also has about eight dinky, en-suite wooden bungalows and serves communal lunch and dinner on its rainbow-painted decks set under the screw palms beside the shore. ❸–❹

Chalee Bar and Bungalows ⓣ081 535 5507. Cute, homely place of just half a dozen simple, rickety but en-suite fan-cooled bamboo bungalows, all with decks and shell mobiles and set in a pretty little garden behind the shorefront bar, which hosts regular live-music parties. ❷

Lanta Nice Beach Resort ⓣ075 697276, ⓦwww.krabidir.com/lantanicebeach. Located on a broad swathe of sand, this place comprises several rows of spacious concrete bungalows, many with sea views and some with air-con, plus a neat arrangement of cheaper bamboo bungalows in a garden across the road from the beach. Air-con ❺–❼

Lanta Paradise ⓣ089 473 3279, ⓦwww.lantaparadiseresort.com. Long-running beachfront accommodation where you can choose between old, pretty cheap, wooden fan huts and big, concrete air-con bungalows nearer the sea. Though the concrete bungalows are packed uncomfortably close together, they feel spacious inside. There's a pool here too. Fan ❷–❹, air-con ❻–❼

Miami Bungalow ⓣ075 697081, ⓦwww.lantamiami.com. Options here range from simple wooden huts with fans to larger concrete versions, some with air-con and sea view. ❺–❼

Nature Beach Bungalow ⓣ081 397 0785, ⓦwww.krabidir.com/lantanaturebeach/index.htm. Has large, high-standard concrete villas with air-con or fan, both on the beachfront and in a garden across the road. Fan ❹–❺, air-con ❻–❼

Hat Khlong Nam Jud

Just over 1km south of Hat Khlong Nin, the road passes the two tiny little bays known as **HAT KHLONG NAM JUD**. The northerly one is the domain of *The Narima* (ⓣ075 607700, ⓦwww.narima-lanta.com; ❼–❽), a very quiet but welcoming, elegantly designed resort of 32 posh but unadorned thatch-roofed bamboo bungalows set in three rows in a palm-filled garden. The bungalows all have polished wood floors, verandas with sea view, and fans as well as air-con (but no TV); there's also a three-tiered pool (with kids' level), a spa and a dive centre, and staff rent out jeeps.

Around the headland to the south, the next tiny cove is rocky in parts but enjoys a swimmable beach and one set of bungalows, *Lanta Coral Beach* (ⓣ075 618073; ❸–❻; closed May–Oct). The twenty good-sized bamboo and concrete huts here are scattered among the palms (some of which are hung with hammocks) and come with fan or air-con; you can rent kayaks here too.

Ao Kantiang

The secluded cove of **AO KANTIANG**, some 7km beyond Hat Khlong Nam Jud, is an impressively curved sweep of long, sandy bay backed by jungle-clad hillsides and fronted by just a few bungalows and one large hotel. The beach is good for swimming, there's some coral at the northern end, and snorkelling and fishing trips are easily arranged. Because it's quite protected it's generally also fine for swimming in the rainy season. The roadside village covers most necessities, including tours, onward transport, motorbike rental and Internet access. There's also a clinic a little further south, between *Kantiang Bay View* and *Pimalai*. Wherever you're staying on Ao Kantiang, it's well worth heading down to *Same Same But Different*, a lovely tranquil haven of a **restaurant** on the beach to the south of *Pimalai*, where the tables are set beneath a tangled growth of shrubs and vines, surrounded by shell-mobiles and driftwood sculptures; it's run by the man behind the renowned *Ruen Mai* restaurant in Krabi, and the mid-priced menu of mainly Thai and seafood dishes is of a similarly high standard.

The thirty or so **bungalows** at *Lanta Marine Park View* (ⓣ081 956 2935, ⓦwww.lantamarine.com; fan ❸, air-con ❼) are ranged up the slope at the northern end of the beach: steps lead down to the shore. The best of the bungalows, though pricey, are great value as they're on stilts and enjoy glorious bay views from their balconies and glass-fronted interiors, and the furnishings are chic and modern. The cheap fan-cooled bamboo bungalows sit further back and are plain and not very interesting for the price. There's also a small cliffside bar affording great views, plus Internet access and a tour agency. Down at sea level, in the middle of the bay, *Kantiang Bay View Resort* (ⓣ081 787 5192; fan ❷–❺, air-con ❺–❼) also offers lots of different accommodation options, in 26 rooms, including plenty of good, cheap bamboo huts, concrete huts (fan and air-con) and rooms in a small block. Weather permitting, they are also one of the few places to run four-island tours throughout the year. The southern end of Ao Kantiang is the province of Ko Lanta's poshest hotel, the *Pimalai Resort and Spa* (ⓣ075 607999, ⓦwww.pimalai.com; ❾; published rates from B8950), which spreads over such an extensive area that guests are shuttled around in golf buggies. All rooms are luxuriously and elegantly designed in contemporary style, and there's a delightful spa, a swimming pool and dive centre. However, only the more expensive accommodation gets a sea view (the walled beach villas are particularly stunning but cost B18,500). From November to April, guests are transferred direct to the resort by boat, landing at the *Pimalai*'s private floating jetty.

Ao Khlong Jaak and Ao Mai Phai

The paved road terminates at the *Pimalai* boundary at the southern end of Ao Kantiang, so from here to Lanta's southern tip, about 4km away, access is via a steeply undulating, rutted and potholed track that's either dusty or muddy depending on the season – take care on a motorbike as it's extremely challenging. The next bay south of Ao Kantiang is **AO KHLONG JAAK**, site of the upscale and pretty pricey *Anda Lanta Resort* (Ⓣ075 607555, Ⓦwww.andalanta.com; ❼–❽), where you have the option of rather cramped bamboo huts, attractive cliffside wooden huts that enjoy fine views, deluxe, quite chic, shorefront concrete bungalows in various sizes and permutations, or rooms in a block. All accommodation is air-con, many rooms have DVD players, and there's a pool, Internet and international phone services, kayak rental and organized boat trips. Sharing the bay, but right at the other end, *Khlong Jaak Bungalows* (Ⓣ089 866 2768; closed May–Oct; ❷–❹) has a range of fan-cooled bamboo huts, from simple en-suite rooms in a line at the back of the compound through to bigger front-row bungalows.

A kilometre south, over the headland from *Klong Jaak Bungalows*, brings you to the lovely white-sand **AO MAI PHAI**, which is extremely peaceful and has good coral close to the shore – though this makes it too rocky for low-tide swimming, when you'll need to kayak up to Ao Klong Jaak instead. At the northern end of the bay, the Danish-Thai-run *Bamboo Bay Resort* (Ⓣ075 618240, Ⓦwww.bamboobay.net; fan ❹–❻, air-con ❼) offers 21 concrete bungalows, with fan or air-con, stepped up the cliffside above the headland, plus a few just across the narrow road. Nearly all have great sea views and interiors are spacious and of a high standard. Its *pièce de resistance* is its idyllically sited deck restaurant and bar, which jut out over the rocks just above the water. Occupying the centre of the bay and deservedly popular is the cute, tasteful and welcoming ✭ *Baan Phu Lae* (Ⓣ081 201 1704, Ⓦwww.baanphulae.net; fan ❹, air-con ❻), which manages to combine an appealing whiff of Bangkok sophistication with laid-back island charm. The bamboo bungalows are stylishly simple, have good beds and come with fan or air-con; nearly all enjoy direct sea views, many of them from the shorefront, and there are plenty of shell mobiles and hammocks around.

The interior and the east coast

Although the **east coast** lacks decent beaches, it's got plenty of other attractions, including an impressive series of caves at **Tham Mai Kaew**, a jaw-droppingly great **view over islands and coastlines** at the viewpoint (worth an early rise), an atmospheric neighbourhood in **Lanta Old Town**, and cultural interest at the **Sea Gypsy Home**. The tiny island of Ko Bubu is also reached from here. Access to the east coast is easy as the road is good: it starts at the Ban Klong Nin junction half way down the west coast at kilometre-stone 13. Alternatively, most tour agencies over guided day-trips covering this area.

Tham Mai Kaew caves

One kilometre beyond the fork, a two-kilometre side road veers off the eastbound road and leads to **Tham Mai Kaew caves**, Ko Lanta's biggest inland attraction. There are myriad chambers here, some of which you can only just crawl into, and they boast stalactites and interesting rock formations as well as a creepy cave pool and the inevitable bats. Access to the cave is regulated by the local family who first properly explored the cave system in the 1980s: they now act as caretakers and guides, in conjunction with the national park authorities, and charge B200 for a two-hour tour. These tours leave frequently throughout the day, year-round and include an easy walk through forest to the mouth of the cave (also possible on elephant for an extra B100), an hour's guided scramble through the most accessible part of the cave system, and the all-important head torch. Guides also lead longer cave trips (B400) and extended all-day jungle treks up the mountain with or without overnight in a jungle hammock (B800/1200). Most of Thailand's countless caves are underwhelming and certainly not worth B200, but this is one of the better ones, not least because the caretakers have resisted the temptation to string it with electric lights so you're left to wonder both at what you catch with your torch and at what you don't see. Among its star features are crystallized waterfalls, fossils and ammonites embedded in the cave walls and overhangs, stalagmites and stalactites young and old and a tangible sense of there being endless passageways to explore. In the rainy season it's a more slippery, challenging experience, with some wading likely and the option of a dip in the wet-season-only lagoon. Even in the dry season it's moderately arduous and best done in sensible shoes and clothes you're happy to get grubby in. If you don't have your own transport, a motorcycle taxi costs B150 each way from Khlong Dao or Ao Phra-Ae.

The viewpoint and Lanta Old Town (Ban Si Raya)

Three kilometres beyond the turn-off to the caves, the eastbound road drops down over the central spine of hills and you pass *Viewpoint* café (daily 6am–9pm), where nearly everyone stops for a drink and a gawp at the stunning panorama. The **view over the east coast** is glorious, encompassing the southeast coast of mangrove-fringed Ko Lanta Noi, dozens of islets – including Ko Bubu and Ko Por – adrift in the milky blue sea, and the hilly profile of the mainland along the horizon. It's an unbeatable spot for a sunrise breakfast.

Once back down at sea level, follow the east-coast road (Route 4245) south for a few kilometres to reach, at kilometre-stone 20, the seductively atmospheric little waterfront settlement of **Lanta Old Town**, officially known as **Ban Si Raya**. Ko Lanta's oldest town, it began life as a sheltered staging post for ships sailing between China and Penang and served as the island's administrative capital from 1901–1998. The government offices have since moved to Ko Lanta Noi, and Ban Sala Dan has assumed the role of harbour, island gateway and commercial hub, so Ban Si Raya has been left much as it was a century ago, with its historic charm intact. There's little more to the Old Town than its peaceful main street, which runs right along the coast and is lined with traditional, one-hundred-year-old sea- and wind-blasted wooden homes and shops, many of them constructed on stilted jetties over the sea, their first-floor overhangs shading the pavements and plant-filled doorways. The Chinese shrine mid-way down the street is evidence of the town's cultural mix: Ban Si Raya is home to a long-established Chinese-Thai community as well as to Muslims.

There are several enticing **restaurants** in the old town: the dining area at locally popular *Kroua Lanta Yai Seafood* is on a jetty over the seafront, while sophisticated little *Mango House Bar and Bistro* is all done out in stylish dark wood and, as well as serving tourist-oriented food and drink, has a small library of English-language books, and a couple of similarly arty **rooms** for rent upstairs (Ⓣ081 677 2866, Ⓦwww.bestofkolanta.com; ❻). There's an Internet centre on the main street but otherwise it's nearly all local general stores. The hourly Krabi minibus service starts from Lanta Old Town.

Sea Gypsy Home and Ban Sang-Ga-U

About 3km south of Lanta Old Town, an inviting hand-painted sign draws you down to a stony mangrove shore and the intriguing, driftwood-architecture **Sea Gypsy Home** (Ⓣ089 467 3312, Ⓔshadowgypsyhome@yahoo.com), which is café, homestay (B100 per person), hand-made handicrafts outlet, art gallery and, most interestingly, a resource centre of *chao ley* ("sea gypsy") culture. Ko Lanta's *chao ley* are **Urak Lawoy** (see the box on p.713 for an introduction to the Urak Lawoy and other *chao ley* groups in Thailand) and are thought to have been the island's first inhabitants, perhaps as long as 500 years ago, living along the shoreline during the monsoon season and setting off along the coast again when the winds abated. Lanta's community of Urak Lawoy have now settled permanently in the village of **Ban Sang-Ga-U**, 1km to the south of the Sea Gypsy Home; other Urak Lawoy living elsewhere in the Andaman Sea, around Trang and beyond, consider Ko Lanta their capital and will always stop at Sang Ga U when making a journey. Though the Sea Gypsy Home is not run by the *chao ley* and doesn't try to be a formal ethnographic museum, it does have lots of information about the Urak Lawoy and is especially strong on their **music**, displaying many of their musical instruments and selling CD recordings. Their music is an interesting fusion of far-flung influences, featuring violins (from the Dutch East Indies), drums (from Persia), and gongs (from China), as well as singing, dancing and ritual elements. The best time to experience their music is at one of their twice-yearly three-day **festivals**, which are held at full moon in the sixth and eleventh lunar months (usually June and November) on a beach close by the centre. This is also when they launch their special *zalacca* boats, a miniature version of which is on permanent display at the Sea Gypsy Home.

South beyond Sang-Ga-U, the road ends at kilometre-stone 26, where a track branches off westwards to a tiny stony bay and the bizarre **hotel** that is *Sang Kha Ou Resort and Spa* (Ⓣ086 952 3244, Ⓦwww.sangkhaouresortspa.com; ❹–❼). Rooms here are designed in a fantasy-kitsch back-to-nature style and include "cave rooms" with boulder-studded walls and pseudo-primitive concrete artwork, plus some more appealing treehouses and Thai-style rooms. There's also a shooting range. The hotel is right on the edge of national park land, and you can walk across to the park headquarters in about an hour.

Ko Bubu

The minuscule, wooded island of **Ko Bubu**, with a radius of just 500m, lies 7km northeast off Lanta Old Town and is the preserve of *Bubu Island Resort* (Ⓣ075 612536; ❸–❹; closed May–Oct), which has a dozen en-suite bungalows and a restaurant. It's twenty minutes' chartered **longtail** ride (B100) from Lanta Old Town.

Travel details

Buses

Cheow Lan Lake (Ratchabrapa Dam, Khao Sok) to: Phunphin (Surat Thani train station; every 2hr; 1hr).

Khao Lak to: Khao Sok (every 90min; 1hr 30min); Phuket (11 daily; 2hr 30min); Ranong (8 daily; 2hr 30min–3hr); Surat Thani (every 90min; 3hr 30min); Takua Pa (every 40min; 30min).

Khao Sok to: Khao Lak (every 90min; 1hr 30min); Surat Thani (every 90min; 2hr); Takua Pa (every 90min; 50min).
Krabi to: Bangkok (7 daily; 12–14hr); Hat Yai (13 daily; 4–5hr); Ko Lanta (hourly; 2hr); Nakhon Si Thammarat (at least hourly; 3–4hr); Phang Nga (every 30min; 1hr 30min–2hr); Phattalung (2 daily; 3hr); Phuket (every 30min; 3–5hr); Ranong (4 daily; 6–7hr); Satun (2 daily; 5hr); Sungai Kolok (3 daily; 9hr); Surat Thani (hourly; 2–3hr); Takua Pa (4 daily; 3hr 30min–4hr 30min); Trang (at least hourly; 2–3hr).
Phang Nga to: Bangkok (6 daily; 11hr–12hr 30min); Krabi (every 30min; 1hr 30min–2hr); Phuket (every 30min; 1hr 30min–2hr 30min); Surat Thani (5 daily; 4hr); Takua Pa (hourly; 2hr); Trang (every 30min; 3hr).
Phuket to: Bangkok (27 daily; 14–15hr); Chumphon (3 daily; 6hr 30min); Hat Yai (16 daily; 6–8hr); Khao Lak (12 daily; 2hr 30min); Khao Sok (at least 2 daily; 3–4hr); Khuraburi (12 daily; 3hr 30min–4hr); Krabi (22 daily; 3–5hr); Nakhon Si Thammarat (27 daily; 7–8hr); Phang Nga (30 daily; 1hr 30min–2hr 30min); Phattalung (2 daily; 6–7hr); Ranong (12 daily; 5–6hr); Satun (3 daily; 7hr); Sungai Kolok (3 daily; 11hr); Surat Thani (21 daily; 4hr 30min–6hr); Takua Pa (20 daily; 2hr 30min–3hr); Trang (20 daily; 5–6hr).
Ranong to: Bangkok (12 daily; 8–10hr); Chumphon (hourly; 2–3hr); Hat Yai (3 daily; 5hr); Khuraburi (8 daily; 1hr 30min–2hr); Krabi (5 daily; 6–7hr); Phang Nga (5 daily; 4–5hr); Phuket (8 daily; 5–6hr); Surat Thani (10 daily; 3–5hr); Takua Pa (8 daily; 2hr 30min–3hr).
Takua Pa to: Bangkok (10 daily; 12–13hr); Khuraburi (at least 8 daily; 1hr); Krabi (at least 4 daily; 3hr); Phuket (hourly; 3hr); Ranong (5 daily; 3hr 30min–4hr); Surat Thani (11 daily; 3hr 15min).

Ferries

Ao Nang to: Ko Lanta Yai (Nov–May 1 daily; 2hr 30min); Ko Phi Phi Don (1 daily; 2hr 30min); Phuket (1 daily; 3hr).
Khuraburi to: Ko Surin (Nov–May 1–2 daily; 1–3hr).
Ko Lanta Yai to: Ao Nang (Nov–May 1 daily; 2hr 30min); Ko Phi Phi Don (Nov–May 2 daily; 1hr 30min); Krabi (mid-Oct to mid-May 2 daily; 2hr 30min); Phuket (Nov–May 2 daily; 4hr 30min).
Ko Phi Phi Don to: Ao Nang and Laem Phra Nang (Nov–May 1 daily; 2hr 30min); Ko Lanta Yai (Nov–May 2 daily; 1hr 30min); Krabi (2 daily; 2hr); Phuket (2 daily; 1hr 30min–2hr 30min).
Ko Yao Noi to: Krabi (Ao Thalen; daily; 1hr); Phang Nga (daily; 90min); Phuket (4 daily; 1hr).
Krabi to: Ko Jum (mid-Oct to mid-May 2 daily; 1hr 30min–2hr); Ko Lanta Yai (mid-Oct to mid-May 2 daily; 2hr 30min); Ko Phi Phi Don (2 daily; 2hr); Ko Yao Noi (departs Ao Thalen; 2 daily; 1hr).
Laem Kruat to: Ban Ko Jum.
Phang Nga (Tha Dan) to: Ko Yao Noi (daily; 90min).
Phuket to: Ao Nang (Nov–May daily; 2–2hr 30min); Ko Lanta Yai (Nov–May 1 daily; 4hr 30min); Ko Phi Phi Don (2 daily; 1hr 30min–2hr 30min); Ko Yao Noi (5 daily; 1hr).
Ranong to: Ko Chang (Nov–May 3–4 daily; 1hr); Ko Phayam (Nov–May 1–4 daily; 40min–3hr).
Thap Lamu (Khao Lak) to: Ko Similan (Nov–May 1 daily; 2hr).

Flights

Krabi to: Bangkok (up to 6 daily; 1hr 20min).
Phuket to: Bangkok (15 daily; 1hr 20min); Ko Samui (2 daily; 50min); Pattaya/ U-Tapao (1–2 daily; 1hr 40min–2hr 20min).

The deep south

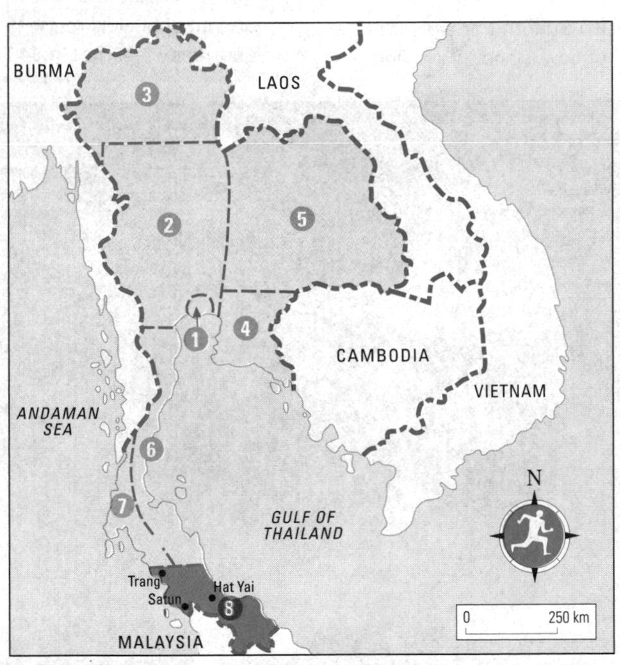

CHAPTER 8

Highlights

* **Thale Noi Waterbird Park** Boating on this fascinating inland lake isn't just for birdwatchers. See p.829

* **Ko Mook** One of the best of the Trang islands, with laid-back resorts and the stunning Emerald Cave. See p.837

* **Ko Sukorn** For a glimpse of how islanders live and an outstanding beach resort. See p.839

* **Ko Tarutao National Marine Park** A largely undisturbed haven of beautiful land- and seascapes. See p.844

* **Ko Lipe** One dazzling beach, fine opportunities for snorkelling and diving, and an appealing rough-and-ready feel. See p.849

△ Ko Tarutao National Marine Park

The deep south

The frontier between Thailand and Malaysia carves across the peninsula six degrees north of the equator, but the cultures of the two countries shade into each other much further north. According to official divisions, the southern Thais – the *thai pak tai* – begin around Chumphon, and as you move further down the peninsula you see ever more sarongs, yashmaks and towering mosques, and hear with increasing frequency a staccato dialect that baffles many Thais. In Trang and Phatthalung provinces, the Muslim population is generally accepted as being Thai, but the inhabitants of the southernmost provinces – Satun, Pattani, Yala, Narathiwat and most of Songkhla – are ethnically more akin to the Malays: most of the 1.5 million followers of Islam here speak Yawi, an old Malay dialect. To add to the ethnic confusion, the deep south has a large urban population of Chinese, whose comparative wealth makes them stand out sharply from the Muslim farmers and fishermen.

On a journey south, the first thing you might be tempted by is an atmospheric boat trip through the **Thale Noi Waterbird Park** near Phatthalung. Over on the beautiful **west coast**, sheer limestone outcrops, pristine sands and fish-laden coral stretch down to the Malaysian border. The spread of tourism outwards

Travel warning

Because of the ongoing **violence** in the deep south (see p.828), all major Western governments are currently advising people **not to travel** to or through Songkhla, Pattani, Yala and Narathiwat provinces, unless essential. This encompasses the city and transport hub of **Hat Yai** and several of the main border crossings to Malaysia: by rail from Hat Yai (and Bangkok) to Butterworth via Padang Besar and to Sungai Kolok; and by road from Hat Yai via Sadao, from Yala via Betong, and down the east coast to Kota Bharu.

The routes to Sungai Kolok, Betong and Kota Bharu pass through particularly volatile territory, with **martial law** declared in Pattani, Yala and Narathiwat provinces; however, martial law is not in effect in Hat Yai itself or the districts of Songkhla province through which the Bangkok–Butterworth rail line or the Hat Yai–Sadao road pass.

The provinces of Phatthalung, Trang and Satun are not affected, and it's still perfectly possible to continue overland via **Satun**: by share-taxi from Satun town to Alor Setar via Thale Ban National Park, or by ferry from nearby Thammalang to Kuala Perlis or the Malaysian island of Langkawi (see p.841); or by irregular boats from Ko Lipe to Langkawi (see p.845). For up-to-the-minute advice, consult your government travel advisory (see p.81).

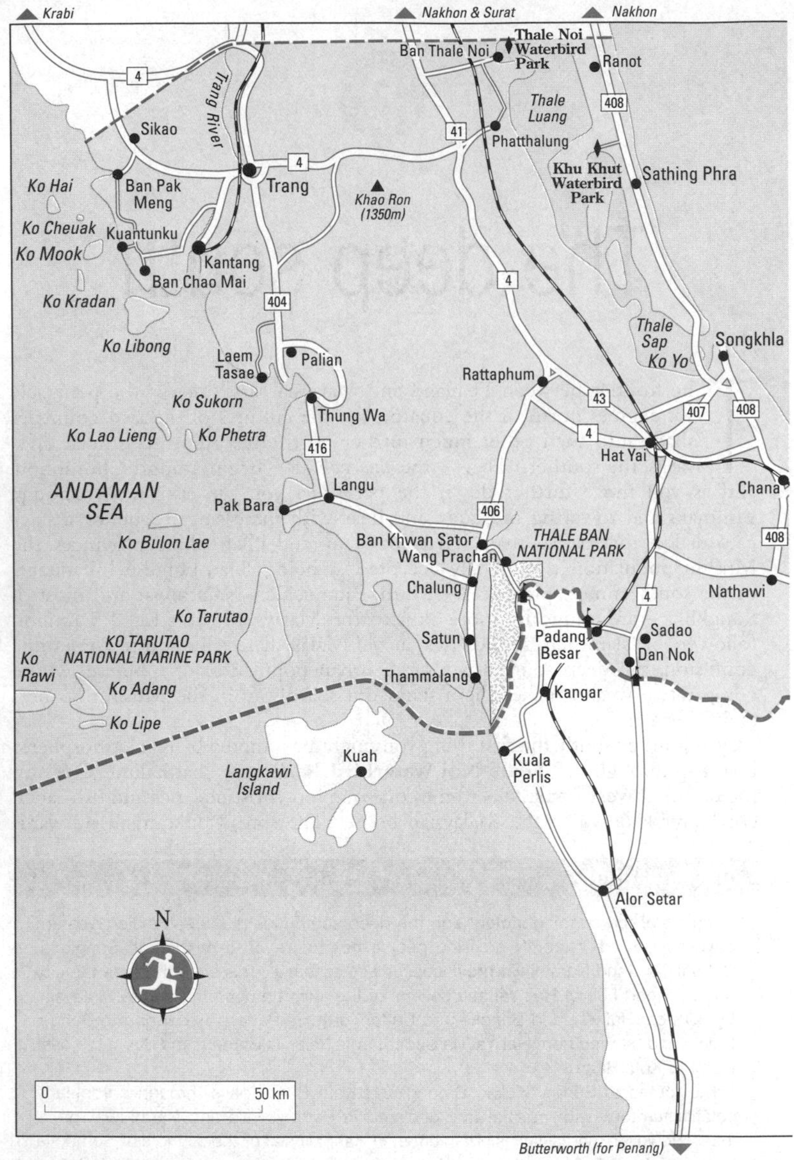

from Phuket has been inching its way south towards **Trang** for some time now, but the province remains largely undeveloped. Along the mainland **coast** here, there's a thirty-kilometre stretch of attractive beaches, dotted with mangroves and impressive caves that can be explored by sea canoe, but the real attraction of the province is the offshore **islands**, which offer gorgeous panoramas and beaches, great snorkelling and at least a modicum of comfort in their small clusters of resorts. Further south in the spectacular **Ko Tarutao National Marine**

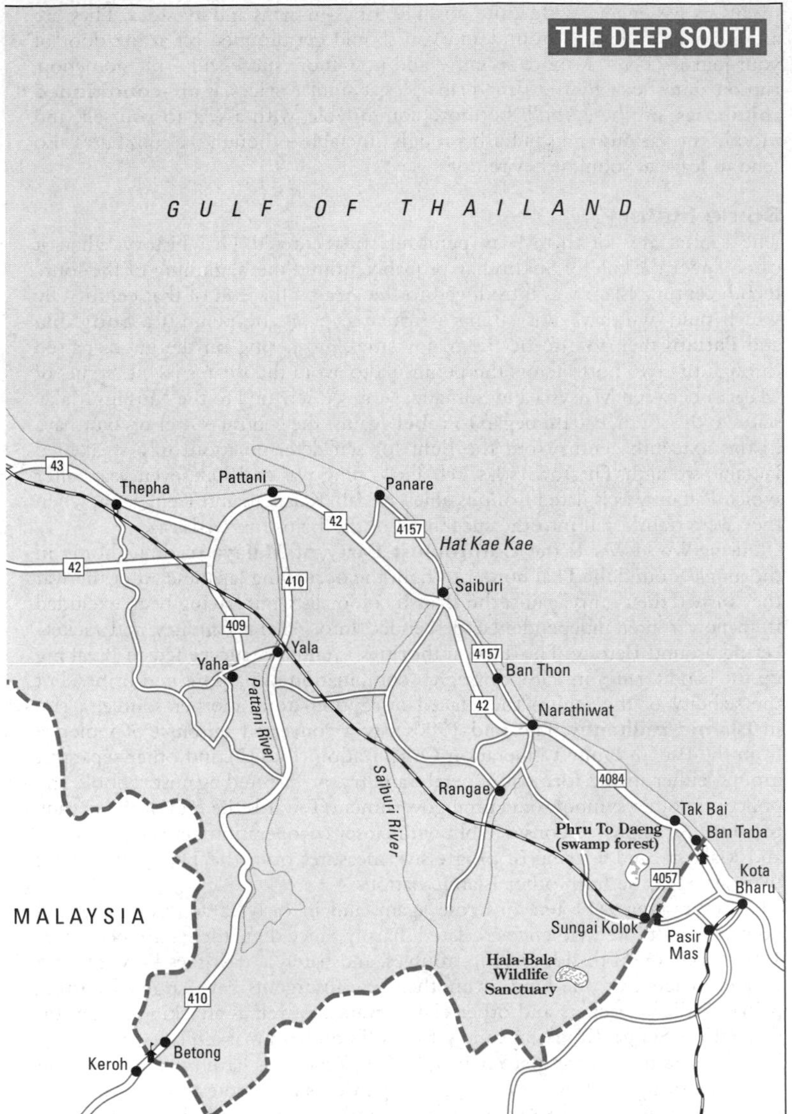

Park, you'll usually have the place much to yourself, although **Ko Lipe** and its beautiful beach of Hat Pattaya have been arousing travellers' interest of late, albeit at a low-key, manageable level.

As well as the usual bus services, the area covered in this chapter is served by flights to Trang and trains to Phatthalung and Trang. The deep south is also the territory of **share-taxis**, which connect all the major towns for about twice the fare of ordinary buses. The cars leave when they're full, which usually means six passengers, with, quite possibly, babes-in-arms and livestock. They are a quick way of getting around and you should get dropped off at the door of your journey's end. A more recent – and now more successful – phenomenon, run on almost exactly the same principles at similar prices, is **air-conditioned minibuses**; on these you'll be more comfortable, with a seat to yourself, and most of the various ranks publish a rough timetable – though the minibuses also tend to leave as soon as they're full.

Some history

The central area of the Malay peninsula first entered Thai history when it came under the rule of Sukhothai, probably around the beginning of the fourteenth century. Islam was introduced to the area by the end of that century, by which time Ayutthaya was taking a firmer grip on the peninsula. **Songkhla** and **Pattani** then rose to be the major cities, prospering on the goods passed through the two ports across the peninsula to avoid the pirates in the Straits of Malacca between Malaysia and Sumatra. More closely tied to the Muslim Malay states to the south, Pattani began to **rebel** against the central power of Ayutthaya in the sixteenth century, but the fight for self-determination only weakened Pattani's strength. The town's last rebellious fling was in 1902, seven years after which Pattani was isolated from its allies, Kedah, Kelantan and Trengganu, when they were transferred into the suzerainty of the British in Malaysia.

During World War II the **Communist Party of Malaya** made its home in the jungle around the Thai border to fight the occupying Japanese. After the war they turned their guns against the British colonialists, but having been excluded from power after independence, descended into general banditry and racketeering around Betong. The Thai authorities eventually succeeded in breaking up the bandit gangs in 1989 through a combination of pardons and bribes, but the stability of the region then faced disruption from another source, a rise in **Islamic militancy**. The mid-1990s saw a concerted outburst of violence from the Pattani United Liberation Organization (PULO) and other separatist groups, either in the form of general banditry, or directed against schools, the police and other symbols of central government. Towards the end of the decade the situation improved considerably, with closer co-operation between Thailand and Malaysia, and a string of progressive measures from the Thai government that earned praise from other Islamic nations.

However, after 9/11 tensions rose again, and in early 2004, criminally and politically motivated violence escalated sharply. Since then, there have been over 1200 deaths on both sides in the troubles, and barely a day goes by without a violent incident of one kind or another. The insurgents have targeted monks, police, soldiers, teachers and other civil servants, as well as attacking a train on the Hat Yai–Sungai Kolok line and setting off bombs in marketplaces, near tourist hotels and bars and at Hat Yai airport. The authorities have inflamed opinion in the south by reacting violently, notably in crushing protests at Tak Bai and the much-revered Krue Se Mosque in Pattani in 2004, in which a total of over two hundred alleged insurgents died. In 2005, the government announced a **serious state of emergency** in Pattani, Yala and Narathiwat provinces, and imposed **martial law** here and in parts of Songkhla province. This, however, has exacerbated economic and unemployment problems in what is Thailand's poorest region.

A large part of the problem is that a wide variety of shadowy groups – with names like the Pattani Islamic Mujahideen, the Barisan Revolusi Nasional-Coordinate and New Pulo – are operating against the government. It's unclear who they are, what they want and how far they are motivated by separatism,

Islamic fundamentalism or just gang-related criminality. Concern is growing that Islamist terrorist networks linked to Al-Qaeda – such as Jemaah Islamiyah, thought to be responsible for the Bali bombings of 2002 and 2005 – could move in to exploit the situation, if they haven't already done so. The authorities have generally maintained that a military solution is attainable, but an inquiry by the **National Reconciliation Commission**, headed by former prime minister Anand Panyarachun, has recently proposed, among other measures, the introduction of Islamic law in the southern provinces, the formation of an unarmed battalion to deal with disputes between the state and the people, and the adoption of ethnic Malay as a second official language. It remains to be seen, however, whether the new government in Bangkok will heed these proposals or how successful they might be.

Phatthalung and Thale Noi

Halfway between Nakhon and Hat Yai, the hot, dusty town of **PHATTHALUNG** is worth a stop only if you're tempted by a boat trip through the nearby Thale Noi Waterbird Park – though even then it's possible to bypass the town altogether, as outlined overleaf. Although its setting among limestone outcrops is dramatic, Phatthalung itself is of little interest, its only claim to fame being *nang thalung*, the Thai shadow puppet theatre to which it probably gave its name (see box on p.686).

Phatthalung is on the major rail line, which crosses the main street, Thanon Ramet, in the centre of town. Out of a poor selection of **hotels**, the best value is the friendly *Thai Hotel*, at 14 Thanon Disara Sakarin, behind the Bangkok Bank on Thanon Ramet (Ⓣ074 611636; fan ❷, air-con ❸); rooms with attached bathrooms and a choice of fan or air-conditioning are clean and reasonably quiet. *Koo Hoo*, around the corner at 9 Thanon Prachabamrung (parallel to and south of Ramet), is an excellent, moderately priced **restaurant** – try the sweet and sour fish or the delicious giant tiger prawns.

Thale Noi Waterbird Park

Thale Noi Waterbird Park isn't just for bird-spotters – even the most recalcitrant city-dweller can appreciate boating through the bizarre freshwater habitat formed at the head of the huge lagoon that spills into the sea at Songkhla. Here, in the "Little Sea" (*thale noi*), which has an average depth of just 1.5m, the distinction between land and water breaks down: the lake is dotted with low, marshy islands, and much of the intervening shallow water is so thickly covered with water vines, lotus pads and reeds that it looks like a field. But the real delight of this area is the hundreds of thousands of birds that breed here – brown teals, loping purple herons, white cattle egrets and nearly two hundred other species. Most are migratory, arriving here from December onwards from as far away as Siberia. March and April provide the widest variety of birds; from October to December you'll generally spot only native species, while June to September is the worst season for spotting. Early morning and late afternoon are the best times to come, when the heat is less searing and when, in the absence of hunters and fishermen, more birds are visible.

To get from Phatthalung to **BAN THALE NOI**, the village on the western shore, take one of the frequent **songthaews** (1hr) from Thanon Nivas, which runs north off Thanon Ramet near the station, or from the Bangkok Bank on Thanon Ramet in front of the *Thai Hotel*. If you're coming from Nakhon or points further north by bus, you can save yourself a trip into Phatthalung by getting out at **Ban Chai Khlong**, 15km from Ban Thale Noi, and waiting for a songthaew there. If you're travelling by train, it's also possible to bypass Phatthalung, by getting out at **Ban Pak Khlong** and catching a songthaew for the last 8km to Ban Thale Noi. **Longtail boats** can be hired at the pier in the village: for B300, the boatman will give you a one-hour trip around the lake. If you want to get a dawn start, stay in one of the few national park **bungalows** built over the lake (donation required; book on ⓣ074 685230).

Trang town

The town of **TRANG** (aka Taptieng), 60km west of Phatthalung, is fast developing as a popular jumping-off point for backpackers drawn south from the crowded sands of Krabi to the pristine beaches and islands of the nearby coast. The town, which prospers on rubber, oil palms, fisheries and – increasingly – tourism, is a sociable place whose wide, clean streets are dotted with crumbling, wooden-shuttered houses. In the evening, restaurant tables sprawl onto the main Thanon Rama VI and Thanon Wisetkul, and during the day, many of the town's Chinese inhabitants hang out in the cafés, drinking the local filtered coffee. Trang's Chinese population makes the **Vegetarian Festival** at the beginning of October almost as frenetic as Phuket's (see box on p.738) – and for veggie travellers it's an opportunity to feast at the stalls set up around the temples. Getting

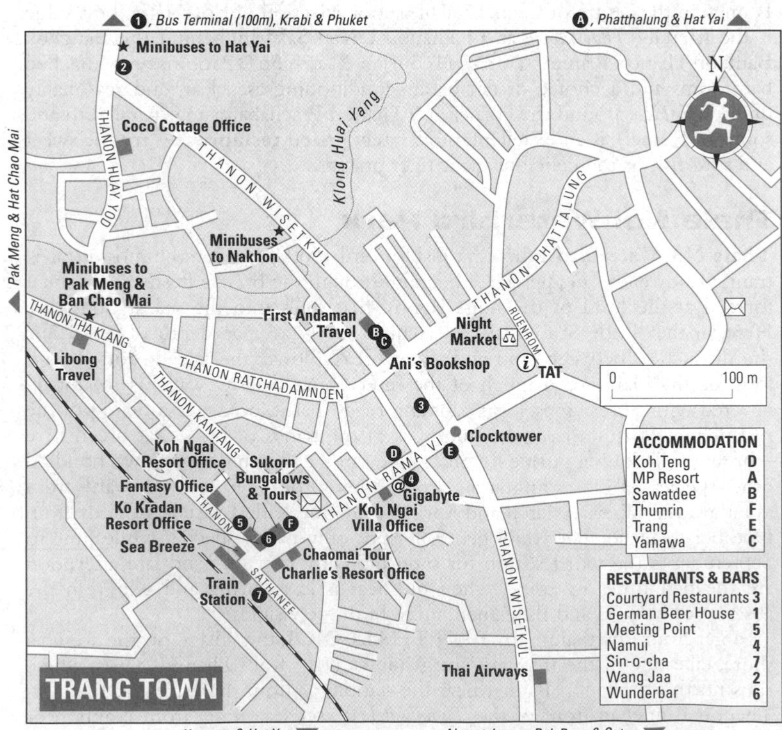

there is easy, as Trang is ninety minutes from Phatthalung and well served by buses and air-con minibuses from all the surrounding provinces.

Practicalities

Nok Air (Ⓣ075 212229, at the airport) run daily **flights** between Bangkok and Trang airport, which is connected to Trang town by B50 air-conditioned minibuses, operated by, for example, World Travel Service, 25/2 Thanon Sathanee (Ⓣ075 214010–1). Two overnight **trains** from the capital run down a branch of the southern line to Trang, stopping at the station at the western end of Thanon Rama VI. Most **buses** arrive at the terminal on Thanon Huay Yod, to the north of the centre, including the air-conditioned service between Satun and Phuket; ordinary buses from Satun stop on Thanon Ratsada out on the southeast side of town. **Air-conditioned minibuses** for Nakhon Si Thammarat have their office on Thanon Wisetkul, those for Surat Thani on Thanon Tha Klang, and those for Hat Yai on Thanon Huay Yod near the main bus terminal. Those for Ban Saladan on Ko Lanta and Pak Bara don't have specific offices, but can be booked through several guest houses and **travel agencies** around town, including Sukorn Beach Bungalows and Tours, 22 Thanon Sathanee (Ⓣ075 211457, Ⓦwww.sukorn-island-trang.com). This well-organized outfit offers a wide range of services – including accommodation booking on any island, boat trips and trekking, rafting and sea-canoeing excursions – in addition to running their own bungalow outfit on Ko Sukorn. The friendly staff are a great source of information on the area, and their office makes a good first stop in town.

TAT have a small **tourist office** on Thanon Ruenrom (daily 8.30am–4.30pm; Ⓣ075 215867–8, Ⓔtattrang@tat.or.th). There's a good **bookshop**, Ani's, at 285 Thanon Ratchadamnoen (Ⓣ081 397 4574), which buys and sells a wide range of second hand books in English, as well as selling handicrafts, beachwear and jewellery. The owners are a good source of information on the area, and also have several **motorbikes**, which they rent out at B150 for the day (B200/24hr, B1000/week). *Sawatdee* guest house (see below) has a **car** for rent, costing from B1800/day, while Sukorn Beach Bungalows and Tours (see above) can arrange hire of an air-con minibus with driver, for around B2000 a day. You can connect to the **Internet** at, for example, *Wunderbar* (see below) and Gigabyte opposite the *Koh Teng Hotel* on Thanon Rama VI.

Accommodation

Trang's **hotels** and **guest houses** are concentrated along Thanon Rama VI and Thanon Wisetkul. The owners of Ani's (see above) also own a quiet, fan-cooled house with an attractive terrace, kitchen and cold-water bathroom, five minutes' walk from the shop; you can rent a room (❸) or the whole house for the night, or rent it for a longer period.

Koh Teng Hotel 77–79 Thanon Rama VI Ⓣ075 218622 or 075 218148. Styling itself, with some justification, as a "Five-Star Backpackers", this 1940s Chinese hotel has been smartly renovated, offering large, clean en-suite rooms, some with cable TV and air-con, above a popular restaurant and coffee shop, serving Thai, Chinese and Western food. Fan ❶, air-con ❷

MP Resort Hotel About 2km east of the centre on the Phatthalung road Ⓣ075 214230–45, Ⓕ075 211177. Among several luxury hotels in Trang town, this grandiose white edifice – built to resemble a cruise liner – stands out, with Thai, Chinese, Japanese and Vietnamese restaurants, a pool, golf driving range, sauna, tennis court and fitness centre on offer. ❻

Sawatdee Thanon Wisetkul Ⓣ089 728 4386. Friendly, helpful, family-style guest house in a concrete shophouse, where you're free to use the kitchen – or you can order Western breakfasts. Rooms come with some nice decorative touches, fans and shared hot-water bathrooms. The owner can organize one-day tours by car to local waterfalls and caves. Decent rates for singles. ❷

Thumrin Hotel Thanon Rama VI near the station ⓣ075 211011–5, ⓦwww.thumrin.co.th. Formerly the top hotel in town, now offering international-standard facilities – air-con, hot water and TV – at bargain prices, in a high-rise block above its popular coffee shop. ❸

Trang Hotel 134/2–5 Thanon Wisetkul ⓣ075 218944, ⓕ075 218451. Good, welcoming choice in the moderate range, on the corner of Thanon Rama VI overlooking the clocktower, with large, comfortable twin rooms with air-con, hot water and TV. ❸

Yamawa Guesthouse Thanon Wisetkul ⓣ075 216617. Large, attractive rooms above a massage shop in the same block as *Sawatdee*, either fan-cooled with shared hot showers or air-conditioned and en-suite, all with cable TV; decent rate for singles. Fan ❷, air-con ❸

Eating and drinking

Trang's streets are dotted with dozens of traditional cafés, which serve up gallons of **kopii** (local filtered coffee) accompanied by various tidbits and light meals. Most famous of these is the local delicacy, **muu yaang**, delicious barbecued pork, which is generally eaten for breakfast. At the excellent **night market**, around the back of the city hall on Thanon Ruenrom, you can try another tasty southern dish, *khanom jiin*, soft noodles topped with hot, sweet or fishy sauces and eaten with crispy greens.

Courtyard restaurants Thanon Wisetkul, north of the clocktower. A good bet at any time of the day or evening – four simple, very cheap restaurants with outdoor tables in a quiet, alley-courtyard, offering tray dishes, noodles, rice, soups and a few more substantial mains.

German Beer House 342 Thanon Huay Yod, on the right, about 1km from the centre beyond the bus terminal ⓣ087 283 0454. Smart farang bolthole, with a small patio out front for the evenings, producing excellent, unpretentious Western food such as steaks, burgers, chicken cordon bleu, German sausages and *sauerkraut*. Imported German and English beers.

The Meeting Point Thanon Sathanee. Smart, well-run spot, catering largely to foreigners, with espresso coffee, pancakes, pasta, burgers, pizzas, steaks and a large menu of seafood and other Thai dishes.

Namui 130 Thanon Rama VI. Large, clean institution serving very tasty and quite reasonably priced Chinese food, with seafood a speciality; ignore the unprepossessing interior and head straight through the restaurant to the creeper-covered patio, waterfall and outdoor seating at the back.

Sin-o-cha Next to the station at 25/25–26 Thanon Sathanee. Very popular, updated traditional café: *kopii* with Thai cakes and main courses, or espresso, various teas, Western breakfasts, and even baguettes and ciabattas. Daily 7am–7pm.

Wang Jaa Thanon Huay Yod, near the Hat Yai minibus office. Simple café renowned for its *muu yaang*, but also serving *salapao* (Chinese buns), dim sum and, of course, *kopii*. Daily 5am–2pm.

Wunderbar Bottom end of Thanon Rama VI, near the station. Multi-purpose farang bar-restaurant that serves a wide selection of drinks (including imported beers), Thai food, and salads, burgers, pizzas and other Western favourites. Also acts as a travel agent, especially for island bookings, and offers Internet and reasonably priced overseas calls.

Mainland Trang

From Ban Pak Meng, 40km due west of Trang town, to the mouth of the Trang River runs a thirty-kilometre stretch of lovely **beaches**, broken only by dramatic limestone outcrops pitted with explorable **caves**. Sea-canoeing day-trips through the mangroves to the impressive cave of Tham Chao Mai can be arranged, notably through *Had Yao Nature Resort* at Ban Chao Mai. Air-conditioned **minibuses** run from Trang to Pak Meng in the north, and via Hat Yao to Ban Chao Mai in the south, but if you want to explore the whole coastline, you'll need to rent a motorbike or car in Trang.

△ Typical Trang scenery of limestone islands and a deserted beach.

Away from the beach, **inland** Trang Province has plenty to offer too, including **trekking** and **rafting** excursions, most taking in some of the myriad caves and waterfalls that are scattered though the province. Libong Travel, 59/1 Thanon Tha Klang (Ⓣ075 217642 or 075 214676, Ⓦwww.libongtravel.net), offer a particularly wide range of trips, including a three-day, two-night jungle trek up to the peak of nearby Phu Pha Mek from Sairoong waterfall (B1800/person, minimum 6 people), and a day-trip to three waterfalls and Tham Le (aka Khao Kob), a dramatic inland system of caverns accessed by boat (B750).

The coast: Pak Meng to Ban Chao Mai

Although it has a fine outlook to the headlands and islands to the west, the beach at **PAK MENG** is certainly not the most attractive on the coast, a rather muddy strip of sand truncated at its northern end by a busy pier and to the south by a promenade and sea wall. However, if it's just a day on the sand you're after, and a meal at one of the many tree-shaded foodstalls and simple eateries that line the back of the beach, it's not at all bad. Getting to Pak Meng takes about an hour on one of the air-con **minibuses** that leave when full (roughly half-hourly; B50) from Thanon Tha Klang in Trang. If you need **to stay**, the nicest place is the *Lay Trang Resort*, a stone's throw from the pier (Ⓣ075 274027–8, Ⓦwww.laytrang.com; fan ❸, air-con ❻); its smart brick rooms with en-suite bathrooms, ranged around a large, peaceful garden, come with fan and cold water or air-con, TV, fridge and hot water, and it has a pleasant, reasonably priced restaurant that's locally renowned for its seafood.

Immediately south of Pak Meng's beach is the white sand of **Hat Chang Lang**, famous for its oysters, which shelters at its north end the finest luxury hotel in the province, *Amari Trang Beach Resort* (Ⓣ075 205888, Ⓦwww.amari.com; ❾). The low-rise blocks of stylish bedrooms with large balconies are set behind a line of casuarina trees, and facilities encompass a beautiful, large pool, an excellent Thai restaurant, a spa and a fitness centre. Watersports on offer include kayaking, windsurfing and sailing rental and lessons, and there's a huge range of other activities laid on, notably yoga, t'ai chi, cooking and Thai-language lessons and some interesting local tours. In addition, the hotel has its own beach club on the main strand on Ko Kradan (see p.838), reached by daily longtail transfer, with watersports available and a great little restaurant. About 1km down Hat Chang Lang is the much simpler *Chang Lang Resort* (Ⓣ075 213369, Ⓕ075 291008; fan ❸, air-con ❹), a pleasant resort with attached restaurant, set back from the beach just off the main road; smallish rooms in well-built concrete bungalows, some air-conditioned, all come with en-suite bathrooms, TVs and verandas.

Three kilometres further on is the turning for the **headquarters** of the **Hat Chao Mai National Park** (entry B200; Ⓣ075 213260), which covers 230 square kilometres, including the islands of Mook and Kradan and the entire stretch of coastline from Pak Meng down to Ban Chao Mai. At the headquarters there's a simple café as well as bungalows for two–six people (B800–1500), or you can rent a two-person (B150) or three-person (B225) tent to pitch under the casuarinas at the back of the sandy beach (bedding B60 extra per person). From HQ a short trail leads to the south end of the beach and a viewpoint part way up a karst pinnacle, from which you can see Ko Mook and occasionally dugong (manatees) in the bay below.

Four kilometres south of Hat Chang Lang, beyond Kuantunku, the pier for Ko Mook, is **Hat Yong Ling**. This quiet and attractive convex beach, which shelters a national park ranger station, is probably the nicest along this stretch of coast, with a large cave which you can swim into at high tide or walk into at low tide. Immediately beyond comes **Hat Yao**, which runs in a broad five-kilometre white-sand strip, backed by casuarina trees and some simple restaurants. Next up is **Hat Chao Mai**, where *Sinchai's Chaomai Resort* (Ⓣ081 396 4838 or 075 203034; fan ❷–❹, air-con ❹–❻) occupies a shady, scenic spot hard up against a great lump of karst at the western end of the beach. It's very relaxed and friendly, but accommodation is mostly ramshackle, including some very basic rooms sharing bathrooms at the back of the compound, though there are some smart, large, new bungalows with air-con. The owners rustle up tasty Thai and Western meals, especially seafood, rent out kayaks and snorkelling equipment, and can arrange boat tours to the nearby islands and caves.

A short walk away from *Sinchai's* is the Muslim village of **BAN CHAO MAI**, a straggle of mostly thatched houses on stilts, which exists on fishing, especially for crabs. Roughly half-hourly air-conditioned **minibuses** (B50) from Thanon Tha Klang (same stand as for Pak Meng) in Trang via Hat Yao take about an hour to reach Ban Chao Mai, from whose harbour boats run regularly across to Ko Libong. By the harbour, the distinctive green tin-roofed *Had Yao Nature Resort* (Ⓣ075 203012, 075 207934 or 081 894 6936, Ⓦwww.trangsea.com; fan ❷, air-con ❹) is an efficiently run, eco-friendly resort whose aims are nature conservation and helping the local communities. The same people own the *Libong Nature Beach Resort*, covered on p.839, and a resort on an organic farm on Highway 4 between Trang and Krabi, where you can learn to make soap, candles, aloe vera, honey and batiks. Dorm beds in the large house cost B200, and there are also some fan-cooled rooms with shared bath, as well as nicer self-contained rooms and bungalows with hot water and air-con, some of which have balconies over the canal. The breezy, waterside **restaurant** serves up Western breakfasts, vegetarian food and excellent squid and other seafood dishes; **bikes** can be rented at the hostel for B200 per day. The owners organize tours to the local islands, including highly recommended trips to Ko Libong, and to **Tham Chao Mai**, a nearby cave which is large enough to enter by boat; inside are impressively huge rock pillars and a natural theatre, its stage framed by rock curtains. Tham Chao Mai can be visited on a fully insured trip with a longtail and local guide (B950, including lunch) or you can rent a **kayak** (B600/day) and guide yourself with a map and torch.

The Trang islands

Much nicer than the mainland beaches – and more geared towards foreign tourists – are the fantastic **islands** off the coast of Trang. Generally blessed with blinding white beaches, great coral and amazing marine life, these islands have managed, with at most a handful of resorts on each, to cling onto that illusory desert-island atmosphere which better-known places like Phuket and Samui lost long ago. **Access** to the islands, as described in the accounts below, is improving all the time, not least in the shape of **day-trip boats from Ko Lanta** (see p.809), which will drop travellers off on **Ko Hai**, **Ko Mook** or **Ko Kradan** for around B400/person. **Accommodation**, much of which is in the moderate price range, is now often fully booked at peak times. Nearly all the resorts open year round, though in practice many can't be reached out of season (roughly June–Oct) due to treacherous seas. It's sensible to phone ahead, either to the place you want to stay or to its office in Trang town, to check whether they're open or have vacancies, and in many cases to arrange transfers to the resort from Trang.

If you just fancy a day exploring the islands, any travel agent in Trang can book you on a **boat trip** (mid-Oct to mid-May only) to the Emerald Cave on Ko Mook, Ko Hai, Ko Cheuak ("Robe Island", so named after its limestone folds) and other small nearby islands for snorkelling, for B1050 per person including admission to Hat Chao Mai National Park, packed lunch and soft drinks; snorkelling gear is available and the boat will drop you off at one of the islands if you wish. **Scuba-diving** is available on Ko Hai and Ko Mook, while Paddle Asia (Ⓣ076 240952, Ⓦwww.paddleasia.com) run four- to six-day **sea-kayaking** trips around the Trang islands costing US$675–850. Bangkok-based adventure travel company X-Site (895 Pornpailin Business Point, Thanon On Nut, Thanon Sukhumvit; Ⓣ02 730 0935, Ⓦwww.xsitediving.com), run three-day **scuba-diving**, **snorkelling** or **rock-climbing** trips to **Ko Lao Lieng**, beautiful, twin desert islands to the south near Ko Sukorn; all-in costs range from US$150–170, including kayaking and fishing in your down time, camping in luxury tents on Lao Lieng and transfers from Trang.

Ko Hai (Ko Ngai)

KO HAI (aka **KO NGAI**), 16km southwest of Pak Meng, is the most developed of the Trang islands, though it's still decidedly low-key. The island's action, such as it is, centres on the east coast, where half a dozen resorts enjoy a dreamy panorama of jagged limestone outcrops, whose crags glow pink and blue against the setting sun, stretching across the sea to the mainland behind. The gently sloping beach of fine, white sand here stretches unbroken for over two kilometres, and there's some good snorkelling in the shallow, clear water off the island's southeastern tip. For the best snorkelling in the region, the resorts run **boat trips** every day in high season (from B400/person) to Ko Cheuak, Ko Maa and Ko Waen, just off Ko Hai to the east, where you can swim into caverns and explore a fantastic variety of multi-coloured soft and hard coral; these trips also take in Ko Mook's Emerald Cave. *Koh Ngai Villa* also runs day-trips to the popular snorkelling and diving site of Ko Rok (see p.809), 30km southwest in the Mu Ko Lanta National Park, for B900/person. You'll find that such boat trips, as well as massages and other extras, are considerably pricier at the island's more upmarket resorts.

As there's no village on Ko Hai, there's no demand for regular, scheduled **boats** to serve the islanders. Instead, the resorts lay on boats from Pak Meng, typically charging B250/person in a longtail (45min–1hr), B450/person in a speedboat (20min), fed by transfers from Trang town or airport for B150 (some also offer pick-ups from Krabi airport).

Snorkelling equipment (around B150/day) and **kayaks** (B500/day for a one-seater, B700 for a two-seater) can be rented at most of the resorts. *Fantasy Resort* has a well-organized **dive shop**, the German-run Rainbow Divers (ⓦ www.rainbow-diver.com), while *Ko Ngai Resort* is home to Sea Breeze (with an office in Trang at 59/1 Thanon Sathanee ⓣ 075 217460, ⓦ www.seabreeze.co.th), which as well as diving and kayaking, offers **windsurfing**.

Accommodation

Ko Hai now has the whole gamut of **accommodation**, from simple, en-suite bamboo bungalows to swanky, air-con cottages, and there are even two-person tents available (B250), erected under thatched, A-frame shelters, at *Ko Hai Seafood*, a restaurant on the south side of *Fantasy Resort*.

Coco Cottage Towards the northern end of the main beach ⓣ 089 724 9225 or 081 693 6457, ⓦ www.coco-cottage.com; Trang office at 80 Thanon Huay Yod. Charming, helpful and family-friendly resort in a palm grove, where the stylish, thatched wooden bungalows sport verandas, mosquito nets and outdoor bathrooms with wooden basins and bamboo showers. Very good restaurant and beach bar, Internet access and occasional yoga courses. Fan ❼, air-con ❽

Fantasy Resort Towards the southern end of the main beach ⓣ 075 206960–2, ⓦ www.kohhai.com; Trang office on Thanon Sathanee ⓣ 075 215923. The largest resort on Ko Hai is rather institutional, without much of an island feel. The swanky rooms and bungalows, all with mini-bars, some with air-con, hot water and TVs, are quite tightly packed but have some nice decorative touches. There's a spa, swimming pool and pricey Internet access. Fan ❼, air-con ❼–❾

Ko Hai Paradise Resort Ao Kauntong on the south coast ⓣ 075 203024, ⓔ kohhaiparadise@yahoo.com; Trang office at *The Meeting Point* ⓣ 075 216420 or 075 218535 (see p.832). With this tranquil bay to themselves, the functional but well-maintained, en-suite bungalows are sheltered by tall palms in spacious, grassy grounds. The food's good and the long, white-sand beach slopes down towards some great coral for snorkelling right in front of the resort. They provide their own longtail transfer from Trang via Kuantunku pier (B300/person). ❸

Ko Ngai Resort On the east coast by the island's jetty ⓣ 075 206924–6, ⓦ www.kohngairesort.com; Trang office on Thanon Sathanee ⓣ 075 590035. This traditional-style resort, the first on the island, occupies its own small, shady, sandy cove, to the south of the main beach (10min walk along a path around the rocky headland). Besides a swimming pool and a good restaurant, it has a spread of upmarket accommodation, some of it in a rather ugly, two-storey block, ranging from fan-cooled en-suite rooms to air-conditioned, thatched beachside bungalows with large wooden verandas, spacious bathrooms, hot water, TVs and mini-bars. Fan ❼, air-con ❼–❾

Koh Ngai Villa Near the centre of the main beach ⓣ 075 203263, ⓦ www.krabidir.com/kohngaivilla; Trang office at 112 Thanon Rama VI ⓣ 075 210496. Friendly, old-style beach resort with plenty of space. Simple, well-organized bamboo bungalows boast verandas and small toilets, or you could opt for a smart concrete bungalow or room in a concrete longhouse, or even a two-person tent (B200, including bedding). ❷–❺

Thapwarin Resort Towards the northern end of the main beach ⓣ 075 203169 or 081 894 3585, ⓦ www.thapwarin.com; Trang office at 140/2 Thanon Rongrien ⓣ 075 220139. Welcoming, shady resort, where you can choose between thatched, bamboo and rattan cottages with outdoor bathrooms, and large, very smart wooden bungalows boasting air-con as well as hot water and miniature gardens in their spacious bathrooms. Internet access, beach bar and good restaurant, serving Thai and Western food and espresso coffee. Fan ❼, air-con ❽

Ko Mook

KO MOOK, about 8km southeast of Ko Hai, supports a comparatively busy fishing village on its eastern side, around which the beaches are disappointing, often reduced to dirty mud flats when the tide goes out. However, across on the island's west coast lies beautiful **Hat Farang**, with gently shelving white sand, crystal-clear water that's good for swimming and snorkelling, and gorgeous sunsets. The island's main source of renown is **Tham Morakhot**, the stunning "Emerald Cave" further north on the west coast, which can only be visited by boat, but shouldn't be missed. An eighty-metre swim through the cave – 10m or so of which is in pitch darkness – brings you to an inland beach of powdery sand open to the sky, at the base of a spectacular natural chimney whose walls are coated with dripping vegetation. Unless you're a nervous swimmer, avoid the organized tours on bigger boats offered by some of the resorts on nearby islands, and charter your own longtail instead: you won't get lifejackets and torches, but the boatman will swim through the cave with you and – if you're lucky – you'll avoid the tours and get the inland beach all to yourself, an experience not to be forgotten.

The easiest way to **get there** is to book a minibus-and-boat package to Hat Farang through one of the resort offices or travel agents in Trang, which cost B300, including the thirty-minute longtail ride; *Charlie's* offer the alternative of a fifteen-minute speedboat transfer (B400 from Trang town, B450 from the airport). Otherwise, there's a pretty reliable boat (B60) at around midday to Ko Mook's village from Kuantunku pier, 8km south of Pak Meng, between Hat Chang Lang and Hat Yong Ling; Ban Chao Mai air-con minibuses from Trang charge around B100 to detour to Kuantunku; once landed at the village, you're left with a thirty-minute walk or B50 motorbike-taxi ride over to Hat Farang.

Accommodation

With most of Hat Farang to itself, the nicest of the **bungalow** outfits here is ⭐ *Charlie's* (Ⓣ075 203281–2; Trang office at 17 Thanon Sathanee Ⓣ075 217671–2; Ⓦwww.kohmook.com; fan ❺–❻, air-con ❼), a well-run establishment offering very smart bamboo huts that share a spotlessly clean shower block, as well as attractive concrete en-suite cottages, some with hot water and air-con. The recommended restaurant serves good coffee and a huge variety of Western and Thai food, including local dishes and plenty of seafood, and there are Internet, exchange and overseas phone facilities. You can rent kayaks, have a massage or take a **boat trip**, either to Tham Morakhot and around Ko Mook or to neighbouring islands (from B400/person); the owners plan to build a freshwater swimming pool, so prices will probably go up. If all that isn't enough for you, there's a **dive shop** (Ⓦwww.princessdivers.com) offering courses, local dives off Ko Mook, Ko Kradan and Ko Waen, and trips by speedboat to sites such as Hin Daeng and Hin Muang.

At the rocky, northern end of the beach, *Sawaddee*'s en-suite concrete or stilted wooden bungalows (Ⓣ075 207964–5, Ⓔsawaddeeresort64@yahoo.com; or contact *Wunderbar* in Trang – see p.832; ❹–❺) are less stylish, but enjoy plenty of shade and largely uninterrupted sea views. There are also a few good places on the attractive, shady slopes behind the beach: friendly *Hat Farang* (Ⓣ087 884 4785; ❸) offers simple but clean en-suite huts, as well as good food, including Western breakfasts and a *matsaman* curry speciality; *Rubber Tree* (Ⓣ075 203284 or 081 270 4148; ❸) has well-maintained, thatched, en-suite bungalows in a small plantation and runs regular, reasonably priced **boat trips to Ko Rok** (see p.809); and at *Mookies*, some enterprising Australians have set up comfortable tents, each pitched under a semi-permanent shelter with a bed and table (❷).

Ko Kradan

About 6km to the southwest of Ko Mook, **KO KRADAN** is the remotest of the inhabited islands off Trang, and one of the most beautiful, with crystal-clear waters. On this slender, hilly triangle of thick jungle, the main beach is a long strand of steeply sloping, powdery sand on the east coast, with fine views of Ko Mook, Ko Libong and the karst-strewn mainland, and an offshore reef to the north with a great variety of hard coral. From the *Amari Trang's* beach club (see p.833) towards the south end of this beach, a path across the island will bring you after about fifteen minutes to Sunset Beach, another lovely stretch of fine, white sand in a cove; a branch off this path at *Paradise Lost* (see below) leads to a beach on the short south coast, which enjoys good reef snorkelling (also about 15min from the *Amari* beach club).

Accommodation

Kradan's best **accommodation** option is *Paradise Lost* (Ⓣ089 587 2409; ❸–❺), in the middle of the island, roughly halfway along the path to Sunset Beach. In a grassy, palm-shaded grove, it offers simple, thatched rattan bungalows with shared bathrooms or larger, wooden, en-suite affairs, as well as massages and good Thai and Western food. Phone to arrange a boat (B700) from Kuantunku pier, which is accessible by air-con minibus from Trang (see p.837). On the east coast lies the uninspiring *Ko Kradan Paradise Beach Resort* (Ⓣ075 211367, Ⓦwww.kradanisland.com; Trang office at 28–30 Thanon Sathanee Ⓣ075 211391; ❹–❻), with poorly maintained concrete rooms and bungalows and little shade. Transfers from their Trang office cost B350/person, and the resort can arrange **boat trips** to the neighbouring islands (from B550/person). At the south end of the main beach there's a Hat Chao Mai National Park ranger station, with a few tents to rent (B300 for two people, B400 for three–four people, including bedding), a couple of basic rooms with shared bathrooms (❹) and plans to build some bungalows (contact the park's headquarters for information – see p.834).

Ko Libong

The largest of the Trang islands, **Ko Libong**, lies 10km southeast of Ko Mook, opposite Ban Chao Mai on the mainland. Less visited than its northern neighbours, it's known mostly for its wildlife, although it has its fair share of golden beaches too. Libong is one of the most significant remaining refuges in Thailand of the **dugong** (also known as the manatee), a large marine mammal which feeds on sea grasses growing on the sea floor – the sea-grass meadow around Libong is reckoned to be the largest in Southeast Asia. Sadly, dugongs are now an endangered species, traditionally hunted for their blubber (used as fuel) and meat, and increasingly affected by fishing practices such as scooping, and by coastal pollution which destroys their source of food. The dugong has now been adopted as one of fifteen "reserved animals" of Thailand and is the official mascot of Trang province, but it remains to be seen how effective methods of conservation will be, especially with tourist interest in the dugong growing all the time.

Libong is also well known for its migratory **birds**, which stop off here on their way south from Siberia, drawn by the island's food-rich mud flats (now protected by the Libong Archipelago Sanctuary, which covers the eastern third of the island). For those seriously interested in ornithology, the best time to come is during March and April, when you can expect to see crab plovers, great knots, Eurasian curlews, bar-tailed godwits, brown-winged kingfishers, masked finfoots and even the rare black-necked stork, not seen elsewhere on the Thai–Malay peninsula.

Libong Nature Beach Resort runs award-winning, environmentally friendly, day-long **boat trips** (B2000/person, or B600/person in a group of six or more), which are also available from their sister resort, *Had Yao Nature Resort*. As well as visiting a *chao ley* village, these give you the chance to kayak into the sanctuary to observe the rare birds and to snorkel at the sea-grass beds – with, they reckon, an eighty percent chance of seeing a dugong.

Practicalities

Boats depart daily year-round from Ban Chao Mai (see p.834) when full (B40–50/person), arriving twenty minutes later at Ban Phrao on Ko Libong; from here motorbike taxis (B80–100) transport you across to Ban Lan Khao and the island's resorts. Alternatively, you can take a boat direct from *Had Yao Nature Resort* in Ban Chao Mai to *Libong Nature Beach Resort* for B200/person.

Ko Libong's two **resorts** are situated on the long, thin strip of golden sand which runs along the southwestern coast, where at low tide the sea retreats for hundreds of metres, exposing rock pools that are great for splashing about in but not so good for a dip. The *Libong Nature Beach Resort* (❹) is run by the same team who operate the *Had Yao Nature Resort*, with the same contact details (see p.834). Its neat, brick en-suite bungalows are set slightly back from a secluded stretch of beach, a ten-minute walk south of the fishing village of Ban Lan Khao; there's a good restaurant attached too, and Internet access is available. At *Libong Beach Resort* (Ⓣ075 225205 or 081 477 8609, Ⓦwww.libongbeachresort.com; fan ❹, air-con ❻), on the opposite, northern, side of Ban Lan Khao, a little closer to the clutter of the village, sturdy and smart en-suite bungalows on stilts come with or without air-con, or you can sleep in a tent (B200/night). There's also a reasonable restaurant and a dive shop, and the owner, a friendly local teacher, organizes boat trips and rents out kayaks.

Ko Sukorn

A good way south of the other Trang islands, low-lying **Ko Sukorn** lacks the white-sand beaches and beautiful coral of its neighbours, but makes up for it with its friendly inhabitants, laid-back ambience and one excellent resort; for a glimpse of how islanders live and work, this is the place to come.

The lush interior of the island is mainly given over to rubber plantations, interspersed with rice paddies, banana and coconut palms, while Hat Talo Yai, the island's main **beach** – 500m of gently shelving brown sand, backed by coconut palms – runs along the southwestern shore. It's here you'll find the outstanding ★ *Sukorn Beach Bungalows* (Ⓣ075 207707; Trang office at 22 Thanon Sathanee Ⓣ075 211457; Ⓦwww.sukorn-island-trang.com; fan ❹–❺, air-con ❻–❼), one of the few Trang resorts that's reliably accessible all year round (discounts of up to sixty percent are available in low season). The clued-up and congenial Thai-Dutch duo who run the place are keen to keep the resort low-key and work with the locals as much as possible, something that's reflected in the friendly welcome you get all over the island. Attractively decorated and well-designed bungalows and rooms – all spotlessly clean and with en-suite bathrooms, some with hot water – are set around a lush garden dotted with deckchairs and umbrellas, and there's an excellent, well-priced **restaurant**. At the resort, you can access the Internet, make overseas calls, exchange money and get a good massage, and you're free to paddle around in kayaks.

△ Sukorn Beach Bungalows

Boat excursions from the resort include trips out to Ko Lao Lieng and Ko Takieng, which are part of the Mu Ko Phetra National Marine Park, for some excellent snorkelling. These run in high season only, when the sea is calm enough; at other times of year you're restricted to fishing trips – and to looking round the island itself, which, at thirty square kilometres, is a good size for exploring. The resort offers **guided tours** (B250 or less per person), or it has motorbikes (half-day B300) and mountain bikes (half-day B150) for rent, as well as a handy map that marks all the sights, including the seafood market and a 150-metre-high viewpoint.

A songthaew-and-boat **transfer to the island** (B130/person) leaves the resort's office in Trang daily at 11am and takes a couple of hours, or you can arrange a private transfer. The resort can also organize pricey longtail-boat transfers to or from any of the nearby islands, and can even put together an all-in island-hopping package, with stays at *Charlie's* on Ko Mook and *Libong Beach Resort*, for B28,900 for two people, most of which goes on your private longtail transfers.

If *Sukorn Beach Bungalows* is not your cup of tea, the best of the rest of the island's handful of resorts is the friendly and peaceful *Ko Sukorn Cabana* (Ⓣ089 724 2326, Ⓦwww.sukorncabana.com; Trang office at 160/3 Moo 10, Thanon Trang–Palian Ⓣ075 225894; ⑤), with large, well-appointed log cabins on a secluded beach to the north of Hat Talo Yai; transfers from Trang can be arranged for B350/person.

Satun province

Satun province may in the coming years be developed as a gateway to Malaysia, away from the troubles further east, but for the moment its sleepy capital, **Satun town**, offers few attractions for the visitor – though it does make a good base for the nearby **Thale Ban National Park**, with its caves, waterfalls and luxuriant jungle. The province's main attraction, however, is the **Ko Tarutao National Marine Park**, with pristine stretches of sand and a fantastic array of marine life, which is served by daily dry-season ferries from the port of **Pak Bara**, which lies off the main Satun–Trang highway. The tiny islands to the north of the national park are much less visited, with the exception of **Ko Bulon Lae**, which has a decent selection of privately run bungalows along its long and beautiful beach.

Satun

Nestling in the last wedge of Thailand's west coast, the remote town of **SATUN** is served by just one road, Highway 406, which approaches through forbidding karst outcrops. Set in a green valley bordered by limestone hills, the town is leafy and relaxing but not especially interesting: the boat services to and from Kuala Perlis and Langkawi in Malaysia are the main reason for foreigners to come here.

If you find yourself with time on your hands in Satun, it's worth seeking out the **National Museum** (Wed–Sun 9am–4pm; B30) on Soi 5, Thanon Satun Thani, on the north side of the centre. It's memorable, as much as anything else, for its setting, in the graceful **Kuden Mansion**, which was built in British colonial style, with some Thai and Malay features, by craftsmen from Penang, and inaugurated in 1902 as the Satun governor's official residence. The exhibits and audiovisuals in English have a distinctive anthropological tone, but are diverting enough, notably concerning Thai Muslims, the *chao ley* on Ko Lipe, and the Sakai, a dwindling band of nomadic hunter-gatherers who still live in the jungle of southern Thailand.

Practicalities

Frequent **buses** depart for Satun from Thanon Ratsada in Trang, and regular buses also come here from Hat Yai, Phuket and Bangkok. These buses are based at three different locations in Satun, as marked on our map; on their way out of town, those heading for Hat Yai or Trang will pick up passengers in the centre, for example outside the *Sinkiat Thani Hotel*. **Share-taxis** and **air-con minibuses** also have a variety of bases in town, depending on their destination, as marked on our map. **Internet access** and overseas calls are available at Satun CyberNet, 136 Thanon Satun Thani. Next to the *Sinkiat Thani Hotel* at 48 Thanon Bureewanit, *On's* restaurant (Ⓣ081 097 9783, Ⓔonmarch13@hotmail.com) can provide **motorbike** (B200–250/day) and **car rental** (B1500/day), as well as local **tourist information**.

Moving on to Malaysia from Satun

From Thammalang pier, 10km south of Satun at the mouth of the river, longtail boats leave when full on regular, 45-minute trips (B100/person) to Kuala Perlis on the north-west tip of Malaysia, from where there are plentiful transport connections down the west coast. Three ferry boats a day cross from Thammalang to the Malaysian island of Langkawi (1hr; B250); you can get information in town from *On's*, or from the ferry office at the pier (Ⓣ074 730510–2). Frequent songthaews (B20) run to Thammalang from near the 7-11 supermarket on Thanon Sulakanukul, while motorbike taxis (B50) can be picked up, for example, near the junction of Thanon Saman Pradit and Thanon Bureewanit; both take around fifteen minutes. It's also possible to cross by road into Malaysia at Thale Ban National Park, either with your own transport or if you take a share-taxi to Alor Setar from Thanon Bureewanit, next to Mambang Mosque in Satun.

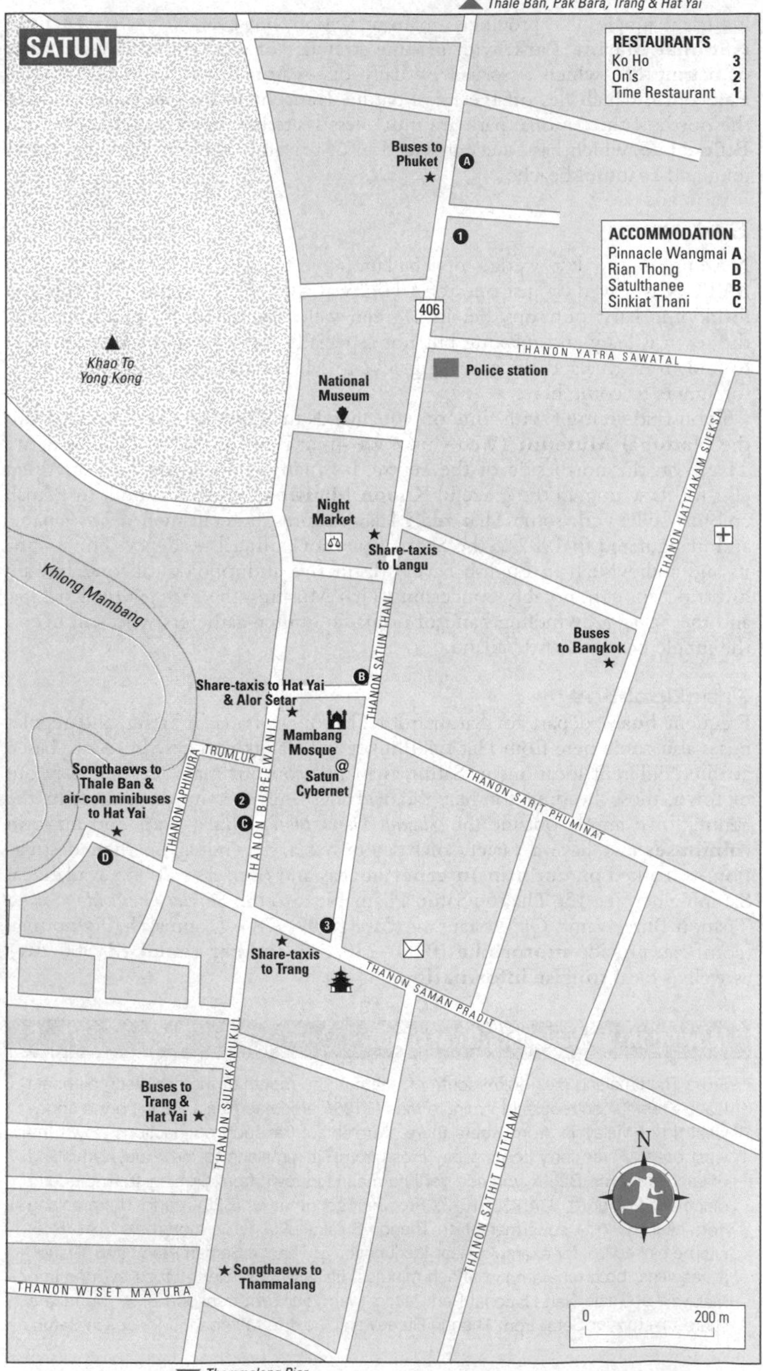
Thale Ban, Pak Bara, Trang & Hat Yai
SATUN
RESTAURANTS
Ko Ho 3
On's 2
Time Restaurant 1
ACCOMMODATION
Pinnacle Wangmai A
Rian Thong D
Satulthanee B
Sinkiat Thani C
Buses to Phuket
406
Thanon Yatra Sawatal
Police station
Khao To Yong Kong
National Museum
Thanon Hatthakam Suksa
Night Market
Share-taxis to Langu
Khlong Mambang
Buses to Bangkok
Thanon Satun Thani
Share-taxis to Hat Yai & Alor Setar
Mambang Mosque
Trumluk
Satun Cybernet
Songthaews to Thale Ban & air-con minibuses to Hat Yai
Thanon Aphinura
Thanon Bureewanit
Thanon Sarit Phuminat
Share-taxis to Trang
Thanon Saman Pradit
Thanon Sulakanukul
Buses to Trang & Hat Yai
Thanon Sathit Utitham
N
Songthaews to Thammalang
Thanon Wiset Mayura
0
200 m
Thammalang Pier

Accommodation

Just on the west side of the centre at 4 Thanon Saman Pradit, *Rian Thong* (the hotel sign mistakenly says "Rain Thong"; ⓣ074 711036; ❶) is the best budget **hotel** in Satun; the owners are friendly, and some of the clean, large, en-suite rooms overlook the canal. Moving up a notch, the *Satulthanee* on Thanon Satun Thani by Mambang Mosque (ⓣ074 712309 or 074 711010; fan ❶, air-con ❷) is a typical Chinese hotel, with spacious, well-kept en-suite rooms, some with air-con and TV and most set back from the main road. The *Pinnacle Wangmai*, north of the centre at 43 Thanon Satun Thani (ⓣ074 711607–8, ⓦwww.pinnaclehotels.com; ❹), fulfils another stereotype, that of a provincial "deluxe" hotel, with air-conditioned rooms in a modern concrete building with hot water, fridges and satellite TV, but no distinctive features. With the same facilities but far more central and preferable is the *Sinkiat Thani*, 50 Thanon Bureewanit (ⓣ074 721055–8, ⓔsinkiathotel@hotmail.com; ❹), where large, carpeted bedrooms offer good views over the surrounding countryside.

Eating and drinking

A good option for moderately priced Thai and Western **food** is the air-conditioned *Time Restaurant*, which is suitably decorated with nostalgic antiques, next door to the *Pinnacle Wangmai Hotel* on Thanon Satun Thani. *On's* simple bar-restaurant (see above) offers good American breakfasts, sandwiches and a short menu of typical Thai dishes. For a meal in the evening, however, you can't do much better than the lively and very popular night market, north of the centre on the west side of Thanon Satun Thani, or try *Ko Ho*, on Thanon Saman Pradit opposite the Chinese temple, a cheap, busy restaurant that serves tasty Thai and Chinese food, including plenty of fish, seafood and salads.

Thale Ban National Park

Spread over rainforested mountains along the Malaysian border, **THALE BAN NATIONAL PARK** is a pristine nature reserve which shelters a breathtaking variety of wildlife: from tapirs, Malayan sun bears, clouded leopards and barking tree frogs, to butterflies, which proliferate in March, and unusual birds such as bat hawks, booted eagles and flamboyant argus pheasants. Unfortunately for naturalists and casual visitors alike, few trails have been marked out through the jungle, but the lush, peaceful setting and the views and bathing pools of the Yaroy waterfall are enough to justify the trip.

Songthaews leave from opposite the *Rian Thong* hotel in Satun when they have enough people (most likely in the early morning), passing through the village of Wang Prachan and reaching Thale Ban **headquarters** (ⓣ074 722736–7), 2km further on, in an hour. Otherwise, get off any bus along Highway 406 between Satun and Hat Yai at Ban Khwan Sator, 19km north of Satun, from where motorbike taxis (B100 one way) make the twenty-kilometre journey along Highway 4184 to Thale Ban.

Hemmed in by steep, verdant hills and spangled with red water lilies, the **lake** by the headquarters is central to the story that gives the park its name. Local legend tells how a villager once put his *ban* (headscarf) on a tree stump to have a rest; this caused a landslide, the lake appeared from nowhere, and he, the stump and the *ban* tumbled into it. The water is now surrounded by **bungalows** with hot showers (B600–2500/night depending on size), a **campsite** (B30/person/night) with showers and toilets, and a decent small **restaurant**.

There used to be an interesting, sixteen-kilometre jungle walk from the headquarters to Yaroy waterfall, but the path has now grown over and is closed, though it may reopen in the future. All that's currently left are two short circular trails (700m and 1300m) from the headquarters, on which you're likely to see birds, gibbons and snakes. A little further afield is **Tham Tondin**, a low, sweaty stalactite cave, about 2km north of headquarters just off the road to Khwan Sator, that gradually slopes down for 800m to deep water. A more compelling jaunt, however, is to **Yaroy waterfall** – bring swimming gear for the pools above the main fall. Take the main road north from the headquarters through the narrow, idyllic valley for 6km (beyond the village of Wang Prachan) and follow the sign to the right. After 700m, you'll find the main, lower fall set in screeching jungle. Climbing the path on the left side, you reach what seems like the top, with fine views of the steep, green peaks to the west. However, there's more: further up the stream are a series of gorgeous shady pools, where you can bathe and shower under the six-metre falls.

Ko Tarutao National Marine Park

The unspoilt **KO TARUTAO NATIONAL MARINE PARK** is probably the most beautiful of all Thailand's accessible beach destinations. Occupying 1400 square kilometres of the Andaman Sea, the park covers 51 mostly uninhabited islands, of which three are easy to reach from the mainland and offer accommodation for visitors. Site of the park headquarters, **Ko Tarutao** offers the widest variety of accommodation and things to do, while **Ko Adang** is much more low-key and a springboard to some excellent snorkelling. Home to a population of around seven hundred *chao ley* (see p.713), **Ko Lipe** is something of a frontier maverick, attracting ever more backpackers with one dazzling beach, ten or so private bungalow resorts and a rough-and-ready atmosphere. The port of **Pak Bara** is currently the only jumping-off point for the park, and houses a **national park visitor centre** (☎074 783485 or 074 783597), set back on the left just before the pier, where you can gather information and book a room before boarding your boat.

The park's forests and seas support an incredible variety of **fauna**: langurs, crab-eating macaques and wild pigs are common on the islands, which also shelter several unique subspecies of squirrel, tree shrew and lesser mouse deer; among the hundred-plus bird species found here, reef egrets and hornbills are regularly seen, while white-bellied sea eagles, frigate birds and pied imperial pigeons are more rarely encountered; and the park is the habitat of about 25

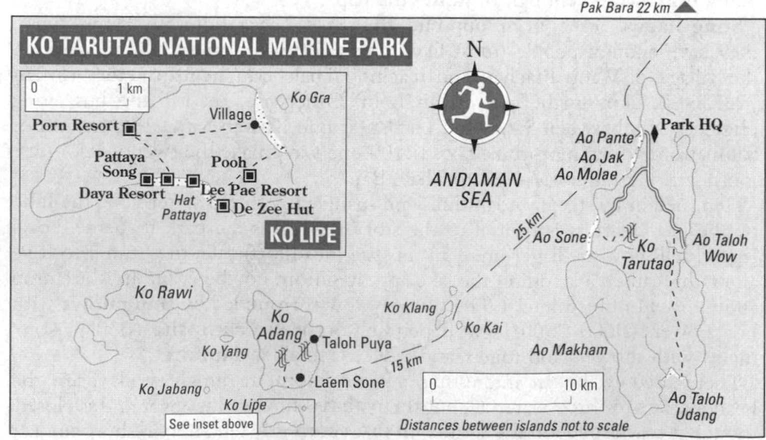

percent of the world's tropical fish species, as well as marine mammals such as the dugong, sperm whale and dolphins. The islands are also home to dwindling populations of Olive Ridley, green, hawksbill and leatherback **turtles** (see box on p.846), with Ao Sone on Ko Tarutao the main nesting beach, especially in January.

The park amenities on Tarutao and Adang are officially **closed** to tourists in the monsoon season from mid-May to mid-November (the exact dates vary from year to year). Most of the resorts on Ko Lipe close at this time too, and the frequency of the ferry service is reduced to one a week. Accommodation is especially likely to get full around the three New Years (Thai, Chinese and Western), when it's best to book national park rooms in advance in Bangkok (see p.51).

The prime **dive sites** in the park are to the west of Ko Tarutao, around Ko Klang, Ko Adang, Ko Rawi and Ko Dong, where encounters with reef and even whale sharks, dolphins, stingrays and turtles are not uncommon. These are now served by two reliable, foreign-run **dive shops** on Ko Lipe, the long-established Sabye Sports at *Porn Resort* (see p.850), and Lotus at *Pooh's* (see p.850), which both offer day-trips to around thirty sites, as well as a wide range of PADI courses. **Snorkelling gear** can be rented at Pak Bara visitor centre or on Ko Adang for B50 per day, and is widely available from the private bungalow outfits or dive shops on Ko Lipe. For watery adventures above the surface, Paddle Asia (see p.835) organizes four- to eight-day, small-group **sea-kayaking** trips around the Tarutao islands, costing US$580–1275 per person.

Ferries

Ferry services into the park seem to change by the year, due to competition between the boat companies and local politicking; there have also been services in the past from Thammalang pier, 10km south of Satun town, which may possibly reappear. For up-to-date **information**, call the Pak Bara National Park Visitor Centre; the friendly and helpful Langu Tourist Boat Association, a co-operative of many of the local boat-owners, which has an office on the left-hand corner right opposite Pak Bara pier (☎089 655 8090 or 081 609 1413); or one of the ferry agents at the pier, such as Andrew Tour (☎074 783459 or 081 897 8482). Note that there is no pier on Adang or Lipe, so boats anchor in the channel between the islands or off Hat Pattaya where they're met by **longtails** (B30–40 to any beach on Lipe or the Adang park station). The pier at Ao Pante on Tarutao is inaccessible at low tide, when longtails (B20) shuttle people to shore.

In season, ferries currently leave **Pak Bara** at around 11am and 2pm daily for Ao Pante on Ko Tarutao (1hr or more on most boats; B250 one way), before continuing to Ko Adang and Ko Lipe (B500–550 from Pak Bara), 40km and about two hours west of Ko Tarutao. There's also a 10.30am ferry via Ko Bulon Lae (see p.850) to Ko Adang and Ko Lipe (about 5hr in total; B500). Coming back to Pak Bara, boats that call in at Ko Tarutao leave Ko Adang and Ko Lipe at around 9am and 10am, those via Ko Bulon Lae at 2pm. On the Pak Bara–Tarutao–Adang route, one fast boat, the *Satun 1*, is currently in operation, cutting the journey time to Tarutao down to thirty minutes or so, to Adang and Lipe to around 2hr. All the operators offer small discounts on return tickets; for the slower boats (not *Satun 1*), you can buy a return ticket to Adang/Lipe for B900 and stop off at Tarutao and/or Bulon Lae. At busy times, there may be additional ferries and speedboats.

At the time of writing, boats **between Ko Lipe and Langkawi**, the large Malaysian island to the southeast, were just starting up. This service, however, is

Turtles in Thailand

Thailand is home to four species of **marine turtle**: the green, the leatherback, the Olive Ridley and the hawksbill. The loggerhead turtle also once swam in Thai waters, until the constant plundering of its eggs rendered it locally extinct. Of the remaining four species, the **green turtle** is the commonest, a mottled brown creature named not for its appearance but for the colour of the soup made from its flesh. Adults weigh up to 180kg and are herbivorous, subsisting on sea grass, mangrove leaves and algae. The **leatherback**, encased in a distinctive ridged shell, is the world's largest turtle, weighing in at between 250kg and 550kg; it eats nothing but jellyfish. The small **Olive Ridley** weighs up to 50kg and feeds mainly on shrimps and crabs. Named for its peculiar beak-like mouth, the **hawksbill** is prized for its spectacular carapace (the sale of which was banned by CITES in 1992); it weighs up to 75kg and lives off a type of sea sponge.

The survival of the remaining four species is by no means assured - prized for their meat, their shells and their eggs, and the frequent victims of trawler nets, all types of marine turtle are now **endangered species**. The worldwide population of female turtles is thought to be as small as 70,000 to 75,000, and only around fifty percent of hatchlings reach adulthood. As a result, several of the Thai beaches most favoured by egg-laying turtles have been protected as **marine parks**, and some are equipped with special hatcheries. The breeding season usually starts in October or November and lasts until February, and the astonishing egg-laying ritual can be witnessed, under national park rangers' supervision, on Ko Surin Tai (see p.712) and Ko Tarutao.

Broody female turtles of all species always return to the beach on which they were born to lay their **eggs**, often travelling hundreds of kilometres to get there – no mean feat, considering that females can wait anything from twenty to fifty years before reproducing. Once *in situ*, the turtles lurk in the water and wait for a cloudy night before wending their laborious way onto and up the beach: at 180kg, the green turtles have a hard enough time, but the 550kg leatherbacks endure an almost impossible uphill struggle. Choosing a spot well above the high-tide mark, each turtle digs a deep nest in the sand into which she lays ninety or more eggs; she then packs the hole with the displaced sand and returns to sea. Tears often stream down the turtle's face at this point, but they're a means of flushing out sand from the eyes and nostrils, not a manifestation of grief.

Many females come back to land three or four times during the nesting season, laying a new batch of ninety-plus eggs at every sitting. Incubation of each batch takes from fifty to sixty days, and the temperature of the sand during this period determines the sex of the hatchling: warm sand results in females, cooler sand in males. When the baby turtles finally emerge from their eggshells, they immediately and instinctively head seawards, guided both by the moonlight on the water – which is why any artificial light, such as torch beams or camera flashes, can disorientate them – and by the downward gradient of the beach.

hampered by the lack of an immigration post on Lipe, so the operators generally have to bring over an immigration officer from the mainland to stamp people out of or into Thailand. *Tarutao Cabana Resort* on the east side of Lipe (Ⓣ089 150 5350) currently does the one-hour trip four times a week, charging B1000 each way. Sabye Sports (see p.850) also covers this route, especially at weekends, charging B1260.

En route to Tarutao and Bulon Lae: Pak Bara

From Trang, agencies such as Sukorn Beach Bungalows and Tours (see p.831) offer regular direct air-con minibuses to **PAK BARA** in high season (2hr);

otherwise you'll need to take a Satun-bound bus (2hr 30min) or share-taxi (1hr 30min) from Thanon Ratsada to the inland town of **Langu** and change there to a red songthaew for the ten-kilometre hop to the port. Frequent buses and taxis **from Satun** make the fifty-kilometre trip to Langu.

Accommodation is available in Pak Bara for people who miss the boats. The best budget choice is the friendly *Bara Guesthouse* (Ⓣ074 783097; ❷), less than 500m before the pier on the west side of the main road, which offers large, tiled, concrete rooms with their own bathrooms in a garden running down to the sea. Another couple of hundred metres from the pier on the same side of the road and a short way upmarket, the motel-like *Grand Villa* (Ⓣ074 783499; ❸) provides air-con and TV in its smart, modern, en-suite rooms. On the right just before the pier, *Cherry Delight* is a charming, little daytime **café**, which serves up Western breakfasts and sandwiches, healthy juices and espresso coffee, as well as tasty southern Thai specialities such as savoury or sweet rotis. There are no banks on the Tarutao islands or Bulon Lae, but Smooth Tours by the pier offers **currency-exchange** facilities, as well as **Internet access**. After a stint on the islands, Pak Bara Travel by the pier (Ⓣ081 776 1271) can arrange **air-con minibus** transfers to Trang, Ko Lanta and Krabi in high season.

Ko Tarutao

The largest of the national park's islands, **KO TARUTAO** offers the greatest natural variety: mountains covered in semi-evergreen rainforest rise steeply to a high point of 700m; limestone caves and mangrove swamps dot the shoreline; and the west coast is lined with perfect beaches for most of its 26-kilometre length.

Boats will drop you off at **Ao Pante**, on the northwestern side of the island, where the admission fee (B200) is collected and where the **park headquarters** (Ⓣ074 729002–3) is situated. Here you'll find the only shop on the island, selling basic supplies, as well as a visitor centre, a library and a **restaurant**. The **bungalows** (B800–1000/bungalow sleeping four to six people, or B600 for a twin room), which are spread over a large, quiet park behind the beach, are for the main part national park standard issue with cold-water bathrooms, but there are also some basic mattress-on-floor four-person rooms in **longhouses**, sharing bathrooms (B500/room). A few two-person **tents** can be rented for B150 per night; campers with their own gear are charged B30 per person per night. The visitor centre can arrange **transport** by car to several of the island's beaches, as detailed below; transfers to the same places by boat cost at least twice as much, though you may be tempted by a **round-island boat trip** for B2500.

Behind the settlement, the steep, half-hour climb to **To-Boo cliff** is a must, especially at sunset, for the view of the surrounding islands and the crocodile's-head cape at the north end of the bay. A fun ninety-minute boat trip (B400/boat; contact the visitor centre to book) can also be made near Ao Pante, up the canal which leads 2km inland from the pier, through a bird-filled mangrove swamp, to **Crocodile Cave** – where you're unlikely to see any of the big snappers, reported sightings being highly dubious.

A half-hour walk south from Ao Pante brings you to the two quiet bays of **Ao Jak** and **Ao Molae**, fringed by coconut palms and filled with fine white sand; the latter now sports some **bungalows** (from B1000 for an en-suite twin room) and a small restaurant. Transfers by car from Ao Pante to Ao Molae are free if you're staying here, B200/car otherwise. Beyond the next headland lies **Ao Sone** (which gets its names from the casuarina trees that fringe the beach), where a pretty freshwater stream runs past the ranger station at the north end

△ Ko Tarutao

of the bay, and there's a simple restaurant, making this a good place for peaceful camping. Transfers to Ao Sone from Ao Pante cost B400/car, or else it's a two-hour walk. A favourite egg-laying site for sea turtles, the main part of the bay is a three-kilometre sweep of flawless sand, with a one-hour trail leading up to Lu Du Waterfall at the north end, a ninety-minute trail to Lo Po Waterfall in the middle and a mangrove swamp at the far south end.

On the east side of the island, **Ao Taloh Wow** is a rocky bay with a ranger station, restaurant and campsite, connected to Ao Pante by a twelve-kilometre road (B600/car transfer) through old rubber plantations and evergreen forest. If you have a tent, you might want to set off along the overgrown, five-hour trail beyond Taloh Wow, which cuts through the forest to **Ao Taloh Udang**, a sandy bay on the south side where you can set up camp. Here the remnants of a penal colony for political prisoners are just visible: the plotters of two failed coup attempts – including the author of the first English–Thai dictionary and a grandson of Rama VII – were imprisoned here in the 1930s before returning to high government posts. The ordinary convicts, who used to be imprisoned here and at Ao Taloh Wow, had a much harsher time, and during World War II, when supplies from the mainland dried up, prisoners and guards ganged together to turn to piracy. This turned into a lucrative business, which was not suppressed until 1946 when the Thai government asked the British in Malaysia to send in three hundred troops. Pirates and smugglers still occasionally hide out in the Tarutao archipelago, but the main problem now is illegal trawlers fishing in national park waters.

Ko Adang

At **KO ADANG**, a wild, rugged island covered in tropical rainforest, the park station is at **Laem Sone** on the southern shore, where the beach is steep and narrow and backed by a thick canopy of pines. There are **rooms** in bamboo longhouses (B400/room sleeping four), as well as three-person rooms in bungalows (B300) and large **bungalows** sleeping up to nine people (B900–1500). Two-person **tents** can be rented (B150/night), as well as comfortable tents in thatched shelters by the beach (B250/night, supposedly sleeping up to five people); or campers can pitch their own tents for B30 per person per night. There's a **restaurant** here, too.

The half-hour climb to **Sha-do** cliff on the steep slope above Laem Sone gives good views over Ko Lipe to the south. About 2km west along the coast from the park station, the small beach is lined with coconut palms and an abandoned customs house, behind which a twenty-minute trail leads to the small **Pirate Waterfall**. You can rent **longtail boats** (as well as snorks and masks) through the rangers for excellent snorkelling trips to nearby islands such as Ko Rawi and Ko Jabang (around B800 for up to 10 people, depending on how far you want to go).

Ko Lipe

KO LIPE, 2km south of Adang, makes a busy contrast to the other islands. A small, flat triangle, it's covered in coconut plantations and inhabited by *chao ley*, with shops, a school and a health centre in the village on the eastern side. By rights, such a settlement should not be allowed within the national park boundaries, but the *chao ley* on Lipe are well entrenched: Satun's governor forced the community to move here from Phuket and Ko Lanta between the world wars, to reinforce the island's Thai character and prevent the British rulers of Malaya from laying claim to it. More recently, an influx of mostly European backpackers has been enticed here by the gorgeous beach of Hat Pattaya, the relaxed, anything-goes atmosphere and mellow nightlife. There's a good, regularly updated **website** dedicated to the island, Ⓦwww.kohlipethailand.com.

There are fifteen or so **bungalow** outfits on the island, generally not very well designed and mostly operated by enterprising newcomers from the mainland rather than the indigenous *chao ley*. Several of them have set up shop on the eastern side of the island near the village, but the beach here is nowhere near as nice as Hat Pattaya, or even Sunset Beach. Nearly all of the resorts can arrange **snorkelling trips** to the best sites around the islands on the west side of Ko Adang, for around B350/person.

Hat Pattaya

The majority of the resorts can be found on **Hat Pattaya**, the prettiest beach on Ko Lipe, a shining crescent of squeaky-soft white sand, 1km from the village on the south side of the island; on its eastern side, it also has a good offshore reef to explore. Towards the east end of the beach lies *De Zee Huts* (Ⓣ085 069 0566; ❸), a friendly, easy-going place that offers thatched and yellow-painted bamboo bungalows (at the lower end of this price code) with mosquito nets and en-suite, outdoor toilets. Towards the western end, the cheery and efficiently run *Lee Pae Resort* (Ⓣ074 724336 or 074 723804, Ⓦwww.leepaeresort.com; ❸–❻) has plenty of shade and dozens of serried bungalows, ranging from en-suite bamboo huts to concrete cottages with air-con and large glass doors facing the beach; also on offer are Internet access and good massages in a *sala* by the beach. At the far west end of the beach is the Italian-run *Pattaya Song* (Ⓣ074 728034, Ⓦwww.pattayasongresort.com; ❷–❺), where basic, en-suite bamboo or concrete bungalows are strung out behind the beach or in a lovely location up on a steep promontory with great views of the bay; **sea-kayaks** can be rented here for B500 per day. *Daya Resort* next door (Ⓣ074 728030; ❷) offers basic concrete rooms or colourful bamboo-and-thatch bungalows, some in a great position right on the beach. Their **restaurant** makes itself very popular with candlelit tables on the beach and excellent grub, notably grilled seafood and southern Thai curries.

About half a dozen **beach bars**, with candlelit tables sprawled on the sand and names like *Time to Chill*, are thinly scattered along Hat Pattaya, while midway along the path that connects the eastern end of the beach to the village, is *Pooh's*, a well-run and welcoming **bar-restaurant-travel agent** that's a hub of touristic activity on Lipe: on offer are great Thai and Western food, including a choice of breakfasts and coffees, Internet access, currency exchange and **diving** with Lotus (Ⓦwww.lotusdive.com). *Pooh's* also has some smart, en-suite concrete **rooms** behind the restaurant (Ⓣ074 728020, Ⓦwww.poohlipe.com; ❸).

Sunset Beach

On the northwest side of Ko Lipe, **Sunset Beach** is not as postcard-perfect as Hat Pattaya, but *Porn* here is probably the most attractive and welcoming resort on the island (Ⓣ089 464 5765; ❷–❸): in a pleasant setting under the trees on the beach are well-kept thatched, bamboo bungalows with verandas and en-suite bathrooms, or there are two-person tents for rent (B100). A path from the back of the resort will bring you to Hat Pattaya, just east of *Daya Resort*, in ten minutes. Attached to *Porn* is Sabye Sports (Ⓣ074 728026, Ⓦwww.sabye-sports.com), Lipe's oldest **dive shop**, which also offers snorkelling trips (B750/person including lunch and gear) and massages. Behind here, under the trees, *Flour Power Bakery* prepares great brownies, apple pie, cookies and iced coffee.

Ko Bulon Lae

The scenery at tiny **KO BULON LAE**, 20km west of Pak Bara, isn't as beautiful as that generally found in Ko Tarutao National Park to the south, but it's not at all bad: a two-kilometre strip of fine white sand runs the length of the casuarina-lined east coast, while *chao ley* fishermen make their ramshackle homes in the tight coves of the rest of the island. A reef of curiously shaped hard coral closely parallels the eastern beach, while **White Rock** to the south of the island has beautifully coloured soft coral and equally dazzling fish. **Snorkelling** gear, as well as **boats** for trips to White Rock, Ko Lao Lieng and other surrounding islands (from around B1200/boat), can be rented at *Pansand* and *Bulon Viewpoint* resorts.

In high season, **ferries** for Ko Bulon Lae currently leave Pak Bara (see p.846) daily at about 10.30am and 3pm (1hr 30min; B250 one way, B400 return); the former continues to Ko Adang and Ko Lipe (3hr; B300 one way). As there's no pier on Bulon Lae, the inter-island boats are met by longtails to transfer visitors to shore (B30). Boats return from Bulon Lae to Pak Bara at around 9am and noon. Services are reduced, sometimes to nothing, during the monsoon season. Contact *Pansand* or First Andaman Travel (see below) for the latest information.

Accommodation

The island's largest and best **resort** is *Pansand* on the east-coast beach (Ⓣ081 397 0802, Ⓦwww.pansand-resort.com; Trang office at First Andaman Travel, 82–84 Thanon Wisetkul Ⓣ075 218035; ❻–❼, breakfast included), where large, smart, white clapboard cottages come with verandas, cold-water bathrooms and plenty of room to breathe. On the beach side of the shady, well-tended grounds, there's a sociable restaurant serving up good seafood and other Thai dishes; Internet access is also available. The best of several budget resorts is friendly *Bulone* (Ⓣ081 897 9084; ❷–❺), a huge grassy compound under the casuarinas at the north end of the main beach. Choose between airy, bamboo-walled bungalows (with or without their own bathrooms) and larger, white, en-suite, clapboard affairs, and be sure to eat at the restaurant, which features a small selection of tasty Italian faves. On the north coast about ten minutes' walk from *Pansand*, *Bulon Viewpoint* (Ⓣ074 728005–6, Ⓔbulon_view_satun@hotmail.com; ❸–❺) doesn't quite live up to its name. In a shady garden, which slopes steeply down to a beach bar and restaurant, stand small, simple, en-suite bungalows, as well as large, sturdy, concrete affairs with verandas and chairs.

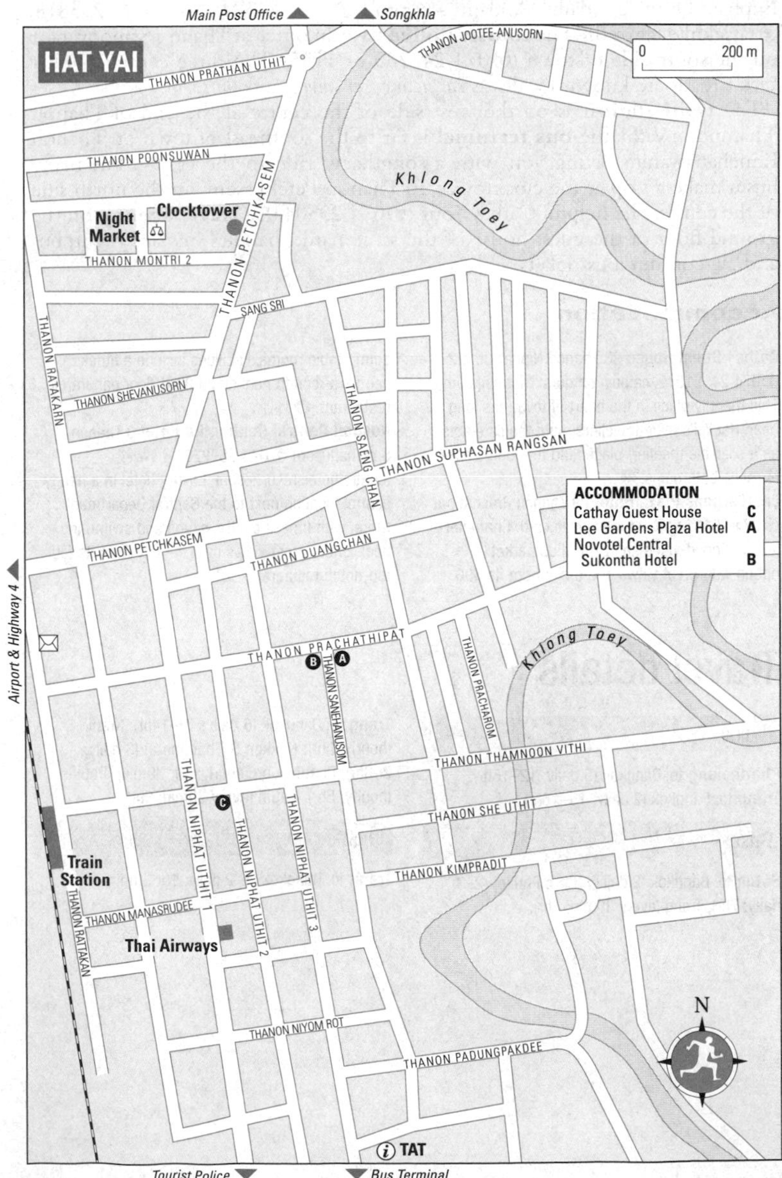

Hat Yai

Travelling to or through **HAT YAI**, the biggest city in the region, is currently **not recommended** because of the troubles in the south (see p.825). However, as it's a major transport axis, we've provided a few, rudimentary practicalities and a map of the city (see p.851), in case you get stuck there.

The **TAT office** for Songkhla and Satun provinces is at 1/1 Soi 2, Thanon Niphat Uthit 3 (daily 8.30am–4.30pm; ⓣ074 243747 or 074 235818, ⓔtatsgkhl@tat.or.th). The **tourist police** have an office at Thanon Sripoovanart on the south side of town (ⓣ074 246733 or 1155). The three central Niphat Uthit roads are known locally as *sai neung*, *sai sawng* and *sai saam*.

The **train station** is on the west side of the centre at the end of Thanon Thamnoon Vithi; the **bus terminal** is far to the southeast of town on Thanon Kanchanawanit, leaving you with a songthaew ride to the centre, but many buses make a stop at the clocktower on Thanon Petchkasem, on the north side of the centre. The helpful Cathay Tour (ⓣ074 235044), a **travel agency** on the ground floor of the guest house of the same name, handles onward flight, bus and air-con minibus tickets.

Accommodation

Cathay Guest House 93 Thanon Niphat Uthit 2 ⓣ074 243815, ⓔcathay_ontours@hotmail.com. This friendly place in the heart of town has long been Hat Yai's main travellers' hub; the café acts as a sociable meeting-place, and the rooms have en-suite bathrooms. ❷

Lee Gardens Plaza Hotel 29 Thanon Prachatipat ⓣ074 261111, ⓦwww.leeplaza.com. Characterless but good-value and central upmarket option with great views of the city from its 400 comfortable rooms. Facilities include a fitness centre, a rooftop pool and a 33rd-floor panoramic restaurant. ❻

Novotel Central Sukhontha Hotel 3 Thanon Sanehanusom ⓣ074 352222, ⓦwww.centralhotelsresorts.com. Luxury hotel in a handy central location next to the Central Department Store, with fitness centre, sauna and swimming pool. Offers great views over the city from its four top-notch restaurants. ❽

Travel details

Trains

Phatthalung to: Bangkok (5 daily; 12–15hr).
Trang to: Bangkok (2 daily; 15–16hr).

Buses

Satun to: Bangkok (2 daily; 16hr); Phuket (2–3 daily; 7hr); Trang (every 30min; 3hr).

Trang to: Bangkok (6 daily; 12–14hr); Krabi (hourly; 2hr); Nakhon Si Thammarat (3 daily; 2–3hr); Phatthalung (hourly; 1hr 30min); Phuket (hourly; 5hr); Satun (every 30min; 3hr).

Flights

Trang to: Bangkok (1–2 daily; 1hr 30min).

Contexts

Contexts

History

As long as forty thousand years ago, Thailand was inhabited by **hunter-gatherers** who lived in semi-permanent settlements and used tools made of wood, bamboo and stone. By the end of the last Ice Age, around ten thousand years ago, these groups had become **farmers**, keeping chickens, pigs and cattle, and – as evidenced by the seeds and plant husks which have been discovered in caves in northern Thailand – cultivating rice and beans. This drift into an agricultural society gave rise to further technological developments: the earliest **pottery** found in Thailand has been dated to 6800 BC, while the recent excavations at **Ban Chiang** in the northeast have shown that **bronze** was being worked at least as early as 2000 BC, putting Thailand on a par with Mesopotamia, which has traditionally been regarded as the earliest Bronze Age culture. By two thousand years ago, the peoples of Southeast Asia had settled in small villages, among which there was regular communication and trade, but they had split into several broad families, differentiated by language and culture. At this time, the ancestors of the Thais, speaking proto-Thai languages, were still far away in southeastern China, whereas Thailand itself was inhabited by Austroasiatic speakers, among whom the Mon were to establish the region's first distinctive civilization, Dvaravati.

Dvaravati and Srivijaya

The history of **Dvaravati** is ill-defined to say the least, but the name is applied to a distinctive culture complex which shared the **Mon** language and **Theravada Buddhism**. This form of religion probably entered Thailand during the second or third centuries BC, when Indian missionaries were sent to Suvarnabhumi, "land of gold", which seems to correspond to the broad swath of fertile land stretching from southern Burma across the north end of the Gulf of Thailand.

From the discovery of monastery boundary stones (*sema*), clay votive tablets and Indian-influenced Buddhist sculpture, it's clear that Dvaravati was an extensive and prosperous Buddhist civilization which had its greatest flourishing between the sixth and ninth centuries AD. No strong evidence has turned up, however, for the existence of a single capital – rather than an empire, Dvaravati seems to have been a collection of city-states, which, at least in their early history, came under the lax suzerainty of **Funan**, a poorly documented kingdom centred in Cambodia. Nakhon Pathom, Lopburi, Si Thep and Muang Sema were among the most important Dvaravati sites, and their concentration around the Chao Phraya valley would seem to show that they gained much of their prosperity, and maintained religious and cultural contacts with India, via the **trade route** from the Indian Ocean over the Three Pagodas Pass.

Although they passed on aspects of their heavily Indianized art, religion and government to later rulers of Thailand, these Mon city-states were politically fragile and from the ninth century onwards succumbed to the domination of the invading Khmers from Cambodia. One northern outpost, the state of **Haripunjaya**, centred on Lamphun, which had been set up on the trade route with southern China, maintained its independence probably until the beginning of the eleventh century.

Meanwhile, to the south of Dvaravati, the shadowy Indianized state of Lankasuka had grown up in the second century, centred on Ligor (now Nakhon Si

Thammarat) and covering an area of the Malay peninsula which included the important trade crossings at Chaiya and Trang. In the eighth century, it came under the control of the **Srivijaya** empire, a Mahayana Buddhist state centred on Sumatra, which had strong ties with India and a complex but uneasy relationship with neighbouring Java. Thriving on seaborne trade between Persia and China, Srivijaya extended its influence as far north as Chaiya, its regional capital, where discoveries of temple remains and some of the finest stone and bronze statues ever produced in Thailand have borne witness to the cultural vitality of this crossroads empire. In the tenth century the northern part of Lankasuka, under the name **Tambralinga**, regained a measure of independence, although it seems still to have come under the influence of Srivijaya as well as owing some form of allegiance to Dvaravati. By the beginning of the eleventh century, however, peninsular Thailand had come under the sway of the Khmer empire, with a Cambodian prince ruling over a community of Khmer settlers and soldiers at Tambralinga.

The Khmers

The history of central Southeast Asia comes into sharper focus with the emergence of the **Khmers**, vigorous empire-builders whose political history can be pieced together from the numerous stone inscriptions they left. Originally vassal subjects of Funan, the Khmers of **Chenla** – to the north of Cambodia – seized power in the latter half of the sixth century during a period of economic decline in the area. Chenla's rise to power was knocked back by a punitive expedition conducted by the Srivijaya empire in the eighth century, but was reconsolidated during the watershed reign of **Jayavarman II** (802–50), who succeeded in conquering the whole of Kambuja, an area which roughly corresponds to modern-day Cambodia. In order to establish the authority of his monarchy and of his country, Jayavarman II had himself initiated as a *chakravartin*, or universal ruler, the living embodiment of the **devaraja**, the divine essence of kingship – a concept which was adopted by later Thai rulers. Taking as the symbol of his authority the phallic lingam, the king was thus identified with the god Shiva, although the Khmer concept of kingship and thus the religious mix of the state as a whole was not confined to Hinduism: elements of ancestor worship were also included, and Mahayana Buddhism gradually increased its hold over the next four centuries.

It was Jayavarman II who moved the Khmer capital to **Angkor** in northern Cambodia, which he and later kings, especially after the eleventh century, embellished with a series of prodigiously beautiful temples. Jayavarman II also recognized the advantages of the lakes around Angkor for irrigating rice fields and providing fish, and thus for feeding a large population. His successors developed this idea and gave the state a sound economic core with a remarkably complex system of **reservoirs** (*baray*) and water channels, which were copied and adapted in later Thai cities.

In the ninth and tenth centuries, Jayavarman II and his imperialistic successors, especially **Yasovarman I** (889–900), confirmed Angkor as the major power in Southeast Asia. They pushed into Vietnam, Laos, southern China and into northeastern Thailand, where the Khmers left dozens of Angkor-style temple complexes, as seen today at Prasat Phanom Rung and Prasat Hin Phimai. To the west and northwest, Angkor took control over central Thailand, with its most important outpost at Lopburi, and even established a strong presence to the south on the Malay peninsula. As a result of this expansion, the Khmers were masters of the most important trade routes between India and China, and indeed nearly every communications link in the region, from which they were able to derive huge income and strength.

The reign of **Jayavarman VII** (1181–1219), a Mahayana Buddhist who firmly believed in his royal destiny as a *bodhisattva*, sowed the seeds of Angkor's downfall. Nearly half of all the extant great religious monuments of the empire were erected under his supervision, but the ambitious scale of these building projects and the upkeep they demanded – some 300,000 priests and temple servants of 20,000 shrines consumed 38,000 tons of rice per year – along with a series of wars against Vietnam, terminally exhausted the economy.

In subsequent reigns, much of the life-giving irrigation system around Angkor turned into malarial swamp through neglect, and the rise of the more democratic creed of Theravada Buddhism undermined the divine authority which the Khmer kings had derived from the hierarchical Mahayana creed. As a result of all these factors, the Khmers were in no position to resist the onslaught between the thirteenth and fifteenth centuries of the vibrant new force in Southeast Asia, the Thais.

The earliest Thais

The earliest traceable history of the **Thai people** picks them up in southern China around the fifth century AD, when they were squeezed by Chinese and Vietnamese expansionism into sparsely inhabited northeastern Laos and neighbouring areas. The first entry of a significant number of Thais onto what is now Thailand's soil seems to have happened in the region of Chiang Saen, where it appears that some time after the seventh century the Thais formed a state in an area then known as **Yonok**. A development which can be more accurately dated and which had immense cultural significance was the spread of Theravada Buddhism to Yonok via Dvaravati around the end of the tenth century, which served not only to unify the Thais but also to link them to Mon civilization and give them a sense of belonging to the community of Buddhists.

The Thais' political development was also assisted by **Nan-chao**, a well-organized military state comprising a huge variety of ethnic groups, which established itself as a major player on the southern fringes of the Chinese empire from the beginning of the eighth century. As far as can be gathered, Nan-chao permitted the rise of Thai *muang* or small principalities on its periphery, especially in the area immediately to the south known as **Sipsong Panna**.

Thai infiltration continued until, by the end of the twelfth century, they seem to have formed the majority of the population in Thailand, then under the control of the Khmer empire. The Khmers' main outpost, at Lopburi, was by then regarded as the administrative capital of a land called "Syam" (possibly from the Sanskrit *syam*, meaning swarthy) – a mid-twelfth-century bas-relief at Angkor Wat, portraying the troops of Lopburi preceded by a large group of self-confident Syam Kuk mercenaries, shows that the Thais were becoming a force to be reckoned with.

Sukhothai

By the middle of the thirteenth century, the Thais, thanks largely to the decline of Angkor and the inspiring effect of Theravada Buddhism, were poised on the verge of autonomous power. The final catalyst was the invasion by Qubilai Khan's Mongol armies of China and Nan-chao, which began around 1215 and was completed in the 1250s. Demanding that the whole world should acknowledge the primacy of the Great Khan, the Mongols set their hearts on the "pacification" of the "barbarians" to the south of China, which obliged the Thais to form a broad power base to meet the threat.

The founding of the first Thai kingdom at **Sukhothai**, now popularly viewed as the cornerstone of the country's development, was in fact a small-scale piece of opportunism which almost fell at the first hurdle. At some time around 1238, the princes of two small Thai principalities in the upper Chao Phraya valley joined forces to capture the main Khmer outpost in the region at Sukhothai. One of the princes, **Intradit**, was crowned king, but for the first forty years Sukhothai remained merely a local power, whose existence was threatened by the ambitions of neighbouring princes. When attacked by the ruler of Mae Sot, Intradit's army was only saved by the grand entrance of Sukhothai's most dynamic leader: the king's nineteen-year-old son, Rama, held his ground and pushed forward to defeat the opposing commander, earning himself the name **Ramkhamhaeng**, "Rama the Bold".

When Ramkhamhaeng came to the throne around 1278, he saw the south as his most promising avenue for expansion and, copying the formidable military organization of the Mongols, seized control of much of the Chao Phraya valley. Over the next twenty years, largely by diplomacy rather than military action, Ramkhamhaeng gained the submission of most of the rulers of Thailand, who entered the **new empire**'s complex tributary system either through the pressure of the Sukhothai king's personal connections or out of recognition of his superior military strength and moral prestige. To the east, Ramkhamhaeng pushed as far as Vientiane in Laos; by marrying his daughter to a Mon ruler to the west, he obtained the allegiance of parts of southern Burma; and to the south his vassals stretched down the peninsula at least as far as Nakhon Si Thammarat. To the north, Sukhothai concluded an alliance with the parallel Thai states of Lanna and Phayao in 1287 for mutual protection against the Mongols – though it appears that Ramkhamhaeng managed to pinch several *muang* on their eastern periphery as tribute states.

Meanwhile **Lopburi**, which had wrested itself free from Angkor sometime in the middle of the thirteenth century, was able to keep its independence and its control of the eastern side of the Chao Phraya valley. Having been first a major cultural and religious centre for the Mon, then the Khmers' provincial capital, and now a state dominated by migrating Thais, Lopburi was a strong and vibrant place mixing the best of the three cultures, as evidenced by the numerous original works of art produced at this time.

Although the empire of Sukhothai extended Thai control over a vast area, its greatest contribution to the Thais' development was at home, in cultural and political matters. A famous **inscription** by Ramkhamhaeng, now housed in the Bangkok National Museum, describes a prosperous era of benevolent rule: "In the time of King Ramkhamhaeng this land of Sukhothai is thriving. There is fish in the water and rice in the fields … [The King] has hung a bell in the opening of the gate over there: if any commoner has a grievance which sickens his belly and gripes his heart … he goes and strikes the bell … [and King Ramkhamhaeng] questions the man, examines the case, and decides it justly for him." Although this plainly smacks of self-promotion, it seems to contain at least a kernel of truth: in deliberate contrast to the Khmer god-kings, Ramkhamhaeng styled himself as a **dhammaraja**, a king who ruled justly according to Theravada Buddhist doctrine and made himself accessible to his people. To honour the state religion, the city's temples were lavishly endowed: as original as Sukhothai's political systems were its religious **architecture and sculpture**, which, though bound to borrow from existing Khmer and Sri Lankan styles, show the greatest leap of creativity at any stage in the history of art in Thailand.

△ Three Kings Monument (Mengrai, Ramkhamhaeng and Ngam Muang), Chiang Mai

A further sign of the Thais' new self-confidence was the invention of a new **script** to make their tonal language understood by the non-Thai inhabitants of the land.

All this was achieved in a remarkably short period of time. After the death of Ramkhamhaeng around 1299, his successors took their Buddhism so seriously that they neglected affairs of state. The empire quickly fell apart, and by 1320 Sukhothai had regressed to being a kingdom of only local significance.

Lanna

Almost simultaneous with the birth of Sukhothai was the establishment of a less momentous but longer-lasting kingdom to the north, called **Lanna**. Its founding father was **Mengrai**, chief of Ngon Yang, a small principality on the banks of the Mekhong near modern-day Chiang Saen. Around 1259 he set out to unify the squabbling Thai principalities of the region, first building a strategically placed city at Chiang Rai in 1262, and then forging alliances with Ngam Muang, the Thai king of Phayao, and with Ramkhamhaeng of Sukhothai.

In 1281, after ten years of guileful preparations, Mengrai conquered the Mon kingdom of Haripunjaya based at Lamphun, and was now master of northern Thailand. Taking advice from Ngam Muang and Ramkhamhaeng, in 1292 he selected a site for an impressive new capital of Lanna at **Chiang Mai**, which remains the centre of the north to the present day. Mengrai concluded further alliances in Burma and Laos, making him strong enough to successfully resist further Mongol attacks, although he was eventually obliged to bow to the superiority of the Mongols by sending them small tributes from 1312 onwards. When Mengrai died after a sixty-year reign in 1317, supposedly struck by a bolt of lightning, he had built up an extensive and powerful kingdom. But although he began a tradition of humane, reasonable laws, probably borrowed from the Mons, he had found little time to set up sound political and administrative institutions. His death severely destabilized Lanna, which quickly shrank in size and influence.

It was only in the reign of **Ku Na** (1355–85) that Lanna's development regained momentum. A well-educated and effective ruler, Ku Na enticed the venerable monk Sumana from Sukhothai, to establish an ascetic Sri Lankan sect in Lanna in 1369. Sumana brought a number of Buddha images with him, inspiring a new school of art that flourished for over a century, but more importantly his sect became a cultural force that had a profound unifying effect on the kingdom. The influence of Buddhism was further strengthened under **King Tilok** (1441–87), who built many great monuments at Chiang Mai and cast huge numbers of bronze seated Buddhas in the style of the central image at Bodh Gaya in India, the scene of the Buddha's enlightenment. Tilok, however, is best remembered as a great warrior, who spent most of his reign resisting the advances of Ayutthaya, by now the strongest Thai kingdom.

Under continuing pressure both from Ayutthaya and from Burma, Lanna went into rapid decline in the second quarter of the sixteenth century. For a short period after 1546, Chiang Mai came under the control of Setthathirat, the king of Lan Sang (Laos), but, unable to cope with Lanna's warring factions, he then abdicated, purloining the talismanic Emerald Buddha for his own capital at Louang Phabang. In 1558, Burma decisively captured Chiang Mai, and the Mengrai dynasty came to an end. For most of the next two centuries, the Burmese maintained control through a succession of puppet rulers, and Lanna again became much as it had been before Mengrai, little more than a chain of competing principalities.

Ayutthaya

While Lanna was fighting for its place as a marginalized kingdom, from the fourteenth century onwards the seeds of a full-blown Thai nation were being sown to the south at **Ayutthaya**. The city of Ayutthaya itself was founded on its present site in 1351 by U Thong, "Prince Golden Cradle", when his own town, Lopburi, was ravaged by smallpox. Taking the title **Ramathibodi**, he soon united the principalities of the lower Chao Phraya valley, which had formed the western provinces of the Khmer empire. When he recruited his bureaucracy from the urban elite of Lopburi, Ramathibodi set the **style of government** at Ayutthaya – the elaborate etiquette, language and rituals of Angkor were adopted, and, most importantly, the conception of the ruler as *devaraja*. The king became sacred and remote, an object of awe and dread, with none of the accessibility of the kings of Sukhothai: when he processed through the town, ordinary people were forbidden to look at him and had to be silent while he passed. This hierarchical system also provided the state with much-needed manpower, as all freemen were obliged to give up six months of each year to the crown either on public works or military service.

The site chosen by Ramathibodi turned out to be the best in the region for an international port, and so began Ayutthaya's rise to prosperity, based on its ability to exploit the upswing in **trade** in the middle of the fourteenth century along the routes between India and China. Flushed with economic success, Ramathibodi's successors were able to expand their control over the ailing states in the region. After a long period of subjugation, Sukhothai became a province of the kingdom of Ayutthaya in 1438, six years after Boromraja II had powerfully demonstrated Ayutthaya's pre-eminence by capturing the once-mighty Angkor, enslaving large numbers of its subjects and looting the Khmer royal regalia. (The Cambodian royal family were forced to abandon the palace forever and to found a new capital near Phnom Penh.)

Although a century of nearly continuous warfare against Lanna was less decisive, success generally bred success, and Ayutthaya's increasing wealth through trade brought ever greater power over its neighbouring states. To streamline the functioning of his unwieldy empire, **Trailok** (1448–88) found it necessary to make reforms of its administration. His **Law of Civil Hierarchy** formally entrenched the inequality of Ayutthayan society, defining the status of every individual by assigning him or her an imaginary number of rice fields – for example, 25 for an ordinary freeman and 10,000 for the highest ministers of state. Trailok's legacy is found in today's unofficial but fiendishly complex status system, by which everyone in Thailand knows their place.

Ramathibodi II (1491–1529), almost at a loss as to what to do with his enormous wealth, undertook an extensive programme of public works. In the 1490s he built several major religious monuments, and between 1500 and 1503 cast the largest standing metal image of the Buddha ever known, the Phra Si Sanphet, which gave its name to the temple of the royal palace. By 1540, the kingdom of Ayutthaya had grown to cover most of the area of modern-day Thailand.

Burmese wars and European trade

In the sixteenth century recurring tensions with Burma led **Chakkraphat** (1548–69) to improve his army and build brick ramparts around the capital. This was to no avail however: in 1568 the Burmese besieged Ayutthaya with a huge army, said by later accounts to have consisted of 1,400,000 men. The Thais held out until August 8, 1569, when treachery within their own ranks helped the Burmese break through the defences. The Burmese looted the city, took thousands of prisoners and installed a vassal king to keep control.

The decisive character who broke the Burmese stranglehold twenty years later and re-established Ayutthaya's economic growth was **Naresuan** (1590–1605), who defied the Burmese by amassing a large army. The enemy sent a punitive expedition which was conclusively defeated at Nong Sarai near modern-day Suphanburi on January 18, 1593, Naresuan himself turning the battle by killing the Burmese crown prince. Historians have praised Naresuan for his personal bravery and his dynamic leadership, although the chronicles of the time record a strong streak of tyranny – in his fifteen years as king he had eighty thousand people killed, excluding the victims of war. A favoured means of punishment was to slice off pieces of the offender's flesh, which he was then made to eat in the king's presence.

The period following Naresuan's reign was characterized by a more sophisticated engagement in **foreign trade**. In 1511 the Portuguese had become the first Western power to trade with Ayutthaya, and Naresuan himself concluded a treaty with Spain in 1598; relations with Holland and England were initiated in 1608 and 1612 respectively. For most of the seventeenth century, European merchants flocked to Thailand, not only to buy Thai products, but also to gain access to Chinese and Japanese goods on sale there. The role of foreigners at Ayutthaya reached its peak under **Narai** (1656–88), but he overstepped the mark in cultivating close links with Louis XIV of France, who secretly harboured the notion of converting Ayutthaya to Christianity. On Narai's death, relations with Westerners were severely cut back.

Despite this reduction of trade and prolonged civil strife over the succession to the throne whenever a king died – then, as now, there wasn't a fixed principle of primogeniture – Ayutthaya continued to flourish for much of the eighteenth century. The reign of **Borommakot** (1733–58) was particularly prosperous, producing many works of drama and poetry. Furthermore, Thai Buddhism had by then achieved such prestige that Sri Lanka, from where the Thais had originally imported their form of religion in the thirteenth century, requested Thai aid in restoring their monastic orders in 1751.

However, immediately after the death of Borommakot the rumbling in the Burmese jungle to the north began to make itself heard again. Alaunghpaya of Burma, apparently a blindly aggressive country bumpkin, first recaptured the south of his country from the Mons, then turned his attentions on Ayutthaya. A siege in 1760 was unsuccessful, with Alaunghpaya dying of wounds sustained there, but the scene was set. In February 1766 the Burmese descended upon Ayutthaya for the last time. The Thais held out for over a year, during which they were afflicted by famine, epidemics and a terrible fire which destroyed ten thousand houses. Finally, in **April 1767**, the walls were breached and the city taken. The Burmese razed everything to the ground and tens of thousands of prisoners were led off to Burma, including most of the royal family. The king, Suriyamarin, is said to have escaped from the city in a boat and starved to death ten days later. As one observer has said, the Burmese laid waste to Ayutthaya "in such a savage manner that it is hard to imagine that they shared the same religion with the Siamese". The city was abandoned to the jungle, but with remarkable speed the Thais regrouped and established a new seat of power, further down the Chao Phraya River at Bangkok.

The early Bangkok empire

As the bulk of the Burmese army was obliged by war with China to withdraw almost immediately, Thailand was left to descend into banditry. Out of this lawless mess several centres of power arose, the most significant being at Chanthaburi, commanded by **Phraya Taksin**. A charismatic, brave and able general who had been unfairly blamed for a failed counter-attack against the Burmese at Ayutthaya, Taksin had anticipated the fall of the besieged city and quietly slipped away with a force of five hundred men. In June 1767 he took control of the east-coast strip around Chanthaburi and very rapidly expanded his power across central Thailand.

Blessed with the financial backing of the Chinese trading community, to whom he was connected through his father, Taksin was crowned king in December 1768 at his new capital of Thonburi, on the opposite bank of the river from modern-day Bangkok. One by one the new king defeated his rivals, and within two years he had restored all of Ayutthaya's territories. More remarkably, by the end of the next decade Taksin had outdone his Ayutthayan predecessors by bringing Lanna, Cambodia and much of Laos into a huge new empire. During this period of expansionism, Taksin left most of the fighting to Thong Duang, an ambitious soldier and descendant of an Ayutthayan noble family, who became the *chakri*, the military commander, and took the title **Chao Phraya Chakri**.

However, by 1779 all was not well with the king. Being an outsider, who had risen from an ordinary family on the fringes of society, Taksin became paranoid about plots against him, a delusion that drove him to imprison and torture even his wife and sons. At the same time he sank into religious excesses, demanding that the monkhood worship him as a god. By March 1782, public outrage at his sadism and dangerously irrational behaviour had reached such fervour that he was ousted in a coup.

Chao Phraya Chakri was invited to take power and had Taksin executed. In accordance with ancient etiquette, this had to be done without royal blood touching the earth: the mad king was duly wrapped in a black velvet sack and struck on the back of the neck with a sandalwood club. (Popular tradition has it that even this form of execution was too much: an unfortunate substitute got the velvet sack treatment, while Taksin was whisked away to a palace in the hills near Nakhon Si Thammarat, where he is said to have lived until 1825.)

Rama I

With the support of the Ayutthayan aristocracy, Chakri – reigning as **Rama I** (1782–1809) – set about consolidating the Thai kingdom. His first act was to move the capital across the river to Bangkok, a better defensive position against any Burmese attack from the west. Borrowing from the layout of Ayutthaya, he built a new royal palace and impressive monasteries, and enshrined in the palace wat the Emerald Buddha, which he had snatched back during his campaigns in Laos.

As all the state records had disappeared in the destruction of Ayutthaya, religious and legal texts had to be written afresh and historical chronicles reconstituted – with some very sketchy guesswork. The monkhood was in such a state of crisis that it was widely held that moral decay had been partly responsible for Ayutthaya's downfall. Within a month of becoming king, Rama I issued a series of religious laws and made appointments to the leadership of the monkhood, to restore discipline and confidence after the excesses of Taksin's reign. Many works of drama and poetry had also been lost in the sacking of Ayutthaya, so Rama I set about rebuilding the Thais' literary heritage, at the same time attempting to make it more cosmopolitan and populist. His main contribution was the *Ramakien*, a dramatic version of the Indian epic *Ramayana*, which is said to have been set to verse by the king himself, with a little help from his courtiers, in 1797. Heavily adapted to its Thai setting, the *Ramakien* served as an affirmation of the new monarchy and its divine links, and has since become the national epic.

In the early part of Rama I's reign, the Burmese reopened hostilities on several occasions, the biggest attempted invasion coming in 1785, but the emphatic manner in which the Thais repulsed them only served to knit together the young kingdom. Trade with China revived, and the king addressed the besetting problem of manpower by ordering every man to be tattooed with the name of his master and his town, so that avoiding royal service became almost impossible. On a more general note, Rama I put the style of government in Thailand on a modern footing: while retaining many of the features of a *devaraja*, he shared more responsibility with his courtiers, as a first among equals.

Rama II and Rama III

The peaceful accession of his son as **Rama II** (1809–24) signalled the establishment of the **Chakri dynasty**, which is still in place today. This Second Reign was a quiet interlude, best remembered as a fertile period for Thai literature. The king, himself one of the great Thai poets, gathered round him a group of writers including the famous Sunthorn Phu, who produced scores of masterly love poems, travel accounts and narrative songs.

In contrast, **Rama III** (1824–51) actively discouraged literary development – probably in reaction against his father – and was a vigorous defender of conservative values. To this end, he embarked on an extraordinary redevelopment of Wat Pho, the oldest temple in Bangkok. Hundreds of educational inscriptions and mural paintings, on all manner of secular and religious subjects, were put on show, apparently to preserve traditional culture against the rapid change which the king saw corroding the country. In foreign affairs, Rama III faced a serious threat from the vassal states of Laos, who in 1827 sent an invading army from Vientiane, which got as far as Saraburi, only three days' march from Bangkok. The king's response was savage: having repelled the initial invasion, he ordered his army to destroy everything in Vientiane apart from Buddhist temples and to forcibly resettle huge numbers of Lao in Isaan. Shortly after, the king was forced to go to war in Cambodia, to save Buddhism and its traditional institutions from the attentions of the newly powerful, non-Buddhist Vietnamese. A series of campaigns in the 1830s and 1840s culminated in the peace treaty of 1845–46, which again established Thailand as the dominant influence in Cambodia.

More significant in the long run was the danger posed by the increase in Western influence which began in the Third Reign. As early as 1825, the Thais were sufficiently alarmed at British colonialism to strengthen Bangkok's defences by stretching a great iron chain across the mouth of the Chao Phraya River, to which every blacksmith in the area had to donate a certain number of links. In 1826 Rama III was obliged to sign a limited trade agreement with the British, the **Burney Treaty**, by which the Thais won some political security in return for reducing their taxes on goods passing through Bangkok. British and American missions in 1850 unsuccessfully demanded more radical concessions, but by this time Rama III was seriously ill, and it was left to his far-sighted and progressive successors to reach a decisive accommodation with the Western powers.

Mongkut and Chulalongkorn

Rama IV, more commonly known as **Mongkut** (1851–68), had been a Buddhist monk for 27 years when he succeeded his brother. But far from leading a cloistered life, Mongkut had travelled widely throughout Thailand, had maintained scholarly contacts with French and American missionaries and, like most of the country's new generation of leaders, had taken an interest in Western learning, studying English, Latin and the sciences. He had also turned his mind to the condition of Buddhism in Thailand, which seemed to him to have descended into little more than popular superstition; indeed, after a study of the Buddhist scriptures in Pali, he was horrified to find that Thai ordinations were probably invalid. So in the late 1830s he set up a rigorously fundamentalist sect called *Thammayutika*, the "Order Adhering to the Teachings of the Buddha", and as abbot of the order he oversaw the training of a generation of scholarly leaders for Thai Buddhism from his base at Bangkok's Wat Bowonniwet, which became a major centre of Western learning.

When his kingship faced its first major test, in the form of a threatening British mission in 1855 led by **Sir John Bowring**, Mongkut dealt with it confidently. Realizing that Thailand was unable to resist the military might of the British, the king reduced import and export taxes, allowed British subjects to live and own land in Thailand and granted them freedom of trade. Of the **government monopolies**, which had long been the mainstay of the Thai economy, only that on opium was retained. After making up the loss in revenue through internal taxation, Mongkut quickly made it known that he would welcome diplomatic contacts from other Western countries: within a decade, agreements similar to the Bowring Treaty had been signed with France, the US and a score of other nations. Thus by skilful diplomacy the king avoided a close relationship with only one power, which could easily have led to Thailand's annexation.

While all around the colonial powers were carving up Southeast Asia amongst themselves, Thailand suffered nothing more than the weakening of its influence over Cambodia, which in 1863 the French brought under their protection. As a result of the open-door policy, foreign trade boomed, financing the redevelopment of Bangkok's waterfront and, for the first time, the building of paved roads. However, Mongkut ran out of time for instituting the far-reaching domestic reforms which he saw were needed to drag Thailand into the modern world.

The modernization of Thailand

Mongkut's son, **Chulalongkorn**, took the throne as Rama V (1868–1910) at the age of only 15, but he was well prepared by an excellent education which mixed traditional Thai and modern Western elements – provided by Mrs Anna Leonowens, subject of *The King and I*. When Chulalongkorn reached his majority after a five-year regency, he set to work on the reforms envisioned by his father. One of his first acts was to scrap the custom by which subjects were required to prostrate themselves in the presence of the king, which he followed up in 1874 with a series of decrees announcing the gradual abolition of slavery. The speed of his financial and administrative reforms, however, proved too much for the "**Ancients**" (*hua boran*), the old guard of ministers and officials inherited from his father. Their opposition culminated in the Front Palace Crisis of 1875, when a show of military strength almost plunged the country into civil war, and, although Chulalongkorn skilfully defused the crisis, many of his reforms had to be quietly shelved for the time being.

An important administrative reform which did go through, necessitated by the threat of colonial expansionism, concerned the former kingdom of Lanna. British exploitation of teak had recently spread into northern Thailand from neighbouring Burma, so in 1874 Chulalongkorn sent a commissioner to Chiang Mai to keep an eye on the prince of Chiang Mai and make sure that he avoided any collision with the British. The commissioner was gradually able to limit the power of the princes and integrate the region more fully into the kingdom.

In the 1880s prospects for reform brightened as many of the "Ancients" died or retired. This allowed Chulalongkorn to **restructure the government** to meet the country's needs: the Royal Audit Office made possible the proper control of revenue and finance; the Department of the Army became the nucleus of a modern armed services; and a host of other departments were set up, for justice, education, public health and the like. To fill these new positions, the king appointed many of his younger brothers, who had all received a modern education, while scores of foreign technicians and advisers were brought in to help with everything from foreign affairs to rail lines.

Throughout this period, however, the Western powers maintained their pressure on the region. The most serious threat to Thai sovereignty was the **Franco-Siamese Crisis** of 1893, which culminated in the French, based in Vietnam, sending gunboats up the Chao Phraya River to Bangkok. Flouting numerous international laws, France claimed control over Laos and made other outrageous demands, which Chulalongkorn had no option but to concede. In 1907 Thailand was also forced to relinquish Cambodia to the French, and in 1909 three Malay states fell to the British. In order to preserve its independence, the country ceded almost half of its territory and forewent huge sums of tax revenue. But from the end of the Fifth Reign, the frontiers were fixed as they are today.

By the time of the king's death in 1910, Thailand could not yet be called a modern nation-state – corruption and nepotism were still grave problems, for example. However, Chulalongkorn had made remarkable advances, and, almost from scratch, had established the political institutions to cope with twentieth-century development.

The end of absolute monarchy

Chulalongkorn was succeeded by a flamboyant, British-educated prince, **Vajiravudh** (1910–25), who was crowned Rama VI. The new king found it difficult to shake the dominance of his father's appointees in the government, who formed an extremely narrow elite, comprised almost entirely of members of Chulalongkorn's family. In an attempt to build up a personal following, Vajiravudh created, in May 1911, the **Wild Tigers**, a nationwide paramilitary corps recruited widely from the civil service. However, in 1912 a group of young army lieutenants, disillusioned by the absolute monarchy and upset at the downgrading of the regular army in favour of the Wild Tigers, plotted a **coup**. The conspirators were easily broken up before any trouble began, but this was something new in Thai history: the country was used to in-fighting among the royal family, but not to military intrigue from men from comparatively ordinary backgrounds.

Vajiravudh's response to the coup was a series of modernizing **reforms**, including the introduction of compulsory primary education and an attempt to better the status of women by supporting monogamy in place of the widespread practice of polygamy. His huge output of writings invariably encouraged people to live as modern Westerners, and he brought large numbers of commoners into high positions in government. Nonetheless, he would not relinquish his strong opposition to constitutional democracy.

When **World War I** broke out in 1914, the Thais were generally sympathetic to the Germans out of resentment over their loss of territory to the French and British. The king, however, was in favour of neutrality, until the US entered the war in 1917, when Thailand followed the expedient policy of joining the winning side and sent an expeditionary force of 1300 men to France in June 1918. The goodwill earned by this gesture enabled the Thais, between 1920 and 1926, to negotiate away the unequal treaties which had been imposed on them by the Western powers. Foreigners on Thai soil were no longer exempted from Thai laws, and the Thais were allowed to set reasonable rates of import and export taxes.

Yet Vajiravudh's extravagant lifestyle – during his reign, royal expenditure amounted to as much as ten percent of the state budget – left severe financial problems for his successor. Vajiravudh died without leaving a son, and as three better-placed contenders to the crown all died in the 1920s, **Prajadhipok** – the seventy-sixth child and last son of Chulalongkorn – was catapulted to the throne as Rama VII (1925–35). Young and inexperienced, he responded to the country's crisis by creating a Supreme Council of State, seen by many as a return to Chulalongkorn's absolutist "government by princes".

Prajadhipok himself seems to have been in favour of constitutional government, but the weakness of his personality and the opposition of the old guard in the Supreme Council prevented him from introducing it. Meanwhile a vigorous community of Western-educated intellectuals had emerged in the lower echelons of the bureaucracy, who were increasingly dissatisfied with the injustices of monarchical government. The final shock to the Thai system came with the Great Depression, which from 1930 onwards ravaged the economy. On June 24, 1932, a small group of middle-ranking officials, led by a lawyer, Pridi Phanomyong, and an army major, Luang Phibunsongkhram, staged a **coup** with only a handful of troops. Prajadhipok weakly submitted to the conspirators, or "Promoters", and 150 years of absolute monarchy in Bangkok came to a sudden end. The king was sidelined to a position of symbolic significance and in 1935 he abdicated in favour of his ten-year-old nephew, **Ananda**, then a schoolboy living in Switzerland.

To the 1957 coup

The success of the 1932 coup was in large measure attributable to the army officers who gave the conspirators credibility, and it was they who were to dominate the constitutional regimes that followed. The Promoters' first worry was that the French or British might attempt to restore the monarchy to full power. To deflect such intervention, they appointed a government under a provisional constitution and espoused a wide range of liberal Western-type reforms, including freedom of the press and social equality, few of which ever saw the light of day.

The regime's first crisis came early in 1933 when **Pridi Phanomyong**, by now leader of the government's civilian faction, put forward a socialist economic plan based on the nationalization of land and labour. The proposal was denounced as communistic by the military, Pridi was forced into temporary exile and an anti-communist law was passed. Then, in October, a royalist coup was mounted which brought the kingdom close to civil war. After intense fighting, the rebels were defeated by Lieutenant-Colonel **Luang Phibunsongkhram** (or Phibun), so strengthening the government and bringing Phibun to the fore as the leading light of the military faction.

Pridi was rehabilitated in 1934 and remained powerful and popular, especially among the intelligentsia, but it was Phibun who became prime minister after the decisive **elections of 1938**, presiding over a cabinet dominated by military men. Phibun encouraged a wave of nationalistic feeling with such measures as the official institution of the name Thailand in 1939 – Siam, it was argued, was a name bestowed by external forces, and the new title made it clear that the country belonged to the Thais rather than the economically dominant Chinese. This latter sentiment was reinforced with a series of harsh laws against the Chinese, who faced discriminatory taxes on income and commerce.

World War II

The outbreak of **World War II** gave the Thais the chance to avenge the humiliation of the 1893 Franco–Siamese Crisis. When France was occupied by Germany in June 1940, Phibun seized the opportunity to invade western Cambodia and the area of Laos lying to the west of the Mekong River. In the following year, however, the threat of a Japanese attack on Thailand loomed. On December 8, 1941, almost at the same time as the assault on Pearl Harbour, the Japanese invaded the country at nine points, most of them along the east coast of the peninsula. The Thais at first resisted fiercely, but realizing that the position was hopeless, Phibun quickly ordered a ceasefire. Meanwhile the British sent a force from Malaysia to try to stop the Japanese at Songkhla, but were held up in a fight with Thai border police. The Japanese had time to establish themselves, before pushing down the peninsula to take Singapore.

The Thai government concluded a military alliance with Japan and declared war against the US and Great Britain in January 1942, probably in the belief that the Japanese would win the war. However, the Thai minister in Washington, Seni Pramoj, refused to deliver the declaration of war against the US and, in co-operation with the Americans, began organizing a resistance movement called **Seri Thai**. Pridi, now acting as regent to the young king, furtively co-ordinated the movement under the noses of the occupying Japanese, smuggling in American agents and housing them in a European prison camp in Bangkok.

By 1944 Japan's final defeat looked likely, and Phibun, who had been most closely associated with them, was forced to resign by the National Assembly in July. A civilian, Khuang Aphaiwong, was chosen as prime minister, while Seri Thai became well established in the government under the control of Pridi. At the end of the war, Thailand was forced to restore the annexed Cambodian and Lao provinces to French Indochina, but American support prevented the British from imposing heavy punishments for the alliance with Japan.

Postwar upheavals

With the fading of the military, the election of January 1946 was for the first time contested by organized political parties, resulting in Pridi becoming prime minister. A new constitution was drafted and the outlook for democratic, civilian government seemed bright.

Hopes were shattered, however, on June 9, 1946, when King Ananda was found dead in his bed, with a bullet wound in his forehead. Three palace servants were hurriedly tried and executed, but the murder has never been satisfactorily explained, and public opinion attached at least indirect responsibility for the killing to Pridi, who had in the past shown strong anti-royalist feeling. He resigned as prime minister, and in April 1948 the military made a decisive return: playing on the threat of communism, with Pridi pictured as a Red bogeyman, Phibun took over the premiership.

After the bloody suppression of two attempted coups in favour of Pridi, the main feature of Phibun's second regime was its heavy involvement with the US. As communism developed its hold in the region, with the takeover of China in 1949 and the French defeat in Indochina in 1954, the US increasingly viewed Thailand as a bulwark against the Red menace. Between 1951 and 1957, when its annual state budget was only about $200 million a year, Thailand received a total $149 million in American economic aid and $222 million in military aid. This strengthened Phibun's dictatorship, while enabling leading military figures to divert American money and other funds into their own pockets.

In 1955, his position threatened by two rival generals, Phibun experienced a sudden conversion to the cause of democracy. He narrowly won a general election in 1957, but only by blatant vote-rigging and coercion. Although there's a strong tradition of foul play in Thai elections, this is remembered as the dirtiest ever: after vehement public outcry, **General Sarit**, the commander-in-chief of the army, overthrew the new government in September 1957.

To the present day

Believing that Thailand would prosper best under a unifying authority – an ideology that still has its supporters – Sarit set about re-establishing the monarchy as the head of the social hierarchy and the source of legitimacy for the government. Ananda's successor, **King Bhumibol** (Rama IX), was pushed into an active role while Sarit ruthlessly silenced critics and pressed ahead with a plan for economic development. These policies achieved a large measure of stability and prosperity at home, although from 1960 onwards the international situation worsened. With the Marxist Pathet Lao making considerable advances in Laos, and Cambodia's ruler, Prince Sihanouk, drawing into closer relations with China, Sarit turned again to the US. The Americans obliged by sharply increasing military aid and by stationing troops in Thailand.

The Vietnam war

Sarit died in 1963, whereupon the military succession passed to **General Thanom**, closely aided by his deputy prime minister, **General Praphas**. Neither man had anything of Sarit's charisma and during a decade in power they followed his political philosophies largely unchanged. Their most pressing problem was the resumption of open hostilities between North and South Vietnam in the early 1960s – the **Vietnam War**. Both Laos and Cambodia became involved on the side of the communists by allowing the North Vietnamese to supply their troops in the south along the Ho Chi Minh Trail, which passed through southern Laos and northeastern Cambodia. The Thais, with the backing of the US, quietly began to conduct military operations in Laos, to which North Vietnam and China responded by supporting anti-government insurgency in Thailand.

The more the Thais felt threatened by the spread of communism, the more they looked to the Americans for help – by 1968 around 45,000 US military personnel were on Thai soil, which became the base for US bombing raids against North Vietnam and Laos, and for covert operations into Laos and beyond.

The effects of the **American presence in Thailand** were profound. The economy swelled with dollars, and hundreds of thousands of Thais became reliant on the Americans for a living, with a consequent proliferation of corruption and prostitution. What's more, the sudden exposure to Western culture led many to question the traditional Thai values and the political status quo.

The democracy movement and civil unrest

At the same time, poor farmers were becoming disillusioned with their lot, and during the 1960s many turned against the Bangkok government. At the end of 1964, the **Communist Party of Thailand** and other groups formed a **broad left coalition** that soon had the support of several thousand insurgents in remote areas of the northeast. By 1967, the problem had spread to Chiang Rai and Nan provinces, and a separate threat had arisen in southern Thailand, involving **Muslim dissidents** and the Chinese-dominated **Communist Party of Malaya**, as well as local Thais.

Thanom was now facing a major security crisis, especially as the war in Vietnam was going badly. In 1969 he held elections which produced a majority for the government party but, still worried about national stability, the general got cold feet. In November 1971 he reimposed repressive military rule, under a triumvirate of himself, his son Colonel Narong and Praphas, who became known as the "Three Tyrants". However, the 1969 experiment with democracy had heightened expectations of power-sharing among the middle classes, especially in the universities. **Student demonstrations** began in June 1973, and in October as many as 500,000 people turned out at Thammasat University in Bangkok to demand a new constitution. King Bhumibol intervened with apparent success, and indeed the demonstrators were starting to disperse on the morning of October 14, when the police tried to control the flow of people away. Tensions quickly mounted and soon a full-scale riot was under way, during which over 350 people were reported killed. The army, however, refused to provide enough troops to suppress this massive uprising, and later the same day, Thanom, Narong and Praphas were forced to resign and leave the country.

In a new climate of openness, **Kukrit Pramoj** managed to form a coalition of seventeen elected parties and secured a promise of US withdrawal from Thailand, but his government was riven with feuding. Meanwhile, the king and much of the middle class, alarmed at the unchecked radicalism of the students, began to support new, often violent, right-wing organizations. In October 1976, the students demonstrated again, protesting against the return of Thanom to Thailand to become a monk at Wat Bowonniwet. Supported by elements of the military and the government, the police and reactionary students launched a massive assault on Thammasat University. On October 6, hundreds of students were brutally beaten, scores were lynched and some even burnt alive; the military took control and suspended the constitution.

General Prem

Soon after, the military-appointed prime minister, **Thanin Kraivichien**, imposed rigid censorship and forced dissidents to undergo anti-communist indoctrination, but his measures seem to have been too repressive even for the military, who forced him to resign in October 1977. General Kriangsak Chomanand took over, and began to break up the insurgency with shrewd offers of amnesty. His power base was weak, however, and although Kriangsak won the elections of 1979, he was displaced in February 1980 by **General Prem Tinsulanonda**, who was backed by a broad parliamentary coalition.

Untainted by corruption, Prem achieved widespread support, including that of the monarchy, which was to prove crucial. In April 1981, a group of disaffected military officers seized government buildings in Bangkok, forcing Prem to flee the capital. However, the rebels' attempt to mobilize the army was hamstrung by a radio message from Queen Sirikit in support of Prem, who was easily able to retake Bangkok. Parliamentary elections in 1983 returned the military to power and legitimized Prem's rule.

Overseeing a period of strong foreign investment and rapid economic growth, Prem maintained the premiership until 1988, with a unique mixture of dictatorship and democracy sometimes called Premocracy: although never standing for parliament himself, Prem was asked by the legislature after every election to become prime minister. He eventually stepped down because, he said, it was time for the country's leader to be chosen from among its elected representatives.

The 1992 demonstrations

The new prime minister was indeed an elected MP, **Chatichai Choonhavan**, a retired general with a long civilian career in public office. He pursued a vigorous policy of economic development, but this fostered widespread corruption, in which members of the government were often implicated. Following an economic downturn and Chatichai's attempts to downgrade the political role of the military, the armed forces staged a bloodless **coup** on February 23, 1991, led by Supreme Commander Sunthorn and General Suchinda, the army commander-in-chief, who became premier.

When Suchinda reneged on promises to make democratic amendments to the constitution, hundreds of thousands of ordinary Thais poured onto the streets around Bangkok's Democracy Monument in **mass demonstrations** between May 17 and 20, 1992. Hopelessly misjudging the mood of the country, Suchinda brutally crushed the protests, leaving hundreds dead or injured. Having justified the massacre on the grounds that he was protecting the king from communist agitators, Suchinda was forced to resign when King Bhumibol expressed his disapproval in a ticking-off that was broadcast on world television.

Chuan, Banharn and Chavalit

In the elections on September 13, 1992, the Democrat Party, led by **Chuan Leekpai**, a noted upholder of democracy and the rule of law, gained the largest number of parliamentary seats. Despite many successes through a period of continued economic growth, he was able to hold onto power only until July 1995, when he was forced to call new elections. Chart Thai and its leader, **Banharn Silpa-archa** – nicknamed by the local press "the walking ATM", a reference to his reputation for buying votes – emerged victorious. Allegations of corruption soon mounted against Banharn and in the following year he was obliged to dissolve parliament.

In November 1996, **General Chavalit Yongchaiyudh**, leader of the New Aspiration Party (NAP), narrowly won what was dubbed the most corrupt election in Thai history, with an estimated 25 million baht spent on vote-buying in rural areas. The most significant positive event of his tenure was the approval of a **new constitution**. Drawn up by an independent drafting assembly, its main points included: direct elections to the senate, rather than appointment of senators by the prime minister; acceptance of the right of assembly as the basis of a democratic society and guarantees of individual rights and freedoms; greater public accountability; and increased popular participation in local administration. The eventual aim of the new charter was to end the traditional system of patronage, vested interests and vote-buying.

The economic crisis

At the start of Chavalit's premiership, the Thai **economy** was already on shaky ground. In February 1997 foreign-exchange dealers began to mount speculative attacks on the baht, alarmed at the size of Thailand's private foreign debt – 250 billion baht in the unproductive property sector alone, much of it accrued through the proliferation of prestigious skyscrapers in Bangkok. The government valiantly defended the pegged exchange rate, spending $23 billion of the country's formerly healthy foreign-exchange reserves, but at the beginning of July was forced to give up the ghost – the baht was floated and soon went into free-fall.

Blaming its traditional allies the Americans for neglecting their obligations, Thailand sought help from Japan; Tokyo suggested the **IMF**, who in August put together a $17-billion **rescue package** for Thailand. Among the conditions of the package, the Thai government was to slash the national budget, control inflation and open up financial institutions to foreign ownership.

Chavalit's performance in the face of the crisis was viewed as inept, more concerned with personal interests and political game-playing than managing the economy properly. In November he resigned, to be succeeded by Chuan Leekpai, who took up what was widely seen as a poisoned chalice for his second term. Chuan immediately took a hard line to try to restore confidence in the economy: he followed the IMF's advice, which involved maintaining cripplingly high interest rates to protect the baht, and pledged to reform the financial system. Although this played well abroad, at home the government encountered increasing hostility. Unemployment, which had been as low as 1 million before the crisis, edged past 2 million by mid-1998, inflation peaked at ten percent, and there were frequent public protests against the IMF.

By the end of 1998, however, Chuan's tough stance was paying off, with the baht stabilizing at just under 40 to the US dollar, and interest rates and inflation starting to fall. Foreign investors slowly began returning to Thailand, and by October 1999 Chuan was confident enough to announce that he was forgoing almost $4 billion of the IMF's planned rescue package.

Thaksin

The year 2000 was dominated by the build-up to the general election in January 2001. It was to be the first such vote held under the 1997 constitution, which was intended to take the traditionally crucial role of money, especially for vote-buying, out of politics. However, this election coincided with the emergence of a new party, **Thai Rak Thai** (Thai Loves Thai), formed by one of Thailand's wealthiest men, **Thaksin Shinawatra**, an ex-policeman who had made a personal fortune from government telecommunications concessions.

Although Thaksin denied the money attraction, over one hundred MPs from other parties, including the ruling Democrats, were drawn to Thai Rak Thai as the dissolution of parliament approached. Thai Rak Thai duly won the election but, instead of a move towards greater democracy, as envisioned by the new constitution, Thaksin's government seemed to represent a full-blown merger between politics and big business, concentrating economic power in even fewer hands. His first cabinet was a motley crew of old-style vested interests, including as deputy premier former PM Chavalit, credited by many with having sparked the 1997 economic crisis. Furthermore, the prime minister began to apply commercial and legal pressure, including several lawsuits, to try to silence critics in the media and parliament, and to manipulate the Senate and supposedly independent institutions such as the Election Commission to consolidate his own power. As his standing became more firmly entrenched, he rejected constitutional reforms designed to rein in his power – famously declaring that "democracy is only a tool" for achieving other goals.

Thaksin did, however, maintain his profile as a populist reformer by carrying through nearly all of his controversial election promises. He issued a three-year loan moratorium for perennially indebted farmers and set up a one-million-baht development fund for each of the country's seventy thousand villages – though many villages just used the money as a lending tool to cover past debts, rather than creating productive projects for the future as intended. To improve public health access, a standard charge of B30 per hospital visit was introduced nationwide. However, too little was invested in the health service to cope with the increased demand that was generated.

In early 2004, politically and criminally motivated violence in the **Islamic southern provinces** escalated sharply, and since then, there have been over 1200 deaths on both sides in the troubles. The insurgents have targeted any representative of central authority, including monks and teachers, as well as setting off bombs in marketplaces and near tourist hotels. The authorities have inflamed opinion in the south by reacting violently, notably in crushing protests at Tak Bai and the much-revered Krue Se Mosque in Pattani in 2004, in which a total of over two hundred alleged insurgents died. In 2005, the government imposed **martial law** in Pattani, Yala and Narathiwat provinces and in parts of Songkhla province – this, however, has exacerbated economic and unemployment problems in what is Thailand's poorest region. Facing a variety of shadowy groups, whose precise aims are unclear, the authorities' natural instinct has been to get tough – which so far has brought the problem no nearer to a solution. Recent, constructive proposals by the **National Reconciliation Commission**, however, headed by former prime minister Anand Panyarachun may, if adopted, hold out some cause for hope.

Despite these problems, but bolstered by his high-profile response to the tsunami on December 26, 2004, in which over eight thousand people died on Thailand's Andaman Coast (see p.722), Thaksin breezed through the **February 2005 election**, becoming the first prime minister in Thai history to win an outright majority at the polls. He promised an end to poverty, ambitious infrastructure projects and privatization of state companies, but the prospect of a one-party state alarmed a wide spectrum of opposition. When Thaksin's relatives sold their shares in the family's Shin Corporation in January 2006 for £1.1 billion, without paying tax, the tipping point was reached: tens of thousands of mostly middle-class Thais flocked to Bangkok to take part in peaceful demonstrations, which went on for weeks on end, under the umbrella of the **People's Alliance for Democracy**. The prime minister was eventually obliged to call a snap general election for April 2, but the three main opposition parties decided to boycott the poll, claiming that Thaksin was unfairly seeking a mandate without having to answer the corruption claims against him. Unsurprisingly, Thai Rak Thai won the election, but three days later, after an audience with King Bhumibol, Thaksin resigned in favour of his deputy, Chitchai Wannasathit. In May, the Constitutional Court ruled that the election had been unconstitutional and ordered a new poll, which will take place in late 2006.

Art and architecture

Aside from pockets of Hindu-inspired statuary and architecture, the vast majority of historical Thai culture takes its inspiration from Theravada Buddhism and, though the country does have some excellent museums, to understand fully the evolution of Thai art you have to visit its temples. For Thailand's architects and sculptors, the act of creation was an act of merit and a representation of unchanging truths, rather than an act of expression, and thus Thai art history is characterized by broad schools rather than individual names. This section, in conjunction with our colour insert on the **wat**, which explains the typical temple layout, is designed to help make sense of the most common aspects of Thai art and architecture at their various stages of development.

Buddhist iconography

In the early days of Buddhism, image-making was considered inadequate to convey the faith's abstract philosophies, so the only approved iconography comprised doctrinal **symbols** such as the *Dharmachakra* (Wheel of Law, also known as Wheel of Doctrine or Wheel of Life). Gradually these symbols were displaced by **images of the Buddha**, construed chiefly as physical embodiments of the Buddha's teachings rather than as portraits of the man (see p.884 for more on the life of the Buddha). Sculptors took their guidance from the Pali texts which ordained the Buddha's most common postures (*asanha*) and gestures (*mudra*).

Of the **four postures** – sitting, standing, walking and reclining – the **seated Buddha**, which represents him in meditation, is the most common in Thailand. A popular variation shows the Buddha seated on a coiled serpent, protected by the serpent's hood – a reference to the story about the Buddha meditating during the rainy season, when a serpent offered to raise him off the wet ground and shelter him from the storms. The **reclining** pose symbolizes the Buddha entering Nirvana at his death, while the **standing** and **walking** images both represent his descent from Tavatimsa heaven.

The most common **hand gestures** include: *Dhyana Mudra* (Meditation), in which the hands rest on the lap, palms upwards; *Bhumisparsa Mudra* (Calling the Earth to Witness, a reference to the Buddha resisting temptation), with the left hand upturned in the lap and the right-hand fingers resting on the right knee and pointing to the earth; *Vitarkha Mudra* (Teaching), with one or both hands held at chest height with the thumb and forefinger touching; and *Abhaya Mudra* (Dispelling Fear), showing the right hand (occasionally both hands) raised in a flat-palmed "stop" gesture.

All three-dimensional Buddha images are objects of reverence, but some are more esteemed than others. Some are alleged to have displayed human attributes or reacted in some way to unusual events, others have performed miracles, or are simply admired for their beauty, their phenomenal size or even their material value – if made of solid gold or of jade, for example. Most Thais are familiar with these exceptional images, all of which have been given special names, always prefixed by the honorific "Phra", and many of which have spawned thousands of miniaturized copies in the form of amulets. Pilgrimages are made to see the most famous originals.

It was in the Sukhothai era that the craze for producing **Buddha footprints** really took off. Harking back to the time when images were allusive rather than representative, these footprints were generally moulded from stucco to depict the 108 auspicious signs or *lakshanas* (which included references to the sixteen Buddhist heavens, the traditional four great continents and seven great rivers and lakes) and housed in a special mondop. Few of the Sukhothai prints remain, but Ayutthaya-Ratanakosin-era examples are found all over the country, the most famous being Phra Phutthabat near Lopburi, the object of pilgrimages throughout the year. The feet of the famous Reclining Buddha in Bangkok's Wat Po are also inscribed with the 108 *lakshanas*, beautifully depicted in mother-of-pearl inlay.

Hindu iconography

Hindu images tend to be a lot livelier than Buddhist ones, partly because there is a panoply of gods to choose from, and partly because these gods have mischievous personalities and reappear in all sorts of bizarre incarnations. Central to the Hindu philosophy is the certainty that any object can be viewed as the temporal residence, embodiment or symbol of the deity; thus its iconography includes abstract representations (such as the phallic lingam for Shiva) as well as figurative images. Though pure Hinduism receded from Thailand with the collapse of the Khmers, the iconography has endured, as Buddhist Thais have incorporated some Hindu and Brahmin concepts into the national belief system and have continued to create statues of the three chief Hindu deities – Brahma, Vishnu and Shiva – as well as using lesser mythological beasts in modern designs.

Vishnu has always been especially popular: his role of "Preserver" has him embodying the status quo, representing both stability and the notion of altruistic love. He is most often depicted as the deity, but frequently crops up in other human and animal incarnations. There are ten of these manifestations in all, of which **Rama** (number seven) is by far the most popular in Thailand. The epitome of ideal manhood, Rama is the super-hero of the epic story the *Ramayana* (see box on p.137) and appears in storytelling reliefs and murals in every Hindu temple in Thailand; in painted portraits you can usually recognize him by his green face. Manifestation number eight is **Krishna**, more widely known than Rama in the West, but slightly less common in Thailand. Krishna is usually characterized as a flirtatious, flute-playing, blue-skinned cowherd whose most famous achievement is the lifting of Mount Govadhana (as depicted in relief at Phimai; see box on opposite), but he is also a crucial moral figure in the *Mahabharata*. Confusingly, Vishnu's ninth avatar is the **Buddha** – a manifestation adopted many centuries ago to minimize defection to the Buddhist faith. When represented as **the deity**, Vishnu is generally shown sporting a crown and four arms, his hands holding a conch shell (whose music wards off demons), a discus (used as a weapon), a club (symbolizing the power of nature and time), and a lotus (symbol of joyful flowering and renewal). The god is often depicted astride a **garuda**, a half-man, half-bird. Even without Vishnu on its back, the garuda is a very important beast – a symbol of strength, it's often shown "supporting" temple buildings.

Statues and representations of **Brahma** (the Creator) are very rare. Confusingly, he too has four arms, but you should recognize him by the fact that he holds no objects, has four faces (sometimes painted red), and is generally borne by a goose-like creature called a *hamsa*.

Shiva (the Destroyer) is the most volatile member of the pantheon. He stands for extreme behaviour, for beginnings and endings (as enacted in his frenzied Dance of Destruction, described in the box on opposite), and for fertility, and is

Hindu legends

Once you've recognized the main characters of the Hindu pantheon, you'll want to know what they're up to in the murals and reliefs that ornament temple walls and ceilings. Of the hundreds of different episodes featured in as many interpretations by painters and sculptors – many taken from the *Ramayana* and *Mahabharata* – the following recur frequently.

The Churning of the Sea of Milk (*in situ* at Khao Phra Viharn, on display at Phimai's National Museum, and in reproduction at Ayutthaya's Historical Study Centre). A creation myth in which Vishnu appears in his second, tortoise, incarnation. The legend describes how the cosmic ocean (or "milk") was churned with a sacred inverted conical mountain to create the universes and all things in them ("the butter"). A naga was used as the churning rope, and the holy tortoise offered his shell to support the mountain – an image which gave rise to the notion of tortoise as the base and foundation stone of the world. The churning also produced a sacred nectar of immortality, which both the gods and the demons were keen to consume. Vishnu craftily encouraged the demons to hold the head-end of the naga rope while helping to make this nectar, giving the gods the tail-end, and encouraging the demons to drink the liquid at its early, alcoholic stage; the friction of the process caused the naga to heat up and breathe fire, burning the demons, who by this stage were so intoxicated that they promptly fell asleep, leaving the distilled nectar for the gods.

Reclining Vishnu Asleep on the Milky Sea of Eternity (the most accessible lintels at Phanom Rung and in the National Museum in Bangkok). Another common creation myth, this time featuring Vishnu as four-armed deity (sometimes referred to as Phra Narai), sleepily reclining on a naga, here representing the Milky Sea of Eternity. Vishnu is dreaming of creating a new universe, shown by the lotus blossoms which spring from his navel, and the four-faced god Brahma who perches atop them; as "Creator", Brahma will be responsible for putting this dream into practice.

Krishna Lifting Mount Govadhana (lintel at Phimai). A story of godly rivalry, in which a community of worshippers suddenly transferred allegiance from the god Indra to the interloping Krishna. Indra, the god of the elements, was so incensed that he attacked the turncoats with a raging storm; they called on Krishna for help, and he obliged by lifting up the mighty Mount Govadhana to provide an enormous umbrella.

Shiva Nataraja: the Dance of Shiva or Shiva's Dance of Destruction (at Phimai, Phanom Rung and Khao Phra Viharn). A very powerful and highly symbolic image in which the multi-armed Shiva, as Nataraja, performs a wild, ecstatic dance that brings about the total destruction (through fire) of the extant world and replaces it with a new epoch (as represented by a double-sided drum). In the northeastern Khmer temples this dance is a fairly common subject of stone reliefs, nearly always set as a lintel above a major gateway into the sanctuary.

How Ganesh Came to Have an Elephant's Head. At the time of Ganesh's birth, his father, Shiva, happened to be away from home. On returning to his wife's apartments, Shiva was enraged to find a strange young man in Parvati's boudoir and rashly decapitated the youth. Of course, the boy turned out to be Ganesh, Shiva's own son; full of remorse, the god immediately despatched a servant to procure the head of the first living being he encountered so that his son could be restored to life. The servant returned with an elephant's head, which is why this endearing Hindu god has the pot-bellied body of a child and the head of a young elephant. An alternative version of the tale has Shiva overreacting after his baby son's cries woke him from a particularly pleasant daydream.

a symbol of great energy and power. His godlike form typically has four, eight or ten arms, sometimes holding a trident (representing creation, protection and destruction) and a drum (to beat the rhythm of creation). In his most famous role, as **Nataraja**, or Lord of the Dance, he is usually shown in stylized standing position with legs bent into a balletic position, and the full complement of arms outstretched above his head. Three stripes on a figure's forehead also indicate Shiva, or one of his followers. In abstract form, he is represented by a **lingam** or phallic pillar (once found at the heart of every Khmer temple in the northeast). Primarily a symbol of energy and godly power, the lingam also embodies fertility, particularly when set upright in a vulva-shaped vessel known as a **yoni**. The yoni doubles as a receptacle for the holy water that worshippers pour over the lingam.

Close associates of Shiva include **Parvati**, his wife, and **Ganesh**, his elephant-headed son (the story of how Ganesh came to look as he does is explained in the box on p.875). Depictions of Ganesh abound, both as statues and, because he is the god of knowledge and overcomer of obstacles (in the path of learning), as the symbol of the Fine Arts Department – which crops up on all entrance tickets to museums and historical parks.

The royal, three-headed elephant, **Erawan**, usually only appears as the favourite mount of the god **Indra**, who is rather unremarkable without the beast but generally figures as the king of the gods, with specific power over the elements (particularly rain) – four statues of the god and his mount grace the base of the prang at Bangkok's Wat Arun.

Lesser mythological figures, which originated as Hindu symbols but feature frequently in wats and other Buddhist contexts, include the **yaksha** giants who ward off evil spirits (like the enormous freestanding ones guarding Bangkok's Wat Phra Kaeo); the graceful half-woman, half-bird **kinnari**; and finally, the ubiquitous **naga**, or serpent king of the underworld – often the proud owner of as many as seven heads, whose reptilian body most frequently appears as staircase balustrades in Hindu and Buddhist temples.

The schools

In the 1920s art historians and academics began compiling a classification system for Thai art and architecture which was modelled along the lines of the country's historical periods – these are the guidelines followed below. The following brief overview starts in the sixth century, when Buddhism began to take a hold on the country; few examples of art from before that time have survived, and there are no known earlier architectural relics.

Dvaravati (sixth to eleventh centuries)

Centred around Nakhon Pathom, U Thong and Lopburi in the Chao Phraya basin and in the smaller northern enclave of Haripunjaya (modern-day Lamphun), the **Dvaravati** state was populated by Theravada Buddhists who were strongly influenced by Indian culture.

Only one, fairly late, known example of a Dvaravati-era **building** remains standing: the pyramidal laterite chedi in the compound of Lamphun's Wat Kukut, which is divided into five tiers with niches for stucco Buddha images on each row. Dvaravati-era **artefacts** are much more common, and the national museums in Nakhon Pathom and Lamphun both house quite extensive collections of Buddha images from that period. In an effort to combat the defects inherent in the poor-quality limestone at their disposal, sculptors made their Buddhas quite stocky, cleverly dressing the figures in a sheet-like drape that dropped down to ankle level from each raised wrist, forming a U-shaped hemline – a style which they used when casting in bronze as well. Nonetheless many **statues** have cracked, leaving them headless or limbless. Where the faces have survived, Dvaravati statues display some of the most naturalistic features ever produced in Thailand, distinguished by their thick lips, flattened noses and wide cheekbones.

Nakhon Pathom, a target of Buddhist missionaries from India since before the first century AD, has also yielded a substantial hoard of **dharmachakra**, originating in the period when the Buddha could not be directly represented. These metre-high carved stone wheels symbolize the cycles of life and reincarnation, and in Dvaravati examples are often accompanied by a small statue of a deer, which refers to the Buddha preaching his first sermon in a deer park.

Srivijaya (eighth to thirteenth centuries)

While Dvaravati's Theravada Buddhists were influencing the central plains and, to a limited extent, areas further to the north, southern Thailand was paying allegiance to the Mahayana Buddhists of the **Srivijayan** empire. The key distinction between Theravada and Mahayana strands of thought is that Mahayanists believe that those who have achieved enlightenment should postpone their entry into Nirvana in order to help others along the way. These stay-behinds, revered like saints both during and after life, are called **bodhisattva**, and **statues** of them were the mainstay of Srivijayan art.

The finest Srivijayan *bodhisattva* statues were cast in bronze and show such grace and sinuosity that they rank among the finest sculpture ever produced in the country. Usually shown in the **tribunga**, or hipshot pose, with right hip thrust out and left knee bent, many are lavishly adorned, and some were even bedecked in real jewels when first made. By far the most popular *bodhisattva* subject was **Avalokitesvara**, worshipped as compassion incarnate. Generally shown with four or more arms and with an animal skin over the left shoulder or tied at the waist, Avalokitesvara is also sometimes depicted with his torso covered in tiny Buddha images. Bangkok's National Museum holds the most beautiful Avalokitesvara, found in Chaiya; most of the other best Srivijayan sculptures have been snapped up by Bangkok's curators as well.

As for Srivijayan **temples**, quite a number have been built over, and so are unviewable. The most typical intact example is the Javanese-style chedi at Chaiya's Wat Phra Boromathat, heavily restored but distinguished from contemporaneous Dvaravati structures by its highly ornamented stepped chedi, with mini chedis at each corner.

Khmer and Lopburi (tenth to fourteenth centuries)

By the end of the ninth century the **Khmers** of Cambodia were starting to expand from their capital at Angkor into the Dvaravati states, bringing with them the Hindu faith and the cult of the god-king (*devaraja*). As lasting testaments to the sacred power of their kings, the Khmers built hundreds of imposing stone **sanctuaries** across their newly acquired territory: the top examples are in southern Isaan, at Phimai, Phanom Rung, and Khao Phra Viharn, though there is also an interesting early one at Muang Singh near Kanchanaburi.

Each magnificent castle-temple – known in Khmer as a **prasat** – was constructed primarily as a shrine for a Shiva lingam, the phallic representation of the god Shiva. They followed a similar pattern, centred on at least one towering structure, or **prang**, which represented Mount Meru (the gods' heavenly abode), and surrounded by concentric rectangular enclosures, within and beyond which were dug artificial lakes and moats – miniature versions of the primordial ocean dividing heaven from earth.

The prasats' most fascinating and superbly crafted features, however, are the **carvings** that ornament almost every surface. Usually gouged from sandstone, but frequently moulded in stucco, these exuberant reliefs depict Hindu deities, incarnations and stories, especially episodes from the *Ramayana* (see box on p.137). Towards the end of the twelfth century, the Khmer leadership became Mahayana Buddhist, commissioning Buddhist carvings to be installed alongside the Hindu ones, and simultaneously replacing the Shiva lingam at the heart of each sanctuary with a Buddha or *bodhisattva* image. (See p.537 for more on the architectural details.)

The temples built in the former Theravada Buddhist principality of **Lopburi** during the Khmer period are much smaller affairs than those in Isaan, and are best represented by the triple-pranged temple of Phra Prang Sam Yot. The Lopburi classification is most usually applied to the Buddha statues that emerged at the tail end of the Khmer period, picking up the Dvaravati sculptural legacy. Broad-faced and muscular, the classic Lopburi Buddha wears a diadem or ornamental headband – a nod to the Khmers' ideological fusion of earthly and heavenly power – and the *ushnisha* (the sign of enlightenment) becomes distinctly conical rather than a mere bump on the head. Early Lopburi Buddhas come garlanded with necklaces and ornamental belts; later examples eschew the jewels. As you'd expect, Lopburi National Museum houses a good selection.

Sukhothai (thirteenth to fifteenth centuries)

Capitalizing on the Khmers' weakening hold over central Thailand, two Thai generals established the first real Thai kingdom in **Sukhothai** in 1238, and over the next two hundred years the artists of this realm produced some of Thailand's most refined art. Sukhothai's artistic reputation rests above all on its **sculpture**. More sinuous even than the Srivijayan images, Sukhothai Buddhas tend towards elegant androgyny, with slim oval faces that show little of the humanistic Dvaravati features or the strength of Lopburi statues, and slender curvaceous bodies usually clad in a plain, skintight robe that fastens with a tassel close to the navel. The sculptors favoured the seated pose, with hands in the *Bhumisparsa Mudra*, most expertly executed in the Phra Buddha Chinnarat image, now housed in Phitsanulok's Wat Si Ratana Mahathat (replicated at Bangkok's Wat Benjamabophit) and in the enormous Phra Sri Sakyamuni, now enshrined in Bangkok's Wat Suthat. They were also the first to represent the **walking Buddha**, a supremely graceful figure with his right leg poised to move forwards and his left arm in the *Vitarkha Mudra*, as seen in the compounds of Sukhothai's Wat Sra Si.

The cities of Sukhothai and nearby Si Satchanalai were already stamped with sturdy relics of the Khmers' presence, but rather than pull down the sacred prangs of their predecessors, Sukhothai builders added bots, viharns and chedis to the existing structures, as well as conceiving quite separate **temple complexes**. Their viharns and bots are the earliest halls of worship still standing in Thailand (the Khmers didn't go in for large public assemblies), but in most cases only the stone pillars and their platforms remain, the wooden roofs having long since disintegrated. The best examples can be seen in the historical park at Sukhothai, with less grandiose structures at the parks in nearby Si Satchanalai and Kamphaeng Phet.

Most of the **chedis**, though, are in much better shape. Many were modelled on the Sri Lankan bell-shaped reliquary tower (symbolizing the Buddha's teachings ringing out far and wide), often set atop a one- or two-tiered square base surrounded by elephant buttresses – Si Satchanalai's Wat Chang Lom is a stylish example. The architects also devised a new type of chedi, as elegant in its way as the images their sculptor colleagues were producing. This was the **lotus-bud chedi**, a slender tower topped with a tapered finial that was to become a hallmark of the Sukhothai era. In Sukhothai both Wat Mahathat and Wat Trapang Ngoen display good examples.

Ancient Sukhothai is also renowned for the skill of its potters, who produced a **ceramic ware** known as Sawankhalok, after the name of one of the nearby kiln towns. Most museum ceramics collections are dominated by Sawankhalok ware, which is distinguished by its grey-green celadon glazes and by the fish and chrysanthemum motifs used to decorate bowls and plates; there's a dedicated Sawankhalok museum in Sukhothai.

Lanna (thirteenth to sixteenth centuries)

Meanwhile, to the north of Sukhothai, the independent Theravada Buddhist kingdom of Lanna was flourishing. Its art styles – known interchangeably as Chiang Saen and Lanna – evolved from an eclectic range of precursors, building on the Dvaravati heritage of Haripunjaya, copying direct from Indian sources and incorporating Sukhothai and Sri Lankan ideas from the south.

The earliest surviving Lanna **monument** is the Dvaravati-style Chedi Si Liam at Wiang Kum Kam near Chiang Mai, built to the pyramidal form characteristic of Mon builders in fairly close imitation of the much earlier Wat Kukut in Lampang. Also in Chiang Mai, Wat Jet Yot replicates the temple built at Bodh Gaya in India to commemorate the seven sites where the Buddha meditated in the first seven weeks after attaining enlightenment – hence the symbolic seven pyramidal chedis, and hence also the name, which means "the temple of seven spires".

Lanna **sculpture** also drew some inspiration from Bodh Gaya: the early Lanna images tend to plumpness, with broad shoulders and prominent hair curls, which are all characteristics of the main Buddha at Bodh Gaya. The later works are slimmer, probably as a result of Sukhothai influence, and one of the most famous examples of this type is the Phra Singh Buddha, enshrined in Chiang Mai's Wat Phra Singh. Other good illustrations of both styles are housed in Chiang Mai's National Museum.

Ayutthaya (fourteenth to eighteenth centuries)

Although the Sukhothai era was artistically fertile, the kingdom had only a short political life and

△ Lotus-bud chedi, Wat Trapang Ngoen, Sukhothai

from 1351 Thailand's central plains came under the thrall of a new power centred on **Ayutthaya** and ruled by a former prince of Lopburi. Over the next four centuries, the Ayutthayan capital became one of the most prosperous and ostentatious cities in Asia, its rulers commissioning some four hundred grand wats as symbols of their wealth and power. Though essentially Theravada Buddhists, the kings also adopted some Hindu and Brahmin beliefs from the Khmers – most significantly the concept of *devaraja* or god-kingship, whereby the monarch became a mediator between the people and the Hindu gods. The religious buildings and sculptures of this era reflected this new composite ideology, both by fusing the architectural styles inherited from the Khmers and from Sukhothai and by dressing their Buddhas to look like regents.

Retaining the concentric layout of the typical Khmer **temple complex**, Ayutthayan builders played around with the component structures, most notably the prang, which they refined and elongated into a **corncob-shaped tower**, rounding it off at the top and introducing vertical incisions around its circumference. As a spire they often added a bronze thunderbolt, and into niches within the prang walls they placed Buddha images. In Ayutthaya itself, the ruined complexes of Wat Phra Mahathat and Wat Ratburana both include these corncob prangs, but the most famous example is Bangkok's Wat Arun, which though built during the subsequent Bangkok period is a classic Ayutthayan structure.

Ayutthaya's architects also adapted the Sri Lankan **chedi** so favoured by their Sukhothai predecessors, stretching the bell-shaped base and tapering it into a very graceful conical spire, as at Wat Sri Sanphet in Ayutthaya. The **viharns** of this era are characterized by walls pierced by slit-like windows, designed to foster a mysterious atmosphere by limiting the amount of light inside the building. As with all of Ayutthaya's buildings, few viharns survived the brutal 1767 sacking, with the notable exception of Wat Na Phra Mane. Phitsanulok's Wat Phra Ratana Si Mahathat was built to a similar plan – and in Phetchaburi, Wat Yai Suwannaram has no windows at all.

From Sukhothai's Buddha **sculptures** the Ayutthayans copied the soft oval face, adding an earthlier demeanour to the features and imbuing them with an hauteur in tune with the *devaraja* ideology. Like the Lopburi images, early Ayutthayan statues wear crowns to associate kingship with Buddhahood; as the court became ever more lavish, so these figures became increasingly adorned, until – as in the monumental bronze at Wat Na Phra Mane – they appeared in earrings, armlets, anklets, bandoliers and coronets. The artists justified these luscious portraits of the Buddha – who was, after all, supposed to have given up worldly possessions – by pointing to an episode when the Buddha transformed himself into a well-dressed nobleman to gain the ear of a proud emperor, whereupon he scolded the man into entering the monkhood.

While a couple of wats in Sukhothai show hints of painted decoration, religious **painting** in Thailand really dates from the Ayutthayan era. Unfortunately most of Ayutthaya's own paintings were destroyed in 1767 and others have suffered badly from damp, but several temples in other parts of the country still have some well-preserved murals, in particular Wat Yai Suwannaram in Phetchaburi. By all accounts typical of late-seventeenth-century painting, Phetchaburi's murals depict rows of *thep*, or divinities, paying homage to the Buddha, in scenes presented without shadow or perspective, and mainly executed in dark reds and cream.

Ratanakosin (eighteenth century to the 1930s)

When **Bangkok** emerged as Ayutthaya's successor in 1782, the new capital's founder was determined to revive the old city's grandeur, and the **Ratanakosin** (or Bangkok) period began by aping what the Ayutthayans had done. Since then neither wat architecture nor religious sculpture has evolved much further.

The first Ratanakosin **building** was the bot of Bangkok's Wat Phra Kaeo, built to enshrine the Emerald Buddha. Designed to a typical Ayutthayan plan, it's coated in glittering mirrors and gold leaf, with roofs ranged in multiple tiers and tiled in green and orange. To this day, most newly built bots and viharns follow a more economical version of this paradigm, whitewashing the outside walls but decorating the pediment in gilded ornaments and mosaics of coloured glass. Tiered temple roofs – an Ayutthayan innovation of which few examples remain in that city – still taper off into the slender bird-like finials called *chofa*, and naga staircases – a Khmer feature inherited by Ayutthaya – have become an almost obligatory feature of any major temple. The result is that modern wats are often almost indistinguishable from each other, though Bangkok does have a few exceptions, including Wat Benjamabophit, which uses marble cladding for its walls and incorporates Victorian-style stained-glass windows, and Wat Rajabophit, which is covered all over in Chinese ceramics. The most dramatic chedi of the Ratanokosin era – the tallest in the world – was constructed in the mid-nineteenth century in Nakhon Pathom to the original Sri Lankan style, but minus the elephant buttresses found in Sukhothai.

Early Ratanakosin sculptors produced adorned **Buddha images** very much in the Ayutthayan vein, sometimes adding real jewels to the figures, and more modern images are notable for their ugliness rather than for any radical departure from type. The obsession with size, first apparent in the Sukhothai period, has plumbed new depths, with graceless concrete statues up to 60m high becoming the norm (as in Roi Et's Wat Burapha), a monumentalism made worse by the routine application of browns and dull yellows. Most small images are cast from or patterned on older models, mostly Sukhothai or Ayutthayan in origin.

Painting has fared much better, with the *Ramayana* murals in Bangkok's Wat Phra Kaeo (see p.137) a shining example of how Ayutthayan techniques and traditional subject matters could be adapted into something fantastic, imaginative and beautiful.

Contemporary

Following the democratization of Thailand in the 1930s, artists increasingly became recognized as individuals, and took to signing their work for the first time. In 1933 the first school of fine art (now Bangkok's Silpakorn University) was established under the Italian sculptor Corrado Feroci, designer of the capital's Democracy Monument and, as the new generation experimented with secular themes and styles adapted from the Western Impressionist, post-Impressionist and Cubist movements, later embracing Abstraction and Expressionism, Thai art began to look a lot more "**modern**". Nonetheless, with a few notable exceptions, the leading artistic preoccupation of the past 75 years has been Thailand's spiritual heritage, with nearly every major figure on the contemporary art scene tackling religious issues at some point. For some artists this has meant a straightforward modernization of Buddhist legends or a reworking of particular symbols, while others have sought to dramatize the moral relevance of their religion in the light of political, social and philosophical trends. A number of Thailand's more established contemporary artists have earned the title **National Artist**, an honour that has been bestowed on one or two artists, of any discipline, nearly every year since 1985.

Bangkok has a near-monopoly on Thailand's **art galleries**. While the permanent collections at the National Gallery are disappointing, regular exhibitions of more challenging contemporary work appear at the Silpakorn University Art Gallery, The Queen's Gallery, and the Queen Sirikit Convention Centre, as well as at smaller gallery spaces around the city. The listings magazine *Bangkok Metro* prints details of current exhibitions, and does features on prominent artists too, or there's the bi-monthly free Art Connection calendar of exhibitions, available from galleries. The headquarters of Bangkok's major banks and securities' companies also display works by modern Thai artists both established and lesser known, and in recent years have made a big show of backing substantial art prizes. For a preview of works by Thailand's best modern artists, visit the Rama IX Art Museum Foundation's website at ⓦwww.rama9art.org.

One of the first modern artists to adapt traditional styles and themes was **Angkarn Kalayanapongsa** (b. 1926), whose work fuses the elegant, two-dimensional styles of Ayutthayan mural painting (of which few original examples remain) with a surrealistic, dreamlike quality. He has been employed as a temple muralist and many of his paintings, some of which are on show in Bangkok's National Gallery, reflect this experience, typically featuring casts of *khon*-like figures and flying *thep* in a setting studded with symbols from both Buddhism and contemporary culture. Angkarn was an early recipient of the title National Artist.

Aiming for the more secular environments of the gallery and the private home, National Artist **Pichai Nirand** (b. 1936) rejects the traditional mural style and makes more selective choices of Buddhist imagery, appropriating religious objects and icons and reinterpreting their significance. He's particularly well known for his fine-detail canvases of Buddha footprints, many of which can be seen in Bangkok galleries and public spaces.

Pratuang Emjaroen (b. 1935) is famous for his social commentary, as epitomized by his huge and powerful canvas *Dharma and Adharma; The Days of Disaster*, which he painted in response to the vicious clashes between the military and students in 1973. The 5m x 2m picture depicts images of severed limbs, screaming faces and bloody gun barrels amid shadowy images of the Buddha's face, a spiked *dharmachakra* and other religious symbols. Many of Pratuang's subsequent works have addressed the issue of social injustice, using his trademark strong shafts of light and bold colour in a mix of Buddhist iconography and abstract imagery.

Prolific traditionalist **Chakrabhand Posayakrit** (b. 1943) is also inspired by Thailand's Buddhist culture; he is famously proud of his country's cultural heritage, which infuses much of his work and has led to him being honoured as a National Artist. He is best known for his series of 33 *Life of the Buddha* paintings, and for his portraits, including many of members of the Thai royal family.

More controversial, and more of a household name, **Thawan Duchanee** (b. 1939) has tended to examine the spiritual tensions of modern life. His surreal juxtaposition of religious icons with fantastical Bosch-like characters and explicitly sexual images prompted a group of fundamentalist students to slash ten of his early paintings in 1971 – an unprecedented reaction to a work of Thai art. Since then, Thawan has continued to produce allegorical investigations into the individual's struggles against the obstacles that dog the Middle Way, prominent among them lust and violence, but since the 1980s his street cred has waned as his saleability has mushroomed. Critics have questioned his integrity at accepting commissions from corporate clients, and his neo-conservative image cannot have been enhanced when he was honoured as a National Artist in 2001.

Complacency is not a criticism that could be levelled at **Vasan Sitthiket** (b. 1957), Thailand's most outspoken and iconoclastic artist, whose uncompromising pictures are shown at – and still occasionally banned from – large and small galleries around the capital. A persistent crusader against the hypocrisies of establishment figures such as monks, politicians and military leaders, Vasan's is one of the loudest and most aggressive political voices on the contemporary art scene, expressed on canvas, in multimedia works and in performance art. His significance is well established and he was one of the seven artists to represent Thailand at the 2003 Venice Biennale, where Thailand had its own pavilion for the first time. Some of Vasan's most famous recent work has taken the form of enormous wooden puppets: typical were his grotesque representations of 49 Thai luminaries in his 2000 show What's In our Head, an exhibit that had to be assembled in just a few days following the banning of his original show for being too provocative.

Equally forthright is fellow Biennale exhibitor, the photographer, performance artist and social activist **Manit Sriwanichpoom** (b. 1961). Manit is best known for his "Pink Man" series of photographs in which he places a Thai man (his collaborator Sompong Thawee), dressed in a flashy pink suit and pushing a pink shopping trolley, into different scenes and situations in Thailand and elsewhere. The Pink Man represents thoughtless, dangerous consumerism and his backdrop might be an impoverished hill-tribe village (*Pink Man on Tour*; 1998), or black-and-white shots from the political violence of 1976 (*Horror in Pink*; 2001).

Thaweesak Srithongdee (b. 1970) is another increasingly important name on the Thai art scene. His style is very accessible, a distinctive blend of surreal, pop, erotic and figurative, often cartoonlike. His subject is generally popular culture, often with a strong dose of sci-fi fantasy: in his 2006 exhibition, Flesh, he explores the way in which popular culture manifests itself through the human body.

Contemporary women artists tend to be less high profile in Thailand, but **Pinaree Santipak** (b. 1961) is known for her focus on gender roles and traditional attitudes and for her recurrent use of a female iconography in the form of vessels and mounds. She works mainly in multimedia, and her Vessels and Mounds show of 2001 featured installations of huge, breast-shaped floor cushions, candles and bowls.

Religion: Thai Buddhism

Over ninety percent of Thais consider themselves Theravada Buddhists, followers of the teachings of a holy man usually referred to as the Buddha (Enlightened One), though more precisely known as Gautama Buddha to distinguish him from three lesser-known Buddhas who preceded him, and from the fifth and final Buddha who is predicted to arrive in the year 4457 AD. Theravada Buddhism is one of the two main schools of Buddhism practised in Asia, and in Thailand it has absorbed an eclectic assortment of animist and Hindu elements into its beliefs as well.

The other ten percent of Thailand's population comprises Mahayana Buddhists, Muslims, Hindus, Sikhs and Christians. Islam is the dominant religion in far southern Thailand.

The Buddha: his life and beliefs

Buddhists believe that Gautama Buddha was the five-hundredth incarnation of a single being: the stories of these five hundred lives, collectively known as the **Jataka**, provide the inspiration for much Thai art. (Hindus also accept Gautama Buddha into their pantheon, perceiving him as the ninth manifestation of their god Vishnu.)

In his last incarnation he was born in Nepal as **Prince Gautama Siddhartha** in either the sixth or seventh century BC, the son of a king and his hitherto barren wife, who finally became pregnant only after having a dream that a white elephant had entered her womb. At the time of his birth astrologers predicted that Gautama was to become universally respected, either as a worldly king or as a spiritual saviour, depending on which way of life he pursued. Much preferring the former idea, the prince's father forbade anyone to let the boy out of the palace grounds, and took it upon himself to educate Gautama in all aspects of the high life. Most statues of the Buddha depict him with elongated earlobes, which is a reference to this early pampered existence, when he would have worn heavy precious stones in his ears.

The prince married and became a father, but at the age of 29 he flouted his father's authority and sneaked out into the world beyond the palace. On this fateful trip he encountered successively an old man, a sick man, a corpse and a hermit, and thus for the first time was made aware that pain and suffering were intrinsic to human life. Contemplation seemed the only means of discovering why this should be so – and therefore Gautama decided to leave the palace and become a **Hindu ascetic**.

For six or seven years he wandered the countryside leading a life of self-denial and self-mortification, but failed to come any closer to the answer. Eventually concluding that the best course of action must be to follow a "Middle Way" – neither indulgent nor over-ascetic – Gautama sat down beneath the famous riverside bodhi tree at **Bodh Gaya** in India, facing the rising sun, to meditate until he achieved enlightenment. For 49 days he sat cross-legged in the "lotus position", contemplating the causes of suffering and wrestling with temptations that materialized to distract him. Most of these were sent by **Mara**, the Evil One, who was finally subdued when Gautama summoned the earth goddess **Mae Toranee** by pointing the fingers of his right hand at the ground – the gesture known as *Bhumisparsa Mudra*, which has been immortalized by hundreds of Thai sculptors. Mae Toranee wrung torrents of water from her hair and engulfed Mara's demonic emissaries in a

△ Wat Yai Chai Mongkol, Ayutthaya

flood, an episode that also features in several sculptures and paintings, most famously in the statue in Bangkok's Sanam Luang.

Temptations dealt with, Gautama soon came to attain **enlightenment** and so become a Buddha. As the place of his enlightenment, the **bodhi tree** (or bo tree) has assumed special significance for Buddhists: not only does it appear in many Buddhist paintings and a few sculptures, but there's often a real bodhi tree (*Ficus religiosa*) planted in temple compounds as well. Furthermore, the bot is nearly always built facing either a body of water or facing east (preferably both).

The Buddha preached his **first sermon** in a deer park in India, where he characterized his Dharma (doctrine) as a wheel. From this episode comes the early Buddhist symbol the **Dharmachakra**, known as the Wheel of Law, Wheel of Doctrine or Wheel of Life, which is often accompanied by a statue of a deer. Thais celebrate this first sermon with a public holiday in July known as Asanha Puja. On another occasion 1250 people spontaneously gathered to hear the Buddha speak, an event remembered in Thailand as Maha Puja and marked by a public holiday in February.

For the next forty-odd years the Buddha travelled the region converting non-believers and performing miracles. One rainy season he even ascended into the Tavatimsa heaven (Heaven of the thirty-three gods) to visit his mother and to preach the doctrine to her. His descent from this heaven is quite a common theme of paintings and sculptures, and the **Standing Buddha** pose of numerous Buddha statues comes from this story. He also went back to his father's palace where he was temporarily reunited with his wife and child: the Khon Kaen museum houses a particularly lovely carving of this event.

The Buddha "died" at the age of eighty on the banks of a river at Kusinari in India – an event often dated to 543 BC, which is why the Thai calendar is 543 years out of synch with the Western one, so that the year 2007 AD becomes 2550 BE (Buddhist Era). Lying on his side, propping up his head on his hand, the Buddha passed into **Nirvana** (giving rise to another classic pose, the Reclining Buddha), the unimaginable state of nothingness which knows no suffering and from which there is no reincarnation. Buddhists believe that the day the Buddha entered Nirvana was the same date on which he was born and on which he achieved enlightenment, a triply significant day that Thais honour with the Visakha Puja festival in May.

Buddhist doctrine

After the Buddha entered Nirvana, his **doctrine** spread relatively quickly across India, and probably was first promulgated in Thailand in about the third century BC. His teachings, the *Tripitaka*, were written down in the Pali language – a derivative of Sanskrit – in a form that became known as Theravada, or "The Doctrine of the Elders".

As taught by the Buddha, **Theravada Buddhism** built on the Hindu theory of perpetual reincarnation in the pursuit of perfection, introducing the notion of life as a cycle of suffering which could only be transcended by enlightened beings able to free themselves from earthly ties and enter into the blissful state of Nirvana. For the well-behaved but unenlightened Buddhist, each reincarnation marks a move up a vague kind of ladder, with animals at the bottom, women figuring lower down than men, and monks coming at the top.

The Buddhist has no hope of enlightenment without acceptance of the **four noble truths**. In encapsulated form, these hold that desire is the root cause of all suffering and can be extinguished only by following the eightfold path or Middle Way. This **Middle Way** is essentially a highly moral mode of life that includes all the usual virtues like compassion, respect and moderation, and eschews vices such as self-indulgence and antisocial behaviour. But the key to it all is an acknowledgement that the physical world is impermanent and ever-changing, and that all things – including the self – are therefore not worth craving. Only by pursuing a condition of complete **detachment** can human beings transcend earthly suffering.

By the beginning of the first millennium, a new movement called **Mahayana** (Great Vehicle) had emerged within the Theravada school, attempting to make Buddhism more accessible by introducing a Hindu-style pantheon of *bodhisattva*, or Buddhist saints, who, although they had achieved enlightenment, nevertheless postponed entering Nirvana in order to inspire the populace. Mahayana Buddhism subsequently spread north into China, Korea, Vietnam and Japan, also entering southern Thailand via the Srivijayan empire around the eighth century and parts of Khmer Cambodia in about the eleventh century. Meanwhile Theravada Buddhism (which the Mahayanists disparagingly renamed "Hinayana" or "Lesser Vehicle") established itself most significantly in Sri Lanka, northern and central Thailand and Burma.

The monkhood

In Thailand it's the duty of the 270,000-strong **Sangha** (monkhood) to set an example to the Theravada Buddhist community by living a life as close to the Middle Way as possible and by preaching the Dharma to the people. A monk's life is governed by 227 strict precepts that include celibacy and the rejection of all personal possessions except gifts.

Each day begins with an alms round in the neighbourhood so that the laity can donate food and thereby gain themselves merit, and then is chiefly spent in meditation, chanting, teaching and study. Always the most respected members of any community, monks act as teachers, counsellors and arbiters in local disputes, and sometimes become spokesmen for villagers' rights. They also perform rituals at cremations, weddings and other events, such as the launching of a new business or even the purchase of a new car. Although some Thai women do become nuns, they belong to no official order and aren't respected as much as the monks. Many young boys from poor families find themselves almost obliged to become **novice monks** because that's the only way they can get accommodation, food and, crucially, an education. This is provided free in exchange for duties around the wat, and novices are required to adhere to ten rather than 227 Buddhist precepts.

Monkhood doesn't have to be for life: a man may leave the Sangha three times without stigma and in fact every Thai male (including royalty) is expected to **enter the monkhood** for a short period at some point in his life, ideally between leaving school and marrying, as a rite of passage into adulthood. So ingrained into the social system is this practice that Thai government departments and some private companies grant their employees paid leave for their time as a monk, but the custom is in decline as young men increasingly have to consider the effect their absence may have on their career prospects. Instead, many men now enter the monkhood for a brief period after the death of a parent, to make merit both for the deceased and for the rest of the family. The most popular time for temporary ordination is the three-month Buddhist retreat period – **Pansa**, sometimes referred to as "Buddhist Lent" – which begins in July and lasts for the duration of the rainy season. (The monks' confinement is said to originate from the earliest years of Buddhist history, when farmers complained that perambulating monks were squashing their sprouting rice crops.) **Ordination ceremonies** take place in almost every wat at this time and make spectacular scenes, with the shaven-headed novice usually clad entirely in white and carried about on friends' or relatives' shoulders, or even on elephants as in Hat Siew near Si Satchanalai (see p.306) and Ban Ta Klang near Surin (see p.550). The boys' parents donate money, food and necessities such as washing powder and mosquito repellent, processing around the temple compound with their gifts, often joined by dancers or travelling players hired for the occasion.

Monks in contemporary society

In recent years, some monks have extended their role as village spokesmen to become influential activists: monks played a key role in the fierce campaign against the Pak Mun dam in Isaan, for example; Wat Tham Krabok near Lopburi and Wat Nong Sam Pran in Kanchanaburi are among a growing number of temples that have established themselves as successful drug rehabilitation centres; monks at Wat Phai Lom near Bangkok have developed the country's largest breeding colony of Asian open-billed storks; and the monks at Wat Pa Luang Ta Bua Yannasampanno in Kanchanaburi (see p.254) have hit the headlines with their tiger sanctuary. Other monks, such as the famous octogenarian Luang Pho Khoon of Wat Ban Rai in Nakhon Ratchasima province, have acquired such a reputation for giving wise counsel and bringing good fortune and prosperity to their followers that they have become national gurus and their temples now generate great wealth through the production of specially blessed amulets and photographs.

Though the increasing involvement of many monks in the secular world has not met with unanimous approval, far more disappointing to the laity are those monks who **flout the precepts** of the Sangha by succumbing to the temptations of a consumer society, flaunting Raybans, Rolexes and Mercedes (in some cases actually bought with temple funds), chain-smoking and flirting, even making pocket money from predicting lottery results and practising faith-healing. With so much national pride and integrity riding on the sanctity of the Sangha, any whiff of a deeper scandal is bound to strike deep into the national psyche, and everyone was shocked when a young monk confessed to robbing and then murdering a British tourist in 1995. Since then Thai monks have been involved in an unprecedented litany of crimes, including several rapes and murders, and there's been an embarrassment of exposés of corrupt, high-ranking abbots caught carousing in disreputable bars, drug-dealing and even gun-running. This has prompted a stream of editorials on the state of the Sangha and the collapse of spiritual values at the heart of Thai society. The inclusivity of the monkhood – which is open to just about any male who wants to join – has been highlighted as a particularly vulnerable aspect, not least because donning saffron robes has always been an accepted way for criminals, reformed or otherwise, to repent of their past deeds.

Interestingly, back in the late 1980s, the influential monk Phra Bodhirak was unceremoniously defrocked after criticizing what he saw as a tide of decadence infecting Thai Buddhism and advocating an all-round purification of the Sangha. He now preaches from his breakaway **Santi Asoke** sect headquarters on the outskirts of Bangkok, but though his ascetic code of anti-materialist behaviour is followed by thousands of devotees across Thailand, it is not sanctioned by the more worldly figures of the Sangha Supreme Council. Nonetheless, Santi Asoke is often vocal on political issues: sect members were active in the democracy movement of 1992 and participated in the 2006 anti-Thaksin demonstrations as the self-fashioned Dharma Army. The sect is also famous across the country for its cheap vegetarian restaurants and for the back-to-basics uniform of the traditional blue farmer's shirt worn by many of its members.

Buddhist practice

A devout Buddhist layperson is expected to adhere to the **five basic precepts**, namely not to kill or steal, to refrain from sexual misconduct and incorrect speech (lies, gossip and abuse) and to eschew intoxicating liquor and drugs. There are three extra precepts for special *wan phra* holy days and for those laypeople including foreign students who study meditation at Thai temples: no eating after noon, no entertainment (including TV and music) and no sleeping on a soft bed; in addition, the no sexual misconduct precept turns into no sex at all.

In practice most Thai Buddhists aim only to be **reborn** higher up the incarnation scale rather than set their sights on the ultimate goal of Nirvana. The rank of the reincarnation is directly related to the good and bad actions performed in the previous life, which accumulate to determine one's **karma** or destiny – hence the Thai obsession with "making merit".

Merit-making (*tham bun*) can be done in all sorts of ways, from giving a monk his breakfast to attending a Buddhist service or donating money to the neighbourhood temple, and most festivals are essentially communal merit-making opportunities. Between the big festivals, the most common days for making merit and visiting the temple are *wan phra* (holy days), which are determined by the phase of the moon and occur four times a month. For a Thai man, temporary ordination is a very important way of accruing merit not only for himself but also for his mother and sisters – wealthier citizens might take things a step further by commissioning the casting of a Buddha statue or even paying for the building of a wat. One of the more bizarre but common merit-making activities involves **releasing caged birds**: worshippers buy one or more tiny finches from vendors at wat compounds and, by liberating them from their cage, prove their Buddhist compassion towards all living things. The fact that the birds were free until netted earlier that morning doesn't seem to detract from the ritual at all. In riverside and seaside wats, birds are sometimes replaced by fish or even baby turtles.

For a detailed introduction to Thai Buddhism, see Ⓦwww.thaibuddhism.net. Details of Thai temples that welcome foreign students of Buddhism and meditation are on p.65.

Spirits and non-Buddhist deities

The complicated history of the area now known as Thailand has, not surprisingly, made Thai Buddhism a strangely syncretic faith, as you'll realize when you enter a Buddhist temple compound to be confronted by a statue of a Hindu deity. While regular Buddhist merit-making insures a Thai for the next life, there are certain **Hindu gods and animist spirits** that most Thais also cultivate for help with more immediate problems. Sophisticated Bangkokians and illiterate farmers alike find no inconsistency in these apparently incompatible practices, and as often as not it's a Buddhist monk who is called in to exorcize a malevolent spirit. Even the Buddhist King Bhumibol employs Brahmin priests and astrologers to determine auspicious days and officiate at certain royal ceremonies and, like his royal predecessors of the Chakri dynasty, he also associates himself with the Hindu god Vishnu by assuming the title Rama IX – Rama, hero of the Hindu epic the *Ramayana*, having been Vishnu's seventh manifestation on earth.

If a Thai wants help in achieving a short-term goal, like passing an exam, becoming pregnant or winning the lottery, then he or she will quite likely turn to the **Hindu pantheon**, visiting an enshrined statue of Brahma, Vishnu, Shiva or Ganesh, and making offerings of flowers, incense and maybe food. If the outcome is favourable, devotees will probably come back to show thanks, bringing more offerings and maybe even hiring a dance troupe to perform a celebratory *lakhon chatri* as well. Built in honour of Brahma, Bangkok's Erawan Shrine is the most famous place of Hindu-inspired worship in the country.

Whereas Hindu deities tend to be benevolent, **spirits** (or *phi*) are not nearly as reliable and need to be mollified more frequently. They come in hundreds of varieties, some more malign than others, and inhabit everything from trees, rivers and caves to public buildings and private homes – even taking over people if they feel like it. So that these *phi* don't pester human inhabitants, each building has a special **spirit house** (*saan phra phum*) in its vicinity, as a dwelling for spirits ousted by the building's construction. Usually raised on a short column to set it at or above eye-level, the spirit house must occupy an auspicious location – not, for example, in the shadow of the main building – so help from the local temple is usually required when deciding on the best position. Spirit houses are generally about the size of a dolls' house and designed to look like a wat or a traditional Thai house, but their ornamentation is supposed to reflect the status of the humans' building, so if that building is enlarged or refurbished, the spirit house should be improved accordingly. And as architects become increasingly bold in their designs, so modernist spirit houses are also beginning to appear, especially in Bangkok where an eyecatching new skyscraper might be graced by a *saan phra phum* of glass or polished concrete. Figurines representing the relevant guardian spirit and his aides are sometimes put inside the little house, and daily offerings of incense, lighted candles and garlands of jasmine are placed alongside them to keep the *phi* happy – a disgruntled spirit is a dangerous spirit, liable to cause sickness, accidents and even death. As with any religious building or icon in Thailand, an unwanted or crumbling spirit house should never be dismantled or destroyed, which is why you'll often see damaged spirit houses placed around the base of a sacred banyan tree, where they are able to rest in peace.

Flora, fauna and environmental issues

Spanning some 1650km north to south, Thailand lies in the heart of Southeast Asia's tropical zone, its northernmost region just a few degrees south of the Tropic of Cancer, its southern border running less than seven degrees north of the Equator. As with other tropical regions across the world, Thailand's climate is characterized by high humidity and even higher temperatures, a very fertile combination which nourishes a huge diversity of flora and fauna in a vast range of habitats, from mixed deciduous and dry dipterocarp forests in the mountainous north to wet tropical rainforests in the steamy south. At least six percent of the world's vascular plants are found here, with over 15,000 species so far recorded.

Thirteen percent of Thailand's land mass is protected as **national park**, and it is in these reserves that the kingdom's natural heritage is best appreciated. The most rewarding of the country's national parks, including Khao Yai in the northeast, Doi Inthanon and Doi Suthep in the north, and Khao Sam Roi Yot, Khao Sok and Ko Tarutao in the south, are described in detail in the guide chapters; general practical information on national parks is given in Basics on p.72.

The geography of Thailand

Thailand has a **tropical monsoon climate**. Most rain is brought from the Indian Ocean by the southwest monsoon from May to October, the so-called rainy season. From November to February the northeast monsoon brings a much cooler and drier climate from China, the cold, dry season. However, this northeastern monsoon hits the peninsular east coast after crossing the South China Sea, loading up with moist air and therefore extending this region's rainy season until January or later. The north–south divide is generally considered to lie just north of Ranong (10°N) – the capital of Thailand's wettest province – at the Kra Isthmus (see p.696).

Agriculture plays a significant role in Thailand's economy, and 46 percent of Thais live off the land. Waterlogged rice paddies characterize the central plains; cassava, tapioca and eucalyptus are grown as cash crops on the scrubby plateau of the northeast; and rubber plantations dominate the commercial land-use of the south. Dotted along Thailand's coastline are mangrove swamps and palm forests; the country's coral reefs are discussed under "Wildlife" (see p.897).

Mixed deciduous and dry dipterocarp forests

An estimated 65 percent of Thailand's forests are **deciduous**, sometimes referred to as monsoon forest because they have to survive periods of up to six months with minimal rainfall, so the trees shed their leaves to conserve water. Deciduous forests are often light and open, with canopies ranging from as low as 10m up to a maximum of about 40m. The undergrowth is usually fairly thick. As they are relatively easy to fell, especially with the notorious slash-and-burn technique, a significant proportion of Thailand's deciduous forest has been cleared for both small and commercial cultivation purposes.

The family **Dipterocarpaceae** dominate these forests, a group of tropical hardwoods prized for their timber and, in places, their resin. The name comes from the Greek and means "two-winged fruit". **Teak** was once a common species in northern deciduous forests, but its solid, unwarpable timber is such a sought-after material for everything from floors to furniture that nearly all the teak forests have been felled. Since teak trees take around two hundred years to attain their full height of 40m, logging them was banned in Thailand in 1989 and thereafter most of the teak used in Thai furniture was brought in from Burma. However there have been several raids proving that some of this so-called Burmese teak actually originated in Thai forests, a practice that allegedly continues to this day.

Another prized local resource is the **aloewood** (sandalwood) tree, whose aromatic oil is such a sought-after ingredient of perfumes and incense that the wood can fetch up to US$1000 per kilogramme. It's said to be more valuable on the black market, gramme for gramme, than cocaine, which makes it a tempting prize for poachers, particularly within national parks such as Khao Yai.

Bamboo thrives in a monsoon climate, shooting up at a remarkable rate during the wet season, often in soils too poor for other species; as a result bamboo often predominates in secondary forests (those where logging or clearing has previously taken place, and a new generation of plants has grown up – the majority of Thailand's forest). The smooth, woody, hollow stem characteristic of all varieties of bamboo is a fantastically adaptable material, used by the Thais for constructing everything from outside walls to chairs to water-pipes (in hill-tribe villages) and musical instruments; and the bamboo shoot is an essential ingredient in Thai-Chinese cuisine.

Tropical rainforests

Thailand's **tropical rainforests** occur in areas of high and prolonged rainfall in the southern peninsula, most accessibly in the national parks of Khao Sok, Tarutao and Khao Luang. Some areas contain as many as two hundred species of tree within a single hectare, along with a host of other flora. Characteristic of a tropical rainforest is the multi-layered series of **canopies**. The uppermost storey of emergent trees sometimes reaches 60m, and these towering trees often have enormous buttressed roots for support; beneath this, the dense canopy of 25–35m is often festooned with climbers and epiphytes such as ferns, lianas, mosses and orchids; then comes an uneven layer 5–10m high consisting of palms, rattans, shrubs and small trees. The forest floor in tropical rainforests tends to be relatively open and free of dense undergrowth, owing to the intense filtering of light by the upper three layers.

Again, members of the Dipterocarpaceae family are dominant, and it is these trees, along with strangling figs, that form some of the most spectacular buttress roots. Though dipterocarps provide little food for fauna, they play an important role as nesting sites for hornbills, as lookout posts for gibbons – and as timber.

Semi-evergreen forests

Semi-evergreen forests are the halfway house between tropical rainforests and dry deciduous forests, showing characteristics of both habitats. It's a classification that includes all lowland and submontane evergreen forests from the plains to about 1000m. Semi-evergreen forests thrive in regions with distinctly seasonal rainfall where the humidity is relatively low; they share many similarities with the southern rainforests, though the canopies are lower and you'll find fewer palms and rattans. Fine examples can be found at Khao Yai and Kaeng Krachan national parks, and all along the Burmese border, all of which are potentially good places to observe large mammals, including elephants, gaurs, tigers and bears.

△ Mangrove swamp, Ao Thalen

Hill evergreen (montane) forests

Above 1000m, the canopy of tall trees gives way to **hill evergreen forest** growth, consisting of oaks, chestnuts, laurels and other shorter temperate-zone tree families, many with twisted trunks and comparatively small leaves. Rainfall is frequent and often continuous at these elevations, so moss usually covers the forest floor and the undergrowth seems a lot denser, particularly with epiphytes, rhododendrons and various types of tree fern. These highland forests are exposed to the harshest winds and coolest temperatures, so only the hardiest, sturdiest tree and plant species survive.

Hill evergreen forest can occur within areas dominated by either monsoon forest or tropical rainforest. Good examples can be seen in Doi Inthanon and Phu Kradung national parks, and in parts of Doi Suthep and Khao Yai national parks. In the higher areas of the north not protected as national park, a lot of the primary hill evergreen forest has been cleared for cultivation, especially by local hill tribespeople who favour the slash-and-burn farming technique.

Mangrove swamps and coastal forests

Mangrove swamps are an important habitat for a wide variety of marine life (including 204 species of bird, 74 species of fish and 54 types of crab) but, like much of Thailand's natural heritage, they have fallen victim to destructive economic policies (see "Environmental issues". Huge swathes of Thailand's coast used to be fringed with mangrove swamps, but now they are mainly found only along the west peninsular coast, between Ranong and Satun. On Phuket, the Thachatchai Nature Trail leads you on a guided tour through a patch of mangrove swamp, but an even better way of exploring the swamps is to paddle through them in a kayak; several tour operators in Phuket and in the Krabi area can arrange this. At high tide only the upper branches of the thirty or so species of mangrove are visible, thick with glossy, dark green leaves, but as the tide recedes, a tangled mass of aerial roots is exposed. These roots not only absorb oxygen, but also trap water-borne debris brought in by the tides, thus gradually extending the swamp area (reclaiming land from the sea) and simultaneously nurturing fertile conditions for the new mangrove seedlings. They also help prevent coastal erosion, and in some areas of the tsunami-hit Andaman coast intact mangrove forest absorbed some of the waves' impact, protecting land and homes from even worse damage.

Nipa palms share the mangrove's penchant for brackish water, and these stubby-stemmed palm trees grow in abundance in southern **coastal areas**, though commercial plantations are now replacing the natural colonies. Like most other species of palm indigenous to Thailand, the nipa is a versatile plant, its components exploited to the full – alcohol is distilled from its sugary sap, for instance, while roofs, sticky-rice baskets and chair-backs are constructed from its fronds.

Taller and more elegant, **coconut palms** grace some of Thailand's most beautiful beaches. On islands such as Ko Kood, they form the backbone of the local economy, with millions of coconuts harvested every month for their milk, their oil, their fibrous husks (used in matting and for brushes and mattress stuffing) and their wood.

Casuarinas also flourish in sandy soils and are common on beaches throughout Thailand; because they are also fast-growing and attain heights of up to 20m, they are quite often used in afforestation programmes along the coast where they make useful wind-breaks. At first glance, the casuarina's feathery profile makes it look like a pine tree of some kind, but it's actually made up of tiny twigs, not needles.

The wildlife

Before World War II, Thailand's landscapes were apparently teeming with **wild animals** such as elephants, wild boar, rhinoceroses, bears and deer. So numerous were these species, in fact, that they were regarded as little more than an impediment to economic progress, an attitude which resulted in a calamitous reduction of Thailand's wildlife and its habitats.

Nonetheless, in zoogeographical terms, Thailand lies in an exceptionally rich "transition zone" of the Indo-Malayan realm, its forests, mountains and national parks attracting creatures from both Indochina and Indonesia. In all, Thailand is home to three hundred species of mammal (36 of which are considered to be endangered) and 971 species of bird (42 of them endangered).

Mammals

In the main national parks of Khao Yai, Doi Inthanon, Khao Sok and the like, the animals you're most likely to encounter – with your ears if not your eyes – are **primates**, particularly macaques and gibbons. The latter spend much of their time foraging for food in the higher reaches of the forest canopy, while the former usually seek their sustenance lower down, often descending closer to the ground to rest and to socialize.

The gibbons are responsible for the unmistakable hooting that echoes through the forests of some of the national parks. Chief noise-maker is the **white-handed** or **lar gibbon**, an appealing beige- or black-bodied, white-faced animal whose appearance, intelligence and dexterity unfortunately make it a popular pet. The poaching and maltreating of lar gibbons has become so severe that several organizations are now dedicated to protecting them (see the box on p.901 for details).

Similarly chatty, macaques hang out in gangs of twenty or more. The **long-tailed** or **crab-eating macaque** lives in the lowlands, near the rivers, lakes and coasts of Ao Phang Nga, Krabi, Ko Tarutao, Ang Thong and Khao Sam Roi Yot, for example. It eats not only crabs, but mussels, other small animals and fruit, transporting and storing food in its big cheek pouch when swimming and diving. The **pig-tailed macaque**, so called because of its short curly tail, excels at scaling the tall trees of Erawan, Khao Yai, Doi Inthanon and other national parks, a skill which has resulted in many of the males being captured and trained to pick coconuts.

You're almost certain to see deer in areas of protected forest, especially the **barking deer**, a medium-sized loner happy in pretty much any type of woodland (easily seen in Khao Yai, Phu Kradung and Erawan) and the large, dark-brown **sambar deer**, which prefers the deciduous forests of the same parks. The tiny **mouse deer** is less often seen, and at only 20cm from ground to shoulder it's Southeast Asia's smallest hoofed animal. Mouse deer live in the dense undergrowth of forests (Khao Yai, Erawan, Ko Surin) but their reputed tastiness could see them heading for the endangered species list.

Commonly sighted on night treks in Khao Yai and Khao Sam Roi Yot national parks, the **civet** – species of which include the common palm and small Indian – is a small mongoose-type animal which hunts smaller mammals in trees and on the ground; it's known in the West for the powerful smell released from its anal glands, a scent used commercially as a perfume base. More elusive is the **Indochinese tiger**, which lives under constant threat from both poachers and the destruction of its habitat by logging interests, both of which have reduced the current population to probably fewer than one hundred; for now Khao Yai and Khao Sok are the two likeliest places for sightings. The medium-sized arboreal **clouded leopard** is also on the endangered list, and is hard to spot anyway as it only comes out to feed on birds and monkeys under cover of darkness, rarely venturing out in moonlight let alone daylight.

The shy, nocturnal **tapir**, an ungulate with three-toed hind legs and four-toed front ones, lives deep in the forest of peninsular Thailand but is occasionally spotted in daylight. A relative of both the horse and the rhino, the tapir is the size of a pony and has a stubby trunk-like snout and distinctive colouring that serves to confuse predators: the front half of its body and all four legs are black, while the rear half is white. Another unusual ungulate is the **gaur**, recognizable by its brown coat, sharp horns, powerful off-white legs and sheer bulk – the largest member of the cattle family, it measures up to 2m at shoulder height and can weigh over a tonne. It feeds mainly at night, and is most frequently spotted at salt licks, for example in Khao Yai.

It's thought there are now as few as two thousand wild **elephants** left in Thailand: small-eared Asian elephants found mainly in Khao Yai and Khao Sok. For more on elephants see the boxes on p.384.

Birds

Even if you don't see many mammals on a trek through a national park, you're certain to spot a satisfying range of **birds**. Because of its location at the zoogeographical crossroads of Southeast Asia, Thailand boasts a huge diversity of bird species. The forests of continental Thailand are home to many of the same birds that inhabit India, Burma and Indochina, while the mountains of the north share species with the Himalayas and Tibet, and the peninsular forests are home to birds found also in Malaysia and Indonesia. Khao Yai and Khao Nor Chuchi are prime year-round sites for bird-spotting, and, during the dry season, Doi Inthanon is a good place for flycatchers and warblers, and Khao Sam Roi Yot and Thale Noi Waterbird Park are rewarding areas to see migrant waders and waterfowl.

There are twelve species of **hornbill** in Thailand, all equally majestic with massive, powerful wings (the flapping of which can be heard for long distances) and huge beaks surmounted by bizarre horny casques. Khao Yai is the easiest place to spot at least two of the species, the plain black-and-white **oriental pied hornbill** and the flashier **great hornbill**, whose monochromic body and head are broken up with jaunty splashes of yellow; the little islands of Ko Phayam and Ko Chang in Ranong province also have some resident oriental pied hornbills.

The shyness of the gorgeous **pitta** makes a sighting all the more rewarding. Usually seen hopping around on the floor of evergreen forests, especially in Doi Inthanon, Doi Suthep and Khao Yai, these plump little birds – varieties of which include the **rusty-naped**, the **blue** and the **eared** – have dazzling markings in iridescent reds, yellows, blues and blacks. The one pitta you might see outside a rainforest is the **blue-winged** pitta, which occasionally migrates to drier bamboo forests. Thailand is also home to the extremely rare **Gurney's pitta**, found only in Khlong Thom National Park, in Krabi province.

Members of the pheasant family can be just as shy as the pittas, and are similarly striking. The black-and-white-chevron-marked **silver pheasant**, and the **green peafowl** are particularly fine birds, and the commonly seen **red jungle fowl** is the ancestor to all domestic chickens.

The striking orange-breasted and red-headed **trogons** live mainly in the middle layer of forests such as Khao Yai, as does the **barbet**, a little lime-green relative of the woodpecker. Less dramatic but more frequently sighted forest residents include the **abbot's babbler**, whose short tail and rounded, apparently ineffectual wings mean it spends most of its time on the forest floor; and the distinctive, deeply fork-tailed, glossy black **drongo**. The noisy, fruit-eating **bulbuls** are also commonly spotted; many bulbuls have confusingly similar green and brown colouring, but two easily recognized species are the yellow-chested olive-backed **black-crested bulbul**, and the black, brown and white **red-whiskered bulbul**. The **black-naped oriole**, small groups of which fly from tree to tree in gardens as well as forests, is also easy to single out, both by its loud chirping and by its yellow body, black head and wing markings and reddish beak.

Thailand's **rice fields** also attract a host of different birds including the various species of **munia**, a chubby relative of the finch, whose chunky, conical beak is ideally suited to cracking unripened rice seeds; the aptly named **scaly breasted** munia and the **white-headed** munia are the most recognizable members of the family, although all members are an assortment of browns and whites. **Egrets** and **herons** also frequent the fields, wading through the waterlogged furrows or perching on the backs of water buffaloes and pecking at cattle insects, while from November to April, thousands of **Asian open-billed storks** – so called because of the gap between the upper and lower mandibles – descend on agricultural land as well, building nests in sugar-palm trees and bamboos and feeding on pira snails – each baby stork polishing off at least half a kilo a day.

Coastal areas also attract storks, egrets and herons, and Thale Noi Waterbird Park and the mud flats of Khao Sam Roi Yot are breeding grounds for the large, long-necked **purple heron**. The magnificent **white-bellied sea eagle** haunts the Thai coast, nesting in the forbidding crags around Krabi, Ao Phang Nga and Ko Tarutao and preying on fish and sea snakes. The tiny **edible nest swiftlet** makes its eponymous nest – the major ingredient of bird's-nest soup and a target for thieves – in the limestone crags, too, though it prefers the caves within these karsts; for more on these swiftlets and their nests see box on p.802.

Snakes

Thailand is home to around 175 different species and subspecies of **snake**, 56 of them dangerously venomous. Death by snakebite is not common, however, but all hospitals should keep a stock of serum, produced at the Snake Farm in Bangkok (see p.175).

Found everywhere and highly venomous, the two-metre, nocturnal, yellow-and-black-striped **banded krait** is one to avoid, as is the shorter but equally poisonous **Thai** or **monocled cobra**, which lurks in low-lying humid areas and close to human habitation. As its name implies, this particular snake sports a distinctive "eye" mark on its hood, the only detail on an otherwise plain brown body. The other most widespread poisonous snake is the sixty-centimetre **Malayan pit viper**, whose dangerousness is compounded by its unnerving ability to change the tone of its pinky-brown and black-marked body according to its surroundings.

The ubiquitous shiny black or brown **common blind snake**, also known as the flowerpot snake, grows to only 17cm, and is as harmless as its worm-like appearance suggests. Also non-venomous but considerably mightier, with an average measurement of 7.5m (maximum 10m) and a top weight of 140kg, the **reticulated python** is Thailand's largest snake, and the second largest in the world after the anaconda. Tan-coloured, with "reticulated" black lines containing whitish oval spots, like eyes, the reticulated python is found near human habitation all over Thailand, especially in the suburbs of Greater Bangkok. It feeds on rats, rabbits, small deer, pigs, cats and dogs which it kills by constriction; if provoked, it can kill humans in the same way.

Other common Thai snakes include the **iridescent earth** or **sunbeam snake**, named after the sheen of its scales which glisten and change from black to a dark brown in the sunlight. Non-venomous and burrowing, this snake reaches a length of 1.2m and is found all over Thailand. South of Chumphon, the **mangrove snake** lives in the humid swamps that fringe the river banks, estuaries and coastal plains. Arboreal, nocturnal and mildly venomous, it can grow to about 2.5m and is black with thin yellow bands set at fairly wide intervals. Finally, the **golden tree snake** is the most common of Thailand's flying snakes, so called because they can glide from tree to ground. Frequently sighted in Greater Bangkok, this mildly venomous tree snake is not golden but green with a dense pattern of black flecks, and grows to about 1.5m.

Quite a few of Thailand's snakes can swim if they have to, but the country is also home to 25 species of **sea snakes**, whose tails are flattened to act as an efficient paddle in water. Most sea snakes are venomous though not aggressive. Of the poisonous ones, the commonest and most easily recognized is the **banded sea snake**, which is silvery grey with thirty to fifty black bands and a slightly yellow underside at its front end. It grows to 1.5m and inhabits shallow coastal waters, coming onto land to lay its eggs.

Marine species

The Indian Ocean (Andaman Sea) and the South China Sea (Gulf of Thailand) together play host to over 850 species of open-water fish, more than one hundred species of reef fish and some 250 species of hard coral.

Forty percent of Thailand's coral reef is protected within **national marine parks**, which are the most rewarding places to observe underwater life. The best of these are detailed in the guide and include Ko Similan, Ko Surin, Ko Tarutao and Ang Thong; Thailand's major diving bases have their headquarters on Phuket, Ko Phi Phi, Ko Lanta and Ko Tao, and in Ao Nang, Khao Lak and Pattaya. (See also "Snorkelling and Diving" in Basics on p.70.)

Coral reefs are living organisms composed of a huge variety of marine life forms, but the foundation of every reef is its ostensibly inanimate **stony coral** – hard constructions such as boulder, mushroom, bushy staghorn and brain coral. Stony coral is composed of whole colonies of polyps – minuscule invertebrates which feed on plankton, depend on algae and direct sunlight for photosynthesis, and extract calcium carbonate (limestone) from sea water in order to reproduce. The polyps use this calcium carbonate to build new skeletons outside their bodies – an asexual reproductive process known as budding – and this is how a reef is formed. It's an extraordinarily slow process, with colony growth averaging somewhere between 5mm and 30mm a year.

The fleshy plant-like **soft coral**, such as dead man's fingers and elephant's ear, generally establishes itself on and around these banks of stony coral, swaying with the currents and using tentacles to trap all sorts of micro-organisms. Soft coral is also composed of polyps, but a variety with flaccid internal skeletons built from protein rather than calcium. **Horny coral**, like sea whips and intricate sea fans, looks like a cross between the stony and the soft varieties, while **sea anemones** have much the most obvious, and poisonous, tentacles of any member of the coral family, using them to trap fish and other large prey.

The algae and plankton that accumulate around coral colonies attract a whole catalogue of fish known collectively as **reef fish**. Most are small in stature, with vibrant colours which serve as camouflage against the coral, flattened bodies and broad tails for easy manoeuvring around the reef, and specially adapted features to help them poke about for food in the tiniest crannies.

Among the most typical and easily recognizable reef fish is the gorgeously coloured **emperor angel fish**, which boasts spectacular horizontal stripes in bright blue and orange, and an orange tail. The **moorish idol** is another fantastic sight, bizarrely shaped with a trailing streamer – or pennant fin – extending from its dorsal fin, a pronounced snout and dramatic black, yellow and white bands of colour. Similarly eye-catching, the ovoid **powder-blue surgeon fish** has a light blue body, a bright yellow dorsal fin and a white "chinstrap". The commonly spotted **long-nosed butterfly fish** is named for the butterfly-like movements of its yellow-banded silver body as it darts in and out of crevices looking for food. The bright orange **clown fish**, so called because the thick white stripes across its body resemble a clown's ruff, is more properly known as the anemone fish because of its mutually protective relationship with the sea anemone, near which it can usually be sighted. Equally predictable is the presence of **cleaner fish**, or cleaner wrasse, on the edges of every shoal of reef fish. Streamlined, with a long snout and jaws that act like tweezers, a cleaner fish spends its days picking parasites off the skins of other fish – a symbiotic relationship essential to both parties.

Some reef fish, among them the ubiquitous turquoise and purple **parrot fish**, eat coral. With the help of a bird-like beak, which is in fact several teeth fused together, the parrot fish scrapes away at the coral and then grinds the fragments down with another set of back teeth – a practice reputedly responsible for the erosion of a great deal of Thailand's reef. The magnificent mauve and burgundy **crown-of-thorns starfish** also feeds on coral, laying waste to as much as fifty square centimetres of stony coral in a 24-hour period. Its appearance is as formidable as its eating habits, with a body that measures up to 50cm in diameter protected by "arms" covered in highly venomous spines.

Larger, less frequent visitors to Thailand's offshore reefs include the **moray eel**, whose elongated jaws of viciously pointed teeth make it a deadly predator, and the similarly equipped **barracuda**, the world's fastest-swimming fish. **Sharks** are quite common off the reefs, where it's also sometimes possible to swim with a **manta ray**, whose extraordinary flatness, strange wing-like fins and massive size – up to 6m across and weighing some 1600kg – make it an astonishing presence. **Turtles** sometimes paddle around reef waters, too, but all four local species – leatherback, Olive Ridley, green and hawksbill – are fast becoming endangered in Thailand, so much so that several of their egg-laying beaches have been placed under national park protection (see p.846), including those at Hat Mai Khao on Phuket, Thai Muang, Ko Surin Tai and Ko Tarutao.

Other commonly spotted creatures are the **sea urchin**, whose evil-looking spines grow up to 35cm in length, and the ugly but harmless **sea cucumber**, which looks like a large slug and lies half-buried on the sea bed. Deceptively slothful in appearance, sea cucumbers are constantly busy ingesting and excreting so much sand and mud that the combined force of those in a three-square-kilometre area can together redistribute one million kilogrammes of sea-bed material a year.

Environmental issues

Predictably, Thailand's rapid economic growth has had a significant effect on its environment. Huge new infrastructure projects, an explosion in real-estate developments and the constantly expanding tourist industry have all played a part, and the effects of the subsequent **deforestation** and pollution have been felt nationwide. Such was the devastation caused by floods and mudslides in Surat Thani in 1988 that the government banned commercial logging the following year, though land continues to be denuded for other purposes. There is also the endemic problem of "influence" so that when a big shot wants to clear a previously pristine area for a new property development, for example, it is virtually impossible for a lowly provincial civil servant to reject their plan, or money. Thailand lost nine percent of its forest cover between 1990 and 2005 (2005 figures show just over 28 percent of Thailand's total land area as forested).

Though flooding has always been a feature of the Thai environment, crucial to the fertility of its soil, and its worst effects obviated by the stilted design of the traditional Thai house, in recent times far more dangerous **flash floods** have recurred with depressing frequency every year. This happened most dramatically around the northern town of Pai in 2005, where many homes and guest houses were washed away, and around Uttaradit, also in the north, in 2006. More mundanely there is now an almost annual inundation of town centres such as Sukhothai and Bangkok to name just a couple, and of roads and railways, particularly along the Gulf coast. The link between deforestation and flash floods is now disputed, though encroaching cement and tarmac on Thai flood plains surely play a part, as does the clogging of exit channels by garbage and other pollutants, and of course climate change.

Infrastructure projects and energy policies

The Electricity Generating Authority of Thailand (EGAT) has harnessed some of the nation's river power for hydro-electric schemes. However, a number of these, along with other large-scale **infrastructure projects**, have caused significant controversy, both because of corrupt practices and loss of forest, and also because of inadequate compensation for displaced villagers. The plight of the three thousand families affected by the 1994 completion of the Pak Mun dam in southern Isaan struck a chord with many poor and disaffected communities across Thailand and resulted in the founding of the **Assembly of the Poor**, now the most powerful grassroots movement in the country. Uniting under the declaration that "the people must be the real beneficiaries of development, and the poor must participate in the decision-making on development projects that will affect them", the Assembly of the Poor has brought numerous development and poverty issues into the headlines and forced the introduction of some new consultative measures.

Hydro-electric projects notwithstanding, Thailand has to date depended on lignite (low-grade coal) for most of its **energy**, and currently less than two percent of its energy output comes from renewable sources. Greenpeace says that, with the right policies, by 2020 a third of the country's power could be produced by renewables, and is calling on the government to phase out its coal-fired plants. As a small step in that direction, the government anticipates a forty-fold increase in the use of solar energy by 2010: a nationwide scheme has already supplied off-the-grid homes on Thailand's less developed islands with solar panels and will have fitted 120,000 homes in other remote rural locations by completion.

The coastal environment

Many of Thailand's **coral reefs** – some of which are thought to be around 450 million years old – are being destroyed by factors attributable to tourism. The main cause of tourism-related destruction is the pollution generated by the hotels and bungalows which have multiplied unchecked at many of the most beautiful sites on the coasts. The demand for coral souvenirs is exploited by unscrupulous divers and local traders, and some irresponsible dive leaders allow their customers to use harpoon guns, which cause terrible damage to reefs. Still, the destruction of coral by tourists is dwarfed by that wreaked by the practice of dynamite fishing and cyanide poisoning, which happen in areas away from the normal tourist haunts.

The 2004 **tsunami** also caused significant damage to coastal and marine environments the length of the Andaman coast. Reefs close to shore were crushed by debris (furniture, machinery, even cars) and buried under displaced soil; the sea was temporarily polluted by extensive damage to sewage systems; and tracts of shorefront farmland were rendered unusable by salt water.

National parks

Although Thailand has since the 1970s been protecting some of its natural resources within **national parks**, these have long been caught between commercial and conservationist aims, an issue which the government addressed in 2002 by establishing a new National Park, Wildlife and Plant Conservation Department (DNP; www.dnp.go.th), separate from the Royal Forestry Department and its parent Ministry of Agriculture.

With 114 national parks across the country, plus 24 national marine parks as well as various other protected zones, over thirteen percent of the country is now, in theory at least, protected from encroachment and hunting (a high proportion compared to other nations, such as Japan at 6.5 percent, and the US at 10.5 percent). However, as parks planner Dr Surachet Chettamart has warned, "Creating parks is not a numbers game, and when degraded areas are included, the whole parks system suffers. Some, such as Ko Phi Phi and Ko Samet, should be excised or reclassified since they have been transformed into holiday resorts."

The **touristification of national parks** such as Ko Phi Phi and Ko Samet is a controversial issue, and was highlighted when the RFD allowed a film crew to "relandscape" part of Ko Phi Phi Leh in 1999 for the movie *The Beach* – to vociferous protest from environmental groups. There is no question that both

Wildlife charities and volunteer projects

Elephant Nature Park near Chiang Mai ⓦwww.elephantnaturepark.org. Famous conservation-education centre and sanctuary for elephants that's open to pre-booked visitors, overnight guests and volunteers. See p.421.

Gibbon Rehabilitation Project Phuket ⓦwww.gibbonproject.org. Resocializes abused pet gibbons before releasing them back into the forests. Visitors and volunteers welcome. See p.760.

Highland Farm Gibbon Sanctuary near Mae Sot ⓦwww.highland-farm.org. Day-trippers and homestay guests are welcome at this haven caring for over forty injured and abandoned gibbons. One-month placements are also possible. See p.317.

Thai Elephant Conservation Centre near Lampang ⓦwww.changthai.com. Government-run centre and hospital that offers rides, shows and a home-stay mahout programme, with profits ploughed back into elephant conservation. See p.383.

Thai Society for the Conservation of Wild Animals ⓦwww.tscwa.org. Bangkok-based animal welfare NGO that welcomes skilled volunteers.

Wild Animal Rescue Foundation of Thailand (WAR) ⓦwww.warthai.org. A campaigning organization that runs animal rescue sanctuaries, hospitals and research centres in various locations across Thailand and is open to unskilled paying volunteers.

WWF Thailand ⓦwww.wwfthai.org. The Thai branch of the international wildlife conservation NGO.

Phi Phi and Samet have suffered huge environmental damage as a direct result of the number of overnight visitors they receive, and the contrast with national parks where the government has put its foot down – for example in Khao Yai, where all tourist businesses were kicked out in the early 1990s – is marked. While most people understand that the role of the national parks is to conserve vulnerable and precious resources, the dramatic hike in entrance fees payable by foreigners to national parks – from B20 up to B200 in 2000 – was greeted with cynicism and anger, not least because there is often little sign of anything tangible being done on site with the money.

Zoos, endangered species and the wildlife trade

Despite the efforts of local and international conservation and wildlife-protection organizations, **animal rights** issues often meet with a confused response in Thailand. The muddled thinking behind the highly publicized new Chiang Mai Night Safari park is typical: not only was this commercial animal park erected on land appropriated from a national park, but early publicity trumpeted the fact that meat from many of the exotic animals kept in the park – including tigers, lions and elephants – would be available in the park's restaurant. Negative comment soon quashed that, but exotic meats from endangered animals are served, albeit clandestinely, all over Thailand.

Some of Thailand's many **zoos**, such as those in Bangkok and Chiang Mai, are legitimate, decent enough places, but a number of the country's other private wildlife theme parks and zoos – especially those majoring in tigers and crocodiles – have more dubious purposes and some have been targeted by international animal welfare organizations such as Born Free. On the positive front, there's an increasing number of **animal sanctuaries** working to look after abused and endangered animals, especially elephants and gibbons (see box above for details), which operate both as safe havens and as educational visitor attractions. The Tiger Temple near Kanchanaburi (see p.254) falls somewhere in between.

The wildlife trade

Though Thailand signed the Convention on the International Trade in Endangered Species – **CITES** – in 1983, and hosted the annual CITES conference in 2004, the business of imported animals and animal products continues.

Most of the trade in **endangered species** is focused along the borders with Cambodia and Burma, where Thai middle-merchants can apparently easily acquire any number of creatures. Some will be sold as pets and to zoos, while others are destined for dining tables and medicine cabinets. **Tiger** body-parts are especially lucrative and mostly end up on the black markets of China, Korea, Taiwan and Hong Kong, where bones, skin, teeth, whiskers and penis are prized for their "medicinal" properties; it's thought that much of Thailand's dwindling tiger population ends up this way. **Bear** paws and gall bladders are considered to have similar potency and are a star feature, along with other endangered species, at certain clandestine restaurants in Thailand catering to "gourmet" tourists from China and Korea; the traditional custom of slicing paws off a living bear and enhancing gall bladder flavour by taking it from an animal that is literally scared to death make this practice particularly vile. The Burmese border market at Thachileik near Mae Sai (see p.435) is a notorious outlet for tiger and bear body-parts, while Chatuchak Weekend Market in Bangkok (see p.179) has long had a thriving trade in live animals – everything from hornbills to slow loris – though this may change following recent crackdowns.

Contributions by Mark Read and Gavin Lewis

Music

Music is an important part of Thai culture, whether related to Buddhist activities in the local temple (still a focal point for many communities), animist rituals, Brahmanic ceremonies or the wide range of popular song styles. While local forms of Thai popular music such as *luk thung* and *mor lam* remain very popular and distinctively Thai in character, a lively, ever-changing rock, indie, DJ and underground scene is also fast developing, with Bangkok now the hub for Southeast Asian pop and rock.

The classical tradition

Thai classical dance and music can be traced back to stone engravings during the Sukhothai period (thirteenth to fifteenth centuries), which show ensembles of musicians playing traditional instruments, called **phipat**. The *phipat* ensembles include many percussion instruments, rather like Indonesian gamelan – gong circles, xylophones and drums – plus a raucous oboe called the *phinai*. The music was developed to accompany classical dance-drama (*khon* or *lakhon*) or shadow-puppet theatre (*nang*): a shadow-puppet show is depicted in the magnificent *Ramayana* murals in Wat Phra Kaeo in Bangkok's Grand Palace complex.

Phipat music sounds strange to Western ears as the seven equal notes of the Thai scale fall between the cracks of the piano keyboard. But heard in the right environment – in a temple, at a dance performance or at a Thai boxing match – it can be entrancing. As there is no notation, everything is memorized. And, as in all Thai music, elements have been assimilated over the years from diverse sources, then synthesized into something new. Check out any of the international albums by the Prasit Thawon Ensemble (Thawon was a National Artist).

Despite the country's rapid Westernization, Thai classical music has been undergoing something of a revival in the past few years, partly as a result of royal patronage. There have been recent experiments, too, at blending Thai classical and Western styles – often jazz or rock – led by adventurous groups like **Kangsadan** and **Fong Naam**. Recently **Boy Thai** have followed their lead, albeit with a more pop-oriented sound, and have had some mainstream success with two albums. The movie *Homrong* (*The Overture*), about a famous *ranat* (xylophone) player in pre-World War II Siam and xylophone duelling between players, proved surprisingly popular in 2004.

There are dance and classical music **performances** in Bangkok at the National Theatre and the Thailand Cultural Centre (see p.201), and you may also come across some more lacklustre examples at the Erawan Shrine on Thanon Rama I and the *lak muang* shrine behind the Grand Palace, where people give thanks to deities by paying for the temple musicians and dancers to go through a routine. A number of Bangkok restaurants also mount music and dance shows for tourists, including regular shows by Fong Naam, the resident band at the *Tawandang German Brewery* (see p.197), and **Duriyapraneet**, the latter being the country's longest-established classical band.

Folk music

Thailand's folk musics are often referred to as **pleng phua bahn**, which encompasses styles from the country's four distinct regions (central, north, northeast and south), with more than eighty languages and dialects. Despite the rapid social change of the past two decades, numerous folk styles are still enthusiastically played, from the hill-tribe New Year dances in the far north to the all-night singing jousts of northeastern *mor lam glawn*, to the haunting Muslim vocals of *likay wolou* in the deep south.

Most Thais are familiar with the exciting central folk styles like *lam tad, pleng choi* and *pleng I-saw*, which often feature raunchy verbal jousting between male and female singers. Styles like these and the ever-popular *mor lam* from the northeast (see p.910) are incorporated into modern popular styles like *luk thung* (see p.909).

One notable folk style to have grown in popularity in recent years is the up-tempo and danceable northeastern instrumental style known as **bong lang** (the name comes from a wooden xylophone that is attached vertically to a tree). *Bong lang* is ancient, predating Indian-Thai culture, and while it is clearly old music, the style continues to be refined. As recently as the late 1970s, the *phin hai*, a jar with rubber stretched across the mouth, was introduced (often only to put a cute young woman up front); its sound, made by plucking the rubber, is similar to that of a double bass. The top *bong lang* outfit is the glitzy Pong-Lang Sa-Orn.

The best place to see *bong lang* is upcountry, especially in Kalasin province in central Isaan between November and March. Folk music also features prominently at the major festivals held in the northeastern cities of Khon Kaen, Ubon Ratchathani and Udon Thani, particularly at Songkhran (April), the Bun Bang Fai rocket festival (May), and the Asanha Puja candle festival (July); check with TAT for specific dates and locations.

Popular styles

Despite the crippling problem of music piracy and a market dominated by two major companies, the Thai **pop scene** remains vibrant and full of surprises. Thailand is the second biggest Southeast Asian music market after Indonesia, and Bangkok is a major and increasingly important regional hub for pop music and popular culture.

Western orchestration for Thai melodies had been introduced in the 1920s and 1930s and this led to the development of *pleng Thai sakon*, or modern Thai music, in the form of big band and swing, country and western, Hollywood film music, rock 'n' roll, and so on. In the early days, two distinctive Thai genres developed: *pleng luk grung*, a schmaltzy romantic ballad form, popularized by Thailand's most beloved composer and bandleader Euah Sunthornsanan and his Suntharaporn band; and *pleng luk thung* (Thai country). **Luk grung**, with its clearly enunciated singing style and romantic fantasies, was long associated with the rich strata of Bangkok society; it's the kind of music that is played by state organs like Radio Thailand. However, it was largely transformed during the 1960s by the popularity of Western stars like Cliff Richard; as musicians started to mimic the new Western music, a new term was coined, *wong shadow* (*wong* meaning group, *shadow* from the British group The Shadows).

String

The term **string** came into use as Thai-language pop music rapidly developed in the economic boom times of the 1980s. *String* encompasses ballads, rock and alternative, indies, disco, techno/house, heavy metal, reggae, ska, rap and underground; whatever trend is popular in the US, UK and increasingly Japan (with a nod to both Taiwan and Korea) gets picked up quickly and reassembled with Thai lyrics and a particular local flavour, often with sweet melodies.

Megastars like veteran **Thongchai "Bird" Macintyre** generally record on either of the two major labels, Grammy and RS Promotion, though another major star, **Tata Young**, is now signed to BEC-Tero and is making waves in other Asian markets like Japan, Hong Kong and the rest of Southeast Asia. Grammy, which controls more than half the market, has an umbrella of labels that releases everything from best-selling soft rockers **LoSo** and **Mai Chareonpura** to *luk thung* star "Got" Chakrapand Arbkornburi. Their most famous Thai rock act, though, are the talented brothers **Asanee & Wasan** (**Chotikul**), now producing a new generation of rockers on their own label.

Since the mid-1990s, Bakery Music, originally an independent label but now owned by BMG, has led the two major developing pop trends. They broke the **alternative/indie** scene with **Modern Dog**, the country's best rock act of the last decade, and helped develop the rap scene with the top-selling Thai language rapper **Joey Boy** (the hip only buy his profane and savage MP3 underground songs). They also picked up on the popularity of Japanese culture and music with Thai youth and started a label, Dohjo, which specializes in **J-pop** (Japanese-influenced pop) and produces a Thai *manga* comic. Several former founders recently left Bakery to form their own label and further develop the popular rock band **Pru**; also look out for Bakery's indie band **Flure**.

Thailand, and in particular Bangkok, is developing its own musical identity, partly as a result of many high-profile **festivals**, like Rock 100, which in 2006 featured local and regional bands along with Franz Ferdinand, Oasis and Placebo, and the Pattaya Music Festival, which showcases Asian bands, and partly because of the explosion of new genres and the emergence of a busy underground and **live scene**. You'll find Thai, foreign and mixed bands playing in Bangkok's many clubs and bars, and dynamic scenes in Chiang Mai, Khorat and Ko Samui. Recently, more Western and Asian musicians have joined their Thai counterparts – as with electro-clash band **Futon** (Thai-Japanese-Western) and power-pop punksters **The Darlings** (US-Thai) – now that Bangkok is a must for any band touring Asia. And no list of current Thai popstars and rockers would be complete without mentioning **Ebola** (metal plus rap), **Big Ass** (hard-core punk/pop), **Bodyslam** (heavy rock), **Thaitanic** (hip hop from US-born Thais) and **Apartment Khun Pa** (funk plus rock).

Campuses like Ramkhamhaeng University are good places to get information on upcoming **events**, as are radio stations (especially Fat Radio FM). Bangkok is the best place to catch gigs – check ⓦwww.bangkokgigguide.com for comprehensive listings, or browse websites and the monthly magazines *Bangkok Metro* and *Untamed Travel* and the *Nation* and *Bangkok Post* newspapers.

Songs for life

Another big genre is **pleng phua chiwit**, or "songs for life", which started as a kind of progressive rock in the early 1970s, with bands like **Caravan** (no relation to the British songsters) blending *pleng phua bahn* (folk songs) with Western folk and rock. Caravan were at the forefront of the left-wing campaign for democracy with songs like *Khon Gap Kwai* (*Human with Buffaloes*):

Greed eats our labour and divides people into classes
The rice farmers fall to the bottom
Insulted as backward and ignorant brutes
With one important and sure thing: death.

Although an elected government survived from 1973 to 1976, the military returned soon after and Caravan, like many of the student activists, went into

Discography

CDs are taking over from cassettes, even in the provinces (where the mix is 70 percent *luk thung*, 25 percent *string* and 5 percent international). In Bangkok, ask the vendors at the day and night markets, or the stores on Thanon Charoen Krung (New Road). Most major *luk thung* or *mor lam* artists release a CD every three months, which is often given an artist's series number. Old-style recordings of Suraphon Sombatjalern and the like can be found on the ground floor of the Mah Boon Krong Shopping Centre at the Bangkok Cassette Co. store or at Panthip Plaza. All the releases listed here are CDs except where stated; the rest are Thai cassettes.

In addition, one **DVD** well worth seeking out is Jeremy Marre's episode on music in Thailand, from his award-winning Beats of the Heart music-TV documentary series *Two Faces of Thailand: A Musical Portrait* (Shanachie, USA).

Classical

Fong Naam *The Hang Hong Suite* (Nimbus, UK). A good introduction to the vivacious and glittering sound of classical Thai music, from one of Thailand's best ensembles. The CD includes some upbeat funeral music and parodies of the musical languages of neighbouring cultures. *The Sleeping Angel* (Nimbus, UK) is also a splendid recording.

The Prasit Thawon Ensemble *Thai Classical Music* (Nimbus, UK). Brilliant playing (and outstanding recording quality) from some of Thailand's best performers, mainly of *piphat* style. Includes the overture Homrong Sornthong and, on Cherd Chin, some scintillating dialogues between different instruments.

Various Thailande (Auvidis/UNESCO, France). An atmospheric disc of three contrasting ensembles from Chiang Mai. Intricate textures that draw you in.

Modern music (Thai sakol)

Euah Suntaraporn *Chabab Derm (Old Songs) Vols 1–5, 6–10* (Bangkok Cassette). Modern Thai music was popularized by the late master Euah. Some of the most popular Thai songs ever were performed by the Suntaraporn band and a bevy of singers.

Hill-tribe music

Various *Thailand: Musiques et Chants des Peuples du Triangle d'Or* (Globe Music, France). Recordings of the traditional music of Thailand's main hill-tribe groups: Meo, Lisu, Shan, Lahu, Yao, Akha and Karen.

Chao ley (sea gypsy) music

Various *Sea Gypsies of the Andaman Sea* (Topic, UK). The traditional music of the nomadic Moken fisherfolk in southern Thailand, mostly recorded in the Surin islands.

Folk music

David Fanshawe *Music From Thailand and Laos: Southeast Asia Recordings* (Arc Music, UK). Excellent range of folk music from different regions of both countries.

Luk thung

If you can't find any of the albums below, go for a compilation of past albums, usually under a title like *Luam Hits* (*Mixed Hits*).

Got Chakrapand Arbkornburi *Jareon, Jareon* (*New, New*) (GMM Grammy, Thailand). Big hit during 2003 and 2004, following his performance in a telenovella on a *likay* troupe. Also check out any of his Greatest Hits compilations.

Pompuang Duangjan In Thailand, the best of many cassettes to go for is *Pompuang Lai Por Sor* (*Pompuang's Many Eras*) (Topline, Thailand). Her early spine-tingling hits can be found on several CD compilations from Bangkok Cassette, some recorded when she was known as Nampung Petsupan (Honey Diamond from Supanburi).

Monsit Khamsoi *Khai Kwai Chuay Mae* (*Sell the Buffalo to Help Mum*) and *Sang Nang* (*While I'm Away*) (both on Sure, Thailand). He came from nowhere and was considered too ugly to make it, but with his humility and that fabulously soft emotive voice, he captured the hearts of the entire nation and proved to be the best male *luk thung* singer to emerge for years.

Sodsai Rungphothong *Rak Nong Porn* (*I Love Young Porn*) (Topline, Thailand). The killer comeback by veteran Sodsai – the title track sold two million. Classic old-style *luk thung* – jangling temple bells and brass blaring, and Sodsai wailing over it all.

Sayan Sanya *Luk Thung Talap Thong* (*Luk Thung from the Golden Tape*) (Onpa, Thailand). Heir to Sombatjalern's throne, sweet-voiced Sanya has never sounded better than on this greatest hits collection.

Suraphon Sombatjalern *Luam Pleng* (*Mixed Songs*) *Vols 1–4* (Bangkok Cassette, Thailand). Greatest hits by the king of *luk thung*. Great voice, great songs, great backing – Siamese soul.

Various *Mon Rak Luk Thung* (*Enchanting Countryside*) (RS Promotion, Thailand). Runaway bestseller from the TV series based on the 1969 movie.

Various *Mon Rak Transistor* (*A Transistor Love Story*) (UFO, Thailand). From the hit movie about a young country boy who tries to make it in the big city as a *luk thung* singer. Includes Surapon's wonderful theme song, *Mai Lerm* (*Don't Forget*). The movie is widely available.

Various *The Rough Guide to the Music of Thailand: Lukthung and Morlam: The Hidden Sounds of Asia* (World Music Network, UK). Good review of some current *mor lam* and *luk thung*, despite confusing liner notes.

Mor lam/northeastern music

Jintara Poonlarp *Luam Hit Baet Pi* (*Mixed Hits from Eight Years*) (Master Tape, Thailand). Poonlarp has conquered *mor lam* over the past decade with her powerful husky voice.

Banyen Rakgan *Luk Thung, Mor Lam Sood Hit* (*Luk Thung, Mor Lam Top Hits*) (Rota, Thailand). Sixteen scorchers from the first national *mor lam* star. Rakgan's voice is a standout. Good example of the big-band *mor lam* sound.

Isan Slété *Songs and Music from North East Thailand* (Globestyle, UK). Excellent selection of traditional *mor lam*. Vocal and instrumental numbers, played by a band of master musicians.

Pornsak Songsaeng *Gaud Mawn Nawn Pur* (*Holding the Pillow in my Delirium*) (Onpa, Thailand). *Mor lam*'s top male act, a fine singer with a deep, distinctive voice.

Various *Instrumental Music of Northeast Thailand* (King, Japan). Wonderful collection of *bong lang* and related instrumental northeastern styles. Lively and fun. Unmissable.

Various, featuring Chaweewan Damnoen *Mor Lam Singing of Northeast Thailand* (King, Japan). The only female *mor lam* National Artist, Chaweewan Damnoen, headlines this fine collection of many *lam* (singing) styles. Most *luk thung glawn* narrative and dance styles, even spirit-possession rituals, are included.

String and Songs for Life

Big Ass *Not Bad* (Music Bugs, Thailand) and *Seven* (GMM Grammy, Thailand). After four albums, Big Ass are huge – hardcore punk/pop.

continued.....

continued.....

Carabao *Made in Thailand* and *Ameri-koi* (both Krabue, Thailand). Two classic albums from the Songs for Life giants. *Made in Thailand* was right in tune with the times and targeted social problems like consumerism, the sex trade and a failing education system. *Ameri-koi* (*Greedy America*) is even more nationalistic than the previous one, but it also hits out at Thai migrant workers exploited by labour brokers.

Ebola *In My Hate* (Hello Records, Thailand) and *Entertain* (Warner, Thailand). New-school metal with rap influences.

Futon *Never Mind the Botox* (Rehab, Thailand). Electro-clash with a punk attitude from the kingdom's favourite underground band. Excellent cover of Iggy Pop's "I Wanna Be Your Dog".

Modern Dog *Modern Dog* (Bakery Music, Thailand). This album of alternative rock marked an important change of direction for the Thai rock scene. Also see albums *Love Me Love My Life* and *That Song*.

Kantrum

Darkie *Darkie, Rock II: Buk Jah* (Movie Music, Thailand). The first-ever *kantrum* crossover album achieved nationwide stardom for the King of Kantrum. Darkie's booming voice moves from rap-like delivery to moans and wails, shadowed closely by the fiddle and some funky riddims. Unmissable.

Darkie *Kantrum Rock Vols I & II* (available on separate cassettes). Benchmark recordings by *kantrum*'s only major star: Darkie's fine wailing voice is featured in rock-*kantrum*, *kantrum* and *kantrum luk thung*.

hiding in the jungle. There they performed to villagers and hill-tribes people and gave the occasional concert. When the government offered an amnesty in 1979, most of the students, and Caravan too, disillusioned with the Communist Party's support for the Khmer Rouge in Cambodia, returned to normal life.

In the 1980s a new group emerged to carry on Caravan's work, **Carabao**. The band split up but has had several reunions; their influence is still strong, with leader Ad Carabao still in the limelight but now more as a businessman hawking his "energy" drink, Carabao Daeng, via the band's gigs and nasty nationalistic TV ad campaigns. However, despite the bloody street riots of 1992 (in protest at the then military-installed government) once again bringing "songs for life" artists out to support the pro-democracy protests, since the 1980s the strong social activism of Caravan's early years has generally been replaced by more individual and personal themes. The current top act is fresh-faced singer-songwriter **Pongsit Kamphee**, whose earnest approach and rise through the ranks (he was reportedly once a stagehand for Caravan) have garnered him a sizeable following.

Musically, the genre has changed little in 25 years, remaining strongly rooted in Western folk-rock styles. Nonetheless, these musicians came out in droves during democracy protests in January 2006 (except the conspicuously absent Ad Carabao), providing concerts to entertain protestors camped outside Government House. In fact, the music scene received a shot in the arm from the protests: a banned music video of savage satire "Ai Na Liem" ("Old Square Face", a reference to controversial prime minister Thaksin Shinawatra) was one of the highlights, as was the five-CD series of satirical Chinese classical opera (*ngieu*) skits, performed live.

Songs for life fans should check out CD stalls at Bangkok's Chatuchak Weekend Market, several of which specialize in this genre.

Luk thung

Go to one of the huge **luk thung** shows held in a temple or local stadium on the outskirts of Bangkok, or to any temple fair in the countryside, and you'll hear one of the great undiscovered popular musics of Asia. The shows, amid the bright lights, foodstalls and fairground games, last several hours and involve dozens of dancers and costume changes. In contrast with *luk grung*, *luk thung* (literally, "child of the field") has always been associated with the rural and urban poor, and because of this has gained nationwide popularity over the past forty years.

According to *luk thung* DJ Jenpope Jobkrabunwan, the term was first coined by Jamnong Rangsitkuhn in 1962, but the first song in the style was *Oh Jow Sow Chao Rai* (Oh, the Vegetable Grower's Bride), recorded in 1937, and the genre's first big singer, **Kamrot Samboonanon**, emerged in the mid-1940s. Originally called *pleng talat* (market songs) or *pleng chiwit* (songs of life), the style blended together folk songs (*pleng phua bahn*), central Thai classical music and Thai folk dances (*ram wong*). Malay strings and fiddles were added in the 1950s, as were Latin brass and rhythms like the cha-cha-cha and mambo (Asian tours by Xavier Cugat influenced many Asian pop styles during the 1950s), as well as elements from Hollywood movie music and "yodelling" country and western vocal styles from the likes of Gene Autry and Hank Williams. In 1952, a new singer, **Suraphon Sombatjalern**, made his debut with a song entitled *Nam Da Sow Vienne* (Tears of the Vientiane Girl) and became the undisputed king of the style until his untimely murder (for serious womanizing, rumour has it) in 1967. Sombatjalern helped develop the music into a mature form, and was known as the "King" of the genre, along with his Queen, sweet-voiced Pongsri Woranut.

Today, *luk thung* is a mix of Thai folk music and traditional entertainment forms like *likay* (travelling popular theatre), as well as a range of Western styles. There are certainly some strong musical affinities with other regional pop styles like Indonesian *dangdut* and Japanese *enka*, but what is distinctly Thai – quite apart from the spectacular live shows – are the singing styles and the content of the lyrics. Vocal styles are full of glissando, wavering grace notes and wailing ornamentation. A singer must have a wide vocal range, as the late *luk thung* megastar **Pompuang Duangjan** explained: "Making the *luk thung* sound is difficult, you must handle well the high and low notes. And because the emotional content is stronger than in *luk grung*, you must also be able to create a strongly charged atmosphere."

Pompuang had the kind of voice that turns the spine to jelly. She rose to prominence during the late 1970s, joining **Sayan Sanya** as the biggest male and female names in the business. Like Sombatjalern, both came from the rural peasantry, making identification with themes and stories that related directly to the audience much easier. Songs narrate mini-novellas, based around typical characters like the lorry driver, peasant lad or girl, poor farmer, prostitute or maid; and the themes are those of going away to the big city, infidelity, grief, tragedy and sexual pleasure. Interestingly, it is not always the lyrics that carry the sexual charge of the song (and if lyrics are deemed too risqué by the authorities the song will be subject to strict censorship) but rather the vocal style and the stage presentation, which can be very bawdy indeed.

With the advent of TV and the rise in popularity of *string*, the number of large upcountry *luk thung* shows has declined. It's not easy, said Pompuang, to tour with over a hundred staff, including the dancers in the *hang kruang* (chorus). "We play for over four hours, but *string* bands, with only a few staff members, play a paltry two hours!" Her response to the advent of *string* and the increasing importance of promotional videos was to develop a dance-floor-oriented sound – **electronic luk thung**. Few *luk thung* singers are capable of this, but Pompuang had the vocal range to tackle both ballad forms and the up-tempo dance numbers. Her musical diversification increased her popularity enormously, and when she died in 1992, aged only 31, up to 200,000 people, ranging from royalty to the rural poor, made their way to her funeral in her home town of Suphanburi.

Since Pompuang's death, the top *luk thung* slot has been occupied by **"Got" Chakrapand Arbkornburi**, whose switch from pop to full-time *luk thung* has brought many younger listeners to the style, while the reigning female singer was **Suranee Ratchasima** but she has been superseded by the perkier **Arpaporn Nakornsawan**. **Mike Piromporn**, originally a *mor lam* man, is Got's main challenger. Bangkok's first 24-hour *luk thung* radio station, Luk Thung FM (at 90 FM), was launched in 1997, and it's even hip for the middle class to like *luk thung* these days. Listeners have been snapping up collections of *luk thung* classics, and several veteran singers have relaunched their careers, including **Sodsai Rungphothong**, who had a monster two-million seller with his *Rak Nong Porn* album. A new generation of singers has also emerged, with artists like **Monsit Kamsoi**, **Yingyong Yodbuangarm**, **Yui Yardyuh, Tai Orathai** and **Fon Thanasunthorn**. There is some truth, however, in the criticism that some new *luk thung* stars are being artificially manufactured just like their pop and rock counterparts, and there's a tendency to rate a pretty face over vocal expertise.

For many years, *luk thung* was sung by performers from the Suphanburi area in the central plains, but more regional voices are being heard in the genre now, with northeasterners now outnumbering these singers. A slightly faster rhythm, *luk thung* Isaan, has developed, led initially by **Pimpa Pornsiri**, who called the style *luk thung prayuk*. The south, too, has its own *luk thung* star, in the enormously popular **Ekachai Srivichai**. But the most surprising development has been the emergence of not one but two blonde-haired, blue-eyed foreigners singing *luk thung* and *mor lam*. First up is Swede **Manat "Jonas" Andersson**, who rose to national prominence with his debut album, *Pom Cheu Jonas* – he's already a fixture on the *luk thung* circuits; meanwhile, Anglo-Dutch singer **Kristy Gibson** sings mainly *luk thung Isaan* and *mor lam*.

Mor lam

Mor lam is the folk style from the poor, dry northeastern region of Isaan, an area famed for droughts, hot spicy food, good boxers and great music. Over the last fifteen years, the modern pop form of this style has risen dramatically, at *luk thung*'s expense. Traditionally, a *mor lam* is a master of the *lam* singing style (sung in the Isaan dialect, which is actually Lao), and is accompanied by the *khaen* (bamboo mouth organ), the *phin* (two- to four-string guitar) and *ching* (small temple bells). Modern **mor lam** developed from *mor lam glawn*, a narrative form where all-night singing jousts are held between male and female singers, and from *mor lam soeng*, the group-dance form. Both still play an important part in many social events like weddings, births and deaths, festivals and temple fairs. A *mor lam* may sing intricate fixed-metre Lao epic poems or may relate current affairs in a spontaneous rap. In the large groups, Western instruments like guitar (replacing the *phin*) and synthesizer (for the *khaen*) are used.

The style came to national prominence more than twenty years ago, when a female *mor lam* singer, **Banyen Rakgan**, appeared on national TV. In the early 1980s the music was heard not only in Isaan but also in the growing slums of Bangkok, as rural migrants poured into the capital in search of work. By the end of the decade stars like **Jintara Poonlarp** (with her hit song "Isaan Woman Far From Home") and **Pornsak Songsaeng** could command the same sell-out concerts as their *luk thung* counterparts. The current bestseller is **Siriporn**

Ampaiporn, whose strong vocals burst upon the scene with the monster-selling *Bor Rak Si Dam* album.

The format of a *mor lam* **performance** is similar to that of *luk thung* shows – lots of dancers in wild costumes, comedy skits and a large backing orchestra – as is the subject matter. The music is definitely hot, especially if you see it live, when bands will often play through the night, never missing the groove for a minute, driven on by the relentless *phin* and *khaen* playing. To some people, the fast plucking style of the *phin* gives a West African or Celtic tinge; the *khaen* has a rich sound – over a bass drone players improvise around the melody, while at the same time vamping the basic rhythm. Male and female singers rotate or duet humorous love songs, which often start with one of the *mor khaen* setting up the beat. They sing about topical issues, bits of news, crack lewd jokes or make fun of the audience – all very tongue-in-cheek.

Musically, however, *mor lam* and *luk thung* are very different; *mor lam* has a much faster, relentless rhythm and the vocal delivery is rapid-fire, rather like a rap. You'll immediately recognize a *mor lam* song with its introductory wailing moan "*Oh la naw*", meaning "fortune". *Mor lam* artists, brought up bilingually, can easily switch from *luk thung* to *mor lam*, but *luk thung* artists, who only speak the national central Thai dialect, cannot branch out so easily.

In the 1990s, *mor lam* musicians headed off the challenge of increasingly popular *string* bands by creating **mor lam sing**, a turbo-charged modern version of *mor lam glawn* played by small electric combos. The number of large touring *luk thung* or *mor lam* shows has declined in recent years, owing to high overheads, TV entertainment and the popularity of *string* bands, so *mor lam sing* satisfies the need for local music with a modern edge.

Mor lam sing was followed quickly by a more rock-oriented *mor lam* sound (this is a little similar to Grand X in the 1980s, which played a mix of rock and *luk thung*), led by funky little combos like **Rocksadert** and **Rock Saleang**, actually much better live than on recordings, although the latter had a hilarious hit in 2006 with "Motorcy Hoy".

Kantrum: Thai-Cambodian pop

"Isaan nua (north) has *mor lam*, Isaan dai (south) has *kantrum*," sings **Darkie**, the first – and so far only – star of **kantrum**, Thai-Cambodian pop, in his song "Isaan Dai Sah Muk Kee" (Southern Isaan Unity). His music is a very specific offshoot, from the southern part of Isaan, where Thai-Cambodians mix with ethnic Lao and Thais. So far *kantrum* is only popular in Isaan, and that seems unlikely to change, as few people outside the region speak either Cambodian or the Thai-Cambodian dialect, Suay, in which the songs are sung.

Modern *kantrum* has developed from Cambodian folk and classical music, played in a small group consisting of fiddle, small hand drums and *krab* (pieces of hardwood bashed together rather like claves). This traditional style is now quite hard to find in Thailand; some ten or so years ago, musicians started to electrify the music, using both traditional and Western instruments. Shunning the synthesizer preferred by his competitors like Khong Khoi, Oh-Yot and Ai Num Muang Surin, Darkie puts the wailing fiddle centre-stage, cranks up the rhythms (*kantrum* has a harder beat than even *mor lam*) and sets off with his deep, distinctive voice. In 1997, he broke new ground with *Darkie Rock II: Buk Jah*, the first *kantrum* crossover album to have success in the mainstream pop market. Sadly, in 2001, at the young age of 35, Darkie passed away.

John Clewley
(Adapted from the *Rough Guide to World Music*)

The hill tribes

Originating in various parts of China and Southeast Asia, the hill tribes are sometimes termed Fourth World people, in that they are migrants who continue to migrate without regard for established national boundaries. Most arrived in Thailand during the last century, and many of the hill peoples are still found in other parts of Southeast Asia – in Vietnam, for example, where the French used the *montagnards* ("mountain dwellers") in their fight against communism. Since 1975, a large percentage of the one million refugees that Thailand has accepted from Burma, Laos and Cambodia has been hill-tribe people. Some, however, have been around for much longer, like the Lawa, who are thought to have been the first settlers in northern Thailand, though these days they have largely been assimilated into mainstream Thai culture.

Called **chao khao** (mountain people) by the Thais, the tribes are mostly pre-literate societies, whose sophisticated systems of customs, laws and beliefs have developed to harmonize relationships between individuals and their environment. In recent years their ancient culture has come under threat, faced with the effects of rapid population growth and the ensuing competition for land, discrimination and exploitation by lowland Thais, and tourism. However, the integrity of their way of life is as yet largely undamaged, and what follows is the briefest of introductions to an immensely complex subject. If you want to learn more, visit the Tribal Museum in Chiang Mai (see p.354), or the Hill Tribe Museum and Handicrafts Shop in Chiang Rai (see p.430) before setting out on a trek.

Agriculture

Although the hill tribes keep some livestock, such as pigs, poultry and elephants, the base of their economy is **swidden agriculture**, a crude form of shifting cultivation also practised by many Thai lowland farmers. At the beginning of the season an area of jungle is cleared and burned, producing ash to fertilize rice, corn, chillies and other vegetables, which are replanted in succeeding years until the soil's nutrients are exhausted. This system is sustainable with a low population density, which allows the jungle time to recover before it is used again. However, with the increase in population over recent decades, ever greater areas are being exhausted, and the decreasing forest cover is leading to erosion and micro-climatic change.

As a result, many villages took up the large-scale production of **opium** to supplement the traditional subsistence crops, though the Thai government has now largely eradicated opium production in the north. However, the cash crops which have been introduced in its place have often led to further environmental damage, as these low-profit crops require larger areas of cultivation, and thus greater deforestation. Furthermore, the water supplies have become polluted with chemical pesticides, and, although more environmentally sensitive agricultural techniques are being introduced, they have yet to achieve widespread acceptance.

Religion and festivals

Although some tribes have taken up Buddhism and others – especially among the Karen, Mien and Lahu – have been converted by Christian missionaries bringing the incentives of education and modern medicine, the hill tribes are predominantly **animists**. In this belief system, all natural objects are inhabited by spirits which, along with the tribe's ancestor spirits and the supreme divine spirit, must be propitiated to prevent harm to the family or village. Most villages have one or more religious leaders, which may include a priest who looks after the ritual life of the community, and at least one shaman who has the power to mediate with the spirits and prescribe what has to be done to keep them happy. If a member of the community is sick, for example, the shaman will be consulted to determine what action has insulted which spirit, and will then carry out the correct sacrifice.

The most important festival, celebrated by all the tribes, is at **New Year**, when whole communities take part in dancing, music and rituals particular to each tribe: Hmong boys and girls, for instance, take part in a courting ritual at this time, while playing catch with a ball. The New Year festivals are not held on fixed dates, but at various times during the cool-season slack period in the agricultural cycle from January to March.

Costumes and handicrafts

The most conspicuous characteristics of the hill tribes are their exquisitely crafted **costumes** and adornments, the styles and colours of which are particular to each group. Although many men and children now adopt Western clothes for everyday wear, with boys in particular more often running around in long shorts and T-shirts with logos, most women and girls still wear the traditional attire at all times. It's the women who make the clothes too – some still spin their own cotton, though many Hmong, Lisu and Mien women are prosperous enough to buy materials from itinerant traders. Other distinctive hill-tribe artefacts – tools, jewellery, weapons and musical instruments – are the domain of the men, and specialist **blacksmiths** and **silversmiths** have such high status that some attract business from villages many kilometres away. Jewellery, the chief outward proof of a family's wealth, is displayed most obviously by Lisu women at the New Year festivals, and is commonly made from silver melted down from Indian and Burmese coins, though brass, copper and aluminium are also used.

Clothing and **handicrafts** were not regarded as marketable products until the early 1980s, when co-operatives were set up to manufacture and market these goods, which are now big business in the shops of Thailand. The hill tribes' deep-dyed coarse cloth, embroidered with simple geometric patterns in bright colours, has become popular among middle-class Thais as well as farang visitors. Mien material, dyed indigo or black with bright snowflake embroidery, is on sale in many shops, as is the simple but very distinctive Akha work – coarse black cotton, with triangular patterns of stitching and small fabric patches in rainbow colours, usually made up into bags and hats. The Hmong's much more sophisticated **embroidery** and **appliqué**, added to jacket lapels and cuffs and skirt hems, is also widely seen – Blue Hmong skirts, made on a base of indigo-dyed cotton with a white geometric batik design and embroidered in loud primary colours, are particularly attractive.

Besides clothing, the hill tribes' other handicrafts, such as knives and wooden or bamboo musical pipes, have found a market amongst farangs, the most saleable product being the intricate engraving work of their silversmiths, especially in the form of chunky bracelets. For a sizeable minority of villages, handicrafts now provide the security of a steady income to supplement what they make from farming.

The main tribes

Within the small geographical area of northern Thailand there are at least ten different hill tribes, many of them divided into distinct subgroups –

the following are the main seven, listed in order of population and under their own names, rather than the sometimes derogatory names used by Thais. (The Thai Yai – or Shan – the dominant group in most of the west of the region, are not a hill tribe, but a subgroup of Thais.) Beyond the broad similarities outlined above, this section sketches their differences in terms of history, economy and religion, and describes elements of dress by which they can be distinguished.

Karen

The **Karen** (called Kaliang or Yang in Thai) form by far the largest hill-tribe group in Thailand with a population of about 500,000, and are the second oldest after the Lawa, having begun to arrive here from Burma and China in the seventeenth century. The Thai Karen, many of them refugees from Burma (see box on p.312), mostly live in a broad tract of land west of Chiang Mai, which stretches along the border from Mae Hong Son province all the way down to Kanchanaburi, with scattered pockets in Chiang Mai, Chiang Rai and Phayao provinces.

The Karen traditionally practise a system of **rotating cultivation** – ecologically far more sensitive than slash-and-burn – in the valleys of this region and on low hills. Their houses, very similar to those of lowland Thais, are small (they do not live in extended family groups), built on stilts and made of bamboo or teak; they're often surrounded by fruit gardens and neat fences. As well as farming their own land, the Karen often hire out their labour to Thais and other hill tribes, and keep a variety of livestock including elephants, which used to be employed in the teak trade but are now often found giving rides to trekking parties.

Unmarried Karen women wear loose white or undyed V-necked shift dresses, often decorated with grass seeds at the seams. Some subgroups decorate them more elaborately, Sgaw girls with a woven red or pink band above the waist, and Pwo girls with woven red patterns in the lower half of the shift. Married women wear blouses and skirts in bold colours, predominantly red or blue. Men generally wear blue, baggy trousers with red or blue shirts, a simplified version of the women's blouse.

Hmong

Called the Meo ("barbarians") by the Thais, the **Hmong** ("free people") originated in central China or Mongolia and are now found widely in northern Thailand; they are still the most widespread minority group in south China. There are two subgroups: the **Blue Hmong**, who live around and to the west of Chiang Mai; and the **White Hmong**, who are found to the east. Their overall population in Thailand is about 110,000, making them the second-largest hill-tribe group.

Of all the hill tribes, the Hmong have been the quickest to move away from subsistence farming. In the past, Hmong people were more involved in opium production than most other tribes in Thailand, though now many have eagerly embraced the newer cash crops. Hmong clothing has become much in demand in Thailand, and Hmong women will often be seen at markets throughout the country selling their handicrafts. The women, in fact, are expected to do most of the work on the land and in the home.

Hmong **villages** are usually built at high altitudes, below the crest of a protecting hill. Although wealthier families sometimes build the more comfortable Thai-style houses, most stick to the traditional house, with its dirt floor and a roof descending almost to ground level. They live together in extended families, with two or more bedrooms and a large guest platform.

The Blue Hmong dress in especially striking **clothes**. The women wear intricately embroidered pleated skirts decorated with parallel horizontal bands of red, pink, blue and white; their jackets are of black satin, with wide orange and yellow embroidered cuffs and lapels. White Hmong women wear black baggy trousers and simple jackets with blue cuffs. Men of both groups generally wear baggy black pants with colourful sashes round the waist, and embroidered jackets closing over the chest with a button at the left shoulder. All the Hmong are famous for their chunky **silver jewellery**, which the women wear every day, the men only on special occasions: they believe silver binds a person's spirits together, and wear a heavy neck ring to keep the spirits weighed down in the body.

Lahu

The **Lahu**, who originated in the Tibetan highlands, migrated to southern China, Burma and Laos centuries ago; only since the end of the nineteenth century did they begin to come into Thailand from northern Burma. They're called Muser – from the Burmese word for "hunter" – by the Thais, because many of the first Lahu to reach northern Thailand were professional hunters. With a population of about 80,000, they are the third-largest hill-tribe group: most of their settlements are concentrated close to the Burmese border, in Chiang Rai, northern Chiang Mai and Mae Hong Son provinces, but families and villages change locations frequently. The Lahu language has become a *lingua franca* among the hill tribes, since the Lahu often hire out their labour. About one-third of Lahu have been converted to Christianity (through exposure in colonial Burma), and many have abandoned their traditional way of life as a result. The remaining animist Lahu believe in a village guardian spirit, who is often worshipped at a central temple that is surrounded by banners and streamers of white and yellow flags. Village houses are built on high stilts with walls of bamboo or wooden planks, thatched with grass. While subsistence farming is still common, sustainable agriculture – plantations of orchards, tea or coffee – is becoming more prevalent, and cash crops such as corn and cotton have taken the place of opium.

Some Lahu women wear a distinctive black cloak with diagonal white stripes, decorated in bold red and yellow at the top of the sleeve, but traditional costume has been supplanted by the Thai shirt and sarong amongst many Lahu groups. The tribe is famous for its richly embroidered **yaam** (shoulder bags), which are widely available in Chiang Mai.

Akha

The poorest of the hill tribes, the **Akha** (Kaw or Eekaw in Thai) migrated from Tibet over two thousand years ago to Yunnan in China, where at some stage they had an organized state and kept written chronicles of their history – these chronicles, like the Akha written language, are now lost. From the 1910s the tribe began to settle in Thailand and is found in four provinces – Chiang Rai, Chiang Mai, Lampang and Phrae – with a population of nearly 50,000 in about 250 villages. The greatest concentration of Akha villages is in Chiang Rai province followed by northern Chiang Mai, near the Burmese border – recently many Akha have fled persecution in politically unstable Burma. A large Akha population still lives in Yunnan and there are communities in neighbouring Laos as well as in Burma.

The Akha are less open to change than the other hill tribes, and have maintained their old agricultural methods of **shifting cultivation**. The Akha's form of animism – *Akhazang*, "the way of life of the Akha" – has also survived in uncompromised form. As well as spirits in the natural world, *Akhazang*

△ Hill-tribe handicrafts

encompasses the worship of ancestor spirits: some Akha can recite the names of over sixty generations of forebears.

Every Akha village is entered through ceremonial **gates** decorated with carvings depicting human activities and attributes – even cars and aeroplanes – to indicate to the spirit world that beyond here only humans should pass. To touch any of these carvings, or to show any lack of respect to them, is punishable by fines or sacrifices. The gates are rebuilt every year, so many villages have a series of gates, the older ones in a state of disintegration. Another characteristic of an Akha villages is its giant **swing** (also replaced each year), and used every August or early September in a swinging festival in which the whole population takes part.

Akha **houses** are recognizable by their low stilts and steeply pitched roofs, though some may use higher stilts to reflect higher status. Even more distinctive is the elaborate **headgear** which women wear all day; it frames the entire face and usually features white beads interspersed with silver coins, topped with plumes of red taffeta and framed by dangling hollow silver balls and other jewellery or strings of beads. The rest of their heavy costume is made up of decorated tube-shaped ankle-to-knee leggings, an above-the-knee black skirt with a white beaded centrepiece, and a loose-fitting black jacket with heavily embroidered cuffs and lapels.

Mien

The **Mien** (called Yao in Thai) consider themselves the aristocrats of the hill tribes. Originating in central China, they began migrating southward more than two thousand years ago to southern China, Vietnam, Laos and Thailand; in southern China they used to have such power that at one time a Mien princess was married to a Chinese emperor. In Thailand today the Mien are widely scattered throughout the north, with concentrations around Nan, Phayao and Chiang Rai, and a population of about 40,000. They are the only hill tribe to have a written language, and a codified religion based on medieval Chinese Taoism, although in recent years there have been many Mien converts to Christianity and Buddhism. In general, the Mien strike a balance between integration into Thai life and maintenance of their separate cultural base. Many earn extra cash by selling exquisite embroidery and religious scrolls, painted in bold Chinese style.

Mien villages are not especially distinctive: their houses are usually built of wooden planks on a dirt floor, with a guest platform of bamboo in the communal living area. The **clothes** of the women, however, are instantly recognizable: long black jackets with glamorous looking stole-like lapels of bright scarlet wool, heavily embroidered loose trousers in intricate designs which can take up to two years to complete, and a similarly embroidered black turban. The caps of babies are also very beautiful, richly embroidered with red or pink pom-poms. On special occasions, like weddings, women and children wear silver neck rings, with silver chains decorated with silver ornaments extending down the back, and even their turbans are crossed with lengths of silver. A Mien woman's wedding headdress is quite extraordinary, a carefully constructed platform with arched supports which are covered with red fabric and heirlooms of embroidered cloth. Two burgundy-coloured fringes create side curtains obscuring her face, and the only concession to modernity is the black insulating tape that holds the structure to her head.

Lisu

The **Lisu** (Lisaw in Thai), who originated in eastern Tibet, first arrived in Thailand in 1921 and are found mostly in the west, particularly between Chiang Mai and Mae Hong Son, but also in western Chiang Rai, Chiang Mai and Phayao provinces, with a population of around 30,000. Whereas the other hill tribes are led by the village headman or shaman, the Lisu are organized into patriarchal clans which have authority over many villages, and their strong sense of clan rivalry often results in public violence.

The Lisu live in extended families at moderate to high altitudes, in houses built on the ground, with dirt floors and bamboo walls. Both men and women dress colourfully; the women wear a blue or green parti-coloured knee-length tunic, split up the sides to the waist, with a wide black belt and blue or green pants. At New Year, the women don dazzling outfits, including waistcoats and belts of intricately fashioned silver and turbans with multicoloured pom-poms and streamers; traditionally, the men wear green, pink or yellow baggy pants and a blue jacket.

Lawa

The history of the **Lawa** people (Lua in Thai) is poorly understood, but it seems very likely that they have inhabited Thailand since at least the eighth century; they were certainly here when the Thais arrived eight hundred years ago. The Lawa people are found only in Thailand; they believe that they migrated from Cambodia and linguistically they are certainly closely related to Mon-Khmer, but some archeologists think that their origins lie in Micronesia, which they left perhaps two thousand years back.

This lengthy cohabitation with the Thais has produced large-scale integration, so that most Lawa villages are indistinguishable from Thai settlements and most Lawa speak Thai as their first language. However, in an area of about 500 square kilometres between Hot, Mae Sariang and Mae Hong Son, the Lawa still live a largely traditional life, although even here the majority have adopted Buddhism and Thai-style houses. The basis of their economy is subsistence agriculture, with rice grown on terraces according to a sophisticated rotation system. Those identified as Lawa number just over 10,000.

Unmarried Lawa women wear distinctive strings of orange and yellow beads, loose white blouses edged with pink, and tight skirts in parallel bands of blue, black, yellow and pink. After marriage, these brightly coloured clothes are replaced with a long fawn dress, but the beads are still worn. All the women wear their hair tied in a turban, and the men wear light-coloured baggy pants and tunics or, more commonly, Western clothes.

Film

Until recently, Thai cinema was almost impenetrable to the outside world. Thai films were shown exclusively in Thailand, in their original language, and considered to be of little interest to a foreign audience. But the West began to take notice of Thai cinema in 2000, when films such as *Iron Ladies*, *Tears of the Black Tiger* and later *The Legend of Suriyothai* showed that Thai directors had the style and wit to entertain non-Thai-speaking audiences. Many larger-budget Thai films are now released outside Thailand and with English subtitles.

A brief history

Thailand's first **cinema** was built in 1905 in Bangkok, behind Wat Tuk on Thanon Charoen Krung, and for a couple of decades screened only short, silent films from America, Europe and Japan. Though nothing remains of the earliest film-theatres, the recently renovated Art-Deco Sala Chalermkrung, which was built in 1933 in Bangkok's Chinatown, is still in use today as a venue for live theatre and the occasional screening.

The **first home-grown film**, *Chok Sorng Chan* (*Double Luck*), made by the Wasuwat brothers of the Bangkok Film Company, didn't emerge until 1927, and it was another five years before *Long Thang* (*Going Astray*), the first Thai film with sound, followed.

During the 1920s, a few foreign film companies came to Thailand to film the local culture and wildlife. One early classic from this period is *Chang* (1927; available on video), which tells the simple story, in documentary style, of a family who live on the edge of the forest in Nan province. *Chang's* American directors Merian Cooper and Ernest B. Schoedsack later drew on their experiences in the Thai jungle for their 1933 classic, *King Kong*.

Outdoor film shows

Before TVs became a standard fixture of every village home, the only way anyone living outside a town could see a movie was when the **travelling cinema** pitched up. These outdoor film shows, or *nang klarng plaeng*, were hugely popular well into the 1980s, when an estimated 2000 travelling screens were regularly staging film shows all over the country. Their popularity has since declined but they are not yet extinct and, if you get the chance, the shows are well worth attending. These days, *nang klarng plaeng* are most common in the northeast, the poorest and least urbanized region of the country. If you spot a large cinema screen in a field, park or temple grounds, then there is probably going to be a film show that night. They're usually staged either as part of a fair, or in honour of a family occasion such as a birthday or funeral. Anyone is welcome to attend the film show and spectators may or may not be charged a small entrance fee. Chances are the movie will be wild kung fu, corny romance, gruesome horror or lurid action melodrama, but you're very unlikely to get English subtitles.

Even if you don't get to witness an outdoor film show first hand, you can see one in action in Pen-Ek's charming tragi-comedy *Mon Rak Transistor* (see p.921). In the film, the heroine attends a *nang klarng plaeng* showing of a Hollywood movie. A voice-over man sits at a microphone translating the dialogue for his audience of northeastern villagers – cheaper than getting the film dubbed into Thai – and manages to direct a few flirtatious lines of his own at the heroine as he does so.

Though Thai film-making continued throughout the 1930s and 1940s, it was virtually suspended during World War II, before re-emerging with a flourish in the 1950s. The **1950s, 1960s and 1970s** were a golden period for the production of large numbers of hastily made but hugely popular low-budget escapist films, mainly action melodramas featuring stereotypical characters, gangsters and corny love interest. Many of these films starred **Mitr Chaibancha**, Thailand's greatest-ever film star. He played the handsome hero in 265 films, in many of them performing opposite former beauty queen **Petchara Chaowarat**. Of the 165 movies they made together, their most famous was *Mon Rak Luk Thung* (*Enchanting Countryside,* 1969), a folk-musical about life and love in the countryside that played continuously in Bangkok for six months and later spawned a bestselling soundtrack album. Nearly every Thai adult can recall the days when Mitr co-starred with Petchara, and when Mitr fell to a dramatic death in 1970 during a stunt involving a rope ladder suspended from a helicopter – it caused nationwide mourning. He was cremated at Wat Thepsirin in Bangkok (off Thanon Luang in Chinatown), where photos of the cremation ceremony and the crowds of fans who attended are still on display. Though non-Thai speakers are denied the pleasure of seeing Mitr and Petchara in action, you can get a good idea of the general tone of their films from the 2000 hit *Tears of the Black Tiger*, described on p.921, which affectionately parodies the films of this period.

For many years after Mitr's death, Thai cinema continued to be dominated by action melodramas, though a notable exception was *Khao Cheu Karn* (*His Name is Karn*), the first Thai film to tackle corruption in the civil service – it was released in 1973, not long before mass student demonstrations led to the ousting of the military government, and was made by Chatri Chalerm Yukol, who went on to direct the 2001 epic *The Legend of Suriyothai*, described on p.921. The other stand-out of film of the 1970s is *Phlae Khao* (*The Old Scar*, 1977), in which director Cherd Songsri uses traditional rural Thailand as a potent setting for a tragic romance that ends with the heroine's death.

With competition from television and large numbers of imported Hollywood films, Thai film production dwindled during the 1980s, but in 1984 the **Thai National Film Archive** was set up to preserve not only Thai films but also many of the wonderful posters used to promote them (see box on p.920 for more on film-poster art). A rare stand-out film from the 1980s is Yuttana Mukdasanit's coming-of-age drama *Butterflies and Flowers* (*Pee Sua Lae Dok Mai,* 1986), which is set in a Muslim community in southern Thailand and looks at the pressures on a poor teenager who ends up smuggling rice across the nearby Malaysian border. The film won an award at the Hawaii International Film Festival.

By the 1990s, the Thai film industry was in a rather sorry state and the few films still produced were mainly trite melodramas aimed at an undiscerning teenage audience. But everything started to change for the better in 1997.

Modern Thai cinema

The Thai film industry is currently enjoying a remarkable re-birth and it all started in 1997 with the release of Pen-Ek Ratanaruang's *Fun Boy Karaoke* and Nonzee Nimibutr's *Daeng Bireley's and the Young Gangsters*. Fuelled by a new wave of talented directors and writers, including Nonzee and Pen-Ek, this resurgence has seen Thai films benefiting from larger budgets and achieving international acclaim. The new breed of Thai film-makers has moved away from traditional action melodramas and soap operas to create films that are

Posters and billboards

Until the 1990s, domestic and foreign films were always promoted in Thailand with **original Thai artwork**, especially commissioned to hang as billboards and to be reproduced on posters. The artists who produced them really poured their hearts into these images, interpreting the film in their own style and always including an extraordinary amount of detail. Unlike the films themselves, Thai film posters were rarely subject to any censorship and as a result they were often far more eye-catchingly graphic and explicit than Western artwork for the same films. Posters for horror films (always very big in Thailand) depicted particularly gruesome, blood-drenched images, while ads for the (illegal) screenings of soft-porn movies often displayed a surprising amount of naked flesh.

The Thai poster for **Apocalypse Now**, painted by Tong Dee Panumas in about 1980, is a classic. Tong Dee used as his starting point the close-up image of Marlon Brando that graced most posters in America and Europe. He re-rendered this in his own style then added an eye-boggling montage of scenes from the film: soldiers standing among ruined Khmer temples, Robert Duvall looking out at the carnage of war, great clouds of napalm-fire, Dennis Hopper photographing it all, Martin Sheen in sweaty close-up, and more.

Locally produced posters are still used to advertise films in Thailand, but for over a decade now they have featured photographic images instead of original artwork. However, there's still a chance to admire the exuberant creativity of Thai cinema art because many provincial cinemas continue to employ local artists to produce their own **billboard** paintings every week. Look for these giant works of art above cinema doors, at key locations around town, and on the sides of the megaphone trucks that circulate around town screeching out the times and plot lines of the next show. In seven days' time they will have been dismantled, reduced to a pile of planks and painted over with the artwork for next week's film.

more imaginative, realistic and stylish. With a new emphasis on production values, they also look very good, yet it is the fresh, distinctly Thai style that most charms Western audiences, a style summed up by one Thai film commentator as "neo-unrealist", and by another as being influenced by the popular *likay* genre of bawdy, over-the-top Thai street-theatre, where actors use song and dance as well as speech to tell their story.

Daeng Bireley's and the Young Gangsters (*Antaphan Krong Muang*) was the surprise hit of 1997; **Nonzee Nimibutr** showed in this story of 1950s gangsters that he was able to appeal to the international festival circuit as well as local cinema-goers. He followed it up with the even more successful *Nang Nak* in 1999, giving the big-budget treatment to a traditional nineteenth-century Thai ghost story about a woman who dies while in labour, along with her unborn child. In *Jan Dara* (2001), the 1930s story of a young man who despises his womanizing stepfather, yet eventually becomes just such a person, Nonzee pushed the envelope of what was acceptable in Thai cinema by including scenes of rape and lesbianism that would not have been permitted a decade earlier. *Okay Betong* (2004) follows a former monk forced to deal with the modern world when, after a bomb attack kills his sister in the politically turbulent deep south, he forsakes his insular northeastern monastery and journeys south to Betong to find his young niece.

In a wry tale of messages received from beyond the grave, **Pen-Ek Ratanaruang**'s first film *Fun Bar Karaoke* (1997) looked at how the lives of modern middle-class Thais are still affected by traditional superstitions. His next film *6ixtynin9* (*Ruang Talok 69,* 1999) was a fast-paced thriller set during the Asian financial crisis, with a down-on-her-luck woman stumbling upon a horde of money. Pen-Ek followed this with *Mon Rak Transistor: A Transistor Love Story* (2003), a bitter-sweet love story about a naïve boy from the country with ambitions to be a *luk thung* singer. It's full of charm and the popular soundtrack is available on CD (see p.907). Pen-Ek's *Last Life in the Universe* (2003) is a much darker, more melancholy affair, following two very different personalities – a suicidal Japanese man and a Thai girl – who are brought together in grief. The tenor of his slow-moving thriller *Invisible Waves* (2006) is also gloomy, and its use of many non-Thai actors, locations and technicians prompted critics to question the film's Thainess.

The scriptwriter on Nonzee's *Daeng Bireley's* and *Nang Nak* was Wisit Sasanatieng who, in 2000, directed **Tears of the Black Tiger** (*Fah Talai Jone*). This gentle send-up of the old Thai action films of the 1960s and 1970s uses exaggerated acting styles and irresistible comic-book colours to tell the story of handsome bandit Dum and his love for upper-class Rumpoey. Writer-director Wisit grew up watching the Spaghetti Westerns of Sergio Leone and includes more than a few passing references to those films. His **Citizen Dog** (*Mah Nakorn*, 2004) is an even more surreal colour-saturated satire, both comic and pointed, about a country boy looking for work and romance in Bangkok.

Another notable name is director Bandit Rittakol, who enjoyed domestic success with a series of comic films in the 1980s and 1990s before tackling the highly sensitive issue of Thailand's radical pro-democracy movement in **The Moon-Hunter** (2001). Based on an autobiographical script by Seksan Prasetkul, one of the student leaders of the October 14 uprising in 1973, the film takes an intelligent look at what happened to the leftist groups after they toppled the corrupt military government.

There have been a number of other recent high-profile international successes. The warm and off-beat comedy **Iron Ladies** (*Satri Lek*, 2000) charts the often hilarious true-life adventures of a Lampang volleyball team made up of transsexuals and transvestites. **Beautiful Boxer** (2003) fashions a sensitive, insightful biopic out of a similar subject – the true story of transvestite *muay thai* champion Nong Toom who fights in order to win money for sex-change surgery. **Bangkok Dangerous** (*Krung Thep Antharai*, 2000) is a riveting thriller directed by brothers Oxide and Danny Pang, effectively counterbalancing a brutal tale about a deaf and dumb hitman with the story of his love affair with a girl who knows nothing about his occupation. Heavily influenced by the fast-paced Hong Kong gangster films of John Woo, it contains a number of chase scenes shot in the streets and alleys of Bangkok. The sixteenth-century epic **The Legend of Suriyothai** (2001) broke the mould in a different way. A visually stunning historical blockbuster whose B400 million budget made it the most expensive Thai film ever made, it tells the true story of a queen of the Ayutthayan court who gave her life defending her husband during a Burmese invasion. Keen to give international appeal to this complex portrait of court intrigue and rather partisan take on Thai-Burmese relations, director Chatri Chalerm Yukol brought in Frances Ford Coppola to edit a shortened version for Western audiences. Tanit Jitnukul's **Bang Rajan: Legend of the Village Warriors** (2000) also tapped the patriotic vein in its bloody, big-budget dramatization of the legendary brave but futile attempt by Thai villagers to repel the Burmese invasion of 1767, which ended in the sacking of Thailand's then-capital, Ayutthaya.

Prachya Pinkaew's martial arts action-flick **Ong Bak** (2003) was such a huge box-office hit around the world that its star **Tony Jaa** – who performed all his own extraordinary stunts – was appointed Cultural Ambassador for Thailand (following in the footsteps of tennis star Paradorn Srichaphan). Director and star teamed up again in the similarly testosterone-fuelled **Tom Yum Goong** (2005), in which Tony Jaa's fight skills lead him to Sydney on the trail of a stolen elephant. At the other end of the spectrum, Thai arthouse also went international with the success of Apichatpong Weerasethakul's challenging **Tropical Malady** (*Sud Pralad*, 2004), which won the Jury Prize at Cannes in 2004. Part gay romance, part trippy jungle ghost story, it was for some a pioneering experiment in Thai storytelling, to others an inaccessible bore.

The films that get widespread international release are, however, often unrepresentative of the pictures that play week in, week out at most Thai cinemas. These crowd-pleasers tend to feature lots of laughs, slapstick, gangsters, likeably corny romance and much poking of fun at authority figures. A few have emerged internationally, albeit sometimes only for brief showings at festivals. These include **Bupah Rahtree: Scent of the Night Flower** (2003), director Yuthlert Sippapak's deliriously over-the-top horror film with affectionate homages to *The Exorcist*; **The Bodyguard** (*Bodyguard Na Liam*, 2004), a crazy mixture of thriller shoot-outs and eccentric characters, with a sense of fun that is uniquely Thai; and **Sars Wars** (*Khun Krabii Hiiroh*, 2004), which managed to treat the Sars virus as a subject for comedy and threw in a costume-clad super hero for good measure. Meanwhile, Yuthlert Sippapak's **Pattaya Maniac** (*Sai Loh Fa*, 2005) reminded us that, despite all the recent advances, you can, happily, still find a Thai film featuring gangsters, sex slaves, unpaid debts and a love-conquers-all ending – just like thirty years ago – and, for non-Thais, it also offers an insight into such local preoccupations as karaoke bars, amulet shops and the Thai mafia.

Interest in Thai films has been so significant over the last few years that since 1998 Thailand has hosted regular film festivals, and the **Bangkok International Film Festival** is now held every February (see ⓦwww.bangkokfilm.org for details). Meanwhile, entire festivals of Thai films have also been held in London and Tokyo and Thai films have been enthusiastically received at many international film festivals, including Cannes. For the latest reviews see ⓦwww.thaicinema.org.

Neil Pettigrew

Books

We have included publishers' details for books that may be hard to find outside Thailand, though some of them can be ordered online through www.dcothai.com. Other titles should be available worldwide. Titles marked are particularly recommended.

Travelogues

Steve Van Beek *Slithering South* (Wind and Water, Hong Kong). An expat writer tells how he single-handedly paddled his wooden boat down the entire 1100-kilometre course of the Chao Phraya River, and reveals a side of Thailand that's rarely written about in English.

Carl Bock *Temples and Elephants* (Orchid Press, Bangkok). Nineteenth-century account of a rough journey from Bangkok to the far north, dotted with vivid descriptions of rural life and court ceremonial.

Karen Connelly *Touch the Dragon* (Silkworm Books, Chiang Mai). Evocative and humorous journal of an impressionable Canadian teenager, sent on an exchange programme to Den Chai in northern Thailand for a year.

Tristan Jones *To Venture Further.* Amazing tale of how the author, a veteran adventurer and an amputee, pioneered the crossing of the Kra Isthmus in a longtail boat staffed by a disabled crew.

Charles Nicholl *Borderlines.* Entertaining adventures and dangerous romance in the "Golden Triangle" form the core of this slightly hackneyed traveller's tale, interwoven with stimulating and well-informed cultural diversions.

James O'Reilly and Larry Habegger (eds) *Travelers' Tales: Thailand.* An absorbing anthology of contemporary writings about Thailand, by Thailand experts, social commentators, travel writers and first-time visitors.

Tom Vater *Beyond the Pancake Trench: Road tales from the Wild East.* Filmically described snapshots of life in twenty-first century Thailand, from a self-confessed seeker after marginal experiences. Also covers exploits in Cambodia, Laos, Vietnam and India.

Culture and society

Michael Carrithers *The Buddha: A Very Short Introduction.* Accessible account of the life of the Buddha, and the development and significance of his thought.

Philip Cornwel-Smith and John Goss *Very Thai.* Why do Thais decant their soft drinks into plastic bags, what lies behind their penchant for Neoclassical architecture, and how does one sniff-kiss? Answers and insights aplenty in this intriguingly observant and highly readable fully illustrated guide to contemporary Thai culture.

James Eckardt *Bangkok People* (Asia Books, Bangkok). The collected articles of a renowned expat journalist, whose interviews and encounters with a gallery of different Bangkokians – from construction-site workers and street vendors to boxers and political candidates – add texture and context to the city.

Sanitsuda Ekachai *Behind the Smile* (Thai Development Support Committee, Bangkok). Compilation of features by a *Bangkok Post* journalist highlighting the effect of Thailand's sudden economic growth on the country's rural poor.

Sandra Gregory with Michael Tierney *Forget You Had A Daughter: Doing Time in the "Bangkok Hilton" – Sandra Gregory's Story*. The frank and shocking account of a young British woman who was imprisoned in Bangkok's notorious Lard Yao prison after being caught trying to smuggle 89 grammes of heroin out of Thailand.

Roger Jones *Culture Smart! Thailand*. Handy little primer on Thailand's social and cultural mores, with plenty of refreshingly up-to-date insights.

Erich Krauss *Wave of Destruction: One Thai Village and its Battle with the Tsunami*. A sad and often shocking, clear-eyed account of what Ban Nam Khen went through before, during and after the tsunami. Fills in many gaps left unanswered by news reports at the time, with depressing revelations about corruption at several levels.

Elaine and Paul Lewis *Peoples of the Golden Triangle*. Hefty, exhaustive work illustrated with excellent photographs, describing every aspect of hill-tribe life.

Father Joe Maier *Welcome To The Bangkok Slaughterhouse: The Battle For Human Dignity In Bangkok's Bleakest Slums*. Catholic priest Father Joe shares the stories of some of the Bangkok street kids and slum-dwellers that his charitable foundation has been supporting since 1972 (see Basics p.78).

Trilok Chandra Majupuria *Erawan Shrine and Brahma Worship in Thailand* (Tecpress, Bangkok). The most concise introduction to the complexities of Thai religion, with a much wider scope than the title implies.

Cleo Odzer *Patpong Sisters*. An American anthropologist's funny and touching account of her life with the prostitutes and bar girls of Bangkok's notorious red-light district.

Phra Peter Pannapadipo *Little Angels: The Real-Life Stories of Twelve Thai Novice Monks*. A dozen young boys, many of them from desperate backgrounds, tell the often poignant stories of why they became novice monks. For some, funding from the Students Education Trust (described on p.78) has changed their lives.

Phra Peter Pannapadipo *Phra Farang: An English Monk in Thailand*. Behind the scenes in a Thai monastery: the frank, funny and illuminating account of a UK-born former businessman's life as a Thai monk.

Pasuk Phongpaichit and Sungsidh Piriyarangsan *Corruption and Democracy in Thailand*. Fascinating academic study, revealing the nuts and bolts of corruption in Thailand and its links with all levels of political life, and suggesting a route to a stronger society. Their sequel, a study of Thailand's illegal economy, *Guns, Girls, Gambling, Ganja*, co-written with Nualnoi Treerat, makes equally eye-opening and depressing reading.

Denis Segaller *Thai Ways* (Silkworm Books, Chiang Mai). Fascinating collection of short pieces on Thai customs and traditions written by a long-term English resident of Bangkok.

Pira Sudham *People of Esarn* (Shire Asia, Bangkok). Wry and touching potted life stories of villagers who live in, leave and return to the poverty-stricken northeast, compiled by a northeastern lad turned author.

Phil Thornton *Restless Souls: Rebels, Refugees, Medics and Misfits on the Thai-Burma Border*. An Australian journalist brings to light the terrible and complicated plight of the Karen, thousands of whom live as refugees in and around his adopted town of Mae Sot on the Thai-Burma border.

Richard Totman *The Third Sex: Kathoey – Thailand's Ladyboys*. As several *kathoey* share their life stories with him, social scientist Totman examines their place in modern Thai society and explores the theory, supported by Buddhist philosophy, that *kathoey* are members of a third sex whose transgendered make-up is pre-determined from birth.

William Warren *Living in Thailand*. Luscious gallery of traditional houses, with an emphasis on the homes of Thailand's rich and famous; seductively photographed by Luca Invernizzi Tettoni.

Daniel Ziv and Guy Sharett *Bangkok Inside Out*. This A-Z of Bangkok quirks and cultural substrates is full of slick photography and sparky observations but was deemed offensive by Thailand's Ministry of Culture and so some Thai bookshops won't stock it.

History

John Hoskin *Falcon*. Part narrative, part fictionalized journal, the tale of the Greek, Constantine Phaulkon, who became prime minister to King Narai in seventeenth-century Ayutthaya (see p.281).

Anna Leonowens *The English Governess at the Siamese Court*. The mendacious memoirs of the nineteenth-century English governess that inspired the infamous Yul Brynner film *The King and I*; low on accuracy, high on inside-palace gossip.

Michael Smithies *Old Bangkok*. Brief, anecdotal history of the capital's early development, emphasizing what remains to be seen of bygone Bangkok.

William Stevenson *The Revolutionary King*. Fascinating biography of the normally secretive King Bhumibol, by a British journalist who was given unprecedented access to the monarch and his family. The overall approach is fairly uncritical, but lots of revealing insights emerge along the way.

John Stewart *To the River Kwai: Two Journeys – 1943, 1979*. A survivor of the horrific World War II POW camps along the River Kwai returns to the region, interlacing his wartime reminiscences with observations on how he feels 36 years later.

William Warren *Jim Thompson: the Legendary American of Thailand*. The engrossing biography of the ex-intelligence agent, art collector and Thai silk magnate whose disappearance in Malaysia in 1967 has never been satisfactorily resolved.

David K. Wyatt *Thailand: A Short History*. An excellent, recently updated treatment, scholarly but highly readable, with a good eye for witty, telling details. Good chapters on the story of the Thais before they reached what's now Thailand, and on recent developments. His *Siam in Mind* (Silkworm Books, Chiang Mai) is a wide-ranging and intriguing collection of sketches and short reflections that point towards an intellectual history of Thailand.

Art, architecture and film

Steve Van Beek *The Arts of Thailand*. Lavish and perfectly pitched introduction to the history of Thai architecture, sculpture and painting, with superb photographs by Luca Invernizzi Tettoni.

Jean Boisselier *The Heritage of Thai Sculpture*. Expensive but accessible seminal tome by influential French art historian.

Susan Conway *Thai Textiles*. A fascinating, richly illustrated work which draws on sculptures and temple murals to trace the evolution of Thai weaving techniques and costume styles, and to examine the functional and ceremonial uses of textiles.

Sumet Jumsai *Naga: Cultural Origins in Siam and the West Pacific*. Wide-ranging discussion of water symbols in Thailand and other parts of Asia – a stimulating mix of architecture, art, mythology and cosmology.

Steven Pettifor *Flavours: Thai Contemporary Art*. Takes up the baton from Poshyananda (see below) to look at the newly invigorated art scene in Thailand from 1992 to 2004, with profiles of 23 leading lights, including painters, multi-media and performance artists.

Apinan Poshyananda *Modern Art In Thailand*. Excellent introduction which extends up to the early 1990s, with very readable discussions on dozens of individual artists, and lots of colour plates.

Dome Sukwong and Sawasdi Suwannapak *A Century of Thai Cinema*. Full-colour tome tracing the history of the Thai film industry and all the promotional artwork (billboards, posters, magazines and cigarette cards) associated with it.

William Warren and Luca Invernizzi Tettoni *Arts and Crafts of Thailand*. Good-value large-format paperback, setting the wealth of Thai arts and crafts in cultural context, with plenty of attractive illustrations and colour photographs.

Natural history and ecology

Ashley J. Boyd and Collin Piprell *Diving in Thailand*. A thorough guide to 84 dive sites, detailing access, weather conditions, visibility, scenery and marine life for each, plus general introductory sections on Thailand's marine life, conservation and photography tips.

Boonsong Lekagul and Philip D. Round *Guide to the Birds of Thailand* (Saha Karn Bheat, Thailand). Worth scouring second-hand outlets for this hard-to-find but unparalleled illustrated guide to Thailand's birds.

Craig Robson *A Field Guide to the Birds of Thailand*. Expert and beautifully illustrated guide to Thailand's top 950 bird species, with locator maps.

Eric Valli and Diane Summers *The Shadow Hunters*. Beautifully photographed photo-essay on the birds'-nest collectors of southern Thailand, with whom the authors spent over a year, together scaling the phenomenal heights of the sheer limestone walls.

Literature

Alastair Dingwall (ed) *Traveller's Literary Companion: Southeast Asia.* A useful though rather dry reference, with a large section on Thailand, including a book list, well-chosen extracts, biographical details of authors and other literary notes.

M.L. Manich Jumsai *Thai Ramayana* (Chalermnit, Bangkok). Slightly stilted abridged prose translation of King Rama I's version of the epic Hindu narrative, full of gleeful descriptions of bizarre mythological characters and supernatural battles. Essential reading for a full appreciation of Thai painting, carving and classical dance.

Khammaan Khonkhai *The Teachers of Mad Dog Swamp* (Silkworm Books, Chiang Mai). The engaging story of a young teacher who encounters opposition to his progressive ideas when he is posted to a remote village school in the northeast. A typical example of the "novels for life" genre, which are known for their strong moral stance.

Chart Korpjitti *The Judgement* (Thai Modern Classics). Sobering modern-day tragedy about a good-hearted Thai villager who is ostracized by his hypocritical neighbours. Contains lots of interesting details on village life and traditions and thought-provoking passages on the stifling conservatism of rural communities. Winner of the S.E.A. Write award in 1982.

Rattawut Lapcharoensap *Sightseeing.* This outstanding debut collection of short stories by a young Thai-born author now living overseas highlights big, pertinent themes – cruelty, corruption, racism, pride – in its neighbourhood tales of randy teenagers, bullyboys, a child's friendship with a Cambodian refugee, a young man who uses family influence to dodge the draft.

Nitaya Masavisut (ed) *The S.E.A. Write Anthology of Thai Short Stories and Poems* (Silkworm Books, Chiang Mai). Interesting medley of short stories and poems by Thai writers who have won Southeast Asian Writers' Awards, providing a good introduction to the contemporary literary scene.

Kukrit Pramoj *Si Phaendin: Four Reigns* (Silkworm Books, Chiang Mai). A kind of historical romance spanning the four reigns of Ramas V to VIII (1892–1946). Written by former prime minister Kukrit Pramoj, the story has become a modern classic in Thailand, made into films, plays and TV dramas, with heroine Ploi as the archetypal feminine role model.

J.C. Shaw *The Ramayana through Western Eyes* (DK Books, Bangkok). The bare bones of the epic tale are retold between tenuously comparable excerpts from Western poets, including Shakespeare, Shelley and Walt Whitman. Much more helpfully, the text is interspersed with key scenes from the murals at Bangkok's Wat Phra Kaeo.

S.P. Somtow *Jasmine Nights.* An engaging and humorous rites-of-passage tale, of an upper-class boy learning what it is to be Thai. *Dragon's Fin Soup and Other Modern Siamese Fables* is an imaginative and entertaining collection of often supernatural short stories, focusing on the collision of East and West.

Khamsing Srinawk *The Politician and Other Stories* (Silkworm Books, Chiang Mai). A collection of brilliantly satiric short stories, full of pithy moral observation and biting irony, which capture the vulnerability of peasant farmers in the north and northeast, as they try to come to grips with the modern world. Written by an insider from a peasant family, who was educated at Chulalongkorn University, became a hero of the left, and joined the communist insurgents after the 1976 clampdown.

Atsiri Thammachoat *Of Time and Tide* (Thai Modern Classics). Set in a fishing village near Hua Hin, this poetically written novella looks at how Thailand's fishing industry is changing, charting the effects on its fisherfolk and their communities.

Klaus Wenk *Thai Literature – An Introduction* (White Lotus, Bangkok). Dry, but useful, short overview of the last seven hundred years by a noted German scholar, with plenty of extracts.

Thailand in foreign literature

Dean Barrett *Kingdom of Make-Believe.* Despite the clichéd ingredients – the Patpong go-go bar scene, opium smuggling in the Golden Triangle, Vietnam veterans – this novel about a return to Thailand following a twenty-year absence turns out to be a rewardingly multi-dimensional take on the farang experience.

Botan *Letters from Thailand* (Silkworm Books, Chiang Mai). Probably the best introduction to the Chinese community in Bangkok, presented in the form of letters written over a twenty-year period by a Chinese emigrant to his mother. Branded as both anti-Chinese and anti-Thai, this 1969 prizewinning book is now mandatory reading in school social studies' classes.

Pierre Boulle *The Bridge Over the River Kwai.* The World War II novel that inspired the David Lean movie and kicked off the Kanchanaburi tourist industry.

John Burdett *Bangkok 8.* Gripping Bangkok thriller that takes in Buddhism, plastic surgery, police corruption, the *yaa baa* drugs trade, hookers, jade-smuggling and the spirit world.

Alex Garland *The Beach.* Gripping cult thriller (made into a film in 1999) that uses a Thai setting to explore the way in which travellers' ceaseless quest for "undiscovered" utopias inevitably leads to them despoiling the idyll.

Spalding Gray *Swimming to Cambodia.* Entertaining and politically acute account of the late actor and monologist's time in Thailand on location for the filming of *The Killing Fields.*

Andrew Hicks *Thai Girl.* A British backpacker falls for a reticent young beach masseuse on Ko Samet but struggles with age-old cross-cultural confusion in this sensitive attempt at a different kind of expat novel.

Michel Houellebecq *Platform.* Sex tourism in Thailand provides the nucleus of this brilliantly provocative (some would say offensive) novel, in which Houellebecq presents a ferocious critique of Western decadence and cultural colonialism, and of radical Islam too.

Christopher G. Moore *God Of Darkness* (Asia Books, Bangkok). Thailand's bestselling expat novelist sets his most intriguing thriller during the economic crisis of 1997 and includes plenty of meat on endemic corruption and the desperate struggle for power within family and society.

Collin Piprell *Yawn: A Thriller* (Asia Books, Bangkok). Enjoyable page-turner that spins a good yarn from the apparently disparate worlds of scuba-diving and Buddhist retreats. Set mainly in Pattaya and a thinly disguised Ko Pha Ngan.

Darin Strauss *Chang & Eng.* An intriguing imagined autobiography of the famous nineteenth-century

Siamese twins (see p.231), from their impoverished Thai childhood via the freak shows of New York and London to married life in smalltown North Carolina. Unfortunately marred by lazy research and a confused grasp of Thai geography and culture.

Food and cookery

Vatcharin Bhumichitr *The Taste of Thailand.* Another glossy introduction to this eminently photogenic country, this time through its food. The author runs a Thai restaurant in London and provides background colour as well as about 150 recipes adapted for Western kitchens.

Jacqueline M. Piper *Fruits of South-East Asia.* An exploration of the bounteous fruits of the region, tracing their role in cooking, medicine, handicrafts and rituals. Well illustrated with photos, watercolours and early botanical drawings.

David Thompson *Thai Food.* Comprehensive, impeccably researched celebration of Thai food, with over 300 recipes, by the owner of the first Thai restaurant ever to earn a Michelin star.

Travel guides

Oliver Hargreave *Exploring Chiang Mai: City, Valley and Mountains* (Within Books, Chiang Mai). Thorough, updated guide to the city and out-of-town trips, with plenty of useful small-scale maps, written by a long-time resident.

Thom Henley *Krabi: Caught in the Spell – A Guide to Thailand's Enchanted Province* (Thai Nature Education, Phuket). Highly readable features and observations on the attractions and people of south Thailand's most beautiful region, written by an expat environmentalist.

William Warren *Bangkok.* An engaging portrait of the unwieldy capital, weaving together anecdotes and character sketches from Bangkok's past and present.

Language

Language

Language

Thai belongs to one of the oldest families of languages in the world, Austro-Thai, and is radically different from most of the other tongues of Southeast Asia. Being tonal, Thai is extremely difficult for Westerners to master, but by building up from a small core of set phrases, you should soon have enough to get by. Most Thais who deal with tourists speak some English, but once you stray off the beaten track you'll probably need at least a little Thai. Anywhere you go, you'll impress and get better treatment if you at least make an effort to speak a few words.

Distinct dialects are spoken in the north, the northeast and the south, which can increase the difficulty of comprehending what's said to you. **Thai script** is even more of a problem to Westerners, with 44 consonants to represent 21 consonant sounds and 32 vowels to deal with 48 different vowel sounds. However, street signs in touristed areas are nearly always written in Roman script as well as Thai, and in other circumstances you're better off asking than trying to unscramble the swirling mess of symbols, signs and accents. For more information on transliteration into Roman script, see the box in this book's introduction.

Among **language books**, *Thai: The Rough Guide Phrasebook* covers the essential phrases and expressions in both Thai script and phonetic equivalents, as well as dipping into grammar and providing a menu reader and fuller vocabulary in dictionary format (English-Thai and Thai-English). Probably the best pocket dictionary is Paiboon Publishing's (ⓦwww.ThaiLao.com) *Thai-English, English-Thai Dictionary*, which lists words in phonetic Thai as well as Thai script, and features a very handy table of the Thai alphabet in a dozen different fonts; it's also available as a searchable dictionary for Palm PDAs. Among the rest, G.H. Allison's *Mini English-Thai and Thai-English Dictionary* (Chalermnit) has the edge over *Robertson's Practical English-Thai Dictionary* (Asia Books), although it's more difficult to find.

The best **teach-yourself course** is the expensive *Linguaphone Thai*, which includes six CDs or six cassettes. *Thai for Beginners* by Benjawan Poomsan Becker (Paiboon Publishing; ⓦwww.ThaiLao.com) is a cheaper, more manageable textbook and is especially good for getting to grips with the Thai writing system; you can also buy accompanying CDs or tapes to help with listening skills. For a more traditional textbook, try Stuart Campbell and Chuan Shaweevongse's *The Fundamentals of the Thai Language*, which is comprehensive, though hard going. G.H. Allison's *Easy Thai* is best for those who feel the urge to learn the alphabet. The **website** ⓦwww.thai-language.com is an amazing free resource, featuring a searchable dictionary of over 27,000 Thai words, complete with Thai script and audio clips, plus a guide to the language and forums.

Pronunciation

Mastering **tones** is probably the most difficult part of learning Thai. Five different tones are used – low, middle, high, falling, and rising – by which the meaning of a single syllable can be altered in five different ways. Thus, using four of the five tones, you can make a sentence just from just one syllable: "mái mài mâi mǎi" meaning "New wood burns, doesn't it?" As well as the natural difficulty in becoming attuned to speaking and listening to these different tones, Western efforts are complicated by our habit of denoting the overall meaning of a sentence by modulating our tones – for example, turning a statement into a question through a shift of stress and tone. Listen to native Thai speakers and you'll soon begin to pick up the different approach to tone.

The pitch of each tone is gauged in relation to your vocal range when speaking, but they should all lie within a narrow band, separated by gaps just big enough to differentiate them. The **low tones** (syllables marked ˋ), **middle tones** (unmarked syllables), and **high tones** (syllables marked ˊ) should each be pronounced evenly and with no inflection. The **falling tone** (syllables marked ^) is spoken with an obvious drop in pitch, as if you were sharply emphasizing a word in English. The **rising tone** (marked ˇ) is pronounced as if you were asking an exaggerated question in English.

As well as the unfamiliar tones, you'll find that, despite the best efforts of the transliterators, there is no precise English equivalent to many **vowel and consonant sounds** in the Thai language. The lists below give a rough idea of pronunciation.

Vowels

a	as in dad.
aa	has no precise equivalent, but is pronounced as it looks, with the vowel elongated.
ae	as in there.
ai	as in buy.
ao	as in now.
aw	as in awe.
e	as in pen.
eu	as in sir, but heavily nasalized.
i	as in tip.
ii	as in feet.
o	as in knock.
oe	as in hurt, but more closed.
oh	as in toe.
u	as in loot.
uay	"u" plus "ay" as in pay.
uu	as in pool.

Consonants

r	as in rip, but with the tongue flapped quickly against the palate – in everyday speech, it's often pronounced like "l".
kh	as in keep.
ph	as in put.
th	as in time.
k	is unaspirated and unvoiced, and closer to "g".
p	is also unaspirated and unvoiced, and closer to "b".
t	is also unaspirated and unvoiced, and closer to "d".

General words and phrases

Greetings and basic phrases

When you speak to a stranger in Thailand, you should generally end your sentence in *khráp* if you're a man, *khâ* if you're a woman – these untranslatable politening syllables will gain goodwill, and are nearly always used after *sawàt dii* (hello/goodbye) and *khàwp khun* (thank you). *Khráp* and *khâ* are also often used to answer "yes" to a question, though the most common way is to repeat the verb of the question (precede it with *mâi* for "no"). *Châi* (yes) and *mâi châi* (no) are less frequently used than their English equivalents.

Hello	sawàt dii
Where are you going?	pai năi? (not always meant literally, but used as a general greeting)
I'm out having fun/ I'm travelling	pai thîaw (answer to pai năi, almost indefinable pleasantry)
Goodbye	sawàt dii/la kàwn
Good luck/cheers	chôk dii
Excuse me	khăw thâwt
Thank you	khàwp khun
It's nothing/it doesn't matter	mâi pen rai
How are you?	sabai dii reŭ?
I'm fine	sabai dii
What's your name?	khun chêu arai?
My name is…	phŏm (men)/ diichăn (women) chêu…
I come from…	phŏm/diichăn maa jàak…
I don't understand	mâi khâo jai
Do you speak English?	khun phûut phasăa angkrìt dâi măi?
Do you have…?	mii…măi?
Is there…?	…mii măi?
Is…possible?	…dâi măi?
Can you help me?	chûay phŏm/ diichăn dâi măi?
(I) want…	ao…
(I) would like to…	yàak jà…
(I) like…	châwp…
What is this called in Thai?	níi phasăa thai rîak wâa arai?

Getting around

Where is the…?	…yùu thîi năi?
How far?	klai thâo rai?
I would like to go to…	yàak jà pai…
Where have you been?	pai năi maa?
Where is this bus going?	rót níi pai năi?
When will the bus leave?	rót jà àwk mêua rai?
What time does the bus arrive in…?	rót theŭng…kìi mohng?
Stop here	jàwt thîi nîi
here	thîi nîi
there/over there	thîi nâan/thîi nôhn
right	khwăa
left	sái
straight	trong
north	neŭa
south	tâi
east	tawan àwk
west	tawan tòk
near/far	klâi/klai
street	thanŏn
train station	sathàanii rót fai
bus station	sathàanii rót meh
airport	sanăam bin
ticket	tŭa
hotel	rohng raem
post office	praisanii
restaurant	raan ahăan
shop	raan
market	talàt
hospital	rohng pha-yaabaan
motorbike	rót mohtoesai
taxi	rót táksîi
boat	reua
bicycle	jàkràyaan

Accommodation and shopping

How much is…?	…thâo rai/kìi bàat?
How much is a room here per night?	hâwng thîi nîi kheun lá thâo rai?

Do you have a cheaper room?	mii hâwng thùuk kwàa măi?
Can I/we look at the room?	duu hâwng dâi măi?
I/We'll stay two nights	jà yùu săwng kheun
Can you reduce the price?	lót raakhaa dâi măi?
Can I store my bag here?	fàak krapăo wái thîi nîi dâi măi?
cheap/expensive	thùuk/phaeng
air-con room	hăwng ae
ordinary room	hăwng thammadaa
telephone	thohrásàp
laundry	sák phâa
blanket	phâa hòm
fan	phát lom

General adjectives

alone	khon diaw
another	ìik...nèung
bad	mâi dii
big	yài
clean	sa-àat
closed	pìt
cold (object)	yen
cold (person or weather)	năo
delicious	aròi
difficult	yâak
dirty	sokaprok
easy	ngâi
fun	sanùk
hot (temperature)	ráwn
hot (spicy)	phèt
hungry	hiŭ khâo
ill	mâi sabai
open	pòet
pretty	sŭay
small	lek
thirsty	hiŭnám
tired	nèu-ai
very	mâak

General nouns

Nouns have no plurals or genders, and don't require an article.

bathroom/toilet	hăwng nám
boyfriend or girlfriend	faen
food	ahăan
foreigner	fàràng
friend	phêuan
money	ngoen
water/liquid	nám

General verbs

Thai verbs do not conjugate at all, and also often double up as nouns and adjectives, which means that foreigners' most unidiomatic attempts to construct sentences are often readily understood.

come	maa
do	tham
eat	kin/thaan khâo
give	hâi
go	pai
sit	nâng
sleep	nawn làp
take	ao
walk	doen pai

Numbers

zero	sŭun
one	nèung
two	săwng
three	săam
four	sìi
five	hâa
six	hòk
seven	jèt

eight	pàet	**twenty-two, twenty-three…**	yîi sìp săwng, yîi sìp săam…
nine	kâo	**thirty, forty, etc**	săam sìp, sìi sìp…
ten	sìp	**one hundred, two hundred…**	nèung rói, săwng rói…
eleven	sìp èt	**one thousand**	nèung phan
twelve, thirteen…	sìp săwng, sìp săam…	**ten thousand**	nèung mèun
twenty	yîi sìp/yiip		
twenty-one	yîi sìp èt		

Time

The commonest system for telling the time, as outlined below, is actually a confusing mix of several different systems. The State Railway and government officials use the 24-hour clock (9am is *kâo naalikaa*, 10am *sìp naalikaa*, and so on), which is always worth trying if you get stuck.

1–5am	tii nèung–tii hâa	**hour**	chûa mohng
6–11am	hòk mohng cháo–sìp èt mohng cháo	**day**	waan
noon	thîang	**week**	aathít
1pm	bài mohng	**month**	deuan
2–4pm	bài săwng mohng–bài sìi mohng	**year**	pii
5–6pm	hâa mohng yen–hòk mohng yen	**today**	wan níi
7–11pm	nèung thûm–hâa thûm	**tomorrow**	phrûng níi
midnight	thîang kheun	**yesterday**	mêua wan
What time is it?	kìi mohng láew?	**now**	diăw níi
How many hours?	kìi chûa mohng?	**next week**	aathít nâa
How long?	naan thâo rai?	**last week**	aathít kàwn
minute	naathii	**morning**	cháo
		afternoon	bài
		evening	yen
		night	kheun

Days

Sunday	wan aathít	**Thursday**	wan pháréuhàt
Monday	wan jan	**Friday**	wan sùk
Tuesday	wan angkhaan	**Saturday**	wan săo
Wednesday	wan phút		

Food and drink

Basic ingredients

Kài	Chicken
Mŭu	Pork
Néua	Beef, meat
Pèt	Duck
Ahăan thaleh	Seafood
Plaa	Fish
Plaa dùk	Catfish
Plaa mèuk	Squid
Kûng	Prawn, shrimp
Hŏy	Shellfish
Hŏy nang rom	Oyster
Puu	Crab
Khài	Egg
Phàk	Vegetables

Vegetables

Makĕua	Aubergine
Makĕua thêt	Tomato
Nàw mái	Bamboo shoots
Tùa ngâwk	Bean sprouts
Phrík	Chilli
Man faràng	Potato
Man faràng thâwt	Chips
Taeng kwaa	Cucumber
Phrík yùak	Green pepper
Krathiam	Garlic
Hèt	Mushroom
Tùa	Peas, beans or lentils
Tôn hŏrm	Spring onions

Noodles

Ba mii	Egg noodles
Kwáy tiăw (sên yai/sên lék)	White rice noodles (wide/thin)
Ba mii kràwp	Crisp fried egg noodles
	Rice noodles/egg noodles fried with egg, small pieces of meat and a few vegetables
Kwáy tiăw/ ba mii haêng	Rice noodle/egg noodles fried with egg, small pieces of meat and a few vegetables
Kwáy tiăw/ba mii nám (mŭu)	Rice noodle/egg noodle soup, made with chicken broth (and pork balls)
Kwáy tiăw/ ba mii rât nâ (mŭu)	Rice noodles/egg noodles fried in gravy-like sauce with vegetables (and pork slices)
Phàt thai	Thin noodles fried with egg, bean sprouts and tofu, topped with ground peanuts
Phàt siyú	Wide or thin noodles fried with soy sauce, egg and meat

Names and descriptions of Thai fruits are given on p.54.

Rice

Khâo	Rice	**Khâo nâ kài/pèt**	Chicken/duck served with sauce over rice
Khâo man kài	Slices of chicken served over marinated rice	**Khâo niăw**	Sticky rice
Khâo mŭu daeng	Red pork with rice	**Khâo phàt**	Fried rice
		Khâo kaeng	Curry over rice
		Khâo tôm	Rice soup (usually for breakfast)

Curries and soups

Kaeng phèt	Hot, red curry	**Kaeng liang**	Aromatic vegetable soup
Kaeng phánaeng	Thick, savoury curry	**Tôm khà kài**	Chicken coconut soup
Kaeng khĭaw wan	Green curry	**Tôm yam kûng**	Hot and sour prawn soup
Kaeng mátsàman	Rich Muslim-style curry, usually with beef and potatoes	**Kaeng jèut**	Mild soup with vegetables and usually pork
Kaeng karìi	Mild, Indian-style curry		
Kaeng sôm	Fish and vegetable curry		

Salads

Lâap	Spicy ground meat salad	**Yam plaa mèuk**	Squid salad
Nám tòk	Grilled beef or pork salad	**Yam sôm oh**	Pomelo salad
Sôm tam	Spicy papaya salad	**Yam plaa dùk foo**	Crispy fried catfish salad
Yam hua plee	Banana flower salad	**Yam thuù phuu**	Wing-bean salad
Yam néua	Grilled beef salad	**Yam wun sen**	Noodle and pork salad

Other dishes

Hâwy thâwt	Omelette stuffed with mussels	**Néua phàt krathiam phrík thai**	Beef fried with garlic and pepper
Kài phàt bai kraprao	Chicken fried with basil leaves	**Néua phàt nám man hâwy**	Beef in oyster sauce
Kài phàt nàw mái	Chicken with bamboo shoots	**Phàt phàk bûng fai daeng**	Morning glory fried in garlic and bean sauce
Kài phàt mét mámûang	Chicken with cashew nuts	**Phàt phàk lăi yàng**	Stir-fried vegetables
Kài phàt khĭng	Chicken with ginger	**Pàw pía**	Spring rolls
Kài yâang	Grilled chicken	**Plaa nêung páe sá**	Whole fish steamed with vegetables and ginger
Khài yát sài	Omelette with pork and vegetables	**Plaa rât phrík**	Whole fish cooked with chillies
Khanŏm jiin nám yaa	Noodles topped with fish curry	**Plaa thâwt**	Fried whole fish
Kûng chúp paêng thâwt	Prawns fried in batter	**Sàté**	Satay
Mŭu prîaw wăan	Sweet and sour pork	**Thâwt man plaa**	Fish cake

Thai desserts (khanŏm)

Khanŏm beuang	Small crispy pancake folded over with coconut cream and strands of sweet egg inside
Khâo lăam	Sticky rice, coconut cream and black beans cooked and served in bamboo tubes
Khâo niăw daeng	Sticky red rice mixed with coconut cream
Khâo niăw thúrian/ mámûang	Sticky rice mixed with coconut cream and durian/mango
Klûay khàek	Fried banana
Lûk taan chêum	Sweet palm kernels served in syrup
Săngkhayaa	Coconut custard
Tàkôh	Squares of transparent jelly (jello) topped with coconut cream

Drinks (khreûang deùm)

Bia	Beer
Chaa ráwn	Hot tea
Chaa yen	Iced tea
Kaafae ráwn	Hot coffee
Kâew	Glass
Khúat	Bottle
Mâekhŏng (or anglicized "Mekong")	Thai brand-name rice whisky
Nám klûay	Banana shake
Nám mánao/sôm	Fresh, bottled or fizzy lemon/orange juice
Nám plào	Drinking water (boiled or filtered)
Nám sŏdaa	Soda water
Nám tan	Sugar
Kleua	Salt
Nám yen	Cold water
Nom jeùd	Milk
Ohlíang	Iced coffee
Thûay	Cup

Ordering

I am vegetarian/vegan	**Phŏm (male)/ diichăn (female) kin ahăan mangsàwirát/jeh**
Can I see the menu?	**Khăw duù menu?**
I would like...	**Khăw...**
With/without...	**Saì/mâi sai...**
Can I have the bill please?	**Khăw check bin?**

Glossary

Amphoe District.
Amphoe muang Provincial capital.
Ao Bay.
Apsara Female deity.
Avalokitesvara Bodhisattva representing compassion.
Avatar Earthly manifestation of a deity.
Ban Village or house.
Bang Village by a river or the sea.
Bencharong Polychromatic ceramics made in China for the Thai market.
Bhumisparsa mudra Most common gesture of Buddha images; symbolizes the Buddha's victory over temptation.
Bodhisattva In Mahayana Buddhism, an enlightened being who postpones his or her entry into Nirvana.
Bot Main sanctuary of a Buddhist temple.
Brahma One of the Hindu trinity – "The Creator". Usually depicted with four faces and four arms.
Celadon Porcelain with distinctive grey-green glaze.
Changwat Province.
Chao ley/chao nam "Sea gypsies" – nomadic fisherfolk of south Thailand.
Chedi Reliquary tower in Buddhist temple.
Chofa Finial on temple roof.
Deva Mythical deity.
Devaraja God-king.
Dharma The teachings or doctrine of the Buddha.
Dharmachakra Buddhist Wheel of Law (also known as Wheel of Doctrine or Wheel of Life).
Doi Mountain.
Erawan Mythical three-headed elephant; Indra's vehicle.
Farang Foreigner/foreign.
Ganesh Hindu elephant-headed deity, remover of obstacles and god of knowledge.
Garuda Mythical Hindu creature – half-man half-bird; Vishnu's vehicle.
Gopura Entrance pavilion to temple precinct (especially Khmer).
Hamsa Sacred mythical goose; Brahma's vehicle.
Hanuman Monkey god and chief of the monkey army in the Ramayana; ally of Rama.
Hat Beach.
Hin Stone.
Hinayana Pejorative term for Theravada school of Buddhism, literally "Lesser Vehicle".
Ho trai A scripture library.
Indra Hindu king of the gods and, in Buddhism, devotee of the Buddha; usually carries a thunderbolt.
Isaan Northeast Thailand.
Jataka Stories of the five hundred lives of the Buddha.
Khaen Reed and wood pipe; the characteristic musical instrument of Isaan.
Khao Hill, mountain.
Khlong Canal.
Khon Classical dance-drama.
Kinnari Mythical creature – half woman, half bird.
Kirtimukha Very powerful deity depicted as a lion-head.
Ko Island.
Ku The Lao word for prang; a tower in a temple complex.
Laem Headland or cape.
Lakhon Classical dance-drama.
Lak muang City pillar; revered home for the city's guardian spirit.
Lakshaman/Phra Lak Rama's younger brother.
Lakshana Auspicious signs or "marks of greatness" displayed by the Buddha.
Lanna Northern Thai kingdom that lasted from the thirteenth to the sixteenth century.
Likay Popular folk theatre.
Longyi Burmese sarong.
Luang Pho Abbot or especially revered m
Maenam River.
Mahathat Chedi containing r
Mahayana School of Buddh
mainly in China, Japan and
"the Great Vehicle".

Mara The Evil One; tempter of the Buddha.

Mawn khwaan Traditional triangular or "axe-head" pillow.

Meru/Sineru Mythical mountain at the centre of Hindu and Buddhist cosmologies.

Mondop Small, square temple building to house minor images or religious texts.

Moo/muu Neighbourhood.

Muang City or town.

Muay thai Thai boxing.

Mudra Symbolic gesture of the Buddha.

Mut mee Tie-dyed cotton or silk.

Naga Mythical dragon-headed serpent in Buddhism and Hinduism.

Nakhon Honorific title for a city.

Nam Water.

Nam tok Waterfall.

Nang thalung Shadow-puppet entertainment, found in southern Thailand.

Nielloware Engraved metalwork.

Nirvana Final liberation from the cycle of rebirths; state of non-being to which Buddhists aspire.

Pak Tai Southern Thailand.

Pali Language of ancient India; the script of the original Buddhist scriptures.

Pha sin Woman's sarong.

Phi Animist spirit.

Phra Honorific term – literally "excellent".

Phu Mountain.

Prang Central tower in a Khmer temple.

Prasat Khmer temple complex or central shrine.

Rama/Phra Ram Human manifestation of Hindu deity Vishnu; hero of the Ramayana.

Ramakien Thai version of the Ramayana.

Ramayana Hindu epic of good versus evil: chief characters include Rama, Sita, Ravana, Hanuman.

Ravana/Totsagan Rama's adversary in the Ramayana; represents evil.

Reua hang yao Longtail boat.

Rishi Ascetic hermit.

Rot ae/rot tua Air-conditioned bus.

Rot thammadaa Ordinary bus.

Sala Meeting hall, pavilion, bus stop – or any open-sided structure.

Samlor Passenger tricycle; literally "three-wheeled".

anskrit Sacred language of Hinduism; also ed in Buddhism.

Sanuk Fun.

Sema Boundary stone to mark consecrated ground within temple complex.

Shiva One of the Hindu trinity – "The Destroyer".

Shiva lingam Phallic representation of Shiva.

Soi Lane or side road.

Songkhran Thai New Year.

Songthaew Pick-up used as public transport; literally "two rows", after the vehicle's two facing benches.

Takraw Game played with a rattan ball.

Talat Market.

Talat nam Floating market.

Talat yen Night market.

Tambon Subdistrict.

Tavatimsa Buddhist heaven.

Tha Pier.

Thale Sea or lake.

Tham Cave.

Thanon Road.

That Chedi.

Thep A divinity.

Theravada Main school of Buddhist thought in Thailand; also known as Hinayana.

Totsagan Rama's evil rival in the Ramayana; also known as Ravana.

Tripitaka Buddhist scriptures.

Trok Alley.

Tuk-tuk Motorized three-wheeled taxi.

Uma Shiva's consort.

Ushnisha Cranial protuberance on Buddha images, signifying an enlightened being.

Viharn Temple assembly hall for the laity; usually contains the principal Buddha image.

Vipassana Buddhist meditation technique; literally "insight".

Vishnu One of the Hindu trinity – "The Preserver". Usually shown with four arms, holding a disc, a conch, a lotus and a club.

Wai Thai greeting expressed by a prayer-like gesture with the hands.

Wang Palace.

Wat Temple.

Wiang Fortified town.

Yaksha Mythical giant.

Yantra Magical combination of numbers and letters, used to ward off danger.

Travel store

ROUGH GUIDES Complete Listing

UK & Ireland
Britain
Devon & Cornwall
Dublin **D**
Edinburgh **D**
England
Ireland
The Lake District
London
London **D**
London Mini Guide
Scotland
Scottish Highlands & Islands
Wales

Europe
Algarve **D**
Amsterdam
Amsterdam **D**
Andalucía
Athens **D**
Austria
The Baltic States
Barcelona
Barcelona **D**
Belgium & Luxembourg
Berlin
Brittany & Normandy
Bruges **D**
Brussels
Budapest
Bulgaria
Copenhagen
Corfu
Corsica
Costa Brava **D**
Crete
Croatia
Cyprus
Czech & Slovak Republics
Dodecanese & East Aegean
Dordogne & The Lot
Europe
Florence & Siena
Florence **D**
France
Germany
Gran Canaria **D**
Greece
Greek Islands
Hungary
Ibiza & Formentera **D**
Iceland
Ionian Islands
Italy
The Italian Lakes
Languedoc & Roussillon
Lanzarote **D**
Lisbon **D**
The Loire
Madeira **D**
Madrid **D**
Mallorca **D**
Mallorca & Menorca
Malta & Gozo **D**
Menorca
Moscow
The Netherlands
Norway
Paris
Paris **D**
Paris Mini Guide
Poland
Portugal
Prague
Prague **D**
Provence & the Côte D'Azur
Pyrenees
Romania
Rome
Rome **D**
Sardinia
Scandinavia
Sicily
Slovenia
Spain
St Petersburg
Sweden
Switzerland
Tenerife & La Gomera **D**
Turkey
Tuscany & Umbria
Venice & The Veneto
Venice **D**
Vienna

Asia
Bali & Lombok
Bangkok
Beijing
Cambodia
China
Goa
Hong Kong & Macau
India
Indonesia
Japan
Laos
Malaysia, Singapore & Brunei
Nepal
The Philippines
Singapore
South India
Southeast Asia
Sri Lanka
Thailand
Thailand's Beaches & Islands
Tokyo
Vietnam

Australasia
Australia
Melbourne
New Zealand
Sydney

North America
Alaska
Baja California
Boston
California
Canada
Chicago
Colorado
Florida
The Grand Canyon
Hawaii
Las Vegas **D**
Los Angeles
Maui **D**
Miami & South Florida
Montréal
New England
New Orleans **D**
New York City
New York City **D**
New York City Mini Guide
Orlando & Walt Disney World® **D**
Pacific Northwest
San Francisco
San Francisco **D**
Seattle
Southwest USA
Toronto
USA
Vancouver
Washington DC
Washington DC **D**
Yosemite

Caribbean & Latin America
Antigua & Barbuda **D**
Argentina
Bahamas
Barbados **D**
Belize
Bolivia
Brazil
Cancùn & Cozumel **D**
Caribbean
Central America
Chile
Costa Rica
Cuba
Dominican Republic
Dominican Republic **D**
Ecuador
Guatemala
Jamaica
Mexico
Peru
St Lucia **D**
South America
Trinidad & Tobago
Yúcatan

Africa & Middle East
Cape Town & the Garden Route
Egypt
The Gambia
Jordan
Kenya
Marrakesh **D**
Morocco
South Africa, Lesotho & Swaziland
Syria
Tanzania
Tunisia
West Africa
Zanzibar

D: Rough Guide **DIRECTIONS** for short breaks

Available from all good bookstores

ROUGH
GUIDES

Small print and

Index

A Rough Guide to Rough Guides

Published in 1982, the first Rough Guide – to Greece – was a student scheme that became a publishing phenomenon. Mark Ellingham, a recent graduate in English from Bristol University, had been travelling in Greece the previous summer and couldn't find the right guidebook. With a small group of friends he wrote his own guide, combining a highly contemporary, journalistic style with a thoroughly practical approach to travellers' needs.

The immediate success of the book spawned a series that rapidly covered dozens of destinations. And, in addition to impecunious backpackers, Rough Guides soon acquired a much broader and older readership that relished the guides' wit and inquisitiveness as much as their enthusiastic, critical approach and value-for-money ethos.

These days, Rough Guides include recommendations from shoestring to luxury and cover more than 200 destinations around the globe, including almost every country in the Americas and Europe, more than half of Africa and most of Asia and Australasia. Our ever-growing team of authors and photographers is spread all over the world, particularly in Europe, the USA and Australia.

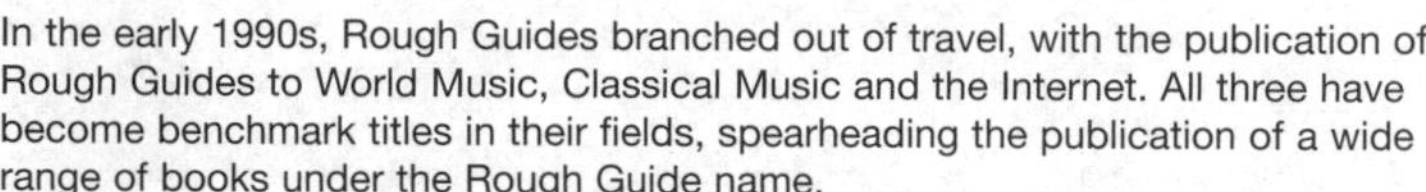

In the early 1990s, Rough Guides branched out of travel, with the publication of Rough Guides to World Music, Classical Music and the Internet. All three have become benchmark titles in their fields, spearheading the publication of a wide range of books under the Rough Guide name.

Including the travel series, Rough Guides now number more than 350 titles, covering: phrasebooks, waterproof maps, music guides from Opera to Heavy Metal, reference works as diverse as Conspiracy Theories and Shakespeare, and popular culture books from iPods to Poker. Rough Guides also produce a series of more than 120 World Music CDs in partnership with World Music Network.

Visit www.roughguides.com to see our latest publications.

Rough Guide travel images are available for commercial licensing at www.roughguidespictures.com

Rough Guide credits

Text editors: Clifton Wilkinson, Alison Murchie, Matthew Teller, Lucy White
Layout: Ajay Verma
Cartography: Jai Prakash Mishra
Picture editor: Siobhan Donoghue
Production: Aimee Hampson
Proofreader: Amanda Jones
Cover design: Chloë Roberts
Photographer: Karen Trist
Editorial: London Kate Berens, Claire Saunders, Geoff Howard, Ruth Blackmore, Polly Thomas, Richard Lim, Karoline Densley, Andy Turner, Keith Drew, Edward Aves, Nikki Birrell, Helen Marsden, Alice Park, Sarah Eno, Jo Kirby, Joe Staines, Duncan Clark, Peter Buckley, Matthew Milton, Tracy Hopkins, David Paul, Ruth Tidball; **New York** Andrew Rosenberg, Steven Horak, April Isaacs, AnneLise Sorensen, Amy Hegarty, Sean Mahoney, Ella Steim
Design & Pictures: London Simon Bracken, Dan May, Diana Jarvis, Mark Thomas, Jj Luck, Harriet Mills; **Delhi** Madhulita Mohapatra, Umesh Aggarwal, Jessica Subramanian, Ankur Guha, Pradeep Thapliyal, Sachin Tanwar, Anita Singh
Production: Sophie Hewat, Katherine Owers
Cartography: London Maxine Repath, Ed Wright, Katie Lloyd-Jones; **Delhi** Rajesh Chhibber, Ashutosh Bharti, Rajesh Mishra, Animesh Pathak, Jasbir Sandhu, Karobi Gogoi, Amod Singh, Alakananda Bhattacharya
Online: New York Jennifer Gold, Suzanne Welles, Kristin Mingrone; **Delhi** Manik Chauhan, Narender Kumar, Rakesh Kumar, Amit Verma, Amit Kumar, Rahul Kumar
Marketing & Publicity: London Richard Trillo, Niki Hanmer, Louise Maher, Jess Carter; **New York** Geoff Colquitt, Megan Kennedy, Katy Ball; **Delhi** Reem Khokhar
Custom publishing and foreign rights: Philippa Hopkins
Manager India: Punita Singh
Series editor: Mark Ellingham
Reference Director: Andrew Lockett
PA to Managing and Publishing Directors: Megan McIntyre
Publishing Director: Martin Dunford

Publishing information

This sixth edition published October 2006 by
Rough Guides Ltd,
80 Strand, London WC2R 0RL
345 Hudson St, 4th Floor,
New York, NY 10014, USA
14 Local Shopping Centre, Panchsheel Park,
New Delhi 110017, India
Distributed by the Penguin Group
Penguin Books Ltd,
80 Strand, London WC2R 0RL
Penguin Putnam, Inc.
375 Hudson Street, NY 10014, USA
Penguin Group (Australia)
250 Camberwell Road, Camberwell,
Victoria 3124, Australia
Penguin Books Canada Ltd,
10 Alcorn Avenue, Toronto, Ontario,
Canada M4V 1E4
Penguin Group (NZ)
67 Apollo Drive, Mairangi Bay, Auckland 1310,
New Zealand
Cover concept by Peter Dyer.

Typeset in Bembo and Helvetica to an original design by Henry Iles.

Printed and bound in Italy by LegoPrint S.p.A

968pp includes index

A catalogue record for this book is available from the British Library

ISBN 1-84353-677-3

ISBN 13: 9-78184-353-677-2

1 3 5 7 9 8 6 4 2

Help us update

We've gone to a lot of effort to ensure that the sixth edition of **The Rough Guide to Thailand** is accurate and up to date. However, things change – places get "discovered", opening hours are notoriously fickle, restaurants and rooms raise prices or lower standards. If you feel we've got it wrong or left something out, we'd like to know, and if you can remember the address, the price, the time, the phone number, so much the better. We'll credit all contributions, and send a copy of the next edition (or any other Rough Guide if you prefer) for the best letters. Everyone who writes to us and isn't already a subscriber will receive a copy of our full-colour thrice-yearly newsletter. Please mark letters: "**Rough Guide Thailand Update**" and send to: Rough Guides, 80 Strand, London WC2R 0RL, or Rough Guides, 4th Floor, 345 Hudson St, New York, NY 10014. Or send an email to **mail@roughguides.com**
Have your questions answered and tell others about your trip at
www.roughguides.atinfopop.com

Acknowledgements

The authors jointly would like to thank: Abigail Batalla and Richard Hume at London TAT; Ron Emmons; Melanie McCoy at Sydney TAT; staff at TAT offices in Phitsanulok, Khorat, Ubon Ratchathani, Udon Thani, Trat, Surat Thani, Ko Samui and Nakhon Si Thammarat; Wijite Tongkham at Mae Hong Son TAT; Felix Hude for the section on cycling; Neil Pettigrew for writing about Thai cinema; John Clewley for his piece on Thai music; Fran Sandham for the feature on Bangkok tailors; Victor Borg for information on drugs penalties; Tom Vater for background on the chao ley; kohjumonline.com for use of their map; Phil Cornwel-Smith; Bangkok Airways and Sandra Gosling and Andrew Hoskins at Aviareps.

From Lucy, thanks to: Jacques Rayner; Apple and Noi; Tan and Michel; Tom and Aroon; Seonai Chongrak; David Knapp; Pirom and Aree; Jaeb in Khuraburi; Serge in Trat; Khun Naa in Sukhothai; Aung and Lizzie on Ko Samet; Brad Cousins; Richard and Walter on Ko Phayam; Ray, Sao and Phil on Ko Jum; Steve Nye.

From Paul, special, belated thanks to Joe de Souza for his much-valued help and companionship. Thanks also to: Bill Gray; Jack Grassby; Jan Galloway; Gerlinde Bankemper on Ko Samui; Rashi and Bambi at the Backpackers' Information Centre on Ko Pha Ngan; staff at Ko Tarutao National Marine Park; Nikki Busuttil of Amari; Shamini Murugan of Anantara/Marriott.

From Ron, thanks to: Annette Kunigagon in Chiang Mai; Watchara Lewpongsawat in Chiang Khong.

SMALL PRINT

Readers' letters

Thanks to all the readers who have taken the time to write in with comments and suggestions (and apologies if we've inadvertently omitted anyone's name):

Philip Ampofo, Roger Baker, Arden Bashforth, Sue Bayliss, Paul Bonner, Andy & Claire Brice, Meredith Byers, Brian Candler, Paula Carter, John Clements, Varry Cocker, Andy Conner, Joanna Cox, B.M. Dobson, Colin Doyle, Don Dunlop, Heather Engley, Mike Fletcher, Johanna Ford and Chris Porter, George, Adrian Greenwood, Joan Gregoire, Lesley & Bob Hamson, Alan Hickey, Paul Jeffries, Monica Kearns, Harm Jan Kinkhorst, Liz Kirby, Alexander MacArthur, Lyn McCoy, Orlaith Mannion, Bill & Sandra Martin, Shelley Mason, Ken Mays, Bernard Nalson, Terry J Nixon, Hubert de Paor, Miranda Pattinson, Bryan Pittman, Geoff Pocket, Sarah Riches, Emily De Ruyter, Rob Samborn, Maya Smith, Jeremy Tilden-Smith, Jim Snaith, Ian Spinney, Allan Tyrer, Sarah Valencik, A Watson, Philip Wong, Helen Williams, Roger S. Windsor, Linda Wylie & Stephen Rodgers.

Photo credits

Front colour section

09 Thai boxing © Tourism Authority of Thailand
15 Khao Yai National Park, Nakhon © Tourism Authority of Thailand
16 Umphang Falls © Zhin Choo
16 Diving and snorkling, Koh Similian © Tourism Authority of Thailand
17 National Museum of Bangkok © Tourism Authority of Thailand
18 Phuket Vegetarian Festival © Bjorn Svensson/Alamy
19 Ko Tarutao National Park, Satun © Tourism Authority of Thailand
20 Thai cooking classes © Chiang Mai Cookery School
21 Nan © Luca I. Tettoni
21 Khao Yai National Park, Nakhon © Tourism Authority of Thailand
22 Koh Tao, Surat Thani- Hat Saike © Tourism Authority of Thailand
22 Songkran Chiang Mai © Tourism Authority of Thailand
23 Mae Hong Song Mai © Tourism Authority of Thailand
23 Thai massage © Tourism Authority of Thailand
24 Wat Phu Tok © Paul Gray

The wat colour section

p.03 Worshippers splash water on the Buddha © Darby Sawchuk/Alamy

Black and whites

p.403 Mai Ong Son wild sunflower field© Tourism Authority of Thailand
p.417 Working elephants walking up the Pai River © Kevin Morris/Corbis
p.469 Tiffany Show; Pattaya Night Life © Tiffany's Show, Pattaya
p.518 Koa Yao NP – Hightlight © WoodyStock/Alamy
p.527 Khao Luuk Chang, wrinkle-tipped bats © WoodyStock/Alamy
p.538 Prasat Hin National Historic Park, Phimai © Cris Haigh/Alamy
p.546 I San elephant © Hemis/Alamy
p.557 Temple façade and roof detail, Ubon Ratchathani © J Marshall/Alamy
p.568 Khon Kaen Wat Nongwang© David Sanger/Alamy
p.578 Masked dancer, Phi Ta Kon Festival © Bjorn Svensson/Alamy
p.584 Mekong River © Terry Whittaker/ Alamy
p.592 Wat Khaek Sala Kaew Ku, Nong Khai © Cris Haigh/Alamy
p.639 Ang Thong NP beach© Tourism Authority of Thailand
p.652 Chaweng Beach, Ko Samui island, Beach Vendor © Andrew Woodley/Alamy
p.665 Ko Phang Nga © Andrew Woodley/Alamy
p.673 Ko Tao underwater image © Tourism Authority of Thailand
p.687 Phra Buddha Sihing of Nakhon Si Thammarat © Luca Tettoni/Alamy
p.716 Cheow Lan Lake- National Park Bungalows © Lucy Ridout
p.824 Tarutao National Park, Satun © Tourism Authority of Thailand
p.833 Trang Beach © Tourism Authority of Thailand
p.840 Sukorn bunglows © Sukorn Island Trang Hotel
p.848 Ko Tarutao © Tourism Authority of Thailand

Index

Map entries are in colour.

C

D

E

F

INDEX

L

M

N

O

P

R

S

T

U

V

Map symbols

maps are listed in the full index using coloured text

International boundary
Chapter division boundary
Road
Unpaved road
Path
Railway
Ferry route
Waterway
Wall
Cable car & station
Point of interest
Accommodation
Restaurants & bars
Campground
Border crossing
Peak
Mountains
Cave
Spring
Waterfall
Rock
Lighthouse
Viewpoint

Gate
Arch
Dam
Statue
Airport
Transport stop
Museum
Internet access
Information office
Telephone
Hospital
Post office
Market
Swimming pool
Mosque
Temple
Chinese temple/pagod
Church
Building
Forest
Christian cemetery
Park
Beach

WHEREVER YOU ARE,

WHEREVER YOU'RE GOING,

COLUMBUS DIRECT
Travel Insurance

ROUGH
GUIDES

G